GABRIEL MANTZ

SOUTH AMERICAN FOOTBALL INTERNATIONAL LINE-UPS & STATISTICS 1902-2013

VOLUME 3

British Library Cataloguing in Publication Data
A catalogue record for this book is available from the British Library

ISBN 978-1-86223-289-1

72 St. Peter's Avenue, Cleethorpes, N.E. Lincolnshire, DN35 8HU, England

Web site www.soccer-books.co.uk
e-mail info@soccer-books.co.uk

Printed in the UK by 4edge Ltd.

Dear Readers,

This book is the third and final volume of a new series which contains statistics for all matches played by South American national teams from the very first game played in 1902 through to the present day. There are 10 national teams in South America and the governing body of association football in South America is CONMEBOL (Confederación Sudamericana de Fútbol – The South American Football Confederation), also the oldest continental confederation in the world. With 10 member football associations, CONMEBOL has the fewest members of all continental confederations belonging to FIFA. However, the national teams belonging to CONMEBOL have won nine of 19 FIFA World Cup tournaments played between 1930 and 2010 (Brazil winning five times, Argentina and Uruguay each with two trophies). In 1916, the first South American continental championship was founded under the name Campeonato Sudamericano de Fútbol. The competition still exists to this day though it is now named the Campeonato Sudamericano Copa América or more simply the Copa América. In this, the oldest of continental football competitions, Uruguay holds the record number of victories after winning the trophy on 15 occasions between 1916 and 2011.

The first international match between two South American national teams was played on 20th July 1902 between Uruguay and Argentina, approximately 3 months earlier than the first European game played between non-British national teams (Austria played Hungary on 12th October 1902). This third volume contains the complete statistical records of the national teams Ecuador, Peru, Uruguay and Venezuela.

The Ecuadorian national team only joined the higher-echelons of football in the last 12 years, qualifying for the FIFA World Cup final for the first time in 2002. They repeated this performance in 2006 and against for the 2014 World Cup Finals in Brazil. It should also be mentioned that Ecuador began their first World Cup qualifying campaign only in 1961 after refusing an invitation to participate in the inaugural 1930 FIFA World Cup competition held in Uruguay. To date, they are one of just three countries – along with Chile and Venezuela – in South America never to win the Copa América.

The Peruvian national team has a glorious past with many achievements but this exceeds the results of recent years. Peru participated in the first World Cup finals held in 1930 in Uruguay but then did not return to the big competition until 40 years later when a strong generation of players lead by Héctor Chumpitaz and Teofilo Cubillas won some great results, mostly in the 1978 World Cup finals tournament in Argentina. Peru won have lifted the Copa América on two occasions, in 1939 and 1975.

Historically, the Uruguayan national football team are one of the key sides in world football. They won Gold Medals at the Summer Olympic Games in 1924 and 1928, before the creation of the World Cup, and were then considered the best team in the World. Uruguay organized the first FIFA World Cup final tournament in 1930 and were the first World Champions, a performance repeated 20 years later in the memorable final at the Estádio Maracanã in Rio de Janeiro when they defeated the home favourites Brazil 2-1 to win their second World Cup title! Uruguay have also won the Copa América on no fewer than 15 occasions. After three decades of failure in the World Cup tournament, Uruguay were back in the finals tournament 2010, unexpectedly finishing in fourth place. Diego Forlan, elected "Best player of the 2010 FIFA World Cup tournament" became a worthy follower of previous Uruguayan greats such José Andrade, Obdulio Varela and Juan Antonio Schiaffino.

The Venezuelan national football team is the only South American national team which has not yet qualified for the World Cup finals. They first played in the competition in 1966 and for many decades only achieved very poor results. The greatest success of the national team was achieved in 2011 when they finished fourth in the Copa América. Improving results over the past ten years bring hope that Venezuela may finally qualify for a World Cup finals tournament in the near future.

This book contains statistics for all the matches played by each country's "A" national team from their first match until the end of 2013. For each match played, besides the names of the players who appear you will find the number of caps and goals for each player achieved by that game. There is also information about the stadium, referee and attendance for each game and, of course, the name of the national team coach. In addition to the individual match information, a second section lists all the players to make an international appearance for each country which shows number of total caps won and goals scored, the period when the player made his international appearances and the club he was playing for at the time. A third section presents information for all the national coaches/managers and a fourth section presents head-to-head statistics for each country versus all opponents faced in international matches. I have to apologise for the lack of complete statistical data for some players, but it can be very difficult to be find this information. I hope that readers will find this work both useful and informative.

The Author

SUMMARY

ABBREVIATIONS

FM/Nr Number of first match played for the national team / Player counter
DOB Date of birth

FIFA COUNTRY CODES – SOUTH AMERICA

Argentina	**ARG**
Bolivia	**BOL**
Brazil	**BRA**
Chile	**CHI**
Colombia	**COL**
Ecuador	**ECU**
Paraguay	**PAR**
Peru	**PER**
Uruguay	**URU**
Venezuela	**VEN**

ECUADOR

The Country:
República del Ecuador (Republic of Ecuador)
Capital: Quito
Surface: 256,370 km²
Inhabitants: 13,800,000
Time: UTC-5 to -6

The FA:
Federación Ecuatoriana de Fútbol
Avenida Las Aguas y Calle Alianza, P.O. Box 09-01-7447, Guayaquíl
Year of Formation: 1925
Member of FIFA since: 1926
Member of CONMEBOL since: 1927

NATIONAL TEAM RECORDS

COPA AMÉRICA	
1916	Did not enter
1917	Did not enter
1919	Did not enter
1920	Did not enter
1921	Did not enter
1922	Did not enter
1923	Did not enter
1924	Did not enter
1925	Did not enter
1926	Did not enter
1927	Did not enter
1929	Did not enter
1935	Did not enter
1937	Did not enter
1939	5th Place
1941	5th Place
1942	7th Place
1945	7th Place
1946	Withdrew
1947	6th Place
1949	7th Place
1953	6th Place
1955	7th Place
1956	Withdrew
1957	7th Place
1959	Withdrew
1959E	4th Place
1963	6th Place
1967	Qualifying Round
1975	Round 1
1979	Round 1
1983	Round 1
1987	Round 1
1989	Round 1
1991	Round 1
1993	4th Place
1995	Round 1
1997	Quarter-Finals
1999	Round 1
2001	Round 1
2004	Round 1
2007	Round 1
2011	Round 1

WORLD CUP	
1930	Did not enter
1934	Did not enter
1938	Did not enter
1950	Withdrew
1954	Did not enter
1958	Did not enter
1962	Qualifiers
1966	Qualifiers
1970	Qualifiers
1974	Qualifiers
1978	Qualifiers
1982	Qualifiers
1986	Qualifiers
1990	Qualifiers
1994	Qualifiers
1998	Qualifiers
2002	Final Tournament (1st Round)
2006	Final Tournament (2nd Round)
2010	Qualifiers
2014	Final Tournament (*to be played*)

OLYMPIC GAMES 1900-2012
None
FIFA CONFEDERATIONS CUP 1992-2013
None
PLAYER WITH MOST INTERNATIONAL CAPS
Iván Jacinto Hurtado Angulo – 167 caps (1992-2010)
PLAYER WITH MOST INTERNATIONAL GOALS
Agustín Javier Delgado Chalá – 31 goals / 72 caps (1994-2011)

FULL INTERNATIONALS (1938-2013)

1. 08.08.1938 **BOLIVIA - ECUADOR** **1-1** 1st Juegos Bolivarianos
Estadio Universitario, Bogotá
ECU: Francisco Martínez Roiz (1/0), J.Naranjo (1/0), Eloy Ronquillo (1/0), Jorge Sola (1/0), Arturo Zambrano (1/0), José Vasconez (1/0), Alfonso Suárez Rizzo (1/0), Antonio Abril (1/0), Enrique Herrera (1/1), Francisco López (1/0), César Augusto Freire (1/1). Trainer: Enrique Lamas (1).
Goal: Enrique Herrera.

2. 10.08.1938 **COLOMBIA - ECUADOR** **1-2(1-0)** 1st Juegos Bolivarianos
Estadio „Nemesio Camacho" 'El Campín', Bogotá; Referee: Carlos Esteva Tejada (Mexico)
ECU: Francisco Martínez Roiz (2/0), Eloy Ronquillo (2/0), Luis Hungría (1/0), Jorge Sola (2/0), Manuel Arenas (1/0), Arturo Zambrano (2/0), José Vasconez (2/0), Alfonso Suárez Rizzo (2/0), Antonio Abril (2/0), Enrique Herrera (2/2), Francisco López (2/0), César Augusto Freire (2/1). Trainer: Enrique Lamas (2).
Goals: Enrique Herrera (68), César Augusto Freire (88).

3. 11.08.1938 **PERU - ECUADOR** **9-1(4-1)** 1st Juegos Bolivarianos
Estadio „Nemesio Camacho" 'El Campín', Bogotá; Referee: Carlos Esteva Tejada (Mexico)
ECU: Francisco Martínez Roiz (3/0), Eloy Ronquillo (3/0), Luis Hungría (2/0), Víctor Sandoval (1/0), Arturo Zambrano (3/0), José Vasconez (3/0), Nicolás Alvarez (1/0), Alfonso Suárez Rizzo (3/1), Manuel Arenas (2/0), Enrique Herrera (3/2), César Augusto Freire (3/1). Trainer: Enrique Lamas (3).
Goal: Alfonso Suárez Rizzo (11).

4. 19.08.1938 **VENEZUELA - ECUADOR** **2-5(2-4)** 1st Juegos Bolivarianos
Estadio „Nemesio Camacho" 'El Campín', Bogotá
ECU: Humberto Vásquez (1/0) [Francisco Martínez Roiz (4/0)], Luis Hungría (3/0), Eloy Ronquillo (4/0), Jorge Sola (3/0), Arturo Zambrano (4/0), José Vasconez (4/0), Nicolás Alvarez (2/0), Alfonso Suárez Rizzo (4/2), Manuel Arenas (3/1), Enrique Herrera (4/4), César Augusto Freire (4/2). Trainer: Enrique Lamas (4).
Goals: Alfonso Suárez Rizzo (14), Manuel Arenas (20), César Augusto Freire (24), Enrique Herrera (30, 70).

5. 22.08.1938 **BOLIVIA - ECUADOR** **2-1(2-0)** 1st Juegos Bolivarianos
Estadio Universitario, Bogotá; Referee: Carlos Esteva Tejada (Mexico)
ECU: Francisco Martínez Roiz (5/0), Eloy Ronquillo (5/0), Luis Hungría (4/0), Jorge Sola (4/0), Arturo Zambrano (5/1), José Vasconez (5/0), Alfonso Suárez Rizzo (5/2), Antonio Abril (3/0), Enrique Herrera (5/4), Francisco López (3/0), César Augusto Freire (5/2). Trainer: Enrique Lamas (5).
Goals: Arturo Zambrano (65).

6. 15.01.1939 **PERU - ECUADOR** **5-2(3-0)** 15th Copa América
Estadio Nacional, Lima; Referee: Carlos Puyol (Uruguay); Attendance: 10,000
ECU: Humberto Vásquez (2/0), Eloy Ronquillo (6/0), Augusto Solís (1/0), José Merino (1/0), Arturo Zambrano (6/1) [José Peralta (1/0)], Luis Arias (1/0) [José Vasconez (6/0)], Ernesto Cevallos (1/0), Ramón Unamuno (1/0) [Marino Alcívar (1/2)], Alfonso Suárez Rizzo (6/2), Enrique Herrera (6/4), César Augusto Freire (6/2). Trainer: Ramón Unamuno (1).
Goals: Marino Alcívar (55, 89).

7. 22.01.1939 **URUGUAY - ECUADOR** **6-0(4-0)** 15th Copa América
Estadio Nacional, Lima (Peru); Referee: Enrique Cuenca (Peru); Attendance: 10,000
ECU: Humberto Vásquez (3/0), Eloy Ronquillo (7/0), Augusto Solís (2/0), José Merino (2/0), José Peralta (2/0) [Arturo Zambrano (7/1)], José Vasconez (7/0), Ernesto Cevallos (2/0), Alfonso Suárez Rizzo (7/2), Manuel Arenas (4/1) [Marino Alcívar (2/2)], Enrique Herrera (7/4) [Fonfredes Bohórquez (1/0], Leónidas Elizalde (1/0). Trainer: Ramón Unamuno (2).

8. 05.02.1939 **CHILE - ECUADOR** **4-1(3-1)** 15th Copa América
Estadio Nacional, Lima (Peru); Referee: Carlos Puyol (Uruguay); Attendance: 10,000
ECU: Francisco Martínez Roiz (6/0), Eloy Ronquillo (8/0), Luis Hungría (5/0), José Peralta (3/0), José Vasconez (8/0), Jorge Laurido (1/0), Ernesto Cevallos (3/0), César Augusto Freire (7/2), Marino Alcívar (3/2), Manuel Arenas (5/2), Alfonso Suárez Rizzo (8/2). Trainer: Ramón Unamuno (3).
Goal: Manuel Arenas (35).

9. 12.02.1939 **PARAGUAY - ECUADOR** **3-1(1-0)** 15th Copa América
Estadio Nacional, Lima (Peru); Referee: Enrique Cuenca (Peru); Attendance: 15,000
ECU: Humberto Vásquez (4/0), Eloy Ronquillo (9/0), Augusto Solís (3/0), José Peralta (4/0), José Vasconez (9/0), Luis Arias (2/0), Ernesto Cevallos (4/0), César Augusto Freire (8/2), Marino Alcívar (4/2) [Alfonso Suárez Rizzo (9/2)], Manuel Arenas (6/3), Enrique Herrera (8/4). Trainer: Ramón Unamuno (4).
Goal: Manuel Arenas (75).

10. 02.02.1941 **CHILE - ECUADOR** **5-0(4-0)** 16th Copa América
Estadio Nacional, Santiago; Referee: José Bartolomé Macías (Argentina); Attendance: 40,000
ECU: Ignacio Molina (1/0), Luis Hungría (6/0), Jorge Laurido (2/0), José Merino (3/0), Alfonso Romo (1/0), Luis Mendoza (1/0), Ernesto Cevallos (5/0), Alfonso Suárez Rizzo (10/2), Enrique Raymondi Chávez (1/0), Marino Alcívar (5/2), César Augusto Freire (9/2). Trainer: Juan Parodi (1).

11. 09.02.1941 **URUGUAY - ECUADOR** **6-0(4-0)** 16th Copa América
Estadio Nacional, Santiago (Chile); Referee: Alfredo Vargas (Chile); Attendance: 70,000
ECU: Ignacio Molina (2/0) [Luis Santoliva (1/0)], Luis Hungría (7/0), Jorge Laurido (3/0), Vicente Aguirre (1/0), José Peralta (5/0) [Alfonso Romo (2/0)], Luis Mendoza (2/0), Ernesto Cevallos (6/0), Alfonso Suárez Rizzo (11/2), Enrique Raymondi Chávez (2/0), Marino Alcívar (6/2), César Augusto Freire (10/2). Trainer: Juan Parodi (2).

12. 16.02.1941 **ARGENTINA - ECUADOR** **6-1(5-0)** 16th Copa América
Estadio Nacional, Santiago (Chile); Referee: Aníbal Tejada (Uruguay); Attendance: 70,000
ECU: Luis Santoliva (2/0) [Ignacio Molina (3/0)], Luis Hungría (8/0) [Clemente Angulo (1/0)], Jorge Laurido (4/0), Carlos Garnica (1/0), José Peralta (6/0), Luis Mendoza (3/0), Ernesto Cevallos (7/0), Alfonso Suárez Rizzo (12/2), Enrique Raymondi Chávez (3/0) [Eduardo Stacey (1/0)], Marino Alcívar (7/2), César Augusto Freire (11/3). Trainer: Juan Parodi (3).
Goal: César Augusto Freire (47).

13. 23.02.1941 **PERU - ECUADOR** **4-0(3-0)** 16th Copa América
Estadio Nacional, Santiago (Chile); Referee: Víctor Francisco Rivas (Chile)
ECU: Ignacio Molina (4/0), Luis Hungría (9/0), Jorge Laurido (5/0), José Merino (4/0), José Peralta (7/0), Luis Mendoza (4/0), Ernesto Cevallos (8/0), Alfonso Suárez Rizzo (13/2), Enrique Raymondi Chávez (4/0), José Herrera (1/0) [Marino Alcívar (8/2)], César Augusto Freire (12/3). Trainer: Juan Parodi (4).

14. 18.01.1942 **URUGUAY – ECUADOR** **7-0(7-0)** 17th Copa América
Estadio Centenario, Montevideo; Referee: Marcos Gerinaldo Rojas (Paraguay); Attendance: 45,000
ECU: Napoleón Medina (1/0) [Humberto Vásquez (5/0)], Eloy Ronquillo (10/0), Luis Hungría (10/0), José Merino (5/0) [Manuel Sempértegui (1/0)], Arturo Zambrano (8/1), Luis Mendoza (5/0), Enrique Alvarez (1/0), José María Jiménez (1/0), José Herrera (2/0), Marino Alcívar (9/2), Pedro Acevedo (1/0). Trainer: Juan Parodi (5).

15. 22.01.1942 **ARGENTINA - ECUADOR** **12-0(6-0)** 17th Copa América
Estadio Centenario, Montevideo (Uruguay); Referee: Manuel Soto (Chile); Attendance: 25,000
ECU: Napoleón Medina (2/0), Romualdo Ronquillo (1/0), Félix Leyton Zurita (1/0), Manuel Sempértegui (2/0), Arturo Zambrano (9/1) [Celso Torres (1/0)], Luis Mendoza (6/0), Enrique Alvarez (2/0), José María Jiménez (2/0), Guillermo Gavilánez (1/0) [José Herrera (3/0)], Marino Alcívar (10/2), Pedro Acevedo (2/0). Trainer: Juan Parodi (6).

16. 25.01.1942 **PARAGUAY - ECUADOR** **3-1(1-0)** 17th Copa América
Estadio Centenario, Montevideo (Uruguay); Referee: Manuel Soto (Chile); Attendance: 12,000
ECU: Napoleón Medina (3/0), Romualdo Ronquillo (2/0), Luis Hungría (11/0) [Félix Leyton Zurita (2/0)], Celso Torres (2/0), Arturo Zambrano (10/1), Luis Mendoza (7/0), Enrique Alvarez (3/0), José María Jiménez (3/1), Antonio Abril (4/0) [José Herrera (4/0)], Marino Alcívar (11/2), Pedro Acevedo (3/0). Trainer: Juan Parodi (7).
Goal: José María Jiménez (46).

17. 28.01.1942 **PERU - ECUADOR** **2-1(1-0)** 17th Copa América
Estadio Centenario, Montevideo (Uruguay); Referee: Aníbal Tejada (Uruguay); Attendance: 40,000
ECU: Napoleón Medina (4/0), Félix Leyton Zurita (3/0), Luis Hungría (12/0), Celso Torres (3/0), Arturo Zambrano (11/1), Luis Mendoza (8/0) [José Merino (6/0)], Enrique Alvarez (4/0), José María Jiménez (4/2), Guillermo Gavilánez (2/0) [José Herrera (5/0)], Marino Alcívar (12/2), Pedro Acevedo (4/0). Trainer: Juan Parodi (8).
Goal: José María Jiménez (52).

18. 31.01.1942 **BRAZIL - ECUADOR** **5-1(3-1)** 17th Copa América
Estadio Centenario, Montevideo (Uruguay); Referee: José Bartolomé Macias (Argentina); Attendance: 40,000
ECU: Napoleón Medina (5/0), Félix Leyton Zurita (4/0), Luis Hungría (13/0), Celso Torres (4/0), Arturo Zambrano (12/1), Manuel Sempértegui (3/0) [Luis Mendoza (9/0)], Enrique Alvarez (5/1), José María Jiménez (5/2), José Herrera (6/0) [José Merino (7/0), Antonio Abril (5/0)], Marino Alcívar (13/2), Pedro Acevedo (5/0). Trainer: Juan Parodi (9).
Goal: Enrique Alvarez (19 penalty).

19. 05.02.1942 **CHILE - ECUADOR** **2-1(2-1)** 17th Copa América
Estadio Centenario, Montevideo (Uruguay); Referee: Marcos Gerinaldo Rojas (Paraguay); Attendance: 15,000
ECU: Napoleón Medina (6/0), Romualdo Ronquillo (3/0) [Félix Leyton Zurita (5/0)], Luis Hungría (14/0), Celso Torres (5/0), Arturo Zambrano (13/1), Luis Mendoza (10/0), Enrique Alvarez (6/1), José María Jiménez (6/2) [Marino Alcívar (14/3)], José Mendoza (1/0), Guillermo Gavilánez (3/0), Pedro Acevedo (6/0). Trainer: Juan Parodi (10).
Goal: Marino Alcívar (5).

20. 14.01.1945 **CHILE - ECUADOR** **6-3(3-2)** 18th Copa América
Estadio Nacional, Santiago; Referee: José Bartolomé Macías (Argentina); Attendance: 65,000
ECU: Napoleón Medina (7/0), Jorge Henríquez (1/0), Félix Leyton Zurita (6/0), Luis Mendoza (11/1), Enrique Alvarez (7/1), Eloy Mejía (1/0), José Mendoza (2/0), José María Jiménez (7/3), Enrique Raymondi Chávez (5/1), Víctor Aguayo (1/0), Pedro Acevedo (7/0). Trainer: Rodolfo Orlandini (1).
Goal: Enrique Raymondi Chávez (30), José María Jiménez (44), Luis Mendoza (51).

21. 24.01.1945 **URUGUAY - ECUADOR** **5-1(2-1)** 18th Copa América
Estadio Nacional, Santiago (Chile); Referee: Mário Gonçalves Vianna (Brazil); Attendance: 70,000
ECU: Napoleón Medina (8/0), Jorge Henríquez (2/0), Félix Leyton Zurita (7/0), Luis Mendoza (12/1), Enrique Alvarez (8/1), Eloy Mejía (2/0), José Mendoza (3/0), José María Jiménez (8/3), Enrique Raymondi Chávez (6/1) [Luis Albán (1/0)], Víctor Aguayo (2/1), Pedro Acevedo (8/0). Trainer: Rodolfo Orlandini (2).
Goal: Víctor Aguayo (39).

22. 31.01.1945 **ARGENTINA - ECUADOR** **4-2(1-0)** 18th Copa América
Estadio Nacional, Santiago (Chile); Referee: Nobel Valentini (Uruguay); Attendance: 60,000
ECU: Napoleón Medina (9/0), Jorge Henríquez (3/0), Félix Leyton Zurita (8/0) [Francisco Villagómez (1/0)], Luis Mendoza (13/1), Enrique Alvarez (9/1), Eloy Mejía (3/0), José Mendoza (4/1), José María Jiménez (9/3), Enrique Raymondi Chávez (7/1), Víctor Aguayo (3/2), Pedro Acevedo (9/0). Trainer: Rodolfo Orlandini (3).
Goals: Víctor Aguayo (53), José Mendoza (62).

23. 11.02.1945 **BOLIVIA - ECUADOR** **0-0** 18th Copa América
Estadio Nacional, Santiago (Chile); Referee: Mário Gonçalves Vianna (Brazil); Attendance: 70,000
ECU: Napoleón Medina (10/0), Jorge Henríquez (4/0), Félix Leyton Zurita (9/0), Luis Mendoza (14/1) [Carlos Garnica (2/0)], Enrique Alvarez (10/1), Eloy Mejía (4/0), José Mendoza (5/1) [Luis Montenegro (1/0)], José María Jiménez (10/3), Enrique Raymondi Chávez (8/1), Víctor Aguayo (4/2), Pedro Acevedo (10/0). Trainer: Rodolfo Orlandini (4).

24. 18.02.1945 **COLOMBIA - ECUADOR** **3-1(1-1)** 18th Copa América
Estadio Nacional, Santiago (Chile); Referee: Nobel Valentini (Uruguay); Attendance: 65,000
ECU: Napoleón Medina (11/0), Jorge Henríquez (5/0), Félix Leyton Zurita (10/0), Carlos Garnica (3/0), Enrique Alvarez (11/1), Eloy Mejía (5/0), Luis Montenegro (2/0), José María Jiménez (11/3), Enrique Raymondi Chávez (9/1), Víctor Aguayo (5/3), Pedro Acevedo (11/0) [José Mendoza (6/1)]. Trainer: Rodolfo Orlandini (5).
Goal: Víctor Aguayo (4).

25. 21.02.1945 **BRAZIL - ECUADOR** **9-2(5-1)** 18th Copa América

Estadio Nacional, Santiago (Chile); Referee: José Bartolomé Macías (Argentina); Attendance: 22,000

ECU: Napoleón Medina (12/0) [Víctor Suárez (1/0)], Félix Leyton Zurita (11/0), Jorge Henríquez (6/0) [Francisco Villagómez (2/0)], Luis Mendoza (15/1), Enrique Alvarez (12/1), Eloy Mejía (6/0), Luis Montenegro (3/0), José María Jiménez (12/3), Guillermo Albornoz (1/1), Víctor Aguayo (6/4), José Mendoza (7/1). Trainer: Rodolfo Orlandini (6).

Goals: Víctor Aguayo (42), Guillermo Albornoz (49).

26. 30.11.1947 **ECUADOR - BOLIVIA** **2-2(2-2)** 20th Copa América

Estadio „George Capwell", Guayaquil; Referee: Luis Alberto Fernández (Uruguay); Attendance: 30,000

ECU: Napoleón Medina (13/0), Jorge Henríquez (7/0), Félix Leyton Zurita (12/0), Celso Torres (6/0), Enrique Alvarez (13/1) [Eduardo Ortiz (1/0)], Luis Mendoza (16/1), Federico Zenck (1/0), José Mendoza (8/1), José María Jiménez (13/5), Víctor Aguayo (7/4) [Enrique Cantos (1/0)], Gonzalo Pozo (1/0). Trainer: Ramón Unamuno (5).

Goals: José María Jiménez (1, 24).

27. 04.12.1947 **ECUADOR - COLOMBIA** **0-0** 20th Copa América

Estadio „George Capwell", Guayaquil; Referee: Mario Rubén Heyn (Paraguay); Attendance: 30,000

ECU: Napoleón Medina (14/0), Jorge Henríquez (8/0), Félix Leyton Zurita (13/0), Heráclides Marín (1/0) [Luis Mendoza (17/1)], Ricardo Riveros (1/0) [Celso Torres (7/0)], Eduardo Ortiz (2/0), Víctor Cevallos (1/0), César Garnica (1/0) [Guillermo Gavilánez (4/0)], José María Jiménez (14/5), Enrique Cantos (2/0), Gonzalo Pozo (2/0). Trainer: Ramón Unamuno (6).

28. 11.12.1947 **ECUADOR - CHILE** **0-3(0-0)** 20th Copa América

Estadio „George Capwell", Guayaquil; Referee: Juan José Alvarez (Argentina); Attendance: 22,000

ECU: Luis Alfredo Carrillo (1/0), Carlos Sánchez (1/0), Félix Leyton Zurita (14/0), Heráclides Marín (2/0), Enrique Alvarez (14/1), Alfredo Molina (1/0), Víctor Cevallos (2/0), Federico Zenck (2/0), José María Jiménez (15/5), José Vargas (1/0), Gonzalo Pozo (3/0). Trainer: Ramón Unamuno (7).

29. 16.12.1947 **ECUADOR - URUGUAY** **1-6(0-5)** 20th Copa América

Estadio „George Capwell", Guayaquil; Referee: Víctor Francisco Rivas (Chile); Attendance: 30,000

ECU: Luis Alfredo Carrillo (2/0), Jorge Henríquez (9/0), Carlos Sánchez (2/0), Celso Torres (8/0) [Ricardo Riveros (2/0)], Eduardo Ortiz (3/0), Luis Mendoza (18/1), César Garnica (2/1), José Mendoza (9/1) [José María Jiménez (16/5)], Guillermo Gavilánez (5/0), Víctor Aguayo (8/4) [Federico Zenck (3/0)], Gonzalo Pozo (4/0). Trainer: Ramón Unamuno (8).

Goal: César Garnica (51).

30. 20.12.1947 **ECUADOR - PERU** **0-0** 20th Copa América

Estadio „George Capwell", Guayaquil; Referee: Mario Rubén Heyn (Paraguay); Attendance: 20,000

ECU: Napoleón Medina (15/0), Jorge Henríquez (10/0), Félix Leyton Zurita (15/0), Ricardo Riveros (3/0) [Enrique Alvarez (15/1)], Eduardo Ortiz (4/0), Luis Mendoza (19/1), César Garnica (3/1), José Mendoza (10/1), José María Jiménez (17/5), Víctor Aguayo (9/4) [Enrique Cantos (3/0)], Guillermo Gavilánez (6/0) [Heráclides Marín (3/0)]. Trainer: Ramón Unamuno (9).

31. 25.12.1947 **ARGENTINA - ECUADOR** **2-0(1-0)** 20th Copa América

Estadio „George Capwell", Guayaquil; Referee: Alfredo Alvarez (Bolivia), from 35' Mario Rubén Heyn (Paraguay)

ECU: Napoleón Medina (16/0), Jorge Henríquez (11/0), Félix Leyton Zurita (16/0), Ricardo Riveros (4/0) [Heráclides Marín (4/0)], Enrique Alvarez (16/1) [Eduardo Ortiz (5/0)], Luis Mendoza (20/1), Víctor Cevallos (3/0), Federico Zenck (4/0) [Guillermo Gavilánez (7/0)], José María Jiménez (18/5), Víctor Aguayo (10/4), Gonzalo Pozo (5/0). Trainer: Ramón Unamuno (10).

32. 29.12.1947 **PARAGUAY - ECUADOR** **4-0** 20th Copa América

Estadio „George Capwell", Guayaquil; Referee: Luis Alberto Fernández (Uruguay); Attendance: 5,000

ECU: Napoleón Medina (17/0), Jorge Henríquez (12/0), Félix Leyton Zurita (17/0), Ricardo Riveros (5/0) [Heráclides Marín (5/0)], Eduardo Ortiz (6/0) [Guillermo Gavilánez (8/0)], Luis Mendoza (21/1), Enrique Alvarez (17/1), José Mendoza (11/1), César Garnica (4/1) [Gonzalo Pozo (6/0)], José María Jiménez (19/5), Víctor Aguayo (11/4). Trainer: Ramón Unamuno (11).

33. 03.04.1949 **BRAZIL – ECUADOR** **9-1(7-1)** 21th Copa América

Estádio São Januario, Rio de Janeiro; Referee: Cyril Jack Barrick (England); Attendance: 70,000

ECU: Luis Alfredo Carrillo (3/0), Mario Lovato (1/0) [Carlos Sánchez (3/0)], Marcos Bermeo (1/0), Luis Torres (1/0), Luis Vásquez (1/0), Heráclides Marín (6/0) [Jorge Cantos (1/0)], Víctor Arteaga (1/0), Enrique Cantos (4/0), Sigfredo Agapito Chuchuca (1/1), José Vargas (2/0), Guido Andrade (1/0). Trainer: José Planas (1).

Goal: Sigfredo Agapito Chuchuca (18).

34. 10.04.1949 **PARAGUAY - ECUADOR** **1-0(0-0)** 21th Copa América

Estádio São Januario, Rio de Janeiro (Brazil); Referee: Juan Carlos Armental (Uruguay); Attendance: 15,000

ECU: Félix Torres (1/0), Carlos Sánchez (4/0), Marcos Bermeo (2/0), Ricardo Riveros (6/0), Luis Vásquez (2/0), Heráclides Marín (7/0), Marcos Spencer (1/0) [Víctor Arteaga (2/0)], Enrique Cantos (5/0), Sigfredo Agapito Chuchuca (2/1) [Rafael Maldonado (1/0)], José Vargas (3/0), Guido Andrade (2/0). Trainer: José Planas (2).

35. 13.04.1949 **URUGUAY - ECUADOR** **3-2(2-2)** 21th Copa América

Estádio São Januario, Rio de Janeiro (Brazil); Referee: Alberto Da Gama Malcher (Brazil); Attendance: 30,000

ECU: Félix Torres (2/0), Carlos Sánchez (5/0), Marcos Bermeo (3/0), Hernán Salgado (1/0), Luis Vásquez (3/1), Heráclides Marín (8/0), Víctor Arteaga (3/1), Enrique Cantos (6/0), Rafael Maldonado (2/0), José Vargas (4/0) [Sigfredo Agapito Chuchuca (3/1)], Gonzalo Pozo (7/0) [Guido Andrade (3/0)]. Trainer: José Planas (3).

Goals: Víctor Arteaga (35), Luis Vásquez (40).

36. 17.04.1949 **CHILE - ECUADOR** **1-0(1-0)** 21th Copa América

Estádio São Januario, Rio de Janeiro (Brazil); Referee: Cyril John Barrick (England); Attendance: 8,000

ECU: Félix Torres (3/0), Carlos Sánchez (6/0), Bolívar Andrade (1/0) [Mario Lovato (2/0)], Hernán Salgado (2/0), Jorge Cantos (2/0) [Luis Vásquez (4/1)], Luis Torres (2/0) [Ricardo Riveros (7/0)], Víctor Arteaga (4/1), Sigfredo Agapito Chuchuca (4/1), Rafael Maldonado (3/0), César Garnica (5/1), Gonzalo Pozo (8/0). Trainer: José Planas (4).

37. 20.04.1949 **PERU - ECUADOR** **4-0(2-0)** 21th Copa América
Estádio São Januario, Rio de Janeiro (Brazil); Referee: Juan Carlos Armental (Uruguay); Attendance: 7,000
ECU: Félix Torres (4/0) [Luis Alfredo Carrillo (4/0)], Carlos Sánchez (7/0), Marcos Bermeo (4/0) [*sent off*], Hernán Salgado (3/0), Luis Vásquez (5/1), Ricardo Riveros (8/0), Enrique Cantos (7/0) [César Garnica (6/1)], Rafael Maldonado (4/0) [Marcos Spencer (2/0)], Víctor Arteaga (5/1), José Vargas (5/0), Guido Andrade (4/0). Trainer: José Planas (5).

38. 25.04.1949 **BOLIVIA – ECUADOR** **2-0(2-0)** 21th Copa América
Estádio Pacaembú, São Paulo (Brazil); Referee: Mario Gardelli (Brazil); Attendance: 14,000
ECU: Félix Torres (5/0), Carlos Sánchez (8/0), Bolívar Andrade (2/0), Luis Vásquez (6/1), Ricardo Riveros (9/0), Heráclides Marín (9/0), Marcos Spencer (3/0), Enrique Cantos (8/0) [Sigfredo Agapito Chuchuca (5/1)], José María Jiménez (20/5), Rafael Maldonado (5/0) [Guido Andrade (5/0)], Gonzalo Pozo (9/0). Trainer: José Planas (6).

39. 03.05.1949 **ECUADOR - COLOMBIA** **4-1(2-1)** 21st Copa América
Estádio São Januario, Rio de Janeiro; Referee: Alfredo Alvarez (Bolivia); Attendance: 3,000
ECU: Félix Torres (6/0), Carlos Sánchez (9/0), Marcos Bermeo (5/0), Ricardo Riveros (10/0), Jorge Cantos (3/0), Hernán Salgado (4/0), Marcos Spencer (4/0) [Víctor Arteaga (6/1)], Enrique Cantos (9/1) [César Garnica (7/1)], Rafael Maldonado (6/1), José Vargas (6/1), Guido Andrade (6/1). Trainer: José Planas (7).
Goals: Enrique Cantos (23), José Vargas (44), Guido Andrade (49), Rafael Maldonado (74).

40. 28.02.1953 **PERU - ECUADOR** **1-0(0-0)** 22nd Copa América
Estadio Nacional, Lima; Referee: George Rhoden (England); Attendance: 50,000
ECU: Alfredo Bonnard (1/0), Carlos Sánchez (10/0), Jorge Henríquez (13/0), Heráclides Marín (10/0) [César Solórzano (1/0)], Jorge Izaguirre (1/0), Ricardo Riveros (11/0) [Orlando Zambrano (1/0)], Víctor Arteaga (7/1), Daniel Pinto (1/0), Sigfredo Agapito Chuchuca (6/1) [Luis Marañón (1/0)], José Vargas (7/1), Eduardo Guzmán (1/0). Trainer: Gregorio Juan Esperón (1).

41. 04.03.1953 **PARAGUAY - ECUADOR** **0-0** 22nd Copa América
Estadio Nacional, Lima (Peru); Referee: Mário Gonçalves Vianna (Brazil); Attendance: 45,000
ECU: Alfredo Bonnard (2/0), Carlos Sánchez (11/0), Jorge Henríquez (14/0), Heráclides Marín (11/0), Jorge Izaguirre (2/0), Ricardo Riveros (12/0), Luis Marañón (2/0), Daniel Pinto (2/0), José Vicente Balseca (1/0), José Vargas (8/1), Raúl Pio de la Torre (1/0) [Eduardo Guzmán (2/0)]. Trainer: Gregorio Juan Esperón (2).

42. 08.03.1953 **BOLIVIA - ECUADOR** **1-1(1-1)** 22nd Copa América
Estadio Nacional, Lima (Peru); Referee: Charles McKenna (England); Attendance: 45,000
ECU: Alfredo Bonnard (3/0), Carlos Sánchez (12/0), Jorge Henríquez (15/0), Heráclides Marín (12/0), Jorge Izaguirre (3/0) [Galo Solís (1/0)], Ricardo Riveros (13/0), Luis Marañón (3/0), Daniel Pinto (3/0) [Víctor Arteaga (8/1)], José Vicente Balseca (2/0), Rafael Maldonado (7/1) [José Vargas (9/1), Eduardo Guzmán (3/1). Trainer: Gregorio Juan Esperón (3).
Goal: Eduardo Guzmán (6).

43. 12.03.1953 **BRAZIL – ECUADOR** **2-0(1-0)** 22nd Copa América
Estadio Nacional, Lima (Peru); Referee: Richard Maddison (England); Attendance: 35,000
ECU: Alfredo Bonnard (4/0), Carlos Sánchez (13/0), Jorge Henríquez (16/0), Mario Lovato (3/0), Heráclides Marín (13/0), Galo Solís (2/0), Sigfredo Agapito Chuchuca (7/1) [Luis Marañón (4/0)], Daniel Pinto (4/0), José Vicente Balseca (3/0), José Vargas (10/1), Eduardo Guzmán (4/1). Trainer: Gregorio Juan Esperón (4).

44. 19.03.1953 **CHILE – ECUADOR** **3-0(1-0)** 22nd Copa América
Estadio Nacional, Lima (Peru); Referee: Richard Maddison (England); Attendance: 44,415
ECU: Alfredo Bonnard (5/0), Carlos Sánchez (14/0), Jorge Henríquez (17/0), Heráclides Marín (14/0), Mario Lovato (4/0) [Jorge Izaguirre (4/0), Ricardo Riveros (14/0)], Galo Solís (3/0), Sigfredo Agapito Chuchuca (8/1) [Luis Marañón (5/0)], Daniel Pinto (5/0), José Vicente Balseca (4/0), José Vargas (11/1), Eduardo Guzmán (5/1). Trainer: Gregorio Juan Esperón (5).

45. 23.03.1953 **URUGUAY - ECUADOR** **6-0(1-0)** 22nd Copa América
Estadio Nacional, Lima (Peru); Referee: David Gregory (England); Attendance: 35,000
ECU: Alfredo Bonnard (6/0), Carlos Sánchez (15/0), Jorge Henríquez (18/0), César Solórzano (2/0) [Orlando Zambrano (2/0)], Jorge Izaguirre (5/0), Ricardo Riveros (15/0) [Galo Solís (4/0)], Luis Marañón (6/0), Víctor Arteaga (9/1), Daniel Pinto (6/0) [José Vargas (12/1)], José Vicente Balseca (5/0), Raúl Pio de la Torre (2/0). Trainer: Gregorio Juan Esperón (6).

46. 27.02.1955 **CHILE - ECUADOR** **7-1(4-0)** 23rd Copa América
Estadio Nacional, Santiago; Referee: Washington Rodríguez (Uruguay); Attendance: 32,450
ECU: Alfredo Bonnard (7/0), Carlos Sánchez (16/0), Gerónimo Gando (1/0), Carlos Alume (1/0), Jorge Izaguirre (6/0) [Washington Villacreses (1/1)], Orlando Zambrano (3/0) [Ricardo Valencia (1/0)], José Vicente Balseca (6/0), Enrique Cantos (10/1) [Daniel Pinto (7/0)], Isidro Matute (1/0), Colón Merizalde (1/0), Simon Climaco Cañarte (1/0). Trainer: José María Díaz Granados (1).
Goal: Washington Villacreses (64).

47. 09.03.1955 **ARGENTINA - ECUADOR** **4-0(3-0)** 23rd Copa América
Estadio Nacional, Santiago (Chile); Referee: Carlos Robles (Chile); Attendance: 40,000
ECU: Alfredo Bonnard (8/0), Carlos Sánchez (17/0), Ricardo Valencia (2/0), Honorato Gonzabay (1/0), Washington Villacreses (2/1), Galo Solís (5/0), José Vicente Balseca (7/0), Enrique Cantos (11/1) [Simon Climaco Cañarte (2/0)], Isidro Matute (2/0), Colón Merizalde (2/0), Mario Saeteros (1/0) [Daniel Pinto (8/0)]. Trainer: José María Díaz Granados (2).

48. 13.03.1955 **PERU - ECUADOR** **4-2(3-1)** 23rd Copa América
Estadio Nacional, Santiago (Chile); Referee: Carlos Robles (Chile); Attendance: 50,000
ECU: Alfredo Bonnard (9/0), Carlos Sánchez (18/0), Ricardo Valencia (3/0), Honorato Gonzabay (2/0), Washington Villacreses (3/1), Galo Solís (6/0), José Vicente Balseca (8/0), Daniel Pinto (9/0), Isidro Matute (3/2), Elías Gereneldo Triviño (1/0), Mario Saeteros (2/0) [Simon Climaco Cañarte (3/0)]. Trainer: José María Díaz Granados (3).
Goals: Isidro Matute (34, 61).

49. 16.03.1955 **PARAGUAY - ECUADOR** **2-0(2-0)** 23rd Copa América
Estadio Nacional, Santiago (Chile); Referee: Carlos Robles (Chile); Attendance: 35,000
ECU: Alfredo Bonnard (10/0), Carlos Sánchez (19/0), Ricardo Valencia (4/0), Honorato Gonzabay (3/0), Washington Villacreses (4/1), Galo Solís (7/0), José Vicente Balseca (9/0), Colón Merizalde (3/0) [Enrique Cantos (12/1)], Isidro Matute (4/2) [Daniel Pinto (10/0)], Elías Gereneldo Triviño (2/0), Mario Saeteros (3/0). Trainer: José María Díaz Granados (4).

50. 23.03.1955 **URUGUAY - ECUADOR** **5-1(3-1)** 23rd Copa América
Estadio Nacional, Santiago (Chile); Referee: Roberto González (Paraguay); Attendance: 25,000
ECU: Alfredo Bonnard (11/0) [Hugo Mejía (1/0)], Carlos Sánchez (20/0), Galo Solís (8/0), Honorato Gonzabay (4/0), Jorge Izaguirre (7/0) [Gerónimo Gando (2/0)], Washington Villacreses (5/1) [Rómulo Gómez (1/0)], José Vicente Balseca (10/0), Elías Gereneldo Triviño (3/0), Isidro Matute (5/3), Simon Climaco Cañarte (4/0), Mario Saeteros (4/0). Trainer: José María Díaz Granados (5).
Goal: Isidro Matute (36).

51. 07.03.1957 **URUGUAY - ECUADOR** **5-2(2-2)** 25th Copa América
Estadio Nacional, Lima (Peru); Referee: Erwin Hieger (Austria); Attendance: 50,000
ECU: Cipriano Yu Lee (1/0), Honorato Gonzabay (5/0), Luciano Macías (1/0), César Solórzano (3/0) [Jaime Galarza (1/0)], Raúl Arguello (1/0) [Ezio Martínez (1/0)], Julio Caisaguano (1/0), Gonzalo Salcedo (1/0), Enrique Cantos (13/2), Jorge Larraz (1/1), José Vargas (13/1) [Colón Merizalde (4/0)], Simon Climaco Cañarte (5/0). Trainer: Eduardo Spandre (1).
Goals: Enrique Cantos (12), Jorge Larraz (40).

52. 10.03.1957 **PERU - ECUADOR** **2-1(1-1)** 25th Copa América
Estadio Nacional, Lima; Referee: Robert Turner (England); Attendance: 55,000
ECU: Alfredo Bonnard (12/0), Raúl Arguello (2/0), César Solórzano (4/0), Luciano Macías (2/0), Jaime Galarza (2/0) [Julio Caisaguano (2/0)], Honorato Gonzabay (6/0), José Vicente Balseca (11/0), Enrique Cantos (14/3) [Gonzalo Salcedo (2/0)], Isidro Matute (6/3) [José Vargas (14/1)], Jorge Larraz (2/1), Simon Climaco Cañarte (6/0). Trainer: Eduardo Spandre (2).
Goal: Enrique Cantos (44).

53. 17.03.1957 **ARGENTINA - ECUADOR** **3-0(3-0)** 25th Copa América
Estadio Nacional, Lima (Peru); Referee: Bertley Cross (England); Attendance: 50,000
ECU: Alfredo Bonnard (13/0), Raúl Arguello (3/0), Julio Caisaguano (3/0) [Hugo Pardo (1/0)], Luciano Macías (3/0), César Solórzano (5/0), Honorato Gonzabay (7/0), Gonzalo Salcedo (3/0), Daniel Pinto (11/0) [Isidro Matute (7/3)], José Vicente Balseca (12/0), Jorge Larraz (3/1), Júpiter Miranda (1/0). Trainer: Eduardo Spandre (3).

54. 21.03.1957 **BRAZIL - ECUADOR** **7-1(4-0)** 25th Copa América
Estadio Nacional, Lima (Peru); Referee: Ronald Lynch (England); Attendance: 45,000
ECU: Alfredo Bonnard (14/0) [Cipriano Yu Lee (2/0)], Raúl Arguello (4/0), Honorato Gonzabay (8/0), Julio Caisaguano (4/0) [Hugo Pardo (2/0)], Luciano Macías (4/0), César Solórzano (6/0), José Vicente Balseca (13/0), Enrique Cantos (15/3), Jorge Larraz (4/2), José Vargas (15/1), Simon Climaco Cañarte (7/0). Trainer: Eduardo Spandre (4).
Goal: Jorge Larraz (80 penalty).

55. 24.03.1957 **CHILE - ECUADOR** **2-2(2-1)** 25th Copa América
Estadio Nacional, Lima (Peru); Referee: Erwin Hieger (Austria); Attendance: 45,000
ECU: Alfredo Bonnard (15/0), Hugo Pardo (3/0), César Solórzano (7/0), Raúl Arguello (5/0), José Vargas (16/1), Carlos Sánchez (21/0), Gonzalo Salcedo (4/0) [Simon Climaco Cañarte (8/0)], Enrique Cantos (16/4) [Isidro Matute (8/3)], José Vicente Balseca (14/0), Jorge Larraz (5/3), Júpiter Miranda (2/0). Trainer: Eduardo Spandre (5).
Goals: Jorge Larraz (25 penalty), Enrique Cantos (59).

56. 01.04.1957 **COLOMBIA - ECUADOR** **4-1** 25th Copa América
Estadio Nacional, Lima (Peru); Referee: Harry Davis (England); Attendance: 40,000
ECU: Alfredo Bonnard (16/0), Carlos Sánchez (22/0), Hugo Pardo (4/0), César Solórzano (8/0) [Rómulo Gómez (2/0)], Raúl Arguello (6/0), José Vargas (17/1), Gonzalo Salcedo (5/0), Enrique Cantos (17/4) [Daniel Pinto (12/0)], José Vicente Balseca (15/0) [Isidro Matute (9/3)], Jorge Larraz (6/4), Júpiter Miranda (3/0). Trainer: Eduardo Spandre (6).
Goal: Jorge Larraz (14 penalty)

57. 06.12.1959 **ECUADOR - URUGUAY** **0-4(0-2)** 25th Copa América
Estadio Modelo, Guayaquil; Referee: José Luis Praddaude (Argentina); Attendance: 55,000
ECU: Alfredo Bonnard (17/0), Raúl Argüello (7/0), Honorato Gonzabay (9/0), Flavio Nall (1/0) [Jorge Izaguirre (8/0)], Jaime Galarza (3/0) [Ruperto Reeves Patterson (1/0)], Rómulo Gómez (3/0), José Vicente Balseca (16/0), Leonardo Palacios (1/0), Alberto Pedro Spencer Herrera (1/0), Carlos Alberto Raffo (1/0), Francisco Almeida (1/0). Trainer: Juan López Fontana (1).

58. 12.12.1959 **ECUADOR – ARGENTINA** **1-1(1-0)** 27th Copa América
Estadio Modelo, Guayaquil; Referee: José Gomes Sobrinho (Brazil); Attendance: 55,000
ECU: Alfredo Bonnard (18/0), Raúl Argüello (8/0), Honorato Gonzabay (10/0), Jorge Izaguirre (9/0), Jaime Galarza (4/0) [Ruperto Reeves Patterson (2/0)], Rómulo Gómez (4/0), José Vicente Balseca (17/0), Leonardo Palacios (2/0), Alberto Pedro Spencer Herrera (2/0), Carlos Alberto Raffo (2/1) [Mario Saeteros (5/0)], Simon Climaco Cañarte (9/0) [Francisco Almeida (2/0)]. Trainer: Juan López Fontana (2).
Goal: Carlos Alberto Raffo (20).

59. 19.12.1959 **ECUADOR – BRAZIL** **1-3(1-3)** 27th Copa América
Estadio Modelo, Guayaquil; Referee: Esteban Marino (Uruguay); Attendance: 55,000
ECU: Alfredo Bonnard (19/0), Raúl Argüello (9/0), Honorato Gonzabay (11/0), Jorge Izaguirre (10/0), Jaime Galarza (5/0) [Ruperto Reeves Patterson (3/0], Rómulo Gómez (5/0), José Vicente Balseca (18/0) [Nelson Vicente Aurea (1/0)], Leonardo Palacios (3/0), Alberto Pedro Spencer Herrera (3/0), Carlos Alberto Raffo (3/2), Simon Climaco Cañarte (10/0). Trainer: Juan López Fontana (3).
Goal: Carlos Alberto Raffo (12).

60. 25.12.1959 **ECUADOR - PARAGUAY** **3-1(2-1)** 27th Copa América
Estadio Modelo, Guayaquil; Referee: José Gomes Sobrinho (Brazil); Attendance: 55,000
ECU: Cipriano Yu Lee (3/0), Raúl Argüello (10/0), Honorato Gonzabay (12/0), Flavio Nall (2/0), Jaime Galarza (6/0), Rómulo Gómez (6/0), José Vicente Balseca (19/1), Leonardo Palacios (4/0) [Ernesto Guerra (1/0)], Alberto Pedro Spencer Herrera (4/1) [Mario Saeteros (6/0)], Carlos Alberto Raffo (4/2), Simon Climaco Cañarte (11/1). Trainer: Juan López Fontana (4).
Goals: Alberto Pedro Spencer Herrera (16), José Vicente Balseca (25), Simon Climaco Cañarte (74).

61. 27.12.1959 **ECUADOR – BRAZIL** **1-2**
Estadio Olimpico, Guayaquil; Referee: José Gomes Sobrinho (Brazil)
ECU: Cipriano Yu Lee (4/0), Raúl Arguello (11/0), Vicente Lecaro (1/0), Flavio Nall (3/0) [Jaime Ubilla (1/0)], Ruperto Reeves Patterson (4/0) [Alberto Cruz Avila (1/0)], Jaime Galarza (7/0) [Rómulo Gómez (7/0)], José Vicente Balseca (20/1), Leonardo Palacios (5/0), Mario Saeteros (7/0), Carlos Alberto Raffo (5/3), Simon Climaco Cañarte (12/1). Trainer: Juan López Fontana (5).
Goal: Carlos Alberto Raffo.

62. 04.12.1960 **ECUADOR - ARGENTINA** **3-6(0-4)** 7th FIFA WC. Qualifiers
Estadio Olimpico, Guayaquil; Referee: Juan Carlos Robles (Chile); Attendance: 60,000
ECU: Cipriano Yu Lee (5/0), Luciano Macías (5/0), Jorge Izaguirre (11/0), Vicente Lecaro (2/0), Jaime Galarza (8/0), Rómulo Gómez (8/0), José Vicente Balseca (21/1), Jorge Washington Bolaños (1/0), Carlos Alberto Raffo (6/5), Alberto Pedro Spencer Herrera (5/2), Simon Climaco Cañarte (13/1). Trainer: Juan López Fontana (6).
Goals: Alberto Pedro Spencer Herrera (81), Carlos Alberto Raffo (83, 85).

63. 17.12.1960 **ARGENTINA - ECUADOR** **5-0(1-0)** 7th FIFA WC. Qualifiers
Estadio „Alberto Armando“, Buenos Aires; Referee: Juan Carlos Robles (Chile); Attendance: 50,000
ECU: Cipriano Yu Lee (6/0), Luciano Macías (6/0), Raúl Arguello (12/0), Vicente Lecaro (3/0), Jaime Galarza (9/0), Rómulo Gómez (9/0), José Vicente Balseca (22/1), Leonardo Palacios (6/0), Jorge Washington Bolaños (2/0), Carlos Alberto Raffo (7/5), Simon Climaco Cañarte (14/1). Trainer: Juan López Fontana (7).

64. 10.03.1963 **BOLIVIA – ECUADOR** **4-4(2-2)** 28th Copa América
Estadio „Hernándo Siles Zuazo“, La Paz; Referee: Arturo Maximo Yamasaki Maldonado (Peru); Attendance: 15,000
ECU: Hugo Mejía (2/0), Jaime Galarza (10/0) [José Johnson (1/0)], Vicente Lecaro (4/0), Ruperto Reeves Patterson (5/0), Alfonso Quijano (1/0), Luciano Macías (7/0), José Vicente Balseca (23/1) [Pedro Gando (1/0)], Jorge Washington Bolaños (3/0), Carlos Alberto Raffo (8/7), Enrique Raymondi Contreras (1/2) [Leonardo Palacios (7/0)], Armando Tito Larrea (1/0). Trainer: Fausto Montalván (1).
Goals: Carlos Alberto Raffo (30), Enrique Raymondi Contreras (44), Carlos Alberto Raffo (47), Enrique Raymondi Contreras (50).

65. 14.03.1963 **PARAGUAY – ECUADOR** **3-1(1-1)** 28th Copa América
Estadio „Hernándo Siles Zuazo“, La Paz (Bolivia); Referee: Luis Ventre (Argentina); Attendance: 15,000
ECU: Hugo Mejía (3/0) [Pablo Ansaldo (1/0)], Luciano Macías (8/0), Carlos Pineda (1/0), Vicente Lecaro (5/0), Jaime Galarza (11/0), Alfonso Quijano (2/0), Pedro Gando (2/0), Jorge Washington Bolaños (4/0), Carlos Alberto Raffo (9/8) [Néstor Azón (1/0)], Enrique Raymondi Contreras (2/2) [José Vicente Balseca (24/1)], Armando Tito Larrea (2/0). Trainer: Fausto Montalván (2).
Goal: Carlos Alberto Raffo (32).

66. 17.03.1963 **PERU – ECUADOR** **2-1(2-1)** 28th Copa América
Estadio „Hernándo Siles Zuazo“, La Paz (Bolivia); Referee: Ovidio Orrego (Colombia); Attendance: 8,000
ECU: Pablo Ansaldo (2/0) [Hugo Mejía (4/0)], Luciano Macías (9/0), Vicente Lecaro (6/0), José Johnson (2/0), Jaime Galarza (12/0), Alfonso Quijano (3/0) [Miguel Bustamante (1/0)], Pedro Gando (3/0), Jorge Washington Bolaños (5/0), Carlos Alberto Raffo (10/9), Enrique Raymondi Contreras (3/2) [Néstor Azón (2/0)], Armando Tito Larrea (3/0). Trainer: Fausto Montalván (3).
Goal: Carlos Alberto Raffo (20).

67. 20.03.1963 **ARGENTINA – ECUADOR** **4-2(1-1)** 28th Copa América
Estadio „Félix Capriles“, Cochabamba (Bolivia); Referee: Arturo Maximo Yamasaki Maldonado (Peru); Attendance: 20,000
ECU: Hugo Mejía (5/0) [Pablo Ansaldo (3/0)], Miguel Bustamante (2/0), Vicente Lecaro (7/0), José Johnson (3/0), Carlos Pineda (2/1) [Jaime Galarza (13/0)], Luciano Macías (10/0), Pedro Gando (4/0), Leonardo Palacios (8/1), Carlos Alberto Raffo (11/9), Enrique Raymondi Contreras (4/2), Armando Tito Larrea (4/0) [Simon Climaco Cañarte (15/1)]. Trainer: Fausto Montalván (4).
Goals: Carlos Pineda (32), Leonardo Palacios (49).

68. 27.03.1963 **BRAZIL – ECUADOR** **2-2(1-0)** 28th Copa América
Estadio „Félix Capriles“, Cochabamba (Bolivia); Referee: José Dimas Larrosa (Paraguay); Attendance: 20,000
ECU: Hugo Mejía (6/0), Miguel Bustamante (3/0), Alfonso Quijano (4/0) [Luciano Macías (11/0)], José Johnson (4/0), Ruperto Reeves Patterson (6/0) [Jaime Galarza (14/0)], Vicente Lecaro (8/0), Pedro Gando (5/0), Bolívar Merizalde (1/0) [Carlos Alberto Raffo (12/10)], Néstor Azón (3/1), Leonardo Palacios (9/1), Armando Tito Larrea (5/0). Trainer: Fausto Montalván (5).
Goals: Néstor Azón (84), Carlos Alberto Raffo (90).

69. 31.03.1963 **ECUADOR - COLOMBIA** **4-3(2-0)** 28th Copa América
Estadio „Hernándo Siles Zuazo“, La Paz (Bolivia); Referee: José Dimas Larrosa (Paraguay); Attendance: 15,000
ECU: Pablo Ansaldo (4/0) [Hugo Mejía (7/0)], Miguel Bustamante (4/0), Luciano Macías (12/0), Carlos Pineda (3/1), José Johnson (5/0), Vicente Lecaro (9/0), Pedro Gando (6/0), Enrique Raymondi Contreras (5/3) [Leonardo Palacios (10/2)], Carlos Alberto Raffo (13/10), Jorge Washington Bolaños (6/0) [Néstor Azón (4/2)], Armando Tito Larrea (6/1). Trainer: Fausto Montalván (6).
Goals: Enrique Raymondi Contreras (30), Armando Larrea (37), Leonardo Palacios (53), Néstor Azón (88).

70. 20.07.1965 **COLOMBIA - ECUADOR** **0-1(0-1)** 8th FIFA WC. Qualifiers
Estadio Municipal, Barranquilla; Referee: Enrique Montes (Peru); Attendance: 10,175
ECU: Pablo Ansaldo (5/0), Alfonso Quijano (5/0), Vicente Lecaro (10/0), Luciano Macías (13/0), Miguel Bustamante (5/0), Rómulo Gómez (10/0), Simon Climaco Cañarte (16/1), Washington Muñoz (1/1), Jorge Washington Bolaños (7/0), Enrique Raymondi Contreras (6/3), Armando Tito Larrea (7/1). Trainer: José María Rodríguez (1).
Goal: Washington Muñoz (18).

71. 25.07.1965 **ECUADOR - COLOMBIA** **2-0(0-0)** 8th FIFA WC. Qualifiers
Estadio Modelo, Guayaquil; Referee: Luis Spinetto (Argentina); Attendance: 48,457
ECU:. Pablo Ansaldo (6/0), Alfonso Quijano (6/0), Vicente Lecaro (11/0), Luciano Macías (14/0), Miguel Bustamante (6/0), Rómulo Gómez (11/0), Washington Muñoz (2/1), Jorge Washington Bolaños (8/0), Enrique Raymondi Contreras (7/5), Mario Zambrano (1/0), Armando Tito Larrea (8/1). Trainer: José María Rodríguez (2).
Goals: Enrique Raymondi Contreras (56, 77).

72. 15.08.1965 **ECUADOR - CHILE** **2-2(1-1)** 8th FIFA WC. Qualifiers
Estadio Modelo, Guayaquil; Referee: Eunápio Gouveia de Queiroz (Brazil); Attendance: 50,041
ECU: Pablo Ansaldo (7/0), Alfonso Quijano (7/0), Vicente Lecaro (12/0), Luciano Macías (15/0), Miguel Bustamante (7/0), Rómulo Gómez (12/0), Simon Climaco Cañarte (17/1), Washington Muñoz (3/1), Alberto Pedro Spencer Herrera (6/3), Jorge Washington Bolaños (9/0), Enrique Raymondi Contreras (8/6). Trainer: José María Rodríguez (3).
Goals: Alberto Pedro Spencer Herrera (15), Enrique Raymondi Contreras (85).

73. 22.08.1965 **CHILE - ECUADOR** **3-1(1-1)** 8th FIFA WC. Qualifiers
Estadio Nacional, Santiago; Referee: José María Codesal (Uruguay); Attendance: 70,602
ECU: Alfredo Bonnard (20/0), Alfonso Quijano (8/0), Vicente Lecaro (13/0), Luciano Macías (16/0), Felipe Mina (1/0), Mario Zambrano (2/0), Washington Muñoz (4/1), Jorge Washington Bolaños (10/0), Alberto Pedro Spencer Herrera (7/4), Simon Climaco Cañarte (18/1), Armando Tito Larrea (9/1). Trainer: José María Rodríguez (4).
Goal: Alberto Pedro Spencer Herrera (36).

74. 12.10.1965 **CHILE - ECUADOR** **2-1(2-0)** 8th FIFA WC. Qualifiers (Play-off)
Estadio Nacional, Lima (Peru); Referee: Roberto Héctor Goicoechea (Argentina); Attendance: 44,864
ECU: Helio Carreira Da Silva "Helinho" (1/0), Alfonso Quijano (9/0), Vicente Lecaro (14/0), Luciano Macías (17/1), Felipe Mina (2/0), Rómulo Gómez (13/0), Washington Muñoz (5/1), Jorge Washington Bolaños (11/0), Alberto Pedro Spencer Herrera (8/4), Carlos Pineda (4/1), Bolívar Merizalde (2/0). Trainer: José María Rodríguez (5).
Goal: Luciano Macías (89).

75. 21.12.1966 **ECUADOR - PARAGUAY** **2-2(0-0)** 29th Copa América (Qualifiers)
Estadio Modelo, Guayaquil; Referee: Duval Goicoechea (Argentina); Attendance: 47,000
ECU: Helio Carreira Da Silva "Helinho" (2/0), Vicente Lecaro (15/0), Miguel Bustamante (8/0), Luciano Macías (18/1), Alfonso Quijano (10/0), Paúl Carrera (1/1), Carlos Pineda (5/1), Jorge Washington Bolaños (12/0), Washington Muñoz (6/2) [Jaime Delgado Mena (1/0)], Félix Lasso (1/0) [Bolívar Merizalde (3/0)], Simon Climaco Cañarte (19/1). Trainer: Fausto Montalván (7).
Goals: Paúl Carrera (56), Washington Muñoz (58).

76. 28.12.1966 **PARAGUAY - ECUADOR** **3-1(2-0)** 29th Copa América (Qualifiers)
Estadio Defensores del Chaco, Asunción; Referee: César Orozco (Peru); Attendance: 25,000
ECU: Helio Carreira Da Silva "Helinho" (3/0), Vicente Lecaro (16/0), Miguel Bustamante (9/0), Luciano Macías (19/1), Alfonso Quijano (11/0), Héctor Morales (1/0) [Enrique José Portilla (1/0)], Paúl Carrera (2/1) [Tom Eugenio Rodríguez (1/0)], Jorge Washington Bolaños (13/0), Washington Muñoz (7/3), Félix Lasso (2/0), Simon Climaco Cañarte (20/1). Trainer: Fausto Montalván (8).
Goal: Washington Muñoz (81).

77. 22.06.1969 **ECUADOR - COLOMBIA** **4-1(2-1)**
Estadio „George Capwell", Guayaquil; Referee: Francisco García
ECU: Fernando Gilberto Maldonado (1/0), Alfonso Quijano (12/0), Enrique José Portilla (2/0), Eulogio Quinteros (1/0), Luciano Macías (20/1), Walter Cardeñas (1/0), Jorge Washington Bolaños (14/0) [Francisco Contreras (1/0)], Simon Bolívar Rangel (1/0) [Washington Muñoz (8/5)], Jorge Ernesto Tapia (1/0), Félix Lasso (3/2) [Servelio Malagon (1/0)], Mario Espinosa (1/0). Trainer: José Gómez Nogueira (1).
Goals: Félix Lasso (4, 34), Washington Muñoz (53, 72).

78. 06.07.1969 **ECUADOR - URUGUAY** **0-2(0-1)** 9th FIFA WC. Qualifiers
Estadio Modelo, Guayaquil; Referee: Romualdo Arppi Filho (Brazil); Attendance: 55,783
ECU: Luis Manuel Ordenana (1/0), Alfonso Quijano (13/0), Ramiro Tobar (1/0), Walter Cardeñas (2/0), Enrique José Portilla (3/0), Eulogio Quinteros (2/0), Washington Muñoz (9/5), Félix Lasso (4/2) [Tom Eugenio Rodríguez (2/0)], Jorge Washington Bolaños (15/0), Jorge Ernesto Tapia (2/0), Mario Espinosa (2/0) [Simon Bolívar Rangel (2/0)]. Trainer: José Gómez Nogueira (2).

79. 20.07.1969 **URUGUAY - ECUADOR** **1-0(0-0)** 9th FIFA WC. Qualifiers
Estadio Centenario, Montevideo; Referee: Rodolfo Pérez Osorio (Paraguay); Attendance: 39,387
ECU: Fernando Gilberto Maldonado (2/0), Alfonso Quijano (14/0), Vicente Lecaro (17/0), Luciano Macías (21/1), Ramiro Tobar (2/0), Eulogio Quinteros (3/0), Washington Muñoz (10/5), Juan Raúl Noriega (1/0), Jorge Washington Bolaños (16/0), Jorge Ernesto Tapia (3/0) [84.Tom Eugenio Rodríguez (3/0)], Mario Espinosa (3/0) [46.Servelio Malagon (2/0)]. Trainer: José Gómez Nogueira (3).

80. 27.07.1969 **CHILE – ECUADOR** **4-1(0-0)** 9th FIFA WC. Qualifiers
Estadio Nacional, Santiago; Referee: Guillermo Velázquez Ramírez (Colombia); Attendance: 71,948
ECU: Fernando Gilberto Maldonado (3/0), Alfonso Enrique Echanique (1/0), Luciano Macías (22/2), Ramiro Tobar (3/0), Enrique José Portilla (4/0), Eulogio Quinteros (4/0), Washington Muñoz (11/5), Juan Raúl Noriega (2/0), Félix Lasso (5/2), Jorge Washington Bolaños (17/0), Jorge Ernesto Tapia (4/0) [34.Walter Cardeñas (3/0)]. Trainer: José Gómez Nogueira (4).
Goal: Luciano Macías (89).

81. 03.08.1969 **ECUADOR - CHILE** **1-1(1-0)** 9th FIFA WC. Qualifiers
Estadio Modelo, Guayaquil; Referee: Carlos Riveros (Peru); Attendance: 11,565
ECU: Fernando Gilberto Maldonado (4/0), Vicente Lecaro (18/0), Luciano Macías (23/2), Ramiro Tobar (4/0), Juan Raúl Noriega (3/0), Alfonso Quijano (15/0), Washington Muñoz (12/5), Jorge Washington Bolaños (18/0), Tom Eugenio Rodríguez (4/1) [64.Servelio Malagon (3/0)], Jorge Ernesto Tapia (5/0) [46.Félix Lasso (6/2)], Mario Espinosa (4/0). Trainer: José Gómez Nogueira (5).
Goal: Tom Eugenio Rodríguez (16).

82. 24.05.1970 **ECUADOR - ENGLAND** **0-2(0-1)**
Estadio Olimpico „Atahualpa", Quito; Referee: Alberto Noriega Tejada (Peru); Attendance: 36,000
ECU: Edwin Roberto Mejía (1/0), Lincoln Utreras (1/0), Carlos German Campoverde (1/0), Enrique José Portilla (5/0), Atahúlfo Valencia (1/0), Jorge Washington Bolaños (19/0), Walter Cardeñas (4/0), Washington Muñoz (13/5) [Marcelo Vicente Cabezas (1/0)], Raúl Patricio Peñaherrera (1/0), Paúl Carrera (3/1) [Tom Eugenio Rodríguez (5/1)], Armando Tito Larrea (10/1). Trainer: Ernesto Guerra (1).

83. 11.06.1972 **PORTUGAL - ECUADOR** **3-0(2-0)** Copa Independencia de Brasil
Estádio "Castelo Branco", Natal (Brazil); Referee: Angel Norberto Coerezza (Argentina)
ECU: Carlos Omar Delgado (1/0), Walter Cardeñas (5/0), Juan Raúl Noriega (4/0) [Rafael Enrique Guerrero (1/0)], Jefferson Donald Camacho (1/0), Víctor Hugo Peláez (1/0), Jorge Washington Bolaños (20/0), Héctor Morales (2/0) [Miguel Angel Coronel (1/0)], Luis Cristóbal Mantilla (1/0), Félix Lasso (7/2), Alberto Pedro Spencer Herrera (9/4), Italo Eugenio Estupiñan (1/0). Trainer: Ernesto Guerra (2).

84. 14.06.1972 **CHILE - ECUADOR** **2-1(0-0)** Copa Independencia de Brasil
Estádio "Castelo Branco", Natal (Brazil); Referee: Romualdo Arppi Filho (Brazil); Attendance: 10,000
ECU: Carlos Omar Delgado (2/0), Walter Cardeñas (6/0), Jefferson Donald Camacho (2/0), Rafael Enrique Guerrero (2/0), Víctor Hugo Peláez (2/0), Jorge Washington Bolaños (21/0) [Héctor Morales (3/0)], Miguel Angel Coronel (2/0), Luis Cristóbal Mantilla (2/0), Félix Lasso (8/2), Alberto Pedro Spencer Herrera (10/4) [Italo Eugenio Estupiñan (2/0)], Marco Antonio Guime (1/1). Trainer: Ernesto Guerra (3).
Goal: Marco Antonio Guime.

85. 18.06.1972 **REPUBLIC OF IRELAND - ECUADOR** **3-2(1-1)** Copa Independencia de Brasil
Estádio "Castelo Branco", Natal (Brazil); Referee: Michel Kitabdjian (France)
ECU: Fernando Gilberto Maldonado (5/0), Víctor Hugo Peláez (3/0), Jefferson Donald Camacho (3/0), Rafael Enrique Guerrero (3/0), Jesús Emilio Ortiz (1/0), Miguel Angel Coronel (3/1), Jorge Washington Bolaños (22/0), Italo Eugenio Estupiñan (3/0), Raúl Patricio Peñaherrera (2/0) [Héctor Morales (4/0)], Félix Lasso (9/3), Marco Antonio Guime (2/1). Trainer: Ernesto Guerra (4).
Goals: Miguel Angel Coronel (35), Félix Lasso (81).

86. 21.06.1972 **ECUADOR – IRAN** **1-1** Copa Independencia de Brasil
Estádio "José do Rego Maciel", Recife (Brazil); Referee: Sebastião Rufino (Brazil)
ECU: Fernando Gilberto Maldonado (6/0), Víctor Hugo Peláez (4/0), Carlos German Campoverde (2/0), Rafael Enrique Guerrero (4/0), Jesús Emilio Ortiz (2/0), Miguel Angel Coronel (4/1), Jorge Washington Bolaños (23/0), Luis Cristóbal Mantilla (3/0) [Marco Antonio Guime (3/1)], Félix Lasso (10/4), Alberto Pedro Spencer Herrera (11/4), Italo Eugenio Estupiñan (4/0). Trainer: Ernesto Guerra (5).
Goal: Félix Lasso (15).

87. 18.02.1973 **ECUADOR – EAST GERMANY** **1-1(0-1)**
Estadio Olimpico „Atahualpa", Quito; Referee: Guillermo Naranja (Ecuador); Attendance: 40,000
ECU: Edwin Roberto Mejía (2/0) [Enrique Aguirre (1/0)], Víctor Hugo Peláez (5/0), Enrique José Portilla (6/0), Jefferson Donald Camacho (4/0), Jesús Emilio Ortiz (3/0), Jorge Ernesto Tapia (6/1), Héctor Morales (5/0), Italo Eugenio Estupiñan (5/0), Félix Lasso (11/4), Paúl Carrera (4/1) [Ramiro Tobar (5/0)], Marco Antonio Guime (4/1) [Rómulo Dudar Mina (1/0)]. Trainer: Jorge Lazo Araque (1).
Goal: Joreg Tapia (74).

88. 24.04.1973 **ECUADOR – CHILE** **1-1(0-1)**
Estadio Modelo, Guayaquil; Referee: Eduardo Rendón (Ecuador); Attendance: 30,000
ECU: Edwin Roberto Mejía (3/0), Víctor Hugo Peláez (6/0), Enrique José Portilla (7/0), Manuel E.Enríquez (1/0), Ramiro Tobar (6/0) [Jesús Emilio Ortiz (4/0)], Jorge Ernesto Tapia (7/1), Belford Parraga (1/0), Luis Cristóbal Mantilla (4/0) [Juan José Tenorio (1/0)], Italo Eugenio Estupiñan (6/0), Gonzalo Castañeda (1/0), Marco Antonio Guime (5/2). Trainer: Jorge Lazo Araque (2).
Goal: Marco Antonio Guime (85).

89. 29.04.1973 **BOLIVIA – ECUADOR** **3-3**
Estadio „Hernándo Siles Zuazo", La Paz; Referee: Juan Oscar Ortubé Vargas (Bolivia)
ECU: Edwin Roberto Mejía (4/0) [Eduardo Enrique Méndez (1/0)], Ramiro Tobar (7/0), Jefferson Donald Camacho (5/0), Enrique José Portilla (8/0), Víctor Hugo Peláez (7/0), Belford Parraga (2/0), Jorge Ernesto Tapia (8/1) [Marcelo Vicente Cabezas (2/0)], Juan José Tenorio (2/0) [Cristóbal Mantilla], Félix Lasso (12/4) [Gonzalo Castañeda], Italo Eugenio Estupiñan (7/2), Marco Antonio Guime (6/3) [Rómulo Dudar Mina]. Trainer: Jorge Lazo Araque (3).
Goals: Italo Eugenio Estupiñan 2, Marco Antonio Guime.

90. 06.05.1973 **ECUADOR – BOLIVIA** **0-0**
Estadio Olimpico „Atahualpa", Quito; Referee: René Torres (Ecuador)
ECU: Eduardo Enrique Méndez (2/0), Víctor Hugo Peláez (8/0), Jefferson Donald Camacho (6/0), Enrique José Portilla (9/0), Ramiro Tobar (8/0) [Jesús Emilio Ortiz (5/0)], Belford Parraga (3/0), Jorge Ernesto Tapia (9/1) [Julio Vicente Bayona (1/0)], Juan José Tenorio (3/0) [Luis Cristóbal Mantilla (5/0)], Félix Lasso (13/4), Italo Eugenio Estupiñan (8/2), Marco Antonio Guime (7/3). Trainer: Jorge Lazo Araque (4).

91. 12.05.1973 **HAITI - ECUADOR** **1-2**
Stade "Sylvio Cator", Port-au-Prince
ECU: Eduardo Enrique Méndez (3/0), Miguel Oswaldo Pérez (1/0), Jefferson Donald Camacho (7/0), Enrique José Portilla (10/0), Jesús Emilio Ortiz (6/0) [Ramiro Tobar (9/0)], Belford Parraga (4/0), Jorge Ernesto Tapia (10/1), Félix Lasso (14/4), Luis Cristóbal Mantilla (6/1) [V. Martínez (1/0)], Italo Eugenio Estupiñan (9/3), Marco Antonio Guime (8/3) [Gonzalo Castañeda (2/0)]. Trainer: Roberto Resquín (1).
Goals: Italo Eugenio Estupiñan, Luis Cristóbal Mantilla.

92. 15.05.1973 **HAITI - ECUADOR** **1-0**
Stade "Sylvio Cator", Port-au-Prince
ECU: Eduardo Enrique Méndez (4/0), Víctor Hugo Peláez (9/0), Jefferson Donald Camacho (8/0), Jesús Emilio Ortiz (7/0), Enrique José Portilla (11/0), Juan Raúl Noriega (5/0) [Rafael Enrique Guerrero (5/0)], Paúl Carrera (5/1), Jorge Washington Bolaños (24/0) [Marco Antonio Guime (9/3)], Félix Lasso (15/4), Italo Eugenio Estupiñan (10/3), Washington Muñoz (14/5). Trainer: Roberto Resquín (2).

93. 21.06.1973 **COLOMBIA - ECUADOR** **1-1(1-0)** 10th FIFA WC. Qualifiers
Estadio „Nemesio Camacho" 'El Campín', Bogotá; Referee: César Augusto Orozco Guerrero (Peru); Attendance: 43,497
ECU: Eduardo Enrique Méndez (5/0), Víctor Hugo Peláez (10/0), Jesús Emilio Ortiz (8/0), Jefferson Donald Camacho (9/0) [Paúl Carrera (6/1)], Enrique José Portilla (12/0), Juan Raúl Noriega (6/0), Marcelo Vicente Cabezas (3/0) [Washington Muñoz (15/5)], Jorge Washington Bolaños (25/0), Félix Lasso (16/4), Italo Eugenio Estupiñan (11/3), Marco Antonio Guime (10/3). Trainer: Roberto Resquín (3).
Goal: Hermenegildo Segrera (72 own goal).

94. 28.06.1973 **ECUADOR - COLOMBIA** **1-1(1-0)** 10th FIFA WC. Qualifiers
Estadio Modelo, Guayaquil; Referee: Luis Pestarino (Argentina); Attendance: 46,979
ECU: Eduardo Enrique Méndez (6/0), Víctor Hugo Peláez (11/0), Enrique José Portilla (13/0), Juan Raúl Noriega (7/0), Jesús Emilio Ortiz (9/0), Jorge Washington Bolaños (26/0), Jefferson Donald Camacho (10/0) [76.Gonzalo Castañeda (3/0)], Washington Muñoz (16/6) [60.Paúl Carrera (7/1)], Félix Lasso (17/4), Italo Eugenio Estupiñan (12/3), Marco Antonio Guime (11/3). Trainer: Roberto Resquín (4).
Goal: Washington Muñoz (29).

95. 01.07.1973 **ECUADOR - URUGUAY** **1-2(1-1)** 10th FIFA WC. Qualifiers
Estadio Olimpico „Atahualpa", Quito; Referee: Romualdo Arppi Filho (Brazil); Attendance: 43,075
ECU: Eduardo Enrique Méndez (7/0), Víctor Hugo Peláez (12/0), Ramiro Tobar (10/0), Jefferson Donald Camacho (11/0), Enrique José Portilla (14/0), Jorge Washington Bolaños (27/0), Félix Lasso (18/4), Italo Eugenio Estupiñan (13/4), Marco Antonio Guime (12/3) [46.Washington Muñoz (17/6)], Juan Raúl Noriega (8/0), Paúl Carrera (8/1) [50.Julio Vicente Bayona (2/0)]. Trainer: Roberto Resquín (5).
Goal: Italo Eugenio Estupiñan (35).

96. 08.07.1973 **URUGUAY - ECUADOR** **4-0(3-0)** 10th FIFA WC. Qualifiers
Estadio Centenario, Montevideo; Referee: José Romei Canete (Paraguay); Attendance: 33,033
ECU: Eduardo Enrique Méndez (8/0), Víctor Hugo Peláez (13/0), Miguel Oswaldo Pérez (2/0) [46.Ramiro Tobar (11/0)], Jefferson Donald Camacho (12/0), Enrique José Portilla (15/0) [60. Félix Lasso (19/4)], Rafael Enrique Guerrero (6/0), Jorge Washington Bolaños (28/0), Italo Eugenio Estupiñan (14/4), Marco Antonio Guime (13/3), Juan Raúl Noriega (9/0), Juan José Tenorio (4/0). Trainer: Roberto Resquín (6).

97. 22.06.1975 **ECUADOR – PERU** **6-0(3-0)**
Estadio Olimpico „Atahualpa", Quito; Referee: René Torres (Ecuador)
ECU: Carlos Omar Delgado (3/0), Víctor Hugo Peláez (14/0) [Washington Guevara (1/0)], Jefferson Donald Camacho (13/0), Fausto Rubén Carrera (1/0), Fausto Klinger (1/0), Carlos René Ron (1/0) [Marcelo Vicente Cabezas (4/0)], Jorge Ernesto Tapia (11/1), Paúl Carrera (9/2), Gonzalo Castañeda (4/1) [Wilmer Alberto Gómez (1/0)], Félix Lasso (20/6), José Fabián Pazymiño (1/2). Trainer: Roque Gaston Máspoli (1).
Goal: José Fabián Pazymiño (15), Gonzalo Castañeda (22), Félix Lasso (35), José Fabián Pazymiño (47), Paúl Carrera (55), Félix Lasso (66).

98. 25.06.1975 **ECUADOR - PERU** **1-0(0-0)**
Estadio Modelo, Guayaquil; Referee: Eduardo Rondón (Ecuador)
ECU: Carlos Omar Delgado (4/0), Víctor Hugo Peláez (15/0), Jefferson Donald Camacho (14/0), Rafael Enrique Guerrero (7/0), Fausto Klinger (2/0), Carlos René Ron (2/1), Jorge Ernesto Tapia (12/1), Gonzalo Castañeda (5/1), Félix Lasso (21/6), Paúl Carrera (10/2), José Fabián Pazymiño (2/2) [Wilmer Alberto Gómez (2/0)]. Trainer: Roque Gaston Máspoli (2).
Goal: Carlos René Ron (80).

99. 01.07.1975 **PERU - ECUADOR** **2-0(1-0)**
Estadio „Alejandro Villanueva", Lima; Referee: Carlos Rivero (Peru)
ECU: Carlos Omar Delgado (5/0), Víctor Hugo Peláez (16/0), Jefferson Donald Camacho (15/0), Fausto Rubén Carrera (2/0) [*sent off 43*], Fausto Klinger (3/0), Marcelo Vicente Cabezas (5/0), Jorge Ernesto Tapia (13/1), Carlos René Ron (3/1), Gonzalo Castañeda (6/1), Félix Lasso (22/6), José Fabián Pazymiño (3/2) [Rafael Enrique Guerrero (8/0)]. Trainer: Roque Gaston Máspoli (3).

100. 09.07.1975 **BOLIVIA – ECUADOR** **1-0(1-0)**
Estadio „Félix Capriles", Cochabamba; Referee: Alberto Albornoz (Bolivia)
ECU: Carlos Omar Delgado (6/0), Víctor Hugo Peláez (17/0), Jefferson Donald Camacho (16/0), Fausto Rubén Carrera (3/0), Fausto Klinger (4/0), Jorge Ernesto Tapia (14/1) [*sent off 89*], Paúl Carrera (11/2), Carlos René Ron (4/1), Gonzalo Castañeda (7/1), Félix Lasso (23/6) [Wilmer Alberto Gómez (3/0)], José Fabián Pazymiño (4/2) [Gustavo Tapia (1/0)]. Trainer: Roque Gaston Máspoli (4).

101. 24.07.1975 **ECUADOR - PARAGUAY** **2-2** 30th Copa América
Estadio Modelo, Guayaquil; Referee: Mario Fiorenza (Venezuela); Attendance: 50,000
ECU: Carlos Omar Delgado (7/0), Víctor Hugo Peláez (18/0), Jefferson Donald Camacho (17/0), Miguel Pérez (3/0), Fausto Klinger (5/0), Carlos René Ron (5/1), Jorge Ernesto Tapia (15/1) [Marcelo Vicente Cabezas (6/0)], Gonzalo Castañeda (8/2), Félix Lasso (24/7), Paúl Carrera (12/2) [Ramiro Tobar (12/0)], Gustavo Tapia (2/0). Trainer: Roque Gastón Máspoli (5).
Goals: Félix Lasso, Gonzalo Castañeda.

102. 27.07.1975 **ECUADOR - COLOMBIA** **1-3(1-1)** 30th Copa América
Estadio Olimpico „Atahualpa", Quito; Referee: Miguel Angel Comesaña (Argentina); Attendance: 45,000
ECU: Carlos Omar Delgado (8/0), Víctor Hugo Peláez (19/0), Jefferson Donald Camacho (18/0), Miguel Oswaldo Pérez (4/0), Fausto Klinger (6/0), Carlos René Ron (6/1), Jorge Ernesto Tapia (16/1) [Marcelo Vicente Cabezas (7/0), Ramiro Tobar (13/0)], Gonzalo Castañeda (9/2), Félix Lasso (25/7), Paúl Carrera (13/3), Gustavo Tapia (3/0). Trainer: Roque Gastón Máspoli (6).
Goal: Paúl Carrera (40).

103. 07.08.1975 **COLOMBIA - ECUADOR** **2-0** 30th Copa América
Estadio „Nemesio Camacho" 'El Campín', Bogotá; Referee: Carlos Robles (Chile); Attendance: 50,000
ECU: Carlos Omar Delgado (9/0), Víctor Hugo Peláez (20/0), Jefferson Donald Camacho (19/0), Fausto Rubén Carrera (4/0), Fausto Klinger (7/0), Jorge Ernesto Tapia (17/1), Marcelo Vicente Cabezas (8/0) [*sent off 8*], Ramiro Tobar (14/0), Paúl Carrera (14/3), Gonzalo Castañeda (10/2), Félix Lasso (26/7) [José Fabián Pazymiño (5/2)]. Trainer: Roque Gastón Máspoli (7).

104. 10.08.1975 **PARAGUAY - ECUADOR** **3-1** 30th Copa América
Estadio Defensores del Chaco, Asunción; Referee: Armando Marques (Brazil); Attendance: 10,000
ECU: Máximo Vera (1/0), Víctor Hugo Peláez (21/0), Jefferson Donald Camacho (20/0), Fausto Rubén Carrera (5/0), Fausto Klinger (8/0), Gustavo Tapia (4/0) [Washington Guevara (2/0)], Ramiro Tobar (15/0), Paúl Carrera (15/3), Gonzalo Castañeda (11/3) [Wilmer Alberto Gómez (4/0)], Félix Lasso (27/7), José Fabián Pazymiño (6/2). Trainer: Roque Gastón Máspoli (8).
Goals: Gonzalo Castañeda (31).

105. 20.10.1976 **ECUADOR - URUGUAY** **2-2(1-0)**
Estadio Olimpico „Atahualpa", Quito; Referee: Oscar Veiró (Argentina); Attendance: 50,000
ECU: Eduardo García (1/0), Washington Méndez (1/0), Ecuador Figueroa (1/0), Fausto Rubén Carrera (6/0), Fausto Klinger (9/0), Juan Carlos Gómez (1/0) [Carlos Torres Garces (1/0)], Carlos René Ron (7/1) [José Daniel Tenorio (1/0)], José Voltaire Villafuerte (1/1), Wilson Nieves (1/0), Angel Luis Liciardi (1/1), José Fabián Pazymiño (7/2) [Luis Cristóbal Mantilla (7/1)]. Trainer: Ernesto Guerra (6).
Goals: Angel Luis Liciardi (50), José Voltaire Villafuerte (87).

106. 04.01.1977 **URUGUAY - ECUADOR** **1-1(0-1)***
Estadio Centenario, Montevideo; Referee: Héctor Rodríguez (Uruguay); Attendance: 35,000
ECU: Carlos Omar Delgado (10/0) [*sent off 50*], Jesús Emilio Ortiz (10/0), Jefferson Donald Camacho (21/0), Fausto Rubén Carrera (7/0), Washington Méndez (2/0), Luis Augusto Granda (1/0) [*sent off 78*], José Voltaire Villafuerte (2/1) [*sent off 78*], Juan Carlos Gómez (2/0) [*sent off 78*], Jorge Vinicio Ron (1/0), Angel Luis Liciardi (2/2) [50.Eduardo García (2/0)][*sent off 78*], Wilson Nieves (2/0). Trainer: Ernesto Guerra (7).
Goal: Angel Luis Liciardi (23).
**The game was abandoned as Ecuador had only 6 players left on the field in the 78th minute.*

107. 09.01.1977 **PARAGUAY - ECUADOR** **2-0**
Estadio Defensores del Chaco, Asunción; Referee: Carlos Alberto Maciel (Paraguay)
ECU: Carlos Omar Delgado (11/0), Washington Méndez (3/0), Fausto Rubén Carrera (8/0), Jefferson Donald Camacho (22/0), Jesús Emilio Ortiz (11/0), Luis Augusto Granda (2/0), José Daniel Tenorio (2/0) [Carlos Torres Garcés (2/0)], José Voltaire Villafuerte (3/1), Jorge Vinicio Ron (2/0) [Luis Cristóbal Mantilla (8/1)], Angel Luis Liciardi (3/2), Wilson Nieves (3/0). Trainer: Ernesto Guerra (8).

108. 16.01.1977 **COLOMBIA – ECUADOR** **0-1(0-1)**
Estadio „Nemesio Camacho“ 'El Campín', Bogotá; Referee: Guillermo Velásquez (Colombia)
ECU: Carlos Omar Delgado (12/0), Washington Méndez (4/0), Jefferson Donald Camacho (23/0), Fernando Villena (1/0), Fausto Klinger (10/0), Juan Carlos Gómez (3/0), Luis Augusto Granda (3/0) [José Daniel Tenorio (3/0)], José Voltaire Villafuerte (4/1), Angel Luis Liciardi (4/3) [José Fabián Pazymiño (8/2)], Jorge Vinicio Ron (3/0), Wilson Nieves (4/0). Trainer: Ernesto Guerra (9).
Goal: Angel Luis Liciardi (44).

109. 20.01.1977 **VENEZUELA – ECUADOR** **1-0(1-0)**
Estadio "José Antonio Páez", Acarigua; Referee: José Varrone (Venezuela), Attendance: 2,500
ECU: Carlos Omar Delgado (13/0), Washington Méndez (5/0), Ecuador Figueroa (2/0), Fernando Villena (2/0) [*sent off 80*], Fausto Klinger (11/0), Juan Carlos Gómez (4/0), Luis Augusto Granda (4/0) [José Fabián Pazymiño (9/2)], José Voltaire Villafuerte (5/1), Jorge Vinicio Ron (4/0), Angel Luis Liciardi (5/3), Wilson Nieves (5/0) [Luis Cristóbal Mantilla (9/1)]. Trainer: Ernesto Guerra (10).

110. 26.01.1977 **ECUADOR – COLOMBIA** **4-1(4-1)**
Estadio Olimpico „Atahualpa“, Quito; Referee: René Torres (Ecuador)
ECU: Carlos Omar Delgado (14/0), Washington Méndez (6/0), Ecuador Figueroa (3/0), Fernando Villena (3/0), Fausto Klinger (12/0), Juan Carlos Gómez (5/0), José Voltaire Villafuerte (6/2) [Luis Augusto Granda (5/0)], Wilson Nieves (6/0), Angel Luis Liciardi (6/5), Jorge Vinicio Ron (5/1), José Fabián Pazymiño (10/2) [Luis Cristóbal Mantilla (10/1)]. Trainer: Ernesto Guerra (11).
Goal: José Voltaire Villafuerte (10), Angel Luis Liciardi (27, 39), Jorge Vinicio Ron (42).

111. 13.02.1977 **ECUADOR – PARAGUAY** **2-1**
Estadio Olimpico „Atahualpa“, Quito; Referee: Hernán Silva Arce (Chile)
ECU: Carlos Omar Delgado (15/0), Washington Méndez (7/0), Fausto Rubén Carrera (9/0), Fernando Villena (4/0), Fausto Klinger (13/0) [Jesús Emilio Ortiz (12/0)], José Daniel Tenorio (4/0) [José Fabián Pazymiño (11/2)], José Voltaire Villafuerte (7/2), Luis Augusto Granda (6/0), Jorge Vinicio Ron (6/1), Angel Luis Liciardi (7/7), Wilson Nieves (7/0) [Luis Cristóbal Mantilla (11/1)]. Trainer: Ernesto Guerra (12).
Goals: Angel Luis Liciardi 2.

112. 20.02.1977 **ECUADOR – PERU** **1-1(0-1)** 11th FIFA WC. Qualifiers
Estadio Olimpico „Atahualpa“, Quito; Referee: Agomar Martins Rohrig (Brazil); Attendance: 39,576
ECU: Carlos Omar Delgado (16/0), Washington Méndez (8/0), Fausto Rubén Carrera (10/0), Fernando Villena (5/0), Fausto Klinger (14/0), Luis Augusto Granda (7/0) [Luis Cristóbal Mantilla (12/1)], José Voltaire Villafuerte (8/2), Juan Carlos Gómez (6/0) [60.José Fabián Pazymiño (12/3)], Jorge Vinicio Ron (7/1), Angel Luis Liciardi (8/7), Wilson Nieves (8/0). Trainer: Ernesto Guerra (13).
Goal: José Fabián Pazymiño (89).

113. 27.02.1977 **ECUADOR – CHILE** **0-1(0-1)** 11th FIFA WC. Qualifiers
Estadio Modelo, Guayaquil; Referee: Jorge Eduardo Romero (Argentina); Attendance: 51,200
ECU: Carlos Omar Delgado (17/0), Washington Méndez (9/0), Fausto Rubén Carrera (11/0), Carlos German Campoverde (3/0), Fausto Klinger (15/0), José Daniel Tenorio (5/0), José Voltaire Villafuerte (9/2) [Luis Augusto Granda (8/0)], Juan Carlos Gómez (7/0), Jorge Vinicio Ron (8/1), Angel Luis Liciardi (9/7) [60.José Fabián Pazymiño (13/3)], Wilson Nieves (9/0). Trainer: Ernesto Guerra (14).

114. 12.03.1977 **PERU - ECUADOR** **4-0(1-0)** 11th FIFA WC. Qualifiers
Estadio Nacional, Lima; Referee: Luis Barrancos Alvarez (Bolivia); Attendance: 43,319
ECU: Eduardo García (3/0), Washington Méndez (10/0), Fausto Rubén Carrera (12/0), Fernando Villena (6/0), Fausto Klinger (16/0), Luis Augusto Granda (9/0), José Voltaire Villafuerte (10/2), Ecuador Figueroa (4/0) [Luis Cristóbal Mantilla (13/1)], José Fabián Pazymiño (14/3), Jorge Vinicio Ron (9/1), Wilson Nieves (10/0). Trainer: Ernesto Guerra (15).

115. 20.03.1977 **CHILE - ECUADOR** **3-0(2-0)** 11th FIFA WC. Qualifiers
Estadio Nacional, Santiago; Referee: Vicente Llobregat Vicedo (Venezuela); Attendance: 15,571
ECU: Walter Pinillos (1/0), Jesús Emilio Ortiz (13/0), Fausto Rubén Carrera (13/0), Fausto Klinger (17/0), Donald Iván Caicedo (1/0), Luis Augusto Granda (10/0) [Ecuador Figueroa (5/0)), José Voltaire Villafuerte (11/2), Juan Carlos Gómez (8/0), José Fabián Pazymiño (15/3) [Wilson Nieves (11/0)], Jorge Vinicio Ron (10/1), Luis Cristóbal Mantilla (14/1). Trainer: Ernesto Guerra (16).

116. 13.06.1979 **CHILE - ECUADOR** **0-0**
Estadio Nacional, Santiago; Referee: Jorge Eduardo Romero (Argentina); Attendance: 19,105
ECU: Milton Rodríguez (1/0), Flavio Perlaza (1/0), Ecuador Figueroa (6/0) [José Julio Bardales (1/0)], Miguel Oswaldo Pérez (5/0), Luis Esteban Escalante (1/0), Carlos René Ron (8/1), Carlos Torres Garcés (3/0) [José Francisco Paes (1/0)], José Voltaire Villafuerte (12/2), Ramiro Aguirre (1/0) [Roque Parraga (1/0)], Jorge Vinicio Ron (11/1), Luis Cristóbal Mantilla (15/1). Trainer: Ernesto Guerra (17).

117. 21.06.1979 **ECUADOR - CHILE** **2-1(1-1)**
Estadio Modelo, Guayaquil; Referee: José Ramírez (Peru); Attendance: 35,000
ECU: Milton Rodríguez (2/0), Flavio Perlaza (2/0), José Julio Bardales (2/0), José Francisco Paes (2/0), Luis Esteban Escalante (2/0), Carlos René Ron (9/1), José Voltaire Villafuerte (13/2) [Jorge Luis Alarcón (1/0)], Carlos Torres Garcés (4/1), Roque Parraga (2/0) [Mario Tenorio (1/0)], Jorge Vinicio Ron (12/2) [Luis Augusto Granda (11/0)], Luis Cristóbal Mantilla (16/1). Trainer: Héctor Morales (1).
Goals: Carlos Torres Garcés (34), Jorge Vinicio Ron (49).

118. 11.07.1979 **PERU - ECUADOR** **2-1(2-1)**
Estadio Nacional, Lima; Referee: Carlos Montalvan (Peru)
ECU: Milton Rodríguez (3/0), Flavio Perlaza (3/0), José Julio Bardales (3/0), José Francisco Paes (3/0), Fausto Klinger (18/0), Carlos Torres Garcés (5/1), Carlos René Ron (10/1), José Voltaire Villafuerte (14/2), Ramiro Aguirre (2/0) [Mario Tenorio (2/0)], Jorge Vinicio Ron (13/2), Luis Cristóbal Mantilla (17/2) [Jorge Luis Alarcón (2/0)]. Trainer: Héctor Morales (2).
Goal: Luis Cristóbal Mantilla (5).

119. 08.08.1979 **ECUADOR - PERU** **2-1(1-1)**
Estadio Olimpico „Atahualpa“, Quito; Referee: Adolfo Quirola (Ecuador)
ECU: Milton Rodríguez (4/0), Flavio Perlaza (4/1), Miguel Pérez (6/0) [Fabian Vicente Burbano (1/0)], Ecuador Figueroa (7/0), Fausto Klinger (19/0), José Francisco Paes (4/0), José Voltaire Villafuerte (15/2) [Juan Eulogio Madruñero (1/0)], Luis Augusto Granda (12/0) [José Julio Bardales (4/0)], Mario Tenorio (3/0), Jorge Luis Alarcón (3/1), Luis Cristóbal Mantilla (18/2). Trainer: Héctor Morales (3).
Goals: Jorge Luis Alarcón (13), Flavio Perlaza (60).

120. 29.08.1979 **ECUADOR - PARAGUAY** **1-2(0-1)** 31st Copa América. Group Stage
Estadio Olimpico „Atahualpa", Quito; Referee: Carlos Alfonso Espósito (Argentina); Attendance: 45,000
ECU: Milton Rodríguez (5/0), Flavio Perlaza (5/1) [Luis Augusto Granda (13/0)], Miguel Oswaldo Pérez (7/0), José Francisco Paes (5/0), Fausto Klinger (20/0), José Voltaire Villafuerte (16/2) [Jorge Luis Alarcón (4/1)], Carlos René Ron (11/1), Carlos Torres Garcés (6/2), Mario Tenorio (4/0), Jorge Vinicio Ron (14/2), Luis Cristóbal Mantilla (19/2). Trainer: Héctor Morales (4).
Goal: Carlos Torres Garcés (64 penalty).

121. 05.09.1979 **ECUADOR - URUGUAY** **2-1(2-0)** 31st Copa América. Group Stage
Estadio Olimpico „Atahualpa", Quito; Referee: Romualdo Arppi Filho (Brazil); Attendance: 30,000
ECU: Milton Rodríguez (6/0), Flavio Perlaza (6/1), Miguel Oswaldo Pérez (8/0), José Francisco Paes (6/0), Fausto Klinger (21/0), Luis Augusto Granda (14/0), Carlos René Ron (12/1), Carlos Torres Garcés (7/2), Mario Tenorio (5/1) [José Voltaire Villafuerte (17/2)], Jorge Luis Alarcón (5/2) [Jorge Vinicio Ron (15/2)], Juan Eulogio Madruñero (2/0). Trainer: Héctor Morales (5).
Goals: Mario Tenorio (6), Jorge Luis Alarcón (9).

122. 13.09.1979 **PARAGUAY - ECUADOR** **2-0** 31st Copa América. Group Stage
Estadio Defensores del Chaco, Asunción; Referee: Abel Gnecco (Argentina); Attendance: 25,000
ECU: Milton Rodríguez (7/0), Flavio Perlaza (7/1), Miguel Oswaldo Pérez (9/0), José Francisco Paes (7/0), Fausto Klinger (22/0), Luis Augusto Granda (15/0), Carlos René Ron (13/1), Carlos Torres Garcés (8/2), Jorge Luis Alarcón (6/2), Mario Tenorio (6/1) [Jorge Vinicio Ron (16/2)], Juan Eulogio Madruñero (3/0) [Luis Cristóbal Mantilla (20/2)]. Trainer: Héctor Morales (6).

123. 16.09.1979 **URUGUAY - ECUADOR** **2-1(1-0)** 31st Copa América. Group Stage
Estadio Centenario, Montevideo; Referee: Oscar Scolfaro (Brazil); Attendance: 25,000
ECU: Milton Rodríguez (8/0), Flavio Perlaza (8/1), José Francisco Paes (8/0), Ecuador Figueroa (8/0), Fausto Klinger (23/1), Luis Augusto Granda (16/0) [*sent off 57*], Carlos René Ron (14/1) [*sent off 81*], Carlos Torres Garcés (9/2) [Jorge Luis Alarcón (7/2)], Mario Tenorio (7/1), Jorge Vinicio Ron (17/2), Luis Cristóbal Mantilla (21/2). Trainer: Héctor Morales (7).
Goal: Fausto Klinger (77).

124. 28.01.1981 **ECUADOR - BULGARIA** **1-3(1-2)**
Estadio Olimpico „Atahualpa", Quito; Referee: Adolfo Quirola (Ecuador); Attendance: 7,000
ECU: Edgar González (1/0), Carlos Quinteros (1/0) [Carlos Carrion (1/0)], Duval Regio Altafuya (1/0), Ecuador Figueroa (9/0) [Luis Corrales (1/0)], Ernesto Mesias (1/1), Luis Augusto Granda (17/0) [Angel Vicuña (1/0)], Carlos Torres Garcés (10/2) [Jesús Jorge Cárdenas (1/0)], José Voltaire Villafuerte (18/2), Jaime Fernando Baldeón (1/0), Jorge Vinicio Ron (18/2), Eddie José Valencia (1/0) [Antonio Arias (1/0)]. Trainer: Otto Vieira (1).
Goal: Ernesto Mesias (34).

125. 14.02.1981 **ECUADOR - BRAZIL** **0-6(0-3)**
Estadio Olimpico „Atahualpa", Quito; Referee: Adolfo Quirola (Ecuador)
ECU: Freddy Valdivieso (1/0), Flavio Perlaza (9/1), Luis Corrales (2/0), John Landeta (1/0), Ernesto Mesias (2/1), Carlos Torres Garcés (11/2) [Luis Augusto Granda (18/0)], José Voltaire Villafuerte (19/2) [Jorge Vinicio Ron (19/2)], Belford Parraga (5/0), Mario Tenorio (8/1), Gorky Eugenio Revelo (1/0) [Lupo Senén Quiñónez (1/0)], Juan Eulogio Madrunero (4/0) [Eddie José Valencia (2/0)]. Trainer: Otto Vieira (2).

126. 17.05.1981 **ECUADOR – PARAGUAY** **1-0(0-0)** 12th FIFA WC. Qualifiers
Estadio Modelo, Guayaquil; Referee: Luis Barrancos Alvarez (Bolivia); Attendance: 55,000
ECU: Carlos Omar Delgado (18/0), Flavio Perlaza (10/1), Ecuador Figueroa (10/0) [46.Orly Klinger (1/1)], José Francisco Paes (9/0), Digner Valencia (1/0), José Voltaire Villafuerte (20/2), Belford Parraga (6/0), Paúl Carrera (16/3) [79.Fabian Vicente Burbano (2/0)], Mario Tenorio (9/1), Lupo Senén Quiñónez (2/0), Wilson Nieves (12/0). Trainer: Juan Eduardo Hohberg (1).
Goal: Orly Klinger (48).

127. 24.05.1981 **ECUADOR – CHILE** **0-0** 12th FIFA WC. Qualifiers
Estadio Modelo, Guayaquil; Referee: Juan Daniel Cardellino de San Vicente (Uruguay); Attendance: 55,000
ECU: Carlos Omar Delgado (19/0), Flavio Perlaza (11/1), Orly Klinger (2/1), José Francisco Paes (10/0), Digner Valencia (2/0), José Voltaire Villafuerte (21/2), Belford Parraga (7/0), Paúl Carrera (17/3) [33.Gorky Eugenio Revelo (2/0)], Mario Tenorio (10/1), Lupo Senén Quiñónez (3/0), Wilson Nieves (13/0) [42.José Fabián Pazymiño (16/3)]. Trainer: Juan Eduardo Hohberg (2).

128. 31.05.1981 **PARAGUAY - ECUADOR** **3-1(0-0)** 12th FIFA WC. Qualifiers
Estadio Puerta Sajonia, Asunción; Referee: Roque Tito Cerullo Giuliano (Uruguay); Attendance: 37,000
ECU: Carlos Omar Delgado (20/0), Flavio Perlaza (12/1), Ecuador Figueroa (11/0), José Francisco Paes (11/0), Orly Klinger (3/1), Digner Valencia (3/0), Belford Parraga (8/0), Paúl Carrera (18/3), Mario Tenorio (11/1) [63.Fabian Vicente Burbano (3/0)], Lupo Senén Quiñónez (4/0), Wilson Nieves (14/1). Trainer: Juan Eduardo Hohberg (3).
Goal: Wilson Nieves (89).

129. 14.06.1981 **CHILE - ECUADOR** **2-0(1-0)** 12th FIFA WC. Qualifiers
Estadio Nacional, Santiago; Referee: Gilberto Aristizábal Murcia (Colombia); Attendance: 72,290
ECU: Carlos Omar Delgado (21/0), Flavio Perlaza (13/1), Ecuador Figueroa (12/0), José Francisco Paes (12/0), Orly Klinger (4/1), Digner Valencia (4/0) [*sent off 86*], Belford Parraga (9/0), José Voltaire Villafuerte (22/2), Mario Tenorio (12/1), Lupo Senén Quiñónez (5/0), Wilson Nieves (15/1). Trainer: Juan Eduardo Hohberg (4).

130. 26.07.1983 **ECUADOR - COLOMBIA** **0-0**
Estadio Olimpico „Atahualpa", Quito; Referee: Jorge Orellana Vimos (Ecuador)
ECU: Carlos Omar Delgado (22/0), Luis Orlando Narváez (1/0), Wilson Antonio Armas (1/0), Orly Klinger (5/1), Carlos Hans Maldonado (1/0), Tulio Quinteros (1/0), José Voltaire Villafuerte (23/2), Paúl Carrera (19/3) [Hamilton Emilio Cuvi Rivera (1/0)], Mario Tenorio (13/1), Lupo Senén Quiñónez (6/0), Gabriel Cantos (1/0). Trainer: Ernesto Guerra (18).

131. 29.07.1983 **COLOMBIA - ECUADOR** **0-0**
Estadio „Nemesio Camacho" 'El Campín', Bogotá; Referee: Octavio Sierra Mesa (Colombia); Attendance: 15,000
ECU: Carlos Omar Delgado (23/0), Luis Orlando Narváez (2/0), Wilson Antonio Armas (2/0), Orly Klinger (6/1), Carlos Hans Maldonado (2/0), José Voltaire Villafuerte (24/2), Bolívar Gustavo Ruiz (1/0), Luis Augusto Granda (19/0) [Galo Fidean Vásquez (1/0)], Mario Tenorio (14/1), Lupo Senén Quiñónez (7/0), Carlos Gorosabel (1/0). Trainer: Ernesto Guerra (19).

132. 10.08.1983 **ECUADOR - ARGENTINA** **2-2(0-1)** 32nd Copa América. Group Stage
Estadio Olimpico „Atahualpa", Quito; Referee: Gilberto Aristizábal (Colombia); Attendance: 50,000
ECU: Carlos Omar Delgado (24/0), Luis Orlando Narváez (3/0), Wilson Antonio Armas (3/0), Orly Klinger (7/1), Carlos Hans Maldonado (3/0), José Jacinto Vega (1/1), José Voltaire Villafuerte (25/2), Paúl Carrera (20/3) [Galo Fidean Vásquez (2/1)], Mario Tenorio (15/1), Lupo Senén Quiñónez (8/0) [Jorge Vinicio Ron (20/2) [*sent off 69*]], Carlos Gorosabel (2/0). Trainer: Ernesto Guerra (20).
Goals: Galo Fidean Vásquez (68), José Jacinto Vega (89).

133. 17.08.1983 **ECUADOR - BRAZIL** **0-1(0-1)** 32nd Copa América. Group Stage
Estadio Olimpico „Atahualpa", Quito; Referee: Jesus Alfonso Postigo Trucios (Peru); Attendance: 50,000
ECU: Carlos Omar Delgado (25/0), Luis Orlando Narváez (4/0), Wilson Antonio Armas (4/0), Orly Klinger (8/1), Carlos Hans Maldonado (4/0), Luis Augusto Granda (20/0), Galo Fidean Vásquez (3/1), José Jacinto Vega (2/1) [Paúlo Carrera (21/3)], Mario Tenorio (16/1), José Voltaire Villafuerte (26/2), Carlos Gorosabel (3/0) [Lupo Senén Quiñónez (9/0)]. Trainer: Ernesto Guerra (21).

134. 01.09.1983 **BRAZIL - ECUADOR** **5-0(1-0)** 32nd Copa América. Group Stage
Estádio Serra Dourada, Goiânia; Referee: Luis Gregorio Da Rosa (Uruguay); Attendance: 35,000
ECU: Carlos Omar Delgado (26/0), Luis Orlando Narváez (5/0) [Alfredo Encalada (1/0)], Wilson Antonio Armas (5/0), Orly Klinger (9/1), Carlos Hans Maldonado (5/0), Galo Fidean Vásquez (4/1) [Hamilton Emilio Cuvi Rivera (2/0)], Luis Augusto Granda (21/0), Tulio Quinteros (2/0), Mario Tenorio (17/1), Lupo Senén Quiñónez (10/0), José Voltaire Villafuerte (27/2). Trainer: Ernesto Guerra (22).

135. 07.09.1983 **ARGENTINA - ECUADOR** **2-2(0-1)** 32nd Copa América. Group Stage
Estadio Monumental „Antonio Vespucio Liberti", Buenos Aires; Referee: Juan Daniel Cardellino de San Vicente (Uruguay); Attendance: 40,000
ECU: Israel Rodríguez (1/0), Alfredo Encalada (2/0), Wilson Antonio Armas (6/0), Orly Klinger (10/1), Carlos Hans Maldonado (6/1), José Jacinto Vega (3/1), Bolívar Gustavo Ruiz (2/0), Tulio Quinteros (3/0), Jorge Vinicio Ron (21/2), Lupo Senén Quiñónez (11/1), Hamilton Emilio Cuvi Rivera (3/0). Trainer: Ernesto Guerra (23).
Goals: Lupo Senén Quiñónez (44), Carlos Hans Maldonado (90 penalty).

136. 30.11.1984 **UNITED STATES - ECUADOR** **0-0**
Giants Stadium, East Rutherford, New York; Referee: David Socha (United States)
ECU: Israel Rodríguez (2/0), Flavio Perlaza (14/1), Orly Klinger (11/1), Luis Preciado (1/0), Carlos Hans Maldonado (7/1), José Elias De Negri (1/0), Carlos Torres Garcés (12/2), José Voltaire Villafuerte (28/2) [Hamilton Emilio Cuvi Rivera (4/0)], Jaime Fernando Baldeón (2/0) [Jorge Vinicio Ron (22/2)], Lupo Senén Quiñónez (12/1) [José Vicente Moreno (1/0)], Hermen De Jesús Benítez (1/0). Trainer: Antônio Ferreira „Antoninho" (1).

137. 02.12.1984 **UNITED STATES - ECUADOR** **2-2**
Orange Bowl, Miami; Referee: David Socha; Attendance: 4,000
ECU: Israel Rodríguez (3/0), Flavio Perlaza (15/1), Orly Klinger (12/1), Luis Preciado (2/0), Carlos Hans Maldonado (8/1), José Voltaire Villafuerte (29/2) [Carlos Torres Garcés (13/2)], Hamilton Emilio Cuvi Rivera (5/1), José Elias De Negri (2/0), Jaime Fernando Baldeón (3/0), Lupo Senén Quiñónez (13/1), Hermen De Jesús Benítez (2/1) [Jorge Vinicio Ron (23/2)]. Trainer: Antônio Ferreira „Antoninho" (2).
Goals: Hamilton Emilio Cuvi Rivera (39), Hermen De Jesús Benítez (48).

138. 04.12.1984 **MEXICO - ECUADOR** **3-2(1-1)**
Memorial Coliseum, Los Angeles (United States); Referee: Luis M. Macías (United States)
ECU: Israel Rodríguez (4/0), Flavio Perlaza (16/1), Orly Klinger (13/1), Luis Preciado (3/0), Carlos Hans Maldonado (9/1), José Elias De Negri (3/1), Marcelo Hurtado (1/0), José Voltaire Villafuerte (30/3), Hamilton Emilio Cuvi Rivera (6/1), Jaime Fernando Baldeón (4/0) [81.Hermen De Jesús Benítez (3/1)], Lupo Senén Quiñónez (14/1). Trainer: Antônio Ferreira „Antoninho" (3).
Goals: José Elias De Negri (3), José Voltaire Villafuerte (62).

139. 07.12.1984 **HONDURAS - ECUADOR** **0-0**
Estadio Nacional, Tegucigalpa; Referee: Rolando Paz (Honduras)
ECU: Pedro Carlos Latino (1/0), Flavio Perlaza (17/1), Orly Klinger (14/1), Holguer Abraham Quiñónez (1/0), Carlos Hans Maldonado (10/1), José Elias De Negri (4/1), Hamilton Emilio Cuvi Rivera (7/1), Carlos Torres Garcés (14/2), José Voltaire Villafuerte (31/3), Jaime Fernando Baldeón (5/0) [Lupo Senén Quiñónez (15/1)], Jorge Vinicio Ron (24/2) [Hermen De Jesús Benítez (4/1)]. Trainer: Antônio Ferreira „Antoninho" (4).

140. 09.12.1984 **GUATEMALA – ECUADOR** **1-0**
Estadio Nacional "Mateo Flores", Ciudad de Guatemala
ECU: Israel Rodríguez (5/0), Flavio Perlaza (18/1), Orly Klinger (15/1), Holguer Abraham Quiñónez (2/0) [*sent off*], Carlos Hans Maldonado (11/1), Marcelo Hurtado (2/0), Hamilton Emilio Cuvi Rivera (8/1), José Voltaire Villafuerte (32/3), Carlos Torres Garcés (15/2) [José Vicente Moreno (2/0)], Jaime Fernando Baldeón (6/0), Lupo Senén Quiñónez (16/1). Trainer: Antônio Ferreira „Antoninho" (5).

141. 12.12.1984 **EL SALVADOR – ECUADOR** **1-1**
Estadio Cuscatlán, San Salvador
ECU: Israel Rodríguez (6/0), Flavio Perlaza (19/1), Orly Klinger (16/1), Luis Preciado (4/0), Carlos Hans Maldonado (12/1), José Elias De Negri (5/1) [Carlos Torres Garcés (16/2)], Marcelo Hurtado (3/0), Hamilton Emilio Cuvi Rivera (9/1), José Voltaire Villafuerte (33/3) [Hermén De Jesús Benítez (5/1)], Jaime Fernando Baldeón (7/0) [José Vicente Moreno (3/0)], Lupo Senén Quiñónez (17/2). Trainer: Antônio Ferreira „Antoninho" (6).
Goal: Lupo Senérn Quiñónez (79).

142. 06.02.1985 **ECUADOR – EAST GERMANY** **2-3(1-2)**
Estadio Modelo, Guayaquil; Referee: Elías Víctoriano Jacomé Guerreiro (Ecuador); Attendance: 26,000
ECU: Israel Rodríguez (7/0), Luis Enrique Capurro Bautista (1/0), Orly Klinger (17/1), Luis Preciado (5/0) [Wilson Antonio Armas (7/0)], Carlos Hans Maldonado (13/1) [José Jacinto Vega (4/1)], José Elias De Negri (6/1), Marcelo Hurtado (4/0) [68.Galo Fidean Vásquez (5/1)], Hamilton Emilio Cuvi Rivera (10/1), José Voltaire Villafuerte (34/3) [Carlos Torres Garcés (17/2)], Jaime Fernando Baldeón (8/1), Hermen De Jesús Benítez (6/2). Trainer: Antônio Ferreira „Antoninho" (7).
Goals: Jaime Fernando Baldeón (18), Hermen De Jesús Benítez (82).

143. 10.02.1985 **ECUADOR – EAST GERMANY** **3-2(1-2)**
Estadio Olimpico „Atahualpa", Quito; Referee: Jorge Orellana Vimos (Ecuador); Attendance: 19,000
ECU: Pedro Carlos Latino (2/0), Luis Enrique Capurro Bautista (2/0), Orly Klinger (18/1) [*sent off*], Wilson Antonio Armas (8/0), Carlos Hans Maldonado (14/2), Hamilton Emilio Cuvi Rivera (11/1), José Voltaire Villafuerte (35/3), José Elias De Negri (7/1), Jaime Fernando Baldeón (9/1), Hermen De Jesús Benítez (7/4) [José Jacinto Vega (5/1)], José Fabián Pazymiño (17/3). Trainer: Antônio Ferreira „Antoninho" (8).
Goals: Hermen De Jesús Benítez (43, 58), Carlos Hans Maldonado (81 penalty).

144. 17.02.1985 **ECUADOR – FINLAND** **3-1(2-0)**

Estadio Bellavista, Ambato; Referee: Jorge Ortiz (Ecuador); Attendance: 12,000

ECU: Pedro Carlos Latino (3/0), Luis Enrique Capurro Bautista (3/0), Holguer Abraham Quiñónez (3/0), Wilson Antonio Armas (9/0), Carlos Hans Maldonado (15/2), Hamilton Emilio Cuvi Rivera (12/1), José Elias De Negri (8/1), José Voltaire Villafuerte (36/3), Jaime Fernando Baldeón (10/1), Hermen De Jesús Benítez (8/6) [Galo Fidean Vásquez (6/1)], José Fabián Pazymiño (18/4) [José Vicente Moreno (4/0)]. Trainer: Antônio Ferreira „Antoninho" (9).

Goals: José Fabián Pazymiño (12), Hermen De Jesús Benítez (34, 85).

145. 21.02.1985 **ECUADOR – BOLIVIA** **3-0(1-0)**

Estadio Olimpico „Atahualpa", Quito; Referee: Alfredo Rodas (Ecuador)

ECU: Pedro Carlos Latino (4/0), Flavio Perlaza (20/1), Holguer Abraham Quiñónez (4/0), Wilson Antonio Armas (10/0), Carlos Hans Maldonado (16/3), Marcelo Hurtado (5/0), José Elias De Negri (9/1) [José Jacinto Vega (6/1)], José Voltaire Villafuerte (37/4), Galo Fidean Vásquez (7/1), Hermen De Jesús Benítez (9/7), José Fabián Pazymiño (19/4) [José Vicente Moreno]. Trainer: Antônio Ferreira „Antoninho" (10).

Goals: Carlos Hans Maldonado (22), Hermen De Jesús Benítez (64), José Voltaire Villafuerte (69).

146. 03.03.1985 **ECUADOR – CHILE** **1-1(1-1)** 13th FIFA WC. Qualifiers

Estadio Olimpico „Atahualpa", Quito; Referee: José Roberto Ramiz Wright (Brazil); Attendance: 40,000

ECU: Israel Rodríguez (8/0), Flavio Perlaza (21/1), Holguer Abraham Quiñónez (5/0) [*sent off*], Wilson Antonio Armas (11/0), Carlos Hans Maldonado (17/4), Marcelo Hurtado (6/0), José Elias De Negri (10/1), José Voltaire Villafuerte (38/4) [Hamilton Emilio Cuvi Rivera (13/1)], Jaime Fernando Baldeón (11/1), Hermen De Jesús Benítez (10/7), José Vicente Moreno (5/0) [Lupo Senén Quiñónez (18/2)]. Trainer: Antônio Ferreira „Antoninho" (11).

Goal: Carlos Hans Maldonado (44 penalty).

147. 10.03.1985 **URUGUAY - ECUADOR** **2-1(1-0)** 13th FIFA WC. Qualifiers

Estadio Centenario, Montevideo; Referee: Edison Pérez Nuñez (Peru); Attendance: 65,000

ECU: Israel Rodríguez (9/0), Flavio Perlaza (22/1), Orly Klinger (19/1), Wilson Antonio Armas (12/0), Carlos Hans Maldonado (18/4), Marcelo Hurtado (7/0), José Elias De Negri (11/1), José Voltaire Villafuerte (39/4), Hamilton Emilio Cuvi Rivera (14/2), Jaime Fernando Baldeón (12/1) [80.Hermen De Jesús Benítez (11/7)], Lupo Senén Quiñónez (19/2) [86.Galo Fidean Vásquez (8/1)]. Trainer: Antônio Ferreira „Antoninho" (12).

Goal: Hamilton Emilio Cuvi Rivera (54).

148. 17.03.1985 **CHILE - ECUADOR** **6-2(4-2)** 13th FIFA WC. Qualifiers

Estadio Nacional, Santiago; Referee: Orázio Di Rosa (Venezuela); Attendance: 60,892

ECU: Israel Rodríguez (10/0), Flavio Perlaza (23/1), Orly Klinger (20/1), Wilson Antonio Armas (13/0), Carlos Hans Maldonado (19/4) [Eddie José Valencia (3/0)], Marcelo Hurtado (8/0), José Elias De Negri (12/1), José Voltaire Villafuerte (40/4), Hamilton Emilio Cuvi Rivera (15/3), Jaime Fernando Baldeón (13/3), Hermen De Jesús Benítez (12/7). Trainer: Antônio Ferreira „Antoninho" (13).

Goal: Jaime Fernando Baldeón (23, 37).

149. 21.03.1985 **PERU - ECUADOR** **1-0(0-0)**

Estadio Nacional, Lima; Referee: Wálter Chatter (Peru); Attendance: 10,000

ECU: Pedro Carlos Latino (5/0), Flavio Perlaza (24/1), Orly Klinger (21/1), Luis Preciado (6/0), Luis Enrique Capurro Bautista (4/0), Galo Fidean Vásquez (9/1) [Jaime Fernando Baldeón (14/3)], Marcelo Hurtado (9/0), José Jacinto Vega (7/1) [56.José Voltaire Villafuerte (41/4)], Hamilton Emilio Cuvi Rivera (16/3) [61.José Elias De Negri (13/1)], Lupo Senén Quiñónez (20/2), Eddie José Valencia (4/0). Trainer: Antônio Ferreira „Antoninho" (14).

150. 31.03.1985 **ECUADOR – URUGUAY** **0-2(0-0)** 13th FIFA WC. Qualifiers

Estadio Olimpico „Atahualpa", Quito; Referee: Juan Francisco Escobar Váldez (Paraguay); Attendance: 30,000

ECU: Israel Rodríguez (11/0) [69.Pedro Carlos Latino (6/0)], Luis Enrique Capurro Bautista (5/0), Orly Klinger (22/1), Wilson Antonio Armas (14/0), Carlos Hans Maldonado (20/4), Marcelo Hurtado (10/0) [46.Eddie José Valencia (5/0)], José Voltaire Villafuerte (42/4), José Elias De Negri (14/1), Hamilton Emilio Cuvi Rivera (17/3), Jaime Fernando Baldeón (15/3), Lupo Senén Quiñónez (21/2). Trainer: Antônio Ferreira „Antoninho" (15).

151. 05.03.1987 **CUBA - ECUADOR** **2-1(0-0)**

Estadio "Pedro Marrero", La Habana; Referee: Ángel Mesa (Cuba)

ECU: Carlos Luis Morales (1/0), Lenin Samaniego (1/0), Kléber Emilson Fajardo Barzola (1/0), Holguer Abraham Quiñónez (6/0), Claudio Alcívar (1/0), Wilson Homero Macías (1/0), Pablo Estebán Marín (1/0) [Edgar Domínguez (1/0)], Pietro Raúl Marsetti (1/0) [Joffre Sánchez (1/0)], Alex Darío Aguinaga Garzón (1/1), Freddy Barreto (1/0) [Ney Raúl Avilés Aguirre (1/0)], Mauricio Arguëllo (1/0). Trainer: Luis Grimaldi (1).

Goal: Alex Darío Aguinaga Garzón (80).

152. 08.03.1987 **CUBA - ECUADOR** **0-0**

Estadio "Pedro Marrero", La Habana

ECU: Héctor Lautaro Chiriboga (1/0), Freddy Egberto Bravo (1/0), Kléber Emilson Fajardo Barzola (2/0), Holguer Abraham Quiñónez (7/0), Luis Bolivar Mosquera (1/0), Wilson Homero Macías (2/0), Edgar Domínguez (2/0), Pietro Raúl Marsetti (2/0) [Freddy Barreto (2/0)], Alex Darío Aguinaga Garzón (2/1), Joffre Sánchez (2/0) [Claudio Alcívar (2/0)], Ney Raúl Avilés Aguirre (2/0). Trainer: Luis Grimaldi (2).

153. 31.03.1987 **ECUADOR - CUBA** **0-1(0-0)**

Estadio 9 de Mayo, Machala; Referee: Medardo Serrano (Ecuador)

ECU: Héctor Lautaro Chiriboga (2/0), Luis Alberto Carrión (1/0), Kléber Emilson Fajardo Barzola (3/0), Holguer Abraham Quiñónez (8/0), Claudio Alcívar (3/0) [Pedro Mauricio Muñoz (1/0)], Edgar Domínguez (3/0), Wilson Homero Macías (3/0), Pietro Raúl Marsetti (3/0) [Pablo Estebán Marín (3/0)], Luis Eduardo Vaca (1/0), Ney Raúl Avilés Aguirre (3/0), Stony Marin Batioja (1/0) [Diego Cordova (1/0)]. Trainer: Luis Grimaldi (3).

154. 02.04.1987 **ECUADOR – CUBA** **0-0**

Estadio Municipal, Azogues; Referee: Jorge Orellana Vimos (Ecuador)

ECU: Carlos Milton Enríquez Garzón (1/0) [Héctor Lautaro Chiriboga (3/0)], Luis Alberto Carrión (2/0), Kléber Emilson Fajardo Barzola (4/0), Wilson Homero Macías (4/0), Pablo Estebán Marín (3/0), Wilfrido Enrique Verduga (1/0), Edgar Domínguez (4/0), Alex Darío Aguinaga Garzón (3/1), Ney Raúl Avilés Aguirre (4/0), Pedro Mauricio Muñoz (2/0) [Diego Cordova (2/0)], Stony Marin Batioja (2/0) [Pietro Raúl Marsetti (4/0)]. Trainer: Luis Grimaldi (4).

155. 11.06.1987 **COLOMBIA - ECUADOR** **1-0(1-0)**

Estadio „Atanasio Girardot", Medellín; Referee: Armando Pérez (Colombia)

ECU: Carlos Luis Morales (2/0), Juan Carlos Jacomé (1/0) [Pietro Raúl Marsetti (5/0)], Urlin Bautista Canga Quintero (1/0) [Wilson Homero Macías (5/0)], Kléber Emilson Fajardo Barzola (5/0), Luis Enrique Capurro Bautista (6/0), Pablo Estebán Marín (4/0), Edgar Domínguez (5/0), Hamilton Emilio Cuvi Rivera (18/3) [Alex Darío Aguinaga Garzón (4/1)], Jaime Fernando Baldeón (16/3) [Geovanny Alfonso Mera (1/0) [*sent off*]], Lupo Senén Quiñónez (22/2), Ney Raúl Avilés Aguirre (5/0). Trainer: Luis Grimaldi (5).

156. 14.06.1987 **ECUADOR - COLOMBIA** **3-0(0-0)**
Estadio Modelo, Guayaquil; Referee: Alfredo Rodas Iñíguez (Ecuador)
ECU: Carlos Luis Morales (3/0), Luis Bolivar Mosquera (2/0), Wilson Homero Macías (6/0), Kléber Emilson Fajardo Barzola (6/0), Luis Enrique Capurro Bautista (7/0), Pablo Estebán Marín (5/0) [Jaime Fernando Baldeón (17/4)], Edgar Domínguez (6/0), Hamilton Emilio Cuvi Rivera (19/3), Alex Darío Aguinaga Garzón (5/1) [Pietro Raúl Marsetti (6/1)], Lupo Senén Quiñónez (23/3), Ney Raúl Avilés Aguirre (6/0) [Urlin Bautista Canga]. Trainer: Luis Grimaldi (6).
Goals: Lupo Senén Quiñónez (49), Jaime Fernando Baldeón (82), Pietro Raúl Marsetti (86).

157. 19.06.1987 **URUGUAY - ECUADOR** **2-1(1-0)**
Estadio Centenario, Montevideo; Referee: José Luis Martínez Bazan (Uruguay); Attendance: 5,000
ECU: Carlos Luis Morales (4/0), Luis Bolivar Mosquera (3/0), Wilson Homero Macías (7/0), Kléber Emilson Fajardo Barzola (7/0), Luis Enrique Capurro Bautista (8/0), Alex Darío Aguinaga Garzón (7/1) [Geovanny Alfonso Mera (2/0)], Pablo Estebán Marín (6/0), Edgar Domínguez (7/0) [Pietro Raúl Marsetti (7/2)], Hamilton Emilio Cuvi Rivera (20/3), Jaime Fernando Baldeón (18/4), Lupo Senén Quiñónez (24/3). Trainer: Luis Grimaldi (7).
Goal: Pietro Raúl Marsetti (49).

158. 21.06.1987 **BRAZIL - ECUADOR** **4-1(1-0)**
Estádio Ressacada, Florianópolis; Referee: José Roberto Ramiz Wright (Brazil); Attendance: 5,000
ECU: Carlos Luis Morales (5/0), Luis Bolivar Mosquera (4/0), Wilson Homero Macías (8/0), Kléber Emilson Fajardo Barzola (8/0), Luis Enrique Capurro Bautista (9/0), Galo Fidean Vásquez (10/1), Pablo Estebán Marín (7/0), Edgar Domínguez (8/0) [Ney Raúl Avilés Aguirre (7/0)], Hamilton Emilio Cuvi Rivera (21/3) [Pietro Raúl Marsetti (8/2)], Lupo Senén Quiñónez (25/3), Jaime Fernando Baldeón (19/4) [Geovanny Alfonso Mera (3/1)]. Trainer: Luis Grimaldi (8).
Goal: Geovanny Alfonso Mera (88).

159. 02.07.1987 **ARGENTINA - ECUADOR** **3-0(0-0)** 33rd Copa América. Group Stage
Estadio Monumental „Antonio Vespucio Liberti“, Buenos Aires; Referee: Romualdo Arppi Filho (Brazil); Attendance: 30,000
ECU: Carlos Luis Morales (6/0), Luis Bolivar Mosquera (5/0), Wilson Homero Macías (9/0), Kléber Emilson Fajardo Barzola (9/0), Luis Enrique Capurro Bautista (10/0), Galo Fidean Vásquez (11/1), Pablo Estebán Marín (8/0), [58.Jaime Fernando Baldeón (20/4)], José Jacinto Vega (8/1), Hamilton Emilio Cuvi Rivera (22/3), Lupo Senén Quiñónez (26/3), Ney Raúl Avilés Aguirre (8/0) [42.Geovanny Alfonso Mera (4/1)]. Trainer: Luis Grimaldi (9).

160. 04.07.1987 **PERU - ECUADOR** **1-1(0-0)** 33rd Copa América. Group Stage
Estadio Monumental „Antonio Vespucio Liberti“, Buenos Aires (Argentina); Referee: Asterio Martínez (Paraguay); Attendance: 30,000
ECU: Héctor Lautaro Chiriboga (4/0), Luis Bolivar Mosquera (6/0), Wilson Homero Macías (10/0), Kléber Emilson Fajardo Barzola (10/0), Luis Enrique Capurro Bautista (11/0), Alex Darío Aguinaga Garzón (8/1) [69.Galo Fidean Vásquez (12/1)], Pablo Estebán Marín (9/0), José Jacinto Vega (9/1), Hamilton Emilio Cuvi Rivera (23/4), Lupo Senén Quiñónez (27/3) [65.Jaime Fernando Baldeón (21/4)], Geovanny Alfonso Mera (5/1). Trainer: Luis Grimaldi (10).
Goal: Hamilton Emilio Cuvi Rivera (72).

161. 07.06.1988 **UNITED STATES - ECUADOR** **0-1(0-1)**
University Stadium, Albuquerque; Referee: Arturo Angeles (United States)
ECU: Carlos Luis Morales (7/0), Carlos Quinteros (2/0) [Kléber Emilson Fajardo Barzola (11/0)], Wilson Homero Macías (11/0), Holguer Abraham Quiñónez (9/0), Luis Enrique Capurro Bautista (12/0), Alex Darío Aguinaga Garzón (9/2), Pablo Estebán Marín (10/0), Hamilton Emilio Cuvi Rivera (24/4), Ney Raúl Avilés Aguirre (9/0), Byron Zózimo Tenorio (1/0), Pedro Mauricio Muñoz (3/0). Trainer: Dušan Drašković (1).
Goal: Alex Darío Aguinaga Garzón (20 penalty).

162. 10.06.1988 **UNITED STATES - ECUADOR** **0-2(0-1)**
Delmar Stadium, Houston; Referee: Julio Salas (United States)
ECU: Héctor Lautaro Chiriboga (5/0), Kléber Emilson Fajardo Barzola (12/0), Wilson Homero Macías (12/0) [*sent off*], Holguer Abraham Quiñónez (10/0), Luis Enrique Capurro Bautista (13/0) [Carlos Quinteros (3/0)], Edgar Domínguez (9/0) [Hamilton Emilio Cuvi Rivera (25/4)], Pablo Estebán Marín (11/0), Pietro Raúl Marsetti (9/2) [Ney Raúl Avilés Aguirre (10/0)], Pedro Mauricio Muñoz (4/1), Byron Zózimo Tenorio (2/0) [Raúl Alfredo Noriega Escobar (1/0)], Nelson Guerrero (1/0) [Alex Darío Aguinaga Garzón (10/3)]. Trainer: Dušan Drašković (2).
Goals: Pedro Mauricio Muñoz (36), Alex Darío Aguinaga Garzón (87).

163. 12.06.1988 **UNITED STATES - ECUADOR** **0-0**
"Herman Clark" Stadium, Fort Worth; Referee: Angelo Bratsis (United States); Attendance: 7,250
ECU: Carlos Luis Morales (8/0), Carlos Quinteros (4/0), Holguer Abraham Quiñónez (11/0), Raúl Alfredo Noriega Escobar (2/0) [Kléber Emilson Fajardo Barzola (13/0)], Luis Enrique Capurro Bautista (14/0), Alex Darío Aguinaga Garzón (11/3), Edgar Domínguez (10/0) [Pablo Estebán Marín (12/0)], Hamilton Emilio Cuvi Rivera (26/4), Ney Raúl Avilés Aguirre (11/0), Byron Zózimo Tenorio (3/0), Nelson Guerrero (2/0) [Pedro Mauricio Muñoz (5/1)]. Trainer: Dušan Drašković (3).

164. 15.06.1988 **HONDURAS – ECUADOR** **1-1**
Estadio "Francisco Morazán", San Pedro Sula; Referee: Salvador Tabora (Honduras)
ECU: Héctor Lautaro Chiriboga (6/0), Carlos Quinteros (5/0), Wilson Homero Macías (13/0), Holguer Abraham Quiñónez (12/0), Luis Enrique Capurro Bautista (15/0), Alex Darío Aguinaga Garzón (12/4) [Pietro Raúl Marsetti (10/2)], Edgar Domínguez (11/0), Hamilton Emilio Cuvi Rivera (27/4), Ney Raúl Avilés Aguirre (12/0), Byron Zózimo Tenorio (4/0) [Pablo Estebán Marín (13/0)], Pedro Mauricio Muñoz (6/1), Nelson Guerrero (3/0). Trainer: Dušan Drašković (4).
Goal: Alex Darío Aguinaga Garzón (74).

165. 17.06.1988 **HONDURAS - ECUADOR** **0-1(0-1)**
Estadio Nacional, Tegucigalpa; Referee: Marcial Gallardo (Honduras)
ECU: Carlos Luis Morales (9/0), Raúl Alfredo Noriega Escobar (3/0) [Carlos Quinteros (6/0)], Holguer Abraham Quiñónez (13/0), Wilson Homero Macías (14/0), Luis Enrique Capurro Bautista (16/0), Kléber Emilson Fajardo Barzola (14/0) [Edgar Domínguez (12/0)], Pablo Estebán Marín (14/0) [Hamilton Emilio Cuvi Rivera (28/4)], Pietro Raúl Marsetti (11/2), Ney Raúl Avilés Aguirre (13/1), Byron Zózimo Tenorio (5/0) [Pedro Mauricio Muñoz (7/1)], Nelson Guerrero (4/0) [Alex Darío Aguinaga Garzón (13/4)]. Trainer: Dušan Drašković (5).
Goal: Ney Raúl Avilés Aguirre (42).

166. 19.06.1988 **COSTA RICA - ECUADOR** **1-0**
Estadio "Alejandro Morera", San José
ECU: Héctor Lautaro Chiriboga, Carlos Quinteros, Wilson Homero Macías, Holguer Abraham Quiñónez, Edgar Domínguez, Alex Darío Aguinaga Garzón [Ney Raúl Avilés Aguirre], Pietro Raúl Marsetti [Luis Enrique Capurro Bautista], Hamilton Emilio Cuvi Rivera, Pedro Mauricio Muñoz, Byron Zózimo Tenorio [Pablo Estebán Marín], Nelson Guerrero. Trainer: Dušan Drašković.
Costa Rica fielded a U-20 Selection so this game is not counted as full international.

167. 07.09.1988 **ECUADOR – PARAGUAY** **1-5(0-3)**
Estadio Monumental de Barcelona, Guayaquil; Referee: Elías Víctoriano Jacomé Guerreiro (Ecuador); Attendance: 30,000
ECU: Alex Bolívar Cevallos (1/0) [Héctor Lautaro Chiriboga (7/0)], Juan Carlos Suárez (1/0), Wilson Homero Macías (15/0), Carlos Quinteros (7/0), Segundo Pazmiño (1/0) [Luis Enrique Capurro Bautista (17/0)], Pietro Raúl Marsetti (12/2), Pablo Estebán Marín (15/0) [Edgar Domínguez (13/0)), Fausto Anibal Delgado (1/0) [Hamilton Emilio Cuvi Rivera (29/5)], Nelson Guerrero (5/0) [Luis Bolivar Mosquera (7/0)], Pedro Mauricio Muñoz (8/1), Byron Zózimo Tenorio (6/0). Trainer: Dušan Drašković (6).
Goal: Hamilton Emilio Cuvi Rivera (79 penalty).

168. 13.09.1988 **CHILE – ECUADOR** **3-1(1-0)**
Estadio La Portada, La Serena; Referee: Pedro Roa (Chile); Attendance: 6,345
ECU: Carlos Luis Morales (10/0), Luis Enrique Capurro Bautista (18/0), Wilson Homero Macías (16/0), Kléber Emilson Fajardo Barzola (15/0), Holguer Abraham Quiñónez (14/0), Pietro Raúl Marsetti (13/2), Edgar Domínguez (14/0), Hamilton Emilio Cuvi Rivera (30/6), Pedro Mauricio Muñoz (9/1) [José Federico Minda (1/0)], Byron Zózimo Tenorio (7/0), Ney Raúl Avilés Aguirre (14/1). Trainer: Dušan Drašković (7).
Goal: Hamilton Emilio Cuvi Rivera (83).

169. 27.09.1988 **URUGUAY – ECUADOR** **2-1(1-0)** Boqueron Cup. Semi-finals
Estadio Defensores del Chaco, Asunción; Referee: Gabriel González (Paraguay); Attendance: 10,000
ECU: Carlos Luis Morales (11/0), Jimmy Izquierdo (1/1), Tulio Quinteros (4/0) [Wilson Homero Macías (17/0)], Holguer Abraham Quiñónez (15/0), Luis Enrique Capurro Bautista (19/0) [*sent off*], Alex Darío Aguinaga Garzón (14/4), Pietro Raúl Marsetti (14/2) [José Federico Minda (2/0)], Kléber Emilson Fajardo Barzola (16/0), Hamilton Emilio Cuvi Rivera (31/6), Byron Zózimo Tenorio (8/0), Ney Raúl Avilés Aguirre (15/1). Trainer: Dušan Drašković (8).
Goal: Jimmy Izquierdo (74).

170. 29.09.1988 **CHILE – ECUADOR** **0-0; 2-3 on penalties** Boqueron Cup. Bronze Medal
Estadio Defensores del Chaco, Asunción; Referee: Artemio Martínez (Paraguay); Attendance: 25,000
ECU: Carlos Luis Morales (12/0), Jimmy Izquierdo (2/1), Wilson Homero Macías (18/0), Carlos Quinteros (8/0), Holguer Abraham Quiñónez (16/0), Alex Darío Aguinaga Garzón (15/4), Pietro Raúl Marsetti (15/2), Kléber Emilson Fajardo Barzola (17/0), Hamilton Emilio Cuvi Rivera (32/6), Byron Zózimo Tenorio (9/0), Ney Raúl Avilés Aguirre (16/1). Trainer: Dušan Drašković (9).
Penalties: Alex Darío Aguinaga Garzón, Jimmy Izquierdo, Carlos Luis Morales (Pietro Raúl Marsetti and Hamilton Emilio Cuvi Rivera missed).

171. 29.01.1989 **ECUADOR – CHILE** **1-0(1-0)**
Estadio Monumental de Barcelona, Guayaquil; Referee: Alfredo Rodas (Ecuador); Attendance: 13,000
ECU: Carlos Luis Morales (13/0), Carlos Quinteros (9/0) [54.Claudio Alcívar (4/0)], Wilson Homero Macías (19/0), Holguer Abraham Quiñónez (17/0), Luis Enrique Capurro Bautista (20/0), Alex Darío Aguinaga Garzón (16/4), Pietro Raúl Marsetti (16/2) [58.Jesús José Cárdenas (2/0)], Kléber Emilson Fajardo Barzola (18/0), Hamilton Emilio Cuvi Rivera (33/6) [58.José Federico Minda (3/0)], Byron Zózimo Tenorio (10/0) [72.Wilfrido Enrique Verduga (2/0)], Ney Raúl Avilés Aguirre (17/2). Trainer: Dušan Drašković (10).
Goal: Ney Raúl Avilés Aguirre (41).

172. 15.03.1989 **BRAZIL – ECUADOR** **1-0(1-0)**
Estádio "José Fragelli", Cuiabá; Referee: Dulcídio Vanderlei Boschilla (Brazil); Attendance: 54,815
ECU: Carlos Luis Morales (14/0), Claudio Alcívar (5/0) [Carlos Quinteros (10/0)], Wilson Homero Macías (20/0), Holguer Abraham Quiñónez (18/0), Luis Enrique Capurro Bautista (21/0), Pietro Raúl Marsetti (17/2) [Nelson Guerrero (6/0)], Wilfrido Enrique Verduga (3/0) [Carlos Antonio Muñoz Martínez (1/0)], Kléber Emilson Fajardo Barzola (19/0) [Jimmy Gustavo Montanero Soledispa (1/0)], Hamilton Emilio Cuvi Rivera (34/6) [Julio César Rosero (1/0)], Byron Zózimo Tenorio (11/0) [*sent off 39*], Ney Raúl Avilés Aguirre (18/2). Trainer: Dušan Drašković (11).

173. 13.04.1989 **ECUADOR – ARGENTINA** **2-2(0-2)**
Estadio Monumental de Barcelona, Guayaquil; Referee: César Cachay (Peru); Attendance: 12,000
ECU: Carlos Luis Morales (15/0), Claudio Alcívar (6/0), Wilson Homero Macías (21/0), Holguer Abraham Quiñónez (19/0), Luis Enrique Capurro Bautista (22/0), Pedro Raúl Marsetti (18/2) [46.Julio César Rosero (2/0)], Kléber Emilson Fajardo Barzola (20/0), Wilfrido Enrique Verduga (4/0) [46.Carlos Quinteros (11/0)], Hamilton Emilio Cuvi Rivera (35/7), Carlos Antonio Muñoz Martínez (2/0) [46.Nelson Guerrero (7/0)], Ney Raúl Avilés Aguirre (19/3). Trainer: Dušan Drašković (12).
Goals: Ney Raúl Avilés Aguirre (50), Hamilton Emilio Cuvi Rivera (58 penalty).

174. 03.05.1989 **URUGUAY – ECUADOR** **3-1(1-0)**
Estadio Centenario, Montevideo; Referee: Jorge Romero (Argentina); Attendance: 15,000
ECU: Carlos Luis Morales (16/0), Jimmy Izquierdo (3/1) [Claudio Alcívar (7/0)], Wilson Homero Macías (22/0), Holguer Abraham Quiñónez (20/0), Luis Enrique Capurro Bautista (23/0), Alex Darío Aguinaga Garzón (17/4), Pietro Raúl Marsetti (19/2) [Julio César Rosero (3/0)], Kléber Emilson Fajardo Barzola (21/0), Hamilton Emilio Cuvi Rivera (36/7), Byron Zózimo Tenorio (12/0) [Carlos Antonio Muñoz Martínez (3/0)], Ney Raúl Avilés Aguirre (20/4). Trainer: Dušan Drašković (13).
Goal: Ney Raúl Avilés Aguirre (85).

175. 23.05.1989 **ECUADOR – URUGUAY** **1-1(0-0)**
Estadio Olimpico „Atahualpa", Quito; Referee: Adolfo Quirola (Ecuador); Attendance: 20,000
ECU: Carlos Luis Morales (17/0), Jimmy Izquierdo (4/1), Wilson Homero Macías (23/0), Holguer Abraham Quiñónez (21/0), Luis Enrique Capurro Bautista (24/0), Alex Darío Aguinaga Garzón (18/4) [Nelson Guerrero (8/0)], Julio César Rosero (4/0), Kléber Emilson Fajardo Barzola (22/0), Hamilton Emilio Cuvi Rivera (37/7) [Carlos Antonio Muñoz Martínez (4/0)], Byron Zózimo Tenorio (13/0), Ney Raúl Avilés Aguirre (21/5). Trainer: Dušan Drašković (14).
Goal: Ney Raúl Avilés Aguirre (58).

176. 20.06.1989 **PERU – ECUADOR** **2-1(1-1)** Soccer Bowl '89
Queen's Park Oval, Port of Spain (Trinidad Tobago)
ECU: Víctor Mendoza Cevallos (1/0), Claudio Alcívar (8/0), Wilson Homero Macías (24/0), Holguer Abraham Quiñónez (22/0), Luis Enrique Capurro Bautista (25/0) [*sent off 82*], Pietro Raúl Marsetti (20/2) [46.Jimmy Gustavo Montanero Soledispa (2/0)], Kléber Emilson Fajardo Barzola (23/0) [46. Ney Raúl Avilés Aguirre (22/5)], Wilfrido Enrique Verduga (5/0) [46.Carlos Antonio Muñoz Martínez (5/0)], Nelson Guerrero (9/1) [*sent off 61*], Hermen De Jesús Benítez (13/7), Byron Zózimo Tenorio (14/0) [46.Hamilton Emilio Cuvi Rivera (38/7)]. Trainer: Dušan Drašković (15).
Goal: Nelson Guerrero (26).

177. 02.07.1989 **ECUADOR – URUGUAY** **1-0(0-0)** 34th Copa América. Group Stage
Estádio Serra Dourada, Goiânia (Brazil); Referee: Carlos Alberto Maciel (Paraguay); Attendance: 19,000
ECU: Carlos Luis Morales (18/0), Jimmy Izquierdo (5/1), Wilson Homero Macías (25/0), Holguer Abraham Quiñónez (23/0), Luis Enrique Capurro Bautista (26/0), Alex Darío Aguinaga Garzón (19/4) [89.Pietro Raúl Marsetti (21/2)], Julio César Rosero (5/0), Kléber Emilson Fajardo Barzola (24/0), Hamilton Emilio Cuvi Rivera (39/7), Byron Zózimo Tenorio (15/0) [77.Hermen De Jesús Benítez (14/8)], Ney Raúl Avilés Aguirre (23/5). Trainer: Dušan Drašković (16).
Goal: Hermen De Jesús Benítez (88).

178. 04.07.1989 **ECUADOR – ARGENTINA** **0-0** 34th Copa América. Group Stage
Estádio Serra Dourada, Goiânia (Brazil); Referee: José Ramírez (Peru); Attendance: 12,000
ECU: Carlos Luis Morales (19/0), Jimmy Izquierdo (6/1), Wilson Homero Macías (26/0), Holguer Abraham Quiñónez (24/0), Luis Enrique Capurro Bautista (27/0) [*sent off 72*], Alex Darío Aguinaga Garzón (20/4), Kléber Emilson Fajardo Barzola (25/0), Julio César Rosero (6/0), Hamilton Emilio Cuvi Rivera (40/7), Byron Zózimo Tenorio (16/0) [75.Hermen De Jesús Benítez (15/8)], Ney Raúl Avilés Aguirre (24/5). Trainer: Dušan Drašković (17).

179. 06.07.1989 **ECUADOR – BOLIVIA** **0-0** 34th Copa América. Group Stage
Estádio Serra Dourada, Goiânia (Brazil); Referee: Jesús Díaz Palacios (Colombia); Attendance: 3,000
ECU: Carlos Luis Morales (20/0), Jimmy Izquierdo (7/1), Wilson Homero Macías (27/0), Holguer Abraham Quiñónez (25/0), Claudio Alcívar (9/0) [61.Hermen De Jesús Benítez (16/8)], Alex Darío Aguinaga Garzón (21/4), Julio César Rosero (7/0), Kléber Emilson Fajardo Barzola (26/0), Hamilton Emilio Cuvi Rivera (41/7), Byron Zózimo Tenorio (17/0) [76.Pietro Raúl Marsetti (22/2)], Ney Raúl Avilés Aguirre (25/5). Trainer: Dušan Drašković (18).

180. 10.07.1989 **CHILE – ECUADOR** **2-1(1-0)** 34th Copa América. Group Stage
Estádio Serra Dourada, Goiânia (Brazil); Referee: Carlos Alberto Maciel (Paraguay); Attendance: 2,000
ECU: Carlos Luis Morales (21/0), Jimmy Izquierdo (8/1), Wilson Homero Macías (28/0), Holguer Abraham Quiñónez (26/0), Luis Enrique Capurro Bautista (28/0), Alex Darío Aguinaga Garzón (22/4), Julio César Rosero (8/0), Kléber Emilson Fajardo Barzola (27/0) [46.Jimmy Gustavo Montanero Soledispa (3/0)], Hamilton Emilio Cuvi Rivera (42/7), Byron Zózimo Tenorio (18/0) [59.Hermen De Jesús Benítez (17/8)], Ney Raúl Avilés Aguirre (26/6). Trainer: Dušan Drašković (19).
Goal: Ney Raúl Avilés Aguirre (89).

181. 20.08.1989 **COLOMBIA – ECUADOR** **2-0(1-0)** 14th FIFA WC. Qualifiers
Estadio Metropolitano „Roberto Meléndez“, Barranquilla; Referee: Romualdo Arppi Filho (Brazil)
ECU: Carlos Luis Morales (22/0), Jimmy Izquierdo (9/1), Wilson Homero Macías (29/0), Holguer Abraham Quiñónez (27/0), Luis Enrique Capurro Bautista (29/0), Alex Darío Aguinaga Garzón (23/4), Julio César Rosero (9/0), Kléber Emilson Fajardo Barzola (28/0), Hamilton Emilio Cuvi Rivera (43/7) [77.Pietro Raúl Marsetti (23/2)], Hermen De Jesús Benítez (18/8) [64.Byron Zózimo Tenorio (19/0)], Ney Raúl Avilés Aguirre (27/6). Trainer: Dušan Drašković (20).

182. 03.09.1989 **ECUADOR – COLOMBIA** **0-0** 14th FIFA WC. Qualifiers
Estadio Monumental de Barcelona, Guayaquil; Referee: Ricardo Calabria (Argentina); Attendance: 55,000
ECU: Carlos Luis Morales (23/0), Jimmy Izquierdo (10/1), Holguer Abraham Quiñónez (28/0), Tulio Quinteros (5/0), Luis Enrique Capurro Bautista (30/0), Alex Darío Aguinaga Garzón (24/4), Julio César Rosero (10/0) [72.Hermen De Jesús Benítez (19/8)], Kléber Emilson Fajardo Barzola (29/0), Hamilton Emilio Cuvi Rivera (44/7) [65.Wilfrido Enrique Verduga (6/0)], Byron Zózimo Tenorio (20/0), Ney Raúl Avilés Aguirre (28/6). Trainer: Dušan Drašković (21).

183. 10.09.1989 **PARAGUAY – ECUADOR** **2-1(1-0)** 14th FIFA WC. Qualifiers
Estadio Defensores del Chaco, Asunción; Referee: José Francisco Ramírez Calle (Peru); Attendance: 60,000
ECU: Carlos Luis Morales (24/0), Freddy Egberto Bravo (2/0), Holguer Abraham Quiñónez (29/0), Tulio Quinteros (6/0), Luis Enrique Capurro Bautista (31/0), Julio César Rosero (11/0) [74.Hamilton Emilio Cuvi Rivera (45/7)], Kléber Emilson Fajardo Barzola (30/0), Carlos Antonio Muñoz Martínez (6/0), Nelson Guerrero (10/1), Alex Darío Aguinaga Garzón (25/4) [67.Byron Zózimo Tenorio (21/0)], Ney Raúl Avilés Aguirre (29/7). Trainer: Dušan Drašković (22).
Goal: Ney Raúl Avilés Aguirre (84).

184. 24.09.1989 **ECUADOR – PARAGUAY** **3-1(1-1)** 14th FIFA WC. Qualifiers
Estadio Monumental de Barcelona, Guayaquil; Referee: Arnaldo César Coelho (Brazil); Attendance: 18,000
ECU: Víctor Mendoza Cevallos (2/0), Freddy Egberto Bravo (3/0), Wilson Homero Macías (30/0), Holguer Abraham Quiñónez (30/0), Luis Enrique Capurro Bautista (32/0), Carlos Antonio Muñoz Martínez (7/0) [*sent off 78*], Kléber Emilson Fajardo Barzola (31/0), Pietro Raúl Marsetti (24/3) [82.Wilfrido Enrique Verduga (7/0)], Nelson Guerrero (11/1) [75.Byron Zózimo Tenorio (22/0)], Alex Darío Aguinaga Garzón (26/5), Ney Raúl Avilés Aguirre (30/8). Trainer: Dušan Drašković (23).
Goals: Alex Darío Aguinaga Garzón (26), Pietro Raúl Marsetti (72), Ney Raúl Avilés Aguirre (82).

185. 06.06.1991 **PERU – ECUADOR** **0-1(0-0)**
Estadio Nacional, Lima; Referee: Fernando Chapell (Peru); Attendance: 10,000
ECU: Erwin Aníbal Ramírez Castro (1/0), Luis Enrique Capurro Bautista (33/0), Jimmy Gustavo Montanero Soledispa (4/0), Carlos Antonio Muñoz Martínez (8/0), Juan Carlos Garay (1/0), José Guerrero (1/0), Nixon Aníbal Carcelén Chalá (1/0) [Wilson Homero Macías (31/0)], Ivo Norman Ron Viver (1/1) [Ángel Oswaldo Fernández Vernaza (1/0)], Byron Zózimo Tenorio (23/0), Freddy Egberto Bravo (4/0), Roberth Javier Burbano (1/0) [Juan Helio Guamán (1/0)]. Trainer: Dušan Drašković (24).
Goal: Ivo Norman Ron Viver (47).

186. 19.06.1991 **ECUADOR – CHILE** **2-1(1-1)**
Estadio Monumental de Barcelona, Guayaquil; Referee: Luis Naranjo Villacres (Ecuador); Attendance: 25,000
ECU: Erwin Aníbal Ramírez Castro (2/0), José Higinio Rivera (1/0), Byron Zózimo Tenorio (24/0), Luis Enrique Capurro Bautista (34/0), José Guerrero (2/1), Freddy Egberto Bravo (5/0), Nixon Aníbal Carcelén Chalá (2/0) [Alex Darío Aguinaga Garzón (27/5)], Ivo Norman Ron Viver (2/1) [Carlos Antonio Muñoz Martínez (9/0)], Juan Carlos Garay (2/1), Roberth Javier Burbano (2/0) [Manuel Antonio Uquillas (1/0)], Edwin Patricio Hurtado Zurita (1/0) [Ney Raúl Avilés Aguirre (31/8)]. Trainer: Dušan Drašković (25).
Goals: Juan Carlos Garay (7), José Guerrero (70).

187. 25.06.1991 **ECUADOR – PERU** **2-2(2-0)**
Estadio Monumental de Barcelona, Guayaquil; Referee: Jorge Orellana Vimos (Ecuador); Attendance: 10,000
ECU: Erwin Aníbal Ramírez Castro (3/0), José Higinio Rivera (2/0), Byron Zózimo Tenorio (25/0), Luis Enrique Capurro Bautista (35/0), José Guerrero (3/1), Freddy Egberto Bravo (6/0), Juan Carlos Garay (3/1) [Manuel Antonio Uquillas (2/0)], Nixon Aníbal Carcelén Chalá (3/1) [Ney Raúl Avilés Aguirre (32/8)], Stony Marin Batioja (3/0) [Wilson Homero Macías (32/0)], Alex Darío Aguinaga Garzón (28/5), Carlos Antonio Muñoz Martínez (10/1) [Roberth Javier Burbano (3/0)]. Trainer: Dušan Drašković (26).
Goals: Nixon Aníbal Carcelén Chalá (2), Carlos Antonio Muñoz Martínez (32).

188. 30.06.1991 **CHILE - ECUADOR** **3-1(3-0)**
Estadio Nacional, Santiago; Referee: Carlos Manuel Robles Mella (Chile); Attendance: 25,000
ECU: Erwin Aníbal Ramírez Castro (4/0), Luis Enrique Capurro Bautista (36/0), Byron Zózimo Tenorio (26/0), José Higinio Rivera (3/0), José Guerrero (4/1) [Manuel Antonio Uquillas (3/0)], Freddy Egberto Bravo (7/0), Carlos Antonio Muñoz Martínez (11/1) [Roberth Javier Burbano (4/0)], Nixon Aníbal Carcelén Chalá (4/1), Juan Carlos Garay (4/1) [Ángel Oswaldo Fernández Vernaza (2/0)], Ney Raúl Avilés Aguirre (33/8) [Holguer Abraham Quiñónez (31/0)], Alex Darío Aguinaga Garzón (29/6). Trainer: Dušan Drašković (27).
Goal: Alex Darío Aguinaga Garzón (49).

189. 07.07.1991 **COLOMBIA - ECUADOR** **1-0(1-0)** 35th Copa América. Group Stage
Estadio Playa Ancha, Valparaíso; Referee: Juan Francisco Escobar (Paraguay); Attendance: 15,000
ECU: Erwin Aníbal Ramírez Castro (5/0), Jimmy Gustavo Montanero Soledispa (5/0), Byron Zózimo Tenorio (27/0), Luis Enrique Capurro Bautista (37/0), Holguer Abraham Quiñónez (32/0), Juan Carlos Garay (5/1), Carlos Antonio Muñoz Martínez (12/1) [75.Manuel Antonio Uquillas (4/0)], Freddy Egberto Bravo (8/0), Nixon Aníbal Carcelén Chalá (5/1), Alex Darío Aguinaga Garzón (30/6), Ney Raúl Avilés Aguirre (34/8) [46.Roberth Javier Burbano (5/0)]. Trainer: Dušan Drašković (28).

190. 09.07.1991 **ECUADOR - URUGUAY** **1-1(1-0)** 35th Copa América. Group Stage
Estadio Sausalito, Viña del Mar (Chile); Referee: Gastón Castro (Chile); Attendance: 18,000
ECU: Erwin Aníbal Ramírez Castro (6/0), Jimmy Gustavo Montanero Soledispa (6/0), Luis Enrique Capurro Bautista (38/0), Byron Zózimo Tenorio (28/0), Holguer Abraham Quiñónez (33/0), Juan Carlos Garay (6/1), Nixon Aníbal Carcelén Chalá (6/1), Freddy Egberto Bravo (9/0), Carlos Antonio Muñoz Martínez (13/1) [78.Roberth Javier Burbano (6/0)], Alex Darío Aguinaga Garzón (31/7), Ney Raúl Avilés Aguirre (35/8) [79.José Guerrero (5/1)]. Trainer: Dušan Drašković (29).
Goal: Alex Darío Aguinaga Garzón (44).

191. 13.07.1991 **ECUADOR - BOLIVIA** **4-0(2-0)** 35th Copa América. Group Stage
Estadio Sausalito, Viña del Mar (Chile); Referee: Gastón Castro (Chile); Attendance: 19,000
ECU: Erwin Aníbal Ramírez Castro (7/1), Jimmy Gustavo Montanero Soledispa (7/0), Byron Zózimo Tenorio (29/0), Luis Enrique Capurro Bautista (39/0), Holguer Abraham Quiñónez (34/0), Freddy Egberto Bravo (10/0), Ivo Norman Ron Viver (3/1), Carlos Antonio Muñoz Martínez (14/1), Nixon Aníbal Carcelén Chalá (7/1) [81.Roberth Javier Burbano (7/0)], Alex Darío Aguinaga Garzón (32/8) [77.Juan Carlos Garay (7/1)], Ney Raúl Avilés Aguirre (36/10). Trainer: Dušan Drašković (30).
Goals: Alex Darío Aguinaga Garzón (32), Ney Raúl Avilés Aguirre (42, 73), Erwin Aníbal Ramírez Castro (80 penalty).

192. 15.07.1991 **BRAZIL - ECUADOR** **3-1(1-1)** 35th Copa América. Group Stage
Estadio Sausalito, Viña del Mar (Chile); Referee: Juan Francisco Escobar (Paraguay); Attendance: 30,000
ECU: Erwin Aníbal Ramírez Castro (8/1), Jimmy Gustavo Montanero Soledispa (8/0), Byron Zózimo Tenorio (30/0), Luis Enrique Capurro Bautista (40/0), Holguer Abraham Quiñónez (35/0), Freddy Egberto Bravo (11/0), Nixon Aníbal Carcelén Chalá (8/1) [65.Juan Carlos Garay (8/1)], Ivo Norman Ron Viver (4/1) [65.Roberth Javier Burbano (8/0)], Carlos Antonio Muñoz Martínez (15/2), Ney Raúl Avilés Aguirre (37/10), Alex Darío Aguinaga Garzón (33/8). Trainer: Dušan Drašković (31).
Goal: Carlos Antonio Muñoz Martínez (12).

193. 24.05.1992 **GUATEMALA - ECUADOR** **1-1**
Estadio Nacional "Mateo Flores", Ciudad de Guatemala; Referee: Freddy Burgos
ECU: Jacinto Alberto Espinoza Castillo (1/0), José Guerrero (6/1), Luis Enrique Capurro Bautista (41/0), Iván Jacinto Hurtado Angulo (1/1), Dannes Arsenio Coronel (1/0), Héctor Jhonny Carabalí Cevallos (1/0), Nixon Aníbal Carcelén Chalá (9/1), Cléber Manuel Chalá Guerrón (1/0) [Edwin Patricio Hurtado Zurita (2/0)], Juan Carlos Garay (9/1) [Oswaldo De la Cruz (1/0], Ángel Oswaldo Fernández Vernaza (3/0), Eduardo Estíguar Hurtado Roa (1/0) [Diego Rodrigo Herrera Larrea (1/0)]. Trainer: Dušan Drašković (32).
Goal: Iván Jacinto Hurtado Angulo (44 penalty).

194. 27.05.1992 **COSTA RICA - ECUADOR** **2-1**
Estadio Nacional, San José; Referee: Ramón Mendez (Costa Rica)
ECU: Jacinto Alberto Espinoza Castillo (2/0), José Guerrero (7/1), Luis Enrique Capurro Bautista (42/0), Iván Jacinto Hurtado Angulo (2/1), Dannes Arsenio Coronel (2/0), Héctor Jhonny Carabalí Cevallos (2/1), Alberto Guillermo Montaño Angulo (1/0) [Ronney Mantilla (1/0)], Nixon Aníbal Carcelén Chalá (10/1), Ángel Oswaldo Fernández Vernaza (4/0), Eduardo Estíguar Hurtado Roa (2/0), Cléber Manuel Chalá Guerrón (2/0). Trainer: Dušan Drašković (33).
Goal: Héctor Jhonny Carabalí Cevallos (90).

195. 04.07.1992 **URUGUAY - ECUADOR** **3-1(1-0)**
Estadio Centenario, Montevideo; Referee: Juan Carlos Crespi (Argentina); Attendance: 15,000
ECU: Jacinto Alberto Espinoza Castillo (3/0), Jimmy Gustavo Montanero Soledispa (9/0), Iván Jacinto Hurtado Angulo (3/1) [43.Dannes Arsenio Coronel (3/0)], Máximo Wilson Tenorio Quiñónez (1/0), Luis Enrique Capurro Bautista (43/0), Holguer Abraham Quiñónez (36/0) [70.Juan Carlos Garay (10/1)], Raúl Alfredo Noriega Escobar (4/0) [46.Héctor Jhonny Carabalí Cevallos (3/1)], Nixon Aníbal Carcelén Chalá (11/1) [62.Cléber Manuel Chalá Guerrón (3/0)], Carlos Antonio Muñoz Martínez (16/2), Ney Raúl Avilés Aguirre (38/10), Ángel Oswaldo Fernández Vernaza (5/1). Trainer: Dušan Drašković (34).
Goal: Ángel Oswaldo Fernández Vernaza (84).

196. 06.08.1992 **ECUADOR - COSTA RICA** **1-1**
Estadio „George Capwell", Guayaquil; Referee: Elías Víctoriano Jacomé Guerreiro (Ecuador)
ECU: Jacinto Alberto Espinoza Castillo (4/0), Raúl Alfredo Noriega Escobar (5/0), Byron Zózimo Tenorio (31/1), Luis Enrique Capurro Bautista (44/0), Dannes Arsenio Coronel (4/0) [Iván Jacinto Hurtado Angulo (4/1)], Héctor Jhonny Carabalí Cevallos (4/1), Nixon Aníbal Carcelén Chalá (12/1), Ivo Norman Ron Viver (5/1) [Oswaldo De la Cruz (2/0)], José Eduardo Gavica Peñafiel (1/0) [Ney Raúl Avilés Aguirre (39/10)], Ángel Oswaldo Fernández Vernaza (6/1) [Diego Rodrigo Herrera Larrea (2/0)], Carlos Antonio Muñoz Martínez (17/2) [Máximo Wilson Tenorio Quiñónez (2/0)]. Trainer: Dušan Drašković (35).
Goal: Byron Zózimo Tenorio (66).

197. 24.11.1992 **PERU - ECUADOR** **1-1(0-1)**
Estadio Nacional, Lima; Referee: José Arana (Peru)
ECU: Jacinto Alberto Espinoza Castillo (5/0), Héctor Américo Ferri (1/0) [*sent off 87*], Iván Jacinto Hurtado Angulo (5/1), Ángel Hurtado (1/0), Luis Enrique Capurro Bautista (45/0), Ángel Oswaldo Fernández Vernaza (7/1), Hjalmar Zambrano (1/1) [68.Dannes Arsenio Coronel (5/0)], Héctor Jhonny Carabalí Cevallos (5/1), Nixon Aníbal Carcelén Chalá (13/1), Ney Raúl Avilés Aguirre (40/10) [67.Carlos Quiñónez (1/0)], David Reascos (1/0). Trainer: Dušan Drašković (36).
Goal: Hjalmar Zambrano (4).

198. 27.01.1993 **ECUADOR – BELARUS** **1-1(1-0)**

Estadio Monumental de Barcelona, Guayaquil; Referee: Elías Víctoriano Jacomé Guerreiro (Ecuador); Attendance: 38,000

ECU: Jacinto Alberto Espinoza Castillo (6/0), Raúl Alfredo Noriega Escobar (6/0), Carlos Antonio Muñoz Martínez (18/2), Héctor Jhonny Carabalí Cevallos (6/1) [65.Iván Jacinto Hurtado Angulo (6/1)], Byron Zózimo Tenorio (32/1), Ángel Oswaldo Fernández Vernaza (8/2), José Guerrero (8/1), Eduardo Estíguar Hurtado Roa (3/0) [71.Máximo Wilson Tenorio Quiñónez (3/0)], Nixon Aníbal Carcelén Chalá (14/1) [59.José Eduardo Gavica Peñafiel (2/0)], Cléber Manuel Chalá Guerrón (4/0) [76.Hjalmar Zambrano (2/1)], Ney Raúl Avilés Aguirre (Cap) (41/10). Trainer: Dušan Drašković (37).

Goal: Ángel Oswaldo Fernández Vernaza (38).

199. 31.01.1993 **ECUADOR – ROMANIA** **3-0(2-0)**

Estadio Monumental de Barcelona, Guayaquil; Referee: Medardo Martínez (Ecuador)

ECU: Víctor Mendoza Cevallos (3/0) [46.Alex Bolívar Cevallos (2/0)], Carlos Antonio Muñoz Martínez (19/2), Iván Jacinto Hurtado Angulo (7/1), Raúl Alfredo Noriega Escobar (7/0), Byron Zózimo Tenorio (33/1), Héctor Jhonny Carabalí Cevallos (7/1), Nixon Aníbal Carcelén Chalá (15/1), Ángel Oswaldo Fernández Vernaza (9/2), José Eduardo Gavica Peñafiel (3/1) [88.Ángel Hurtado (2/0)], Ney Raúl Avilés Aguirre (42/11) [78.Diego Rodrigo Herrera Larrea (3/0)], Eduardo Estíguar Hurtado Roa (4/1). Trainer: Dušan Drašković (38).

Goals: Eduardo Estíguar Hurtado Roa (32), José Eduardo Gavica Peñafiel (43), Ney Raúl Avilés Aguirre (82).

200. 30.05.1993 **ECUADOR – PERU** **1-0(1-0)**

Estadio Olimpico „Atahualpa“, Quito; Referee: Marco Aguas (Ecuador)

ECU: Jacinto Alberto Espinoza Castillo (7/0), Carlos Antonio Muñoz Martínez (20/2), Raúl Alfredo Noriega Escobar (8/0), Luis Enrique Capurro Bautista (46/0), Jimmy Gustavo Montanero Soledispa (10/0) [46.Holguer Abraham Quiñónez (37/0)], Héctor Jhonny Carabalí Cevallos (8/1), Nixon Aníbal Carcelén Chalá (16/1), José Eduardo Gavica Peñafiel (4/1) [Dannes Arsenio Coronel (6/0)], Ángel Oswaldo Fernández Vernaza (10/3) [54.Juan Carlos Garay (11/1)], Cléber Manuel Chalá Guerrón (5/0) [46.Alex Darío Aguinaga Garzón (34/8)], Luis Anibal Chérrez (1/0) [46.Eduardo Estíguar Hurtado Roa (5/1)]. Trainer: Dušan Drašković (39).

Goal: Ángel Oswaldo Fernández Vernaza (24).

201. 09.06.1993 **ECUADOR – CHILE** **1-2(1-2)**

Estadio Olimpico „Atahualpa“, Quito; Referee: José Carpio Guevara (Ecuador); Attendance: 45,000

ECU: Jacinto Alberto Espinoza Castillo (8/0), Carlos Antonio Muñoz Martínez (21/2), Byron Zózimo Tenorio (34/1), Luis Enrique Capurro Bautista (47/0) [Raúl Alfredo Noriega Escobar (9/0)], José Guerrero (9/1), Nixon Aníbal Carcelén Chalá (17/1), Héctor Jhonny Carabalí Cevallos (9/1), Holguer Abraham Quiñónez (38/0) [José Eduardo Gavica Peñafiel (5/1)], Cléber Manuel Chalá Guerrón (6/0) [Luis Anibal Chérrez (2/0)], Ney Raúl Avilés Aguirre (43/12) [Ángel Oswaldo Fernández Vernaza (11/3)], Eduardo Estíguar Hurtado Roa (6/1). Trainer: Dušan Drašković (40).

Goal: Ney Raúl Avilés Aguirre (29).

202. 15.06.1993 **ECUADOR – VENEZUELA** **6-1(2-0)** 36th Copa América. Group Stage

Estadio Olimpico „Atahualpa“, Quito; Referee: Francisco Lamolina (Argentina); Attendance: 45,000

ECU: Jacinto Alberto Espinoza Castillo (9/0), Jimmy Gustavo Montanero Soledispa (11/0) [75.Iván Jacinto Hurtado Angulo (8/1)], Raúl Alfredo Noriega Escobar (10/1), Luis Enrique Capurro Bautista (48/0), Carlos Antonio Muñoz Martínez (22/3), Héctor Jhonny Carabalí Cevallos (10/1), Nixon Aníbal Carcelén Chalá (18/1), Alex Darío Aguinaga Garzón (35/9), Ángel Oswaldo Fernández Vernaza (12/5), Eduardo Estíguar Hurtado Roa (7/2), Ney Raúl Avilés Aguirre (44/12) [70.José Eduardo Gavica Peñafiel (6/1)]. Trainer: Dušan Drašković (41).

Goals: Carlos Antonio Muñoz Martínez (19), Raúl Alfredo Noriega Escobar (32), Ángel Oswaldo Fernández Vernaza (57), Eduardo Estíguar Hurtado Roa (65), Ángel Oswaldo Fernández Vernaza (81), Alex Darío Aguinaga Garzón (84).

203. 19.06.1993 **ECUADOR – UNITED STATES** **2-0(2-0)** 36th Copa América. Group Stage

Estadio Olimpico „Atahualpa“, Quito; Referee: Iván Enrique Guerrero Levancini (Chile); Attendance: 45,000

ECU: Jacinto Alberto Espinoza Castillo (10/0), Luis Enrique Capurro Bautista (49/0), Jimmy Gustavo Montanero Soledispa (12/0), Héctor Jhonny Carabalí Cevallos (11/1), Raúl Alfredo Noriega Escobar (11/1) [40.Byron Zózimo Tenorio (35/1)], Carlos Antonio Muñoz Martínez (23/3), Nixon Aníbal Carcelén Chalá (19/1), Ángel Oswaldo Fernández Vernaza (13/5), Alex Darío Aguinaga Garzón (36/9), Eduardo Estíguar Hurtado Roa (8/3), Ney Raúl Avilés Aguirre (45/13) [64.José Eduardo Gavica Peñafiel (7/1)]. Trainer: Dušan Drašković (42).

Goals: Ney Raúl Avilés Aguirre (11), Eduardo Estíguar Hurtado Roa (35).

204. 22.06.1993 **ECUADOR – URUGUAY** **2-1(1-0)** 36th Copa América. Group Stage

Estadio Olimpico „Atahualpa“, Quito; Referee: Francisco Oscar Lamolina (Argentina); Attendance: 45,000

ECU: Jacinto Alberto Espinoza Castillo (11/0), Jimmy Gustavo Montanero Soledispa (13/0), Raúl Alfredo Noriega Escobar (12/1), Luis Enrique Capurro Bautista (50/0), Carlos Antonio Muñoz Martínez (24/3), Héctor Jhonny Carabalí Cevallos (12/1), Nixon Aníbal Carcelén Chalá (20/1), Alex Darío Aguinaga Garzón (37/10), Ángel Oswaldo Fernández Vernaza (14/5) [79.Máximo Wilson Tenorio Quiñónez (4/0)], Eduardo Estíguar Hurtado Roa (9/3), Ney Raúl Avilés Aguirre (46/14) [59.Byron Zózimo Tenorio (36/1)]. Trainer: Dušan Drašković (43).

Goals: Ney Raúl Avilés Aguirre (28), Alex Darío Aguinaga Garzón (87).

205. 26.06.1993 **ECUADOR – PARAGUAY** **3-0(2-0)** 36th Copa América. Quarter-Finals

Estadio Olimpico „Atahualpa“, Quito; Referee: Márcio Rezende de Freitas (Brazil); Attendance: 45,000

ECU: Víctor Mendoza Cevallos (4/0), Jimmy Gustavo Montanero Soledispa (14/0), Raúl Alfredo Noriega Escobar (13/1), Luis Enrique Capurro Bautista (51/0), Carlos Antonio Muñoz Martínez (25/3), Héctor Jhonny Carabalí Cevallos (13/1), Nixon Aníbal Carcelén Chalá (21/1), Alex Darío Aguinaga Garzón (38/10) [77.José Eduardo Gavica Peñafiel (8/1)], Ángel Oswaldo Fernández Vernaza (15/5) [79.Iván Jacinto Hurtado Angulo (9/1)], Eduardo Estíguar Hurtado Roa (10/4), Ney Raúl Avilés Aguirre (47/15). Trainer: Dušan Drašković (44).

Goals: Eduardo Estíguar Hurtado Roa (33), Mario Ramírez (43 own goal), Ney Raúl Avilés Aguirre (81).

206. 30.06.1993 **ECUADOR – MEXICO** **0-2(0-1)** 36th Copa América. Semi-Finals

Estadio Olimpico „Atahualpa“, Quito; Referee: Alberto Tejada (Peru); Attendance: 47,000

ECU: Jacinto Alberto Espinoza Castillo (12/0), Carlos Antonio Muñoz Martínez (26/3), Raúl Alfredo Noriega Escobar (14/1), Luis Enrique Capurro Bautista (52/0), Iván Jacinto Hurtado Angulo (10/1), Ángel Oswaldo Fernández Vernaza (16/5) [68.José Eduardo Gavica Peñafiel (9/1)], Héctor Jhonny Carabalí Cevallos (14/1), Nixon Aníbal Carcelén Chalá (22/1), Alex Darío Aguinaga Garzón (39/10), Eduardo Estíguar Hurtado Roa (11/4), Ney Raúl Avilés Aguirre (48/15) [55.Cléber Manuel Chalá Guerrón (7/0)]. Trainer: Dušan Drašković (45).

207. 03.07.1993 **ECUADOR – COLOMBIA** **0-1(0-0)** 36th Copa América. 3rd Place Play-Off

Estadio Reales Tamarindos, Portoviejo; Referee: Álvaro Arboleda (Venezuela); Attendance: 18,000

ECU: Jacinto Alberto Espinoza Castillo (13/0), Jimmy Gustavo Montanero Soledispa (15/0), Raúl Alfredo Noriega Escobar (15/1), Luis Enrique Capurro Bautista (53/0), Carlos Antonio Muñoz Martínez (27/3), Héctor Jhonny Carabalí Cevallos (15/1), Nixon Aníbal Carcelén Chalá (23/1), Alex Darío Aguinaga Garzón (40/10), Ángel Oswaldo Fernández Vernaza (17/5) [64.Byron Zózimo Tenorio (37/1)], Eduardo Estíguar Hurtado Roa (12/4) [61.Cléber Manuel Chalá Guerrón (8/0)], Ney Raúl Avilés Aguirre (49/15). Trainer: Dušan Drašković (46).

208. 18.07.1993 **ECUADOR - BRAZIL** **0-0** 15th FIFA WC. Qualifiers
Estadio „Isidro Romero", Guayaquil; Referee: Juan Carlos Lostau (Argentina); Attendance: 40,000
ECU: Jacinto Alberto Espinoza Castillo (14/0), Dannes Arsenio Coronel (7/0), Raúl Alfredo Noriega Escobar (16/1), Byron Zózimo Tenorio (38/1), Luis Enrique Capurro Bautista (54/0), Héctor Jhonny Carabalí Cevallos (16/1) [64.Iván Jacinto Hurtado Angulo (11/1)], Máximo Wilson Tenorio Quiñónez (5/0), Nixon Aníbal Carcelén Chalá (24/1), Alex Darío Aguinaga Garzón (41/10), Cléber Manuel Chalá Guerrón (9/0) [67.Eduardo Estíguar Hurtado Roa (13/4)], Carlos Antonio Muñoz Martínez (28/3). Trainer: Dušan Drašković (47).

209. 01.08.1993 **URUGUAY - ECUADOR** **0-0** 15th FIFA WC. Qualifiers
Estadio Centenario, Montevideo; Referee: Alberto Tejada Noriega (Peru); Attendance: 45,000
ECU: Jacinto Alberto Espinoza Castillo (15/0), Raúl Alfredo Noriega Escobar (17/1), Luis Enrique Capurro Bautista (55/0) (Cap), Byron Zózimo Tenorio (39/1) [82.Héctor Jhonny Carabalí Cevallos (17/1)], Nixon Aníbal Carcelén Chalá (25/1), Máximo Wilson Tenorio Quiñónez (6/0), Iván Jacinto Hurtado Angulo (12/1), Dannes Arsenio Coronel (8/0), Alex Darío Aguinaga Garzón (42/10) [33.Cléber Manuel Chalá Guerrón (10/0)], Eduardo Estíguar Hurtado Roa (14/4), Carlos Antonio Muñoz Martínez (29/3). Trainer: Dušan Drašković (48).

210. 08.08.1993 **ECUADOR - VENEZUELA** **5-0(2-0)** 15th FIFA WC. Qualifiers
Estadio Olimpico „Atahualpa", Quito; Referee: Francisco Oscar Lamolina (Argentina); Attendance: 35,000
ECU: Jacinto Alberto Espinoza Castillo (16/0), Jimmy Gustavo Montanero Soledispa (16/0), Luis Enrique Capurro Bautista (56/0), Héctor Jhonny Carabalí Cevallos (18/1), Nixon Aníbal Carcelén Chalá (26/1), Iván Jacinto Hurtado Angulo (13/1), Eduardo Estíguar Hurtado Roa (15/7), Dannes Arsenio Coronel (9/0) [69.Eduardo Zambrano (1/0)], Ángel Oswaldo Fernández Vernaza (18/5), Carlos Antonio Muñoz Martínez (30/4), Cléber Manuel Chalá Guerrón (11/1) [69.Ney Raúl Avilés Aguirre (50/15)]. Trainer: Dušan Drašković (49).
Goals: Carlos Antonio Muñoz Martínez (23), Eduardo Estíguar Hurtado Roa (40, 50), Cléber Manuel Chalá Guerrón (60), Eduardo Estíguar Hurtado Roa (76).

211. 15.08.1993 **BOLIVIA - ECUADOR** **1-0(1-0)** 15th FIFA WC. Qualifiers
Estadio „Hernándo Siles Zuazo", La Paz; Referee: Hernán Silva Arce (Chile); Attendance: 48,000
ECU: Jacinto Alberto Espinoza Castillo (17/0), Dannes Arsenio Coronel (10/0), Luis Enrique Capurro Bautista (57/0), Byron Zózimo Tenorio (40/1), Raúl Alfredo Noriega Escobar (18/1) [*sent off 88*], Héctor Jhonny Carabalí Cevallos (19/1), Nixon Aníbal Carcelén Chalá (27/1), Iván Jacinto Hurtado Angulo (14/1), Alex Darío Aguinaga Garzón (43/10) [60.Ángel Oswaldo Fernández Vernaza (19/5)], Carlos Antonio Muñoz Martínez (31/4) [53.Cléber Manuel Chalá Guerrón (12/1)], Eduardo Estíguar Hurtado Roa (16/7). Trainer: Dušan Drašković (50).

212. 22.08.1993 **BRAZIL - ECUADOR** **2-0(1-0)** 15th FIFA WC. Qualifiers
Estádio "Cicero Pompeu de Toledo" (Morumbi), São Paulo; Referee: José Joaquín Torres Cadena (Colombia); Attendance: 77,916
ECU: Jacinto Alberto Espinoza Castillo (18/0), Dannes Arsenio Coronel (11/0), Luis Enrique Capurro Bautista (58/0), Máximo Wilson Tenorio Quiñónez (7/0), Iván Jacinto Hurtado Angulo (15/1), Héctor Jhonny Carabalí Cevallos (20/1), Nixon Aníbal Carcelén Chalá (28/1), Ángel Oswaldo Fernández Vernaza (20/5) [64.Ney Raúl Avilés Aguirre (51/15)], Carlos Antonio Muñoz Martínez (32/4) [78.José Eduardo Gavica Peñafiel (10/1)], Cléber Manuel Chalá Guerrón (13/1), Eduardo Estíguar Hurtado Roa (17/7). Trainer: Dušan Drašković (51).

213. 05.09.1993 **ECUADOR - URUGUAY** **0-1(0-1)** 15th FIFA WC. Qualifiers
Estadio „Isidro Romero", Guayaquil; Referee: Enrique Marín Gallo (Chile); Attendance: 65,000
ECU: Jacinto Alberto Espinoza Castillo (19/0), Luis Enrique Capurro Bautista (59/0), Byron Zózimo Tenorio (41/1), Raúl Alfredo Noriega Escobar (19/1), Iván Jacinto Hurtado Angulo (16/1) [63.Ney Raúl Avilés Aguirre (52/15)], Nixon Aníbal Carcelén Chalá (29/1) [76.Cléber Manuel Chalá Guerrón (14/1)], Héctor Jhonny Carabalí Cevallos (21/1), José Eduardo Gavica Peñafiel (11/1), Alex Darío Aguinaga Garzón (44/10), Eduardo Estíguar Hurtado Roa (18/7), Carlos Antonio Muñoz Martínez (33/4). Trainer: Dušan Drašković (52).

214. 12.09.1993 **VENEZUELA - ECUADOR** **2-1(1-1)** 15th FIFA WC. Qualifiers
Estadio Polideportivo Cachamay, Puerto Ordaz; Referee: Fernando Chappel Merino (Peru); Attendance: 2,000
ECU: Jacinto Alberto Espinoza Castillo (20/0), Carlos Antonio Muñoz Martínez (34/4) [58.Ney Raúl Avilés Aguirre (53/15)], Luis Enrique Capurro Bautista (60/0), Raúl Alfredo Noriega Escobar (20/1), Iván Jacinto Hurtado Angulo (17/1), Dannes Arsenio Coronel (12/0), Cléber Manuel Chalá Guerrón (15/1) [58.José Eduardo Gavica Peñafiel (12/1)], Nixon Aníbal Carcelén Chalá (30/1), Ángel Oswaldo Fernández Vernaza (21/5), Byron Zózimo Tenorio (42/2), Eduardo Estíguar Hurtado Roa (19/7),. Trainer: Dušan Drašković (53).
Goal: Byron Zózimo Tenorio (1).

215. 19.09.1993 **ECUADOR - BOLIVIA** **1-1(0-1)** 15th FIFA WC. Qualifiers
Estadio „Isidro Romero", Guayaquil; Referee: John Jairo Toro Rendón (Colombia); Attendance: 5,000
ECU: Jacinto Alberto Espinoza Castillo (21/0), Dannes Arsenio Coronel (13/0), Raúl Alfredo Noriega Escobar (21/2), Luis Enrique Capurro Bautista (61/0), Iván Jacinto Hurtado Angulo (18/1), Ángel Oswaldo Fernández Vernaza (22/5), Máximo Wilson Tenorio Quiñónez (8/0), Cléber Manuel Chalá Guerrón (16/1) [54.Nixon Aníbal Carcelén Chalá (31/1)], Alex Darío Aguinaga Garzón (45/10), Ney Raúl Avilés Aguirre (54/15), Carlos Antonio Muñoz Martínez (35/4) [43.José Eduardo Gavica Peñafiel (13/1)]. Trainer: Dušan Drašković (54).
Goal: Raúl Alfredo Noriega Escobar (82).

216. 25.05.1994 **ECUADOR - ARGENTINA** **1-0(0-0)**
Estadio „Isidro Romero", Guayaquil; Referee: Jorge Orellana Vimos (Ecuador); Attendance: 35,000
ECU: Jacinto Alberto Espinoza Castillo (22/0), Luis Enrique Capurro Bautista (62/0), Dannes Arsenio Coronel (14/0), Byron Zózimo Tenorio (43/3), Alberto Guillermo Montaño Angulo (2/0), Juan Carlos Garay (12/1), Kléber Emilson Fajardo Barzola (32/0) [46.José Eduardo Gavica Peñafiel (14/1)], Ivo Norman Ron Viver (6/1), Héctor Jhonny Carabalí Cevallos (22/1) [87.José Germán Carcelén (1/0)], Máximo Wilson Tenorio Quiñónez (9/0), Cléber Manuel Chalá Guerrón (17/1) [66.Carlos Vernaza (1/0)]. Trainer: Carlos Torres Garcés (1).
Goal: Byron Zózimo Tenorio (72).

217. 05.06.1994 **ECUADOR - SOUTH KOREA** **2-1(1-0)**
Wakefield High School Field, Wakefield (United States); Referee: Edwin Resendes (United States); Attendance: 3,000
ECU: Jacinto Alberto Espinoza Castillo (23/0), Dannes Arsenio Coronel (15/0), Byron Zózimo Tenorio (44/3), Máximo Wilson Tenorio Quiñónez (10/0), Alberto Guillermo Montaño Angulo (3/0), Luis Enrique Capurro Bautista (Cap) (63/0), Juan Carlos Garay (13/1), Kléber Emilson Fajardo Barzola (33/0) [77.José Eduardo Gavica Peñafiel (15/1)], Cléber Manuel Chalá Guerrón (18/1), Ivo Norman Ron Viver (7/2), Carlos Vernaza (2/1) [69.Wilson Iván Carabalí González (1/0)]. Trainer: Dušan Drašković (55).
Goals: Carlos Vernaza (34), Ivo Norman Ron Viver (77).

218. 17.08.1994 **ECUADOR - PERU** **0-2(0-1)**
Estadio Nacional, Lima; Referee: Luis Ángel Seminario Maura (Peru); Attendance: 12,000
ECU: Jacinto Alberto Espinoza Castillo (24/0), Dannes Arsenio Coronel (16/0) [Wilson Iván Carabalí González (2/0)], Bryon Zózimo Tenorio (45/3), Alberto Guillermo Montaño Angulo (4/0), Luis Enrique Capurro Bautista (64/0), Jimmy Achille (1/0), Kléber Emilson Fajardo Barzola (34/0), Héctor Jhonny Carabalí Cevallos (23/1), Ivo Norman Ron Viver (8/2) [César Fabián Cubero Guerra (1/0)], Eduardo Estíguar Hurtado Roa (20/7) [Édison Maldonado (1/0)], Agustín Javier Delgado Chalá (1/0). Trainer: Carlos René Ron (1).

219. 21.09.1994 **ECUADOR - PERU** **0-0**
Nueve de Marzo, Machala (Colombia), Ref: Jorge Orellana Vimos (Ecuador)
ECU: José Francisco Cevallos Villavicencio (1/0), Dannes Arsenio Coronel (17/0), Byron Zózimo Tenorio (46/3), Raúl Alfredo Noriega Escobar (22/2), Wilson Iván Carabalí González (3/0) [Kléber Emilson Fajardo Barzola (35/0)], Luis Enrique Capurro Bautista (65/0), Héctor Jhonny Carabalí Cevallos (24/1), Iván Jacinto Hurtado Angulo (19/1), Ángel Oswaldo Fernández Vernaza (23/5) [68.Wellington Eduardo Sánchez Luzuriaga (1/0)], Eduardo Estíguar Hurtado Roa (21/7) [68.Luis Anibal Chérrez (3/0)], Manuel Antonio Uquillas (5/0). Trainer: Carlos René Ron (2).

220. 24.05.1995 **SCOTLAND - ECUADOR** **2-1(0-0)** Kirin Cup
Toyama Park, Toyama (Japan); Referee: Masayoshi Okada (Japan); Attendance: 5,669
ECU: José Francisco Cevallos Villavicencio (2/0), Luis Enrique Capurro Bautista (66/0), Raúl Alfredo Noriega Escobar (23/2), Iván Jacinto Hurtado Angulo (20/2), Wilfrido Enrique Verduga (8/0), Juan Helio Guamán (2/0), Nixon Aníbal Carcelén Chalá (32/1), Juan Carlos Garay (14/1) [46.Agustín Javier Delgado Chalá (2/0)), Hjalmar Zambrano (3/1), Diego Rodrigo Herrera Larrea (4/0) [71.José Marcos Mora Calderón (1/0)], Eduardo Estíguar Hurtado Roa (22/7). Trainer: Francisco Maturana (1).
Goal: Iván Jacinto Hurtado Angulo (79 penalty).

221. 28.05.1995 **JAPAN - ECUADOR** **3-0(1-0)** Kirin Cup
Nacional Stadium, Tokyo; Referee: Lutz Michael Fröhlich (Germany); Attendance: 50,000
ECU: José Francisco Cevallos Villavicencio (3/0), Raúl Alfredo Noriega Escobar (24/2) [68.Nixon Aníbal Carcelén Chalá (33/1)], Juan Helio Guamán (3/0) [46.Ulises Hernán de la Cruz Bernardo (1/0)], Iván Jacinto Hurtado Angulo (21/2), Luis Enrique Capurro Bautista (67/0), Máximo Wilson Tenorio Quiñónez (11/0), Wilfrido Enrique Verduga (9/0), Juan Carlos Garay (15/1), José Marcos Mora Calderón (2/0) [Hjalmar Zambrano (4/1)], Eduardo Estíguar Hurtado Roa (23/7), Agustín Javier Delgado Chalá (3/0). Trainer: Francisco Maturana (2).

222. 04.06.1995 **ECUADOR - ZAMBIA** **4-1(1-0)** Korea Cup
Civil Stadium, Changwon (South Korea); Referee: Lee Sang-Kwon (South Korea); Attendance: 12,013
ECU: José Francisco Cevallos Villavicencio (4/0), Iván Jacinto Hurtado Angulo (22/2) [64.Juan Helio Guamán (4/0)], Máximo Wilson Tenorio Quiñónez (12/0), Luis Enrique Capurro Bautista (68/0), Ulises Hernán de la Cruz Bernardo (2/0), Nixon Aníbal Carcelén Chalá (34/1), Wilfrido Enrique Verduga (10/0) [63.José Marcos Mora Calderón (3/0)], Juan Carlos Garay (16/1), Diego Rodrigo Herrera Larrea (5/0), Hjalmar Zambrano (5/1) [69.Energio Díaz (1/0)], Eduardo Estíguar Hurtado Roa (24/11). Trainer: Francisco Maturana (3).
Goals: Eduardo Estíguar Hurtado Roa (19, 66, 78, 81).

223. 10.06.1995 **ECUADOR - COSTA RICA** **2-1(1-0)** Korea Cup
Dongdaemun Stadium, Seoul (South Korea); Referee: Cha Deok-Hwan (South Korea); Attendance: 26,328
ECU: José Francisco Cevallos Villavicencio (5/0), Iván Jacinto Hurtado Angulo (23/2), Máximo Wilson Tenorio Quiñónez (13/0) [46.Raúl Alfredo Noriega Escobar (25/2)], Luis Enrique Capurro Bautista (69/0), Juan Helio Guamán (5/0), José Guerrero (10/1) [46.José Marcos Mora Calderón (4/0)], Nixon Aníbal Carcelén Chalá (35/1), Juan Carlos Garay (17/1), Diego Rodrigo Herrera Larrea (6/0) [Wilfrido Enrique Verduga (11/0)], Eduardo Estíguar Hurtado Roa (25/12), Energio Díaz (2/1). Trainer: Francisco Maturana (4).
Goals: Eduardo Estíguar Hurtado Roa (37), Energio Díaz (69).

224. 12.06.1995 **ECUADOR - ZAMBIA** **1-0(0-0)** Korea Cup
Dongdaemun Stadium, Seoul (South Korea); Referee: Kim Kwang-Taek (South Korea); Attendance: 18,724
ECU: José Francisco Cevallos Villavicencio (6/0), Iván Jacinto Hurtado Angulo (24/2), Máximo Wilson Tenorio Quiñónez (14/0), Luis Enrique Capurro Bautista (Cap) (70/0), Juan Helio Guamán (6/0), Nixon Aníbal Carcelén Chalá (36/1), Juan Carlos Garay (18/1), José Marcos Mora Calderón (5/0), Diego Rodrigo Herrera Larrea (7/0), Eduardo Estíguar Hurtado Roa (26/12), Energio Díaz (3/2). Trainer: Francisco Maturana (5).
Goal: Energio Díaz (46).

225. 30.06.1995 **PARAGUAY - ECUADOR** **1-0(0-0)**
Estadio Defensores del Chaco, Asunción; Referee: Carlos Manuel Robles Mella (Chile); Attendance: 10,000
ECU: José Francisco Cevallos Villavicencio (7/0) [Carlos Luis Morales (25/0)], Juan Helio Guamán (7/0), Máximo Wilson Tenorio Quiñónez (15/0), Iván Jacinto Hurtado Angulo (25/2), Luis Enrique Capurro Bautista (71/0), Nixon Aníbal Carcelén Chalá (37/1) [Héctor Jhonny Carabalí Cevallos (25/1)], Holguer Abraham Quiñónez (39/0), Ivo Norman Ron Viver (9/2) [Diego Rodrigo Herrera Larrea (8/0)], Edwin Patricio Hurtado Zurita (3/0), Nicolás Geovanny Asencio Espinoza (1/0) [Alex Darío Aguinaga Garzón (46/10)], Eduardo Estíguar Hurtado Roa (27/12). Trainer: Francisco Maturana (6).

226. 07.07.1995 **BRAZIL - ECUADOR** **1-0(0-0)** 37th Copa América. Group Stage
Estadio „Atilio Paiva Olivera", Rivera (Uruguay); Referee: Javier Alberto Castrilli (Argentina); Attendance: 10,000
ECU: Carlos Luis Morales (26/0), Juan Helio Guamán (8/0) [*sent off*], Máximo Wilson Tenorio Quiñónez (16/0), Iván Jacinto Hurtado Angulo (26/2), Luis Enrique Capurro Bautista (72/0), Héctor Jhonny Carabalí Cevallos (26/1), Holguer Abraham Quiñónez (40/0), José Marcos Mora Calderón (6/0) [77.Nicolás Geovanny Asencio Espinoza (2/0)], Alex Darío Aguinaga Garzón (47/10), Energio Díaz (4/2) [62.Edwin Patricio Hurtado Zurita (4/0)], Eduardo Estíguar Hurtado Roa (28/12). Trainer: Francisco Maturana (7).

227. 10.07.1995 **COLOMBIA - ECUADOR** **1-0(1-0)** 37th Copa América. Group Stage
Estadio „Atilio Paiva Olivera", Rivera (Uruguay); Referee: Pablo Peña (Bolivia); Attendance: 8,000
ECU: Carlos Luis Morales (27/0), Dannes Arsenio Coronel (18/0), Iván Jacinto Hurtado Angulo (27/2), Máximo Wilson Tenorio Quiñónez (17/0), Luis Enrique Capurro Bautista (73/0), Héctor Jhonny Carabalí Cevallos (27/1) [71.José Marcos Mora Calderón (7/0)], Holguer Abraham Quiñónez (41/0), Diego Rodrigo Herrera Larrea (9/0) [46.Juan Carlos Garay (19/1)], Alex Darío Aguinaga Garzón (48/10), Edwin Patricio Hurtado Zurita (5/0) [71.Nicolás Geovanny Asencio Espinoza (3/0)], Eduardo Estíguar Hurtado Roa (29/12). Trainer: Francisco Maturana (8).

228. 13.07.1995 **ECUADOR - PERU** **2-1(0-0)** 37th Copa América. Group Stage
Estadio „Atilio Paiva Olivera", Rivera (Uruguay); Referee: Eduardo Dluzniewski (Uruguay); Attendance: 10,000
ECU: Carlos Luis Morales (28/0), Juan Helio Guamán (9/0), Máximo Wilson Tenorio Quiñónez (18/0), Iván Jacinto Hurtado Angulo (28/2), Luis Enrique Capurro Bautista (74/0), Juan Carlos Garay (20/1) [83.Raúl Alfredo Noriega Escobar (26/2)], Holguer Abraham Quiñónez (42/0) [46.José Marcos Mora Calderón (8/1)], Nixon Aníbal Carcelén Chalá (38/1) [*sent off 66*], Alex Darío Aguinaga Garzón (49/10), Energio Díaz (5/3) [67.Ivo Norman Ron Viver (10/2)], Eduardo Estíguar Hurtado Roa (30/12). Trainer: Francisco Maturana (9).
Goals: Energio Díaz (61), José Marcos Mora Calderón (75).

229. 25.10.1995 **BOLIVIA - ECUADOR** **2-2(2-1)**
Estadio „Ramón 'Tahuichi' Aguilera", Santa Cruz; Referee: Pablo Peña Durán (Bolivia); Attendance: 32,000
ECU: Carlos Luis Morales (29/0) [Jacinto Alberto Espinoza Castillo (25/0)], Juan Helio Guamán (10/0) [Wágner Apolinario Rivera Cortazar (1/0)], Iván Jacinto Hurtado Angulo (29/2), Alfonso Andrés Obregón Cancino (1/0) [Juan Carlos Garay (21/1)], Máximo Wilson Tenorio Quiñónez (19/1), Roberth Javier Burbano (9/0) [Ángel Oswaldo Fernández Vernaza (24/6)], Wellington Eduardo Sánchez Luzuriaga (2/0), Alex Darío Aguinaga Garzón (50/10), Roberth Macías (1/0), Eduardo Estíguar Hurtado Roa (31/13), Rolando Santiago Jacomé Ponce (1/0). Trainer: Francisco Maturana (10).
Goals: Máximo Wilson Tenorio Quiñónez (41), Eduardo Estíguar Hurtado Roa (89).

230. 02.02.1996 **VENEZUELA - ECUADOR** **0-1(0-0)**
Estadio „Brígido Iriarte", Caracas; Referee: Lenin David Rodríguez Aguilera (Venezuela); Attendance: 6,000
ECU: José Francisco Cevallos Villavicencio (8/0), Wágner Apolinario Rivera Cortazar (2/0), Máximo Wilson Tenorio Quiñónez (20/1), Alberto Guillermo Montaño Angulo (5/0), Wilson Iván Carabalí González (4/0), Cléber Manuel Chalá Guerrón (19/1) [46.Luis Ernesto González (1/0)], Roberth Macías (2/0), Alfonso Andrés Obregón Cancino (2/0) [75.Roberth Javier Burbano (10/0)], Jorge Batallas (1/0) [46.Ángel Oswaldo Fernández Vernaza (25/6)], Oswaldo De la Cruz (3/0) [73.Juan Carlos Garay (22/1)], Eduardo Estíguar Hurtado Roa (32/13). Trainer: Francisco Maturana (11).
Goal: Ángel Oswaldo Fernández Vernaza (55).

231. 11.02.1996 **LEBANON - ECUADOR** **1-0(1-0)**
Bourj Hammound Stadium, Beirut; Referee: Ahmad Nabil Ayad (Lebanon); Attendance: 6,000
ECU: José Francisco Cevallos Villavicencio (9/0), Wágner Apolinario Rivera Cortazar (3/0), Alfonso Andrés Obregón Cancino (3/0) [Juan Carlos Garay (23/1)], Máximo Wilson Tenorio Quiñónez (21/1), Alberto Guillermo Montaño Angulo (6/0), Wilson Iván Carabalí González (5/0) [Carlos Pazmiño (1/0)], Roberth Macías (3/0) [Luis Ernesto González (2/0)], Jorge Batallas (2/0), Cléber Manuel Chalá Guerrón (20/1) [Edwin Patricio Hurtado Zurita (6/0)], Ángel Oswaldo Fernández Vernaza (26/6), Eduardo Estíguar Hurtado Roa (33/13). Trainer: Francisco Maturana (12).

232. 16.02.1996 **ECUADOR - OMAN** **2-0(1-0)**
Riyad (Saudi Arabia); Referee: Ali Khalifi (Qatar); Attendance: 1,000
ECU: Jacinto Alberto Espinoza Castillo (26/0), Wágner Apolinario Rivera Cortazar (4/0), Máximo Wilson Tenorio Quiñónez (22/1) [Byron Zózimo Tenorio (47/3)], Alberto Guillermo Montaño Angulo (7/0), Carlos Pazmiño (2/0), Juan Carlos Garay (24/1), Wilson Iván Carabalí González (6/0) [Cléber Manuel Chalá Guerrón (21/1)], Luis Ernesto González (3/0), Jorge Batallas (3/0), Ángel Oswaldo Fernández Vernaza (27/7), Eduardo Estíguar Hurtado Roa (34/14) [Edwin Patricio Hurtado Zurita (7/0)]. Trainer: Francisco Maturana (13).
Goals: Eduardo Estíguar Hurtado Roa (24), Ángel Oswaldo Fernández Vernaza (70).

233. 18.02.1996 **QATAR - ECUADOR** **1-1(0-1)**
Al Assad Stadium, Doha; Referee: Jassen Al Kari (Saudi Arabia); Attendance: 1,000
ECU: Jacinto Alberto Espinoza Castillo (27/0), Wágner Apolinario Rivera Cortazar (5/0), Máximo Wilson Tenorio Quiñónez (23/1), Alberto Guillermo Montaño Angulo (8/0), Carlos Pazmiño (3/0), Juan Carlos Garay (25/1) [Roberth Macías (4/0)], Wilson Iván Carabalí González (7/0) [Cléber Manuel Chalá Guerrón (22/1)], Luis Ernesto González (4/0), Jorge Batallas (4/0), Ángel Oswaldo Fernández Vernaza (28/7) [Roberth Javier Burbano (11/0)], Eduardo Estíguar Hurtado Roa (35/15). Trainer: Francisco Maturana (14).
Goal: Eduardo Estíguar Hurtado Roa (3).

234. 23.02.1996 **KUWAIT - ECUADOR** **0-3(0-1)**
Al-Kuwait; Referee: Hassan Johar; Attendance: 1,000
ECU: José Francisco Cevallos Villavicencio (10/0), Wágner Apolinario Rivera Cortazar (6/0), Máximo Wilson Tenorio Quiñónez (24/2) [77.Byron Zózimo Tenorio (48/3)], Alberto Guillermo Montaño Angulo (9/0), Carlos Pazmiño (4/0), Juan Carlos Garay (26/1), Wilson Iván Carabalí González (8/0), Luis Ernesto González (5/0) [84.Oswaldo De la Cruz (4/0)], Jorge Batallas (5/1), Ángel Oswaldo Fernández Vernaza (29/7), Eduardo Estíguar Hurtado Roa (36/16) [77.Edwin Patricio Hurtado Zurita (8/0)]. Trainer: Francisco Maturana (15).
Goals: Máximo Wilson Tenorio Quiñónez (5), Eduardo Estíguar Hurtado Roa (70), Jorge Batallas (80).

235. 25.02.1996 **QATAR - ECUADOR** **1-2(1-0)**
Al Salah Stadium, Doha; Referee: Jumaa Al Ali (Qatar)
ECU: José Francisco Cevallos Villavicencio (11/0), Wágner Apolinario Rivera Cortazar (7/0), Máximo Wilson Tenorio Quiñónez (25/2), Alberto Guillermo Montaño Angulo (10/0) [84.Byron Zózimo Tenorio (49/3)], Carlos Pazmiño (5/0), Luis Ernesto González (6/0), Wilson Iván Carabalí González (9/0) [80.Roberth Macías (5/0)], Juan Carlos Garay (27/1), Jorge Batallas (6/1) [80.Roberth Javier Burbano (12/0)], Ángel Oswaldo Fernández Vernaza (30/8), Eduardo Estíguar Hurtado Roa (37/17). Trainer: Francisco Maturana (16).
Goals: Eduardo Estíguar Hurtado Roa (46), Ángel Oswaldo Fernández Vernaza (73).

236. 06.03.1996 **JAPAN - ECUADOR** **0-1(0-0)**
Nagaragawa Stadium, Gifu (Japan)
ECU: Jacinto Alberto Espinoza Castillo (28/0), Wágner Apolinario Rivera Cortazar (8/0), Máximo Wilson Tenorio Quiñónez (26/2), Alberto Guillermo Montaño Angulo (11/0), Carlos Pazmiño (6/0), Wilson Iván Carabalí González (10/0), Luis Ernesto González (7/0), Juan Carlos Garay (28/1) [Alfonso Andrés Obregón Cancino (4/0)], Gilson Simões de Souza (1/0), Ángel Oswaldo Fernández Vernaza (31/8), Eduardo Estíguar Hurtado Roa (38/18). Trainer: Francisco Maturana (17).
Goal: Eduardo Estíguar Hurtado Roa (89).

237. 24.04.1996 **ECUADOR - PERU** **4-1(0-0)** 16th FIFA WC. Qualifiers
Estadio „Isidro Romero", Guayaquil; Referee: Julio Matto (Uruguay); Attendance: 60,000
ECU: Carlos Luis Morales (30/0), Iván Jacinto Hurtado Angulo (30/2) [84.Alfonso Andrés Obregón Cancino (5/0)), Wágner Apolinario Rivera Cortazar (9/0), Luis Enrique Capurro Bautista (75/0), Máximo Wilson Tenorio Quiñónez (27/3), Alberto Guillermo Montaño Angulo (12/0), Wilson Iván Carabalí González (11/0) [46.Héctor Jhonny Carabalí Cevallos (28/1)], Gilson Simões de Souza (2/0), Alex Darío Aguinaga Garzón (51/10), Eduardo Estíguar Hurtado Roa (39/20), Ángel Oswaldo Fernández Vernaza (32/8) [76.José Eduardo Gavica Peñafiel (16/2)]. Trainer: Francisco Maturana (18).
Goals: Eduardo Estíguar Hurtado Roa (54), Máximo Wilson Tenorio Quiñónez (65), José Eduardo Gavica Peñafiel (78), Eduardo Estíguar Hurtado Roa (88).

238. 02.06.1996 **ECUADOR - ARGENTINA** **2-0(0-0)** 16th FIFA WC. Qualifiers
Estadio Olimpico „Atahualpa", Quito; Referee: Armando Pérez Hoyos (Colombia); Attendance: 41,500
ECU: Carlos Luis Morales (31/0), Iván Jacinto Hurtado Angulo (31/2) [Alfonso Andrés Obregón Cancino (6/0)], Wágner Apolinario Rivera Cortazar (10/0), Luis Enrique Capurro Bautista (76/0), Máximo Wilson Tenorio Quiñónez (28/3), Alberto Guillermo Montaño Angulo (13/1), Héctor Jhonny Carabalí Cevallos (29/1), Gilson Simões de Souza (3/0), Alex Darío Aguinaga Garzón (52/10), Eduardo Estíguar Hurtado Roa (40/21), José Eduardo Gavica Peñafiel (17/2) [46.Ángel Oswaldo Fernández Vernaza (33/8)]. Trainer: Francisco Maturana (19).
Goals: Alberto Guillermo Montaño Angulo (51), Eduardo Estíguar Hurtado Roa (89).

239. 30.06.1996 **ECUADOR – ARMENIA** **3-0(1-0)**
Estadio Reales Tamarindos, Porto Viejo; Referee: Roger Zambrano (Ecuador); Attendance: 12,000
ECU: Carlos Luis Morales (32/0) [Jacinto Alberto Espinoza Castillo (29/0)], Dannes Arsenio Coronel (19/0), Byron Zózimo Tenorio (50/3), Alberto Guillermo Montaño Angulo (14/1) [Segundo Manuel Matamba Cabezas (1/0)], Luis Enrique Capurro Bautista (77/0), Alfonso Andrés Obregón Cancino (7/0) [Jorge Díaz (1/0)], Luis Ernesto González (8/0), José Eduardo Gavica Peñafiel (18/3), Gilson Simões de Souza (4/1), Ángel Oswaldo Fernández Vernaza (34/9), Manuel Antonio Uquillas (6/0) [Wellington Eduardo Sánchez Luzuriaga (3/0)]. Trainer: Francisco Maturana (20).
Goals: Gilson Simões de Souza (23), Ángel Oswaldo Fernández Vernaza (48), José Eduardo Gavica Peñafiel (75).

240. 06.07.1996 **CHILE – ECUADOR** **4-1(1-0)** 16th FIFA WC. Qualifiers
Estadio Nacional, Santiago; Referee: Pablo Peña Durán (Bolivia); Attendance: 74,905
ECU: Carlos Luis Morales (33/0), Iván Jacinto Hurtado Angulo (32/2), Wágner Apolinario Rivera Cortazar (11/0), Máximo Wilson Tenorio Quiñónez (29/3) [79.Luis Ernesto González (9/0)], Alfonso Andrés Obregón Cancino (8/0) [46.Byron Zózimo Tenorio (51/3)], Luis Enrique Capurro Bautista (78/0), Gilson Simões de Souza (5/1), Héctor Jhonny Carabalí Cevallos (30/1), Alex Darío Aguinaga Garzón (53/11), Alberto Guillermo Montaño Angulo (15/1) [46.Ángel Oswaldo Fernández Vernaza (35/9)], Eduardo Estíguar Hurtado Roa (41/21). Trainer: Francisco Maturana (21).
Goal: Alex Darío Aguinaga Garzón (73).

241. 16.08.1996 **ECUADOR – COSTA RICA** **1-1(1-0)**
Estadio „Alejandro Serrano", Cuenca; Referee: Jorge Orellana Vimos (Ecuador); Attendance: 6,000
ECU: Alex Bolívar Cevallos (3/0), Juan Carlos Burbano de Lara Torres (1/0), Máximo Wilson Tenorio Quiñónez (30/3), Holguer Abraham Quiñónez (43/0), Luis Enrique Capurro Bautista (79/0), Alfonso Andrés Obregón Cancino (9/0) [Evelio Agustín Ordóñez Martínez (1/0)], Héctor Jhonny Carabalí Cevallos (31/1), Wellington Eduardo Sánchez Luzuriaga (4/0) [Eduardo Fabián Smith Chávez (1/0)], Gabriel Yepez Salazar (1/0) [José Oleas Gómez (1/0)], José Eduardo Gavica Peñafiel (19/3), Ángel Oswaldo Fernández Vernaza (36/10). Trainer: Francisco Maturana (22).
Goal: Ángel Oswaldo Fernández Vernaza (18).

242. 01.09.1996 **ECUADOR – VENEZUELA** **1-0(1-0)** 16th FIFA WC. Qualifiers
Estadio Olimpico „Atahualpa", Quito; Referee: Carlos Manuel Robles Mella (Chile); Attendance: 36,889
ECU: Carlos Luis Morales (34/0), Iván Jacinto Hurtado Angulo (33/2), Wágner Apolinario Rivera Cortazar (12/0), Máximo Wilson Tenorio Quiñónez (31/3), Jorge Díaz (2/0) [75.Alfonso Andrés Obregón Cancino (10/0)], Luis Enrique Capurro Bautista (80/0), Gilson Simões de Souza (6/1), Héctor Jhonny Carabalí Cevallos (32/1), Alex Darío Aguinaga Garzón (54/12), Eduardo Estíguar Hurtado Roa (42/21), José Eduardo Gavica Peñafiel (20/3) [46.Ángel Oswaldo Fernández Vernaza (37/10)]. Trainer: Francisco Maturana (23).
Goal: Alex Darío Aguinaga Garzón (4).

243. 04.10.1996 **ECUADOR – JAMAICA** **2-1(1-1)**
Estadio Bellavista, Ambato; Referee: Mauricio Reinoso (Ecuador); Attendance: 18,000
ECU: Carlos Luis Morales (35/0) [46.Alex Bolívar Cevallos (4/0)], Juan Carlos Burbano de Lara Torres (2/0), Máximo Wilson Tenorio Quiñónez (32/3) [46.Eduardo Fabián Smith Chávez (2/0)], Alberto Guillermo Montaño Angulo (16/1), Edmundo Marcelo Méndez (1/0), Iván Jacinto Hurtado Angulo (34/2) [46.Alfonso Andrés Obregón Cancino (11/0)], Gilson Simões de Souza (7/1), Oswaldo De la Cruz (5/0), Héctor Jhonny Carabalí Cevallos (33/1) [60.Jorge Díaz (3/0)], Ángel Oswaldo Fernández Vernaza (38/10), Agustín Javier Delgado Chalá (4/2). Trainer: Francisco Maturana (24).
Goals: Agustín Javier Delgado Chalá (19, 90).

244. 09.10.1996 **ECUADOR – COLOMBIA** **0-1(0-0)** 16th FIFA WC. Qualifiers
Estadio Olimpico „Atahualpa", Quito; Referee: Horacio Marcelo Elizondo (Argentina); Attendance: 45,000
ECU: Carlos Luis Morales (36/0), Iván Jacinto Hurtado Angulo (35/2) [62.Alfonso Andrés Obregón Cancino (12/0)], Wágner Apolinario Rivera Cortazar (13/0), Alberto Guillermo Montaño Angulo (17/1), Máximo Wilson Tenorio Quiñónez (33/3), Luis Enrique Capurro Bautista (81/0), Gilson Simões de Souza (8/1) [75.Ángel Oswaldo Fernández Vernaza (39/10)], Héctor Jhonny Carabalí Cevallos (34/1), Eduardo Estíguar Hurtado Roa (43/21), Alex Darío Aguinaga Garzón (55/12), Agustín Javier Delgado Chalá (5/2). Trainer: Francisco Maturana (25).

245. 23.10.1996 **MEXICO – ECUADOR** **0-1(0-0)**
Coliseum Stadium, Oakland (United States); Referee: Brian Hall (United States); Attendance: 27,528
ECU: Carlos Luis Morales (37/0), Juan Carlos Burbano de Lara Torres (3/0) [52.Edmundo Marcelo Méndez (2/0)], Byron Zózimo Tenorio (52/3), Holguer Abraham Quiñónez (44/0), Alberto Guillermo Montaño Angulo (18/1), Jorge Díaz (4/0), Héctor Jhonny Carabalí Cevallos (35/2), Oswaldo De la Cruz (6/0), Gilson Simões de Souza (9/1), Agustín Javier Delgado Chalá (6/2) [70.Evelio Agustín Ordóñez Martínez (2/0)], César Fabián Cubero Guerra (2/0). Trainer: Francisco Maturana (26).
Goal: Héctor Jhonny Carabalí Cevallos (61).

246. 10.11.1996 **PARAGUAY – ECUADOR** **1-0(1-0)** 16th FIFA WC. Qualifiers
Estadio Defensores del Chaco, Asunción; Referee: Daniel Orlando Giménez (Argentina); Attendance: 31,002
ECU: Carlos Luis Morales (38/0), Iván Jacinto Hurtado Angulo (36/2), Wágner Apolinario Rivera Cortazar (14/0), Byron Zózimo Tenorio (53/3), Alberto Guillermo Montaño Angulo (19/1), Gilson Simões de Souza (10/1) [76.Ángel Oswaldo Fernández Vernaza (40/10)], Oswaldo De La Cruz (7/0), Alex Darío Aguinaga Garzón (56/12), Holguer Abraham Quiñónez (45/0), Eduardo Estíguar Hurtado Roa (44/21), Eduardo Fabián Smith Chávez (3/0). Trainer: Francisco Maturana (27).

247. 12.01.1997 **BOLIVIA – ECUADOR** **2-0(2-0)** 16th FIFA WC. Qualifiers
Estadio „Hernándo Siles Zuazo", La Paz; Referee: Oscar Julián Ruíz Acosta (Colombia); Attendance: 39,968
ECU: Carlos Luis Morales (39/0), Iván Jacinto Hurtado Angulo (37/2), Wágner Apolinario Rivera Cortazar (15/0), Byron Zózimo Tenorio (54/3), Alberto Guillermo Montaño Angulo (20/1), Holguer Abraham Quiñónez (46/0), Ángel Oswaldo Fernández Vernaza (41/10 [46.Eduardo Estíguar Hurtado Roa (45/21)], Oswaldo De La Cruz (8/0) [46.Gilson Simões de Souza (11/1)], Cléber Manuel Chalá Guerrón (23/1) [64.Agustín Javier Delgado Chalá (7/2)], Alex Darío Aguinaga Garzón (57/12), Héctor Jhonny Carabalí Cevallos (36/2) [*sent off 73*]. Trainer: Francisco Maturana (28).

248. 05.02.1997 **MEXICO – ECUADOR** **3-1(2-0)**
Estadio Azteca, Ciudad de México; Referee: Benito Armando Archundia Téllez (Mexico); Attendance: 15,000
ECU: Geovanny Oswaldo Ibarra (1/0), Wágner Apolinario Rivera Cortazar (16/0), Máximo Wilson Tenorio Quiñónez (34/3), Alberto Guillermo Montaño Angulo (21/1), Luis Enrique Capurro Bautista (82/0), Simón Patricio Ruíz (1/0), Jimmy Roberto Blandón Quiñónez (1/0), Gilson Simões de Souza (12/1), Oswaldo De la Cruz (9/0), Cléber Manuel Chalá Guerrón (24/1) [59.Ángel Oswaldo Fernández Vernaza (42/10)], Agustín Javier Delgado Chalá (8/3). Trainer: Francisco Maturana (29).
Goal: Agustin Javier Delgado (82).

249. 12.02.1997 **ECUADOR – URUGUAY** **4-0(1-0)** 16th FIFA WC. Qualifiers
Estadio Olimpico „Atahualpa“, Quito; Referee: Javier Alberto Castrilli (Argentina); Attendance: 18,000
ECU: Geovanny Oswaldo Ibarra (2/0), Wágner Apolinario Rivera Cortazar (17/0), Iván Jacinto Hurtado Angulo (38/2), Alberto Guillermo Montaño Angulo (22/1), Luis Enrique Capurro Bautista (83/0), Simón Patricio Ruíz (2/0), Jimmy Roberto Blandón Quiñónez (2/0), Gilson Simões de Souza (13/1) [81.Ángel Oswaldo Fernández Vernaza (43/10)], Alex Darío Aguinaga Garzón (58/13), Oswaldo De La Cruz (10/0) [61.Cléber Manuel Chalá Guerrón (25/2)], Agustín Javier Delgado Chalá (9/5). Trainer: Francisco Maturana (30).
Goals: Alex Darío Aguinaga Garzón (6), Agustín Javier Delgado Chalá (68, 76), Cléber Chalá (87).

250. 25.03.1997 **GUATEMALA – ECUADOR** **0-0**
Estadio La Pedrera, Ciudad de Guatemala; Referee: Mijangos (Guatemala); Attendance: 8,000
ECU: Geovanny Oswaldo Ibarra (3/0), Wágner Apolinario Rivera Cortazar (18/0), Alberto Guillermo Montaño Angulo (23/1), Eduardo Fabián Smith Chávez (4/0), Luis Enrique Capurro Bautista (84/0), Simón Patricio Ruíz (3/0), Jimmy Roberto Blandón Quiñónez (3/0), Héctor Jhonny Carabalí Cevallos (37/2), Agustín Javier Delgado Chalá (10/5), Oswaldo De la Cruz (11/0) [Edmundo Marcelo Méndez (3/0)], Cléber Manuel Chalá Guerrón (26/2) [Ángel Oswaldo Fernández Vernaza (44/10)]. Trainer: Francisco Maturana (31).

251. 02.04.1997 **PERU – ECUADOR** **1-1(0-0)** 16th FIFA WC. Qualifiers
Estadio Nacional, Lima; Referee: John Jairo Toro Rendón (Colombia); Attendance: 42,299
ECU: Geovanny Oswaldo Ibarra (4/0), Wágner Apolinario Rivera Cortazar (19/0), Iván Jacinto Hurtado Angulo (39/2), Alberto Guillermo Montaño Angulo (24/1), Luis Enrique Capurro Bautista (85/0) [*sent off 85*], Simón Patricio Ruíz (4/0) [62.Cléber Manuel Chalá Guerrón (27/2)], Jimmy Roberto Blandón Quiñónez (4/0), Héctor Jhonny Carabalí Cevallos (38/2), Alex Darío Aguinaga Garzón (59/14), Agustín Javier Delgado Chalá (11/5), Ariel José Graziani Lentini (1/0) [46.Eduardo Estíguar Hurtado Roa (46/21)]. Trainer: Francisco Maturana (32).
Goal: Alex Darío Aguinaga Garzón (78).

252. 30.04.1997 **ARGENTINA – ECUADOR** **2-1(2-0)** 16th FIFA WC. Qualifiers
Estadio Monumental „Antonio Vespucio Liberti“, Buenos Aires; Referee: Félix Ramón Benegas Caballero (Paraguay); Attendance: 62,300
ECU: Geovanny Oswaldo Ibarra (5/0), Wágner Apolinario Rivera Cortazar (20/0) [76.Juan Carlos Burbano de Lara Torres (4/0)], Raúl Alfredo Noriega Escobar (27/2), Alberto Guillermo Montaño Angulo (25/1), Gilson Simões de Souza (14/1), Eduardo Estíguar Hurtado Roa (47/21), Jimmy Roberto Blandón Quiñónez (5/0), Héctor Jhonny Carabalí Cevallos (39/2), Alex Darío Aguinaga Garzón (60/15), Cléber Manuel Chalá Guerrón (28/2) [63.Oswaldo De La Cruz (12/0)], Edmundo Marcelo Méndez (4/0). Trainer: Francisco Maturana (33).
Goal: Alex Darío Aguinaga Garzón (73).

253. 28.05.1997 **EL SALVADOR – ECUADOR** **0-2(0-1)**
Estadio Cuscatlán, San Salvador; Referee: Neri Zepada; Attendance: 8,000
ECU: Geovanny Oswaldo Ibarra (6/0), Ulises Hernán de la Cruz Bernardo (3/0), Iván Jacinto Hurtado Angulo (40/2), Alberto Guillermo Montaño Angulo (26/1), Edmundo Marcelo Méndez (5/0), Marco Vinicius Constante (1/0) [Eduardo Fabián Smith Chávez (5/0)], Jimmy Roberto Blandón Quiñónez (6/0), Wellington Eduardo Sánchez Luzuriaga (5/0), Gilson Simões de Souza (15/1)], Oswaldo De La Cruz (13/1), Agustín Javier Delgado Chalá (12/5) [Héctor González (1/0)], Ariel José Graziani Lentini (2/1). Trainer: Francisco Maturana (34).
Goals: Ariel José Graziani Lentini (9), Oswaldo De la Cruz (66).

254. 08.06.1997 **ECUADOR – CHILE** **1-1(1-0)** 16th FIFA WC. Qualifiers
Estadio Olimpico „Atahualpa“, Quito; Referee: Benito Armando Archundia Téllez (Mexico); Attendance: 42,225
ECU: Geovanny Oswaldo Ibarra (7/0), Iván Jacinto Hurtado Angulo (41/2), Oswaldo De La Cruz (14/1) [60.Eduardo Estíguar Hurtado Roa (48/21)], Alberto Guillermo Montaño Angulo (27/1), Ulises Hernán de la Cruz Bernardo (4/0), Alex Darío Aguinaga Garzón (61/15), Edmundo Marcelo Méndez (6/0), Jimmy Roberto Blandón Quiñónez (7/0), Marco Vinicius Constante (2/0), Agustín Javier Delgado Chalá (13/5 [60.Gilson Simões de Souza (16/1)], Ariel José Graziani Lentini (3/2) [68.Ángel Oswaldo Fernández Vernaza (45/10)]. Trainer: Francisco Maturana (35).
Goal: Ariel José Graziani Lentini (43).

255. 11.06.1997 **ECUADOR – ARGENTINA** **0-0** 38th Copa América. Group Stage
Estadio „Félix Capriles“, Cochabamba (Bolivia); Referee: Jorge Nieves (Uruguay); Attendance: 17,000
ECU: José Francisco Cevallos Villavicencio (12/0), Edmundo Marcelo Méndez (7/0), Luis Enrique Capurro Bautista (86/0), Juan Carlos Burbano de Lara Torres (5/0), Máximo Wilson Tenorio Quiñónez (35/3), Eduardo Fabián Smith Chávez (6/0), Héctor Jhonny Carabalí Cevallos (40/2), Wellington Eduardo Sánchez Luzuriaga (6/0), José Eduardo Gavica Peñafiel (21/3) [75.Hidrobo Vilson Rosero Rodríguez (1/0)], Cléber Manuel Chalá Guerrón (29/2) [46.Ariel José Graziani Lentini (4/2)], Édison Maldonado (2/0) [46.Eduardo Estíguar Hurtado Roa (49/21)]. Trainer: Francisco Maturana (36).

256. 14.06.1997 **ECUADOR – PARAGUAY** **2-0(0-0)** 38th Copa América. Group Stage
Estadio „Félix Capriles“, Cochabamba (Bolivia); Referee: Paolo Borgosano (Venezuela); Attendance: 5,000
ECU: José Francisco Cevallos Villavicencio (13/0), Edmundo Marcelo Méndez (8/0), Luis Enrique Capurro Bautista (87/0), Máximo Wilson Tenorio Quiñónez (36/3), Ulises Hernán de la Cruz Bernardo (5/0), Wellington Eduardo Sánchez Luzuriaga (7/1), Héctor Jhonny Carabalí Cevallos (41/2), Eduardo Fabián Smith Chávez (7/0), José Eduardo Gavica Peñafiel (22/3) [58.Hidrobo Vilson Rosero Rodríguez (2/0)], Eduardo Estíguar Hurtado Roa (50/21), Agustín Javier Delgado Chalá (14/5) [46.Ariel José Graziani Lentini (5/3)]. Trainer: Francisco Maturana (37).
Goals: Wellington Eduardo Sánchez Luzuriaga (71), Ariel José Graziani Lentini (86).

257. 17.06.1997 **ECUADOR – CHILE** **2-1(1-0)** 38th Copa América. Group Stage
Estadio „Félix Capriles“, Cochabamba (Bolivia); Referee: Rafael Sanabria Díaz (Colombia); Attendance: 8,000
ECU: Geovanny Oswaldo Ibarra (8/0), Edmundo Marcelo Méndez (9/0), Luis Enrique Capurro Bautista (88/0), Alberto Guillermo Montaño Angulo (28/1), Ulises Hernán de la Cruz Bernardo (6/0), Eduardo Fabián Smith Chávez (8/0), Héctor Jhonny Carabalí Cevallos (42/2), Wellington Eduardo Sánchez Luzuriaga (8/1), José Eduardo Gavica Peñafiel (23/4) [66.Hidrobo Vilson Rosero Rodríguez (3/0)], Eduardo Estíguar Hurtado Roa (51/21) [75.Agustín Javier Delgado Chalá (15/5)], Ariel José Graziani Lentini (6/4) [79.Édison Maldonado (3/0)]. Trainer: Francisco Maturana (38).
Goals: Ariel José Graziani Lentini (32), José Eduardo Gavica Peñafiel (55).

258. 22.06.1997 **ECUADOR – MEXICO** **1-1(1-1,1-1); 3-4 on penalties** 38th Copa América. Quarter-Finals
Estadio „Félix Capriles“, Cochabamba (Bolivia); Referee: Antônio Pereira (Brazil); Attendance: 15,000
ECU: Geovanny Oswaldo Ibarra (9/0), Edmundo Marcelo Méndez (10/0), Luis Enrique Capurro Bautista (89/1), Máximo Wilson Tenorio Quiñónez (37/3) [46.Alberto Guillermo Montaño Angulo (29/1)], Ulises Hernán de la Cruz Bernardo (7/0), Wellington Eduardo Sánchez Luzuriaga (9/1) [81.Hidrobo Vilson Rosero Rodríguez (4/0)], Marco Vinicius Constante (3/0), Héctor Jhonny Carabalí Cevallos (43/2), José Eduardo Gavica Peñafiel (24/4) [73.Ángel Oswaldo Fernández Vernaza (46/10)], Ariel José Graziani Lentini (7/4), Eduardo Estíguar Hurtado Roa (52/21). Trainer: Francisco Maturana (39).
Goal: Luis Enrique Capurro Bautista (6 penalty).
Penalties: 1-0 Alberto Guillermo Montaño Angulo, 1-1 Luis Enrique Capurro Bautista (saved), 1-2 Ulises Hernán de la Cruz Bernardo (saved), 2-2 Ariel José Graziani Lentini, 3-3 Ángel Oswaldo Fernández Vernaza, 3-3 Hidrobo Vilson Rosero Rodríguez (saved)

259. 06.07.1997 **VENEZUELA - ECUADOR** **1-1(0-0)** 16th FIFA WC. Qualifiers
Estadio "José Encarnación 'Pachenco' Romero", Maracaibo; Referee: Arturo Angeles (United States); Attendance: 4,729
ECU: Geovanny Oswaldo Ibarra (10/0), Iván Jacinto Hurtado Angulo (42/3), Alberto Guillermo Montaño Angulo (30/1), Juan Carlos Burbano de Lara Torres (6/0), Edmundo Marcelo Méndez (11/0), Jimmy Roberto Blandón Quiñónez (8/0), Héctor Jhonny Carabalí Cevallos (44/2) [85.Eduardo Fabián Smith Chávez (9/0)], Alex Darío Aguinaga Garzón (62/15), José Eduardo Gavica Peñafiel (25/4) [73.Gilson Simões de Souza (17/1)], Eduardo Estíguar Hurtado Roa (53/21), Ariel José Graziani Lentini (8/4). Trainer: Francisco Maturana (40).
Goal: Iván Jacinto Hurtado Angulo (55).

260. 20.07.1997 **COLOMBIA - ECUADOR** **1-0(0-0)** 16th FIFA WC. Qualifiers
Estadio Metropolitano, Barranquilla; Referee: Márcio Rezende de Freitas (Brazil); Attendance: 35,000
ECU: José Francisco Cevallos Villavicencio (14/0), Iván Jacinto Hurtado Angulo (43/3), Alberto Guillermo Montaño Angulo (31/1), Wágner Apolinario Rivera Cortazar (21/0), Luis Enrique Capurro Bautista (90/1), Jimmy Roberto Blandón Quiñónez (9/0), Héctor Jhonny Carabalí Cevallos (45/2), Alex Darío Aguinaga Garzón (63/15), José Eduardo Gavica Peñafiel (26/4), Eduardo Estíguar Hurtado Roa (54/21) [57.Ariel José Graziani Lentini (9/4)], Wellington Eduardo Sánchez Luzuriaga (10/1) [87.Édison Maldonado (4/0)]. Trainer: Francisco Maturana (41).

261. 07.08.1997 **UNITED STATES - ECUADOR** **0-1(0-0)**
Memorial Stadium, Baltimore; Referee: Raúl Domínguez (United States); Attendance: 13,629
ECU: José Francisco Cevallos Villavicencio (15/0), Wágner Apolinario Rivera Cortazar (22/0), Ulises Hernán de la Cruz Bernardo (8/0), Eduardo Fabián Smith Chávez (10/0), Luis Enrique Capurro Bautista (91/0), Alberto Guillermo Montaño Angulo (32/1), Jimmy Roberto Blandón Quiñónez (10/0), José Eduardo Gavica Peñafiel (27/4), Wellington Eduardo Sánchez Luzuriaga (11/2), Édison Maldonado (5/0) [Cléber Manuel Chalá Guerrón (30/2)], Ariel José Graziani Lentini (10/4). Trainer: Francisco Maturana (42).
Goal: Wellington Eduardo Sánchez Luzuriaga (83).

262. 20.08.1997 **ECUADOR - PARAGUAY** **2-1(0-1)** 16th FIFA WC. Qualifiers
Estadio Olimpico „Atahualpa", Quito; Referee: Rodrigo Badilla Sequeira (Costa Rica)
ECU: José Francisco Cevallos Villavicencio (16/0), Iván Jacinto Hurtado Angulo (44/3), Alberto Guillermo Montaño Angulo (33/1) [46.Wágner Apolinario Rivera Cortazar (23/0)], Ulises Hernán de la Cruz Bernardo (9/0), Luis Enrique Capurro Bautista (92/1), Jimmy Roberto Blandón Quiñónez (11/0), Héctor Jhonny Carabalí Cevallos (46/2), Alex Darío Aguinaga Garzón (64/16), Ariel José Graziani Lentini (11/5), Eduardo Estíguar Hurtado Roa (55/21) [46.José Eduardo Gavica Peñafiel (28/4)], Wellington Eduardo Sánchez Luzuriaga (12/2) [73.Édison Maldonado (6/0)]. Trainer: Francisco Maturana (43).
Goals: Alex Darío Aguinaga Garzón (53), Ariel José Graziani Lentini (72).

263. 10.09.1997 **BRAZIL - ECUADOR** **4-2(3-0)**
Estádio Fonte Nova, Salvador; Referee: Jorge Luis Nieves Parra (Uruguay); Attendance: 40,000
ECU: José Francisco Cevallos Villavicencio (17/0), Wágner Apolinario Rivera Cortazar (24/0) [46.Dannes Arsenio Coronel (20/0)], Alberto Guillermo Montaño Angulo (34/1) [Eduardo Fabián Smith Chávez (11/0)], Máximo Wilson Tenorio Quiñónez (38/3), Ulises Hernán de la Cruz Bernardo (10/0), Jimmy Roberto Blandón Quiñónez (12/0), Héctor Jhonny Carabalí Cevallos (47/2), Wellington Eduardo Sánchez Luzuriaga (13/2), José Eduardo Gavica Peñafiel (29/4) [55.Alex Darío Aguinaga Garzón (65/17)], Ariel José Graziani Lentini (12/5) [70.Édison Maldonado (7/1)], Oswaldo De La Cruz (15/1) [46.Pedro Pablo Valencia (1/0)]. Trainer: Francisco Maturana (44).
Goals: Alex Darío Aguinaga Garzón (66), Édison Maldonado (76).

264. 12.10.1997 **ECUADOR - BOLIVIA** **1-0(1-0)** 16th FIFA WC. Qualifiers
Estadio „Isidro Romero", Guayaquil; Referee: Arturo Pablo Brizio Carter (Mexico); Attendance: 14,568
ECU: José Francisco Cevallos Villavicencio (18/0), Iván Jacinto Hurtado Angulo (45/3), Alberto Guillermo Montaño Angulo (35/1), Ulises Hernán de la Cruz Bernardo (11/0), Luis Enrique Capurro Bautista (93/1), Jimmy Roberto Blandón Quiñónez (13/0), Héctor Jhonny Carabalí Cevallos (48/2), José Eduardo Gavica Peñafiel (30/4) [46.Alex Darío Aguinaga Garzón (66/17)], Wellington Eduardo Sánchez Luzuriaga (14/2) [75.Ángel Oswaldo Fernández Vernaza (47/10)], Ariel José Graziani Lentini (13/6), Eduardo Estíguar Hurtado Roa (56/21) [75.Eduardo Fabián Smith Chávez (12/0)]. Trainer: Francisco Maturana (45).
Goal: Ariel José Graziani Lentini (27).

265. 16.11.1997 **URUGUAY - ECUADOR** **5-3(2-1)** 16th FIFA WC. Qualifiers
Estadio "Domingo Burgueño", Maldonado; Referee: Antonio Marrufo Mendoza (Mexico); Attendance: 4,000
ECU: José Francisco Cevallos Villavicencio (19/0), Iván Jacinto Hurtado Angulo (46/3) [63.Dannes Arsenio Coronel (21/0)], Alberto Guillermo Montaño Angulo (36/1), Ulises Hernán de la Cruz Bernardo (12/0), Jimmy Roberto Blandón Quiñónez (14/0), Héctor Jhonny Carabalí Cevallos (49/2), José Eduardo Gavica Peñafiel (31/4), Alex Darío Aguinaga Garzón (67/17), Raúl Alfredo Noriega Escobar (28/2), Ariel José Graziani Lentini (14/9), Eduardo Estíguar Hurtado Roa (57/21) [63.Ángel Oswaldo Fernández Vernaza (48/10)]. Trainer: Francisco Maturana (46).
Goals: Ariel José Graziani Lentini (2, 59, 68).

266. 14.10.1998 **BRAZIL - ECUADOR** **5-1(2-0)**
"Robert F. Kennedy" Memorial Stadium, Washington (United States); Referee: Bryan Hall (United States); Attendance: 18,116
ECU: Jacinto Alberto Espinoza Castillo (30/0), Ulises Hernán de la Cruz Bernardo (13/1), Alberto Guillermo Montaño Angulo (37/1), Holguer Abraham Quiñónez (47/0), Néicer Reasco Yano (1/0), Héctor Jhonny Carabalí Cevallos (50/2) [46.Julio Briones (1/0)], Marlon Ritter Ayoví Mosquera (1/0), Edwin Rolando Tenorio Montaño (1/0), Alex Darío Aguinaga Garzón (68/17) [46.José Eduardo Gavica Peñafiel (32/4)], Jaime Iván Kaviedes Llorenty (1/0) [57.Nicolás Geovanny Asencio Espinoza (4/0)], Ariel José Graziani Lentini (15/9) [78.Carlos Armando Grueso Quiñónez (1/0)]. Trainer: Paúl Fernando Carrera Velasteguí (1).
Goal: Ulises Hernán de la Cruz Bernardo (67).

267. 27.01.1999 **ECUADOR - COSTA RICA** **0-0**
Estadio „Alejandro Morera Soto", Alajuela; Referee: Rónald Cedeño (Costa Rica); Attendance: 15,000
ECU: José Francisco Cevallos Villavicencio (20/0), Ulises Hernán de la Cruz Bernardo (14/1), Augusto Jesús Poroso Caicedo (1/0), Pavel Cipriano Caicedo Renteria (1/0), Marlon Ritter Ayoví Mosquera (2/0), Alberto Guillermo Montaño Angulo (38/1), Héctor Jhonny Carabalí Cevallos (51/2), Nixon Aníbal Carcelén Chalá (39/1) [76.Edwin Rolando Tenorio Montaño (2/0)], Moisés Antonio Candelario Díaz (1/0) [46.Ángel Oswaldo Fernández Vernaza (49/10)], Francisco Correa (1/0) [67.Rafael Alberto Capurro Bautista (1/0)], Eduardo Estíguar Hurtado Roa (58/21) [58.Wellington Eduardo Sánchez Luzuriaga (15/2)]. Trainer: Carlos Edmundo Sevilla (1).

268. 31.01.1999 **ECUADOR - DENMARK XI** **1-1(0-0)**
Estadio Modelo, Guayaquil; Referee: José Patricio Carpio (Ecuador); Attendance: 3,000
ECU: José Francisco Cevallos Villavicencio (21/0), Omar Andrés De Jesús Borja (1/0) [57.Ángel Valencia (1/0)], Alberto Guillermo Montaño Angulo (39/1), Pavel Cipriano Caicedo Renteria (2/0), Marlon Ritter Ayoví Mosquera (3/0), Augusto Jesús Poroso Caicedo (2/0) [78.Renán Calle Camacho (1/0)], Héctor Jhonny Carabalí Cevallos (52/2), Moisés Antonio Candelario Díaz (2/0), Ángel Oswaldo Fernández Vernaza (50/10) [73.Wellington Eduardo Sánchez Luzuriaga (16/2)], Eduardo Estíguar Hurtado Roa (59/22), Francisco Correa (2/0) [71.Rafael Alberto Capurro Bautista (2/0)]. Trainer: Carlos Edmundo Sevilla (2).

Goal: Eduardo Estíguar Hurtado Roa (73).

269. 03.02.1999 **GUATEMALA - ECUADOR** **0-0**
Estadio "Mateo Flores", Ciudad de Guatemala; Referee: Hugo Rolando Castillo (Guatemala); Attendance: 7,000
ECU: José Francisco Cevallos Villavicencio (22/0), Pavel Cipriano Caicedo Renteria (3/0), Augusto Jesús Poroso Caicedo (3/0), Alberto Guillermo Montaño Angulo (40/1), Marlon Ritter Ayoví Mosquera (4/0), Ángel Valencia (2/0) [Omar Andrés De Jesús Borja (2/0)], Héctor Jhonny Carabalí Cevallos (53/2) [Edwin Rolando Tenorio Montaño (3/0)], Wellington Eduardo Sánchez Luzuriaga (17/2) [Édison Maldonado (8/1)], Moisés Antonio Candelario Díaz (3/0), Héctor Américo Ferri (2/0) [Ángel Oswaldo Fernández Vernaza (51/10)], Eduardo Estíguar Hurtado Roa (60/22). Trainer: Carlos Edmundo Sevilla (3).

270. 10.02.1999 **PERU - ECUADOR** **1-2(1-0)**
Estadio Nacional, Lima; Referee: Ángel Ziani Bailetti (Peru); Attendance: 10,000
ECU: José Francisco Cevallos Villavicencio (23/0), Ulises Hernán de la Cruz Bernardo (15/1), Alberto Guillermo Montaño Angulo (41/1), Augusto Jesús Poroso Caicedo (4/0), Iván Jacinto Hurtado Angulo (47/3), Marlon Ritter Ayoví Mosquera (5/0) [70.Angel Valencia (3/0)], Nixon Aníbal Carcelén Chalá (40/1), Edwin Rolando Tenorio Montaño (4/0) [74.Renán Calle Camacho (2/0)], Francisco Correa (3/0) [59.Édison Maldonado (9/1)], Wellington Eduardo Sánchez Luzuriaga (18/2) [46.Héctor Américo Ferri (3/0)], Eduardo Estíguar Hurtado Roa (61/24) [90.Rafael Alberto Capurro Bautista (3/0)]. Trainer: Carlos Edmundo Sevilla (4).
Goals: Eduardo Estíguar Hurtado Roa (66, 75).

271. 17.02.1999 **ECUADOR - PERU** **1-2(0-1)**
Estadio „Isidro Romero", Guayaquil; Referee: Roger Zambrano (Ecuador); Attendance: 15,000
ECU: José Francisco Cevallos Villavicencio (24/0), Renán Calle Camacho (3/0) [Angel Valencia (4/0)], Alberto Guillermo Montaño Angulo (42/1), Augusto Jesús Poroso Caicedo (5/0), Omar Andrés De Jesús Borja (3/0) [Héctor Américo Ferri (4/0)], Edwin Rolando Tenorio Montaño (5/0), Héctor Jhonny Carabalí Cevallos (54/2) [Édison Maldonado (10/1)], Alex Darío Aguinaga Garzón (69/17), Marlon Ritter Ayoví Mosquera (6/0), Nicolás Geovanny Asencio Espinoza (5/0) [Cléber Manuel Chalá Guerrón (31/3)], Eduardo Estíguar Hurtado Roa (62/24). Trainer: Carlos Edmundo Sevilla (5).
Goal: Cléber Manuel Chalá Guerrón (68).

272. 14.04.1999 **MEXICO - ECUADOR** **0-0**
Estadio Universitario, Monterrey; Referee: Kevin Stott (United States); Attendance: 25,000
ECU: José Francisco Cevallos Villavicencio (25/0), Marlon Ritter Ayoví Mosquera (7/0) [69.Omar Andrés De Jesús Borja (4/0)], Iván Jacinto Hurtado Angulo (48/3), Franklin Anangonó (1/0), Alberto Guillermo Montaño Angulo (43/1), John Patricio Cagua Padilla (1/0), Jimmy Roberto Blandón Quiñónez (15/0), Héctor Jhonny Carabalí Cevallos (55/2), Alex Darío Aguinaga Garzón (70/17) [46.Cléber Manuel Chalá Guerrón (32/3)], Jaime Iván Kaviedes Llorenty (2/0) [46.Eduardo Estíguar Hurtado Roa (63/24)], Ariel José Graziani Lentini (16/9) [46.Agustín Javier Delgado Chalá (16/5)]. Trainer: Carlos Edmundo Sevilla (6).

273. 19.05.1999 **ECUADOR - VENEZUELA** **0-2(0-1)**
Estadio Reales Tamarindos, Porto Viejo; Referee: Byron Moreno (Ecuador); Attendance: 26,000
ECU: José Francisco Cevallos Villavicencio (26/0), Iván Jacinto Hurtado Angulo (49/3), Alberto Guillermo Montaño Angulo (44/1), Augusto Jesús Poroso Caicedo (6/0) [62.Wellington Eduardo Sánchez Luzuriaga (19/2)], Ulises Hernán de la Cruz Bernardo (16/1) [68.Dannes Arsenio Coronel (22/0)], Néicer Reasco Yano (2/0), Jimmy Roberto Blandón Quiñónez (16/0), Moisés Antonio Candelario Díaz (4/0) [68.Luis Ernesto González (10/0)], Cléber Manuel Chalá Guerrón (33/3) [81.Héctor Américo Ferri (5/0)], Edwin Patricio Hurtado Zurita (9/0), Diego Rodrigo Herrera Larrea (10/0) [46.César Fabián Cubero Guerra (3/0)]. Trainer: Carlos Edmundo Sevilla (7).

274. 02.06.1999 **ECUADOR - IRAN** **1-1(1-0)** 2nd Canada Cup
Commonwealth Stadium, Edmonton (Canada); Referee: Mike Seifert (Canada); Attendance: 5,386
ECU: Geovanny Oswaldo Ibarra (11/0), Iván Jacinto Hurtado Angulo (50/3), Franklin Anangonó (2/0), Alberto Guillermo Montaño Angulo (45/2), Ulises Hernán de la Cruz Bernardo (17/1), Jimmy Roberto Blandón Quiñónez (17/0), Ariel José Graziani Lentini (17/9), John Patricio Cagua Padilla (2/0), Luis Ernesto González (11/0), Eduardo Estíguar Hurtado Roa (64/24) [70.Luis Heberthson Moreira Ibarra (1/0)], Agustín Javier Delgado Chalá (17/5). Trainer: Carlos Edmundo Sevilla (8).
Goal: Alberto Guillermo Montaño Angulo (39).

275. 04.06.1999 **ECUADOR - GUATEMALA** **3-1(1-1)** 2nd Canada Cup
Commonwealth Stadium, Edmonton (Canada); Referee: Jerry Proctor (Canada); Attendance: 8865
ECU: José Francisco Cevallos Villavicencio (27/0), Iván Jacinto Hurtado Angulo (51/3), Alberto Guillermo Montaño Angulo (46/2), Ulises Hernán de la Cruz Bernardo (18/1), John Patricio Cagua Padilla (3/0) [56.Dannes Arsenio Coronel (23/0)], Jimmy Roberto Blandón Quiñónez (18/0), Luis Ernesto González (12/0), Alex Darío Aguinaga Garzón (71/17) [62.Nicolás Geovanny Asencio Espinoza (6/0)], Ariel José Graziani Lentini (18/11), Eduardo Estíguar Hurtado Roa (65/24) [46.Franklin Anangonó (3/0)], Agustín Javier Delgado Chalá (18/6). Trainer: Carlos Edmundo Sevilla (9)
Goals: Ariel José Graziani Lentini (15), Agustín Javier Delgado Chalá (48), Ariel José Graziani Lentini (56).

276. 06.06.1999 **CANADA "U 23" - ECUADOR** **1-2(0-1)** 2nd Canada Cup
Commonwealth Stadium, Edmonton; Referee: Antonio Maruffo Mendoza (Mexico); Attendance: 10,026
ECU: Geovanny Oswaldo Ibarra (12/0) [46.José Francisco Cevallos Villavicencio (28/0)], Iván Jacinto Hurtado Angulo (52/3), Frankin Anangonó (4/0), Alberto Guillermo Montaño Angulo (47/2), Ulises Hernán de la Cruz Bernardo (19/1), Luis Heberthson Moreira Ibarra (2/0), Jimmy Roberto Blandón Quiñónez (19/0), Ariel José Graziani Lentini (19/12), Nicolás Geovanny Asencio Espinoza (7/0) [57.Dannes Arsenio Coronel (24/0)], Luis Ernesto González (13/0) [54.Jairon Leonel Zamora Narváez (1/0)], John Patricio Cagua Padilla (4/0). Trainer: Carlos Edmundo Sevilla (10)
Goals: Ariel José Graziani Lentini (17), Jason De Vos (54 own goal).

277. 15.06.1999 **VENEZUELA - ECUADOR** **3-2(0-2)**
Estadio Pueblo Nuevo, San Cristóbal; Referee: Édison Ibarra (Venezuela); Attendance: 9,000
ECU: José Francisco Cevallos Villavicencio (29/0) [46.Geovanny Oswaldo Ibarra (13/0)], Rolando Santiago Jacomé Ponce (2/0), Franklin Anangonó (5/0), Alberto Guillermo Montaño Angulo (48/3), Ulises Hernán de la Cruz Bernardo (20/1), Jimmy Roberto Blandón Quiñónez (20/0), Fricson Vinicio George Tenorio (1/0) [75.Néicer Reasco Yano (3/0)], Jairon Leonel Zamora Narváez (2/0) [31.Luis Ernesto González (14/0)], Luis Heberthson Moreira Ibarra (3/0) [54.Cléber Manuel Chalá Guerrón (34/3)], Ariel José Graziani Lentini (20/12) [72.Augusto Jesús Poroso Caicedo (7/0)], Agustín Javier Delgado Chalá (19/7). Trainer: Carlos Edmundo Sevilla (11).
Goals: Alberto Guillermo Montaño Angulo (15), Agustín Javier Delgado Chalá (22).

278. 23.06.1999 **CHILE - ECUADOR** **0-0**
Estadio Nacional, Santiago; Referee: Daniel Orlando Giménez (Argentina); Attendance: 23,282
ECU: José Francisco Cevallos Villavicencio (30/0), Iván Jacinto Hurtado Angulo (53/3), Franklin Anangonó (6/0), Holguer Abraham Quiñónez (48/0), Ulises Hernán de la Cruz Bernardo (21/1), Fricson Vinicio George Tenorio (2/0) [61.Dannes Arsenio Coronel (25/0)], Jimmy Roberto Blandón Quiñónez (21/0), Marlon Ritter Ayoví Mosquera (8/0), Luis Heberthson Moreira Ibarra (4/0) [65.Wellington Eduardo Sánchez Luzuriaga (20/2)], Agustín Javier Delgado Chalá (20/7) [87.Nicolás Geovanny Asencio Espinoza (8/0)], Ariel José Graziani Lentini (21/12) [70.Jaime Iván Kaviedes Llorenty (3/0)]. Trainer: Carlos Edmundo Sevilla (12).

279. 01.07.1999 **ARGENTINA - ECUADOR** **3-1(1-0)** 39th Copa América. Group Stage
Estadio „Feliciano Cáceres", Luque (Paraguay); Referee: Gilberto Hildalgo (Peru); Attendance: 20,000
ECU: José Francisco Cevallos Villavicencio (31/0), Iván Jacinto Hurtado Angulo (54/3), Alberto Guillermo Montaño Angulo (49/3), Holguer Abraham Quiñónez (49/0), Ulises Hernán de la Cruz Bernardo (22/1), Fricson Vinicio George Tenorio (3/0), Jimmy Roberto Blandón Quiñónez (22/0), Héctor Jhonny Carabalí Cevallos (56/2) [59.Alex Darío Aguinaga Garzón (72/17)], Luis Heberthson Moreira Ibarra (5/0) [59.Jairon Leonel Zamora Narváez (3/0)], Agustín Javier Delgado Chalá (21/7) [46.Jaime Iván Kaviedes Llorenty (4/1)), Ariel José Graziani Lentini (22/12). Trainer: Carlos Edmundo Sevilla (13).
Goal: Jaime Iván Kaviedes Llorenty (77).

280. 04.07.1999 **URUGUAY - ECUADOR** **2-1(0-0)** 39th Copa América. Group Stage
Estadio „Feliciano Cáceres", Luque (Paraguay); Referee: Mario Sánchez (Chile); Attendance: 18,000
ECU: José Francisco Cevallos Villavicencio (32/0), Iván Jacinto Hurtado Angulo (55/3), Alberto Guillermo Montaño Angulo (50/3), Holguer Abraham Quiñónez (50/0), Ulises Hernán de la Cruz Bernardo (23/1), Fricson Vinicio George Tenorio (4/0) [66.Luis Heberthson Moreira Ibarra (6/0)], Jimmy Roberto Blandón Quiñónez (23/0), Héctor Jhonny Carabalí Cevallos (57/2) [61.Jairon Leonel Zamora Narváez (4/0)], Alex Darío Aguinaga Garzón (Cap) (73/17), Jaime Iván Kaviedes Llorenty (5/2), Ariel José Graziani Lentini (23/12) [65.Agustín Javier Delgado Chalá (22/7)]. Trainer: Carlos Edmundo Sevilla (14).
Goal: Jaime Iván Kaviedes Llorenty (78).

281. 07.07.1999 **COLOMBIA - ECUADOR** **2-1(2-0)** 39th Copa América. Group Stage
Estadio „Feliciano Cáceres", Luque (Paraguay); Referee: Masayoshi Okada (Japan); Attendance: 12,000
ECU: José Francisco Cevallos Villavicencio (33/0), Iván Jacinto Hurtado Angulo (56/3), Frankin Anangonó (7/0), Alberto Guillermo Montaño Angulo (51/3), Ulises Hernán de la Cruz Bernardo (24/1), Dannes Arsenio Coronel (26/0), Héctor Jhonny Carabalí Cevallos (58/2) [46.Marlon Ritter Ayoví Mosquera (9/0)], Alex Darío Aguinaga Garzón (74/17) [70.Wellington Eduardo Sánchez Luzuriaga (21/2)], Jimmy Roberto Blandón Quiñónez (24/0), Ariel José Graziani Lentini (24/13), Jaime Iván Kaviedes Llorenty (6/2) [86.Nicolás Geovanny Asencio Espinoza (9/0)]. Trainer: Carlos Edmundo Sevilla (15).
Goal: Ariel José Graziani Lentini (50).

282. 12.10.1999 **URUGUAY - ECUADOR** **0-0**
Estadio Centenario, Montevideo; Referee: Carlos Arencio Amarilla Demarqui (Paraguay); Attendance: 3,779
ECU: José Francisco Cevallos Villavicencio (34/0), John Patricio Cagua Padilla (5/0), Iván Jacinto Hurtado Angulo (57/3), Alberto Guillermo Montaño Angulo (52/3), Marlon Ritter Ayoví Mosquera (10/0), Jairon Leonel Zamora Narváez (5/0), Wellington Eduardo Sánchez Luzuriaga (Cap) (22/2) [76.Christian Fernando Quiñónez Cangá (1/0)], Edwin Rolando Tenorio Montaño (6/0), Cléber Manuel Chalá Guerrón (35/3), Eduardo Estíguar Hurtado Roa (66/24), Ariel José Graziani Lentini (25/13) [46.Jaime Iván Kaviedes Llorenty (7/2)]. Trainer: Hernán Darío Gómez (1).

283. 27.10.1999 **MEXICO - ECUADOR** **0-0**
Robertson Stadium, Houston (United States); Referee: Ali Saheli (United States); Attendance: 30.000
ECU: Carlos Luis Morales (40/0) [17.Héctor Rolando Carabalí Pabón (1/0)], Marlon Ritter Ayoví Mosquera (11/0), Iván Jacinto Hurtado Angulo (58/3), Alberto Guillermo Montaño Angulo (53/3), John Patricio Cagua Padilla (6/0), Edwin Rolando Tenorio Montaño (7/0), Jairon Leonel Zamora Narváez (6/0), Wellington Eduardo Sánchez Luzuriaga (23/2) [46.César Fabián Cubero Guerra (4/0)], Cléber Manuel Chalá Guerrón (36/3), Agustín Javier Delgado Chalá (23/7) [64.Santiago Damián Morales Montenegro (1/0)], Eduardo Estíguar Hurtado Roa (67/24) [74.Carlos García (1/0)]. Trainer: Hernán Darío Gómez (2).

284. 27.01.2000 **HONDURAS - ECUADOR** **1-1(0-1)**
Estadio Metropolitano, San Pedro Sula; Referee: Evaristo Soriano (Honduras); Attendance: 12,000
ECU: Geovanny Oswaldo Ibarra (14/0), Dannes Arsenio Coronel (27/0) [Santiago Damián Morales Montenegro (2/0)], Rolando Santiago Jacomé Ponce (3/0), John Patricio Cagua Padilla (7/0), Alberto Guillermo Montaño Angulo (54/3), Marlon Ritter Ayoví Mosquera (12/0) [Luis Alberto Zambrano (1/0)], Edwin Rolando Tenorio Montaño (8/0), Héctor Américo Ferri (6/0) [Roberth Javier Burbano (13/0)], César Fabián Cubero Guerra (5/0) [Edwin Patricio Hurtado Zurita (10/0)], Cléber Manuel Chalá Guerrón (37/3), Ariel José Graziani Lentini (26/14). Trainer: Hernán Darío Gómez (3).
Goal: Ariel José Graziani Lentini (10).

285. 08.03.2000 **ECUADOR - HONDURAS** **1-3(1-0)**
Estadio Casa Blanca de LDU, Quito; Referee: Segundo Díaz (Ecuador); Attendance: 1,000
ECU: José Francisco Cevallos Villavicencio (35/0), Marlon Ritter Ayoví Mosquera (13/0) [71.Ulises Hernán de la Cruz Bernardo (25/1)], Iván Jacinto Hurtado Angulo (59/3), Alberto Guillermo Montaño Angulo (55/3), John Patricio Cagua Padilla (8/0), Christian Fernando Quiñónez Cangá (2/0) [65.Édison Vicente Méndez Méndez (1/0)], Edwin Rolando Tenorio Montaño (9/0), Cléber Manuel Chalá Guerrón (38/3), César Fabián Cubero Guerra (6/0) [65.Héctor Américo Ferri (7/0)], Jaime Iván Kaviedes Llorenty (8/2), Eduardo Estíguar Hurtado Roa (68/25). Trainer: Hernán Darío Gómez (4).
Goal: Eduardo Estíguar Hurtado Roa (24).

286. 29.03.2000 **ECUADOR - VENEZUELA** **2-0(1-0)** 17th FIFA WC. Qualifiers
Estadio Casa Blanca de LDU, Quito; Referee: Eduardo Gamboa (Chile); Attendance: 37,288
ECU: José Francisco Cevallos Villavicencio (36/0), Ulises Hernán de la Cruz Bernardo (26/1), Rolando Santiago Jacomé Ponce (4/0), Alberto Guillermo Montaño Angulo (56/3) [*sent off 27*], John Patricio Cagua Padilla (9/0) [49. Marlon Ritter Ayoví Mosquera (14/0)], Jimmy Roberto Blandón Quiñónez (25/0), Edwin Rolando Tenorio Montaño (10/0) [73.Cléber Manuel Chalá Guerrón (39/3)], Alex Darío Aguinaga Garzón (75/18), Alfonso Andrés Obregón Cancino (13/0), Ariel José Graziani Lentini (27/14) [38.Augusto Jesús Poroso Caicedo (8/0)], Agustín Javier Delgado Chalá (24/8). Trainer: Hernán Darío Gómez (5).
Goals: Agustín Javier Delgado Chalá (17), Alex Darío Aguinaga Garzón (51).

287. 26.04.2000 **BRAZIL - ECUADOR** **3-2(2-1)** 17th FIFA WC. Qualifiers
Estádio „Cícero Pompeu de Toledo" (Morumbi), São Paulo; Referee: Henry Cervantes Jiménez (Colombia); Attendance: 64.738
ECU: José Francisco Cevallos Villavicencio (37/0), Ulises Hernán de la Cruz Bernardo (27/2), Iván Jacinto Hurtado Angulo (60/3), Augusto Jesús Poroso Caicedo (9/0), Luis Enrique Capurro Bautista (94/1), Jimmy Roberto Blandón Quiñónez (26/0), Edwin Rolando Tenorio Montaño (11/0), Alfonso Andrés Obregón Cancino (14/0), Alex Darío Aguinaga Garzón (76/19) [40.Marlon Ritter Ayoví Mosquera (15/0), 88.Jaime Iván Kaviedes Llorenty (9/2)], Agustín Javier Delgado Chalá (25/8), Ariel José Graziani Lentini (28/14) [65.Eduardo Estíguar Hurtado Roa (69/25)]. Trainer: Hernán Darío Gómez (6).
Goals: Alex Darío Aguinaga Garzón (12), Ulises Hernán de la Cruz Bernardo (76).

288. 03.06.2000 **PARAGUAY - ECUADOR** **3-1(2-0)** 17th FIFA WC. Qualifiers
Estadio Defensores del Chaco, Asunción; Referee: Gustavo Adolfo Gallesio Greco (Uruguay); Attendance: 22,000
ECU: José Francisco Cevallos Villavicencio (38/0), Ulises Hernán de la Cruz Bernardo (28/2), Alberto Guillermo Montaño Angulo (57/3), Augusto Jesús Poroso Caicedo (10/0) [65.Jaime Iván Kaviedes Llorenty (10/2)], Luis Enrique Capurro Bautista (95/1), Edwin Rolando Tenorio Montaño (12/0) [46.Cléber Manuel Chalá Guerrón (40/3)], Jimmy Roberto Blandón Quiñónez (27/0), Iván Jacinto Hurtado Angulo (61/3), Alex Darío Aguinaga Garzón (77/19), Carlos Alberto Juárez Devico (1/0), Agustín Javier Delgado Chalá (26/8) [61.Ariel José Graziani Lentini (29/15)]. Trainer: Hernán Darío Gómez (7).
Goal: Ariel José Graziani Lentini (85).

289. 25.06.2000 **ECUADOR - PANAMA** **5-0(4-0)**
Estadio Olimpico „Atahualpa", Quito; Referee: Luis Enrique Vasco (Ecuador); Attendance: 2,000
ECU: José Francisco Cevallos Villavicencio (39/0) [46.Jacinto Alberto Espinoza Castillo (31/0)], Ulises Hernán de la Cruz Bernardo (29/2), Iván Jacinto Hurtado Angulo (62/3), Augusto Jesús Poroso Caicedo (11/0) [59.Giovanny Patricio Espinoza Pavón (1/0)], John Patricio Cagua Padilla (10/0) [66.Marlon Ritter Ayoví Mosquera (16/0)], Jimmy Roberto Blandón Quiñónez (28/0), Alfonso Andrés Obregón Cancino (15/0), Roberth Javier Burbano (14/0) [46.Cléber Manuel Chalá Guerrón (41/3)], Jaime Iván Kaviedes Llorenty (11/5), Agustín Javier Delgado Chalá (27/10), Eduardo Estíguar Hurtado Roa (70/25) [46.Carlos Alberto Juárez Devico (2/0)]. Trainer: Hernán Darío Gómez (8).
Goals: Agustín Javier Delgado Chalá (22), Jaime Iván Kaviedes Llorenty (25), Agustín Javier Delgado Chalá (34), Jaime Iván Kaviedes Llorenty (44, 55).

290. 29.06.2000 **ECUADOR - PERU** **2-1(1-0)** 17th FIFA WC. Qualifiers
Estadio Olimpico „Atahualpa", Quito; Referee: Carlos Eugênio Simon (Brazil); Attendance: 40,167
ECU: José Francisco Cevallos Villavicencio (40/0), Ulises Hernán de la Cruz Bernardo (30/2), Iván Jacinto Hurtado Angulo (63/3), Augusto Jesús Poroso Caicedo (12/0), Marlon Ritter Ayoví Mosquera (17/0), Alfonso Andrés Obregón Cancino (16/0), Jimmy Roberto Blandón Quiñónez (29/0), Alex Darío Aguinaga Garzón (78/19) [71.Roberth Javier Burbano (15/0)], Cléber Manuel Chalá Guerrón (42/4), Agustín Javier Delgado Chalá (28/10) [71.Ariel José Graziani Lentini (30/15)], Eduardo Estíguar Hurtado Roa (71/26) [71.Jaime Iván Kaviedes Llorenty (12/5)]. Trainer: Hernán Darío Gómez (9).
Goals: Cléber Manuel Chalá Guerrón (14), Eduardo Estíguar Hurtado Roa (51).

291. 19.07.2000 **ARGENTINA - ECUADOR** **2-0(1-0)** 17th FIFA WC. Qualifiers
Estadio Monumental „Antonio Vespucio Liberti", Buenos Aires; Referee: Daniel Bello (Uruguay); Attendance: 44,199
ECU: José Francisco Cevallos Villavicencio (41/0), Ulises Hernán de la Cruz Bernardo (31/2), Iván Jacinto Hurtado Angulo (64/3), Augusto Jesús Poroso Caicedo (13/0), Marlon Ritter Ayoví Mosquera (18/0), Edwin Rolando Tenorio Montaño (13/0), Jimmy Roberto Blandón Quiñónez (30/0), Alfonso Andrés Obregón Cancino (17/0), Alex Darío Aguinaga Garzón (79/19) [88.Cléber Manuel Chalá Guerrón (43/4)], Eduardo Estíguar Hurtado Roa (72/26), Agustín Javier Delgado Chalá (29/10) [73.Ariel José Graziani Lentini (31/15)]. Trainer: Hernán Darío Gómez (10).

292. 25.07.2000 **ECUADOR - COLOMBIA** **0-0** 17th FIFA WC. Qualifiers
Estadio Olimpico „Atahualpa", Quito; Referee: Ubaldo Aquino Valenzano (Paraguay); Attendance: 43,000
ECU: José Francisco Cevallos Villavicencio (42/0), Ulises Hernán de la Cruz Bernardo (32/2), Iván Jacinto Hurtado Angulo (65/3), Augusto Jesús Poroso Caicedo (14/0), Marlon Ritter Ayoví Mosquera (19/0), Alfonso Andrés Obregón Cancino (18/0), Cléber Manuel Chalá Guerrón (44/4) [68.Diego Rodrigo Herrera Larrea (11/0)], Edwin Rolando Tenorio Montaño (14/0), Alex Darío Aguinaga Garzón (80/19), Eduardo Estíguar Hurtado Roa (73/26) [76.Carlos Alberto Juárez Devico (3/0)], Ariel José Graziani Lentini (32/15) [68.Agustín Javier Delgado Chalá (30/10)]. Trainer: Hernán Darío Gómez (11).

293. 11.08.2000 **PANAMA - ECUADOR** **0-0**
Estadio „Rommel Fernández", Ciudad de Panamá; Referee: de León (Panama)
ECU: Jorge Wilber Corozo (1/0), Omar Andrés De Jesús Borja (5/0), Giovanny Patricio Espinoza Pavón (2/0), Raúl Fernando Guerrón Méndez (1/0), Wellington Pinta Paredes Mejía (1/0), Édison Vicente Méndez Méndez (2/0), Santiago Damián Morales Montenegro (3/0), Jorge Enrique Justavino (1/0), Franklin Agustín Salas Narváez (1/0), Gustavo Omar Figueroa Cáceres (1/0) [Camilo David Hurtado Hurtado (1/0)], Rafael Alberto Capurro Bautista (4/0) [Joel Aurelio Vernaza Valencia (1/0)]. Trainer: Hernán Darío Gómez (12).

294. 16.08.2000 **ECUADOR - BOLIVIA** **2-0(1-0)** 17th FIFA WC. Qualifiers
Estadio Casa Blanca de LDU, Quito; Referee: Luis Solórzano Torres (Venezuela); Attendance: 21,526
ECU: Geovanny Oswaldo Ibarra (15/0), Ulises Hernán de la Cruz Bernardo (33/2), Iván Jacinto Hurtado Angulo (66/3), Augusto Jesús Poroso Caicedo (15/0), Marlon Ritter Ayoví Mosquera (20/0) [46.Néicer Reasco Yano (4/0)], Alex Darío Aguinaga Garzón (81/19), Alfonso Andrés Obregón Cancino (19/0), Edwin Rolando Tenorio Montaño (15/0), Cléber Manuel Chalá Guerrón (45/4), Ariel José Graziani Lentini (33/15) [62.Carlos Alberto Juárez Devico (4/0)], Agustín Javier Delgado Chalá (31/12). Trainer: Hernán Darío Gómez (13).
Goals: Agustín Javier Delgado Chalá (17, 59).

295. 03.09.2000 **URUGUAY - ECUADOR** **4-0(2-0)** 17th FIFA WC. Qualifiers
Estadio Centenario, Montevideo; Referee: Henry Cervantes Jiménez (Colombia); Attendance: 62,000
ECU: José Francisco Cevallos Villavicencio (43/0), Ulises Hernán de la Cruz Bernardo (34/2), Augusto Jesús Poroso Caicedo (16/0) [*sent off 85*], Iván Jacinto Hurtado Angulo (67/3), Luis Enrique Capurro Bautista (96/1), Alfonso Andrés Obregón Cancino (20/0), Edwin Rolando Tenorio Montaño (16/0) [56.Juan Carlos Burbano de Lara Torres (7/0)], Cléber Manuel Chalá Guerrón (46/4) [46.Moisés Antonio Candelario Díaz (5/0)], Alex Darío Aguinaga Garzón (82/19), Carlos Alberto Juárez Devico (5/0), Ariel José Graziani Lentini (34/15). Trainer: Hernán Darío Gómez (14).

296. 20.09.2000 **MEXICO - ECUADOR** **2-0(1-0)**
Qualcomm Stadium, San Diego (United States); Referee: Kevin Stott (United States)
ECU: José Francisco Cevallos Villavicencio (44/0), Omar Andrés De Jesús Borja (6/0), Giovanny Patricio Espinoza Pavón (3/0), Raúl Fernando Guerrón Méndez (2/0), Wellington Pinta Paredes Mejía (2/0), Alfonso Andrés Obregón Cancino (21/0) [69.Jorge Enrique Justavino (2/0)], Richard Alfonso Borja Moreno (1/0), Marlon Ritter Ayoví Mosquera (21/0) [56.Édison Vicente Méndez Méndez (3/0)], Wellington Eduardo Sánchez Luzuriaga (24/2), Eduardo Estíguar Hurtado Roa (74/26) [69.Rafael Alberto Capurro Bautista (5/0)], Gustavo Omar Figueroa Cáceres (2/0). Trainer: Hernán Darío Gómez (15).

297. 08.10.2000 **ECUADOR - CHILE** **1-0(0-0)** 17th FIFA WC. Qualifiers
Estadio Olimpico „Atahualpa", Quito; Referee: John Jairo Toro Rendón (Colombia); Attendance: 28,566
ECU: José Francisco Cevallos Villavicencio (45/0), Ulises Hernán de la Cruz Bernardo (35/2), Giovanny Patricio Espinoza Pavón (4/0), Iván Jacinto Hurtado Angulo (68/3), Raúl Fernando Guerrón Méndez (3/0), Edwin Rolando Tenorio Montaño (17/0) [62.Ángel Oswaldo Fernández Vernaza (52/10)], Alfonso Andrés Obregón Cancino (22/0), Cléber Manuel Chalá Guerrón (47/4) [58.Wellington Eduardo Sánchez Luzuriaga (25/2)], Alex Darío Aguinaga Garzón (83/19), Jaime Iván Kaviedes Llorenty (13/5) [75.Evelio Agustín Ordóñez Martínez (3/0)], Agustín Javier Delgado Chalá (32/13). Trainer: Hernán Darío Gómez (16).
Goal: Agustín Javier Delgado Chalá (76).

298. 15.11.2000 **VENEZUELA - ECUADOR** **1-2(0-2)** 17th FIFA WC. Qualifiers

Estadio „José Encarnación ‚Pachencho' Romero", Maracaibo; Referee: Eduardo Abel Lecca Betancourt (Peru); Attendance: 6,500

ECU: José Francisco Cevallos Villavicencio (46/0), Iván Jacinto Hurtado Angulo (69/3), Augusto Jesús Poroso Caicedo (17/0), Raúl Fernando Guerrón Méndez (4/0), Ulises Hernán de la Cruz Bernardo (36/2), Édison Vicente Méndez Méndez (4/0) [72.Jairon Leonel Zamora Narváez (7/0)], Juan Carlos Burbano de Lara Torres (8/0), Cléber Manuel Chalá Guerrón (48/4), Wellington Eduardo Sánchez Luzuriaga (26/3), Jaime Iván Kaviedes Llorenty (14/6) [68.Ángel Oswaldo Fernández Vernaza (53/10)], Agustín Javier Delgado Chalá (33/13). Trainer: Hernán Darío Gómez (17).

Goals: Jaime Iván Kaviedes Llorenty (3), Wellington Eduardo Sánchez Luzuriaga (23).

299. 28.03.2001 **ECUADOR - BRAZIL** **1-0(0-0)** 17th FIFA WC. Qualifiers

Estadio Olimpico „Atahualpa", Quito; Referee: Felipe Ramos Rizzo (Mexico); Attendance: 40,800

ECU: José Francisco Cevallos Villavicencio (47/0), Augusto Jesús Poroso Caicedo (18/0), Iván Jacinto Hurtado Angulo (70/3), Ulises Hernán de la Cruz Bernardo (37/2), Raúl Fernando Guerrón Méndez (5/0), Jaime Iván Kaviedes Llorenty (15/6) [88.Alfonso Andrés Obregón Cancino (23/0)], Alex Darío Aguinaga Garzón (84/19), Agustín Javier Delgado Chalá (34/14), Juan Carlos Burbano de Lara Torres (9/0), Édison Vicente Méndez Méndez (5/0), Edwin Rolando Tenorio Montaño (18/0) [69.Wellington Eduardo Sánchez Luzuriaga (27/3)]. Trainer: Hernán Darío Gómez (18).

Goal: Agustín Javier Delgado Chalá (49).

300. 24.04.2001 **ECUADOR - PARAGUAY** **2-1(1-1)** 17th FIFA WC. Qualifiers

Estadio Olimpico „Atahualpa", Quito; Referee: Ángel Oswaldo Sánchez (Argentina); Attendance: 30,145

ECU: José Francisco Cevallos Villavicencio (48/0), Augusto Jesús Poroso Caicedo (19/0) [*sent off 18*], Iván Jacinto Hurtado Angulo (71/3), Ulises Hernán de la Cruz Bernardo (38/2), Raúl Fernando Guerrón Méndez (6/0), Jaime Iván Kaviedes Llorenty (16/6), Alex Darío Aguinaga Garzón (85/19) [44.Édison Vicente Méndez Méndez (6/0)], Agustín Javier Delgado Chalá (35/16), Juan Carlos Burbano de Lara Torres (10/0) [46.Giovanny Patricio Espinoza Pavón (5/0)], Cléber Manuel Chalá Guerrón (49/4) [68.Wellington Eduardo Sánchez Luzuriaga (28/3) [*sent off 90*]], Edwin Rolando Tenorio Montaño (19/0). Trainer: Hernán Darío Gómez (19).

Goals: Agustín Javier Delgado Chalá (44, 52).

301. 02.06.2001 **PERU - ECUADOR** **1-2(1-1)** 17th FIFA WC. Qualifiers

Estadio Nacional, Lima; Referee: Antonio Marrufo Mendoza (Mexico); Attendance: 54,236

ECU: José Francisco Cevallos Villavicencio (49/0), Ulises Hernán de la Cruz Bernardo (39/2), Iván Jacinto Hurtado Angulo (72/3), Giovanny Patricio Espinoza Pavón (6/0), Raúl Fernando Guerrón Méndez (7/0), Édison Vicente Méndez Méndez (7/1) [*sent off 82*], Edwin Rolando Tenorio Montaño (20/0), Alfonso Andrés Obregón Cancino (24/0) [73.Jorge Daniel Guagua Tamayo (1/0)], Cléber Manuel Chalá Guerrón (50/4) [85.Juan Francisco Aguinaga Garzón (1/0)], Jaime Iván Kaviedes Llorenty (17/6) [80.Ángel Oswaldo Fernández Vernaza (54/10)], Agustín Javier Delgado Chalá (36/17). Trainer: Hernán Darío Gómez (20).

Goals: Édison Vicente Méndez Méndez (11), Agustín Javier Delgado Chalá (90).

302. 07.06.2001 **UNITED STATES - ECUADOR** **0-0**

Columbus Crew Stadium, Columbus (United States); Referee: José Farias Martínez (Canada); Attendance: 12,572

ECU: Geovanny Oswaldo Ibarra (16/0), Ulises Hernán de la Cruz Bernardo (40/2), Iván Jacinto Hurtado Angulo (73/3), Giovanny Patricio Espinoza Pavón (7/0), Raúl Fernando Guerrón Méndez (8/0), Juan Francisco Aguinaga Garzón (2/0), Wellington Eduardo Sánchez Luzuriaga (29/3) [63.Walter Orlando Ayoví Corozo (1/0)], Cléber Manuel Chalá Guerrón (51/4), Édison Vicente Méndez Méndez (8/1), Edwin Rolando Tenorio Montaño (21/0), Agustín Javier Delgado Chalá (37/17). Trainer: Hernán Darío Gómez (21).

303. 02.07.2001 **ECUADOR - EL SALVADOR** **1-0(0-0)**

Giants Stadium, East Rutherford, New York (United States)

ECU: Geovanny Oswaldo Ibarra (17/0), Marlon Ritter Ayoví Mosquera (22/0), Iván Jacinto Hurtado Angulo (74/3), Giovanny Patricio Espinoza Pavón (8/0), Raúl Fernando Guerrón Méndez (9/0), Alfonso Andrés Obregón Cancino (25/0) [Édison Vicente Méndez Méndez (9/1)], Juan Carlos Burbano de Lara Torres (11/0), Juan Francisco Aguinaga Garzón (3/0) [Cléber Manuel Chalá Guerrón (52/5)], Wellington Eduardo Sánchez Luzuriaga (30/3), Ángel Oswaldo Fernández Vernaza (55/10), Jaime Iván Kaviedes Llorenty (18/6) [Evelio Agustín Ordóñez Martínez (4/0)]. Trainer: Hernán Darío Gómez (22).

Goal: Cléber Manuel Chalá Guerrón (87).

304. 07.07.2001 **ECUADOR - HONDURAS** **1-1(0-0)**

Orange Bowl, Miami (United States); Referee: Richard Green (United States); Attendance: 10,000

ECU: José Francisco Cevallos Villavicencio (50/0), Ángel Oswaldo Fernández Vernaza (56/10), Iván Jacinto Hurtado Angulo (75/3), Raúl Fernando Guerrón Méndez (10/0) [73.Walter Orlando Ayoví Corozo (2/0)], Marlon Ritter Ayoví Mosquera (23/0), Cléber Manuel Chalá Guerrón (53/5), Giovanny Patricio Espinoza Pavón (9/1), Édison Vicente Méndez Méndez (10/1), Edwin Rolando Tenorio Montaño (22/0) [46.Alfonso Andrés Obregón Cancino (26/0)], Jaime Iván Kaviedes Llorenty (19/6) [68. Evelio Agustín Ordóñez Martínez (5/0)], Wellington Eduardo Sánchez Luzuriaga (31/3) [*sent off*]. Trainer: Hernán Darío Gómez (23).

Goal: Giovanny Patricio Espinoza Pavón (90).

305. 11.07.2001 **CHILE - ECUADOR** **4-1(1-0)** 40th Copa América.Group Stage.

Estadio Metropolitano „Roberto Meléndez", Barranquilla (Colombia); Referee: René Ortubé Betancourt (Bolivia); Attendance: 33,511

ECU: Geovanny Oswaldo Ibarra (18/0), Ulises Hernán de la Cruz Bernardo (41/2), Iván Jacinto Hurtado Angulo (76/6), Giovanny Patricio Espinoza Pavón (10/1), Raúl Fernando Guerrón Méndez (11/0), Édison Vicente Méndez Méndez (11/1) [46.Alfonso Andrés Obregón Cancino (27/0)], Edwin Rolando Tenorio Montaño (23/0) [84.Evelio Agustín Ordóñez Martínez (6/0)], Alex Darío Aguinaga Garzón (86/19) [64.Wellington Eduardo Sánchez Luzuriaga (32/3)], Cléber Manuel Chalá Guerrón (54/6) [*sent off 77*], Ángel Oswaldo Fernández Vernaza (57/10), Agustín Javier Delgado Chalá (38/17). Trainer: Hernán Darío Gómez (24).

Goal: Cléber Manuel Chalá Guerrón (53).

306. 14.07.2001 **COLOMBIA - ECUADOR** **1-0(1-0)** 40th Copa América.Group Stage.

Estadio Metropolitano „Roberto Meléndez", Barranquilla; Referee: Ubaldo Aquino Valenzano (Paraguay); Attendance: 26,150

ECU: José Francisco Cevallos Villavicencio (51/0), Ulises Hernán de la Cruz Bernardo (42/2), Iván Jacinto Hurtado Angulo (77/3), Giovanny Patricio Espinoza Pavón (11/1), Raúl Fernando Guerrón Méndez (12/0), Juan Carlos Burbano de Lara Torres (12/0) [46.Edwin Rolando Tenorio Montaño (24/0)], Alex Darío Aguinaga Garzón (87/19) [*sent off 81*], Agustín Javier Delgado Chalá (39/17), Ángel Oswaldo Fernández Vernaza (58/10), Alfonso Andrés Obregón Cancino (28/0) [46.Wellington Eduardo Sánchez Luzuriaga (33/3)], Édison Vicente Méndez Méndez (12/1). Trainer: Hernán Darío Gómez (25).

307. 17.07.2001 **ECUADOR - VENEZUELA** **4-0(2-0)** 40th Copa América.Group Stage.

Estadio Metropolitano „Roberto Meléndez", Barranquilla (Colombia); Referee: Gilberto Hidalgo Zamora (Peru); Attendance: 21,818

ECU: Geovanny Oswaldo Ibarra (19/0), Iván Jacinto Hurtado Angulo (78/3), Ulises Hernán de la Cruz Bernardo (43/2), Juan Carlos Burbano de Lara Torres (13/0), Raúl Fernando Guerrón Méndez (13/0), Agustín Javier Delgado Chalá (40/19), Ángel Oswaldo Fernández Vernaza (59/11), Cléber Manuel Chalá Guerrón (55/6) [78.Alfonso Andrés Obregón Cancino (29/0)], Giovanny Patricio Espinoza Pavón (12/1), Édison Vicente Méndez Méndez (13/2), Wellington Eduardo Sánchez Luzuriaga (34/3) [76.Juan Francisco Aguinaga Garzón (4/0)]. Trainer: Hernán Darío Gómez (26).

Goals: Agustín Javier Delgado Chalá (19), Ángel Oswaldo Fernández Vernaza (29), Édison Vicente Méndez Méndez (60), Agustín Javier Delgado Chalá (63).

308. 15.08.2001 **ECUADOR – ARGENTINA** **0-2(0-2)** 17th FIFA WC. Qualifiers
Estadio Olimpico „Atahualpa", Quito; Referee: Stefano Braschi (Italy); Attendance: 38,156
ECU: Geovanny Oswaldo Ibarra (20/0), Jorge Daniel Guagua Tamayo (2/0) [53.Ángel Oswaldo Fernández Vernaza (60/11)], Iván Jacinto Hurtado Angulo (79/3), Ulises Hernán de la Cruz Bernardo (44/2), Raúl Fernando Guerrón Méndez (14/0), Jaime Iván Kaviedes Llorenty (20/6), Agustín Javier Delgado Chalá (41/19), Juan Carlos Burbano de Lara Torres (14/0) [46.Juan Francisco Aguinaga Garzón (5/0)], Cléber Manuel Chalá Guerrón (56/6) [*sent off 34*], Giovanny Patricio Espinoza Pavón (13/1), Wellington Eduardo Sánchez Luzuriaga (35/3) [46.Alex Darío Aguinaga Garzón (88/19)]. Trainer: Hernán Darío Gómez (27).

309. 05.09.2001 **COLOMBIA – ECUADOR** **0-0** 17th FIFA WC. Qualifiers
Estadio "Nemesio Camacho" 'El Campín', Bogotá; Referee: Youssuf Al Aqily (Saudi Arabia); Attendance: 28,487
ECU: José Francisco Cevallos Villavicencio (52/0), Iván Jacinto Hurtado Angulo (80/3), Ulises Hernán de la Cruz Bernardo (45/2), Alfonso Andrés Obregón Cancino (30/0), Raúl Fernando Guerrón Méndez (15/0), Luis Oswaldo Gómez Cáceres (1/0) [65.Juan Francisco Aguinaga Garzón (6/0)], Jaime Iván Kaviedes Llorenty (21/6) [55.Ángel Oswaldo Fernández Vernaza (61/11)], Agustín Javier Delgado Chalá (42/19), Giovanny Patricio Espinoza Pavón (14/1), Édison Vicente Méndez Méndez (14/2), Edwin Rolando Tenorio Montaño (25/0). Trainer: Hernán Darío Gómez (28).

310. 06.10.2001 **BOLIVIA – ECUADOR** **1-5(0-2)** 17th FIFA WC. Qualifiers
Estadio „Hernándo Siles Zuazo", La Paz; Referee: Ángel Oswaldo Sánchez (Argentina); Attendance: 8,000
ECU: José Francisco Cevallos Villavicencio (53/0), Ulises Hernán de la Cruz Bernardo (46/3), Iván Jacinto Hurtado Angulo (81/3), Giovanny Patricio Espinoza Pavón (15/1), Raúl Fernando Guerrón Méndez (16/0), Alfonso Andrés Obregón Cancino (31/0) [89.Luis Oswaldo Gómez Cáceres (2/1)], Edwin Rolando Tenorio Montaño (26/0) [89.Juan Carlos Burbano de Lara Torres (15/0)], Édison Vicente Méndez Méndez (15/2), Cléber Manuel Chalá Guerrón (57/6), Jaime Iván Kaviedes Llorenty (22/7) [77.Ángel Oswaldo Fernández Vernaza (62/12)], Agustín Javier Delgado Chalá (43/20). Trainer: Hernán Darío Gómez (29).
Goals: Ulises Hernán de la Cruz Bernardo (13), Agustín Javier Delgado Chalá (23), Jaime Iván Kaviedes Llorenty (56), Ángel Oswaldo Fernández Vernaza (89), Luis Oswaldo Gómez Cáceres (90).

311. 07.11.2001 **ECUADOR – URUGUAY** **1-1(0-1)** 17th FIFA WC. Qualifiers
Estadio Olimpico „Atahualpa", Quito; Referee: Felipe Ramos Rizzo (Mexico); Attendance: 40,000
ECU: José Francisco Cevallos Villavicencio (54/0), Iván Jacinto Hurtado Angulo (82/3), Ulises Hernán de la Cruz Bernardo (47/3), Alfonso Andrés Obregón Cancino (32/0), Raúl Fernando Guerrón Méndez (17/0) [67.Ángel Oswaldo Fernández Vernaza (63/12)], Jaime Iván Kaviedes Llorenty (23/8) [78.Luis Oswaldo Gómez Cáceres (3/1)], Agustín Javier Delgado Chalá (44/20), Cléber Manuel Chalá Guerrón (58/6) [57.Alex Darío Aguinaga Garzón (89/19)], Giovanny Patricio Espinoza Pavón (16/1), Édison Vicente Méndez Méndez (16/2), Edwin Rolando Tenorio Montaño (27/0). Trainer: Hernán Darío Gómez (30).
Goal: Jaime Iván Kaviedes Llorenty (72).

312. 14.11.2001 **CHILE – ECUADOR** **0-0** 17th FIFA WC. Qualifiers
Estadio Nacional, Santiago; Referee: Juan Carlos Paniagua Arandia (Bolivia); Attendance: 19,237
ECU: José Francisco Cevallos Villavicencio (55/0), Iván Jacinto Hurtado Angulo (83/3), Ulises Hernán de la Cruz Bernardo (48/3), Alfonso Andrés Obregón Cancino (33/0), Luis Oswaldo Gómez Cáceres (4/1), Jaime Iván Kaviedes Llorenty (24/8) [70.Carlos Vicente Tenorio Medina (1/0)], Ángel Oswaldo Fernández Vernaza (64/12), Juan Carlos Burbano de Lara Torres (16/0), Marlon Ritter Ayoví Mosquera (24/0), Giovanny Patricio Espinoza Pavón (17/1), Édison Vicente Méndez Méndez (17/2). Trainer: Hernán Darío Gómez (31).

313. 12.01.2002 **ECUADOR – GUATEMALA** **1-0(0-0)**
Estadio Modelo, Guayaquil; Referee: Rogger Zambrano (Ecuador); Attendance: 45,000
ECU: José Francisco Cevallos Villavicencio (56/0), Orfilio Octavio Mercado Ortíz (1/0) [65.Marlon Ritter Ayoví Mosquera (25/0)], Augusto Jesús Poroso Caicedo (20/0), Iván Jacinto Hurtado Angulo (84/4), Luis Enrique Capurro Bautista (97/1) [59.Hugo Stalin Guerrón Méndez (1/0)], Carlos Ramón Hidalgo (1/0), Edwin Rolando Tenorio Montaño (28/0) [65.Luis Oswaldo Gómez Cáceres (5/1)], Moisés Antonio Candelario Díaz (6/0) [65.Édison Vicente Méndez Méndez (18/2)], Christian Rolando Lara Anangonó (1/0), Carlos Vicente Tenorio Medina (2/0), Nicolás Geovanny Asencio Espinoza (10/0) [88.Juan Carlos Burbano de Lara Torres (17/0)]. Trainer: Hernán Darío Gómez (32).
Goal: Iván Jacinto Hurtado Angulo (83).

314. 20.01.2002 **HAITI – ECUADOR** **2-0(2-0)** Gold Cup
Orange Bowl, Miami (United States); Referee: Carlos Alberto Batres González (Guatemala); Attendance: 12,253
ECU: José Francisco Cevallos Villavicencio (57/0), Giovanny Patricio Espinoza Pavón (18/1), Iván Jacinto Hurtado Angulo (85/4), Alfonso Andrés Obregón Cancino (34/0) [56.Nicolás Geovanny Asencio Espinoza (11/0)], Raúl Fernando Guerrón Méndez (18/0), Carlos Vicente Tenorio Medina (3/0), Alex Darío Aguinaga Garzón (90/19) (Cap) [56.Luis Oswaldo Gómez Cáceres (6/1)], Ángel Oswaldo Fernández Vernaza (65/12), Cléber Manuel Chalá Guerrón (59/6) [46.Christian Rolando Lara Anangonó (2/0)], Édison Vicente Méndez Méndez (19/2), Edwin Rolando Tenorio Montaño (29/0). Trainer: Hernán Darío Gómez (33).

315. 22.01.2002 **ECUADOR – CANADA** **2-0(0-0)** Gold Cup
Orange Bowl, Miami (United States); Referee: Brian Hall (United States); Attendance: 3,827
ECU: José Francisco Cevallos Villavicencio (58/0), Augusto Jesús Poroso Caicedo (21/0), Iván Jacinto Hurtado Angulo (86/4), Marlon Ritter Ayoví Mosquera (26/0), Alfonso Andrés Obregón Cancino (35/0), Luis Oswaldo Gómez Cáceres (7/1), Carlos Vicente Tenorio Medina (4/0) [76.Nicolás Geovanny Asencio Espinoza (12/0)], Alex Darío Aguinaga Garzón (Cap) (91/21), Cléber Manuel Chalá Guerrón (60/6), Édison Vicente Méndez Méndez (20/2), Edwin Rolando Tenorio Montaño (30/0) [69.Ángel Oswaldo Fernández Vernaza (66/12)]. Trainer: Hernán Darío Gómez (34).
Goals: Alex Darío Aguinaga Garzón (85 penalty, 90).

316. 12.02.2002 **ECUADOR – TURKEY** **1-0(0-0)**
Fuji Film Stadium, Breda (Holland); Referee: Jack van Hulten (Holland); Attendance: 6,000
ECU: José Francisco Cevallos Villavicencio (59/0), Augusto Jesús Poroso Caicedo (22/0), Iván Jacinto Hurtado Angulo (87/4), Ulises Hernán de la Cruz Bernardo (49/3), Alfonso Andrés Obregón Cancino (36/0), Raúl Fernando Guerrón Méndez (19/0), Jaime Iván Kaviedes Llorenty (25/8) [61.Carlos Vicente Tenorio Medina (5/1)], Alex Darío Aguinaga Garzón (92/21), Cléber Manuel Chalá Guerrón (61/6), Édison Vicente Méndez Méndez (21/2), Edwin Rolando Tenorio Montaño (31/0). Trainer: Hernán Darío Gómez (35).
Goal: Carlos Vicente Tenorio Medina (65).

317. 10.03.2002 **UNITED STATES – ECUADOR** **1-0(1-0)**
Legion Field, Birmingham (United States); Referee: Rodolfo Sibrián (El Salvador); Attendance: 24,133
ECU: José Francisco Cevallos Villavicencio (60/0), Édison Vicente Méndez Méndez (22/2), Augusto Jesús Poroso Caicedo (Cap) (23/0), Raúl Fernando Guerrón Méndez (20/0), Marlon Ritter Ayoví Mosquera (27/0), Giovanny Patricio Espinoza Pavón (19/1), Edwin Rolando Tenorio Montaño (32/0), Cléber Manuel Chalá Guerrón (62/6) [66.Luis Oswaldo Gómez Cáceres (8/1)], Alfonso Andrés Obregón Cancino (37/0), Nicolás Geovanny Asencio Espinoza (13/0), Carlos Vicente Tenorio Medina (6/1). Trainer: Hernán Darío Gómez (36).

318. 27.03.2002 **ECUADOR – BULGARIA** **3-0(1-0)**
Giants Stadium, East Rutherford, New York; Referee: Michael Kennedy (USA); Attendance: 45,511
ECU: José Francisco Cevallos Villavicencio (61/0), Iván Jacinto Hurtado Angulo (88/4), Ulises Hernán de la Cruz Bernardo (50/3), Raúl Fernando Guerrón Méndez (21/0), Augusto Jesús Poroso Caicedo (24/0), Édison Vicente Méndez Méndez (23/2), Alfonso Andrés Obregón Cancino (38/0), Cléber Manuel Chalá Guerrón (63/6), Edwin Rolando Tenorio Montaño (33/0) [77.Ángel Oswaldo Fernández Vernaza (67/12)], Jaime Iván Kaviedes Llorenty (26/10) [84.Evelio Agustín Ordóñez Martínez (7/0)], Carlos Vicente Tenorio Medina (7/2) [72.Alex Darío Aguinaga Garzón (93/21)]. Trainer: Hernán Darío Gómez (37).
Goals: Jaime Iván Kaviedes Llorenty (24), Carlos Vicente Tenorio Medina (49). Jaime Iván Kaviedes Llorenty (82).

319. 17.04.2002 **ECUADOR – SOUTH AFRICA** **0-0**
Estadio La Condomina, Murcia (Spain); Referee: Rodríguez Santiago (Spain); Attendance: 6,000
ECU: Geovanny Oswaldo Ibarra (21/0), Iván Jacinto Hurtado Angulo (89/4), Augusto Jesús Poroso Caicedo (25/0), Ulises Hernán de la Cruz Bernardo (51/3), Raúl Fernando Guerrón Méndez (22/0), Alfonso Andrés Obregón Cancino (39/0), Édison Vicente Méndez Méndez (24/2), Cléber Manuel Chalá Guerrón (64/6), Alex Darío Aguinaga Garzón (94/21) [46.Agustín Javier Delgado Chalá (45/20)], Juan Carlos Burbano de Lara Torres (18/0), Carlos Vicente Tenorio Medina (8/2). Trainer: Hernán Darío Gómez (38).

320. 08.05.2002 **ECUADOR – YUGOSLAVIA** **1-0(0-0)**
Giants Stadium, East Rutherford, New York; Referee: Rich Grady (United States); Attendance: 36,540
ECU: José Francisco Cevallos Villavicencio (62/0), Augusto Jesús Poroso Caicedo (26/0), Iván Jacinto Hurtado Angulo (90/4), Ulises Hernán de la Cruz Bernardo (52/3), Alfonso Andrés Obregón Cancino (40/0), Raúl Fernando Guerrón Méndez (23/0), Alex Darío Aguinaga Garzón (95/21), Agustín Javier Delgado Chalá (46/21), Cléber Manuel Chalá Guerrón (65/6) [46.Carlos Vicente Tenorio Medina (9/2) [*sent off 53*], Édison Vicente Méndez Méndez (25/2), Edwin Rolando Tenorio Montaño (34/0) [61.Ángel Oswaldo Fernández Vernaza (68/12)]. Trainer: Hernán Darío Gómez (39).
Goal: Agustín Javier Delgado Chalá (69).

321. 23.05.2002 **SENEGAL – ECUADOR** **1-0(0-0)**
Bird Park, Tottori (Japan); Referee: Kazuhiko Matsumura (Japan); Attendance: 8,533
ECU: José Francisco Cevallos Villavicencio (63/0), Luis Oswaldo Gómez Cáceres (9/1) [46.Ulises Hernán de la Cruz Bernardo (53/3)], Augusto Jesús Poroso Caicedo (27/0), Giovanny Patricio Espinoza Pavón (20/1) [46.Iván Jacinto Hurtado Angulo (91/4)], Raúl Fernando Guerrón Méndez (24/0), Cléber Manuel Chalá Guerrón (66/6), Alex Darío Aguinaga Garzón (96/21) [74.Ángel Oswaldo Fernández Vernaza (69/12)], Wellington Eduardo Sánchez Luzuriaga (36/3) [46.Édison Vicente Méndez Méndez (26/2)], Edwin Rolando Tenorio Montaño (35/0) [46.Alfonso Andrés Obregón Cancino (41/0)], Jaime Iván Kaviedes Llorenty (27/10) [74.Nicolás Geovanny Asencio Espinoza (14/0)], Carlos Vicente Tenorio Medina (10/2). Trainer: Hernán Darío Gómez (40).

322. 03.06.2002 **ITALY – ECUADOR** **2-0(2-0)** 17th FIFA WC. Group Stage.
Sapporo Dome, Sapporo (Japan); Referee: Brian Hall (United States); Attendance: 31,081
ECU: José Francisco Cevallos Villavicencio (64/0), Augusto Jesús Poroso Caicedo (28/0), Iván Jacinto Hurtado Angulo (Cap) (92/4), Ulises Hernán de la Cruz Bernardo (54/3), Alfonso Andrés Obregón Cancino (42/0), Raúl Fernando Guerrón Méndez (25/0), Alex Darío Aguinaga Garzón (97/21) [46.Carlos Vicente Tenorio Medina (11/2)], Agustín Javier Delgado Chalá (47/21), Cléber Manuel Chalá Guerrón (67/6) [85.Nicolás Geovanny Asencio Espinoza (15/0)], Édison Vicente Méndez Méndez (27/2), Edwin Rolando Tenorio Montaño (36/0) [59.Marlon Ritter Ayoví Mosquera (28/0)]. Trainer: Hernán Darío Gómez (41).

323. 09.06.2002 **MEXICO – ECUADOR** **2-1(1-1)** 17th FIFA WC. Group Stage.
Miyagi Stadium, Miyagi (Japan); Referee: Mourad Daami (Tunisia); Attendance: 45,610
ECU: José Francisco Cevallos Villavicencio (65/0), Augusto Jesús Poroso Caicedo (29/0), Iván Jacinto Hurtado Angulo (Cap) (93/4), Ulises Hernán de la Cruz Bernardo (55/3), Alfonso Andrés Obregón Cancino (43/0) [58.Alex Darío Aguinaga Garzón (98/21)], Raúl Fernando Guerrón Méndez (26/0), Jaime Iván Kaviedes Llorenty (28/10) [53.Carlos Vicente Tenorio Medina (12/2)], Agustín Javier Delgado Chalá (48/22), Cléber Manuel Chalá Guerrón (68/6), Édison Vicente Méndez Méndez (28/2), Edwin Rolando Tenorio Montaño (37/0) [35.Marlon Ritter Ayoví Mosquera (29/0)]. Trainer: Hernán Darío Gómez (42).
Goals: Agustín Javier Delgado Chalá (5).

324. 13.06.2002 **ECUADOR – CROATIA** **1-0(0-0)** 17th FIFA WC. Group Stage.
Yokohama International Stadium, Yokohama; Referee: Wílliam Mattus Vega (Costa Rica); Attendance: 65,862
ECU: José Francisco Cevallos Villavicencio (66/0), Augusto Jesús Poroso Caicedo (30/0), Iván Jacinto Hurtado Angulo (Cap) (94/4), Ulises Hernán de la Cruz Bernardo (56/3), Alfonso Andrés Obregón Cancino (44/0) [40.Alex Darío Aguinaga Garzón (99/21)], Raúl Fernando Guerrón Méndez (27/0), Agustín Javier Delgado Chalá (49/22), Marlon Ritter Ayoví Mosquera (30/0), Cléber Manuel Chalá Guerrón (69/6), Carlos Vicente Tenorio Medina (13/2) [76.Jaime Iván Kaviedes Llorenty (29/10)], Édison Vicente Méndez Méndez (29/3). Trainer: Hernán Darío Gómez (43).
Goal: Édison Vicente Méndez Méndez (48).

325. 16.10.2002 **COSTA RICA – ECUADOR** **1-1(0-0)**
Estadio „Ricardo Saprissa“, San José; Referee: Rodrigo Sequeira Badilla (Costa Rica); Attendance: 8,000
ECU: Geovanny Oswaldo Ibarra (22/0), Luis Oswaldo Gómez Cáceres (10/1), Iván Jacinto Hurtado Angulo (95/4), Augusto Jesús Poroso Caicedo (31/0), Marlon Ritter Ayoví Mosquera (31/0) [80.Luis Enrique Capurro Bautista (98/1)], Alfonso Andrés Obregón Cancino (45/0), Édison Vicente Méndez Méndez (30/3), Wellington Eduardo Sánchez Luzuriaga (37/3) [72.Franklin Agustín Salas Narváez (2/0)], Carlos Vicente Tenorio Medina (14/3), Nicolás Geovanny Asencio Espinoza (16/0) [67.Walter Orlando Ayoví Corozo (3/0)], Edwin Rolando Tenorio Montaño (38/0) [61.Otelino George Tenorio Bastidas (1/0)]. Trainer: Hernán Darío Gómez (44).
Goal: Carlos Vicente Tenorio Medina (82).

326. 20.10.2002 **VENEZUELA – ECUADOR** **2-0(1-0)**
Estadio Olímpico „Ciudad Universitaria“, Caracas; Referee: Gustavo Brand (Venezuela); Attendance: 28,000
ECU: Geovanny Oswaldo Ibarra (23/0), Luis Oswaldo Gómez Cáceres (11/1) [56.Walter Orlando Ayoví Corozo (4/0)], Iván Jacinto Hurtado Angulo (96/4), Augusto Jesús Poroso Caicedo (32/0), Marlon Ritter Ayoví Mosquera (32/0) [81.Luis Enrique Capurro Bautista (99/1)], Edwin Rolando Tenorio Montaño (39/0), Alfonso Andrés Obregón Cancino (46/0), Wellington Eduardo Sánchez Luzuriaga (38/3) [59.Otelino George Tenorio Bastidas (2/0)], Édison Vicente Méndez Méndez (31/3) [81.Franklin Agustín Salas Narváez (3/0)], Carlos Vicente Tenorio Medina (15/3), Nicolás Geovanny Asencio Espinoza (17/0) [69.Johnny Alejandro Baldeón Parreño (1/0)]. Trainer: Hernán Darío Gómez (45).

327. 20.11.2002 **ECUADOR – COSTA RICA** **2-2(0-2)**
Estadio Olimpico „Atahualpa", Quito; Referee: Pedro Senatore Ramos (Ecuador); Attendance: 35,000
ECU: Geovanny Oswaldo Ibarra (24/0), Ulises Hernán de la Cruz Bernardo (57/3), Augusto Jesús Poroso Caicedo (33/0), Iván Jacinto Hurtado Angulo (97/4), Raúl Fernando Guerrón Méndez (28/0) [53.Carlos Vicente Tenorio Medina (16/3)], Cléber Manuel Chalá Guerrón (70/6), Marlon Ritter Ayoví Mosquera (33/0), Edwin Rolando Tenorio Montaño (40/0) [71.Wellington Eduardo Sánchez Luzuriaga (39/3)], Alex Darío Aguinaga Garzón (Cap) (**100**/22), Nicolás Geovanny Asencio Espinoza (18/0) [71.Walter Orlando Ayoví Corozo (5/0)], Jaime Iván Kaviedes Llorenty (30/11). Trainer: Hernán Darío Gómez (46).
Goals: Alex Darío Aguinaga Garzón (75 penalty), Jaime Iván Kaviedes Llorenty (85).

328. 09.02.2003 **ECUADOR – ESTONIA** **1-0(0-0)**
Estadio „Isidro Romero", Guayaquil; Referee: Pedro Senatore Ramos (Ecuador); Attendance: 12,000
ECU: José Francisco Cevallos Villavicencio (67/0), Marlon Ritter Ayoví Mosquera (34/0), Iván Jacinto Hurtado Angulo (98/5), Augusto Jesús Poroso Caicedo (34/0), Luis Enrique Capurro Bautista (**100**/1) [42.Fricson Vinicio George Tenorio (5/0)], Edwin Rolando Tenorio Montaño (41/0), Wellington Eduardo Sánchez Luzuriaga (40/3) [70.Édison Vicente Méndez Méndez (32/3)], Walter Orlando Ayoví Corozo (6/0) [70.Johnny Alejandro Baldeón Parreño (2/0)], José Eduardo Gavica Peñafiel (33/4) [72.Cléber Manuel Chalá Guerrón (71/6)], Otelino George Tenorio Bastidas (3/0) [89.Walter Richard Calderón Carcelén (1/0)], Nicolás Geovanny Asencio Espinoza (19/0) [46.Roberto Javier Mina Mercado (1/0)]. Trainer: Hernán Darío Gómez (47).
Goal: Iván Jacinto Hurtado Angulo (90 penalty).

329. 12.02.2003 **ECUADOR – ESTONIA** **2-1(1-0)**
Estadio Olimpico „Atahualpa", Quito; Referee: Luis Enrique Vasco (Ecuador); Attendance: 3,000
ECU: José Francisco Cevallos Villavicencio (68/0), Marlon Ritter Ayoví Mosquera (35/0), Iván Jacinto Hurtado Angulo (99/5), Giovanny Patricio Espinoza Pavón (21/1), Fricson Vinicio George Tenorio (6/0), Edwin Rolando Tenorio Montaño (42/0), Édison Vicente Méndez Méndez (33/3) [63.José Eduardo Gavica Peñafiel (34/4)], Alfonso Andrés Obregón Cancino (47/0), Cléber Manuel Chalá Guerrón (72/6) [82.Segundo Alejandro Castillo Nazareno (1/0)], Roberto Javier Mina Mercado (2/0) [22.Franklin Agustín Salas Narváez (4/0)], Johnny Alejandro Baldeón Parreño (3/2) [80.Walter Richard Calderón Carcelén (2/0)]. Trainer: Hernán Darío Gómez (48).
Goals: Johnny Alejandro Baldeón Parreño (24, 48).

330. 30.04.2003 **SPAIN – ECUADOR** **4-0(3-0)**
Estadio "Vicente Calderón", Madrid; Referee: Sergo Kvaratskhelia (Georgia); Attendance: 45,000
ECU: José Francisco Cevallos Villavicencio (69/0), Ulises Hernán de la Cruz Bernardo (58/3), Augusto Jesús Poroso Caicedo (35/0) [27.Giovanny Patricio Espinoza Pavón (22/1)], Iván Jacinto Hurtado Angulo (**100**/5), Fricson Vinicio George Tenorio (7/0), Edwin Rolando Tenorio Montaño (43/0) [27.Jaime Iván Kaviedes Llorenty (31/11), 75.Wellington Eduardo Sánchez Luzuriaga (41/3)], Cléber Manuel Chalá Guerrón (73/6) [81.Franklin Agustín Salas Narváez (5/0)], Édison Vicente Méndez Méndez (34/3), Marlon Ritter Ayoví Mosquera (36/0), Alex Darío Aguinaga Garzón (101/22) [75.Ángel Oswaldo Fernández Vernaza (70/12)], Carlos Vicente Tenorio Medina (17/3) [75.Nicolás Geovanny Asencio Espinoza (20/0)]. Trainer: Hernán Darío Gómez (49).

331. 08.06.2003 **COLOMBIA – ECUADOR** **0-0**
Estadio "Vicente Calderón", Madrid; Referee: Antonio Rubinos Pérez (Spain); Attendance: 6,000
ECU: Jacinto Alberto Espinoza Castillo (32/0), Ulises Hernán de la Cruz Bernardo (59/3), Iván Jacinto Hurtado Angulo (101/5), Giovanny Patricio Espinoza Pavón (23/1) [*sent off 70*], Fricson Vinicio George Tenorio (8/0), Marlon Ritter Ayoví Mosquera (37/0), Alfonso Andrés Obregón Cancino (48/0), Édison Vicente Méndez Méndez (35/3), Cléber Manuel Chalá Guerrón (74/6), Johnny Alejandro Baldeón Parreño (4/2) [46.Carlos Vicente Tenorio Medina (18/3)], Otelino George Tenorio Bastidas (4/0) [71.Augusto Jesús Poroso Caicedo (36/0)]. Trainer: Hernán Darío Gómez (50).

332. 11.06.2003 **ECUADOR – PERU** **2-2(1-1)**
Giants Stadium, East Rutherford, New York (United States); Referee: Kevin Terry (USA); Attendance: 35,000
ECU: Jacinto Alberto Espinoza Castillo (33/0), Ulises Hernán de la Cruz Bernardo (60/3), Iván Jacinto Hurtado Angulo (102/5), Giovanny Patricio Espinoza Pavón (24/1), Fricson Vinicio George Tenorio (9/0), Marlon Ritter Ayoví Mosquera (38/0), Alfonso Andrés Obregón Cancino (49/0), Édison Vicente Méndez Méndez (36/3) [75.Alex Darío Aguinaga Garzón (102/22)], Cléber Manuel Chalá Guerrón (75/6) [46.Luis Fernando Saritama Padilla (1/0)], Jaime Iván Kaviedes Llorenty (32/11) [77.Evelio Agustín Ordóñez Martínez (8/0)], Otelino George Tenorio Bastidas (5/2) [86.Carlos Vicente Tenorio Medina (19/3)]. Trainer: Hernán Darío Gómez (51).
Goals: Otelino George Tenorio Bastidas (27, 74).

333. 20.08.2003 **ECUADOR – GUATEMALA** **2-0(1-0)**
Estadio Bellavista, Ambato; Referee: Segundo Jackson Díaz (Ecuador); Attendance: 25,023
ECU: José Francisco Cevallos Villavicencio (70/0), Néicer Reasco Yano (5/0), Iván Jacinto Hurtado Angulo (103/5), Giovanny Patricio Espinoza Pavón (25/1), Kléber Gutemberg Corozo Mosquera (1/0) [46. Fricson Vinicio George Tenorio (10/0)], Luis Fernando Saritama Padilla (2/0) [46.Alfonso Andrés Obregón Cancino (50/0)], Édison Vicente Méndez Méndez (37/3), Santiago Damián Morales Montenegro (4/0) [46.Marlon Ritter Ayoví Mosquera (39/0)], Alex Darío Aguinaga Garzón (103/23) [62.Vicente Paúl Ambrosi Zambrano (1/0)], Johnny Alejandro Baldeón Parreño (5/3) [46.Ángel Oswaldo Fernández Vernaza (71/12)], Franklin Agustín Salas Narváez (6/0) [46.Evelio Agustín Ordóñez Martínez (9/0)]. Trainer: Hernán Darío Gómez (52).
Goals: Johnny Alejandro Baldeón Parreño (6), Alex Darío Aguinaga Garzón (50).

334. 06.09.2003 **ECUADOR – VENEZUELA** **2-0(1-0)** 18th FIFA WC. Qualifiers
Estadio Olimpico „Atahualpa", Quito; Referee: Rubén Selmán (Chile); Attendance: 14,997
ECU: José Francisco Cevallos Villavicencio (71/0), Ulises Hernán de la Cruz Bernardo (61/3), Iván Jacinto Hurtado Angulo (104/5), Giovanny Patricio Espinoza Pavón (26/2), Néicer Reasco Yano (6/0), Alex Darío Aguinaga Garzón (104/23) [43.Otelino George Tenorio Bastidas (6/2)], Alfonso Andrés Obregón Cancino (51/0), Édison Vicente Méndez Méndez (38/3), Marlon Ritter Ayoví Mosquera (40/0), Carlos Vicente Tenorio Medina (20/4), Cléber Manuel Chalá Guerrón (76/6). Trainer: Hernán Darío Gómez (53).
Goals: Giovanny Patricio Espinoza Pavón (6), Carlos Vicente Tenorio Medina (72).

335. 10.09.2003 **BRAZIL – ECUADOR** **1-0(1-0)** 18th FIFA WC. Qualifiers
Estádio "Vivaldo Lima", Manaus; Referee: Luis Solórzano Torres (Venezuela); Attendance: 36,601
ECU: José Francisco Cevallos Villavicencio (72/0), Ulises Hernán de la Cruz Bernardo (62/3), Iván Jacinto Hurtado Angulo (105/5), Giovanny Patricio Espinoza Pavón (27/2), Néicer Reasco Yano (7/0), Edwin Rolando Tenorio Montaño (44/0), Alfonso Andrés Obregón Cancino (52/0), Édison Vicente Méndez Méndez (39/3), Marlon Ritter Ayoví Mosquera (41/0), Carlos Vicente Tenorio Medina (21/4) [83.Otelino George Tenorio Bastidas (7/2)], Cléber Manuel Chalá Guerrón (77/6). Trainer: Hernán Darío Gómez (54).

336. 15.11.2003 **PARAGUAY - ECUADOR** **2-1(1-0)** 18th FIFA WC. Qualifiers
Estadio Defensores del Chaco, Asunción; Referee: Juan Carlos Paniagua Arandia (Bolivia); Attendance: 12,000
ECU: José Francisco Cevallos Villavicencio (73/0), Ulises Hernán de la Cruz Bernardo (63/3), Iván Jacinto Hurtado Angulo (106/5), Giovanny Patricio Espinoza Pavón (28/2), Kléber Gutemberg Corozo Mosquera (2/0), Luis Oswaldo Gómez Cáceres (12/1), Edwin Rolando Tenorio Montaño (45/0) [83.Ángel Oswaldo Fernández Vernaza (72/12)], Édison Vicente Méndez Méndez (40/4), Vicente Paúl Ambrosi Zambrano (2/0) [73.Franklin Agustín Salas Narváez (7/0)], Evelio Agustín Ordóñez Martínez (10/0), Cléber Manuel Chalá Guerrón (78/6). Trainer: Hernán Darío Gómez (55).
Goal: Édison Vicente Méndez Méndez (59).

337. 19.11.2003 **ECUADOR - PERU** **0-0** 18th FIFA WC. Qualifiers
Estadio Olimpico „Atahualpa", Quito; Referee: Epifanio González Chavéz (Paraguay); Attendance: 34,361
ECU: José Francisco Cevallos Villavicencio (74/0), Ulises Hernán de la Cruz Bernardo (64/3), Iván Jacinto Hurtado Angulo (107/5), Giovanny Patricio Espinoza Pavón (29/2), Néicer Reasco Yano (8/0), Marlon Ritter Ayoví Mosquera (42/0), Alfonso Andrés Obregón Cancino (53/0) [66.Ángel Oswaldo Fernández Vernaza (73/12)], Édison Vicente Méndez Méndez (41/4), Cléber Manuel Chalá Guerrón (79/6) [79.Alex Darío Aguinaga Garzón (105/23)], Carlos Vicente Tenorio Medina (22/4), Evelio Agustín Ordóñez Martínez (11/0) [46.Franklin Agustín Salas Narváez (8/0)]. Trainer: Hernán Darío Gómez (56).

338. 10.03.2004 **MEXICO - ECUADOR** **2-1(2-1)**
Estadio „Víctor Manuel Reina", Tuxtla Gutiérrez; Referee: Carlos Alberto Batres González (Guatemala)
ECU: Geovanny Oswaldo Ibarra (25/0), Kléber Gutemberg Corozo Mosquera (3/0), Iván Jacinto Hurtado Angulo (108/5), José Luis Perlaza Napa (1/0) [46.Ángel Oswaldo Fernández Vernaza (74/12)], Raúl Fernando Guerrón Méndez (29/0) [46.Mario David Quiroz Villón (1/0)], Édison Vicente Méndez Méndez (42/5), Marlon Ritter Ayoví Mosquera (43/0) [75.Evelio Agustín Ordóñez Martínez (12/0)], Jorge Daniel Guagua Tamayo (3/0) [63.Jairo Rolando Campos León (1/0)], Hidrobo Vilson Rosero Rodríguez (5/0) [61.Luis Fernando Saritama Padilla (3/0)], Cléber Manuel Chalá Guerrón (80/6), Agustín Javier Delgado Chalá (50/22). Trainer: Hernán Darío Gómez (57).
Goal: Édison Vicente Méndez Méndez (32 penalty).

339. 30.03.2004 **ARGENTINA - ECUADOR** **1-0(0-0)** 18th FIFA WC. Qualifiers
Estadio Monumental „Antonio Vespucio Liberti", Buenos Aires; Referee: Martín Vásquez (Uruguay); Attendance: 55,000
ECU: José Francisco Cevallos Villavicencio (75/0), Ulises Hernán de la Cruz Bernardo (65/3), Iván Jacinto Hurtado Angulo (109/5), Giovanny Patricio Espinoza Pavón (30/2), Néicer Reasco Yano (9/0), Édison Vicente Méndez Méndez (43/5), Edwin Rolando Tenorio Montaño (46/0) [68.Jaime Iván Kaviedes Llorenty (33/11)], Alfonso Andrés Obregón Cancino (54/0), Marlon Ritter Ayoví Mosquera (44/0), Carlos Vicente Tenorio Medina (23/4) [74.Franklin Agustín Salas Narváez (9/0)], Cléber Manuel Chalá Guerrón (81/6) [64.Agustín Javier Delgado Chalá (51/22)]. Trainer: Hernán Darío Gómez (58).

340. 28.04.2004 **ECUADOR - HONDURAS** **1-1(0-1)**
Lockhart Stadium, Fort Lauderdale (United States); Referee: Ali Saheli (United States); Attendance: 15,000
ECU: Jacinto Alberto Espinoza Castillo (34/0), Erick Rolando de Jesús Delgado (1/0), Jorge Daniel Guagua Tamayo (4/0), Giovanny Patricio Espinoza Pavón (31/2), Néicer Reasco Yano (10/0), Luis Antonio Valencia Mosquera (1/0) [Ángel Oswaldo Fernández Vernaza (75/12)], Alfonso Andrés Obregón Cancino (55/0) [Mario David Quiroz Villón (2/0)], Marlon Ritter Ayoví Mosquera (45/0) [Evelio Agustín Ordóñez Martínez (13/1)], Vicente Paúl Ambrosi Zambrano (3/0) [Cléber Manuel Chalá Guerrón (82/6)], Agustín Javier Delgado Chalá (52/22), Franklin Agustín Salas Narváez (10/0). Trainer: Hernán Darío Gómez (59).
Goal: Evelio Agustín Ordóñez Martínez (82).

341. 02.06.2004 **ECUADOR - COLOMBIA** **2-1(1-0)** 18th FIFA WC. Qualifiers
Estadio Olimpico „Atahualpa", Quito; Referee: Héctor Walter Baldassi (Argentina); Attendance: 31,784
ECU: Jacinto Alberto Espinoza Castillo (35/0), Ulises Hernán de la Cruz Bernardo (66/3), Iván Jacinto Hurtado Angulo (110/5), Giovanny Patricio Espinoza Pavón (32/2), Vicente Paúl Ambrosi Zambrano (4/0), Édison Vicente Méndez Méndez (44/5) [65.Alex Darío Aguinaga Garzón (106/23)], Edwin Rolando Tenorio Montaño (47/0), Marlon Ritter Ayoví Mosquera (46/0) [87.Mario Roberto Lastra Mina (1/0)], Cléber Manuel Chalá Guerrón (83/6), Agustín Javier Delgado Chalá (53/23), Gustavo Omar Figueroa Cáceres (3/0) [50.Franklin Agustín Salas Narváez (11/1)]. Trainer: Hernán Darío Gómez (60).
Goals: Agustín Javier Delgado Chalá (3), Franklin Agustín Salas Narváez (66).

342. 05.06.2004 **ECUADOR - BOLIVIA** **3-2(3-0)** 18th FIFA WC. Qualifiers
Estadio Olimpico „Atahualpa", Quito; Referee: Gustavo Brand (Venezuela); Attendance: 30,020
ECU: Jacinto Alberto Espinoza Castillo (36/0), Ulises Hernán de la Cruz Bernardo (67/4), Iván Jacinto Hurtado Angulo (111/5), Giovanny Patricio Espinoza Pavón (33/2), Néicer Reasco Yano (11/0), Cléber Manuel Chalá Guerrón (84/6) [66.Édison Vicente Méndez Méndez (45/5)], Edwin Rolando Tenorio Montaño (48/0), Alfonso Andrés Obregón Cancino (56/0) [70.Alex Darío Aguinaga Garzón (107/23)], Vicente Paúl Ambrosi Zambrano (5/0) [80.Marlon Ritter Ayoví Mosquera (47/0)], Agustín Javier Delgado Chalá (54/24), Franklin Agustín Salas Narváez (12/1). Trainer: Hernán Darío Gómez (61).
Goals: Hernán Soliz (27 own goal), Agustín Javier Delgado Chalá (32), Ulises Hernán de la Cruz Bernardo (39).

343. 07.07.2004 **ARGENTINA - ECUADOR** **6-1(1-0)** 41st Copa América. Group Stage
Estadio "Elías Aguirre", Chiclayo (Peru); Referee: Carlos Arencio Amarilla Demarqui (Paraguay); Attendance: 24,000
ECU: Geovanny Oswaldo Ibarra (26/0), Ulises Hernán de la Cruz Bernardo (68/4) [54.Édison Vicente Méndez Méndez (46/5)], Iván Jacinto Hurtado Angulo (112/5), Giovanny Patricio Espinoza Pavón (34/2), Néicer Reasco Yano (12/0), Edwin Rolando Tenorio Montaño (49/0) [31.Franklin Agustín Salas Narváez (13/1)], Alfonso Andrés Obregón Cancino (57/0), Marlon Ritter Ayoví Mosquera (48/0), Vicente Paúl Ambrosi Zambrano (6/0), Cléber Manuel Chalá Guerrón (85/6), Evelio Agustín Ordóñez Martínez (14/1) [46.Agustín Javier Delgado Chalá (55/25)]. Trainer: Hernán Darío Gómez (62).
Goal: Agustín Javier Delgado Chalá (62).

344. 10.07.2004 **URUGUAY - ECUADOR** **2-1(0-0)** 41st Copa América. Group Stage
Estadio "Elías Aguirre", Chiclayo (Peru); Referee: Gustavo Brand (Venezuela); Attendance: 25,000
ECU: Geovanny Oswaldo Ibarra (27/0), Ulises Hernán de la Cruz Bernardo (69/4), Iván Jacinto Hurtado Angulo (113/5), Giovanny Patricio Espinoza Pavón (35/2), Néicer Reasco Yano (13/0), Édison Vicente Méndez Méndez (47/5) [83.Evelio Agustín Ordóñez Martínez (15/1)], Alfonso Andrés Obregón Cancino (58/0), Edwin Rolando Tenorio Montaño (50/0) [64.Franklin Agustín Salas Narváez (14/2)], Cléber Manuel Chalá Guerrón (86/6), Alex Darío Aguinaga Garzón (108/23), Agustín Javier Delgado Chalá (56/25). Trainer: Hernán Darío Gómez (63).
Goal: Franklin Agustín Salas Narváez (73).

345. 13.07.2004 **MEXICO - ECUADOR** **2-1(2-0)** 41st Copa América. Group Stage
Estadio "Miguel Grau", Piura (Peru); Referee: Eduardo Abel Lecca Betancourt (Peru); Attendance: 21,000
ECU: Jacinto Alberto Espinoza Castillo (37/0) [46.Damián Enrique Lanza Moyano (1/0)], Ulises Hernán de la Cruz Bernardo (70/4), Iván Jacinto Hurtado Angulo (114/5), Giovanny Patricio Espinoza Pavón (36/2), Néicer Reasco Yano (14/0), Cléber Manuel Chalá Guerrón (87/6) [46.Franklin Agustín Salas Narváez (15/2)], Marlon Ritter Ayoví Mosquera (49/0), Leonardo Javier Soledispa Cortés (1/0), Luis Fernando Saritama Padilla (4/0), Alex Darío Aguinaga Garzón (109/23) [65.Gustavo Omar Figueroa Cáceres (4/0)], Agustín Javier Delgado Chalá (57/26). Trainer: Hernán Darío Gómez (64).
Goal: Agustín Javier Delgado Chalá (71).

346. 05.09.2004 **URUGUAY – ECUADOR** **1-0(0-0)** 18th FIFA WC. Qualifiers
Estadio Centenario, Montevideo; Referee: Gilberto Hidalgo Zamora (Peru); Attendance: 28,000
ECU: Edwin Alberto Villafuerte Posliuga (1/0), Ulises Hernán de la Cruz Bernardo (71/4), Iván Jacinto Hurtado Angulo (115/5), Giovanny Patricio Espinoza Pavón (37/2), Néicer Reasco Yano (15/0), Édison Vicente Méndez Méndez (48/5), Leonardo Javier Soledispa Cortés (2/0) [71.Carlos Quiñónez (1/0)], Marlon Ritter Ayoví Mosquera (50/0), Walter Orlando Ayoví Corozo (7/0) [83.Luis Antonio Valencia Mosquera (2/0)], Carlos Vicente Tenorio Medina (24/4), Johnny Alejandro Baldeón Parreño (6/3) [60.Agustín Javier Delgado Chalá (58/26)]. Trainer: Luis Fernando Suárez (1).

347. 10.10.2004 **ECUADOR – CHILE** **2-0(0-0)** 18th FIFA WC. Qualifiers
Estadio Olimpico „Atahualpa“, Quito; Referee: René Ortubé Betancourt (Bolivia); Attendance: 27,956
ECU: Edwin Alberto Villafuerte Posliuga (2/0), Ulises Hernán de la Cruz Bernardo (72/4), Iván Jacinto Hurtado Angulo (116/5), Giovanny Patricio Espinoza Pavón (38/2), Raúl Fernando Guerrón Méndez (30/0), Édison Vicente Méndez Méndez (49/6), Edwin Rolando Tenorio Montaño (51/0), Marlon Ritter Ayoví Mosquera (51/0), Walter Orlando Ayoví Corozo (8/0) [46.Franklin Agustín Salas Narváez (16/2)], Jaime Iván Kaviedes Llorenty (34/12) [88.Ángel Oswaldo Fernández Vernaza (76/12)], Evelio Agustín Ordóñez Martínez (16/1) [61.Vicente Paúl Ambrosi Zambrano (7/0)]. Trainer: Luis Fernando Suárez (2).
Goals: Jaime Iván Kaviedes Llorenty (49), Édison Vicente Méndez Méndez (64).

348. 14.10.2004 **VENEZUELA – ECUADOR** **3-1(1-1)** 18th FIFA WC. Qualifiers
Estadio Pueblo Nuevo, San Cristóbal; Referee: Eduardo Lecca (Peru); Attendance: 13,800
ECU: Edwin Alberto Villafuerte Posliuga (3/0), Néicer Reasco Yano (16/0), Iván Jacinto Hurtado Angulo (117/5), Giovanny Patricio Espinoza Pavón (39/2), Raúl Fernando Guerrón Méndez (31/0), Édison Vicente Méndez Méndez (50/6), Edwin Rolando Tenorio Montaño (52/0), Marlon Ritter Ayoví Mosquera (52/1), Vicente Paúl Ambrosi Zambrano (8/0) [75.Evelio Agustín Ordóñez Martínez (17/1)], Jaime Iván Kaviedes Llorenty (35/12), Franklin Agustín Salas Narváez (17/2) [71.Johnny Alejandro Baldeón Parreño (7/3)]. Trainer: Luis Fernando Suárez (3).
Goal: Marlon Ritter Ayoví Mosquera (42 penalty).

349. 20.10.2004 **JORDAN – ECUADOR** **3-0(1-0)** LG Cup
Stade 11 June, Tripoli (Libya); Referee: Jamel Ambaya (Libya)
ECU: José Francisco Cevallos Villavicencio (76/0), Erick Rolando de Jesús Delgado (2/0), Augusto Jesús Poroso Caicedo (37/0), Geovanny Banner Caicedo Quiñonez (1/0), Raúl Fernando Guerrón Méndez (32/0), Mario David Quiroz Villón (3/0) [Juan Ignacio Triviño Burgos (1/0)], Marlon Ritter Ayoví Mosquera (53/1), Moisés Antonio Candelario Díaz (7/0) [Juan Pablo Romero (1/0)], Wellington Eduardo Sánchez Luzuriaga (42/3), Mario Roberto Lastra Mina (2/0), Roberto Javier Mina Mercado (3/0). Trainer: Luis Fernando Suárez (4).

350. 22.10.2004 **ECUADOR – NIGERIA** **2-2; 4-3 on penalties** LG Cup
Stade 11 Juin, Tripoli (Libya); Referee: Jamal Ambaya (Libya)
ECU: Damián Enrique Lanza Moyano (2/0), Erick Rolando de Jesús Delgado (3/0), Augusto Jesús Poroso Caicedo (38/1), Geovanny Banner Caicedo Quiñonez (2/0), Raúl Fernando Guerrón Méndez (33/0), Juan Ignacio Triviño Burgos (2/0), Juan Pablo Romero (2/0), Wellington Eduardo Sánchez Luzuriaga (43/3), Marlon Ritter Ayoví Mosquera (54/2), Moisés Antonio Candelario Díaz (8/0), Roberto Javier Mina Mercado (4/0). Trainer: Luis Fernando Suárez (5).
Goals: Marlon Ritter Ayoví Mosquera (penalty), Augusto Jesús Poroso Caicedo (65).
Penalties: Marlon Ritter Ayoví Mosquera, Moisés Antonio Candelario Díaz, Raúl Fernando Guerrón Méndez, Geovanny Caicedo, Augusto Jesús Poroso Caicedo (miss).

351. 27.10.2004 **MEXICO – ECUADOR** **2-1(1-0)**
Giants Stadium, East Rutherford, New York (United States); Referee: Arkadiusz Prus (United States)
ECU: Damián Enrique Lanza Moyano (3/0), Néicer Reasco Yano (17/0), Renán Calle Camacho (4/1), Giovanny Patricio Espinoza Pavón (40/2), Raúl Fernando Guerrón Méndez (34/0) [46.Mario Roberto Lastra Mina (3/0)], Édison Vicente Méndez Méndez (51/6), Edwin Rolando Tenorio Montaño (53/0) [63.Wellington Eduardo Sánchez Luzuriaga (44/3)], Marlon Ritter Ayoví Mosquera (55/2), Walter Orlando Ayoví Corozo (9/0) [82.Moisés Antonio Candelario Díaz (9/0)], Roberto Javier Mina Mercado (5/0) [46.Evelio Agustín Ordóñez Martínez (18/1)], Franklin Agustín Salas Narváez (18/2). Trainer: Luis Fernando Suárez (6).
Goal: Renán Calle Camacho (80).

352. 17.11.2004 **ECUADOR – BRAZIL** **1-0(0-0)** 18th FIFA WC. Qualifiers
Estadio Olimpico „Atahualpa“, Quito; Referee: Oscar Julián Ruíz (Colombia); Attendance: 38,308
ECU: Edwin Alberto Villafuerte Posliuga (4/0), Ulises Hernán de la Cruz Bernardo (73/4), Iván Jacinto Hurtado Angulo (118/5), Giovanny Patricio Espinoza Pavón (41/2), Vicente Paúl Ambrosi Zambrano (9/0), Édison Vicente Méndez Méndez (52/7), Edwin Rolando Tenorio Montaño (54/0), Marlon Ritter Ayoví Mosquera (56/2), Patricio Javier Urrutia Espinoza (1/0) [46.Franklin Agustín Salas Narváez (19/2)], Agustín Javier Delgado Chalá (59/26) [90.Néicer Reasco Yano (18/0)], Jaime Iván Kaviedes Llorenty (36/12) [75.Walter Orlando Ayoví Corozo (10/0)]. Trainer: Luis Fernando Suárez (7).
Goal: Édison Vicente Méndez Méndez (77).

353. 26.01.2005 **ECUADOR – PANAMA** **2-0(0-0)**
Estadio Bellavista, Ambato; Referee: Luis Enrique Vasco (Ecuador)
ECU: Edwin Alberto Villafuerte Posliuga (5/0), Erick Rolando de Jesús Delgado (4/0), Iván Jacinto Hurtado Angulo (Cap) (119/5) [60.Jorge Daniel Guagua Tamayo (5/0)], Renán Calle Camacho (5/1) [60.Juan Ignacio Triviño Burgos (3/0)], Óscar Dalmiro Bagüí Angulo (1/0) [61.Leonardo Javier Soledispa Cortés (3/0)], Marlon Ritter Ayoví Mosquera (57/2) [51.Luis Andrés Caicedo de la Cruz (1/0)], Edwin Rolando Tenorio Montaño (55/0) [46.Fricson Vinicio George Tenorio (11/0)], Luis Fernando Saritama Padilla (5/0) [46.Luis Antonio Valencia Mosquera (3/0)], Christian Rolando Lara Anangonó (3/0), Jaime Iván Kaviedes Llorenty (37/12) [46.Otelino George Tenorio Bastidas (8/4)], Walter Richard Calderón Carcelén (3/0) [54.Roberto Javier Mina Mercado (6/0)]. Trainer: Luis Fernando Suárez (8).
Goals: Otelino George Tenorio Bastidas (86, 90).

354. 29.01.2005 **ECUADOR – PANAMA** **2-0(2-0)**
Estadio “Rafael Vera Yepez”, Babahoyo; Referee: Pedro Senarore Ramos (Ecuador)
ECU: Damián Enrique Lanza Moyano (4/0), Erick Rolando de Jesús Delgado (5/0) [Juan Ignacio Triviño Burgos (4/0)], Iván Jacinto Hurtado Angulo (Cap) (120/5), Jorge Daniel Guagua Tamayo (6/0) [Renán Calle Camacho (6/1)], Fricson Vinicio George Tenorio (12/0), Edwin Rolando Tenorio Montaño (56/0), Marlon Ritter Ayoví Mosquera (58/2) [Luis Andrés Caicedo de la Cruz (2/0)], Luis Antonio Valencia Mosquera (4/0) [Luis Fernando Saritama Padilla (6/0)], Jaime Iván Kaviedes Llorenty (38/12) [Óscar Dalmiro Bagüí Angulo (2/0)], Otelino George Tenorio Bastidas (9/6), Roberto Javier Mina Mercado (7/0) [Christian Rolando Lara Anangonó (4/0)]. Trainer: Luis Fernando Suárez (9).
Goals: Otelino George Tenorio Bastidas (45, 53).

355. 09.02.2005 **CHILE – ECUADOR** **3-0(2-0)**
Estadio Sausalito, Viña del Mar; Referee: Gabriel Favale (Argentina); Attendance: 17,171
ECU: José Francisco Cevallos Villavicencio (Cap) (77/0), Erick Rolando de Jesús Delgado (6/0), Jorge Daniel Guagua Tamayo (7/0), Renán Calle Camacho (7/1), Fricson Vinicio George Tenorio (13/0), Edwin Rolando Tenorio Montaño (57/0) [75.Juan Ignacio Triviño Burgos (5/0)], Marlon Ritter Ayoví Mosquera (59/2) [65.Luis Fernando Saritama Padilla (7/0)], Christian Rolando Lara Anangonó (5/0) [46.Luis Andrés Caicedo de la Cruz (3/0)], Walter Orlando Ayoví Corozo (11/0) [65.Óscar Dalmiro Bagüí Angulo (3/0)], Jaime Iván Kaviedes Llorenty (39/12) [46.Walter Richard Calderón Carcelén (4/0)], Otelino George Tenorio Bastidas (10/6). Trainer: Luis Fernando Suárez (10).

356. 16.02.2005 **COSTA RICA – ECUADOR** **1-2(0-0)**
Estadio "Eladio Rosabal Cordero", Heredia; Referee: Edgar Duran (Costa Rica)
ECU: Edwin Alberto Villafuerte Posliuga (6/0), Néicer Reasco Yano (19/0), Jorge Daniel Guagua Tamayo (8/1), Giovanny Patricio Espinoza Pavón (42/2), Vicente Paúl Ambrosi Zambrano (10/0), Edwin Rolando Tenorio Montaño (58/0) [55.Wilfrido Antonio Vinces Mendoza (1/0)], Marlon Ritter Ayoví Mosquera (Cap) (60/3) [81.Luis Fernando Saritama Padilla (8/0)], Luis Antonio Valencia Mosquera (5/0), Édison Vicente Méndez Méndez (53/7), Walter Orlando Ayoví Corozo (12/0), Otelino George Tenorio Bastidas (11/6) [88.Christian Rolando Lara Anangonó (6/0)]. Trainer: Luis Fernando Suárez (11).
Goals: Marlon Ritter Ayoví Mosquera (61 penalty), Jorge Daniel Guagua Tamayo (87).

357. 27.03.2005 **ECUADOR – PARAGUAY** **5-2(2-2)** 18th FIFA WC. Qualifiers
Estadio Olimpico "Atahualpa", Quito; Referee: Gustavo Méndez González (Uruguay); Attendance: 32,449
ECU: Edwin Alberto Villafuerte Posliuga (7/0), Ulises Hernán de la Cruz Bernardo (74/4), Iván Jacinto Hurtado Angulo (Cap) (121/5), Giovanny Patricio Espinoza Pavón (43/2), Vicente Paúl Ambrosi Zambrano (11/0), Edwin Rolando Tenorio Montaño (59/0) [79.Luis Andrés Caicedo de la Cruz (4/0)], Marlon Ritter Ayoví Mosquera (61/4), Luis Antonio Valencia Mosquera (6/2), Édison Vicente Méndez Méndez (54/9), Otelino George Tenorio Bastidas (12/6) [56.Franklin Agustín Salas Narváez (20/2)], Agustín Javier Delgado Chalá (60/26) [79.Jaime Iván Kaviedes Llorenty (40/12)]. Trainer: Luis Fernando Suárez (12).
Goals: Luis Antonio Valencia Mosquera (32), Édison Vicente Méndez Méndez (45, 48), Luis Antonio Valencia Mosquera (50), Marlon Ritter Ayoví Mosquera (77 penalty).

358. 30.03.2005 **PERU – ECUADOR** **2-2(1-2)** 18th FIFA WC. Qualifiers
Estadio Nacional "José Díaz", Lima; Referee: Carlos Chandía Alarcón (Chile); Attendance: 40,000
ECU: Edwin Alberto Villafuerte Posliuga (8/0), Ulises Hernán de la Cruz Bernardo (75/5), Iván Jacinto Hurtado Angulo (Cap) (122/5), Giovanny Patricio Espinoza Pavón (44/2), Vicente Paúl Ambrosi Zambrano (12/0), Edwin Rolando Tenorio Montaño (60/0), Marlon Ritter Ayoví Mosquera (62/4) [71.Luis Andrés Caicedo de la Cruz (5/0)], Luis Antonio Valencia Mosquera (7/3), Édison Vicente Méndez Méndez (55/9) [86.Walter Orlando Ayoví Corozo (13/0)], Johnny Alejandro Baldeón Parreño (8/3) [46.Franklin Agustín Salas Narváez (21/2)], Agustín Javier Delgado Chalá (61/26). Trainer: Luis Fernando Suárez (13).
Goals: Ulises Hernán de la Cruz Bernardo (3), Luis Antonio Valencia Mosquera (45).

359. 04.05.2005 **ECUADOR – PARAGUAY** **1-0(0-0)**
Giants Stadium, East Rutherford, New York (United States); Referee: Terry Deughn (United States); Attendance: 20,000
ECU: Edwin Alberto Villafuerte Posliuga (9/0), Néicer Reasco Yano (20/0), Jorge Daniel Guagua Tamayo (9/1), Giovanny Patricio Espinoza Pavón (45/2), Vicente Paúl Ambrosi Zambrano (13/0) [84.José Luis Cortéz Arroyo (1/0)], Mario David Quiroz Villón (4/0), Marlon Ritter Ayoví Mosquera (Cap) (63/4), Luis Antonio Valencia Mosquera (8/3) [79.Walter Orlando Ayoví Corozo (14/0)], Édison Vicente Méndez Méndez (56/10), Johnny Alejandro Baldeón Parreño (9/3) [63.Wilfrido Antonio Vinces Mendoza (2/0)], Otelino George Tenorio Bastidas (13/6) [63.Felipe Salvador Caicedo Corozo (1/0)]. Trainer: Luis Fernando Suárez (14).
Goal: Édison Vicente Méndez Méndez (50).

360. 04.06.2005 **ECUADOR – ARGENTINA** **2-0(0-0)** 18th FIFA WC. Qualifiers
Estadio Olimpico „Atahualpa", Quito; Referee: Rubén Marcos Selman (Chile); Attendance: 37,583
ECU: Edwin Alberto Villafuerte Posliuga (10/0), Ulises Hernán de la Cruz Bernardo (76/5), Iván Jacinto Hurtado Angulo (Cap) (123/5), Giovanny Patricio Espinoza Pavón (46/2), Néicer Reasco Yano (21/0) [76.Mario David Quiroz Villón (5/0)], Edwin Rolando Tenorio Montaño (61/0), Marlon Ritter Ayoví Mosquera (64/4), Vicente Paúl Ambrosi Zambrano (14/0), Luis Antonio Valencia Mosquera (9/3) [84.Carlos Vicente Tenorio Medina (25/4)], Christian Adrián Gómez Ledesma (1/0) [46.Christian Rolando Lara Anangonó (7/1)], Agustín Javier Delgado Chalá (62/27). Trainer: Luis Fernando Suárez (15).
Goals: Christian Rolando Lara Anangonó (54), Agustín Javier Delgado Chalá (90).

361. 08.06.2005 **COLOMBIA – ECUADOR** **3-0(2-0)** 18th FIFA WC. Qualifiers
Estadio Metropolitano „Roberto Meléndez", Barranquilla; Referee: Carlos Eugênio Simón (Brazil); Attendance: 20,402
ECU: Edwin Alberto Villafuerte Posliuga (11/0), Ulises Hernán de la Cruz Bernardo (77/5), Iván Jacinto Hurtado Angulo (Cap) (124/5), Giovanny Patricio Espinoza Pavón (47/2), Vicente Paúl Ambrosi Zambrano (15/0) [60.Christian Rolando Lara Anangonó (8/1)], Mario David Quiroz Villón (6/0), Marlon Ritter Ayoví Mosquera (65/4) [46.Luis Andrés Caicedo de la Cruz (6/0)], Néicer Reasco Yano (22/0), Luis Antonio Valencia Mosquera (10/3) [54.Walter Orlando Ayoví Corozo (15/0)], Carlos Vicente Tenorio Medina (26/4), Agustín Javier Delgado Chalá (63/27). Trainer: Luis Fernando Suárez (16).

362. 11.06.2005 **ECUADOR – ITALY** **1-1(1-1)**
Giants Stadium, East Rutherford, New York (United States); Referee: Terry Vaughn (United States); Attendance: 27,583
ECU: Cristian Rafael Mora Medrano (1/0), Ulises Hernán de la Cruz Bernardo (78/5) [80.Mario David Quiroz Villón (7/0)], Iván Jacinto Hurtado Angulo (Cap) (125/5), Giovanny Patricio Espinoza Pavón (48/2) [80.Jorge Daniel Guagua Tamayo (10/1)], Néicer Reasco Yano (23/0), Marlon Ritter Ayoví Mosquera (66/5) [80.Vicente Paúl Ambrosi Zambrano (16/0)], Edwin Rolando Tenorio Montaño (62/0), Christian Rolando Lara Anangonó (9/1) [50.Christian Adrián Gómez Ledesma (2/0)], Walter Orlando Ayoví Corozo (16/0), Johnny Alejandro Baldeón Parreño (10/3) [46.Luis Antonio Valencia Mosquera (11/3)], Carlos Vicente Tenorio Medina (27/4) [46.Agustín Javier Delgado Chalá (64/27)]. Trainer: Luis Fernando Suárez (17).
Goal: Marlon Ritter Ayoví Mosquera (18 penalty).

363. 17.08.2005 **ECUADOR – VENEZUELA** **3-1(2-0)**
Estadio Federativo, Loja; Referee: Luis Enrique Vasco (Ecuador); Attendance: 10,000
ECU: Cristian Rafael Mora Medrano (2/0), Néicer Reasco Yano (24/0), Giovanny Patricio Espinoza Pavón (49/2) [63.Jairo Rolando Campos León (2/0)], Jorge Daniel Guagua Tamayo (11/1), Vicente Paúl Ambrosi Zambrano (17/0) [63.Ángel Gabriel Escobar Arce (1/0)], Patricio Javier Urrutia Espinoza (2/0) [59.Segundo Alejandro Castillo Nazareno (2/0)], Marlon Ritter Ayoví Mosquera (Cap) (67/5), Édison Vicente Méndez Méndez (57/10) [78.Armando Aquiles Paredes Duarte (1/0)], Christian Rolando Lara Anangonó (10/3) [69.Walter Orlando Ayoví Corozo (17/0)], Franklin Agustín Salas Narváez (22/2) [59.Christian Rogelio Benítez Betancourt (1/0)], Félix Alexander Borja Valencia (1/1) [73.Walter Richard Calderón Carcelén (5/0)]. Trainer: Luis Fernando Suárez (18).
Goals: Félix Alexander Borja Valencia (7), Christian Rolando Lara Anangonó (40, 67).

364. 03.09.2005 **BOLIVIA - ECUADOR** **1-2(1-1)** 18th FIFA WC. Qualifiers

Estadio „Hernándo Siles Zuazo", La Paz; Referee: Héctor Walter Baldassi (Argentina); Attendance: 11,000

ECU: Cristian Rafael Mora Medrano (3/0), Ulises Hernán de la Cruz Bernardo (79/5), Iván Jacinto Hurtado Angulo (Cap) (126/5), Giovanny Patricio Espinoza Pavón (50/2), Vicente Paúl Ambrosi Zambrano (18/0), Edwin Rolando Tenorio Montaño (63/0), Marlon Ritter Ayoví Mosquera (68/5) [89.Segundo Alejandro Castillo Nazareno (3/0)], Luis Antonio Valencia Mosquera (12/3) [45.Franklin Agustín Salas Narváez (23/2)], Néicer Reasco Yano (25/0) [77.Christian Rolando Lara Anangonó (11/3)], Édison Vicente Méndez Méndez (58/10), Agustín Javier Delgado Chalá (65/29). Trainer: Luis Fernando Suárez (19).

Goals: Agustín Javier Delgado Chalá (8, 49).

365. 08.10.2005 **ECUADOR - URUGUAY** **0-0** 18th FIFA WC. Qualifiers

Estadio Olimpico „Atahualpa", Quito; Referee: Marcio Rezende (Brazil); Attendance: 37,270

ECU: Cristian Rafael Mora Medrano (4/0), Ulises Hernán de la Cruz Bernardo (80/5), Iván Jacinto Hurtado Angulo (Cap) (127/5), Giovanny Patricio Espinoza Pavón (51/2), Vicente Paúl Ambrosi Zambrano (19/0), Edwin Rolando Tenorio Montaño (64/0), Marlon Ritter Ayoví Mosquera (69/5), Luis Antonio Valencia Mosquera (13/3) [56.Christian Rolando Lara Anangonó (12/3)], Édison Vicente Méndez Méndez (59/10), Agustín Javier Delgado Chalá (66/29), Félix Alexander Borja Valencia (2/1) [76.Roberto Javier Mina Mercado (8/0)]. Trainer: Luis Fernando Suárez (20).

366. 12.10.2005 **CHILE - ECUADOR** **0-0** 18th FIFA WC. Qualifiers

Estadio Nacional, Santiago; Referee: Horacio Marcelo Elizondo (Argentina); Attendance: 49,530

ECU: Edwin Alberto Villafuerte Posliuga (12/0), Néicer Reasco Yano (26/0), Giovanny Patricio Espinoza Pavón (Cap) (52/2), Jorge Daniel Guagua Tamayo (12/1), José Luis Cortéz Arroyo (2/0) [58.Ulises Hernán de la Cruz Bernardo (81/5)], Luis Andrés Caicedo de la Cruz (7/0), Edwin Rolando Tenorio Montaño (65/0), Segundo Alejandro Castillo Nazareno (4/0), Luis Fernando Saritama Padilla (9/0), Christian Rolando Lara Anangonó (13/3) [69.Vicente Paúl Ambrosi Zambrano (20/0)], Félix Alexander Borja Valencia (3/1) [81.Roberto Javier Mina Mercado (9/0)]. Trainer: Luis Fernando Suárez (21).

367. 13.11.2005 **POLAND - ECUADOR** **3-0(1-0)**

Estadio Ministadi, Barcelona (Spain); Referee: Xavier Moreno Delgado (Spain); Attendance: 9,000

ECU: Damián Enrique Lanza Moyano (5/0), Ulises Hernán de la Cruz Bernardo (82/5) [79.Luis Fernando Saritama Padilla (10/0)], Segundo Alejandro Castillo Nazareno (5/0), José Luis Cortéz Arroyo (3/0), Vicente Paúl Ambrosi Zambrano (21/0) [65.Fricson Vinicio George Tenorio (14/0)], Edwin Rolando Tenorio Montaño (66/0) [75.Luis Andrés Caicedo de la Cruz (8/0)], Marlon Ritter Ayoví Mosquera (Cap) (70/5), Édison Vicente Méndez Méndez (60/10) [73.Christian Rolando Lara Anangonó (14/3)], Luis Antonio Valencia Mosquera (14/3) [56.Néicer Reasco Yano (27/0)], Agustín Javier Delgado Chalá (67/29), Félix Alexander Borja Valencia (4/1) [56.Walter Richard Calderón Carcelén (6/0)]. Trainer: Luis Fernando Suárez (22).

368. 27.12.2005 **SENEGAL - ECUADOR** **2-1(1-1)** LG Cup

Cairo International Stadium, Cairo (Egypt)

ECU: Edwin Alberto Villafuerte Posliuga (13/0), Erick Rolando de Jesús Delgado (7/0), Jorge Daniel Guagua Tamayo (13/1), Carlos Ernesto Castro Cadena (1/0) [Renán Calle Camacho (8/1)], Fricson Vinicio George Tenorio (15/0) [Leonardo Javier Soledispa Cortés (4/0)], Segundo Alejandro Castillo Nazareno (6/0), Luis Andrés Caicedo de la Cruz (9/0) [Mario David Quiroz Villón (8/0)], Christian Rolando Lara Anangonó (15/3) [Christian Rogelio Benítez Betancourt (2/0)], Luis Fernando Saritama Padilla (11/0) [Roberto Javier Mina Mercado (10/0)], Jaime Iván Kaviedes Llorenty (41/12), Félix Alexander Borja Valencia (5/2) [Pablo David Palacios Herreria (1/0)]. Trainer: Luis Fernando Suárez (23).

Goal: Félix Alexander Borja Valencia (40).

369. 29.12.2005 **UGANDA - ECUADOR** **2-1(0-1)** LG Cup

Cairo International Stadium, Cairo

ECU: Edwin Alberto Villafuerte Posliuga (14/0), Erick Rolando de Jesús Delgado (8/0) [64.Renán Calle Camacho (9/1)], Jorge Daniel Guagua Tamayo (14/1), Carlos Ernesto Castro Cadena (2/0), Leonardo Javier Soledispa Cortés (5/0), Luis Andrés Caicedo de la Cruz (10/0), Segundo Alejandro Castillo Nazareno (7/0) [62.Mario David Quiroz Villón (9/0)], Luis Fernando Saritama Padilla (12/0) [54.Christian Rolando Lara Anangonó (16/3)], Christian Rogelio Benítez Betancourt (3/0) [54.Pablo David Palacios Herreria (2/0)], Jaime Iván Kaviedes Llorenty (42/13) [77.Roberto Javier Mina Mercado (11/0)], Félix Alexander Borja Valencia (6/2). Trainer: Luis Fernando Suárez (24).

Goal: Jaime Iván Kaviedes Llorenty (2).

370. 25.01.2006 **ECUADOR - HONDURAS** **1-0(0-0)**

Estadio Modelo, Guayaquil; Referee: Pedro Senatore Ramos (Ecuador); Attendance: 10,000

ECU: Cristian Rafael Mora Medrano (5/0), Néicer Reasco Yano (28/0), Giovanny Patricio Espinoza Pavón (53/2), Jorge Daniel Guagua Tamayo (15/1), Vicente Paúl Ambrosi Zambrano (22/0) [83.Luis Andrés Caicedo de la Cruz (11/0)], Marlon Ritter Ayoví Mosquera (Cap) (71/5), Segundo Alejandro Castillo Nazareno (8/0) [46.Luis Miguel Garcés Prado (1/0)], Luis Fernando Saritama Padilla (13/0) [57.Erick Rolando de Jesús Delgado (9/0)], Édison Vicente Méndez Méndez (61/10), Johnny Alejandro Baldeón Parreño (11/3) [72.Leonardo Javier Soledispa Cortés (6/0)], Roberto Javier Mina Mercado (12/0) [46.Darwin Deivis Caicedo Wila (1/1)]. Trainer: Luis Fernando Suárez (25).

Goal: Darwin Deivis Caicedo Wila (67).

371. 01.03.2006 **HOLLAND - ECUADOR** **1-0(0-0)**

ArenA, Amsterdam; Referee: Olegário Manuel Bartolo Faustino Benquerença (Portugal); Attendance: 32,000

ECU: Cristian Rafael Mora Medrano (6/0), Ulises Hernán de la Cruz Bernardo (83/5), Iván Jacinto Hurtado Angulo (Cap) (128/5) [73.Jorge Daniel Guagua Tamayo (16/1)], Giovanny Patricio Espinoza Pavón (54/2), Néicer Reasco Yano (29/0), Patricio Javier Urrutia Espinoza (3/0), Marlon Ritter Ayoví Mosquera (Cap) (72/5) [83.Walter Richard Calderón Carcelén (7/0)], Luis Antonio Valencia Mosquera (15/3) [68.Segundo Alejandro Castillo Nazareno (9/0)], Christian Rogelio Benítez Betancourt (4/0) [46.Christian Rolando Lara Anangonó (17/3)], Édison Vicente Méndez Méndez (62/10), Carlos Vicente Tenorio Medina (28/4) [68.Félix Alexander Borja Valencia (7/2)]. Trainer: Luis Fernando Suárez (26).

372. 30.03.2006 **JAPAN - ECUADOR** **1-0(0-0)**

Big Eye Stadium, Oita; Referee: Shamsul Maidin (Singapore); Attendance: 36,507

ECU: Cristian Rafael Mora Medrano (7/0), José Luis Cortéz Arroyo (4/0), Giovanny Patricio Espinoza Pavón (55/2), José Luis Perlaza Napa (2/0), Fricson Vinicio George Tenorio (16/0), Edwin Rolando Tenorio Montaño (67/0), Marlon Ritter Ayoví Mosquera (Cap) (73/5), Leonardo Javier Soledispa Cortés (7/0) [67.Luis Andrés Caicedo de la Cruz (12/0)], Patricio Javier Urrutia Espinoza (4/0) [85.Luis Fernando Saritama Padilla (14/0)], Johnny Alejandro Baldeón Parreño (12/3), Walter Richard Calderón Carcelén (8/0) [67.Gustavo Omar Figueroa Cáceres (5/0)]. Trainer: Luis Fernando Suárez (27).

373. 25.05.2006 **ECUADOR - COLOMBIA** **1-1(0-0)**
Giants Stadium, East Rutherford, New York; Referee: Terry Vaughn (United States); Attendance: 52,425
ECU: Cristian Rafael Mora Medrano (8/0), Jorge Daniel Guagua Tamayo (17/1), Iván Jacinto Hurtado Angulo (129/5), Vicente Paúl Ambrosi Zambrano (23/0), Néicer Reasco Yano (30/0), Edwin Rolando Tenorio Montaño (68/0) [78.Patricio Javier Urrutia Espinoza (5/0)], Segundo Alejandro Castillo Nazareno (10/1), Luis Antonio Valencia Mosquera (16/3) [81.Luis Fernando Saritama Padilla (15/0)], Édison Vicente Méndez Méndez (63/10) [70.Christian Rolando Lara Anangonó (18/3)], Félix Alexander Borja Valencia (8/2), Jaime Iván Kaviedes Llorenty (43/13) [63.Christian Rogelio Benítez Betancourt (5/0)]. Trainer: Luis Fernando Suárez (28).
Goal: Segundo Alejandro Castillo Nazareno (52).

374. 28.05.2006 **MACEDONIA - ECUADOR** **2-1(1-1)**
Estadio "Alfonso Pérez", Getafe (Spain); Referee: Carlos del Cerro Grande (Spain); Attendance: 4,000
ECU: Edwin Alberto Villafuerte Posliuga (15/0), Iván Jacinto Hurtado Angulo (130/5), Néicer Reasco Yano (31/0), Giovanny Patricio Espinoza Pavón (56/2) [61.José Luis Perlaza Napa (3/0)], Vicente Paúl Ambrosi Zambrano (24/0), Marlon Ritter Ayoví Mosquera (74/5) [46.Jaime Iván Kaviedes Llorenty (44/13)], Édison Vicente Méndez Méndez (64/10) [46.Jorge Daniel Guagua Tamayo (18/1)], Segundo Alejandro Castillo Nazareno (11/1), Luis Antonio Valencia Mosquera (17/3) [46.Patricio Javier Urrutia Espinoza (6/0)], Agustín Javier Delgado Chalá (68/29) [46.Christian Rolando Lara Anangonó (19/3)], Carlos Vicente Tenorio Medina (29/5) [65.Ulises Hernán de la Cruz Bernardo (84/5)] . Trainer: Luis Fernando Suárez (29).
Goal: Carlos Vicente Tenorio Medina (18).

375. 09.06.2006 **POLAND - ECUADOR** **0-2(0-1)** 18th FIFA WC. Group Stage
FIFA World Cup Stadion (Veltins-Arena), Gelsenkirchen (Germany); Referee: Toru Kamikawa (Japan); Attendance: 48,426
ECU: Cristian Rafael Mora (9/0), Ulises Hernán de la Cruz Bernardo (85/5), Iván Jacinto Hurtado Angulo (Cap) (131/5) [69.Jorge Daniel Guagua Tamayo (19/1)], Giovanny Patricio Espinoza Pavón (57/2), Néicer Reasco Yano (32/0), Édison Vicente Méndez Méndez (65/10), Segundo Alejandro Castillo Nazareno (12/1), Edwin Rolando Tenorio Montaño (69/0), Luis Antonio Valencia Mosquera (18/3), Agustín Javier Delgado Chalá (69/30) [83.Patricio Javier Urrutia Espinoza (7/0)], Carlos Vicente Tenorio Medina (30/6) [65.Jaime Iván Kaviedes Llorenty (45/13)].Trainer: Luis Fernando Suárez (30).
Goals: Carlos Vicente Tenorio Medina (24), Agustín Javier Delgado Chalá (80).

376. 14.06.2006 **ECUADOR – COSTA RICA** **3-0(1-0)** 18th FIFA WC. Group Stage
FIFA World Cup Stadion, Hamburg (Germany); Referee: Coffi Codjia (Benin); Attendance: 50,000
ECU: Cristian Rafael Mora (10/0), Ulises Hernán de la Cruz Bernardo (86/5), Iván Jacinto Hurtado Angulo (Cap) (132/5), Giovanny Patricio Espinoza Pavón (58/2) [68.Jorge Daniel Guagua Tamayo (20/1)], Néicer Reasco Yano (33/0), Édison Vicente Méndez Méndez (66/10), Edwin Rolando Tenorio Montaño (70/0), Segundo Alejandro Castillo Nazareno (13/1), Luis Antonio Valencia Mosquera (19/3) [69.Patricio Javier Urrutia Espinoza (8/0)], Agustín Javier Delgado Chalá (70/31), Carlos Vicente Tenorio Medina (31/7) [46.Jaime Iván Kaviedes Llorenty (46/14)]. Trainer: Luis Fernando Suárez (31).
Goals: Carlos Vicente Tenorio Medina (8), Agustín Javier Delgado Chalá (54), Jaime Iván Kaviedes Llorenty (90)

377. 20.06.2006 **GERMANY - ECUADOR** **3-0(2-0)** 18th FIFA WC. Group Stage
Olympiastadion, Berlin; Referee: Valentin Ivanov (Russia); Attendance: 72,000
ECU: Cristian Rafael Mora (11/0), Ulises Hernán de la Cruz Bernardo (87/5), Jorge Daniel Guagua Tamayo (21/1), Giovanny Patricio Espinoza Pavón (59/2), Vicente Paúl Ambrosi Zambrano (25/0), Édison Vicente Méndez Méndez (67/10), Edwin Rolando Tenorio Montaño (71/0), Marlon Ritter Ayoví Mosquera (Cap) (75/5) [68.Patricio Javier Urrutia Espinoza (9/0)], Luis Antonio Valencia Mosquera (20/3) [63.Christian Rolando Lara Anangonó (20/3)], Félix Alexander Borja Valencia (9/2) [46.Christian Rogelio Benítez Betancourt (6/0)], Jaime Iván Kaviedes Llorenty (47/14). Trainer: Luis Fernando Suárez (32).

378. 25.06.2006 **ENGLAND - ECUADOR** **1-0(0-0)** 18th FIFA WC. 2nd Round
Olympiastadion, Berlin (Germany); Referee: Frank De Bleeckere (Belgium); Attendance: 52,000
ECU: Cristian Rafael Mora (12/0), Ulises Hernán de la Cruz Bernardo (88/5), Iván Jacinto Hurtado Angulo (Cap) (133/5), Giovanny Patricio Espinoza Pavón (60/2), Néicer Reasco Yano (34/0), Édison Vicente Méndez Méndez (68/10), Edwin Rolando Tenorio Montaño (72/0) [69.Christian Rolando Lara Anangonó (21/3)], Segundo Alejandro Castillo Nazareno (14/1), Luis Antonio Valencia Mosquera (21/3), Agustín Javier Delgado Chalá (71/31), Carlos Vicente Tenorio Medina (32/7) [71.Jaime Iván Kaviedes Llorenty (48/14)]. Trainer: Luis Fernando Suárez (33).

379. 06.09.2006 **ECUADOR - PERU** **1-1(1-0)**
Giants Stadium, East Rutherford, New York (United States); Referee: Terry Vaughn (United States); Attendance: 20,556
ECU: Cristian Rafael Mora Medrano (13/0), Jairo Eliecer Montaño Quiñónez (1/0) [90.José Luis Perlaza Napa (4/0)], Jorge Daniel Guagua Tamayo (22/1), Giovanny Patricio Espinoza Pavón (61/2), Vicente Paúl Ambrosi Zambrano (26/0), Leonardo Javier Soledispa Cortés (8/0), Edwin Rolando Tenorio Montaño (73/0), Patricio Javier Urrutia Espinoza (10/0) [82.José Ramón Aguirre Icaza (1/0)], Jaime Iván Kaviedes Llorenty (49/14) [88.Jorge Washington Ladines Garcés (1/0)], Christian Rogelio Benítez Betancourt (7/1) [75.Franklin Agustín Salas Narváez (24/2)], Felipe Salvador Caicedo Corozo (2/0) [71.Armando Aquiles Paredes Duarte (2/0)]. Trainer: Luis Fernando Suárez (34).
Goal: Christian Rogelio Benítez Betancourt (14).

380. 10.10.2006 **BRAZIL - ECUADOR** **2-1(1-1)**
Råsundastadion, Stockholm (Sweden); Referee: Stefan Johannesson (Sweden); Attendance: 34,592
ECU: Cristian Rafael Mora Medrano (14/0), Ulises Hernán de la Cruz Bernardo (89/5), Iván Jacinto Hurtado Angulo (Cap) (134/5), Giovanny Patricio Espinoza Pavón (62/2), Vicente Paúl Ambrosi Zambrano (27/0), Luis Antonio Valencia Mosquera (22/3) [*sent off 79*], Segundo Alejandro Castillo Nazareno (15/1), Edwin Rolando Tenorio Montaño (74/0) [82.Jairo Eliecer Montaño Quiñónez (2/0)], Édison Vicente Méndez Méndez (69/10) [77.Patricio Javier Urrutia Espinoza (11/0)], Félix Alexander Borja Valencia (10/3) [63.Edmundo Salomón Zura De Jesús (1/0)], Felipe Salvador Caicedo Corozo (3/0) [46.Luis Fernando Saritama Padilla (16/0)]. Trainer: Luis Fernando Suárez (35).
Goal: Félix Alexander Borja Valencia (23).

381. 18.01.2007 **ECUADOR - SWEDEN** **2-1(2-0)**
Estadio "Alejandro Serrano Aguilar", Cuenca; Referee: Víctor Hugo Carrillo (Peru); Attendance: 20,000
ECU: Geovanny Francisco Camacho Paredes (1/0), Jairo Eliecer Montaño Quiñónez (3/0) [67.Omar Andrés de Jesús Borja (7/0)], Renán Calle Camacho (10/1), Fricson Vinicio George Tenorio (17/0), Óscar Dalmiro Bagüí Angulo (4/0) [67.Fernando Alexander Guerrero Vásquez (1/0)], Luis Andres Caicedo de la Cruz (13/0), Alex Leonardo Bolaños Reascos (1/0), Éder Javier Vaca Quinde (1/1) [46.Walter Orlando Ayoví Corozo (18/0)], Christian Rolando Lara Anangonó (22/3) [59.Mario David Quiroz Villón (10/0)], Edmundo Salomón Zura De Jesús (2/0) [46.Felipe Salvador Caicedo Corozo (4/0)], Carlos Vicente Tenorio Medina (33/8) [59.Danny Alejandro Vera Carpio (1/0)]. Trainer: Luis Fernando Suárez (36).
Goals: Éder Javier Vaca Quinde (16), Carlos Vicente Tenorio Medina (24).

382. 21.01.2007 **ECUADOR - SWEDEN** **1-1(0-0)**
Estadio Olimpico "Atahualpa", Quito; Referee: Manuel Garay (Peru); Attendance: 18,000
ECU: Daniel Jimmy Viteri Vinces (1/0), Iván Jacinto Hurtado Angulo (135/5), Marco Antonio Quinóñez Angulo (1/0) [46.Renán Calle Camacho (11/1)], Fricson Vinicio George Tenorio (18/0) [77.Óscar Dalmiro Bagüí Angulo (5/0)], Omar Andrés de Jesús Borja (8/0), Jorge Washington Ladines Garcés (2/0) [46.Luis Andres Caicedo de la Cruz (14/0)], Walter Orlando Ayoví Corozo (19/0), Mario David Quiroz Villón (11/0), Marlon Ritter Ayoví Mosquera (76/5) [67.Fernando Alexander Guerrero Vásquez (2/0)], Danny Alejandro Vera Carpio (2/0) [46.Felipe Salvador Caicedo Corozo (5/0)], Carlos Vicente Tenorio Medina (34/8) [80.Edmundo Salomón Zura De Jesús (3/1)]. Trainer: Luis Fernando Suárez (37).
Goal: Edmundo Salomón Zura De Jesús (82).

383. 25.03.2007 **UNITED STATES - ECUADOR** **3-1(1-1)**
"Raymond James" Stadium, Tampa; Referee: Silviu Petrescu (Canada); Attendance: 31,547
ECU: Rorys Andrés Aragón Espinoza (1/0), Iván Jacinto Hurtado Angulo (136/5) [78.Jorge Daniel Guagua Tamayo (23/1)], Ulises Hernán de la Cruz Bernardo (90/5), Giovanny Patricio Espinoza Pavón (63/2), Néicer Reasco Yano (35/0) [90+1.Óscar Dalmiro Bagüí Angulo (6/0)], Édison Vicente Méndez Méndez (70/10), Segundo Alejandro Castillo Nazareno (16/1), Luis Antonio Valencia Mosquera (23/3), Luis Andres Caicedo de la Cruz (15/0) [64.Luis Fernando Saritama Padilla (17/0)], Felipe Salvador Caicedo Corozo (6/1) [72.Edmundo Salomón Zura De Jesús (4/1)], Carlos Vicente Tenorio Medina (35/8) [78.Félix Alexander Borja Valencia (11/3)]. Trainer: Luis Fernando Suárez (38).
Goal: Felipe Salvador Caicedo Corozo (11).

384. 28.03.2007 **ECUADOR - MEXICO** **2-4(1-1)**
McAfee Coliseum, Oakland (United States); Referee: Baldomero Toledo (United States); Attendance: 47,416
ECU: Rorys Andrés Aragón Espinoza (2/0), Ulises Hernán de la Cruz Bernardo (91/5), Iván Jacinto Hurtado Angulo (137/5) [49.Jorge Daniel Guagua Tamayo (24/1)], Giovanny Patricio Espinoza Pavón (64/3), Néicer Reasco Yano (36/0), Luis Andres Caicedo de la Cruz (16/0), Édison Vicente Méndez Méndez (71/10), Segundo Alejandro Castillo Nazareno (17/1), Luis Antonio Valencia Mosquera (24/3) [88.Óscar Dalmiro Bagüí Angulo (7/0)], Carlos Vicente Tenorio Medina (36/9) [46.Félix Alexander Borja Valencia (12/3)], Felipe Salvador Caicedo Corozo (7/1) [59.Edmundo Salomón Zura De Jesús (5/1); 68.Luis Fernando Saritama Padilla (18/0)]. Trainer: Luis Fernando Suárez (39).
Goals: Carlos Vicente Tenorio Medina (43), Giovanny Patricio Espinoza Pavón (56).

385. 23.05.2007 **ECUADOR – REPUBLIC OF IRELAND** **1-1(1-1)**
Giants Stadium, East Rutherford, New York (United States); Referee: n/a; Attendance: 20,823
ECU: Marcelo Ramón Elizaga Ferrero (1/0), Jairo Eliecer Montaño Quiñónez (4/0), Carlos Ernesto Castro Cadena (3/0) [*sent off 90*], Jairo Rolando Campos León (3/0), Óscar Dalmiro Bagüí Angulo (8/0), Mario David Quiroz Villón (12/0) [65.Franklin Agustín Salas Narváez (25/2)], Luis Andres Caicedo de la Cruz (17/0), Patricio Javier Urrutia Espinoza (12/0), Walter Orlando Ayoví Corozo (20/0), Jaime Iván Kaviedes Llorenty (50/14) [81.Pablo David Palacios Herreria (3/0)], Christian Rogelio Benítez Betancourt (8/2). Trainer: Luis Fernando Suárez (40).
Goal: Christian Rogelio Benítez Betancourt (13).

386. 03.06.2007 **PERU - ECUADOR** **2-1(1-1)**
Estadio "Vicente Calderón", Madrid (Spain); Referee: Hugo López Huerta (Spain); Attendance: 25,000
ECU: Daniel Jimmy Viteri Vinces (2/0), Ulises Hernán de la Cruz Bernardo (92/5), Iván Jacinto Hurtado Angulo (138/5), Renán Calle Camacho (12/1), Néicer Reasco Yano (37/0) [82.Félix Alexander Borja Valencia (13/3)], Luis Alberto Bolaños León (1/0) [55.Óscar Dalmiro Bagüí Angulo (9/0)], Patricio Javier Urrutia Espinoza (13/0), Segundo Alejandro Castillo Nazareno (18/1), Walter Orlando Ayoví Corozo (21/0) [70.Felipe Salvador Caicedo Corozo (8/1)], Carlos Vicente Tenorio Medina (37/10), Christian Rogelio Benítez Betancourt (9/2). Trainer: Luis Fernando Suárez (41).
Goal: Carlos Vicente Tenorio Medina (10 penalty).

387. 06.06.2007 **ECUADOR - PERU** **2-0(0-0)**
Miniestadi, Barcelona (Spain); Referee: Felipe Crespo García (Spain); Attendance: 10,000
ECU: Javier Hernán Klimowicz Laganá (1/0), Ulises Hernán de la Cruz Bernardo (93/6), Iván Jacinto Hurtado Angulo (139/5), Jairo Rolando Campos León (4/0), Óscar Dalmiro Bagüí Angulo (10/0), Edwin Rolando Tenorio Montaño (75/0), Segundo Alejandro Castillo Nazareno (19/1) [74.Patricio Javier Urrutia Espinoza (14/0)], Vicente Paúl Ambrosi Zambrano (28/0) [68.Walter Orlando Ayoví Corozo (22/0)], Jaime Iván Kaviedes Llorenty (51/14) [46.Néicer Reasco Yano (38/0)], Felipe Salvador Caicedo Corozo (9/1) [58.Christian Rogelio Benítez Betancourt (10/3)], Félix Alexander Borja Valencia (14/3) [72.Carlos Vicente Tenorio Medina (38/10)]. Trainer: Luis Fernando Suárez (42).
Goals: Christian Rogelio Benítez Betancourt (83), Ulises Hernán de la Cruz Bernardo (90+3).

388. 23.06.2007 **COLOMBIA - ECUADOR** **3-1(2-1)**
Estadio Metropolitano „Roberto Meléndez", Barranquilla; Referee: Mayker Alain Gómez (Venezuela); Attendance: 40,000
ECU: Cristian Rafael Mora Medrano (15/0), Néicer Reasco Yano (39/0), Renán Calle Camacho (13/1) [46.Giovanny Patricio Espinoza Pavón (65/3)], Jorge Daniel Guagua Tamayo (25/1), Óscar Dalmiro Bagüí Angulo (11/0) [46.Ulises Hernán de la Cruz Bernardo (94/6)], Mario David Quiroz Villón (13/0) [46.Luis Antonio Valencia Mosquera (25/3)], Pedro Ángel Quiñónez Rodríguez (1/0) [46.Segundo Alejandro Castillo Nazareno (20/1)], Edwin Rolando Tenorio Montaño (76/0), Walter Orlando Ayoví Corozo (23/1) [46.Édison Vicente Méndez Méndez (72/10)], Félix Alexander Borja Valencia (15/3) [72.Pablo David Palacios Herreria (4/0)], Felipe Salvador Caicedo Corozo (10/1). Trainer: Luis Fernando Suárez (43).
Goal: Walter Orlando Ayoví Corozo (11).

389. 27.06.2007 **ECUADOR - CHILE** **2-3(2-1)** 42nd Copa América. Group Stage
Estadio Polideportivo Cachamay, Puerto Ordaz (Venezuela); Referee: Óscar Julián Ruiz Acosta (Colombia); Attendance: 25,000
ECU: Cristian Rafael Mora Medrano (16/0), Ulises Hernán de la Cruz Bernardo (95/6), Giovanny Patricio Espinoza Pavón (66/3), Iván Jacinto Hurtado Angulo (140/5), Óscar Dalmiro Bagüí Angulo (12/0), Segundo Alejandro Castillo Nazareno (21/1), Edwin Rolando Tenorio Montaño (77/0), Édison Vicente Méndez Méndez (73/10), Luis Antonio Valencia Mosquera (26/4), Carlos Vicente Tenorio Medina (39/10) [76.Felipe Salvador Caicedo Corozo (11/1)], Christian Rogelio Benítez Betancourt (11/4). Trainer: Luis Fernando Suárez (44).
Goals: Luis Antonio Valencia Mosquera (16), Christian Rogelio Benítez Betancourt (23).

390. 01.07.2007 **MEXICO - ECUADOR** **2-1(0-0)** 42nd Copa América. Group Stage
Estadio Monumental „Juana la Avanzadora", Maturín (Venezuela); Referee: René Ortubé Betancourt (Bolivia); Attendance: 42,000
ECU: Cristian Rafael Mora Medrano (17/0), Ulises Hernán de la Cruz Bernardo (96/6), Giovanny Patricio Espinoza Pavón (67/3), Iván Jacinto Hurtado Angulo (141/5), Óscar Dalmiro Bagüí Angulo (13/0) [72.Walter Orlando Ayoví Corozo (24/1)], Segundo Alejandro Castillo Nazareno (22/1), Edwin Rolando Tenorio Montaño (78/0) [46.Néicer Reasco Yano (40/0)], Édison Vicente Méndez Méndez (74/11), Luis Antonio Valencia Mosquera (27/4), Carlos Vicente Tenorio Medina (40/10) [79.Félix Alexander Borja Valencia (16/3)], Christian Rogelio Benítez Betancourt (12/4). Trainer: Luis Fernando Suárez (45).
Goal: Édison Vicente Méndez Méndez (85).

391. 04.07.2007 **BRAZIL - ECUADOR** **1-0(0-0)** 42nd Copa América. Group Stage
Estadio "General José Antonio Anzoátegui", Puerto La Cruz (Venezuela); Referee: Sergio Fabián Pezzotta (Argentina); Attendance: 34,000
ECU: Marcelo Ramón Elizaga Ferrero (2/0), Néicer Reasco Yano (41/0), Giovanny Patricio Espinoza Pavón (68/3), Jorge Daniel Guagua Tamayo (26/1), Óscar Dalmiro Bagüí Angulo (14/0), Segundo Alejandro Castillo Nazareno (23/1), Luis Antonio Valencia Mosquera (28/4), Walter Orlando Ayoví Corozo (25/1) [76.Felipe Salvador Caicedo Corozo (12/1)], Édison Vicente Méndez Méndez (75/11), Félix Alexander Borja Valencia (17/3) [60.Carlos Vicente Tenorio Medina (41/10)], Christian Rogelio Benítez Betancourt (13/4). Trainer: Luis Fernando Suárez (46).

392. 22.08.2007 **ECUADOR - BOLIVIA** **1-0(1-0)**
Estadio Olímpico „Atahualpa", Quito; Referee: Albert Duarte (Colombia); Attendance: 18,000
ECU: Marcelo Ramón Elizaga Ferrero (3/0), Jairo Eliecer Montaño Quiñónez (5/0), Giovanny Patricio Espinoza Pavón (69/3), Iván Jacinto Hurtado Angulo (142/5), José Ramón Aguirre Icaza (2/0), Patricio Javier Urrutia Espinoza (15/1) [78.Alex Leonardo Bolaños Reascos (2/0)], Jimmy Alfredo Bran Orozco (1/0), Édison Vicente Méndez Méndez (76/11) [83.Éder Javier Vaca Quinde (2/1)], Christian Rolando Lara Anangonó (23/3) [82.Fernando Roberto Hidalgo Maldonado (1/0)], Christian Rogelio Benítez Betancourt (14/4) [76.Joffre David Guerrón Méndez (1/0)], Felipe Salvador Caicedo Corozo (13/1) [46.Edmundo Salomón Zura De Jesús (6/1); 56.Luis Alberto Bolaños León (2/0) [*sent off 90+1*]]. Trainer: Luis Fernando Suárez (47).
Goal: Patricio Javier Urrutia Espinoza (35 penalty).

393. 08.09.2007 **ECUADOR – EL SALVADOR** **5-1(3-1)**
Estadio Olimpico "Atahualpa", Quito; Referee: Víctor Hugo Rivera (Peru); Attendance: 8,000
ECU: Javier Hernán Klimowicz Laganá (2/0), Jairo Rolando Campos León (5/0), Iván Jacinto Hurtado Angulo (143/5) [57.Giovanny Patricio Espinoza Pavón (70/3)], Jorge Daniel Guagua Tamayo (27/1), Vicente Paúl Ambrosi Zambrano (29/0), Segundo Alejandro Castillo Nazareno (24/1), Patricio Javier Urrutia Espinoza (16/2) [81.José Ramón Aguirre Icaza (3/0)], Édison Vicente Méndez Méndez (77/11) [57.Luis Alberto Bolaños León (3/0)], Christian Rolando Lara Anangonó (24/4) [67.Éder Javier Vaca Quinde (3/1)], Christian Rogelio Benítez Betancourt (15/6) [67.Jorge Washington Ladines Garcés (3/0)], Felipe Salvador Caicedo Corozo (14/2) [67.Joffre David Guerrón Méndez (2/0)]. Trainer: Luis Fernando Suárez (48).
Goals: Christian Rolando Lara Anangonó (14), Christian Rogelio Benítez Betancourt (30), Felipe Salvador Caicedo Corozo (45), Christian Rogelio Benítez Betancourt (49), Patricio Javier Urrutia Espinoza (54 penalty).

394. 12.09.2007 **HONDURAS - ECUADOR** **2-1(0-0)**
Estadio Olimpico Metropolitano, San Pedro Sula; Referee: Carlos Alberto Batrés González (Guatemala); Attendance: 25,000
ECU: Daniel Jimmy Viteri Vinces (3/0), Jairo Rolando Campos León (6/0), Giovanny Patricio Espinoza Pavón (71/3), Jorge Daniel Guagua Tamayo (28/2), Vicente Paúl Ambrosi Zambrano (30/0), Segundo Alejandro Castillo Nazareno (25/1), Patricio Javier Urrutia Espinoza (17/2) [85.Alex Leonardo Bolaños Reascos (3/0)], José Ramón Aguirre Icaza (4/0) [58.Luis Alberto Bolaños León (4/0)], Christian Rolando Lara Anangonó (25/4) [80.Jorge Washington Ladines Garcés (4/0)], Edmundo Salomón Zura De Jesús (7/1) [46.Felipe Salvador Caicedo Corozo (15/2)], Christian Rogelio Benítez Betancourt (16/6) [85.Joffre David Guerrón Méndez (3/0)]. Trainer: Luis Fernando Suárez (49).
Goal: Jorge Daniel Guagua Tamayo (87 penalty).

395. 13.10.2007 **ECUADOR - VENEZUELA** **0-1(0-0)** 19th FIFA WC. Qualifiers
Estadio Olimpico "Atahualpa", Quito; Referee: René Ortubé Betancourt (Bolivia); Attendance: 37,000
ECU: Daniel Jimmy Viteri Vinces (4/0), Ulises Hernán de la Cruz Bernardo (97/6), Iván Jacinto Hurtado Angulo (144/5), Giovanny Patricio Espinoza Pavón (72/3), Óscar Dalmiro Bagüí Angulo (15/0) [76.Mario David Quiroz Villón (14/0)], Luis Antonio Valencia Mosquera (29/4) [71.Félix Alexander Borja Valencia (18/3)], Segundo Alejandro Castillo Nazareno (26/1), Édison Vicente Méndez Méndez (78/11), Christian Rolando Lara Anangonó (26/4) [46.Walter Orlando Ayoví Corozo (26/1)], Christian Rogelio Benítez Betancourt (17/6), Carlos Vicente Tenorio Medina (42/10). Trainer: Luis Fernando Suárez (50).

396. 17.10.2007 **BRAZIL - ECUADOR** **5-0(1-0)** 19th FIFA WC. Qualifiers
Estádio „Jornalista Mário Filho" (Maracanã), Rio de Janeiro; Referee: Jorge Luis Larrionda Pietrafiesa (Uruguay); Attendance: 76,657
ECU: Daniel Jimmy Viteri Vinces (5/0), Ulises Hernán de la Cruz Bernardo (98/6), Iván Jacinto Hurtado Angulo (145/5), Giovanny Patricio Espinoza Pavón (73/3), Óscar Dalmiro Bagüí Angulo (16/0), Mario David Quiroz Villón (15/0) [46.Carlos Vicente Tenorio Medina (43/10)], Segundo Alejandro Castillo Nazareno (27/1), Patricio Javier Urrutia Espinoza (18/2), Édison Vicente Méndez Méndez (79/11), Walter Orlando Ayoví Corozo (27/1) [76.Joffre David Guerrón Méndez (4/0)], Christian Rogelio Benítez Betancourt (18/6) [82.Christian Rolando Lara Anangonó (27/4)]. Trainer: Luis Fernando Suárez (51).

397. 17.11.2007 **PARAGUAY - ECUADOR** **5-1(2-0)** 19th FIFA WC. Qualifiers
Estadio Defensores del Chaco, Asunción; Referee: Héber Lopes (Brazil); Attendance: 30,000
ECU: Marcelo Ramón Elizaga Ferrero (4/0), Jairo Eliecer Montaño Quiñonez (6/0), Giovanny Patricio Espinoza Pavón (74/3), Jorge Daniel Guagua Tamayo (29/2), Óscar Dalmiro Bagüí Angulo (17/0), Patricio Javier Urrutia Espinoza (19/2) [46.Jairo Rolando Campos León (7/0)], Segundo Alejandro Castillo Nazareno (28/1), Édison Vicente Méndez Méndez (80/11), Walter Orlando Ayoví Corozo (28/1), Christian Rogelio Benítez Betancourt (19/6) [77.Felipe Salvador Caicedo Corozo (16/2)], Evelio Agustín Ordóñez Martínez (19/1) [64.Jaime Iván Kaviedes Llorenty (52/15)]. Trainer: Luis Fernando Suárez (52).
Goal: Jaime Iván Kaviedes Llorenty (80).

398. 21.11.2007 **ECUADOR - PERU** **5-1(3-0)** 19th FIFA WC. Qualifiers
Estadio Olimpico "Atahualpa", Quito; Referee: Carlos Chandía Alarcón (Chile); Attendance: 35,000
ECU: Marcelo Ramón Elizaga Ferrero (5/0) [67.Edwin Alberto Villafuerte Posligua (1/0)], Omar Andrés de Jesús Borja (9/0), Giovanny Patricio Espinoza Pavón (75/3), Iván Jacinto Hurtado Angulo (146/5), Vicente Paúl Ambrosi Zambrano (31/0), Mario David Quiroz Villón (16/0), Segundo Alejandro Castillo Nazareno (29/1), Édison Vicente Méndez Méndez (81/13), Walter Orlando Ayoví Corozo (29/3), Christian Rogelio Benítez Betancourt (20/6) [85.Jefferson Antonio Montero Vite (1/0)], Jaime Iván Kaviedes Llorenty (53/16) [69.Patricio Javier Urrutia Espinoza (20/2)]. Trainer: Sixto Rafael Vizuete Toapanta (1).
Goals: Walter Orlando Ayoví Corozo (10), Jaime Iván Kaviedes Llorenty (24), Édison Vicente Méndez Méndez (44), Walter Orlando Ayoví Corozo (48), Édison Vicente Méndez Méndez (62).

399. 26.03.2008 **ECUADOR - HAITI** **3-1(1-1)**
Estadio La Cocha, Latacunga; Referee: n/a; Attendance: 9,000
ECU: Marcelo Ramón Elizaga Ferrero (6/0) [71.Máximo Orlando Banguera Valdivieso (1/0)], Erick Rolando De Jesús Delgado (10/0), Iván Jacinto Hurtado Angulo (147/5), Giovanny Patricio Espinoza Pavón (76/3) [73.Carlos Ernesto Castro Cadena (4/0)], Gabriel Eduardo Achilier Zurita (1/0) [59.Isaac Bryan Mina Arboleda (1/0)], Segundo Alejandro Castillo Nazareno (30/2), Mario David Quiroz Villón (17/0) [66.Christian Rolando Lara Anangonó (28/4)], Luis Antonio Valencia Mosquera (30/4), Walter Orlando Ayoví Corozo (30/4) [71.Carlos Ramón Hidalgo Ortega (1/0)], Carlos Vicente Tenorio Medina (44/11), Felipe Salvador Caicedo Corozo (17/2) [54.Christian Rogelio Benítez Betancourt (21/6)]. Trainer: Sixto Rafael Vizuete Toapanta (2).
Goals: Segundo Alejandro Castillo Nazareno (45), Walter Orlando Ayoví Corozo (58), Carlos Vicente Tenorio Medina (61 penalty).

400. 27.05.2008 **FRANCE - ECUADOR** **2-0(0-0)**

Stade des Alpes, Grenoble; Referee: Paul Allaerts (Belgium); Attendance: 20,000

ECU: Marcelo Ramón Elizaga Ferrero (7/0), Omar Andrés de Jesús Borja (10/0), Iván Jacinto Hurtado Angulo (148/5), Carlos Ernesto Castro Cadena (5/0), Isaac Bryan Mina Arboleda (2/0), Mario David Quiroz Villón (18/0) [63.Félix Alexander Borja Valencia (19/3)], José Luis Cortéz Arroyo (5/0), Segundo Alejandro Castillo Nazareno (31/2), Walter Orlando Ayoví Corozo (31/4), Luis Antonio Valencia Mosquera (31/4), Carlos Vicente Tenorio Medina (45/11) [86.Felipe Salvador Caicedo Corozo (18/2)]. Trainer: Sixto Rafael Vizuete Toapanta (3).

401. 15.06.2008 **ARGENTINA - ECUADOR** **1-1(0-0)** 19th FIFA WC. Qualifiers

Estadio Monumental „Antonio Vespucio Liberti“, Buenos Aires; Referee: René Ortubé Betancourt (Bolivia); Attendance: 41,167

ECU: José Francisco Cevallos Villavicencio (78/0), Omar Andrés de Jesús Borja (11/0), Iván Jacinto Hurtado Angulo (149/5), Giovanny Patricio Espinoza Pavón (77/3), Isaac Bryan Mina Arboleda (3/0), Segundo Alejandro Castillo Nazareno (32/2), Patricio Javier Urrutia Espinoza (21/3), Luis Antonio Valencia Mosquera (32/4), Joffre David Guerrón Méndez (5/0) [90+2.Ulises Hernán de la Cruz Bernardo (99/6)], Walter Orlando Ayoví Corozo (32/4) [85.Luis Alberto Bolaños León (5/0)], Carlos Vicente Tenorio Medina (46/11) [88.Christian Rogelio Benítez Betancourt (22/6)]. Trainer: Sixto Rafael Vizuete Toapanta (4).

Goal: Patricio Javier Urrutia Espinoza (69).

402. 18.06.2008 **ECUADOR - COLOMBIA** **0-0** 19th FIFA WC. Qualifiers

Estadio Olimpico "Atahualpa", Quito; Referee: Héctor Walter Baldassi (Argentina); Attendance: 33,588

ECU: José Francisco Cevallos Villavicencio (79/0), Omar Andrés de Jesús Borja (12/0), Iván Jacinto Hurtado Angulo (150/5), Giovanny Patricio Espinoza Pavón (78/3), Vicente Paúl Ambrosi Zambrano (32/0), Segundo Alejandro Castillo Nazareno (33/2), Patricio Javier Urrutia Espinoza (22/3) [46.Joffre David Guerrón Méndez (6/0)], Luis Antonio Valencia Mosquera (33/4), Walter Orlando Ayoví Corozo (33/4) [72.Luis Alberto Bolaños León (6/0)], Carlos Vicente Tenorio Medina (47/11) [81.Felipe Salvador Caicedo Corozo (19/2)], Christian Rogelio Benítez Betancourt (23/6). Trainer: Sixto Rafael Vizuete Toapanta (5).

403. 20.08.2008 **COLOMBIA - ECUADOR** **0-1(0-1)**

Giants Stadium, East Rutherford, New York (United States); Referee: Arkadiusz Prus (United States); Attendance: 32,439

ECU: José Francisco Cevallos Villavicencio (80/0) [46.Marcelo Ramón Elizaga Ferrero (8/0)], Giovanny Patricio Espinoza Pavón (79/3) [54.Carlos Ernesto Castro Cadena (6/0)], Iván Jacinto Hurtado Angulo (151/5), Isaac Bryan Mina Arboleda (4/0), Joffre David Guerrón Méndez (7/0), Walter Orlando Ayoví Corozo (34/4), Segundo Alejandro Castillo Nazareno (34/2) [58.Fernando Roberto Hidalgo Maldonado (2/0)], Patricio Javier Urrutia Espinoza (23/3) [17.Jose Luis Cortéz Arroyo (6/0)], Luis Alberto Bolaños León (7/0) [82.Omar Andrés de Jesús Borja (13/0)], Christian Rogelio Benítez Betancourt (24/7), Felipe Salvador Caicedo Corozo (20/2) [77.Pablo David Palacios Herreria (5/0)]. Trainer: Sixto Rafael Vizuete Toapanta (6).

Goal: Christian Rogelio Benítez Betancourt (40).

404. 06.09.2008 **ECUADOR - BOLIVIA** **3-1(1-1)** 19th FIFA WC. Qualifiers

Estadio Olímpico "Atahualpa", Quito; Referee: Pablo Antonio Pozo Quinteros (Chile); Attendance: 28,000

ECU: José Francisco Cevallos Villavicencio (81/0), Néicer Reasco Yano (42/0) [28.Omar Andrés de Jesús Borja (14/0)], Iván Jacinto Hurtado Angulo (152/5), Giovanny Patricio Espinoza Pavón (80/3), Walter Orlando Ayoví Corozo (35/4), Segundo Alejandro Castillo Nazareno (35/2), Joffre David Guerrón Méndez (8/0), Édison Vicente Méndez Méndez (82/14), Luis Alberto Bolaños León (8/0) [75.Patricio Javier Urrutia Espinoza (24/3)], Christian Rogelio Benítez Betancourt (25/8), Felipe Salvador Caicedo Corozo (21/3) [76.Pablo David Palacios Herreria (6/0)]. Trainer: Sixto Rafael Vizuete Toapanta (7).

Goals: Felipe Salvador Caicedo Corozo (21), Édison Vicente Méndez Méndez (51 penalty), Christian Rogelio Benítez Betancourt (72).

405. 10.09.2008 **URUGUAY - ECUADOR** **0-0** 19th FIFA WC. Qualifiers

Estadio Centenario, Montevideo; Referee: Óscar Julián Ruiz Acosta (Colombia); Attendance: 43,392

ECU: José Francisco Cevallos Villavicencio (82/0), Omar Andrés de Jesús Borja (15/0), Iván Jacinto Hurtado Angulo (153/5), Giovanny Patricio Espinoza Pavón (81/3), Isaac Bryan Mina Arboleda (5/0), Segundo Alejandro Castillo Nazareno (36/2), Luis Antonio Valencia Mosquera (34/4), Édison Vicente Méndez Méndez (83/14), Walter Orlando Ayoví Corozo (36/4), Joffre David Guerrón Méndez (9/0) [82.José Luis Cortéz Arroyo (7/0)], Felipe Salvador Caicedo Corozo (22/3) [79.Félix Alexander Borja Valencia (20/3)]. Trainer: Sixto Rafael Vizuete Toapanta (8).

406. 12.10.2008 **ECUADOR - CHILE** **1-0(0-0)** 19th FIFA WC. Qualifiers

Estadio Olimpico "Atahualpa", Quito; Referee: Martín Emilio Vázquez Broquetas (Uruguay); Attendance: 33,079

ECU: Marcelo Ramón Elizaga Ferrero (9/0), Omar Andrés de Jesús Borja (16/0), Iván Jacinto Hurtado Angulo (154/5), Giovanny Patricio Espinoza Pavón (82/3), Vicente Paúl Ambrosi Zambrano (33/0) [46.Luis Alberto Bolaños León (9/0)], Segundo Alejandro Castillo Nazareno (37/2) [43.Patricio Javier Urrutia Espinoza (25/3)], Walter Orlando Ayoví Corozo (37/4), Joffre David Guerrón Méndez (10/0), Luis Antonio Valencia Mosquera (35/4) [*sent off 75*], Christian Rogelio Benítez Betancourt (26/9), Felipe Salvador Caicedo Corozo (23/3) [85.Fernando Roberto Hidalgo Maldonado (3/0)]. Trainer: Sixto Rafael Vizuete Toapanta (9).

Goal: Christian Rogelio Benítez Betancourt (70).

407. 15.10.2008 **VENEZUELA - ECUADOR** **3-1(0-1)** 19th FIFA WC. Qualifiers

Estadio "General José Antonio Anzoategui", Puerto La Cruz; Referee: Enrique Marcos Osses Zencovich (Chile); Attendance: 10,581

ECU: José Francisco Cevallos Villavicencio (83/0), Isaac Bryan Mina Arboleda (6/1), Iván Jacinto Hurtado Angulo (155/5) [36.Carlos Ernesto Castro Cadena (7/0)], Giovanny Patricio Espinoza Pavón (83/3), Omar Andrés de Jesús Borja (17/0), José Luis Cortéz Arroyo (8/0), Édison Vicente Méndez Méndez (84/14), Patricio Javier Urrutia Espinoza (26/3), Walter Orlando Ayoví Corozo (38/4) [60.Luis Alberto Bolaños León (10/0)], Joffre David Guerrón Méndez (11/0) [65.Félix Alexander Borja Valencia (21/3)], Felipe Salvador Caicedo Corozo (24/3). Trainer: Sixto Rafael Vizuete Toapanta (10).

Goal: Isaac Bryan Mina Arboleda (12).

408. 12.11.2008 **ECUADOR - MEXICO** **1-2(1-0)**

Chase Field, Phoenix (United States); Referee: Arkadiusz Prus (United States); Attendance: 47,861

ECU: Máximo Orlando Banguera Valdivieso (2/0), Enrique Roberto Gámez Quintero (1/0), Luis Armando Checa Villamar (1/0), Isaac Bryan Mina Arboleda (7/2) [46.Arrinton Narciso Mina Villalba (1/0)], Jorge Daniel Guagua Tamayo (30/2), Pedro Ángel Quiñónez Rodríguez (2/0), Fernando Roberto Hidalgo Maldonado (4/0), Luis Alberto Bolaños León (11/0) [86.Giovanny Enrique Nazareno Simisterra (1/0)], Luis Fernando Saritama Padilla (19/0) [90.Fabricio Jonathan Guevara Cangá (1/0)], Walter Orlando Ayoví Corozo (39/4) [90.Jefferson David Pinto Quiróz (1/0)], Pablo David Palacios Herreria (7/0) [89.Joao Robin Rojas Mendoza (1/0)]. Trainer: Sixto Rafael Vizuete Toapanta (11).

Goals: Isaac Bryan Mina Arboleda (7).

409. 17.12.2008 **IRAN - ECUADOR** **0-1(0-0)** International Tournament
Sultan Qaboos Sports Complex, Muscat (Oman); Referee: Mahmood Mohammed Juma'a Al Ghatrifi (Oman); Attendance: 2,500
ECU: Cristian Rafael Mora Medrano (18/0), Franklin Orlando Corozo Quiñónez (1/0), Jorge Daniel Guagua Tamayo (31/2), Iván Jacinto Hurtado Angulo (156/5), Isaac Bryan Mina Arboleda (8/2) [85.Luis Armando Checa Villamar (2/0)], Fernando Roberto Hidalgo Maldonado (5/0), Tilson Oswaldo Minda Suscal (1/0), Jefferson Antonio Montero Vite (2/0), Fidel Francisco Martínez Tenorio (1/1) [88.Arrinton Narciso Mina Villalba (2/0)], Walter Richard Calderón Carcelén (9/0), Edmundo Salomón Zura De Jesús (8/1) [78.Ángel Gabriel Escobar Arce (2/0)]. Trainer: Sixto Rafael Vizuete Toapanta (12).
Goal: Fidel Francisco Martínez Tenorio (54).

410. 19.12.2008 **OMAN - ECUADOR** **2-0(1-0)** International Tournament
Sultan Qaboos Sports Complex, Muscat; Referee: Mahmood Merdas (Oman); Attendance: 2,500
ECU: Cristian Rafael Mora Medrano (19/0) [46.Máximo Orlando Banguera Valdivieso (3/0)], Franklin Orlando Corozo Quiñónez (2/0) [46.Enrique Roberto Gámez Quintero (2/0)], Iván Jacinto Hurtado Angulo (157/5), Jorge Daniel Guagua Tamayo (32/2), Isaac Bryan Mina Arboleda (9/2), Tilson Oswaldo Minda Suscal (2/0), Fernando Roberto Hidalgo Maldonado (6/0), Fidel Francisco Martínez Tenorio (2/1), Jefferson Antonio Montero Vite (3/0), Walter Richard Calderón Carcelén (10/0) [46.Arrinton Narciso Mina Villalba (3/0)], Edmundo Salomón Zura De Jesús (9/1). Trainer: Sixto Rafael Vizuete Toapanta (13).

411. 29.03.2009 **ECUADOR - BRAZIL** **1-1(0-0)** 19th FIFA WC. Qualifiers
Estadio Olimpico "Atahualpa", Quito; Referee: Carlos Chandía Alarcón (Chile); Attendance: 40,000
ECU: José Francisco Cevallos Villavicencio (84/0), Giovanny Patricio Espinoza Pavón (84/3), Iván Jacinto Hurtado Angulo (158/5), Néicer Reasco Yano (43/0), Segundo Alejandro Castillo Nazareno (38/2), Walter Orlando Ayoví Corozo (40/4), Luis Antonio Valencia Mosquera (36/4), Édison Vicente Méndez Méndez (85/14), Felipe Salvador Caicedo Corozo (25/3) [90+2.Pablo David Palacios Herreria (8/0)], Christian Rogelio Benítez Betancourt (27/9), Joffre David Guerrón Méndez (12/0) [75.Christian Fernando Noboa Tello (1/1)]. Trainer: Sixto Rafael Vizuete Toapanta (14).
Goal: Christian Fernando Noboa Tello (89).

412. 01.04.2009 **ECUADOR - PARAGUAY** **1-1(0-0)** 19th FIFA WC. Qualifiers
Estadio Olimpico "Atahualpa", Quito; Referee: Wilmar Roldán Pérez (Colombia); Attendance: 36,953
ECU: José Francisco Cevallos Villavicencio (85/0), Giovanny Patricio Espinoza Pavón (85/3), Iván Jacinto Hurtado Angulo (159/5), Vicente Paúl Ambrosi Zambrano (34/0), Néicer Reasco Yano (44/0), Segundo Alejandro Castillo Nazareno (39/2), Luis Antonio Valencia Mosquera (37/4) [85.Patricio Javier Urrutia Espinoza (27/3)], Édison Vicente Méndez Méndez (86/14), Felipe Salvador Caicedo Corozo (26/3) [46.Walter Richard Calderón Carcelén (11/0)], Christian Rogelio Benítez Betancourt (28/9), Joffre David Guerrón Méndez (13/0) [61.Christian Fernando Noboa Tello (2/2)]. Trainer: Sixto Rafael Vizuete Toapanta (15).
Goal: Christian Fernando Noboa Tello (63).

413. 27.05.2009 **ECUADOR – EL SALVADOR** **1-3(1-1)**
Memorial Coliseum Stadium, Los Angeles (United States); Referee: Ricardo Salazar (United States); Attendance: 28,793
ECU: José Francisco Cevallos Villavicencio (86/0) [68.Cristian Rafael Mora Medrano (20/0)], Miguel Washington Ibarra Tixe (1/0) [54.Edmundo Salomón Zura de Jesús (10/1)], Jairo Rolando Campos León (8/0), Isaac Bryan Mina Arboleda (10/2), Jorge Daniel Guagua Tamayo (33/2), Mario David Quiroz Villón (19/0) [*sent off 58*], Fernando Roberto Hidalgo Maldonado (7/0), Jefferson Antonio Montero Vite (4/1), Walter Orlando Ayoví Corozo (41/4), Joao Robin Rojas Mendoza (2/0), Pablo David Palacios Herreria (9/0) [54.Michael Jackson Quiñónez Cabeza (1/0)]. Trainer: Sixto Rafael Vizuete Toapanta (16).
Goal: Jefferson Antonio Montero Vite (9).

414. 07.06.2009 **PERU - ECUADOR** **1-2(0-1)** 19th FIFA WC. Qualifiers
Estadio Monumental, Lima; Referee: Carlos Manuel Torres (Paraguay); Attendance: 17,050
ECU: Marcelo Ramón Elizaga Ferrero (10/0), Julio Marcelo Fleitas Silveira (1/0), Jorge Daniel Guagua Tamayo (34/2), Néicer Reasco Yano (45/0), Segundo Alejandro Castillo Nazareno (40/2), Walter Orlando Ayoví Corozo (42/4), Christian Fernando Noboa Tello (3/2), Édison Vicente Méndez Méndez (87/14), Jefferson Antonio Montero Vite (5/2) [83.Isaac Bryan Mina Arboleda (11/2)], Pablo David Palacios Herreria (10/0) [60.Joffre David Guerrón Méndez (14/0)], Carlos Vicente Tenorio Medina (48/12) [87.Fernando Roberto Hidalgo Maldonado (8/0)]. Trainer: Sixto Rafael Vizuete Toapanta (17).
Goals: Jefferson Antonio Montero Vite (38), Carlos Vicente Tenorio Medina (59).

415. 10.06.2009 **ECUADOR - ARGENTINA** **2-0(0-0)** 19th FIFA WC. Qualifiers
Estadio Olimpico "Atahualpa", Quito; Referee: Carlos Chandía Alarcón (Chile); Attendance: 36,359
ECU: Marcelo Ramón Elizaga Ferrero (11/0), Giovanny Patricio Espinoza Pavón (86/3), Iván Jacinto Hurtado Angulo (160/5), Néicer Reasco Yano (46/0), Segundo Alejandro Castillo Nazareno (41/2), Walter Orlando Ayoví Corozo (43/5), Christian Fernando Noboa Tello (4/2) [46.Pablo David Palacios Herreria (11/1)], Édison Vicente Méndez Méndez (88/14), Luis Antonio Valencia Mosquera (38/4), Felipe Salvador Caicedo Corozo (27/3) [79.Joffre David Guerrón Méndez (15/0)], Carlos Vicente Tenorio Medina (49/12) [13.Jefferson Antonio Montero Vite (6/2)]. Trainer: Sixto Rafael Vizuete Toapanta (18).
Goals: Walter Orlando Ayoví Corozo (72), Pablo David Palacios Herreria (83).

416. 12.08.2009 **ECUADOR - JAMAICA** **0-0**
Giants Stadium, East Rutherford, New York (United States); Referee: Jair Marrufo (United States); Attendance: n/a
ECU: José Francisco Cevallos Villavicencio (87/0) [46.Marcelo Ramón Elizaga Ferrero (12/0)], Miguel Washington Ibarra Tixe (2/0) [80.Jorge Daniel Guagua Tamayo (35/2)], Julio Marcelo Fleitas Silveira (2/0), Iván Jacinto Hurtado Angulo (161/5), Walter Orlando Ayoví Corozo (44/5), Segundo Alejandro Castillo Nazareno (42/2), Mario David Quiroz Villón (20/0) [51.Pablo David Palacios Herreria (12/1)], Christian Fernando Noboa Tello (5/2), Jefferson Antonio Montero Vite (7/2) [75.Isaac Bryan Mina Arboleda (12/2)], Joao Robin Rojas Mendoza (3/0) [90.Fernando Roberto Hidalgo Maldonado (9/0)], Carlos Vicente Tenorio Medina (50/12) [65.Hólger Eduardo Matamoros Chunga (1/0)]. Trainer: Sixto Rafael Vizuete Toapanta (19).

417. 05.09.2009 **COLOMBIA - ECUADOR** **2-0(0-0)** 19th FIFA WC. Qualifiers
Estadio „Atanasio Girardot“, Medellín; Referee: Sergio Fabián Pezzotta (Argentina); Attendance: 42,000
ECU: José Francisco Cevallos Villavicencio (88/0), Giovanny Patricio Espinoza Pavón (87/3), Iván Jacinto Hurtado Angulo (162/5), Néicer Reasco Yano (47/0), Segundo Alejandro Castillo Nazareno (43/2), Walter Orlando Ayoví Corozo (45/5), Christian Fernando Noboa Tello (6/2), Édison Vicente Méndez Méndez (89/14) [90.Jefferson Antonio Montero Vite (8/2)], Luis Antonio Valencia Mosquera (39/4), Christian Rogelio Benítez Betancourt (29/9), Carlos Vicente Tenorio Medina (51/12) [23.Pablo David Palacios Herreria (13/1) [*sent off 49*]]. Trainer: Sixto Rafael Vizuete Toapanta (20).

418. 09.09.2009 **BOLIVIA - ECUADOR** **1-3(0-1)** 19th FIFA WC. Qualifiers
Estadio „Hernándo Siles Zuazo“, La Paz; Referee: Héctor Walter Baldassi (Argentina); Attendance: 10,200
ECU: Marcelo Ramón Elizaga Ferrero (13/0), Giovanny Patricio Espinoza Pavón (88/3) [61.Jorge Daniel Guagua Tamayo (36/2)], Julio Marcelo Fleitas Silveira (3/0), Iván Jacinto Hurtado Angulo (163/5), Segundo Alejandro Castillo Nazareno (44/2), Walter Orlando Ayoví Corozo (46/5), Christian Fernando Noboa Tello (7/2), Édison Vicente Méndez Méndez (90/15), Luis Antonio Valencia Mosquera (40/5) [80.Fernando Roberto Hidalgo Maldonado (10/0)], Jefferson Antonio Montero Vite (9/2) [75.Vicente Paúl Ambrosi Zambrano (35/0)], Christian Rogelio Benítez Betancourt (30/10). Trainer: Sixto Rafael Vizuete Toapanta (21).
Goals: Édison Vicente Méndez Méndez (4), Luis Antonio Valencia Mosquera (46), Christian Rogelio Benítez Betancourt (66).

419. 10.10.2009 **ECUADOR - URUGUAY** **1-2(0-0)** 19th FIFA WC. Qualifiers
Estadio Olimpico "Atahualpa", Quito; Referee: Sálvio Spínola Fagundes Filho (Brazil); Attendance: 42,700
ECU: Marcelo Ramón Elizaga Ferrero (14/0), Giovanny Patricio Espinoza Pavón (89/3) [79.Jorge Daniel Guagua Tamayo (37/2)], Iván Jacinto Hurtado Angulo (164/5), Néicer Reasco Yano (48/0), Segundo Alejandro Castillo Nazareno (45/2), Walter Orlando Ayoví Corozo (47/5), Christian Fernando Noboa Tello (8/2) [58.Jefferson Antonio Montero Vite (10/2)], Édison Vicente Méndez Méndez (91/15), Luis Antonio Valencia Mosquera (41/6), Felipe Salvador Caicedo Corozo (28/3) [66.Edmundo Salomón Zura de Jesús (11/1)], Christian Rogelio Benítez Betancourt (31/10). Trainer: Sixto Rafael Vizuete Toapanta (22).
Goal: Luis Antonio Valencia Mosquera (68).

420. 14.10.2009 **CHILE - ECUADOR** **1-0(0-0)** 19th FIFA WC. Qualifiers
Estadio Monumental „David Arellano", Santiago; Referee: Carlos Arecio Amarilla Demarqui (Paraguay); Attendance: 47,000
ECU: Marcelo Ramón Elizaga Ferrero (15/0), Néicer Reasco Yano (49/0), Iván Jacinto Hurtado Angulo (165/5), Jorge Daniel Guagua Tamayo (38/2), Walter Orlando Ayoví Corozo (48/5), Segundo Alejandro Castillo Nazareno (46/2) [*sent off 84*], Édison Vicente Méndez Méndez (92/15) [76.Edmundo Salomón Zura de Jesús (12/1)], Fernando Roberto Hidalgo Maldonado (11/0), Christian Rolando Lara Anangonó (29/4) [57.Joao Robin Rojas Mendoza (4/0)], Christian Rogelio Benítez Betancourt (32/10), Jefferson Antonio Montero Vite (11/2). Trainer: Sixto Rafael Vizuete Toapanta (23).

421. 07.05.2010 **ECUADOR - MEXICO** **0-0**
Meadowlands Stadium, East Rutherford (United States); Referee: Steven Depiero (Canada); Attendance: 77,507
ECU: Marcelo Ramón Elizaga Ferrero (16/0), Julio Marcelo Fleitas Silveira (4/0), Iván Jacinto Hurtado Angulo (166/5), Ulises Hernán de la Cruz Bernardo (**100**/6), Miguel Washington Ibarra Tixe (3/0), Geovanny Enrique Nazareno Simisterra (2/0), Fernando Roberto Hidalgo Maldonado (12/0), Tilson Oswaldo Minda Suscal (3/0), Michael Antonio Arroyo Mina (1/0) [90.Pedro Ángel Quiñónez Rodríguez (3/0)], Michael Jackson Quiñónez Cabeza (2/0) [68.Joao Robin Rojas Mendoza (5/0)], Jaime Iván Kaviedes Llorenty (54/16) [86.Édison Andres Preciado Bravo (1/0)]. Trainer: Sixto Rafael Vizuete Toapanta (24).

422. 16.05.2010 **SOUTH KOREA - ECUADOR** **2-0(0-0)**
Seoul World Cup Stadium, Seoul; Referee: Porached Wongkamdee (Thailand); Attendance: 62,209
ECU: Marcelo Ramón Elizaga Ferrero (17/0), Julio Marcelo Fleitas Silveira (5/0), Iván Jacinto Hurtado Angulo (167/5), Miguel Washington Ibarra Tixe (4/0), Geovanny Enrique Nazareno Simisterra (3/0), Tilson Oswaldo Minda Suscal (4/0) [78.Joao Robin Rojas Mendoza (6/0)], Fernando Roberto Hidalgo Maldonado (13/0), Ulises Hernán de la Cruz Bernardo (101/6) [77.Pedro Ángel Quiñónez Rodríguez (4/0)], Michael Antonio Arroyo Mina (2/0), Jaime Iván Kaviedes Llorenty (55/16), Michael Jackson Quiñónez Cabeza (3/0) [46.Édison Andres Preciado Bravo (2/0)]. Trainer: Sixto Rafael Vizuete Toapanta (25).

423. 04.09.2010 **MEXICO - ECUADOR** **1-2(1-1)**
Estadio Omnilife, Guadalajara; Referee: Walter Quesada Cordero (Costa Rica); Attendance: 43,800
ECU: Máximo Orlando Banguera Valdivieso (4/0), Luis Armando Checa Villamar (3/0), Mario David Quiroz Villón (21/0), Geovanny Banner Caicedo Quiñónez (3/0), Walter Orlando Ayoví Corozo (49/5), Michael Antonio Arroyo Mina (3/0) [79.Geovanny Enrique Nazareno Simisterra (4/0)], Christian Fernando Noboa Tello (9/2) [90.Tilson Oswaldo Minda Suscal (5/0)], Juan Carlos Paredes Reasco (1/0), Luis Antonio Valencia Mosquera (42/6), Christian Rogelio Benítez Betancourt (33/11) [70.Marlon Jonathan de Jesús Pavón (1/0)], Jaime Javier Ayoví Corozo (1/1) [72.Joao Robin Rojas Mendoza (7/0)]. Trainer: Reinaldo Rueda Rivera (1).
Goals: Christian Rogelio Benítez Betancourt (1), Jaime Javier Ayoví Corozo (58).

424. 07.09.2010 **VENEZUELA - ECUADOR** **1-0(0-0)**
Estadio Metropolitano, Barquisimeto; Referee: Juan Torres (Panama); Attendance: 37,262
ECU: Máximo Orlando Banguera Valdivieso (5/0) [51.Rorys Andrés Aragón Espinoza (3/0)], Geovanny Banner Caicedo Quiñónez (4/0), Luis Armando Checa Villamar (4/0), Mario David Quiroz Villón (22/0), Walter Orlando Ayoví Corozo (50/5), Christian Fernando Noboa Tello (10/2), Michael Antonio Arroyo Mina (4/0) [60.Joao Robin Rojas Mendoza (8/0)], Luis Antonio Valencia Mosquera (43/6), Jefferson Antonio Montero Vite (12/2) [78.Geovanny Enrique Nazareno Simisterra (5/0)], Jaime Javier Ayoví Corozo (2/1), Juan Carlos Paredes Reasco (2/0). Trainer: Reinaldo Rueda Rivera (2).

425. 08.10.2010 **COLOMBIA - ECUADOR** **1-0(0-0)**
Red Bull Arena, New Jersey (United States); Referee: Andrew Chapin (United States); Attendance: 25,000
ECU: Máximo Orlando Banguera Valdivieso (6/0), Jorge Daniel Guagua Tamayo (39/2), Isaac Bryan Mina Arboleda (13/2), Néicer Reasco Yano (50/0), Mario David Quiroz Villón (23/0), Walter Orlando Ayoví Corozo (51/5), Christian Fernando Noboa Tello (11/2), Michael Antonio Arroyo Mina (5/0) [84.Cristian Andrés Suárez Valencia (1/0); 90+1.Juan Carlos Paredes Reasco (3/0)], Jaime Javier Ayoví Corozo (3/1), Christian Rogelio Benítez Betancourt (34/11) [74.Luis Fernando Saritama Padilla (20/0)], Joffre David Guerrón Méndez (16/0) [64.Joao Robin Rojas Mendoza (9/0)]. Trainer: Reinaldo Rueda Rivera (3).

426. 12.10.2010 **ECUADOR - POLAND** **2-2(1-0)**
Stade Saputo, Montréal (Canada); Referee: Mauricio Navarro (Canada); Attendance: 1,000
ECU: Máximo Orlando Banguera Valdivieso (7/0), Juan Carlos Paredes Reasco (4/0), Jairo Rolando Campos León (9/0), Luis Armando Checa Villamar (5/0), Walter Orlando Ayoví Corozo (52/5), Tilson Oswaldo Minda Suscal (6/0), Luis Fernando Saritama Padilla (21/0), Christian Fernando Noboa Tello (12/2), Joffre David Guerrón Méndez (17/0) [85.Isaac Bryan Mina Arboleda (14/2)], Michael Antonio Arroyo Mina (6/0), Christian Rogelio Benítez Betancourt (35/13). Trainer: Reinaldo Rueda Rivera (4).
Goals: Christian Rogelio Benítez Betancourt (31, 78)

427. 17.11.2010 **ECUADOR - VENEZUELA** **4-1(3-1)**
Estadio Olimpico "Atahualpa", Quito; Referee: Ibrahim Chaibou (Niger); Attendance: 9,000
ECU: Máximo Orlando Banguera Valdivieso (8/0), Juan Carlos Paredes Reasco (5/0) [71.Luis Armando Checa Villamar (6/0)], Jairo Rolando Campos León (10/0), Isaac Bryan Mina Arboleda (15/2), Walter Orlando Ayoví Corozo (53/7) [88.Geovanny Banner Caicedo Quiñónez (5/0)], Segundo Alejandro Castillo Nazareno (47/2), Mario David Quiroz Villón (24/0), Luis Fernando Saritama Padilla (22/0), Michael Antonio Arroyo Mina (7/0) [68.Jaime Javier Ayoví Corozo (4/1)], Joao Robin Rojas Mendoza (10/0) [54.Jefferson Antonio Montero Vite (13/2)], Christian Rogelio Benítez Betancourt (36/15) [79.Fernando Alexander Guerrero Vásquez (3/0)]. Trainer: Reinaldo Rueda Rivera (5).
Goals: Christian Rogelio Benítez Betancourt (2, 4), Walter Orlando Ayoví Corozo (45, 46).

428. 09.02.2011 **HONDURAS - ECUADOR** **1-1(1-1,1-1,1-1); 4-5 on penalties** Copa Municipal de La Ceiba
Estadio Nilmo Edwards, La Ceiba; Referee: Walter Alexander López Castellanos (Honduras); Attendance: 15,000
ECU: Marcelo Ramón Elizaga Ferrero (18/0), Juan Carlos Paredes Reasco (6/0), Geovanny Banner Caicedo Quiñónez (6/0) [52.Isaac Bryan Mina Arboleda (16/2)], Jorge Daniel Guagua Tamayo (40/2), Segundo Alejandro Castillo Nazareno (48/2) [60.Michael Jackson Quiñónez Cabeza (4/0)], Walter Orlando Ayoví Corozo (54/7), Christian Fernando Noboa Tello (13/2), Luis Fernando Saritama Padilla (23/0) [67.Geovanny Enrique Nazareno Simisterra (6/0)], Michael Antonio Arroyo Mina (8/0) [81.Tilson Oswaldo Minda Suscal (7/0)], Pablo David Palacios Herreria (14/2) [64.Joao Robin Rojas Mendoza (11/0)], Jaime Javier Ayoví Corozo (5/1). Trainer: Reinaldo Rueda Rivera (6).
Goal: Pablo David Palacios Herreria (12).
Penalties: Jorge Daniel Guagua Tamayo, Christian Fernando Noboa Tello, Jaime Javier Ayoví Corozo, Michael Jackson Quiñónez Cabeza (miss), Walter Orlando Ayoví Corozo, Tilson Oswaldo Minda Suscal.

429. 26.03.2011 **COLOMBIA - ECUADOR** **2-0(1-0)**
Estadio „Vicente Calderón", Madrid (Spain); Referee: Antonio Miguel Mateu Lahoz (Spain); Attendance: 15,000
ECU: Alexander Domínguez Carabalí (1/0), Juan Carlos Paredes Reasco (7/0), Jairo Rolando Campos León (11/0), Isaac Bryan Mina Arboleda (17/2), Geovanny Enrique Nazareno Simisterra (7/0), Segundo Alejandro Castillo Nazareno (49/2) [76.Edson Eli Montaño Angulo (1/0)], Walter Orlando Ayoví Corozo (55/7) [66.Jefferson Antonio Montero Vite (14/2)], Christian Fernando Noboa Tello (14/2), Luis Fernando Saritama Padilla (24/0), Luis Antonio Valencia Mosquera (44/6) [76.Pablo David Palacios Herreria (15/2)], Jaime Javier Ayoví Corozo (6/1). Trainer: Reinaldo Rueda Rivera (7).

430. 29.03.2011 **ECUADOR - PERU** **0-0**
Kyocera Stadion, Den Haag (Holland); Referee: Oscar Eric Braamhaar (Holland); Attendance: n/a
ECU: Máximo Orlando Banguera Valdivieso (9/0), Jorge Daniel Guagua Tamayo (41/2), Isaac Bryan Mina Arboleda (18/2), Christian Fernando Noboa Tello (15/2) [69.Juan Carlos Paredes Reasco (8/0)], Tilson Oswaldo Minda Suscal (8/0), Mario David Quiroz Villón (25/0), Luis Fernando Saritama Padilla (25/0), Walter Orlando Ayoví Corozo (56/7) [69.Geovanny Enrique Nazareno Simisterra (8/0)], Jefferson Antonio Montero Vite (15/2) [84.Pablo David Palacios Herreria (16/2)], Edson Eli Montaño Angulo (2/0), Jaime Javier Ayoví Corozo (7/1). Trainer: Reinaldo Rueda Rivera (8).

431. 20.04.2011 **ARGENTINA - ECUADOR** **2-2(2-1)**
Estadio "José María Minella", Mar del Plata; Referee: Roberto Carlos Silvera (Uruguay); Attendance: n/a
ECU: Marcelo Ramón Elizaga Ferrero (19/0), Juan Carlos Paredes Reasco (9/0), Luis Armando Checa Villamar (7/0), Isaac Bryan Mina Arboleda (19/2), Geovanny Enrique Nazareno Simisterra (9/0) [90.José Enrique Madrid (1/0)], Segundo Alejandro Castillo Nazareno (50/3), Tilson Oswaldo Minda Suscal (9/0) [72.Flavio David Caicedo Gracia (1/0)], Michael Jackson Quiñónez Cabeza (5/1) [74.Marlon Jonathan de Jesús Pavón (2/0)], Alex Renato Ibarra Mina (1/0) [83.Dennys Andrés Quiñónez Espinoza (1/0)], Arrinton Narciso Mina Villalba (4/0) [65.Juan José Govea Tenorio (1/0)], Franklin Agustín Salas Narváez (26/2) [65.Frickson Rafael Erazo Vivero (1/0)]. Trainer: Reinaldo Rueda Rivera (9).
Goals: Michael Jackson Quiñónez Cabeza (26), Segundo Alejandro Castillo Nazareno (68 penalty).

432. 28.05.2011 **MEXICO - ECUADOR** **1-1(1-1)**
Qwest Field, Seattle (United States); Referee: Edvin Jurisevic (United States); Attendance: 50,305
ECU: Máximo Orlando Banguera Valdivieso (10/0), Néicer Reasco Yano (51/0), Geovanny Banner Caicedo Quiñónez (7/0), Frickson Rafael Erazo Vivero (2/0), Walter Orlando Ayoví Corozo (57/7) [80.Diego Armando Calderón Espinoza (1/0)], Luis Fernando Saritama Padilla (26/0), Segundo Alejandro Castillo Nazareno (51/3), Michael Antonio Arroyo Mina (9/1) [81.Isaac Bryan Mina Arboleda (20/2)], Édison Vicente Méndez Méndez (93/15) [70.Tilson Oswaldo Minda Suscal (10/0)], Christian Rogelio Benítez Betancourt (37/15) [88.Flavio David Caicedo Gracia (2/0)], Jaime Javier Ayoví Corozo (8/1). Trainer: Reinaldo Rueda Rivera (10).
Goal: Michael Antonio Arroyo Mina (37).

433. 01.06.2011 **CANADA - ECUADOR** **2-2(1-0)**
BMO Field, Toronto; Referee: Raymond Bogle (Jamaica); Attendance: 14,356
ECU: Marcelo Ramón Elizaga Ferrero (20/0), Geovanny Banner Caicedo Quiñónez (8/0), Frickson Rafael Erazo Vivero (3/0), Néicer Reasco Yano (52/0), Segundo Alejandro Castillo Nazareno (52/3), Walter Orlando Ayoví Corozo (58/7), Christian Fernando Noboa Tello (16/2) [52.Édison Vicente Méndez Méndez (94/15)], Luis Fernando Saritama Padilla (27/0) [77.Tilson Oswaldo Minda Suscal (11/0)], Michael Antonio Arroyo Mina (10/2) [90.Joao Jimmy Plata Cotera (1/0)], Jaime Javier Ayoví Corozo (9/1), Christian Rogelio Benítez Betancourt (38/16). Trainer: Reinaldo Rueda Rivera (11).
Goals: Christian Rogelio Benítez Betancourt (61), Michael Antonio Arroyo Mina (63).

434. 07.06.2011 **GREECE - ECUADOR** **1-1(1-0)**
Citi Field, New York (United States); Referee: Mark Geiger (United States); Attendance: 39,656
ECU: Máximo Orlando Banguera Valdivieso (11/0), Luis Armando Checa Villamar (8/0), Frickson Rafael Erazo Vivero (4/1), Néicer Reasco Yano (53/0), Walter Orlando Ayoví Corozo (59/7), Christian Fernando Noboa Tello (17/2) [73.Segundo Alejandro Castillo Nazareno (53/3)], Luis Fernando Saritama Padilla (28/0) [61.Tilson Oswaldo Minda Suscal (12/0)], Michael Antonio Arroyo Mina (11/2), Édison Vicente Méndez Méndez (95/15) [82.Diego Armando Calderón Espinoza (2/0)], Jaime Javier Ayoví Corozo (10/1) [80.Isaac Bryan Mina Arboleda (21/2)], Christian Rogelio Benítez Betancourt (39/16). Trainer: Reinaldo Rueda Rivera (12).
Goal: Frickson Rafael Erazo Vivero (58).

435. 03.07.2011 **PARAGUAY - ECUADOR** **0-0** 43rd Copa América. Group Stage
Estadio "Brigadier General Estanislao López", Santa Fe (Argentina); Referee: Sergio Fabián Pezzotta (Argentina); Attendance: 12,000
ECU: Marcelo Ramón Elizaga Ferrero (21/0), Néicer Reasco Yano (54/0), Norberto Carlos Araujo López (1/0), Frickson Rafael Erazo Vivero (5/1), Walter Orlando Ayoví Corozo (60/7), Luis Antonio Valencia Mosquera [46.Michael Antonio Arroyo Mina (12/2)], Christian Fernando Noboa Tello (18/2), Segundo Alejandro Castillo Nazareno (54/3), Édison Vicente Méndez Méndez (96/15) [82.Mario David Quiroz Villón (26/0)], Christian Rogelio Benítez Betancourt (40/16), Felipe Salvador Caicedo Corozo (29/3). Trainer: Reinaldo Rueda Rivera (13).

436. 09.07.2011 **VENEZUELA - ECUADOR** **1-0(0-0)** 43rd Copa América. Group Stage
Estadio "Padre Ernesto Martearena", Salta (Argentina); Referee: Wálter Enrique Quesada Cordero (Costa Rica); Attendance: n/a
ECU: Marcelo Ramón Elizaga Ferrero (22/0), Néicer Reasco Yano (55/0), Norberto Carlos Araujo López (2/0), Frickson Rafael Erazo Vivero (6/1), Christian Fernando Noboa Tello (19/2), Segundo Alejandro Castillo Nazareno (55/3) [76.Mario David Quiroz Villón (27/0)], Michael Antonio Arroyo Mina (13/2) [72.Edson Eli Montaño Angulo (3/0)], Walter Orlando Ayoví Corozo (61/7), Édison Vicente Méndez Méndez (97/15), Christian Rogelio Benítez Betancourt (41/16), Felipe Salvador Caicedo Corozo (30/3). Trainer: Reinaldo Rueda Rivera (14).

437. 13.07.2011 **BRAZIL - ECUADOR** **4-2(1-1)** 43rd Copa América. Group Stage
Estadio "Mario Alberto Kempes", Córdoba (Argentina); Referee: Roberto Carlos Silvera Calcerrada (Uruguay); Attendance: n/a
ECU: Marcelo Ramón Elizaga Ferrero (23/0), Néicer Reasco Yano (56/0) [82.Gabriel Eduardo Achilier Zurita (2/0)], Norberto Carlos Araujo López (3/0), Frickson Rafael Erazo Vivero (7/1), Walter Orlando Ayoví Corozo (62/7), Christian Fernando Noboa Tello (20/2) [90+1.Edson Eli Montaño Angulo (4/0)], Tilson Oswaldo Minda Suscal (13/0), Édison Vicente Méndez Méndez (98/15) [77.Arrinton Narciso Mina Villalba (5/0)], Michael Antonio Arroyo Mina (14/2), Christian Rogelio Benítez Betancourt (42/16), Felipe Salvador Caicedo Corozo (31/5). Trainer: Reinaldo Rueda Rivera (15).
Goals: Felipe Salvador Caicedo Corozo (36, 58).

438. 10.08.2011 **COSTA RICA - ECUADOR** **0-2(0-0)**
Estadio Nacional, San José; Referee: Joel Antonio Aguilar Chicas (El Salvador); Attendance: 15,000
ECU: Máximo Orlando Banguera Valdivieso (12/0), Frickson Rafael Erazo Vivero (8/1), Eduardo Javier Morante Rosas (1/0), Mario David Quiroz Villón (28/0) [46.Segundo Alejandro Castillo Nazareno (56/3)], Christian Andrés Suárez Valencia (2/1) [80.Flavio David Caicedo Gracia (3/0)], Walter Orlando Ayoví Corozo (63/7), Tilson Oswaldo Minda Suscal (14/0), Luis Fernando Saritama Padilla (29/0) [60.Gabriel Eduardo Achilier Zurita (3/0)], Jaime Javier Ayoví Corozo (11/1) [58.Édison Vicente Méndez Méndez (99/16)], Christian Rogelio Benítez Betancourt (43/16) [70.Félix Alexander Borja Valencia (22/3)], Juan Carlos Paredes Reasco (10/0). Trainer: Reinaldo Rueda Rivera (16).
Goals: Christian Andrés Suárez Valencia (53), Édison Vicente Méndez Méndez (66).

439. 02.09.2011 **ECUADOR - JAMAICA** **5-2(3-0)**
Estadio Olímpico "Atahualpa", Quito; Referee: José Hernando Buitrago Arango (Colombia); Attendance: 1,000
ECU: Adrián Javier Bone Sánchez (1/0), Geovanny Banner Caicedo Quiñónez (9/0), Frickson Rafael Erazo Vivero (9/1), Segundo Alejandro Castillo Nazareno (57/4) [75.Alex Leonardo Bolaños Reascos (4/0)], Christian Andrés Suárez Valencia (3/2) [61.Gabriel Eduardo Achilier Zurita (4/0)], Walter Orlando Ayoví Corozo (64/7) [70.Mario David Quiroz Villón (29/0)], Luis Fernando Saritama Padilla (30/0) [75.Marwin Jonathan Pita Mora (1/0)], Édison Vicente Méndez Méndez (**100**/16) [61.Isaac Bryan Mina Arboleda (22/2)], Jaime Javier Ayoví Corozo (12/2), Christian Rogelio Benítez Betancourt (44/18) [72.Jaime Iván Kaviedes Llorenty (56/16)], Juan Carlos Paredes Reasco (11/0). Trainer: Reinaldo Rueda Rivera (17).
Goals: Jaime Javier Ayoví Corozo (20), Christian Andrés Suárez Valencia (38), Christian Rogelio Benítez Betancourt (45, 51), Segundo Alejandro Castillo Nazareno (65).

440. 06.09.2011 **ECUADOR – COSTA RICA** **4-0(2-0)**
Estadio Olímpico "Atahualpa", Quito; Referee: Wilmar Alexander Roldán Pérez (Colombia); Attendance: 2,000
ECU: Adrián Javier Bone Sánchez (2/0), Frickson Rafael Erazo Vivero (10/1), Gabriel Eduardo Achilier Zurita (5/0), Segundo Alejandro Castillo Nazareno (58/5), Christian Andrés Suárez Valencia (4/3) [73.Édison Vicente Méndez Méndez (101/16)], Walter Orlando Ayoví Corozo (65/7) [81.Diego Armando Calderón Espinoza (3/0)], Alex Leonardo Bolaños Reascos (5/0) [68.Mario David Quiroz Villón (30/0)], Luis Fernando Saritama Padilla (31/0) [83.Brayan José de la Torre Martínez (1/0)], Jaime Javier Ayoví Corozo (13/3) [80.Jaime Iván Kaviedes Llorenty (57/16)], Christian Rogelio Benítez Betancourt (45/19) [87.Agustín Javier Delgado Chalá (72/31)], Juan Carlos Paredes Reasco (12/0). Trainer: Reinaldo Rueda Rivera (18).
Goals: Christian Andrés Suárez Valencia (21), Jaime Javier Ayoví Corozo (28), Segundo Alejandro Castillo Nazareno (58), Christian Rogelio Benítez Betancourt (75).

441. 07.10.2011 **ECUADOR - VENEZUELA** **2-0(2-0)** 20th FIFA WC. Qualifiers
Estadio Olímpico "Atahualpa", Quito; Referee: Enrique Roberto Osses Zencovich (Chile); Attendance: 32,278
ECU: Máximo Orlando Banguera Valdivieso (13/0), Jairo Rolando Campos León (12/0), Frickson Rafael Erazo Vivero (11/1), Christian Andrés Suárez Valencia (5/3) [69.Alex Leonardo Bolaños Reascos (6/0)], Walter Orlando Ayoví Corozo (66/7), Christian Fernando Noboa Tello (21/2) [77.Michael Antonio Arroyo Mina (15/2)], Luis Fernando Saritama Padilla (32/0), Luis Antonio Valencia Mosquera (45/6), Jaime Javier Ayoví Corozo (14/4), Christian Rogelio Benítez Betancourt (46/20) [83.Édison Vicente Méndez Méndez (102/16)], Juan Carlos Paredes Reasco (13/0). Trainer: Reinaldo Rueda Rivera (19).
Goals: Jaime Javier Ayoví Corozo (15), Christian Rogelio Benítez Betancourt (28).

442. 11.10.2011 **UNITED STATES - ECUADOR** **0-1(0-0)**
Red Bull Arena, Harrison, New Jersey (United States); Referee: Joel Antonio Aguilar Chicas (El Salvador); Attendance: 20,707
ECU: Máximo Orlando Banguera Valdivieso (14/0), Frickson Rafael Erazo Vivero (12/1), Gabriel Eduardo Achilier Zurita (6/0), Eduardo Javier Morante Rosas (2/0), Segundo Alejandro Castillo Nazareno (59/5), Walter Orlando Ayoví Corozo (67/7), Luis Antonio Valencia Mosquera (46/6) [74.Christian Andrés Suárez Valencia (6/3)], Michael Antonio Arroyo Mina (16/2) [86.Juan Carlos Paredes Reasco (14/0)], Édison Vicente Méndez Méndez (103/16) [80.Luis Fernando Saritama Padilla (33/0)], Jefferson Antonio Montero Vite (16/2) [60.Jaime Javier Ayoví Corozo (15/5)], Christian Rogelio Benítez Betancourt (47/20). Trainer: Reinaldo Rueda Rivera (20).
Goal: Jaime Javier Ayoví Corozo (79).

443. 11.11.2011 **PARAGUAY - ECUADOR** **2-1(0-0)** 20th FIFA WC. Qualifiers
Estadio Defensores del Chaco, Asunción; Referee: José Hernando Buitrago Arango (Colombia); Attendance: 11,173
ECU: Máximo Orlando Banguera Valdivieso (15/0), Frickson Rafael Erazo Vivero (13/1), Gabriel Eduardo Achilier Zurita (7/0), Eduardo Javier Morante Rosas (3/0), Christian Andrés Suárez Valencia (7/3) [60.Jefferson Antonio Montero Vite (17/2)], Walter Orlando Ayoví Corozo (68/7), Christian Fernando Noboa Tello (22/2), Luis Fernando Saritama Padilla (34/0) [78.Joao Robin Rojas Mendoza (12/1)], Luis Antonio Valencia Mosquera (47/6), Jaime Javier Ayoví Corozo (16/5), Félix Alexander Borja Valencia (23/3) [70.Édison Vicente Méndez Méndez (104/16)]. Trainer: Reinaldo Rueda Rivera (21).
Goal: Joao Robin Rojas Mendoza (90+2).

444. 15.11.2011 **ECUADOR - PERU** **2-0(0-0)** 20th FIFA WC. Qualifiers
Estadio Olímpico "Atahualpa", Quito; Referee: Jorge Luis Larrionda Pietrafesa (Uruguay); Attendance: 34,481
ECU: Máximo Orlando Banguera Valdivieso (16/0), Jairo Rolando Campos León (13/0), Frickson Rafael Erazo Vivero (14/1) [37.Eduardo Javier Morante Rosas (4/0)], Segundo Alejandro Castillo Nazareno (60/5), Walter Orlando Ayoví Corozo (69/7), Luis Fernando Saritama Padilla (35/0) [81.Tilson Oswaldo Minda Suscal (15/0)], Luis Antonio Valencia Mosquera (48/6), Jaime Javier Ayoví Corozo (17/5), Christian Rogelio Benítez Betancourt (48/21), Juan Carlos Paredes Reasco (15/0), Joao Robin Rojas Mendoza (13/1) [46.Édison Vicente Méndez Méndez (105/17)]. Trainer: Reinaldo Rueda Rivera (22).
Goals: Édison Vicente Méndez Méndez (69), Christian Rogelio Benítez Betancourt (88).

445. 29.02.2012 **ECUADOR - HONDURAS** **2-0(1-0)**
Estadio "George Capwell", Guayaquil; Referee: Ímer Lemuel Machado Barrera (Colombia); Attendance: n/a
ECU: Alexander Domínguez Carabalí (2/0), Frickson Rafael Erazo Vivero (15/1), Jorge Daniel Guagua Tamayo (42/2) [69.Jairo Rolando Campos León (14/0)], Gabriel Eduardo Achilier Zurita (8/0), Diego Armando Calderón Espinoza (4/0), Segundo Alejandro Castillo Nazareno (61/5) [70.Alex Leonardo Bolaños Reascos (7/0)], Mario David Quiroz Villón (31/0) [61.Christian Andrés Suárez Valencia (8/3)], Jefferson Antonio Montero Vite (18/2) [81.Enner Remberto Valencia Lastra (1/0)], Jaime Javier Ayoví Corozo (18/7), Christian Rogelio Benítez Betancourt (49/21) [75.Arrinton Narciso Mina Villalba (6/0)], Joao Robin Rojas Mendoza (14/1) [61.Walter Orlando Ayoví Corozo (70/7)]. Trainer: Reinaldo Rueda Rivera (23).
Goals: Jaime Javier Ayoví Corozo (16, 70).

446. 02.06.2012 **ARGENTINA - ECUADOR** **4-0(3-0)** 20th FIFA WC. Qualifiers
Estadio Monumental „Antonio Vespucio Liberti", Buenos Aires; Referee: Víctor Hugo Rivera Chávez (Peru); Attendance: 50,000
ECU: Alexander Domínguez Carabalí (3/0), Jorge Daniel Guagua Tamayo (43/2), Jairo Rolando Campos León (15/0), Gabriel Eduardo Achilier Zurita (9/0), Luis Fernando Saritama Padilla (36/0) [40.Jaime Javier Ayoví Corozo (19/7)], Luis Antonio Valencia Mosquera (49/6), Christian Fernando Noboa Tello (23/2), Pedro Ángel Quiñónez Rodríguez (5/0), Walter Orlando Ayoví Corozo (71/7), Christian Rogelio Benítez Betancourt (50/21) [84.Alex Renato Ibarra Mina (2/0)], Cristian Andrés Suárez Valencia (9/3) [46.Jefferson Antonio Montero Vite (19/2)]. Trainer: Reinaldo Rueda Rivera (24).

447. 10.06.2012 **ECUADOR - COLOMBIA** **1-0(0-0)** 20th FIFA WC. Qualifiers
Estadio Olímpico "Atahualpa", Quito; Referee: Wilson Luiz Seneme (Brazil); Attendance: 37,352
ECU: Alexander Domínguez Carabalí (4/0), Jairo Rolando Campos León (16/0), Frickson Rafael Erazo Vivero (16/1), Segundo Alejandro Castillo Nazareno (62/5), Luis Antonio Valencia Mosquera (50/6), Christian Fernando Noboa Tello (24/2) [*sent off 86*], Joao Robin Rojas Mendoza (15/1) [72.Édison Vicente Méndez Méndez (106/17)], Walter Orlando Ayoví Corozo (72/7), Juan Carlos Paredes Reasco (16/0), Jefferson Antonio Montero Vite (20/2) [78.Luis Fernando Saritama Padilla (37/0)], Christian Rogelio Benítez Betancourt (51/22) [90+4.Tilson Oswaldo Minda Suscal (16/0)]. Trainer: Reinaldo Rueda Rivera (25).
Goal: Christian Rogelio Benítez Betancourt (54).

448. 15.08.2012 **ECUADOR - CHILE** **3-0(2-0)**
Citi Field, New York (United States); Referee: Terry Vaughn (United States); Attendance: 31,901
ECU: Alexander Domínguez Carabalí (5/0), Jayro Rolando Campos León (17/0) [46.Jorge Daniel Guagua Tamayo (43/2)], Frickson Rafael Erazo Vivero (17/1), Segundo Alejandro Castillo Nazareno (63/5), Luis Fernando Saritama Padilla (38/0), Luis Antonio Valencia Mosquera (51/6), Walter Orlando Ayoví Corozo (73/7) [76.Diego Armando Calderón Espinoza (5/0)], Juan Carlos Paredes Reasco (17/0) [85.Gabriel Eduardo Achilier Zurita (10/0)], Jefferson Antonio Montero Vite (21/3) [85.Juan Luis Anangonó León (1/0)], Jaime Javier Ayoví Corozo (20/8) [65.Dennys Andrés Quiñonez Espinoza (2/0)], Arrinton Narciso Mina Villalba (7/1) [46.Christian Rogelio Benítez Betancourt (52/22)]. Trainer: Reinaldo Rueda Rivera (26).
Goals: Arrinton Narciso Mina Villalba (9), Jaime Javier Ayoví Corozo (13), Jefferson Antonio Montero Vite (67).

449. 07.09.2012 **ECUADOR - BOLIVIA** **1-0(0-0)** 20th FIFA WC. Qualifiers
Estadio Olímpico Atahualpa, Quito; Referee: Juan Ernesto Soto Arevalo (Venezuela); Attendance: 32,213
ECU: Alexander Domínguez Carabalí (6/0), Jayro Rolando Campos León (18/0), Frickson Rafael Erazo Vivero (18/1), Segundo Alejandro Castillo Nazareno (64/5), Luis Fernando Saritama Padilla (39/0), Luis Antonio Valencia Mosquera (52/6), Walter Orlando Ayoví Corozo (74/7), Juan Carlos Paredes Reasco (18/0), Jefferson Antonio Montero Vite (22/3) [46.Michael Antonio Arroyo Mina (17/2)], Jaime Javier Ayoví Corozo (21/8) [57.Felipe Salvador Caicedo Corozo (32/6)], Arrinton Narciso Mina Villalba (8/1) [87.Dennys Andrés Quiñonez Espinoza (3/0)]. Trainer: Reinaldo Rueda Rivera (27).
Goal: Felipe Salvador Caicedo Corozo (73 penalty).

450. 11.09.2012 **URUGUAY - ECUADOR** **1-1(0-1)** 20th FIFA WC. Qualifiers
Estadio Centenario, Montevideo; Referee: Carlos Arecio Amarilla Demarqui (Paraguay); Attendance: 38,000
ECU: Alexander Domínguez Carabalí (7/0), Jayro Rolando Campos León (19/0), Frickson Rafael Erazo Vivero (19/1), Segundo Alejandro Castillo Nazareno (65/5), Luis Fernando Saritama Padilla (40/0) [84.Alex Renato Ibarra Mina (3/0)], Luis Antonio Valencia Mosquera (53/6) [*sent off 90+4*], Walter Orlando Ayoví Corozo (75/7), Tilson Oswaldo Minda Suscal (17/0), Juan Carlos Paredes Reasco (19/0), Christian Rogelio Benítez Betancourt (53/22) [90+2.Gabriel Eduardo Achilier Zurita (11/0)], Felipe Salvador Caicedo Corozo (33/7) [58.Jaime Javier Ayoví Corozo (22/8)]. Trainer: Reinaldo Rueda Rivera (28).
Goal: Felipe Salvador Caicedo Corozo (7 penalty).

451. 12.10.2012 **ECUADOR - CHILE** **3-1(1-1)** 20th FIFA WC. Qualifiers
Estadio Olímpico Atahualpa, Quito; Referee: Héber Roberto Lopes (Brazil); Attendance: 32,600
ECU: Alexander Domínguez Carabalí (8/0), Gabriel Eduardo Achilier Zurita (12/0), Frickson Rafael Erazo Vivero (20/1), Segundo Alejandro Castillo Nazareno (66/6), Luis Fernando Saritama Padilla (41/0), Walter Orlando Ayoví Corozo (76/7), Juan Carlos Paredes Reasco (20/0), Alex Renato Ibarra Mina (4/0) [78.Jefferson Antonio Montero Vite (23/3)], Christian Rogelio Benítez Betancourt (54/22), Joao Robin Rojas Mendoza (16/1) [74.Christian Fernando Noboa Tello (25/2)], Felipe Salvador Caicedo Corozo (34/9) [68.Jaime Javier Ayoví Corozo (23/8)]. Trainer: Reinaldo Rueda Rivera (29).
Goals: Felipe Salvador Caicedo Corozo (33, 57 penalty), Segundo Alejandro Castillo Nazareno (90+3).

452. 16.10.2012 **VENEZUELA - ECUADOR** **1-1(1-1)** 20th FIFA WC. Qualifiers
Estadio "José Antonio Anzoátegui", Puerto La Cruz; Referee: Néstor Fabián Pitana (Argentina); Attendance: 35,076
ECU: Alexander Domínguez Carabalí (9/0), Gabriel Eduardo Achilier Zurita (13/0), Frickson Rafael Erazo Vivero (21/1), Segundo Alejandro Castillo Nazareno (67/7), Luis Antonio Valencia Mosquera (54/6), Christian Fernando Noboa Tello (26/2) [80.Jefferson Antonio Montero Vite (24/3)], Walter Orlando Ayoví Corozo (77/7), Michael Antonio Arroyo Mina (18/2) [88.Joao Robin Rojas Mendoza (17/1)], Juan Carlos Paredes Reasco (21/0), Christian Rogelio Benítez Betancourt (55/22), Jaime Javier Ayoví Corozo (24/8) [71.Tilson Oswaldo Minda Suscal (18/0)]. Trainer: Reinaldo Rueda Rivera (30).
Goal: Segundo Alejandro Castillo Nazareno (23).

453. 06.02.2013 **PORTUGAL - ECUADOR** **2-3(1-1)**
Estádio "Dom Afonso Henriques", Guimarães; Referee: Marijo Strahonja (Croatia); Attendance: 20,288
ECU: Máximo Orlando Banguera Valdivieso (17/0), Gabriel Eduardo Achilier Zurita (14/0), Óscar Dalmiro Bagüí Angulo (18/0), Frickson Rafael Erazo Vivero (22/1), Segundo Alejandro Castillo Nazareno (68/7) [77.Henry Geovanny León León (1/0)], Luis Antonio Valencia Mosquera (55/7) [85.Eduardo Javier Morante Rosas (5/0)], Christian Fernando Noboa Tello (27/2) [61.Luis Fernando Saritama Padilla (42/0)], Juan Carlos Paredes Reasco (22/0), Jefferson Antonio Montero Vite (25/3) [61.Pedro Ángel Quiñónez Rodríguez (6/0)], Christian Rogelio Benítez Betancourt (56/22), Felipe Salvador Caicedo Corozo (35/10) [71.Alex Renato Ibarra Mina (5/0)]. Trainer: Reinaldo Rueda Rivera (31).
Goals: Luis Antonio Valencia Mosquera (2), João Pedro da Silva Pereira (61 own goal), Felipe Salvador Caicedo Corozo (70).

454. 21.03.2013 **ECUADOR - EL SALVADOR** **5-0(2-0)**
Estadio Olimpico Atahualpa, Quito; Referee: Miguel Santibáñez (Peru); Attendance: n/a
ECU: Máximo Orlando Banguera Valdivieso (18/0) [46.Alexander Domínguez Carabalí (10/0)], Gabriel Eduardo Achilier Zurita (15/0) [58.Jorge Daniel Guagua Tamayo (44/2)], Frickson Rafael Erazo Vivero (23/1), Christian Fernando Noboa Tello (28/2) [56.Luis Fernando Saritama Padilla (43/0)], Pedro Ángel Quiñónez Rodríguez (7/0), Walter Orlando Ayoví Corozo (78/7), Luis Antonio Valencia Mosquera (56/7) [63.Alex Renato Ibarra Mina (6/0)], Juan Carlos Paredes Reasco (23/0), Jefferson Antonio Montero Vite (26/4), Christian Rogelio Benítez Betancourt (57/23) [70.Joao Robin Rojas Mendoza (18/2)], Felipe Salvador Caicedo Corozo (36/12) [57.Christian Andrés Suárez Valencia (10/3)]. Trainer: Reinaldo Rueda Rivera (32).
Goals: Felipe Salvador Caicedo Corozo (18), Christian Rogelio Benítez Betancourt (36), Felipe Salvador Caicedo Corozo (46), Jefferson Antonio Montero Vite (64), Joao Robin Rojas Mendoza (89).

455. 26.03.2013 **ECUADOR - PARAGUAY** **4-1(1-1)** 20th FIFA WC. Qualifiers
Estadio Olímpico Atahualpa, Quito; Referee: Sandro Meira Ricci (Brazil); Attendance: 33,048
ECU: Alexander Domínguez Carabalí (11/0), Gabriel Eduardo Achilier Zurita (16/0), Frickson Rafael Erazo Vivero (24/1), Luis Antonio Valencia Mosquera (57/7), Christian Fernando Noboa Tello (29/2), Pedro Ángel Quiñónez Rodríguez (8/0) [70.Luis Fernando Saritama Padilla (44/0)], Walter Orlando Ayoví Corozo (79/7), Juan Carlos Paredes Reasco (24/0), Jefferson Antonio Montero Vite (27/6) [84.Alex Renato Ibarra Mina (7/0)], Christian Rogelio Benítez Betancourt (58/24), Felipe Salvador Caicedo Corozo (37/13) [80.Joao Robin Rojas Mendoza (19/2)]. Trainer: Reinaldo Rueda Rivera (33).
Goals: Felipe Salvador Caicedo Corozo (38), Jefferson Antonio Montero Vite (50), Christian Rogelio Benítez Betancourt (54), Jefferson Antonio Montero Vite (75).

456. 29.05.2013 **ECUADOR - GERMANY** **2-4(1-4)**
FAU Football Stadium, Boca Raton (United States); Referee: Ricardo Salazar (United States); Attendance: 9,000
ECU: Máximo Orlando Banguera Valdivieso (19/0), Gabriel Eduardo Achilier Zurita (17/0) [67.Jorge Daniel Guagua Tamayo (45/2)], Frickson Rafael Erazo Vivero (25/1), Segundo Alejandro Castillo Nazareno (69/7) [70.Luis Fernando Saritama Padilla (45/0)], Luis Antonio Valencia Mosquera (58/8), Christian Fernando Noboa Tello (30/2) [60.Pedro Ángel Quiñónez Rodríguez (9/0)], Walter Orlando Ayoví Corozo (80/8), Juan Carlos Paredes Reasco (25/0), Jefferson Antonio Montero Vite (28/6) [81.Marlon Jonathan de Jesús Pavón (3/0)], Christian Rogelio Benítez Betancourt (59/24) [60.Joao Robin Rojas Mendoza (20/2)], Felipe Salvador Caicedo Corozo (38/13) [35.Alex Renato Ibarra Mina (8/0)]. Trainer: Reinaldo Rueda Rivera (34).
Goals: Luis Antonio Valencia Mosquera (45), Walter Orlando Ayoví Corozo (84).

457. 07.06.2013 **PERU - ECUADOR** **1-0(1-0)** 20th FIFA WC. Qualifiers
Estadio Nacional, Lima; Referee: Marcelo de Lima Henrique (Brazil); Attendance: 37,000
ECU: Alexander Domínguez Carabalí (12/0), Jorge Daniel Guagua Tamayo (46/2), Frickson Rafael Erazo Vivero (26/1), Segundo Alejandro Castillo Nazareno (70/7), Luis Antonio Valencia Mosquera (59/8), Christian Fernando Noboa Tello (31/2), Walter Orlando Ayoví Corozo (81/8), Juan Carlos Paredes Reasco (26/0) [75.Alex Renato Ibarra Mina (9/0)], Jefferson Antonio Montero Vite (29/6), Christian Rogelio Benítez Betancourt (60/24) [87.Marlon Jonathan de Jesús Pavón (4/0)], Joao Robin Rojas Mendoza (21/2) [64.Felipe Salvador Caicedo Corozo] (39/13). Trainer: Reinaldo Rueda Rivera (35).

458. 11.06.2013 **ECUADOR - ARGENTINA** **1-1(1-1)** 20th FIFA WC. Qualifiers
Estadio Olímpico Atahualpa, Quito Referee: Enrique Cáceres Villafante (Paraguay); ; Attendance: 35,000
ECU: Alexander Domínguez Carabalí (13/0), Jorge Daniel Guagua Tamayo (47/2), Frickson Rafael Erazo Vivero (27/1), Segundo Alejandro Castillo Nazareno (71/8), Luis Antonio Valencia Mosquera (60/8), Christian Fernando Noboa Tello (32/2) [69.Luis Fernando Saritama Padilla (46/0)], Walter Orlando Ayoví Corozo (82/8), Juan Carlos Paredes Reasco (27/0) [70.Alex Renato Ibarra Mina (10/0)], Jefferson Antonio Montero Vite (30/6), Joao Robin Rojas Mendoza (22/2) [88.Juan Luis Anangonó León (2/0)], Felipe Salvador Caicedo Corozo (40/13). Trainer: Reinaldo Rueda Rivera (36).
Goal: Segundo Alejandro Castillo Nazareno (17).

459. 14.08.2013 **ECUADOR - SPAIN** **0-2(0-1)**
Estadio Monumental "Isidro Romero Carbo", Guayaquil; Referee: Wilmar Alexander Roldán Pérez (Colombia); Attendance: 45,000
ECU: Máximo Orlando Banguera Valdivieso (20/0), Jorge Daniel Guagua Tamayo (48/2), Gabriel Eduardo Achilier Zurita (18/0), Walter Orlando Ayoví Corozo (83/8), Juan Carlos Paredes Reasco (28/0), Segundo Alejandro Castillo Nazareno (72/8) [83.Óscar Dalmiro Bagüí Angulo (19/0)], Édison Vicente Méndez Méndez (107/17) [62.Michael Antonio Arroyo Mina (19/2)], Pedro Ángel Quiñónez Rodríguez (10/0) [52.Christian Fernando Noboa Tello (33/2)], Enner Remberto Valencia Lastra (2/0) [62.Alex Renato Ibarra Mina (11/0)], Joao Robin Rojas Mendoza (23/2) [70.Luis Fernando Saritama Padilla (47/0)], Felipe Salvador Caicedo Corozo (41/13) [62.Arrinton Narciso Mina Villalba (9/1)]. Trainer: Reinaldo Rueda Rivera (37).

460. 07.09.2013 **COLOMBIA - ECUADOR** **1-0(1-0)** 20th FIFA WC. Qualifiers
Estadio Metropolitano "Roberto Meléndez", Barranquilla; Referee: Héber Roberto Lopes (Brazil); Attendance: 46,000
ECU: Máximo Orlando Banguera Valdivieso (21/0), Gabriel Eduardo Achilier Zurita (19/0) [*sent off* 28], Walter Orlando Ayoví Corozo (84/8), Juan Carlos Paredes Reasco (29/0), Frickson Rafael Erazo Vivero (28/1), Segundo Alejandro Castillo Nazareno (73/8), Édison Vicente Méndez Méndez (108/17) [46.Jorge Daniel Guagua Tamayo (49/2)], Luis Antonio Valencia Mosquera (61/8), Christian Fernando Noboa Tello (34/2), Enner Remberto Valencia Lastra (3/0) [69.Joao Robin Rojas Mendoza (24/2)], Jefferson Antonio Montero Vite (31/6) [77.Alex Renato Ibarra Mina (12/0)]. Trainer: Reinaldo Rueda Rivera (38).

461. 10.09.2013 **BOLIVIA - ECUADOR** **1-1(0-0)** 20th FIFA WC. Qualifiers
Estadio "Hernando Siles Zuazo", La Paz; Referee: Paulo César de Oliveira (Brazil); Attendance: 12,043
ECU: Alexander Domínguez Carabalí (14/0), Jorge Daniel Guagua Tamayo (50/2), Walter Orlando Ayoví Corozo (85/8), Juan Carlos Paredes Reasco (30/0), Frickson Rafael Erazo Vivero (29/1), Segundo Alejandro Castillo Nazareno (74/8) [65.Christian Fernando Noboa Tello (35/2)], Luis Fernando Saritama Padilla (48/0), Luis Antonio Valencia Mosquera (62/8), Jaime Javier Ayoví Corozo (25/8) [50.Alex Renato Ibarra Mina (13/0)], Felipe Salvador Caicedo Corozo (42/14) [73.Joffre David Guerrón Méndez (18/0)], Jefferson Antonio Montero Vite (32/6). Trainer: Reinaldo Rueda Rivera (39).
Goal: Felipe Salvador Caicedo Corozo (58).

462. 11.10.2013 **ECUADOR - URUGUAY** **1-0(1-0)** 20th FIFA WC. Qualifiers
Estadio Olimpico "Atahualpa", Quito; Referee: Sandro Meira Ricci (Brazil); Attendance: 32,996
ECU: Alexander Domínguez Carabalí (15/0), Jorge Daniel Guagua Tamayo (51/2), Walter Orlando Ayoví Corozo (86/8), Juan Carlos Paredes Reasco (31/0), Frickson Rafael Erazo Vivero (30/1), Segundo Alejandro Castillo Nazareno (75/8), Luis Antonio Valencia Mosquera (63/8), Christian Fernando Noboa Tello (36/2), Enner Remberto Valencia Lastra (4/0) [71.Joao Robin Rojas Mendoza (25/2); 90.Alex Leonardo Bolaños Reascos (8/0)], Felipe Salvador Caicedo Corozo (43/14), Jefferson Antonio Montero Vite (33/7) [82.Alex Renato Ibarra Mina (14/0)]. Trainer: Reinaldo Rueda Rivera (40).
Goals: Jefferson Antonio Montero Vite (30).

463. 16.10.2013 **CHILE - ECUADOR** **2-1(2-0)** 20th FIFA WC. Qualifiers
Estadio Nacional „Julio Martínez Prádanos", Santiago; Referee: Leandro Pedro Vuaden (Brazil); Attendance: 47,458
ECU: Alexander Domínguez Carabalí (16/0), Jorge Daniel Guagua Tamayo (52/2), Walter Orlando Ayoví Corozo (87/8), Juan Carlos Paredes Reasco (32/0), Frickson Rafael Erazo Vivero (31/1), Segundo Alejandro Castillo Nazareno (76/8), Luis Antonio Valencia Mosquera (64/8), Christian Fernando Noboa Tello (37/2), Enner Remberto Valencia Lastra (5/0) [72.Jaime Javier Ayoví Corozo (26/8)], Felipe Salvador Caicedo Corozo (44/15) [89.Alex Renato Ibarra Mina (15/0)], Jefferson Antonio Montero Vite (34/7) [84.Fidel Francisco Martínez Tenorio (3/1)]. Trainer: Reinaldo Rueda Rivera (41).
Goal: Felipe Salvador Caicedo Corozo (66).

464. 15.11.2013 **ECUADOR - ARGENTINA** **0-0**
MetLife Stadium, East Rutherford, New Jersey (United States); Referee: Silviu Petrescu (Canada); Attendance: n/a
ECU: Alexander Domínguez Carabalí (17/0), Jorge Daniel Guagua Tamayo (53/2), Walter Orlando Ayoví Corozo (88/8), Juan Carlos Paredes Reasco (33/0), Frickson Rafael Erazo Vivero (32/1), Segundo Alejandro Castillo Nazareno (77/8), Luis Antonio Valencia Mosquera (65/8) [89.Joao Robin Rojas Mendoza (26/2)], Christian Fernando Noboa Tello (38/2) [84.Fernando Vicente Gaibor Orellana (1/0)], Enner Remberto Valencia Lastra (6/0) [60.Alex Renato Ibarra Mina (16/0)], Felipe Salvador Caicedo Corozo (45/15) [73.Jaime Javier Ayoví Corozo (27/8)], Jefferson Antonio Montero Vite (35/7) [73.Fidel Francisco Martínez Tenorio (4/1)]. Trainer: Reinaldo Rueda Rivera (42).

465. 19.11.2013 **HONDURAS - ECUADOR** **2-2(0-1)**
BBVA Compass Stadium, Houston (United States); Referee: Ricardo Salazar (United States); Attendance: 10,000
ECU: Máximo Orlando Banguera Valdivieso (22/0), Jorge Daniel Guagua Tamayo (54/2), Walter Orlando Ayoví Corozo (89/8), Juan Carlos Paredes Reasco (34/0) [*sent off* 76], Frickson Rafael Erazo Vivero (33/1), Segundo Alejandro Castillo Nazareno (78/8) [73.Fernando Vicente Gaibor Orellana (2/0)], Luis Antonio Valencia Mosquera (66/8) [46.Joao Robin Rojas Mendoza (27/2)], Christian Fernando Noboa Tello (39/2) [89.Luis Fernando Saritama Padilla (49/0)], Alex Renato Ibarra Mina (17/0) [82.Cristian Leonel Ramírez Zambrano (1/0)], Fidel Francisco Martínez Tenorio (5/1) [73.Enner Remberto Valencia Lastra (7/1)], Jaime Javier Ayoví Corozo (28/9) [59.Jefferson Antonio Montero Vite (36/7)].Trainer: Reinaldo Rueda Rivera (43).
Goals: Jaime Javier Ayoví Corozo (15), Enner Remberto Valencia Lastra (89).

INTERNATIONAL PLAYERS

FM/Nr	Name	DOB	Caps	Goals	Period, Club
(1/008)	ABRIL Antonio		5	0	1938-1942
(14/041)	ACEVEDO Pedro		11	0	1942-1945
(399/460)	ACHILIER ZURITA Gabriel Eduardo	24.03.1985	19	0	2008-2013, Deportivo Azogues (1/0), CS Emelec Guayaquil (18/0).
(218/323)	ACHILLE Jimmy	30.07.1968	1	0	1994, CD Espoli Quito (1/0).
(20/049)	AGUAYO Víctor		11	4	1945-1947
(151/258)	AGUINAGA GARZÓN Alex Darío	09.07.1968	109	23	1987-2004, Sociedad Deportivo Quito (26/5), Club Impulsora del Deportivo Necaxa (76/17), CDSC Cruz Azul Ciudad de México (3/1), LDU de Quito (4/0).
(301/394)	AGUINAGA GARZÓN Juan Francisco	04.01.1978	5	1	2001, CD Espoli Quito (5/1).
(87/171)	AGUIRRE Enrique		1	0	1973, Club Deportivo Cuenca (1/0).
(379/440)	AGUIRRE ICAZA José Ramón	05.01.1983	4	0	2006-2007, CS Emelec Guayaquil (4/0).
(116/206)	AGUIRRE Ramiro		2	0	1979, CD Técnico Universitario Ambato (2/0).
(11/031)	AGUIRRE Vicente		1	0	1941, Italia
(117/210)	ALARCÓN Jorge Luis		7	2	1979, LDU de Quito (7/2).
(21/050)	ALBÁN Luis		1	0	1945
(25/053)	ALBORNOZ Guillermo		1	1	1945
(151/254)	ALCÍVAR Claudio G.	15.07.1966	9	0	1987-1989, Barcelona SC Guayaquil (9/0).
(6/023)	ALCÍVAR Marino		14	3	1939-1942, Panamá SC Guayaquil
(57/116)	ALMEIDA Francisco		2	0	1959
(124/216)	ALTAFUYA Duval Regio		1	0	1981, CS Everest Guayaquil (1/0).
(46/091)	ALUME Carlos		1	0	1955
(14/037)	ALVAREZ Enrique		17	1	1941-1947
(3/015)	ALVAREZ Nicolás		2	0	1938
(333/409)	AMBROSI ZAMBRANO Vicente Paúl	14.10.1980	35	0	2003-2009, LDU de Quito (34/0), CA Rosario Central (1/0).
(272/371)	ANANGONÓ Franklin	12.12.1974	7	0	1999, Truenos Cuautitlán (7/0).
(448/501)	ANANGONÓ LEÓN Juan Luis	13.04.1989	2	0	2012-2013, CD El Nacional Quito (1/0), AA Argentinos Juniors Buenos Aires (1/0).
(36/079)	ANDRADE Bolívar		2	0	1949, CS Norte America Guayaquil (2/0).
(33/073)	ANDRADE Guido		6	1	1949, Barcelona SC Guayaquil (6/1).
(12/034)	ANGULO Clemente		1	0	1941, Titan
(65/130)	ANSALDO Pablo		7	0	1963-1965, Barcelona SC Guayaquil (7/0).
(383/450)	ARAGÓN ESPINOZA Rorys Andrés	28.06.1982	3	0	2007-2010, R Standard Liège (2/0), CD El Nacional Quito (1/0).
(435/495)	ARAUJO LÓPEZ Norberto Carlos	13.10.1978	3	0	2011, LDU de Quito (3/0).
(2/013)	ARENAS Manuel		6	3	1938-1939
(151/260)	ARGUËLLO Mauricio		1	0	1987, Barcelona SC Guayaquil (1/0).
(51/104)	ARGUELLO Raúl		12	0	1957-1960, CS Emelec Guayaquil (6/0)
(124/224)	ARIAS Antonio		1	0	1981, CD Universidad Católica Quito (1/0).
(6/019)	ARIAS Luis		2	0	1939
(130/232)	ARMAS Wilson Antonio		14	0	1983-1985, CD El Nacional Quito (14/0).
(421/479)	ARROYO MINA Michael Antonio	23.04.1987	19	2	2010-2013, Sociedad Deportivo Quito (2/0), San Luis FC (14/2), Barcelona SC Guayaquil (3/0).
(33/071)	ARTEAGA Víctor		9	1	1949-1953, CS Norte America Guayaquil (9/1).
(225/332)	ASENCIO ESPINOZA Nicolás Geovanny	26.04.1975	20	0	1995-2003, SD Aucas Quito (3/0), Barcelona SC Guayaquil (1/0), Universidad Autónoma de Guadalajara (5/0), Barcelona SC Guayaquil (11/0).
(59/118)	AUREA Nelson Vicente		1	0	1959
(151/263)	AVILÉS AGUIRRE Ney Raúl	17.02.1965	54	15	1987-1993, CS Emelec Guayaquil (37/10), Club Sporting Cristal Lima (3/0), Barcelona SC Guayaquil (14/5).
(423/482)	AYOVÍ COROZO Jaime Javier	21.02.1988	28	9	2010-2013, CS Emelec Guayaquil (4/1), Deportivo Toluca FC (6/0), CF Pachuca (14/7), LDU de Quito (4/1).
(302/395)	AYOVÍ COROZO Walter Orlando	11.08.1979	89	8	2001-2013, CS Emelec Guayaquil (5/0), Barcelona SC Guayaquil (12/0), CD El Nacional Quito (22/4), CF Monterrey (43/4), CF Pachuca (7/0).
(266/358)	AYOVÍ MOSQUERA Marlon Ritter	27.09.1971	76	5	1998-2007, Sociedad Deportivo Quito (75/5), Barcelona SC Guayaquil (1/0).
(65/131)	AZÓN Néstor		4	2	1963, CS Everest Guayaquil (4/2).
(353/424)	BAGÜÍ ANGULO Óscar Dalmiro	10.12.1982	19	0	2005-2013, CD Olmedo Riobamba (17/0), CS Emelec Guayaquil (2/0).
(124/218)	BALDEÓN Jaime Fernando		21	4	1981-1987, Sociedad Deportivo Quito (1/0), CD El Nacional Quito (20/4).
(326/403)	BALDEÓN PARREÑO Johnny Alejandro	15.06.1981	12	3	2002-2006, Sociedad Deportivo Quito (12/3).
(41/087)	BALSECA José Vicente		24	1	1953-1963, CS Emelec Guayaquil (24/1).
(399/462)	BANGUERA VALDIVIESO Máximo Orlando	16.12.1985	22	0	2008-2013, Club Espoli Quito (3/0), Barcelona SC Guayaquil (19/0).
(116/207)	BARDALES José Julio		4	0	1979, Barcelona SC Guayaquil (4/0).
(151/259)	BARRETO Freddy		2	0	1987, Sociedad Deportivo Quito (2/0).
(230/337)	BATALLAS Jorge	15.04.1969	6	1	1996, CS Emelec Guayaquil (6/1).
(153/268)	BATIOJA Stony Marin	20.04.1964	3	0	1987-1991, Club Deportivo Cuenca (2/0), Valdez SC Guayaquil (1/0).
(90/178)	BAYONA Julio Vicente	05.12.1948	2	0	1973, CS Emelec Guayaquil (2/0).
(363/432)	BENÍTEZ BETANCOURT Christian Rogelio	01.05.1986	60	24	2005-2013, CD El Nacional Quito (13/4), Club Santos Laguna Torreón (15/5), Birmingham City FC (4/1), Club Santos Laguna Torreón (4/5), CF América Ciudad de México (24/9).

(136/245)	BENÍTEZ Hermen De Jesús	04.05.1961	**19**	**8**	1984-1989, CD El Nacional Quito (19/8).
(33/068)	BERMEO Marcos		**5**	**0**	1949, SD Aucas Quito (5/0).
(248/351)	BLANDÓN QUIÑÓNEZ Jimmy Roberto	20.11.1969	**30**	**0**	1997-2000, Club Deportivo Cuenca (24/0), Club Blooming Santa Cruz (3/0), Barcelona SC Guayaquil (3/0).
(7/025)	BOHÓRQUEZ Fonfredes		**1**	**0**	1939
(62/123)	BOLAÑOS Jorge Washington	26.09.1943	**28**	**0**	1960-1973, CS Emelec Guayaquil (19/0), Barcelona SC Guayaquil (9/0).
(386/452)	BOLAÑOS LEÓN Luis Alberto	27.03.1985	**11**	**0**	2007, LDU de Quito (11/0).
(381/444)	BOLAÑOS REASCOS Alex Leonardo	22.01.1985	**8**	**0**	2007-2013, Barcelona SC Guayaquil (3/0), Sociedad Deportivo Quito (5/0).
(439/497)	BONE SÁNCHEZ Adrián Javier	08.09.1988	**2**	**0**	2011, Sociedad Deportivo Quito (2/0).
(40/080)	BONNARD Alfredo		**20**	**0**	1953-1965, CS Norte America Guayaquil (6/0), UD Valdes (5/0), (8/0), CS Patria Guayaquil (1/0).
(296/392)	BORJA MORENO Richard Alfonso	23.07.1980	**1**	**0**	2000, CS Emelec Guayaquil (1/0).
(363/431)	BORJA VALENCIA Félix Alexander	02.04.1983	**23**	**3**	2005-2011, CD El Nacional Quito (6/2), Olympiakos SFP Peiraiás (2/0), CD El Nacional Quito (2/0), Olympiakos SFP Peiraiás (7/1), 1.FSV Mainz 05 (4/0), CF Pachuca (2/0).
(392/455)	BRAN OROZCO Jimmy Alfredo	15.07.1979	**1**	**0**	2007, Deportivo Azogues (1/0).
(152/265)	BRAVO Freddy Egberto	12.04.1962	**11**	**0**	1987-1991, CD Filanbanco Guayaquil (3/0), Barcelona SC Guayaquil (8/0)
(266/361)	BRIONES Julio	01.07.1975	**1**	**0**	1998, Delfin SC Manta (1/0).
(241/343)	BURBANO de LARA TORRES Juan Carlos	15.02.1969	**18**	**0**	1996-2002, CD El Nacional Quito (18/0).
(119/213)	BURBANO Fabian Vicente		**3**	**0**	1979-1981, CD Técnico Universitario Ambato (3/0).
(185/295)	BURBANO Roberth Javier	27.09.1970	**15**	**0**	1991-2000, CD Universidad Católica Quito (8/0), LDU de Quito (1/0), Club Deportivo Cuenca (3/0), CD El Nacional Quito (3/0).
(66/132)	BUSTAMANTE Miguel	17.02.1940	**9**	**0**	1963, CS Everest Guayaquil (4/0), Barcelona SC Guayaquil (5/0).

(82/161)	CABEZAS Marcelo Vicente	05.04.1945	**8**	**0**	1970-1975, CD El Nacional Quito (8/0).
(272/372)	CAGUA PADILLA John Patricio	29.09.1979	**10**	**0**	1999-2000, Sociedad Deportivo Quito (6/0), Barcelona SC Guayaquil (4/0).
(359/427)	CAICEDO COROZO Felipe Salvador	05.09.1988	**45**	**15**	2005-2013, Rocafuerte FC Guayaquil (1/0), FC Basel (15/2), Manchester City FC (11/1), Sporting Clubde de Portugal Lisboa (1/0), Levante UD Valencia (3/2), FK Lokomotiv Moskva (14/10).
(370/438)	CAICEDO Darwin Deivis	25.05.1983	**1**	**0**	2006, CS Emelec Guayaquil (1/0).
(353/425)	CAICEDO DE LA CRUZ Luis Andrés	12.05.1979	**17**	**0**	2005-2007, CD Olmedo Riobamba (17/0).
(115/202)	CAICEDO Donald Iván	15.01.1949	**1**	**0**	1977, Club Deportivo Cuenca (1/0).
(431/490)	CAICEDO GRACIA Flavio David	28.02.1988	**3**	**0**	2011, CD El Nacional Quito (3/0).
(349/420)	CAICEDO QUIÑONEZ Geovanny Banner	28.03.1981	**9**	**0**	2004-2011, Barcelona SC Guayaquil (2/0), Sociedad Deportivo Quito (3/0), LDU de Quito (4/0).
(267/363)	CAICEDO RENTERIA Pavel Cipriano	15.06.1977	**3**	**0**	1999, CS Emelec Guayaquil (3/0).
(51/105)	CAISAGUANO Julio		**4**	**0**	1957
(328/405)	CALDERÓN CARCELÉN Walter Richard	17.10.1977	**11**	**0**	2003-2009, Club Deportivo Cuenca (8/0), LDU de Quito (3/0).
(432/493)	CALDERÓN ESPINOZA Diego Armando	26.10.1986	**5**	**0**	2011-2012, LDU de Quito (5/0).
(268/369)	CALLE CAMACHO Renán	09.08.1976	**13**	**1**	1999-2007, SD Aucas Quito (9/1), CD El Nacional Quito (2/0), LDU de Quito (2/0).
(83/163)	CAMACHO Jefferson Donald	18.05.1949	**23**	**0**	1972-1977, CS Emelec Guayaquil (23/0).
(381/443)	CAMACHO PAREDES Geovanny Francisco	15.12.1984	**1**	**0**	2007, Barcelona SC Guayaquil (1/0).
(338/412)	CAMPOS LEÓN Jairo Rolando	19.07.1984	**19**	**0**	2004-2012, SD Aucas Quito (1/0), LDU de Quito (7/0), Clube Atletico Mineiro Belo Horizonte (2/0), Sociedad Deportivo Quito (3/0), Barcelona SC Guayaquil (6/0).
(82/158)	CAMPOVERDE Carlos German		**3**	**0**	1970-1977, CD El Nacional Quito (3/0).
(46/094)	CAÑARTE Sorin Climaco		**20**	**1**	1955-1966, (4/0), Barcelona SC Guayaquil (16/1).
(267/365)	CANDELARIO DÍAZ Moisés Antonio	24.08.1978	**9**	**0**	1999-2004, CS Emelec Guayaquil (9/0).
(155/275)	CANGA QUINTERO Urlin Bautista	29.08.1959	**1**	**0**	1987, CS Emelec Guayaquil (1/0).
(26/059)	CANTOS Enrique		**17**	**4**	1947-1957, Barcelona SC Guayaquil (17/4).
(130/235)	CANTOS Gabriel		**1**	**0**	1983, LDU de Portoviejo (1/0).
(33/074)	CANTOS Jorge		**3**	**0**	1949, Barcelona SC Guayaquil (3/0).
(142/250)	CAPURRO BAUTISTA Luis Enrique	01.05.1961	**100**	**1**	1985-2003, CD Filanbanco Guayaquil (19/0), CS Emelec Guayaquil (26/0), Club Cerro Porteño (16/0), CS Emelec Guayaquil (20/0), Barcelona SC Guayaquil (12/1), LDU de Quito (3/0), *unattached* (4/0).
(267/367)	CAPURRO BAUTISTA Rafael Alberto	24.10.1970	**5**	**0**	1999-2000, CD Espoli Quito (5/0).
(193/304)	CARABALÍ CEVALLOS Héctor Jhonny	15.02.1972	**58**	**2**	1992-1999, Valdez SC Guayaquil (5/1), Barcelona SC Guayaquil (47/1), São Paulo FC (6/0).
(217/322)	CARABALÍ GONZÁLEZ Wilson Iván	11.08.1972	**11**	**0**	1994-1996, Barcelona SC Guayaquil (3/0), CS Emelec Guayaquil (8/0).
(283/377)	CARABALÍ PABÓN Héctor Rolando	18.04.1977	**1**	**0**	1999, Sociedad Deportivo Quito (1/0).
(185/293)	CARCELÉN CHALÁ Nixon Aníbal	27.09.1969	**40**	**1**	1991-1999, Sociedad Deportivo Quito (37/1), LDU de Quito (3/0).
(216/320)	CARCELÉN José Germán	02.02.1968	**1**	**0**	1994, CD El Nacional Quito (1/0).
(124/223)	CÁRDENAS Jesús José	04.04.1959	**1**	**0**	1981, CS Emelec Guayaquil (1/0).
(77/146)	CARDEÑAS Walter	17.01.1944	**6**	**0**	1969-1972, Barcelona SC Guayaquil (6/0).
(97/181)	CARRERA Fausto Rubén	12.03.1950	**13**	**0**	1975-1977, CD Universidad Católica Quito (13/0).
(75/138)	CARRERA Paúl "Polo"		**21**	**3**	1966-1983, LDU de Quito (2/0), CD El Nacional Quito (6/1), LDU de Quito (7/2), CD América Quito (3/0), Sociedad Deportivo Quito (3/0).

(28/063)	CARRILLO Luis Alfredo		**4**	**0**	1947-1949, CSD Macará Ambato
(124/220)	CARRION Carlos		**1**	**0**	1981, CD América Quito (1/0).
(153/267)	CARRIÓN Luis Alberto		**2**	**0**	1987, CD Filanbanco Guayaquil (2/0).
(88/175)	CASTAÑEDA Gonzalo	10.01.1948	**11**	**3**	1973-1975, CS Emelec Guayaquil (3/0), Club Deportivo Cuenca (8/3).
(329/406)	CASTILLO NAZARENO Segundo Alejandro	15.05.1982	**78**	**8**	2003-2013, CD El Nacional Quito (14/1), FK Crvena zvezda Beograd (19/1), Everton FC Liverpool (8/0), Wolverhampton Wanderers FC (5/0), Sociedad Deportivo Quito (7/1), CF Pachuca (14/4), CF Puebla (4/1), Al Hilal Saudi FC Riyadh (7/0).
(368/435)	CASTRO CADENA Carlos Ernesto	24.09.1978	**7**	**0**	2005-2008, CD El Nacional Quito (3/0), Barcelona SC Guayaquil (4/0).
(167/280)	CEVALLOS Alex Bolívar	03.08.1967	**4**	**0**	1988-1996, CD Filanbanco Guayaquil (1/0), CS Emelec Guayaquil (30).
(6/020)	CEVALLOS Ernesto		**8**	**0**	1939-1941, Panamá SC Guayaquil
(27/062)	CEVALLOS Víctor		**3**	**0**	1947
(219/327)	CEVALLOS VILLAVICENCIO José Francisco	17.04.1971	**88**	**0**	1994-2009, Barcelona SC Guayaquil (76/0), CD Once Caldas Manizales (1/0), LDU de Quito (11/0).
(193/305)	CHALÁ GUERRÒN Cléber Manuel	29.06.1971	**87**	**6**	1992-2004, CD El Nacional Quito (55/6), Southampton FC (7/0), CD El Nacional Quito (17/0), Sociedad Deportivo Quito (8/0).
(408/465)	CHECA VILLAMAR Luis Armando	21.12.1983	**8**	**0**	2008-2011, Sociedad Deportivo Quito (8/0).
(200/318)	CHÉRREZ Luis Anibal	19.01.1968	**3**	**0**	1993-1994, CD El Nacional Quito (2/0), Sociedad Deportivo Quito (1/0).
(152/264)	CHIRIBOGA Héctor Lautaro	23.03.1966	**7**	**0**	1987-1988, LDU de Quito (8/0).
(33/072)	CHUCHUCA Sigfredo Agapito		**8**	**1**	1949-1953, Barcelona SC Guayaquil (8/1).
(253/353)	CONSTANTE Marco Vinicius	20.03.1967	**3**	**0**	1997, CD El Nacional Quito (3/0).
(77/150)	CONTRERAS Francisco		**1**	**0**	1969, Sociedad Deportivo Quito (1/0).
(153/271)	CORDOVA Diego		**2**	**0**	1987, CA River Plate Buenos Aires (2/0).
(193/303)	CORONEL Dannes Arsenio	04.05.1973	**27**	**0**	1992-2000, CS Emelec Guayaquil (26/0), CD El Nacional Quito (1/0).
(83/168)	CORONEL Miguel Angel	30.09.1952	**4**	**1**	1972, Barcelona SC Guayaquil (4/1).
(293/384)	COROZO Jorge Wilber	24.04.1965	**1**	**0**	2000, CD Olmedo Riobamba (1/0).
(333/408)	COROZO MOSQUERA Kléber Gutemberg	16.09.1975	**3**	**0**	2003-2004, CD El Nacional Quito (3/0).
(409/471)	COROZO QUINÓÑEZ Franklin Orlando	15.02.1981	**2**	**0**	2008, Sociedad Deportivo Quito (2/0).
(124/221)	CORRALES Luis		**2**	**0**	1981, LDU de Quito (2/0).
(267/366)	CORREA Francisco	29.10.1974	**3**	**0**	1999, SD Aucas Quito (3/0).
(359/428)	CORTÉZ ARROYO José Luis	21.11.1979	**8**	**0**	2005-2008, SD Aucas Quito (3/0), CD Espoli Quito (1/0), Sociedad Deportivo Quito (4/0).
(61/122)	CRUZ AVILA, Alberto		**1**	**0**	1959
(218/325)	CUBERO GUERRA César Fabián	29.04.1971	**6**	**0**	1994-2000, Sociedad Deportivo Quito (2/0), CD Espoli Quito (4/0).
(130/236)	CUVI RIVERA Hamilton Emilio	8.05.1960	**45**	**7**	1983-1989, AD 9 de Octubre Guayaquil (9/1), CD Filanbanco Guayaquil (36/6).
(74/137)	DA SILVA "HELINHO" Helio Carreira		**3**	**0**	1965-1966, Barcelona SC Guayaquil (3/0).
(268/368)	DE JESÚS BORJA Omar Andrés	19.02.1977	**17**	**0**	1999-2008, SD Aucas Quito (6/0), CD El Nacional Quito (3/0), Barcelona SC Guayaquil (8/0).
(340/413)	DE JESÚS DELGADO Erick Rolando	08.11.1982	**10**	**0**	2004-2008, CD El Nacional Quito (10/0).
(423/483)	DE JESÚS PAVÓN Marlon Jonathan	09.04.1991	**4**	**0**	2010-2013, CD El Nacional Quito (1/0), Sociedad Deportivo Quito (1/0), CS Emelec Guayaquil (2/0).
(221/330)	DE LA CRUZ BERNARDO Ulises Hernán	08.02.1974	**101**	**6**	1995-2010, Barcelona SC Guayaquil (2/0), LDU de Quito (34/2), Barcelona SC Guayaquil (4/0), Hibernian FC Edinburgh (16/1), Aston Villa FC Birmingham (32/2), Reading FC London (11/1), LDU de Quito (2/0).
(193/307)	DE LA CRUZ Oswaldo	13.12.1968	**15**	**1**	1992-1997, CD El Nacional Quito (15/1).
(440/499)	DE LA TORRE MARTÍNEZ Brayan José	11.01.1991	**1**	**0**	2011, Barcelona SC Guayaquil (1/0).
(41/088)	DE LA TORRE Raúl Pio		**2**	**0**	1953, CS Norte America Guayaquil (2/0).
(136/244)	DE NEGRI José Elias	20.06.1954	**14**	**1**	1984-1987, CD El Nacional Quito (14/1).
(83/162)	DELGADO Carlos Omar	07.02.1950	**26**	**0**	1972-1983, CS Emelec Guayaquil (2/0), CD El Nacional Quito (24/0).
(218/324)	DELGADO CHALÁ Agustín Javier	23.12.1974	**72**	**31**	1994-2011, Barcelona SC Guayaquil (1/0), CD El Nacional Quito (5/2), Deportivo Independiente Medellín (9/3), CDSC Cruz Azul Ciudad de México (7/2), Club Impulsora del Deportivo Necaxa (21/13), Southampton FC (6/2), SD Aucas Quito (8/4), Club Universidad Nacional Ciudad de México(2/0), Barcelona SC Guayaquil (8/3), LDU de Quito (4/2), *unattached* (1/0).
(167/283)	DELGADO Fausto Anibal	20.05.1960	**1**	**0**	1988, CD Técnico Universitario Ambato (1/0).
(75/140)	DELGADO MENA Jaime		**1**	**0**	1966, CS Emelec Guayaquil (1/0).
(222/331)	DÍAZ Energio	15.09.1969	**5**	**3**	1995, Club Deportivo Cuenca (5/3).
(239/342)	DÍAZ Jorge	24.02.1973	**4**	**0**	1996, CD Espoli Quito (4/0).
(429/485)	DOMÍNGUEZ CARABALÍ Alexander	05.06.1987	**17**	**0**	2011-2013, LDU de Quito (17/0).
(151/261)	DOMÍNGUEZ Edgar	23.12.1962	**14**	**0**	1987-1988, CD Filanbanco Guayaquil (14/0).
(80/155)	ECHANIQUE Alfonso Enrique	10.09.1945	**1**	**0**	1969, CS Everest Guayaquil (1/0).
(385/451)	ELIZAGA FERRERO Marcelo Ramón	19.04.1972	**23**	**0**	2007-2011, CS Emelec Guayaquil (17/0), Sociedad Deportivo Quito (6/0).
(7/024)	ELIZALDE Leónidas		**1**	**0**	1939
(134/241)	ENCALADA Alfredo		**2**	**0**	1983, Sociedad Deportivo Quito (2/0).
(154/272)	ENRÍQUEZ GARZÓN Carlos Milton	22.05.1966	**1**	**0**	1987, Sociedad Deportivo Quito (1/0).
(88/173)	ENRÍQUEZ Manuel E.	12.10.1946	**1**	**0**	1973, CD El Nacional Quito (1/0).

(431/489)	ERAZO VIVERO Frickson Rafael	05.05.1988	33	1	2011-2013, CD El Nacional Quito (14/1), Barcelona SC Guayaquil (19/0).
(116/205)	ESCALANTE Luis Esteban	12.01.1945	2	0	1979, CD El Nacional Quito (2/0).
(363/433)	ESCOBAR ARCE Ángel Gabriel	30.03.1981	2	0	2005-2008, Barcelona SC Guayaquil (1/0), CSD Macará Ambato (1/0).
(77/149)	ESPINOSA Mario		4	0	1969, Barcelona SC Guayaquil (4/0).
(193/301)	ESPINOZA CASTILLO Jacinto Alberto	24.11.1969	37	0	1992-2004, CS Emelec Guayaquil (5/0), Delfín SC Manta (16/0), CS Emelec Guayaquil (8/0), LDU de Quito (8/0).
(289/383)	ESPINOZA PAVÓN Giovanny Patricio	12.04.1977	89	3	2000-2009, SD Aucas Quito (12/1), CF Monterrey (5/0), SD Aucas Quito (3/0), LDU de Quito (42/1), SBV Vitesse Arnhem (13/1), Cruzeiro EH Belo Horizonte (8/0), Barcelona SC Guayaquil (3/0), Birmingham City FC (3/0).
(83/166)	ESTUPIÑAN Italo Eugenio	01.01.1952	14	4	1972-1973, CSD Macará Ambato (4/0), CD El Nacional Quito (10/4).
(151/253)	FAJARDO BARZOLA Kléber Emilson	04.01.1965	35	0	1987-1994, CS Emelec Guayaquil (35/0).
(185/296)	FERNÁNDEZ VERNAZA Angel Oswaldo	02.08.1971	76	12	1991-2004, CD Green Cross Manta (2/0), CS Emelec Guayaquil (49/10), CD El Nacional Quito (25/2).
(197/313)	FERRI Héctor Americo	17.10.1968	7	0	1992-2000, SD Aucas Quito (1/0), CD El Nacional Quito (6/0).
(293/389)	FIGUEROA CÁCERES Gustavo Omar	30.08.1978	5	0	2000-2006, SD Aucas Quito (4/0), CD El Nacional Quito (1/0).
(105/189)	FIGUEROA Ecuador		12	0	1976-1981, CS Emelec Guayaquil (5/0), (3/0), LDU de Quito (4/0).
(414/477)	FLEITAS SILVEIRA Julio Marcelo	01.09.1973	5	0	2009-2010, CS Emelec Guayaquil (5).
(1/011)	FREIRE César Augusto		12	3	1938-1941, Gimnástico Guayaquil
(464/503)	GAIBOR ORELLANA Fernando Vicente	08.10.1991	2	0	2013, CS Emelec Guayaquil (2/0).
(51/108)	GALARZA Jaime		14	0	1957-1963
(408/464)	GÁMEZ QUINTERO Enrique Roberto	13.07.1981	2	0	2008, CSD Macará Ambato (2/0).
(46/090)	GANDO Gerónimo		2	0	1955
(64/128)	GANDO Pedro		6	0	1963, CS Everest Guayaquil (6/0).
(185/292)	GARAY Juan Carlos	15.09.1968	28	1	1991-1996, CD El Nacional Quito (13/1), LDU de Quito (15/0).
(370/437)	GARCÉS PRADO Luis Miguel	12.08.1982	1	0	2006, CSD Macará Ambato (1/0).
(283/379)	GARCÍA Carlos	24.09.1978	1	0	1999, CS Emelec Guayaquil (1/0).
(105/190)	GARCÍA Eduardo		3	0	1976-1977, CS Emelec Guayaquil (3/0).
(12/033)	GARNICA Carlos		3	0	1941-1945, Titan
(26/055)	GARNICA César		7	1	1947-1949, SD Aucas Quito
(196/312)	GAVICA José Eduardo	08.01.1969	34	4	1992-2003, Barcelona SC Guayaquil (31/4), Delfin SC Manta (1/0), Barcelona SC Guayaquil (2/0).
(15/044)	GAVILÁNEZ Guillermo		8	0	1942-1947
(277/375)	GEORGE TENORIO Fricson Vinicio	15.10.1976	18	0	1999-2007, Barcelona SC Guayaquil (18/0).
(309/396)	GÓMEZ CACERES Luis Oswaldo	20.04.1972	12	1	2001-2003, Barcelona SC Guayaquil (12/1).
(105/191)	GÓMEZ Juan Carlos		8	0	1976-1977, LDU de Quito (2/0),
(360/429)	GÓMEZ LEDESMA Christian Adrián	29.10.1979	2	0	2005, CD Olmedo Riobamba (2/0).
(50/100)	GÓMEZ Rómulo		13	0	1955-1965, (9/0), Barcelona SC Guayaquil (4/0).
(97/186)	GÓMEZ Wilmer Alberto	15.05.1951	4	0	1975, CS Emelec Guayaquil (4/0).
(47/097)	GONZABAY Honorato		12	0	1955-1959
(124/214)	GONZÁLEZ Edgar		1	0	1981, CS Everest Guayaquil (1/0).
(253/354)	GONZÁLEZ Héctor	05.04.1972	1	0	1997, CD Olmedo Riobamba (1/0).
(230/338)	GONZÁLEZ Luis Ernesto	25.11.1972	14	0	1996-1999, LDU de Quito (14/0).
(131/238)	GOROSABEL Carlos		3	0	1983, LDU de Portoviejo (3/0).
(431/488)	GOVEA TENORIO Juan José	27.01.1990	1	0	2011, Club Deportivo Cuenca (1/0).
(106/199)	GRANDA Luis Augusto		21	0	1977-1983, CD El Nacional Quito (21/0).
(251/352)	GRAZIANI LENTINI Ariel José	07.06.1971	34	15	1997-2000, CS Emelec Guayaquil (14/9), CA Atletico Morelia (11/4), Dallas Burns (9/2).
(266/362)	GRUESO QUIÑÓNEZ Carlos Armando	18.09.1975	1	0	1998, CD Espoli Quito (1/0).
(301/393)	GUAGUA TAMAYO Jorge Daniel	28.09.1981	54	2	2001-2013, CD El Nacional Quito (22/1), CA Colón de Santa Fé (4/0), CS Emelec Guayaquil (3/1), Barcelona SC Guayaquil (3/0), CD El Nacional Quito (6/0), LDU de Quito (3/0), CF Atlante Cancún (3/0), Sociedad Deportivo Quito (11/0).
(185/297)	GUAMÁN Juan Helio	27.06.1965	10	0	1991-1995, LDU de Quito (10/0).
(60/119)	GUERRA Ernesto		1	0	1959, Sociedad Deportivo Quito (1/0).
(184/290)	GUERRERO José F. "Lupo"	17.09.1967	10	1	1987-1995, CD El Nacional Quito (9/1), Barcelona SC Guayaquil (1/0).
(162/278)	GUERRERO Nelson	12.09.1962	11	1	1988-1989, SD Aucas Quito (5/0), LDU de Quito (6/1).
(83/167)	GUERRERO Rafael Enrique	28.12.1951	8	0	1972-1975, CS Emelec Guayaquil (4/0)
(381/447)	GUERRERO VÁSQUEZ Fernando Alexander	30.09.1989	3	0	2007-2010, Real Madrid CF (2/0), CSD Independiente José Terán (1/0).
(313/401)	GUERRÓN MÉNDEZ Hugo Stalin	01.01.1978	1	0	2002, Sociedad Deportivo Quito (1/0).
(392/456)	GUERRÓN MÉNDEZ Joffre David	28.04.1985	18	0	2007-2013, LDU de Quito (6/0), Getafe CF (5/0), Cruzeiro EC Belo Horizonte (5/0), Club Atlético Paranaense (1/0), Beijing Guoan FC (1/0).
(293/385)	GUERRÓN MÉNDEZ Raúl Fernando	12.10.1976	34	0	2000-2004, Sociedad Deportivo Quito (34/0).
(408/469)	GUEVARA CANGÁ Fabricio Jonathan	16.02.1989	1	0	2008, CD El Nacional Quito (1/0).
(97/185)	GUEVARA Washington		2	0	1975, LDU de Quito (2/0).
(84/169)	GUIME Marco Antonio	25.04.1949	13	3	1972-1973, CS Emelec Guayaquil (13/3).
(40/083)	GUZMÁN Eduardo		5	1	1953, CS Everest Guayaquil (5/1).

(20/047)	HENRÍQUEZ Jorge		**18**	**0**	1945-1953
(1/009)	HERRERA Enrique		**8**	**4**	1938-1939
(13/036)	HERRERA José		**6**	**0**	1941-1942, Daring
(193/308)	HERRERA LARREA Diego Rodrigo	20.04.1969	**11**	**0**	1992-2000, LDU de Quito (9/0), CD El Nacional Quito (2/0).
(313/399)	HIDALGO Carlos Ramón	09.02.1979	**1**	**0**	2002, CS Emelec Guayaquil (1/0).
(392/457)	HIDALGO MALDONADO Fernando Roberto	20.05.1985	**13**	**0**	2007-2010, Sociedad Deportivo Quito (1/0), Barcelona SC Guayaquil (12/0).
(399/463)	HIDALGO ORTEGA Carlos Ramón	09.02.1979	**1**	**0**	2008, Barcelona SC Guayaquil (1/0).
(2/012)	HUNGRÍA Luis		**14**	**0**	1938-1942, Panamá SC Guayaquil
(197/314)	HURTADO Ángel	07.11.1967	**2**	**0**	1992-1993, CD Green Cross Manta (1/0), CS Emelec Guayaquil (1/0)
(193/302)	HURTADO ANGULO Iván Jacinto	16.08.1974	**167**	**5**	1992-2010, CS Emelec Guayaquil (29/2), Club Atlético Celaya (17/1), Universidad Autónoma de Nuevo León (32/0), CF La Piedad (10/1), Barcelona SC Guayaquil (19/1), Real Murcia CF (4/0), Universidad Autónoma de Nuevo León (3/0), CF Pachuca (11/0), Al-Arabi SC Doha (8/0), Al-Ahli SC Jeddah (2/0), CD Club Atlético Nacional Medellín (11/0), Barcelona SC Guayaquil (4/0), CD Los Millonários Bogotá (10/0), Sociedad Deportivo Quito (7/0).
(293/390)	HURTADO HURTADO Camilo David	14.03.1981	**1**	**0**	2000, LDU de Quito (1/0).
(138/247)	HURTADO Marcelo	10.11.1959	**10**	**0**	1984-1985, CD Filanbanco Guayaquil (10/0)
(193/306)	HURTADO ROA Eduardo Estíguar	12.01.1969	**74**	**26**	1992-2000,Valdez SC Guayaquil (2/0), CSD Colo Colo Santiago (19/7), CS Emelec Guayaquil (10/6), Los Angeles Galaxy (26/8), New York Metro Stars (8/3), LDU de Quito (2/0), New England Revolution (2/1), LDU de Quito (5/1).
(186/299)	HURTADO ZURITA Edwin Patricio	09.08.1970	**10**	**0**	1991-2000, CD El Nacional Quito (2/0), LDU de Quito (8/0),
(248/349)	IBARRA Geovanny Oswaldo	08.09.1969	**27**	**0**	1997-2004, CD El Nacional Quito (27/0).
(431/487)	IBARRA MINA Alex Renato	20.01.1991	**17**	**0**	2011-2013, CD El Nacional Quito (1/0), SBV Vitesse Arnhem (16/0).
(413/475)	IBARRA TIXE Miguel Washington	08.09.1984	**4**	**0**	2009-2010, Club Espoli Quito (2/0), CDP Universidad Católica de Ecuador Quito (2/0).
(40/081)	IZAGUIRRE Jorge		**11**	**0**	1953-1960, AD 9 de Octubre Guayaquil
(169/285)	IZQUIERDO Jimmy	28.05.1961	**10**	**1**	1988-1989, Barcelona SC Guayaquil (10/1).
(155/274)	JACOMÉ Juan Carlos	06.11.1960	**1**	**0**	1987, LDU de Quito (1/0).
(229/335)	JACOMÉ PONCE Rolando Santiago	04.04.1974	**4**	**0**	1995-2000, LDU de Quito (4/0).
(14/040)	JIMÉNEZ José María		**20**	**5**	1942-1949
(64/127)	JOHNSON José		**5**	**0**	1963, CS Everest Guayaquil (5/0).
(288/382)	JUÁREZ DEVICO Carlos Alberto	24.04.1972	**5**	**0**	2000, CS Emelec Guayaquil (5/0).
(293/387)	JUSTAVINO Jorge Enrique	26.03.1978	**2**	**0**	2000, CD Espoli Quito (2/0).
(266/360)	KAVIEDES LLORENTY Jaime Iván	24.10.1977	**57**	**16**	1998-2011, CS Emelec Guayaquil (1/0), Perugia Calcio (5/2), RC Celta de Vigo (6/3), Real Valladolid CF (7/1), RC Celta de Vigo (5/2), FC do Porto (1/0), Barcelona SC Guayaquil (4/2), RC Celta de Vigo (1/1), Sociedad Deportivo Quito (2/0), Barcelona SC Guayaquil (1/0), Crystal Palace FC London (3/1), Barcelona SC Guayaquil (4/0), AA Argentinos Juniors Buenos Aires (9/2), CD El Nacional Quito (4/2), CSD Macará Ambato (2/0), CD El Nacional Quito (2/0).
(387/453)	KLIMOWICZ LAGANÁ Javier Hernán	10.03.1977	**2**	**0**	2007, Club Deportivo Cuenca (2/0).
(97/182)	KLINGER Fausto	15.04.1953	**23**	**1**	1975-1979, Club Deportivo Cuenca (17/0), Barcelona SC Guayaquil (6/1).
(126/230)	KLINGER Orly		**22**	**1**	1981-1985, LDU de Portoviejo (10/1)
(379/441)	LADINES GARCÉS Jorge Washington	21.09.1986	**4**	**0**	2006-2007, CS Emelec Guayaquil (4/0).
(125/226)	LANDETA John		**1**	**0**	1981, CD Universidad Católica Quito (1/0).
(345/417)	LANZA MOYANO Damian Enrique	10.04.1982	**5**	**0**	2004-2005, Club Deportivo Cuenca (5/0).
(313/400)	LARA ANANGONÓ Christian Rolando	27.04.1980	**28**	**4**	2002-2009, CD El Nacional Quito (21/3), LDU de Quito (6/1), Barcelona SC Guayaquil (1/0), LDU de Quito (.
(51/107)	LARRAZ Jorge		**6**	**4**	1957
(64/126)	LARREA Armando Tito	11.05.1943	**10**	**1**	1963-1965, CS Everest Guayaquil (6/1), LDU de Quito (3/0).
(75/139)	LASSO GARCÍA José Félix	28.05.1945	**27**	**7**	1966-1975, Barcelona SC Guayaquil (6/2), CS Emelec Guayaquil (13/2), CD El Nacional Quito (14/3).
(341/415)	LASTRA MINA Mario Roberto	30.04.1979	**3**	**0**	2004, SD Aucas Quito (3/0).
(139/248)	LATINO Pedro Carlos		**6**	**0**	1984-1985, Sociedad Deportivo Quito (1/0), CD Filanbanco Guayaquil (5/0).
(8/026)	LAURIDO Jorge		**5**	**0**	1939-1941, Panamá SC Guayaquil
(61/120)	LECARO Vicente		**18**	**0**	1959-1969, Barcelona SC Guayaquil (18/0).
(453/502)	LEÓN LEÓN Henry Geovanny	20.04.1983	**1**	**0**	2013, CSD Independiente José Terán Sangolquí (1/0).
(105/192)	LICIARDI Angel Luis	02.03.1947	**9**	**7**	1976-1977, Club Deportivo Cuenca (9/7).
(1/010)	LÓPEZ Francisco		**3**	**0**	1938
(33/067)	LOVATO Mario		**4**	**0**	1949-1953, SD Aucas Quito (4/0).
(51/103)	MACÍAS Luciano		**23**	**2**	1957-1969, Barcelona SC Guayaquil (23/2).
(229/333)	MACÍAS Roberth	12.07.1969	**5**	**0**	1995-1996, LDU de Portoviejo (1/0), LDU de Quito (4/0).
(151/255)	MACÍAS Wilson Homero	30.09.1962	**32**	**0**	1987-1991, CD Filanbanco Guayaquil (30/0), Barcelona SC Guayaquil (2/0).
(431/492)	MADRID José Enrique	21.04.1988	**1**	**0**	2011, CD El Nacional Quito (1/0).
(119/212)	MADRUÑERO Juan Eulogio	26.04.1954	**4**	**0**	1979-1981, Barcelona SC Guayaquil (4/0).
(77/151)	MALAGON Servelio		**3**	**0**	1969, Barcelona SC Guayaquil (3/0).
(130/233)	MALDONADO Carlos Hans	25.07.1957	**20**	**4**	1983-1985, CD El Nacional Quito (20/4).

(218/326)	MALDONADO Édison	07.06.1972	**10**	**1**	1994-1999, SD Aucas Quito (10/1).
(77/144)	MALDONADO Fernando Gilberto	21.01.1945	**6**	**0**	1969-1972, CD El Nacional Quito (6/0).
(34/077)	MALDONADO Rafael		**7**	**1**	1949-1953, SD Aucas Quito (6/1), CS Patria Guayaquil (1/0).
(83/165)	MANTILLA Luis Cristóbal	28.11.1949	**21**	**2**	1972-1979, CD Universidad Católica Quito (21/2).
(194/310)	MANTILLA Ronney	20.10.1967	**1**	**0**	1992, LDU de Quito (1/0).
(40/084)	MARAÑÓN Luis		**6**	**0**	1953, CS Everest Guayaquil (6/0).
(27/060)	MARÍN Heráclides		**14**	**0**	1947-1953, LDU de Guayaquil (9/0), Barcelona SC Guayaquil (5/0).
(151/256)	MARÍN Pablo Estebán	22.08.1965	**15**	**0**	1987-1988, Club Deportivo Cuenca (15/0).
(151/257)	MARSETTI Pietro Raúl	22.02.1965	**24**	**3**	1987-1989, LDU de Quito (24/3).
(51/109)	MARTÍNEZ Ezio		**1**	**0**	1957
(1/001)	MARTÍNEZ ROIZ Francisco A.		**6**	**0**	1938
(409/473)	MARTÍNEZ TENORIO Fidel Francisco	15.02.1990	**5**	**1**	2008-2013, Cruzeiro EH Belo Horizonte (2/1), Club Tijuana Xoloitzcuintles de Caliente (3/0).
(91/180)	MARTÍNEZ V.		**1**	**0**	1973,
(239/341)	MATAMBA CABEZAS Segundo Manuel	19.05.1976	**1**	**0**	1996, Club Deportivo Cuenca (1/0).
(416/478)	MATAMOROS CHUNGA Hólger Eduardo	04.01.1985	**1**	**0**	2009, Club Deportivo Cuenca (1/0).
(46/092)	MATUTE Isidro		**9**	**3**	1955-1957
(14/038)	MEDINA Napoleón		**17**	**0**	1942-1947
(82/156)	MEJÍA Edwin Roberto	05.09.1944	**4**	**0**	1970-1973, CD América Quito (4/0).
(20/048)	MEJÍA Eloy		**6**	**0**	1945
(50/101)	MEJÍA Hugo		**7**	**0**	1955-1963, (1/0), CS Everest Guayaquil (6/0).
(243/348)	MÉNDEZ Edmundo Marcelo	05.12.1968	**11**	**0**	1996-1997, Club Deportivo Cuenca (11/0).
(89/177)	MÉNDEZ Eduardo Enrique	13.01.1947	**8**	**0**	1973, CD El Nacional Quito (8/0).
(285/381)	MÉNDEZ MÉNDEZ Édison Vicente	16.03.1979	**108**	**17**	2000-2013, Sociedad Deportivo Quito (31/3), CD El Nacional Quito (10/1), Irapuato FC (6/1), FC Santos Laguna Torreón (5/2), LDU de Quito (17/3), PSV Eindhoven (19/4), LDU de Quito (4/1), CS Emelec Guayaquil (13/2), LDU de Quito (3/0).
(105/193)	MÉNDEZ Washington	17.02.1952	**10**	**0**	1976-1977, Universidad Catolica Quito (10/0).
(176/289)	MENDOZA CEVALLOS Víctor	24.08.1961	**4**	**0**	1989-1993, SD Aucas Quito (2/0), Barcelona SC Guayaquil (2/0).
(19/046)	MENDOZA José		**11**	**1**	1942-1947
(10/029)	MENDOZA Luis		**21**	**1**	1941-1947, Panamá SC Guayaquil
(155/276)	MERA Geovanny Alfonso	16.08.1962	**5**	**1**	1987, CD El Nacional Quito (5/1).
(313/398)	MERCADO ORTÍZ Orfilio Octavio	23.04.1974	**1**	**0**	2002, CD Olmedo Riobamba (1/0)
(6/018)	MERINO José		**7**	**0**	1939-1942, Panamá SC Guayaquil
(68/133)	MERIZALDE Bolívar		**3**	**0**	1963-1966, CS Everest Guayaquil (1/0), CS Emelec Guayaquil (2/0).
(46/093)	MERIZALDE Colón		**4**	**0**	1955-1957
(124/217)	MESIAS Ernesto		**2**	**1**	1981, CS Everest Guayaquil (2/1).
(399/461)	MINA ARBOLEDA Isaac Bryan	17.10.1980	**22**	**2**	2008-2011, Sociedad Deportivo Quito (22/2).
(72/136)	MINA Felipe		**2**	**0**	1965, CS Emelec Guayaquil (2/0).
(328/404)	MINA MERCADO Roberto Javier	07.11.1984	**12**	**0**	2003-2006, CA Huracán Buenos Aires (2/0), CD El Nacional Quito (5/0), Dallas FC (5/0).
(87/172)	MINA Rómulo Dúdar	05.09.1949	**1**	**0**	1973, CSD Macará Ambato (1/0).
(408/466)	MINA VILLALBA Arrinton Narciso	25.11.1982	**9**	**1**	2008-2013, Manta FC (3/0), CSD Independiente José Terran Sangolquí (2/0), Barcelona SC Guayaquil (3/1), CF América Ciudad de México (1/0).
(168/284)	MINDA José Federico	10.11.1961	**3**	**0**	1988-1989, CS Emelec Guayaquil (3/0).
(409/472)	MINDA SUSCAL Tilson Oswaldo	26.07.1983	**18**	**0**	2008-2012, Sociedad Deportivo Quito (15/0), CD Chivas Carson (3/0).
(53/110)	MIRANDA Júpiter		**3**	**0**	1957
(28/065)	MOLINA Alfredo		**1**	**0**	1947
(10/027)	MOLINA Ignacio		**4**	**0**	1941, AD 9 de Octubre Guayaquil
(172/286)	MONTANERO SOLEDISPA Jimmy Gustavo	24.08.1960	**16**	**0**	1989-1993, Barcelona SC Guayaquil (16/0).
(194/309)	MONTAÑO ANGULO Alberto Guillermo	23.03.1970	**57**	**3**	1992-2000, CD Green Cross Manta (1/0), Barcelona SC Guayaquil (35/1), CD Santiago Wanderers Valparaíso (1/0), Barcelona SC Guayaquil (20/2)
(429/486)	MONTAÑO ANGULO Edson Eli	15.03.1991	**4**	**0**	2011, KAA Gent (4/0).
(379/439)	MONTAÑO QUIÑÓNEZ Jairo Eliecer	08.07.1979	**6**	**0**	2006-2007, Barcelona SC Guayaquil (6/0).
(23/052)	MONTENEGRO Luis		**3**	**0**	1945
(397/459)	MONTERO VITE Jefferson Antonio	01.09.1989	**36**	**7**	2007-2013, CS Emelec Guayaquil (1/0), CSD Independiente José Terán (5/2), Villarreal CF (7/0), Levante UD Valencia (2/0), Real Betis Balompié Sevilla (5/0), CA Monarcas Morelia (16/5).
(220/329)	MORA CALDERÓN José Marco	8.08.1975	**8**	**1**	1995, Barcelona SC Guayaquil (8/1).
(362/430)	MORA MEDRANO Cristian Rafael	28.08.1982	**20**	**0**	2005-2009, LDU de Quito (17/0), CD El Nacional Quito (3/0).
(151/251)	MORALES Carlos Luis	12.06.1965	**40**	**0**	1987-1999, Barcelona SC Guayaquil (24/0), CA Independiente Avellaneda (5/0), Barcelona SC Guayaquil (9/0), CS Emelec Guayaquil (1/0), CD Espoli Quito (1/0).
(76/141)	MORALES Héctor	15.07.1944	**5**	**0**	1966-1973, LDU de Quito (1/0), CD Universidad Católica Quito (2/0), CD El Nacional Quito (2/0).
(283/378)	MORALES MONTENEGRO Santiago Damián	03.05.1979	**4**	**0**	1999-2003, CD El Nacional Quito (3/0), Sociedad Deportivo Quito (1/0).
(438/496)	MORANTE ROSAS Eduardo Javier	01.06.1987	**5**	**0**	2011-2013, CS Emelec Guayaquil (4/0), LDU de Quito (1/0).
(274/373)	MOREIRA IBARRA Luis Heberthson	23.09.1978	**6**	**0**	1999, CS Emelec Guayaquil (6/0).
(136/246)	MORENO José Vicente	25.05.1962	**5**	**0**	1984-1985, LDU de Quito (5/0).
(152/266)	MOSQUERA Luis Bolivar	14.12.1964	**7**	**0**	1987-1988, CD El Nacional Quito (7/0).
(172/287)	MUÑOZ MARTÍNEZ Carlos Antonio	13.11.1964	**35**	**4**	1989-1993, CD Filanbanco Guayaquil (7/0), Barcelona SC Guayaquil (28/4).
(153/270)	MUÑOZ Pedro Mauricio	13.02.1965	**9**	**1**	1987-1988, CD Filanbanco Guayaquil (2/0), LDU de Quito (7/1).

(70/134)	MUÑOZ Washington Liben	26.06.1945	**17**	**6**	1965-1973, Barcelona SC Guayaquil (17/6).
(57/112)	NALL Flavio		**3**	**0**	1959
(1/002)	NARANJO J		**1**	**0**	1938
(130/231)	NARVÁEZ Luis Orlando		**5**	**0**	1983, CD El Nacional Quito (5/0).
(408/467)	NAZARENO SIMISTERRA Geovanny Enrique	17.01.1988	**9**	**0**	2008-2011, Sociedad Deportivo Quito (1/0), Barcelona SC Guayaquil (8/0).
(105/194)	NIEVES Wilson		**15**	**1**	1976-1981, CD El Nacional Quito (11/0), Barcelona SC Guayaquil (4/1).
(411/474)	NOBOA TELLO Christian Fernando	09.04.1985	**39**	**2**	2009-2013, FK Rubin Kazan (22/2), FK Dinamo Moskva (17/0).
(162/279)	NORIEGA ESCOBAR Raúl Alfredo	04.01.1970	**28**	**2**	1988-1997, Barcelona SC Guayaquil (28/2).
(79/154)	NORIEGA Juan Raúl	02.02.1943	**9**	**0**	1969-1973, Barcelona SC Guayaquil (9/0).
(229/334)	OBREGÓN CANCINO Alfonso Andrés	12.05.1972	**58**	**0**	1995-2004, CD Espoli Quito (12/0), LDU de Quito (10/0), Delfín SC Manta (11/0), LDU de Quito (25/0).
(241/347)	OLEAS GÓMEZ José	11.02.1969	**1**	**0**	1996, CD Espoli Quito (1/0).
(78/152)	ORDENANA Luis Manuel		**1**	**0**	1969, CS Emelec Guayaquil (1/0).
(241/345)	ORDÓÑEZ MARTÍNEZ Evelio Agustín	03.11.1973	**19**	**1**	1996-2004, CD Técnico Universitario Ambato (2/0), CD El Nacional Quito (17/1).
(26/058)	ORTIZ Eduardo		**6**	**0**	1947
(85/170)	ORTIZ Jesús Emilio	25.12.1947	**13**	**0**	1972-1977, CS Emelec Guayaquil (13/0).
(116/208)	PAES José Francisco	26.03.1946	**12**	**0**	1979-1981, Barcelona SC Guayaquil (12/0).
(368/436)	PALACIOS HERRERIA Pablo David	05.02.1982	**16**	**2**	2005-2011, SD Aucas Quito (2/0), Sociedad Deportivo Quito (2/0), Barcelona SC Guayaquil (12/2).
(57/113)	PALACIOS Leonardo		**10**	**2**	1959-1963, SD Aucas Quito (6/0), CS Everest Guayaquil (4/2).
(53/111)	PARDO Hugo		**4**	**0**	1957
(363/434)	PAREDES DUARTE Armando Aquiles	18.06.1984	**2**	**0**	2005-2006, Barcelona SC Guayaquil (1/0), CS Emelec Guayaquil (1/0).
(293/386)	PAREDES MEJÍA Wellington Pinta	06.11.1974	**2**	**0**	2000, CD Olmedo Riobamba (2/0)
(423/481)	PAREDES REASCO Juan Carlos	08.07.1987	**34**	**0**	2010-2013, Sociedad Deportivo Quito (21/0), Barcelona SC Guayaquil (13/0).
(88/174)	PARRAGA Belford		**9**	**0**	1973-1981, Club Deportivo Cuenca (4/0), AD 9 de Octubre Guayaquil (5/0).
(116/209)	PARRAGA Roque		**2**	**0**	1979, CD Técnico Universitario Ambato (2/0).
(231/339)	PAZMIÑO Carlos	10.07.1970	**6**	**0**	1996, CD Espoli Quito (6/0).
(167/282)	PAZMIÑO Segundo	25.04.1964	**1**	**0**	1988, SD Aucas Quito (1/0).
(97/184)	PAZYMIÑO José Fabián	16.03.1953	**19**	**4**	1975-1985, CD El Nacional Quito (19/4).
(83/164)	PELÁEZ Víctor Hugo	12.02.1947	**21**	**0**	1972-1975, Barcelona SC Guayaquil (21/0).
(82/160)	PEÑAHERRERA Raúl Patricio	15.03.1947	**2**	**0**	1970-1972, CD El Nacional Quito (2/0).
(6/022)	PERALTA José		**7**	**0**	1939-1941, Daring
(91/179)	PÉREZ Miguel Oswaldo	08.03.1945	**9**	**0**	1973-1979, CD El Nacional Quito (9/0).
(116/204)	PERLAZA Flavio		**24**	**1**	1979-1985, CD El Nacional Quito (8/1), Barcelona SC Guayaquil (16/0).
(338/410)	PERLAZA NAPA José Luis	06.10.1981	**4**	**0**	2004-2006, CD Olmedo Riobamba (4/0).
(65/129)	PINEDA Carlos		**5**	**1**	1963-1966, CS Emelec Guayaquil (5/1).
(115/201)	PINILLOS Walter		**1**	**0**	1977, SD Aucas Quito (1/0).
(40/082)	PINTO Daniel		**12**	**0**	1953-1957, CS Norte America Guayaquil (6/0), CS Emelec Guayaquil (2/0).
(408/470)	PINTO QUIRÓZ Jefferson David	23.03.1990	**1**	**0**	2008, CS Emelec Guayaquil (1/0).
(439/498)	PITA MORA Marwin Jonathan	17.04.1985	**1**	**0**	2011, CD El Nacional Quito (1/0).
(433/494)	PLATA COTERA Joao Jimmy	01.03.1992	**1**	**0**	2011, Toronto FC (1/0).
(267/364)	POROSO CAICEDO Augusto Jesús	13.04.1974	**38**	**1**	1999-2004, CS Emelec Guayaquil (38/1).
(76/142)	PORTILLA Enrique José	14.05.1944	**15**	**0**	1966-1973, LDU de Quito (5/0), CD Universidad Católica Quito (10/0).
(26/057)	POZO Gonzalo		**9**	**0**	1947-1949, SD Aucas Quito
(421/480)	PRECIADO BRAVO Édison Andres	18.04.1986	**2**	**0**	2010, CD El Nacional Quito (2/0).
(136/243)	PRECIADO Luis		**6**	**0**	1984-1985, CD Filanbanco Guayaquil (6/0).
(64/124)	QUIJANO Alfonso	01.08.1943	**15**	**0**	1963-1969, Barcelona SC Guayaquil (15/0).
(382/449)	QUINÓÑEZ ANGULO Marco Antonio	28.09.1977	**1**	**0**	2007, CS Emelec Guayaquil (1/0).
(413/476)	QUIÑÓNEZ CABEZA Michael Jackson	21.06.1984	**5**	**1**	2009-2011, CD El Nacional Quito (3/0), Sociedad Deportivo Quito (2/1).
(282/376)	QUIÑÓNEZ CANGÁ Christian Fernando	12.09.1981	**2**	**0**	1999-2000, Barcelona SC Guayaquil (2/0).
(197/317)	QUIÑÓNEZ Carlos		**1**	**0**	1992, CD Universidad Católica Quito (1/0).
(346/419)	QUIÑÓNEZ Carlos	04.11.1975	**1**	**0**	2004, Club Deportivo Cuenca (1/0).
(431/491)	QUIÑÓNEZ ESPINOZA Dennys Andrés	12.03.1992	**3**	**0**	2011-2012, Barcelona SC Guayaquil (1/0), CD El Nacional Quito (2/0).
(139/249)	QUIÑÓNEZ Holguer Abraham	18.09.1962	**50**	**0**	1984-1999, Barcelona SC Guayaquil (30/0), CS Emelec Guayaquil (5/0), Club Deportivo Pereira (7/0), Barcelona SC Guayaquil (8/0).
(125/228)	QUIÑÓNEZ Lupo Senén	12.02.1957	**27**	**3**	1981-1987, CS Emelec Guayaquil (5/0), Manta Sporting Club (6/1), Barcelona SC Guayaquil (16/2).
(388/454)	QUIÑÓNEZ RODRÍGUEZ Pedro Ángel	04.03.1986	**10**	**0**	2007-2013, CD el Nacional Quito (2/0), CS Emelec Guayaquil (8/0).
(124/215)	QUINTEROS Carlos		**11**	**0**	1981-1989, SD Aucas Quito (8/0), CD Filanbanco Guayaquil (3/0).
(77/145)	QUINTEROS Eulogio	07.04.1942	**4**	**0**	1969, CD El Nacional Quito (4/0).
(130/234)	QUINTEROS Tulio		**6**	**0**	1983-1989, Barcelona SC Guayaquil (6/0).
(338/411)	QUIROZ VILLÓN Mario David	08.09.1982	**31**	**0**	2004-2012, CD El Nacional Quito (16/0), Barcelona SC Guayaquil (2/0), CS Emelec Guayaquil (12/0), LDU de Quito (1/0).

(57/115)	RAFFO Carlos Alberto		**13**	**10**	1959-1963, CS Emelec Guayaquil (13/10).
(185/291)	RAMÍREZ CASTRO Erwin Aníbal	13.11.1971	**8**	**1**	1991, CD Green Cross Manta (8/1).
(465/504)	RAMÍREZ ZAMBRANO Cristian Leonel	12.08.1994	**1**	**0**	2013, TSV Fortuna Düsseldorf (1/0).
(77/147)	RANGEL Simon Bolívar	24.07.1940	**2**	**0**	1969, CD El Nacional Quito (2/0).
(10/030)	RAYMONDI CHÁVEZ, Enrique		**9**	**1**	1941-1945, Panamá SC Guayaquil
(64/125)	RAYMONDI CONTRERAS, Enrique		**8**	**6**	1963-1965, CS Emelec Guayaquil (8/6).
(266/357)	REASCO YANO Néicer	23.07.1977	**56**	**0**	1999-2011, LDU de Quito (34/0), São Paulo FC (7/0), LDU de Quito (15/0).
(197/316)	REASCOS David		**1**	**0**	1992, CD Técnico Universitario Ambato (1/0).
(57/117)	REEVES PATTERSON, Ruperto		**6**	**0**	1959-1963, Barcelona SC Guayaquil (6/0).
(125/227)	REVELO Gorky Eugenio	06.08.1957	**2**	**0**	1981, CD Técnico Universitario Ambato (2/0).
(229/336)	RIVERA CORTAZAR Wágner Apolinario	18.09.1972	**24**	**0**	1996-1997, CD Espoli Quito (11/0), CR Flamengo Rio de Janeiro (3/0), Barcelona SC Guayaquil (10/0).
(186/298)	RIVERA José Higinio	11.01.1963	**3**	**0**	1991, Sociedad Deportivo Quito (3/0).
(27/061)	RIVEROS Ricardo		**15**	**0**	1947-1953, CS Emelec Guayaquil
(135/242)	RODRÍGUEZ Israel	16.11.1960	**11**	**0**	1983-1985, CS Emelec Guayaquil (11/0).
(116/203)	RODRÍGUEZ Milton		**8**	**0**	1979, CD El Nacional Quito (8/0).
(76/143)	RODRÍGUEZ Tom Eugenio	23.01.1945	**5**	**1**	1966-1970, Deportivo Español Guayaquil (1/0), CD El Nacional Quito (4/1).
(408/468)	ROJAS MENDOZA Joao Robin	14.07.1989	**27**	**2**	2008-2013, CD River Plate Ecuador Guayaquil (1/0), CS Emelec Guayaquil (9/0), CA Monarcas Morelia (12/2), Cruz Azul FC Ciudad de México (5/0).
(349/422)	ROMERO Juan Pablo	24.10.1979	**2**	**0**	2004, LDU de Quito (2/0).
(10/028)	ROMO Alfonso		**2**	**0**	1941, AD 9 de Octubre Guayaquil
(97/183)	RON Carlos René		**14**	**1**	1975-1979, CD El Nacional Quito (14/1).
(106/195)	RON IBARRA Jorge Vinicio	06.02.1954	**24**	**2**	1976-1984, CD El Nacional Quito (17/2), CD Universidad Católica Quito (7/0).
(185/294)	RON VIVER Ivo Norman	17.02.1968	**10**	**2**	1991-1995, CS Emelec Guayaquil (10/2).
(1/003)	RONQUILLO Eloy		**10**	**0**	1938-1939
(14/039)	RONQUILLO Romualdo		**3**	**0**	1942
(172/288)	ROSERO Julio César	11.06.1964	**11**	**0**	1989, CD El Nacional Quito (11/0).
(255/355)	ROSERO RODRÍGUEZ Hidrobo Vilson	24.08.1974	**5**	**0**	1997-2004, CD El Nacional Quito (4/0), SD Aucas Quito (1/0).
(131/237)	RUÍZ Bolívar Gustavo	29.04.1959	**2**	**0**	1983, LDU de Quito (2/0).
(248/350)	RUÍZ Simón Patricio	14.03.1965	**4**	**0**	1997, CD El Nacional Quito (4/0).
(47/098)	SAETEROS Mario		**7**	**0**	1955-1959
(293/388)	SALAS NARVÁEZ Franklin Agustín	30.08.1981	**26**	**2**	2000-2011, LDU de Quito (25/2), Imbabura SC Ibarra (1/0).
(51/106)	SALCEDO Gonzalo		**5**	**0**	1957
(35/078)	SALGADO Hernán		**4**	**0**	1949, SD Aucas Quito (4/0).
(151/252)	SAMANIEGO Lenin		**1**	**0**	1987, LDU de Quito (1/0).
(28/064)	SÁNCHEZ Carlos		**22**	**0**	1947-1957, Barcelona SC Guayaquil
(151/262)	SÁNCHEZ Joffre		**2**	**0**	1987, Barcelona SC Guayaquil (2/0).
(219/328)	SÁNCHEZ LUZURIAGA Wellington Eduardo	19.06.1974	**44**	**3**	1994-2004, CD El Nacional Quito (14/2), Los Angeles Galaxy (4/0), CS Emelec Guayaquil (26/1).
(3/014)	SANDOVAL Víctor		**1**	**0**	1938
(11/032)	SANTOLIVA Luis		**2**	**0**	1941, Gimnástico Guayaquil
(332/407)	SARITAMA PADILLA Luis Fernando	20.10.1983	**49**	**0**	2003-2013, Sociedad Deportivo Quito (15/0), Tigres de la Universidad Autónoma de Nuevo León (1/0), CF América Ciudad de Mexico (2/0), Sociedad Deportivo Quito (23/0), LDU de Quito (8/0).
(14/042)	SEMPÉRTEGUI Manuel		**3**	**0**	1942
(236/340)	SIMÕES DE SOUSA Gilson	25.03.1967	**17**	**1**	1996-1997, Barcelona SC Guayaquil (17/1).
(241/346)	SMITH CHÁVEZ Eduardo Fabián	23.02.1966	**12**	**0**	1996-1997, CS Emelec Guayaquil (12/0).
(1/004)	SOLA Jorge		**4**	**0**	1938
(345/416)	SOLEDISPA CORTÉS Leonardo Javier	15.01.1983	**8**	**0**	2004-2006, Barcelona SC Guayaquil (8/0).
(6/017)	SOLÍS Augusto		**3**	**0**	1939
(42/089)	SOLÍS Galo		**8**	**0**	1953-1955, Barcelona SC Guayaquil
(40/085)	SOLÓRZANO César		**8**	**0**	1953-1957, Barcelona SC Guayaquil
(57/114)	SPENCER HERRERA Alberto Pedro	06.12.1937	**11**	**4**	1959-1972, CS Everest Guayaquil (4/1), CA Peñarol Montevideo (4/3), Barcelona SC Guayaquil (3/0).
(34/076)	SPENCER Marcos		**4**	**0**	1949, Panamá SC Guayaquil (4/0).
(12/035)	STACEY Eduardo		**1**	**0**	1941, Gimnástico Guayaquil
(167/281)	SUÁREZ Juan Carlos		**1**	**0**	1988, CSD Macará Ambato (1/0).
(1/007)	SUÁREZ RIZZO Alfonso		**13**	**2**	1938-1941, Panamá SC Guayaquil
(425/484)	SUÁREZ VALENCIA Cristian Andrés	02.11.1985	**9**	**3**	2010-2013, CD El Nacional Quito (1/0), Club Santos Laguna Torreón (8/3), CF Pachuca (1/0).
(25/054)	SUÁREZ Víctor		**1**	**0**	1945
(100/187)	TAPIA Gustavo		**4**	**0**	1975, LDU de Quito (4/0).
(77/148)	TAPIA Jorge Ernesto		**17**	**1**	1969-1975, LDU de Quito (17/1).
(325/402)	TENORIO BASTIDAS Otelino George	01.02.1980	**13**	**6**	2002-2005, CS Emelec Guayaquil (5/2), Al Nassr ASC Riyadh (2/0), CD El Nacional Quito (6/4).
(161/277)	TENORIO Byron Zózimo	14.06.1965	**54**	**3**	1988-1997, CD El Nacional Quito (30/0), Barcelona SC Guayaquil (23/3), CS Emelec Guayaquil (1/0).
(105/197)	TENORIO José Daniel	23.10.1952	**5**	**0**	1976-1977,
(88/176)	TENORIO Juan José	27.06.1949	**4**	**0**	1973, CS Emelec Guayaquil (4/0).
(117/211)	TENORIO Mario		**17**	**1**	1979-1983, Club Deportivo Cuenca (7/1), Barcelona SC Guayaquil (10/0).

(312/397)	TENORIO MEDINA Carlos Vicente	14.05.1979	**51**	**12**	2001-2009, LDU de Quito (16/3), Al Nassr ASC Riyadh (3/0), Al Sadd SC Doha (28/8), Al-Nasr SC Dubai (4/1).
(266/359)	TENORIO MONTAÑO Edwin Rolando	16.06.1976	**78**	**0**	1998-2007, SD Aucas Quito (3/0), Club Jorge Wilstermann Cochabamba (4/0), SD Aucas Quito (6/0), Tiburones Rojos de Veracruz (11/0), *unattached* (2/0), Barcelona SC Guayaquil (48/0), LDU de Quito (4/0).
(195/311)	TENORIO QUIÑÓNEZ Máximo Wilson	30.09.1969	**38**	**3**	1992-1997, CS Emelec Guayaquil (33/3), Barcelona SC Guayaquil (5/0).
(78/153)	TOBAR Ramiro		**15**	**0**	1969-1975, LDU de Quito (15/0)
(15/045)	TORRES Celso		**8**	**0**	1942-1947
(34/075)	TORRES Félix		**6**	**0**	1949, CS Emelec Guayaquil (6/0).
(105/198)	TORRES GARCÉS Carlos		**17**	**2**	1976-1985, CS Emelec Guayaquil (9/2), Barcelona SC Guayaquil (2/0), 9 de Octubre Milagro (6/0).
(33/069)	TORRES Luis		**2**	**0**	1949, SD Aucas Quito (2/0).
(349/421)	TRIVIÑO BURGOS Juan Ignacio	03.09.1980	**5**	**0**	2004-2005, CS Emelec Guayaquil (5/0).
(48/099)	TRIVIÑO Elías Gereneldo		**3**	**0**	1955
(61/121)	UBILLA Jaime		**1**	**0**	1959
(6/021)	UNAMUNO Ramón		**1**	**0**	1939
(186/300)	UQUILLAS Manuel Antonio	19.11.1963	**6**	**0**	1991-1996, Barcelona SC Guayaquil (4/0), CD Espoli Quito (1/0), Barcelona SC Guayaquil (1/0).
(352/423)	URRUTIA ESPINOZA Patricio Javier	15.10.1977	**27**	**3**	2004-2009, LDU de Quito (27/3).
(82/157)	UTRERAS Lincoln	26.12.1946	**1**	**0**	1970, Sociedad Deportivo Quito (1/0).
(153/269)	VACA Luis Eduardo		**1**	**0**	1987, Barcelona SC Guayaquil (1/0).
(381/445)	VACA QUINDE Éder Javier	25.12.1985	**3**	**1**	2007, Sociedad Deportivo Quito (3/1).
(125/225)	VALDIVIESO Freddy		**1**	**0**	1981, CD América Quito (1/0).
(268/370)	VALENCIA Ángel	27.01.1977	**4**	**0**	1999, CD Espoli Quito (4/0).
(82/159)	VALENCIA Atahúlfo	01.07.1944	**1**	**0**	1970, CD América Quito (1/0).
(126/229)	VALENCIA Digner		**4**	**0**	1981, Barcelona SC Guayaquil (4/0).
(124/219)	VALENCIA Eddie José	27.09.1959	**5**	**0**	1981-1985, AD 9 de Octubre Guayaquil (2/0), CD Filanbanco Guayaquil (3/0).
(445/500)	VALENCIA LASTRA Enner Remberto	11.04.1989	**7**	**1**	2012-2013, CS Emelec Guayaquil (7/1).
(340/414)	VALENCIA MOSQUERA Luis Antonio	04.08.1985	**66**	**8**	2004-2013, CD El Nacional Quito (11/3), Villarreal CF (3/0), CD Recreativo Huelva (7/0), Wigan Athletic FC (17/1), Manchester United FC (28/4).
(263/356)	VALENCIA Pedro Pablo	29.06.1969	**1**	**0**	1997, Club Deportivo Cuenca (1/0).
(46/095)	VALENCIA Ricardo		**4**	**0**	1955
(28/066)	VARGAS José		**17**	**1**	1947-1957, Barcelona SC Guayaquil
(1/006)	VASCONEZ José M		**9**	**0**	1938-1939
(131/239)	VÁSQUEZ Galo Fidean		**12**	**1**	1983-1987, Barcelona SC Guayaquil (9/1), Sociedad Deportivo Quito (1/0), Barcelona SC Guayaquil (2/0).
(4/016)	VÁSQUEZ Humberto		**5**	**0**	1938-1942
(33/070)	VÁSQUEZ Luis		**6**	**1**	1949, SD Aucas Quito (6/1).
(132/240)	VEGA José Jacinto	28.10.1958	**9**	**1**	1983-1987, CD El Nacional Quito (3/1), LDU de Quito (4/0), Barcelona SC Guayaquil (2/0).
(381/446)	VERA CARPIO Danny Alejandro	08.08.1980	**2**	**0**	2007, Barcelona SC Guayaquil (2/0).
(104/188)	VERA Máximo		**1**	**0**	1975, Barcelona SC Guayaquil (1/0).
(154/273)	VERDUGA Wilfrido Enrique	19.01.1964	**11**	**0**	1987-1995, CS Emelec Guayaquil (11/0).
(216/321)	VERNAZA Carlos	06.08.1968	**2**	**1**	1994, CD El Nacional Quito (2/1).
(293/391)	VERNAZA VALENCIA Joel Aurelio	02.08.1976	**1**	**0**	2000, Sociedad Deportivo Quito (1/0).
(124/222)	VICUÑA Angel		**1**	**0**	1981
(46/096)	VILLACRESES Washington		**5**	**1**	1955
(105/196)	VILLAFUERTE José Voltaire	07.11.1956	**42**	**4**	1976-1985, CD El Nacional Quito (42/4).
(397/458)	VILLAFUERTE POSLIGUA Edwin Alberto	12.03.1979	**1**	**0**	2007, Barcelona SC Guayaquil (1/0).
(346/418)	VILLAFUERTE POSLIUGA Edwin Alberto	12.03.1979	**15**	**0**	2004-2006, Barcelona SC Guayaquil (14/0), Sociedad Deportivo Quito (1/0).
(22/051)	VILLAGÓMEZ Francisco		**2**	**0**	1945
(108/200)	VILLENA Fernando		**6**	**0**	1977, LDU de Quito (6/0).
(356/426)	VINCES MENDOZA Wilfrido Antonio	05.12.1983	**2**	**0**	2005, Sociedad Deportivo Quito (2/0).
(382/448)	VITERI VINCES Daniel Jimmy	12.09.1981	**5**	**0**	2007, Sociedad Deportivo Quito (5/0).
(241/344)	YEPEZ SALAZAR Gabriel	02.05.1963	**1**	**0**	1996, CD Espoli Quito (1/0).
(51/102)	YU LEE Cipriano		**6**	**0**	1957-1960, CS Emelec Guayaquil (6/0).
(1/005)	ZAMBRANO Arturo		**13**	**1**	1938-1942
(210/319)	ZAMBRANO Eduardo	24.03.1967	**1**	**0**	1993, LDU de Quito (1/0).
(197/315)	ZAMBRANO Hjalmar	23.04.1971	**5**	**1**	1992-1995, Valdez SC Guayaquil (1/1), Barcelona SC Guayaquil (1/0), LDU de Quito (3/0).
(284/380)	ZAMBRANO Luis Alberto	28.11.1970	**1**	**0**	2000, CD Espoli Quito (1/0).
(71/135)	ZAMBRANO Mario		**2**	**0**	1965, LDU de Quito (2/0).
(40/086)	ZAMBRANO Orlando		**3**	**0**	1953-1955, CS Norte America Guayaquil
(276/374)	ZAMORA Jairon Leonel	05.02.1978	**7**	**0**	1999-2000, CD El Nacional Quito (7/0).
(26/056)	ZENCK Federico		**4**	**0**	1947
(380/442)	ZURA DE JESÚS Edmundo Salomón	12.01.1983	**12**	**1**	2006-2009, Imbabura SC Ibarra (7/1), Newcastle United Jets FC (2/0), CD El Nacional Quito (3/0).
(15/043)	ZURITA Félix Leyton		**17**	**0**	1942-1947

NATIONAL COACHES

Name	Period	Matches	P	W	D	L		GF	-	GA	
Enrique LAMAS (*Chile*)	08.08.1938 – 22.08.1938	[1-5]	5	2	1	2		10	-	15	50.00 %
Ramón UNAMUNO	15.01.1939 – 12.02.1939	[6-9]	4	0	0	4		4	-	18	0.00 %
Juan PARODI (*Argentina*)	02.02.1941 – 05.02.1942	[10-19]	10	0	0	10		5	-	52	0.00 %
Rodolfo ORLANDINI (*Argentina*)	14.01.1945 – 21.02.1945	[20-25]	6	0	1	5		9	-	27	8.33 %
Ramón UNAMUNO	30.11.1947 – 29.12.1947	[26-32]	7	0	3	4		3	-	17	21.42 %
José PLANAS (*Spain*)	03.04.1949 – 03.05.1949	[33-39]	7	1	0	6		7	-	21	14.28 %
Gregorio Juan ESPERÓN (*Argentina*)	28.02.1953 – 23.03.1953	[40-45]	6	0	2	4		1	-	13	16.66 %
José María DÍAZ GRANADOS	27.02.1955 – 23.03.1955	[46-50]	5	0	0	5		4	-	22	0.00 %
Eduardo SPANDRE (*Argentina*)	07.03.1957 – 01.04.1957	[51-56]	6	0	1	5		7	-	23	8.33 %
Juan LÓPEZ FONTANA (*Uruguay*)	06.12.1959 – 17.12.1960	[57-63]	7	1	1	5		9	-	32	21.42 %
Fausto MONTALVÁN	10.03.1963 – 31.03.1963	[64-69]	6	1	2	3		14	-	18	33.33 %
José María RODRÍGUEZ (*Uruguay*)	20.07.1965 – 12.10.1965	[70-74]	5	2	1	2		7	-	7	50.00 %
Fausto MONTALVÁN	21.12.1966 – 28.12.1966	[75-76]	2	0	1	1		3	-	5	25.00 %
José Gómez NOGUEIRA (*Brazil*)	22.06.1969 – 03.08.1969	[77-81]	5	1	1	3		6	-	9	30.00 %
Ernesto GUERRA	24.05.1970 – 21.06.1972	[82-86]	5	0	1	4		4	-	11	10.00 %
Jorge LAZO ARAQUE	18.02.1973 – 06.05.1973	[87-90]	4	0	4	0		5	-	5	50.00 %
Roberto RESQUIN (*Argentina*)	12.05.1973 – 08.07.1973	[91-96]	6	1	3	2		5	-	10	41.66 %
Roque Gastón MÁSPOLI (*Uruguay*)	22.06.1975 – 10.08.1975	[97-104]	8	2	1	5		11	-	13	31.25 %
Ernesto GUERRA	20.10.1976 – 13.06.1979	[105-116]	12	3	4	5		11	-	17	41.66 %
Héctor MORALES	21.06.1979 – 16.09.1979	[117-123]	7	3	0	4		9	-	11	42.85 %
Otto VIEIRA (*Brazil*)	28.01.1981 – 14.02.1981	[124-125]	2	0	0	2		1	-	9	0.00 %
Juan Eduardo HOHBERG (*Uruguay*)	17.05.1981 – 14.06.1981	[126-129]	4	1	1	2		2	-	5	37.50 %
Ernesto GUERRA	26.07.1983 – 07.09.1983	[130-135]	6	0	4	2		4	-	10	33.33 %
Antônio Ferreira"ANTONINHO" (*Brazil*)	30.11.1984 – 31.03.1985	[136-150]	15	3	5	7		20	-	25	36.66 %
Luis GRIMALDI (*Uruguay*)	05.03.1987 – 04.07.1987	[151-160]	10	1	3	6		7	-	14	25.00 %
Dušan DRAŠKOVIĆ (*Yugoslavia*)	07.06.1988 – 19.09.1993	[161-215]	54	16	17	21		63	-	61	45.37 %
Carlos TORRES GARCÉS	25.05.1994	[216]	1	1	0	0		1	-	0	100.00 %
Dušan DRAŠKOVIĆ (*Yugoslavia*)	05.06.1994	[217]	1	1	0	0		2	-	1	100.00 %
Carlos René RON	17.08.1994 – 21.09.1994	[218-219]	2	0	1	1		0	-	2	25.00 %
Francisco MATURANA (*Colombia*)	24.05.1995 – 16.11.1997	[220-265]	46	22	9	15		62	-	48	57.60 %
Paúl Fernando CARRERA VELASTEGUÍ	14.10.1998	[266]	1	0	0	1		1	-	5	0.00 %
Carlos Edmundo SEVILLA	27.01.1999 – 07.07.1999	[267-281]	15	3	6	6		15	-	19	40.00 %
Hernán Darío GÓMEZ (*Colombia*)	12.10.1999 – 13.07.2004	[282-345]	64	24	17	23		70	-	72	50.78 %
Luis Fernando SUÁREZ (*Colombia*)	05.09.2004 – 17.11.2007	[346-397]	52	18	9	25		65	-	77	43.26 %
Sixto Rafael VIZUETE TOAPANTA	21.11.2007 – 16.05.2010	[398-422]	25	9	7	9		28	-	27	50.00 %
Reinaldo RUEDA RIVERA (*Colombia*)	04.09.2010 –>	[423->	43	17	14	12		66	-	48	

National coaches several times in charge:

Name	How often	Matches	M	W	D	L		GF	-	GA	
Ramón UNAMUNO	2x	[6-9], [26-32]	11	0	3	8		7	-	35	13.63 %
Fausto MONTALVÁN	2x	[64-69], [75-76]	8	1	3	4		17	-	23	31.25 %
Ernesto GUERRA	3x	[82-86], [105-116], [130-135]	23	3	9	11		19	-	38	32.60
Dušan DRAŠKOVIĆ (*Yugoslavia*)	2x	[161-215], [217]	55	17	17	21		65	-	62	46.36 %

HEAD-TO-HEAD STATISTICS

	HOME					AWAY					NEUTRAL					TOTAL				
	P	W	D	L	Goals	P	W	D	L	Goals	P	W	D	L	Goals	P	W	D	L	Goals
Argentina	11	4	4	3	16 : 16	9	0	3	6	6 : 22	11	0	3	8	7 : 42	31	4	10	17	29 : 80
Armenia	1	1	0	0	3 : 0											1	1	0	0	3 : 0
Belarus	1	0	1	0	1 : 1											1	0	1	0	1 : 1
Bolivia	10	7	3	0	17 : 6	10	3	4	3	20 : 17	7	1	4	2	7 : 6	27	11	11	5	44 : 29
Brazil	8	2	2	4	5 : 13	9	0	0	9	6 : 34	11	0	1	10	11 : 41	28	2	3	23	22 : 88
Cameroon	1	0	0	1	1 : 3						1	1	0	0	3 : 0	2	1	0	1	4 : 3
Canada						1	0	1	0	2 : 2	1	1	0	0	2 : 0	2	1	1	0	4 : 2
Canada "U23"						1	1	0	0	2 : 1						1	1	0	0	2 : 1
Chile	16	7	6	3	19 : 15	18	0	4	14	12 : 52	13	2	2	9	15 : 26	47	9	12	26	46 : 93
Colombia	15	6	6	3	18 : 9	15	3	3	9	6 : 18	12	3	2	7	13 : 19	42	12	11	19	37 : 46
Costa Rica	5	1	4	0	8 : 4	5	2	1	2	6 : 5	2	2	0	0	5 : 1	12	5	5	2	19 : 10
Croatia											1	1	0	0	1 : 0	1	1	0	0	1 : 0
Cuba	2	0	1	1	0 : 1	2	0	1	1	1 : 2						4	0	2	2	1 : 3
Denmark	1	0	1	0	1 : 1											1	0	1	0	1 : 1
East Germany	3	1	1	1	6 : 6											3	1	1	1	6 : 6
El Salvador	2	2	0	0	10 : 1	2	1	1	0	3 : 1	2	1	0	1	2 : 3	6	4	1	1	15 : 5
England	1	0	0	1	0 : 2						1	0	0	1	0 : 1	2	0	0	2	0 : 3
Estonia	2	2	0	0	3 : 1											2	2	0	0	3 : 1
Finland	1	1	0	0	3 : 1											1	1	0	0	3 : 1
France						1	0	0	1	0 : 2						1	0	0	1	0 : 2
Germany						1	0	0	1	0 : 3						1	0	0	1	0 : 3
Greece											1	0	1	0	1 : 1	1	0	1	0	1 : 1
Guatemala	2	2	0	0	3 : 0	4	0	3	1	1 : 2	1	1	0	0	3 : 1	7	3	3	1	7 : 3
Haiti	1	1	0	0	3 : 1	2	1	0	1	2 : 2	1	0	0	1	0 : 2	4	2	0	2	5 : 5
Holland						1	0	0	1	0 : 1						1	0	0	1	0 : 1
Honduras	3	2	0	1	4 : 3	6	1	4	1	5 : 5	3	0	3	0	4 : 4	12	3	7	2	13 : 12
Iran											3	1	2	0	3 : 2	3	1	2	0	3 : 2
Italy											2	0	1	1	1 : 3	2	0	1	1	1 : 3
Jamaica	2	2	0	0	7 : 3						1	0	1	0	0 : 0	3	2	1	0	7 : 3
Japan						2	1	0	1	1 : 1	1	0	0	1	0 : 3	3	1	0	2	1 : 4
Jordan											1	0	0	1	0 : 3	1	0	0	1	0 : 3
Kuwait						1	1	0	0	3 : 0						1	1	0	0	3 : 0
Lebanon						1	0	0	1	0 : 1						1	0	0	1	0 : 1
Macedonia											1	0	0	1	1 : 2	1	0	0	1	1 : 2
Mexico	1	0	0	1	0 : 2	3	1	1	1	3 : 4	14	1	4	9	13 : 23	18	2	5	11	16 : 29
Nigeria											1	0	1	0	2 : 2	1	0	1	0	2 : 2
Oman						1	0	0	1	0 : 2	1	1	0	0	2 : 0	2	1	0	1	2 : 2
Panama	3	3	0	0	9 : 0	1	0	1	0	0 : 0						4	3	1	0	9 : 0
Paraguay	15	9	3	3	32 : 24	12	0	0	12	8 : 29	9	2	2	5	6 : 12	36	11	5	20	46 : 65
Peru	14	8	5	1	27 : 9	16	4	3	9	15 : 26	14	2	4	8	15 : 34	44	14	12	18	57 : 69
Poland											3	1	1	1	4 : 5	3	1	1	1	4 : 5
Portugal						1	1	0	0	3 : 2	1	0	0	1	0 : 3	2	1	0	1	3 : 5
Republic of Ireland											2	0	1	1	3 : 4	2	0	1	1	3 : 4
Qatar						2	1	1	0	3 : 2						2	1	1	0	3 : 2
Romania	1	1	0	0	3 : 0											1	1	0	0	3 : 0
Scotland											1	0	0	1	1 : 2	1	0	0	1	1 : 2
Senegal											2	0	0	2	1 : 3	2	0	0	2	1 : 3
South Africa											1	0	1	0	0 : 0	1	0	1	0	0 : 0
South Korea						1	0	0	1	0 : 2	1	1	0	0	2 : 1	2	1	0	1	2 : 3
Spain	1	0	0	1	0 : 2	1	0	0	1	0 : 4						2	0	0	2	0 : 6
Sweden	2	1	1	0	3 : 2											2	1	1	0	3 : 2
Turkey											1	1	0	0	1 : 0	1	1	0	0	1 : 0
Uganda											1	0	0	1	1 : 2	1	0	0	1	1 : 2
United States	1	1	0	0	2 : 0	10	4	4	2	8 : 6						11	5	4	2	10 : 6
Uruguay	15	4	4	7	16 : 25	16	0	5	11	10 : 26	12	1	1	10	11 : 43	43	5	10	28	37 : 94
Venezuela	10	8	0	2	25 : 6	11	2	2	7	10 : 18	3	2	0	1	9 : 3	24	12	2	10	44 : 27
Yugoslavia											1	1	0	0	1 : 0	1	1	0	0	1 : 0
Zambia											2	2	0	0	5 : 1	2	2	0	0	5 : 1
TOTAL	**151**	**76**	**42**	**33**	**245 : 157**	**166**	**27**	**42**	**97**	**136 : 292**	**148**	**29**	**35**	**84**	**158 : 302**	**465**	**132**	**119**	**214**	**539 : 751**

PERU

The Country:
República del Perú (Republic of Peru)
Capital: Lima
Surface: 1,285,216 km²
Inhabitants: 30,475,144
Time: UTC-5

The FA:
Federación Peruana de Fútbol
Avenida Aviación 2085 San Luis, Lima 30
Year of Formation: 1922
Member of FIFA since: 1924
Member of CONMEBOL since: 1925

NATIONAL TEAM RECORDS

COPA AMÉRICA	
1916	Did not enter
1917	Did not enter
1919	Did not enter
1920	Did not enter
1921	Did not enter
1922	Did not enter
1923	Did not enter
1924	Did not enter
1925	Did not enter
1926	Did not enter
1927	3rd Place
1929	4th Place
1935	3rd Place
1937	6th Place
1939	**Winners**
1941	4th Place
1942	5th Place
1945	Withdrew
1946	Withdrew
1947	5th Place
1949	3rd Place
1953	5th Place
1955	3rd Place
1956	6th Place
1957	4th Place
1959	4th Place
1959E	Did not enter
1963	5th Place
1967	Withdrew
1975	**Winners**
1979	Semi-Finals
1983	Semi-Finals
1987	Round 1
1989	Round 1
1991	Round 1
1993	Quarter-Finals
1995	Round 1
1997	4th Place
1999	Quarter-Finals
2001	Quarter-Finals
2004	Quarter-Finals
2007	Quarter-Finals
2011	3rd Place

WORLD CUP	
1930	Final Tournament (1st Round)
1934	Withdrew
1938	Qualifiers
1950	Withdrew
1954	Withdrew
1958	Qualifiers
1962	Qualifiers
1966	Qualifiers
1970	Final Tournament (Quarter-Finals)
1974	Qualifiers
1978	Final Tournament (2nd Round)
1982	Final Tournament (1st Round)
1986	Qualifiers
1990	Qualifiers
1994	Qualifiers
1998	Qualifiers
2002	Qualifiers
2006	Qualifiers
2010	Qualifiers
2014	Qualifiers

OLYMPIC GAMES 1900-2012
1936, 1960
FIFA CONFEDERATIONS CUP 1992-2013
None
PLAYER WITH MOST INTERNATIONAL CAPS
Roberto Carlos Palacios Mestas – 128 caps (1992-2009)
PLAYER WITH MOST INTERNATIONAL GOALS
Teófilo Juan Cubillas Arizaga – 26 goals / 81 caps (1968-1982)

FULL INTERNATIONALS (1927-2013)

1. 01.11.1927 **PERU - URUGUAY** **0-4(0-0)** 11th Copa América
Estadio Nacional, Lima; Referee: Consolato Nay Foino (Argentina); Attendance: 19,367
PER: Jorge Hernesto Pardón García (1/0), Carlos Moscoso (1/0), Alfonso Saldarriaga (1/0), Santiago Ulloa (1/0), Filomeno García (1/0), Leopoldo Basurto (Cap) (1/0), José María Lavalle (1/0), Alberto Montellanos (1/0), Segundo Aranda (1/0), Carlos Alejandro Villanueva Martínez (1/0), Adolfo Muro (1/0). Trainer: Pedro Olivieri, Raúl Blanco, Romeo Parravicini (1).

2. 13.11.1927 **PERU - BOLIVIA** **3-2(3-2)** 11th Copa América
Estadio Nacional, Lima; Referee: Consolato Nay Foino (Argentina); Attendance: 9,687
PER: Jorge Hernesto Pardón García (2/0), Antonio Maquilón Badaracco (1/0), Carlos Moscoso (Cap) (2/0), Esteban Danino (1/0), Alfonso Saldarriaga (2/0), Santiago Ulloa (2/0), José María Lavalle (2/0), Alberto Montellanos (2/1), Segundo Aranda (2/0), Demetrio Neyra (1/1), Jorge Sarmiento (1/1). Trainer: Pedro Olivieri, Raúl Blanco, Romeo Parravicini (2).
Goals: Demetrio Neyra (31), Jorge Sarmiento (40), Alberto Montellanos (43).

3. 27.11.1927 **PERU - ARGENTINA** **1-5(1-5)** 11th Copa América
Estadio Nacional, Lima; Referee: Victorio Gariboni (Bolivia); Attendance: 15,000
PER: Jorge Hernesto Pardón García (3/0), Antonio Maquilón Badaracco (2/0), Carlos Moscoso (3/0), Leopoldo Basurto (2/0), Alfonso Saldarriaga (3/0), Esteban Danino (2/0), José María Lavalle (3/0), Alberto Montellanos (3/1), Carlos Alejandro Villanueva Martínez (2/1), Demetrio Neyra (2/1), Jorge Sarmiento (2/1). Trainer: Pedro Olivieri, Raúl Blanco, Romeo Parravicini (3).
Goal: Carlos Alejandro Villanueva Martínez (5).

4. 03.11.1929 **ARGENTINA - PERU** **3-0(2-0)** 12th Copa América
Estadio Gasómetro de Boedo, Buenos Aires; Referee: Aníbal Tejada (Uruguay); Attendance: 20,000
PER: Jorge Hernesto Pardón García (4/0), Antonio Maquilón Badaracco (3/0), Alfonso Saldarriaga (4/0), Luis Alberto Denegri (1/0), Plácido Reynaldo Galindo Pardo (1/0), Eduardo Astengo (1/0), Rodolfo Ortega (1/0), Juan Bulnes (1/0), Jorge Góngora Montalván (1/0), Miguel Rostaing (1/0), Julio Ramírez (1/0). Trainer: Julio Borelli (1).

5. 11.11.1929 **URUGUAY - PERU** **4-1(3-0)** 12th Copa América
Estadio Alvear y Tagle, Buenos Aires (Argentina); Referee: Mario Barba (Paraguay); Attendance: 22,000
PER: Jorge Hernesto Pardón García (5/0), Alfonso Saldarriaga (5/0), Antonio Maquilón Badaracco (4/0), Luis Alberto Denegri (2/0), Eduardo Astengo (2/0), Enrique Salas (1/0), Julio Ramírez (2/0), Augusto Lizarbe (1/1), Miguel Rostaing (2/0), Juan Bulnes (2/0), Rodolfo Ortega (2/0). Trainer: Julio Borelli (2).
Goal: Augusto Lizarbe (81).

6. 16.11.1929 **PARAGUAY - PERU** **5-0(1-0)** 12th Copa América
Estadio Independiente, Avellaneda (Argentina); Referee: José Galli (Argentina); Attendance: 8,000
PER: Eugenio Segala (1/0), Alfonso Saldarriaga (6/0), Antonio Maquilón Badaracco (5/0), Luis Alberto Denegri (3/0), Adolfo Muro (2/0), Faustino Mustafich (1/0), Julio Ramírez (3/0), Augusto Lizarbe (2/1), Juan Bulnes (3/0), Miguel Rostaing (3/0), Rodolfo Ortega (3/0). Trainer: Julio Borelli (3).

7. 14.07.1930 **ROMANIA - PERU** **3-1(1-0)** 1st FIFA WC. Group Stage
Estadio Pocitos, Montevideo (Uruguay); Referee: Alberto Warnken (Chile); Attendance: 300
PER: Juan Valdivieso Padilla (1/0), Mario de las Casas Ramírez (1/0), Alberto Soria (1/0), Luis Alberto Denegri (4/0), Plácido Reynaldo Galindo Pardo (Cap) (2/0), Domingo García Heredia (1/0), José María Lavalle (4/0), Julio Víctor Lores Colán (1/0), Carlos Alejandro Villanueva Martínez (3/1), Demetrio Neyra (3/1), Luis Alfonso de Souza Ferreira Huby (1/0). Trainer: Francisco Bru Sanz (1).
Goal: Luis Alfonso de Souza Ferreira Huby (60).

8. 18.07.1930 **URUGUAY - PERU** **1-0(0-0)** 1st FIFA WC. Group Stage
Estadio Centenario, Montevideo; Referee: John Langenus (Belgium); Attendance: 45,000
PER: Jorge Hernesto Pardón García (6/0), Mario de las Casas Ramírez (2/0), Antonio Maquilón Badaracco (Cap) (6/0), Luis Alberto Denegri (5/0), Plácido Reynaldo Galindo Pardo (3/0), Eduardo Astengo (3/0), José María Lavalle (5/0), Carlos Alejandro Villanueva Martínez (4/1), Julio Víctor Lores Colán (2/0), Demetrio Neyra (4/1), Luis Alfonso de Souza Ferreira Huby (2/0). Trainer: Francisco Bru Sanz (2).

9. 13.01.1935 **PERU - URUGUAY** **0-1(0-1)** 13th Copa América
Estadio Nacional, Lima; Referee: Humberto Reginato (Chile); Attendance: 25,000
PER: Juan Valdivieso Padilla (2/0), Narciso León (1/0), Arturo Fernández (1/0), Luis Alberto Denegri (6/0), Vicente Arce (1/0), Domingo García Heredia (2/0), José María Lavalle (6/0), Carlos Alejandro Villanueva Martínez (5/1), Teodoro Fernández (1/0), Carlos Tovar (1/0) [75.Lizandro Rodríguez Nué (1/0)], José Morales (1/0). Trainer: Termo Carbajo (1).

10. 20.01.1935 **PERU - ARGENTINA** **1-4(1-1)** 13th Copa América
Estadio Nacional, Lima; Referee: César Pioli (Uruguay); Attendance: 21,000
PER: Juan Valdivieso Padilla (3/0), Narciso León (2/0) [46.Mario de las Casas Ramírez (3/0)], Arturo Fernández (2/0), Luis Alberto Denegri (7/0) [46.Juan Rivero (1/0)], Vicente Arce (2/0), Domingo García Heredia (3/0), José María Lavalle (7/0), Jorge Alcalde (1/0), Teodoro Fernández (2/1) [13.Jorge Góngora Montalván (2/0)], Carlos Alejandro Villanueva Martínez (6/1), José Morales (2/0). Trainer: Termo Carbajo (2).
Goal: Teodoro Fernández (2).

11. 26.01.1935 **PERU - CHILE** **1-0(1-0)** 13th Copa América
Estadio Nacional, Lima; Referee: Eduardo Forte (Argentina); Attendance: 12,000
PER: Juan Valdivieso Padilla (4/0), Narciso León (3/0), Arturo Fernández (3/0), Luis Alberto Denegri (8/0), Vicente Arce (3/0) [46.Eulogio García (1/0)], Domingo García Heredia (4/0), José María Lavalle (8/0) [46.Mario Pacheco (1/0)], Carlos Alejandro Villanueva Martínez (7/1), Teodoro Fernández (3/1), Carlos Tovar (2/0) [25.Alberto Montellanos (4/2)], José Morales (3/0). Trainer: Termo Carbajo (3).
Goal: Alberto Montellanos (5).

12. 06.08.1936 **PERU - FINLAND** **7-3(3-1)** Olympic Games
Hertha-Platz, Berlin (Germany); Referee: Rinaldo Barlassina (Italy); Attendance: 2,500
PER: Juan Valdivieso Padilla (Cap) (5/0), Arturo Fernández (4/0), Víctor Lavalle (1/0), Carlos Tovar (3/0), Segundo Castillo (1/0), Orestes Jordán (1/0), Adelfo Magallanes (1/0), Teodoro Alcalde (1/0), Teodoro Fernández (4/6), Carlos Alejandro Villanueva Martínez (8/3), José Morales (4/0). Trainer: Luis Alberto Denegri (1).
Goal: Teodoro Fernández (17), Carlos Alejandro Villanueva Martínez (22), Teodoro Fernández (33, 47, 49), Carlos Alejandro Villanueva Martínez (67), Teodoro Fernández (70).

13. 08.08.1936 **PERU - AUSTRIA** **4-2(0-2,2-2)** Olympic Games

Hertha-Platz, Berlin (Germany); Referee: Thoralf Kristiansen (Norway); Attendance: 5,000

PER: Juan Valdivieso Padilla (Cap) (6/0), Víctor Lavalle (2/0), Arturo Fernández (5/0), Carlos Tovar (4/0), Segundo Castillo (2/0), Orestes Jordán (2/0), Adelfo Magallanes (2/0), Jorge Alcalde (2/1), Teodoro Fernández (5/7), Carlos Alejandro Villanueva Martínez (9/5), José Morales (5/0). Trainer: Luis Alberto Denegri (2).

Goal: Jorge Alcalde (75), Carlos Alejandro Villanueva Martínez (81, 99), Teodoro Fernández (102).

Upon protest by Austria this match was cancelled by the jury of appeal because peruvian fans had invaded the field to celebrate after Villanueva scored the 4th goal in the last minute of the overtime, FIFA ordered the match replayed and Peru did not show because all their Olympia delegation had returned home in disagreement with the ruling.

14. 27.12.1936 **BRAZIL - PERU** **3-2(3-0)** 14th Copa América

Estadio Gasómetro de Boedo, Buenos Aires (Argentina); Referee: Alfredo Vargas Ascui (Chile); Attendance: 20,000

PER: Juan Valdivieso Padilla (7/0), Arturo Fernández (6/0), Alberto Soria (2/0), Carlos Tovar (5/0), Vicente Arce (4/0) [52.Segundo Castillo (3/0)], Orestes Jordán (3/0), José María Lavalle (9/0), Adelfo Magallanes (3/0) [46.Jorge Alcalde (3/1)], Teodoro Fernández (6/8), Carlos Alejandro Villanueva Martínez (10/6) [Andrés Álvarez (1/0)], José Morales (6/0). Trainer: Luis Alberto Denegri (3).

Goals: Teodoro Fernández (53), Carlos Alejandro Villanueva Martínez (80).

15. 06.01.1937 **URUGUAY - PERU** **4-2(2-2)** 14th Copa América

Estadio Gasómetro de Boedo, Buenos Aires (Argentina); Referee: Alfredo Vargas Ascui (Chile); Attendance: 20,000

PER: Marcos Huby (1/0), Arturo Fernández (7/0), Alberto Soria (3/0) [55.Ricardo Del Rio (1/0)], Carlos Tovar (6/0), Segundo Castillo (4/0), Orestes Jordán (4/0), José María Lavalle (10/0), Jorge Alcalde (4/1), Teodoro Fernández (7/9), Adelfo Magallanes (4/1), José Morales (7/0). Trainer: Luis Alberto Denegri (4).

Goals: Teodoro Fernández (29), Adelfo Magallanes (40).

16. 16.01.1937 **ARGENTINA - PERU** **1-0(0-0)** 14th Copa América

Estadio Gasómetro de Boedo, Buenos Aires; Referee: Aníbal Tejada (Uruguay); Attendance: 40,000

PER: Juan Honores (1/0), Arturo Fernández (8/0) [53.Teodoro Fernández (8/9)], Alberto Soria (4/0), Carlos Tovar (7/0), Segundo Castillo (5/0), Orestes Jordán (5/0), Teodoro Alcalde (2/0), Pedro Ibáñez (1/0) [75.Vicente Arce (5/0)], Jorge Alcalde (5/1), Andrés Álvarez (2/0), Arturo Paredes (1/0). Trainer: Luis Alberto Denegri (5).

17. 21.01.1937 **CHILE - PERU** **2-2(1-2)** 14th Copa América

Estadio Gasómetro de Boedo, Buenos Aires (Argentina); Referee: José Bartolomé Macías (Argentina); Attendance: 12,000

PER: Juan Honores (2/0), Arturo Fernández (9/0), Alberto Soria (5/0), Carlos Tovar (8/0), Segundo Castillo (6/0), Orestes Jordán (6/0) [65.Carlos Portal (1/0)], Teodoro Alcalde (3/0), Pedro Ibáñez (2/0), Teodoro Fernández (9/9) [65.Adelfo Magallanes (5/1)], Jorge Alcalde (6/3), Arturo Paredes (2/0). Trainer: Luis Alberto Denegri (6).

Goals: Jorge Alcalde (1, 26).

18. 24.01.1937 **PERU - PARAGUAY** **1-0(0-0)** 14th Copa América

Estadio Monumental „Antonio Vespucio Liberti“, Buenos Aires (Argentina); Referee: Aníbal Tejada (Uruguay); Attendance: 8,000

PER: Juan Honores (3/0), Arturo Fernández (10/0), Alberto Soria (6/0), Carlos Tovar (9/0), Vicente Arce (6/0), Orestes Jordán (7/0), José María Lavalle (11/0), Pedro Ibáñez (3/0) [46.Adelfo Magallanes (6/2)], Jorge Alcalde (7/3) [70.Arturo Paredes (3/0)], Andrés Álvarez (3/0), José Morales (8/0). Trainer: Luis Alberto Denegri (7).

Goal: Adelfo Magallanes (84).

19. 08.08.1938 **COLOMBIA - PERU** **2-4(0-2)** 1st Juegos Bolivarianos

Estadio Universitario, Bogotá; Referee: Carlos Esteva Tejada (Mexico)

PER: Juan Valdivieso Padilla (8/0), Arturo Fernández (11/0), Raúl Chapell (1/0), Carlos Tovar (10/0) [*sent off 74*], Segundo Castillo (7/0), Orestes Jordán (8/0), Teodoro Alcalde (4/0), Pedro Ibáñez (4/2), Teodoro Fernández (10/10), Jorge Alcalde (8/4), Arturo Paredes (4/0). Trainer: John Richard Greenwell (1).

Goals: Pedro Ibáñez (10), Teodoro Fernández (40), Jorge Alcalde (57), Pedro Ibáñez (60).

20. 11.08.1938 **PERU - ECUADOR** **9-1(4-1)** 1st Juegos Bolivarianos

Estadio Universitario, Bogotá (Colombia); Referee: Carlos Esteva Tejada (Mexico)

PER: Víctor Marchena (1/0), Arturo Fernández (12/0), Raúl Chapell (2/0), Carlos Portal (2/0), Pablo Pasache (1/0), Carlos Tovar (11/0), Oscar Espinar (1/3), Víctor Bielich (1/2), Teodoro Fernández (11/10), Jorge Alcalde (9/8), José Morales (9/0). Trainer: John Richard Greenwell (2).

Goals: Oscar Espinar (14, 24), Jorge Alcalde (40, 42), Oscar Espinar (50), Jorge Alcalde (60), Víctor Bielich (65, 68), Jorge Alcalde (88).

21. 14.08.1938 **PERU - BOLIVIA** **3-0(2-0)** 1st Juegos Bolivarianos

Estadio Universitario, Bogotá (Colombia); Referee: Carlos Esteva Tejada (Mexico)

PER: Juan Valdivieso Padilla (9/0), Arturo Fernández (13/0), Raúl Chapell (3/0), Orestes Jordán (9/0), Segundo Castillo (8/0), Jorge Parró (1/0), Leopoldo Quiñónes (1/0), Jorge Alcalde (10/9), Teodoro Fernández (12/12), Carlos Alejandro Villanueva Martínez (11/6), José Morales (10/0). Trainer: John Richard Greenwell (3).

Goals: Teodoro Fernández (18), Jorge Alcalde (33), Teodoro Fernández (85).

22. 17.08.1938 **PERU - VENEZUELA** **2-1(1-0)** 1st Juegos Bolivarianos

Estadio Universitario, Bogotá (Colombia); Referee: Carlos Esteva Tejada (Mexico)

PER: Juan Valdivieso Padilla (10/0), Arturo Fernández (14/0), Raúl Chapell (4/0), Orestes Jordán (10/0), Pablo Pasache (2/0), Carlos Portal (3/0), Teodoro Alcalde (5/0), Víctor Bielich (2/3), Oscar Espinar (2/3), Jorge Alcalde (11/9), Arturo Paredes (5/1). Trainer: John Richard Greenwell (4).

Goals: Víctor Bielich (45 penalty), Arturo Paredes (47).

23. 15.01.1939 **PERU – ECUADOR** **5-2(3-0)** 15th Copa América

Estadio Nacional, Lima; Referee: Carlos Puyol (Uruguay); Attendance: 10,000

PER: Juan Honores (4/0), Arturo Fernández (15/0), Juan Quispe (1/0), Enrique Perales (1/0), Segundo Castillo (9/0), Carlos Tovar (12/0), Arturo Paredes (6/1), Jorge Alcalde (12/11), Teodoro Fernández (13/14), Pedro Ibáñez (5/3), Adelfo Magallanes (7/2) [67.Teodoro Alcalde (6/0)]. Trainer: John Richard Greenwell (5).

Goals: Teodoro Fernández (6), Jorge Alcalde (30), Pedro Ibáñez (34), Jorge Alcalde (47), Teodoro Fernández (77).

24. 22.01.1939 **PERU – CHILE** **3-1(0-0)** 15th Copa América
Estadio Nacional, Lima; Referee: Carlos Puyol (Uruguay); Attendance: 6,000
PER: Juan Honores (5/0), Arturo Fernández (16/0), Raúl Chapell (5/0), Enrique Perales (2/0) [46.Segundo Castillo (10/0)], Pablo Pasache (3/0), Carlos Tovar (13/0), Arturo Paredes (7/1), Jorge Alcalde (13/11), Teodoro Fernández (14/17), Víctor Bielich (3/3), Teodoro Alcalde (7/0) [46.Adelfo Magallanes (8/2)]. Trainer: John Richard Greenwell (6).
Goals: Teodoro Fernández (46, 65 penalty, 70).

25. 29.01.1939 **PERU - PARAGUAY** **3-0(2-0)** 15th Copa América
Estadio Nacional, Lima; Referee: Alfredo Vargas Ascui (Chile); Attendance: 15,000
PER: Juan Honores (6/0), Arturo Fernández (17/0), Raúl Chapell (6/0), Pablo Pasache (4/0) [70.Orestes Jordán (11/0)], Segundo Castillo (11/0), Carlos Tovar (14/0), Teodoro Alcalde (8/0) [57.Adelfo Magallanes (9/2)], Víctor Bielich (4/3), Teodoro Fernández (15/19), Jorge Alcalde (14/12), Arturo Paredes (8/1). Trainer: John Richard Greenwell (7).
Goals: Teodoro Fernández (11, 30), Jorge Alcalde (79).

26. 12.02.1939 **PERU - URUGUAY** **2-1(2-1)** 15th Copa América
Estadio Nacional, Lima; Referee: Alfredo Vargas Ascui (Chile); Attendance: 40,000
PER: Juan Honores (7/0), Arturo Fernández (18/0), Raúl Chapell (7/0), Pablo Pasache (5/0), Segundo Castillo (12/0), Carlos Tovar (15/0), Teodoro Alcalde (9/0), Víctor Bielich (5/4) [63.Pedro Ibáñez (6/3), 72.Juan Quispe (2/0)], Teodoro Fernández (16/19), Jorge Alcalde (15/13), Arturo Paredes (9/1). Trainer: John Richard Greenwell (8).
Goals: Jorge Alcalde (6), Víctor Bielich (35).

27. 19.01.1941 **PERU - ARGENTINA** **1-1(0-0)** Copa Roque Sáenz Peña
Estadio Nacional, Lima; Referee: Lizardo López Torres (Argentina); Attendance: 35,000
PER: Juan Honores (8/0), Juan Quispe (3/0), Enrique Perales (3/0), Orestes Jordán (12/0), Guillermo Sayers (1/0) [65.Guillermo Andrade (1/0)], Máximo Lobatón (1/0), Pedro Magán (1/0), Luis Guzmán (1/0) [53.César Socarraz (1/0)], Teodoro Fernández (17/19), Adelfo Magallanes (10/2), Leopoldo Quiñónes (2/0) [53.Marcial Hurtado (1/1)]. Trainer: Domingo Arrillaga (1).
Goal: Marcial Hurtado (87).

28. 26.01.1941 **PERU - ARGENTINA** **1-1(1-1)** Copa Roque Sáenz Peña
Estadio Nacional, Lima; Referee: Enrique Cuenca (Peru); Attendance: 30,000
PER: Juan Honores (9/0), Pedro Luna (1/0), Juan Quispe (4/0), Orestes Jordán (13/0), Guillermo Sayers (2/0) [Guillermo Andrade (2/0)], Máximo Lobatón (2/0) [30.Guillermo Janneau (1/0)], Pedro Magán (2/0), César Socarraz (2/0), Teodoro Fernández (18/19) [Roberto Morales (1/0)], Adelfo Magallanes (11/3) [77.Robles (1/0)], Leopoldo Quiñónes (3/0). Trainer: Domingo Arrillaga (2).
Goal: Adelfo Magallanes (42).

29. 29.01.1941 **PERU - ARGENTINA** **0-3(0-0)** Copa Roque Sáenz Peña
Estadio Nacional, Lima; Referee: Enrique Cuenca (Peru); Attendance: 20,000
PER: Juan Honores (10/0), Pedro Luna (2/0), Juan Quispe (5/0), Máximo Lobatón (3/0), Vicente Arce (7/0) [70.Guillermo Sayers (3/0)], Carlos Portal (4/0), Pedro Magán (3/0) [46.Manuel Vallejos (1/0)], César Socarraz (3/0), Teodoro Fernández (19/19) [76.Roberto Morales (2/0)], Adelfo Magallanes (12/3), Leopoldo Quiñónes (4/0) [46.Marcial Hurtado (2/1)]. Trainer: Domingo Arrillaga (3).

30. 09.02.1941 **CHILE - PERU** **1-0(1-0)** 16th Copa América
Estadio Nacional, Santiago; Referee: José Bartolomé Macías (Argentina); Attendance: 51,709
PER: Juan Honores (11/0), Pedro Luna (3/0), Enrique Perales (4/0), Vicente Arce (8/0), Carlos Portal (5/0), Máximo Lobatón (4/0), Pedro Magán (4/0), Roberto Morales (3/0), Teodoro Fernández (20/19), Adelfo Magallanes (13/3), Leopoldo Quiñónes (5/0) [67.Marcial Hurtado (3/1)],. Trainer: Domingo Arrillaga (4).

31. 12.02.1941 **ARGENTINA - PERU** **2-1(1-0)** 16th Copa América
Estadio Nacional, Santiago (Chile); Referee: Alfredo Vargas Ascui (Chile); Attendance: 45,000
PER: Juan Honores (12/0), Enrique Perales (5/0), Juan Quispe (6/0), Vicente Arce (9/0), Carlos Portal (6/0) [88.Orestes Jordán (14/0)], Guillermo Janneau (2/0) [46.Máximo Lobatón (5/0)], Manuel Vallejos (2/0), César Socarraz (4/1), Teodoro Fernández (21/19), Roberto Morales (4/0) [88.Adelfo Magallanes (14/3)], Leopoldo Quiñónes (6/0). Trainer: Domingo Arrillaga (5).
Goal: César Socarraz (53).

32. 23.02.1941 **PERU – ECUADOR** **4-0(3-0)** 16th Copa América
Estadio Nacional, Santiago (Chile); Referee: Víctor Francisco Rivas (Chile); Attendance: 48,000
PER: Juan Honores (13/0), Enrique Perales (6/0), Juan Quispe (7/0), Vicente Arce (10/0), Carlos Portal (7/0), Máximo Lobatón (6/0), Marcial Hurtado (4/1), César Socarraz (5/1), Teodoro Fernández (22/22), Adelfo Magallanes (15/3), Manuel Vallejos (3/1). Trainer: Domingo Arrillaga (6).
Goals: Teodoro Fernández (25, 32), Manuel Vallejos (36), Teodoro Fernández (48).

33. 26.02.1941 **URUGUAY - PERU** **2-0(1-0)** 16th Copa América
Estadio Nacional, Santiago (Chile); Referee: José Bartolomé Macías (Argentina); Attendance: 20,000
PER: Juan Honores (14/0), Enrique Perales (7/0), Juan Quispe (8/0), Orestes Jordán (15/0), Vicente Arce (11/0) [65.Alejandro Gonzáles (1/0)], Máximo Lobatón (7/0), Pedro Magán (5/0), César Socarraz (6/1), Teodoro Fernández (23/22), Adelfo Magallanes (16/3), Leopoldo Quiñónes (7/0). Trainer: Domingo Arrillaga (7).

34. 18.01.1942 **PERU - PARAGUAY** **1-1(1-1)** 17th Copa América
Estadio Centenario, Montevideo (Uruguay); Referee: José Bartolomé Macías (Argentina); Attendance: 45,000
PER: Juan Honores (15/0), Enrique Perales (8/0), Juan Quispe (9/0), Teobaldo Guzmán (1/0), Pablo Pasache (6/0), Máximo Lobatón (8/0) [88.Orestes Jordán (16/0)], Pedro Magán (6/0) [80.Armando Agurto (1/0)], Luis Guzmán (2/0) [70.Roberto Morales (5/0)], Teodoro Fernández (24/22), Adelfo Magallanes (17/4), Leopoldo Quiñónes (8/0). Trainer: Angel Fernández (1).
Goal: Adelfo Magallanes (1).

35. 21.01.1942 **BRAZIL - PERU** **2-1(1-0)** 17th Copa América
Estadio Centenario, Montevideo (Uruguay); Referee: Marcos Gerinaldo Rojas (Paraguay); Attendance: 10,000
PER: Juan Honores (16/0), Enrique Perales (9/0), Juan Quispe (10/0), Orestes Jordán (17/0) [77.Carlos Portal (8/0)], Teobaldo Guzmán (2/0), Pablo Pasache (7/0), Pedro Magán (7/0) [80.Armando Agurto (2/0)], Alberto Delgado (1/0) [46.Luis Guzmán (3/0)], Teodoro Fernández (25/23), Adelfo Magallanes (18/4), Leopoldo Quiñónes (9/0). Trainer: Angel Fernández (2).
Goal: Teodoro Fernández (72).

36. 25.01.1942 **ARGENTINA - PERU** **3-1(1-1)** 17th Copa América
Estadio Centenario, Montevideo (Uruguay); Referee: Aníbal Tejada (Uruguay); Attendance: 12,000
PER: Juan Soriano (1/0), Pedro Luna (4/0), Juan Quispe (11/0), Teobaldo Guzmán (3/0), Antonio Biffi (1/0), Máximo Lobatón (9/0) [46.Carlos Portal (9/0)], Pedro Magán (8/0) [46.Marcial Hurtado (5/1)], Luis Guzmán (4/0) [70.Antonio Zegarra (1/0)], Teodoro Fernández (26/24), Adelfo Magallanes (19/4), Leopoldo Quiñónes (10/0). Trainer: Angel Fernández (3).
Goal: Teodoro Fernández (19).

37. 28.01.1942 **PERU - ECUADOR** **2-1(1-0)** 17th Copa América
Estadio Centenario, Montevideo (Uruguay); Referee: Aníbal Tejada (Uruguay); Attendance: 40,000
PER: Juan Honores (17/0), Enrique Perales (10/0), Tulio Obando (1/0), Pablo Pasache (8/0), Carlos Portal (10/0), Máximo Lobatón (10/0), Marcial Hurtado (6/1), Luis Guzmán (5/1), Teodoro Fernández (27/24), Adelfo Magallanes (20/4) [46.Roberto Morales (6/0)], Leopoldo Quiñónes (11/1). Trainer: Angel Fernández (4).
Goals: Leopoldo Quiñónes (32), Luis Guzmán (69).

38. 01.02.1942 **URUGUAY - PERU** **3-0(2-0)** 17th Copa América
Estadio Centenario, Montevideo; Referee: José Bartolomé Macías (Argentina); Attendance: 40,000
PER: Juan Honores (18/0), Enrique Perales (11/0), Juan Quispe (12/0), Teobaldo Guzmán (4/0), Pablo Pasache (9/0), Máximo Lobatón (11/0), Marcial Hurtado (7/1) [57.Pedro Magán (9/0)], Luis Guzmán (6/1) [62.Antonio Zegarra (2/0)], Teodoro Fernández (28/24) [62.Adelfo Magallanes (21/4)], Roberto Morales (7/0), Leopoldo Quiñónes (12/1). Trainer: Angel Fernández (5).

39. 07.02.1942 **PERU - CHILE** **0-0** 17th Copa América
Estadio Centenario, Montevideo (Uruguay); Referee: José Bartolomé Macías (Argentina); Attendance: 70,000
PER: Juan Honores (19/0), Enrique Perales (12/0), Juan Quispe (13/0), Teobaldo Guzmán (5/0), Pablo Pasache (10/0) [46.Antonio Biffi (2/0)], Máximo Lobatón (12/0), Pedro Magán (10/0), Luis Guzmán (7/1), Teodoro Fernández (29/24), Adelfo Magallanes (22/4), Leopoldo Quiñónes (13/1). Trainer: Angel Fernández (6).

40. 06.12.1947 **PERU - PARAGUAY** **2-2(1-1)** 20th Copa América
Estadio „George Capwell", Guayaquil (Ecuador); Referee: Luis Alberto Fernández (Uruguay); Attendance: 20,000
PER: Luis Suárez (1/0), Eliseo Morales (1/0), Andrés Da Silva (1/0), Juan Castillo (1/0), Alejandro Gonzáles (2/0), Cornelio Heredia (1/0), Félix Castillo (1/1), Guillermo Barbadillo (1/0) [60.Máximo Mosquera (1/1)], Teodoro Fernández (30/24) [60.Valeriano López (1/0)], Carlos Gómez Sánchez (1/0) [70.Luis Guzmán (8/1)], Guillermo Valdivieso (1/0). Trainer: José Arana (1).
Goals: Félix Castillo (17), Máximo Mosquera (63).

41. 09.12.1947 **CHILE - PERU** **2-1(1-0)** 20th Copa América
Estadio „George Capwell", Guayaquil (Ecuador); Referee: Juan José Álvarez (Argentina); Attendance: 15,000
PER: Rafael Asca (1/0), Eliseo Morales (2/0), Enrique Perales (13/0), Juan Castillo (2/0) [68.Lorenzo Pacheco (1/0)], Domingo Raffo (1/0) [46.Alejandro Gonzáles (3/0)], René Rosasco (1/0), Marin Reyna (1/0), Guillermo Barbadillo (2/0), Valeriano López (2/1), Carlos Gómez Sánchez (2/0), Ernesto Morales (1/0) [63.Carlos Torres (1/0)]. Trainer: José Arana (2).
Goal: Valeriano López (72).

42. 11.12.1947 **ARGENTINA - PERU** **3-2(1-1)** 20th Copa América
Estadio „George Capwell", Guayaquil (Ecuador); Referee: Luis Alberto Fernández (Uruguay); Attendance: 22,000
PER: Rafael Asca (2/0) [46.Luis Suárez (2/0)], Eliseo Morales (3/0), Enrique Perales (14/0), Lorenzo Pacheco (2/0) [70.Juan Castillo (3/0)], Carlos Torres (2/0), Cornelio Heredia (2/0), Marin Reyna (2/0) [46.Teodoro Fernández (31/24)], Máximo Mosquera (2/1), Valeriano López (3/2), Luis Guzmán (9/1), Carlos Gómez Sánchez (3/1). Trainer: José Arana (3).
Goals: Carlos Gómez Sánchez (26), Valeriano López (65).

43. 20.12.1947 **ECUADOR - PERU** **0-0** 20th Copa América
Estadio „George Capwell", Guayaquil; Referee: Mario Rubén Heyn (Paraguay); Attendance: 20,000
PER: Luis Suárez (3/0), Eliseo Morales (4/0), Enrique Perales (15/0), Lorenzo Pacheco (3/0), Alejandro Gonzáles (4/0) [65.Rene Rosasco (2/0)], Cornelio Heredia (3/0), Marin Reyna (3/0), Máximo Mosquera (3/1), Teodoro Fernández (32/24) [46.Guillermo Barbadillo (3/0)], Luis Guzmán (10/1), Félix Castillo (2/1). Trainer: José Arana (4).

44. 23.12.1947 **PERU - COLOMBIA** **5-1(1-0)** 20th Copa América
Estadio „George Capwell", Guayaquil (Ecuador); Referee: Mario Rubén Heyn (Paraguay); Attendance: 5,000
PER: Luis Suárez (4/0), Andrés Da Silva (2/0), Enrique Perales (16/0), Juan Castillo (4/0), Alejandro Gonzáles (5/0), Cornelio Heredia (4/0), Guillermo Valdivieso (2/0) [55.Valeriano López (4/2)], Máximo Mosquera (4/2), Luis Guzmán (11/3), Félix Castillo (3/1), Carlos Gómez Sánchez (4/3). Trainer: José Arana (5) .
Goal: Carlos Gómez Sánchez (3), Máximo Mosquera (53), Luis Guzmán (67, 79), Carlos Gómez Sánchez (81).

45. 25.12.1947 **URUGUAY - PERU** **1-0(0-0)** 20th Copa América
Estadio „George Capwell", Guayaquil (Ecuador); Referee: Víctor Francisco Rivas (Chile); Attendance: 6,000
PER: Luis Suárez (5/0), Andrés Da Silva (3/0) [Eliseo Morales (5/0)], Enrique Perales (17/0), Lorenzo Pacheco (4/0), Alejandro Gonzáles (6/0), Cornelio Heredia (5/0), Félix Castillo (4/1), Máximo Mosquera (5/2), Carlos Gómez Sánchez (5/3), Luis Guzmán (12/3), Guillermo Valdivieso (3/0) [30.Valeriano López (5/2)]. Trainer: José Arana (6).

46. 27.12.1947 **PERU - BOLIVIA** **2-0(0-0)** 20th Copa América
Estadio „George Capwell", Guayaquil (Ecuador); Referee: Mario Rubén Heyn (Paraguay); Attendance: 5,000
PER: Luis Suárez (6/0), Eliseo Morales (6/0), Domingo Raffo (2/0), Lorenzo Pacheco (5/0), Alejandro Gonzáles (7/0), Cornelio Heredia (6/0), Félix Castillo (5/2), Guillermo Barbadillo (4/0) [46.Máximo Mosquera (6/2)], Valeriano López (6/2), Luis Guzmán (13/4), Carlos Gómez Sánchez (6/3) [64.Juan Castillo (5/0)]. Trainer: José Arana (7)
Goals: Luis Guzmán (75), Félix Castillo (82).

47. 10.04.1949 **PERU - COLOMBIA** **4-0(1-0)** 21st Copa América
Estádio São Januario, Río de Janeiro (Brazil); Referee: Mario Rubén Heyn (Paraguay); Attendance: 15,000
PER: Walter Ormeño (1/0), Andrés Da Silva (4/0), Félix Fuentes (1/0), Gerardo Arce (1/0), Lorenzo Pacheco (6/0), Germán Colunga (1/0), Félix Castillo (6/2), Manuel Drago (1/1), Juan Emilio Salinas (1/1), Alfredo Mosquera (1/0), Víctor Pedraza (1/2) [73.Pedro Valdivieso (1/0)]. Trainer: Arturo Fernández (1).
Goals: Víctor Pedraza (24), Manuel Drago (47), Juan Emilio Salinas (84), Víctor Pedraza (89).

48. 13.04.1949 **PARAGUAY – PERU** **3-1(1-0)** 21st Copa América
Estádio São Januario, Río de Janeiro (Brazil); Referee: Cyril Jack Barrick (England); Attendance: 30,000
PER: Walter Ormeño (2/0), Gerardo Arce (2/0) [56.Andrés Da Silva (5/0)], Félix Fuentes (2/0), Alejandro Gonzáles (8/0) [46.Germán Colunga (2/0)], Lorenzo Pacheco (7/0), Luis Calderón (1/0), Félix Castillo (7/2), Roberto Drago (1/1), Carlos Gómez Sánchez (7/3) [62.Juan Emilio Salinas (2/1)], Alfredo Mosquera (2/0), Víctor Pedraza (2/2). Trainer: Arturo Fernández (2).
Goal: Roberto Drago (88).

49. 20.04.1949 **PERU - ECUADOR** **4-0(2-0)** 21st Copa América
Estádio São Januario, Río de Janeiro (Brazil); Referee: Juan Carlos Armental (Uruguay); Attendance: 7,000
PER: Walter Ormeño (3/0), Gerardo Arce (3/0), Félix Fuentes (3/0), Luis Calderón (2/0) [70.Cornelio Heredia (7/0)], Lorenzo Pacheco (8/0), Alejandro Gonzáles (9/0), Félix Castillo (8/3) [65.Roberto Drago (2/1)], Manuel Drago (2/1), Juan Emilio Salinas (3/2), Alfredo Mosquera (3/0), Víctor Pedraza (3/3). Trainer: Arturo Fernández (3).
Goals: Juan Emilio Salinas (26), Marcos Bermeo (36 own goal), Félix Castillo (50), Víctor Pedraza (85).

50. 24.04.1949 **BRAZIL – PERU** **7-1(4-1)** 21st Copa América
Estádio São Januario, Río de Janeiro; Referee: Cyril John Barrick (England); Attendance: 45,000
PER: Walter Ormeño (4/0), Gerardo Arce (4/0) [46.Andrés Da Silva (6/0)], Félix Fuentes (4/0), Luis Calderón (3/0), Germán Colunga (3/0), Alejandro Gonzáles (10/0), Leonidas Mendoza (1/0) [46.Manuel Drago (3/1)], Juan Emilio Salinas (4/3) [46.Alfredo Mosquera (4/0)], Carlos Gómez Sánchez (8/3), Víctor Pedraza (4/3), Félix Castillo (9/3). Trainer: Arturo Fernández (4).
Goal: Juan Emilio Salinas (44).

51. 27.04.1949 **PERU – BOLIVIA** **3-0(1-0)** 21st Copa América
Estádio Villa Belmiro, Santos (Brazil); Referee: Alberto Monard da Gama Malcher (Brazil); Attendance: 12,000
PER: Walter Ormeño (5/0), Andrés Da Silva (7/0), Félix Fuentes (5/0), Germán Colunga (4/0), Dagoberto Lavalle (1/0) [58.Alejandro Gonzáles (11/0)], Cornelio Heredia (8/1), Félix Castillo (10/3), Roberto Drago (3/3) [65.Leonidas Mendoza (2/0)], Carlos Gómez Sánchez (9/3), Alfredo Mosquera (5/0) [71.Pedro Valdivieso (2/0)], Víctor Pedraza (5/3). Trainer: Arturo Fernández (5).
Goals: Roberto Drago (31, 74), Cornelio Heredia (77 penalty).

52. 30.04.1949 **PERU – CHILE** **3-0(1-0)** 21st Copa América
Estádio Pacaembú, São Paulo (Brazil); Referee: Mario Gardelli (Brazil); Attendance: 1,000
PER: Walter Ormeño (6/0), Andrés Da Silva (8/0), Félix Fuentes (6/0), Cornelio Heredia (9/1), Germán Colunga (5/0), Alejandro Gonzáles (12/0) [73.Dagoberto Lavalle (2/0)], Roberto Drago (4/3), Alfredo Mosquera (6/1), Carlos Gómez Sánchez (10/3), Víctor Pedraza (6/3), Félix Castillo (11/5). Trainer: Arturo Fernández (6).
Goals: Félix Castillo (28, 58), Alfredo Mosquera (73).

53. 04.05.1949 **PERU – URUGUAY** **4-3(2-0)** 21st Copa América
Estádio Botafogo, Rio de Janeiro (Brazil); Referee: Alfredo Álvarez (Bolivia); Attendance: 30,000
PER: Walter Ormeño (7/0), Andrés Da Silva (9/0), Félix Fuentes (7/0) [75.Gerardo Arce (5/0)], Cornelio Heredia (10/1), Germán Colunga (6/0), Alejandro Gonzáles (13/0), Roberto Drago (5/3), Alfredo Mosquera (7/2), Carlos Gómez Sánchez (11/5), Víctor Pedraza (7/3) [71.Ernesto Morales (2/0)], Félix Castillo (12/6). Trainer: Arturo Fernández (7).
Goals: Alfredo Mosquera (16), Félix Castillo (43), Carlos Gómez Sánchez (57, 60).

54. 23.03.1952 **PERU - PANAMA** **7-1(4-0)** Campeonato Panamericano
Estadio Nacional, Santiago (Chile); Referee: Geoffrey Sunderland (England)
PER: Walter Ormeño (8/0), Diego Agurto (1/0), Guillermo Delgado (1/0), Luis Calderón (4/0), Cornelio Heredia (11/1), Lorenzo Pacheco (9/0), Gilberto Torres (1/0) [46.Roberto Castillo (1/0)], Roberto Drago (6/4), Valeraiano López (7/7) [80.Carlos Lazón (1/0)], Guillermo Barbadillo (5/0), Ernesto Morales (3/1). Trainer: Alfonso Huapaya (1).
Goal: Valeriano López (4, 9, 17), Roberto Drago (42), Ernesto Morales (60), Valeriano López (86, 88).

55. 30.03.1952 **URUGUAY – PERU** **5-2(3-1)** Campeonato Panamericano
Estadio Nacional, Santiago (Chile); Referee: William Crawford (England)
PER: Walter Ormeño (9/0), Diego Agurto (2/0), Guillermo Delgado (2/0), Luis Calderón (5/0), Dagoberto Lavalle (3/0) [60.Cornelio Heredia (12/1)], Lorenzo Pacheco (10/0), Roberto Castillo (2/0), Roberto Drago (7/4) [55.Máximo Mosquera (7/2)], Valeriano López (8/8), Guillermo Barbadillo (6/1), Ernesto Morales (4/1) [60.René Rosasco (3/0)]. Trainer: Alfonso Huapaya (2).
Goal: Guillermo Barbadillo (21), Valeriano López (71).

56. 02.04.1952 **CHILE - PERU** **3-2(1-0)** Campeonato Panamericano
Estadio Nacional, Santiago; Referee: John Aldrige (England); Attendance: 47,000
PER: Walter Ormeño (10/0), César Brusch (1/0), Guillermo Delgado (3/0), Rene Rosasco (4/0) [62.Dagoberto Lavalle (4/0)], Cornelio Heredia (13/1), Rafael Goyoneche (1/0), Gilberto Torres (2/0), Roberto Drago (8/4) [69.Roberto Castillo (3/0)], Valeriano López (9/9), Carlos Lazón (2/0), Guillermo Barbadillo (7/2). Trainer: Alfonso Huapaya (3).
Goal: Guillermo Barbadillo (55), Valeriano López (74 penalty).

57. 10.04.1952 **PERU – BRAZIL** **0-0** Campeonato Panamericano
Estadio Nacional, Santiago (Chile); Referee: Charles McKenna (England)
PER: Walter Ormeño (11/0), César Brusch (2/0), Guillermo Delgado (4/0) [76.Adolfo Cabada (1/0)], Rene Rosasco (5/0), Cornelio Heredia (14/1), Rafael Goyoneche (2/0), Gilberto Torres (3/0), Máximo Mosquera (8/2) [56.Valeriano López (10/9)], Manuel Rivera (1/0), Roberto Drago (9/4), Ernesto Morales (5/1). Trainer: Alfonso Huapaya (4).

58. 20.04.1952 **PERU – MEXICO** **3-0(1-0)** Campeonato Panamericano
Estadio Nacional, Santiago (Chile); Referee: Charles McKenna (England)
PER: Walter Ormeño (12/0), César Brusch (3/0), Guillermo Delgado (5/0), Rene Rosasco (6/0), Cornelio Heredia (15/1), Rafael Goyoneche (3/0), Gilberto Torres (4/1), Máximo Mosquera (9/2) [55.Valeriano López (11/9)], Manuel Rivera (2/1), Roberto Drago (10/5), Ernesto Morales (6/1). Trainer: Alfonso Huapaya (5).
Goals: Manuel Rivera (6), Roberto Drago (16), Gilberto Torres (85).

59. 22.02.1953 **PERU – BOLIVIA** **0-1(0-0)** 22nd Copa América
Estadio Nacional, Lima; Referee: George Rhoden (England); Attendance: 50,000
PER: Rafael Asca (3/0), César Brusch (4/0), Guillermo Delgado (6/0), Luis Calderón (6/0), Rafael Goyoneche (4/0) [46.Ernesto Villamares (1/0)], Cornelio Heredia (16/1), Gilberto Torres (5/1), Roberto Drago (11/5) [Luis Dávalos (1/0)], Roberto Castillo (4/0) [60.Alberto Reyes (1/0)], Guillermo Barbadillo (8/2) [66.Juan Bassa (1/0)], Luis Navarrete (1/0). Trainer: William Cook (1).

60. 28.02.1953 **PERU - ECUADOR** **1-0(0-0)** 22nd Copa América
Estadio Nacional, Lima; Referee: George Rhoden (England); Attendance: 50,000
PER: Rafael Asca (4/0), José Allen (1/0), Guillermo Delgado (7/0), Luis Calderón (7/0), Rafael Goyoneche (5/0) [46.Ernesto Villamares (2/0)], Cornelio Heredia (17/1), Gilberto Torres (6/1), Roberto Drago (12/5) [46.Roberto Castillo (5/0)], Manuel Rivera (3/1), Guillermo Barbadillo (9/2) [65.Juan Bassa (2/0)], Oscar Gómez Sánchez (1/1). Trainer: William Cook (2).
Goal: Oscar Gómez Sánchez (78).

61. 04.03.1953 **PERU – CHILE** **0-0** 22nd Copa América
Estadio Nacional, Lima; Referee: Richard Maddison (England); Attendance: 42,737
PER: Rafael Asca (5/0), José Allen (2/0), Guillermo Delgado (8/0), Luis Calderón (8/0), Ernesto Villamares (3/0), Cornelio Heredia (18/1), Gilberto Torres (7/1) [46.Luis Navarrete (2/0)], Roberto Drago (13/5), Roberto Castillo (6/0) [55.Guillermo Barbadillo (10/2)], Manuel Rivera (4/1), Oscar Gómez Sánchez (2/1). Trainer: Angel Fernández (7).

62. 08.03.1953 **PERU – PARAGUAY** **2-2(1-1)** 22nd Copa América
Estadio Nacional, Lima; Referee: Richard Maddison (England); Attendance: 45,000
PER: Rafael Asca (6/0), José Allen (3/0), Guillermo Delgado (9/0), Luis Calderón (9/0), Ernesto Villamares (4/1), Cornelio Heredia (19/1), Oscar Gómez Sánchez (3/1) [65.Alberto Reyes (2/0)], Roberto Drago (14/5), Alberto Terry (1/1) [58.Gilberto Torres (8/1)], Guillermo Barbadillo (11/2) [46.Juan Bassa (3/0)], Luis Navarrete (3/0). Trainer: Angel Fernández (8).
Goals: Alberto Terry (21), Ernesto Villamares (76).
Match awarded to Peru due to unsportsmanlike behaviour of Paraguayan players by making one extra change. Ayala was banned for three years for kicking the referee.

63. 19.03.1953 **PERU – BRAZIL** **1-0(0-0)** 22nd Copa América
Estadio Nacional, Lima; Referee: Charles McKenna (England); Attendance: 55,000
PER: Rafael Asca (7/0), José Allen (4/0), Guillermo Delgado (10/0), Luis Calderón (10/0), Ernesto Villamares (5/1), Cornelio Heredia (20/1), Gilberto Torres (9/1), Roberto Drago (15/5) [66.Juan Bassa (4/0)], Alberto Terry (2/1) [50.Manuel Rivera (5/1)], Guillermo Barbadillo (12/2), Luis Navarrete (4/1),. Trainer: Angel Fernández (9).
Goal: Luis Navarrete (61).

64. 28.03.1953 **URUGUAY – PERU** **3-0(1-0)** 22nd Copa América
Estadio Nacional, Lima; Referee: Mário Silveira Vianna (Brazil); Attendance: 45,000
PER: Rafael Asca (8/0), José Allen (5/0), Guillermo Delgado (11/0), Luis Calderón (11/0), Ernesto Villamares (6/1), Cornelio Heredia (21/1), Gilberto Torres (10/1) [Roberto Castillo (7/0)], Roberto Drago (16/5) [Juan Bassa (5/0)], Alberto Terry (3/1) [Manuel Rivera (6/1)], Guillermo Barbadillo (13/2), Luis Navarrete (5/1). Trainer: Angel Fernández (10).

65. 26.07.1953 **PERU – CHILE** **1-2(1-1)** Copa del Pacífico
Estadio Nacional, Lima; Referee: Charles McKenna (England); Attendance: 33,175
PER: Clemente Velásquez (1/0), Enrique Velásquez (1/0), Guillermo Delgado (12/0) [65.Adolfo Donayre (1/0)], Luis Calderón (12/0), Dagoberto Lavalle (5/0), Cornelio Heredia (22/1), Luis Navarrete (6/2), Roberto Drago (17/5) [77.Emilio Vargas (1/0)], Alberto Terry (4/1), Guillermo Barbadillo (14/2) [50.Félix Castillo (13/6)], Gilberto Torres (11/1). Trainer: Angel Fernández (11).
Goal: Luis Navarrete (57).

66. 28.07.1953 **PERU – CHILE** **5-0(2-0)** Copa del Pacífico
Estadio Nacional, Lima; Referee: Charles McKenna (England); Attendance: 29,377
PER: Clemente Velásquez (2/0), Enrique Velásquez (2/0), Guillermo Delgado (13/0), Luis Calderón (13/0), Dagoberto Lavalle (6/0), Cornelio Heredia (23/3) [77.René Rosasco (7/0)], Luis Navarrete (7/2), Roberto Drago (18/6), Félix Castillo (14/6), Alberto Terry (5/3) [73.Guillermo Barbadillo (15/2)], Raúl Da Giau (1/0) [46.Tulio Quiñónes (1/0)]. Trainer: Angel Fernández (12).
Goals: Alberto Terry (8), Cornelio Heredia (49), Roberto Drago (52), Alberto Terry (55), Cornelio Heredia (67 penalty).

67. 17.09.1954 **CHILE – PERU** **2-1(1-1)** Copa del Pacífico
Estadio Nacional, Santiago; Referee: Juan Carlos Robles (Chile); Attendance: 21,116
PER: Luis Suárez (7/0), Andrés Bedoya (1/0), Guillermo Delgado (14/0), Luis Calderón (14/0), Dagoberto Lavalle (7/0), Cornelio Heredia (24/3), Félix Castillo (15/6) [60.Carlos Lazón (3/0)], Roberto Drago (19/6) [46.Guillermo Barbadillo (16/2)], Manuel Rivera (7/1), Alberto Terry (6/3), Oscar Gómez Sánchez (4/2). Trainer: Juan Valdivieso Padilla (1).
Goal: Oscar Gómez Sánchez (14).

68. 19.09.1954 **CHILE – PERU** **2-4(1-4)** Copa del Pacífico
Estadio Nacional, Santiago; Referee: Juan Carlos Robles (Chile); Attendance: 21,051
PER: Luis Suárez (8/0), Andrés Bedoya (2/0), Guillermo Delgado (15/0), Alfonso Garrido (1/0), Germán Colunga (7/0), Cornelio Heredia (25/3), Carlos Lazón (4/0) [80.Félix Castillo (16/6)], Máximo Mosquera (10/2), Guillermo Barbadillo (17/2), Roberto Castillo (8/0) [46.Alberto Terry (7/4)], Oscar Gómez Sánchez (5/4). Trainer: Juan Valdivieso Padilla (2).
Goal: Alberto Terry (60), Sergio Roberto Livingstone (68 own goal), Oscar Gómez Sánchez (73, 78).

69. 06.03.1955 **CHILE – PERU** **5-4(2-1)** 23rd Copa América
Estadio Nacional, Santiago; Referee: Harry Dykes (England); Attendance: 42,833
PER: Luis Suárez (9/0), Andrés Bedoya (3/0), Guillermo Delgado (16/0), Alfonso Garrido (2/0), Germán Colunga (8/0) [65.Dagoberto Lavalle (8/0)], Cornelio Heredia (26/4), Félix Castillo (17/7) [55.Luis Navarrete (8/2)], Guillermo Barbadillo (18/3), Roberto Castillo (9/0), Máximo Mosquera (11/2) [65.Alberto Terry (8/4)], Oscar Gómez Sánchez (6/5). Trainer: Juan Valdivieso Padilla (3).
Goals: Félix Castillo (35), Guillermo Barbadillo (61), Cornelio Heredia (64 penalty), Oscar Gómez Sánchez (83).

70. 13.03.1955 **PERU – ECUADOR** **4-2(3-1)** 23rd Copa América
Estadio Nacional, Santiago (Chile); Referee: Juan Carlos Robles (Chile); Attendance: 50,000
PER: Luis Suárez (10/0), Andrés Bedoya (4/0) [62.Carlos Lazón (5/0)], Agapito Perales (1/0) [79.Guillermo Delgado (17/0)], Víctor Salas (1/0), Luis Calderón (15/0), Cornelio Heredia (27/4), Félix Castillo (18/7), Guillermo Barbadillo (19/3), Roberto Castillo (10/0) [57.Alberto Loret de Mola (1/0)], Máximo Mosquera (12/3), Oscar Gómez Sánchez (7/7). Trainer: Juan Valdivieso Padilla (4).
Goals: Oscar Gómez Sánchez (11, 27), Honorato Gonzabay (29 own goal), Máximo Mosquera (88).

71. 16.03.1955 **ARGENTINA - PERU** **2-2(2-1)** 23rd Copa América
Estadio Nacional, Santiago (Chile); Referee: Washington Rodríguez (Uruguay); Attendance: 23,000
PER: Luis Suárez (11/0), Carlos Lazón (6/0), Guillermo Delgado (18/0), Víctor Salas (2/0), Germán Colunga (9/0), Cornelio Heredia (28/4), Luis Navarrete (9/2), Roberto Drago (20/6) [Félix Castillo (19/7)], Alberto Loret de Mola (2/0) [Alberto Terry (9/4)], Máximo Mosquera (13/3), Oscar Gómez Sánchez (8/9). Trainer: Juan Valdivieso Padilla (5).
Goal: Oscar Gómez Sánchez (25, 60).

72. 23.03.1955 **PARAGUAY - PERU** **1-1(0-1)** 23rd Copa América
Estadio Nacional, Santiago (Chile); Referee: Juan Regis Brozzi (Argentina); Attendance: 25,000
PER: Luis Suárez (12/0), Carlos Lazón (7/0) [67.Andrés Bedoya (5/0)], Guillermo Delgado (19/0), Víctor Salas (3/0), Germán Colunga (10/0), Cornelio Heredia (29/4), Luis Navarrete (10/2), Roberto Drago (21/6), Alberto Loret de Mola (3/0) [55.Guillermo Barbadillo (20/3)], Alberto Terry (10/5) [65.Félix Castillo (20/7)], Oscar Gómez Sánchez (9/9). Trainer: Juan Valdivieso Padilla (6).
Goal: Alberto Terry (33).

73. 30.03.1955 **PERU – URUGUAY** **2-1(1-0)** 23rd Copa América
Estadio Nacional, Santiago (Chile); Referee: Juan Carlos Robles (Chile); Attendance: 65,000
PER: Luis Suárez (13/0), Andrés Bedoya (6/0), Guillermo Delgado (20/0), Víctor Salas (4/0), Germán Colunga (11/0), Cornelio Heredia (30/4), Félix Castillo (21/7) [65.Luis Navarrete (11/2)], Guillermo Barbadillo (21/3), Roberto Castillo (11/1) [73.Alberto Loret de Mola (4/0)], Máximo Mosquera (14/3), Oscar Gómez Sánchez (10/10). Trainer: Juan Valdivieso Padilla (7).
Goal: Roberto Castillo (11), Oscar Gómez Sánchez (69).

74. 22.01.1956 **ARGENTINA - PERU** **2-1(1-0)** 24th Copa América
Estadio Centenario, Montevideo (Uruguay); Referee: Washington Rodríguez (Uruguay); Attendance: 16,000
PER: Dimas Zegarra (1/0), Guillermo Delgado (21/0), Carlos Lazón (8/0), Víctor Salas (5/0), Luis Calderón (16/0), Cornelio Heredia (31/4), Félix Castillo (22/7), Roberto Drago (22/7), Alberto Loret de Mola (5/0) [55.Alberto Terry (11/5)], Máximo Mosquera (15/3), Oscar Gómez Sánchez (11/10). Trainer: Arturo Fernández (8).
Goal: Roberto Drago (55).

75. 28.01.1956 **URUGUAY – PERU** **2-0(1-0)** 24th Copa América
Estadio Centenario, Montevideo; Referee: Cayetano De Nicola (Paraguay); Attendance: 70,000
PER: Dimas Zegarra (2/0), Guillermo Delgado (22/0), Carlos Lazón (9/0), Víctor Salas (6/0), Luis Calderón (17/0), Cornelio Heredia (32/4) [65.René Gutiérrez (1/0)], Félix Castillo (23/7), Roberto Castillo (12/1), Guillermo Barbadillo (22/3) [46.Roberto Drago (23/7)], Máximo Mosquera (16/3) [75.Alberto Loret de Mola (6/0)], Juan Seminario (1/0). Trainer: Arturo Fernández (9).

76. 01.02.1956 **BRAZIL – PERU** **2-1(1-1)** 24th Copa América
Estadio Centenario, Montevideo (Uruguay); Referee: Washington Rodríguez (Uruguay); Attendance: 20,000
PER: Dimas Zegarra (3/0), Guillermo Delgado (23/0), Carlos Lazón (10/0), Víctor Salas (7/0) [60.Isaac Andrade (1/0)], Luis Calderón (18/0) [46.Germán Colunga (12/0)], René Gutiérrez (2/0), Félix Castillo (24/7), Roberto Drago (24/8), Roberto Castillo (13/1), Guillermo Barbadillo (23/3), Juan Seminario (2/0) [77.Jacinto Villalba (1/0)]. Trainer: Arturo Fernández (10).
Goal: Roberto Drago (42).

77. 05.02.1956 **PERU – PARAGUAY** **1-1(0-0)** 24th Copa América
Estadio Centenario, Montevideo (Uruguay); Referee: Juan Regis Brozzi (Argentina); Attendance: 25,000
PER: Dimas Zegarra (4/0), Guillermo Delgado (24/0), Carlos Lazón (11/1), Isaac Andrade (2/0), Luis Calderón (19/0), René Gutiérrez (3/0), Félix Castillo (25/7), Roberto Drago (25/8), Roberto Castillo (14/1) [75.Alberto Terry (12/5)], Máximo Mosquera (17/3), Oscar Gómez Sánchez (12/10). Trainer: Arturo Fernández (11).
Goal: Carlos Lazón (61).

78. 09.02.1956 **CHILE - PERU** **4-3(2-1)** 24th Copa América
Estadio Centenario, Montevideo (Uruguay); Referee: Juan Regis Brozzi (Argentina); Attendance: 5,000
PER: Dimas Zegarra (5/0), Guillermo Delgado (25/0), Carlos Lazón (12/1), Víctor Salas (8/0) [69.Isaac Andrade (3/0)], Luis Calderón (20/0), Cornelio Heredia (33/4) [61.René Gutiérrez (4/0)], Félix Castillo (26/8), Roberto Drago (26/8), Alberto Loret de Mola (7/0) [46.Roberto Castillo (15/1)], Máximo Mosquera (18/4), Oscar Gómez Sánchez (13/11). Trainer: Arturo Fernández (12).
Goals: Félix Castillo (15), Máximo Mosquera (79), Oscar Gómez Sánchez (84).

79. 28.02.1956 **ARGENTINA – PERU** **0-0** Campeonato Panamericano
Estadio Olímpico de Centro Universitário, Ciudad de México (Mexico); Referee: Alberto Monard de Gama Malcher (Brazil); Attendance: 60,000
PER: Rigoberto Felandro (1/0), Carlos Lazón (13/1), Guillermo Delgado (26/0), Víctor Salas (9/0), Luis Calderón (21/0), Cornelio Heredia (34/4), Félix Castillo (27/8), Guillermo Barbadillo (24/3), Jorge Lama (1/0), Máximo Mosquera (19/4), Oscar Gómez Sánchez (14/11). Trainer: Arturo Fernández (13).

80. 04.03.1956 **MEXICO - PERU** **0-2(0-1)** Campeonato Panamericano
Estadio Olímpico de Centro Universitário, Ciudad de México; Referee: Alberto Monard de Gama Malcher (Brazil)
PER: Rigoberto Felandro (2/0), Carlos Lazón (14/1), Guillermo Delgado (27/0), Víctor Salas (10/0), Dagoberto Lavalle (9/0), Luis Calderón (22/0) [88.Humberto Del Valle (1/0)], Félix Castillo (28/8), Roberto Drago (27/9) [63.Ernesto Morales (7/1)], Jorge Lama (2/0) [50.Juan Emilio Salinas (5/3)], Máximo Mosquera (20/4), Oscar Gómez Sánchez (15/12). Trainer: Arturo Fernández (14).
Goals: Roberto Drago (44), Oscar Gómez Sánchez (72).

81. 06.03.1956 **BRAZIL – PERU** **1-0(1-0)** Campeonato Panamericano
Estadio Olímpico de Centro Universitário, Ciudad de México (Mexico); Referee: Alfredo Rossi (Argentina)
PER: Rigoberto Felandro (3/0), Carlos Lazón (15/1), Guillermo Delgado (28/0), Víctor Salas (11/0), Dagoberto Lavalle (10/0) [80.Enrique Velásquez (3/0)], Luis Calderón (23/0), Félix Castillo (29/8), Roberto Drago (28/9) [*sent off*], Jorge Lama (3/0) [55.Juan Emilio Salinas (6/3)], Máximo Mosquera (21/4), Oscar Gómez Sánchez (16/12) [77.Juan Seminario (3/0)]. Trainer: Arturo Fernández (15).

82. 15.03.1956 **PERU – CHILE** **2-2(1-1)** Campeonato Panamericano

Estadio Olímpico de Centro Universitário, Ciudad de México (Mexico); Referee: Danilo Alfaro (Costa Rica)

PER: Rigoberto Felandro (4/0), Carlos Lazón (16/1), Guillermo Delgado (29/0), Alberto Del Solar (1/0), Cornelio Heredia (35/4), Luis Calderón (24/0), Félix Castillo (30/8), Guillermo Barbadillo (25/3) [50.Ernesto Morales (8/1)], Jorge Lama (4/1), Máximo Mosquera (22/5), Oscar Gómez Sánchez (17/12) [65.Juan Seminario (4/0)]. Trainer: Arturo Fernández (16).

Goals: Jorge Lama (21), Máximo Mosquera (73).

83. 17.03.1956 **COSTA RICA - PERU** **4-2(3-0)** Campeonato Panamericano

Estadio Olímpico de Centro Universitário, Ciudad de México (Mexico); Referee: Fernando Buergo (Mexico)

PER: Rigoberto Felandro (5/0), Carlos Lazón (17/1), Guillermo Delgado (30/0), Alberto Del Solar (2/0), Cornelio Heredia (36/4), Dagoberto Lavalle (11/0) [46.Luis Calderón (25/0)], Félix Castillo (31/8), Roberto Drago (29/9), Juan Emilio Salinas (7/5), Ernesto Morales (9/1) [70.Máximo Mosquera (23/5)], Juan Seminario (5/0). Trainer: Arturo Fernández (17).

Goals: Juan Emilio Salinas (55, 69).

84. 10.03.1957 **PERU - ECUADOR** **2-1(1-1)** 25th Copa América

Estadio Nacional, Lima; Referee: Robert Turner (England); Attendance: 55,000

PER: Rafael Asca (9/0), Guillermo Fleming (1/0), Guillermo Delgado (31/0), Víctor Salas (12/0), Carlos Lazón (18/1), Luis Calderón (26/0), Jacinto Villalba (2/0) [46.Roberto Castillo (16/1)], Alberto Terry (13/7), Valeriano López (12/9), Máximo Mosquera (24/5), Juan Joya (1/0) [78.Juan Seminario (6/0)]. Trainer: György Orth (1).

Goals: Alberto Terry (38, 61).

85. 16.03.1957 **PERU – CHILE** **1-0(0-0)** 25th Copa América

Estadio Nacional, Lima; Referee: Ronald Lynch (England); Attendance: 60,000

PER: Rigoberto Felandro (6/0), Guillermo Fleming (2/0) [55.Alfredo Cavero (1/0)], Guillermo Delgado (32/0), Víctor Salas (13/0) [Dante Rovay (1/0)], Carlos Lazón (19/1), René Gutiérrez (5/0) [Luis Calderón (27/0)], Jacinto Villalba (3/0), Alberto Terry (14/7), Daniel Ruiz (1/0) [Valeriano López (13/9)], Máximo Mosquera (25/6), Juan Seminario (7/0). Trainer: György Orth (2).

Goal: Máximo Mosquera (56).

86. 23.03.1957 **PERU – URUGUAY** **3-5(1-2)** 25th Copa América

Estadio Nacional, Lima; Referee: Bertley Cross (England); Attendance: 55,000

PER: Rigoberto Felandro (7/0), Alfredo Cavero (2/0), Guillermo Delgado (33/0), Víctor Salas (14/0) [46.Dante Rovay (2/0)], Carlos Lazón (20/1), René Gutiérrez (6/0) [46.Luis Calderón (28/0)], Jacinto Villalba (4/0), Alberto Terry (15/8), Daniel Ruiz (2/0) [46.Valeriano López (14/9)], Máximo Mosquera (26/7), Juan Seminario (8/1). Trainer: György Orth (3).

Goals: Alberto Terry (3), Juan Seminario (71), Máximo Mosquera (72).

87. 27.03.1957 **PERU - COLOMBIA** **4-1(3-0)** 25th Copa América

Estadio Nacional, Lima; Referee: Ronald Lynch (England); Attendance: 55,000

PER: Rafael Asca (10/0), Guillermo Fleming (3/0), Guillermo Delgado (34/0), Dante Rovay (3/0), Carlos Lazón (21/1), Luis Calderón (29/0), Roberto Castillo (17/1), Alberto Terry (16/9) [62.Juan Bassa (6/1)], Manuel Rivera (8/3), Máximo Mosquera (27/7), Juan Seminario (9/1). Trainer: György Orth (4).

Goals: Alberto Terry (34), Manuel Rivera (35, 37), Juan Bassa (83).

88. 31.03.1957 **PERU - BRAZIL** **0-1(0-0)** 25th Copa América

Estadio Nacional, Lima; Referee: Ronald Lynch (England); Attendance: 55,000

PER: Rafael Asca (11/0), Guillermo Fleming (4/0), Guillermo Delgado (35/0) [*sent off*], Víctor Salas (15/0), Carlos Lazón (22/1) [*sent off*], Luis Calderón (30/0), Roberto Castillo (18/1) [69.Juan Bassa (7/1)], Alberto Terry (17/9), Manuel Rivera (9/3), Máximo Mosquera (28/7), Juan Seminario (10/1). Trainer: György Orth (5).

The match was stopped after 74 minutes

89. 06.04.1957 **PERU - ARGENTINA** **2-1(1-0)** 25th Copa América

Estadio Nacional, Lima; Referee: Bertley Cross (England); Attendance: 50,000

PER: Rafael Asca (12/0), Guillermo Fleming (5/0), Guillermo Delgado (36/0) [58.Alfredo Cavero (3/0)], Dante Rovay (4/0), Mario Minaya (1/0) [76.Víctor Benítez (1/0)], Luis Calderón (31/0), Juan Bassa (8/1), Alberto Terry (18/10), Manuel Rivera (10/3), Máximo Mosquera (29/8), Juan Seminario (11/1). Trainer: György Orth (6).

Goals: Máximo Mosquera (15), Alberto Terry (81).

90. 09.04.1957 **PERU - ARGENTINA** **1-4(0-1)**

Estadio Nacional, Lima; Referee: Diego De Leo (Italy); Attendance: 40,000

PER: Walter Ormeño (13/0), Alfredo Cavero (4/0), Víctor Benítez (2/0), Víctor Salas (16/0) [65.Dante Rovay (5/0)], Carlos Lazón (23/1) [55.René Gutiérrez (7/0)], Mario Minaya (2/1), Faustino Delgado (1/0) [46.Juan Joya (2/0)], Juan Bassa (9/1), Daniel Ruiz (3/0), Manuel Márquez (1/0), Oscar Gómez Sánchez (18/12). Trainer: György Orth (7).

Goal: Mario Minaya (85).

91. 13.04.1957 **PERU – BRAZIL** **1-1(1-0)** 6th FIFA WC. Qualifiers

Estadio Nacional, Lima; Referee: Washington Rodríguez (Uruguay)

PER: Rafael Asca (13/0), Guillermo Fleming (6/0), Víctor Benítez (3/0), Víctor Salas (17/0), Carlos Lazón (24/1), Luis Calderón (Cap) (32/0), Juan Bassa (10/1), Máximo Mosquera (30/8), Alberto Terry (19/11), Mamuel Rivera (11/3), Oscar Gómez Sánchez (19/12). Trainer: György Orth (8).

Goal: Alberto Terry (38).

92. 21.04.1957 **BRAZIL - PERU** **1-0(1-0)** 6th FIFA WC. Qualifiers

Estádio „Jornalista Mario Filho“ (Maracanã), Rio de Janeiro; Referee: Estebán Marino (Uruguay)

PER: Rafael Asca (14/0), Guillermo Fleming (7/0), Víctor Benítez (4/0), Dante Rovay (6/0), Carlos Lazón (25/1), Luis Calderón (Cap) (33/0), Juan Seminario (12/1), Máximo Mosquera (31/8), Alberto Terry (20/11), Manuel Rivera (12/3), Oscar Gómez Sánchez (20/12),. Trainer: György Orth (9).

93. 10.03.1959 **PERU - BRAZIL** **2-2(0-1)** 26th Copa América

Estadio Monumental „Antonio Vespucio Liberti“, Buenos Aires (Argentina); Referee: Juan Carlos Robles (Chile); Attendance: 45,000

PER: Rafael Asca (15/0), Guillermo Fleming (8/0), Víctor Benítez (5/0), José Antonio Fernández Santini (1/0), Manuel Grimaldo (1/0), Juan De La Vega (1/0), Oscar Gómez Sánchez (21/12), Miguel Loayza (1/0) [68.José Carrasco (1/0)], Juan Joya (3/0), Alberto Terry (21/11), Juan Seminario (13/3). Trainer: György Orth (10).

Goals: Juan Seminario (80, 82).

94. 14.03.1959 **PERU - URUGUAY** **5-3(3-1)** 26th Copa América

Estadio Monumental „Antonio Vespucio Liberti", Buenos Aires (Argentina); Referee: Juan Carlos Robles (Chile); Attendance: 40,000

PER: Rafael Asca (16/0), Guillermo Fleming (9/0), Víctor Benítez (6/0), José Antonio Fernández Santini (2/0), Manuel Grimaldo (2/0) [74.Lorenzo Flores (1/0)], Juan De La Vega (2/0), Oscar Gómez Sánchez (22/13), Miguel Loayza (2/3) [88.José Carrasco (2/0)], Juan Joya (4/1), Alberto Terry (22/11) [59.Oscar Montalvo (1/0], Juan Seminario (14/3). Trainer: György Orth (11).

Goals: Miguel Loayza (4, 21), Oscar Gómez Sánchez (30), Juan Joya (80), Miguel Loayza (87).

95. 18.03.1959 **ARGENTINA - PERU** **3-1(2-0)** 26th Copa América

Estadio Monumental „Antonio Vespucio Liberti", Buenos Aires; Referee: Alberto Monard de Gama Malcher (Brazil); Attendance: 70,000

PER: Rafael Asca (17/0), Guillermo Fleming (10/0), Víctor Benítez (7/0), José Antonio Fernández Santini (3/0), Manuel Grimaldo (3/0) [63.Lorenzo Flores (2/0], Juan De La Vega (3/0), Oscar Gómez Sánchez (23/13), Miguel Loayza (3/4) [Tomás Iwasaki (1/0)], Juan Joya (5/1), Alberto Terry (23/11) [69.José Carrasco (3/0)], Juan Seminario (15/3). Trainer: György Orth (12).

Goal: Miguel Loayza (38).

96. 21.03.1959 **PERU - CHILE** **1-1(1-0)** 26th Copa América

Estadio Monumental „Antonio Vespucio Liberti", Buenos Aires (Argentina); Referee: Washington Rodríguez (Uruguay); Attendance: 50,000

PER: Rafael Asca (18/0), Lorenzo Flores (3/0), Víctor Benítez (8/0), José Antonio Fernández Santini (4/0), Juan De La Vega (4/0), Claudio Lostanau (1/0), Oscar Gómez Sánchez (24/13), Miguel Loayza (4/5), Juan Joya (6/1), Alberto Terry (24/11) [75.José Carrasco (4/0)], Juan Seminario (16/3). Trainer: György Orth (13).

Goal: Miguel Loayza (48).

97. 29.03.1959 **PERU - BOLIVIA** **0-0** 26th Copa América

Estadio Monumental „Antonio Vespucio Liberti", Buenos Aires (Argentina); Referee: Washington Rodríguez (Uruguay); Attendance: 40,000

PER: Rafael Asca (19/0), Lorenzo Flores (4/0) [79.Adolfo Calenzani (1/0)], Víctor Benítez (9/0), José Antonio Fernández Santini (5/0), Juan De La Vega (5/0), Manuel Grimaldo (4/0), Oscar Gómez Sánchez (25/13), Miguel Loayza (5/5) [69.José Carrasco (5/0)], Juan Joya (7/1), Alberto Terry (25/11) [80.Alonso Urdániga (1/0)], Juan Seminario (17/3). Trainer: György Orth (14).

98. 02.04.1959 **PARAGUAY – PERU** **2-1(1-1)** 26th Copa América

Estadio Monumental „Antonio Vespucio Liberti", Buenos Aires (Argentina); Referee: Alberto Monard de Gama Malcher (Brazil); Attendance: 5,000

PER: Rafael Asca (20/0), Lorenzo Flores (5/0), Víctor Benítez (10/0), José Antonio Fernández Santini (6/0), Juan De La Vega (6/0), Manuel Grimaldo (5/0), Oscar Gómez Sánchez (26/14), Miguel Loayza (6/5) [42.Tomás Iwasaki (2/0)], Juan Joya (8/1) [53.Alonso Urdániga (2/0)], José Carrasco (6/0), Juan Seminario (18/3). Trainer: György Orth (15).

Goal: Oscar Gómez Sánchez (21).

99. 17.05.1959 **PERU – ENGLAND** **4-1(2-0)**

Estadio Nacional, Lima; Referee: Erwin Hiegger (Austria); Attendance: 50,306

PER: Rafael Asca (Cap) (21/0), Guillermo Fleming (11/0), José Antonio Fernández Santini (7/0), Isaac Andrade (4/0), Juan De La Vega (7/0), Víctor Benítez (11/0), Oscar Montalvo (2/0), Miguel Loayza (7/5), Juan Joya (9/2), José Carrasco (7/0), Juan Seminario (19/6). Trainer: György Orth (16).

Goals: Juan Seminario (10, 40), Juan Joya (70), Juan Seminario (80).

100. 10.07.1960 **PERU - SPAIN** **1-3(0-2)**

Estadio Nacional, Lima; Referee: Juan Carlos Robles (Chile); Attendance: 49,957

PER: Dimas Zegarra (6/0), Guillermo Fleming (12/0), José Antonio Fernández Santini (8/0), Isaac Andrade (5/0) [71.Humberto Arguedas (1/0)], Juan De La Vega (8/0), Luis Calderón (Cap) (34/0), Neptalí Briceño (1/0) [71.Enrique Tenemás (1/0)], Enrique García (1/0) [46.Manuel Márquez (2/0)], Angel Uribe (1/0), José Carrasco (8/1), Oscar Montalvo (3/0). Trainer: György Orth (17).

Goal: José Carrasco (54).

101. 19.03.1961 **CHILE – PERU** **5-2(1-2)**

Estadio Nacional, Santiago; Referee: Juan Regis Brozzi (Argentina); Attendance: 24,735

PER: Dimas Zegarra (7/0), Carlos Bravo (1/0), José Antonio Fernández Santini (9/0), Guillermo Fleming (13/0), Juan De La Vega (9/0), Manuel Grimaldo (6/0) [52.Mario Gonzáles (1/0)], Oscar Montalvo (4/0), José Carrasco (9/2), Eduardo Flores (1/1), Angel Uribe (2/0) [69.Luis Fernando Cruzado Sánchez (1/0)], Oscar Huapaya (1/0). Trainer: Marcos Calderón Medrano (1).

Goal: Eduardo Flores (27), José Carrasco (28).

102. 30.04.1961 **COLOMBIA - PERU** **1-0(1-0)** 7th FIFA WC. Qualifiers

Estadio „Nemesio Camacho" 'El Campín', Bogotá; Referee: Luis Praddaude (Argentina)

PER: Rigoberto Felandro (8/0), Guillermo Fleming (14/0), José Antonio Fernández Santini (10/0), Luis Fernando Cruzado Sánchez (2/0), Juan De La Vega (10/0), Luis Calderón (35/0), Oscar Montalvo (5/0), Roberto Drago (30/9), Angel Uribe (3/0), José Carrasco (10/2), Oscar Huapaya (2/0). Trainer: Marcos Calderón Medrano (2).

103. 07.05.1961 **PERU - COLOMBIA** **1-1(1-1)** 7th FIFA WC. Qualifiers

Estadio Nacional, Lima; Referee: Esteban Marino (Uruguay)

PER: Fernando Cárpena (1/0), Adolfo Calenzani (2/0), José Antonio Fernández Santini (11/0), Luis Fernando Cruzado Sánchez (3/0), Juan De La Vega (11/0), Luis Calderón (36/0), Oscar Montalvo (6/0), Eduardo Flores (2/1), Angel Uribe (4/0), Manuel Márquez (3/0), Faustino Delgado (2/1). Trainer: Marcos Calderón Medrano (3).

Goal: Faustino Delgado (3 penalty)

104. 20.05.1962 **PERU - ENGLAND** **0-4(0-4)**

Estadio Nacional, Lima; Referee: Erwin Hiegger (Austria); Attendance: 32,565

PER: Rodolfo Bazán (1/0), Guillermo Fleming (15/0), Adolfo Donayre (2/0), Rodolfo Guzmán (1/0), Juan De La Vega (Cap) (12/0) [59.Humberto Arguedas (2/0)], Manuel Grimaldo (7/0) [*sent off 89*], Nicolás Nieri (1/0), Víctor Zegarra (1/0) [Nemesio Mosquera (1/0], Hugo Lobatón (1/0), Alejandro Zevallos (1/0), Oscar Montalvo (7/0). Trainer: Jaime De Almeyda (1).

105. 10.03.1963 **BRAZIL – PERU** **1-0(1-0)** 28th Copa América

Estadio „Félix Capriles", Cochabamba (Bolivia); Referee: José Dimas Larrosa (Paraguay); Attendance: 18,000

PER: Rodolfo Bazán (2/0), Ángel Eloy Campos (1/0), Pedro Anselmo Ruiz (1/0), Roberto Elías (1/0), Adolfo Donayre (3/0), Juan De La Vega (13/0), Nemesio Mosquera (2/0), Víctor Zegarra (2/0), Pedro Pablo León García (1/0), Víctor Rostaing (1/0) [60.Enrique Tenemás (2/0)], Félix Alberto Gallardo Mendoza (1/0). Trainer: Juan Valdivieso Padilla (8).

106. 13.03.1963 **ARGENTINA - PERU** **1-2(0-0)** 28th Copa América
Estadio „Félix Capriles", Cochabamba (Bolivia); Referee: José Dimas Larrosa (Paraguay); Attendance: 10,000
PER: Rodolfo Bazán (3/0), Ángel Eloy Campos (2/0) [71.Carlos Bravo (2/0)], Pedro Anselmo Ruiz (2/0), Roberto Elías (2/0), Adolfo Donayre (4/0), Juan De La Vega (14/0) [66.Héctor Ladrón de Guevara (1/0)], Enrique Tenemás (3/1), Víctor Zegarra (3/0), Pedro Pablo León García (2/0), Nemesio Mosquera (3/0), Félix Alberto Gallardo Mendoza (2/1). Trainer: Juan Valdivieso Padilla (9).
Goal: Enrique Tenemás (63), Félix Alberto Gallardo Mendoza (76).

107. 17.03.1963 **PERU – ECUADOR** **2-1(2-1)** 28th Copa América
Estadio „Hernándo Siles Zuazo", La Paz (Bolivia); Referee: Ovidio Orrego (Colombia); Attendance: 8,000
PER: Rodolfo Bazán (4/0) [Luis Rubiños Cerna (1/0)], Carlos Bravo (3/0), Pedro Anselmo Ruiz (3/0), Roberto Elías (3/0) [74.Mario Yacsetick (1/0)], Adolfo Donayre (5/0), Héctor Ladrón De Guevara (2/0), Enrique Tenemás (4/1), Víctor Zegarra (4/0) [82.Jesús Peláez (1/0)], Pedro Pablo León García (3/1), Nemesio Mosquera (4/1), Félix Alberto Gallardo Mendoza (3/1) [Jorge Vázquez (1/0)]. Trainer: Juan Valdivieso Padilla (10).
Goal: Pedro Pablo León García (34), Nemesio Mosquera (43).

108. 21.03.1963 **BOLIVIA – PERU** **3-2(1-1)** 28th Copa América
Estadio „Hernándo Siles Zuazo", La Paz; Referee: João Etzel Filho (Brazil); Attendance: 20,000
PER: Luis Rubiños Cerna (2/0) [Rodolfo Bazán (5/0)], Ángel Eloy Campos (3/0), Pedro Anselmo Ruiz (4/0), Roberto Elías (4/0) [60.Mario Yacsetick (2/0)], Adolfo Donayre (6/0), Héctor Ladrón De Guevara (3/0), Enrique Tenemás (5/1) [49.Juan De La Vega (15/0)], Víctor Zegarra (5/0), Pedro Pablo León García (4/2) [46.Jesús Peláez (2/0)], Nemesio Mosquera (5/1), Félix Alberto Gallardo Mendoza (4/2). Trainer: Juan Valdivieso Padilla (11)
Goals: Félix Alberto Gallardo Mendoza (12), Pedro Pablo León García (62).

109. 24.03.1963 **PERU – COLOMBIA** **1-1(1-1)** 28th Copa América
Estadio „Hernándo Siles Zuazo", La Paz (Bolivia); Referee: Luis Ventre (Argentina); Attendance: 10,000
PER: Rodolfo Bazán (6/0), Carlos Bravo (4/0), Pedro Anselmo Ruiz (5/0), Mario Yacsetick (3/0), Adolfo Donayre (7/0), Juan De La Vega (16/0), Enrique Tenemás (6/1) [64.Héctor Ladrón De Guevara (4/0)], Víctor Zegarra (6/0), Pedro Pablo León García (5/2), Nemesio Mosquera (6/1), Félix Alberto Gallardo Mendoza (5/3) [72.Jesús Peláez (3/0)]. Trainer: Juan Valdivieso Padilla (12).
Goal: Félix Alberto Gallardo Mendoza (25).

110. 27.03.1963 **PARAGUAY - PERU** **4-1(4-0)** 28th Copa América
Estadio „Félix Capriles", Cochabamba (Bolivia); Referee: Luis Ventre (Argentina); Attendance: 20,000
PER: Rodolfo Bazán (7/0), Ángel Eloy Campos (4/0), Pedro Anselmo Ruiz (6/0), Roberto Elías (5/0), Adolfo Donayre (8/0), Juan De La Vega (17/0), Enrique Tenemás (7/1), Víctor Zegarra (7/0) [46.Jesús Peláez (4/0)], Pedro Pablo León García (6/2) [46.Jorge Vázquez (2/0)], Félix Alberto Gallardo Mendoza (6/4), Félix Escobar (1/0) [46.Nemesio Mosquera (7/1)]. Trainer: Juan Valdivieso Padilla (13).
Goal: Félix Alberto Gallardo Mendoza (70).

111. 03.04.1965 **PERU – PARAGUAY** **0-1(0-1)**
Estadio Nacional, Lima; Referee: Arturo Máximo Yamasaki Maldonado (Peru)
PER: Rodolfo Bazán (8/0), Ángel Eloy Campos (5/0), José Antonio Fernández Santini (12/0), Nicolás Fuentes Zegarra (1/0), Luis Fernando Cruzado Sánchez (4/0) [60.Manuel Grimaldo (8/0)], Héctor Eduardo Chumpitaz González (1/0), José Del Castillo (1/0), Víctor Zegarra (8/0), Alejandro Guzmán (1/0), Angel Uribe (5/0) [60.Pedro Pablo León García (7/2)], Tomás Iwasaki (3/0) [46.Nemesio Mosquera (8/1)]. Trainer: Marcos Calderón Medrano (4).

112. 15.04.1965 **CHILE – PERU** **4-1(3-1)** Copa del Pacífico
Estadio Nacional, Santiago; Referee: Cláudio Vicuña Larrain (Chile); Attendance: 47,589
PER: Rodolfo Bazán (9/0) [46.Dimas Zegarra (8/0)], Ángel Eloy Campos (6/0) [51.Humberto Arguedas (3/0)], Julio Meléndez (1/0), Mario Gonzáles (2/0), José Antonio Fernández Santini (13/0), Luis Fernando Cruzado Sánchez (5/0) [77.Manuel Grimaldo (9/0)], Víctor Calatayud (1/0) [46.José Del Castillo (2/0)], Víctor Zegarra (9/1), Pedro Pablo León García (8/2), Angel Uribe (6/0), Nemesio Mosquera (9/1). Trainer: Marcos Calderón Medrano (5).
Goal: Víctor Zegarra (8).

113. 28.04.1965 **PERU – CHILE** **0-1(0-0)** Copa del Pacífico
Estadio Nacional, Lima; Referee: Arturo Máximo Yamasaki Maldonado (Peru); Attendance: 45,000
PER: Luis Rubiños Cerna (3/0), Ángel Eloy Campos (7/0), José Antonio Fernández Santini (14/0), Rodolfo Guzmán (2/0), Luis Fernando Cruzado Sánchez (6/0) [66.Manuel Grimaldo (10/0)], Pedro Anselmo Ruiz (7/0), Víctor Calatayud (2/0), Luis Zavala (1/0), Hugo Lobatón (2/0) [46.Pedro Pablo León García (9/2)], Angel Uribe (7/0) [50.Víctor Zegarra (10/1)], Enrique Rodríguez (1/0). Trainer: Marcos Calderón Medrano (6).

114. 16.05.1965 **PERU – VENEZUELA** **1-0(1-0)** 8th FIFA WC. Qualifiers
Estadio Nacional, Lima; Referee: Adolfo Reginato (Chile); Attendance: 43,990
PER: Luis Rubiños Cerna (4/0), Ángel Eloy Campos (8/0), José Antonio Fernández Santini (15/0), Rodolfo Guzmán (3/0), Manuel Grimaldo (11/0), Héctor Eduardo Chumpitaz González (2/0), Víctor Calatayud (3/0), Víctor Zegarra (11/2), Pedro Pablo León García (10/2), Luis Zavala (2/0), Nemesio Mosquera (10/1). Trainer: Marcos Calderón Medrano (7).
Goal: Víctor Zegarra (37 penalty).

115. 02.06.1965 **VENEZUELA – PERU** **3-6((2-3)** 8th FIFA WC. Qualifiers
Estadio Olímpico, Caracas; Referee: José Antonio Sundheim (Colombia); Attendance: 6,245
PER: Luis Rubiños Cerna (5/0), Ángel Eloy Campos (9/0), José Antonio Fernández Santini (16/0), Rodolfo Guzmán (4/0), Luis Fernando Cruzado Sánchez (7/0), Héctor Eduardo Chumpitaz González (3/0), Víctor Calatayud (4/0), Víctor Zegarra (12/2), Pedro Pablo León García (11/5), Luis Zavala (3/2), Nemesio Mosquera (11/2). Trainer: Marcos Calderón Medrano (8).
Goals: Nemesio Mosquera (10), Luis Zavala (40), Pedro Pablo León García (43, 62, 68), Luis Zavala (81).

116. 06.06.1965 **PERU – URUGUAY** **0-1(0-0)** 8th FIFA WC. Qualifiers
Estadio Nacional, Lima; Referee: Claudio Vicuña (Chile); Attendance: 44,033
PER: Luis Rubiños Cerna (6/0), Ángel Eloy Campos (10/0), José Antonio Fernández Santini (17/0), Rodolfo Guzmán (5/0), Luis Fernando Cruzado Sánchez (8/0), Héctor Eduardo Chumpitaz González (4/0), Víctor Calatayud (5/0), Víctor Zegarra (13/2), Pedro Pablo León García (12/5), Luis Zavala (4/2), Nemesio Mosquera (12/2). Trainer: Marcos Calderón Medrano (9).

117. 13.06.1965 **URUGUAY – PERU** **2-1(1-1)** 8th FIFA WC. Qualifiers
Estadio Centenario, Montevideo; Referee: Armando Nunes Castanheiras da Rosa Marques (Brazil); Attendance: 58,413
PER: Rodolfo Bazán (10/0), Ángel Eloy Campos (11/0), José Antonio Fernández Santini (18/0), Rodolfo Guzmán (6/0), Luis Fernando Cruzado Sánchez (9/0), Héctor Eduardo Chumpitaz González (5/0), Italo Cavagnari (1/0), Angel Uribe (8/1), Pedro Pablo León García (13/5), Jesús Peláez (5/0), Nemesio Mosquera (13/2). Trainer: Marcos Calderón Medrano (10).
Goal: Angel Uribe (3).

118. 04.06.1966 **BRAZIL - PERU** **4-0(2-0)**
Estádio „Cicero Pompeu de Toledo“ Morumbi, São Paulo; Referee: Archibald F. Wester (Scotland)
PER: Luis Rubiños Cerna (7/0), Ángel Eloy Campos (12/0), Julio Meléndez (2/0), Luis Pau (1/0), Roberto Elías (6/0), Nicolás Nieri (2/0), Ramón Antonio Mifflin Páez (1/0), Italo Cavagnari (2/0) [46.Andrés Herrera (1/0)], Tomás Iwasaki (4/0), Carlos Urrunaga (1/0) [46.Napoleón Rodríguez (1/0)], Carlos Gonzáles Pajuelo (1/0). Trainer: José Gomes Nogueira (1).

119. 08.06.1966 **BRAZIL - PERU** **3-1(2-0)**
Estádio „Jornalista Mario Filho“ (Maracanã), Rio de Janeiro; Referee: William Syme (Scotland)
PER: Ottorino Sartor Espinoza (1/0), Ángel Eloy Campos (13/0) [Walter Milera (1/0)], Julio Meléndez (3/0), Roberto Elías (7/0), Juan Leturia (1/0) [Nicolás Nieri (3/0)), Luis Pau (2/0) [Pedro Anselmo Ruiz (8/0)], Ramón Antonio Mifflin Páez (2/0), Andrés Herrera (2/1) [Italo Cavagnari (3/0)], Napoleón Rodríguez (2/0) [Rómulo Ferreti (1/0)], Tomás Iwasaki (5/0) [Carlos Urrunaga (2/0), Mario Aquije (1/0)], Carlos Gonzáles Pajuelo (2/0) [Carlos Solís]. Trainer: José Gomes Nogueira (2).
Goal: Andrés Herrera (65).

120. 28.07.1967 **PERU - URUGUAY** **0-1(0-0)**
Estadio Nacional, Lima; Referee: Erwin Hiegger (Austria)
PER: Rubén David Correa Montenegro (1/0), Pedro Gonzáles Zavala (1/0), Luis La Fuente (1/0), Nicolás Fuentes Zegarra (2/0), Luis Fernando Cruzado Sánchez (10/0), Héctor Eduardo Chumpitaz González (6/0) [30.José Javier González (1/0)], Roberto Federico Chale Olarte (1/0), Víctor Calatayud (6/0) [46.Andrés Zegarra (1/0], Napoleón Rodríguez (3/0) [55.Andrés Herrera (3/1)], Angel Uribe (9/1), Víctor Lobatón (1/0). Trainer: Marcos Calderón Medrano (11).

121. 28.07.1967 **PERU - JAPAN** **1-0(1-0)**
Estadio Nacional, Lima; Referee: Arturo Máximo Yamasaki Maldonado (Peru)
PER: .Luis Rubiños Cerna (8/0), Ángel Eloy Campos (14/0), Julio Meléndez (4/0), Orlando de la Torre Castro (1/0), Roberto Elías (8/0) [86.José Gonzáles (1/0)], Matías Quintos (1/0), Ramón Antonio Mifflin Páez (3/0), Juan José Muñante López (1/0), Mario Aquije (2/0), Carlos Gonzáles Pajuelo (3/1), José Del Castillo (3/0). Trainer: Marcos Calderón Medrano (12).
Goal: Carlos Gonzáles Pajuelo (31).

122. 30.07.1967 **PERU - JAPAN** **0-0**
Estadio Nacional, Lima; Referee: Arturo Máximo Yamasaki Maldonado (Peru)
PER: Alberto Párraga (1/0), Ángel Eloy Campos (15/0), Julio Meléndez (5/0), Orlando de la Torre Castro (2/0), Roberto Elías (9/0), Matías Quintos (2/0) [46.José Villanueva (1/0)], Ramón Antonio Mifflin Páez (4/0), Juan José Muñante López (2/0), Mario Aquije (3/0), Carlos Gonzáles Pajuelo (4/1), José Del Castillo (4/0). Trainer: Marcos Calderón Medrano (13).

123. 30.07.1967 **PERU - URUGUAY** **1-2(1-1)**
Estadio Nacional, Lima; Referee: Erwin Hiegger (Austria)
PER: Rubén David Correa Montenegro (2/0) [Luis Rubiños Cerna (9/0)], Pedro Gonzáles Zavala (2/0), Luis La Fuente (2/0), Nicolás Fuentes Zegarra (3/0) [78.Walter Milera (2/0)], José Javier González (2/0), Luis Fernando Cruzado Sánchez (11/0), Roberto Federico Chale Olarte (2/0), Andrés Zegarra (2/0) [64.Andrés Herrera (4/1)], Napoleón Rodríguez (4/0), Angel Uribe (10/2), Víctor Lobatón (2/0). Trainer: Marcos Calderón Medrano (14).
Goal: Angel Uribe (14).

124. 14.07.1968 **PERU - BRAZIL** **3-4(2-1)**
Estadio Nacional, Lima; Referee: Miguel Angel Francisco Comesaña (Argentina); Attendance: 43,095
PER: Luis Rubiños Cerna (10/0) [54.Román Villanueva (1/0)], Ángel Eloy Campos (16/0), Fernando Mellán (1/0), Héctor Eduardo Chumpitaz González (7/0), Roberto Elías (10/0), Ramón Antonio Mifflin Páez (5/0), Roberto Federico Chale Olarte (3/0), Julio Alberto Temistocles Baylón Aragonés (1/0), Víctor Zegarra (14/3), Pedro Pablo León García (14/7), Félix Alberto Gallardo Mendoza (7/4). Trainers: Roberto Drago (1).
Goal: Pedro Pablo León García (33, 38), Víctor Zegarra (64).

125. 17.07.1968 **PERU - BRAZIL** **0-4(0-3)**
Estadio Nacional, Lima; Referee: Miguel Angel Francisco Comesaña (Argentina); Attendance: 42,994
PER: Román Villanueva (2/0) [39.Walter Flores (1/0)], Ángel Eloy Campos (17/0), Fernando Mellán (2/0), Héctor Eduardo Chumpitaz González (8/0), Roberto Elías (11/0), Ramón Antonio Mifflin Páez (6/0), Roberto Federico Chale Olarte (4/0) [46.José Antonio Fernández Santini (19/0)], Julio Alberto Temistocles Baylón Aragonés (2/0), Víctor Zegarra (15/3), Pedro Pablo León García (15/7), Félix Alberto Gallardo Mendoza (8/4) [46.Teófilo Juan Cubillas Arizaga (1/0)]. Trainers: Roberto Drago (2).

126. 18.08.1968 **PERU - CHILE** **1-2(0-2)** Copa del Pacífico
Estadio Nacional, Lima; Referee: César Orozco (Peru); Attendance: 26,008
PER: Luis Rubiños Cerna (11/0), Ángel Eloy Campos (18/0), Fernando Mellán (3/0), Orlando de la Torre Castro (3/0), José Javier González (3/0), Juan De La Vega (Cap) (18/0), Ramón Antonio Mifflin Páez (7/0) [46.Eladio Máximo Reyes Caraza (1/0)], Andrés Zegarra (3/0) [46.Nemesio Mosquera (14/2)], Jorge Charún (1/0), Mariano Loo (1/0), Héctor Bailetti (1/1). Trainer: Waldyr Pereira „Didi“ (1).
Goal: Héctor Bailetti (68).

127. 21.08.1968 **PERU - CHILE** **0-0** Copa del Pacífico
Estadio Nacional, Lima; Referee: Erwin Hiegger (Austria); Attendance: 13,142
PER: Dimas Zegarra (9/0), Ángel Eloy Campos (19/0), Fernando Mellán (4/0), Orlando de la Torre Castro (4/0), José Javier González (4/0), Ramón Antonio Mifflin Páez (8/0), Juan Leturia (2/0), Antonio Franco (1/0) [46.Andrés Zegarra (4/0)], Alejandro Zevallos (2/0), Héctor Bailetti (2/1) [74.Eladio Máximo Reyes Caraza (2/0)], Nemesio Mosquera (15/2). Trainer: Waldyr Pereira „Didi“ (2).

128. 29.08.1968 **PERU - ARGENTINA** **2-2(1-1)**
Estadio Nacional, Lima; Referee: Erwin Hiegger (Austria); Attendance: 29,975
PER: Dimas Zegarra (10/0), Ángel Eloy Campos (20/0), José Antonio Fernández Santini (20/0), Héctor Eduardo Chumpitaz González (9/0), Nicolás Fuentes Zegarra (4/0), Víctor Zegarra (16/3), Teófilo Juan Cubillas Arizaga (2/0), Julio Alberto Temistocles Baylón Aragonés (3/0), Pedro Pablo León García (16/7), Enrique Cassaretto (1/2) [86.Roberto Federico Chale Olarte (5/0)], José Del Castillo (5/0) [78.Héctor Bailetti (3/1)]. Trainer: Waldyr Pereira „Didi“ (3).
Goals: Enrique Cassaretto (40, 63).

129. 01.09.1968 **PERU – ARGENTINA** **1-1(1-1)**
Estadio Nacional, Lima; Referee: José Varrone (Venezuela); Attendance: 33,371
PER: Dimas Zegarra (11/0), Ángel Eloy Campos (21/0), José Antonio Fernández Santini (21/0), Héctor Eduardo Chumpitaz González (10/0), Nicolás Fuentes Zegarra (5/0), Víctor Zegarra (17/3) [63.Roberto Federico Chale Olarte (6/0)], Teófilo Juan Cubillas Arizaga (3/0), Julio Alberto Temistocles Baylón Aragonés (4/0) [76.Héctor Bailetti (4/1)], Pedro Pablo León García (17/7), Enrique Cassaretto (2/3), José Del Castillo (6/0) [84.Carlos Solis (2/0)]. Trainer: Waldyr Pereira „Didi“ (4).
Goal: Enrique Cassaretto (23).

130. 20.10.1968 **PERU – MEXICO** **3-3(3-0)**
Estadio Nacional, Lima; Referee: Alberto Tejada Burga (Peru)
PER: Luis Rubiños Cerna (12/0), Ángel Eloy Campos (22/0), Orlando de la Torre Castro (5/0), Héctor Eduardo Chumpitaz González (11/0), Nicolás Fuentes Zegarra (6/0), Roberto Federico Chale Olarte (7/0), Teófilo Juan Cubillas Arizaga (4/0) [46.Ramón Antonio Mifflin Páez (9/0)], Julio Alberto Temistocles Baylón Aragonés (5/0) [*sent off 57*], Pedro Pablo León García (18/7), Enrique Cassaretto (3/6), José Del Castillo (7/0) [46.Víctor Zegarra (18/3)]. Trainer: Waldyr Pereira „Didi“ (5).
Goals: Enrique Cassaretto (8, 26, 32).

131. 07.04.1969 **BRAZIL – PERU** **2-1(2-1)**
Estádio Beira Rio, Porto Alegre; Referee: Alberto Tejada Burga (Peru)
PER: Ottorino Sartor Espinoza (2/0), José Antonio Fernández Santini (22/0), Orlando de la Torre Castro (6/0), Héctor Eduardo Chumpitaz González (12/0), José Javier González (5/0), Ramón Antonio Mifflin Páez (10/0), Teófilo Juan Cubillas Arizaga (5/0) [62.Roberto Federico Chale Olarte (8/0)], Julio Alberto Temistocles Baylón Aragonés (6/0) [51.Juan José Muñante López (3/0)], Pedro Pablo León García (19/7), Víctor Zegarra (19/3) [78.Oswaldo Felipe Ramírez Salcedo (1/0)], Félix Alberto Gallardo Mendoza (9/5). Trainer: Waldyr Pereira „Didi“ (6).
Goal: Félix Alberto Gallardo Mendoza (9).

132. 09.04.1969 **BRAZIL – PERU** **3-2(2-2)**
Estádio „Jornalista Mario Filho“ (Maracanã), Rio de Janeiro; Referee: Alberto Tejada Burga (Peru)
PER: Ottorino Sartor Espinoza (3/0), Pedro Gonzáles Zavala (3/0), Orlando de la Torre Castro (7/0) [46.José Antonio Fernández Santini (23/0)], Héctor Eduardo Chumpitaz González (13/0), José Javier González (6/0), Ramón Antonio Mifflin Páez (11/0), Teófilo Juan Cubillas Arizaga (6/0), Julio Alberto Temistocles Baylón Aragonés (7/1), Pedro Pablo León García (20/7), Enrique Cassaretto (4/6) [46.Jorge Barreto (1/0)], Félix Alberto Gallardo Mendoza (10/6) [60.Oswaldo Felipe Ramírez Salcedo (2/0]. Trainer: Waldyr Pereira „Didi“ (7).
Goals: Félix Alberto Gallardo Mendoza (4), Julio Alberto Temistocles Baylón Aragonés (8).

133. 08.05.1969 **COLOMBIA – PERU** **1-3(1-1)**
Estadio „Nemesio Camacho“ 'El Campín', Bogotá; Referee: Mario Canessa (Chile); Attendance: 32,000
PER: Ottorino Sartor Espinoza (4/0), Ángel Eloy Campos (23/0) [85.Pedro Gonzáles Zavala (4/0)], Orlando de la Torre Castro (8/0), Héctor Eduardo Chumpitaz González (14/0), José Javier González (7/0), Ramón Antonio Mifflin Páez (12/0), Teófilo Juan Cubillas Arizaga (7/1), Julio Alberto Temistocles Baylón Aragonés (8/1) [64.Juan José Muñante López (4/0)], Pedro Pablo León García (21/8), Enrique Cassaretto (5/6) [55.Roberto Federico Chale Olarte (9/0)], Oswaldo Felipe Ramírez Salcedo (3/1). Trainer: Waldyr Pereira „Didi“ (8).
Goals: Oswaldo Felipe Ramírez Salcedo (37), Teófilo Juan Cubillas Arizaga (55), Pedro Pablo León García (88).

134. 14.05.1969 **EL SALVADOR – PERU** **1-4(1-2)**
Estadio Flor Blanca, San Salvador; Referee: Leonel Bohórquez (El Salvador)
PER: Dimas Zegarra (12/0), Ángel Eloy Campos (24/0), Orlando de la Torre Castro (9/0), Héctor Eduardo Chumpitaz González (15/0), Roberto Elías (12/0), Ramón Antonio Mifflin Páez (13/0) [50.Roberto Federico Chale Olarte (10/0)], Teófilo Juan Cubillas Arizaga (8/1), Juan José Muñante López (5/0), Pedro Pablo León García (22/8), Eladio Máximo Reyes Caraza (3/0) [53.Hernán Castañeda (1/1)], Oswaldo Felipe Ramírez Salcedo (4/3). Trainer: Waldyr Pereira „Didi“ (9).
Goals: Guillermo Castro (27 own goal), Oswaldo Felipe Ramírez Salcedo (44), Hernán Castañeda (70), Oswaldo Felipe Ramírez Salcedo (72).

135. 20.05.1969 **MEXICO – PERU** **0-1(0-0)**
Estadio Azteca, Ciudad de México; Referee: Juan Carlos Robles (Chile)
PER: Luis Rubiños Cerna (13/0), Ángel Eloy Campos (25/0), Orlando de la Torre Castro (10/0) [*sent off 87*], Héctor Eduardo Chumpitaz González (16/0), José Javier González (8/0), Ramón Antonio Mifflin Páez (14/0), Teófilo Juan Cubillas Arizaga (9/1), Julio Alberto Temistocles Baylón Aragonés (9/1) [76.Juan José Muñante López (6/0), 86.José Antonio Fernández Santini (24/0)], Pedro Pablo León García (23/9), Enrique Cassaretto (6/6) [57.Roberto Federico Chale Olarte (11/0)], Oswaldo Felipe Ramírez Salcedo (5/3). Trainer: Waldyr Pereira „Didi“ (10).
Goal: Pedro Pablo León García (79).

136. 22.05.1969 **MEXICO – PERU** **3-0(3-0)**
Estadio Nou Camp, León; Referee: Juan Carlos Robles (Chile)
PER: Ottorino Sartor Espinoza (5/0), Ángel Eloy Campos (26/0), Orlando de la Torre Castro (11/0), Héctor Eduardo Chumpitaz González (17/0), José Javier González (9/0), Ramón Antonio Mifflin Páez (15/0), Teófilo Juan Cubillas Arizaga (10/1), Julio Alberto Temistocles Baylón Aragonés (10/1), Pedro Pablo León García (24/9), Enrique Cassaretto (7/6) [29.Roberto Federico Chale Olarte (12/0)], Oswaldo Felipe Ramírez Salcedo (6/3) [56.Juan José Muñante López (7/0)]. Trainer: Waldyr Pereira „Didi“ (11).

137. 18.06.1969 **PERU – COLOMBIA** **1-1(0-1)**
Estadio Nacional, Lima; Referee: Erwin Hiegger (Austria); Attendance: 42,977
PER: Luis Rubiños Cerna (14/0), Pedro Gonzáles Zavala (5/0), Orlando de la Torre Castro (12/0), Héctor Eduardo Chumpitaz González (18/1), Nicolás Fuentes Zegarra (7/0), Ramón Antonio Mifflin Páez (16/0) [70.Hernán Castañeda (2/1], Roberto Federico Chale Olarte (13/0), Andrés Zegarra (5/0), Pedro Pablo León García (25/9) [59.Percy Rojas Montero (1/0)], Teófilo Juan Cubillas Arizaga (11/1), Félix Alberto Gallardo Mendoza (11/6) [80.Oswaldo Felipe Ramírez Salcedo (7/3)]. Trainer: Waldyr Pereira „Didi“ (12).
Goal: Héctor Eduardo Chumpitaz González (78).

138. 27.06.1969 **PERU – URUGUAY** **1-0(0-0)**
Estadio Nacional, Lima; Referee: Erwin Hiegger (Austria); Attendance: 42,754
PER: Luis Rubiños Cerna (15/0), Pedro Gonzáles Zavala (6/0), Orlando de la Torre Castro (13/0), Héctor Eduardo Chumpitaz González (19/1), Nicolás Fuentes Zegarra (8/0), Ramón Antonio Mifflin Páez (17/0), Roberto Federico Chale Olarte (14/0), Julio Alberto Temistocles Baylón Aragonés (11/1), Pedro Pablo León García (26/10), Teófilo Juan Cubillas Arizaga (12/1) [76.Hernán Castañeda (3/1)], Félix Alberto Gallardo Mendoza (12/6). Trainer: Waldyr Pereira „Didi“ (13).
Goal: Pedro Pablo León García (83).

139. 09.07.1969 **PERU – PARAGUAY** **2-1(1-1)**
Estadio Nacional, Lima; Referee: Enrique Montes (Peru); Attendance: 31,293
PER: Luis Rubiños Cerna (16/0) [75.Rubén David Correa Montenegro (3/0)], Pedro Gonzáles Zavala (7/0), José Antonio Fernández Santini (25/0), Héctor Eduardo Chumpitaz González (20/1), Nicolás Fuentes Zegarra (9/0), Ramón Antonio Mifflin Páez (18/0), Roberto Federico Chale Olarte (15/0), Julio Alberto Temistocles Baylón Aragonés (12/1), Percy Rojas Montero (2/0), Teófilo Juan Cubillas Arizaga (13/3), Félix Alberto Gallardo Mendoza (13/6). Trainer: Waldyr Pereira „Didi" (14).
Goals: Teófilo Juan Cubillas Arizaga (45 penalty, 50 penalty).

140. 18.07.1969 **PERU – PARAGUAY** **2-1(1-0)**
Estadio Nacional, Lima; Referee: Erwin Hiegger (Austria); Attendance: 26,648
PER: Luis Rubiños Cerna (17/0), Pedro Gonzáles Zavala (8/0) [80.Ángel Eloy Campos (27/0)], José Antonio Fernández Santini (26/0), Héctor Eduardo Chumpitaz González (21/1), Nicolás Fuentes Zegarra (10/0), Ramón Antonio Mifflin Páez (19/0), Roberto Federico Chale Olarte (16/0), Julio Alberto Temistocles Baylón Aragonés (13/1), Pedro Pablo León García (27/11), Teófilo Juan Cubillas Arizaga (14/3), Félix Alberto Gallardo Mendoza (14/6). Trainer: Waldyr Pereira „Didi" (15).
Goals: Sergio Rojas (7 own goal), Pedro Pablo León García (75).

141. 03.08.1969 **PERU – ARGENTINA** **1-0(0-0)** 9th FIFA WC. Qualifiers
Estadio Nacional, Lima; Referee: Aírton Vieira de Moraes (Brazil); Attendance: 43,147
PER: Luis Rubiños Cerna (18/0), Pedro Gonzáles Zavala (9/0), Orlando de la Torre Castro (14/0), Héctor Eduardo Chumpitaz González (22/1), Nicolás Fuentes Zegarra (11/0), Roberto Federico Chale Olarte (17/0), Ramón Antonio Mifflin Páez (20/0), Julio Alberto Temistocles Baylón Aragonés (14/1), Pedro Pablo León García (28/12), Teófilo Juan Cubillas Arizaga (15/3), Félix Alberto Gallardo Mendoza (15/6). Trainer: Waldyr Pereira „Didi" (16).
Goal: Pedro Pablo León García (52).

142. 10.08.1969 **BOLIVIA – PERU** **2-1(0-0)** 9th FIFA WC. Qualifiers
Estadio „Hernándo Siles Zuazo", La Paz; Referee: Sergey Chechelev (Soviet Union); Attendance: 20,670
PER: Luis Rubiños Cerna (19/0), Pedro Gonzáles Zavala (10/0) [80.José Antonio Fernández Santini (27/0)], Orlando de la Torre Castro (15/0), Héctor Eduardo Chumpitaz González (23/1), Nicolás Fuentes Zegarra (12/0), Ramón Antonio Mifflin Páez (21/0), Roberto Federico Chale Olarte (18/1), Julio Alberto Temistocles Baylón Aragonés (15/1), Pedro Pablo León García (29/12), Teófilo Juan Cubillas Arizaga (16/3), Félix Alberto Gallardo Mendoza (16/6). Trainer: Waldyr Pereira „Didi" (17).
Goal: Roberto Federico Chale Olarte (51).

143. 17.08.1969 **PERU – BOLIVIA** **3-0(2-0)** 9th FIFA WC. Qualifiers
Estadio Nacional, Lima; Referee: Guillermo Velázquez Ramírez (Colombia); Attendance: 43,148
PER: Luis Rubiños Cerna (20/0), Ángel Eloy Campos (28/0), Orlando de la Torre Castro (16/0), Héctor Eduardo Chumpitaz González (24/1), Rafael Risco (1/0), Roberto Federico Chale Olarte (19/1), Luis Fernando Cruzado Sánchez (12/1), Julio Alberto Temistocles Baylón Aragonés (16/1), Pedro Pablo León García (30/12), Teófilo Juan Cubillas Arizaga (17/4), Félix Alberto Gallardo Mendoza (17/7) [62.Andrés Zegarra (6/0)]. Trainer: Waldyr Pereira „Didi" (18)
Goals: Teófilo Juan Cubillas Arizaga (36), Luis Fernando Cruzado Sánchez (40 penalty), Félix Alberto Gallardo Mendoza (58).

144. 31.08.1969 **ARGENTINA – PERU** **2-2(0-0)** 9th FIFA WC. Qualifiers
Estadio „Alberto Armando", Buenos Aires; Referee: Rafael Hormazábal Díaz (Chile); Attendance: 53,627
PER: Luis Rubiños Cerna (21/0), Ángel Eloy Campos (29/0), Orlando de la Torre Castro (17/0), Héctor Eduardo Chumpitaz González (25/1), Rafael Risco (2/0), Roberto Federico Chale Olarte (20/1), Luis Fernando Cruzado Sánchez (13/1), Julio Alberto Temistocles Baylón Aragonés (17/1) [90.José Antonio Fernández Santini (28/0)], Pedro Pablo León García (31/12), Teófilo Juan Cubillas Arizaga (18/4), Oswaldo Felipe Ramírez Salcedo (8/5). Trainer: Waldyr Pereira „Didi" (19).
Goals: Oswaldo Felipe Ramírez Salcedo (64, 83).

145. 04.02.1970 **PERU – CZECHOSLOVAKIA** **0-2(0-2)**
Estadio Nacional, Lima; Referee: Alberto Tejada Burga (Peru)
PER: Luis Rubiños Cerna (22/0), Ángel Eloy Campos (30/0), Orlando de la Torre Castro (18/0), Héctor Eduardo Chumpitaz González (26/1), Félix Salinas (1/0), Roberto Federico Chale Olarte (21/1) [57.Luis Fernando Cruzado Sánchez (14/1)], Hernán Castañeda (4/1) [46.Hugo Alejandro Sotil Yerén (1/0)], Julio Alberto Temistocles Baylón Aragonés (18/1), Pedro Pablo León García (32/12), Teófilo Juan Cubillas Arizaga (19/4), Félix Alberto Gallardo Mendoza (18/7) [63.Oswaldo Felipe Ramírez Salcedo (9/5)]. Trainer: Waldyr Pereira „Didi" (20).

146. 07.02.1970 **PERU – CZECHOSLOVAKIA** **2-1(1-0)**
Estadio Nacional, Lima; Referee: Erwin Hiegger (Austria)
PER: Dimas Zegarra (13/0), Pedro Gonzáles Zavala (11/0), José Antonio Fernández Santini (29/0), José Javier González (10/0), Rafael Risco (3/0), Roberto Federico Chale Olarte (22/1), Luis Fernando Cruzado Sánchez (15/1), Juan José Muñante López (8/0), Hugo Alejandro Sotil Yerén (2/1), Teófilo Juan Cubillas Arizaga (20/5) [60.Pedro Pablo León García (33/12)], Oswaldo Felipe Ramírez Salcedo (10/5) [60.José Del Castillo (8/0)]. Trainer: Waldyr Pereira „Didi" (21).
Goals: Hugo Alejandro Sotil Yerén (29), Teófilo Juan Cubillas Arizaga (57).

147. 09.02.1970 **PERU – ROMANIA** **1-1(0-1)**
Estadio Nacional, Lima; Referee: César Augusto Orozco Guerrero (Peru); Attendance: 35,000
PER: Ottorino Sartor Espinoza (6/0), Ángel Eloy Campos (31/0), José Javier González (11/0), Héctor Eduardo Chumpitaz González (27/1), Félix Salinas (2/0), Luis Fernando Cruzado Sánchez (16/1), Hernán Castañeda (5/1) [46.Hugo Alejandro Sotil Yerén (3/1)], Julio Alberto Temistocles Baylón Aragonés (19/1) [73.Andrés Zegarra (7/0)], Pedro Pablo León García (34/12), Teófilo Juan Cubillas Arizaga (21/6), Félix Alberto Gallardo Mendoza (19/7). Trainer: Waldyr Pereira „Didi" (22).
Goal: Teófilo Juan Cubillas Arizaga (55).

148. 14.02.1970 **PERU – SOVIET UNION** **0-0**
Estadio Nacional, Lima; Referee: Alberto Tejada Burga (Peru); Attendance: 42,000
PER: Luis Rubiños Cerna (23/0), Ángel Eloy Campos (32/0), Orlando de la Torre Castro (19/0), Héctor Eduardo Chumpitaz González (28/1), Félix Salinas (3/0), Roberto Federico Chale Olarte (23/1), Luis Fernando Cruzado Sánchez (17/1) [65.Hugo Alejandro Sotil Yerén (4/1)], Julio Alberto Temistocles Baylón Aragonés (20/1), Pedro Pablo León García (35/12), Teófilo Juan Cubillas Arizaga (22/6), Félix Alberto Gallardo Mendoza (20/7). Trainer: Waldyr Pereira „Didi" (23).

149. 20.02.1970 **PERU – SOVIET UNION** **0-2(0-0)**

Estadio Nacional, Lima; Referee: César Augusto Orozco Guerrero (Peru); Attendance: 27,000

PER: Dimas Zegarra (14/0), Ángel Eloy Campos (33/0), Orlando de la Torre Castro (20/0), Héctor Eduardo Chumpitaz González (29/1), Félix Salinas (4/0), Roberto Federico Chale Olarte (24/1), Luis Fernando Cruzado Sánchez (18/1), Julio Alberto Temistocles Baylón Aragonés (21/1) [66.Andrés Zegarra (8/0)], Pedro Pablo León García (36/12), Teófilo Juan Cubillas Arizaga (23/6), Félix Alberto Gallardo Mendoza (21/7). Trainer: Waldyr Pereira „Didi" (24).

150. 21.02.1970 **PERU – BULGARIA** **1-3(1-0)**

Estadio Nacional, Lima; Referee: Carlos Rivero (Peru); Attendance: 25,000

PER: Ottorino Sartor Espinoza (7/0), Pedro Gonzáles Zavala (12/0), José Antonio Fernández Santini (30/0), José Javier González (12/0), Rafael Risco (4/0), Carlos Oliva (1/0), Hernán Castañeda (6/1), Andrés Zegarra (9/0) [73.Juan José Muñante López (9/0)], Percy Rojas Montero (3/0), Hugo Alejandro Sotil Yerén (5/2), Oswaldo Felipe Ramírez Salcedo (11/5). Trainer: Waldyr Pereira „Didi" (25).

Goal: Hugo Alejandro Sotil Yerén (28).

151. 24.02.1970 **PERU – BULGARIA** **5-3(0-1)**

Estadio Nacional, Lima; Referee: Erwin Hiegger (Peru); Attendance: 30,000

PER: Rubén David Correa Montenegro (4/0), Ángel Eloy Campos (34/0), Orlando de la Torre Castro (21/0), Héctor Eduardo Chumpitaz González (30/1), Félix Salinas (5/0), Roberto Federico Chale Olarte (25/2), Luis Fernando Cruzado Sánchez (19/1) [46.Hugo Alejandro Sotil Yerén (6/5)], Julio Alberto Temistocles Baylón Aragonés (22/1), Pedro Pablo León García (37/12), Teófilo Juan Cubillas Arizaga (24/7), Félix Alberto Gallardo Mendoza (22/7) [40.José Del Castillo (9/0)]. Trainer: Waldyr Pereira „Didi" (26).

Goals: Hugo Alejandro Sotil Yerén (55), Roberto Federico Chale Olarte (63), Teófilo Juan Cubillas Arizaga (82), Hugo Alejandro Sotil Yerén (84, 88).

152. 05.03.1970 **PERU – MEXICO** **0-1(0-1)**

Estadio Nacional, Lima; Referee: Erwin Hiegger (Austria)

PER: Luis Rubiños Cerna (24/0), Ángel Eloy Campos (35/0), Orlando de la Torre Castro (22/0), Héctor Eduardo Chumpitaz González (31/1), Félix Salinas (6/0), Luis Fernando Cruzado Sánchez (20/1) [46.Hugo Alejandro Sotil Yerén (7/5)], Roberto Federico Chale Olarte (26/2), Julio Alberto Temistocles Baylón Aragonés (23/1) [54.José Del Castillo (10/0)], Pedro Pablo León García (38/12), Teófilo Juan Cubillas Arizaga (25/7), Félix Alberto Gallardo Mendoza (23/7). Trainer: Waldyr Pereira „Didi" (27).

153. 08.03.1970 **PERU – MEXICO** **1-0(0-0)**

Estadio Nacional, Lima; Referee: Alberto Tejada Burga (Peru)

PER: Luis Rubiños Cerna (25/0), Ángel Eloy Campos (36/0), Orlando de la Torre Castro (23/0) [76.José Javier González (13/0)], Héctor Eduardo Chumpitaz González (32/1), Rafael Risco (5/0), Roberto Federico Chale Olarte (27/2), Teófilo Juan Cubillas Arizaga (26/7), José Del Castillo (11/0) [46.Julio Alberto Temistocles Baylón Aragonés (24/1)], Pedro Pablo León García (39/13) [67.Eladio Máximo Reyes Caraza (4/0)], Hugo Alejandro Sotil Yerén (8/5), Félix Alberto Gallardo Mendoza (24/7). Trainer: Waldyr Pereira „Didi" (28).

Goal: Pedro Pablo León García (63).

154. 15.03.1970 **MEXICO – PERU** **3-1(2-1)**

Estadio Azteca, Ciudad de México; Referee: Diego de Leo (Mexico)

PER: Luis Rubiños Cerna (26/0), Ángel Eloy Campos (37/0), Orlando de la Torre Castro (24/0), Héctor Eduardo Chumpitaz González (33/1), Rafael Risco (6/0), Roberto Federico Chale Olarte (28/3), Luis Fernando Cruzado Sánchez (21/1) [63.Hugo Alejandro Sotil Yerén (9/5)], Julio Alberto Temistocles Baylón Aragonés (25/1) [57.Eladio Máximo Reyes Caraza (5/0)], Pedro Pablo León García (40/13) [79.Oswaldo Felipe Ramírez Salcedo (12/5)], Teófilo Juan Cubillas Arizaga (27/7), Félix Alberto Gallardo Mendoza (25/7). Trainer: Waldyr Pereira „Didi" (29).

Goal: Roberto Federico Chale Olarte (40).

155. 18.03.1970 **MEXICO – PERU** **3-3(2-1)**

Estadio Nou Camp, León; Referee: Abel Aguilar (Mexico)

PER: Luis Rubiños Cerna (27/0), Ángel Eloy Campos (38/0), Orlando de la Torre Castro (25/0), Héctor Eduardo Chumpitaz González (34/1) [*sent off 37*], Félix Salinas (7/0), Roberto Federico Chale Olarte (29/3), Luis Fernando Cruzado Sánchez (22/1) [42.José Javier González (14/0)], Julio Alberto Temistocles Baylón Aragonés (26/2) [75.Hugo Alejandro Sotil Yerén (10/5)], Pedro Pablo León García (41/15), Teófilo Juan Cubillas Arizaga (28/7), Félix Alberto Gallardo Mendoza (26/7). Trainer: Waldyr Pereira „Didi" (30).

Goals: Pedro Pablo León García (10), Julio Alberto Temistocles Baylón Aragonés (51), Pedro Pablo León García (80).

156. 31.03.1970 **URUGUAY – PERU** **2-0(2-0)**

Estadio Centenario, Montevideo; Referee: Pablo Vega (Uruguay)

PER: Luis Rubiños Cerna (28/0), Ángel Eloy Campos (39/0), Orlando de la Torre Castro (26/0), José Javier González (15/0), Félix Salinas (8/0), Roberto Federico Chale Olarte (30/3), Hernán Castañeda (7/1), Julio Alberto Temistocles Baylón Aragonés (27/2), Pedro Pablo León García (42/15) [46.Hugo Alejandro Sotil Yerén (11/5)], Teófilo Juan Cubillas Arizaga (29/7) [67.José Del Castillo (12/0)], Félix Alberto Gallardo Mendoza (27/7). Trainer: Waldyr Pereira „Didi" (31).

157. 21.04.1970 **PERU – EL SALVADOR** **3-0(0-0)**

Estadio Nacional, Lima; Referee: César Augusto Orozco Guerrero (Peru)

PER: Luis Rubiños Cerna (29/0) [81.Pedro Pablo León García (43/15)], Ángel Eloy Campos (40/0), Orlando de la Torre Castro (27/0), Héctor Eduardo Chumpitaz González (35/1), Rafael Risco (7/0), Luis Fernando Cruzado Sánchez (23/1), Hernán Castañeda (8/1), Julio Alberto Temistocles Baylón Aragonés (28/2), Eladio Máximo Reyes Caraza (6/0), Hugo Alejandro Sotil Yerén (12/6), Félix Alberto Gallardo Mendoza (28/8) [69.José Del Castillo (13/1)]. Trainer: Waldyr Pereira „Didi" (32).

Goals: Félix Alberto Gallardo Mendoza (48), Hugo Alejandro Sotil Yerén (55), José Del Castillo (79).

158. 02.06.1970 **PERU – BULGARIA** **3-2(0-1)** 9th FIFA WC. Group Stage

Estadio Nou Camp, León (Mexico); Referee: Antonio Sbardella (Italy); Attendance: 13,765

PER: Luis Rubiños Cerna (30/0), Ángel Eloy Campos (41/0) [28.José Javier González (16/0)], Orlando de la Torre Castro (28/0), Héctor Eduardo Chumpitaz González (Cap) (36/2), Nicolás Fuentes Zegarra (13/0), Roberto Federico Chale Olarte (31/3), Ramón Antonio Mifflin Páez (22/0), Julio Alberto Temistocles Baylón Aragonés (29/2) [46.Hugo Alejandro Sotil Yerén (13/6)], Pedro Pablo León García (44/15), Teófilo Juan Cubillas Arizaga (30/8), Félix Alberto Gallardo Mendoza (29/9). Trainer: Waldyr Pereira „Didi" (33).

Goals: Félix Alberto Gallardo Mendoza (51), Héctor Eduardo Chumpitaz González (56), Teófilo Juan Cubillas Arizaga (74).

159. 06.06.1970 **PERU – MOROCCO** **3-0(0-0)** 9th FIFA WC. Group Stage
Estadio Nou Camp, León (Mexico); Referee: Tofik Bahramov (Soviet Union); Attendance: 14,000
PER: Luis Rubiños Cerna (31/0), Pedro Gonzáles Zavala (13/0), Orlando de la Torre Castro (29/0), Héctor Eduardo Chumpitaz González (Cap) (37/2), Nicolás Fuentes Zegarra (14/0), Roberto Federico Chale Olarte (32/4), Ramón Antonio Mifflin Páez (23/0) [56.Luis Fernando Cruzado Sánchez (24/1)], Hugo Alejandro Sotil Yerén (14/6), Pedro Pablo León García (45/15), Teófilo Juan Cubillas Arizaga (31/10), Félix Alberto Gallardo Mendoza (30/9) [76.Oswaldo Felipe Ramírez Salcedo (13/5)]. Trainer: Waldyr Pereira „Didi" (34).
Goals: Teófilo Juan Cubillas Arizaga (65), Roberto Federico Chale Olarte (67), Teófilo Juan Cubillas Arizaga (75).

160. 10.06.1970 **WEST GERMANY – PERU** **3-1(3-1)** 9th FIFA WC. Group Stage
Estadio Nou Camp, León (Mexico); Referee: Abel Aguilar Elizalde (Mexico); Attendance: 17,875
PER: Luis Rubiños Cerna (32/0), Pedro Gonzáles Zavala (14/0), Héctor Eduardo Chumpitaz González (Cap) (38/2), Orlando de la Torre Castro (30/0), Nicolás Fuentes Zegarra (15/0), Roberto Federico Chale Olarte (33/4), Ramón Antonio Mifflin Páez (24/0) [71.Luis Fernando Cruzado Sánchez (25/1)], Hugo Alejandro Sotil Yerén (15/6), Pedro Pablo León García (46/15) [56.Oswaldo Felipe Ramírez Salcedo (14/5)], Teófilo Juan Cubillas Arizaga (32/11), Félix Alberto Gallardo Mendoza (31/9). Trainer: Waldyr Pereira „Didi" (35).
Goal: Teófilo Juan Cubillas Arizaga (44).

161. 14.06.1970 **BRAZIL – PERU** **4-2(2-1)** 9th FIFA WC. Quarter-Finals
Estadio Monumental Jalisco, Guadalajara (Mexico); Referee: Vital Loraux (Belgium); Attendance: 54,233
PER: Luis Rubiños Cerna (33/0), Ángel Eloy Campos (42/0), José Antonio Fernández Santini (31/0), Héctor Eduardo Chumpitaz González (Cap) (39/2), Nicolás Fuentes Zegarra (16/0), Ramón Antonio Mifflin Páez (25/0), Roberto Federico Chale Olarte (34/4), Teófilo Juan Cubillas Arizaga (33/12), Julio Alberto Temistocles Baylón Aragonés (30/2) [54.Hugo Alejandro Sotil Yerén (16/6)], Pedro Pablo León García (47/15) [61.Eladio Máximo Reyes Caraza (7/0)], Félix Alberto Gallardo Mendoza (32/10). Trainer: Waldyr Pereira „Didi" (36).
Goals: Félix Alberto Gallardo Mendoza (27), Teófilo Juan Cubillas Arizaga (64).

162. 27.07.1971 **PERU – PARAGUAY** **0-0**
Estadio Nacional, Lima; Referee: Edison Pérez Nuñez (Peru)
PER: Ottorino Sartor Espinoza (8/0), Ángel Eloy Campos (43/0) [77.Moisés Palacios (1/0)], Fernando Cárdenas (1/0), Héctor Eduardo Chumpitaz González (40/2), Nicolás Fuentes Zegarra (17/0), Ramón Antonio Mifflin Páez (26/0), Roberto Federico Chale Olarte (35/4), Alfredo Quesada Farías (1/0) [54.Héctor Bailetti (5/1)], Hugo Alejandro Sotil Yerén (17/6), Teófilo Juan Cubillas Arizaga (34/12), Félix Alberto Gallardo Mendoza (33/10). Trainer: Alejandro Heredia (1).

163. 11.08.1971 **PERU – CHILE** **1-0(0-0)** Copa del Pacífico
Estadio Nacional, Lima; Referee: Alberto Tejada Burga (Peru); Attendance: 40,000
PER: Jesús Goyzueta (1/0), Moisés Palacios (2/0), Orlando de la Torre Castro (31/0), Héctor Eduardo Chumpitaz González (41/2), Félix Salinas (9/0), Roberto Federico Chale Olarte (36/4) [Luis Fernando Cruzado Sánchez (26/1)], Ramón Antonio Mifflin Páez (27/0), Teófilo Juan Cubillas Arizaga (35/12), Juan José Muñante López (10/0), Juan Rivero (1/0) [Hugo Alejandro Sotil Yerén (18/7)], Oswaldo Felipe Ramírez Salcedo (15/5) [Héctor Bailetti (6/1)]. Trainer: Alejandro Heredia (2).
Goal: Hugo Alejandro Sotil Yerén (86).

164. 15.08.1971 **PARAGUAY – PERU** **2-0(0-0)**
Estadio Defensores del Chaco, Asunción; Referee: José Romei (Paraguay)
PER: Jesús Goyzueta (2/0), Moisés Palacios (3/0), Orlando de la Torre Castro (32/0), Héctor Eduardo Chumpitaz González (42/2), Félix Salinas (10/0), Ramón Antonio Mifflin Páez (28/0), Roberto Federico Chale Olarte (37/4), Juan José Muñante López (11/0), Juan Rivero (2/0) [46.Hugo Alejandro Sotil Yerén (19/7)], Teófilo Juan Cubillas Arizaga (36/12), Héctor Bailetti (7/1). Trainer: Alejandro Heredia (3).

165. 18.08.1971 **CHILE – PERU** **1-0(0-0)** Copa del Pacífico
Estadio Nacional, Santiago; Referee: Jaime Amor (Chile); Attendance: 55,000
PER: Ottorino Sartor Espinoza (9/0), Ángel Eloy Campos (44/0), Orlando de la Torre Castro (33/0) [*sent off 64*], Héctor Eduardo Chumpitaz González (43/2), Félix Salinas (11/0), Augusto Palacios (1/0), Ramón Antonio Mifflin Páez (29/0), Juan José Muñante López (12/0), Hugo Alejandro Sotil Yerén (20/7), Teófilo Juan Cubillas Arizaga (37/12), Héctor Bailetti (8/1) [65.Fernando Cuéllar (1/0)]. Trainer: Alejandro Heredia (4).

166. 29.03.1972 **COLOMBIA – PERU** **1-1(1-0)**
Estadio „Nemesio Camacho" 'El Campín', Bogotá; Referee: Omar Delgado Piedrahita (Colombia)
PER: Manuel Uribe (1/0), Antonio Trigueros (1/0), Rodolfo Manzo Audante (1/0), José Manuel Velásquez Castillo (1/0), Rubén Toribio Díaz Rivas (1/0), Ramón Antonio Mifflin Páez (30/0), Roberto Federico Chale Olarte (38/4) [23.Alfredo Quesada Farías (2/0)], Juan José Muñante López (13/1), Hugo Alejandro Sotil Yerén (21/7), Percy Rojas Montero (4/0), Héctor Bailetti (9/1) [46.Teófilo Juan Cubillas Arizaga (38/12)]. Trainer: Lajos Baróti (1).
Goal: Juan José Muñante López (68).

167. 05.04.1972 **MEXICO – PERU** **2-1(0-1)**
Estadio Azteca, Ciudad de México; Referee: Javier Galindo (Mexico)
PER: Manuel Uribe (2/0), Antonio Trigueros (2/0), Héctor Eduardo Chumpitaz González (44/2), José Manuel Velásquez Castillo (2/0), Rubén Toribio Díaz Rivas (2/0) [65.Rodolfo Manzo Audante (2/0)], Alfredo Quesada Farías (3/0), Ramón Antonio Mifflin Páez (31/0), Juan José Muñante López (14/1), Hugo Alejandro Sotil Yerén (22/7), Teófilo Juan Cubillas Arizaga (39/13), Percy Rojas Montero (5/0) [63.Héctor Bailetti (10/1)]. Trainer: Lajos Baróti (2).
Goal: Teófilo Juan Cubillas Arizaga (39).

168. 19.04.1972 **SOVIET UNION – PERU** **2-0(2-0)**
Centralniy Stadium, Kiev; Referee: Wolfgang Riedel (East Germany); Attendance: 48,000
PER: Manuel Uribe (3/0), Rodolfo Manzo Audante (3/0), José Manuel Velásquez Castillo (3/0), Héctor Eduardo Chumpitaz González (45/2), Antonio Trigueros (3/0), Ramón Antonio Mifflin Páez (32/0), Alfredo Quesada Farías (4/0), Juan José Muñante López (15/1), Percy Rojas Montero (6/0), Teófilo Juan Cubillas Arizaga (40/13), Héctor Bailetti (11/1) [46.Hugo Alejandro Sotil Yerén (23/7)]. Trainer: Lajos Baróti (3).

169. 23.04.1972 **ROMANIA – PERU** **2-2(0-1)**
Stadionul 23 August, Bucureşti; Referee: Nikolaos Zlatanos (Greece); Attendance: 6,000
PER: Manuel Uribe (4/0), Antonio Trigueros (4/0), Héctor Eduardo Chumpitaz González (46/2), José Manuel Velásquez Castillo (4/0), Rodolfo Manzo Audante (4/0), Alfredo Quesada Farías (5/0), Teófilo Juan Cubillas Arizaga (41/14), Ramón Antonio Mifflin Páez (33/0), Juan José Muñante López (16/1), Percy Rojas Montero (7/1) [46.Hugo Alejandro Sotil Yerén (24/7)], Héctor Bailetti (12/1) [55.Juan Orbegoso (1/0)]. Trainer: Lajos Baróti (4).
Goals: Percy Rojas Montero (22), Teófilo Juan Cubillas Arizaga (52).

170. 26.04.1972 **SCOTLAND - PERU** **2-0(0-0)**
Hampden Park, Glasgow; Referee: Patrick Partridge (England); Attendance: 21,001
PER: Manuel Uribe (5/0), Rodolfo Manzo Audante (5/0), José Manuel Velásquez Castillo (5/0), Héctor Eduardo Chumpitaz González (47/2), Antonio Trigueros (5/0), Ramón Antonio Mifflin Páez (34/0), Alfredo Quesada Farías (6/0), Juan José Muñante López (17/1), Percy Rojas Montero (8/1) [46.Hugo Alejandro Sotil Yerén (25/7)], Teófilo Juan Cubillas Arizaga (42/14), Juan Orbegoso (2/0). Trainer: Lajos Baróti (5).

171. 03.05.1972 **HOLLAND - PERU** **3-0(2-0)**
Feijenoord Stadion, Rotterdam; Referee: Mario Clematide (Switzerland); Attendance: 22,000
PER: Manuel Uribe (6/0), Rodolfo Manzo Audante (6/0), Héctor Eduardo Chumpitaz González (48/2), Rubén Toribio Díaz Rivas (3/0), Alfredo Quesada Farías (7/0), José Manuel Velásquez Castillo (6/0), Ramón Antonio Mifflin Páez (35/0), Juan José Muñante López (18/1) [48.Percy Rojas Montero (9/1)], Roberto Drago Jr. (1/0) [73.Gerónimo Barbadillo González (1/0)], Teófilo Juan Cubillas Arizaga (43/14), Hugo Alejandro Sotil Yerén (26/7). Trainer: Lajos Baróti (6).

172. 06.06.1972 **PERU - COLOMBIA** **0-0**
Estadio Nacional, Lima; Referee: Edison Pérez Nuñez (Peru)
PER: Luis Rubiños Cerna (34/0), Ángel Eloy Campos (45/0), Fernando Cuéllar (2/0), Orlando de la Torre Castro (34/0), Julio Luna (1/0), Ramón Antonio Mifflin Páez (36/0) [60.Hernán Castañeda (9/1)], Alfredo Quesada Farías (8/0), Juan José Muñante López (19/1) [60.Oswaldo Felipe Ramírez Salcedo (16/5)], Percy Rojas Montero (10/1) [46.César Augusto Cueto Villa (1/0)], Hugo Alejandro Sotil Yerén (27/7), Félix Alberto Gallardo Mendoza (34/10). Trainer: Roberto Scarone (1).

173. 11.06.1972 **PERU - BOLIVIA** **3-0(3-0)** Copa Independencia de Brasil
Estádio „Belfort Duarte“, Curitiba (Brazil); Referee: Keith Edwin Walker (England); Attendance: 18,000
PER: Luis Rubiños Cerna (35/0), Ángel Eloy Campos (46/0), Fernando Cuéllar (3/0), Orlando de la Torre Castro (35/0), Julio Luna (2/0), Manuel Mayorga (1/0), Hernán Castañeda (10/2) [52.Ramón Antonio Mifflin Páez (37/0)], Juan José Muñante López (20/1), César Augusto Cueto Villa (2/0), Hugo Alejandro Sotil Yerén (28/8), Félix Alberto Gallardo Mendoza (35/11) [55.Oswaldo Felipe Ramírez Salcedo (17/5)]. Trainer: Roberto Scarone (2).
Goals: Félix Alberto Gallardo Mendoza (7 penalty), Hernán Castañeda (16), Hugo Alejandro Sotil Yerén (31).

174. 14.06.1972 **PARAGUAY - PERU** **1-0(0-0)** Copa Independencia de Brasil
Estádio „Pedro Pedrossian“, Campo Grande (Brazil); Referee: Abraham Klein (Israel)
PER: Luis Rubiños Cerna (36/0), José Manuel Velásquez Castillo (7/0), Fernando Cuéllar (4/0), Orlando de la Torre Castro (36/0), Julio Luna (3/0), Manuel Mayorga (2/0), Hernán Castañeda (11/2), Juan José Muñante López (21/1), César Augusto Cueto Villa (3/0) [46.Percy Rojas Montero (11/1)], Hugo Alejandro Sotil Yerén (29/8), Félix Alberto Gallardo Mendoza (36/11) [60.Héctor Bailetti (13/1)]. Trainer: Roberto Scarone (3).

175. 18.06.1972 **PERU - VENEZUELA** **1-0(0-0)** Copa Independencia de Brasil
Estádio „Vivaldo Lima“, Manaus (Brazil); Referee: Armando Coelho (Brazil); Attendance: 20,000
PER: Luis Rubiños Cerna (37/0), Eleazar Soria (1/0), Fernando Cuéllar (5/0), Héctor Eduardo Chumpitaz González (49/2), Julio Luna (4/0), Ramón Antonio Mifflin Páez (38/0), Manuel Mayorga (3/0), Juan José Muñante López (22/1) [46.Oswaldo Felipe Ramírez Salcedo (18/6)], Percy Rojas Montero (12/1) [58.César Augusto Cueto Villa (4/0)], Hugo Alejandro Sotil Yerén (30/8), Héctor Bailetti (14/1). Trainer: Roberto Scarone (4).
Goal: Oswaldo Felipe Ramírez Salcedo (65).

176. 25.06.1972 **YUGOSLAVIA - PERU** **2-1(2-1)** Copa Independencia de Brasil
Estádio „Vivaldo Lima“, Manaus (Brazil); Referee: Alfonso Archundia Gonzáles (Mexico); Attendance: 20,000
PER: Luis Rubiños Cerna (38/0), Eleazar Soria (2/0), Fernando Cuéllar (6/0), Héctor Eduardo Chumpitaz González (50/2), Julio Luna (5/0), Manuel Mayorga (4/0), Alfredo Quesada Farías (9/0), Ramón Antonio Mifflin Páez (39/0), Juan José Muñante López (23/1) [63.Félix Alberto Gallardo Mendoza (37/11)], Hugo Alejandro Sotil Yerén (31/8) [63.Percy Rojas Montero (13/1)], Oswaldo Felipe Ramírez Salcedo (19/7). Trainer: Roberto Scarone (5).
Goal: Oswaldo Felipe Ramírez Salcedo (11).

177. 09.08.1972 **PERU - MEXICO** **3-2(2-2)**
Estadio Nacional, Lima; Referee: Carlos Rivero (Peru); Attendance: 45,000
PER: Carlos Burela (1/0), José Navarro Aramburu (1/0), Fernando Cuéllar (7/0), José Manuel Velásquez Castillo (8/0), Félix Salinas (12/0) [46.Rafael Risco (8/0)], Manuel Mayorga (5/0), José Antonio Fernández Santini (32/2), Julio Alberto Temistocles Baylón Aragonés (31/2), Teófilo Juan Cubillas Arizaga (44/14), Hugo Alejandro Sotil Yerén (32/8) [61.Percy Rojas Montero (14/1)], Juan José Muñante López (24/2) [72.Walter Daga (1/0)]. Trainer: Roberto Scarone (6).
Goals: Juan José Muñante López (35), José Antonio Fernández Santini (41, 75).

178. 25.10.1972 **PERU - ARGENTINA** **0-2(0-2)** Copa Ramón Castilla
Estadio Nacional, Lima; Referee: Carlos Rivero (Peru); Attendance: 20,000
PER: Carlos Burela (2/0), Rodolfo Manzo Audante (7/0), Julio Meléndez (6/0) [72.Fernando Cuéllar (8/0)], Héctor Eduardo Chumpitaz González (51/2), Julio Luna (6/0), Manuel Mayorga (6/0), Ramón Antonio Mifflin Páez (40/0) [55.Alfredo Quesada Farías (10/0)], Teófilo Juan Cubillas Arizaga (45/14), Julio Alberto Temistocles Baylón Aragonés (32/2) [52.Oswaldo Felipe Ramírez Salcedo (20/7)], Hugo Alejandro Sotil Yerén (33/8), Juan José Muñante López (25/2). Trainer: Roberto Scarone (7).

179. 04.03.1973 **PERU - GUATEMALA** **5-1(2-0)**
Estadio Nacional, Lima; Referee: Pedro Reyes (Peru); Attendance: 20,353
PER: Ottorino Sartor Espinoza (10/0), José Navarro Aramburu (2/0), Luis La Fuente (3/0), Héctor Eduardo Chumpitaz González (52/2), Julio Luna (7/0), Roberto Federico Chale Olarte (39/4), José Antonio Fernández Santini (33/2), Teófilo Juan Cubillas Arizaga (46/16), Juan José Muñante López (26/4), Pedro Pablo León García (48/15) [76.Oswaldo Felipe Ramírez Salcedo (21/7)], Hugo Alejandro Sotil Yerén (34/9) [76.Juan Carlos Oblitas Saba (1/0)]. Trainer: Roberto Scarone (8).
Goals: Teófilo Juan Cubillas Arizaga (23, 32), Juan José Muñante López (50), Hugo Alejandro Sotil Yerén (60), Juan José Muñante López (70).

180. 24.03.1973 **PERU - BOLIVIA** **2-0(2-0)** Copa Mariscal Sucre
Estadio Nacional, Lima; Referee: Pedro Reyes (Peru); Attendance: 14,219
PER: Manuel Uribe (7/0), José Navarro Aramburu (3/0), Luis La Fuente (4/0), Rodolfo Manzo Audante (8/0), Antonio Trigueros (6/0), Manuel Mayorga (7/0), Roberto Federico Chale Olarte (40/4), Alfredo Quesada Farías (11/0), Juan José Muñante López (27/4) [71.Gerónimo Barbadillo González (2/0)], Percy Rojas Montero (15/1) [71.Teófilo Juan Cubillas Arizaga (47/16)], Hugo Alejandro Sotil Yerén (35/10). Trainer: Roberto Scarone (9).
Goals: Luis Iriondo Angola (20 own goal), Hugo Alejandro Sotil Yerén (35).

181. 28.03.1973 **PERU – PARAGUAY** **1-0(1-0)**

Estadio Nacional, Lima; Referee: Carlos Rivero (Peru); Attendance: 36,516

PER: Manuel Uribe (8/0), José Navarro Aramburu (4/0), Luis La Fuente (5/0), Rodolfo Manzo Audante (9/0), Antonio Trigueros (7/0) [61.Julio Luna (8/0)], Manuel Mayorga (8/0), Roberto Federico Chale Olarte (41/4) [50.Pedro Pablo León García (49/15)], Alfredo Quesada Farías (12/0) [46.José Antonio Fernández Santini (34/2)], Juan José Muñante López (28/4), Teófilo Juan Cubillas Arizaga (48/16), Hugo Alejandro Sotil Yerén (36/11). Trainer: Roberto Scarone (10).

Goal: Hugo Alejandro Sotil Yerén (40).

182. 08.04.1973 **PARAGUAY – PERU** **1-1(1-0)**

Estadio Defensores del Chaco, Asunción; Referee: José Larrosa (Paraguay)

PER: Ottorino Sartor Espinoza (11/0), José Navarro Aramburu (5/0), Rodolfo Manzo Audante (10/0), Héctor Eduardo Chumpitaz González (53/2), Antonio Trigueros (8/0), Alfredo Quesada Farías (13/0), Manuel Mayorga (9/0), Percy Rojas Montero (16/1) [63.Pedro Gonzáles Zavala (15/0)], Oswaldo Felipe Ramírez Salcedo (22/7), José Antonio Fernández Santini (35/2) [46.Teófilo Juan Cubillas Arizaga (49/16)], Hugo Alejandro Sotil Yerén (37/12). Trainer: Roberto Scarone (11).

Goal: Hugo Alejandro Sotil Yerén (88).

183. 23.04.1973 **PERU – PANAMA** **4-0(2-0)**

Estadio Nacional, Lima; Referee: Enrique Labó (Peru)

PER: Manuel Uribe (9/0), Pedro Gonzáles Zavala (16/0), Rodolfo Manzo Audante (11/0), Héctor Eduardo Chumpitaz González (54/2), Julio Luna (9/0) [46.Antonio Trigueros (9/0)], Roberto Federico Chale Olarte (42/4), Manuel Mayorga (10/1) [71.José Antonio Fernández Santini (36/2)], Teófilo Juan Cubillas Arizaga (50/17), Juan José Muñante López (29/5), Hugo Alejandro Sotil Yerén (38/12), Oswaldo Felipe Ramírez Salcedo (23/8). Trainer: Roberto Scarone (12).

Goals: Teófilo Juan Cubillas Arizaga (16), Juan José Muñante López (26), Oswaldo Felipe Ramírez Salcedo (56), Manuel Mayorga (65).

184. 29.04.1973 **PERU – CHILE** **2-0(1-0)** 10th FIFA WC. Qualifiers

Estadio Nacional, Lima; Referee: Armando Nunes Castanheiras da Rosa Marques (Brazil); Attendance: 42,947

PER: Manuel Uribe (10/0), José Navarro Aramburu (6/0), Rodolfo Manzo Audante (12/0), Héctor Eduardo Chumpitaz González (55/2), Julio Luna (10/0), Manuel Mayorga (11/1) [Juan José Muñante López (30/5)], Roberto Federico Chale Olarte (43/4), Alfredo Quesada Farías (14/0), Hugo Alejandro Sotil Yerén (39/14), Teófilo Juan Cubillas Arizaga (51/17) [66.José Antonio Fernández Santini (37/2)], Oswaldo Felipe Ramírez Salcedo (24/8). Trainer: Roberto Scarone (13).

Goals: Hugo Alejandro Sotil Yerén (43, 63).

185. 13.05.1973 **CHILE – PERU** **2-0(0-0)** 10th FIFA WC. Qualifiers

Estadio Nacional, Santiago; Referee: Ramón Ivannoe Barreto Ruíz (Uruguay); Attendance: 69,881

PER: Manuel Uribe (11/0), José Navarro Aramburu (7/0), Rodolfo Manzo Audante (13/0), Héctor Eduardo Chumpitaz González (56/2), Julio Luna (11/0), Manuel Mayorga (12/1), Roberto Federico Chale Olarte (44/4), Alfredo Quesada Farías (15/0) [46.José Manuel Velásquez Castillo (9/0)], Oswaldo Felipe Ramírez Salcedo (25/8), Teófilo Juan Cubillas Arizaga (52/17) [57.Juan José Muñante López (31/5)], Hugo Alejandro Sotil Yerén (40/14). Trainer: Roberto Scarone (14).

186. 01.07.1973 **PERU – COLOMBIA** **3-1(1-0)**

Estadio Nacional, Lima; Referee: Enrique Labó (Peru)

PER: Manuel Uribe (12/0), José Navarro Aramburu (8/0), Rodolfo Manzo Audante (14/0) [69.Héctor Eduardo Chumpitaz González (57/2)], Orlando de la Torre Castro (37/0), Carlos Carbonell (1/0), Ramón Antonio Mifflin Páez (41/0), Roberto Federico Chale Olarte (45/4), Manuel Mayorga (13/1) [54.Hugo Alejandro Sotil Yerén (41/14)], Juan José Muñante López (32/5), Héctor Bailetti (15/3), Oswaldo Felipe Ramírez Salcedo (26/9). Trainer: Roberto Scarone (15).

Goals: Héctor Bailetti (31, 49), Oswaldo Felipe Ramírez Salcedo (68).

187. 15.07.1973 **BOLIVIA – PERU** **2-0(0-0)** Copa Mariscal Sucre

Estadio „Hernándo Siles Zuazo“, La Paz; Referee: Juan Oscar Ortubé Vargas (Bolivia)

PER: Ottorino Sartor Espinoza (12/0), Eleazar Soria (3/0), Rodolfo Manzo Audante (15/0), Héctor Eduardo Chumpitaz González (58/2), Antonio Trigueros (10/0), Manuel Mayorga (14/1), Juan José Muñante López (33/5) [62.Héctor Bailetti (16/3)], Ramón Antonio Mifflin Páez (42/0) [46.Roberto Federico Chale Olarte (46/4)], Juan Rivero (3/0) [52.Oswaldo Felipe Ramírez Salcedo (27/9)], Teófilo Juan Cubillas Arizaga (53/17), Juan Carlos Oblitas Saba (2/0). Trainer: Roberto Scarone (16).

188. 27.07.1973 **ARGENTINA – PERU** **3-1(1-1)** Copa Ramón Castilla

Estadio „Alberto Armando“, Buenos Aires; Referee: Arturo Andrés Ithurralde (Argentina); Attendance: 20,000

PER: Manuel Uribe (13/0), José Navarro Aramburu (9/0) [73.Eleazar Soria (4/0)], Orlando de la Torre Castro (38/0), Héctor Eduardo Chumpitaz González (59/2), Carlos Carbonell (2/0), Roberto Federico Chale Olarte (47/4), Ramón Antonio Mifflin Páez (43/0), Juan José Muñante López (34/5) [80.Juan Rivero (4/0)], Héctor Bailetti (17/4), Hugo Alejandro Sotil Yerén (42/14), Oswaldo Felipe Ramírez Salcedo (28/9) [46.Manuel Mayorga (15/1)]. Trainer: Roberto Scarone (17).

Goal: Héctor Bailetti (39).

189. 05.08.1973 **CHILE – PERU** **2-1(1-1)** 10th FIFA WC. Qualifiers (Play-Off)

Estadio Centenario, Montevideo; Referee: Néstor Gregorio Da Rosa Caraballo (Uruguay); Attendance: 57,933

PER: Manuel Uribe (14/0), José Navarro Aramburu (10/0), Orlando de la Torre Castro (39/0), Héctor Eduardo Chumpitaz González (60/2), Carlos Carbonell (3/0), Roberto Federico Chale Olarte (48/4), Ramón Antonio Mifflin Páez (44/0), Juan José Muñante López (35/5), Hugo Alejandro Sotil Yerén (43/14) [46.Juan Carlos Oblitas Saba (3/0)], Héctor Bailetti (18/5), Oswaldo Felipe Ramírez Salcedo (29/9). Trainer: Roberto Scarone (18).

Goal: Héctor Bailetti (42).

190. 22.06.1975 **ECUADOR – PERU** **6-0(3-0)**

Estadio Olimpico „Atahualpa“, Quito; Referee: René Torres (Ecuador)

PER: Juan José Cáceres Palomares (1/0) [62.Ottorino Sartor Espinoza (13/0)], Eleazar Soria (5/0), Fernando Cuéllar (9/0), Héctor Eduardo Chumpitaz González (61/2) [58.Julio Meléndez (7/0)], Rubén Toribio Díaz Rivas (4/0), Julio Aparicio (1/0), Pedro Anselmo Ruiz (1/0), Alfredo Quesada Farías (16/0), Andrés Zegarra (10/0) [46.Reynaldo Jaime (1/0)], Juan Rivero (5/0) [65.Guillermo La Rosa Laguna (1/0)], Juan Carlos Oblitas Saba (4/0). Trainer: Marcos Calderón Medrano (15).

191. 25.06.1975 **ECUADOR - PERU** **1-0(0-0)**
Estadio Modelo, Guayaquil; Referee: Eduardo Rondón (Ecuador)
PER: Ottorino Sartor Espinoza (14/0), Eleazar Soria (6/0), Julio Meléndez (8/0), Héctor Eduardo Chumpitaz González (62/2), Rubén Toribio Díaz Rivas (5/0), Raúl Párraga (1/0), Alfredo Quesada Farías (17/0), César Augusto Cueto Villa (5/0), Andrés Zegarra (11/0) [64.Reynaldo Jaime (2/0)], Juan Rivero (6/0) [60.Guillermo La Rosa Laguna (2/0)], Juan Carlos Oblitas Saba (5/0). Trainer: Marcos Calderón Medrano (16).

192. 01.07.1975 **PERU - ECUADOR** **2-0(1-0)**
Estadio „Alejandro Villanueva", Lima; Referee: Carlos Rivero (Peru)
PER: Ottorino Sartor Espinoza (15/0), Eleazar Soria (7/0), Julio Meléndez (9/0), Jaime Eduardo Duarte Huerta (1/0), Rubén Toribio Díaz Rivas (6/1), Raúl Párraga (2/0), Alfredo Quesada Farías (18/0), César Augusto Cueto Villa (6/0) [46.Juan Rivero (7/0)], Reynaldo Jaime (3/0) [70.Carlos Gómez Laynez (1/0)], Oswaldo Felipe Ramírez Salcedo (30/9), Juan Carlos Oblitas Saba (6/1). Trainer: Marcos Calderón Medrano (17).
Goals: Juan Carlos Oblitas Saba (14), Rubén Toribio Díaz Rivas (76).

193. 10.07.1975 **PERU - PARAGUAY** **2-0(2-0)**
Estadio „Alejandro Villanueva", Lima; Referee: Enrique Labó (Peru)
PER: José Manuel Gonzáles Ganoza (1/0), José Navarro Aramburu (11/0), Julio Meléndez (10/0), Jaime Eduardo Duarte Huerta (2/0), Rubén Toribio Díaz Rivas (7/1), José Manuel Velásquez Castillo (10/0), Alfredo Quesada Farías (19/0), Oswaldo Felipe Ramírez Salcedo (31/11) [68.Carlos Gómez Laynez (2/0)], Teófilo Juan Cubillas Arizaga (54/17), Percy Rojas Montero (17/1) [50.César Augusto Cueto Villa (7/0)], Juan Carlos Oblitas Saba (7/1). Trainer: Marcos Calderón Medrano (18).
Goals: Oswaldo Felipe Ramírez Salcedo (13, 26).

194. 16.07.1975 **CHILE - PERU** **1-1(1-0)** 30th Copa América. Group Stage
Estadio Nacional, Santiago; Referee: Omar Delgado Piedrahita (Colombia); Attendance: 13,651
PER: Ottorino Sartor Espinoza (16/0), Eleazar Soria (8/0), Julio Meléndez (11/0), Héctor Eduardo Chumpitaz González (63/2), Rubén Toribio Díaz Rivas (8/1), Alfredo Quesada Farías (20/0), Teófilo Juan Cubillas Arizaga (55/17), José Manuel Velásquez Castillo (11/0) [66.Raúl Párraga (3/0)], Oswaldo Felipe Ramírez Salcedo (32/11), Percy Rojas Montero (18/2), Juan Carlos Oblitas Saba (8/1). Trainer: Marcos Calderón Medrano (19).
Goal: Percy Rojas Montero (72).

195. 27.07.1975 **BOLIVIA - PERU** **0-1(0-1)** 30th Copa América. Group Stage
Estadio „Jesús Bermúdez", Oruro; Referee: Alberto Ducatelli (Argentina); Attendance: 18,000
PER: Ottorino Sartor Espinoza (17/0), Eleazar Soria (9/0), Julio Meléndez (12/0), Héctor Eduardo Chumpitaz González (64/2), Rubén Toribio Díaz Rivas (9/1), Raúl Párraga (4/0), Alfredo Quesada Farías (21/0), Teófilo Juan Cubillas Arizaga (56/17), Oswaldo Felipe Ramírez Salcedo (33/12), Percy Rojas Montero (19/2) [57.Julio Aparicio (2/0)], Juan Carlos Oblitas Saba (9/1). Trainer: Marcos Calderón Medrano (20).
Goal: Oswaldo Felipe Ramírez Salcedo (16).

196. 07.08.1975 **PERU - BOLIVIA** **3-1(2-0)** 30th Copa América. Group Stage
Estadio „Alejandro Villanueva", Lima; Referee: Romualdo Arppi Filho (Brazil); Attendance: 40,000
PER: Ottorino Sartor Espinoza (18/0), Eleazar Soria (10/0), Julio Meléndez (13/0), Héctor Eduardo Chumpitaz González (65/2), Rubén Toribio Díaz Rivas (10/1), Alfredo Quesada Farías (22/0), Raúl Párraga (5/0), César Augusto Cueto Villa (8/1) [65.Julio Aparicio (3/0)], Oswaldo Felipe Ramírez Salcedo (34/13), Percy Rojas Montero (20/2), Juan Carlos Oblitas Saba (10/2). Trainer: Marcos Calderón Medrano (21).
Goals: Oswaldo Felipe Ramírez Salcedo (7), César Augusto Cueto Villa (26 penalty), Juan Carlos Oblitas Saba (52).

197. 20.08.1975 **PERU - CHILE** **3-1(3-0)** 30th Copa América. Group Stage
Estadio „Alejandro Villanueva", Lima; Referee: Juan José Fortunato (Uruguay); Attendance: 40,000
PER: Ottorino Sartor Espinoza (19/0), Eleazar Soria (11/0), Julio Meléndez (14/0), Héctor Eduardo Chumpitaz González (66/2), Rubén Toribio Díaz Rivas (11/1) [73.José Navarro Aramburu (12/0)], Alfredo Quesada Farías (23/0), Raúl Párraga (6/0), Teófilo Juan Cubillas Arizaga (57/18), Oswaldo Felipe Ramírez Salcedo (35/13), Percy Rojas Montero (21/3), Juan Carlos Oblitas Saba (11/3). Trainer: Marcos Calderón Medrano (22).
Goals: Percy Rojas Montero (3), Juan Carlos Oblitas Saba (32), Teófilo Juan Cubillas Arizaga (39).

198. 30.09.1975 **BRAZIL - PERU** **1-3(0-1)** 30th Copa América. Semi-Finals
Estádio Mineirão, Belo Horizonte; Referee: Miguel Angel Francisco Comesaña (Argentina); Attendance: 25,000
PER: Ottorino Sartor Espinoza (20/0), Eleazar Soria (12/0) [62.José Navarro Aramburu (13/0)], Julio Meléndez (15/0), Héctor Eduardo Chumpitaz González (67/2), Rubén Toribio Díaz Rivas (12/1), Alfredo Quesada Farías (24/0), Santiago Ojeda (1/0), Teófilo Juan Cubillas Arizaga (58/19), Oswaldo Felipe Ramírez Salcedo (36/13), Enrique Cassaretto (8/8), Juan Carlos Oblitas Saba (12/3). Trainer: Marcos Calderón Medrano (23).
Goal: Enrique Cassaretto (19), Teófilo Juan Cubillas Arizaga (82), Enrique Cassaretto (89).

199. 04.10.1975 **PERU - BRAZIL** **0-2(0-1)** 30th Copa América. Semi-Finals
Estadio „Alejandro Villanueva", Lima; Referee: Arturo Andrés Ithurralde (Argentina); Attendance: 55,000
PER: Ottorino Sartor Espinoza (21/0), Eleazar Soria (13/0), Julio Meléndez (16/0), Héctor Eduardo Chumpitaz González (68/2), Rubén Toribio Díaz Rivas (13/1), Alfredo Quesada Farías (25/0), Teófilo Juan Cubillas Arizaga (59/19), Percy Rojas Montero (22/3) [58.Pedro Anselmo Ruiz (2/0)], Oswaldo Felipe Ramírez Salcedo (37/13) [50.Santiago Ojeda (2/0)], Enrique Cassaretto (9/8), Juan Carlos Oblitas Saba (13/3). Trainer: Marcos Calderón Medrano (24).

200. 16.10.1975 **COLOMBIA - PERU** **1-0(1-0)** 30th Copa América. Final
Estadio „Nemesio Camacho" 'El Campín', Bogotá; Referee: Miguel Angel Comesaña (Argentina); Attendance: 50,000
PER: Ottorino Sartor Espinoza (22/0), Eleazar Soria (14/0), Héctor Eduardo Chumpitaz González (69/2), Julio Meléndez (17/0), Rubén Toribio Díaz Rivas (14/1), Alfredo Quesada Farías (26/0), Santiago Ojeda (3/0), Percy Rojas Montero (23/3) [77.Pedro Anselmo Ruiz (3/0)], Gerónimo Barbadillo González (3/0), Juan Carlos Oblitas Saba (14/3), Oswaldo Felipe Ramírez Salcedo (38/13) [60.Enrique Cassaretto (10/8)]. Trainer: Marcos Calderón Medrano (25).

201. 22.10.1975 **PERU - COLOMBIA** **2-0(2-0)** 30th Copa América. Final
Estadio „Alejandro Villanueva", Lima; Referee: Juan Ambrosio Silvagno Cavanna (Chile); Attendance: 50,000
PER: Ottorino Sartor Espinoza (23/0), Eleazar Soria (15/0), Julio Meléndez (18/0), Héctor Eduardo Chumpitaz González (70/2), Rubén Toribio Díaz Rivas (15/1), Alfredo Quesada Farías (27/0), Santiago Ojeda (4/0), Gerónimo Barbadillo González (4/0) [67.Pedro Anselmo Ruiz (4/0)], Percy Rojas Montero (24/3), Oswaldo Felipe Ramírez Salcedo (39/14), Juan Carlos Oblitas Saba (15/4). Trainer: Marcos Calderón Medrano (26).
Goals: Juan Carlos Oblitas Saba (18), Oswaldo Felipe Ramírez Salcedo (44).

202. 28.10.1975 **PERU – COLOMBIA** **1-0(0-0)** 30th Copa América.Final.
Estadio Olímpico, Caracas; Referee: Ramón Ivannoe Barreto Ruíz (Uruguay); Attendance: 30,000
PER: Ottorino Sartor Espinoza (24/0), Eleazar Soria (16/0), Julio Meléndez (19/0), Héctor Eduardo Chumpitaz González (71/2), Rubén Toribio Díaz Rivas (16/1), Alfredo Quesada Farías (28/0), Teófilo Juan Cubillas Arizaga (60/19), Santiago Ojeda (5/0), Percy Rojas Montero (25/3) [46.Oswaldo Felipe Ramírez Salcedo (40/14)], Hugo Alejandro Sotil Yerén (44/15), Juan Carlos Oblitas Saba (16/4). Trainer: Marcos Calderón Medrano (27).
Goal: Hugo Alejandro Sotil Yerén (25).

203. 12.10.1976 **PERU – URUGUAY** **0-0**
Estadio Nacional, Lima; Referee: César Pagano (Peru)
PER: José Manuel Gonzáles Ganoza (2/0), Moisés Palacios (4/0), Julio Meléndez (20/0), Rafael Salvador Salguero González (1/0), Antonio Trigueros (11/0), Alfredo Quesada Farías (29/0), Pedro Anselmo Ruiz (5/0) [67.David Zuluaga (1/0)], José Manuel Velásquez Castillo (12/0), Ernesto Neyra (1/0) [46.José Carranza (1/0)], Guillermo La Rosa Laguna (3/0) [46.Jorge Ramírez Salcedo (1/0)], Roberto Zevallos (1/0). Trainer: Alejandro Heredia (5).

204. 28.10.1976 **PERU – ARGENTINA** **1-3(0-0)** Copa Ramón Castilla
Estadio Nacional, Lima; Referee: José Ramírez (Peru); Attendance: 25,000
PER: José Manuel Gonzáles Ganoza (3/0), Eleazar Soria (17/0) [62.Moisés Palacios (5/0), 83.Jaime Eduardo Duarte Huerta (3/0)], Julio Meléndez (21/0), Rubén Toribio Díaz Rivas (17/1), Antonio Trigueros (12/0), Alfredo Quesada Farías (30/1), José Manuel Velásquez Castillo (13/0), Percy Rojas Montero (26/3), Henry Perales (1/0) [70.José Carranza (2/0)], Guillermo La Rosa Laguna (4/0), Roberto Zevallos (2/0). Trainer: Alejandro Heredia (6).
Goal: Alfredo Quesada Farías (58).

205. 10.11.1976 **ARGENTINA – PERU** **1-0(0-0)** Copa Ramón Castilla
Estadio „José Amalfitani“, Buenos Aires; Referee: Jorge Eduardo Romero (Argentina); Attendance: 38,446
PER: Humberto Ballesteros (1/0), Eleazar Soria (18/0), Julio Meléndez (22/0), Rubén Toribio Díaz Rivas (18/1), Antonio Trigueros (13/0), José Manuel Velásquez Castillo (14/0), Alfredo Quesada Farías (31/1), Henry Perales (2/0) [60.Jorge Ramírez Salcedo (2/0)], Percy Rojas Montero (27/3), Guillermo La Rosa Laguna (5/0), Roberto Zevallos (3/0). Trainer: Alejandro Heredia (7).

206. 24.11.1976 **URUGUAY – PERU** **0-0**
Estadio Centenario, Montevideo; Referee: Roque Tito Cerullo Giuliano (Uruguay); Attendance: 15,000
PER: Humberto Ballesteros (2/0), Moisés Palacios (6/0), Rubén Toribio Díaz Rivas (19/1), Julio Meléndez (23/0), Antonio Trigueros (14/0), José Manuel Velásquez Castillo (15/0), Raúl Enrique Gorriti Dragó (1/0), Alfredo Quesada Farías (32/1), Henry Perales (3/0), Guillermo La Rosa Laguna (6/0), Roberto Zevallos (4/0). Trainer: Alejandro Heredia (8).

207. 09.02.1977 **PERU – HUNGARY** **3-2(2-1)**
Estadio Nacional, Lima; Referee: Edison Pérez Nuñez (Peru); Attendance: 43,500
PER: José Manuel Gonzáles Ganoza (4/0) [46.Ramón Quiroga Arancibia (1/0)], Eleazar Soria (19/0) [74.José Navarro Aramburu (14/0)], Julio Meléndez (24/0), Rafael Salvador Salguero González (2/0), Rubén Toribio Díaz Rivas (20/1), Alfredo Quesada Farías (33/1), Teófilo Juan Cubillas Arizaga (61/19), José Manuel Velásquez Castillo (16/2), Augusto Palacios (2/0) [46.Hugo Alejandro Sotil Yerén (45/16)], Percy Rojas Montero (28/3), Oswaldo Felipe Ramírez Salcedo (41/14) [64.Alejandro Luces (1/0)]. Trainer: Marcos Calderón Medrano (28).
Goals: José Manuel Velásquez Castillo (35, 42), Hugo Alejandro Sotil Yerén (87).

208. 20.02.1977 **ECUADOR – PERU** **1-1(0-1)** 11th FIFA WC. Qualifiers
Estadio Olimpico „Atahualpa“, Quito; Referee: Agomar Martins Rohrig (Brazil); Attendance: 39,576
PER: Ramón Quiroga Arancibia (2/0), Eleazar Soria (20/0), Julio Meléndez (25/0), Héctor Eduardo Chumpitaz González (72/2), Rubén Toribio Díaz Rivas (21/1), Alfredo Quesada Farías (34/1), José Manuel Velásquez Castillo (17/2), Juan José Muñante López (36/5) [60.Oswaldo Felipe Ramírez Salcedo (42/14)], Hugo Alejandro Sotil Yerén (46/16), Teófilo Juan Cubillas Arizaga (62/19) [46.Percy Rojas Montero (29/3)], Juan Carlos Oblitas Saba (17/5). Trainer: Marcos Calderón Medrano (29).
Goal: Juan Carlos Oblitas Saba (42).

209. 06.03.1977 **CHILE – PERU** **1-1(1-0)** 11th FIFA WC. Qualifiers
Estadio Nacional, Santiago; Referee: José Faville Neto (Brazil); Attendance: 67,983
PER: Ramón Quiroga Arancibia (3/0), Eleazar Soria (21/0), Julio Meléndez (26/0), Héctor Eduardo Chumpitaz González (73/2), Rubén Toribio Díaz Rivas (22/1), José Manuel Velásquez Castillo (18/2), Alfredo Quesada Farías (35/1), Teófilo Juan Cubillas Arizaga (63/19) [18.Hugo Alejandro Sotil Yerén (47/16)], Juan José Muñante López (37/6), Percy Rojas Montero (30/3) [67.Alejandro Luces (2/0)], Juan Carlos Oblitas Saba (18/5). Trainer: Marcos Calderón Medrano (30).
Goal: Juan José Muñante López (73).

210. 12.03.1977 **PERU – ECUADOR** **4-0(1-0)** 11th FIFA WC. Qualifiers
Estadio Nacional, Lima; Referee: Luis Barrancos Álvarez (Bolivia); Attendance: 43,319
PER: Ramón Quiroga Arancibia (4/0), Eleazar Soria (22/0), Julio Meléndez (27/0), Héctor Eduardo Chumpitaz González (74/2), Rubén Toribio Díaz Rivas (23/1), Alfredo Quesada Farías (36/1), José Manuel Velásquez Castillo (19/3), Juan José Muñante López (38/6), Percy Rojas Montero (31/3) [68.Augusto Palacios (3/0)], Hugo Alejandro Sotil Yerén (48/16) [58.Alejandro Luces (3/1)], Juan Carlos Oblitas Saba (19/7). Trainer: Marcos Calderón Medrano (31).
Goals: José Manuel Velásquez Castillo (19), Juan Carlos Oblitas Saba (48, 50), Alejandro Luces (63).

211. 26.03.1977 **PERU – CHILE** **2-0(0-0)** 11th FIFA WC. Qualifiers
Estadio Nacional, Lima; Referee: Arnaldo David César Coelho (Brazil); Attendance: 52,000
PER: Ramón Quiroga Arancibia (5/0), José Navarro Aramburu (15/0), Julio Meléndez (28/0), Héctor Eduardo Chumpitaz González (75/2), Rubén Toribio Díaz Rivas (24/1), Alfredo Quesada Farías (37/1), José Manuel Velásquez Castillo (20/3), Percy Rojas Montero (32/3) [60.Oswaldo Felipe Ramírez Salcedo (43/14)], Juan José Muñante López (39/6) [64.Alejandro Luces (4/1)], Hugo Alejandro Sotil Yerén (49/17), Juan Carlos Oblitas Saba (20/8). Trainer: Marcos Calderón Medrano (32).
Goals: Hugo Alejandro Sotil Yerén (49), Juan Carlos Oblitas Saba (55).

212. 17.05.1977 **MEXICO – PERU** **1-1(1-1)**
Estadio Azteca, Ciudad de México; Referee: Javier Galindo (Mexico)
PER: Ramón Quiroga Arancibia (6/0), Eleazar Soria (23/0) [70.José Navarro Aramburu (16/0)], Julio Meléndez (29/0), Héctor Eduardo Chumpitaz González (76/2), Rubén Toribio Díaz Rivas (25/1) [67.Jaime Eduardo Duarte Huerta (4/0)], Julio Aparicio (4/0), José Manuel Velásquez Castillo (21/3), Hugo Alejandro Sotil Yerén (50/17), Oswaldo Felipe Ramírez Salcedo (44/15), Percy Rojas Montero (33/3) [77.Alfredo Quesada Farías (38/1)], Juan Carlos Oblitas Saba (21/8). Trainer: Marcos Calderón Medrano (33).
Goal: Oswaldo Felipe Ramírez Salcedo (33).

213. 24.05.1977 **MEXICO - PERU** **2-1(1-1)**
Estadio Universitario, Monterrey; Referee: Enrique Mendoza Guillén (Mexico)
PER: Ramón Quiroga Arancibia (7/0), José Navarro Aramburu (17/0), Julio Meléndez (30/0), Héctor Eduardo Chumpitaz González (77/2), Rubén Toribio Díaz Rivas (26/1), Alfredo Quesada Farías (39/1), José Manuel Velásquez Castillo (22/3), Oswaldo Felipe Ramírez Salcedo (45/15) [88.Alejandro Luces (5/1)], Percy Rojas Montero (34/4) [75.Julio Aparicio (5/0)], Hugo Alejandro Sotil Yerén (51/17), Juan Carlos Oblitas Saba (22/8) [83.Augusto Palacios (4/0)]. Trainer: Marcos Calderón Medrano (34).
Goal: Percy Rojas Montero (35).

214. 26.05.1977 **HAITI - PERU** **1-2(1-1)**
Stade „Sylvio Cator", Port au Prince; Referee: Pajotte (Haiti); Attendance: 9,000
PER: Ramón Quiroga Arancibia (8/0) [46.José Manuel Gonzáles Ganoza (5/0)], Eleazar Soria (24/0), Rafael Salvador Salguero González (3/0) [71.Julio Meléndez (31/0)], Jaime Eduardo Duarte Huerta (5/0), Rubén Toribio Díaz Rivas (27/1), Alfredo Quesada Farías (40/1), José Manuel Velásquez Castillo (23/3), Percy Rojas Montero (35/4) [52.Oswaldo Felipe Ramírez Salcedo (46/15)], Augusto Palacios (5/0), Hugo Alejandro Sotil Yerén (52/18) [57.Alejandro Luces (6/2)], Juan Carlos Oblitas Saba (23/8). Trainer: Marcos Calderón Medrano (35).
Goals: Hugo Alejandro Sotil Yerén (37), Alejandro Luces (65).

215. 29.05.1977 **HAITI - PERU** **2-2(1-0)**
Stade „Sylvio Cator", Port au Prince
PER: José Manuel Gonzáles Ganoza (6/0), Eleazar Soria (25/0), Julio Meléndez (32/0), Jaime Eduardo Duarte Huerta (6/0), Rubén Toribio Díaz Rivas (28/1), José Manuel Velásquez Castillo (24/4), Alfredo Quesada Farías (41/1), Percy Rojas Montero (36/4), Augusto Palacios (6/0) [52.Oswaldo Felipe Ramírez Salcedo (47/16)], Hugo Alejandro Sotil Yerén (53/18), Juan Carlos Oblitas Saba (24/8) [Alejandro Luces (7/2)]. Trainer: Marcos Calderón Medrano (36).
Goal: José Manuel Velásquez Castillo (68), Oswaldo Felipe Ramírez Salcedo (73 penalty).

216. 10.06.1977 **PERU - POLAND** **1-3(0-2)**
Estadio Nacional, Lima; Referee: César Augusto Orozco Guerrero (Peru); Attendance: 35,000
PER: Ramón Quiroga Arancibia (9/0), Eleazar Soria (26/0) [54.José Navarro Aramburu (18/0)], Julio Meléndez (33/0), Jaime Eduardo Duarte Huerta (7/0), Rubén Toribio Díaz Rivas (29/1) [75.Walter Escobar (1/0)], José Manuel Velásquez Castillo (25/4), Alfredo Quesada Farías (42/1), Percy Rojas Montero (37/4), Oswaldo Felipe Ramírez Salcedo (48/16), Hugo Alejandro Sotil Yerén (54/18) [58.Alejandro Luces (8/3)], Juan Carlos Oblitas Saba (25/8). Trainer: Marcos Calderón Medrano (37).
Goal: Alejandro Luces (62).

217. 10.07.1977 **BRAZIL - PERU** **1-0(0-0)** 11th FIFA WC. Qualifiers
Estadio „Pascual Guerrero", Cali (Colombia); Referee: Miguel Angel Francisco Comesaña (Argentina); Attendance: 50,345
PER: Ramón Quiroga Arancibia (10/0), José Navarro Aramburu (19/0), Julio Meléndez (34/0), Héctor Eduardo Chumpitaz González (78/2), Rubén Toribio Díaz Rivas (30/1), Alfredo Quesada Farías (43/1), José Manuel Velásquez Castillo (26/4), Teófilo Juan Cubillas Arizaga (64/19), Juan José Muñante López (40/6), Hugo Alejandro Sotil Yerén (55/18) [61.Percy Rojas Montero (38/4)], Juan Carlos Oblitas Saba (26/8). Trainer: Marcos Calderón Medrano (38).

218. 17.07.1977 **PERU - BOLIVIA** **5-0(2-0)** 11th FIFA WC. Qualifiers
Estadio „Pascual Guerrero", Cali (Colombia); Referee: Ramón Ivanoe Barreto Ruíz (Uruguay); Attendance: 32,511
PER: Ramón Quiroga Arancibia (11/0), José Navarro Aramburu (20/0), Julio Meléndez (35/0), Héctor Eduardo Chumpitaz González (79/2), Rubén Toribio Díaz Rivas (31/1), José Manuel Velásquez Castillo (27/6), Julio Aparicio (6/0), Teófilo Juan Cubillas Arizaga (65/21) [61.Oswaldo Felipe Ramírez Salcedo (49/16)], Juan José Muñante López (41/6), Hugo Alejandro Sotil Yerén (56/18) [46.Percy Rojas Montero (39/5)], Juan Carlos Oblitas Saba (27/8). Trainer: Marcos Calderón Medrano (39).
Goals: Teófilo Juan Cubillas Arizaga (32, 44), José Manuel Velásquez Castillo (64), Percy Rojas Montero (75), José Manuel Velásquez Castillo (89).

219. 19.03.1978 **ARGENTINA - PERU** **2-1(1-0)** Copa Ramón Castilla
Estadio „Alberto Armando", Buenos Aires; Referee: Juan José Fortunato (Uruguay); Attendance: 35,000
PER: Ramón Quiroga Arancibia (12/0), José Navarro Aramburu (21/0), Germán Carlos Leguía Dragó (1/0), Héctor Eduardo Chumpitaz González (80/2), Rubén Toribio Díaz Rivas (32/1), Raúl Enrique Gorriti Dragó (2/0) [46.Alfredo Quesada Farías (44/1)], José Manuel Velásquez Castillo (28/6) [58.Jaime Eduardo Duarte Huerta (8/0)], Teófilo Juan Cubillas Arizaga (66/21) [68.César Augusto Cueto Villa (9/1)], Roberto Orlando Mosquera Vera (1/0) [46.Oswaldo Felipe Ramírez Salcedo (50/16)], Percy Rojas Montero (40/6), Juan Carlos Oblitas Saba (28/8). Trainer: Marcos Calderón Medrano (40).
Goal: Percy Rojas Montero (89).

220. 23.03.1978 **PERU - ARGENTINA** **1-3(0-3)** Copa Ramón Castilla
Estadio Nacional, Lima; Referee: Edison Pérez Nuñez (Peru); Attendance: 43,490
PER: Ramón Quiroga Arancibia (13/0), José Navarro Aramburu (22/0) [50.Eleazar Soria (27/0)], Germán Carlos Leguía Dragó (2/0) [35.Víctor Reyna (1/0)], Héctor Eduardo Chumpitaz González (81/2), Rubén Toribio Díaz Rivas (33/1), José Manuel Velásquez Castillo (29/6) [58.Raúl Enrique Gorriti Dragó (3/0)], Teófilo Juan Cubillas Arizaga (67/21) [46.Oswaldo Felipe Ramírez Salcedo (51/16)], Alfredo Quesada Farías (45/1), Roberto Orlando Mosquera Vera (2/0), Percy Rojas Montero (41/6), Juan Carlos Oblitas Saba (29/9). Trainer: Marcos Calderón Medrano (41).
Goal: Juan Carlos Oblitas Saba (53).

221. 01.04.1978 **PERU - BULGARIA** **1-1(0-1)**
Estadio Nacional, Lima; Referee: César Pagano (Peru); Attendance: 30,000
PER: Ramón Quiroga Arancibia (14/0), Eleazar Soria (28/0) [46.José Navarro Aramburu (23/0)], Víctor Reyna (2/0), Héctor Eduardo Chumpitaz González (82/2), Rubén Toribio Díaz Rivas (34/1), Raúl Enrique Gorriti Dragó (4/0), Alfredo Quesada Farías (46/1) [46.Arturo Bisetti (1/0)], Percy Rojas Montero (42/6) [59.César Augusto Cueto Villa (10/1)], Roberto Orlando Mosquera Vera (3/0), Oswaldo Felipe Ramírez Salcedo (52/17), Juan Carlos Oblitas Saba (30/9). Trainer: Marcos Calderón Medrano (42).
Goal: Oswaldo Felipe Ramírez Salcedo (62).

222. 11.04.1978 **MEXICO - PERU** **0-1(0-0)**
Memorial Coliseum, Los Angeles (United States); Referee: Toros Kibritjian (United States); Attendance: 38,016
PER: Ramón Quiroga Arancibia (15/0), José Navarro Aramburu (24/0), Jaime Eduardo Duarte Huerta (9/0), Héctor Eduardo Chumpitaz González (83/2), Rubén Toribio Díaz Rivas (35/1), José Manuel Velásquez Castillo (30/6), Teófilo Juan Cubillas Arizaga (68/21), Percy Rojas Montero (43/6), Roberto Orlando Mosquera Vera (4/0) [57.Raúl Enrique Gorriti Dragó (5/1)], Oswaldo Felipe Ramírez Salcedo (53/17), Juan Carlos Oblitas Saba (31/9). Trainer: Marcos Calderón Medrano (43).
Goal: Raúl Enrique Gorriti Dragó (74).

223. 22.04.1978 **PERU – CHINA P.R.** **2-1(1-0)**
Estadio Nacional, Lima; Referee: César Pagano (Peru)
PER: Ottorino Sartor Espinoza (25/0), Eleazar Soria (29/0), Germán Carlos Leguía Dragó (3/0), Héctor Eduardo Chumpitaz González (84/2), Roberto Rojas Tardío (1/0) [55.Jaime Eduardo Duarte Huerta (10/0), 85.Víctor Reyna (3/0)], Raúl Enrique Gorriti Dragó (6/1), Alfredo Quesada Farías (47/1), Teófilo Juan Cubillas Arizaga (69/21), Roberto Orlando Mosquera Vera (5/1) [80.César Augusto Cueto Villa (11/1)], Percy Rojas Montero (44/7), Oswaldo Felipe Ramírez Salcedo (54/17). Trainer: Marcos Calderón Medrano (44).
Goal: Roberto Orlando Mosquera Vera (25), Percy Rojas Montero (64).

224. 01.05.1978 **BRAZIL – PERU** **3-0(1-0)**
Estádio „Jornalista Mario Filho“ (Maracanã), Rio de Janeiro; Referee: Roque Tito Cerullo Giuliano (Uruguay); Attendance: 145,000
PER: Ramón Quiroga Arancibia (16/0), José Navarro Aramburu (25/0), Rodolfo Manzo Audante (16/0), Héctor Eduardo Chumpitaz González (85/2), Rubén Toribio Díaz Rivas (36/1), Alfredo Quesada Farías (48/1) [57.Raúl Enrique Gorriti Dragó (7/1)], José Manuel Velásquez Castillo (31/6), Teófilo Juan Cubillas Arizaga (70/21), Juan José Muñante López (42/6) [70.Roberto Orlando Mosquera Vera (6/1)], Percy Rojas Montero (45/7) [85.Guillermo La Rosa Laguna (7/0)], Juan Carlos Oblitas Saba (32/9). Trainer: Marcos Calderón Medrano (45).

225. 03.06.1978 **PERU – SCOTLAND** **3-1(1-1)** 11th FIFA WC. Group Stage
Estadio Chateau Carreras, Córdoba (Argentina); Referee: Ulf Eriksson (Sweden); Attendance: 37,792
PER: Ramón Quiroga Arancibia (17/0), Jaime Eduardo Duarte Huerta (11/0), Rodolfo Manzo Audante (17/0), Héctor Eduardo Chumpitaz González (Cap) (86/2), Rubén Toribio Díaz Rivas (37/1), José Manuel Velásquez Castillo (32/6), César Augusto Cueto Villa (12/2) [82.Percy Rojas Montero (46/7)], Teófilo Juan Cubillas Arizaga (71/23), Juan José Muñante López (43/6), Guillermo La Rosa Laguna (8/0) [62.Hugo Alejandro Sotil Yerén (57/18)], Juan Carlos Oblitas Saba (33/9). Trainer: Marcos Calderón Medrano (46).
Goals: César Augusto Cueto Villa (42), Teófilo Juan Cubillas Arizaga (71, 77).

226. 07.06.1978 **PERU – HOLLAND** **0-0** 11th FIFA WC. Group Stage
Estadio „General San Martín“, Mendoza (Argentina); Referee: Adolf Prokop (East Germany); Attendance: 28,125
PER: Ramón Quiroga Arancibia (18/0), Jaime Eduardo Duarte Huerta (12/0), Rodolfo Manzo Audante (18/0), Héctor Eduardo Chumpitaz González (Cap) (87/2), Rubén Toribio Díaz Rivas (38/1), César Augusto Cueto Villa (13/2), José Manuel Velásquez Castillo (33/6), Teófilo Juan Cubillas Arizaga (72/23), Juan José Muñante López (44/6), Guillermo La Rosa Laguna (9/0) [62.Hugo Alejandro Sotil Yerén (58/18)], Juan Carlos Oblitas Saba (34/9). Trainer: Marcos Calderón Medrano (47).

227. 11.06.1978 **PERU – IRAN** **4-1(3-1)** 11th FIFA WC. Group Stage
Estadio Chateau Carreras, Córdoba (Argentina); Referee: Alojzy Jarguz (Poland); Attendance: 21,000
PER: Ramón Quiroga Arancibia (19/0), Jaime Eduardo Duarte Huerta (13/0), Rodolfo Manzo Audante (19/0) [67.Germán Carlos Leguía Dragó (4/0)], Héctor Eduardo Chumpitaz González (Cap) (88/2), Rubén Toribio Díaz Rivas (39/1), José Manuel Velásquez Castillo (34/7), César Augusto Cueto Villa (14/2), Teófilo Juan Cubillas Arizaga (73/26), Juan José Muñante López (45/6), Guillermo La Rosa Laguna (10/0) [60.Hugo Alejandro Sotil Yerén (59/18)], Juan Carlos Oblitas Saba (35/9). Trainer: Marcos Calderón Medrano (48).
Goal: José Manuel Velásquez Castillo (2), Teófilo Juan Cubillas Arizaga (36 penalty, 39 penalty, 79).

228. 14.06.1978 **BRAZIL – PERU** **3-0(2-0)** 11th FIFA WC. 2nd Round
Estadio „General San Martín“, Mendoza (Argentina); Referee: Nicolae Rainea (România); Attendance: 31,278
PER: Ramón Quiroga Arancibia (20/0), Jaime Eduardo Duarte Huerta (14/0), Rodolfo Manzo Audante (20/0), Héctor Eduardo Chumpitaz González (Cap) (89/2), Rubén Toribio Díaz Rivas (40/1) [11.José Navarro Aramburu (26/0)], José Manuel Velásquez Castillo (35/7), César Augusto Cueto Villa (15/2), Juan José Muñante López (46/6), Teófilo Juan Cubillas Arizaga (74/26), Guillermo La Rosa Laguna (11/0), Juan Carlos Oblitas Saba (36/9) [46.Percy Rojas Montero (47/7)]. Trainer: Marcos Calderón Medrano (49).

229. 18.06.1978 **POLAND – PERU** **1-0(0-0)** 11th FIFA WC. 2nd Round
Estadio „General San Martín“, Mendoza (Argentina); Referee: Patrick Partridge (England); Attendance: 35,288
PER: Ramón Quiroga Arancibia (21/0), Jaime Eduardo Duarte Huerta (15/0), Rodolfo Manzo Audante (21/0), Héctor Eduardo Chumpitaz González (Cap) (90/2), José Navarro Aramburu (27/0), César Augusto Cueto Villa (16/2), Alfredo Quesada Farías (49/1), Teófilo Juan Cubillas Arizaga (75/26), Juan José Muñante López (47/6) [46.Percy Rojas Montero (48/7)], Guillermo La Rosa Laguna (12/0) [74.Hugo Alejandro Sotil Yerén (60/18)], Juan Carlos Oblitas Saba (37/9). Trainer: Marcos Calderón Medrano (50).

230. 21.06.1978 **ARGENTINA – PERU** **6-0(2-0)** 11th FIFA WC. 2nd Round.
Estadio Central (Doctor Lisandro de la Torre), Rosario; Referee: Robert Charles Paul Wurtz (France); Attendance: 38,000
PER: Ramón Quiroga Arancibia (22/0), Jaime Eduardo Duarte Huerta (16/0), Rodolfo Manzo Audante (22/0), Héctor Eduardo Chumpitaz González (Cap) (91/2), Roberto Rojas Tardío (2/0), Alfredo Quesada Farías (50/1), José Manuel Velásquez Castillo (36/7) [51.Raúl Enrique Gorriti Dragó (8/1)], César Augusto Cueto Villa (17/2), Juan José Muñante López (48/6), Teófilo Juan Cubillas Arizaga (76/26), Juan Carlos Oblitas Saba (38/9). Trainer: Marcos Calderón Medrano (51).

231. 11.07.1979 **PERU – ECUADOR** **2-1(2-1)**
Estadio Nacional, Lima; Referee: Carlos Montalván (Peru)
PER: Ottorino Sartor Espinoza (26/0), José Navarro Aramburu (28/0), Jorge Andrés Olaechea Quijandría (1/0), Héctor Eduardo Chumpitaz González (92/2), Roberto Rojas Tardío (3/0), Arturo Vargas (1/0), Germán Carlos Leguía Dragó (5/0) [76.Gerardo Baigorria (1/0)], Pedro Anselmo Ruiz (6/0) [65.David Zuluaga (2/0)], Roberto Orlando Mosquera Vera (7/2) [50.Abel Lobatón (1/0)], Juan José Oré (1/1) [55.Ernesto Neyra (2/0)], Víctor Hurtado (1/0). Trainer: José Chiarella (1).
Goals: Juan José Oré (18), Roberto Orlando Mosquera Vera (30).

232. 18.07.1979 **PERU – COLOMBIA** **0-1(0-1)**
Estadio Nacional, Lima; Referee: Edison Pérez Nuñez (Peru)
PER: Ottorino Sartor Espinoza (27/0) [60.Darío Herrera (1/0)], Jaime Eduardo Duarte Huerta (17/0) [78.Alejandro Hugo Gastulo Ramírez (1/0)], Gerardo Baigorria (2/0), Héctor Eduardo Chumpitaz González (93/2) [46.Arturo Vargas (2/0)], Roberto Rojas Tardío (4/0), Germán Carlos Leguía Dragó (6/0), Jorge Andrés Olaechea Quijandría (2/0), Pedro Anselmo Ruiz (7/0) [70.David Zuluaga (3/0)], Roberto Orlando Mosquera Vera (8/2), Juan José Oré (2/1), Freddy Ravello (1/0) [70.Víctor Hurtado (2/0)]. Trainer: José Chiarella (2).

233. 25.07.1979 **COLOMBIA – PERU** **1-2(1-1)**
Estadio „Nemesio Camacho“ 'El Campín', Bogotá; Referee: Guillermo Velásquez (Colombia)
PER: Eusebio Alfredo Acasuzo Colán (1/0), Jaime Eduardo Duarte Huerta (18/1), Jorge Andrés Olaechea Quijandría (3/0), Rafael Salvador Salguero González (4/0), Roberto Rojas Tardío (5/0), Germán Carlos Leguía Dragó (7/0) [69.David Zuluaga (4/0)], César Augusto Cueto Villa (18/3), José Manuel Velásquez Castillo (37/7), Guillermo La Rosa Laguna (13/0), Hugo Alejandro Sotil Yerén (61/18), Freddy Ravello (2/0) [73.Víctor Hurtado (3/0)]. Trainer: José Chiarella (3).
Goals: Jaime Eduardo Duarte Huerta (44), César Augusto Cueto Villa (49).

234. 08.08.1979 **ECUADOR – PERU** **2-1(1-1)**
Estadio Olimpico „Atahualpa“, Quito; Referee: Adolfo Quirola (Ecuador)
PER: Eusebio Alfredo Acasuzo Colán (2/0), Jaime Eduardo Duarte Huerta (19/1), Jorge Andrés Olaechea Quijandría (4/0), Héctor Eduardo Chumpitaz González (94/2), Roberto Rojas Tardío (6/0), José Manuel Velásquez Castillo (38/7), Germán Carlos Leguía Dragó (8/0), César Augusto Cueto Villa (19/3), Guillermo La Rosa Laguna (14/0) [62.Abel Lobatón (2/0)], Hugo Alejandro Sotil Yerén (62/18) [62.Juan José Oré (3/1)], Freddy Ravello (3/1). Trainer: José Chiarella (4).
Goal: Freddy Ravello (27).

235. 30.08.1979 **PERU – URUGUAY** **2-0(1-0)**
Estadio Nacional, Lima; Referee: César Pagano (Peru)
PER: Eusebio Alfredo Acasuzo Colán (3/0), Jaime Eduardo Duarte Huerta (20/1), Eduardo Aguilar (1/0), Rubén Toribio Díaz Rivas (41/1) [75.Eduardo Hugo Malásquez Maldonado (1/0)], Alejandro Hugo Gastulo Ramírez (2/0), Germán Carlos Leguía Dragó (9/1), Arturo Vargas (3/0) [46.Rafael Salvador Salguero González (5/0)], David Zuluaga (5/0), Roberto Orlando Mosquera Vera (9/3), Juan José Oré (4/1) [46.Abel Lobatón (3/0)], Ernesto Labarthe Flores (1/0) [63.Víctor Hurtado (4/0)]. Trainer: José Chiarella (5).
Goals: Roberto Orlando Mosquera Vera (41), Germán Carlos Leguía Dragó (72).

236. 12.09.1979 **SCOTLAND – PERU** **1-1(1-0)**
Hampden Park, Glasgow; Referee: George Courtney (England); Attendance: 41,035
PER: Eusebio Alfredo Acasuzo Colán (4/0), Alejandro Hugo Gastulo Ramírez (3/0), Jorge Andrés Olaechea Quijandría (5/0), Héctor Eduardo Chumpitaz González (95/2), Rubén Toribio Díaz Rivas (42/1), José Manuel Velásquez Castillo (39/7), Germán Carlos Leguía Dragó (10/2), César Augusto Cueto Villa (20/3), Roberto Orlando Mosquera Vera (10/3), Guillermo La Rosa Laguna (15/0), Ernesto Labarthe Flores (2/0) [73.Freddy Ravello (4/1)]. Trainer: José Chiarella (6).
Goal: Germán Carlos Leguía Dragó (85).

237. 10.10.1979 **PERU – PARAGUAY** **2-3(1-2)**
Estadio Nacional, Lima; Referee: César Pagano (Peru)
PER: Eusebio Alfredo Acasuzo Colán (5/0), Alejandro Hugo Gastulo Ramírez (4/0), Rafael Salvador Salguero González (6/0), Héctor Eduardo Chumpitaz González (96/3), Rubén Toribio Díaz Rivas (43/1), Raúl Enrique Gorriti Dragó (9/1), Eduardo Aguilar (2/0) [46.Eduardo Hugo Malásquez Maldonado (2/0)], David Zuluaga (6/0), Abel Lobatón (4/1), Julio César Uribe Flores (1/0), Ernesto Labarthe Flores (3/0) [75.Freddy Ravello (5/1)]. Trainer: José Chiarella (7).
Goal: Héctor Eduardo Chumpitaz González (27), Abel Lobatón (68).

238. 17.10.1979 **PERU – CHILE** **1-2(0-1)** 31st Copa América. Semi-Finals
Estadio Nacional, Lima; Referee: Romualdo Arppi Filho (Brazil); Attendance: 43,724
PER: Eusebio Alfredo Acasuzo Colán (6/0), Jaime Eduardo Duarte Huerta (21/1), Jorge Andrés Olaechea Quijandría (6/0), Héctor Eduardo Chumpitaz González (97/3), Rubén Toribio Díaz Rivas (44/1), José Manuel Velásquez Castillo (40/7), César Augusto Cueto Villa (21/3), Germán Carlos Leguía Dragó (11/2), Roberto Orlando Mosquera Vera (11/4), Guillermo La Rosa Laguna (16/0), Freddy Ravello (6/1) [59.Ernesto Labarthe Flores (4/0)]. Trainer: José Chiarella (8).
Goal: Roberto Orlando Mosquera Vera (71).

239. 24.10.1979 **CHILE – PERU** **0-0** 31st Copa América. Semi-Finals
Estadio Nacional, Santiago; Referee: Juan Daniel Cardellino de San Vicente (Uruguay); Attendance: 75,681
PER: Eusebio Alfredo Acasuzo Colán (7/0), José Navarro Aramburu (29/0), Jorge Andrés Olaechea Quijandría (7/0), Héctor Eduardo Chumpitaz González (98/3), Rubén Toribio Díaz Rivas (45/1), José Manuel Velásquez Castillo (41/7), Germán Carlos Leguía Dragó (12/2) [68.Raúl Enrique Gorriti Dragó (10/1)], César Augusto Cueto Villa (22/3) [8.Percy Rojas Montero (49/7)], Roberto Orlando Mosquera Vera (12/4), Guillermo La Rosa Laguna (17/0), Freddy Ravello (7/1). Trainer: José Chiarella (9).

240. 01.11.1979 **MEXICO – PERU** **1-0(1-0)**
Estadio Universitario, Monterrey; Referee: Manuel Ceja (Mexico)
PER: Eusebio Alfredo Acasuzo Colán (8/0), José Navarro Aramburu (30/0), Jorge Andrés Olaechea Quijandría (8/0), Héctor Eduardo Chumpitaz González (99/3), Rubén Toribio Díaz Rivas (46/1), Germán Carlos Leguía Dragó (13/2), Raúl Enrique Gorriti Dragó (11/1) [63.Eduardo Hugo Malásquez Maldonado (3/0)], Rafael Salvador Salguero González (7/0), Roberto Orlando Mosquera Vera (13/4), Julio César Uribe Flores (2/0) [70.Jaime Drago (1/0)], Freddy Ravello (8/1). Trainer: José Chiarella (10).

241. 18.07.1980 **URUGUAY – PERU** **0-0** 50 years of Centenario
Estadio Centenario, Montevideo; Referee: Edison Pérez Nuñez (Peru)
PER: Eusebio Alfredo Acasuzo Colán (9/0), Jaime Eduardo Duarte Huerta (22/1), Óscar Gilberto Arizaga (1/0), Rubén Toribio Díaz Rivas (47/1), Jorge Andrés Olaechea Quijandría (9/0), Roberto Rojas Tardío (7/0), Eduardo Hugo Malásquez Maldonado (4/0), Miguel Seminario (1/0) [73.José Zapata (1/0)], Roberto Orlando Mosquera Vera (14/4), Oswaldo Felipe Ramírez Salcedo (55/17) [61.Franco Enrique Navarro Monteiro (1/0)], Eduardo Rey Muñoz (1/0). Trainer: Juan José Tan (1).

242. 12.11.1980 **PERU – URUGUAY** **1-1(1-1)**
Estadio „Alejandro Villanueva“, Lima; Referee: Artemio Sención (Uruguay)
PER: Ramón Quiroga Arancibia (23/0), Alejandro Hugo Gastulo Ramírez (5/0), Rubén Toribio Díaz Rivas (48/1), Jaime Eduardo Duarte Huerta (23/1), Miguel Ángel Gutiérrez (1/0) [63.Roberto Rojas Tardío (8/0)], Luis Alberto Reyna Navarro (1/0), Pedro Chinchay (1/0), Julio César Uribe Flores (3/1), Roberto Orlando Mosquera Vera (15/4), Franco Enrique Navarro Monteiro (2/0) [46.Oswaldo Felipe Ramírez Salcedo (56/17), 62.Eduardo Rey Muñoz (2/0)], Miguel Seminario (2/0) [53.Juan Caballero (1/0)]. Trainer: Juan José Tan (2).
Goal: Julio César Uribe Flores (14).

243. 04.02.1981 **PERU – CZECHOSLOVAKIA** **1-3(0-1)**
Estadio „Alejandro Villanueva", Lima; Referee: Pedro Reyes (Peru)
PER: Eusebio Alfredo Acasuzo Colán (10/0), Jaime Eduardo Duarte Huerta (24/1), Rafael Salvador Salguero González (8/0) [67.Alejandro Hugo Gastulo Ramírez (6/0)], Jorge Andrés Olaechea Quijandría (10/0), Roberto Rojas Tardío (9/0), Luis Alberto Reyna Navarro (2/0), Julio César Uribe Flores (4/2), José Zapata (2/0), Miguel Seminario (3/0), José Leyva (1/0) [61.Marcos Echegaray (1/0)], Humberto Correa (1/0). Trainer: Alejandro Heredia (9).
Goal: Julio César Uribe Flores (58).

244. 11.02.1981 **PERU – BULGARIA** **1-2(1-1)**
Estadio „Alejandro Villanueva", Lima; Referee: Carlos Montalván (Peru); Attendance: 15,000
PER: José Manuel Gonzáles Ganoza (7/0), Jaime Eduardo Duarte Huerta (25/1), Jorge Andrés Olaechea Quijandría (11/0), Rubén Toribio Díaz Rivas (49/1), Miguel Ángel Gutiérrez (2/0), Luis Alberto Reyna Navarro (3/0), Germán Carlos Leguía Dragó (14/2), Julio César Uribe Flores (5/2), Roberto Orlando Mosquera Vera (16/4) [67.Miguel Seminario (4/0)], Franco Enrique Navarro Monteiro (3/0), Humberto Correa (2/1). Trainer: Alejandro Heredia (10).
Goal: Humberto Correa (29).

245. 19.04.1981 **CHILE – PERU** **3-0(1-0)**
Estadio Nacional, Santiago; Referee: Arturo Andrés Ithurralde (Argentina); Attendance: 20,692
PER: José Manuel Gonzáles Ganoza (8/0), Jaime Eduardo Duarte Huerta (26/1), Rafael Salvador Salguero González (9/0), Héctor Eduardo Chumpitaz González (100/3), Miguel Ángel Gutiérrez (3/0), Luis Alberto Reyna Navarro (4/0), Jorge Andrés Olaechea Quijandría (12/0), Julio César Uribe Flores (6/2), Miguel Seminario (5/0) [56.Víctor Hurtado (5/0)], Franco Enrique Navarro Monteiro (4/0), Freddy Ravello (9/1). Trainer: Alejandro Heredia (11).

246. 26.07.1981 **COLOMBIA – PERU** **1-1(0-0)** 12th FIFA WC. Qualifiers
Estadio „Nemesio Camacho" 'El Campín', Bogotá; Referee: Arturo Andrés Ithurralde (Argentina); Attendance: 60,000
PER: Ramón Quiroga Arancibia (24/0), Jaime Eduardo Duarte Huerta (27/1), Rubén Toribio Díaz Rivas (50/1), Héctor Eduardo Chumpitaz González (101/3), Roberto Rojas Tardío (10/0), José Manuel Velásquez Castillo (42/7) [73.Jorge Andrés Olaechea Quijandría (13/0)], César Augusto Cueto Villa (23/3), Julio César Uribe Flores (7/2) [63.Guillermo La Rosa Laguna (18/1)], Gerónimo Barbadillo González (5/0), Teófilo Juan Cubillas Arizaga (77/26), Juan Carlos Oblitas Saba (39/9). Trainer: Elba de Padua Lima "Tim" (1).
Goal: Guillermo La Rosa Laguna (86).

247. 05.08.1981 **PERU – CHILE** **1-2(0-2)**
Estadio Nacional, Lima; Referee: Sérgio Leiblinger (Peru); Attendance: 45,000
PER: Ramón Quiroga Arancibia (25/0), Jaime Eduardo Duarte Huerta (28/1), Rubén Toribio Díaz Rivas (51/1), Héctor Eduardo Chumpitaz González (102/3), Roberto Rojas Tardío (11/0) [74.Miguel Ángel Gutiérrez (4/0)], José Manuel Velásquez Castillo (43/7) [68.Jorge Andrés Olaechea Quijandría (14/1)], César Augusto Cueto Villa (24/3), Julio César Uribe Flores (8/2), Gerónimo Barbadillo González (6/0), Guillermo La Rosa Laguna (19/1), Freddy Ravello (10/1) [67.Luis Alberto Reyna Navarro (5/0)]. Trainer: Elba de Padua Lima "Tim" (2).
Goal: Jorge Andrés Olaechea Quijandría (63).

248. 16.08.1981 **PERU – COLOMBIA** **2-0(1-0)** 12th FIFA WC. Qualifiers
Estadio Nacional, Lima; Referee: Vicente Llobregat Vicedo (Venezuela); Attendance: 43,942
PER: Ramón Quiroga Arancibia (26/0), Jaime Eduardo Duarte Huerta (29/1), Rubén Toribio Díaz Rivas (52/1), Héctor Eduardo Chumpitaz González (103/3), Roberto Rojas Tardío (12/0), José Manuel Velásquez Castillo (44/7) [69.Jorge Andrés Olaechea Quijandría (15/1)], César Augusto Cueto Villa (25/3), Julio César Uribe Flores (9/3), Gerónimo Barbadillo González (7/1), Guillermo La Rosa Laguna (20/1), Juan Carlos Oblitas Saba (40/9). Trainer: Elba de Padua Lima "Tim" (3).
Goal: Gerónimo Barbadillo González (7), Julio César Uribe Flores (71 penalty).

249. 23.08.1981 **URUGUAUY – PERU** **1-2(0-1)**
Estadio Centenario, Montevideo; Referee: Juan Ambrosio Silvagno Cavanna (Chile); Attendance: 75,000
PER: Ramón Quiroga Arancibia (27/0), Jaime Eduardo Duarte Huerta (30/1), Rubén Toribio Díaz Rivas (53/1), Héctor Eduardo Chumpitaz González (Cap) (104/3), Roberto Rojas Tardío (13/0), José Manuel Velásquez Castillo (45/7), César Augusto Cueto Villa (26/3), Julio César Uribe Flores (10/4), Gerónimo Barbadillo González (8/1), Guillermo La Rosa Laguna (21/2) [60.Jorge Andrés Olaechea Quijandría (16/1)], Juan Carlos Oblitas Saba (41/9). Trainer: Elba de Padua Lima "Tim" (4).
Goal: Guillermo La Rosa Laguna (40), Julio César Uribe Flores (47).

250. 06.09.1981 **PERU – URUGUAY** **0-0** 12th FIFA WC. Qualifiers
Estadio Nacional, Lima; Referee: Arnaldo David César Coelho (Brazil); Attendance: 45,000
PER: Ramón Quiroga Arancibia (28/0), Jaime Eduardo Duarte Huerta (31/1), Rubén Toribio Díaz Rivas (54/1), Héctor Eduardo Chumpitaz González (Cap) (105/3), Roberto Rojas Tardío (14/0), José Manuel Velásquez Castillo (46/7), César Augusto Cueto Villa (27/3), Julio César Uribe Flores (11/4), Gerónimo Barbadillo González (9/1), Guillermo La Rosa Laguna (22/2), Juan Carlos Oblitas Saba (42/9) [67.Jorge Andrés Olaechea Quijandría (17/1)]. Trainer: Elba de Padua Lima "Tim" (5).

251. 23.03.1982 **CHILE – PERU** **2-1(2-1)**
Estadio Nacional, Santiago; Referee: Edison Pérez Nuñez (Peru); Attendance: 49,800
PER: Ramón Quiroga Arancibia (29/0), Jaime Eduardo Duarte Huerta (32/1), Rubén Toribio Díaz Rivas (55/1), Jorge Andrés Olaechea Quijandría (18/1), Roberto Rojas Tardío (15/0), José Manuel Velásquez Castillo (47/7), César Augusto Cueto Villa (28/3), Germán Carlos Leguía Dragó (15/2) [61.Luis Alberto Reyna Navarro (6/0)], Eduardo Hugo Malásquez Maldonado (5/1), Guillermo La Rosa Laguna (23/2) [52.Franco Enrique Navarro Monteiro (5/0)], Julio César Uribe Flores (12/4). Trainer: Elba de Padua Lima "Tim" (6).
Goal: Eduardo Hugo Malásquez Maldonado (17).

252. 30.03.1982 **PERU – CHILE** **1-0(1-0)** Copa del Pacífico
Estadio Nacional, Lima; Referee: Víctor Ojeda (Chile); Attendance: 38,000
PER: Ramón Quiroga Arancibia (30/0), Alejandro Hugo Gastulo Ramírez (7/0), Rubén Toribio Díaz Rivas (56/1), Jorge Andrés Olaechea Quijandría (19/1), Roberto Rojas Tardío (16/0), José Manuel Velásquez Castillo (48/7), César Augusto Cueto Villa (29/3), Germán Carlos Leguía Dragó (16/2), Eduardo Hugo Malásquez Maldonado (6/1), Oswaldo Felipe Ramírez Salcedo (57/17) [10.Franco Enrique Navarro Monteiro (6/1), 69.Juan Caballero (2/0)], Guillermo La Rosa Laguna (24/2). Trainer: Elba de Padua Lima "Tim" (7).
Goal: Franco Enrique Navarro Monteiro (38).

253. 18.04.1982 **HUNGARY - PERU** **1-2(1-0)**
Népstadion, Budapest; Referee: Horst Brummeier (Austria); Attendance: 25,000
PER: Ramón Quiroga Arancibia (31/0), Jaime Eduardo Duarte Huerta (33/1), Jorge Andrés Olaechea Quijandría (20/1), Rubén Toribio Díaz Rivas (57/1), Roberto Rojas Tardío (17/0), José Manuel Velásquez Castillo (49/7), César Augusto Cueto Villa (30/3), Julio César Uribe Flores (13/6), Eduardo Hugo Malásquez Maldonado (7/1), Guillermo La Rosa Laguna (25/2) [65.Franco Enrique Navarro Monteiro (7/1)], Germán Carlos Leguía Dragó (17/2). Trainer: Elba de Padua Lima "Tim" (8).
Goal: Julio César Uribe Flores (55, 81).

254. 25.04.1982 **ALGERIA - PERU** **1-1(0-1)**
Stade 5 Juillet, Alger; Referee: Belaïd Lacarne (Algeria)
PER: Ramón Quiroga Arancibia (32/0), Jaime Eduardo Duarte Huerta (34/1), Rubén Toribio Díaz Rivas (58/1), Jorge Andrés Olaechea Quijandría (21/1), Roberto Rojas Tardío (18/0) [50.Miguel Ángel Gutiérrez (5/0)], José Manuel Velásquez Castillo (50/7), César Augusto Cueto Villa (31/4), Germán Carlos Leguía Dragó (18/2) [63.Freddy Ravello (11/1)], Eduardo Hugo Malásquez Maldonado (8/1) [Juan Caballero (3/0)], Guillermo La Rosa Laguna (26/2), Julio César Uribe Flores (14/6). Trainer: Elba de Padua Lima "Tim" (9).
Goal: César Augusto Cueto Villa (32).

255. 28.04.1982 **FRANCE - PERU** **0-1(0-0)**
Stade Parc des Princes, Paris; Referee: André Daina (Switzerland); Attendance: 46,429
PER: Ramón Quiroga Arancibia (33/0), Jaime Eduardo Duarte Huerta (35/1), Jorge Andrés Olaechea Quijandría (22/1), Rubén Toribio Díaz Rivas (59/1), Miguel Ángel Gutiérrez (6/0), José Manuel Velásquez Castillo (51/7), César Augusto Cueto Villa (32/4), Germán Carlos Leguía Dragó (19/2) [68.Eduardo Hugo Malásquez Maldonado (9/1)], Guillermo La Rosa Laguna (27/2), Julio César Uribe Flores (15/6), Juan Carlos Oblitas Saba (43/10). Trainer: Elba de Padua Lima "Tim" (10).
Goal: Juan Carlos Oblitas Saba (37).

256. 16.05.1982 **PERU - ROMANIA** **2-0(1-0)**
Estadio Nacional, Lima; Referee: Sergio Leiblinger (Peru); Attendance: 45,000
PER: Ramón Quiroga Arancibia (34/0), Jaime Eduardo Duarte Huerta (36/1), Rafael Salvador Salguero González (10/0), Rubén Toribio Díaz Rivas (60/1), Jorge Andrés Olaechea Quijandría (23/1), José Manuel Velásquez Castillo (52/8), César Augusto Cueto Villa (33/4), Teófilo Juan Cubillas Arizaga (78/26) [73.Franco Enrique Navarro Monteiro (8/1)], Germán Carlos Leguía Dragó (20/2), Julio César Uribe Flores (16/7) [67.Guillermo La Rosa Laguna (28/2)], Juan Carlos Oblitas Saba (44/10). Trainer: Elba de Padua Lima "Tim" (11).
Goals: Julio César Uribe Flores (44 penalty), José Manuel Velásquez Castillo (87).

257. 15.06.1982 **PERU - CAMEROON** **0-0** 12th FIFA WC. Group Stage
Estadio Riazor, La Coruña (Spain); Referee: Franz Woehrer (Austria); Attendance: 11,000
PER: Ramón Quiroga Arancibia (35/0), Jaime Eduardo Duarte Huerta (37/1), Rubén Toribio Díaz Rivas (Cap) (61/1), Rafael Salvador Salguero González (11/0), Jorge Andrés Olaechea Quijandría (24/1), José Manuel Velásquez Castillo (53/8), César Augusto Cueto Villa (34/4), Teófilo Juan Cubillas Arizaga (79/26) [56.Guillermo La Rosa Laguna (29/2)], Germán Carlos Leguía Dragó (21/2) [66.Gerónimo Barbadillo González (10/1)], Julio César Uribe Flores (17/7), Juan Carlos Oblitas Saba (45/10). Trainer: Elba de Padua Lima "Tim" (12).

258. 18.06.1982 **PERU - ITALY** **1-1(1-0)** 12th FIFA WC. Group Stage
Estadio Balaídos, Vigo (Spain); Referee: Werner Eschweiler (West Germany); Attendance: 25,000
PER: Ramón Quiroga Arancibia (36/0), Jaime Eduardo Duarte Huerta (38/1), Rubén Toribio Díaz Rivas (Cap) (62/1), Rafael Salvador Salguero González (12/0), Jorge Andrés Olaechea Quijandría (25/1), José Manuel Velásquez Castillo (54/8), César Augusto Cueto Villa (35/4), Teófilo Juan Cubillas Arizaga (80/26), Gerónimo Barbadillo González (11/1) [65.Guillermo La Rosa Laguna (30/2)], Julio César Uribe Flores (18/7) [65.Germán Carlos Leguía Dragó (22/2)], Juan Carlos Oblitas Saba (46/10). Trainer: Elba de Padua Lima "Tim" (13).
Goal: Fulvio Collovati (84 own goal).

259. 22.06.1982 **POLAND - PERU** **5-1(0-0)** 12th FIFA WC. Group Stage
Estadio Riazor, La Coruña (Spain); Referee: Lamberto Mario Rubio Vásquez (Mexico); Attendance: 25,000
PER: Ramón Quiroga Arancibia (37/0), Jaime Eduardo Duarte Huerta (39/1), Rubén Toribio Díaz Rivas (Cap) (63/1), Rafael Salvador Salguero González (13/0), Jorge Andrés Olaechea Quijandría (26/1), César Augusto Cueto Villa (36/4), José Manuel Velásquez Castillo (55/8), Teófilo Juan Cubillas Arizaga (81/26) [49.Julio César Uribe Flores (19/7)], Germán Carlos Leguía Dragó (23/2), Guillermo La Rosa Laguna (31/3), Juan Carlos Oblitas Saba (47/10) [49.Gerónimo Barbadillo González (12/1)]. Trainer: Elba de Padua Lima "Tim" (14).
Goal: Guillermo La Rosa Laguna (83).

260. 18.07.1983 **URUGUAY - PERU** **1-1(0-1)**
Estadio Centenario, Montevideo; Referee: Claudio Busca (Chile); Attendance: 55,000
PER: José Manuel Gonzáles Ganoza (9/0), Jorge Ramírez (1/0), Jaime Eduardo Duarte Huerta (40/1), Pedro Requena (1/0), Roberto Rojas Tardío (19/0), José Manuel Velásquez Castillo (56/8), Germán Carlos Leguía Dragó (24/2), Luis Alberto Reyna Navarro (7/0), Eduardo Hugo Malásquez Maldonado (10/1), Juan Caballero (4/1) [78.Eduardo Rey Muñoz (3/0)], Franco Enrique Navarro Monteiro (9/1). Trainer: Juan José Tan (3).
Goal: Juan Caballero (29).

261. 21.07.1983 **PERU - CHILE** **0-1(0-1)** Copa del Pacífico
Estadio Nacional, Lima; Referee: Enrique Labó Revoredo (Peru); Attendance: 20,000
PER: José Manuel Gonzáles Ganoza (10/0), Jorge Ramírez (2/0), Jaime Eduardo Duarte Huerta (41/1), Pedro Requena (2/0), Roberto Rojas Tardío (20/0), Luis Alberto Reyna Navarro (8/0), Eduardo Hugo Malásquez Maldonado (11/1), Pedro Bonelli (1/0), Genaro Neyra (1/0) [57.Alberto Castillo (1/0)], Juan Caballero (5/1), Eduardo Rey Muñoz (4/0). Trainer: Juan José Tan (4).

262. 03.08.1983 **CHILE - PERU** **2-0(2-0)** Copa del Pacífico
Estadio „Carlos Dittborn", Arica; Referee: Juan Ambrosio Silvagno Cavanna (Chile); Attendance: 18,802
PER: José Manuel Gonzáles Ganoza (11/0), Jorge Ramírez (3/0), Rubén Toribio Díaz Rivas (64/1), Pedro Requena (3/0), Roberto Rojas Tardío (21/0), José Manuel Velásquez Castillo (57/8), Germán Carlos Leguía Dragó (25/2), Jaime Eduardo Duarte Huerta (42/1) [46.Luis Alberto Reyna Navarro (9/0)], Eduardo Rey Muñoz (5/0) [72.Alberto Mora (1/0)], Franco Enrique Navarro Monteiro (10/1), Eduardo Hugo Malásquez Maldonado (12/1). Trainer: Juan José Tan (5).

263. 11.08.1983 **PERU – URUGUAY** **1-1(1-1)**
Estadio Nacional, Lima; Referee: Sergio Leiblinger (Peru); Attendance: 2,000
PER: Eusebio Alfredo Acasuzo Colán (11/0), Jorge Ramírez (4/0), José Casanova (1/0), Pedro Requena (4/0), Roberto Rojas Tardío (22/0), Germán Carlos Leguía Dragó (26/2), José Manuel Velásquez Castillo (58/8), Luis Alberto Reyna Navarro (10/0) [Pedro Bonelli (2/0)], Juan Caballero (6/1) [Alberto Mora (2/0)], Franco Enrique Navarro Monteiro (11/2) [Eduardo Rey Muñoz (6/0)], Eduardo Hugo Malásquez Maldonado (13/1). Trainer: Juan José Tan (6).
Goal: Franco Enrique Navarro Monteiro (40).

264. 17.08.1983 **PERU – COLOMBIA** **1-0(0-0)** 32nd Copa América. Group Stage
Estadio Nacional, Lima; Referee: José Luis Martínez Bazán (Uruguay); Attendance: 30,000
PER: Eusebio Alfredo Acasuzo Colán (12/0), Jorge Ramírez (5/0), Pedro Requena (5/0), Rubén Toribio Díaz Rivas (65/1) [69.José Casanova (2/0)], Roberto Rojas Tardío (23/0), José Manuel Velásquez Castillo (59/8), Luis Alberto Reyna Navarro (11/0) [65.Pedro Bonelli (3/0)], Germán Carlos Leguía Dragó (27/2), Eduardo Hugo Malásquez Maldonado (14/1), Franco Enrique Navarro Monteiro (12/3), Eduardo Rey Muñoz (7/0). Trainer: Juan José Tan (7).
Goal: Franco Enrique Navarro Monteiro (80).

265. 21.08.1983 **BOLIVIA – PERU** **1-1(0-0)** 32nd Copa América. Group Stage
Estadio „Hernándo Siles Zuazo", La Paz; Referee: Jorge Eduardo Romero (Argentina); Attendance: 45,000
PER: Eusebio Alfredo Acasuzo Colán (13/0), Jorge Ramírez (6/0), Jaime Eduardo Duarte Huerta (43/1) [70.José Casanova (3/0)], Pedro Requena (6/0), José Aguayo (1/0), Pedro Bonelli (4/0), José Manuel Velásquez Castillo (60/8), Germán Carlos Leguía Dragó (28/2) [76.Alberto Mora (3/0)], Genaro Neyra (2/0), Franco Enrique Navarro Monteiro (13/4), Eduardo Hugo Malásquez Maldonado (15/1). Trainer: Juan José Tan (8).
Goal: Franco Enrique Navarro Monteiro (89).

266. 28.08.1983 **COLOMBIA – PERU** **2-2(0-1)** 32nd Copa América. Group Stage
Estadio „Nemesio Camacho" 'El Campín', Bogotá; Referee: Arnaldo David César Coelho (Brazil); Attendance: 50,000
PER: Eusebiuo Acasuzo (14/0), Jorge Ramírez (7/0), Pedro Requena (7/0), Jaime Eduardo Duarte Huerta (44/1), Roberto Rojas Tardío (24/0), Luis Alberto Reyna Navarro (12/0) [75.Alberto Mora (4/0)], José Manuel Velásquez Castillo (61/8), Germán Carlos Leguía Dragó (29/2), Franco Enrique Navarro Monteiro (14/4), Juan Caballero (7/2), Eduardo Hugo Malásquez Maldonado (16/2). Trainer: Juan José Tan (9).
Goal: Eduardo Hugo Malásquez Maldonado (25 penalty), Juan Caballero (84).

267. 04.09.1983 **PERU – BOLIVIA** **2-1(2-0)** 32nd Copa América. Group Stage
Estadio Nacional, Lima; Referee: Guillermo Budge Aguirre (Chile) ; Attendance: 50,000
PER: Eusebio Alfredo Acasuzo Colán (15/0), Jaime Eduardo Duarte Huerta (45/1) [46.Jorge Ramírez (8/0)], Rubén Toribio Díaz Rivas (66/1), Pedro Requena (8/0), Roberto Rojas Tardío (25/0), Luis Alberto Reyna Navarro (13/0) [68.José Casanova (4/0)], José Manuel Velásquez Castillo (62/8), Germán Carlos Leguía Dragó (30/3), Eduardo Hugo Malásquez Maldonado (17/2), Franco Enrique Navarro Monteiro (15/4), Juan Caballero (8/3). Trainer: Juan José Tan (10).
Goal: Germán Carlos Leguía Dragó (5), Juan Caballero (22).

268. 05.10.1983 **PERU – PARAGUAY** **0-2(0-1)**
Estadio Nacional, Lima; Referee: Alfonso Postigo (Peru)
PER: Enrique Bravo (1/0), Jorge Ramírez (9/0), Jaime Eduardo Duarte Huerta (46/1), Pedro Requena (9/0), José Aguayo (2/0), Luis Alberto Reyna Navarro (14/0) [66.Roberto Rojas Tardío (26/0)], José Casanova (5/0), Rodolfo Chávarri (1/0), Eduardo Rey Muñoz (8/0) [57.Juan Caballero (9/3)], Franco Enrique Navarro Monteiro (16/4), Alberto Mora (5/0). Trainer: Juan José Tan (11).

269. 07.10.1983 **PARAGUAY – PERU** **4-1(3-1)**
Estadio Defensores del Chaco, Asunción; Referee: Gabriel González (Paraguay)
PER: José Manuel Gonzáles Ganoza (12/0) [Enrique Bravo (2/0)], Jorge Ramírez (10/0), Pedro Requena (10/0), Rubén Toribio Díaz Rivas (67/1), Roberto Rojas Tardío (27/0), Luis Alberto Reyna Navarro (15/0) [José Aguayo (3/0)], Jaime Eduardo Duarte Huerta (47/1), Jorge Andrés Olaechea Quijandría (27/1), Pedro Bonelli (5/0) [Rodolfo Chávarri (2/0)], Juan Caballero (10/4) [Alberto Mora (6/0)], Franco Enrique Navarro Monteiro (17/4). Trainer: Juan José Tan (12).
Goal: Juan Caballero (40).

270. 13.10.1983 **PERU – URUGUAY** **0-1(0-0)** 32nd Copa América. Semi-Finals
Estadio Nacional, Lima; Referee: Sergio Vázquez (Chile); Attendance: 28,000
PER: Eusebio Alfredo Acasuzo Colán (16/0), Jaime Eduardo Duarte Huerta (48/1), Pedro Requena (11/0), Rubén Toribio Díaz Rivas (68/1), José Aguayo (4/0), José Manuel Velásquez Castillo (63/8), Luis Alberto Reyna Navarro (16/0) [73.José Casanova (6/0)], Jorge Andrés Olaechea Quijandría (28/1), Eduardo Rey Muñoz (9/0) [58.Eduardo Hugo Malásquez Maldonado (18/2)], Franco Enrique Navarro Monteiro (18/4), Juan Caballero (11/4). Trainer: Juan José Tan (13).

271. 20.10.1983 **URUGUAY – PERU** **1-1(0-1)** 32nd Copa América. Semi-Finals
Estadio Centenario, Montevideo; Referee: Arturo Andrés Ithurralde (Argentina); Attendance: 58,000
PER: Eusebio Alfredo Acasuzo Colán (17/0), Jaime Eduardo Duarte Huerta (49/1) [*sent off 79*], Pedro Requena (12/0), Rubén Toribio Díaz Rivas (69/1), José Aguayo (5/0), Germán Carlos Leguía Dragó (31/3), José Manuel Velásquez Castillo (64/8), Jorge Andrés Olaechea Quijandría (29/1), Eduardo Hugo Malásquez Maldonado (19/3), Franco Enrique Navarro Monteiro (19/4), Juan Caballero (12/4). Trainer: Juan José Tan (14).
Goal: Eduardo Hugo Malásquez Maldonado (23).

272. 26.02.1984 **PERU – HONDURAS** **1-3(0-2)**
Estadio „Alejandro Villanueva", Lima; Referee: Edison Pérez Nuñez (Peru)
PER: Eusebio Alfredo Acasuzo Colán (18/0), Jorge Ramírez (11/0), Jaime Eduardo Duarte Huerta (50/1), Pedro Requena (13/0), Felipe Uculmana (1/0) [54.Angel Gutiérrez (1/0)], José Manuel Velásquez Castillo (65/8), Luis Alberto Reyna Navarro (17/0) [71.José Casanova (7/0)], Eduardo Hugo Malásquez Maldonado (20/3), Jorge Hirano (1/1) [67.Julio Aliaga (1/0)], César Loyola (1/0) [61.José Zapata (3/0)], Franco Enrique Navarro Monteiro (20/4). Trainer: Moisés Barack (1).
Goal: Jorge Hirano (48).

273. 26.07.1984 **COLOMBIA – PERU** **1-1(1-0)**
Estadio „Atanasio Girardot", Medellín; Referee: Armando Pérez Hoyos (Colombia); Attendance: 22,000
PER: José Manuel Gonzáles Ganoza (13/0), Leonardo Rojas (1/0), Pedro Requena (14/0), Rubén Toribio Díaz Rivas (70/1), Raúl García (1/0) [68.Jaime Eduardo Duarte Huerta (51/1)], Wilmar Valencia (1/0), Luis Alberto Reyna Navarro (18/0) [72.José Casanova (8/0)], Jorge Olaechea (30/1), Abel Lobatón (5/2), Franco Enrique Navarro Monteiro (21/4), Jorge Hirano (2/1) [75.Fidel Suárez (1/0)]. Trainer: Moisés Barack (2).
Goal: Abel Lobatón (62).

274. 09.08.1984 **PERU – COLOMBIA** **0-0**

Estadio Nacional, Lima; Referee: Enrique Labó (Peru); Attendance: 16,000

PER: José Manuel Gonzáles Ganoza (14/0), Leonardo Rojas (2/0), Pedro Requena (15/0), Rubén Toribio Díaz Rivas (71/1), Jaime Eduardo Duarte Huerta (52/1), Wilmar Valencia (2/0), Luis Alberto Reyna Navarro (19/0), Jorge Andrés Olaechea Quijandría (31/1), Jorge Hirano (3/1), Franco Enrique Navarro Monteiro (22/4), Juan Carlos Oblitas Saba (48/10). Trainer: Moisés Barack (3).

275. 19.09.1984 **URUGUAY – PERU** **2-0(1-0)**

Estadio Centenario, Montevideo; Referee: Carlos Rojas Martins (Brazil); Attendance: 560

PER: José Manuel Gonzáles Ganoza (15/0), Leonardo Rojas (3/0), Samuel Eugenio (1/0), Rubén Toribio Díaz Rivas (72/1), César Espino (1/0), Wilmar Valencia (3/0), Luis Alberto Reyna Navarro (20/0) [46.Pedro Requena (16/0)], Juan Carlos Cabanillas (1/0), Eugenio La Rosa (1/0), Fidel Suárez (2/0), Juan Carlos Oblitas Saba (49/10). Trainer: Moisés Barack (4).

276. 03.10.1984 **PERU – URUGUAY** **1-3(0-1)**

Estadio Nacional, Lima; Referee: Abel Gnecco (Argentina); Attendance: 15,000

PER: Eusebio Alfredo Acasuzo Colán (19/0) [73.José Manuel Gonzáles Ganoza (16/0)], Leonardo Rojas (4/0), Samuel Eugenio (2/0), Rubén Toribio Díaz Rivas (73/1) [*sent off 76*], Jaime Eduardo Duarte Huerta (53/1) [67.Raúl García (2/0)], Wilmar Valencia (4/0), Luis Alberto Reyna Navarro (21/0), Juan Carlos Cabanillas (2/0), Abel Lobatón (6/3) [77.Tomás Farfán (1/0)], Fidel Suárez (3/0), Jorge Hirano (4/1). Trainer: Moisés Barack (5).

Goal: Abel Lobatón (55).

277. 17.02.1985 **PERU – BOLIVIA** **3-0(2-0)**

Estadio Nacional, Lima; Referee: Enrique Labó Revoredo (Peru)

PER: José Manuel Gonzáles Ganoza (17/0), Leonardo Rojas (5/0), Pedro Requena (17/0), Samuel Eugenio (3/0), César Adriazola (1/0) [46.César Espino (2/0)], Eduardo Hugo Malásquez Maldonado (21/3) [60.Juan Carlos Cabanillas (3/0)], José Manuel Velásquez Castillo (66/8), Javier Chirinos (1/0), Abel Lobatón (7/3) [46.Jorge Hirano (5/1)], Franco Enrique Navarro Monteiro (23/7), Juan Carlos Oblitas Saba (50/10). Trainer: Moisés Barack (6).

Goal: Franco Enrique Navarro Monteiro (30, 44, 70).

278. 24.02.1985 **CHILE – PERU** **1-2(0-1)**

Estadio Nacional, Santiago; Referee: Mario Líra Gonzáles (Chile); Attendance: 61,294

PER: José Manuel Gonzáles Ganoza (18/0), Leonardo Rojas (6/0), Pedro Requena (18/0), Rubén Toribio Díaz Rivas (74/1), Jorge Andrés Olaechea Quijandría (32/1), Eduardo Hugo Malásquez Maldonado (22/3), José Manuel Velásquez Castillo (67/9), Javier Chirinos (2/0), Eugenio La Rosa (2/0), Franco Enrique Navarro Monteiro (24/8) [58.Abel Lobatón (8/3)], Juan Carlos Oblitas Saba (51/10). Trainer: Moisés Barack (7).

Goal: José Manuel Velásquez Castillo (10), Franco Enrique Navarro Monteiro (54).

279. 27.02.1985 **URUGUAY – PERU** **2-2(1-1)**

Estadio Centenario, Montevideo; Referee: Ernesto Filippi (Uruguay); Attendance: 48,699

PER: José Manuel Gonzáles Ganoza (19/0), Leonardo Rojas (7/0), Pedro Requena (19/0), Rubén Toribio Díaz Rivas (75/1), Jorge Andrés Olaechea Quijandría (33/1), Eduardo Hugo Malásquez Maldonado (23/3), José Manuel Velásquez Castillo (68/10), Javier Chirinos (3/0), Eugenio La Rosa (3/0) [*sent off 35*], Franco Enrique Navarro Monteiro (25/9), Juan Carlos Oblitas Saba (52/10). Trainer: Moisés Barack (8).

Goals: Franco Enrique Navarro Monteiro (8), José Manuel Velásquez Castillo (50).

280. 09.03.1985 **PERU – CHILE** **1-1(1-0)**

Estadio Nacional, Lima; Referee: José Francisco Ramírez Calle (Peru); Attendance: 50,000

PER: José Manuel Gonzáles Ganoza (20/0), Leonardo Rojas (8/0), Pedro Requena (20/0), Rubén Toribio Díaz Rivas (76/1), Jorge Andrés Olaechea Quijandría (34/1), Eduardo Hugo Malásquez Maldonado (24/3), José Manuel Velásquez Castillo (69/10), Javier Chirinos (4/0), Abel Lobatón (9/3), Franco Enrique Navarro Monteiro (26/9) [46.Juan Caballero (13/4)], Jorge Hirano (6/2) [61.Juan Carlos Cabanillas (4/0)]. Trainer: Moisés Barack (9).

Goal: Jorge Hirano (30).

281. 21.03.1985 **PERU – ECUADOR** **1-0(0-0)**

Estadio Nacional, Lima; Referee: Wálter Chatter (Peru); Attendance: 10,000

PER: Eusebio Alfredo Acasuzo Colán (20/0), Jorge Ramírez (12/0), Pedro Requena (21/0), Rubén Toribio Díaz Rivas (77/1), Jorge Andrés Olaechea Quijandría (35/1), Eduardo Hugo Malásquez Maldonado (25/3), Luis Alberto Reyna Navarro (22/0), César Augusto Cueto Villa (37/4), Jorge Hirano (7/3) [80.Guillermo La Rosa Laguna (32/3)], Franco Enrique Navarro Monteiro (27/9), Juan Carlos Oblitas Saba (53/10). Trainer: Moisés Barack (10).

Goal: Jorge Hirano (47).

282. 23.04.1985 **PERU – URUGUAY** **2-1(1-1)**

Estadio Nacional, Lima; Referee: Edison Pérez Nuñez (Peru); Attendance: 70,000

PER: Eusebio Alfredo Acasuzo Colán (21/0), Leonardo Rojas (9/0), Pedro Requena (22/0), Rubén Toribio Díaz Rivas (78/1) [67.Samuel Eugenio (4/0)], Alejandro Hugo Gastulo Ramírez (8/0) [50.Jorge Andrés Olaechea Quijandría (36/1)], César Augusto Cueto Villa (38/5), José Manuel Velásquez Castillo (70/11), Javier Chirinos (5/0), Guillermo La Rosa Laguna (33/3), Franco Enrique Navarro Monteiro (28/9) [72.Eduardo Hugo Malásquez Maldonado (26/3)], Juan Carlos Oblitas Saba (54/10) [60.Julio César Uribe Flores (20/7)]. Trainer: Moisés Barack (11).

Goals: José Manuel Velásquez Castillo (26), César Augusto Cueto Villa (75).

283. 28.04.1985 **BRAZIL – PERU** **0-1(0-0)**

Estádio „Mané Garrincha“, Brasilia; Referee: Jesús Díaz Palácios (Colombia); Attendance: 65,000

PER: Eusebio Alfredo Acasuzo Colán (22/0), Leonardo Rojas (10/0), Pedro Requena (23/0), Rubén Toribio Díaz Rivas (79/1), Alejandro Hugo Gastulo Ramírez (9/0) [Jorge Andrés Olaechea Quijandría (37/1)], César Augusto Cueto Villa (39/5), José Manuel Velásquez Castillo (71/11), Javier Chirinos (6/0), Guillermo La Rosa Laguna (34/3), Franco Enrique Navarro Monteiro (29/9) [Eduardo Hugo Malásquez Maldonado (27/3)], Juan Carlos Oblitas Saba (55/10) [46.Julio César Uribe Flores (21/8)]. Trainer: Moisés Barack (12).

Goal: Julio César Uribe Flores (61).

284. 01.05.1985 **BOLIVIA – PERU** **0-0**

Estadio „Ramón 'Tahuichi' Aguilera“, Santa Cruz de la Sierra; Referee: Jorge Antequera (Bolivia); Attendance: 20,000

PER: Eusebio Alfredo Acasuzo Colán (23/0), Leonardo Rojas (11/0), Pedro Requena (24/0), Rubén Toribio Díaz Rivas (80/1), Alejandro Hugo Gastulo Ramírez (10/0), César Augusto Cueto Villa (40/5), José Manuel Velásquez Castillo (72/11), Javier Chirinos (7/0), Julio César Uribe Flores (22/8), Guillermo La Rosa Laguna (35/3) [52.Franco Enrique Navarro Monteiro (30/9)], Juan Caballero (14/4) [70.Eduardo Hugo Malásquez Maldonado (28/3)]. Trainer: Moisés Barack (13)

285. 26.05.1985 **COLOMBIA - PERU** **1-0(1-0)** 13th FIFA WC. Qualifiers
Estadio „Nemesio Camacho“ ‘El Campín’, Bogotá; Referee: Luis Barrancos Álvarez (Bolivia); Attendance: 53,000
PER: Eusebio Alfredo Acasuzo Colán (24/0), Leonardo Rojas (12/0), Pedro Requena (25/0) [16.Hugo Gástulo (11/0)], Rubén Toribio Díaz Rivas (81/1) [*sent off 50*], Jorge Andrés Olaechea Quijandría (38/1), César Augusto Cueto Villa (41/5), José Manuel Velásquez Castillo (73/11), Javier Chirinos (8/0), Gerónimo Barbadillo González (13/1), Franco Enrique Navarro Monteiro (31/9), Juan Carlos Oblitas Saba (56/10) [69.Julio César Uribe Flores (23/8)]. Trainer: Moisés Barack (14).

286. 02.06.1985 **VENEZUELA - PERU** **0-1(0-0)** 13th FIFA WC. Qualifiers
Estadio Pueblo Nuevo, San Cristóbal; Referee: Jorge Orellana (Ecuador); Attendance: 16,000
PER: Eusebio Alfredo Acasuzo Colán (25/0), Leonardo Rojas (13/0), Javier Chirinos (9/0), Jorge Andrés Olaechea Quijandría (39/1), Alejandro Hugo Gastulo Ramírez (12/0), César Augusto Cueto Villa (42/5), José Manuel Velásquez Castillo (74/11), Julio César Uribe Flores (24/9), Gerónimo Barbadillo González (14/1), Franco Enrique Navarro Monteiro (32/9), Juan Carlos Oblitas Saba (57/10). Trainer: Moisés Barack (15).
Goal: Julio César Uribe Flores (78).

287. 09.06.1985 **PERU - COLOMBIA** **0-0** 13th FIFA WC. Qualifiers
Estadio Nacional, Lima; Referee: Juan Daniel Cardellino (Uruguay); Attendance: 45,000
PER: Eusebio Alfredo Acasuzo Colán (26/0), Leonardo Rojas (14/0), Jorge Andrés Olaechea Quijandría (40/1), Rubén Toribio Díaz Rivas (82/1), Alejandro Hugo Gastulo Ramírez (13/0), César Augusto Cueto Villa (43/5), Javier Chirinos (10/0), Julio César Uribe Flores (25/9), Gerónimo Barbadillo González (15/1) [57.Eduardo Hugo Malásquez Maldonado (29/3)], Franco Enrique Navarro Monteiro (33/9), Jorge Hirano (8/3) [75.Guillermo La Rosa Laguna (36/3)]. Trainer: Moisés Barack (16).

288. 16.06.1985 **PERU - VENEZUELA** **4-1(2-1)** 13th FIFA WC. Qualifiers
Estadio Nacional, Lima; Referee: Luis Carlos Ferreira (Brazil); Attendance: 10,327
PER: Eusebio Alfredo Acasuzo Colán (27/0), Leonardo Rojas (15/0), Jorge Andrés Olaechea Quijandría (41/1), Rubén Toribio Díaz Rivas (83/1), Alejandro Hugo Gastulo Ramírez (14/0), Eduardo Hugo Malásquez Maldonado (30/3) [64.Jorge Hirano (9/4)], José Manuel Velásquez Castillo (75/11), César Augusto Cueto Villa (44/6), Gerónimo Barbadillo González (16/2), Franco Enrique Navarro Monteiro (34/10) [70.Guillermo La Rosa Laguna (37/3)], Juan Carlos Oblitas (58/10). Trainer: Roberto Federico Chale Olarte (1).
Goal: Franco Enrique Navarro Monteiro (15), Gerónimo Barbadillo González (19), Jorge Hirano (79), César Augusto Cueto Villa (81).

289. 23.06.1985 **PERU - ARGENTINA** **1-0(1-0)** 13th FIFA WC. Qualifiers
Estadio Nacional, Lima; Referee: Hernán Silva Arce (Chile); Attendance: 43,000
PER: Eusebio Alfredo Acasuzo Colán (28/0), Leonardo Rojas (16/0), Jorge Andrés Olaechea Quijandría (42/1), Rubén Toribio Díaz Rivas (84/1), Alejandro Hugo Gastulo Ramírez (15/0), Luis Alberto Reyna Navarro (23/0) [76.Javier Chirinos (11/0)], José Manuel Velásquez Castillo (76/11), César Augusto Cueto Villa (45/6), Gerónimo Barbadillo González (17/2) [54.Julio César Uribe Flores (26/9)], Franco Enrique Navarro Monteiro (35/10), Juan Carlos Oblitas Saba (59/11). Trainer: Roberto Federico Chale Olarte (2).
Goal: Juan Carlos Oblitas Saba (7).

290. 30.06.1985 **ARGENTINA - PERU** **2-2(1-2)** 13th FIFA WC. Qualifiers
Estadio Monumental „Antonio Vespucio Liberti“, Buenos Aires; Referee: Romualdo Arppi Filho (Brazil); Attendance: 65,457
PER: Eusebio Alfredo Acasuzo Colán (29/0), Leonardo Rojas (17/0), Jorge Andrés Olaechea Quijandría (43/1), Rubén Toribio Díaz Rivas (85/1), Alejandro Hugo Gastulo Ramírez (16/0), Luis Alberto Reyna Navarro (24/0) [68.Javier Chirinos (12/0)], José Manuel Velásquez Castillo (77/12), César Augusto Cueto Villa (46/6), Gerónimo Barbadillo González (18/3), Franco Enrique Navarro Monteiro (36/10) [5.Julio César Uribe Flores (27/9)], Juan Carlos Oblitas Saba (60/11). Trainer: Roberto Federico Chale Olarte (3).
Goals: José Manuel Velásquez Castillo (24), Gerónimo Barbadillo González (38).

291. 20.09.1985 **MEXICO - PERU** **0-0**
Memorial Coliseum, Los Angeles (United States); Referee: Edward Elio (United States); Attendance: 25,645
PER: José Manuel Gonzáles Ganoza (21/0), Leonardo Rojas (18/0), Rubén Toribio Díaz Rivas (86/1), Jorge Andrés Olaechea Quijandría (44/1), Alejandro Hugo Gastulo Ramírez (17/0), José Manuel Velásquez Castillo (78/12) [80.Javier Chirinos (13/0)], César Augusto Cueto Villa (47/6), Luis Alberto Reyna Navarro (25/0) [65.José Casanova (9/0)], Guillermo La Rosa Laguna (38/3) [59.Eugenio La Rosa (4/0)], Julio César Uribe Flores (28/9), Juan Carlos Oblitas Saba (61/11) [89.Jorge Hirano (10/4)]. Trainer: Roberto Federico Chale Olarte (4).

292. 22.09.1985 **MEXICO - PERU** **1-0(0-0)**
Spartans Stadium, San José; Referee: Edward Elio (United States)
PER: José Manuel Gonzáles Ganoza (22/0), Leonardo Rojas (19/0), Rubén Toribio Díaz Rivas (87/1), Jorge Andrés Olaechea Quijandría (45/1), Alejandro Hugo Gastulo Ramírez (18/0), José Manuel Velásquez Castillo (79/12), Luis Alberto Reyna Navarro (26/0), Eduardo Hugo Malásquez Maldonado (31/3) [46.enio La Rosa (5/0)], Julio César Uribe Flores (29/9), Guillermo La Rosa Laguna (39/3), Juan Carlos Oblitas Saba (62/11) [46.ge Hirano (11/4)]. Trainer: Roberto Federico Chale Olarte (5).

293. 16.10.1985 **PERU - PARAGUAY** **0-1(0-1)**
Estadio Nacional, Lima; Referee: Alfonso Postigo (Peru)
PER: Ramón Quiroga Arancibia (38/0), Leonardo Rojas (20/0), Pedro Requena (26/0), Rubén Toribio Díaz Rivas (88/1) [70.Javier Chirinos (14/0)], Alejandro Hugo Gastulo Ramírez (19/0), César Augusto Cueto Villa (48/6), José Manuel Velásquez Castillo (80/12), José Casanova (10/0) [46.Jorge Hirano (12/4)], Eugenio La Rosa (6/0), Franco Enrique Navarro Monteiro (37/10), Luis Antonio Escobar (1/0) [46.Luis Alberto Reyna Navarro (27/0)]. Trainer: Roberto Federico Chale Olarte (6).

294. 27.10.1985 **CHILE - PERU** **4-2(3-0)** 13th FIFA WC. Qualifiers
Estadio Nacional, Santiago; Referee: José Luis Martínez Bazán (Uruguay); Attendance: 40,340
PER: Eusebio Alfredo Acasuzo Colán (30/0) [18.Ramón Quiroga Arancibia (39/0)], Leonardo Rojas (21/0), Pedro Requena (27/0), Rubén Toribio Díaz Rivas (89/1) [*sent off 68*], Alejandro Hugo Gastulo Ramírez (20/0), César Augusto Cueto Villa (49/6) [67.Eugenio La Rosa (7/0)], José Manuel Velásquez Castillo (81/12), Jorge Andrés Olaechea Quijandría (46/1), Gerónimo Barbadillo González (19/3), Franco Enrique Navarro Monteiro (38/12), Juan Carlos Oblitas Saba (63/11). Trainer: Roberto Federico Chale Olarte (7).
Goals: Franco Enrique Navarro Monteiro (45, 76).

295. 03.11.1985 **PERU - CHILE** **0-1(0-0)** 13th FIFA WC. Qualifiers
Estadio Nacional, Lima; Referee: Arnaldo David César Coelho (Brazil); Attendance: 45,244
PER: Ramón Quiroga Arancibia (40/0), Leonardo Rojas (22/0), Pedro Requena (28/0), Jaime Eduardo Duarte Huerta (54/1), Alejandro Hugo Gastulo Ramírez (21/0), César Augusto Cueto Villa (50/6) [65.Eduardo Hugo Malásquez Maldonado (32/3)], José Manuel Velásquez Castillo (82/12), Julio César Uribe Flores (30/9), Gerónimo Barbadillo González (20/3), Franco Enrique Navarro Monteiro (39/12), Juan Carlos Oblitas Saba (64/11) [62.Jorge Hirano (13/4)]. Trainer: Roberto Federico Chale Olarte (8).

296. 28.01.1986 **CHINA - PERU** **3-1(3-1)** Nehru Cup

Kerala Stadium, Trivandrum

PER: César Chávez Riva (1/0), Jorge Talavera (1/1), Daniel Reyes (1/0), Juan Máximo Reynoso Guzmán (1/0), Víctor Alcázar (1/0), Cedric Vásquez (1/0) [José Guillermo del Solar Alvarez-Calderón (1/0)], Alvaro Barco (1/0), Roberto Martínez (1/0), Jorge Navas (1/0), Carlos Guillén (1/0), Franco Enrique Navarro Monteiro (Cap) (40/12). Trainer: Luis Fernando Cruzado Sánchez (1).

Goal: Jorge Talavera

297. 30.01.1986 **INDIA - PERU** **0-1(0-0)** Nehru Cup

Kerala Stadium, Trivandrum

PER: César Chávez Riva (2/0), Jorge Talavera (2/1), Daniel Reyes (2/0), Juan Máximo Reynoso Guzmán (2/0), Víctor Alcázar (2/0), Cedric Vásquez (2/0) [José Guillermo del Solar Alvarez-Calderón (2/0)], Alvaro Barco (2/0), Roberto Martínez (2/0), Jorge Navas (2/0), Carlos Guillén (2/0), Franco Enrique Navarro Monteiro (Cap) (41/13). Trainer: Luis Fernando Cruzado Sánchez (2).

Goal: Franco Enrique Navarro Monteiro

298. 01.04.1986 **BRAZIL - PERU** **4-0(1-0)**

Estádio "João Castelo", São Luis; Referee: Arnaldo David César Coelho (Brazil); Attendance: 50,000

PER: Humberto Valdettaro (1/0), Carlos Castro (1/0), Carlos Isusqui (1/0), Juan Máximo Reynoso Guzmán (3/0), Víctor Alcázar (3/0), Roberto Martínez (3/0), Cedric Vásquez (3/0), Juan Carlos Cabanillas (5/0), César Loyola (2/0), Jesús Torrealba (1/0) [82.Rubén Correa (1/0)], Juan Caballero (15/4). Trainer: Manuel Mayorga (1).

299. 19.06.1987 **PERU - CHILE** **1-3(0-0)**

Estadio Nacional, Lima; Referee: Samuel Alarcón (Peru); Attendance: 2,223

PER: José Manuel Gonzáles Ganoza (23/0), Leonardo Rojas (23/0), Pedro Requena (29/0), Martín Duffóo (1/0), Percy Celso Olivares Polanco (1/0), Cedric Vásquez (4/0), Luis Alberto Reyna Navarro (28/0), Eduardo Hugo Malásquez Maldonado (33/3) [35.Roberto Martínez (4/0)], Javier Chirinos (15/0), [César Loyola (3/0)], Franco Enrique Navarro Monteiro (42/14), Jorge Hirano (14/4). Trainer: Fernando Cuéllar Ávalos (1).

Goal: Franco Enrique Navarro Monteiro (54).

300. 21.06.1987 **PERU - CHILE** **2-0(1-0)**

Estadio Nacional, Lima; Referee: José Ramírez Calle (Peru); Attendance: 12,000

PER: José Manuel Gonzáles Ganoza (24/0), Leonardo Rojas (24/0), Pedro Requena (30/0), Javier Chirinos (16/0), Percy Celso Olivares Polanco (2/0), Roberto Martínez (5/0), Juan Máximo Reynoso Guzmán (4/0) [78.Cedric Vásquez (5/0)], Luis Alberto Reyna Navarro (29/0) [60.Jorge Cordero (1/0)], Eugenio La Rosa (8/0) [51.Julio César Uribe Flores (31/9)], José Anselmo Soto (1/1), Jorge Hirano (15/5). Trainer: Fernando Cuéllar Ávalos (2).

Goals: José Anselmo Soto (20), Jorge Hirano (70).

301. 24.06.1987 **CHILE - PERU** **1-0(1-0)**

Estadio Nacional, Santiago; Referee: Guillermo Ojeda (Chile); Attendance: 3,583

PER: José Manuel Gonzáles Ganoza (25/0), Leonardo Rojas (25/0), Pedro Requena (31/0), Jorge Andrés Olaechea Quijandría (47/1), Percy Celso Olivares Polanco (3/0), Roberto Martínez (6/0) [75.José Guillermo del Solar Alvarez-Calderón (3/0)], Javier Chirinos (17/0) [70.Juan Máximo Reynoso Guzmán (5/0)], Luis Alberto Reyna Navarro (30/0), Jorge Hirano (16/5), Eugenio La Rosa (9/0) [67.José Anselmo Soto (2/1)], Franco Enrique Navarro Monteiro (43/14). Trainer: Fernando Cuéllar Ávalos (3).

302. 27.06.1987 **ARGENTINA - PERU** **1-1(0-0)** 33rd Copa America. Group Stage

Estadio Monumental „Antonio Vespucio Liberti", Buenos Aires; Referee: Armando Pérez Hoyos (Colombia); Attendance: 27,479

PER: José Manuel Gonzáles Ganoza (26/0), Leonardo Rojas (26/0), Pedro Requena (32/0), Jorge Andrés Olaechea Quijandría (48/1), Cedric Vásquez (6/0), Roberto Martínez (7/0) [66.Eugenio La Rosa (10/0)], Luis Alberto Reyna Navarro (31/1), Javier Chirinos (18/0), Julio César Uribe Flores (32/9) [*sent off 68*], Franco Enrique Navarro Monteiro (44/14), Jorge Hirano (17/5) [87.José Guillermo del Solar Alvarez-Calderón (4/0)]. Trainer: Fernando Cuéllar Ávalos (4).

Goal: Luis Alberto Reyna Navarro (59).

303. 04.07.1987 **PERU - ECUADOR** **1-1(0-0)** 33rd Copa America. Group Stage

Estadio Monumental „Antonio Vespucio Liberti", Buenos Aires (Argentina); Referee: Asterio Martínez (Paraguay); Attendance: 5,000

PER: José Manuel Gonzáles Ganoza (27/0), Leonardo Rojas (27/0), Pedro Requena (33/0), Jorge Andrés Olaechea Quijandría (49/1), Cedric Vásquez (7/0) [*sent off 83*], Eugenio La Rosa (11/1), Juan Máximo Reynoso Guzmán (6/0), Javier Chirinos (19/0), Eduardo Hugo Malásquez Maldonado (34/3), Franco Enrique Navarro Monteiro (45/14), Jorge Hirano (18/5) [61.César Loyola (4/0)]. Trainer: Fernando Cuéllar Ávalos (5).

Goal: Eugenio La Rosa (89).

304. 21.09.1988 **PERU - PARAGUAY** **0-1(0-1)**

Estadio Nacional, Lima; Referee: Alberto Tejada (Peru); Attendance: 1,642

PER: César Chávez Riva (3/0), Leonardo Rojas (28/0), Pedro Requena (34/0), José Guillermo del Solar Alvarez-Calderón (5/0), Percy Celso Olivares Polanco (4/0), Jorge Cordero (2/0), Juan Máximo Reynoso Guzmán (7/0) [46.José Luis Carranza (1/0)], Francesco Manassero (1/0) [61.Luis Alberto Reyna Navarro (32/1)], César Loyola (5/0) [71.Wilson Ramírez (1/0)], Domingo Farfán (1/0), Humberto Rey Muñoz (1/0). Trainer: José Antonio Fernández Santini (1).

305. 25.10.1988 **CHILE - PERU** **2-0(1-0)** Copa del Pacífico

Estadio „Carlos Dittborn", Arica; Referee: Juan Pablo Torrens (Chile); Attendance: 7,656

PER: César Chávez Riva (4/0), Leonardo Rojas (29/0), Juan Máximo Reynoso Guzmán (8/0), José Guillermo del Solar Alvarez-Calderón (6/0), Percy Celso Olivares Polanco (5/0), Wilmar Valencia (5/0) [*sent off 39*], José Luis Carranza (2/0), Julio César Antón Reyes (1/0) [69.Jesús Torrealba (2/0)], Luis Alberto Reyna Navarro (33/1) [58.Jorge Cordero (3/0)], César Loyola (6/0) [57.Humberto Rey Muñoz (2/0)], Víctor Hurtado (6/0). Trainer: José Antonio Fernández Santini (2).

306. 23.11.1988 **PERU - CHILE** **1-1(0-1)** Copa del Pacífico

Estadio Nacional, Lima; Referee: Walter Barrios (Peru); Attendance: 28,774

PER: Héctor Martín Yupanqui (1/0), Leonardo Rojas (30/0), Pedro Requena (35/0), José Guillermo del Solar Alvarez-Calderón (7/0), Percy Celso Olivares Polanco (6/0), Jorge Cordero (4/0), Juan Máximo Reynoso Guzmán (9/0) [65.José Luis Carranza (3/0)], Julio César Uribe Flores (33/9), César Loyola (7/0) [70.Humberto Rey Muñoz (3/0)], Franco Enrique Navarro Monteiro (46/14) [35.Domingo Farfán (2/1)], Wilson Ramírez (2/0). Trainer: José Antonio Fernández Santini (3).

Goal: Domingo Farfan (57).

307. 14.12.1988 **URUGUAY - PERU** **3-0(3-0)**
Estadio Centenario, Montevideo; Referee: Ricardo Calabria (Argentina); Attendance: 9,000
PER: Jesús Purizaga (1/0), Jorge Talavera (3/1), Juan Máximo Reynoso Guzmán (10/0), José Guillermo del Solar Alvarez-Calderón (8/0), Percy Celso Olivares Polanco (7/0), Juan Carlos Cabanillas (6/0) [55.Jorge Cordero (5/0)], José Luis Carranza (4/0), Luis Alberto Reyna Navarro (34/1) [69.Wilson Ramírez (3/0)], Julio César Uribe Flores (34/9), Domingo Farfán (3/1) [55.Eduardo Rey Muñoz (10/0)], Humberto Rey Muñoz (4/0). Trainer: José Antonio Fernández Santini (4).

308. 01.02.1989 **PERU - CHILE** **0-0** Copa Centenario de Arménia
Estadio Centenario, Arménia (Colombia); Referee: Armando Pérez Hoyos (Colombia); Attendance: 10,024
PER: Jesús Purizaga (2/0), Leonardo Rojas (31/0), Pedro Requena (36/0), José Guillermo del Solar Alvarez-Calderón (9/0), Percy Celso Olivares Polanco (8/0), Wilmar Valencia (6/0), Juan Máximo Reynoso Guzmán (11/0), Jorge Andrés Olaechea Quijandría (50/1), Roberto Martínez (8/0) [66.Jorge Cordero (6/0)], Ramón Anchisi (1/0), Domingo Farfán (4/1) [74.Eduardo Rey Muñoz (11/0)]. Trainer: José Antonio Fernández Santini (5).

309. 03.02.1989 **COLOMBIA - PERU** **1-0(0-0)** Copa Centenario de Arménia
Estadio "Hernán Ramírez Villegas", Pereira; Referee: Jesús Díaz (Colombia); Attendance: 16,200
PER: César Chávez Riva (5/0), Leonardo Rojas (32/0), Pedro Requena (37/0), José Guillermo del Solar Alvarez-Calderón (10/0), Percy Celso Olivares Polanco (9/0), Wilmar Valencia (7/0), Jorge Cordero (7/0), Miguel Elguera (1/0) [65.Roberto Martínez (9/0)], Jorge Andrés Olaechea Quijandría (51/1), Ramón Anchisi (2/0) [74.Eduardo Rey Muñoz (12/0)], Domingo Farfán (5/1). Trainer: José Antonio Fernández Santini (6).

310. 10.05.1989 **BRAZIL - PERU** **4-1(2-0)**
Estádio "Plácido Castelão", Fortaleza; Referee: Carlos Espósito (Argentina); Attendance: 73,000
PER: César Chávez Riva (6/0), Leonardo Rojas (33/0), Pedro Requena (38/0), José Guillermo del Solar Alvarez-Calderón (11/0), Octavio Vidales (1/0) [32.Jorge Talavera (4/1)], Javier Chirinos (20/0) [56.Juan Carlos Bazalar Cruzado (1/0)], José Luis Carranza (5/0) [*sent off 48*], Leoncio Cervera (1/0) [63.César Eduardo Rodríguez (1/0)], Luis Alberto Reyna Navarro (35/1) [72.Martín Ramírez (1/0)], Eduardo Rey Muñoz (13/0) [85.Luis Falcón (1/0)], Carlos Torres (1/1). Trainer: José Macia „Pepe“ (1).
Goal: Carlos Torres (61).

311. 15.05.1989 **PARAGUAY - PERU** **1-1(0-0)**
Estadio Defensores del Chaco, Asunción; Referee: Estanislao Barrientos (Paraguay); Attendance: 20,000
PER: Jesús Purizaga (3/0), José Luis Carranza (6/0), Pedro Requena (39/1), José Guillermo del Solar Alvarez-Calderón (12/0), Jorge Talavera (5/1), Luis Alberto Reyna Navarro (36/1), Juan Carlos Bazalar Cruzado (2/0), Leoncio Cervera (2/0), César Eduardo Rodríguez (2/0), Ricardo Zegarra (1/0) [65.Eduardo Rey Muñoz (14/0)], Carlos Torres (2/1). Trainer: José Macia „Pepe“ (2).
Goal: Pedro Requena (76 penalty).

312. 18.05.1989 **PERU - VENEZUELA** **2-1(0-0)**
Estadio Nacional, Lima; Referee: Walter Barrios (Peru); Attendance: 4,065
PER: Jesús Purizaga (4/0), Jorge Talavera (6/1), Pedro Requena (40/1), José Guillermo del Solar Alvarez-Calderón (13/0), Carlos Guido (1/0), Jorge Cordero (8/0) [46.Ricardo Zegarra (2/0)], Juan Carlos Bazalar Cruzado (3/0) [63.Alfonso Orlando Yáñez (1/0)], Juan Máximo Reynoso Guzmán (12/0), César Eduardo Rodríguez (3/0) [85.Antonio Alguedas (1/0)], Eduardo Rey Muñoz (15/1), Carlos Torres (3/1) [74.Luis Alberto Reyna Navarro (37/1)]. Trainer: José Macia „Pepe“ (3).
Goals: Ricardo Zagarra (63), Eduardo Rey Muñoz (83).

313. 24.05.1989 **PERU - BRAZIL** **1-1(0-1)**
Estadio Nacional, Lima; Referee: Sérgio Leiblinger (Peru); Attendance: 9,815
PER: Jesús Purizaga (5/0), Jorge Talavera (7/1) [71.Carlos Guido (2/0)], Pedro Requena (41/1), Jorge Andrés Olaechea Quijandría (52/1), Percy Celso Olivares Polanco (10/0), Francesco Manassero (2/0) [77.Jorge Cordero (9/0)], Juan Máximo Reynoso Guzmán (13/0), José Guillermo del Solar Alvarez-Calderón (14/0), César Eduardo Rodríguez (4/0), Martín Dall'Orso (1/1), Eduardo Rey Muñoz (16/1). Trainer: José Macia „Pepe“ (4).
Goal: Martin Dall' Orso (76).

314. 04.06.1989 **UNITED STATES - PERU** **3-0(3-0)** Marlboro Cup
Giants Stadium, East Rutherford, New York; Referee: Derek Douglas (Canada); Attendance: 33,133
PER: Gustavo Gonzáles (1/0) [46.Jesús Purizaga (6/0)], Percy Celso Olivares Polanco (11/0), Jorge Andrés Olaechea Quijandría (53/1), Jorge Arteaga (1/0), Carlos Guido (3/0), Francesco Manassero (3/0) [54.Luis Alberto Reyna Navarro (38/1)], Juan Máximo Reynoso Guzmán (14/0) [46.Alfonso Orlando Yáñez (2/0)], José Guillermo del Solar Alvarez-Calderón (15/0), César Eduardo Rodríguez (5/0), Martín Dall'Orso (2/1) [69.César Loyola (8/0)], Eduardo Rey Muñoz (17/1) [80.Carlos Torres (4/1)]. Trainer: José Macia „Pepe“ (5).

315. 16.06.1989 **TRINIDAD & TOBAGO - PERU** **2-1(2-1)** Soccer Bowl '89
Queen's Park Oval Stadium, Port of Spain; Referee: Hubert Tromp (Aruba); Attendance: 5,000
PER: Jesús Purizaga (7/0) [46.César Chávez Riva (7/0)], Pedro Sanjinez (1/0), Jorge Andrés Olaechea Quijandría (54/1), Jorge Arteaga (2/0), Percy Celso Olivares Polanco (12/0), Francesco Manassero (4/1) [70.Martín Dall'Orso (3/1)], Juan Máximo Reynoso Guzmán (15/0), José Guillermo del Solar Alvarez-Calderón (16/0), César Eduardo Rodríguez (6/0) [46.Alfonso Orlando Yáñez (3/0)], Eduardo Rey Muñoz (18/1) [80.César Loyola (9/0)], Franco Enrique Navarro Monteiro (47/14). Trainer: José Macia „Pepe“ (6).
Goal: Francesco Manassero (7).

316. 20.06.1989 **PERU - ECUADOR** **2-1(1-1)** Soccer Bowl '89
Queen's Park Oval Stadium, Port of Spain (Trinidad Tobago)
PER: César Chávez Riva (8/0), Percy Celso Olivares Polanco (13/0), Jorge Arteaga (3/0), José Guillermo del Solar Alvarez-Calderón (17/0), Carlos Guido (4/0), Francesco Manassero (5/1), Juan Máximo Reynoso Guzmán (16/0), Jorge Andrés Olaechea Quijandría (55/2), César Eduardo Rodríguez (7/0) [65.Jorge Cordero (10/0)], Eduardo Rey Muñoz (19/1) [83.César Loyola (10/0)], Franco Enrique Navarro Monteiro (48/15) [61.Martín Dall'Orso (4/1)]. Trainer: José Macia „Pepe“ (7).
Goals: Jorge Andrés Olaechea Quijandría (45 penalty), Franco Enrique Navarro Monteiro (58).

317. 25.06.1989 **VENEZUELA - PERU** **3-1(0-0)**
Estadio Pueblo Nuevo, San Cristóbal; Referee: Arnaldo Gómez (Colombia); Attendance: 20,000
PER: César Chávez Riva (9/0), Pedro Sanjinez (2/0), Jorge Arteaga (4/0), José Guillermo del Solar Alvarez-Calderón (18/0), Carlos Guido (5/0), Francesco Manassero (6/1) [88.Pedro Requena (42/1)], Wilmar Valencia (8/0) [46.César Eduardo Rodríguez (8/1)], Juan Máximo Reynoso Guzmán (17/0), Jorge Andrés Olaechea Quijandría (56/2) [*sent off 57*], Franco Enrique Navarro Monteiro (49/15) [70.Martín Dall'Orso (5/1)], Jorge Hirano (19/5) [77.César Loyola (11/0)]. Trainer: José Macia „Pepe“ (8).
Goal: César Rodríguez (78).

318. 01.07.1989 **PARAGUAY – PERU** **5-2(2-1)** 34th Copa América. Group Stage
Estádio Fonte Nova, Salvador; Referee: Juan Carlos Loustau (Argentina); Attendance: 5,000
PER: César Chávez Riva (10/0), José Luis Carranza (7/0) [70.Jorge Talavera (8/1)], Jorge Arteaga (5/0), José Guillermo del Solar Alvarez-Calderón (19/0), Percy Celso Olivares Polanco (14/0), Francesco Manassero (7/1), Wilmar Valencia (9/0) [63.Eduardo Rey Muñoz (20/1)], Juan Máximo Reynoso Guzmán (18/1), Julio César Uribe Flores (35/9), Franco Enrique Navarro Monteiro (50/15), Jorge Hirano (20/6). Trainer: José Macia „Pepe“ (9).
Goals: Jorge Hirano (30), Juan Máximo Reynoso Guzmán (80).

319. 03.07.1989 **BRAZIL – PERU** **0-0** 34th Copa América. Group Stage
Estádio Fonte Nova, Salvador; Referee: Hernán Silva Arce (Chile); Attendance: 8,223
PER: Jesús Purizaga (8/0) [*sent off 84*], José Luis Carranza (8/0), Jorge Andrés Olaechea Quijandría (57/2), Pedro Requena (43/1), Percy Celso Olivares Polanco (15/0), Wilmar Valencia (10/0), Juan Máximo Reynoso Guzmán (19/1), José Guillermo del Solar Alvarez-Calderón (20/0), Julio César Uribe Flores (36/9), Franco Enrique Navarro Monteiro (51/15) [84.César Chávez Riva (11/0)], Jorge Hirano (21/6) [55.Francesco Manassero (8/1)]. Trainer: José Macia „Pepe“ (10).

320. 05.07.1989 **PERU – VENEZUELA** **1-1(0-0)** 34th Copa América. Group Stage
Estádio Fonte Nova, Salvador; Referee: Vincent Mauro (United States); Attendance: 1,500
PER: César Chávez Riva (12/0), José Luis Carranza (9/0), José Guillermo del Solar Alvarez-Calderón (21/0), Pedro Requena (44/1), Percy Celso Olivares Polanco (16/0), Francesco Manassero (9/1), Wilmar Valencia (11/0) [46.Eduardo Rey Muñoz (21/1)], Juan Máximo Reynoso Guzmán (20/1), Julio César Uribe Flores (37/9), Franco Enrique Navarro Monteiro (52/16), Jorge Hirano (22/6) [61.César Eduardo Rodríguez (9/1)]. Trainer: José Macia „Pepe“ (11).
Goal: Franco Enrique Navarro Monteiro (75).

321. 09.07.1989 **COLOMBIA – PERU** **1-1(1-1)** 34th Copa América. Group Stage
Estádio Arruda, Recife; Referee: Juan Carlos Loustau (Argentina); Attendance: 30,000
PER: Jesús Purizaga (9/0), José Luis Carranza (10/0) [70.Carlos Guido (6/0), 86.Jorge Arteaga (6/0)], Jorge Andrés Olaechea Quijandría (58/2), Pedro Requena (45/1), Percy Celso Olivares Polanco (17/0), Wilmar Valencia (12/0), Juan Máximo Reynoso Guzmán (21/1), José Guillermo del Solar Alvarez-Calderón (22/0), Julio César Uribe Flores (38/9), Franco Enrique Navarro Monteiro (53/16), Jorge Hirano (23/7). Trainer: José Macia „Pepe“ (12).
Goal: Jorge Hirano (42).

322. 25.07.1989 **CHILE – PERU** **2-1(1-0)**
Estadio „Carlos Dittborn“, Arica; Referee: Juan Oscar Ortubé Vargas (Bolivia); Attendance: 10,430
PER: Jesús Purizaga (10/0), José Luis Carranza (11/0) [62.Pedro Sanjinez (3/0)], Pedro Requena (46/1), Jorge Andrés Olaechea Quijandría (59/2), Percy Celso Olivares Polanco (18/0), Wilmar Valencia (13/0) [46.Juan Carlos Bazalar Cruzado (4/0)], Juan Máximo Reynoso Guzmán (22/2), José Guillermo del Solar Alvarez-Calderón (23/0), Francesco Manassero (10/1), Franco Enrique Navarro Monteiro (54/16) [78.Martín Dall'Orso (6/1) [*sent off 87*]], Jorge Hirano (24/7). Trainer: José Macia „Pepe“ (13).
Goal: Juan Máximo Reynoso Guzmán (86).

323. 20.08.1989 **BOLIVIA – PERU** **2-1(1-1)** 14th FIFA WC. Qualifiers
Estadio „Hernándo Siles Zuazo“, La Paz; Referee: Armando Pérez Hoyos (Colombia); Attendance: 43,000
PER: Jesús Purizaga (11/0), José Luis Carranza (12/0), Jorge Andrés Olaechea Quijandría (60/2), Pedro Requena (47/1), Percy Celso Olivares Polanco (19/0), Wilmar Valencia (14/0), Juan Máximo Reynoso Guzmán (23/2) [67.Jesús Torrealba (3/0)], José Guillermo del Solar Alvarez-Calderón (24/1), Fidel Suárez (4/0), Franco Enrique Navarro Monteiro (55/16) [77.Eduardo Rey Muñoz (22/1)], Jorge Hirano (25/7). Trainer: José Macia „Pepe“ (14).
Goal: José Guillermo del Solar Alvarez-Calderón (43).

324. 27.08.1989 **PERU – URUGUAY** **0-2(0-0)** 14th FIFA WC. Qualifiers
Estadio Nacional, Lima; Referee: Carlos Espósito (Argentina); Attendance: 35,000
PER: Jesús Purizaga (12/0), Jorge Arteaga (7/0), Pedro Requena (48/1), José Guillermo del Solar Alvarez-Calderón (25/1), Percy Celso Olivares Polanco (20/0), José Luis Carranza (13/0), Juan Máximo Reynoso Guzmán (24/2), Julio César Uribe Flores (39/9), Jorge Hirano (26/7) [73.Francesco Manassero (11/1)], Martín Dall'Orso (7/1), Franco Enrique Navarro Monteiro (56/16). Trainer: José Macia „Pepe“ (15).

325. 10.09.1989 **PERU – BOLIVIA** **1-2(0-1)** 14th FIFA WC. Qualifiers
Estadio Nacional, Lima; Referee: Carlos Alberto Maciel (Paraguay); Attendance: 9,500
PER: Jesús Purizaga (13/0), Jorge Arteaga (8/0), Pedro Requena (49/1), José Guillermo del Solar Alvarez-Calderón (26/1), Percy Celso Olivares Polanco (21/0), Francesco Manassero (12/1 [46.Alfonso Orlando Yáñez (4/0)], Juan Máximo Reynoso Guzmán (25/2) [*sent off 33*], Luis Alberto Reyna Navarro (39/1) [46.Carlos Torres (5/1)], Jorge Hirano (27/7), Eduardo Rey Muñoz (23/1), Andrés Gonzáles (1/1). Trainer: José Macia „Pepe“ (16).
Goal: Andrés Gonzáles (53).

326. 24.09.1989 **URUGUAY – PERU** **2-0(1-0)** 14th FIFA WC. Qualifiers
Estadio Centenario, Montevideo; Referee: José Roberto Wright (Brazil); Attendance: 57,000
PER: Jesús Purizaga (14/0), Pedro Sanjinez (4/0), Jorge Arteaga (9/0), Pedro Requena (50/1), Carlos Guido (7/0), José Luis Carranza (14/0), Juan Máximo Reynoso Guzmán (26/2) [*sent off 34*], José Guillermo del Solar Alvarez-Calderón (27/1), Alfonso Orlando Yáñez (5/0) [62.Francesco Manassero (13/1)], Andrés Gonzáles (2/1), Jorge Hirano (28/7) [53.Juan Carlos Bazalar Cruzado (5/0)]. Trainer: Percy Rojas Montero (1).

327. 06.06.1991 **PERU – ECUADOR** **0-1(0-0)**
Estadio Nacional, Lima; Referee: Fernando Chapell (Peru); Attendance: 10,000
PER: Jesús Purizaga (15/0), Percy Celso Olivares Polanco (22/0), Jorge Arteaga (10/0), Álvaro Barco (3/0), Carlos Guido (8/0), José Luis Carranza (15/0), Jorge Cordero (11/0) [66.Martín Rodríguez (1/0)], Alfonso Orlando Yáñez (6/0), César Eduardo Rodríguez (10/1), Andrés Gonzáles (3/1) [66.Ernesto Aguirre (1/0)], Jorge Hirano (29/7) [66.Isidro Fuentes (1/0)]. Trainer: Miguel Alejandro Company Chumpitazi (1).

328. 12.06.1991 **PERU – URUGUAY** **1-0(0-0)**
Estadio Nacional, Lima; Referee: José Ramírez (Peru); Attendance: 16,500
PER: Jesús Purizaga (16/0), Percy Celso Olivares Polanco (23/0), Jorge Arteaga (11/0), Álvaro Barco (4/0), Octavio Vidales (2/0), José Luis Carranza (16/0) [46.Roberto Martínez (10/0)], Jorge Cordero (12/0) [46.Martín Rodríguez (2/0)], Alfonso Orlando Yáñez (7/0), César Eduardo Rodríguez (11/1), Ernesto Aguirre (2/0), Jorge Hirano (30/8) [57.Eugenio La Rosa (12/1)]. Trainer: Miguel Alejandro Company Chumpitazi (2).
Goal: Jorge Hirano (51).

329. 20.06.1991 **URUGUAY – PERU** **0-0**
Estadio Centenario, Montevideo; Referee: Roberto Otello (Uruguay); Attendance: 12,000
PER: Jesús Purizaga (17/0), Ricardo Alberto Bravo (1/0), Percy Celso Olivares Polanco (24/0), Jorge Arteaga (12/0), José Guillermo del Solar Alvarez-Calderón (28/1), Alfonso Orlando Yáñez (8/0) [72.Jorge Cordero (13/0)], Álvaro Barco (5/0), Martín Rodríguez (3/0), Roberto Martínez (11/0) [*sent off 68*], Andrés Gonzáles (4/1) [*sent off 64*], Jorge Hirano (31/8) [76.Ernesto Aguirre (3/0)]. Trainer: Miguel Alejandro Company Chumpitazi (3).

330. 25.06.1991 **ECUADOR - PERU** **2-2(2-0)**

Estadio Monumental de Barcelona, Guayaquil; Referee: Jorge Orellana (Ecuador); Attendance: 10,000

PER: Jesús Purizaga (18/0), Percy Celso Olivares Polanco (25/0), José Guillermo del Solar Alvarez-Calderón (29/1), Jorge Arteaga (13/0), Ricardo Alberto Bravo (2/0), Álvaro Barco (6/0), Alfonso Orlando Yáñez (9/0) [64.Martín Ramírez (2/0)], César Eduardo Rodríguez (12/2) [83.Jorge Cordero (14/0)], Martín Rodríguez (4/0), Isidro Fuentes (2/0) [Flavio Francisco Maestri Andrade (1/0)], Jorge Hirano (32/9). Trainer: Miguel Alejandro Company Chumpitazi (4).

Goals: Jorge Hirano (53), César Eduardo Rodríguez (79).

331. 06.07.1991 **PARAGUAY - PERU** **1-0(1-0)** 35th Copa América. Group Stage

Estadio Nacional, Santiago; Referee: Oscar Ortubé (Bolivia); Attendance: 42,779

PER: Jesús Purizaga (19/0), Ricardo Alberto Bravo (3/0), José Guillermo del Solar Alvarez-Calderón (30/1), Jorge Arteaga (14/0), Percy Celso Olivares Polanco (26/0), Álvaro Barco (7/0), Martín Rodríguez (5/0), César Eduardo Rodríguez (13/2) [46.Flavio Francisco Maestri Andrade (2/0)], Alfonso Orlando Yáñez (10/0), Roberto Martínez (12/0), Jorge Hirano (33/9). Trainer: Miguel Alejandro Company Chumpitazi (5).

332. 08.07.1991 **CHILE - PERU** **4-2(1-0)** 35th Copa América. Group Stage

Estadio Municipal de Collao, Concepción; Referee: Ernesto Filippi Cavani (Uruguay); Attendance: 21,520

PER: Jesús Purizaga (20/0), Ricardo Alberto Bravo (4/0), José Guillermo del Solar Alvarez-Calderón (31/2), Jorge Arteaga (15/0), Percy Celso Olivares Polanco (27/0), Álvaro Barco (8/0), Martín Rodríguez (6/0), Eugenio La Rosa (13/1), Jorge Hirano (34/9), Flavio Francisco Maestri Andrade (3/1) [67.César Eduardo Rodríguez (14/2)], Alfonso Orlando Yáñez (11/0). Trainer: Miguel Alejandro Company Chumpitazi (6).

Goals: Flavio Francisco Maestri Andrade (59), José Guillermo del Solar Alvarez-Calderón (71).

333. 12.07.1991 **PERU - VENEZUELA** **5-1(2-1)** 35th Copa América. Group Stage

Estadio Nacional, Santiago; Referee: Armando Pérez Hoyos (Colombia); Attendance: 13,876

PER: Jesús Purizaga (21/0), Ricardo Alberto Bravo (5/0), José Guillermo del Solar Alvarez-Calderón (32/3), Jorge Arteaga (16/0), Percy Celso Olivares Polanco (28/0) [34.Octavio Vidales (3/0)], Álvaro Barco (9/0), Martín Rodríguez (7/0), Alfonso Orlando Yáñez (12/0), César Eduardo Rodríguez (15/3) [57.Roberto Martínez (13/0)], Eugenio La Rosa (14/3), Jorge Hirano (35/10). Trainer: Miguel Alejandro Company Chumpitazi (7).

Goals: Eugenio La Rosa (9), César Eduardo Rodríguez (21), Eugenio La Rosa (55), José Guillermo del Solar Alvarez-Calderón (58), Jorge Hirano (62).

334. 14.07.1991 **ARGENTINA - PERU** **3-2(1-1)** 35th Copa América. Group Stage

Estadio Nacional, Santiago; Referee: Juan Oscar Ortubé Vargas (Bolivia); Attendance: 67,902

PER: Jesús Purizaga (22/0) [55.Diosdada Palma (1/0)], Ricardo Alberto Bravo (6/0), José Guillermo del Solar Alvarez-Calderón (33/3), Jorge Arteaga (17/0), Octavio Vidales (4/0), Álvaro Barco (10/0), Martín Rodríguez (8/0), César Eduardo Rodríguez (16/3), Alfonso Orlando Yáñez (13/1), Jorge Hirano (36/11), Eugenio La Rosa (15/3) [66.Ernesto Aguirre (4/0)]. Trainer: Miguel Alejandro Company Chumpitazi (8).

Goals: Alfonso Orlando Yáñez (35 penalty), Jorge Hirano (65).

335. 25.11.1992 **PERU - ECUADOR** **1-1(0-1)**

Estadio Nacional, Lima; Referee: José Arana (Peru); Attendance: 7,000

PER: Carlos Marrou (1/0), Jorge Antonio Soto Gómez (1/0), Juan Máximo Reynoso Guzmán (27/2), Pedro Requena (Cap) (51/1), Germán Ernesto Pinillos Rioja (1/0), José Luis Carranza (17/0), Álvaro Barco (11/0) [83.José Alberto Soto Gómez (1/0)], Roberto Martínez (14/0), Roberto Carlos Palacios Mestas (1/0), Julio César Rivera (1/0), Alberto Ramírez (1/1) [80.Flavio Francisco Maestri Andrade (4/1)]. Trainer: Vladimir Popović (1).

Goal: Alberto Ramírez (49).

336. 23.01.1993 **VENEZUELA - PERU** **0-0**

Estadio Polideportivo Cachamay, Puerto Ordaz; Referee: Juan José Torres (Venezuela); Attendance: 15,000

PER: Rafael Alfredo Quesada Parodi (1/0), Jorge Antonio Soto Gómez (2/0), Juan Máximo Reynoso Guzmán (28/2), Martín Duffóo (2/0), Germán Ernesto Pinillos Rioja (2/0), José Luis Carranza (18/0), Roberto Martínez (15/0), José Alberto Soto Gómez (2/0) [60.Mario Rodríguez (1/0)], Roberto Carlos Palacios Mestas (2/0), Julio César Rivera (2/0) [65.Ronald Pablo Baroni Ambrosi (1/0)], Flavio Francisco Maestri Andrade (5/1) [70.Raúl Hurtado (1/0)]. Trainer: Vladimir Popović (2).

337. 27.01.1993 **PERU - HONDURAS** **1-1(1-0)**

Estadio Nacional, Lima; Referee: Alberto Tejada (Peru)

PER: Agapito Rodríguez (1/0), César Augusto Charún Pastor (1/0) [65.Mario Rodríguez (2/0)], Jorge Arteaga (18/0), Juan Máximo Reynoso Guzmán (29/2), Germán Ernesto Pinillos Rioja (3/0), Jorge Antonio Soto Gómez (3/0), Roberto Carlos Palacios Mestas (3/0) [66.Marco Valencia (1/0)], José Luis Carranza (19/1), Roberto Martínez (16/0), Julio César Rivera (3/0) [57.Darío Teodoro Muchotrigo Carrillo (1/0)], Flavio Francisco Maestri Andrade (6/1) [57.Ronald Pablo Baroni Ambrosi (2/0)]. Trainer: Vladimir Popović (3).

Goal: José Luis Carranza (39).

338. 30.01.1993 **PERU - BELARUS** **1-1(1-1)**

Estadio Nacional, Lima; Referee: Antonio Arnao Ortega (Peru); Attendance: 10,000

PER: Carlos Marrou (2/0), Germán Ernesto Pinillos Rioja (4/0), Jorge Antonio Soto Gómez (4/0), Jorge Arteaga (19/0), Juan Máximo Reynoso Guzmán (30/2), Mario Rodríguez (3/0), José Luis Carranza (20/1), Roberto Martínez (17/0) [64.Roberto Carlos Palacios Mestas (4/0)], Alberto Ramírez (Cap) (2/1), Ronald Pablo Baroni Ambrosi (3/1), Julio César Rivera (4/0) [61.Darío Teodoro Muchotrigo Carrillo (2/0)]. Trainer: Vladimir Popović (4).

Goal: Ronald Pablo Baroni Ambrosi (14).

339. 03.02.1993 **PERU - ROMANIA** **0-2(0-1)**

Estadio Nacional, Lima; Referee: Fernando Chappel Merino (Peru); Attendance: 10,000

PER: Rafael Alfredo Quesada Parodi (2/0), César Augusto Charún Pastor (2/0), Martín Duffóo (3/0), Juan Máximo Reynoso Guzmán (31/2) [40.Manuel Earl (1/0)], Germán Ernesto Pinillos Rioja (5/0), Jorge Antonio Soto Gómez (5/0) [60.Mario Rodríguez (4/0)], José Luis Carranza (21/1), Freddy Torrealba (1/0) [57.Roberto Carlos Palacios Mestas (5/0)], Julio César Rivera (5/0), Raúl Hurtado (2/0) [70.Alberto Ramírez (3/1)], Ronald Pablo Baroni Ambrosi (4/1) [65.Darío Teodoro Muchotrigo Carrillo (3/0)]. Trainer: Vladimir Popović (5).

340. 26.05.1993 **UNITED STATES - PERU** **0-0**

Trabucco Hills Stadium, Mission Viejo; Referee: Arturo Angeles (United States); Attendance: 5,500

PER: Miguel Eduardo Miranda Campos (1/0), Jorge Antonio Soto Gómez (6/0), Juan Máximo Reynoso Guzmán (32/2), Percy Celso Olivares Polanco (29/0), José Alberto Soto Gómez (3/0), José Luis Carranza (22/1), Juan Carlos Bazalar Cruzado (6/0), Pablo César Zegarra Zamora (1/0), Álvaro Barco (12/0) [69.Mario Rodríguez (5/0)], Flavio Francisco Maestri Andrade (7/1) [50.Andrés Gonzáles (5/1)], Julio César Rivera (6/0). Trainer: Vladimir Popović (6).

341. 30.05.1993 **ECUADOR – PERU** **1-0(1-0)**
Estadio Olimpico „Atahualpa", Quito; Referee: Marco Aguas (Ecuador); Attendance: 24,000
PER: Miguel Eduardo Miranda Campos (2/0), Jorge Antonio Soto Gómez (7/0), José Alberto Soto Gómez (4/0), Juan Máximo Reynoso Guzmán (33/2), Percy Celso Olivares Polanco (30/0), José Luis Carranza (23/1) [70.Mario Rodríguez (6/0)], Juan Carlos Bazalar Cruzado (7/0), Roberto Martínez (18/0) [66.Waldir Alejandro Sáenz Pérez (1/0)], Pablo César Zegarra Zamora (2/0), Andrés Gonzáles (6/1), Julio César Rivera (7/0). Trainer: Vladimir Popović (7).

342. 06.06.1993 **PERU – BOLIVIA** **1-0(1-0)**
Estadio Nacional, Lima; Referee: Luis Seminario (Peru)
PER: Miguel Eduardo Miranda Campos (3/0), Jorge Antonio Soto Gómez (8/0) [69.Álvaro Barco (13/0)], José Alberto Soto Gómez (5/0), Juan Máximo Reynoso Guzmán (34/2), Percy Celso Olivares Polanco (31/0), José Luis Carranza (24/1), Mario Rodríguez (7/0) [63.César Augusto Charún Pastor (3/0)], Pablo César Zegarra Zamora (3/0) [46.Roberto Martínez (19/0)], Julio César Rivera (8/0), Andrés Gonzáles (7/2) [72.Waldir Alejandro Sáenz Pérez (2/0)], Flavio Francisco Maestri Andrade (8/1). Trainer: Vladimir Popović (8).
Goal: Andrés Gonzáles (22).

343. 11.06.1993 **PERU – VENEZUELA** **3-1(2-0)**
Estadio Centenario, Arequipa; Referee: Antonio Arnao Ortega (Peru); Attendance: 18,000
PER: Miguel Eduardo Miranda Campos (4/0), Jorge Antonio Soto Gómez (9/0) [70.César Augusto Charún Pastor (4/0)], José Alberto Soto Gómez (6/0), Juan Máximo Reynoso Guzmán (35/2), Percy Celso Olivares Polanco (32/0), José Luis Carranza (25/1) [Álvaro Barco (14/0)], Pablo César Zegarra Zamora (4/0), José Guillermo del Solar Alvarez-Calderón (34/3), Roberto Martínez (20/1), Julio César Rivera (9/0), Flavio Francisco Maestri Andrade (9/3) [59.Andrés Gonzáles (8/2)]. Trainer: Vladimir Popović (9).
Goals: Flavio Francisco Maestri Andrade (13), Roberto Martínez (42), Flavio Francisco Maestri Andrade (63).

344. 18.06.1993 **PERU – BRAZIL** **0-0** 36th Copa América. Group Stage
Estadio „Alejandro Serrano Aguilar", Cuenca (Ecuador); Referee: Arturo Pablo Brizio Carter (Mexico); Attendance: 20,000
PER: Miguel Eduardo Miranda Campos (5/0), César Augusto Charún Pastor (5/0), Juan Máximo Reynoso Guzmán (36/2), José Alberto Soto Gómez (7/0), Percy Celso Olivares Polanco (33/0), Álvaro Barco (15/0), José Guillermo del Solar Alvarez-Calderón (35/3), José Luis Carranza (26/1), Pablo César Zegarra Zamora (5/0) [46.Roberto Carlos Palacios Mestas (6/0)], Julio César Rivera (10/0), Flavio Francisco Maestri Andrade (10/3) [79.Andrés Gonzáles (9/2)]. Trainer: Vladimir Popović (10).

345. 21.06.1993 **PERU – PARAGUAY** **1-1(0-1)** 36th Copa América. Group Stage
Estadio „Alejandro Serrano Aguilar", Cuenca (Ecuador); Referee: Ángel Guevara (Ecuador); Attendance: 20,000
PER: Miguel Eduardo Miranda Campos (6/0), César Augusto Charún Pastor (6/0) [57.Roberto Martínez (21/1)], Juan Máximo Reynoso Guzmán (37/2), José Alberto Soto Gómez (8/0), Percy Celso Olivares Polanco (34/0), Álvaro Barco (16/0), José Guillermo del Solar Alvarez-Calderón (36/4), José Luis Carranza (27/1), Pablo César Zegarra Zamora (6/0) [57.Andrés Gonzáles (10/2)], Julio César Rivera (11/0), Flavio Francisco Maestri Andrade (11/3). Trainer: Vladimir Popović (11).
Goal: José Guillermo del Solar Alvarez-Calderón (77).

346. 24.06.1993 **PERU – CHILE** **1-0(1-0)** 36th Copa América. Group Stage
Estadio „Alejandro Serrano Aguilar", Cuenca (Ecuador); Referee: José Joaquín Torres Cadena (Colombia); Attendance: 25,000
PER: Miguel Eduardo Miranda Campos (7/0), César Augusto Charún Pastor (7/0), Juan Máximo Reynoso Guzmán (38/2), José Alberto Soto Gómez (9/0), Percy Celso Olivares Polanco (35/0), Álvaro Barco (17/0), José Guillermo del Solar Alvarez-Calderón (37/5), Roberto Martínez (22/1), Pablo César Zegarra Zamora (7/0) [76.Roberto Carlos Palacios Mestas (7/0)], Julio César Rivera (12/0), Flavio Francisco Maestri Andrade (12/3) [66.Andrés Gonzáles (11/2)]. Trainer: Vladimir Popović (12).
Goal: José Guillermo del Solar Alvarez-Calderón (14 penalty).

347. 27.06.1993 **MEXICO – PERU** **4-2(3-0)** 36th Copa América. Quarter-Finals
Estadio Olimpico „Atahualpa", Quito (Ecuador); Referee: Iván Guerrero (Chile); Attendance: 35,000
PER: Miguel Eduardo Miranda Campos (8/0), César Augusto Charún Pastor (8/0), Juan Máximo Reynoso Guzmán (39/3), José Alberto Soto Gómez (10/0), Percy Celso Olivares Polanco (36/0), Álvaro Barco (18/0), José Guillermo del Solar Alvarez-Calderón (38/6), Pablo César Zegarra Zamora (8/0), Roberto Martínez (23/1) [46.Roberto Carlos Palacios Mestas (8/0)], Julio César Rivera (13/0), Flavio Francisco Maestri Andrade (13/3) [53.Luis Germán del Carmen Carty Monserrate (1/0)]. Trainer: Vladimir Popović (13).
Goals: José Guillermo del Solar Alvarez-Calderón (63 penalty), Juan Máximo Reynoso Guzmán (77).

348. 13.07.1993 **PERU – URUGUAY** **1-2(0-1)**
Estadio Nacional, Lima; Referee: Luis Ángel Seminario (Peru); Attendance: 16,050
PER: Miguel Eduardo Miranda Campos (9/0), Carlos Gonzáles (1/0) [60.Darío Teodoro Muchotrigo Carrillo (4/0)], Juan Máximo Reynoso Guzmán (Cap) (40/3), José Alberto Soto Gómez (11/0), Percy Celso Olivares Polanco (37/0), Álvaro Barco (19/0), José Guillermo del Solar Alvarez-Calderón (39/6), Roberto Carlos Palacios Mestas (9/0), Marco Valencia (2/0) [60.Pablo César Zegarra Zamora (9/0)], Waldir Alejandro Sáenz Pérez (3/1), Andrés Gonzáles (12/2). Trainer: Vladimir Popović (14).
Goal: Waldir Alejandro Sáenz Pérez (88).

349. 17.07.1993 **URUGUAY – PERU** **3-0(3-0)**
Estadio Centenario, Montevideo; Referee: Daniel Bello (Uruguay); Attendance: 60,000
PER: Miguel Eduardo Miranda Campos (10/0), Mario Rodríguez (8/0) [62.César Augusto Charún Pastor (9/0)], Juan Máximo Reynoso Guzmán (Cap) (41/3), José Alberto Soto Gómez (12/0), Percy Celso Olivares Polanco (38/0), Álvaro Barco (20/0), José Guillermo del Solar Alvarez-Calderón (40/6), Roberto Carlos Palacios Mestas (10/0), Marco Valencia (3/0) [62.Pablo César Zegarra Zamora (10/0)], Andrés Gonzáles (13/2) [77.Luis Germán del Carmen Carty Monserrate (2/0)], Waldir Alejandro Sáenz Pérez (4/1) [46.Darío Teodoro Muchotrigo Carrillo (5/0)]. Trainer: Vladimir Popović (15).

350. 01.08.1993 **PERU – ARGENTINA** **0-1(0-1)** 15th FIFA WC. Qualifiers
Estadio Nacional, Lima; Referee: Enrique Marín Gallo (Ecuador); Attendance: 27,000
PER: Miguel Eduardo Miranda Campos (11/0), Álvaro Barco (21/0), Jorge Antonio Soto Gómez (10/0) [*sent off 81*], Percy Celso Olivares Polanco (39/0), Juan Máximo Reynoso Guzmán (42/3) [*sent off 55*], José Luis Carranza (28/1), Roberto Martínez (24/1) [59.Darío Teodoro Muchotrigo Carrillo (6/0)], José Guillermo del Solar Alvarez-Calderón (41/6), Roberto Carlos Palacios Mestas (11/0), Andrés Gonzáles (14/2) [59.Flavio Francisco Maestri Andrade (14/3)], Julio César Rivera (14/0). Trainer: Vladimir Popović (16).

351. 08.08.1993 **PERU – COLOMBIA** **0-1(0-1)** 15th FIFA WC. Qualifiers
Estadio Nacional, Lima; Referee: Alfredo Rodas Iniguez (Ecuador); Attendance: 21,500
PER: Miguel Eduardo Miranda Campos (12/0), Julio César Rivera (15/0) [14.César Augusto Charún Pastor (10/0)], José Alberto Soto Gómez (13/0), Álvaro Barco (22/0), Percy Celso Olivares Polanco (40/0), José Luis Carranza (29/1), Roberto Carlos Palacios Mestas (12/0), José Guillermo del Solar Alvarez-Calderón (42/6), Pablo César Zegarra Zamora (11/0) [65.Waldir Alejandro Sáenz Pérez (5/1)], Darío Teodoro Muchotrigo Carrillo (7/0), Flavio Francisco Maestri Andrade (15/3). Trainer: Vladimir Popović (17).

352. 15.08.1993 **PARAGUAY – PERU** **2-1(2-1)** 15th FIFA WC. Qualifiers
Estadio Defensores del Chaco, Asunción; Referee: Francisco D'Abreu Faria (Venezuela); Attendance: 30,000
PER: Miguel Eduardo Miranda Campos (13/0), César Augusto Charún Pastor (11/0) [49.Marco Valencia (4/0)], Álvaro Barco (23/0), José Alberto Soto Gómez (14/0), Percy Celso Olivares Polanco (41/0), José Luis Carranza (30/1), Pablo César Zegarra Zamora (12/0), José Guillermo del Solar Alvarez-Calderón (43/7), Juan Máximo Reynoso Guzmán (43/3), Ronald Pablo Baroni Ambrosi (5/1) [65.Darío Teodoro Muchotrigo Carrillo (8/0)], Luis Germán del Carmen Carty Monserrate (3/0). Trainer: Vladimir Popović (18).
Goal: José Guillermo del Solar Alvarez-Calderón (45 penalty).

353. 22.08.1993 **ARGENTINA – PERU** **2-1(2-0)** 15th FIFA WC. Qualifiers
Estadio Monumental „Antonio Vespucio Liberti", Buenos Aires; Referee: Jorge Luis Nieves Parra (Uruguay); Attendance: 47,730
PER: Miguel Eduardo Miranda Campos (14/0), José Alberto Soto Gómez (15/0), Percy Celso Olivares Polanco (42/0), José Luis Carranza (31/1), Álvaro Barco (24/0), Juan Máximo Reynoso Guzmán (44/3), Pablo César Zegarra Zamora (13/0), José Guillermo del Solar Alvarez-Calderón (44/7), Roberto Carlos Palacios Mestas (13/1), Andrés Gonzáles (15/2) [64.Darío Teodoro Muchotrigo Carrillo (9/0)], Ronald Pablo Baroni Ambrosi (6/1) [55.Flavio Francisco Maestri Andrade (16/3)]. Trainer: Vladimir Popović (19).
Goal: Roberto Carlos Palacios Mestas (66).

354. 29.08.1993 **COLOMBIA – PERU** **4-0(2-0)** 15th FIFA WC. Qualifiers
Estadio Metropolitano „Roberto Meléndez", Barranquilla; Referee: Pablo Peña Durán (Bolivia); Attendance: 70,000
PER: Miguel Eduardo Miranda Campos (15/0), Jorge Antonio Soto Gómez (11/0), José Alberto Soto Gómez (16/0), Álvaro Barco (25/0), Percy Celso Olivares Polanco (43/0) [74.César Augusto Charún Pastor (12/0)], José Luis Carranza (32/1), Juan Máximo Reynoso Guzmán (45/3), José Guillermo del Solar Alvarez-Calderón (45/7), Pablo César Zegarra Zamora (14/0), Andrés Gonzáles (16/2) [46.Darío Teodoro Muchotrigo Carrillo (10/0)], Ronald Pablo Baroni Ambrosi (7/1). Trainer: Vladimir Popović (20).

355. 05.09.1993 **PERU – PARAGUAY** **2-2(1-0)** 15th FIFA WC. Qualifiers
Estadio Nacional, Lima; Referee: José Larrosa (Uruguay); Attendance: 40,000
PER: Miguel Eduardo Miranda Campos (16/0), Jorge Antonio Soto Gómez (12/1), Juan Máximo Reynoso Guzmán (46/3), José Alberto Soto Gómez (17/0), Percy Celso Olivares Polanco (44/0), Álvaro Barco (26/0), José Guillermo del Solar Alvarez-Calderón (46/7), Pablo César Zegarra Zamora (15/0), Marco Valencia (5/0), Darío Teodoro Muchotrigo Carrillo (11/1), Ronald Pablo Baroni Ambrosi (8/1). Trainer: Vladimir Popović (21).
Goals: Darío Teodoro Muchotrigo Carrillo (31), Jorge Antonio Soto Gómez (77).

356. 03.05.1994 **PERU – COLOMBIA** **0-1(0-0)** Miami Cup
„Joe Robbie" Stadium, Miami (United States),Ref: H. Díaz (United States); Attendance: 10,000
PER: Miguel Eduardo Miranda Campos (17/0), Carlos Alberto Basombrío Ormeño (1/0) [*sent off 28*], Juan Máximo Reynoso Guzmán (47/3), Nolberto Albino Solano Todco (1/0), José Alberto Soto Gómez (18/0), Germán Muñoz (1/0), Ronald Pablo Baroni Ambrosi (9/1), Roberto Carlos Palacios Mestas (14/1), Percy Aguilar (1/0) [30.Juan Alexis Ubillús Calmet (1/0)], Martín Rodríguez (9/0), Julio César Rivera (16/0). Trainer: Miguel Alejandro Company Chumpitazi (9).

357. 05.05.1994 **HONDURAS – PERU** **2-1(0-1)** Miami Cup
„Joe Robbie" Stadium, Miami (United States); Referee: Arturo Angeles (United States); Attendance: 8,000
PER: Miguel Eduardo Miranda Campos (18/0), Carlos Alberto Basombrío Ormeño (2/0) [57.Alfonso Antonio Dulanto Corzo (1/0)], Juan Máximo Reynoso Guzmán (48/3), José Alberto Soto Gómez (19/0), Nolberto Albino Solano Todco (2/0), Germán Muñoz (2/0), Martín Rodríguez (10/0), Roberto Carlos Palacios Mestas (15/1), Julio César Rivera (17/0) [46.Manuel López (1/0)], Percy Aguilar (2/1) [64.Freddy Hidalgo (1/0)], Ronald Pablo Baroni Ambrosi (10/1). Trainer: Miguel Alejandro Company Chumpitazi (10).
Goal: Percy Aguilar (31).

358. 25.05.1994 **CHILE – PERU** **2-1(2-1)**
Estadio Nacional, Santiago; Referee: Sabino Fariña (Paraguay); Attendance: 23,892
PER: Francisco Pizarro (1/0), Jorge Antonio Soto Gómez (13/1), Juan Máximo Reynoso Guzmán (49/3) [7.Alfonso Antonio Dulanto Corzo (2/0)], José Alberto Soto Gómez (20/1), Percy Celso Olivares Polanco (45/0), Frank Palomino (1/0) [46.Germán Muñoz (3/0), José Luis Carranza (33/1), Martín Rodríguez (11/0), Roberto Carlos Palacios Mestas (16/1), Ronald Pablo Baroni Ambrosi (11/1) [46.Flavio Francisco Maestri Andrade (17/3)], Julio César Rivera (18/0) [62.Nolberto Albino Solano Todco (3/0)]. Trainer: Miguel Alejandro Company Chumpitazi (11).
Goal: José Alberto Soto Gómez (14).

359. 08.06.1994 **BOLIVIA – PERU** **0-0**
Estadio „Ramón 'Tahuichi' Aguilera", Santa Cruz de la Sierra; Referee: Pedro Saucedo Rodríguez (Bolivia); Attendance: 35,000
PER: Francisco Pizarro (2/0), Jorge Antonio Soto Gómez (14/1), Frank Ruiz (1/0), José Alberto Soto Gómez (21/1), Percy Celso Olivares Polanco (46/0), Roberto Carlos Palacios Mestas (17/1), Mario Rodríguez (9/0), Nolberto Albino Solano Todco (4/0), Juan José Jayo Legario (1/0), Julio César Rivera (19/0) [73.Martín Dall'Orso (8/1)], Flavio Francisco Maestri Andrade (18/3). Trainer: Miguel Alejandro Company Chumpitazi (12).

360. 17.08.1994 **PERU - ECUADOR** **2-0(1-0)**
Estadio Nacional, Lima; Referee: Luis Ángel Seminario Maura (Peru); Attendance: 12,000
PER: Francisco Pizarro (3/0), Jorge Antonio Soto Gómez (15/1), Alfonso Antonio Dulanto Corzo (3/0), José Alberto Soto Gómez (22/1), Juan Alexis Ubillús Calmet (2/0), José Luis Carranza (34/1), Juan José Jayo Legario (2/0), Nolberto Albino Solano Todco (5/0) [71.Julio César Rivera (20/0)], Roberto Carlos Palacios Mestas (18/2), Darío Teodoro Muchotrigo Carrillo (12/1) [62.Frank Palomino (2/0)], Waldir Alejandro Sáenz Pérez (6/2). Trainer: Miguel Alejandro Company Chumpitazi (13).
Goals: Roberto Carlos Palacios Mestas (31), Waldir Alejandro Sáenz Pérez (67).

361. 21.09.1994 **ECUADOR – PERU** **0-0**
Estadio Nueve de Marzo, Machala (Colombia); Referee: Jorge Orellana (Ecuador)
PER: Francisco Pizarro (4/0), Jorge Antonio Soto Gómez (16/1), José Alberto Soto Gómez (23/1), Alfonso Antonio Dulanto Corzo (4/0), Juan Alexis Ubillús Calmet (3/0), César Miguel Rosales Tardío (1/0) [46.Juan José Jayo Legario (3/0)], José Luis Carranza (35/1), Nolberto Albino Solano Todco (6/0) [70.Alfredo Enrique Carmona Hurtado (1/0)], Roberto Carlos Palacios Mestas (19/2), Darío Teodoro Muchotrigo Carrillo (13/1), Waldir Alejandro Sáenz Pérez (7/2) [46.Julio César Rivera (21/0)]. Trainer: Miguel Alejandro Company Chumpitazi (14).

362. 19.10.1994 **PERU – URUGUAY** **0-1(0-1)**
Estadio Nacional, Lima; Referee: Antonio Arnao Ortega (Peru); Attendance: 8,000
PER: Francisco Pizarro (5/0), José Alberto Soto Gómez (24/1), Jorge Antonio Soto Gómez (17/1), Alfonso Antonio Dulanto Corzo (5/0), Marcial Salazar (1/0), Juan José Jayo Legario (4/0) [76.César Miguel Rosales Tardío (2/0)], Roberto Carlos Palacios Mestas (20/2), José Luis Carranza (36/1), Nolberto Albino Solano Todco (7/0) [76.Alfredo Enrique Carmona Hurtado (2/0)], Waldir Alejandro Sáenz Pérez (8/2) [34.Julio César Rivera (22/0)], Darío Teodoro Muchotrigo Carrillo (14/1) [63.Carlos Dolorier (1/0)]. Trainer: Miguel Alejandro Company Chumpitazi (15).

363. 05.04.1995 **URUGUAY – PERU** **1-0(0-0)** El Inca Cup
Estadio Centenario, Montevideo; Referee: Gustavo Gallesio (Uruguay); Attendance: 10,000
PER: Miguel Eduardo Miranda Campos (19/0), Jorge Antonio Soto Gómez (18/1), José Alberto Soto Gómez (25/1), Alfonso Antonio Dulanto Corzo (6/0), Juan Alexis Ubillús Calmet (4/0), José Luis Carranza (37/1), Martín Rodríguez (12/0), Roberto Carlos Palacios Mestas (21/2), Álex Segundo Magallanes Jaimes (1/0) [70.Julio César Rivera (23/0)], Flavio Francisco Maestri Andrade (19/3), Ronald Pablo Baroni Ambrosi (12/1) [62.Nolberto Albino Solano Todco (8/0)]. Trainer: Miguel Alejandro Company Chumpitazi (16).

364. 19.04.1995 **PERU – CHILE** **6-0(4-0)**
Estadio Nacional, Lima; Referee: Juan Carlos Lugones (Bolivia); Attendance: 15,000
PER: Miguel Eduardo Miranda Campos (20/0), Jorge Antonio Soto Gómez (19/1), José Alberto Soto Gómez (26/1), Alfonso Antonio Dulanto Corzo (7/0), Juan Alexis Ubillús Calmet (5/0), Martín Rodríguez (13/0), José Luis Carranza (38/1), Álex Segundo Magallanes Jaimes (2/0) [61.Nolberto Albino Solano Todco (9/0)], Roberto Carlos Palacios Mestas (22/2) [76.Alessandro Morán Torres (1/0)], Flavio Francisco Maestri Andrade (20/6) [69.Alberto Ramírez (4/1)], Ronald Pablo Baroni Ambrosi (13/4). Trainer: Miguel Alejandro Company Chumpitazi (17).
Goals: Flavio Francisco Maestri Andrade (2, 6), Ronald Pablo Baroni Ambrosi (28), Flavio Francisco Maestri Andrade (39), Ronald Pablo Baroni Ambrosi (66, 77).

365. 31.05.1995 **ARGENTINA – PERU** **1-0(1-0)** Copa de Municipalidad Córdoba
Estadio Chateau Carreras, Córdoba; Referee: Daniel Bello Rotunno (Uruguay); Attendance: 15,000
PER: Miguel Eduardo Miranda Campos (21/0), Nolberto Albino Solano Todco (10/0), José Alberto Soto Gómez (27/1), Alfonso Antonio Dulanto Corzo (8/0), Juan Alexis Ubillús Calmet (6/0), Martín Rodríguez (14/0), José Luis Carranza (39/1), Roberto Carlos Palacios Mestas (23/2), Álex Segundo Magallanes Jaimes (3/0) [46.Alfredo Enrique Carmona Hurtado (3/0), 72.Germán Ernesto Pinillos Rioja (6/0)], Ronald Pablo Baroni Ambrosi (14/4), Julio César Rivera (24/0) [46.Martín García (1/0)]. Trainer: Miguel Alejandro Company Chumpitazi (18).

366. 25.06.1995 **PERU – SLOVAKIA** **1-0(0-0)**
Estadio Nacional, Lima; Referee: César Córdoba Nue (Peru); Attendance: 10,000
PER: Miguel Eduardo Miranda Campos (22/0), Jorge Antonio Soto Gómez (20/1), Juan Máximo Reynoso Guzmán (50/3) [46.Alberto Ramírez (5/1)], José Guillermo del Solar Alvarez-Calderón (47/7), Percy Celso Olivares Polanco (47/0) [70.Marcial Salazar (2/0)], José Alberto Soto Gómez (28/1), Nolberto Albino Solano Todco (11/1), Roberto Carlos Palacios Mestas (24/2), José Luis Carranza (40/1), Ronald Pablo Baroni Ambrosi (15/4), Julio César Rivera (25/0) [72.Martín Rodríguez (15/0)]. Trainer: Miguel Alejandro Company Chumpitazi (19).
Goal: Nolberto Albino Solano Todco (59 penalty).

367. 01.07.1995 **PERU – BOLIVIA** **4-1(2-1)**
Estadio Nacional, Lima; Referee: José Antonio Arana Villamonte (Peru); Attendance: 6,362
PER: Miguel Eduardo Miranda Campos (23/0), Jorge Antonio Soto Gómez (21/1) [67.Nolberto Albino Solano Todco (12/2)], Alfonso Antonio Dulanto Corzo (9/0), José Alberto Soto Gómez (29/1), Juan Alexis Ubillús Calmet (7/0), José Guillermo del Solar Alvarez-Calderón (48/7), José Luis Carranza (41/1), Germán Ernesto Pinillos Rioja (7/1) [74.Martín Rodríguez (16/0)], Roberto Carlos Palacios Mestas (25/2), Alberto Ramírez (6/3) [70.Julio César Rivera (26/0)], Ronald Pablo Baroni Ambrosi (16/4) [66.Luis Germán del Carmen Carty Monserrate (4/0)]. Trainer: Miguel Alejandro Company Chumpitazi (20).
Goals: Alberto Ramírez (26), Germán Ernesto Pinillos Rioja (43), Alberto Ramírez (66), Nolberto Albino Solano Todco (84).

368. 07.07.1995 **PERU – COLOMBIA** **1-1(0-0)** 37th Copa América. Group Stage
Estadio „Atilio Paiva Olivera", Rivera (Uruguay); Referee: Ernesto Filippi (Uruguay); Attendance: 5,000
PER: Miguel Eduardo Miranda Campos (24/0), Jorge Antonio Soto Gómez (22/1), Alfonso Antonio Dulanto Corzo (10/0), José Alberto Soto Gómez (30/1), Juan Alexis Ubillús Calmet (8/0) [73.Percy Celso Olivares Polanco (48/0)], José Luis Carranza (42/1), José Guillermo del Solar Alvarez-Calderón (49/7), Martin Rodríguez (17/0) [70.Germán Ernesto Pinillos Rioja (8/1)], Roberto Carlos Palacios Mestas (26/3), Ronald Pablo Baroni Ambrosi (17/4), Alberto Ramírez (7/3) [80.Luis Germán del Carmen Carty Monserrate (5/0)]. Trainer: Miguel Alejandro Company Chumpitazi (21).
Goal: Roberto Carlos Palacios Mestas (80).

369. 10.07.1995 **BRAZIL – PERU** **2-0(0-0)** 37th Copa América. Group Stage
Estadio „Atilio Paiva Olivera", Rivera (Uruguay); Referee: Félix Ramón Benegas Caballero (Paraguay); Attendance: 8,000
PER: Miguel Eduardo Miranda Campos (25/0), José Luis Carranza (43/1), José Alberto Soto Gómez (31/1), Alfonso Antonio Dulanto Corzo (11/0), Percy Celso Olivares Polanco (49/0), Germán Ernesto Pinillos Rioja (9/1) [84.Alberto Ramírez (8/3)], José Guillermo del Solar Alvarez-Calderón (50/7), Roberto Carlos Palacios Mestas (27/3), Martín Rodríguez (18/0) [46.Julio César Rivera (27/0)], Ronald Pablo Baroni Ambrosi (18/4), Luis Germán del Carmen Carty Monserrate (6/0) [46.Jorge Antonio Soto Gómez (23/1)]. Trainer: Miguel Alejandro Company Chumpitazi (22).

370. 13.07.1995 **ECUADOR – PERU** **2-1(0-0)** 37th Copa América. Group Stage
Estadio „Atilio Paiva Olivera", Rivera (Uruguay); Referee: Eduardo Dluzniewski (Uruguay); Attendance: 10,000
PER: Miguel Eduardo Miranda Campos (26/0), Julio César Rivera (28/0), Alfonso Antonio Dulanto Corzo (12/0), José Alberto Soto Gómez (32/1), Percy Celso Olivares Polanco (50/0), José Luis Carranza (44/1), José Guillermo del Solar Alvarez-Calderón (51/7), Alberto Ramírez (9/3) [46.Luis Germán del Carmen Carty Monserrate (7/0)], Nolberto Albino Solano Todco (13/2) [46.Martín Rodríguez (19/0)], Roberto Carlos Palacios Mestas (28/3), Ronald Pablo Baroni Ambrosi (19/4). Trainer: Miguel Alejandro Company Chumpitazi (23).
Goal: Iván Hurtado (82 own goal).

371. 11.02.1996 **PERU – BOLIVIA** **1-3(0-1)**
Estadio Nacional, Lima; Referee: José Antonio Arana Villamonte (Peru); Attendance: 10,000
PER: Héctor Martín Yupanqui (1/0), José Luis Reyna (1/0) [71.Juan Carlos Ormeño (1/0)], José Alberto Soto Gómez (33/1), Alfonso Antonio Dulanto Corzo (13/0), Juan Alexis Ubillús Calmet (9/0), Jorge Antonio Soto Gómez (24/1), Mario Rodríguez (10/0), Germán Ernesto Pinillos Rioja (10/2), Darío Teodoro Muchotrigo Carrillo (15/1) [64.Alfredo Enrique Carmona Hurtado (4/0)], Roberto Carlos Palacios Mestas (29/3), Flavio Francisco Maestri Andrade (21/6) [69.Ricardo Zegarra (3/1)]. Trainer: Juan Carlos Oblitas Saba (1).
Goal: Germán Ernesto Pinillos Rioja (72 penalty).

372. 14.02.1996 **CHILE - PERU** **4-0(2-0)**
Estadio "Francisco Sánchez Rumoroso", Coquimbo; Referee: Luis Héctor Olivetto (Argentina); Attendance: 14,000
PER: Rafael Alfredo Quesada Parodi (3/0), Jorge Antonio Soto Gómez (25/1), Juan Máximo Reynoso Guzmán (51/3), Alfonso Antonio Dulanto Corzo (14/0), Juan Alexis Ubillús Calmet (10/0), José Alberto Soto Gómez (34/1), Mario Rodríguez (11/0) [46.Julio César Rivera (29/0)], Germán Ernesto Pinillos Rioja (11/2), Roberto Carlos Palacios Mestas (30/3) [65.Alfredo Enrique Carmona Hurtado (5/0)], Pablo César Zegarra Zamora (16/0) [90.Juan Carlos Ormeño (2/0)], Ricardo Zegarra (4/1) [46.Alberto Ramírez (10/3)]. Trainer: Juan Carlos Oblitas Saba (2).

373. 07.03.1996 **BOLIVIA - PERU** **2-0(0-0)**
Estadio „Ramón 'Tahuichi' Aguilera", Santa Cruz de la Sierra; Referee: Juan Luna Humerez (Bolivia); Attendance: 8,000
PER: Francisco Pizarro (6/0), Nolberto Albino Solano Todco (14/2), Alfonso Antonio Dulanto Corzo (15/0), Emilio Martín Hidalgo Conde (1/0), José Luis Carranza (45/1) [48.Jean Franco Ferrari Chiabra (1/0)], José Alberto Soto Gómez (35/1), José Guillermo del Solar Alvarez-Calderón (52/7), Juan José Jayo Legario (5/0), Roberto Carlos Palacios Mestas (31/3) [67.Darío Teodoro Muchotrigo Carrillo (16/1)], Luis Alberto Guadalupe Rivadeneyra (1/0), Alberto Ramírez (11/3) [48.Jorge Lazo (1/0)]. Trainer: Juan Carlos Oblitas Saba (3).

374. 24.04.1996 **ECUADOR - PERU** **4-1(0-0)** 16th FIFA WC. Qualifiers
Estadio „Isidro Romero", Guayaquil; Referee: Julio Matto (Uruguay); Attendance: 60,000
PER: Miguel Eduardo Miranda Campos (27/0), Luis Manuel Carmelo Marengo Ramos (1/0), Juan Máximo Reynoso Guzmán (52/3), Jean Franco Ferrari Chiabra (2/0) [66.Álex Segundo Magallanes Jaimes (4/0)], Juan José Jayo Legario (6/0), José Luis Carranza (46/1), Nolberto Albino Solano Todco (15/2), José Guillermo del Solar Alvarez-Calderón (53/7), Flavio Francisco Maestri Andrade (22/6) [85.Eddie Carazas (1/0)], Roberto Carlos Palacios Mestas (32/4), Luis Alberto Guadalupe Rivadeneyra (2/0) [66.Jorge Ramírez (1/0)]. Trainer: Juan Carlos Oblitas Saba (4).
Goal: Roberto Carlos Palacios Mestas (62).

375. 02.06.1996 **PERU - COLOMBIA** **1-1(0-0)** 16th FIFA WC. Qualifiers
Estadio Nacional, Lima; Referee: Alfredo Rodas Iniquez (Ecuador); Attendance: 43,345
PER: Julio César Balerio Correa (1/0), Luis Manuel Carmelo Marengo Ramos (2/0), Juan Máximo Reynoso Guzmán (53/4), Percy Celso Olivares Polanco (51/0), Juan José Jayo Legario (7/0), José Luis Carranza (47/1) [75.Luis Alberto Guadalupe Rivadeneyra (3/0)], Nolberto Albino Solano Todco (16/2), José Guillermo del Solar Alvarez-Calderón (54/7), Flavio Francisco Maestri Andrade (23/6), Roberto Carlos Palacios Mestas (33/4), Pablo César Zegarra Zamora (17/0) [78.Álex Segundo Magallanes Jaimes (5/0)]. Trainer: Juan Carlos Oblitas Saba (5).
Goal: Juan Máximo Reynoso Guzmán (47).

376. 20.06.1996 **PERU - ARMENIA** **4-0(1-0)**
Estadio Nacional, Lima; Referee: Jorge Luis Torres Prada (Peru); Attendance: 5,600
PER: Miguel Eduardo Miranda Campos (28/0), Álvaro Barco (27/0), Luis Manuel Carmelo Marengo Ramos (3/0) [46.José Alberto Soto Gómez (36/1)], Juan Máximo Reynoso Guzmán (54/4) [70.Álex Segundo Magallanes Jaimes (6/0)], Nolberto Albino Solano Todco (17/3), José Luis Reyna (2/0) [46.Jorge Antonio Soto Gómez (26/1)], José Luis Carranza (48/1), Juan José Jayo Legario (8/0), Pablo César Zegarra Zamora (18/1) [46.Jorge Ramírez (2/0)], Roberto Carlos Palacios Mestas (34/5), Andrés Gonzáles (17/2) [46.Roberto Carlos Farfán Quispe (1/1)]. Trainer: Juan Carlos Oblitas Saba (6).
Goals: Pablo César Zegarra Zamora (24), Roberto Carlos Farfán Quispe (56), Roberto Carlos Palacios Mestas (58), Nolberto Albino Solano Todco (87 penalty).

377. 07.07.1996 **PERU - ARGENTINA** **0-0** 16th FIFA WC. Qualifiers
Estadio Nacional, Lima; Referee: Wilson De Souza Mendonça (Brazil); Attendance: 43,675
PER: Julio César Balerio Correa (2/0), José Alberto Soto Gómez (37/1), Juan Máximo Reynoso Guzmán (55/4), Percy Celso Olivares Polanco (52/0), Juan José Jayo Legario (9/0), José Luis Carranza (49/1) [83.Roberto Carlos Farfán Quispe (2/1)], Nolberto Albino Solano Todco (18/3), Julio De Andrade „Julinho" (1/0), Roberto Carlos Palacios Mestas (35/5), Flavio Francisco Maestri Andrade (24/6), Pablo César Zegarra Zamora (19/1) [67.Álex Segundo Magallanes Jaimes (7/0)]. Trainer: Juan Carlos Oblitas Saba (7).

378. 14.08.1996 **PERU - COSTA RICA** **3-0(0-0)**
Estadio Monumental, Arequipa; Referee: César Córdova (Peru); Attendance: 15,000
PER: Julio César Balerio Correa (3/0), Alvaro Barco (28/0), Luis Manuel Carmelo Marengo Ramos (4/0), Jorge Antonio Soto Gómez (27/1), Percy Celso Olivares Polanco (53/0), José Antonio Pereda Maruyama (1/0), Paolo Freddy Maldonado Farje (1/1) [62.Nolberto Albino Solano Todco (19/3)], José Luis Carranza (50/1) [46.Roger Alberto Serrano Ruiz (1/0)], Juan José Jayo Legario (10/0), Roberto Carlos Palacios Mestas (36/6), Andrés Gonzáles (18/2) [46.Roberto Carlos Farfán Quispe (3/2)]. Trainer: Juan Carlos Oblitas Saba (8).
Goals: Paolo Freddy Maldonado Farje (55), Roberto Carlos Palacios Mestas (70), Roberto Carlos Farfán Quispe (90).

379. 01.09.1996 **BOLIVIA - PERU** **0-0** 16th FIFA WC. Qualifiers
Estadio „Hernándo Siles Zuazo", La Paz; Referee: Oscar Velázquez Alvarenga (Paraguay); Attendance: 48,304
PER: Julio César Balerio Correa (4/0), Luis Manuel Carmelo Marengo Ramos (5/0), Juan Máximo Reynoso Guzmán (56/4), Percy Celso Olivares Polanco (54/0), Juan José Jayo Legario (11/0), Roger Alberto Serrano Ruiz (2/0) [49.Julio De Andrade „Julinho" (2/0)], José Antonio Pereda Maruyama (2/0), José Alberto Soto Gómez (38/1), Flavio Francisco Maestri Andrade (25/6) [80.Luis Germán del Carmen Carty Monserrate (8/0)], Roberto Carlos Palacios Mestas (37/6) [82.Jorge Antonio Soto Gómez (28/1)], Pablo César Zegarra Zamora (20/1). Trainer: Juan Carlos Oblitas Saba (9).

380. 16.10.1996 **PERU - UNITED STATES** **4-1(1-1)**
Estadio Nacional, Lima; Referee: Juan Luna Humerez (Bolivia); Attendance: 8,019
PER: Miguel Eduardo Miranda Campos (29/0), Nolberto Albino Solano Todco (20/4), Juan Máximo Reynoso Guzmán (57/4), Alvaro Barco (29/0) [46.Luis Manuel Carmelo Marengo Ramos (6/0)], Percy Celso Olivares Polanco (55/1), Roger Alberto Serrano Ruiz (3/0) [75.Juan Carlos Bazalar Cruzado (8/0)], Juan José Jayo Legario (12/0), Roberto Carlos Palacios Mestas (38/7) [69.Jorge Antonio Soto Gómez (29/1)], Paolo Freddy Maldonado Farje (2/2), Luis Germán del Carmen Carty Monserrate (9/0), Waldir Alejandro Sáenz Pérez (9/2) [69.Roberto Carlos Farfán Quispe (4/2)]. Trainer: Juan Carlos Oblitas Saba (10).
Goals: Roberto Carlos Palacios Mestas (33), Percy Celso Olivares Polanco (68), Paolo Freddy Maldonado Farje (73), Nolberto Albino Solano Todco (83).

381. 10.11.1996 **PERU - VENEZUELA** **4-1(2-0)** 16th FIFA WC. Qualifiers
Estadio Nacional, Lima; Referee: Rene Ortube Betancourt (Bolivia); Attendance: 31,036
PER: Julio César Balerio Correa (5/0), Roger Alberto Serrano Ruiz (4/0) [64.Luis Germán del Carmen Carty Monserrate (10/0)], Juan Máximo Reynoso Guzmán (58/5), Percy Celso Olivares Polanco (56/1), José Alberto Soto Gómez (39/1), Juan José Jayo Legario (13/0), Nolberto Albino Solano Todco (21/4), Roberto Carlos Palacios Mestas (39/9), Julio De Andrade „Julinho" (3/1) [76.Waldir Alejandro Sáenz Pérez (10/2)], Flavio Francisco Maestri Andrade (26/6) [64.Paolo Freddy Maldonado Farje (3/2)], Pablo César Zegarra Zamora (21/1). Trainer: Juan Carlos Oblitas Saba (11).
Goals: Juan Máximo Reynoso Guzmán (4), Julio De Andrade „Julinho" (21), Roberto Carlos Palacios Mestas (49, 83).

382. 15.12.1996 **URUGUAY - PERU** **2-0(2-0)** 16th FIFA WC. Qualifiers
Estadio Centenario, Montevideo; Referee: Felipe Eduardo Russi Páez (Colombia); Attendance: 42,630
PER: Julio César Balerio Correa (6/0), Roger Alberto Serrano Ruiz (5/0), Luis Manuel Carmelo Marengo Ramos (7/0) [46.Alfonso Antonio Dulanto Corzo (16/0)], Percy Celso Olivares Polanco (57/1), José Alberto Soto Gómez (40/1), Juan José Jayo Legario (14/0), Juan Máximo Reynoso Guzmán (59/5), Roberto Carlos Palacios Mestas (40/9), Julio De Andrade „Julinho" (4/1) [64.Waldir Alejandro Sáenz Pérez (11/2)], Flavio Francisco Maestri Andrade (27/6), Pablo César Zegarra Zamora (22/1) [79.Luis Germán del Carmen Carty Monserrate (11/0)]. Trainer: Juan Carlos Oblitas Saba (12).

383. 12.01.1997 **PERU - CHILE** **2-1(2-0)** 16th FIFA WC. Qualifiers
Estadio Nacional, Lima; Referee: José Luis Da Rosa Varela (Uruguay); Attendance: 35,373
PER: Miguel Eduardo Miranda Campos (30/0), Roger Alberto Serrano Ruiz (6/0), Percy Celso Olivares Polanco (58/1), Juan Máximo Reynoso Guzmán (60/5), José Alberto Soto Gómez (41/1), Nolberto Albino Solano Todco (22/4), Juan José Jayo Legario (15/0), Roberto Carlos Palacios Mestas (41/10), Julio De Andrade „Julinho" (5/1) [76.Luis Germán del Carmen Carty Monserrate (12/0)], Flavio Francisco Maestri Andrade (28/7) [79.Jorge Antonio Soto Gómez (30/1)], Paolo Freddy Maldonado Farje (4/2) [46.José Antonio Pereda Maruyama (3/0)]. Trainer: Juan Carlos Oblitas Saba (13).
Goal: Flavio Francisco Maestri Andrade (15), Roberto Carlos Palacios Mestas (34).

384. 17.01.1997 **UNITED STATES - PERU** **0-1(0-1)** US Cup
„Jack Murphy" Stadium, San Diego; Referee: Arturo Brizio Carter (Mexico); Attendance: 35,232
PER: Julio César Balerio Correa (7/0), Alfonso Antonio Dulanto Corzo (17/0), Juan Máximo Reynoso Guzmán (61/5), Percy Celso Olivares Polanco (59/1), Nolberto Albino Solano Todco (23/4), Roger Alberto Serrano Ruiz (7/0), Juan José Jayo Legario (16/0), Paolo Freddy Maldonado Farje (5/2), José Antonio Pereda Maruyama (4/0), Álex Segundo Magallanes Jaimes (8/0) [58.Waldir Alejandro Sáenz Pérez (12/2)], Luis Germán del Carmen Carty Monserrate (13/1) [68.Roberto Carlos Farfán Quispe (5/2)]. Trainer: Juan Carlos Oblitas Saba (14).
Goal: Luis Germán del Carmen Carty Monserrate (8).

385. 19.01.1997 **DENMARK - PERU** **2-1(1-0)** US Cup
Rose Bowl, Pasadena (United States); Referee: Kevin Scott (United States); Attendance: 35,232
PER: Miguel Eduardo Miranda Campos (31/0), Nolberto Albino Solano Todco (24/5), Alvaro Barco (30/0), Alfonso Antonio Dulanto Corzo (18/0), Percy Celso Olivares Polanco (60/1), Juan José Jayo Legario (17/0), Juan Carlos Bazalar Cruzado (9/0), José Antonio Pereda Maruyama (5/0), Álex Segundo Magallanes Jaimes (9/0) [67.Roberto Carlos Farfán Quispe (6/2)], Paolo Freddy Maldonado Farje (6/2) [46.Waldir Alejandro Sáenz Pérez (13/2)], Luis Germán del Carmen Carty Monserrate (14/1). Trainer: Juan Carlos Oblitas Saba (15).
Goal: Nolberto Albino Solano Todco (50).

386. 22.01.1997 **MEXICO - PERU** **0-0** US Cup
Rose Bowl, Pasadena (United States); Referee: Esfandiar Baharmast (United States); Attendance: 17,342
PER: Julio César Balerio Correa (8/0), Nolberto Albino Solano Todco (25/5), Juan Máximo Reynoso Guzmán (62/5), José Alberto Soto Gómez (42/1), Percy Celso Olivares Polanco (61/1), Roger Alberto Serrano Ruiz (8/0), Juan José Jayo Legario (18/0), Álex Segundo Magallanes Jaimes (10/0) [67.Paolo Freddy Maldonado Farje (7/2)], José Antonio Pereda Maruyama (6/0) [81.Juan Carlos Bazalar Cruzado (10/0)], Roberto Carlos Farfán Quispe (7/2), Waldir Alejandro Sáenz Pérez (14/2). Trainer: Juan Carlos Oblitas Saba (16).

387. 12.02.1997 **PARAGUAY - PERU** **2-1(2-1)** 16th FIFA WC. Qualifiers
Estadio Defensores del Chaco, Asunción; Referee: Mario Sánchez Yanten (Chile); Attendance: 32,000
PER: Julio César Balerio Correa (9/0), Juan Máximo Reynoso Guzmán (63/5), Percy Celso Olivares Polanco (62/1), Roger Alberto Serrano Ruiz (9/0) [61.Luis Germán del Carmen Carty Monserrate (15/1)], José Alberto Soto Gómez (43/1), Nolberto Albino Solano Todco (26/5), Juan José Jayo Legario (19/0), José Antonio Pereda Maruyama (7/1), Roberto Carlos Palacios Mestas (42/10) [77.Waldir Alejandro Sáenz Pérez (15/2)], Flavio Francisco Maestri Andrade (29/7), Pablo César Zegarra Zamora (23/1) [69.Álex Segundo Magallanes Jaimes (11/0)]. Trainer: Juan Carlos Oblitas Saba (17).
Goal: José Antonio Pereda Maruyama (33).

388. 02.04.1997 **PERU - ECUADOR** **1-1(0-0)** 16th FIFA WC. Qualifiers
Estadio Nacional, Lima; Referee: John Jairo Toro Rendón (Colombia); Attendance: 42,299
PER: Julio César Balerio Correa (10/0), Juan Máximo Reynoso Guzmán (64/5), Percy Celso Olivares Polanco (63/1), José Alberto Soto Gómez (44/1), José Luis Carranza (51/1), Eddie Carazas (2/0), Nolberto Albino Solano Todco (27/5), Roberto Carlos Palacios Mestas (43/11), Julio De Andrade „Julinho" (6/1) [62.Waldir Alejandro Sáenz Pérez (16/2)], Flavio Francisco Maestri Andrade (30/7), Pablo César Zegarra Zamora (24/1) [81.Luis Germán del Carmen Carty Monserrate (16/1)]. Trainer: Juan Carlos Oblitas Saba (18).
Goal: Roberto Carlos Palacios Mestas (58).

389. 30.04.1997 **COLOMBIA - PERU** **0-1(0-0)** 16th FIFA WC. Qualifiers
Estadio Metropolitano „Roberto Meléndez", Barranquilla; Referee: Márcio Rezende de Freitas (Brazil); Attendance: 22,172
PER: Julio César Balerio Correa (11/0), Juan Máximo Reynoso Guzmán (65/5), Percy Celso Olivares Polanco (64/1), José Alberto Soto Gómez (45/1), Eddie Carazas (3/0) [68.Jorge Antonio Soto Gómez (31/1)], Nolberto Albino Solano Todco (28/5), Roger Alberto Serrano Ruiz (10/0) [80.Juan Carlos Bazalar Cruzado (11/0)], Juan José Jayo Legario (20/0), Roberto Carlos Palacios Mestas (44/11), José Antonio Pereda Maruyama (8/2), Luis Germán del Carmen Carty Monserrate (17/1) [88. Julio De Andrade „Julinho" (7/1)]. Trainer: Juan Carlos Oblitas Saba (19).
Goal: José Antonio Pereda Maruyama (62).

390. 08.06.1997 **ARGENTINA - PERU** **2-0(1-0)** 16th FIFA WC. Qualifiers
Estadio Monumental „Antonio Vespucio Liberti", Buenos Aires; Referee: Claudio Vinicius Cerdeira (Brazil); Attendance: 56,069
PER: Julio César Balerio Correa (12/0), Nolberto Albino Solano Todco (29/5), Juan Máximo Reynoso Guzmán (66/5), Percy Celso Olivares Polanco (65/1), José Alberto Soto Gómez (46/1), Waldir Alejandro Sáenz Pérez (17/2) [46.Julio De Andrade „Julinho" (8/1)], Roger Alberto Serrano Ruiz (11/0) [77.José Luis Carranza (52/1)], Juan José Jayo Legario (21/0), Roberto Carlos Palacios Mestas (45/11), Jorge Antonio Soto Gómez (32/1), Flavio Francisco Maestri Andrade (31/7) [67.Luis Germán del Carmen Carty Monserrate (18/1)]. Trainer: Juan Carlos Oblitas Saba (20).

391. 12.06.1997 **PERU - URUGUAY** **1-0(0-0)** 38th Copa América. Group Stage
Estadio Patria, Sucre (Bolivia); Referee: Antonio Marrufo (Mexico); Attendance: 6,000
PER: Miguel Eduardo Miranda Campos (32/0), José Luis Reyna (3/0), César Miguel Rebosio Compans (1/0), Alfonso Antonio Dulanto Corzo (19/0), Emilio Martín Hidalgo Conde (2/1), Erick Omar Torres Arias (1/0), Germán Muñoz (4/0), César Miguel Rosales Tardío (3/0) [63.Álex Segundo Magallanes Jaimes (12/0)], Roberto Carlos Palacios Mestas (46/11) [82.Waldir Alejandro Sáenz Pérez (18/2)], Paul Manuel Cominges Mayorca (1/0) [63.Frank Palomino (3/0)], Eddie Carazas (4/0) [*sent off 85*]. Trainer: Freddy Santos Ternero Corrales (1).
Goal: Emilio Martín Hidalgo Conde (75).

392. 15.06.1997 **BOLIVIA - PERU** **2-0(1-0)** 38th Copa América. Group Stage
Estadio „Hernándo Siles Zuazo", La Paz; Referee: Rodrigo Badilla Sequeira (Costa Rica); Attendance: 20,000
PER: Miguel Eduardo Miranda Campos (33/0), José Luis Reyna (4/0) [*sent off 20*], César Miguel Rebosio Compans (2/0), Alfonso Antonio Dulanto Corzo (20/0), Emilio Martín Hidalgo Conde (3/1), Erick Omar Torres Arias (2/0), Germán Muñoz (5/0), Frank Palomino (4/0) [59.Waldir Alejandro Sáenz Pérez (19/2)], Roberto Carlos Palacios Mestas (47/11) [56.Orlando Prado (1/0)], Álex Segundo Magallanes Jaimes (13/0), Paul Manuel Cominges Mayorca (2/0) [67.Aldo Jair Cavero Carozzi (1/0)]. Trainer: Freddy Santos Ternero Corrales (2).

393. 18.06.1997 **PERU - VENEZUELA** **2-0(1-0)** 38th Copa América. Group Stage
Estadio Patria, Sucre (Bolivia); Referee: Byron Aldemar Moreno Ruales (Ecuador); Attendance: 1,500
PER: Miguel Eduardo Miranda Campos (34/0), Giuliano Santiago Portilla Castillo (1/0), César Miguel Rebosio Compans (3/0), Alfonso Antonio Dulanto Corzo (21/0), Emilio Martín Hidalgo Conde (4/1) [72.Orlando Prado (2/0)], Erick Omar Torres Arias (3/0), Germán Muñoz (6/0), Álex Segundo Magallanes Jaimes (14/0), Roberto Carlos Palacios Mestas (48/11) [72.Eddie Carazas (5/0)], Waldir Alejandro Sáenz Pérez (20/2), Paul Manuel Cominges Mayorca (3/2) [65.Frank Palomino (5/0)]. Trainer: Freddy Santos Ternero Corrales (3).
Goals: Paul Manuel Cominges Mayorca (13, 59).

394. 21.06.1997 **PERU - ARGENTINA** **2-1(1-0)** 38th Copa América. Quarter-Finals
Estadio Patria, Sucre (Bolivia); Referee: Byron Aldemar Moreno Ruales (Ecuador); Attendance: 9,000
PER: Miguel Eduardo Miranda Campos (35/0), José Luis Reyna (5/0), Alfonso Antonio Dulanto Corzo (22/0), César Miguel Rebosio Compans (4/0), Emilio Martín Hidalgo Conde (5/2), Erick Omar Torres Arias (4/0), Germán Muñoz (7/0), Eddie Carazas (6/1) [52.Orlando Prado (3/0)], Roberto Carlos Palacios Mestas (49/11), Paul Manuel Cominges Mayorca (4/2) [73.Aldo Jair Cavero Carozzi (2/0)], Waldir Alejandro Sáenz Pérez (21/2) [62.Frank Palomino (6/0)]. Trainer: Freddy Santos Ternero Corrales (4).
Goals: Eddie Carazas (30), Emilio Martín Hidalgo Conde (61).

395. 26.06.1997 **BRAZIL - PERU** **7-0(3-0)** 38th Copa América. Semi-Finals
Estadio „Ramón ‚Tahuichi' Aguilera", Santa Cruz de la Sierra (Bolivia); Referee: Rodrigo Badilla Sequeira (Costa Rica); Attendance: 20,000
PER: Miguel Eduardo Miranda Campos (36/0), José Luis Reyna (6/0) [57.Orlando Prado (4/0)], Alfonso Antonio Dulanto Corzo (23/0), César Miguel Rebosio Compans (5/0), Emilio Martín Hidalgo Conde (6/2), Erick Omar Torres Arias (5/0), Germán Muñoz (8/0), Álex Segundo Magallanes Jaimes (15/0), Roberto Carlos Palacios Mestas (50/11) [57.Waldir Alejandro Sáenz Pérez (22/2)], Eddie Carazas (7/1) [57.Frank Palomino (7/0)], Paul Manuel Cominges Mayorca (5/2). Trainer: Freddy Santos Ternero Corrales (5).

396. 28.06.1997 **PERU - MEXICO** **0-1(0-0)** 38th Copa América. 3rd Place Play-off
Estadio „Jesús Bermúdez", Oruro (Bolivia); Referee: Paolo Borgosano (Venezuela); Attendance: 8,000
PER: Miguel Eduardo Miranda Campos (37/0), José Luis Reyna (7/0), Alfonso Antonio Dulanto Corzo (24/0), César Miguel Rebosio Compans (6/0), Giuliano Santiago Portilla Castillo (2/0), Orlando Prado (5/0), Erick Omar Torres Arias (6/0) [71.Germán Muñoz (9/0)], César Miguel Rosales Tardío (4/0) [14.Emilio Martín Hidalgo Conde (7/2)], Roberto Carlos Palacios Mestas (51/11), Frank Palomino (8/0), Paul Manuel Cominges Mayorca (6/2) [20.Álex Segundo Magallanes Jaimes (16/0)]. Trainer: Freddy Santos Ternero Corrales (6).

397. 06.07.1997 **PERU - BOLIVIA** **2-1(1-0)** 16th FIFA WC. Qualifiers
Estadio Nacional, Lima; Referee: Wilson De Souza Mendonça (Brazil); Attendance: 31,489
PER: Julio César Balerio Correa (13/0), Juan Máximo Reynoso Guzmán (67/5), Percy Celso Olivares Polanco (66/1), José Alberto Soto Gómez (47/1), José Luis Carranza (53/1) [88.Juan Carlos Bazalar Cruzado (12/0)], Eddie Carazas (8/1) [60.Roger Alberto Serrano Ruiz (12/0)], Jorge Antonio Soto Gómez (33/2), Juan José Jayo Legario (22/0), Pablo César Zegarra Zamora (25/1), Flavio Francisco Maestri Andrade (32/7) [68.Julio César Rivera (30/0)], Luis Germán del Carmen Carty Monserrate (19/2). Trainer: Juan Carlos Oblitas Saba (21).
Goals: Luis Germán del Carmen Carty Monserrate (9), Jorge Antonio Soto Gómez (53).

398. 20.08.1997 **VENEZUELA - PERU** **0-3(0-1)** 16th FIFA WC. Qualifiers
Estadio La Carolina, Barinas; Referee: Peter Prendergast (Jamaica); Attendance: 10,000
PER: Julio César Balerio Correa (14/0), Juan Máximo Reynoso Guzmán (68/5), Luis Manuel Carmelo Marengo Ramos (8/1), José Alberto Soto Gómez (48/1), Nolberto Albino Solano Todco (30/5), Juan José Jayo Legario (23/0), Jorge Antonio Soto Gómez (34/2), Roberto Carlos Palacios Mestas (52/11) [75.Julio César Rivera (31/0)], Julio De Andrade „Julinho" (9/2) [84.Juan Carlos Bazalar Cruzado (13/0)], Luis Germán del Carmen Carty Monserrate (20/2) [54.Flavio Francisco Maestri Andrade (33/8)], Pablo César Zegarra Zamora (26/1). Trainer: Juan Carlos Oblitas Saba (22).
Goals: Luis Manuel Carmelo Marengo Ramos (14), Julio De Andrade „Julinho" (54), Flavio Francisco Maestri Andrade (81).

399. 24.08.1997 **PERU - COLOMBIA** **2-1(2-1)** 75th Anniversary FPF
Estadio Nacional, Lima; Referee: Víctor Manuel Mayorga (Peru); Attendance: 15,000
PER: Miguel Eduardo Miranda Campos (38/0), Jorge Antonio Soto Gómez (35/2) [60.Julio César Rivera (32/0)], Luis Manuel Carmelo Marengo Ramos (9/1), Alfonso Antonio Dulanto Corzo (25/0), Giuliano Santiago Portilla Castillo (3/0), Juan José Jayo Legario (24/0) [46.Roger Alberto Serrano Ruiz (13/0)], José Antonio Pereda Maruyama (9/3), Roberto Carlos Palacios Mestas (53/11), César Augusto Cueto Villa (51/6) [40.Juan Carlos Bazalar Cruzado (14/0)], Roberto Carlos Farfán Quispe (8/3) [83.Eddie Carrazas (9/1)], Julio De Andrade „Julinho" (10/2). Trainer: Juan Carlos Oblitas Saba (23).
Goals: José Antonio Pereda Maruyama (25), Roberto Carlos Farfán Quispe (40).

400. 10.09.1997 **PERU - URUGUAY** **2-1(0-1)** 16th FIFA WC. Qualifiers
Estadio Nacional, Lima; Referee: Esfandiar Baharmast (United States); Attendance: 34,721
PER: Julio César Balerio Correa (15/0), Percy Celso Olivares Polanco (67/1), Luis Manuel Carmelo Marengo Ramos (10/1), José Alberto Soto Gómez (49/1), José Antonio Pereda Maruyama (10/3) [80.José Luis Carranza (54/1)], Nolberto Albino Solano Todco (31/5), Juan José Jayo Legario (25/0), Roberto Carlos Palacios Mestas (54/12), Luis Germán del Carmen Carty Monserrate (21/3), Flavio Francisco Maestri Andrade (34/8) [76.Julio César Rivera (33/0)], Pablo César Zegarra Zamora (27/1) [46.Jorge Antonio Soto Gómez (36/2)]. Trainer: Juan Carlos Oblitas Saba (24).
Goals: Roberto Carlos Palacios Mestas (57), Luis Germán del Carmen Carty Monserrate (60).

401. 12.10.1997 **CHILE - PERU** **4-0(1-0)** 16th FIFA WC. Qualifiers
Estadio Nacional, Santiago; Referee: Márcio Rezende de Freitas (Brazil); Attendance: 74,219
PER: Julio César Balerio Correa (16/0), Percy Celso Olivares Polanco (68/1), Juan Máximo Reynoso Guzmán (69/5), José Alberto Soto Gómez (50/1), José Antonio Pereda Maruyama (11/3) [60.Julio César Rivera (34/0)], Nolberto Albino Solano Todco (32/5), Juan José Jayo Legario (26/0) [*sent off 63*], Jorge Antonio Soto Gómez (37/2), Roberto Carlos Palacios Mestas (55/12) [78.Pablo César Zegarra Zamora (28/1)], Luis Germán del Carmen Carty Monserrate (22/3) [60. Julio De Andrade „Julinho" (11/2)], Flavio Francisco Maestri Andrade (35/8). Trainer: Juan Carlos Oblitas Saba (25).

402. 16.11.1997 **PERU – PARAGUAY** **1-0(1-0)** 16th FIFA WC. Qualifiers

Estadio Nacional, Lima; Referee: Francisco Mourao Dacildo (Brazil); Attendance: 30,000

PER: Julio César Balerio Correa (17/0), Juan Máximo Reynoso Guzmán (70/5), José Alberto Soto Gómez (51/1), José Antonio Pereda Maruyama (12/3) [46.César Miguel Rebosio Compans (7/0)], Nolberto Albino Solano Todco (33/5), Pablo César Zegarra Zamora (29/1), José Luis Carranza (55/1), Jorge Antonio Soto Gómez (38/3), Roberto Carlos Palacios Mestas (56/12) [65.Juan Carlos Bazalar Cruzado (15/0)], Julio De Andrade „Julinho" (12/2) [56.Luis Germán del Carmen Carty Monserrate (23/3)], Flavio Francisco Maestri Andrade (36/8). Trainer: Juan Carlos Oblitas Saba (26).

Goal: Jorge Antonio Soto Gómez (37).

403. 15.04.1998 **MEXICO – PERU** **1-0(0-0)**

Memorial Coliseum, Los Angeles; Referee: Arturo Angeles (United States); Attendance: 22,650

PER: Óscar Manuel Ibañez Holzmann (1/0), Jorge Antonio Soto Gómez (39/3), César Miguel Rebosio Compans (8/0), Juan Máximo Reynoso Guzmán (Cap) (71/5) [46.Santiago Roberto Salazar Peña (1/0)], Nolberto Albino Solano Todco (34/5), Juan Carlos Bazalar Cruzado (16/0) [72.Jorge Raúl Huamán Salinas (1/0)], Juan José Jayo Legario (27/0), Roberto Carlos Palacios Mestas (57/12), Erick Omar Torres Arias (7/0) [62.Julio Penalillo (1/0)], Roberto Carlos Farfán Quispe (9/3) [46.David Fernando Chévez Solano (1/0)], Waldir Alejandro Sáenz Pérez (23/2). Trainer: Juan Carlos Oblitas Saba (27).

404. 10.10.1998 **HOLLAND – PERU** **2-0(0-0)**

Philips Stadion, Eindhoven; Referee: Fritz Stuchlik (Austria); Attendance: 10,000

PER: Óscar Manuel Ibañez Holzmann (2/0), Jorge Antonio Soto Gómez (40/3), Santiago Roberto Salazar Peña (2/0), Juan Máximo Reynoso Guzmán (Cap) (72/5), Nolberto Albino Solano Todco (35/5), José Antonio Pereda Maruyama (13/3), Roberto Carlos Palacios Mestas (58/12), Carlos Antonio Flores Murillo (1/0) [58.Jorge Raúl Huamán Salinas (2/0)], Juan José Jayo Legario (28/0), Flavio Francisco Maestri Andrade (37/8), Gregorio Abel Bernales Francia (1/0) [77.Paul Manuel Cominges Mayorca (7/2)]. Trainer: Juan Carlos Oblitas Saba (28).

405. 10.02.1999 **PERU – ECUADOR** **1-2(1-0)**

Estadio Nacional, Lima; Referee: Ángel Ziani Bailetti (Peru); Attendance: 10,000

PER: Christian Del Mar (1/0), José Luis Chacón Chávez (1/0), Santiago Roberto Salazar Peña (3/0), César Miguel Rebosio Compans (9/0), Jorge Antonio Soto Gómez (41/3), Emilio Martín Hidalgo Conde (8/2) [77.Mario Augusto Gómez Urbina (1/0)], Gregorio Abel Bernales Francia (2/0), José Antonio Pereda Maruyama (14/3) [77.Erick Omar Torres Arias (8/0)], Roberto Carlos Palacios Mestas (59/12), Claudio Miguel Pizarro Bosio (1/0), Andrés Augusto Mendoza Azevedo (1/1). Trainer: Juan Carlos Oblitas Saba (29).

Goal: Andrés Augusto Mendoza Azevedo (39).

406. 17.02.1999 **ECUADOR – PERU** **1-2(0-1)**

Estadio Monumental "Isidro Romero Carbo", Guayaquil; Referee: Roger Zambrano (Ecuador); Attendance: 15,000

PER: Juan Ángel Flores Ascencio (1/0), Jorge Antonio Soto Gómez (42/3), César Miguel Rebosio Compans (10/0), Juan Máximo Reynoso Guzmán (73/5), Mario Augusto Gómez Urbina (2/0) [68.Emilio Martín Hidalgo Conde (9/2)], Gregorio Abel Bernales Francia (3/0), Erick Omar Torres Arias (9/0), José Antonio Pereda Maruyama (15/3), Roberto Carlos Palacios Mestas (60/12) [74.Santiago Roberto Salazar Peña (4/0)], Claudio Miguel Pizarro Bosio (2/1), Andrés Augusto Mendoza Azevedo (2/2) [69.Waldir Alejandro Sáenz Pérez (24/2)]. Trainer: Juan Carlos Oblitas Saba (30).

Goals: Claudio Miguel Pizarro Bosio (28), Andrés Augusto Mendoza Azevedo (48).

407. 30.05.1999 **PERU – BELGIUM** **1-1(1-1)** Kirin Cup

Nishikyoguku Stadium, Kyoto (Japan); Referee: Naotsugu Fuse (Japan); Attendance: 9,262

PER: Óscar Manuel Ibañez Holzmann (3/0), Luis Alberto Guadalupe Rivadeneyra (4/0), Juan Máximo Reynoso Guzmán (74/5), César Miguel Rebosio Compans (11/0), Jorge Antonio Soto Gómez (43/3), Juan José Jayo Legario (29/0), Nolberto Albino Solano Todco (36/5), José Antonio Pereda Maruyama (16/3) [75.Juan José Manuel Velásquez Castillo (1/0)], Roberto Carlos Palacios Mestas (61/12), Flavio Francisco Maestri Andrade (38/9), Claudio Miguel Pizarro Bosio (3/1) [60.Andrés Augusto Mendoza Azevedo (3/2)]. Trainer: Juan Carlos Oblitas Saba (31).

Goal: Flavio Francisco Maestri Andrade (6).

408. 06.06.1999 **JAPAN – PERU** **0-0** Kirin Cup

International Stadium, Yokohama; Referee: Penya Hanlumyaung (Thailand); Attendance: 67,354

PER: Óscar Manuel Ibañez Holzmann (4/0), Luis Alberto Guadalupe Rivadeneyra (5/0) [73.José Luis Chacón Chávez (2/0)], Juan Máximo Reynoso Guzmán (75/5), César Miguel Rebosio Compans (12/0), Jorge Antonio Soto Gómez (44/3), Juan José Jayo Legario (30/0), Nolberto Albino Solano Todco (37/5), José Antonio Pereda Maruyama (17/3), Roberto Carlos Palacios Mestas (62/12), Flavio Francisco Maestri Andrade (39/9) [90.Andrés Augusto Mendoza Azevedo (4/2)], Claudio Miguel Pizarro Bosio (4/1) [59.Roberto Carlos Holsen Alvarado (1/0)]. Trainer: Juan Carlos Oblitas Saba (32).

409. 17.06.1999 **COLOMBIA – PERU** **3-3(0-2)**

Estadio Palogrande, Manizales; Referee: John Jairo Toro Rendon (Colombia); Attendance: 30,000

PER: Óscar Manuel Ibañez Holzmann (5/0), Luis Alberto Guadalupe Rivadeneyra (6/0), Juan Máximo Reynoso Guzmán (76/5), César Miguel Rebosio Compans (13/0), Percy Celso Olivares Polanco (69/1), Juan José Jayo Legario (31/0), Nolberto Albino Solano Todco (38/6) [70.Juan José Manuel Velásquez Castillo (2/0)], José Antonio Pereda Maruyama (18/3), Roberto Carlos Palacios Mestas (63/12) [67.Jorge Antonio Soto Gómez (45/3)], Roberto Carlos Holsen Alvarado (2/1) [67.Herlyn Ysrael Zúñiga Yañez (1/0)], Claudio Miguel Pizarro Bosio (5/2) [87.José Alberto Soto Gómez (52/1)]. Trainer: Juan Carlos Oblitas Saba (33).

Goals: Nolberto Albino Solano Todco (36 penalty), Roberto Carlos Holsen Alvarado (44), Claudio Miguel Pizarro Bosio (56).

410. 20.06.1999 **VENEZUELA – PERU** **3-0(2-0)**

Estadio „Misael Delgado", Valencia; Referee: Paolo Borgosano (Venezuela); Attendance: 10,853

PER: Óscar Manuel Ibañez Holzmann (6/0), Luis Alberto Guadalupe Rivadeneyra (7/0) [46.Jorge Antonio Soto Gómez (46/3)], José Luis Chacón Chávez (3/0), César Miguel Rebosio Compans (14/0), Percy Celso Olivares Polanco (70/1), Juan José Jayo Legario (32/0), José Antonio Pereda Maruyama (19/3) [46.Juan José Manuel Velásquez Castillo (3/0)], Nolberto Albino Solano Todco (39/6), Roberto Carlos Palacios Mestas (64/12) [*sent off 33*], Roberto Carlos Holsen Alvarado (3/1) [65.Andrés Augusto Mendoza Azevedo (5/2)], Claudio Miguel Pizarro Bosio (6/2) [65.Herlyn Ysrael Zúñiga Yañez (2/0)]. Trainer: Juan Carlos Oblitas Saba (34).

411. 23.06.1999 **PERU – VENEZUELA** **3-0(0-0)**

Estadio „Alejandro Villaneuva", Lima; Referee: José Arana (Peru); Attendance: 13,989

PER: Óscar Manuel Ibañez Holzmann (7/0), Juan Máximo Reynoso Guzmán (77/5), José Alberto Soto Gómez (53/1), César Miguel Rebosio Compans (15/0), Juan José Jayo Legario (33/0), José Antonio Pereda Maruyama (20/3), Jorge Antonio Soto Gómez (47/4), Percy Celso Olivares Polanco (71/1) [46.Claudio Miguel Pizarro Bosio (7/3)], Nolberto Albino Solano Todco (40/7), Flavio Francisco Maestri Andrade (40/9), Roberto Carlos Holsen Alvarado (4/1) [74.Herlyn Ysrael Zúñiga Yañez (3/0)]. Trainer: Juan Carlos Oblitas Saba (35).

Goals: Claudio Miguel Pizarro Bosio (58), Jorge Antonio Soto Gómez (67), Nolberto Albino Solano Todco (79).

412. 29.06.1999 **PERU – JAPAN** **3-2(0-2)** 39th Copa América. Group Stage
Estadio Defensores del Chaco, Asunción (Paraguay); Referee: Byron Aldemar Moreno Ruales (Ecuador); Attendance: 45,000
PER: Óscar Manuel Ibañez Holzmann (8/0), José Alberto Soto Gómez (54/1), Juan Máximo Reynoso Guzmán (78/5), César Miguel Rebosio Compans (16/0), Jorge Antonio Soto Gómez (48/5), José Antonio Pereda Maruyama (21/3) [82.Marko Gustavo Ciurlizza Rodríguez (1/0)], Roberto Carlos Palacios Mestas (65/12) [46.Roberto Carlos Holsen Alvarado (5/3)], Juan José Jayo Legario (34/0), Nolberto Albino Solano Todco (41/7), Flavio Francisco Maestri Andrade (41/9) [88.Juan José Manuel Velásquez Castillo (4/0)], Claudio Miguel Pizarro Bosio (8/3). Trainer: Juan Carlos Oblitas Saba (36).
Goals: Jorge Antonio Soto Gómez (70), Roberto Carlos Holsen Alvarado (74, 81).

413. 02.07.1999 **PERU – BOLIVIA** **1-0(0-0)** 39th Copa América. Group Stage
Estadio Defensores del Chaco, Asunción (Paraguay); Referee: Luis Solórzano (Venezuela); Attendance: 30,000
PER: Óscar Manuel Ibañez Holzmann (9/0), José Alberto Soto Gómez (55/1), César Miguel Rebosio Compans (17/0), Juan Máximo Reynoso Guzmán (79/5), Jorge Antonio Soto Gómez (49/5), José Antonio Pereda Maruyama (22/3) [46.Marko Gustavo Ciurlizza Rodríguez (2/0)], Roberto Carlos Palacios Mestas (66/12), Juan José Jayo Legario (35/0), Nolberto Albino Solano Todco (42/7), Flavio Francisco Maestri Andrade (42/9) [85.Herlyn Ysrael Zúñiga Yañez (4/1)] [*sent off 90*], Claudio Miguel Pizarro Bosio (9/3) [57.Roberto Carlos Holsen Alvarado (6/3)]. Trainer: Juan Carlos Oblitas Saba (37).
Goal: Herlyn Ysrael Zúñiga Yañez (87).

414. 05.07.1999 **PARAGUAY – PERU** **1-0(0-0)** 39th Copa América. Group Stage
Estadio Río Parapití, Pedro Juan Caballero; Referee: Oscar Julián Ruiz (Colombia); Attendance: 23,000
PER: Óscar Manuel Ibañez Holzmann (10/0), Luis Alberto Guadalupe Rivadeneyra (8/0), José Alberto Soto Gómez (56/1), César Miguel Rebosio Compans (18/0), Percy Celso Olivares Polanco (72/1), Marko Gustavo Ciurlizza Rodríguez (3/0), Juan José Manuel Velásquez Castillo (5/0), José Antonio Pereda Maruyama (23/3) [82.Jorge Antonio Soto Gómez (50/5)], Roberto Carlos Palacios Mestas (67/12) [68.Roberto Carlos Holsen Alvarado (7/3)], Claudio Miguel Pizarro Bosio (10/3), Andrés Augusto Mendoza Azevedo (6/2). Trainer: Juan Carlos Oblitas Saba (38).

415. 10.07.1999 **PERU – MEXICO** **3-3(2-3), 2-4 penalties** 39th Copa América. Quarter-Finals
Estadio Defensores del Chaco, Asunción (Paraguay); Referee: Wilson De Souza Mendonça (Brazil); Attendance: 45,000
PER: Óscar Manuel Ibañez Holzmann (11/0), José Alberto Soto Gómez (57/1), Juan Máximo Reynoso Guzmán (80/5), César Miguel Rebosio Compans (19/0), Jorge Antonio Soto Gómez (51/5), Juan José Jayo Legario (36/0), José Antonio Pereda Maruyama (24/4), Nolberto Albino Solano Todco (43/8), Roberto Carlos Palacios Mestas (68/13) [25.Herlyn Ysrael Zúñiga Yañez (5/1), 66.Marko Gustavo Ciurlizza Rodríguez (4/0)], Roberto Carlos Holsen Alvarado (8/3), Flavio Francisco Maestri Andrade (43/9) [79.Claudio Miguel Pizarro Bosio (11/3)]. Trainer: Juan Carlos Oblitas Saba (39).
Goals: Roberto Carlos Palacios Mestas (6), José Antonio Pereda Maruyama (15), Nolberto Albino Solano Todco (40).
Penalties: 1-1 Nolberto Albino Solano Todco, 2-2 Jorge Antonio Soto Gómez, José Alberto Soto Gómez (missed), Juan Máximo Reynoso Guzmán (missed).

416. 17.11.1999 **PERU – SLOVAKIA** **2-1(2-1)**
Estadio Nacional, Lima; Referee: Eduardo Gamboa Martínez (Chile); Attendance: 29,089
PER: Óscar Manuel Ibañez Holzmann (12/0), Jorge Antonio Soto Gómez (52/5), Sandro Paulo Baylón Capcha (1/0), César Miguel Rebosio Compans (20/0), Marcial Salazar (3/0), Juan José Jayo Legario (37/0), Germán Ernesto Pinillos Rioja (12/2), Nolberto Albino Solano Todco (44/9) [62.Eddie Carazas (10/1)], Roberto Carlos Palacios Mestas (69/14) [78.John Christopher Hinostroza Guzmán (1/0)], Roberto Carlos Holsen Alvarado (9/3), Abel Augusto Lobatón Espejo (1/0) [60.Herlyn Ysrael Zúñiga Yañez (6/1)]. Trainer: Francisco Maturana (1).
Goals: Roberto Carlos Palacios Mestas (25), Nolberto Albino Solano Todco (41).

417. 01.12.1999 **PERU – HONDURAS** **0-0**
Estadio Nacional, Lima; Referee: Luis Mariano Peña (Chile); Attendance: 12,668
PER: Óscar Manuel Ibañez Holzmann (13/0), Jorge Antonio Soto Gómez (53/5), José Alberto Soto Gómez (58/1), Juan Luciano Pajuelo Chávez (1/0), Percy Celso Olivares Polanco (73/1), Juan José Jayo Legario (38/0), Germán Ernesto Pinillos Rioja (13/2) [65.Freddy Suárez (1/0)], Pablo César Zegarra Zamora (30/1), Rafael Fabio Villanueva Salazar (1/0) [46.Jorge Raúl Huamán Salinas (3/0)], Abel Augusto Lobatón Espejo (2/0), Herlyn Ysrael Zúñiga Yañez (7/1) [67.Andrés Augusto Mendoza Azevedo (7/2)]. Trainer: Francisco Maturana (2).

418. 14.02.2000 **PERU – HAITI** **1-1(0-0)** 5th CONCACAF Gold Cup. Group Stage
Orange Bowl, Miami (United States); Referee: Carlos Batres (Guatemala); Attendance: 23,795
PER: Óscar Manuel Ibañez Holzmann (14/0), Juan Máximo Reynoso Guzmán (Cap) (81/5), Marcial Salazar (4/0) [65.Herlyn Ysrael Zúñiga Yañez (8/2)], César Miguel Rebosio Compans (21/0), Nolberto Albino Solano Todco (45/9) [86.Jorge Raúl Huamán Salinas (4/0)], Juan José Jayo Legario (39/0), Roberto Carlos Palacios Mestas (70/14), Roberto Carlos Holsen Alvarado (10/3), Jorge Antonio Soto Gómez (54/5), Waldir Alejandro Sáenz Pérez (25/2) [46.Abel Augusto Lobatón Espejo (3/0)], José Guillermo del Solar Alvarez-Calderón (55/7). Trainer: Francisco Maturana (3).
Goal: Herlyn Ysrael Zúñiga Yañez (69).

419. 16.02.2000 **UNITED STATES – PERU** **1-0(0-0)** 5th CONCACAF Gold Cup. Group Stage
Orange Bowl, Miami (United States); Referee: Felipe Ramos (Mexico); Attendance: 36,000
PER: Óscar Manuel Ibañez Holzmann (15/0), Juan Máximo Reynoso Guzmán (Cap) (82/5), Marcial Salazar (5/0) [65.Herlyn Ysrael Zúñiga Yañez (9/2) [*sent off 77*], César Miguel Rebosio Compans (22/0), Juan José Jayo Legario (40/0), Roberto Carlos Palacios Mestas (71/14), Roberto Carlos Holsen Alvarado (11/3) [71.Germán Ernesto Pinillos Rioja (14/2)], Jorge Antonio Soto Gómez (55/5), Abel Augusto Lobatón Espejo (4/0), José Guillermo del Solar Alvarez-Calderón (56/7), Henry Edson Quinteros Sánchez (1/0). Trainer: Francisco Maturana (4).

420. 19.02.2000 **PERU – HONDURAS** **5-3(2-1)** 5th CONCACAF Gold Cup. Quarter-Finals
Orange Bowl, Miami (United States); Referee: Mario Sánchez (Chile); Attendance: 32,972
PER: Óscar Manuel Ibañez Holzmann (16/0), Juan Máximo Reynoso Guzmán (Cap) (83/5), José Alberto Soto Gómez (59/1), César Miguel Rebosio Compans (23/0), Roberto Carlos Palacios Mestas (72/15), Roberto Carlos Holsen Alvarado (12/4) [76.Waldir Alejandro Sáenz Pérez (26/3)], Jorge Antonio Soto Gómez (56/6), Freddy Suárez (2/0) [46.Marcial Salazar (6/0)], Abel Augusto Lobatón Espejo (5/0), José Guillermo del Solar Alvarez-Calderón (57/8), Henry Edson Quinteros Sánchez (2/0) [46.Marko Gustavo Ciurlizza Rodríguez (5/0)]. Trainer: Francisco Maturana (5).
Goals: Roberto Carlos Holsen Alvarado (7), Jorge Antonio Soto Gómez (14 penalty), José Guillermo del Solar Alvarez-Calderón (50), Roberto Carlos Palacios Mestas (52), Waldir Alejandro Sáenz Pérez (87).

421. 23.02.2000 **COLOMBIA – PERU** **2-1(1-0)** 5th CONCACAF Gold Cup. Semi-Finals
Qualcomm Stadium, San Diego (United States); Referee: Rafael Rodríguez (El Salvador); Attendance: 3,402
PER: Óscar Manuel Ibañez Holzmann (17/0), Jorge Antonio Soto Gómez (57/6), Jorge Raúl Huamán Salinas (5/0) [68.Waldir Alejandro Sáenz Pérez (27/3)], José Guillermo del Solar Alvarez-Calderón (58/8), Juan Máximo Reynoso Guzmán (Cap) (84/5), Marcial Salazar (7/0) [46.Henry Edson Quinteros Sánchez (3/0)], César Miguel Rebosio Compans (24/0), Juan José Jayo Legario (41/0), Roberto Carlos Palacios Mestas (73/16), Roberto Carlos Holsen Alvarado (13/4), Abel Augusto Lobatón Espejo (6/0). Trainer: Francisco Maturana (6).
Goal: Roberto Carlos Palacios Mestas (70).

422. 29.03.2000 **PERU – PARAGUAY** **2-0(0-0)** 17th FIFA WC. Qualifiers

Estadio Nacional, Lima; Referee: Horacio Elizondo (Argentina); Attendance: 45,042

PER: Óscar Manuel Ibañez Holzmann (18/0), Jorge Antonio Soto Gómez (58/6), César Miguel Rebosio Compans (25/0), Juan Luciano Pajuelo Chávez (2/0), Percy Celso Olivares Polanco (74/1) [72.Jorge Raúl Huamán Salinas (6/0)], Juan José Jayo Legario (42/0), Roberto Carlos Palacios Mestas (74/17), José Guillermo del Solar Alvarez-Calderón (59/8), Nolberto Albino Solano Todco (46/10), Claudio Miguel Pizarro Bosio (12/3) [80.Marko Gustavo Ciurlizza Rodríguez (6/0)], Herlyn Ysrael Zúñiga Yañez (10/2) [58.Roberto Carlos Holsen Alvarado (14/4)]. Trainer: Francisco Maturana (7).

Goals: Nolberto Albino Solano Todco (55 penalty), Roberto Carlos Palacios Mestas (60).

423. 26.04.2000 **CHILE – PERU** **1-1(1-1)**

Estadio Nacional, Santiago; Referee: Epifanio Gonzáles Chávez (Paraguay); Attendance: 44,979

PER: Óscar Manuel Ibañez Holzmann (19/0), Jorge Antonio Soto Gómez (59/6), César Miguel Rebosio Compans (26/0), Juan Luciano Pajuelo Chávez (3/0), Percy Celso Olivares Polanco (75/1), Juan José Jayo Legario (43/1), José Guillermo del Solar Alvarez-Calderón (60/8), Nolberto Albino Solano Todco (47/10), Roberto Carlos Palacios Mestas (75/17), David Soria Yoshinari (1/0) [58.Herlyn Ysrael Zúñiga Yañez (11/2)], Claudio Miguel Pizarro Bosio (13/3). Trainer: Francisco Maturana (8).

Goal: Juan José Jayo Legario (38).

424. 04.06.2000 **PERU – BRAZIL** **0-1(0-1)** 17th FIFA WC. Qualifiers

Estadio Nacional, Lima; Referee: Daniel Orlando Giménez (Argentina); Attendance: 45,529

PER: Miguel Eduardo Miranda Campos (39/0), Jorge Raúl Huamán Salinas (7/0) [45.Marko Gustavo Ciurlizza Rodríguez (7/0)], César Miguel Rebosio Compans (27/0), Juan Luciano Pajuelo Chávez (4/0), Percy Celso Olivares Polanco (76/1), Jorge Antonio Soto Gómez (60/6), Juan José Jayo Legario (44/1) [50.Roger Alberto Serrano Ruiz (14/0)], José Guillermo del Solar Alvarez-Calderón (61/8), Roberto Carlos Palacios Mestas (76/17), Herlyn Ysrael Zúñiga Yañez (12/2), Roberto Carlos Holsen Alvarado (15/4) [45.Paolo Freddy Maldonado Farje (8/2)]. Trainer: Francisco Maturana (9).

425. 29.06.2000 **ECUADOR – PERU** **2-1(1-0)** 17th FIFA WC. Qualifiers

Estadio Olimpico „Atahualpa", Quito; Referee: Carlos Eugênio Simón (Brazil); Attendance: 40,167

PER: Óscar Manuel Ibañez Holzmann (20/0), Jorge Antonio Soto Gómez (61/6), Juan Luciano Pajuelo Chávez (5/1), César Miguel Rebosio Compans (28/0), Percy Celso Olivares Polanco (77/1) [46.Herlyn Ysrael Zúñiga Yañez (13/2)], Nolberto Albino Solano Todco (48/10), Juan José Jayo Legario (45/1) [78.Marko Gustavo Ciurlizza Rodríguez (8/0)], Roberto Carlos Palacios Mestas (77/17), Roger Alberto Serrano Ruiz (15/0) [20.David Soria Yoshinari (2/0)], José Guillermo del Solar Alvarez-Calderón (62/8), Claudio Miguel Pizarro Bosio (14/3). Trainer: Francisco Maturana (10).

Goal: Juan Luciano Pajuelo Chávez (75).

426. 19.07.2000 **PERU – COLOMBIA** **0-1(0-0)** 17th FIFA WC. Qualifiers

Estadio Nacional, Lima; Referee: Mario Sánchez (Chile); Attendance: 32,207

PER: Jhonny Vegas (1/0), Jorge Antonio Soto Gómez (62/6) [55.Carlos Antonio Flores Murillo (2/0)], César Miguel Rebosio Compans (29/0), Juan Luciano Pajuelo Chávez (6/1), Percy Celso Olivares Polanco (78/1), Juan José Jayo Legario (46/1), José Guillermo del Solar Alvarez-Calderón (63/8), Nolberto Albino Solano Todco (49/10), Roberto Carlos Palacios Mestas (78/17), Claudio Miguel Pizarro Bosio (15/3), Herlyn Ysrael Zúñiga Yañez (14/2) [55.Abel Augusto Lobatón Espejo (7/0)]. Trainer: Francisco Maturana (11).

427. 26.07.2000 **URUGUAY – PERU** **0-0** 17th FIFA WC. Qualifiers

Estadio Centenario, Montevideo; Referee: Oscar Godoi (Brazil); Attendance: 54,345

PER: Jhonny Vegas (2/0), Jorge Antonio Soto Gómez (63/6), César Miguel Rebosio Compans (30/0), Juan Luciano Pajuelo Chávez (7/1), Percy Celso Olivares Polanco (79/1), Juan José Jayo Legario (47/1), Nolberto Albino Solano Todco (50/10), Roger Alberto Serrano Ruiz (16/0) [80.Erick Omar Torres Arias (10/0)], Marko Gustavo Ciurlizza Rodríguez (9/0), Roberto Carlos Palacios Mestas (79/17), Claudio Miguel Pizarro Bosio (16/3). Trainer: Francisco Maturana (12).

428. 16.08.2000 **PERU – VENEZUELA** **1-0(0-0)** 17th FIFA WC. Qualifiers

Estadio Nacional, Lima; Referee: Byron Aldemar Moreno Ruales (Ecuador); Attendance: 41,084

PER: Óscar Manuel Ibañez Holzmann (21/0), Jorge Antonio Soto Gómez (64/6), Juan Luciano Pajuelo Chávez (8/1) [40.Luis Manuel Carmelo Marengo Ramos (11/1)], José Alberto Soto Gómez (60/1), David Soria Yoshinari (3/0), Nolberto Albino Solano Todco (51/10) [66.Paolo Freddy Maldonado Farje (9/2)], Juan José Jayo Legario (48/1), José Guillermo del Solar Alvarez-Calderón (64/8), Roberto Carlos Palacios Mestas (80/18), Claudio Miguel Pizarro Bosio (17/3), Herlyn Ysrael Zúñiga Yañez (15/2). Trainer: Francisco Maturana (13).

Goal: Roberto Carlos Palacios Mestas (68).

429. 03.09.2000 **PERU – ARGENTINA** **1-2(0-2)** 17th FIFA WC. Qualifiers

Estadio Nacional, Lima; Referee: Oscar Julián Ruíz Acosta (Colombia); Attendance: 43,951

PER: Jhonny Vegas (3/0), Nolberto Albino Solano Todco (52/10), Juan Luciano Pajuelo Chávez (9/1), José Alberto Soto Gómez (61/1), Percy Celso Olivares Polanco (80/1) [78.Herlyn Ysrael Zúñiga Yañez (16/2)], Juan José Jayo Legario (49/1), José Guillermo del Solar Alvarez-Calderón (65/8) [46.Gustavo Marcelo Tempone Manterola (1/0)], José Antonio Pereda Maruyama (25/4), Roberto Carlos Palacios Mestas (81/18), Andrés Augusto Mendoza Azevedo (8/2), Claudio Miguel Pizarro Bosio (18/3). Trainer: Francisco Maturana (14).

Goal: Walter Samuel (68 own goal).

430. 08.10.2000 **BOLIVIA – PERU** **1-0(1-0)** 17th FIFA WC. Qualifiers

Estadio „Hernándo Siles Zuazo", La Paz; Referee: José Patricio Carpio Guevara (Ecuador); Attendance: 21,791

PER: Óscar Manuel Ibañez Holzmann (22/0), Franco Walter Zeballos (1/0), Juan Luciano Pajuelo Chávez (10/1), César Miguel Rebosio Compans (31/0), Nolberto Albino Solano Todco (53/10) [46.Alfredo Enrique Carmona Hurtado (6/0], David Soria Yoshinari (4/0), Gregorio Abel Bernales Francia (4/0), Juan José Jayo Legario (50/1), Roberto Carlos Palacios Mestas (82/18), Claudio Miguel Pizarro Bosio (19/3) [57.Abel Augusto Lobatón Espejo (8/0)], Herlyn Ysrael Zúñiga Yañez (17/2) [57.Piero Fernando Alva Niezen (1/0)]. Trainer: Julio César Uribe Flores (1).

431. 15.11.2000 **PARAGUAY – PERU** **5-1(3-0)** 17th FIFA WC. Qualifiers

Estadio Defensores del Chaco, Asunción; Referee: Daniel Giménez (Argentina); Attendance: 30,000

PER: Óscar Manuel Ibañez Holzmann (23/0), César Miguel Rebosio Compans (32/0), Juan Luciano Pajuelo Chávez (11/1) [22.Juan José Manuel Velásquez Castillo (6/0)], David Soria Yoshinari (5/0), Franco Walter Zeballos (2/0) [58.Pedro Alejandro García de la Cruz (1/1)], José Guillermo del Solar Alvarez-Calderón (66/8), José Antonio Pereda Maruyama (26/4) [45.Abel Augusto Lobatón Espejo (9/0)], Gregorio Abel Bernales Francia (5/0), Roberto Carlos Palacios Mestas (83/18), Darío Teodoro Muchotrigo Carrillo (17/1), Piero Fernando Alva Niezen (2/0). Trainer: Julio César Uribe Flores (2).

Goal: Pedro Alejandro García de la Cruz (76).

432. 07.03.2001 **PERU – HONDURAS** **0-0**
Orange Bowl, Miami; Referee: Kevin Terry (United States); Attendance: 17,790
PER: Óscar Manuel Ibañez Holzmann (24/0) [46.Leao Butrón Gotuzzo (1/0)], Juan Luciano Pajuelo Chávez (12/1), César Miguel Rebosio Compans (33/0) [79.José Alberto Soto Gómez (62/1)], Juan Alexis Ubillús Calmet (11/0), Emilio Martín Hidalgo Conde (10/2), José Guillermo del Solar Alvarez-Calderón (67/8) [46.Juan Carlos Bazalar Cruzado (17/0)], Roberto Carlos Palacios Mestas (84/18), Marko Gustavo Ciurlizza Rodríguez (10/0), Roberto Carlos Holsen Alvarado (16/4) [46.Piero Fernando Alva Niezen (3/0)], Darío Teodoro Muchotrigo Carrillo (18/1), Roberto Enrique Silva Pro (1/0) [67.Paolo Freddy Maldonado Farje (10/2)]. Trainer: Julio César Uribe Flores (3).

433. 27.03.2001 **PERU – CHILE** **3-1(0-0)** 17th FIFA WC. Qualifiers
Estadio Nacional, Lima; Referee: Ángel Osvaldo Sánchez (Argentina); Attendance: 38,901
PER: Miguel Eduardo Miranda Campos (40/0), César Miguel Rebosio Compans (34/0), Percy Celso Olivares Polanco (81/1) [41.Emilio Martín Hidalgo Conde (11/2)], Juan Luciano Pajuelo Chávez (13/1), Nolberto Albino Solano Todco (54/10), Juan José Jayo Legario (51/1), Roberto Carlos Palacios Mestas (85/18), Darío Teodoro Muchotrigo Carrillo (19/1) [74.Marko Gustavo Ciurlizza Rodríguez (11/0)], Andrés Augusto Mendoza Azevedo (9/3), Claudio Miguel Pizarro Bosio (20/4), José Guillermo del Solar Alvarez-Calderón (68/8) [46.Flavio Francisco Maestri Andrade (44/10)]. Trainer: Julio César Uribe Flores (4).
Goals: Flavio Francisco Maestri Andrade (53), Andrés Augusto Mendoza Azevedo (72), Claudio Miguel Pizarro Bosio (81).

434. 25.04.2001 **BRAZIL – PERU** **1-1(0-0)** 17th FIFA WC. Qualifiers
Estádio „Cicero Pompeu de Toledo“ Morumbi, São Paulo; Referee: Abdul Rahman Al Zaid (Saudi Arabia); Attendance: 55,000
PER: Miguel Eduardo Miranda Campos (41/0), César Miguel Rebosio Compans (35/0), Percy Celso Olivares Polanco (82/1) [75.Gustavo Marcelo Tempone Manterola (2/0)], Juan Luciano Pajuelo Chávez (14/2), Nolberto Albino Solano Todco (55/10), Juan José Jayo Legario (52/1), Flavio Francisco Maestri Andrade (45/10) [46.Claudio Miguel Pizarro Bosio (21/4)], Roberto Carlos Palacios Mestas (86/18), Darío Teodoro Muchotrigo Carrillo (20/1) [85.Andrés Augusto Mendoza Azevedo (10/3)], Emilio Martín Hidalgo Conde (12/2), Marko Gustavo Ciurlizza Rodríguez (12/0). Trainer: Julio César Uribe Flores (5).
Goal: Juan Luciano Pajuelo Chávez (77).

435. 02.06.2001 **PERU – ECUADOR** **1-2(1-1)** 17th FIFA WC. Qualifiers
Estadio Monumental, Lima; Referee: Antonio Marrufo Mendoza (Mexico); Attendance: 54,236
PER: Miguel Eduardo Miranda Campos (42/0), Nolberto Albino Solano Todco (56/10), César Miguel Rebosio Compans (36/0), Juan Luciano Pajuelo Chávez (15/2), Percy Celso Olivares Polanco (83/1) [61.Emilio Martín Hidalgo Conde (13/2)], Juan José Jayo Legario (53/1), Marko Gustavo Ciurlizza Rodríguez (13/0), Roberto Carlos Palacios Mestas (87/18), Claudio Miguel Pizarro Bosio (22/5), Flavio Francisco Maestri Andrade (46/10) [46.Roberto Enrique Silva Pro (2/0)], Andrés Augusto Mendoza Azevedo (11/3) [72.Darío Teodoro Muchotrigo Carrillo (21/1)]. Trainer: Julio César Uribe Flores (6).
Goal: Claudio Miguel Pizarro Bosio (2).

436. 12.07.2001 **PERU – PARAGUAY** **3-3(1-1)** 40th Copa América. Group Stage
Estadio „Pascual Guerrero“, Cali (Colombia); Referee: Ángel Sánchez (Argentina); Attendance: 27,878
PER: Óscar Manuel Ibañez Holzmann (25/0), Jorge Antonio Soto Gómez (65/6) [68.Julio Edson Uribe Elera (1/0)], José Alberto Soto Gómez (63/1), Santiago Roberto Salazar Peña (5/0), Juan Luciano Pajuelo Chávez (16/3), Emilio Martín Hidalgo Conde (14/2), Juan José Jayo Legario (54/1), José Guillermo del Solar Alvarez-Calderón (69/9) [*sent off 79*], Gustavo Marcelo Tempone Manterola (3/0) [68.Pedro Luis Ascoy Cortez (1/0)], Abel Augusto Lobatón Espejo (10/1) [76.Roberto Carlos Holsen Alvarado (17/4)], Darío Teodoro Muchotrigo Carrillo (22/1). Trainer: Julio César Uribe Flores (7).
Goals: Abel Augusto Lobatón Espejo (16), Juan Luciano Pajuelo Chávez (57), José Guillermo del Solar Alvarez-Calderón (72).

437. 15.07.2001 **BRAZIL – PERU** **2-0(1-0)** 40th Copa América. Group Stage
Estadio „Pascual Guerrero“, Cali (Colombia); Referee: Jorge Larrionda Pietrafiesa (Uruguay); Attendance: 25,711
PER: Óscar Manuel Ibañez Holzmann (26/0), Jorge Antonio Soto Gómez (66/6), José Alberto Soto Gómez (64/1), Santiago Roberto Salazar Peña (6/0) [*sent off 67*], Juan Luciano Pajuelo Chávez (17/3), Emilio Martín Hidalgo Conde (15/2), Juan José Jayo Legario (55/1), Luis Alberto Hernández Díaz (1/0) [46.Franco Walter Zeballos (3/0)], Pedro Alejandro García de la Cruz (2/1) [60.Roberto Carlos Holsen Alvarado (18/4)], Darío Teodoro Muchotrigo Carrillo (23/1), Abel Augusto Lobatón Espejo (11/1) [69.Juan Francisco Hernández Díaz (1/0)]. Trainer: Julio César Uribe Flores (8).

438. 18.07.2001 **PERU – MEXICO** **1-0(0-0)** 40th Copa América. Group Stage
Estadio „Pascual Guerrero“, Cali (Colombia); Referee: René Ortubé (Bolivia); Attendance: 24,105
PER: Óscar Manuel Ibañez Holzmann (27/0), Franco Walter Zeballos (4/0) [46.Pedro Alejandro García de la Cruz (3/1)], José Alberto Soto Gómez (65/1), Emilio Martín Hidalgo Conde (16/2), Juan Luciano Pajuelo Chávez (18/3), Juan José Jayo Legario (56/1), José Guillermo del Solar Alvarez-Calderón (70/9), Jorge Antonio Soto Gómez (67/6), Darío Teodoro Muchotrigo Carrillo (24/1) [*sent off 62*], Roberto Carlos Holsen Alvarado (19/5) [89.Pedro Luis Ascoy Cortez (2/0)], Abel Augusto Lobatón Espejo (12/1) [63.Gustavo Marcelo Tempone Manterola (4/0)]. Trainer: Julio César Uribe Flores (9).
Goal: Roberto Carlos Holsen Alvarado (48).

439. 23.07.2001 **COLOMBIA – PERU** **3-0(0-0)** 40th Copa América. Quarter-Finals
Estadio Centenario, Arménia; Referee: Gilberto Alcalà (Mexico); Attendance: 22,458
PER: Óscar Manuel Ibañez Holzmann (28/0), Pedro Alejandro García de la Cruz (4/1), Franco Walter Zeballos (5/0), Juan Luciano Pajuelo Chávez (19/3), Santiago Roberto Salazar Peña (7/0), José Alberto Soto Gómez (66/1), Juan Francisco Hernández Díaz (2/0) [65.Walter Ricardo Vílchez Soto (1/0)], Juan José Jayo Legario (57/1), José Guillermo del Solar Alvarez-Calderón (71/9) [77.Gustavo Marcelo Tempone Manterola (5/0)], Jorge Antonio Soto Gómez (68/6) [74.Julio Julio Edson Uribe Elera (2/0)], Roberto Carlos Holsen Alvarado (20/5). Trainer: Julio César Uribe Flores (10).

440. 16.08.2001 **COLOMBIA – PERU** **0-1(0-0)** 17th FIFA WC. Qualifiers
Estadio „Nemesio Camacho“ 'El Campín', Bogotá; Referee: Felipe Ramos Rizzo (Mexico); Attendance: 33,875
PER: Miguel Eduardo Miranda Campos (43/0), César Miguel Rebosio Compans (37/0), Emilio Martín Hidalgo Conde (17/2), Juan Luciano Pajuelo Chávez (20/3), Nolberto Albino Solano Todco (57/11), Juan José Jayo Legario (58/1) [73.Santiago Roberto Salazar Peña (8/0)], Claudio Miguel Pizarro Bosio (23/5) [82.José Alberto Soto Gómez (67/1)], Roberto Carlos Palacios Mestas (88/18), Jorge Antonio Soto Gómez (69/6), Andrés Augusto Mendoza Azevedo (12/3) [87.Roberto Carlos Holsen Alvarado (21/5)], José Guillermo del Solar Alvarez-Calderón (72/9). Trainer: Julio César Uribe Flores (11).
Goal: Nolberto Albino Solano Todco (47).

441. 04.09.2001 **PERU – URUGUAY** **0-2(0-2)** 17th FIFA WC. Qualifiers
Estadio Nacional, Lima; Referee: Anders Frisk (Sweden); Attendance: 40,524
PER: Miguel Eduardo Miranda Campos (44/0), Emilio Martín Hidalgo Conde (18/2), Juan Luciano Pajuelo Chávez (21/3), José Alberto Soto Gómez (68/1), Nolberto Albino Solano Todco (58/11), Juan José Jayo Legario (59/1), Claudio Miguel Pizarro Bosio (24/5) [46.Flavio Francisco Maestri Andrade (47/10)], Roberto Carlos Palacios Mestas (89/18), Jorge Antonio Soto Gómez (70/6), Andrés Augusto Mendoza Azevedo (13/3), José Guillermo del Solar Alvarez-Calderón (73/9) [70.José Antonio Pereda Maruyama (27/4)]. Trainer: Julio César Uribe Flores (12).

442. 06.10.2001 **VENEZUELA - PERU** **3-0(0-0)** 17th FIFA WC. Qualifiers

Estadio Pueblo Nuevo, San Cristóbal; Referee: Mario Sánchez (Chile); Attendance: 17,220

PER: Miguel Eduardo Miranda Campos (45/0), Jorge Raúl Huamán Salinas (8/0) [55.Jorge Ramírez (3/0)], César Miguel Rebosio Compans (38/0) [*sent off 44*], Emilio Martín Hidalgo Conde (19/2), Juan Luciano Pajuelo Chávez (22/3), Juan José Jayo Legario (60/1), Flavio Francisco Maestri Andrade (48/10) [75.Pedro Alejandro García de la Cruz (5/1)], Roberto Carlos Palacios Mestas (90/18), Jorge Antonio Soto Gómez (71/6), Andrés Augusto Mendoza Azevedo (14/3) [46.Ernesto Seiko Arakaki Arakaki (1/0) [*sent off 72*], Marko Gustavo Ciurlizza Rodríguez (14/0). Trainer: Julio César Uribe Flores (13).

443. 08.11.2001 **ARGENTINA - PERU** **2-0(0-0)** 17th FIFA WC. Qualifiers

Estadio Monumental „Antonio Vespucio Liberti“, Buenos Aires; Referee: Jorge Luis Larrionda Pietrafiesa (Uruguay); Attendance: 18,901

PER: Miguel Eduardo Miranda Campos (46/0), Emilio Martín Hidalgo Conde (20/2) [61.Jorge Raúl Huamán Salinas (9/0)], Juan Luciano Pajuelo Chávez (23/3), Juan José Jayo Legario (61/1), Flavio Francisco Maestri Andrade (49/10), Roberto Carlos Palacios Mestas (91/18), Jorge Antonio Soto Gómez (72/6), Santiago Roberto Salazar Peña (9/0), Claudio Miguel Pizarro Bosio (25/5) [*sent off 76*], José Guillermo del Solar Alvarez-Calderón (74/9) [60.Andrés Augusto Mendoza Azevedo (15/3)], Marko Gustavo Ciurlizza Rodríguez (15/0). Trainer: Julio César Uribe Flores (14).

444. 14.11.2001 **PERU - BOLIVIA** **1-1(1-0)** 17th FIFA WC. Qualifiers

Estadio Monumental, Lima; Referee: Héctor Walter Baldassi (Argentina); Attendance: 2,374

PER: Miguel Eduardo Miranda Campos (47/0), Jorge Raúl Huamán Salinas (10/0), Emilio Martín Hidalgo Conde (21/2), Juan Luciano Pajuelo Chávez (24/3), Juan José Jayo Legario (62/1), Roberto Carlos Palacios Mestas (92/18), Andrés Augusto Mendoza Azevedo (16/3), Jorge Antonio Soto Gómez (73/6) [46.Frank Palomino (9/0)], Santiago Roberto Salazar Peña (10/0), Marko Gustavo Ciurlizza Rodríguez (16/0) [69.Jean Franco Ferrari Chiabra (1/0)], Piero Fernando Alva Niezen (4/1) [76.Luis Germán del Carmen Carty Monserrate (24/3)]. Trainer: Julio César Uribe Flores (15).

Goal: Piero Fernando Alva Niezen (8).

445. 23.02.2003 **PERU - HAITI** **5-1(3-0)**

Estadio „Alejandro Villanueva“, Lima; Referee: Víctor Hugo Rivera (Peru); Attendance: 5,500

PER: Óscar Manuel Ibañez Holzmann (29/0), Jorge Antonio Soto Gómez (74/7), Miguel Angel Villalta Hurtado (1/0) [61.Jorge Martín Araujo Paredes (1/0)], José Alberto Soto Gómez (69/3), José Alberto Moisella Huapaya (1/0) [59.Guillermo Sandro Salas Suárez (1/0)], Henry Edson Quinteros Sánchez (4/0) [69.Alfredo Enrique Carmona Hurtado (7/0)], Juan José Jayo Legario (63/1), Fernando Daniel del Solar Álvarez Calderón (1/0) [59.Aldo Ítalo Olcese Vasallo (1/0)], Carlos Alberto Zegarra Zamora (1/0), Jefferson Agustín Farfán Guadalupe (1/1) [89.Miguel Ángel Mostto Fernández-Prada (1/0)], Antonio Serrano (1/1) [61.Johan Joussep Sotil Eche (1/0)]. Trainer: Paulo César Autuori (1).

Goals: José Alberto Soto Gómez (13 penalty), Antonio Serrano (19), Jorge Antonio Soto Gómez (26), José Alberto Soto Gómez (83), Jefferson Agustín Farfán Guadalupe (84).

446. 30.03.2003 **CHILE - PERU** **2-0(1-0)**

Estadio Nacional, Santiago; Referee: Carlos Amarilla Demarqui (Paraguay); Attendance: 39,662

PER: Óscar Manuel Ibañez Holzmann (30/0), Guillermo Sandro Salas Suárez (2/0), Miguel Angel Villalta Hurtado (2/0), John Christian Galliquio Castro (1/0), Emilio Martín Hidalgo Conde (22/2), Henry Edson Quinteros Sánchez (5/0) [57.Jefferson Agustín Farfán Guadalupe (2/1)], Juan José Jayo Legario (64/1), Carlos Alberto Zegarra Zamora (2/0) [82.José Alberto Corcuera Valdiviezo (1/0)], Roberto Carlos Palacios Mestas (93/18) [85.Aldo Ítalo Olcese Vasallo (2/0)], Andrés Augusto Mendoza Azevedo (17/3) [81.Flavio Francisco Maestri Andrade (50/10)], Claudio Miguel Pizarro Bosio (26/5). Trainer: Paulo César Autuori (2).

447. 02.04.2003 **PERU - CHILE** **3-0(1-0)**

Estadio Nacional, Lima; Referee: Oscar Julián Ruíz Acosta (Colombia); Attendance: 20,700

PER: Erick Guillermo Delgado Vásquez (1/0), Jorge Antonio Soto Gómez (75/7), Miguel Angel Villalta Hurtado (3/0), César Miguel Rebosio Compans (39/0) [83.Alberto Junior Rodríguez Valdelomar (1/0)], Emilio Martín Hidalgo Conde (23/2) [59.Guillermo Sandro Salas Suárez (3/0)], Henry Edson Quinteros Sánchez (6/1), Juan José Jayo Legario (65/1), Carlos Alberto Zegarra Zamora (3/0) [46.Aldo Ítalo Olcese Vasallo (3/0)], Roberto Carlos Palacios Mestas (94/18) [74.José Alberto Corcuera Valdiviezo (2/0)], Claudio Miguel Pizarro Bosio (27/7), Andrés Augusto Mendoza Azevedo (18/3) [74.Flavio Francisco Maestri Andrade (51/10) [*sent off 89*]]. Trainer: Paulo César Autuori (3).

Goals: Henry Edson Quinteros Sánchez (17), Claudio Miguel Pizarro Bosio (48, 49).

448. 30.04.2003 **PERU - PARAGUAY** **0-1(0-0)**

Estadio Monumental, Lima; Referee: Carlos López (Colombia); Attendance: 18,000

PER: Erick Guillermo Delgado Vásquez (2/0), Jorge Antonio Soto Gómez (76/7), Miguel Angel Villalta Hurtado (4/0) [46.John Christian Galliquio Castro (2/0)], César Miguel Rebosio Compans (40/0), Emilio Martín Hidalgo Conde (24/2), Henry Edson Quinteros Sánchez (7/1) [58.Guillermo Sandro Salas Suárez (4/0)], Juan José Jayo Legario (66/1) [58.César Camilo Ccahuantico Meza (1/0)], Carlos Alberto Zegarra Zamora (4/0), Jefferson Agustín Farfán Guadalupe (3/1) [46.Aldo Ítalo Olcese Vasallo (4/0)], Claudio Miguel Pizarro Bosio (28/7), Andrés Augusto Mendoza Azevedo (19/3) [67.Roberto Enrique Silva Pro (3/0)]. Trainer: Paulo César Autuori (4).

449. 11.06.2003 **ECUADOR - PERU** **2-2(1-1)**

Giants Stadium, East Rutherford, New York (United States); Referee: Kevin Terry (United States); Attendance: 35,000

PER: Erick Guillermo Delgado Vásquez (3/0), Jorge Antonio Soto Gómez (77/7), César Miguel Rebosio Compans (41/0), José Alberto Soto Gómez (70/3), Emilio Martín Hidalgo Conde (25/2), Jefferson Agustín Farfán Guadalupe (4/1), Juan José Jayo Legario (67/1) [70.Marko Gustavo Ciurlizza Rodríguez (17/0)], Carlos Alberto Zegarra Zamora (5/0) [84.John Christian Galliquio Castro (3/0)], Alfredo Enrique Carmona Hurtado (8/0) [60.Aldo Ítalo Olcese Vasallo (5/0)], Andrés Augusto Mendoza Azevedo (20/4) [87.José Alberto Corcuera Valdiviezo (3/0)], Roberto Enrique Silva Pro (4/1). Trainer: Paulo César Autuori (5).

Goals: Roberto Enrique Silva Pro (42), Andrés Augusto Mendoza Azevedo (52).

450. 26.06.2003 **PERU - VENEZUELA** **1-0(0-0)**

Orange Bowl, Miami; Referee: Michael Kennedy (United States)

PER: Erick Guillermo Delgado Vásquez (4/0) [46.Óscar Manuel Ibañez Holzmann (31/0)], Jorge Antonio Soto Gómez (78/7), John Christian Galliquio Castro (4/0), José Alberto Soto Gómez (Cap) (71/3) [72.Luis Manuel Carmelo Marengo Ramos (12/1)], Martín Vásquez (1/0), Henry Edson Quinteros Sánchez (8/1) [72.Alfredo Enrique Carmona Hurtado (9/1)], Juan José Jayo Legario (68/1) [71.Gregorio Abel Bernales Francia (6/0)], Marko Gustavo Ciurlizza Rodríguez (18/0), Carlos Alberto Zegarra Zamora (6/0) [46.Aldo Ítalo Olcese Vasallo (6/0)], Jefferson Agustín Farfán Guadalupe (5/1), Roberto Enrique Silva Pro (5/1) [75.Carlos Alberto Orejuela Pita (1/0)]. Trainer: Paulo César Autuori (6).

Goal: Alfredo Enrique Carmona Hurtado (74).

451. 02.07.2003 **PERU – GUATEMALA** **2-1(2-0)**
Candlestick Park, San Francisco (United States); Referee: Brian Hall (United States); Attendance: 20,000
PER: Erick Guillermo Delgado Vásquez (5/0) [46.Leao Butrón Gotuzzo (2/0)], Jorge Antonio Soto Gómez (79/7) [77.José Alberto Corcuera Valdiviezo (4/0)], John Christian Galliquio Castro (5/0) [66.Miguel Angel Villalta Hurtado (5/0)], José Alberto Soto Gómez (72/3), Martín Vásquez (2/0) [46.Guillermo Sandro Salas Suárez (5/0)], Henry Edson Quinteros Sánchez (9/1) [46.Aldo Ítalo Olcese Vasallo (7/0)], Juan José Jayo Legario (69/1) [77.Carlos Alberto Zegarra Zamora (7/0)], Marko Gustavo Ciurlizza Rodríguez (19/0) [46.Gregorio Abel Bernales Francia (7/0)], Alfredo Enrique Carmona Hurtado (10/1), Carlos Alberto Orejuela Pita (2/1), Roberto Enrique Silva Pro (6/2). Trainer: Paulo César Autuori (7).
Goals: Roberto Enrique Silva Pro (15), Carlos Alberto Orejuela Pita (35).

452. 24.07.2003 **PERU – URUGUAY** **3-4(1-1)**
Estadio Nacional, Lima; Referee: Manuel Garay (Peru); Attendance: 7,500
PER: Óscar Manuel Ibañez Holzmann (32/0), Guillermo Sandro Salas Suárez (6/0), Luis Manuel Carmelo Marengo Ramos (13/2), Miguel Angel Villalta Hurtado (6/0), Martín Vásquez (3/0), Aldo Ítalo Olcese Vasallo (8/0) [60.Gregorio Abel Bernales Francia (8/0)], Juan José Jayo Legario (70/1) [*sent off 84*], Carlos Alberto Zegarra Zamora (8/0), Roberto Carlos Palacios Mestas (95/18), Jefferson Agustín Farfán Guadalupe (6/3), Roberto Enrique Silva Pro (7/2) [67.Carlos Alberto Orejuela Pita (3/1)]. Trainer: Paulo César Autuori (8).
Goals: Jefferson Agustín Farfán Guadalupe (27), Luis Manuel Carmelo Marengo Ramos (46), Jefferson Agustín Farfán Guadalupe (56).

453. 30.07.2003 **URUGUAY – PERU** **1-0(0-0)**
Estadio Centenario, Montevideo; Referee: Gustavo Méndez (Uruguay); Attendance: 6,800
PER: Erick Guillermo Delgado Vásquez (6/0), Omar Alberto Zegarra Tejada (1/0) [84.Martín Vásquez (4/0)], Miguel Angel Villalta Hurtado (7/0), Alberto Junior Rodríguez Valdelomar (2/0), Guillermo Sandro Salas Suárez (7/0), Henry Edson Quinteros Sánchez (10/1) [81.Carlos Alberto Orejuela Pita (4/1)], Marko Gustavo Ciurlizza Rodríguez (20/0) [61.Gregorio Abel Bernales Francia (9/0)], Carlos Alberto Zegarra Zamora (9/0), Luis Alberto Hernández Díaz (2/0) [70.Aldo Ítalo Olcese Vasallo (9/0)], Jefferson Agustín Farfán Guadalupe (7/3), Roberto Carlos Holsen Alvarado (22/5) [70.Juan Elías Cominges Mayorga (1/0)]. Trainer: Paulo César Autuori (9).

454. 20.08.2003 **PERU – MEXICO** **3-1(3-0)**
Giants Stadium, East Rutherford (United States); Referee: Brian Hall (United States); Attendance: 35,000
PER: Erick Guillermo Delgado Vásquez (7/0), Jorge Antonio Soto Gómez (80/7), César Miguel Rebosio Compans (42/0), John Christian Galliquio Castro (6/0) [*sent off 69*], Emilio Martín Hidalgo Conde (26/2), Nolberto Albino Solano Todco (59/12), Juan José Jayo Legario (71/1), Carlos Alberto Zegarra Zamora (10/1), Roberto Carlos Palacios Mestas (96/18) [80.José Alberto Soto Gómez (73/3)], Andrés Augusto Mendoza Azevedo (21/4) [80.Jefferson Agustín Farfán Guadalupe (8/3)], Claudio Miguel Pizarro Bosio (29/8) [*sent off 69*]. Trainer: Paulo César Autuori (10).
Goals: Claudio Miguel Pizarro Bosio (1), Carlos Alberto Zegarra Zamora (31), Nolberto Albino Solano Todco (33).

455. 27.08.2003 **PERU – GUATEMALA** **0-0**
Estadio Nacional, Lima; Referee: Eduardo Lecca (Peru); Attendance: 2,047
PER: Leao Butrón Gotuzzo (3/0), Paolo Giancarlo de la Haza Urquiza (1/0), Juan Luciano Pajuelo Chávez (25/3) [46.Wílder Édison Galliquio Castro (1/0)], Alberto Junior Rodríguez Valdelomar (3/0), Martín Vásquez (5/0) [46.Guillermo Alejandro Guizasola la Rosa (1/0)], Henry Edson Quinteros Sánchez (11/1) [67.César Eduardo Balbín Valles (1/0)], Marco Antonio Ruíz (1/0) [46.José Alberto Corcuera Valdiviezo (5/0)], Luis Alberto Hernández Díaz (3/0), Juan Elías Cominges Mayorga (2/0) [67.Paulo Rinaldo Cruzado Durand (1/0)], Carlos Alberto Orejuela Pita (5/1), Herlyn Ysrael Zúñiga Yañez (18/2) [46.Johan Javier Fano Espinoza (1/0)]. Trainer: Paulo César Autuori (11).

456. 06.09.2003 **PERU – PARAGUAY** **4-1(2-1)** 18th FIFA WC. Qualifiers
Estadio Nacional, Lima; Referee: Héctor Baldassi (Argentina); Attendance: 42,557
PER: Erick Guillermo Delgado Vásquez (8/0), Jorge Antonio Soto Gómez (81/8), César Miguel Rebosio Compans (43/0), John Christian Galliquio Castro (7/0), Emilio Martín Hidalgo Conde (27/2), Nolberto Albino Solano Todco (60/13) [89.José Alberto Soto Gómez (74/3)], Juan José Jayo Legario (72/1), Carlos Alberto Zegarra Zamora (11/1), Roberto Carlos Palacios Mestas (97/18) [76.Marko Gustavo Ciurlizza Rodríguez (21/0)], Claudio Miguel Pizarro Bosio (30/8), Andrés Augusto Mendoza Azevedo (22/5) [70.Jefferson Agustín Farfán Guadalupe (9/4)]. Trainer: Paulo César Autuori (12).
Goals: Nolberto Albino Solano Todco (34), Andrés Augusto Mendoza Azevedo (42), Jorge Antonio Soto Gómez (83), Jefferson Agustín Farfán Guadalupe (90).

457. 09.09.2003 **CHILE – PERU** **2-1(1-0)** 18th FIFA WC. Qualifiers
Estadio Nacional, Santiago; Referee: Horacio Marcelo Elizondo (Argentina); Attendance: 54,303
PER: Erick Guillermo Delgado Vásquez (9/0), Jorge Antonio Soto Gómez (82/8), César Miguel Rebosio Compans (44/0), John Christian Galliquio Castro (8/0), Emilio Martín Hidalgo Conde (28/2), Nolberto Albino Solano Todco (61/13) [81.José Alberto Soto Gómez (75/3)], Juan José Jayo Legario (73/1), Carlos Alberto Zegarra Zamora (12/1), Roberto Carlos Palacios Mestas (98/18) [75.Jefferson Agustín Farfán Guadalupe (10/4)], Claudio Miguel Pizarro Bosio (31/8), Andrés Augusto Mendoza Azevedo (23/6). Trainer: Paulo César Autuori (13).
Goal: Andrés Augusto Mendoza Azevedo (57).

458. 16.11.2003 **PERU – BRAZIL** **1-1(0-1)**
Estadio Monumental, Lima; Referee: Oscar Julián Ruíz Acosta (Colombia); Attendance: 70,000
PER: Óscar Manuel Ibañez Holzmann (33/0), Jorge Antonio Soto Gómez (83/8), César Miguel Rebosio Compans (45/0), John Christian Galliquio Castro (9/0), Emilio Martín Hidalgo Conde (29/2) [52.Guillermo Sandro Salas Suárez (8/0)], Nolberto Albino Solano Todco (62/14), Juan José Jayo Legario (74/1), Marko Gustavo Ciurlizza Rodríguez (22/0), Roberto Carlos Palacios Mestas (99/18) [75.Julio César García Mesones (1/0)], Andrés Augusto Mendoza Azevedo (24/6), Claudio Miguel Pizarro Bosio (32/8). Trainer: Paulo César Autuori (14).
Goal: Nolberto Albino Solano Todco (59).

459. 19.11.2003 **ECUADOR – PERU** **0-0** 18th FIFA WC. Qualifiers
Estadio Olimpico „Atahualpa“, Quito; Referee: Epifanio Gonzáles Chavéz (Paraguay); Attendance: 34,361
PER: Óscar Manuel Ibañez Holzmann (34/0), Jorge Antonio Soto Gómez (84/8), César Miguel Rebosio Compans (46/0), John Christian Galliquio Castro (10/0), Guillermo Sandro Salas Suárez (9/0), Julio César García Mesones (2/0), Juan José Jayo Legario (75/1), Marko Gustavo Ciurlizza Rodríguez (23/0), Roberto Carlos Palacios Mestas (100/18) [54.Alessandro Morán Torres (2/0)], Claudio Miguel Pizarro Bosio (33/8), Andrés Augusto Mendoza Azevedo (25/6) [46.Jefferson Agustín Farfán Guadalupe (11/4)]. Trainer: Paulo César Autuori (15).

460. 18.02.2004 **SPAIN – PERU** **2-1(2-1)**
Estadio Olímpico „Lluís Companys", Barcelona; Referee: Bertrand Layec (France); Attendance: 23,580
PER: Óscar Manuel Ibañez Holzmann (35/0), Jorge Antonio Soto Gómez (85/8) [46.Guillermo Sandro Salas Suárez (10/0)], John Christian Galliquio Castro (11/0) [71.Wilmer Santiago Acasiete Ariadela (1/0)], César Miguel Rebosio Compans (47/0), Emilio Martín Hidalgo Conde (30/2), Nolberto Albino Solano Todco (63/15) [83.Julio César García Mesones (3/0)], Marko Gustavo Ciurlizza Rodríguez (24/0), Carlos Alberto Zegarra Zamora (13/1) [65.Juan Carlos La Rosa Llontrop (1/0)], Roberto Carlos Palacios Mestas (101/18) [74.Henry Edson Quinteros Sánchez (12/1)], Andrés Augusto Mendoza Azevedo (26/6) [67.Roberto Enrique Silva Pro (8/2)], Claudio Miguel Pizarro Bosio (34/8) [67.Jefferson Agustín Farfán Guadalupe (12/4)]. Trainer: Paulo César Autuori (16).
Goal: Nolberto Albino Solano Todco (21).

461. 31.03.2004 **PERU – COLOMBIA** **0-2(0-2)** 18th FIFA WC. Qualifiers
Estadio Nacional, Lima; Referee: Márcio Rezende de Freitas (Brazil); Attendance: 29,325
PER: Óscar Manuel Ibañez Holzmann (36/0), Jorge Antonio Soto Gómez (86/8), John Christian Galliquio Castro (12/0), César Miguel Rebosio Compans (48/0), Emilio Martín Hidalgo Conde (31/2) [46.Guillermo Sandro Salas Suárez (11/0)], Henry Edson Quinteros Sánchez (13/1) [46.Jefferson Agustín Farfán Guadalupe (13/4)], Juan José Jayo Legario (76/1), Marko Gustavo Ciurlizza Rodríguez (25/0), Roberto Carlos Palacios Mestas (102/18) [58.Roberto Enrique Silva Pro (9/2)], Andrés Augusto Mendoza Azevedo (27/6), Claudio Miguel Pizarro Bosio (35/8). Trainer: Paulo César Autuori (17).

462. 28.04.2004 **CHILE – PERU** **1-1(0-0)**
Estadio Regional, Antofagasta; Referee: Carlos Amarilla Demarqui (Paraguay); Attendance: 23,000
PER: Óscar Manuel Ibañez Holzmann (37/0) [71.Leao Butrón Gotuzzo (4/0)], Guillermo Sandro Salas Suárez (12/0), Wilmer Santiago Acasiete Ariadela (2/0), Walter Ricardo Vílchez Soto (2/0), Emilio Martín Hidalgo Conde (32/2) [65.John Christian Galliquio Castro (13/0)], Henry Edson Quinteros Sánchez (14/1) [65.William Medardo Chiroque Távara (1/0)], Juan Carlos La Rosa Llontrop (2/0), Carlos Alberto Zegarra Zamora (14/1), Julio César García Mesones (4/0) [68.Carlos Alberto Orejuela Pita (6/1)], Roberto Carlos Palacios Mestas (103/18) [65.Pedro Alejandro García de la Cruz (6/1)], Roberto Enrique Silva Pro (10/2) [68.Herlyn Ysrael Zúñiga Yañez (19/3)]. Trainer: Paulo César Autuori (18).
Goal: Herlyn Ysrael Zúñiga Yañez (90).

463. 01.06.2004 **URUGUAY – PERU** **1-3(0-2)** 18th FIFA WC. Qualifiers
Estadio Centenario, Montevideo; Referee: Rubén Selman (Chile); Attendance: 23,000
PER: Óscar Manuel Ibañez Holzmann (38/0), John Christian Galliquio Castro (14/0), César Miguel Rebosio Compans (49/0) [81.Julio César García Mesones (5/0)], Wilmer Santiago Acasiete Ariadela (3/0), Walter Ricardo Vílchez Soto (3/0), Nolberto Albino Solano Todco (64/16), Juan José Jayo Legario (77/1), Carlos Alberto Zegarra Zamora (15/1), Roberto Carlos Palacios Mestas (104/18) [58.Jorge Antonio Soto Gómez (87/8)], Claudio Miguel Pizarro Bosio (36/9) [46.Andrés Augusto Mendoza Azevedo (28/6)], Jefferson Agustín Farfán Guadalupe (14/5). Trainer: Paulo César Autuori (19).
Goals: Nolberto Albino Solano Todco (14), Claudio Miguel Pizarro Bosio (19), Jefferson Agustín Farfán Guadalupe (62).

464. 06.06.2004 **PERU – VENEZUELA** **0-0** 18th FIFA WC. Qualifiers
Estadio Nacional, Lima; Referee: Jorge Larrionda Pietrafiesa (Uruguay); Attendance: 39,912
PER: Óscar Manuel Ibañez Holzmann (39/0), Jorge Antonio Soto Gómez (88/8), César Miguel Rebosio Compans (50/0), Wilmer Santiago Acasiete Ariadela (4/0), Emilio Martín Hidalgo Conde (33/2) [67.Walter Ricardo Vílchez Soto (4/0)], Nolberto Albino Solano Todco (65/16), Juan José Jayo Legario (78/1), Carlos Alberto Zegarra Zamora (16/1), Roberto Carlos Palacios Mestas (105/18) [67.Carlos Alberto Orejuela Pita (7/1)], Andrés Augusto Mendoza Azevedo (29/6) [79.Roberto Enrique Silva Pro (11/2)], Jefferson Agustín Farfán Guadalupe (15/5). Trainer: Paulo César Autuori (20).

465. 30.06.2004 **ARGENTINA – PERU** **2-1(1-1)**
Giants Stadium, East Rutherford, New York (United States); Referee: Kevin Stott (United States); Attendance: 41,013
PER: Óscar Manuel Ibañez Holzmann (40/0), Jorge Antonio Soto Gómez (89/8), César Miguel Rebosio Compans (51/0), Wilmer Santiago Acasiete Ariadela (5/0), Walter Ricardo Vílchez Soto (5/0), Nolberto Albino Solano Todco (66/17) [63.John Christian Galliquio Castro (15/0), 85.Pedro Alejandro García de la Cruz (7/1)], Juan Carlos La Rosa Llontrop (3/0), Carlos Alberto Zegarra Zamora (17/1) [79.Guillermo Sandro Salas Suárez (13/0)], Julio César García Mesones (6/0), Flavio Francisco Maestri Andrade (52/10), Andrés Augusto Mendoza Azevedo (30/6) [63.Jefferson Agustín Farfán Guadalupe (16/5)]. Trainer: Paulo César Autuori (21).
Goal: Nolberto Albino Solano Todco (36 penalty).

466. 06.07.2004 **PERU – BOLIVIA** **2-2(0-1)** 41st Copa América. Group Stage
Estadio Nacional, Lima; Referee: Héctor Baldassi (Argentina); Attendance: 41,073
PER: Óscar Manuel Ibañez Holzmann (41/0), Jorge Antonio Soto Gómez (90/8), César Miguel Rebosio Compans (52/0), Wilmer Santiago Acasiete Ariadela (6/0), Walter Ricardo Vílchez Soto (6/0), Nolberto Albino Solano Todco (67/17) [61.Roberto Carlos Palacios Mestas (106/19)], Juan José Jayo Legario (79/1), Carlos Alberto Zegarra Zamora (18/1) [80.Aldo Ítalo Olcese Vasallo (10/0)], Flavio Francisco Maestri Andrade (53/10) [61.Andrés Augusto Mendoza Azevedo (31/6)], Claudio Miguel Pizarro Bosio (37/10), Jefferson Agustín Farfán Guadalupe (17/5). Trainer: Paulo César Autuori (22).
Goals: Claudio Miguel Pizarro Bosio (68 penalty), Roberto Carlos Palacios Mestas (86).

467. 09.07.2004 **PERU – VENEZUELA** **3-1(1-0)** 41st Copa América. Group Stage
Estadio Nacional, Lima; Referee: Rubén Selman (Chile); Attendance: 42,054
PER: Óscar Manuel Ibañez Holzmann (42/0), Guillermo Sandro Salas Suárez (14/0), César Miguel Rebosio Compans (53/0), Wilmer Santiago Acasiete Ariadela (7/1), Walter Ricardo Vílchez Soto (7/0), Nolberto Albino Solano Todco (68/18) [75.Jorge Antonio Soto Gómez (91/8)], Juan José Jayo Legario (80/1), Roberto Carlos Palacios Mestas (107/19) [81.Marko Gustavo Ciurlizza Rodríguez (26/0)], Andrés Augusto Mendoza Azevedo (32/6) [90.Flavio Francisco Maestri Andrade (54/10)], Claudio Miguel Pizarro Bosio (38/10) [*sent off 82*], Jefferson Agustín Farfán Guadalupe (18/6). Trainer: Paulo César Autuori (23).
Goals: Jefferson Agustín Farfán Guadalupe (34), Nolberto Albino Solano Todco (62), Wilmer Santiago Acasiete Ariadela (72).

468. 12.07.2004 **PERU – COLOMBIA** **2-2(0-1)** 41st Copa América. Group Stage
Estadio Mansiche, Trujillo; Referee: Marco Rodríguez (Mexico); Attendance: 19,522
PER: Óscar Manuel Ibañez Holzmann (43/0), Guillermo Sandro Salas Suárez (15/0), César Miguel Rebosio Compans (54/0) [14.Jorge Antonio Soto Gómez (92/8)], Wilmer Santiago Acasiete Ariadela (8/1), Walter Ricardo Vílchez Soto (8/0), Nolberto Albino Solano Todco (69/19) [90.Marko Gustavo Ciurlizza Rodríguez (27/0)], Juan José Jayo Legario (81/1), Roberto Carlos Palacios Mestas (108/19), Flavio Francisco Maestri Andrade (55/11) [76.Pedro Alejandro García de la Cruz (8/1)], Andrés Augusto Mendoza Azevedo (33/6), Jefferson Agustín Farfán Guadalupe (19/6). Trainer: Paulo César Autuori (24).
Goals: Nolberto Albino Solano Todco (58), Flavio Francisco Maestri Andrade (61).

469. 17.07.2004 **PERU - ARGENTINA** **0-1(0-0)** 41st Copa América. Quarter-Finals
Estadio „Elías Aguirre", Chiclayo; Referee: Carlos Amarilla Demarqui (Paraguay); Attendance: 25,000
PER: Óscar Manuel Ibañez Holzmann (44/0), Guillermo Sandro Salas Suárez (16/0), César Miguel Rebosio Compans (55/0), Wilmer Santiago Acasiete Ariadela (9/1), Walter Ricardo Vílchez Soto (9/0) [87.Juan Carlos La Rosa Llontrop (4/0)], Nolberto Albino Solano Todco (70/19), Juan José Jayo Legario (82/1) [86.Aldo Ítalo Olcese Vasallo (11/0)], Carlos Alberto Zegarra Zamora (19/1) [67.Pedro Alejandro García de la Cruz (9/1)], Jorge Antonio Soto Gómez (93/8), Roberto Carlos Palacios Mestas (109/19), Andrés Augusto Mendoza Azevedo (34/6). Trainer: Paulo César Autuori (25).

470. 04.09.2004 **PERU – ARGENTINA** **1-3(0-1)** 18th FIFA WC. Qualifiers
Estadio Monumental, Lima; Referee: Carlos Eugenio Simón (Brazil); Attendance: 28,000
PER: Óscar Manuel Ibañez Holzmann (45/0), Guillermo Sandro Salas Suárez (17/0), John Christian Galliquio Castro (16/0), Wilmer Santiago Acasiete Ariadela (10/1), Walter Ricardo Vílchez Soto (10/0), Nolberto Albino Solano Todco (71/19), Juan José Jayo Legario (83/1), Jorge Antonio Soto Gómez (94/9) [77.Julio César García Mesones (7/0)], Roberto Carlos Palacios Mestas (110/19) [77.Aldo Ítalo Olcese Vasallo (12/0)], Andrés Augusto Mendoza Azevedo (35/6) [27.Flavio Francisco Maestri Andrade (56/11) [*sent off 45*], Jefferson Agustín Farfán Guadalupe (20/6). Trainer: Paulo César Autuori (26).
Goal: Jorge Antonio Soto Gómez (63).

471. 09.10.2004 **BOLIVIA – PERU** **1-0(0-0)** 18th FIFA WC. Qualifiers
Estadio „Hernándo Siles Zuazo", La Paz; Referee: Mauricio Reynoso (Ecuador); Attendance: 23,729
PER: Óscar Manuel Ibañez Holzmann (46/0), John Christian Galliquio Castro (17/0) [72.Juan Carlos La Rosa Llontrop (5/0)], Alberto Junior Rodríguez Valdelomar (4/0), Wilmer Santiago Acasiete Ariadela (11/1), Guillermo Sandro Salas Suárez (18/0), Julio César García Mesones (8/0) [56.Roberto Carlos Palacios Mestas (111/19)], Juan José Jayo Legario (84/1), Marko Gustavo Ciurlizza Rodríguez (28/0) [63.Luis Germán del Carmen Carty Monserrate (25/3)], Jorge Antonio Soto Gómez (95/9), José Paolo Guerrero Gonzales (1/0), Jefferson Agustín Farfán Guadalupe (21/6). Trainer: Paulo César Autuori (27).

472. 13.10.2004 **PARAGUAY – PERU** **1-1(1-0)** 18th FIFA WC. Qualifiers
Estadio Defensores del Chaco, Asunción; Referee: Oscar Julián Ruiz (Colombia); Attendance: 30,000
PER: Óscar Manuel Ibañez Holzmann (47/0), John Christian Galliquio Castro (18/0) [46.Marko Gustavo Ciurlizza Rodríguez (29/0)], César Miguel Rebosio Compans (56/0), Wilmer Santiago Acasiete Ariadela (12/1), Juan Manuel Vargas Risco (1/0), Nolberto Albino Solano Todco (72/20) [86.Juan Elías Cominges Mayorga (3/0)], Juan José Jayo Legario (85/1), Roberto Carlos Palacios Mestas (112/19), Jorge Antonio Soto Gómez (96/9), Andrés Augusto Mendoza Azevedo (36/6) [67.José Paolo Guerrero Gonzales (2/0)], Jefferson Agustín Farfán Guadalupe (22/6). Trainer: Paulo César Autuori (28).
Goal: Nolberto Albino Solano Todco (74 penalty).

473. 17.11.2004 **PERU – CHILE** **2-1(0-0)** 18th FIFA WC. Qualifiers
Estadio Nacional, Lima; Referee: Héctor Baldassi (Argentina); Attendance: 39,752
PER: Óscar Manuel Ibañez Holzmann (48/0), Jorge Antonio Soto Gómez (97/9), Alberto Junior Rodríguez Valdelomar (5/0), Wilmer Santiago Acasiete Ariadela (13/1) [*sent off 41*], Juan Manuel Vargas Risco (2/0), Nolberto Albino Solano Todco (73/20), Juan José Jayo Legario (86/1), Marko Gustavo Ciurlizza Rodríguez (30/0) [37.Carlos Alberto Zegarra Zamora (20/1), 63.Miguel Angel Villalta Hurtado (8/0)], Roberto Carlos Palacios Mestas (113/19), Claudio Miguel Pizarro Bosio (39/10) [72.José Paolo Guerrero Gonzales (3/1)], Jefferson Agustín Farfán Guadalupe (23/7). Trainer: Paulo César Autuori (29).
Goals: Jefferson Agustín Farfán Guadalupe (56), José Paolo Guerrero Gonzales (86).

474. 27.03.2005 **BRAZIL – PERU** **1-0(0-0)** 18th FIFA WC. Qualifiers
Estádio Serra Dourada, Goiânia; Referee: Carlos Amarilla Demarqui (Paraguay); Attendance: 49,163
PER: Óscar Manuel Ibañez Holzmann (49/0), Jorge Antonio Soto Gómez (98/9), César Miguel Rebosio Compans (57/0), Alberto Junior Rodríguez Valdelomar (6/0) [73.Luis Alberto Guadalupe Rivadeneyra (9/0)], Walter Ricardo Vílchez Soto (11/0), Nolberto Albino Solano Todco (74/20) [68.Juan Elías Cominges Mayorga (4/0)], Juan José Jayo Legario (87/1), Carlos Alberto Zegarra Zamora (21/1), Roberto Carlos Palacios Mestas (114/19) [46.Aldo Ítalo Olcese Vasallo (13/0)], Jefferson Agustín Farfán Guadalupe (24/7), Claudio Miguel Pizarro Bosio (40/10). Trainer: Paulo César Autuori (30).

475. 30.03.2005 **PERU – ECUADOR** **2-2(1-2)** 18th FIFA WC. Qualifiers
Estadio Nacional, Lima; Referee: Carlos Chandia (Chile); Attendance: 40,000
PER: Óscar Manuel Ibañez Holzmann (50/0), Jorge Antonio Soto Gómez (99/9) [60.Guillermo Sandro Salas Suárez (19/0)], César Miguel Rebosio Compans (58/0), Wilmer Santiago Acasiete Ariadela (14/1), Juan Manuel Vargas Risco (3/0), Juan José Jayo Legario (88/1), Carlos Alberto Zegarra Zamora (22/1) [62. Roberto Carlos Palacios Mestas (115/19)], Nolberto Albino Solano Todco (75/20) [85.Andrés Augusto Mendoza Azevedo (37/6)], Jefferson Agustín Farfán Guadalupe (25/8), José Paolo Guerrero Gonzales (4/2), Claudio Miguel Pizarro Bosio (41/10). Trainer: Paulo César Autuori (31).
Goals: José Paolo Guerrero Gonzales (1), Jefferson Agustín Farfán Guadalupe (58).

476. 22.05.2005 **JAPAN – PERU** **0-1(0-0)** Kirin Cup
Big Swan Stadium, Niigata; Referee: Lubos Michel (Slovakia); Attendance: 39,856
PER: Juan Ángel Flores Ascencio (2/0), Giuliano Santiago Portilla Castillo (4/0), Luis Alberto Guadalupe Rivadeneyra (10/0), Miguel Angel Villalta Hurtado (9/0), Javier Martín Tenemás Gutiérrez (1/0) [61.Miguel Angel Cevasco Abad (1/0)], Juan Carlos Bazalar Cruzado (Cap) (18/0), Juan Carlos La Rosa Llontrop (6/0) [90.Carlos Enrique Ismodes (1/0)], Carlos Augusto Lobatón Espejo (1/0) [48.William Medardo Chiroque Távara (2/0)], José Adolfo Mendoza (1/0), Miguel Ángel Mostto Fernández-Prada (2/0) [84.Gustavo Enrique Vassallo Ferrari (1/1)], Piero Fernando Alva Niezen (5/1) [79.Hilden Salas Castillo (1/0)]. Trainer: Freddy Santos Ternero Corrales (7).
Goal: Gustavo Enrique Vassallo Ferrari (90).

477. 24.05.2005 **UNITED ARAB EMIRATES – PERU** **0-0** Kirin Cup
Toyota Stadium, Toyota City; Referee: Yuichi Nishimura (Japan); Attendance: 6,536
PER: Juan Ángel Flores Ascencio (3/0), Giuliano Santiago Portilla Castillo (5/0), Luis Alberto Guadalupe Rivadeneyra (11/0), Miguel Angel Villalta Hurtado (10/0), Juan Carlos Bazalar Cruzado (Cap) (19/0), Juan Carlos La Rosa Llontrop (7/0), Carlos Augusto Lobatón Espejo (2/0) [46.Miguel Angel Cevasco Abad (2/0)], William Medardo Chiroque Távara (3/0) [46.Carlos Enrique Ismodes (2/0)], José Adolfo Mendoza (2/0), Gustavo Enrique Vassallo Ferrari (2/1) [78. Miguel Ángel Mostto Fernández-Prada (3/0)], Piero Fernando Alva Niezen (6/1) [72.Hilden Salas Castillo (2/0)]. Trainer: Freddy Santos Ternero Corrales (8).

478. 04.06.2005 **COLOMBIA – PERU** **5-0(1-0)** 18th FIFA WC. Qualifiers
Estadio Metropolitano „Roberto Meléndez", Barranquilla; Referee: Carlos Torres (Paraguay); Attendance: 15,000
PER: Juan Ángel Flores Ascencio (4/0), Wilmer Santiago Acasiete Ariadela (15/1), César Miguel Rebosio Compans (59/0), Walter Ricardo Vílchez Soto (12/0) [46.José Paolo Guerrero Gonzales (5/2)], Nolberto Albino Solano Todco (76/20), Juan José Jayo Legario (89/1) [*sent off 59*], Juan Carlos La Rosa Llontrop (8/0), Jefferson Agustín Farfán Guadalupe (26/8) [63.José Adolfo Mendoza (3/0)], Roberto Carlos Palacios Mestas (116/19) [63.Juan Elías Cominges Mayorga (5/0)], Juan Manuel Vargas Risco (4/0), Claudio Miguel Pizarro Bosio (42/10). Trainer: Freddy Santos Ternero Corrales (9).

479. 07.06.2005 **PERU – URUGUAY** **0-0** 18th FIFA WC. Qualifiers

Estadio Nacional, Lima; Referee: Héctor Baldassi (Argentina); Attendance: 31,515

PER: Juan Ángel Flores Ascencio (5/0), César Miguel Rebosio Compans (60/0), Luis Alberto Guadalupe Rivadeneyra (12/0), Miguel Angel Villalta Hurtado (11/0), Walter Ricardo Vílchez Soto (13/0), José Adolfo Mendoza (4/0), Juan Carlos La Rosa Llontrop (9/0) [86.Nolberto Albino Solano Todco (77/20)], Juan Elías Cominges Mayorga (6/0) [63.Roberto Carlos Palacios Mestas (117/19)], Claudio Miguel Pizarro Bosio (43/10), Jefferson Agustín Farfán Guadalupe (27/8), José Paolo Guerrero Gonzales (6/2). Trainer: Freddy Santos Ternero Corrales (10).

480. 17.08.2005 **PERU – CHILE** **3-1(1-1)**

Estadio „Jorge Basadre", Tacna; Referee: René M. Ortubé Betancourt (Bolivia)

PER: Leao Butrón Gotuzzo (5/0), Jorge Raúl Huamán Salinas (11/0), Luis Alberto Guadalupe Rivadeneyra (Cap) (13/0), Miguel Angel Villalta Hurtado (12/1) [73.Alberto Junior Rodríguez Valdelomar (7/0)], Walter Ricardo Vílchez Soto (14/1), Juan Carlos La Rosa Llontrop (10/0), José Mendoza (5/0) [88.Paolo Giancarlo de la Haza Urquiza (2/0)], Juan Elías Cominges Mayorga (7/0) [90.Carlos Fernández (1/0)], Juan Manuel Vargas Risco (5/0) [85.Luis Alberto Ramírez Lucay (1/0)], Miguel Ángel Mostto Fernández-Prada (4/0) [73.Douglas Junior Ross Santillana (1/0)], José Paolo Guerrero Gonzales (7/3) [85.Hernán Rengifo Trigoso (1/0)]. Trainer: Freddy Santos Ternero Corrales (11).

Goals: Walter Ricardo Vílchez Soto (28), José Paolo Guerrero Gonzales (59), Miguel Angel Villalta Hurtado (63).

481. 03.09.2005 **VENEZUELA – PERU** **4-1(1-0)** 18th FIFA WC. Qualifiers

Estadio „José 'Encarnación' Romero", Maracaibo; Referee: Márcio Rezende (Brazil); Attendance: 12,000

PER: Erick Guillermo Delgado Vásquez (10/0), Jorge Raúl Huamán Salinas (12/0), Luis Alberto Guadalupe Rivadeneyra (14/0), Miguel Angel Villalta Hurtado (13/1), Walter Ricardo Vílchez Soto (15/1) [46.Piero Fernando Alva Niezen (7/1)], Edwin Alberto Pérez León (1/0), Juan Carlos La Rosa Llontrop (11/0) [*sent off 90*], Juan Elías Cominges Mayorga (8/0) [76.Miguel Ángel Mostto Fernández-Prada (5/0) [*sent off 90*], Juan Manuel Vargas Risco (6/0), Jefferson Agustín Farfán Guadalupe (28/9), José Paolo Guerrero Gonzales (8/3). Trainer: Freddy Santos Ternero Corrales (12).

Goal: Jefferson Agustín Farfán Guadalupe (63).

482. 09.10.2005 **ARGENTINA – PERU** **2-0(0-0)** 18th FIFA WC. Qualifiers

Estadio Monumental „Antonio Vespucio Liberti", Buenos Aires; Referee: Carlos Torres (Paraguay); Attendance: 36,977

PER: Leao Butrón Gotuzzo (6/0) [*sent off 78*], John Christian Galliquio Castro (19/0) [90.Douglas Junior Ross Santillana (2/0)], Alberto Junior Rodríguez Valdelomar (8/0), Luis Alberto Guadalupe Rivadeneyra (15/0), Emilio Martín Hidalgo Conde (34/2), Marko Gustavo Ciurlizza Rodríguez (31/0), Rainer Torres Salas (1/0), Jorge Antonio Soto Gómez (**100**/9), Julio César García Mesones (9/0) [80.Erick Guillermo Delgado Vásquez (11/0)], Jefferson Agustín Farfán Guadalupe (29/9) [82.Juan Elías Cominges Mayorga (9/0)], José Paolo Guerrero Gonzales (9/3). Trainer: Freddy Santos Ternero Corrales (13).

483. 12.10.2005 **PERU – BOLIVIA** **4-1(3-0)** 18th FIFA WC. Qualifiers

Estadio „Jorge Basadre", Tacna; Referee: Oscar Sequeira (Argentina); Attendance: 14,744

PER: Erick Guillermo Delgado Vásquez (12/0), John Christian Galliquio Castro (20/0) [46.José Mendoza (6/0)], Luis Alberto Guadalupe Rivadeneyra (16/0), Wilmer Santiago Acasiete Ariadela (16/2), Emilio Martín Hidalgo Conde (35/2), Marko Gustavo Ciurlizza Rodríguez (32/0) [*sent off 74*], Rainer Torres Salas (2/0), Jorge Antonio Soto Gómez (101/9), Juan Elías Cominges Mayorga (10/0) [83.Julio César García Mesones (10/0)], Jefferson Agustín Farfán Guadalupe (30/11), Gustavo Enrique Vassallo Ferrari (3/2) [63.Douglas Junior Ross Santillana (3/0)]. Trainer: Freddy Santos Ternero Corrales (14).

Goals: Gustavo Enrique Vassallo Ferrari (10), Wilmer Santiago Acasiete Ariadela (38), Jefferson Agustín Farfán Guadalupe (45, 82).

484. 10.05.2006 **TRINIDAD TOBAGO – PERU** **1-1(0-1)**

"Hasely Crawford" Stadium, Port of Spain; Referee: Peter Prendergast (Jamaica); Attendance: 20,000

PER: Leao Butrón Gotuzzo (Cap) (7/0), Miguel Angel Villalta Hurtado (14/1), Amilton Jair Prado Barrón (1/0), Wenceslao Ernesto Fernández Donayre (1/0), Santiago Roberto Salazar Peña (11/0), Aldo Ítalo Olcese Vasallo (14/0), Rainer Torres Salas (3/0), Paulo Rinaldo Cruzado Durand (2/0), Pedro Alejandro García de la Cruz (10/1) [56.Junior Douglas Ross (4/0)], Wilmer Alexander Aguirre Vásquez (1/0) [66.Manuel Alejandro Corrales Gonzáles (1/0)], Gustavo Enrique Vassallo Ferrari (4/3) [77.Roberto Carlos Jiménez (1/0)]. Trainer: Franco Enrique Navarro Monteiro (1).

Goal: Gustavo Enrique Vassallo Ferrari (31).

485. 16.08.2006 **PERU – PANAMA** **0-2(0-1)**

Estadio Nacional, Lima; Referee: Manuel Garay (Peru); Attendance: 1,921

PER: Leao Butrón Gotuzzo (8/0) [35.Diego Alonso Penny Valdez (1/0)], Amilton Jair Prado Barrón (2/0), Santiago Roberto Salazar Peña (12/0), John Christian Galliquio Castro (21/0), Emilio Martín Hidalgo Conde (36/2), Rainer Torres Salas (4/0), Paulo Rinaldo Cruzado Durand (3/0), Henry Edson Quinteros Sánchez (15/1), Juan Elías Cominges Mayorga (11/0) [46.Pedro Alejandro García de la Cruz (11/1); 67.Douglas Junior Ross Santillana (5/0)], Gustavo Enrique Vassallo Ferrari (5/3), Roberto Carlos Jiménez (2/0) [67.Miguel Ángel Mostto Fernández-Prada (6/0)]. Trainer: Franco Enrique Navarro Monteiro (2).

486. 06.09.2006 **ECUADOR - PERU** **1-1(1-0)**

Giants Stadium, East Rutherford, New York (United States); Referee: Terry Vaughn (United States); Attendance: 20,556

PER: Leao Butrón Gotuzzo (9/0), Amilton Jair Prado Barrón (3/0), Santiago Roberto Salazar Peña (13/0), Miguel Ángel Villalta Hurtado (15/1), Wenceslao Ernesto Fernández Donayre (2/0), Rainer Torres Salas (5/0), Paulo Rinaldo Cruzado Durand (4/0), Roberto Carlos Palacios Mestas (Cap) (118/19) [82.Douglas Junior Ross Santillana (6/0)], Jefferson Agustín Farfán Guadalupe (31/11), Claudio Miguel Pizarro Bosio (44/10), José Paolo Guerrero Gonzalés (10/4). Trainer: Franco Enrique Navarro Monteiro (3).

Goal: José Paolo Guerrero Gonzales (76).

487. 07.10.2006 **CHILE - PERU** **3-2(1-1)** Copa del Pacífico

Estadio Sausalito, Viña del Mar; Referee: Olivier Viera (Uruguay); Attendance: 20,000

PER: Leao Butrón Gotuzzo (10/0), Amilton Jair Prado Barrón (4/0), Miguel Ángel Villalta Hurtado (16/1), Walter Ricardo Vílchez Soto (16/1), Emilio Martín Hidalgo Conde (37/2) [*sent off 87*], Alexander Gustavo Sánchez Reyes (1/0) [63.Douglas Junior Ross Santillana (7/0)], Miguel Ángel Cevasco Abad (3/0) [*sent off 72*], Paulo Rinaldo Cruzado Durand (5/0) [46.Carlos Alberto Zegarra Zamora (23/1)], Juan Manuel Vargas Risco (7/0) [*sent off 42*], Roberto Carlos Palacios Mestas (Cap) (119/19) [63.Claudio Miguel Pizarro Bosio (45/11)], José Paolo Guerrero Gonzales (11/5). Trainer: Franco Enrique Navarro Monteiro (4).

Goals: José Paolo Guerrero Gonzales (8), Claudio Miguel Pizarro Bosio (84).

488. 11.10.2006 **PERU - CHILE** **0-1(0-1)** Copa del Pacífico

Estadio „José Basadre", Tacna; Referee: Samuel Haro (Ecuador); Attendance: 12,000

PER: Diego Alonso Penny Valdez (2/0), Amilton Jair Prado Barrón (5/0), Miguel Ángel Villalta Hurtado (17/1), Walter Ricardo Vílchez Soto (17/1), Luis Daniel Benito Hernández Alfaro (1/0), Alexander Gustavo Sánchez Reyes (2/0) [77.César Junior Viza Seminario (1/0)], Erick Omar Torres Arias (11/0), Paulo Rinaldo Cruzado Durand (6/0), Roberto Carlos Palacios Mestas (Cap) (120/19) [63.Douglas Junior Ross Santillana (8/0)], Miguel Ángel Mostto Fernández-Prada (7/0) [46.Piero Fernando Alva Niezen (8/1)], José Paolo Guerrero Gonzales (12/5). Trainer: Franco Enrique Navarro Monteiro (5).

489. 15.11.2006 **JAMAICA - PERU** **1-1(0-0)**
National Stadium, Kingston; Referee: Alfredo Whittaker (Cayman Islands); Attendance: n/a
PER: Leao Butrón Gotuzzo (11/0), Amilton Jair Prado Barrón (6/0), Alberto Junior Rodríguez Valdelomar (9/0), Emilio Martín Hidalgo Conde (38/2), Walter Ricardo Vílchez Soto (18/1), Juan Manuel Vargas Risco (8/0), Paulo Paulo Rinaldo Cruzado Durand (7/0), Miguel Ángel Cevasco Abad (4/0), Juan Carlos Mariño Márquez (1/0) [60.Alexander Gustavo Sánchez Reyes (3/1)], Jefferson Agustín Farfán Guadalupe (32/11), Miguel Ángel Mostto Fernández-Prada (8/0) [75.Piero Fernando Alva Niezen (9/1)]. Trainer: Franco Enrique Navarro Monteiro (6).
Goal: Alexander Gustavo Sánchez Reyes (64).

490. 19.11.2006 **PANAMA - PERU** **1-2(1-1)**
Estadio „Rommel Fernández", Ciudad de Panamá; Referee: Rolando Vidal (Panama); Attendance: 2,000
PER: Diego Alonso Penny Valdez (3/0), Amilton Jair Prado Barrón (7/0), Alberto Junior Rodríguez Valdelomar (10/0), Walter Ricardo Vílchez Soto (19/1), Miguel Ángel Cevasco Abad (5/0), Fernando Daniel del Solar Álvarez Calderón (2/0) [80.Paulo Rinaldo Cruzado Durand (8/0)], Luis Daniel Benito Hernández Alfaro (2/0) [46.Wenceslao Ernesto Fernández Donayre (3/0)], Juan Carlos Mariño Márquez (2/0) [60.Pedro Alejandro García de la Cruz (12/1)], Miguel Ángel Torres Quintana (1/0) [60.Alexander Gustavo Sánchez Reyes (4/1) [*sent off 85*]], Piero Fernando Alva Niezen (10/2) [81.César Junior Viza Seminario (2/0)], Miguel Ángel Mostto Fernández-Prada (9/1) [60.Douglas Douglas Junior Ross Santillana (9/0)]. Trainer: Franco Enrique Navarro Monteiro (7).
Goals: Miguel Ángel Mostto Fernández-Prada (41), Piero Fernando Alva Niezen (80).

491. 24.03.2007 **JAPAN - PERU** **2-0(1-0)**
International Stadium, Yokohama; Referee: Angelo Nardi (Australia); Attendance: 60,400
PER: Juan Ángel Flores Ascencio (6/0) [46.George Patrick Forsyth Sommer (1/0)], Ismael Enrique Alvarado Quiñones (1/0), Wálter Ricardo Vílchez Soto (20/1), Jhoel Alexander Herrera Zegarra (1/0), Paolo Giancarlo De La Haza Urquiza (3/0), Emilio Martín Hidalgo Conde (39/2), Juan Carlos Bazalar Cruzado (20/0) [69.Rainer Torres Salas (6/0)], Juan Carlos Mariño Márquez (3/0), Alexander Gustavo Sánchez Reyes (5/1), Jair Edson Céspedes Zegarra (1/0), Roberto Carlos Jiménez (3/0) [68.Miguel Ángel Mostto Fernández-Prada (10/1)]. Trainer: Julio César Uribe Flores (16).

492. 03.06.2007 **PERU - ECUADOR** **2-1(1-1)**
Estadio "Vicente Calderón", Madrid (Spain); Referee: Hugo López Huerta (Spain); Attendance: 25,000
PER: George Patrick Forsyth Sommer (2/0), Miguel Ángel Villalta Hurtado (18/1), Alberto Junior Rodríguez Valdelomar (11/0) [90+1.Wálter Ricardo Vílchez Soto (21/1)], Wilmer Santiago Acasiete Ariadela (17/2), Amilton Jair Prado Barrón (8/0) [46.John Christian Galliquio Castro (22/0)], Damián Diego Ísmodes Saravia (1/0) [74.Jhoel Alexander Herrera Zegarra (2/0)], Juan Carlos Bazalar Cruzado (21/0), Jefferson Agustín Farfán Guadalupe (33/12), Emilio Martín Hidalgo Conde (40/2) [46.Juan Manuel Vargas Risco (9/0)], Andrés Augusto Mendoza Azevedo (38/6) [67.Paolo Giancarlo De La Haza Urquiza (4/0)], José Paolo Guerrero Gonzales (13/5). Trainer: Julio César Uribe Flores (17).
Goals: Jefferson Agustín Farfán Guadalupe (4), Ulises Hernán de la Cruz Bernardo (50 own goal).

493. 06.06.2007 **ECUADOR - PERU** **2-0(0-0)**
Miniestadi, Barcelona (Spain); Referee: Felipe Crespo García (Spain); Attendance: 10,000
PER: George Patrick Forsyth Sommer (3/0), John Christian Galliquio Castro (23/0), Miguel Ángel Villalta Hurtado (19/1), Wilmer Santiago Acasiete Ariadela (18/2), Wálter Ricardo Vílchez Soto (22/1), Juan Carlos Bazalar Cruzado (22/0) [62.Paolo Giancarlo De La Haza Urquiza (5/0)], Amilton Jair Prado Barrón (9/0), Damián Diego Ísmodes Saravia (2/0) [63.Jhoel Alexander Herrera Zegarra (3/0)], Jefferson Agustín Farfán Guadalupe (34/12), Andrés Augusto Mendoza Azevedo (39/6) [74.Hernán Rengifo Trigoso (2/0)], José Paolo Guerrero Gonzales (14/5). Trainer: Julio César Uribe Flores (18).

494. 26.06.2007 **URUGUAY - PERU** **0-3(0-1)** 42nd Copa América. Group Stage
Estadio Metropolitano, Mérida (Venezuela); Referee: Carlos Arecio Amarilla Demarqui (Paraguay); Attendance: 23,000
PER: Leao Butrón Gotuzzo (12/0), John Christian Galliquio Castro (24/0), Miguel Ángel Villalta Hurtado (20/2), Alberto Junior Rodríguez Valdelomar (12/0), Wilmer Santiago Acasiete Ariadela (19/2), Wálter Ricardo Vílchez Soto (23/1), Juan Carlos Bazalar Cruzado (23/0), Pedro Alejandro García de la Cruz (13/1) [57.Juan Carlos Mariño Márquez (4/1)], Jefferson Agustín Farfán Guadalupe (35/12) [80.Paolo Giancarlo De La Haza Urquiza (6/0)], José Paolo Guerrero Gonzales (15/6), Claudio Miguel Pizarro Bosio (46/11) [77.Andrés Augusto Mendoza Azevedo (40/6)]. Trainer: Julio César Uribe Flores (19).
Goals: Miguel Ángel Villalta Hurtado (27), Juan Carlos Mariño Márquez (69), José Paolo Guerrero Gonzales (88).

495. 30.06.2007 **VENEZUELA - PERU** **2-0(0-0)** 42nd Copa América. Group Stage
Estadio Polideportivo de Pablo Nuevo, San Cristóbal; Referee: Benito Armando Archundia Téllez (Mexico); Attendance: 42,000
PER: Leao Butrón Gotuzzo (13/0), Alberto Junior Rodríguez Valdelomar (13/0), John Christian Galliquio Castro (25/0) [76.Andrés Augusto Mendoza Azevedo (41/6)], Miguel Ángel Villalta Hurtado (21/2) [52.Juan Carlos Mariño Márquez (5/1)], Wilmer Santiago Acasiete Ariadela (20/2), Wálter Ricardo Vílchez Soto (24/1), Pedro Alejandro García de la Cruz (14/1), Juan Carlos Bazalar Cruzado (24/0), Jefferson Agustín Farfán Guadalupe (36/12), Claudio Miguel Pizarro Bosio (47/11) [67.Damián Diego Ísmodes Saravia (3/0)], José Paolo Guerrero Gonzales (16/6). Trainer: Julio César Uribe Flores (20).

496. 03.07.2007 **BOLIVIA - PERU** **2-2(2-1)** 42nd Copa América. Group Stage
Estadio Metropolitano, Mérida (Venezuela); Referee: Carlos Luis Chandía Alarcón (Chile); Attendance: 35,000
PER: Leao Butrón Gotuzzo (14/0), John Christian Galliquio Castro (26/0) [56.Jhoel Alexander Herrera Zegarra (4/0)], Alberto Junior Rodríguez Valdelomar (14/0), Edgar Harry Villamarín Arguedas (1/0), Wálter Ricardo Vílchez Soto (25/1), Paolo Giancarlo De La Haza Urquiza (7/0), Damián Diego Ísmodes Saravia (4/0) [70.Roberto Carlos Jiménez (4/0)], Juan Carlos Mariño Márquez (6/1), Jefferson Agustín Farfán Guadalupe (37/12) [46.Herlyn Ysrael Zúñiga Yañez (20/3)], José Paolo Guerrero Gonzales (17/6), Claudio Miguel Pizarro Bosio (48/13). Trainer: Julio César Uribe Flores (21).
Goals: Claudio Miguel Pizarro Bosio (34, 85).

497. 08.07.2007 **ARGENTINA - PERU** **4-0(0-0)** 42nd Copa América. Quarter-Finals
Estadio Metropolitano de Fútbol de Lara, Barquisimeto (Venezuela); Referee: Carlos Eugênio Simon (Brazil); Attendance: 37,000
PER: Leao Butrón Gotuzzo (15/0), John Christian Galliquio Castro (27/0), Miguel Ángel Villalta Hurtado (22/2), Wilmer Santiago Acasiete Ariadela (21/2), Edgar Harry Villamarín Arguedas (2/0) [64.Herlyn Ysrael Zúñiga Yañez (21/3)], Wálter Ricardo Vílchez Soto (26/1), Paolo Giancarlo De La Haza Urquiza (8/0), Juan Carlos Bazalar Cruzado (25/0), Juan Carlos Mariño Márquez (7/1) [74.Andrés Augusto Mendoza Azevedo (42/6)], José Paolo Guerrero Gonzales (18/6) [55.Pedro Alejandro García de la Cruz (15/1)], Claudio Miguel Pizarro Bosio (49/13). Trainer: Julio César Uribe Flores (22).

498. 22.08.2007 **COSTA RICA - PERU** **1-1(1-0)**
Estadio "Ricardo Saprissa", San José; Referee: Víctor Mena (Costa Rica); Attendance: 5,000
PER: Leao Butrón Gotuzzo (16/0), Amilton Jair Prado Barrón (10/0), Miguel Ángel Villalta Hurtado (23/2), Wálter Ricardo Vílchez Soto (27/1), Wenceslao Ernesto Fernández Donayre (4/0) [69.Edgar Harry Villamarín Arguedas (3/0)], Rainer Torres Salas (7/0), Juan José Jayo Legario (90/1) [65.Ernesto Seiko Arakaki Arakaki (2/0)], Pedro Alejandro García de la Cruz (16/2) [87.Renato Gianfranco Espejo Reyes (1/0)], Emilio Martín Hidalgo Conde (41/2) [58.Damián Diego Ísmodes Saravia (5/0)], Juan Diego González-Vigil Bentin (1/0) [65.Roberto Carlos Jiménez (5/0)], Johan Javier Fano Espinoza (2/0) [55.William Medardo Chiroque Távara (4/0)]. Trainer: José Guillermo del Solar Alvarez-Calderón (1).
Goal: Pedro Alejandro García de la Cruz (56).

499. 08.09.2007 **PERU - COLOMBIA** **2-2(0-1)**
Estadio Monumental, Lima; Referee: José Patricio Carpio Guevara (Ecuador); Attendance: 50,000
PER: Leao Butrón Gotuzzo (17/0), Amilton Jair Prado Barrón (11/0), Alberto Junior Rodríguez Valdelomar (15/0) [82.Wálter Ricardo Vílchez Soto (28/1)], Wilmer Santiago Acasiete Ariadela (22/2), Juan Manuel Vargas Risco (10/0) [89.Wenceslao Ernesto Fernández Donayre (5/0)], Wilmer Alexander Aguirre Vásquez (2/0) [46.Henry Edson Quinteros Sánchez (16/1)], Nolberto Albino Solano Todco (78/20) [77.Pedro Alejandro García de la Cruz (17/2)], Juan José Jayo Legario (91/1), Emilio Martín Hidalgo Conde (42/2) [62.William Medardo Chiroque Távara (5/0)], Claudio Miguel Pizarro Bosio (50/13), José Paolo Guerrero Gonzales (19/8). Trainer: José Guillermo del Solar Alvarez-Calderón (2).
Goals: José Paolo Guerrero Gonzales (49, 90+3).

500. 12.09.2007 **PERU - BOLIVIA** **2-0(2-0)**
Estadio Monumental, Lima; Referee: Víctor Hugo Rivera (Peru); Attendance: 20,000
PER: Diego Alonso Penny Valdez (4/0) [46.José Aurelio Carvallo Alonso (1/0)], Amilton Jair Prado Barrón (12/0), Alberto Junior Rodríguez Valdelomar (16/0), Wilmer Santiago Acasiete Ariadela (23/2), Emilio Martín Hidalgo Conde (43/2) [47.Wálter Ricardo Vílchez Soto (29/1)], Paolo Giancarlo De La Haza Urquiza (9/0), Henry Edson Quinteros Sánchez (17/1) [65.Juan José Jayo Legario (92/1)], Nolberto Albino Solano Todco (79/20) [75.Wilmer Alexander Aguirre Vásquez (3/0)], Juan Manuel Vargas Risco (11/1), José Paolo Guerrero Gonzales (20/9) [65.Juan Carlos Mariño Márquez (8/1)], Claudio Miguel Pizarro Bosio (51/13) [82.Juan Diego González-Vigil Bentin (2/0)]. Trainer: José Guillermo del Solar Alvarez-Calderón (3).
Goals: Juan Manuel Vargas Risco (15), José Paolo Guerrero Gonzales (36).

501. 13.10.2007 **PERU - PARAGUAY** **0-0** 19th FIFA WC. Qualifiers
Estadio Monumental, Lima; Referee: Carlos Eugênio Simon (Brazil); Attendance: 50,000
PER: Leao Butrón Gotuzzo (18/0), John Christian Galliquio Castro (28/0) [74.Flavio Francisco Maestri Andrade (57/11)], Alberto Junior Rodríguez Valdelomar (17/0), Wilmer Santiago Acasiete Ariadela (24/2), Wálter Ricardo Vílchez Soto (30/1), Paolo Giancarlo De La Haza Urquiza (10/0), Henry Edson Quinteros Sánchez (18/1) [86.Juan José Jayo Legario (93/1)], Nolberto Albino Solano Todco (80/20), Juan Manuel Vargas Risco (12/1) [84.William Medardo Chiroque Távara (6/0)], Claudio Miguel Pizarro Bosio (52/13), Jefferson Agustín Farfán Guadalupe (38/12). Trainer: José Guillermo del Solar Alvarez-Calderón (4).

502. 17.10.2007 **CHILE - PERU** **2-0(1-0)** 19th FIFA WC. Qualifiers
Estadio Nacional, Santiago; Referee: Óscar Julián Ruiz Acosta (Colombia); Attendance: 60,000
PER: Leao Butrón Gotuzzo (19/0), John Christian Galliquio Castro (29/0), Alberto Junior Rodríguez Valdelomar (18/0), Wilmer Santiago Acasiete Ariadela (25/2), Wálter Ricardo Vílchez Soto (31/1) [73.Paulo Rinaldo Cruzado Durand (9/0)], Paolo Giancarlo De La Haza Urquiza (11/0) [46.Henry Edson Quinteros Sánchez (19/1)], Juan José Jayo Legario (94/1), Nolberto Albino Solano Todco (81/20), Juan Manuel Vargas Risco (13/1), Claudio Miguel Pizarro Bosio (53/13), Jefferson Agustín Farfán Guadalupe (39/12). Trainer: José Guillermo del Solar Alvarez-Calderón (5).

503. 18.11.2007 **PERU - BRAZIL** **1-1(0-1)** 19th FIFA WC. Qualifiers
Estadio Monumental, Lima; Referee: Carlos Torres (Paraguay); Attendance: 45,847
PER: Diego Alonso Penny Valdez (5/0), Guillermo Sandro Salas Suárez (20/0), Wilmer Santiago Acasiete Ariadela (26/2), Alberto Junior Rodríguez Valdelomar (19/0), Juan Manuel Vargas Risco (14/2), Juan José Jayo Legario (95/1) [62.Andrés Augusto Mendoza Azevedo (43/6)], Carlos Augusto Lobatón Espejo (3/0) [65.Paolo Giancarlo De La Haza Urquiza (12/0)], Nolberto Albino Solano Todco (82/20), Jefferson Agustín Farfán Guadalupe (40/12), Claudio Miguel Pizarro Bosio (54/13), José Paolo Guerrero Gonzales (21/9) [46.Roberto Carlos Palacios Mestas (121/19)]. Trainer: José Guillermo del Solar Alvarez-Calderón (6).
Goal: Juan Manuel Vargas Risco (72).

504. 21.11.2007 **ECUADOR - PERU** **5-1(3-0)** 19th FIFA WC. Qualifiers
Estadio Olimpico "Atahualpa", Quito; Referee: Carlos Chandía Alarcón (Chile); Attendance: 35,000
PER: Diego Alonso Penny Valdez (6/0), Guillermo Sandro Salas Suárez (21/0), Wilmer Santiago Acasiete Ariadela (27/2), Wálter Ricardo Vílchez Soto (32/1) [9.Carlos Javier Solís Alvarado (1/0)], Mario Augusto Gómez Urbina (3/0), Juan Carlos Bazalar Cruzado (26/0) [58.Jefferson Agustín Farfán Guadalupe (41/12)], Carlos Augusto Lobatón Espejo (4/0), Julio César García Mesones (11/0), Roberto Carlos Palacios Mestas (122/19), Miguel Ángel Mostto Fernández-Prada (11/1), Claudio Miguel Pizarro Bosio (55/13) [58.Andrés Augusto Mendoza Azevedo (44/7)]. Trainer: José Guillermo del Solar Alvarez-Calderón (7).
Goal: Andrés Augusto Mendoza Azevedo (86).

505. 06.02.2008 **BOLIVIA - PERU** **2-1(0-0)**
Estadio „Hernándo Siles Zuazo", La Paz; Referee: René Ortube Betancourt (Bolivia); Attendance: 35,000
PER: Leao Butrón Gotuzzo (20/0), Amilton Jair Prado Barrón (13/0) [46.Guillermo Sandro Salas Suárez (22/0)], Orlando Contreras Collantes (1/0), Miguel Ángel Villalta Hurtado (24/2), Luis Daniel Benito Hernández Alfaro (3/0), Juan José Jayo Legario (96/1), Miguel Ángel Cevasco Abad (6/1), Pedro Alejandro García de la Cruz (18/2), Sidney Enrique Faiffer Ames (1/0) [63.Reimond Orángel Manco Albarracín (1/0)], Douglas Junior Ross Santillana (10/0) [46.Jorge Johan Vásquez Rosales (1/0)], Roberto Carlos Jiménez (6/0) [74.Juan Diego González-Vigil Bentin (3/0)]. Trainer: José Guillermo del Solar Alvarez-Calderón (8).
Goal: Miguel Ángel Cevasco Abad (71).

506. 26.03.2008 **PERU – COSTA RICA** **3-1(1-1)**
Estadio „Max Augustín", Iquitos; Referee: George Buckley (Peru); Attendance: n/a
PER: George Patrick Forsyth Sommer (4/0) [83.Raúl Omar Fernández Valverde (1/0)], Amilton Jair Prado Barrón (14/0), Carlos Augusto Zambrano Ochandarte (1/1) [86.Miguel Ángel Villalta Hurtado (25/2)], Ernesto Seiko Arakaki Arakaki (3/0), Emilio Martín Hidalgo Conde (44/3), Juan José Jayo Legario (97/1) [46.Rainer Torres Salas (8/0)], Donny Renzo Neyra Ferrada (1/0) [65.Marko Gustavo Ciurlizza Rodríguez (33/0)], Miguel Ángel Torres Quintana (2/0) [46.Luis Daniel Benito Hernández Alfaro (4/0)], Juan Elías Cominges Mayorga (12/0), Daniel Mackensi Chávez Castillo (1/0), Hernán Rengifo Trigoso (3/1) [78.Reimond Orángel Manco Albarracín (2/0)]. Trainer: José Guillermo del Solar Alvarez-Calderón (9).
Goals: Hernán Rengifo Trigoso (32), Carlos Augusto Zambrano Ochandarte (46), Emilio Martín Hidalgo Conde (51).

507. 31.05.2008 **SPAIN - PERU** **2-1(1-0)**
Estadio Nuevo Colombino, Huelva; Referee: Dimitar Mečkarovski (Macedonia); Attendance: n/a
PER: Leao Butrón Gotuzzo (21/0), Guillermo Sandro Salas Suárez (23/0), Alberto Junior Rodríguez Valdelomar (20/0) [43.Miguel Ángel Villalta Hurtado (26/2)], Wálter Ricardo Vílchez Soto (33/1), Luis Daniel Benito Hernández Alfaro (5/0), Nolberto Albino Solano Todco (83/20) [90.Miguel Ángel Cevasco Abad (7/1)], Rainer Torres Salas (9/0), Paulo Rinaldo Cruzado Durand (10/0) [46.Juan Carlos Mariño Márquez (9/1)], Emilio Martín Hidalgo Conde (45/3) [75.Donny Renzo Neyra Ferrada (2/0)], José Paolo Guerrero Gonzales (22/9), Daniel Mackensi Chávez Castillo (2/0) [65.Hernán Rengifo Trigoso (4/2)]. Trainer: José Guillermo del Solar Alvarez-Calderón (10).
Goal: Hernán Rengifo Trigoso (73).

508. 08.06.2008 **MEXICO - PERU** **4-0(4-0)**

Soldier Field, Chicago (United States); Referee: Mark Geiger (United States); Attendance: n/a

PER: George Patrick Forsyth Sommer (5/0), Guillermo Sandro Salas Suárez (24/0) [59.Amilton Jair Prado Barrón (15/0)], Miguel Ángel Villalta Hurtado (27/2), Wálter Ricardo Vílchez Soto (34/1), Luis Daniel Benito Hernández Alfaro (6/0) [46.Donny Renzo Neyra Ferrada (3/0)], Rainer Torres Salas (10/0) [43.Miguel Ángel Cevasco Abad (8/1)], Nolberto Albino Solano Todco (84/20), Juan Elías Cominges Mayorga (13/0) [61.Hernán Rengifo Trigoso (5/2)], Juan Carlos Mariño Márquez (10/1) [70.Paulo Rinaldo Cruzado Durand (11/0)], Daniel Mackensi Chávez Castillo (3/0) [46.Juan Manuel Vargas Risco (15/2)], José Paolo Guerrero Gonzales (23/9). Trainer: José Guillermo del Solar Alvarez-Calderón (11).

509. 14.06.2008 **PERU - COLOMBIA** **1-1(1-1)** 19th FIFA WC. Qualifiers

Estadio Monumental, Lima; Referee: Carlos Manuel Torres (Paraguay); Attendance: 25,000

PER: Leao Butrón Gotuzzo (22/0), Amilton Jair Prado Barrón (16/0), Alberto Junior Rodríguez Valdelomar (21/0), Wálter Ricardo Vílchez Soto (35/1), Juan Manuel Vargas Risco (16/2), Donny Renzo Neyra Ferrada (4/0) [76.Hernán Rengifo Trigoso (6/2)], Rainer Torres Salas (11/0), Nolberto Albino Solano Todco (85/20), Emilio Martín Hidalgo Conde (46/3) [60.Juan Elías Cominges Mayorga (14/0)], Juan Carlos Mariño Márquez (11/2), José Paolo Guerrero Gonzales (24/9). Trainer: José Guillermo del Solar Alvarez-Calderón (12).

Goal: Juan Carlos Mariño Márquez (40).

510. 17.06.2008 **URUGUAY - PERU** **6-0(2-0)** 19th FIFA WC. Qualifiers

Estadio Centenario, Montevideo; Referee: Pablo Antonio Pozo Quinteros (Chile); Attendance: 20,016

PER: Leao Butrón Gotuzzo (23/0), Amilton Jair Prado Barrón (17/0), Alberto Junior Rodríguez Valdelomar (22/0), Miguel Ángel Villalta Hurtado (28/2), Juan Manuel Vargas Risco (17/2) [46.Hernán Rengifo Trigoso (7/2)], Nolberto Albino Solano Todco (86/20), Rainer Torres Salas (12/0), Miguel Ángel Cevasco Abad (9/1), Emilio Martín Hidalgo Conde (47/3) [67.Guillermo Sandro Salas Suárez (25/0)], Juan Carlos Mariño Márquez (12/2) [71.Paulo Rinaldo Cruzado Durand (12/0)], José Paolo Guerrero Gonzales (25/9). Trainer: José Guillermo del Solar Alvarez-Calderón (13).

511. 06.09.2008 **PERU - VENEZUELA** **1-0(1-0)** 19th FIFA WC. Qualifiers

Estadio Monumental, Lima; Referee: Óscar Maldonado (Bolivia); Attendance: 15,000

PER: Leao Butrón Gotuzzo (24/0), Amilton Jair Prado Barrón (18/0), Alberto Junior Rodríguez Valdelomar (23/0), Carlos Augusto Zambrano Ochandarte (2/1), Juan Manuel Vargas Risco (18/2), Paolo Giancarlo De La Haza Urquiza (13/0), Daniel Mackensi Chávez Castillo (4/0) [90+1.Juan Carlos La Rosa Llontop (1/0)], Nolberto Albino Solano Todco (87/20) [62.Henry Edson Quinteros Sánchez (20/1)], Rainer Torres Salas (13/0), Piero Fernando Alva Niezen (11/3), Johan Javier Fano Espinoza (3/0) [80.Hernán Rengifo Trigoso (8/2)]. Trainer: José Guillermo del Solar Alvarez-Calderón (14).

Goal: Piero Fernando Alva Niezen (39).

512. 10.09.2008 **PERU - ARGENTINA** **1-1(0-0)** 19th FIFA WC. Qualifiers

Estadio Monumental, Lima; Referee: Carlos Arecio Amarilla Demarqui (Paraguay); Attendance: 40,000

PER: Leao Butrón Gotuzzo (25/0), Amilton Jair Prado Barrón (19/0), Carlos Augusto Zambrano Ochandarte (3/1), Wálter Ricardo Vílchez Soto (36/1), Juan Manuel Vargas Risco (19/2), Rainer Torres Salas (14/0), Paolo Giancarlo De La Haza Urquiza (14/0), Nolberto Albino Solano Todco (88/20), Daniel Mackensi Chávez Castillo (5/0) [75.Hernán Rengifo Trigoso (9/2)], Piero Fernando Alva Niezen (12/3) [66.Guillermo Sandro Salas Suárez (26/0)], Johan Javier Fano Espinoza (4/1). Trainer: José Guillermo del Solar Alvarez-Calderón (15).

Goal: Johan Javier Fano Espinoza (90+3).

513. 11.10.2008 **BOLIVIA - PERU** **3-0(2-0)** 19th FIFA WC. Qualifiers

Estadio „Hernándo Siles Zuazo", La Paz; Referee: José Hernando Buitrago Arango (Colombia); Attendance: 23,147

PER: Leao Butrón Gotuzzo (26/0), Amilton Jair Prado Barrón (20/0), Carlos Augusto Zambrano Ochandarte (4/1), Wálter Ricardo Vílchez Soto (37/1), Juan Manuel Vargas Risco (20/2), Rainer Torres Salas (15/0), Paolo Giancarlo De La Haza Urquiza (15/0), Juan Carlos Mariño Márquez (13/2), Daniel Mackensi Chávez Castillo (6/0) [46.Roberto Carlos Guizasola La Rosa (1/0)], Johan Javier Fano Espinoza (5/1) [Hernán Rengifo Trigoso (10/2)], Piero Fernando Alva Niezen (13/3) [62.Wilmer Alexander Aguirre Vásquez (4/0)]. Trainer: José Guillermo del Solar Alvarez-Calderón (16).

514. 15.10.2008 **PARAGUAY - PERU** **1-0(0-0)** 19th FIFA WC. Qualifiers

Estadio Defensores del Chaco, Asunción; Referee: Sálvio Spínola Fagundes Filho (Brazil); Attendance: 25,587

PER: Leao Butrón Gotuzzo (27/0), Amilton Jair Prado Barrón (21/0), Orlando Contreras Collantes (2/0), Wálter Ricardo Vílchez Soto (38/1), Juan Manuel Vargas Risco (21/2), Nolberto Albino Solano Todco (89/20), Paolo Giancarlo De La Haza Urquiza (16/0) [85.Henry Edson Quinteros Sánchez (21/1)], Rainer Torres Salas (16/0), Juan Carlos Mariño Márquez (14/2) [70.Piero Fernando Alva Niezen (14/3)], Johan Javier Fano Espinoza (6/1) [84.Daniel Mackensi Chávez Castillo (7/0)], Hernán Rengifo Trigoso (11/2). Trainer: José Guillermo del Solar Alvarez-Calderón (17).

515. 06.02.2009 **EL SALVADOR - PERU** **1-0(1-0)**

Memorial Coliseum Stadium, Los Angeles (United States); Referee: n/a; Attendance: 3,000

PER: Leao Butrón Gotuzzo (28/0) [46.Raúl Omar Fernández Valverde (2/0)], Renzo Revoredo Zuazo (1/0) [46.Aldo Sebastián Corzo Chávez (1/0)], Orlando Contreras Collantes (3/0), John Christian Galliquio Castro (30/0), Edgar Harry Villamarín Arguedas (4/0), Paolo Giancarlo De La Haza Urquiza (17/0), Rainer Torres Salas (17/0), Juan Carlos Mariño Márquez (15/2) [64.Ronald Jhonatan Quinteros Sánchez (1/0)], Alexander Gustavo Sánchez Reyes (6/1), Miguel Ángel Torres Quintana (3/0) [78.Luis Enrique Trujillo Ortíz (1/0)], Piero Fernando Alva Niezen (15/3) [46.Juan José Barros Araujo (1/0)]. Trainer: José Guillermo del Solar Alvarez-Calderón (18).

516. 11.02.2009 **PERU - PARAGUAY** **0-1(0-1)**

Estadio „Alejandro Villanueva", Lima; Referee: Georges Buckley (Peru); Attendance: n/a

PER: Manuel Alexander Heredia Rojas (1/0), Aldo Sebastián Corzo Chávez (2/0), Orlando Contreras Collantes (4/0), Walter Ricardo Vílchez Soto (39/1), Wenceslao Ernesto Fernández Donayre (6/0), Paolo Giancarlo De La Haza Urquiza (18/0), Henry Edson Quinteros Sánchez (22/1) [83.Marko Gustavo Ciurlizza Rodríguez (34/0)], Miguel Ángel Torres Quintana (4/0) [75.Juan José Barros Araujo (2/0)], Juan Carlos Mariño Márquez (16/2) [54.Daniel Alonso Sánchez Albújar (1/0)], Alexander Gustavo Sánchez Reyes (7/1), Johan Javier Fano Espinoza (7/1). Trainer: José Guillermo del Solar Alvarez-Calderón (19).

517. 29.03.2009 **PERU - CHILE** **1-3(1-2)** 19th FIFA WC. Qualifiers

Estadio Monumental, Lima; Referee: Carlos Arecio Amarilla Demarqui (Paraguay); Attendance: 48,700

PER: Leao Butrón Gotuzzo (29/0), Alberto Junior Rodríguez Valdelomar (24/0), Ámilton Jair Prado Barrón (22/0), Carlos Augusto Zambrano Ochandarte (5/1), Juan Manuel Vargas Risco (22/2), Nolberto Albino Solano Todco (90/20) [78.Alexander Gustavo Sánchez Reyes (8/1)], Luis Alberto Ramírez Lucay (2/0), Rainer Torres Salas (18/0), Miguel Ángel Torres Quintana (5/0) [46.Paolo Giancarlo De La Haza Urquiza (19/0)], Daniel Mackensi Chávez Castillo (8/0) [59.Piero Fernando Alva Niezen (16/3)], Johan Javier Fano Espinoza (8/2). Trainer: José Guillermo del Solar Alvarez-Calderón (20).

Goal: Johan Javier Fano Espinoza (34).

518. 01.04.2009 **BRAZIL - PERU** **3-0(2-0)** 19th FIFA WC. Qualifiers

Estádio „José Pinheiro Borda", Porto Alegre; Referee: Sergio Fabián Pezzotta (Argentina); Attendance: 55,000

PER: Leao Butrón Gotuzzo (30/0), Alberto Junior Rodríguez Valdelomar (25/0), Ámilton Jair Prado Barrón (23/0), Walter Ricardo Vílchez Soto (40/1), Carlos Augusto Zambrano Ochandarte (6/1), Nolberto Albino Solano Todco (91/20) [70.José Carlos Fernández Piedra (1/0)], Pedro Alejandro García de la Cruz (19/2) [63.Alexander Gustavo Sánchez Reyes (9/1)], Juan Carlos La Rosa Llontop (2/0), Luis Alberto Ramírez Lucay (3/0) [80.Piero Fernando Alva Niezen (17/3)], Rainer Torres Salas (19/0), Johan Javier Fano Espinoza (9/2). Trainer: Trainer: José Guillermo del Solar Alvarez-Calderón (21).

519. 07.06.2009 **PERU - ECUADOR** **1-2(0-1)** 19th FIFA WC. Qualifiers

Estadio Monumental, Lima; Referee: Carlos Manuel Torres (Paraguay); Attendance: 17,050

PER: Raúl Omar Fernández Valverde (3/0), Alberto Junior Rodríguez Valdelomar (26/0), Ámilton Jair Prado Barrón (24/0) [62.Alexander Gustavo Sánchez Reyes (10/1)], Walter Ricardo Vílchez Soto (41/1), Carlos Augusto Zambrano Ochandarte (7/1), Juan Manuel Vargas Risco (23/3), Paolo Giancarlo De La Haza Urquiza (20/0), Luis Alberto Ramírez Lucay (4/0) [46.Roberto Merino Ramírez (1/0)], Rainer Torres Salas (20/0) [79.Josepmir Aarón Ballón Villacorta (1/0)], José Paolo Guerrero Gonzales (26/9), Johan Javier Fano Espinoza (10/2). Trainer: Trainer: José Guillermo del Solar Alvarez-Calderón (22).

Goal: Juan Manuel Vargas Risco (52).

520. 10.06.2009 **COLOMBIA - PERU** **1-0(1-0)** 19th FIFA WC. Qualifiers

Estadio „Atanasio Girardot", Medellín; Referee: Carlos Eugênio Simon (Brazil); Attendance: 32,300

PER: Leao Butrón Gotuzzo (31/0), Alberto Junior Rodríguez Valdelomar (27/0), Walter Ricardo Vílchez Soto (42/1), Carlos Augusto Zambrano Ochandarte (8/1), Juan Manuel Vargas Risco (24/3) [21.Luis Enrique Trujillo Ortíz (2/0)], Paolo Giancarlo De La Haza Urquiza (21/0), Josepmir Aarón Ballón Villacorta (2/0) [81.Alexander Gustavo Sánchez Reyes (11/1)], Juan Carlos La Rosa Llontop (3/0), Luis Alberto Ramírez Lucay (5/0), Johan Javier Fano Espinoza (11/2), José Paolo Guerrero Gonzales (27/9) [87.Hernán Rengifo Trigoso (12/2)]. Trainer: Trainer: José Guillermo del Solar Alvarez-Calderón (23).

521. 05.09.2009 **PERU - URUGUAY** **1-0(0-0)** 19th FIFA WC. Qualifiers

Estadio Monumental, Lima; Referee: Carlos Chandía Alarcón (Chile); Attendance: 15,000

PER: Leao Butrón Gotuzzo (32/0), Alberto Junior Rodríguez Valdelomar (28/0), Walter Ricardo Vílchez Soto (43/1), Carlos Augusto Zambrano Ochandarte (9/1), Juan Manuel Vargas Risco (25/3), Nolberto Albino Solano Todco (92/20) [78.Rainer Torres Salas (21/0)], Josepmir Aarón Ballón Villacorta (3/0), Paolo Giancarlo De La Haza Urquiza (22/0) [46.Ámilton Jair Prado Barrón (25/0)], Roberto Carlos Palacios Mestas (123/19), Daniel Mackensi Chávez Castillo (9/0) [59.Irven Beybe Ávila Acero (1/0)], Hernán Rengifo Trigoso (13/3). Trainer: Trainer: José Guillermo del Solar Alvarez-Calderón (24).

Goal: Hernán Rengifo Trigoso (86).

522. 09.09.2009 **VENEZUELA - PERU** **3-1(1-1)** 19th FIFA WC. Qualifiers

Estadio Olímpico „Luis Ramos", Puerto la Cruz; Referee: Carlos Vera (Ecuador); Attendance: 31,703

PER: Leao Butrón Gotuzzo (33/0), Alberto Junior Rodríguez Valdelomar (29/0), Christian Guillermo Martín Ramos Garagay (1/0), Ámilton Jair Prado Barrón (26/0), Walter Ricardo Vílchez Soto (44/1), Nolberto Albino Solano Todco (93/20) [68.Joel Melchor Sánchez Alegría (1/0)], Josepmir Aarón Ballón Villacorta (4/0), Rainer Torres Salas (22/0) [67.Henry Edson Quinteros Sánchez (23/1)], Roberto Carlos Palacios Mestas (124/19), José Paolo Guerrero Gonzales (28/9) [15.Hernán Rengifo Trigoso (14/3)], Johan Javier Fano Espinoza (12/2). Trainer: Trainer: José Guillermo del Solar Alvarez-Calderón (25).

Goal: Juan José Fuenmayor Núñez (41 own goal)

523. 10.10.2009 **ARGENTINA - PERU** **2-1(0-0)** 19th FIFA WC. Qualifiers

Estadio Monumental „Antonio Vespucio Liberti", Buenos Aires; Referee: René Ortubé Betancourt (Bolivia); Attendance: 38,019

PER: Leao Butrón Gotuzzo (34/0), Alberto Junior Rodríguez Valdelomar (30/0), Ámilton Jair Prado Barrón (27/0), Walter Ricardo Vílchez Soto (45/1), Carlos Augusto Zambrano Ochandarte (10/1), Juan Manuel Vargas Risco (26/3), Nolberto Albino Solano Todco (94/20) [65.Roberto Carlos Palacios Mestas (125/19)], Josepmir Aarón Ballón Villacorta (5/0), Luis Alberto Ramírez Lucay (6/0) [90.Juan Carlos La Rosa Llontop (4/0)], Rainer Torres Salas (23/0), Johan Javier Fano Espinoza (13/2) [71.Hernán Rengifo Trigoso (15/4)]. Trainer: Trainer: José Guillermo del Solar Alvarez-Calderón (26).

Goal: Hernán Rengifo Trigoso (89).

524. 14.10.2009 **PERU - BOLIVIA** **1-0(0-0)** 19th FIFA WC. Qualifiers

Estadio „Alejandro Villanueva", Lima; Referee: Juan Soto (Venezuela); Attendance: 4,373

PER: Leao Butrón Gotuzzo (35/0), Alberto Junior Rodríguez Valdelomar (31/0), Ámilton Jair Prado Barrón (28/0) [87.Marcio André Valverde Zamora (1/0)], Walter Ricardo Vílchez Soto (46/1), Carlos Augusto Zambrano Ochandarte (11/1), Juan Manuel Vargas Risco (27/3), Nolberto Albino Solano Todco (95/20) [69.Henry Edson Quinteros Sánchez (24/1)], Josepmir Aarón Ballón Villacorta (6/0), Luis Alberto Ramírez Lucay (7/0) [61.Roberto Carlos Palacios Mestas (126/19)], Johan Javier Fano Espinoza (14/3), Hernán Rengifo Trigoso (16/4). Trainer: Trainer: José Guillermo del Solar Alvarez-Calderón (27).

Goals: Johan Javier Fano Espinoza (54).

525. 18.11.2009 **HONDURAS - PERU** **1-2(0-1)**

Sun Life Stadium, Miami (United States); Referee: Edvin Jurisevic (United States); Attendance: n/a

PER: Raúl Omar Fernández Valverde (4/0) [46.Leao Butrón Gotuzzo (36/0)], Orlando Contreras Collantes (5/0), Christian Guillermo Martín Ramos Garagay (2/0), John Christian Galliquio Castro (31/0), Damián Ísmodes Saravia (6/0) [89.Kerwin Junior Peixoto Chiclayo (1/0)], Josepmir Aarón Ballón Villacorta (7/0), Roberto Carlos Palacios Mestas (127/19), Rainer Torres Salas (24/0) [81.Juan Carlos La Rosa Llontop (5/0)], Marcio André Valverde Zamora (2/0) [66.Aldo Sebastián Corzo Chávez (3/0)], Johan Javier Fano Espinoza (15/3) [67.Alexander Gustavo Sánchez Reyes (12/1)], Hernán Rengifo Trigoso (17/5) [81.Irven Beybe Ávila Acero (2/0)]. Trainer: Trainer: José Guillermo del Solar Alvarez-Calderón (28).

Goals: Emilio Arturo Izaguirre Girón (40 own goal), Hernán Rengifo Trigoso (64).

526. 04.09.2010 **CANADA - PERU** **0-2(0-0)**

BMO Field, Toronto; Referee: Edvin Jurisevic (United States); Attendance: 10,619

PER: Raúl Omar Fernández Valverde (5/0), Wilmer Santiago Acasiete Ariadela (28/2), Walter Ricardo Vílchez Soto (47/1) [82.Jesús Giancarlos Rabanal Dávila (1/0)], Roberto Carlos Guizasola La Rosa (2/0), Carlos Augusto Zambrano Ochandarte (12/1), Juan Manuel Vargas Risco (28/3) [63.Reimond Orángel Manco Albarracín (3/0)], Josepmir Aarón Ballón Villacorta (8/0) [89.Rainer Torres Salas (25/0)], Luis Alberto Ramírez Lucay (8/0) [84.Antonio Emiliano Gonzáles Canchari (1/0)], Luis Jan Piers Advíncula Castrillón (1/0) [46.Jean Carlo Tragodara Gálvez (1/1); 73.John Christian Galliquio Castro (32/0)], Jefferson Agustín Farfán Guadalupe (42/12), José Carlos Fernández Piedra (2/1). Trainer: Sergio Apraham Markarián Abrahamian (1).

Goals: José Carlos Fernández Piedra (67), Jean Carlo Tragodara Gálvez (71).

527. 07.09.2010 **JAMAICA - PERU** **1-2(1-1)**

Lockhart Stadium, Fort Lauderdale (United States); Referee: Terry Vaughn (United States); Attendance: n/a

PER: Salomón Alexis Libman Pastor (1/0), Wilmer Santiago Acasiete Ariadela (29/2) [46.Walter Ricardo Vílchez Soto (48/1)], John Christian Galliquio Castro (33/0), Jesús Giancarlos Rabanal Dávila (2/0), Carlos Augusto Zambrano Ochandarte (13/1) [46.Roberto Carlos Guizasola La Rosa (3/0)], Juan Manuel Vargas Risco (29/3), Antonio Emiliano Gonzáles Canchari (2/0) [65.Josepmir Aarón Ballón Villacorta (9/0)], Rainer Torres Salas (26/0) [64.Luis Jan Piers Advíncula Castrillón (2/0)], Reimond Orángel Manco Albarracín (4/0) [46.Jean Carlo Tragodara Gálvez (2/1)], Jefferson Agustín Farfán Guadalupe (43/12), Hernán Rengifo Trigoso (18/5) [84.José Carlos Fernández Piedra (3/2)]. Trainer: Sergio Apraham Markarián Abrahamian (2).

Goals: Demar Philips (4 own goal), José Carlos Fernández Piedra (85).

528. 08.10.2010 **PERU – COSTA RICA** **2-0(2-0)**
Estadio „Alejandro Villanueva", Lima; Referee: Omar Ponce (Ecuador); Attendance: 15,000
PER: Salomón Alexis Libman Pastor (2/0), Christian Guillermo Martín Ramos Garagay (3/0), Walter Ricardo Vílchez Soto (49/1), Roberto Carlos Guizasola La Rosa (4/0) [57.Willy Alexander Rivas Asin (1/0)], Carlos Augusto Zambrano Ochandarte (14/1) [68.John Christian Galliquio Castro (34/0)], Josepmir Aarón Ballón Villacorta (10/0) [68.Rainer Torres Salas (27/0)], Luis Alberto Ramírez Lucay (9/1) [81.Paolo Giancarlo de la Haza Urquiza (23/0)], Reimond Orángel Manco Albarracín (5/0) [57.Jean Carlo Tragodara Gálvez (3/1)], Daniel Mackensi Chávez Castillo (10/0) [57.Luis Jan Piers Advíncula Castrillón (3/0)], Jefferson Agustín Farfán Guadalupe (44/12), Hernán Rengifo Trigoso (19/6). Trainer: Sergio Apraham Markarián Abrahamian (3).
Goals: Luis Alberto Ramírez Lucay (3), Hernán Rengifo Trigoso (5).

529. 12.10.2010 **PANAMA - PERU** **1-0(0-0)**
Estadio „Rommel Fernández", Ciudad de Panamá; Referee: Ricardo Cerdas Sánchez (Costa Rica); Attendance: 5,000
PER: Raúl Omar Fernández Valverde (6/0), Christian Guillermo Martín Ramos Garagay (4/0) [46.John Christian Galliquio Castro (35/0)], Walter Ricardo Vílchez Soto (50/1), Jesús Giancarlos Rabanal Dávila (3/0), Willy Alexander Rivas Asin (2/0), Carlos Augusto Zambrano Ochandarte (15/1) [*sent off 23*], Josepmir Aarón Ballón Villacorta (11/0), Jean Carlo Tragodara Gálvez (4/1) [68.Rainer Torres Salas (28/0)], Luis Alberto Ramírez Lucay (10/1) [81.Luis Jan Piers Advíncula Castrillón (4/0)], Johan Javier Fano Espinoza (16/3) [57.Hernán Rengifo Trigoso (20/6)], Jefferson Agustín Farfán Guadalupe (45/12). Trainer: Sergio Apraham Markarián Abrahamian (4).

530. 17.11.2010 **COLOMBIA - PERU** **1-1(0-1)**
Estadio „Nemesio Camacho" ‚El Campín", Bogotá; Referee: Saúl Esteban Laverni (Argentina); Attendance: 6,900
PER: Erick Guillermo Delgado Vásquez (13/0), Christian Guillermo Martín Ramos Garagay (5/0), Walter Ricardo Vílchez Soto (51/1), Roberto Carlos Guizasola La Rosa (5/0), Jesús Giancarlos Rabanal Dávila (4/0), Juan Manuel Vargas Risco (30/3) [74.Luis Enrique Trujillo Ortíz (3/0)], Josepmir Aarón Ballón Villacorta (12/0) [87.Adán Adolfo Balbín Silva (1/0)], Carlos Augusto Lobatón Espejo (5/0) [58.Jean Carlo Tragodara Gálvez (5/1)], Renzo Santiago Sheput Rodríguez (1/0) [58.Luis Jan Piers Advíncula Castrillón (5/0)], Luis Alberto Ramírez Lucay (11/2) [78.Paulo Rinaldo Cruzado Durand (13/0)], José Carlos Fernández Piedra (4/2) [66.Juan Diego González-Vigil Bentin (4/0)]. Trainer: Sergio Apraham Markarián Abrahamian (5).
Goal: Luis Alberto Ramírez Lucay (32).

531. 08.02.2011 **PERU - PANAMA** **1-0(1-0)**
Estadio 25 de Noviembre, Moquegua; Referee: Darío Ubriaco (Uruguay); Attendance: 15,000
PER: Erick Guillermo Delgado Vásquez (14/0), Christian Guillermo Martín Ramos Garagay (6/0) [62.Gianfranco Roberto Espinoza (1/0)], Orlando Contreras Collantes (6/1), Walter Ricardo Vílchez Soto (52/1), Renzo Revoredo Zuazo (2/0), Paulo Rinaldo Cruzado Durand (14/0) [46.Antonio Emiliano Gonzáles Canchari (3/0)], Jean Carlo Tragodara Gálvez (6/1) [46.Johan Joussep Sotil Eche (1/0)], Michael Fidel Guevara Legua (1/0) [46.Víctor Yoshimar Yotún Flores (1/0)], Luis Jan Piers Advíncula Castrillón (6/0) [46.Carlos Augusto Lobatón Espejo (6/0)], Wilmer Alexander Aguirre Vásquez (5/0) [90.Víctor Alfonso Rossel Del Mar (1/0)], Johan Javier Fano Espinoza (17/3). Trainer: Sergio Apraham Markarián Abrahamian (6).
Goal: Orlando Contreras Collantes (40).

532. 29.03.2011 **ECUADOR - PERU** **0-0**
Kyocera Stadion, Den Haag (Holland); Referee: Oscar Eric Braamhaar (Holland); Attendance: n/a
PER: Salomón Alexis Libman Pastor (3/0), Christian Guillermo Martín Ramos Garagay (7/0) [*sent off 22*], Wilmer Santiago Acasiete Ariadela (30/2), Walter Ricardo Vílchez Soto (53/1), Giancarlo Carmona Maldonado (1/0) [60.Renzo Revoredo Zuazo (3/0)], Juan Manuel Vargas Risco (31/3) [60.Antonio Emiliano Gonzáles Canchari (4/0)], Paulo Rinaldo Cruzado Durand (15/0), Jean Carlo Tragodara Gálvez (7/1) [60.Carlos Augusto Lobatón Espejo (7/0)], Michael Fidel Guevara Legua (2/0) [30.Jesús Giancarlos Rabanal Dávila (5/0)], José Paolo Guerrero Gonzales (29/9) [75.Luis Jan Piers Advíncula Castrillón (7/0)], Claudio Miguel Pizarro Bosio (56/13). Trainer: Sergio Apraham Markarián Abrahamian (7).

533. 01.06.2011 **JAPAN - PERU** **0-0** Kirin Cup
Niigata Stadium, Niigata; Referee: Howard Melton Webb (England); Attendance: 39,048
PER: Salomón Alexis Libman Pastor (4/0), Wilmer Santiago Acasiete Ariadela (31/2), Walter Ricardo Vílchez Soto (54/1), Jesús Giancarlos Rabanal Dávila (6/0) [62.Víctor Yoshimar Yotún Flores (2/0)], Renzo Revoredo Zuazo (4/0), Adan Adolfo Balbín Silva (2/0) [62.Josepmir Aarón Ballón Villacorta (13/0)], Paulo Rinaldo Cruzado Durand (16/0) [73.Carlos Augusto Lobatón Espejo (8/0)], Christian Alberto Cueva Bravo (1/0) [61.William Medardo Chiroque Távara (7/0)], Luis Alberto Ramírez Lucay (12/2), Luis Jan Piers Advíncula Castrillón (8/0), Jefferson Agustín Farfán Guadalupe (46/12) [67.Raúl Mario Ruidíaz Misitich (1/0)]. Trainer: Sergio Apraham Markarián Abrahamian (8).

534. 04.06.2011 **CZECH REPUBLIC - PERU** **0-0** Kirin Cup
Matsumoto Stadium, Matsumoto (Japan); Referee: Ryuji Sato (Japan); Attendance: 7,592
PER: Raúl Omar Fernández Valverde (7/0), Wilmer Santiago Acasiete Ariadela (32/2) [60.Walter Ricardo Vílchez Soto (55/1)], Christian Guillermo Martín Ramos Garagay (8/0), Giancarlo Carmona Maldonado (2/0), Víctor Yoshimar Yotún Flores (3/0) [68.Jesús Giancarlos Rabanal Dávila (7/0)], Adan Adolfo Balbín Silva (3/0), Paulo Rinaldo Cruzado Durand (17/0), Michael Fidel Guevara Legua (3/0) [73.Luis Alberto Ramírez Lucay (13/2)], Luis Jan Piers Advíncula Castrillón (9/0) [75.Carlos Augusto Lobatón Espejo (9/0)], William Medardo Chiroque Távara (8/0) [60.Christian Alberto Cueva Bravo (2/0)], Raúl Mario Ruidíaz Misitich (2/0) [60.Jefferson Agustín Farfán Guadalupe (47/12)]. Trainer: Sergio Apraham Markarián Abrahamian (9).

535. 28.06.2011 **PERU - SENEGAL** **1-0(0-0)**
Estadio „Alejandro Villanueva", Lima; Referee: Leandro Vuaden (Brazil); Attendance: 20,000
PER: Raúl Omar Fernández Valverde (8/0), Wilmer Santiago Acasiete Ariadela (33/2), Alberto Junior Rodríguez Valdelomar (32/0) [46.Carlos Augusto Zambrano Ochandarte (16/1); 63.Christian Guillermo Martín Ramos Garagay (9/0)], Walter Ricardo Vílchez Soto (56/1), Aldo Sebastián Corzo Chávez (4/0), Josepmir Aarón Ballón Villacorta (14/0) [62.Adan Adolfo Balbín Silva (4/0)], Paulo Rinaldo Cruzado Durand (18/0) [62.Carlos Augusto Lobatón Espejo (10/0)], Luis Alberto Ramírez Lucay (14/2), Luis Jan Piers Advíncula Castrillón (10/0) [77.Raúl Mario Ruidíaz Misitich (3/0)], André Martín Carrillo Díaz (1/0) [62.Michael Fidel Guevara Legua (4/0)], José Paolo Guerrero Gonzales (30/10). Trainer: Sergio Apraham Markarián Abrahamian (10).
Goal: José Paolo Guerrero Gonzales (89).

536. 04.07.2011 **URUGUAY - PERU** **1-1(1-1)** 43rd Copa América. Group Stage
Estadio del Bicentenario, San Juan (Argentina); Referee: Wilmar Alexander Roldán Pérez (Colombia); Attendance: 25,000
PER: Raúl Omar Fernández Valverde (9/0), Renzo Revoredo Zuazo (5/0), Wilmer Santiago Acasiete Ariadela (34/2), Alberto Junior Rodríguez Valdelomar (33/0), Walter Ricardo Vílchez Soto (57/1), Adan Adolfo Balbín Silva (5/0), Michael Fidel Guevara Legua (5/0) [58.Carlos Augusto Lobatón Espejo (11/0)], Paulo Rinaldo Cruzado Durand (19/0), Víctor Yoshimar Yotún Flores (4/0) [60.Juan Manuel Vargas Risco (32/3)], Luis Jan Piers Advíncula Castrillón (11/0) [90+1.William Medardo Chiroque Távara (9/0)], José Paolo Guerrero Gonzales (31/11). Trainer: Sergio Apraham Markarián Abrahamian (11).
Goal: José Paolo Guerrero Gonzales (23).

537. 08.07.2011 **PERU - MEXICO** **1-0(0-0)** 43rd Copa América. Group Stage

Estadio Malvinas Argentinas, Mendoza (Argentina); Referee: Sergio Fabián Pezzotta (Argentina); Attendance: n/a

PER: Raúl Omar Fernández Valverde (10/0), Giancarlo Carmona Maldonado (3/0), Wilmer Santiago Acasiete Ariadela (35/2), Alberto Junior Rodríguez Valdelomar (34/0), Walter Ricardo Vílchez Soto (58/1), Adan Adolfo Balbín Silva (6/0), Paulo Rinaldo Cruzado Durand (20/0) [77.Michael Fidel Guevara Legua (6/0)], Carlos Augusto Lobatón Espejo (12/0) [86.Josepmir Aarón Ballón Villacorta (15/0)], José Paolo Guerrero Gonzales (32/12), Luis Jan Piers Advíncula Castrillón (12/0) [46.Víctor Yoshimar Yotún Flores (5/0)], Juan Manuel Vargas Risco (33/3). Trainer: Sergio Apraham Markarián Abrahamian (12).

Goal: José Paolo Guerrero Gonzales (82).

538. 12.07.2011 **CHILE - PERU** **1-0(0-0)** 43rd Copa América. Group Stage

Estadio Malvinas Argentinas, Mendoza (Argentina); Referee: Sálvio Spínola Fagundes Filho (Brazil); Attendance: n/a

PER: Salomón Alexis Libman Pastor (5/0), Renzo Revoredo Zuazo (6/0), Wilmer Santiago Acasiete Ariadela (36/2) [46.Walter Ricardo Vílchez Soto (59/1)], Christian Guillermo Martín Ramos Garagay (10/0), Giancarlo Carmona Maldonado (4/0) [*sent off 62*], Josepmir Aarón Ballón Villacorta (16/0), Michael Fidel Guevara Legua (7/0) [70.Carlos Augusto Lobatón Espejo (13/0)], Antonio Emiliano Gonzáles Canchari (5/0) [77.André Martín Carrillo Díaz (2/0)], Aldo Sebastián Corzo Chávez (5/0), William Medardo Chiroque Távara (10/0), Raúl Mario Ruidíaz Misitich (4/0). Trainer: Sergio Apraham Markarián Abrahamian (13).

539. 16.07.2011 **COLOMBIA - PERU** **0-2(0-0,0-0)** 43rd Copa América. Quarter-Finals

Estadio "Mario Alberto Kempes", Córdoba (Argentina); Referee: Francisco Chacón Gutiérrez (Mexico); Attendance: n/a

PER: Raúl Omar Fernández Valverde (11/0), Renzo Revoredo Zuazo (7/0), Christian Guillermo Martín Ramos Garagay (11/0), Alberto Junior Rodríguez Valdelomar (35/0), Walter Ricardo Vílchez Soto (60/1), Adan Adolfo Balbín Silva (7/0), Paulo Rinaldo Cruzado Durand (21/0) [118.Josepmir Aarón Ballón Villacorta (17/0)], Luis Jan Piers Advíncula Castrillón (13/0) [46.Carlos Augusto Lobatón Espejo (14/1)], Juan Manuel Vargas Risco (34/4), William Medardo Chiroque Távara (11/0) [96.Víctor Yoshimar Yotún Flores (6/0)], José Paolo Guerrero Gonzales (33/12). Trainer: Sergio Apraham Markarián Abrahamian (14).

Goals: Carlos Augusto Lobatón Espejo (101), Juan Manuel Vargas Risco (111).

540. 19.07.2011 **PERU - URUGUAY** **0-2(0-0)** 43rd Copa América. Semi-Finals.

Estadio Ciudad de La Plata, La Plata (Argentina); Referee: Raúl Orosco Delgadillo (Bolivia); Attendance: 35,000

PER: Raúl Omar Fernández Valverde (12/0), Giancarlo Carmona Maldonado (5/0), Wilmer Santiago Acasiete Ariadela (37/2), Alberto Junior Rodríguez Valdelomar (36/0), Walter Ricardo Vílchez Soto (61/1), Adan Adolfo Balbín Silva (8/0) [90+2.Josepmir Aarón Ballón Villacorta (18/0)], Paulo Rinaldo Cruzado Durand (22/0), Luis Jan Piers Advíncula Castrillón (14/0) [60.Carlos Augusto Lobatón Espejo (15/1)], Juan Manuel Vargas Risco (35/4) [*sent off 68*], Víctor Yoshimar Yotún Flores (7/0) [53.William Medardo Chiroque Távara (12/0)], José Paolo Guerrero Gonzales (34/12). Trainer: Sergio Apraham Markarián Abrahamian (15).

541. 23.07.2011 **PERU - VENEZUELA** **4-1(1-0)** 43rd Copa América. 3rd Place Play-off

Estadio Ciudad de La Plata, La Plata (Argentina); Referee: Wilmar Alexander Roldán Pérez (Colombia); Attendance: n/a

PER: Raúl Omar Fernández Valverde (13/0), Christian Guillermo Martín Ramos Garagay (12/0), Alberto Junior Rodríguez Valdelomar (37/0), Aldo Sebastián Corzo Chávez (6/0), Renzo Revoredo Zuazo (8/0), Víctor Yoshimar Yotún Flores (8/0), Adan Adolfo Balbín Silva (9/0), Paulo Rinaldo Cruzado Durand (23/0) [78.Luis Jan Piers Advíncula Castrillón (15/0)], Carlos Augusto Lobatón Espejo (16/1) [60.Michael Fidel Guevara Legua (8/0)], William Medardo Chiroque Távara (13/1), José Paolo Guerrero Gonzales (35/15). Trainer: Sergio Apraham Markarián Abrahamian (16).

Goals: William Medardo Chiroque Távara (41), José Paolo Guerrero Gonzales (63, 89, 90+2).

542. 02.09.2011 **PERU - BOLIVIA** **2-2(1-1)**

Estadio Nacional „José Díaz", Lima; Referee: Juan Ernesto Soto Arevalo (Venezuela); Attendance: 35,000

PER: Leao Butrón Gotuzzo (37/0), Walter Ricardo Vílchez Soto (62/1), Roberto Carlos Guizasola La Rosa (6/0) [46.Aldo Sebastián Corzo Chávez (7/0); 75.Cristopher Paolo César Hurtado Huertas (1/0)], Renzo Revoredo Zuazo (9/0), Víctor Yoshimar Yotún Flores (9/0) [46.Luis Enrique Trujillo Ortíz (4/0)], Adan Adolfo Balbín Silva (10/0), Paulo Rinaldo Cruzado Durand (24/1), Carlos Augusto Lobatón Espejo (17/1) [46.Josepmir Aarón Ballón Villacorta (19/0)], Wilmer Alexander Aguirre Vásquez (6/0) [62.Michael Fidel Guevara Legua (9/0)], Jefferson Agustín Farfán Guadalupe (48/12) [90.Irven Beybe Ávila Acero (3/0)], Claudio Miguel Pizarro Bosio (57/14). Trainer: Sergio Apraham Markarián Abrahamian (17).

Goals: Paulo Rinaldo Cruzado Durand (36), Claudio Miguel Pizarro Bosio (81 penalty).

543. 05.09.2011 **BOLIVIA - PERU** **0-0**

Estadio „Hernándo Siles Zuazo", La Paz; Referee: Julio César Quintana Rodríguez (Paraguay); Attendance: n/a

PER: Leao Butrón Gotuzzo (38/0), Wilmer Santiago Acasiete Ariadela (38/2), Christian Guillermo Martín Ramos Garagay (13/0), Aldo Sebastián Corzo Chávez (8/0) [46.Renzo Revoredo Zuazo (10/0)], Víctor Yoshimar Yotún Flores (10/0), Edwin Retamoso Palomino (1/0), Carlos Augusto Lobatón Espejo (18/1) [75.Josepmir Aarón Ballón Villacorta (20/0)], Cristopher Paolo César Hurtado Huertas (2/0) [59.Wilmer Alexander Aguirre Vásquez (7/0)], Juan Carlos Mariño Márquez (17/2) [67.Luis Enrique Trujillo Ortíz (5/0)], Luis Jan Piers Advíncula Castrillón (16/0) [81.Michael Fidel Guevara Legua (10/0)], Irven Beybe Ávila Acero (4/0) [90.Claudio Miguel Pizarro Bosio (58/14)]. Trainer: Sergio Apraham Markarián Abrahamian (18).

544. 07.10.2011 **PERU - PARAGUAY** **2-0(1-0)** 20th FIFA WC. Qualifiers

Estadio Nacional „José Díaz", Lima; Referee: Sergio Fabián Pezzotta (Argentina); Attendance: 39,600

PER: Raúl Omar Fernández Valverde (14/0), Wilmer Santiago Acasiete Ariadela (39/2), Alberto Junior Rodríguez Valdelomar (38/0), Roberto Carlos Guizasola La Rosa (7/0), Juan Manuel Vargas Risco (36/4), Víctor Yoshimar Yotún Flores (11/0), Adan Adolfo Balbín Silva (11/0), Paulo Rinaldo Cruzado Durand (25/1) [90.Carlos Augusto Lobatón Espejo (19/1)], Jefferson Agustín Farfán Guadalupe (49/12), José Paolo Guerrero Gonzales (36/17) [91.Luis Jan Piers Advíncula Castrillón (17/0)], Claudio Miguel Pizarro Bosio (59/14). Trainer: Sergio Apraham Markarián Abrahamian (19).

Goals: José Paolo Guerrero Gonzales (47, 73).

545. 11.10.2011 **CHILE - PERU** **4-2(2-0)** 20th FIFA WC. Qualifiers

Estadio Monumental „David Arellano", Santiago; Referee: Raúl Orosco Delgadillo (Bolivia); Attendance: 39,000

PER: Raúl Omar Fernández Valverde (15/0), Wilmer Santiago Acasiete Ariadela (40/2) [87.William Medardo Chiroque Távara (14/1)], Alberto Junior Rodríguez Valdelomar (39/0), Renzo Revoredo Zuazo (11/0), Juan Manuel Vargas Risco (37/4), Víctor Yoshimar Yotún Flores (12/0) [46.Roberto Carlos Guizasola La Rosa (8/0)], Adan Adolfo Balbín Silva (12/0) [46.Carlos Augusto Lobatón Espejo (20/1)], Paulo Rinaldo Cruzado Durand (26/1), Jefferson Agustín Farfán Guadalupe (50/13), José Paolo Guerrero Gonzales (37/17), Claudio Miguel Pizarro Bosio (60/15). Trainer: Sergio Apraham Markarián Abrahamian (20).

Goals: Claudio Miguel Pizarro Bosio (49), Jefferson Agustín Farfán Guadalupe (59).

546. 15.11.2011 **ECUADOR - PERU** **2-0(0-0)** 20th FIFA WC. Qualifiers

Estadio Olimpico "Atahualpa", Quito; Referee: Jorge Luis Larrionda Pietrafesa (Uruguay); Attendance: 34,481

PER: Raúl Omar Fernández Valverde (16/0), Wilmer Santiago Acasiete Ariadela (41/2), Christian Guillermo Martín Ramos Garagay (14/0), Walter Ricardo Vílchez Soto (63/1), Renzo Revoredo Zuazo (12/0), Juan Manuel Vargas Risco (38/4), Edwin Retamoso Palomino (2/0), Carlos Augusto Lobatón Espejo (21/1) [46.Michael Fidel Guevara Legua (11/0)], Jefferson Agustín Farfán Guadalupe (51/13) [66.Luis Jan Piers Advíncula Castrillón (18/0)], José Paolo Guerrero Gonzales (38/18), Claudio Miguel Pizarro Bosio (61/15) [63.William Medardo Chiroque Távara (15/1)]. Trainer: Sergio Apraham Markarián Abrahamian (21).

547. 29.02.1012 **TUNISIA - PERU** **1-1(1-1)**

Stade El Menzah, Tunis; Referee: Cecil Fleischer (Ghana); Attendance: 5,000

PER: Diego Alonso Penny Valdez (7/0), Wilmer Santiago Acasiete Ariadela (42/2) [46.Walter Ricardo Vílchez Soto (64/1)], Roberto Carlos Guizasola La Rosa (9/0) [46.Renzo Revoredo Zuazo (13/0)], Carlos Augusto Zambrano Ochandarte (17/1) [78.Christian Guillermo Martín Ramos Garagay (15/0)], Juan Manuel Vargas Risco (39/4) [62.André Martín Carrillo Díaz (3/0)], Víctor Yoshimar Yotún Flores (13/0), Paulo Rinaldo Cruzado Durand (27/1) [62.Jefferson Agustín Farfán Guadalupe (52/13)], Antonio Emiliano Gonzáles Canchari (6/0) [72.Edwin Retamoso Palomino (3/0)], Luis Alberto Ramírez Lucay (15/2) [71.Carlos Augusto Lobatón Espejo (22/1)], José Paolo Guerrero Gonzales (39/18) [77.Michael Fidel Guevara Legua (12/0)], Claudio Miguel Pizarro Bosio (62/16). Trainer: Sergio Apraham Markarián Abrahamian (22).

Goal: Claudio Miguel Pizarro Bosio (45+2).

548. 21.03.2012 **CHILE - PERU** **3-1(2-1)** Copa del Pacífico

Estadio „Carlos Dittborn", Arica; Referee: Julio César Quintana Rodríguez (Paraguay); Attendance: 12,000

PER: Salomón Alexis Libman Pastor (6/0), John Christian Galliquio Castro (36/1), Walter Ricardo Vílchez Soto (65/1), Aldo Sebastián Corzo Chávez (9/0) [46.Luis Jan Piers Advíncula Castrillón (19/0)], Christian Guillermo Martín Ramos Garagay (16/0) [81.Néstor Alonso Duarte Carassa (1/0)], Antonio Emiliano Gonzáles Canchari (7/0), Michael Fidel Guevara Legua (13/0) [63.Ronald Jhonatan Quinteros Sánchez (2/0)], Víctor Yoshimar Yotún Flores (14/0), Álvaro Francisco Ampuero García-Rosell (1/0) [63.Carlos Oswaldo Fernández Maldonado (1/0)], Hernán Rengifo Trigoso (21/6) [76.Cristopher Paolo César Hurtado Huertas (3/0)], Irven Beybe Ávila Acero (5/0) [46.José Carlos Fernández Piedra (5/2)]. Trainer: Sergio Apraham Markarián Abrahamian (23).

Goal: John Christian Galliquio Castro (21).

549. 11.04.2012 **PERU - CHILE** **0-3(0-0)** Copa del Pacífico

Estadio „Jorge Basadre", Tacna; Referee: Enrique Cáceres (Paraguay); Attendance: 15,000

PER: Leao Butrón Gotuzzo (39/0), John Christian Galliquio Castro (37/1), Christian Guillermo Martín Ramos Garagay (17/0), Jaime Vásquez Ramírez (1/0), Ronald Jhonatan Quinteros Sánchez (3/0) [46.Paolo Giancarlo de la Haza Urquiza (24/0) [*sent off 51*]], Renzo Santiago Sheput Rodríguez (2/0) [71.Jair Edson Céspedes Zegarra (2/0)], Antonio Emiliano Gonzáles Canchari (8/0), Víctor Yoshimar Yotún Flores (15/0), Christian Alberto Cueva Bravo (3/0) [46.William Medardo Chiroque Távara (16/1)], Álvaro Francisco Ampuero García-Rosell (2/0) [60.Juan Carlos Mariño Márquez (18/2)], Hernán Rengifo Trigoso (22/6) [60.Daniel Mackensi Chávez Castillo (11/0)]. Trainer: Sergio Apraham Markarián Abrahamian (24).

550. 23.05.2012 **PERU - NIGERIA** **0-1(0-1)**

Estadio Nacional „José Díaz", Lima; Referee: José Luis Espinel Mena (Ecuador); Attendance: 30,000

PER: Diego Alonso Penny Valdez (8/0), John Christian Galliquio Castro (38/1) [46.Jesús Martín Álvarez Hurtado (1/0)], Renzo Revoredo Zuazo (14/0), Christian Guillermo Martín Ramos Garagay (18/0), Carlos Augusto Lobatón Espejo (23/1) [46.Michael Fidel Guevara Legua (14/0)], Roberto Carlos Palacios Mestas (128/19) [10.Luis Alberto Ramírez Lucay (16/2)], Antonio Emiliano Gonzáles Canchari (9/0) [73.Carlos Alberto Zegarra Zamora (24/1)], Víctor Yoshimar Yotún Flores (16/0) [46.Álvaro Francisco Ampuero García-Rosell (3/0)], Jefferson Agustín Farfán Guadalupe (53/13), José Paolo Guerrero Gonzales (40/19), Claudio Miguel Pizarro Bosio (63/16) [62.José Carlos Fernández Piedra (6/2)]. Trainer: Sergio Apraham Markarián Abrahamian (25).

Goal: José Paolo Guerrero Gonzales (36).

551. 03.06.2012 **PERU - COLOMBIA** **0-1(0-0)** 20th FIFA WC. Qualifiers

Estadio Nacional, Lima; Referee: Néstor Fabián Pitana (Argentina); Attendance: 35,724

PER: Diego Alonso Penny Valdez (9/0), John Christian Galliquio Castro (39/1), Jesús Martín Álvarez Hurtado (2/0), Renzo Revoredo Zuazo (15/0) [69.Raúl Mario Ruidíaz Misitich (5/0)], Víctor Yoshimar Yotún Flores (17/0), Christian Guillermo Martín Ramos Garagay (19/0), Paulo Rinaldo Cruzado Durand (28/1), Luis Alberto Ramírez Lucay (17/2), Carlos Augusto Lobatón Espejo (24/1) [58.William Medardo Chiroque Távara (17/1)], José Paolo Guerrero Gonzales (41/19), André Martín Carrillo Díaz (4/0) [85.Jefferson Agustín Farfán Guadalupe (54/13)]. Trainer: Sergio Apraham Markarián Abrahamian (26).

552. 10.06.2012 **URUGUAY - PERU** **4-2(2-1)** 20th FIFA WC. Qualifiers

Estadio Centenario, Montevideo; Referee: Leandro Pedro Vuaden (Brazil), Attendance: 55,000

PER: Diego Alonso Penny Valdez (10/0), John Christian Galliquio Castro (40/1), Jesús Martín Álvarez Hurtado (3/0), Christian Guillermo Martín Ramos Garagay (20/0), Víctor Yoshimar Yotún Flores (18/0), Paulo Rinaldo Cruzado Durand (29/1), Luis Alberto Ramírez Lucay (18/2), Antonio Emiliano Gonzáles Canchari (10/0) [46.Carlos Augusto Lobatón Espejo (25/1)], Luis Jan Piers Advíncula Castrillón (20/0) [69.Christian Alberto Cueva Bravo (4/0)], José Paolo Guerrero Gonzales (42/20), José Carlos Fernández Piedra (7/2) [77.André Martín Carrillo Díaz (5/0)]. Trainer: Sergio Apraham Markarián Abrahamian (27).

Goals: Diego Roberto Godín Leal (40 own goal), José Paolo Guerrero Gonzales (48).

553. 15.08.2012 **COSTA RICA - PERU** **0-1(0-1)**

Estadio Nacional, San José; Referee: Armando Isai Castro Oviedo (Honduras); Attendance: 10,000

PER: Raúl Omar Fernández Valverde (17/0), John Christian Galliquio Castro (41/1) [77.José Vladimir Canova Hernández (1/0)], Renzo Revoredo Zuazo (16/0), Carlos Augusto Zambrano Ochandarte (18/1) [46.Christian Guillermo Martín Ramos Garagay (21/0)], Paulo Rinaldo Cruzado Durand (30/1), Luis Alberto Ramírez Lucay (19/2) [*sent off 45+2*], Edwin Retamoso Palomino (4/0) [61.Juan Gustavo Waldemar Morales Coronado (1/0)], Víctor Yoshimar Yotún Flores (19/0) [59.Rafael Nicanor Farfán Quispe (1/0)], Juan Manuel Vargas Risco (40/4), José Paolo Guerrero Gonzáles (43/20) [83.Juan Carlos Mariño Márquez (19/2)], André Martín Carrillo Díaz (6/1) [46.Douglas Junior Ross Santillana (11/0)]. Trainer: Sergio Apraham Markarián Abrahamian (28).

Goal: André Martín Carrillo Díaz (8).

554. 07.09.2012 **PERU - VENEZUELA** **2-1(0-1)** 20th FIFA WC. Qualifiers

Estadio Nacional, Lima; Referee: Martín Emilio Vázquez Broquetas (Uruguay); Attendance: 34,703

PER: Raúl Omar Fernández Valverde (18/0), Alberto Junior Rodríguez Valdelomar (40/0), Renzo Revoredo Zuazo (17/0) [73.Roberto Carlos Guizasola La Rosa (10/0)], Carlos Augusto Zambrano Ochandarte (19/1), Paulo Rinaldo Cruzado Durand (31/1), Luis Alberto Ramírez Lucay (20/2), Víctor Yoshimar Yotún Flores (20/0), Juan Manuel Vargas Risco (41/4), José Paolo Guerrero Gonzáles (44/20) [49.André Martín Carrillo Díaz (7/1)], Claudio Miguel Pizarro Bosio (64/16), Jefferson Agustín Farfán Guadalupe (55/15) [79.Carlos Augusto Lobatón Espejo (26/1)]. Trainer: Sergio Apraham Markarián Abrahamian (29).

Goals: Jefferson Agustín Farfán Guadalupe (47, 59).

555. 11.09.2012 **PERU - ARGENTINA** **1-1(1-1)** 20th FIFA WC. Qualifiers

Estadio Nacional, Lima; Referee: Wilmar Alexander Roldán Pérez (Colombia); Attendance: 34,111

PER: Raúl Omar Fernández Valverde (19/0), Alberto Junior Rodríguez Valdelomar (41/0), Carlos Augusto Zambrano Ochandarte (20/2), Luis Jan Piers Advíncula Castrillón (21/0), Paulo Rinaldo Cruzado Durand (32/1), Luis Alberto Ramírez Lucay (21/2) [87.José Paolo Guerrero Gonzáles (45/20)], Carlos Augusto Lobatón Espejo (27/1) [46.Josepmir Aarón Ballón Villacorta (21/0)], Víctor Yoshimar Yotún Flores (21/0), Claudio Miguel Pizarro Bosio (65/16), Jefferson Agustín Farfán Guadalupe (56/15), André Martín Carrillo Díaz (8/1) [77.Cristopher Paolo César Hurtado Huertas (4/0)]. Trainer: Sergio Apraham Markarián Abrahamian (30).

Goal: Carlos Augusto Zambrano Ochandarte (22).

556. 12.10.2012 **BOLIVIA - PERU** **1-1(0-1)**

Estadio "Hernando Siles Zuazo", La Paz; Referee: Carlos Alfredo Vera Rodríguez (Ecuador); Attendance: 36,500

PER: José Aurelio Carvallo Alonso (2/0), Wilmer Santiago Acasiete Ariadela (43/2), Jhoel Alexander Herrera Zegarra (5/0), Rafael Nicanor Farfán Quispe (2/0), Christian Guillermo Martín Ramos Garagay (22/0), Juan Carlos Mariño Márquez (20/3) [79.Christian Alberto Cueva Bravo (5/0)], Juan Elías Cominges Mayorga (15/0) [60.Álvaro Francisco Ampuero García-Rossell (4/0)], William Medardo Chiroque Távara (18/1), Edwin Retamoso Palomino (5/0), Joel Melchor Sánchez Alegría (2/0), Irven Beybe Ávila Acero (6/0) [61.Wilmer Alexander Aguirre Vásquez (8/0)]. Trainer: Sergio Apraham Markarián Abrahamian (31).

Goal: Juan Carlos Mariño Márquez (22).

557. 16.10.2012 **PARAGUAY - PERU** **1-0(0-0)** 20th FIFA WC. Qualifiers

Estadio Defensores del Chaco, Asunción; Referee: Pablo Alejandro Lunati (Argentina); Attendance: 10,114

PER: Raúl Omar Fernández Valverde (20/0), Alberto Junior Rodríguez Valdelomar (42/0) [16.Christian Guillermo Martín Ramos Garagay (23/0)], Carlos Augusto Zambrano Ochandarte (21/2), Luis Jan Piers Advíncula Castrillón (22/0), Paulo Rinaldo Cruzado Durand (33/1), Luis Alberto Ramírez Lucay (22/2), Víctor Yoshimar Yotún Flores (22/0) [81.Raúl Mario Ruidíaz Misitich (6/0)], Juan Manuel Vargas Risco (42/4), José Paolo Guerrero Gonzáles (46/20) [66.André Martín Carrillo Díaz (9/1)], Claudio Miguel Pizarro Bosio (66/16), Jefferson Agustín Farfán Guadalupe (57/15). Trainer: Sergio Apraham Markarián Abrahamian (32).

558. 14.11.2012 **PERU - HONDURAS** **0-0**

BBVA Compass Stadium, Houston (United States); Referee: David Gantar (Canada); Attendance: n/a

PER: Raúl Omar Fernández Valverde (21/0), Christian Guillermo Martín Ramos Garagay (24/0), Néstor Alonso Duarte Carassa (2/0), Luis Jan Piers Advíncula Castrillón (23/0) [46.Werner Luis Schuler Gamarra (1/0)], Paulo Rinaldo Cruzado Durand (34/1), Christian Alberto Cueva Bravo (6/0) [60.Jhonny Víctor Vidales Lature (1/0)], Juan Gustavo Waldemar Morales Coronado (2/0), Alfredo Junior Rojas Pajuelo (1/0), Álvaro Francisco Ampuero García-Rossell (5/0) [82.Víctor Yoshimar Yotún Flores (23/0)], Irven Beybe Ávila Acero (7/0) [46.Osnar Noronha Montani (1/0)], Raúl Mario Ruidíaz Misitich (7/0) [69.Daniel Mackensi Chávez Castillo (12/0)]. Trainer: Sergio Apraham Markarián Abrahamian (33).

559. 06.02.2013 **TRINIDAD AND TOBAGO - PERU** **0-2(0-1)**

"Ato Boldon Stadium", Couva; Referee: Adrian Skeete (Barbados); Attendance: n/a

PER: Raúl Omar Fernández Valverde (22/0) [46.Diego Alonso Penny Valdez (11/0)], Renzo Revoredo Zuazo (18/0) [46.Roberto Carlos Guizasola La Rosa (11/0)], Carlos Augusto Zambrano Ochandarte (22/2), Alberto Junior Rodríguez Valdelomar (43/0) [43.Christian Guillermo Martín Ramos Garagay (25/0)], Víctor Yoshimar Yotún Flores (24/0), Luis Alberto Ramírez Lucay (23/2), Carlos Augusto Lobatón Espejo (28/1) [73.Edwin Retamoso Palomino (6/0)], Paulo Rinaldo Cruzado Durand (35/2), Jefferson Agustín Farfán Guadalupe (58/15) [60.Juan Carlos Mariño Márquez (21/3)], Douglas Junior Ross Santillana (12/0) [46.José Paolo Guerrero Gonzáles (47/20)], Claudio Miguel Pizarro Bosio (67/17) [60.André Martín Carrillo Díaz (10/1)]. Trainer: Sergio Apraham Markarián Abrahamian (34).

Goals: Claudio Miguel Pizarro Bosio (29), Paulo Rinaldo Cruzado Durand (88).

560. 22.03.2013 **PERU - CHILE** **1-0(0-0)** 20th FIFA WC. Qualifiers

Estadio Nacional, Lima; Referee: Diego Hernán Abal (Argentina); Attendance: 43,000

PER: Raúl Omar Fernández Valverde (23/0), Alberto Junior Rodríguez Valdelomar (44/0), Jhoel Alexander Herrera Zegarra (6/0), Christian Guillermo Martín Ramos Garagay (26/0) [23.Jesús Martín Álvarez Hurtado (4/0)], Paulo Rinaldo Cruzado Durand (36/2), Luis Alberto Ramírez Lucay (24/2), Cristopher Paolo César Hurtado Huertas (5/0), Carlos Augusto Lobatón Espejo (29/1) [46.Juan Carlos Mariño Márquez (22/3)], Víctor Yoshimar Yotún Flores (25/0), Claudio Miguel Pizarro Bosio (68/17) [79.José Yordy Reyna Serna (1/0)], Jefferson Agustín Farfán Guadalupe (59/16). Trainer: Sergio Apraham Markarián Abrahamian (35).

Goal: Jefferson Agustín Farfán Guadalupe (87).

561. 26.03.2013 **PERU - TRINIDAD AND TOBAGO** **3-0(1-0)**

Estadio Nacional, Lima; Referee: Diego Jefferson Lara León (Ecuador); Attendance: 20,000

PER: Diego Alonso Penny Valdez (12/0), Jesús Martín Álvarez Hurtado (5/0), Néstor Alonso Duarte Carassa (3/0), Luis Jan Piers Advíncula Castrillón (24/0), Edwin Alexi Gómez Gutiérrez (1/0) [60.Cristopher Paolo César Hurtado Huertas (6/1)], Paulo César Albarracín García (1/0), Luis Gabriel García Uribe (1/0) [46.Daniel Mackensi Chávez Castillo (13/0)], Alfredo Junior Rojas Pajuelo (2/0), Álvaro Francisco Ampuero García-Rossell (6/0) [46.Víctor Yoshimar Yotún Flores (26/0)], Irven Beybe Ávila Acero (8/0) [82.Christofer Gonzáles Crespo (1/1)], José Yordy Reyna Serna (2/1) [73.Jefferson Agustín Farfán Guadalupe (60/16)]. Trainer: Sergio Apraham Markarián Abrahamian (36).

Goals: José Yordy Reyna Serna (39), Cristopher Paolo César Hurtado Huertas (81), Christofer Gonzáles Crespo (83).

562. 17.04.2013 **PERU - MEXICO** **0-0**

Candlestick Park, San Francisco (United States); Referee: Ricardo Salazar (United States); Attendance: 46,288

PER: José Aurelio Carvallo Alonso (3/0), Orlando Contreras Collantes (7/1) [75.Alexander Martín Callens Asín (1/0)], Christian Guillermo Martín Ramos Garagay (27/0), Luis Jan Piers Advíncula Castrillón (25/0), Néstor Alonso Duarte Carassa (4/0), Edwin Alexi Gómez Gutiérrez (2/0), Jair Edson Céspedes Zegarra (3/0) [68.Luis Gabriel García Uribe (2/0)], Josepmir Aarón Ballón Villacorta (22/0) [67.Josimar Hugo Vargas García (1/0)], Michael Fidel Guevara Legua (15/0) [46.Cristian Benavente Bristol (1/0)], Paulo César Albarracín García (2/0) [75.Christofer Gonzáles Crespo (2/1)], José Yordy Reyna Serna (3/1) [46.Raúl Mario Ruidíaz Misitich (8/0)]. Trainer: Sergio Apraham Markarián Abrahamian (37).

563. 01.06.2013 **PANAMA - PERU** **1-2(0-0)**

Estadio "Rommel Fernández", Ciudad de Panamá; Referee: Henry Bejarano (Costa Rica); Attendance: 4,000

PER: José Aurelio Carvallo Alonso (4/0), Alberto Junior Rodríguez Valdelomar (45/0) [79.Wilmer Santiago Acasiete Ariadela (44/2)], Carlos Augusto Zambrano Ochandarte (23/2) [46.Christian Guillermo Martín Ramos Garagay (28/0)], Luis Alberto Ramírez Lucay (25/2), Luis Jan Piers Advíncula Castrillón (26/0), Cristopher Paolo César Hurtado Huertas (7/1) [60.André Martín Carrillo Díaz (11/1)], Carlos Augusto Lobatón Espejo (30/1) [60.Cristian Benavente Bristol (2/1)], Edwin Retamoso Palomino (7/0), Juan Manuel Vargas Risco (43/4), Álvaro Francisco Ampuero García-Rossell (7/0) [70.Alexander Martín Marquinho Callens Asín (2/0)], José Yordy Reyna Serna (4/2) [60.Juan Carlos Mariño Márquez (23/3)]. Trainer: Sergio Apraham Markarián Abrahamian (38).

Goals: José Yordy Reyna Serna (50), Cristian Benavente Bristol (84).

564. 07.06.2013 **PERU - ECUADOR** **1-0(1-0)** 20th FIFA WC. Qualifiers
Estadio Nacional, Lima; Referee: Marcelo de Lima Henrique (Brazil); Attendance: 37,000
PER: Raúl Omar Fernández Valverde (24/0), Alberto Junior Rodríguez Valdelomar (46/0), Jhoel Alexander Herrera Zegarra (7/0), Carlos Augusto Zambrano Ochandarte (24/2), Luis Alberto Ramírez Lucay (26/2), Edwin Retamoso Palomino (8/0), Víctor Yoshimar Yotún Flores (27/0), Juan Manuel Vargas Risco (44/4) [81.Álvaro Francisco Ampuero García-Rossell (8/0)], José Paolo Guerrero Gonzáles (48/20), Claudio Miguel Pizarro Bosio (69/18) [90+2.Christian Guillermo Martín Ramos Garagay (29/0)], Jefferson Agustín Farfán Guadalupe (61/16) [89.Luis Jan Piers Advíncula Castrillón (27/0)]. Trainer: Sergio Apraham Markarián Abrahamian (39).
Goal: Claudio Miguel Pizarro Bosio (11).

565. 11.06.2013 **COLOMBIA - PERU** **2-0(2-0)** 20th FIFA WC. Qualifiers
Estadio Metropolitano "Roberto Meléndez", Barranquilla; Referee: Sandro Meira Ricci (Brazil); Attendance: 42,265
PER: Raúl Omar Fernández Valverde (25/0), Alberto Junior Rodríguez Valdelomar (47/0), Jhoel Alexander Herrera Zegarra (8/0) [32.Jefferson Agustín Farfán Guadalupe (62/16)], Carlos Augusto Zambrano Ochandarte (25/2) [*sent off 70*], Luis Jan Piers Advíncula Castrillón (28/0), Josepmir Aarón Ballón Villacorta (23/0), Edwin Retamoso Palomino (9/0) [64.Carlos Augusto Lobatón Espejo (31/1)], Víctor Yoshimar Yotún Flores (28/0) [31.André Martín Carrillo Díaz (12/1)], Juan Manuel Vargas Risco (45/4), José Paolo Guerrero Gonzáles (49/20), Claudio Miguel Pizarro Bosio (70/18). Trainer: Sergio Apraham Markarián Abrahamian (40).

566. 14.08.2013 **KOREA REPUBLIC - PERU** **0-0**
Suwon World Cup Stadium, Suwon; Referee: Abdul Malik Bin Abdul Bashir (Singapore); Attendance: 34,000
PER: Raúl Omar Fernández Valverde (26/0), Alberto Junior Rodríguez Valdelomar (48/0) [46.Édison Michael Flores Peralta (1/0)], Christian Guillermo Martín Ramos Garagay (30/0), Luis Jan Piers Advíncula Castrillón (29/0), Paulo Rinaldo Cruzado Durand (37/2), Luis Alberto Ramírez Lucay (27/2) [74.Carlos Augusto Lobatón Espejo (32/1)], Edwin Retamoso Palomino (10/0) [46.Cristopher Paolo César Hurtado Huertas (8/1)], Víctor Yoshimar Yotún Flores (29/0), José Paolo Guerrero Gonzáles (50/20) [68.Jefferson Agustín Farfán Guadalupe (63/16)], Claudio Miguel Pizarro Bosio (71/18), Reimond Orángel Manco Albarracín (6/0) [46.Jesús Martín Álvarez Hurtado (6/0)]. Trainer: Sergio Apraham Markarián Abrahamian (41).

567. 07.09.2013 **PERU - URUGUAY** **1-2(0-1)** 20th FIFA WC. Qualifiers
Estadio Monumental, Lima; Referee: Patricio Loustau (Argentina); Attendance: 39,222
PER: Raúl Omar Fernández Valverde (27/0), Alberto Junior Rodríguez Valdelomar (49/0), Christian Guillermo Martín Ramos Garagay (31/0), Luis Jan Piers Advíncula Castrillón (30/0) [65.Jhoel Alexander Herrera Zegarra (9/0)], Paulo Rinaldo Cruzado Durand (38/2), Josepmir Aarón Ballón Villacorta (24/0) [46.Juan Manuel Vargas Risco (46/4)], Luis Alberto Ramírez Lucay (28/2) [66.Cristopher Paolo César Hurtado Huertas (9/1)], Víctor Yoshimar Yotún Flores (30/0) [*sent off 45+2*], Jefferson Agustín Farfán Guadalupe (64/17), José Paolo Guerrero Gonzáles (51/20), Claudio Miguel Pizarro Bosio (72/18). Trainer: Sergio Apraham Markarián Abrahamian (42).
Goals: Jefferson Agustín Farfán Guadalupe (84).

568. 10.09.2013 **VENEZUELA - PERU** **3-2(1-1)** 20th FIFA WC. Qualifiers
Estadio Olímpico "General José Antonio Anzoátegui", Puerto la Cruz; Referee: Néstor Fabián Pitana (Argentina); Attendance: 20,049
PER: Raúl Omar Fernández Valverde (28/0), Alberto Junior Rodríguez Valdelomar (50/0), Jhoel Alexander Herrera Zegarra (10/0) [14.Luis Jan Piers Advíncula Castrillón (31/0)], Carlos Augusto Zambrano Ochandarte (26/3), Paulo Rinaldo Cruzado Durand (39/2) [63.Luis Alberto Ramírez Lucay (29/2)], Cristopher Paolo César Hurtado Huertas (10/2), Carlos Augusto Lobatón Espejo (33/1), Edwin Retamoso Palomino (11/0), Juan Manuel Vargas Risco (47/4), Claudio Miguel Pizarro Bosio (73/18) [64.José Paolo Guerrero Gonzáles (52/20)], André Martín Carrillo Díaz (13/1). Trainer: Sergio Apraham Markarián Abrahamian (43).
Goals: Cristopher Paolo César Hurtado Huertas (20), Carlos Augusto Zambrano Ochandarte (87).

569. 11.10.2013 **ARGENTINA - PERU** **3-1(2-1)** 20th FIFA WC. Qualifiers
Estadio Monumental „Antonio Vespucio Liberti", Buenos Aires; Referee: Carlos Alfredo Vera Rodríguez (Ecuador); Attendance: 28,977
PER: Diego Alonso Penny Valdez (13/0), Néstor Alonso Duarte Carassa (5/0), Gianmarco Gambetta Sponza (1/0), Edwin Alexi Gómez Gutiérrez (3/0) [46.Cristian Benavente Bristol (3/1)], Roberto Efraín Koichi Aparicio Mori (1/0), Josepmir Aarón Ballón Villacorta (25/0), Luis Alberto Ramírez Lucay (30/2) [84.José Yordy Reyna Serna (5/2)], Cristopher Paolo César Hurtado Huertas (11/2), Juan Manuel Vargas Risco (48/4), Claudio Miguel Pizarro Bosio (74/19), André Martín Carrillo Díaz (14/1) [69.Óscar Christopher Vílchez Soto (1/0)]. Trainer: Sergio Apraham Markarián Abrahamian (44).
Goal: Claudio Miguel Pizarro Bosio (21).

570. 15.10.2013 **PERU - BOLIVIA** **1-1(1-1)** 20th FIFA WC. Qualifiers
Estadio Nacional, Lima; Referee: Enrique Cáceres Villafante (Paraguay); Attendance: *played behind closed doors*
PER: Diego Alonso Penny Valdez (14/0), Néstor Alonso Duarte Carassa (6/0), Carlos Augusto Zambrano Ochandarte (27/3), Luis Jan Piers Advíncula Castrillón (32/0), Josepmir Aarón Ballón Villacorta (26/0), Carlos Augusto Lobatón Espejo (34/1), Víctor Yoshimar Yotún Flores (31/1), Juan Manuel Vargas Risco (49/4), Cristian Benavente Bristol (4/1) [46.José Yordy Reyna Serna (6/2)], Claudio Miguel Pizarro Bosio (75/19), Irven Beybe Ávila Acero (9/0) [60.André Martín Carrillo Díaz (15/1)]. Trainer: Sergio Apraham Markarián Abrahamian (45).
Goal: Víctor Yoshimar Yotún Flores (19).

INTERNATIONAL PLAYERS

FM/Nr	Name	DOB	Caps	Goals	Period, Club
(460/543)	ACASIETE ARIADELA Wilmer Santiago	22.11.1977	44	2	2004-2013, ADC Unión Ciencano (10/1), UD Almería (32/1), CS Cienciano Cuzco (2/0).
(233/317)	ACASUZO COLÁN Eusebio Alfredo	08.04.1952	30	0	1979-1985, Club Universitario de Deportes Lima (17/0), Huancayo FC (2/0), Club Bolívar La Paz (11/0).
(277/359)	ADRIAZOLA César		1	0	1985, ID Colegio Nacional de Iquitos (1/0).
(526/606)	ADVÍNCULA CASTRILLÓN Luis Jan Piers	02.03.1990	32	0	2010-2013, Club Sporting Cristal Lima (23/0), TSG 1899 Hoffenheim (5/0), AA Ponte Preta (4/0).
(265/342)	AGUAYO José	25.10.1955	5	0	1983, FBC Melgar Arequipa (5/0).
(235/318)	AGUILAR Eduardo	21.12.1948	2	0	1979, Club Universitario de Deportes Lima (2/0).
(356/439)	AGUILAR Percy	14.01.1967	2	1	1994, Ciclista Lima Association (2/1).
(327/408)	AGUIRRE Ernesto	10.09.1963	4	0	1991, CS Unión Huaral (4/0).
(484/562)	AGUIRRE VÁSQUEZ Wilmer Alexander	05.10.1983	8	0	2006-2012, Club Alianza Lima (1/0), FC Metz (2/0), Club Alianza Lima (1/0), San Luís FC (4/0).
(34/080)	AGURTO Armando		4	0	1942,
(54/117)	AGURTO Diego	13.11.1927	2	0	1952, Sport Boys Association Callao (2/0).
(561/639)	ALBARRACÍN GARCÍA Paulo César	30.11.1989	2	0	2012-2013, Club Alianza Lima (2/0).
(10/041)	ALCALDE MILLOS Jorge		15	13	1935-1939, Sport Boys Association Callao (15/13).
(12/048)	ALCALDE MILLOS Prisco Teodoro		9	0	1936-1939, Sport Boys Association Callao (1/0).
(296/366)	ALCÁZAR Víctor		3	0	1986, CD Colegio San Agustín (3/0).
(312/402)	ALGUEDAS Antonio	17.05.1968	1	0	1989, Club Alianza Lima (1/0).
(272/349)	ALIAGA Julio		1	0	1984, Club Sporting Cristal Lima (1/0).
(60/131)	ALLEN José		5	0	1953, Centro Iqueño Lima (5/0).
(430/504)	ALVA NIEZEN Piero Fernando	14.02.1979	17	3	2000-2009, Club Universitario de Deportes Lima (2/0), Club Sporting Cristal Lima (2/1), Club Universitario de Deportes Lima (6/1), CS Cienciano Cuzco (4/1), Club Universitario de Deportes Lima (3/0).
(491/571)	ALVARADO QUIÑONES Ismael Enrique	22.10.1980	1	0	2007, Club Alianza Lima (1/0).
(14/050)	ÁLVAREZ Andrés		3	0	1936
(550/629)	ÁLVAREZ HURTADO Jesús Martín	26.08.1981	6	0	2012-2013, CD Universidad San Martín de Porres (3/0), Club Sporting Cristal Lima (3/0).
(548/625)	AMPUERO GARCÍA-ROSELL Álvaro Francisco	25.09.1992	8	0	2012-2013, Club Universitario de Deportes Lima (5/0), Parma FC (3/0).
(308/390)	ANCHISI Ramón	25.11.1964	2	0	1989, Sport Boys Association Callao (2/0).
(27/070)	ANDRADE Guillermo		2	0	1941, Club Centro Deportivo Municipal Lima (2/0).
(76/148)	ANDRADE Isaac	13.07.1937	5	0	1956-1960, Sport Boys Association Callao (5/0).
(305/387)	ANTÓN REYES Julio César	07.07.1959	1	0	1988, Club Sporting Cristal Lima (1/0).
(190/284)	APARICIO Julio	30.01.1955	6	0	1975-1977, Club Universitario de Deportes Lima (6/0).
(119/223)	AQUIJE Mario		3	0	1966-1967, Club Sporting Cristal Lima (3/0).
(442/513)	ARAKAKI ARAKAKI Ernesto Seiko	13.06.1979	3	0	2001-2008, Club Alianza Lima (3/0).
(1/009)	ARANDA Segundo		2	0	1927, Association FBC (2/0).
(445/522)	ARAUJO PAREDES Jorge Martín	30.11.1979	1	0	2003, Club Alianza Atlético Sullana (1/0).
(47/104)	ARCE Gerardo	24.09.1921	5	0	1949, Club Alianza Lima (5/0).
(9/036)	ARCE Vicente		11	0	1935-1941, Club Universitario de Deportes Lima
(100/177)	ARGUEDAS Humberto		3	0	1960-1965, Club Universitario de Deportes Lima (3/0).
(241/323)	ARIZAGA Óscar Gilberto	20.08.1957	1	0	1980, Club Atlético Chalaco Callao (1/0).
(314/405)	ARTEAGA Jorge Fausto	29.11.1966	19	0	1989-1993, Club Sporting Cristal Lima (19/0).
(41/097)	ASCA Rafael		21	0	1947-1959
(436/508)	ASCOY CORTEZ Pedro Luis	10.08.1980	2	0	2001, Club Juan Aurich de Chiclayo (2/0).
(4/018)	ASTENGO Eduardo	29.09.1904	3	0	1929-1930, Federación Universitaria Lima (3/0).
(521/601)	ÁVILA ACERO Irven Beybe	02.07.1990	9	0	2009-2013, CSD Sport Huancayo (4/0), Club Sporting Cristal Lima (5/0).
(231/312)	BAIGORRIA Gerardo	19.01.1950	2	0	1979, Coronel Bolognesi FC Tacna (2/0).
(126/244)	BAILETTI Héctor	27.11.1947	18	5	1968-1973, Porvenir Miraflores Lima (4/1), Club Universitario de Deportes Lima (14/4).
(530/613)	BALBÍN SILVA Adán Adolfo	13.10.1986	12	0	2010-2011, CD Universidad San Martín de Porres (12/0).
(455/539)	BALBÍN VALLES César Eduardo	18.05.1981	1	0	2003, CD Wanka Huancayo (1/0).
(375/464)	BALERIO CORREA Julio César	19.04.1958	17	0	1996-1997, Club Sporting Cristal Lima (17/0).
(205/298)	BALLESTEROS Humberto		2	0	1976, Club Atlético Chalaco Callao (2/0).
(519/600)	BALLÓN VILLACORTA Josepmir Aarón	21.03.1988	26	0	2009-2013, CD Universidad San Martín de Porres (7/0), CA River Plate Buenos Aires (7/0), Club Universidad San Martín de Porres (12/0).
(171/271)	BARBADILLO GONZÁLEZ Gerónimo	24.09.1952	20	3	1972-1985, Sport Boys Association Callao (1/0), CA Defensor Lima (1/0), Universidad Autonoma de Nuevo León (10/1), US Avellino (6/2), Udinese Calcio (2/0).
(40/092)	BARBADILLO Guillermo	09.01.1925	25	3	1947-1956
(296/368)	BARCO Alvaro	27.06.1967	30	0	1986-1997, Club Universitario de Deportes Lima (10/0), CD Cobreola Calama (15/0), Club Universitario de Deportes Lima (4/0).
(336/423)	BARONI AMBROSI Ronald Pablo	08.04.1966	19	4	1993-1995, Club Universitario de Deportes Lima (8/1), Club Centro Deportivo Municipal Lima (3/0), FC do Porto (8/3).
(132/250)	BARRETO Jorge	05.02.1945	1	0	1969, Club Alianza Lima (1/0).
(515/593)	BARROS ARAUJO Juan José	24.06.1989	2	0	2009, Coronel Bolognesi FC Tacna (2/0).
(356/436)	BASOMBRÍO ORMEÑO Carlos Alberto	21.10.1971	2	0	1994, Club Alianza Lima (2/0).

(59/130)	BASSA Juan		10	1	1953-1957,
(1/006)	BASURTO Leopoldo "Lipo"		2	0	1927, Association FBC (2/0).
(124/239)	BAYLÓN ARAGONÉS Julio Alberto Temistocles	10.12.1947	32	2	1968-1972, Club Alianza Lima (32/2).
(416/493)	BAYLÓN CAPCHA Sandro Paulo	11.04.1977	1	0	1999, Club Alianza Lima (1/0).
(310/396)	BAZALAR CRUZADO Juan Carlos	23.02.1968	26	0	1989-2007, Club Universitario de Deportes Lima (7/0), Sport Boys Association Callao (1/0), Club Alianza Lima (9/0), CS Cienciano Cuzco (9/0).
(104/185)	BAZÁN Rodolfo	14.12.1938	10	0	1962-1965, Club Alianza Lima (10/0).
(67/140)	BEDOYA Andrés		6	0	1954-1955, Club Atlético Chalaco Callao (6/0).
(562/642)	BENAVENTE BRISTOL Cristian	19.05.1994	4	1	2012-2013, Real Madrid CF "B" (4/1).
(89/160)	BENÍTEZ Víctor	20.10.1935	11	0	1957-1959, Club Alianza Lima (11/0).
(404/481)	BERNALES FRANCIA Gregorio Abel	08.11.1976	9	0	1998-2003, Deportivo Pesquero (1/0), Club Universitario de Deportes Lima (4/0), Club Sporting Cristal Lima (4/0).
(20/060)	BIELICH Víctor	07.08.1917	5	4	1938-1939, Club Centro Deportivo Municipal Lima (5/4).
(36/083)	BIFFI Antonio		2	0	1942, Club Universitario de Deportes Lima (2/0).
(221/306)	BISETTI Arturo	18.01.1953	1	0	1978, Coronel Bolognesi FC Tacna (1/0).
(261/337)	BONELLI Pedro	20.10.1956	5	0	1983, Club Centro Deportivo Municipal Lima (5/0).
(101/179)	BRAVO Carlos		4	0	1961-1963, Club Centro Deportivo Municipal Lima (4/0).
(268/343)	BRAVO Enrique		2	0	1983, Club Centro Deportivo Municipal Lima (2/0).
(329/411)	BRAVO Ricardo Alberto	26.06.1970	6	0	1991, Club Universitario de Deportes Lima (6/0).
(100/174)	BRICEÑO Neptalí		1	0	1960, Sport Boys Association Callao (1/0).
(56/122)	BRUSCH César		4	0	1952-1953,
(4/020)	BULNES Juan		3	0	1929, Club Atlético Chalaco Callao (3/0).
(177/276)	BURELA Carlos	12.07.1943	2	0	1972, CA Defensor Lima (2/0).
(432/507)	BUTRÓN GOTUZZO Leao	06.03.1977	39	0	2001-2012, Club Sporting Cristal Lima (1/0), Club Alianza Atlético Sullana (2/0), Club Alianza Lima (3/0), CD Universidad San Martín de Porres (33/0).

(57/125)	CABADA Adolfo		1	0	1952,
(242/331)	CABALLERO Juan	17.06.1956	15	4	1980-1986, Sport Boys Association Callao (3/0), Club Sporting Cristal Lima (11/4), Club Universitario de Deportes Lima (1/0).
(275/356)	CABANILLAS Juan Carlos	02.05.1963	6	0	1984-1988, Sport Boys Association Callao (4/0), Club Universitario de Deportes Lima (1/0), Wanderers FC Montevideo (1/0).
(190/281)	CÁCERES PALOMARES Juan José	27.12.1949	1	0	1975, Club Universitario de Deportes Lima (1/0).
(112/209)	CALATAYUD Víctor		6	0	1965-1967, Club Universitario de Deportes Lima (6/0).
(48/113)	CALDERÓN Luis	21.06.1926	36	0	1949-1961, Sport Boys Association Callao (25/0), Club Universitario de Deportes Lima (9/0), (2/0).
(97/172)	CALENZANI Adolfo		2	0	1959-1961, Sport Boys Association Callao (2/0).
(562/644)	CALLENS ASÍN Alexander Martín Marquinho	04.05.1992	2	0	2012-2013, Real Sociedad de Fútbol San Sebastián "B" (2/0).
(105/192)	CAMPOS Ángel Eloy	31.05.1942	46	0	1963-1972, Club Sporting Cristal Lima (46/0).
(553/632)	CANOVA HERNÁNDEZ José Vladimir	30.09.1992	1	0	2012, Club Alianza Lima (1/0).
(374/463)	CARAZAS Eddie	22.02.1974	10	1	1996-1999, Club Universitario de Deportes Lima (9/1), CA Belgrano (1/0).
(186/280)	CARBONELL Carlos	14.11.1951	3	0	1973, Club Universitario de Deportes Lima (3/0).
(162/257)	CÁRDENAS Fernando		1	0	1971, Club Centro Deportivo Municipal Lima (1/0).
(361/449)	CARMONA HURTADO Alfredo Enrique	10.05.1971	10	1	1994-2003, Club Centro Deportivo Municipal Lima (5/0), FBC Melgar Arequipa (1/0), Sport Boys Association Callao (4/1).
(532/619)	CARMONA MALDONADO Giancarlo	08.10.1985	5	0	2011, CA San Lorenzo de Almagro (5/0).
(103/184)	CÁRPENA Fernando		1	0	1961, Sport Boys Association Callao (1/0).
(203/295)	CARRANZA Ernesto		2	0	1976, CA Defensor Lima (2/0).
(304/385)	CARRANZA José Luis	08.01.1964	55	1	1988-1997, Club Universitario de Deportes Lima (55/1).
(93/167)	CARRASCO José		10	2	1959-1961, Club Centro Deportivo Municipal Lima (8/1),
(535/622)	CARRILLO DÍAZ André Martín	14.06.1992	15	1	2011-2013, Club Alianza Lima (2/0), Sporting Clube de Portugal Lisboa (13/1).
(347/434)	CARTY MONSERRATE Luis Germán del Carmen	16.07.1968	25	3	1993-2004, Sport Boys Association Callao (3/0), Club Universitario de Deportes Lima (4/0), Sport Boys Association Callao (4/0), CF Atlante Mexico City (12/3), CSD Estudiantes de Medicina Ica (1/0), CS Cienciano Cuzco (1/0).
(500/579)	CARVALLO ALONSO José Aurelio	01.03.1986	4	0	2007-2013, Club Sporting Cristal Lima (1/0), Foot Ball Club Melgar Arequipa (1/0), Club Universitario de Deportes Lima (2/0).
(263/341)	CASANOVA José		10	0	1983-1985, Club Alianza Lima (10/0).
(128/248)	CASSARETTO Enrique	29.04.1945	10	8	1968-1975, Club Universitario de Deportes Lima (7/6), Club Sporting Cristal Lima (3/2).
(134/251)	CASTAÑEDA Hernán		11	2	1969-1972, Club Juan Aurich de Chiclayo (3/1), Club Universitario de Deportes Lima (8/1).
(261/339)	CASTILLO Alberto	05.05.1960	1	0	1983, Club Centro Deportivo Municipal Lima (1/0).
(40/091)	CASTILLO Félix	21.02.1928	31	8	1947-1956, Club Alianza Lima (31/8).
(40/089)	CASTILLO Juan		5	0	1947, Club Atlético Chalaco Callao (5/0).
(54/120)	CASTILLO Roberto	29.04.1929	18	1	1952-1957, (7/0), Club Alianza Lima (11/1).
(12/046)	CASTILLO VARELA Segundo		12	0	1936-1939, Sport Boys Association Callao (12/0).
(298/374)	CASTRO Carlos		1	0	1986, CD Colegio San Agustín (1/0).
(117/212)	CAVAGNARI Italo		3	0	1965-1966, Defensor Arica (3/0).
(85/156)	CAVERO Alfredo		4	0	1957, Club Sporting Cristal Lima (4/0).
(392/474)	CAVERO CAROZZI Aldo Jair	24.10.1971	2	0	1997, CS Cienciano Cuzco (2/0).
(448/529)	CCAHUANTICO MEZA César Camilo	16.07.1980	1	0	2003, ADC Unión Ciencano (1/0).
(310/393)	CERVERA Leoncio	12.09.1965	2	0	1989, Club Universitario de Deportes Lima (2/0).

(491/573)	CÉSPEDES ZEGARRA Jair Edson	22.05.1984	**3**	**0**	2007-2013, Sport Boys Association Callao (1/0), CD Universidad San Martín de Porres (1/0), Club Juan Aurich de Chiclayo (1/0).
(477/549)	CEVASCO ABAD Miguel Angel	27.04.1986	**9**	**1**	2005-2008, Club Universitario de Deportes Lima (9/1).
(405/484)	CHACÓN CHÁVEZ José Luis	06.11.1971	**3**	**0**	1999, Club Alianza Lima (3/0).
(120/228)	CHALE OLARTE Roberto Federico (CHALLE)	24.11.1946	**48**	**4**	1967-1973, Club Universitario de Deportes Lima (34/4), CA Defensor Lima (14/0).
(19/057)	CHAPELL Raúl	23.07.1911	**7**	**0**	1938-1939, Sport Boys Association Callao (7/0).
(126/243)	CHARÚN Jorge		**1**	**0**	1968, Club Juan Aurich de Chiclayo (1/0).
(337/426)	CHARÚN PASTOR César Augusto	25.10.1970	**12**	**0**	1993, Club Universitario de Deportes Lima (12/0).
(268/344)	CHÁVARRI Rodolfo	05.02.1961	**2**	**0**	1983, Club Universitario de Deportes Lima (2/0).
(506/587)	CHÁVEZ CASTILLO Daniel Mackensi	08.01.1988	**13**	**0**	2008-2013, Club Brügge KV (9/0), KVC Westerlo (2/0), CD Unión Comercio Nueva Cajamarca (1/0), CSCD Universidad César Vallejo Trujillo (1/0).
(296/362)	CHÁVEZ RIVA César	22.11.1964	**12**	**0**	1986-1989, Club Universitario de Deportes Lima (12/0).
(403/478)	CHÉVEZ SOLANO David Fernando	23.06.1976	**1**	**0**	1998, Club Alianza Lima (1/0).
(242/330)	CHINCHAY Pedro	09.10.1958	**1**	**0**	1980, Club Sporting Cristal Lima (1/0).
(277/360)	CHIRINOS Javier	08.05.1960	**20**	**0**	1985-1989, Club Universitario de Deportes Lima (19/0), CA Defensor Lima (1/0).
(462/544)	CHIROQUE TÁVARA William Medardo	10.05.1980	**18**	**1**	2004-2012, Club Alianza Atlético Sullana (3/0), CS Cienciano Cuzco (3/0), Club Juan Aurich de Chiclayo (12/1).
(111/205)	CHUMPITAZ GONZÁLEZ Héctor Eduardo	12.04.1944	**105**	**3**	1965-1981, Club Centro Deportivo Municipal Lima (5/0), Club Universitario de Deportes Lima (66/2), Club Sporting Cristal Lima (34/1).
(412/492)	CIURLIZZA RODRÍGUEZ Marko Gustavo	22.02.1978	**34**	**0**	1999-2009, Club Universitario de Deportes Lima (9/0), Club Alianza Lima (4/0), Botafogo FR Rio de Janeiro (3/0), Club Alianza Lima (18/0).
(47/111)	COLUNGA Germán	28.05.1922	**12**	**0**	1949-1956, Sucre FBC (6/0), Club Universitario de Deportes Lima (6/0).
(391/472)	COMINGES MAYORCA Paul Manuel	24.07.1975	**7**	**2**	1997-1998, FBC Melgar Arequipa (6/2), PAOK Thessaloníki (1/0).
(453/533)	COMINGES MAYORGA Juan Elías	01.10.1983	**15**	**0**	2003-2012, Club Universitario de Deportes Lima (2/0), Club Sporting Cristal Lima (1/0), Club Atlético Colón Santa Fé (7/0), Club Estudiantes de La Plata (1/0), Caracas FC (3/0), Club Sportivo Cienciano Cuzco (1/0).
(505/581)	CONTRERAS COLLANTES Orlando	06.03.1982	**7**	**1**	2008-2013, CD Universidad San Martín de Porres (2/0), Club Alianza Lima (3/0), CD Universidad San Martín de Porres (1/1), CSCD Universidad César Vallejo Trujillo (1/0).
(446/526)	CORCUERA VALDIVIEZO José Alberto	06.08.1981	**5**	**0**	2003, Sport Boys Association Callao (5/0).
(300/380)	CORDERO Jorge	06.01.1962	**14**	**0**	1987-1991, CS Unión Huaral (10/0), Club Gimnasia y Esgrima La Plata (4/0).
(484/563)	CORRALES GONZÁLES Manuel Alejandro	03.08.1982	**1**	**0**	2006, Club Alianza Lima (1/0).
(243/333)	CORREA Humberto		**2**	**1**	1981, Club Atlético Torino Talara (2/1).
(120/225)	CORREA MONTENEGRO Rubén David	25.07.1941	**4**	**0**	1967-1970, Club Universitario de Deportes Lima (4/0).
(298/377)	CORREA Rubén		**1**	**0**	1986, CD Colegio San Agustín (1/0).
(515/592)	CORZO CHÁVEZ Aldo Sebastián	20.04.1989	**9**	**0**	2009-2012, Club Alianza Lima (3/0), CD Universidad San Martín de Porres (6/0).
(455/540)	CRUZADO DURAND Paulo Rinaldo	21.09.1984	**39**	**2**	2003-2013, Club Alianza Lima (8/0), Grasshopper-Club Zürich (4/0), Club Juan Aurich de Chiclayo (11/0), AC Chievo Verona (13/2), CA Newell's Old Boys Rosario (3/0).
(101/183)	CRUZADO SÁNCHEZ Luis Fernando	06.07.1941	**26**	**1**	1961-1971, Club Universitario de Deportes Lima (26/1).
(125/242)	CUBILLAS ARIZAGA Teófilo Juan	08.03.1949	**81**	**26**	1968-1982, Club Alianza Lima (53/17), FC do Porto (10/2), Club Alianza Lima (13/7), Fort Lauderdale Strikers (5/0).
(165/263)	CUÉLLAR Fernando	27.08.1949	**9**	**0**	1971-1975, Club Universitario de Deportes Lima (9/0).
(172/273)	CUETO VILLA César Augusto	16.06.1952	**51**	**6**	1972-1997, Club Alianza Lima (17/2), Atlético Nacional Medellín (33/4), *unattached* (1/0).
(533/620)	CUEVA BRAVO Christian Alberto	23.11.1991	**6**	**0**	2011-2012, CD Universidad San Martín de Porres (4/0), CSCD Universidad César Vallejo Trujillo (2/0).

(66/138)	DA GIAU Raúl		**1**	**0**	1953,
(40/088)	DA SILVA Andrés	21.03.1921	**9**	**0**	1947-1949, Club Universitario de Deportes Lima (9/0).
(177/278)	DAGA Walter	04.05.1951	**1**	**0**	1972, Sport Boys Association Callao (1/0).
(313/403)	DALL'ORSO Martín	01.09.1966	**8**	**1**	1989-1994, Club Sporting Cristal Lima (7/1), Club Universitario de Deportes Lima (1/0).
(2/013)	DANINO Esteban		**2**	**0**	1927, Club Atlético Chalaco Callao (2/0).
(59/128)	DÁVALOS Luis		**1**	**0**	1953,
(377/466)	DE ANDRADE "JULINHO" Julio	31.10.1965	**12**	**2**	1996-1997, Club Sporting Cristal Lima (12/2).
(455/534)	DE LA HAZA URQUIZA Paolo Giancarlo	30.11.1983	**24**	**0**	2003-2012, Sport Boys Association Callao (1/0), CS Cienciano Cuzco (7/0), FK Chornomorets Odessa (8/0), Club Alianza Lima (5/0), Beitar Jerusalem FC (1/0), Club Alianza Lima (1/0), CD Universidad César Vallejo Trujillo (1/0).
(121/232)	DE LA TORRE CASTRO Orlando	21.11.1943	**39**	**0**	1967-1973, Club Sporting Cristal Lima (39/0).
(93/164)	DE LA VEGA Juan		**18**	**0**	1959-1968, Mariscal Castilla (7/0), Club Alianza Lima (11/0).
(7/029)	DE LAS CASAS RAMÍREZ Mario	31.01.1901	**3**	**0**	1930-1935, Club Universitario de Deportes Lima (3/0).
(7/033)	DE SOUZA FERREIRA HUBY Luis Alfonso	06.10.1908	**2**	**1**	1930, Club Universitario de Deportes Lima (2/1).
(111/206)	DEL CASTILLO José	28.03.1949	**13**	**1**	1965-1970, Club Sporting Cristal Lima (13/1).
(405/483)	DEL MAR Christian	21.02.1972	**1**	**0**	1999, Club Alianza Lima (1/0).
(15/052)	DEL RIO Ricardo		**1**	**0**	1937, Club Universitario de Deportes Lima (1/0).

(82/153)	DEL SOLAR Alberto		**2**	**0**	1956, Club Sporting Cristal Lima (2/0).
(445/516)	DEL SOLAR ÁLVAREZ CALDERÓN Fernando Daniel	27.04.1977	**2**	**0**	2003-2006, Club Universitario de Deportes Lima (1/0), Club Deportivo USMP Callao (1/0).
(296/372)	DEL SOLAR ALVAREZ-CALDERÓN José Guillermo	27.11.1967	**74**	**9**	1986-2001, CD Colegio San Agustín (4/0), Club Universitario de Deportes Lima (23/1), CD Universidad Católica de Chile Santiago (6/2), CD Tenerife (18/4), UD Salamanca (3/0), Club Universitario de Deportes Lima (9/1), KV Mechelen (5/0), *unattached* (1/0), Club Universitario de Deportes Lima (6/1).
(80/152)	DEL VALLE Humberto		**1**	**0**	1956, Centro Iqueño Lima (1/0).
(35/081)	DELGADO Alberto		**1**	**0**	1942, Sport Boys Association Callao (1/0).
(90/161)	DELGADO Faustino		**2**	**1**	1957-1961, Club Sporting Cristal Lima (2/1).
(54/118)	DELGADO Guillermo	11.02.1931	**36**	**0**	1952-1957, (13/0), Club Alianza Lima (23/0).
(447/527)	DELGADO VÁSQUEZ Erick Guillermo	30.06.1982	**14**	**0**	2003-2011, Club Sporting Cristal Lima (14/0).
(4/016)	DENEGRI Alberto Luis		**8**	**0**	1929-1935
(166/268)	DÍAZ RIVAS Rubén Toribio	17.04.1952	**89**	**1**	1972-1985, Club Centro Deportivo Municipal Lima (3/0), Club Universitario de Deportes Lima (28/1), Club Sporting Cristal Lima (58/1).
(362/451)	DOLORIER Carlos	14.10.1966	**1**	**0**	1994, CA Defensor Lima (1/0).
(65/136)	DONAYRE Adolfo	10.12.1932	**8**	**0**	1953-1963, (1/0), Club Alianza Lima (7/0).
(240/322)	DRAGO Jaime	14.01.1959	**1**	**0**	1979, Club Centro Deportivo Municipal Lima (1/0).
(171/270)	DRAGO Jr. Roberto	12.09.1951	**1**	**0**	1972, Club Centro Deportivo Municipal Lima (1/0).
(47/107)	DRAGO Manuel	14.11.1924	**2**	**0**	1949, Sport Boys Association Callao (2/0).
(48/114)	DRAGO Roberto	28.07.1923	**30**	**9**	1949-1961, Club Centro Deportivo Municipal Lima (29/9),
(548/627)	DUARTE CARASSA Néstor Alonso	08.09.1990	**6**	**0**	2012-2013, CD Universitario de Deportes Lima (6/0).
(192/287)	DUARTE HUERTA Jaime Eduardo	27.02.1955	**54**	**1**	1975-1985, Club Alianza Lima (54/1).
(299/378)	DUFFÓO Martín	02.01.1963	**3**	**0**	1987-1993, Juventud La Palma (1/0), Club Sporting Cristal Lima (2/0).
(357/441)	DULANTO CORZO Alfonso Antonio	22.07.1969	**25**	**0**	1994-1997, Club Universitario de Deportes Lima (15/0), Club UNAM Ciudad de México (10/0).

(339/430)	EARL Manuel	20.03.1968	**1**	**0**	1993, Club Sporting Cristal Lima (1/0).
(243/334)	ECHEGARAY Marcos		**1**	**0**	1981, Asociación Deportiva Tarma (1/0).
(309/391)	ELGUERA Miguel		**1**	**0**	1989, CS Unión Huaral (1/0).
(105/194)	ELÍAS Roberto	07.06.1940	**12**	**0**	1963-1969, Club Sporting Cristal Lima (12/0).
(110/203)	ESCOBAR Félix		**1**	**0**	1963,
(293/361)	ESCOBAR Luis Antonio	19.06.1969	**1**	**0**	1985, Club Alianza Lima (1/0).
(216/302)	ESCOBAR Walter	26.01.1949	**1**	**0**	1977, CS Unión Huaral (1/0).
(498/578)	ESPEJO REYES Renato Gianfranco	04.03.1988	**1**	**0**	2007, Club Sporting Cristal Lima (1/0).
(20/061)	ESPINAR Oscar		**2**	**3**	1938, Club Centro Deportivo Municipal Lima (2/3).
(275/355)	ESPINO César		**2**	**0**	1984-1985, Sport Boys Association Callao (2/0).
(531/617)	ESPINOZA Gianfranco Roberto	28.08.1986	**1**	**0**	2011, CSD Sport Huancayo (1/0).
(275/354)	EUGENIO Samuel		**4**	**0**	1984-1985, Club Universitario de Deportes Lima (4/0).

(505/582)	FAIFFER AMES Sidney Enrique	12.05.1980	**1**	**0**	2008, Club Alianza Lima (1/0).
(310/398)	FALCÓN Luis	17.09.1968	**1**	**0**	1989, CSD Octavio Espinoza Ica (1/0).
(455/538)	FANO ESPINOZA Johan Javier	09.08.1978	**17**	**3**	2003-2011, Coronel Bolognesi FC Tacna (1/0), Club Universitario de Deportes Lima (1/0), CD Once Caldas Manizales (13/3), CF Atlante Cancún (1/0), Club Universitario de Deportes Lima (1/0).
(304/382)	FARFÁN Domingo		**5**	**1**	1988-1989, CS Unión Huaral (5/1).
(445/518)	FARFÁN GUADALUPE Jefferson Agustín	28.10.1984	**64**	**17**	2003-2013, Club Alianza Lima (16/5), PSV Eindhoven (25/7), FC Schalke 04 Gelsenkirchen (23/5).
(553/630)	FARFÁN QUISPE Rafael Nicanor	28.12.1975	**2**	**0**	2012-2013, Deportivo Sport Huancayo (2/0).
(376/465)	FARFÁN QUISPE Roberto Carlos	16.12.1973	**9**	**3**	1996-1998, Club Centro Deportivo Municipal Lima (4/2), Club Universitario de Deportes Lima (5/1).
(276/358)	FARFÁN Tomás Lorenzo	10.08.1961	**1**	**0**	1984, Club Alianza Lima (1/0).
(79/150)	FELANDRO Rigoberto	04.01.1924	**8**	**0**	1956-1961,
(480/557)	FERNÁNDEZ Carlos	01.11.1984	**1**	**0**	2005, Club Alianza Lima (1/0).
(484/561)	FERNÁNDEZ DONAYRE Wenceslao Ernesto	14.08.1979	**6**	**0**	2006-2009, CD Universidad San Martín de Porres (5/0), Club Sporting Cristal Lima (1/0).
(548/626)	FERNÁNDEZ MALDONADO Carlos Oswaldo	01.11.1984	**1**	**0**	2012, CD Universidad San Martín de Porres (1/0).
(9/035)	FERNÁNDEZ MEYZÁN Arturo	03.02.1906	**18**	**0**	1935-1939, Club Universitario de Deportes Lima
(9/037)	FERNÁNDEZ MEYZÁN Teodoro	20.05.1913	**32**	**24**	1935-1947, Club Universitario de Deportes Lima
(518/598)	FERNÁNDEZ PIEDRA José Carlos	14.05.1983	**7**	**2**	2009-2012, KSV Cercle Brügge (1/0), Sociedad Deportivo Quito (3/2), Club Alianza Lima (3/0).
(93/163)	FERNÁNDEZ SANTINI José Antonio	14.02.1939	**37**	**2**	1959-1973, Club Universitario de Deportes Lima (8/0), Association Chorrillos (3/0), Club Universitario de Deportes Lima (20/0), CA Defensor Lima (6/2).
(506/588)	FERNÁNDEZ VALVERDE Raúl Omar	06.10.1985	**28**	**0**	2008-2013, Club Universitario de Deportes Lima (13/0), OGC Nice (8/0), FC Dallas (7/0).
(373/459)	FERRARI CHIABRA Jean Franco	29.07.1975	**3**	**0**	1996-2001, Club Universitario de Deportes Lima (2/0), Club Sporting Cristal Lima (1/0).
(119/222)	FERRETI Rómulo	04.08.1949	**1**	**0**	1966, Sport Boys Association Callao (1/0).
(84/154)	FLEMING Guillermo		**15**	**0**	1957-1962, Club Centro Deportivo Municipal Lima (12/0), Ciclista Lima Association (1/0).
(406/488)	FLORES ASCENCIO Juan Ángel	25.02.1976	**6**	**0**	1999-2007, Club Universitario de Deportes Lima (5/0), CS Cienciano Cuzco (1/0).
(101/180)	FLORES Eduardo	13.10.1941	**2**	**1**	1961, Club Alianza Lima (2/1).
(94/168)	FLORES Lorenzo		**5**	**0**	1959, Club Alianza Lima (5/0).

(404/482)	FLORES MURILLO Carlos Antonio	04.08.1974	2	0	1998-2000, Aris Thessaloníki (1/0), Sport Boys Association Callao (1/0).
(566/645)	FLORES PERALTA Édison Michael	15.05.1994	1	0	2013, Villarreal CF "B" (1/0).
(125/241)	FLORES Walter	05.11.1945	1	0	1968, Sport Boys Association Callao (1/0).
(491/574)	FORSYTH SOMMER George Patrick	20.06.1982	5	0	2007-2008, Club Alianza Lima (3/0), Atalanta Bergamasca Calcio (2/0).
(127/247)	FRANCO Antonio		1	0	1968, CSD Octavio Espinoza Ica (1/0).
(47/106)	FUENTES Félix	25.04.1922	7	0	1949, Club Alianza Lima (7/0).
(327/409)	FUENTES Isidro	04.04.1965	2	0	1991, Club Unión Minas Cerro de Pasco (2/0).
(111/204)	FUENTES ZEGARRA Nicolás	20.02.1941	17	0	1965-1971, Club Universitario de Deportes Lima (16/0), CA Defensor Lima (1/0).
(4/017)	GALINDO PARDO Plácido Reynaldo	09.03.1906	3	0	1929-1930, Federación Universitaria Lima (3/0).
(105/195)	GALLARDO MENDOZA Félix Alberto	28.11.1940	37	11	1963-1972, Club Sporting Cristal Lima (37/11).
(446/525)	GALLIQUIO CASTRO John Christian	12.01.1979	41	1	2003-2012, CDSC Cruz Azul Ciudad de México (5/0), Racing Club Avellaneda (5/0), Club Universitario de Deportes Lima (10/0), CD Universidad San Martín de Porres (1/0), Club Universitario de Deportes Lima (6/0), FC Dinamo Bucureşti (2/0), Club Universitario de Deportes Lima (12/1).
(455/536)	GALLIQUIO CASTRO Wílder Édison	25.06.1981	1	0	2003, Club Universitario de Deportes Lima (1/0).
(569/646)	GAMBETTA SPONZA Gianmarco	02.05.1991	1	0	2013, CD Universidad San Martín de Porres (1/0).
(431/505)	GARCÍA DE LA CRUZ Pedro Alexandro	14.03.1974	19	2	2000-2009, Club Alianza Atlético Sullana (9/1), CD Universidad San Martín de Porres (10/1).
(100/175)	GARCÍA Enrique		1	0	1960, Club Centro Deportivo Municipal Lima (1/0).
(11/043)	GARCÍA Eulogio		1	0	1935, Club Alianza Lima (1/0).
(1/005)	GARCÍA Filomeno		1	0	1927
(7/031)	GARCÍA HEREDIA Domingo	1907	4	0	1930-1935, Club Alianza Lima
(365/454)	GARCÍA Martín	04.06.1970	1	0	1995, Deportivo Sipesa (1/0).
(458/541)	GARCÍA MESONES Julio César	16.06.1981	11	0	2003-2007, CS Cienciano Cuzco (6/0), Club Atlético Morelia (2/0), CS Cienciano Cuzco (3/0).
(273/351)	GARCÍA Raúl	21.09.1959	2	0	1984, Club Universitario de Deportes Lima (2/0).
(561/640)	GARCÍA URIBE Luis Gabriel	05.06.1988	2	0	2013, CD Unión Comercio Nueva Cajamarca (2/0).
(68/141)	GARRIDO Alfonso		2	0	1954-1955, Club Alianza Lima (2/0).
(232/316)	GASTULO RAMÍREZ Alejandro Hugo	09.01.1958	21	0	1979-1985, Club Universitario de Deportes Lima (21/0).
(561/638)	GÓMEZ GUTIÉRREZ Edwin Alexi	04.03.1993	3	0	2013, Club Universitario de Deportes Lima (3/0).
(192/288)	GÓMEZ LAYNEZ Carlos		2	0	1975, Club Alianza Lima (2/0).
(40/093)	GÓMEZ SÁNCHEZ Carlos	04.10.1923	11	5	1947-1949
(60/132)	GÓMEZ SÁNCHEZ Oscar	31.10.1935	26	14	1953-1959, Club Alianza Lima (26/14).
(405/487)	GÓMEZ URBINA Mario Augusto	27.05.1981	3	0	1999-2007, Club Universitario de Deportes Lima (2/0), Sport Boys Association Callao (1/0).
(4/021)	GÓNGORA MONTALVÁN Jorge	12.10.1906	2	0	1929-1935, Federación Universitaria Lima,
(33/078)	GONZÁLES Alejandro	1916	13	0	1941-1949
(325/407)	GONZÁLES Andrés	08.04.1968	18	2	1989-1996, Club Universitario de Deportes Lima (18/2).
(526/609)	GONZÁLES CANCHARI Antonio Emiliano	16.05.1986	10	0	2010-2012, Club Universitario de Deportes Lima (10/0).
(348/435)	GONZÁLES Carlos	09.08.1969	1	0	1993, Club Alianza Lima (1/0).
(561/641)	GONZÁLES CRESPO Christofer	12.10.1992	2	1	2013, Club Universitario de Deportes Lima (2/1).
(193/289)	GONZÁLES GANOZA José Manuel	10.07.1954	27	0	1975-1987, Club Alianza Lima (27/0).
(314/404)	GONZÁLES Gustavo	15.09.1964	1	0	1989, Club Sporting Cristal Lima (1/0).
(121/235)	GONZÁLES José		1	0	1967, Sport Boys Association Callao (1/0).
(120/230)	GONZÁLES José Javier	11.05.1939	16	0	1967-1970, Sport Boys Association Callao (2/0), Club Alianza Lima (14/0).
(101/182)	GONZÁLES Mario		2	0	1961-1965
(118/216)	GONZÁLES PAJUELO Carlos		4	1	1966-1967, Club Sporting Cristal Lima (4/1).
(120/226)	GONZÁLES ZAVALA Pedro	19.05.1943	16	0	1967-1973, Club Universitario de Deportes Lima (14/0), CA Defensor Lima (2/0).
(498/577)	GONZÁLEZ VIGIL-BENTIN Juan Diego	18.02.1985	4	0	2007-2010, Club Universitario de Deportes Lima (2/0), Coronel Bolognesi FC Tacna (1/0), Sociedad Deportivo Quito (1/0).
(206/299)	GORRITI DRAGÓ Raúl Enrique	10.10.1956	11	1	1976-1979, CD León de Huánuco (1/0), Club Sporting Cristal Lima (7/1), Club Centro Deportivo Municipal Lima (3/0).
(56/123)	GOYONECHE Rafael		5	0	1952-1953, Club Alianza Lima (5/0).
(163/260)	GOYZUETA Jesús	1947	2	0	1971, Club Universitario de Deportes Lima (2/0).
(93/165)	GRIMALDO Manuel		11	0	1959-1965, Club Alianza Lima (11/0).
(373/458)	GUADALUPE RIVADENEYRA Luis Alberto	03.04.1976	16	0	1996-2005, Club Universitario de Deportes Lima (16/0).
(471/545)	GUERRERO GONZALES José Paolo	01.01.1984	52	20	2004-2013, FC Bayern München (9/3), Hamburger SV (33/17), SC Corinthians Paulista São Paulo (10/0).
(531/614)	GUEVARA LEGUA Michael Fidel	10.06.1984	15	0	2011-2013, Sport Boys Association Callao (11/0), CD Universidad San Martín de Porres (3/0), Club Juan Aurich de Chiclayo (1/0).
(312/400)	GUIDO Carlos	18.04.1966	8	0	1989-1991, Club Sporting Cristal Lima (8/0).
(296/371)	GUILLÉN Carlos		2	0	1986, Club Centro Deportivo Municipal Lima (2/0).
(455/537)	GUIZASOLA LA ROSA Guillermo Alejandro	08.02.1982	1	0	2003, Club Alianza Lima (1/0)
(513/590)	GUIZASOLA LA ROSA Roberto Carlos	21.08.1984	11	0	2008-2013, CS Cienciano Cuzco (1/0), CA Rosario Central (4/0), Club Juan Aurich de Chiclayo (6/0).
(272/348)	GUTIÉRREZ Angel		1	0	1984, FBC Melgar Arequipa (1/0).
(242/328)	GUTIÉRREZ Miguel Ángel	19.11.1956	6	0	1980-1982, Club Sporting Cristal Lima (6/0).
(75/147)	GUTIÉRREZ René		7	0	1956-1957, Club Universitario de Deportes Lima (7/0).
(111/207)	GUZMÁN Alejandro	21.01.1942	1	0	1965, Club Universitario de Deportes Lima (1/0).

(27/069)	GUZMÁN Luis		13	4	1941-1947, Club Centro Deportivo Municipal Lima (13/4).
(104/186)	GUZMÁN Rodolfo		6	0	1962-1965, Club Alianza Lima (6/0).
(34/079)	GUZMÁN Teobaldo		5	0	1942, CA Banfield (5/0).
(40/090)	HEREDIA Cornelio	16.10.1920	36	4	1947-1956, Club Alianza Lima (36/4).
(516/596)	HEREDIA ROJAS Manuel Alexander	01.09.1986	1	0	2009, Club Sporting Cristal Lima (1/0).
(488/567)	HERNÁNDEZ ALFARO Luis Daniel Benito	20.12.1977	6	0	2006-2008, Club Universitario de Deportes Lima (2/0), Club Sporting Cristal Lima (4/0).
(437/511)	HERNÁNDEZ DÍAZ Juan Francisco	26.06.1978	2	0	2001, Club Juan Aurich de Chiclayo (2/0).
(437/510)	HERNÁNDEZ DÍAZ Luis Alberto	15.02.1981	3	0	2001, Club Alianza Lima (1/0), Coronel Bolognesi FC Tacna (2/0)
(118/217)	HERRERA Andrés		4	1	1966-1967, Sport Boys Association Callao (2/1), Defensor Arica (2/0).
(232/315)	HERRERA Darío	28.05.1955	1	0	1979, Sport Boys Association Callao (1/0).
(491/572)	HERRERA ZEGARRA Jhoel Alexander	09.07.1980	10	0	2007-2013, Club Alianza Lima (4/0), Asociación Civil Real Atlético Garcilaso (6/0).
(373/457)	HIDALGO CONDE Emilio Martín	15.06.1976	47	3	1996-2008, Club Sporting Cristal Lima (7/2), UD Las Palmas (2/0), Club Sporting Cristal Lima (7/0), CA Vélez Sarsfield (5/0), FK Saturn Ramenskoe (8/0), Club Alianza Lima (4/0), Club Libertad Asunción (3/0), SC Internacional Porto Alegre (4/0), Grêmio Foot-Ball Porto Alegrense (11/1).
(357/443)	HIDALGO Freddy	25.10.1967	1	0	1994, Deportivo Sipesa (1/0).
(416/495)	HINOSTROZA GUZMÁN John Christopher	22.02.1980	1	0	1999, Club Alianza Lima (1/0).
(272/346)	HIRANO Jorge Alberto	17.12.1959	36	11	1984-1991, Club Sporting Cristal Lima (13/4), Bolívar (23/7).
(408/490)	HOLSEN ALVARADO Roberto Carlos	10.08.1976	22	5	1999-2003, Club Alianza Atlético Sullana (8/3), Club Sporting Cristal Lima (7/1), Club Alianza Lima (6/1), CS Cienciano Cuzco (1/0).
(16/053)	HONORES Juan	04.03.1918	19	0	1937-1942
(403/480)	HUAMÁN SALINAS Jorge Raúl	11.04.1977	12	0	1998-2005, Sport Boys Association Callao (2/0), PAE Veria (5/0), Club Sporting Cristal Lima (3/0), CD Universidad San Martín de Porres (2/0).
(101/181)	HUAPAYA Oscar		2	0	1961, Club Centro Deportivo Municipal Lima (2/0).
(15/051)	HUBY Marcos		1	0	1937
(542/623)	HURTADO HUERTAS Christopher Paolo César	27.07.1990	11	2	2011-2013, Club Alianza Lima (3/0), FC Paços de Ferreira (8/2).
(27/072)	HURTADO Marcial		7	1	1941-1942
(336/424)	HURTADO Raúl	06.03.1966	2	0	1993, Club Sporting Cristal Lima (2/0).
(231/311)	HURTADO Víctor		6	0	1979-1988, Sport Boys Association Callao (5/0), Club Sporting Cristal Lima (1/0).
(403/476)	IBAÑEZ HOLZMANN Óscar Manuel	08.08.1967	50	0	1998-2005, Club Universitario de Deportes Lima (28/0), CS Cienciano Cuzco (22/0).
(16/054)	IBÁÑEZ Pedro		6	3	1937-1939
(476/553)	ISMODES Carlos Enrique	09.02.1983	2	0	2005, CD Universidad San Martín de Porres (2/0).
(492/575)	ÍSMODES SARAVIA Damián Diego	10.03.1989	6	0	2007-2009, Club Sporting Cristal Lima (6/0).
(298/375)	ISUSQUI Carlos		1	0	1986, Sport Boys Association Callao (1/0).
(95/170)	IWASAKI Tomás		5	0	1959-1966, Club Universitario de Deportes Lima (2/0), Club Centro Deportivo Municipal Lima (5/0).
(190/283)	JAIME Reynaldo		3	0	1975, Club Sporting Cristal Lima (3/0).
(28/074)	JANNEAU Guillermo		2	0	1941
(359/447)	JAYO LEGARIO Juan José	20.01.1973	97	1	1994-2008, Club Alianza Lima (28/0), Union de Santa Fè (22/1), Celta de Vigo (9/0), UD Las Palmas (3/0), Club Alianza Lima (35/0).
(484/564)	JIMÉNEZ Roberto Carlos	17.04.1983	6	0	2006-2008, Club Alianza Atlético Sullana (1/0), CA San Lorenzo de Almagro (3/0), CA Lanús (1/0), Club Universitario de Deportes Lima (1/0).
(12/047)	JORDÁN CANEPA Orestes		17	0	1936-1942, Club Universitario de Deportes Lima (17/0).
(84/155)	JOYA CORDERO Juan	25.02.1937	9	2	1957-1959, Club Alianza Lima (9/2).
(569/647)	KOICHI APARICIO MORI Roberto Efraín	06.06.1993	1	0	2013, Club Alianza Linma (1/0).
(120/227)	LA FUENTE Luis	08.06.1947	5	0	1967-1973, Club Universitario de Deportes Lima (2/0), CA Defensor Lima (3/0).
(275/357)	LA ROSA Eugenio	20.12.1961	15	3	1984-1991, Club Alianza Lima (11/1), Club Sporting Cristal Lima (4/2).
(190/282)	LA ROSA LAGUNA Guillermo	06.06.1952	39	3	1975-1985, CA Defensor Lima (2/0), Sport Boys Association Callao (4/0), Club Alianza Lima (6/0), Atlético Nacional Medellín (19/3), *unattached* (8/0).
(511/589)	LA ROSA LLONTOP Juan Carlos	03.03.1980	5	0	2008-2009, Club Alianza Lima (1/0), Club Juan Aurich de Chiclayo (4/0).
(460/542)	LA ROSA LLONTROP Juan Carlos	03.02.1980	11	0	2004-2005, ADC Unión Ciencano (11/0).
(235/319)	LABARTHE FLORES Ernesto	02.06.1956	4	0	1979, Sport Boys Association Callao (4/0).
(106/198)	LADRÓN DE GUEVARA Héctor		4	0	1963, Sport Boys Association Callao (4/0).
(79/151)	LAMA Jorge		4	1	1956,
(51/116)	LAVALLE Dagoberto	09.03.1925	11	0	1949-1956, Sport Boys Association Callao (11/0).
(1/007)	LAVALLE José María	21.04.1902	11	0	1927-1937, Club Alianza Lima (5/0),
(12/045)	LAVALLE Víctor		2	0	1936, Club Alianza Lima (2/0).
(373/460)	LAZO Jorge	25.10.1973	1	0	1996, Club Sporting Cristal Lima (1/0).
(54/121)	LAZÓN Carlos	05.10.1929	25	1	1952-1957, (2/0), Club Alianza Lima (23/1).

(219/303)	LEGUÍA DRAGÓ Germán Carlos	02.01.1954	31	3	1978-1983, Club Centro Deportivo Municipal Lima (1/0), Club Alianza Lima (1/0), Club Centro Deportivo Municipal Lima (2/0), Club Universitario de Deportes Lima (27/2).
(105/196)	LEÓN GARCÍA Pedro Pablo	26.03.1943	49	15	1963-1973, Club Alianza Lima (49/15).
(9/034)	LEÓN Narciso		3	0	1935,
(119/220)	LETURIA Juan		2	0	1966-1968, Mariscal Sucre FC (1/0), Sport Boys Association Callao (1/0).
(243/332)	LEYVA José		1	0	1981, CD Alfonso Ugarte Puno (1/0).
(527/610)	LIBMAN PASTOR Salomón Alexis	25.02.1984	6	0	2010-2012, Club Alianza Lima (2/0).
(5/025)	LIZARBE Augusto		2	1	1929, Hidroaviación Lima (2/1).
(93/166)	LOAYZA Miguel	21.06.1938	7	5	1959, Ciclista Lima Association (7/5).
(231/313)	LOBATÓN Abel		9	3	1979-1985, Sport Boys Association Callao (4/1), CS Unión Huaral (2/2), *unattached* (3/0).
(416/494)	LOBATÓN ESPEJO Abel Augusto	06.02.1980	12	1	1999-2001, Sport Boys Association Callao (7/0), Club Atlético Paranense (2/0), Club Universitario de Deportes Lima (3/1).
(477/547)	LOBATÓN ESPEJO Carlos Augusto	06.02.1980	34	1	2005-2012, CS Cienciano Cuzco (2/0), Club Sporting Cristal Lima (32/1).
(104/189)	LOBATÓN Hugo		2	0	1962-1965, Club Sporting Cristal Lima (2/0).
(27/067)	LOBATÓN Máximo		12	0	1941-1942
(120/229)	LOBATÓN Víctor		2	0	1967, Club Universitario de Deportes Lima (2/0).
(126/245)	LOO Mariano		1	0	1968, Club Atlético Grau Piura (1/0).
(357/442)	LÓPEZ Manuel	13.06.1970	1	0	1994, Ciclista Lima Association (1/0).
(40/096)	LÓPEZ Valeriano	04.05.1926	14	9	1947-1957
(7/032)	LORES COLÁN Julio Víctor	15.09.1908	2	0	1930, Necaxa Ciudad de Mexico (2/0).
(70/144)	LORET DE MOLA Alberto	13.01.1928	7	0	1955-1956, Club Universitario de Deportes Lima (4/0),
(96/171)	LOSTANAU Claudio		1	0	1959, Club Universitario de Deportes Lima (1/0).
(272/347)	LOYOLA César	13.05.1965	11	0	1984-1989, Club Sporting Cristal Lima (11/0).
(207/301)	LUCES Alejandro	20.01.1950	8	3	1977, CS Unión Huaral (8/3).
(172/272)	LUNA Julio		11	0	1972-1973, Club Universitario de Deportes Lima (11/0).
(28/073)	LUNA Pedro		4	0	1941-1942
(330/412)	MAESTRI ANDRADE Flavio Francisco	21.01.1973	57	11	1991-2007, Club Sporting Cristal Lima (24/6), CF Hércules Alicante (12/1), CD Universidad de Chile Santiago (13/3), Club Sporting Cristal Lima (2/0), EC Vitória Bahia (4/1), Club Alianza Lima (2/0).
(12/049)	MAGALLANES CAMPOS Adelfo	1913	22	4	1936-1942, Club Alianza Lima (22/4).
(363/452)	MAGALLANES JAIMES Álex Segundo	01.03.1974	16	0	1995-1997, Club Sporting Cristal Lima (16/0).
(27/068)	MAGÁN Pedro		10	0	1941-1942, Club Centro Deportivo Municipal Lima (1/0).
(235/320)	MALÁSQUEZ MALDONADO Eduardo Hugo	13.10.1957	34	3	1979-1987, Club Centro Deportivo Municipal Lima (19/3), CD Independiente Medellin (13/0), Club Universitario de Deportes Lima (2/0).
(378/468)	MALDONADO FARJE Paolo Freddy	12.08.1973	10	2	1996-2001, Club Universitario de Deportes Lima (10/2).
(304/383)	MANASSERO Francesco	04.12.1965	13	1	1988-1989, Club Sporting Cristal Lima (13/1).
(505/584)	MANCO ALBARRACÍN Reimond Orángel	23.08.1990	6	0	2008-2013, Club Alianza Lima (2/0), Club Juan Aurich de Chiclayo (3/0), Universidad Técnica de Cajamarca (1/0).
(166/266)	MANZO Rodolfo	05.06.1949	22	0	1972-1978, CA Defensor Lima (15/0), Club Centro Deportivo Municipal Lima (7/0).
(2/012)	MAQUILÓN BADARACCO Antonio	29.11.1902	6	0	1927-1930, Association FBC (2/0), Club Atlético Chalaco Callao (4/0).
(20/058)	MARCHENA Víctor		1	0	1938, Sport Boys Association Callao (1/0).
(374/461)	MARENGO Manuel	16.07.1973	13	2	1996-2003, Club Alianza Atlético Sullana (7/0), Club Sporting Cristal Lima (4/1), Coronel Bolognesi FC Tacna (2/1).
(489/569)	MARIÑO MÁRQUEZ Juan Carlos	02.01.1982	23	3	2006-2009, CS Cienciano Cuzco (7/1), Hércules CF Alicante (5/1), CS Cienciano Cuzco (2/0), CD Atlético Nacional Medellín (2/0), Club Sportivo Cienciano Cuzco (1/0), Club Sporting Cristal Lima (3/1), Querétaro FC (3/0).
(90/162)	MÁRQUEZ Manuel		3	0	1957-1961, Club Universitario de Deportes Lima (3/0).
(335/414)	MARROU Carlos	03.02.1970	2	0	1992-1993, Club Universitario de Deportes Lima (2/0).
(296/369)	MARTÍNEZ Roberto	03.12.1967	24	1	1986-1993, CD Colegio San Agustín (7/0), Club Universitario de Deportes Lima (17/1).
(173/274)	MAYORGA Manuel		15	1	1972-1973, Club Alianza Lima (15/1).
(112/208)	MELÉNDEZ Julio	08.03.1949	35	0	1965-1977, Defensor Arica (5/0), CA Boca Juniors Buenos Aires (1/0), Club Juan Aurich de Chiclayo (29/0).
(124/238)	MELLÁN Fernando	20.05.1942	4	0	1968, Club Sporting Cristal Lima (4/0).
(405/486)	MENDOZA AZEVEDO Andrés Augusto	26.04.1978	44	7	1999-2007, Club Sporting Cristal Lima (7/2), Club Brugge KV (22/4), FK Metalurg Donetsk (15/1).
(477/548)	MENDOZA José Adolfo	24.08.1982	6	0	2005, Club Universitario de Deportes Lima (6/0).
(50/115)	MENDOZA Leonidas	01.04.1925	2	0	1949, Sporting Tabaco (2/0).
(519/599)	MERINO RAMÍREZ Roberto	19.05.1982	1	0	2009, Salernitana Calcio 1919 (1/0).
(118/214)	MIFFLIN PÁEZ Ramón Antonio	05.04.1947	44	0	1966-1973, Defensor Arica (4/0), Club Sporting Cristal Lima (36/0), Racing Club Avellaneda (4/0).
(119/221)	MILERA Walter		2	0	1966-1967, Sport Boys Association Callao (2/0).
(89/159)	MINAYA Mario		2	1	1957, Club Universitario de Deportes Lima (2/1).
(340/431)	MIRANDA CAMPOS Miguel Eduardo	13.08.1966	47	0	1993-2001, Club Sporting Cristal Lima (16/0), Club Universitario de Deportes Lima (2/0), Deportivo Sipesa (8/0), Club Juan Aurich de Chiclayo (3/0), Club Centro Deportivo Municipal Lima (9/0), Shenyang FC (1/0), Club Sporting Cristal Lima (8/0).
(445/515)	MOISELLA HUAPAYA José Alberto	25.06.1980	1	0	2003, Club Sporting Cristal Lima (1/0).
(94/169)	MONTALVO Oscar	20.03.1937	7	0	1959-1962, Club Centro Deportivo Municipal Lima (6/0), Ciclista Lima Association (1/0).
(1/008)	MONTELLANOS Alberto	1899	4	2	1927-1935, Club Alianza Lima (4/2).

(262/340)	MORA Alberto		**6**	**0**	1983, Club Sporting Cristal Lima (6/0).
(9/039)	MORALES ALCÁZAR José		**10**	**0**	1935-1938
(553/631)	MORALES CORONADO Juan Gustavo Waldemar	06.03.1989	**2**	**0**	2012-2013, CSCD Universidad César Vallejo Trujillo (2/0).
(40/087)	MORALES Eliseo	13.06.1921	**6**	**0**	1947
(41/101)	MORALES Ernesto	17.05.1925	**9**	**1**	1947-1956
(28/075)	MORALES Roberto		**7**	**0**	1941-1942
(364/453)	MORÁN TORRES Alessandro	30.11.1972	**2**	**0**	1995-2003, Club Universitario de Deportes Lima (1/0), ADC Unión Ciencano (1/0).
(1/002)	MOSCOSO Carlos		**3**	**0**	1927, Association FBC (3/0).
(47/108)	MOSQUERA Alfredo	15.02.1923	**7**	**2**	1949, Sporting Tabaco (7/2).
(40/095)	MOSQUERA Máximo	08.01.1928	**31**	**8**	1947-1957
(104/191)	MOSQUERA Nemesio		**15**	**2**	1962-1968, Ciclista Lima Association (1/0), Club Centro Deportivo Municipal Lima (12/2), Club Juan Aurich de Chiclayo (2/0).
(219/304)	MOSQUERA VERA Roberto Orlando	21.06.1956	**16**	**4**	1978-1981, Club Sporting Cristal Lima (15/4), CA Talleres de Córdoba (1/0).
(445/524)	MOSTTO-PRADA FERNÁNDEZ Miguel Ángel	11.11.1977	**11**	**1**	2003-2006, Coronel Bolognesi FC Tacna (1/0), CS Cienciano Cuzco (9/1), Barnsley FC (1/0).
(337/428)	MUCHOTRIGO CARRILLO Darío Teodoro	17.12.1970	**24**	**1**	1993-2001, Club Alianza Lima (16/1), Ionikos Nikea FC (8/0).
(121/234)	MUÑANTE LÓPEZ Juan José	12.07.1948	**48**	**6**	1967-1978, Sport Boys Association Callao (2/0), Club Universitario de Deportes Lima (33/5), Club UNAM Ciudad de México (13/1).
(356/438)	MUÑOZ Germán	23.06.1973	**9**	**0**	1994-1997, Club Universitario de Deportes Lima (3/0), CS Cienciano Cuzco (6/0).
(1/011)	MURO Adolfo		**1**	**0**	1927-1929
(6/027)	MUSTAFICH Faustino		**1**	**0**	1929, Club Atlético Chalaco Callao (1/0).
(59/126)	NAVARRETE Luis		**11**	**2**	1953-1955,
(177/277)	NAVARRO ARAMBURU José	24.09.1948	**30**	**0**	1972-1979, Club Centro Deportivo Municipal Lima (1/0), CA Defensor Lima (9/0), Club Sporting Cristal Lima (20/0).
(241/327)	NAVARRO MONTEIRO Franco Enrique	10.11.1961	**56**	**16**	1980-1989, Club Centro Deportivo Municipal Lima (19/4), CD Independiente Medellin (22/9), CA Indepensiente Avellaneda (4/0), Tecos UA de Guadalajara (1/0), FC Wettingen (10/3).
(296/370)	NAVAS Jorge		**2**	**0**	1986, CD Hungaritos Agustinos Iquitos (2/0).
(2/014)	NEYRA Demetrio	1906	**4**	**1**	1927-1930, Club Alianza Lima (4/1).
(203/292)	NEYRA Ernesto		**2**	**0**	1976-1979, CD Alfonso Ugarte Puno (1/0), Club Universitario de Deportes Lima (1/0).
(506/586)	NEYRA FERRADA Donny Renzo	12.01.1984	**4**	**0**	2008, Club Universitario de Deportes Lima (4/0).
(261/338)	NEYRA Genaro		**2**	**0**	1983, FBC Melgar Arequipa (2/0).
(104/188)	NIERI Nicolás		**3**	**0**	1962-1966, Club Sporting Cristal Lima (3/0).
(558/635)	NORONHA MONTANI Osnar	17.12.1991	**1**	**0**	2012, Club Juan Aurich de Chiclayo (1/0).
(37/085)	OBANDO Tulio		**1**	**0**	1942, Club Universitario de Deportes Lima (1/0).
(179/279)	OBLITAS SABA Juan Carlos	16.02.1951	**64**	**11**	1973-1985, Club Universitario de Deportes Lima (16/4), Veracruz (11/4), Club Sporting Cristal Lima (11/1), RFC Seraing (9/1), Club Universitario de Deportes Lima (17/1).
(198/290)	OJEDA Santiago		**5**	**0**	1975, Club Atlético Chalaco Callao (5/0).
(231/308)	OLAECHEA QUIJANDRÍA Jorge Andrés	27.08.1956	**60**	**2**	1979-1989, Club Alianza Lima (29/1), CD Independiente Medellin (17/0), Asociación Deportivo Cali (3/0), Club Sporting Cristal Lima (11/1).
(445/520)	OLCESE VASALLO Aldo Ítalo	23.10.1974	**14**	**0**	2003-2006, Club Alianza Lima (14/0).
(150/256)	OLIVA Carlos		**1**	**0**	1970, Defensor Arica (1/0).
(299/379)	OLIVARES POLANCO Percy Celso	05.06.1968	**83**	**1**	1987-2001, Club Sporting Cristal Lima (44/0), CD Tenerife (6/0), Fluminense FC Rio de Janeiro (7/1), CDSC Cruz Azul Ciudad de México (8/0), PAOK Thessaloníki (7/0), Panathinaikos AO Athína (11/0).
(169/269)	ORBEGOSO Juan		**2**	**0**	1972, Club Sporting Cristal Lima (2/0).
(231/310)	ORÉ Juan José	12.06.1954	**4**	**1**	1979, Club Universitario de Deportes Lima (4/1).
(450/531)	OREJUELA Carlos	04.04.1980	**7**	**1**	2003-2004, Sport Boys Association Callao (5/1), Club Sporting Cristal Lima (2/0).
(371/456)	ORMEÑO Juan Carlos	01.08.1970	**2**	**0**	1996, CS Cienciano Cuzco (2/0).
(47/105)	ORMEÑO Walter	03.12.1927	**13**	**0**	1949-1957, Club Universitario de Deportes Lima (13/0).
(4/019)	ORTEGA Rodolfo		**3**	**0**	1929, Hidroaviación Lima (3/0).
(41/102)	PACHECO Lorenzo	10.08.1919	**10**	**0**	1947-1952
(11/044)	PACHECO Mario		**1**	**0**	1935, Club Universitario de Deportes Lima (1/0).
(417/496)	PAJUELO CHÁVEZ Juan Luciano	23.09.1974	**25**	**3**	1999-2003, Club Universitario de Deportes Lima (11/1), CA Los Andes (8/2), CD Atlas Guadalajara (5/0), Club Universitario de Deportes Lima (1/0).
(165/262)	PALACIOS Augusto	23.12.1951	**6**	**0**	1971-1977, Club Sporting Cristal Lima (1/0), Club Centro Deportivo Municipal Lima (5/0).
(335/417)	PALACIOS MESTAS Roberto Carlos	28.12.1972	**128**	**19**	1992-2009, Club Sporting Cristal Lima (40/9), Puebla FC (11/2), Universidad Autonoma de Guadalajara (4/1), Cruzeiro EC Belo Horizonte (1/0), Universidad Autonoma de Guadalajara (31/6), Club Sporting Cristal Lima (5/0), Club Atlético Morelia (2/0), CD Atlas Guadalajara (6/0), Club Atlético Morelia (9/1), Asociación Deportivo Cali (4/0), LDU de Quito (7/0), Club Sporting Cristal Lima (8/0).
(162/259)	PALACIOS Moisés		**6**	**0**	1971-1976, CA Defensor Lima (3/0), Club Alianza Lima (3/0).
(334/413)	PALMA Diosdada	29.03.1965	**1**	**0**	1991, CA Defensor Lima (1/0).
(358/445)	PALOMINO Frank	01.12.1970	**9**	**0**	1994-2001, Ciclista Lima Association (2/0), FBC Melgar Arequipa (6/0), CS Cienciano Cuzco (1/0).

(1/001)	PARDÓN GARCÍA Jorge Hernesto	19.12.1909	6	0	1927-1930, Club Atlético Chalaco Callao (6/0).
(16/055)	PAREDES Arturo	06.10.1915	9	1	1937-1939
(122/236)	PÁRRAGA Alberto		1	0	1967, Sport Boys Association Callao (1/0).
(191/286)	PÁRRAGA Raúl		6	0	1975, Club Universitario de Deportes Lima (6/0).
(21/062)	PARRÓ Jorge		1	0	1938, Club Centro Deportivo Municipal Lima (1/0).
(20/059)	PASACHE Pablo	01.02.1915	10	0	1938-1942, Club Centro Deportivo Municipal Lima (10/0:
(118/213)	PAU Luis		2	0	1966, Defensor Arica (2/0).
(47/109)	PEDRAZA Víctor	24.05.1923	7	3	1949, Club Alianza Lima (7/3).
(525/605)	PEIXOTO CHICLAYO Kerwin Junior	21.02.1988	1	0	2009, Club Alianza Atlético Sullana (1/0).
(107/199)	PELÁEZ Jesús		5	0	1963-1965
(403/477)	PENALILLO Julio	22.05.1975	1	0	1998, Club Centro Deportivo Municipal Lima (1/0).
(485/565)	PENNY VALDEZ Diego Alonso	22.04.1984	14	0	2006-2013, Coronel Bolognesi FC Tacna (6/0), Club Juan Aurich de Chiclayo (4/0), Club Sporting Cristal Lima (4/0).
(70/142)	PERALES Agapito		1	0	1955, Sporting Tabaco (1/0).
(23/065)	PERALES Enrique	1914	17	0	1939-1947
(204/297)	PERALES Henry	30.03.1950	3	0	1976, ID Colegio Nacional de Iquitos (3/0).
(378/467)	PEREDA MARUYAMA José Antonio	08.09.1973	27	4	1996-2001, Club Universitario de Deportes Lima (12/3), CA Boca Juniors Buenos Aires (15/1).
(481/558)	PÉREZ LEÓN Edwin Alberto	28.09.1974	1	0	2005, CD Universidad San Martín de Porres (1/0).
(335/416)	PINILLOS RIOJA Germán Ernesto	06.04.1972	14	2	1992-2000, Club Sporting Cristal Lima (11/2), Sport Boys Association Callao (2/0), Club Sporting Cristal Lima (1/0).
(405/485)	PIZARRO BOSIO Claudio Miguel	03.10.1978	75	19	1999-2013, Club Alianza Lima (11/3), SV Werder Bremen (11/2), FC Bayern München (27/8), Chelsea FC London (6/0), SV Werder Bremen (8/3), FC Bayern München (12/3).
(358/444)	PIZARRO Francisco	03.03.1971	6	0	1994-1996, Club Alianza Lima (6/0).
(17/056)	PORTAL Carlos		10	0	1937-1942
(393/475)	PORTILLA CASTILLO Giuliano Santiago	25.05.1973	5	0	1997-2005, Club Universitario de Deportes Lima (2/0), Club Sporting Cristal Lima (1/0), CS Cienciano Cuzco (2/0).
(484/560)	PRADO BARRÓN Amilton Jair	06.05.1979	28	0	2006-2009, Club Sporting Cristal Lima (28/0).
(392/473)	PRADO Orlando	16.02.1972	5	0	1997, Deportivo Pesquero (5/0).
(307/389)	PURIZAGA Jesús	05.12.1960	22	0	1988-1991, Club Sporting Cristal Lima (14/0), Club Alianza Lima (8/0).

(162/258)	QUESADA FARÍAS Alfredo	22.09.1949	50	1	1971-1978, Club Sporting Cristal Lima (50/1).
(336/421)	QUESADA PARODI Rafael Alfredo	16.08.1971	3	0	1993-1996, Club Sporting Cristal Lima (3/0).
(21/063)	QUIÑÓNES Leopoldo		13	1	1938-1942
(66/139)	QUIÑÓNES Tulio		1	0	1953, Necaxa (Mexico) (1/0).
(419/499)	QUINTEROS SÁNCHEZ Henry Edson	12.10.1977	24	1	2000-2009, Club Alianza Lima (9/1), Club Sporting Cristal Lima (6/0), KKS Lech Poznań (4/0), Club Alianza Lima (5/0).
(515/594)	QUINTEROS SÁNCHEZ Ronald Jhonatan	28.06.1985	1	0	2009-2012, CD Universidad San Martín de Porres (3/0).
(121/233)	QUINTOS Matías		2	0	1967, Defensor Arica (2/0).
(207/300)	QUIROGA ARANCIBIA Ramón	23.07.1950	40	0	1977-1985, Club Sporting Cristal Lima (37/0), Club Universitario de Deportes Lima (3/0).
(23/064)	QUISPE Juan	03.10.1914	13	0	1939-1942

(526/608)	RABANAL DÁVILA Jesús Giancarlos	25.12.1984	7	0	2010-2011, Club Universitario de Deportes Lima (7/0).
(41/098)	RAFFO Domingo		2	0	1947, Club Atlético Chalaco Callao (2/0).
(335/419)	RAMÍREZ Alberto	05.11.1968	11	3	1992-1996, Club Alianza Atlético Sullana (1/1), Club Sporting Cristal Lima (2/0), Deportivo Sipesa (6/2), Club Universitario de Deportes Lima (2/0).
(260/335)	RAMÍREZ Jorge		12	0	1983-1985, FBC Melgar Arequipa (11/0), Club Centro Deportivo Municipal Lima (1/0).
(374/462)	RAMÍREZ Jorge	07.09.1975	3	0	1996-2001, Club Alianza Lima (2/0), CD Wanka Huancayo (1/0).
(4/023)	RAMÍREZ Julio		3	0	1929, Association FBC (3/0).
(480/555)	RAMÍREZ LUCAY Luis Alberto	10.11.1984	30	2	2005-2013, Coronel Bolognesi FC Tacna (1/0), Club Libertad Asunción (4/0), Coronel Bolognesi FC Tacna (2/0), Club Universitario de Deportes Lima (4/2), SC Corinthians Paulista São Paulo (11/0), AA Ponte Preta (8/0).
(310/395)	RAMÍREZ Martín	08.08.1969	2	0	1989-1991, CD Colegio San Agustín (2/0).
(203/296)	RAMÍREZ SALCEDO Jorge		2	0	1976, Club Centro Deportivo Municipal Lima (2/0).
(131/249)	RAMÍREZ SALCEDO Oswaldo Felipe	29.03.1947	57	17	1969-1982, Sport Boys Association Callao (7/3), Club Sporting Cristal Lima (1/2), Sport Boys Association Callao (6/0), Club Universitario de Deportes Lima (15/4), Atlético Español FC (20/7), Club Sporting Cristal Lima (8/1).
(304/386)	RAMÍREZ Wilson		3	0	1988, FBC Melgar Arequipa (3/0).
(522/602)	RAMOS GARAGAY Christian Guillermo Martín	04.11.1988	31	0	2009-2013, CD Universidad San Martín de Porres (5/0), Club Alianza Lima (9/0), Club Universidad San Martín de Porres (10/0), Club Juan Aurich de Chiclayo (7/0).
(232/314)	RAVELLO Freddy	28.01.1955	11	1	1979-1982, Club Alianza Lima (11/1).
(391/470)	REBOSIO COMPANS César Miguel	20.10.1976	60	0	1997-2005, Club Sporting Cristal Lima (28/0), CD Real Zaragoza (27/0), UD Almería (5/0).
(480/556)	RENGIFO TRIGOSO Hernán	18.04.1983	22	6	2005-2012, CD Universidad San Martín de Porres (2/0), KKS Lech Poznań (15/5), AC Omonia Nicosia (3/1), Club Sporting Cristal Lima (2/0).
(260/336)	REQUENA Pedro	15.10.1960	51	1	1983-1992, Sport Boys Association Callao (28/0), Club Universitario de Deportes Lima (22/1), FBC Melgar Arequipa (1/0).
(543/624)	RETAMOSO PALOMINO Edwin	23.02.1982	11	0	2011-2013, Club Sportivo Cienciano Cuzco (5/0), Asociación Civil Real Atlético Garcilaso (6/0).

(515/591)	REVOREDO ZUAZO Renzo	11.05.1986	**18**	**0**	2009-2013, Club Universitario de Deportes Lima (8/0), Club Sporting Cristal Lima (4/0), Club Olimpia Asunción (3/0), Barcelona SC Guayaquil (2/0), Club Sporting Cristal Lima (1/0).
(241/325)	REY MUÑOZ Eduardo	07.08.1957	**23**	**1**	1980-1989, Club Universitario de Deportes Lima (23/1).
(304/384)	REY MUÑOZ Humberto		**4**	**0**	1988, CS Unión Huaral (4/0).
(59/129)	REYES Alberto		**2**	**0**	1953,
(126/246)	REYES CARAZA Eladio Máximo	08.01.1948	**7**	**0**	1968-1970, Club Juan Aurich de Chiclayo (7/0).
(296/364)	REYES Daniel	02.04.1966	**2**	**0**	1986, Club Alianza Lima (2/0).
(371/455)	REYNA José Luis	19.01.1972	**7**	**0**	1996-1997, Club Alianza Lima (7/0).
(41/100)	REYNA Marin		**3**	**0**	1947, Sucre FBC (3/0).
(242/329)	REYNA NAVARRO Luis Alberto	16.05.1959	**39**	**1**	1980-1989, Club Sporting Cristal Lima (17/0), Club Universitario de Deportes Lima (1/0), Club Sporting Cristal Lima (3/0), Club Universitario de Deportes Lima (18/1).
(560/637)	REYNA SERNA José Yordy	17.09.1993	**6**	**2**	2013, Club Alianza Lima (4/2), FC Red Bull Salzburg (2/0).
(220/305)	REYNA Víctor		**3**	**0**	1978
(296/365)	REYNOSO GUZMÁN Juan Máximo	28.12.1969	**84**	**5**	1986-2000, Club Alianza Lima (27/2), Club Universitario de Deportes Lima (22/1), CDSC Cruz Azul Ciudad de México (35/0).
(143/253)	RISCO Rafael		**8**	**0**	1969-1972, Defensor Arica (2/0), Club Alianza Lima (6/0).
(528/611)	RIVAS ASIN Willy Alexander	04.06.1985	**2**	**0**	2010, Club Juan Aurich de Chiclayo (2/0).
(335/418)	RIVERA Julio César	12.04.1968	**34**	**0**	1992-1997, FBC Melgar Arequipa (1/0), Club Sporting Cristal Lima (33/0).
(57/124)	RIVERA Manuel	22.05.1922	**12**	**3**	1952-1957, (6/1), Club Centro Deportivo Municipal Lima (6/2).
(163/261)	RIVERO Juan	08.10.1950	**7**	**0**	1971-1975, Club Alianza Lima (7/0).
(10/042)	RIVERO Juan		**1**	**0**	1935
(28/076)	ROBLES		**1**	**0**	1941
(337/425)	RODRÍGUEZ Agapito	16.03.1966	**1**	**0**	1993, Club Alianza Lima (1/0).
(310/397)	RODRÍGUEZ César Eduardo	21.09.1967	**16**	**3**	1989-1991, Club Centro Deportivo Municipal Lima (9/1), Club Alianza Lima (7/2).
(113/211)	RODRÍGUEZ Enrique		**1**	**0**	1965, Club Universitario de Deportes Lima (1/0).
(336/422)	RODRÍGUEZ Mario	18.03.1972	**11**	**0**	1993-1996, Club Alianza Lima (11/0).
(327/410)	RODRÍGUEZ Martín	24.09.1968	**19**	**0**	1991-1995, Internacional (8/0), Club Universitario de Deportes Lima (11/0).
(118/218)	RODRÍGUEZ Napoleón		**4**	**0**	1966-1967, Defensor Arica (4/0).
(9/040)	RODRÍGUEZ NUÉ Lizandro	30.08.1910	**1**	**0**	1935
(447/528)	RODRÍGUEZ VALDELOMAR Alberto Junior	31.03.1984	**50**	**0**	2003-2013, Club Sporting Cristal Lima (10/0), Sporting Clube de Braga (27/0), Sporting Clube de Portugal Lisboa (2/0), Rio Ave FC Vila do Conde (11/0).
(273/350)	ROJAS Leonardo	09.10.1962	**33**	**0**	1984-1989, Club Universitario de Deportes Lima (33/0).
(137/252)	ROJAS MONTERO Percy	16.09.1949	**49**	**7**	1969-1979, Club Universitario de Deportes Lima (16/1), CA Independiente Buenos Aires (11/2), Club Sporting Cristal Lima (22/4).
(558/633)	ROJAS PAJUELO Alfredo Junior	01.05.1991	**2**	**0**	2012-2013, Club Juan Aurich de Chiclayo (2/0).
(223/307)	ROJAS TARDÍO Roberto	26.10.1955	**27**	**0**	1978-1983, Club Alianza Lima (27/0).
(361/448)	ROSALES TARDÍO César Miguel	09.11.1970	**4**	**0**	1994-1997, Ciclista Lima Association (2/0), Club Alianza Lima (2/0).
(41/099)	ROSASCO René		**7**	**0**	1947-1953
(480/554)	ROSS SANTILLANA Douglas Junior	19.02.1986	**12**	**0**	2005-2013, Coronel Bolognesi FC Tacna (3/0), CS Cienciano Cuzco (1/0), Coronel Bolognesi FC Tacna (6/0), Club Sporting Cristal Lima (2/0).
(531/618)	ROSSEL DEL MAR Víctor Alfonso	05.11.1985	**1**	**0**	2011, CD Universidad César Vallejo Trujillo (1/0).
(4/022)	ROSTAING Miguel	03.07.1900	**3**	**0**	1929, Club Atlético Chalaco Callao (3/0).
(105/197)	ROSTAING Víctor	17.11.1942	**1**	**0**	1963, Club Alianza Lima (1/0).
(85/158)	ROVAY Dante		**6**	**0**	1957, Club Sporting Cristal Lima (6/0).
(107/200)	RUBIÑOS CERNA Luis	31.12.1940	**38**	**0**	1963-1972, Club Sporting Cristal Lima (38/0).
(533/621)	RUIDÍAZ MISITICH Raúl Mario	25.07.1990	**8**	**0**	2011-2013, Club Universitario de Deportes Lima (4/0), Club Universidad de Chile Santiago (1/0), Coritiba FC (2/0), Club Universitario de Deportes Lima (1/0).
(85/157)	RUIZ Daniel		**3**	**0**	1957, Club Universitario de Deportes Lima (3/0).
(359/446)	RUIZ Frank	30.11.1967	**1**	**0**	1994, Club Alianza Lima (1/0).
(455/535)	RUÍZ Marco Antonio	22.09.1979	**1**	**0**	2003, Coronel Bolognesi FC Tacna (1/0).
(105/193)	RUIZ Pedro Anselmo		**8**	**0**	1963-1966, Club Sporting Cristal Lima (6/0), Defensor Arica (1/0), Club Sporting Cristal Lima (1/0).
(190/285)	RUIZ Pedro Anselmo	06.06.1948	**7**	**0**	1975-1979, CS Unión Huaral (7/0).

(341/433)	SÁENZ PÉREZ Waldir Alejandro	15.05.1973	**27**	**3**	1993-2000, Club Alianza Lima (22/1), Colorado Rapids (1/0), Club Atlético Unión de Santa Fé (1/0), Club Sporting Cristal Lima (3/1).
(476/551)	SALAS CASTILLO Hilden	19.07.1980	**2**	**0**	2005, FBC Melgar Arequipa (2/0).
(5/024)	SALAS Enrique		**1**	**0**	1929, Federación Universitaria Lima (1/0).
(445/521)	SALAS SUÁREZ Guillermo Sandro	21.10.1974	**26**	**0**	2003-2008, Club Alianza Lima (21/0), CD Universidad San Martín de Porres (5/0).
(70/143)	SALAS Víctor		**16**	**0**	1955-1957, Club Universitario de Deportes Lima (16/0).
(362/450)	SALAZAR ORBE Marcial	08.09.1967	**7**	**0**	1994-2000, Club Centro Deportivo Municipal Lima (2/0), Club Alianza Lima (5/0).
(403/479)	SALAZAR PEÑA Santiago Roberto	02.11.1974	**13**	**0**	1998-2006, Sport Boys Association Callao (2/0), Club Sporting Cristal Lima (5/0), Trabzonspor Kulübü (3/0), Club Alianza Lima (3/0).
(1/003)	SALDARRIAGA Alfonso	23.01.1902	**6**	**0**	1927-1929, Club Atlético Chalaco Callao (6/0).
(203/291)	SALGUERO GONZÁLEZ Rafael Salvador	10.08.1951	**13**	**0**	1976-1982, Club Alianza Lima (13/0).
(145/254)	SALINAS Félix		**12**	**0**	1970-1972, Club Universitario de Deportes Lima (12/0).
(47/110)	SALINAS Juan Emilio	12.07.1925	**7**	**5**	1949-1956, Club Alianza Lima (6/3),

(516/597)	SÁNCHEZ ALBÚJAR Daniel Alonso	02.05.1990	1	0	2009, Club Sporting Cristal Lima (1/0).
(522/603)	SÁNCHEZ ALEGRÍA Joel Melchor	11.07.1989	2	0	2009-2012, Total Chalaco FBC Callao (1/0), CD Universidad San Martín de Porres (1/0).
(487/566)	SÁNCHEZ REYES Alexander Gustavo	06.06.1984	12	1	2006-2010, Club José Gálvez Chimbote (4/1), Club Alianza Lima (/),
(315/406)	SANJINEZ Pedro	29.06.1966	4	0	1989, Club Alianza Atlético Sullana (4/0).
(2/015)	SARMIENTO Jorge	02.11.1900	2	1	1927, Club Alianza Lima (2/1).
(119/219)	SARTOR ESPINOZA Ottorino	18.09.1945	27	0	1966-1979, Defensor Arica (9/0), Club Centro Deportivo Municipal Lima (3/0), Club Universitario de Deportes Lima (12/0), ID Colegio Nacional de Iquitos (1/0), Coronel Bolognesi FC Tacna (2/0).
(27/066)	SAYERS Guillermo		3	0	1941
(558/634)	SCHULER GAMARRA Werner Luis	27.06.1990	1	0	2012, Club Universitario de Deportes Lima (1/0).
(6/026)	SEGALA Eugenio	1900	1	0	1929, Circolo Sportivo Italiano Lima (1/0).
(75/146)	SEMINARIO Juan Roberto	22.01.1936	19	6	1956-1959, Club Centro Deportivo Municipal Lima (19/6).
(241/324)	SEMINARIO Miguel	29.09.1959	5	0	1980-1981, Sport Boys Association Callao (5/0).
(445/519)	SERRANO Antonio	14.03.1979	1	1	2003, Club Alianza Lima (1/1).
(378/469)	SERRANO RUIZ Roger Alberto	23.07.1970	16	0	1996-2000, Sport Boys Association Callao (5/0), Club Sporting Cristal Lima (8/0), Club Ciencano Cuzco (3/0).
(530/612)	SHEPUT RODRÍGUEZ Renzo Santiago	08.11.1980	2	0	2010-2012, Equidad CD Bogotá (1/0), Club Sporting Cristal Lima (1/0).
(432/506)	SILVA PRO Roberto Enrique	01.06.1976	11	2	2001-2004, Club Sporting Cristal Lima (2/0), San Luis FC (5/2), Club Alianza Lima (4/0).
(27/071)	SOCARRAZ César		6	1	1941, Club Universitario de Deportes Lima (6/1).
(356/437)	SOLANO TODCO Nolberto Albino	12.12.1974	95	20	1994-2009, Club Sporting Cristal Lima (29/5), CA Boca Juniors Buenos Aires (5/0), Newcastle United FC (28/9), Aston Villa FC Birmingham (15/6), West Ham United FC London (9/0), PAE Larissa (3/0), Club Universitario de Deportes Lima (6/0).
(504/580)	SOLÍS ALVARADO Carlos Javier	22.10.1981	1	0	2007, CS Cienciano Cuzco (1/0).
(119/224)	SOLÍS Carlos		2	0	1966-1968, Sport Boys Association Callao (2/0).
(7/030)	SORIA Alberto	10.03.1906	6	0	1930-1937, Club Alianza Lima
(175/275)	SORIA Eleazar	11.01.1949	29	0	1972-1978, Club Universitario de Deportes Lima (11/0), CA Independiente Buenos Aires (7/0), Club Sporting Cristal Lima (11/0).
(423/500)	SORIA YOSHINARI David	18.09.1977	5	0	2000, Club Sporting Cristal Lima (5/0).
(36/082)	SORIANO Juan	18.04.1918	1	0	1942
(445/523)	SOTIL ECHE Johan Joussep	29.08.1982	1	0	2003, Club Universitario de Deportes Lima (1/0).
(531/615)	SOTIL ELCHE Johan Joussep	29.08.1982	1	0	2011, CSD Sport Huancayo (1/0).
(145/255)	SOTIL YERÉN Hugo Alejandro	08.03.1949	62	18	1970-1979, Club Centro Deportivo Municipal Lima (43/14), FC Barcelona (1/1), Club Alianza Lima (16/3), Deportivo Independiente Medellin (2/0).
(335/415)	SOTO GÓMEZ Jorge Antonio	27.10.1971	101	9	1992-2005, Club Centro Deportivo Municipal Lima (1/0), Club Sporting Cristal Lima (50/5), CA Lanus (2/0), CR Flamengo Rio de Janeiro (5/1), Club Sporting Cristal Lima (21/1), San Luis FC (5/1), Club Sporting Cristal Lima (17/1).
(335/420)	SOTO GÓMEZ José Alberto	11.01.1970	75	3	1992-2003, Club Centro Deportivo Municipal Lima (1/0), Club Alianza Lima (23/1), Club Sporting Cristal Lima (12/0), Puebla CF (15/0), Club Alianza Lima (6/0), Club Atlético Celaya (4/0), Club Alianza Lima (14/2).
(300/381)	SOTO José Anselmo	21.04.1965	2	1	1987, Club Universidad Técnica de Cajamarca (2/1).
(273/353)	SUÁREZ Fidel		4	0	1984-1989, Club Atlético Torino Talara (3/0), Club Universitario de Deportes Lima (1/0).
(417/498)	SUÁREZ Freddy	07.05.1970	2	0	1999-2000, FBC Melgar Arequipa (2/0).
(40/086)	SUÁREZ Luis	17.05.1926	13	0	1947-1955

(296/363)	TALAVERA Jorge	31.12.1963	8	1	1986-1989, Club Centro Deportivo Municipal Lima (3/1), Internacional (5/0).
(429/502)	TEMPONE MANTEROLA Gustavo Marcelo	14.04.1971	5	0	2000, Sport Boys Association Callao (5/0).
(100/178)	TENEMÁS Enrique		7	1	1960-1963, Ciclista Lima Association (1/0), Club Alianza Lima (6/1).
(476/550)	TENEMÁS GUTIÉRREZ Javier Martín	19.07.1985	1	0	2005, Atlético Universidad Arequipa (1/0).
(62/133)	TERRY Alberto	16.05.1929	25	11	1953-1959, Club Universitario de Deportes Lima (25/11).
(339/429)	TORREALBA Freddy	01.09.1967	1	0	1993, Club Universitario de Deportes Lima (1/0)
(298/376)	TORREALBA Jesús	15.10.1960	3	0	1986-1989, CSD Octavio Espinoza Ica (1/0), Club Universitario de Deportes Lima (2/0).
(391/471)	TORRES ARIAS Erick Omar	16.05.1975	11	0	1997-2006, Club Sporting Cristal Lima (10/0), Club José Gálvez Chimbote (1/0).
(310/394)	TORRES Carlos	25.05.1966	5	1	1989, Internacional (5/1).
(41/103)	TORRES Carlos		2	0	1947, Club Atlético Chalaco Callao (2/0).
(54/119)	TORRES Gilberto	15.08.1928	11	1	1952-1953,
(490/570)	TORRES QUINTANA Miguel Ángel	17.01.1982	5	0	2006-2009, CS Cienciano Cuzco (1/0), Club Universitario de Deportes Lima (4/0).
(482/559)	TORRES SALAS Rainer	12.01.1980	28	0	2005-2010, Club Sporting Cristal Lima (7/0), Club Universitario de Deportes Lima (21/0).
(9/038)	TOVAR VENEGAS Carlos	02.04.1915	15	0	1935-1939, Club Universitario de Deportes Lima
(526/607)	TRAGODARA GÁLVEZ Jean Carlo	16.12.1985	7	1	2010-2011, Club Alianza Lima (7/1).
(166/265)	TRIGUEROS Antonio	17.01.1948	14	0	1972-1976, CA Defensor Lima (10/0), Club Universitario de Deportes Lima (4/0).
(515/595)	TRUJILLO ORTÍZ Luis Enrique	27.12.1990	5	0	2009-2011, Club Alianza Lima (5/0).

(356/440)	UBILLÚS CALMET Juan Alexis	30.12.1972	11	0	1994-2001, Club Sporting Cristal Lima (1/0), Club Universitario de Deportes Lima (7/0), Club Sporting Cristal Lima (2/0), Club Alianza Lima (1/0).
(272/345)	UCULMANA Felipe		1	0	1984, Club Sporting Cristal Lima (1/0).
(1/004)	ULLOA Santiago		2	0	1927, Sportivo Tarapacá (2/0).
(97/173)	URDÁNIGA Alonso		2	0	1959, Sport Boys Association Callao (2/0).
(100/176)	URIBE Angel	25.11.1939	10	2	1960-1967, Club Universitario de Deportes Lima (10/2).
(436/509)	URIBE ELERA Julio Edson	09.05.1982	2	0	2001, Club Deportivo Maldonado (2/0).
(237/321)	URIBE FLORES Julio César	09.05.1958	39	9	1979-1989, Club Sporting Cristal Lima (19/7), Cagliari Calcio (8/2), Atlético Junior Barranquilla (3/0), CD América de Cali (2/0), Club Sporting Cristal Lima (2/0), CD América de Cali (5/0).
(166/264)	URIBE Manuel		14	0	1972-1973, Sport Boya Callao (6/0), CA Defensor Lima (8/0).
(118/215)	URRUNAGA Carlos	06.06.1946	2	0	1966, CA Defensor Lima (2/0).

(298/373)	VALDETTARO Humberto		1	0	1986, Club Sporting Cristal Lima (1/0).
(40/094)	VALDIVIESO Guillermo		3	0	1947
(7/028)	VALDIVIESO PADILLA Juan	06.05.1910	10	0	1930-1938, Club Alianza Lima (10/0).
(47/112)	VALDIVIESO Pedro		2	0	1947-1949
(337/427)	VALENCIA Marco	23.09.1971	5	0	1993, Club Alianza Lima (5/0).
(273/352)	VALENCIA Wilmar	27.10.1962	14	0	1984-1989, Club Alianza Lima (7/0), Blooming (Bolivia) (7/0).
(29/077)	VALLEJOS Manuel		3	1	1941, Club Universitario de Deportes Lima (3/1).
(524/604)	VALVERDE ZAMORA Marcio André	23.10.1987	2	0	2009, Club Alianza Atlético Sullana (2/0).
(231/309)	VARGAS Arturo		3	0	1979, Club Alianza Lima (3/0).
(65/137)	VARGAS Emilio	27.05.1927	1	0	1953, Club Alianza Lima (1/0).
(562/643)	VARGAS GARCÍA Josimar Hugo	06.04.1990	1	0	2013, Club Universitario de Deportes Lima (1/0).
(472/546)	VARGAS RISCO Juan Manuel	05.10.1983	49	4	2004-2013, Club Universitario de Deportes Lima (2/0), Club Atlético Colón Santa Fé (4/0), Calcio Catania (11/2), AC Fiorentina Firenze (22/2), Genoa CFC (6/0), AC Fiorentina Firenze (4/0).
(296/367)	VÁSQUEZ Cedric		7	0	1986-1987, CD Colegio San Agustín (7/0).
(107/202)	VASQUEZ Jorge	29.07.1941	2	0	1963, Club Sporting Cristal Lima (2/0).
(450/530)	VÁSQUEZ Martín	10.08.1974	5	0	2003, Club Sporting Cristal Lima (5/0).
(549/628)	VÁSQUEZ RAMÍREZ Jaime	21.02.1991	1	0	2012, CD Unión Comercio Nueva Cajamarca (1/0).
(505/583)	VÁSQUEZ ROSALES Jorge Johan	08.10.1984	1	0	2008, Coronel Bolognesi FC Tacna (1/0).
(476/552)	VASSALLO FERRARI Gustavo Enrique	06.09.1978	5	3	2005-2006, Sport Boys Association Callao (3/2), Club Sporting Cristal Lima (2/1).
(426/501)	VEGAS Jhonny	09.02.1976	3	0	2000, Sport Boys Association Callao (3/0).
(166/267)	VELÁSQUEZ CASTILLO José Manuel	04.06.1952	82	12	1972-1985, Club Alianza Lima (36/7), CD Independiente Medellín (5/0), Toronto Blizzard (5/0), CD Independiente Medellín (9/1), Club Alianza Lima (27/4).
(407/489)	VELÁSQUEZ CASTILLO Juan José Manuel	20.03.1971	6	0	1999-2000, Deportivo Pesquero (5/0), Club Alianza Atlético Sullana (1/0).
(65/134)	VELÁSQUEZ Clemente		2	0	1953,
(65/135)	VELÁSQUEZ Enrique	31.12.1930	3	0	1953-1956, (2/0), Club Alianza Lima (1/0).
(558/636)	VIDALES LATURE Jhonny Víctor	22.04.1992	1	0	2012, Club Alianza Lima (1/0).
(310/392)	VIDALES Octavio	02.04.1965	4	0	1989-1991, Club Universitario de Deportes Lima (4/0).
(569/648)	VÍLCHEZ SOTO Óscar Christopher	24.02.1986	1	0	2013, Club Juan Aurich de Chiclayo (1/0).
(439/512)	VÍLCHEZ SOTO Walter Ricardo	19.02.1982	65	1	2001-2012, Club Unión Minas Cerro de Pasco (1/0), Club Alianza Lima (9/0), CA Olimpo (3/0), Club Sporting Cristal Lima (6/1), CDSC Cruz Azul Ciudad de México (7/0), CF Puebla (16/0), CS Cienciano Cuzco (4/0), Club Alianza Lima (5/0), Club Sporting Cristal Lima (14/0).
(76/149)	VILLALBA Jacinto		4	0	1956-1957, Club Universitario de Deportes Lima (4/0).
(445/514)	VILLALTA HURTADO Miguel Angel	16.06.1981	28	2	2003-2008, Club Sporting Cristal Lima (13/1), CS Cienciano Cuzco (4/0), Club Sporting Cristal Lima (11/1).
(59/127)	VILLAMARES Ernesto		6	1	1953, Sporting Tabacco (6/1).
(496/576)	VILLAMARÍN ARGUEDAS Edgar Harry	01.04.1982	4	0	2007-2009, CS Cienciano Cuzco (2/0), Club Universitario de Deportes Lima (1/0).
(122/237)	VILLANUEVA José		1	0	1967, Club Sporting Cristal Lima (1/0).
(1/010)	VILLANUEVA MARTÍNEZ Carlos Alejandro	04.06.1908	11	6	1927-1938, Club Alianza Lima (11/6).
(124/240)	VILLANUEVA Román		2	0	1968, Club Alianza Lima (2/0).
(417/497)	VILLANUEVA SALAZAR Rafael Fabio	17.09.1975	1	0	1999, Sport Boys Association Callao (1/0).
(488/568)	VIZA SEMINARIO César Junior	03.04.1985	2	0	2006, Club Alianza Lima (2/0).

(107/201)	YACSETICK Mario		3	0	1963, Club Centro Deportivo Municipal Lima (3/0).
(312/401)	YÁÑEZ Alfonso Orlando	20.03.1970	13	1	1989-1991, Club Universitario de Deportes Lima (13/1).
(531/616)	YOTÚN FLORES Víctor Yoshimar	07.04.1990	31	1	2011-2013, Club Sporting Cristal Lima (23/0), CR Vasco da Gama Rio de Janeiro (8/1).
(306/388)	YUPANQUI Héctor Martín	20.10.1962	2	0	1988-1996, CD Colegio San Agustín (1/0), Club Universitario de Deportes Lima (1/0).

(506/585)	ZAMBRANO OCHANDARTE Carlos Augusto	10.07.1989	27	3	2008-2013, FC Schalke 04 Gelsenkirchen (11/1), FC St. Pauli Hamburg (6/0), SG Eintracht Frankfurt (10/2).
(241/326)	ZAPATA José		3	0	1980-1984, Club Atlético Torino Talara (3/0).
(113/210)	ZAVALA Luis		4	2	1965, Club Universitario de Deportes Lima (4/2).
(430/503)	ZEBALLOS Franco Walter	15.04.1973	5	0	2000-2001, FBC Melgar Arequipa (5/0).
(120/231)	ZEGARRA Andrés	15.03.1947	11	0	1967-1975, Defensor Arica (9/0), Club Alianza Lima (2/0).
(36/084)	ZEGARRA Antonio		2	0	1942

(74/145)	ZEGARRA Dimas		**14**	**0**	1956-1970, Club Universitario de Deportes Lima (8/0), Porvenir Miraflores (6/0).
(311/399)	ZEGARRA Ricardo	30.04.1967	**4**	**1**	1989-1996, CA Defensor Lima (2/1), Club Sporting Cristal Lima (2/0).
(104/187)	ZEGARRA SALÉ Alejandro Víctor	18.03.1940	**19**	**3**	1962-1969, Club Alianza Lima (19/3).
(453/532)	ZEGARRA TEJADA Omar Alberto	06.08.1980	**1**	**0**	2003, Club Sporting Cristal Lima (1/0).
(445/517)	ZEGARRA ZAMORA Carlos Alberto	02.03.1977	**24**	**1**	2003-2012, Club Sporting Cristal Lima (22/1), PAOK Thessaloníki (1/0), CSD León de Huánuco (1/0).
(340/432)	ZEGARRA ZAMORA Pablo César	11.04.1973	**30**	**1**	1993-1999, Club Sporting Cristal Lima (15/0), CF Badajoz (3/1), UD Salamanca (12/0).
(104/190)	ZEVALLOS Alejandro	30.03.1943	**2**	**0**	1962-1968, Centro Iqueño Lima (1/0), CSD Octavio Espinoza Ica (1/0).
(203/293)	ZEVALLOS Roberto		**4**	**0**	1976, Club Universitario de Deportes Lima (4/0).
(203/294)	ZULUAGA David	18.03.1956	**6**	**0**	1976-1979, Club Universitario de Deportes Lima (6/0).
(409/491)	ZÚÑIGA YAÑEZ Herlyn Ysrael	27.08.1976	**21**	**3**	1999-2007, FBC Melgar Arequipa (9/2), Coventry City FC (8/0), Club Universitario de Deportes Lima (2/1), FCB Melgar Arequipa (2/0).

NATIONAL COACHES

Name	Period	Matches	P	W	D	L		GF	-	GA	
Pedro OLIVIERI (*Uruguay*)	01.11.1927 – 27.11.1927	[1-3]	3	1	0	2		4	-	11	33.33 %
Julio BORELLI (*Uruguay*)	03.11.1929 – 16.11.1929	[4-6]	3	0	0	3		1	-	12	0.00 %
Francisco BRU SANZ (*Spain*)	14.07.1930 – 18.07.1930	[7-8]	2	0	0	2		1	-	4	0.00 %
Telmo CARBAJO	13.01.1935 – 26.01.1935	[9-11]	3	1	0	2		2	-	5	33.33 %
Alberto DENEGRI	06.08.1935 – 24.01.1937	[12-18]	7	3	1	3		18	-	15	50.00 %
John Richard „Jack" GREENWELL (*England*)	08.08.1938 – 12.02.1939	[19-26]	8	8	0	0		31	-	8	100.00 %
Domingo ARRILLAGA	19.01.1941 – 26.02.1941	[27-33]	7	1	2	4		7	-	10	28.57 %
Angel FERNÁNDEZ (*Argentina*)	18.01.1942 – 07.02.1942	[34-39]	6	1	2	3		5	-	10	33.33 %
José ARANA	06.12.1947 – 27.12.1947	[40-46]	7	2	2	3		12	-	9	42.85 %
Arturo FERNÁNDEZ (*Argentina*)	10.04.1949 – 04.05.1949	[47-53]	7	5	0	2		20	-	13	71.42 %
Alfonso HUAPAYA	23.03.1952 – 20.04.1952	[54-58]	5	2	1	2		14	-	9	50.00 %
William COOK (*England*)	22.02.1953 – 28.02.1953	[59-60]	2	1	0	1		1	-	1	50.00 %
Angel FERNÁNDEZ	04.03.1953 – 28.07.1953	[61-66]	6	2	2	2		9	-	7	50.00 %
Juan VALDIVIESO PADILLA	17.09.1954 – 30.03.1955	[67-73]	7	3	2	2		18	-	15	57.14 %
Arturo FERNÁNDEZ	22.01.1956 – 17.03.1956	[74-83]	10	1	3	6		12	-	18	25.00 %
György ORTH (*Hungary*)	10.03.1957 – 17.05.1959	[84-100]	17	6	4	7		29	-	30	47.05 %
Marcos CALDERÓN	19.03.1961 – 07.05.1961	[101-103]	3	0	1	2		3	-	7	16.66 %
Jaime DE ALMEYDA (*Brazil*)	20.05.1962	[104]	1	0	0	1		0	-	4	0.00 %
Juan VALDIVIESO PADILLA	10.03.1963 – 27.03.1963	[105-110]	6	2	1	3		8	-	11	41.66 %
Marcos CALDERÓN	03.04.1965 – 13.06.1965	[111-117]	7	2	0	5		9	-	11	28.57 %
José GOMES NOGUEIRA (*Brazil*)	04.06.1966 – 08.06.1966	[118-119]	2	0	0	2		1	-	7	0.00 %
Marcos CALDERÓN	28.07.1967 – 30.07.1967	[120-123]	4	1	1	2		2	-	3	37.50 %
Roberto DRAGO	14.07.1968 – 17.07.1968	[124-125]	2	0	0	2		3	-	8	0.00 %
Waldir Perreira "DIDI" (*Brazil*)	18.08.1968 – 14.06.1970	[126-161]	36	14	9	13		57	-	55	51.38 %
Alejandro HEREDIA	27.07.1971 – 18.08.1971	[162-165]	4	1	1	2		1	-	3	37.50 %
Lajos BARÓTI (*Hungary*)	29.03.1972 – 03.05.1972	[166-171]	6	0	2	4		4	-	12	16.66 %
Roberto SCARONE (*Uruguay*)	06.06.1972 – 05.08.1973	[172-189]	18	9	2	7		28	-	19	55.55 %
Marcos CALDERÓN	22.06.1975 – 28.10.1975	[190-202]	13	8	1	4		18	-	14	65.38 %
Alejandro HEREDIA	12.10.1976 – 24.11.1976	[203-206]	4	0	2	2		1	-	4	25.00 %
Marcos CALDERÓN	09.02.1977 – 21.06.1978	[207-230]	24	9	6	9		36	-	36	50.00 %
José CHIARELLA	11.07.1979 – 01.11.1979	[231-240]	10	3	2	5		11	-	12	40.00 %
Juan José TAN	18.07.1980 – 12.11.1980	[241-242]	2	0	2	0		1	-	1	50.00 %
Alejandro HEREDIA	04.02.1981 – 19.04.1981	[243-245]	3	0	0	3		2	-	8	0.00 %
Elba de Padua Lima "TIM" (*Brazil*)	26.07.1981 – 22.06.1982	[246-259]	14	6	5	3		16	-	14	60.71 %
Juan José TAN	18.07.1983 – 20.10.1983	[260-271]	12	2	5	5		10	-	17	37.50 %
Moisés BARACK	26.02.1984 – 09.06.1985	[272-287]	16	6	6	4		16	-	15	56.25 %
Roberto Federico CHALE OLARTE (CHALLE)	16.06.1985 – 03.11.1985	[288-295]	8	2	2	4		9	-	10	37.50 %
Luis CRUZADO	28.01.1986 – 30.01.1986	[296-297]	2	1	0	1		2	-	3	50.00 %
Manuel MAYORGA	01.04.1986	[298]	1	0	0	1		0	-	4	0.00 %
Fernando CUÉLLAR ÁVALOS	19.06.1987 – 04.07.1987	[299-303]	5	1	2	2		5	-	6	40.00 %
José FERNÁNDEZ	21.09.1988 – 03.02.1989	[304-309]	6	0	2	4		1	-	8	16.66 %
José Macia "PEPE" (*Brazil*)	10.05.1989 - 10.09.1989	[310-325]	16	2	5	9		16	-	41	28.12 %
Percy ROJAS MONTERO	24.09.1989	[326]	1	0	0	1		0	-	2	0.00 %
Miguel Alejandro COMPANY CHUMPITAZI	06.06.1991 – 14.07.1991	[327-334]	8	2	2	4		12	-	12	37.50 %
Vladimir POPOVIĆ (*Yugoslavia*)	24.11.1992– 05.09.1993	[335-355]	21	3	8	10		16	-	29	33.33 %
Miguel Alejandro COMPANY CHUMPITAZI	03.05.1994 – 13.07.1995	[356-370]	15	4	3	8		17	-	14	36.66 %
Juan Carlos OBLITAS SABA	11.02.1996 – 08.06.1997	[371-390]	20	7	5	8		25	-	26	47.50 %
Freddy Santos TERNERO CORRALES	12.06.1997 – 28.06.1997	[391-396]	6	3	0	3		5	-	11	50.00 %
Juan Carlos OBLITAS SABA	06.07.1997 – 10.07.1999	[397-415]	19	9	4	6		27	-	26	57.89 %
Francisco MATURANA (*Colombia*)	17.11.1999 – 03.09.2000	[416-429]	14	4	4	6		15	-	15	42.85 %
Julio César URIBE FLORES	08.10.2000 – 14.11.2001	[430-444]	15	3	4	8		12	-	26	33.33 %
Paul César AUTUORI (*Brazil*)	23.02.2003 – 30.03.1975	[445-475]	31	9	10	12		44	-	40	45.16 %
Freddy Santos TERNERO CORRALES	22.05.2005 – 12.10.2005	[476-483]	8	3	2	3		9	-	13	50.00 %
Franco Enrique NAVARRO MONTEIRO	10.05.2006 – 19.11.2006	[484-490]	7	1	3	3		7	-	10	35.71 %
Julio César URIBE FLORES	24.03.2007 – 08.07.2007	[491-497]	7	2	1	4		7	-	13	35.71 %
José Guillermo DEL SOLAR ALVAREZ-CALDERÓN	22.08.2007 – 18.11.2009	[498-525]	28	5	6	17		21	-	51	28.57 %
Sergio Apraham MARKARIÁN ABRAHAMIAN (*Uruguay*)	04.09.2010 –>	[526->	45	16	14	15		46	-	45	

National coaches several times in charge:

Name	How often	Matches	M	W	D	L		GF	-	GA	
Marcos CALDERÓN	5x	[101-103], [111-117], [120-123], [190-202], [207-230]	51	20	9	22		68	-	71	48.03 %
Alejandro HEREDIA	3x	[162-165], [203-206], [243-245]	11	1	3	7		4	-	15	22.72 %
Angel FERNÁNDEZ (*Argentina*)	2x	[34-39], [61-66]	12	3	4	5		14	-	17	41.66 %
Arturo FERNÁNDEZ	2x	[47-53], [74-83]	19	6	3	8		32	-	31	39.47 %
Juan VALDIVIESO PADILLA	2x	[67-73], [105-110]	13	5	3	5		26	-	26	50.00 %
Juan José TAN	2x	[241-242], [260-271]	14	2	7	5		11	-	18	39.28 %
Miguel Alejandro COMPANY CHUMPITAZI	2x	[327-334], [356-370]	23	6	5	12		29	-	26	36.95 %
Juan Carlos OBLITAS SABA	2x	[371-390], [397-415]	39	16	9	14		52	-	52	52.56 %
Freddy Santos TERNERO CORRALES	2x	[391-396], [476-483]	14	6	2	6		14	-	24	50.00 %
Julio César URIBE FLORES	2x	[430-444],[491-497]	22	5	5	12		19	-	39	34.09 %

HEAD-TO-HEAD STATISTICS

	HOME					AWAY					NEUTRAL					TOTAL				
Algeria						1	0	1	0	1 : 1						1	0	1	0	1 : 1
Argentina	21	3	7	11	18 : 39	17	0	3	14	11 : 38	11	2	2	7	14 : 23	49	5	12	32	43 : 100
Armenia	1	1	0	0	4 : 0											1	1	0	0	4 : 0
Austria											1	1	0	0	4 : 2	1	1	0	0	4 : 2
Belarus	1	0	1	0	1 : 1											1	0	1	0	1 : 1
Belgium											1	0	1	0	1 : 1	1	0	1	0	1 : 1
Bolivia	19	12	4	3	38 : 19	17	1	6	10	8 : 22	8	6	2	0	19 : 2	44	19	12	13	65 : 43
Brazil	10	1	4	5	8 : 16	14	2	2	10	10 : 30	15	0	3	12	9 : 37	39	3	9	27	27 : 83
Bulgaria	4	1	1	2	8 : 9						1	1	0	0	3 : 2	5	2	1	2	11 : 11
Cameroon											1	0	1	0	0 : 0	1	0	1	0	0 : 0
Canada						1	1	0	0	2 : 0						1	1	0	0	2 : 0
Chile	32	17	4	11	49 : 29	32	2	5	25	33 : 76	11	2	5	4	14 : 14	75	21	14	40	96 : 119
China P.R.	1	1	0	0	2 : 1						1	0	0	1	1 : 3	2	1	0	1	3 : 4
Colombia	20	6	9	5	22 : 17	20	5	6	9	20 : 32	9	4	3	2	16 : 7	49	15	18	16	58 : 56
Costa Rica	3	3	0	0	8 : 1	2	1	1	0	2 : 1	1	0	0	1	2 : 4	6	4	1	1	12 : 6
Czech Republic	3	1	0	2	3 : 6						1	0	1	0	0 : 0	4	1	1	2	3 : 6
Denmark											1	0	0	1	1 : 2	1	0	0	1	1 : 2
Ecuador	16	9	3	4	27 : 15	13	1	4	8	9 : 27	15	8	5	2	34 : 15	44	18	12	14	70 : 57
El Salvador	1	1	0	0	3 : 0	1	1	0	0	4 : 1	1	0	0	1	0 : 1	3	2	0	1	7 : 2
England	2	1	0	1	4 : 5											2	1	0	1	4 : 5
Finland											1	1	0	0	7 : 3	1	1	0	0	7 : 3
France						1	1	0	0	1 : 0						1	1	0	0	1 : 0
Germany											1	0	0	1	1 : 3	1	0	0	1	1 : 3
Guatemala	2	1	1	0	5 : 1						1	1	0	0	2 : 1	3	2	1	0	7 : 2
Haiti	1	1	0	0	5 : 1	3	1	2	0	5 : 4						4	2	2	0	10 : 5
Holland						2	0	0	2	0 : 5	1	0	1	0	0 : 0	3	0	1	2	0 : 5
Honduras	3	0	2	1	2 : 4						5	2	2	1	8 : 6	8	2	4	2	10 : 10
Hungary	1	1	0	0	3 : 2	1	1	0	0	2 : 1						2	2	0	0	5 : 3
India						1	1	0	0	1 : 0						1	1	0	0	1 : 0
Iran											1	1	0	0	4 : 1	1	1	0	0	4 : 1
Italy											1	0	1	0	1 : 1	1	0	1	0	1 : 1
Jamaica						1	0	1	0	1 : 1	1	1	0	0	2 : 1	2	1	1	0	3 : 2
Japan	2	1	1	0	1 : 0	4	1	2	1	1 : 2	1	1	0	0	3 : 2	7	3	3	1	5 : 4
Korea Republic						1	0	1	0	0 : 0						1	0	1	0	0 : 0
Mexico	4	2	1	1	7 : 6	9	2	2	5	10 : 15	14	5	4	5	14 : 15	27	9	7	11	31 : 36
Morocco											1	1	0	0	3 : 0	1	1	0	0	3 : 0
Nigeria	1	0	0	1	0 : 1											1	0	0	1	0 : 1
Panama	3	2	0	1	5 : 2	3	2	0	1	4 : 3	1	1	0	0	7 : 1	7	5	0	2	16 : 6
Paraguay	20	9	4	7	25 : 17	11	0	3	8	7 : 21	14	1	6	7	15 : 30	45	10	13	22	47 : 68
Poland	1	0	0	1	1 : 3						2	0	0	2	1 : 6	3	0	0	3	2 : 9
Romania	3	1	1	1	3 : 3	1	0	1	0	2 : 2	1	0	0	1	1 : 3	5	1	2	2	6 : 8
Scotland						2	0	1	1	1 : 3	1	1	0	0	3 : 1	3	1	1	1	4 : 4
Senegal	1	1	0	0	1 : 0											1	1	0	0	1 : 0
Slovakia	2	2	0	0	3 : 1											2	2	0	0	3 : 1
Soviet Union	2	0	1	1	0 : 2	1	0	0	1	0 : 2						3	0	1	2	0 : 4
Spain	1	0	0	1	1 : 3	2	0	0	2	2 : 4						3	0	0	3	3 : 7
Trinidad and Tobago	1	1	0	0	3 : 0	3	1	1	1	4 : 3						4	2	1	1	7 : 3
Tunisia						1	0	1	0	1 : 1						1	0	1	0	1 : 1
United Arab Emirates											1	0	1	0	0 : 0	1	0	1	0	0 : 0
United States	1	1	0	0	4 : 1	4	1	1	2	1 : 4						5	2	1	2	5 : 5
Uruguay	27	7	5	15	23 : 39	22	2	7	13	12 : 38	13	5	1	7	21 : 28	62	14	13	35	56 : 105
Venezuela	11	10	1	0	24 : 6	11	3	1	7	15 : 24	7	6	1	0	16 : 4	29	19	3	7	55 : 34
Yugoslavia											1	0	0	1	1 : 2	1	0	0	1	1 : 2
TOTAL	**221**	**97**	**50**	**74**	**311 : 250**	**202**	**30**	**52**	**120**	**170 : 361**	**147**	**51**	**40**	**56**	**228 : 221**	**570**	**178**	**142**	**250**	**709 : 832**

URUGUAY

The Country:
República Oriental del Uruguay
(Oriental Republic of Uruguay)
Capital: Montevideo
Surface: 176,215 km²
Inhabitants: 3,318,535
Time: UTC-3

The FA:
Asociación Uruguaya de Fútbol
Guayabo 1531, Montevideo 11200
Year of Formation: 1900
Member of FIFA since: 1923
Member of CONMEBOL since: 1916

NATIONAL TEAM RECORDS

COPA AMÉRICA	
1916	**Winners**
1917	**Winners**
1919	Runners-up
1920	**Winners**
1921	3rd Place
1922	3rd Place
1923	**Winners**
1924	**Winners**
1925	Withdrew
1926	**Winners**
1927	Runners-up
1929	3rd Place
1935	**Winners**
1937	3rd Place
1939	Runners-up
1941	Runners-up
1942	**Winners**
1945	4th Place
1946	4th Place
1947	3rd Place
1949	6th Place
1953	3rd Place
1955	4th Place
1956	**Winners**
1957	3rd Place
1959	5th Place
1959E	**Winners**
1963	Withdrew
1967	**Winners**
1975	Semi-Finals
1979	Round 1
1983	**Winners**
1987	**Winners**
1989	Runners-up
1991	Round 1
1993	Quarter-Finals
1995	**Winners**
1997	Round 1
1999	Runners-up
2001	Semi-Finals
2004	3rd Place
2007	Semi-Finals
2011	**Winners**

WORLD CUP	
1930	**Final Tournament (Winners)**
1934	Withdrew
1938	Did not enter
1950	**Final Tournament (Winners)**
1954	Final Tournament (Semi-Finals)
1958	Qualifiers
1962	Final Tournament (1st Round)
1966	Final Tournament (Quarter-Finals)
1970	Final Tournament (Semi-Finals)
1974	Final Tournament (1st Round)
1978	Qualifiers
1982	Qualifiers
1986	Final Tournament (2nd Round)
1990	Final Tournament (2nd Round)
1994	Qualifiers
1998	Qualifiers
2002	Final Tournament (1st Round)
2006	Qualifiers
2010	Final Tournament (4th Place)
2014	Final Tournament (*to be played*)

OLYMPIC GAMES 1900-2012
1924 (Winners), 1928 (Winners), 2012
FIFA CONFEDERATIONS CUP 1992-2013
1997, 2013
PLAYER WITH MOST INTERNATIONAL CAPS
Diego Martín Forlán Corazo – 107 caps (2002-2013)
PLAYER WITH MOST INTERNATIONAL GOALS
Luis Alberto Suárez Díaz – 38 goals / 76 caps (2007-2013)

FULL INTERNATIONALS (1902-2013)

1. 20.07.1902 **URUGUAY - ARGENTINA** **0-6(0-2)**
Estadio Paso del Molino, Montevideo; Referee: Roberto Whall Rudd (Argentina), Attendance: 8,000
URU: Enrique Sardeson (1/0), Carlos Carve Urioste (1/0), Germán Arímalo (1/0), Miguel Nebel (1/0), Luis Carbone (1/0), Alberto Peixoto (1/0), Bolivar Céspedes (1/0), Gonzalo Rincón (1/0), Juan Sardeson (1/0), Ernesto Boutón Reyes (1/0), Carlos Céspedes (1/0).

2. 13.09.1903 **ARGENTINA - URUGUAY** **2-3(0-1)**
Estadio Sociedad Hípica, Buenos Aires; Referee: Roberto Whall Rudd (Argentina), Attendance: 4,000
URU: Amílcar Céspedes (1/0), Carlos Carve Urioste (2/0), Ernesto Boutón Reyes (2/0), Miguel Nebel (2/0), Luis Carbone (2/0), Gaudencio Pigni (1/0), Bolívar Céspedes (2/1), Gonzalo Rincón (2/0), Carlos Céspedes (2/2), Alejandro Cordero (1/0), Eduardo De Castro (1/0).
Goals: Carlos Céspedes (22, 58), Bolívar Céspedes (61).

3. 15.08.1905 **ARGENTINA - URUGUAY** **0-0 a.e.t** Copa Lipton
Estadio Campo de la Sociedad Sportiva, Buenos Aires; Referee: Guillermo Jordán (Argentina), Attendance: 5,000
URU: Cayetano Saporiti (1/0), Carlos Carve Urioste (3/0), Ernesto Boutón Reyes (3/0), Ceferino Camacho (1/0), Luis Carbone (3/0), Arturo Rovegno (1/0), Carlos María Cuadra (1/0), Juan Pena (1/0), Aniceto Camacho (1/0), Alejandro Cordero (2/0), Cándido Hernández Betancor (1/0).

4. 15.08.1906 **URUGUAY - ARGENTINA** **0-2(0-1)** Copa Lipton
Estadio Parque Central, Montevideo; Referee: Guillermo McFarlane (Argentina), Attendance: 5,000
URU: Cayetano Saporiti (2/0), Carlos Carve Urioste (4/0), Ernesto Boutón Reyes (4/0), Ceferino Camacho (2/0), Félix Lourtet (1/0), Carlos Cibils Juárez (1/0), Pedro Zibechi (1/0), Juan Pena (2/0), Aniceto Camacho (2/0), Alejandro Cordero (3/0), Cándido Hernández Betancor (2/0).

5. 21.10.1906 **ARGENTINA - URUGUAY** **2-1(1-0)** Copa Newton
Estadio Campo de la Sociedad Sportiva, Buenos Aires; Referee: Guillermo Jordán (Argentina), Attendance: 4,000
URU: Cayetano Saporiti (3/0), Martín Aphesteguy (1/0), Juan Carlos Bertone (1/0), Luis Piñeyro Carve (1/0), Francisco Branda (1/0), Enrique Sanderson (1/0), Rafael De Miquelerena (1/0), Juan Pena (3/0), Gilberto Peralta (1/1), Alberto Zumarán (1/0), Cándido Hernández Betancor (3/0).
Goal: Gilberto Peralta (87).

6. 15.08.1907 **ARGENTINA - URUGUAY** **2-1(2-0)** Copa Lipton
Estadio Estudiantes, Buenos Aires; Referee: Guillermo Leslie (Argentina), Attendance: 7,000
URU: Santiago Demarchi (1/0), Juan Carlos Bertone (2/0), Marcos Frommel (1/0), Ceferino Camacho (3/0), Francisco Branda (2/0), Pedro Zuazú (1/0), Rafael De Miquelerena (2/0), Juan Pena (4/0), Aniceto Camacho (3/0), Eugenio Mañana (1/0), Pedro Zibechi (2/2).
Goal: Pedro Zibechi (68).

7. 06.10.1907 **URUGUAY - ARGENTINA** **1-2(0-1)** Copa Newton
Estadio Parque Central, Montevideo; Referee: Cecil Poole (Uruguay), Attendance: 9,000
URU: Santiago Demarchi (2/0), Juan Fernández de la Sierra (1/0), Juan Carlos Bertone (3/0), Luis Piñeyro Carve (2/0), Francisco Branda (3/0), Pedro Zuazú (2/0), Rafael De Miquelerena (3/0), Alberto Cantury (1/0), Luis Panizzi (1/0), Alberto Zumarán (2/1), Pedro Zibechi (3/2).
Goal: Alberto Zumarán (55).

8. 15.08.1908 **URUGUAY - ARGENTINA** **2-2(1-1)** Copa Lipton
Estadio Parque Central, Montevideo; Referee: Léon Peyrou (Uruguay), Attendance: 7,000
URU: Cayetano Saporiti (4/0), Juan Carlos Bertone (4/1), Marcos Frommel (2/0), Carlos Marques Castro (1/0), Luis Carbone (4/0), Ceferino Camacho (4/0), Vicente Módena (1/0), Pablo Dacal (1/0), Alberto Cantury (2/0), Raúl Ribeyro (1/0), Alberto Zumarán (3/2).
Goals: Alberto Zumarán (28), Juan Carlos Bertone (75).

9. 13.09.1908 **ARGENTINA - URUGUAY** **2-1(1-0)** Copa Newton
Estadio Club Gymnasia y Esgrima, Buenos Aires; Referee: Mariano Reyna (Argentina), Attendance: 7,000
URU: Cayetano Saporiti (5/0), Juan Carlos Bertone (5/1), Marcos Frommel (3/0), Ceferino Camacho (5/0), Luis Carbone (5/0), Guillermo Manito (1/0), Vicente Módena (2/0), Pablo Dacal (2/0), Alberto Cantury (3/0), Alberto Zumarán (4/2), José Brachi (1/1).
Goal: José Brachi (82).

10. 04.10.1908 **ARGENTINA - URUGUAY** **0-1(0-0)** Premio de Honor Argentino
Estadio Club Gymnasia y Esgrima, Buenos Aires; Referee: Mariano Reyna (Argentina), Attendance: 7,000
URU: Cayetano Saporiti (6/0), Aníbal Zapicán Falco (1/0), Federico Crocker (1/0), Ceferino Camacho (6/0), Luis Carbone (6/0), Pedro Zuazú (3/0), Vicente Módena (3/0), Pablo Dacal (3/0), Alberto Cantury (4/0), Juan Pena (5/0), José Brachi (2/2).
Goal: José Brachi (82).

11. 15.08.1909 **ARGENTINA - URUGUAY** **2-1(2-0)** Copa Lipton
Estadio Club Gymnasia y Esgrima, Buenos Aires; Referee: Guillermo Jordán (Argentina), Attendance: 4,000
URU: Cayetano Saporiti (7/0), Aníbal Zapicán Falco (2/0), Juan Carlos Bertone (6/1), Félix Lourtet (2/0), Pedro Zuazú (4/0), Carlos Ronzoni (1/0), Vicente Módena (4/0), Pablo Dacal (4/0), Carlos Scarone (1/0), Alberto Zumarán (5/3), José Brachi (3/2).
Goal: Alberto Zumarán (88).

12. 19.09.1909 **URUGUAY - ARGENTINA** **2-2(0-2)** Copa Newton
Estadio Parque Belvedere, Montevideo; Referee: Juan Dall'Orto (Uruguay), Attendance: 9,000
URU: Cayetano Saporiti (8/0), Aníbal Zapicán Falco (3/0), Juan Carlos Bertone (7/1), Alberto García (1/0), Juan Harley (1/0), Pedro Zuazú (5/0), Robert Sidney Buck (1/1), Felipe Canavessi (1/0), Santiago Raymonda (1/1), Juan Pena (6/0), José Brachi (4/2).
Goals: Santiago Raymonda (59), Robert Sidney Buck (68).

13. 10.10.1909 **ARGENTINA - URUGUAY** **3-1(2-1)** Premio de Honor Argentino
Estadio Club Gymnasia y Esgrima, Buenos Aires; Referee: Apeles Bordabehere (Uruguay), Attendance: 6,500
URU: Ángel Cavallotti (1/0), Aníbal Zapicán Falco (4/0), Juan Carlos Bertone (8/1), Félix Lourtet (3/0), Pedro Zuazú (6/0), Alberto García (2/0), Felipe Canavessi (2/0), Juan Pena (7/0), José Piendibene (1/0), Santiago Raymonda (2/2), José Brachi (5/2).
Goal: Santiago Raymonda (35).

14. 29.05.1910 **URUGUAY - CHILE** **3-0(1-0)** May Revolution Centenary Cup
Estadio Colegiales en Palermo, Buenos Aires; Referee: Maximiliano Susan (Argentina), Attendance: 6,000
URU: Cayetano Saporiti (9/0), Juan Carlos Bertone (9/1), Federico Crocker (2/0), Juan Pena (8/0), Juan Harley (2/0), Pedro Zuazú (7/0), Robert Sidney Buck (2/2), Pablo Dacal (5/0), José Piendibene (2/1), Santiago Raymonda (3/2), José Brachi (6/3).
Goals: José Piendibene (5), José Brachi (75), Robert Sidney Buck (85).

15. 12.06.1910 **ARGENTINA - URUGUAY** **4-1(2-0)** May Revolution Centenary Cup
Estadio Club Gymnasia y Esgrima, Buenos Aires; Referee: Armando Bergalli (Chile), Attendance: 8,000
URU: Cayetano Saporiti (10/0), Juan Carlos Bertone (10/1), José Benincasa (1/0), Juan Pena (9/0), Martín Aphesteguy (2/0), Pedro Zuazú (8/0), Robert Sidney Buck (3/2), Pablo Dacal (6/0), José Piendibene (3/2), Santiago Raymonda (4/2), José Brachi (7/3).
Goals: José Piendibene (58).

16. 15.08.1910 **URUGUAY - ARGENTINA** **3-1(1-0)** Copa Lipton
Estadio Parque Belvedere, Montevideo; Referee: Léon Peyrou (Uruguay), Attendance: 8,000
URU: Cayetano Saporiti (11/0), Juan Carlos Bertone (11/1), José Benincasa (2/0), Jorge Germán Pacheco (1/0), Oscar Sanz (1/0), Juan Pena (10/0), Vicente Módena (5/0), Pablo Dacal (7/1), José Piendibene (4/2), Carlos Scarone (2/1), Pedro Zibechi (4/1).
Goals: Pablo Dacal (22), Pedro Ziberchi (49), Carlos Scarone (63).

17. 13.11.1910 **ARGENTINA - URUGUAY** **1-1(0-0,1-1)** Premio de Honor Argentino
Estadio Club Gymnasia y Esgrima, Buenos Aires; Referee: Héctor Alfano (Argentina), Attendance: 5,000
URU: Cayetano Saporiti (12/0), Martín Aphestegui (3/0), José Benincasa (3/0), Jorge Germán Pacheco (2/0), Juan Harley (3/0), Pedro Zuazú (9/0), Vicente Módena (6/0), Luis Quaglia (1/0), José Piendibene (5/3), Carlos Scarone (3/1), Pedro Seoane (1/0).
Goal: José Piendibene (49).

18. 27.11.1910 **ARGENTINA - URUGUAY** **2-6(1-5)** Premio de Honor Argentino
Estadio Club Gymnasia y Esgrima, Buenos Aires; Referee: Héctor Alfano (Argentina), Attendance: 10,000
URU: Leonardo Crossley (1/0), Martín Aphesteguy (4/0), José Benincasa (4/0), Jorge Germán Pacheco (3/0), Juan Harley (4/0), Pedro Zuazú (10/0), Vicente Módena (7/0), Luis Quaglia (2/1), José Piendibene (6/4), Carlos Scarone (4/3), Pedro Seoane (2/2).
Goals: Luis Quaglia (4), Pedro Seoane (35), José Piendibene (37), Carlos Scarone (40, 44), Pedro Seoane (65).

19. 15.08.1911 **ARGENTINA - URUGUAY** **0-2(0-0)** Copa Lipton
Estadio Club Gymnasia y Esgrima, Buenos Aires; Referee: Héctor Alfano (Argentina), Attendance: 15,000
URU: Cayetano Saporiti (13/0), Carlos Ronzoni (2/0), José Benincasa (5/0), Jorge Germán Pacheco (4/0), José Maria Durán Guani (1/0), Ramón Ríos (1/0), José Brachi (8/3), Pablo Dacal (8/1), José Piendibene (7/5), Ángel Romano (1/1), Pascual Somma (1/0).
Goals: José Piendibene (84), Ángel Romano (88).

20. 17.09.1911 **URUGUAY - ARGENTINA** **2-3(0-1)** Copa Newton
Estadio Parque Central, Montevideo; Referee: Álvaro Saralegui (Uruguay), Attendance: 15,000
URU: Cayetano Saporiti (14/0), Carlos Ronzoni (3/0), Martín Aphesteguy (5/0), Jorge Germán Pacheco (5/0), Juan Harley (5/0), Ramón Ríos (2/0), José Brachi (9/3), Felipe Canavessi (3/1), José Piendibene (8/5), Ángel Romano (2/2), Pascual Somma (2/0).
Goals: Felipe Canavessi (58), Ángel Romano (60).

21. 08.10.1911 **URUGUAY - ARGENTINA** **1-1(0-1,1-1)** Premio de Honor Uruguayo
Estadio Parque Central, Montevideo; Referee: Léon Peyrou (Uruguay), Attendance: 12,000
URU: Cayetano Saporiti (15/0), Carlos Ronzoni (4/0), Martín Aphesteguy (6/0), Jorge Germán Pacheco (6/0), Juan Harley (6/0), Ramón Ríos (3/0), Vicente Módena (8/0), Pablo Dacal (9/1), José Piendibene (9/6), Felipe Canavessi (4/1), Ángel Romano (3/2).
Goal: José Piendibene (68).

22. 22.10.1911 **ARGENTINA - URUGUAY** **2-0(2-0)** Premio de Honor Argentino
Estadio Club Gymnasia y Esgrima, Buenos Aires; Referee: Héctor Alfano (Argentina), Attendance: 18,000
URU: Cayetano Saporiti (16/0), Edmundo Novoa (1/0), Miguel Aphesteguy (1/0), Jorge Germán Pacheco (7/0), Juan Harley (7/0), Ramón Ríos (4/0), Vicente Módena (9/0), Pablo Dacal (10/1), José Piendibene (10/6), Felipe Canavessi (5/1), Ángel Romano (4/2).

23. 29.10.1911 **URUGUAY - ARGENTINA** **3-0(1-0)** Premio de Honor Uruguayo
Estadio Parque Central, Montevideo; Referee: Juan Dall'Orto (Uruguay), Attendance: 15,000
URU: Cayetano Saporiti (17/0), Miguel Aphesteguy (2/0), Martín Aphesteguy (7/0), Jorge Germán Pacheco (8/0), Juan Harley (8/0), Ramón Ríos (5/0), Vicente Módena (10/0), Pablo Dacal (11/1), José Piendibene (11/8), Felipe Canavessi (6/2), Ángel Romano (5/2).
Goals: José Piendibene (13, 74), Felipe Canavessi (81).

24. 15.08.1912 **URUGUAY - ARGENTINA** **2-0(1-0)** Copa Lipton
Estadio Parque Central, Montevideo; Referee: Álvaro Saralegui (Uruguay), Attendance: 18,000
URU: Cayetano Saporiti (18/0), José Benincasa (6/0), Martín Aphesteguy (8/0), Jorge Germán Pacheco (9/0), José Maria Durán Guani (2/0), Alfredo Foglino (1/0), Vicente Módena (11/0), Pablo Dacal (12/2), José Piendibene (12/8), Carlos Scarone (5/4), Ángel Romano (6/2).
Goals: Pablo Dacal (24), Carlos Scarone (56).

25. 25.08.1912 **URUGUAY - ARGENTINA** **3-0(2-0)** Premio de Honor Uruguayo
Estadio Parque Central, Montevideo; Referee: Álvaro Saralegui (Uruguay), Attendance: 18,000
URU: Cayetano Saporiti (19/0), José Benincasa (7/0), Martín Aphesteguy (9/0), Jorge Germán Pacheco (10/0), José María Durán Guani (3/0), Alfredo Foglino (2/0), Vicente Módena (12/0), Pablo Dacal (13/3), José Piendibene (13/8), Carlos Scarone (6/5), Ángel Romano (7/3).
Goals: Pablo Dacal (33), Carlos Scarone (43), Ángel Romano (77).

26. 22.09.1912 **ARGENTINA - URUGUAY** **0-1(0-0)** Premio de Honor Uruguayo
Estadio Club Gymnasia y Esgrima, Buenos Aires; Referee: Guillermo Jordán (Argentina), Attendance: 18,000
URU: Cayetano Saporiti (20/0), José Benincasa (8/0), Martín Aphesteguy (10/0), Jorge Germán Pacheco (11/0), José María Durán Guani (4/0), Alfredo Foglino (3/0), Vicente Módena (13/0), Pablo Dacal (14/3), José Piendibene (14/8), Carlos Scarone (7/5), Ángel Romano (8/3).
Goal: Arturo Reparaz (79 own goal).

27. 06.10.1912 **ARGENTINA - URUGUAY** **3-3(1-2)** Copa Newton
Estadio Racing Club, Avellaneda; Referee: Héctor Alfano (Argentina), Attendance: 12,000
URU: Cayetano Saporiti (21/0), José Benincasa (9/0), Martín Aphesteguy (11/0), Jorge Germán Pacheco (12/0), José María Durán Guani (5/0), Alfredo Foglino (4/0), Vicente Módena (14/0), Pablo Dacal (15/4), José Piendibene (15/8), Carlos Scarone (8/6), Ángel Romano (9/4).
Goals: Ángel Romano (17), Pablo Dacal (38), Carlos Scarone (78).

28. 01.12.1912 **URUGUAY - ARGENTINA** **1-3(1-1,1-1)** Copa Montevideo
Estadio Parque Central, Montevideo; Referee: Juan Bartolazzo (Uruguay), Attendance: 12,000
URU: Cayetano Saporiti (22/0), Francisco Castellino (1/0), Martín Aphesteguy (12/0), Jorge Germán Pacheco (13/0), José Maria Durán Guani (6/0), Alfredo Foglino (5/0), Antonio Marques Castro (1/0), Pablo Dacal (16/4), Luis Quaglia (3/1), Carlos Scarone (9/7), Ángel Romano (10/4).
Goal: Carlos Scarone (28).

29. 15.06.1913 **ARGENTINA - URUGUAY** **1-1(0-1,1-1)*** Copa Presídente Roque Sáenz Peña
Estadio Racing Club, Avellaneda; Referee: Héctor Alfano (Argentina), Attendance: 12,000
URU: Santiago Demarchi (3/0), Miguel Aphesteguy (3/0), Alfredo Granja (1/0), Jorge Germán Pacheco (14/0), José Maria Durán Guani (7/0), Bernardo Savio (1/0), Ángel Romano (11/4), Pablo Dacal (17/4), Lucio Gorla (1/1), Pedro Seoane (3/2), Antonio Farinasso (1/0).
Goal: Lucio Gorla (31).
**After 17 mins extra-time, the match was stopped due to nightfall*

30. 09.07.1913 **ARGENTINA - URUGUAY** **2-1(1-1)** Copa Presídente Roque Sáenz Peña
Estadio Racing Club, Avellaneda; Referee: Héctor Alfano (Argentina), Attendance: 12,000
URU: Cayetano Saporiti (23/0), José Benincasa (10/0), Martín Aphesteguy (13/0), Jorge Germán Pacheco (15/0), José Maria Durán Guani (8/0), Bernardo Savio (2/0), Vicente Módena (15/0) [30.Juan Delgado (1/0)], Carlos Bastos (1/1), José Piendibene (16/8) [46.Luis Altamirano (1/0)], Pedro Seoane (4/2), Antonio Farinasso (2/0).
Goal: Carlos Bastos (7).

31. 15.08.1913 **ARGENTINA - URUGUAY** **4-0(2-0)** Copa Lipton
Estadio Racing Club, Avellaneda; Referee: José Susán (Argentina), Attendance: 15,000
URU: Cayetano Saporiti (24/0), José Benincasa (11/0), Martín Aphesteguy (14/0), Jorge Germán Pacheco (16/0), José Maria Durán Guani (9/0), Bernardo Savio (3/0), José Pérez (1/0), Pablo Dacal (18/4), José Piendibene (17/8), Ricardo Vallarino (1/0), Luis Altamirano (2/0).

32. 31.08.1913 **ARGENTINA - URUGUAY** **2-0(0-0)** Premio de Honor Uruguayo
Estadio Club Gymnasia y Esgrima, Buenos Aires; Referee: Carlos Aerst (Argentina), Attendance: 8,500
URU: Cayetano Saporiti (25/0), José Benincasa (12/0), Alfredo Granja (2/0), Jorge Germán Pacheco (17/0), Juan Delgado (2/0), Alfredo Foglino (6/0), José Pérez (2/0), Lucio Gorla (2/1), José Tognola (1/0), Antonio Farinasso (3/0), Alberto Landeira (1/0).

33. 05.10.1913 **URUGUAY - ARGENTINA** **1-0(0-0)** Premio de Honor Uruguayo
Estadio Parque Central, Montevideo; Referee: Hugo Gondra (Argentina), Attendance: 10,000
URU: Cayetano Saporiti (26/0), José Benincasa (13/0), Martín Aphesteguy (15/0), Jorge Germán Pacheco (18/0), Juan Harley (9/0), Alfredo Foglino (7/0), Antonio Retta (1/0), Pablo Dacal (19/4), Lucio Gorla (3/1), Ricardo Vallarino (2/1), Pedro Zibechi (5/2).
Goal: Ricardo Vallarino (80).

34. 26.10.1913 **URUGUAY - ARGENTINA** **1-0(0-0)** Copa Newton
Estadio Parque Central, Montevideo; Referee: Hugo Gondra (Argentina), Attendance: 12,000
URU: Cayetano Saporiti (27/0), José Benincasa (14/0), Martín Aphesteguy (16/0), Jorge Germán Pacheco (19/0), Juan Harley (10/0), Alfredo Foglino (8/0), Manuel Lázaro (1/0), Pablo Dacal (20/4), Lucio Gorla (4/2), Ricardo Vallarino (3/1), Luis Altamirano (3/0).
Goal: Lucio Gorla (62).

35. 30.08.1914 **URUGUAY - ARGENTINA** **3-2(1-1)** Premio de Honor Uruguayo
Estadio Parque Central, Montevideo; Referee: Luis Farinasso (Uruguay), Attendance: 8,000
URU: Ángel Cavallotti (2/0), José Benincasa (15/0), Alfredo Granja (3/0), Fausto Broncini (1/0), Juan Harley (11/0), Alfredo Foglino (9/0), Carlos Bastos (2/1), Pablo Dacal (21/5), José Piendibene (18/8), Ricardo Vallarino (4/2), Manuel Lázaro (2/0).
Goals: Ricardo Vallarino (29), Pablo Dacal (49), Antonio Bruno (53 own goal).

36. 13.09.1914 **ARGENTINA - URUGUAY** **2-1(1-0)** Premio de Honor Argentino
Estadio Club Gymnasia y Esgrima, Buenos Aires; Referee: Ángel Landoni (Uruguay), Attendance: 12,500
URU: Cayetano Saporiti (28/0), José Benincasa (16/0), Alfredo Granja (4/0), Fausto Broncini (2/0), Juan Harley (12/0), Alfredo Foglino (10/0), José Pérez (3/0), Pablo Dacal (22/5), José Piendibene (19/8), Ricardo Vallarino (5/3), Antonio Farinasso (4/0).
Goal: Ricardo Vallarino (51).

37. 18.07.1915 **URUGUAY - ARGENTINA** **2-3(0-1)** Premio de Honor Uruguayo
Estadio Parque Central, Montevideo; Referee: Carlos Williams (Argentina), Attendance: 12,000
URU: Cayetano Saporiti (29/0), José Benincasa (17/0), Martín Aphesteguy (17/0), Bernardo Savio (4/0), Juan Harley (13/0), Manuel Varela (1/0), José Pérez (4/0), Pablo Dacal (23/6), José Tognola (2/0), Isabelino Gradín (1/0), Manuel Lázaro (3/1).
Goals: Pablo Dacal (59), Manuel Lázaro (79).

38. 15.08.1915 **ARGENTINA - URUGUAY** **2-1(0-1)** Copa Lipton
Estadio Club Gymnasia y Esgrima, Buenos Aires; Referee: Héctor Alfano (Argentina), Attendance: 18,000
URU: Cayetano Saporiti (30/0), José Benincasa (18/0), Manuel Varela (2/0), Jorge Germán Pacheco (20/0), Bernardo Savio (5/0), José Vanzzino (1/0), José Pérez (5/0), Pablo Dacal (24/6), José Piendibene (20/9), Ángel Romano (12/4), Manuel Lázaro (4/1).
Goal: José Piendibene (25).

39. 12.09.1915 **URUGUAY - ARGENTINA** **2-0(1-0)** Copa Newton
Estadio Parque Central, Montevideo; Referee: Carlos Williams (Argentina), Attendance: 12,000
URU: Dionisio Eguía (1/0), José Benincasa (19/0), Alfredo Foglino (11/0), Alfredo Zibechi (1/0), Juan Harley (14/0), José Vanzzino (2/0), José Pérez (6/0), Pablo Dacal (25/6), José Piendibene (21/11), Carlos Scarone (10/7), José Brachi (10/3).
Goals: José Piendibene (2, 62).

40. 02.07.1916 **URUGUAY - CHILE** **4-0(1-0)** 1st Copa América
Estadio Club Gymnasia y Esgrima, Buenos Aires (Argentina); Referee: Hugo Gronda (Argentina), Attendance: 3,000
URU: Cayetano Saporiti (31/0), Francisco Castellino (2/0), Alfredo Foglino (12/0), Jorge Germán Pacheco (21/0), Juan Delgado (3/0), Manuel Varela (3/0), Pascual Somma (3/0), Ángel Romano (13/4), José Piendibene (22/13), Isabelino Gradín (2/2), José Brachi (11/3).
Goals: José Piendibene (44), Isabelino Gradín (55, 70), José Piendibene (75).

41. 12.07.1916 **URUGUAY – BRAZIL** **2-1(0-1)** 1st Copa América
Estadio Club Gymnasia y Esgrima, Buenos Aires (Argentina); Referee: Carlos Fanta (Chile), Attendance: 20,000
URU: Cayetano Saporiti (32/0), Manuel Varela (4/0), Alfredo Foglino (13/0), Jorge Germán Pacheco (22/0), Juan Delgado (4/0), José Vanzzino (3/0), Pascual Somma (4/0), José Tognola (3/1), José Piendibene (23/13), Isabelino Gradín (3/3), Ángel Romano (14/4).
Goals: Isabelino Gradín (58), José Tognola (77).

42. 14.07.1916 **URUGUAY - CHILE** **4-1(2-0)**
Estadio Parque Central, Montevideo; Referee: Ángel Minoli (Uruguay), Attendance: 6,000
URU: Antonio Marques Castro (2/0), José Benincasa (20/0), Miguel Benincasa (1/0), Pedro Olivieri (1/0), Abdón Porta (1/1), Domingo Melogno (1/0), José Pérez (7/1), Pablo Dacal (26/6), Carlos Bastos (3/1), Carlos Scarone (11/9), Rodolfo Marán (1/0).
Goals: Carlos Scarone (14, 26), José Pérez (53), Abdón Porta (62).

43. 17.07.1916 **ARGENTINA - URUGUAY** **0-0** 1st Copa América
Estadio Racing Club, Avellaneda; Referee: Carlos Fanta (Chile), Attendance: 17,000
URU: Cayetano Saporiti (33/0), Miguel Benincasa (2/0), Alfredo Foglino (14/0), Juan Delgado (5/0), Alfredo Zibechi (2/0), Manuel Varela (5/0), Pascual Somma (5/0), José Tognola (4/1), José Piendibene (24/13), Isabelino Gradín (4/3), Rodolfo Marán (2/0).

44. 18.07.1916 **URUGUAY – BRAZIL** **0-1(0-1)**
Estadio Parque Central, Montevideo; Referee: Carlos Fanta (Chile), Attendance: 8,000
URU: Antonio Marques Castro (3/0), Antonio Urdinarán (1/0), Alfredo Foglino (15/0), Pedro Olivieri (2/0), Juan Harley (15/0), Pascual Pascuariello (1/0), José Pérez (8/1), Pablo Dacal (27/6), Alberto Broncini (1/0), Carlos Scarone (12/9), José Brachi (12/3).

45. 15.08.1916 **URUGUAY - ARGENTINA** **1-2(1-1)** Copa Lipton
Estadio Parque Central, Montevideo; Referee: José Di Lucca (Argentina), Attendance: 5,000
URU: Cayetano Saporiti (34/0), Manuel Marenco (1/0), Alfredo Foglino (16/0), Alfredo Zibechi (3/0), Juan Delgado (6/0), Pascual Pascuariello (2/0), Pascual Somma (6/0), Ángel Romano (15/4), José Piendibene (25/13), Isabelino Gradín (5/4), Rodolfo Marán (3/0).
Goals: Isabelino Gradín (28).

46. 15.08.1916 **ARGENTINA - URUGUAY** **3-1(0-1)** Copa Newton
Estadio Racing Club, Avellaneda; Referee: Luis Gil (Argentina), Attendance: 16,000
URU: Antonio Marques Castro (4/0), Antonio Urdinarán (2/0), Miguel Benincasa (3/0), Fausto Broncini (3/0), Juan Harley (16/0), Domingo Melogno (2/0), José Pérez (9/1), Pablo Dacal (28/6), Antonio Brienza (1/0), Carlos Scarone (13/9), Antonio Farinasso (5/1).
Goal: Antonio Farinasso (23).

47. 01.10.1916 **URUGUAY - ARGENTINA** **0-1(0-1)** Premio de Honor Uruguayo
Estadio Parque Belvedere, Montevideo; Referee: Ángel Minoli (Uruguay), Attendance: 7,000
URU: Cayetano Saporiti (35/0), Alfredo Granja (5/0), Alfredo Foglino (17/0), Pedro Olivieri (3/0), Juan Delgado (7/0), Bernardo Savio (6/0), Pascual Somma (7/0), Carlos Scarone (14/9), José Piendibene (26/13), Isabelino Gradín (6/4), Ángel Romano (16/4).

48. 01.10.1916 **ARGENTINA - URUGUAY** **7-2(2-0)** Copa Prensa
Estadio Racing Club, Avellaneda; Referee: Guillermo Jordán (Argentina), Attendance: 11,000
URU: Santiago Demarchi (4/0), José Benincasa (21/0), Antonio Urdinarán (3/0), Gregorio Rodríguez (1/0), Juan Harley (17/0), Pascual Pascuariello (3/0), José Pérez (10/1), Felipe Buffoni (1/1), Carlos Mongelar (1/1), Antonio Farinasso (6/1), Rodolfo Marán (4/0).
Goals: Felipe Buffoni (51), Carlos Mongelar (75).

49. 29.10.1916 **URUGUAY - ARGENTINA** **3-1(1-1)** Copa Prensa
Estadio Parque Central, Montevideo; Referee: Ricardo Vallarino (Uruguay), Attendance: 12,000
URU: Cayetano Saporiti (36/0), José Benincasa (22/0), Alfredo Foglino (18/0), Pedro Olivieri (4/0), Bernardo Savio (7/0), José Vanzzino (4/0), Pascual Somma (8/0), Carlos Mongelar (2/2), José Piendibene (27/13), Isabelino Gradín (7/6), Ángel Romano (17/4).
Goals: Isabelino Gradín (30), Carlos Mongelar (55), Isabelino Gradín (65).

50. 18.07.1917 **URUGUAY - ARGENTINA** **0-2(0-2)** Premio de Honor Uruguayo
Estadio Parque Central, Montevideo; Referee: Álvaro Saralegui (Uruguay), Attendance: 12,000
URU: Cayetano Saporiti (37/0), Manuel Varela (6/0), Alfredo Foglino (19/0), Jorge Germán Pacheco (23/0), Gregorio Rodríguez (2/0), José Vanzzino (5/0), Pascual Somma (9/0), Américo Carbone (1/0), Carlos Mongelar (3/2), Isabelino Gradín (8/6), Rodolfo Marán (5/0).

51. 15.08.1917 **ARGENTINA - URUGUAY** **1-0(1-0)** Copa Lipton
Estadio Racing Club, Avellaneda; Referee: Germán Guassone (Argentina), Attendance: 11,000
URU: Alfredo Balmelli (1/0), Antonio Urdinarán (4/0), Manuel Varela (7/0), Jorge Germán Pacheco (24/0), Juan Delgado (8/0), José Vanzzino (6/0), José Pérez (11/1), Carlos Scarone (15/9), Ángel Romano (18/4), Isabelino Gradín (9/6), Rodolfo Marán (6/0). Trainer: Ramón Platero (1).

52. 02.09.1917 **URUGUAY – ARGENTINA** **1-0(0-0)** Copa Newton
Estadio Parque Central, Montevideo; Referee: Ricardo Vallarino (Uruguay), Attendance: 15,000
URU: Cayetano Saporiti (38/0), Antonio Urdinarán (5/0), Manuel Varela (8/0), Jorge Germán Pacheco (25/0), Gregorio Rodríguez (3/0), José Vanzzino (7/0), José Pérez (12/1), Héctor Pedro Scarone (1/0), Ángel Romano (19/5), Carlos Scarone (16/9), Pascual Somma (10/0). Trainer: Ramón Platero (2).
Goal: Ángel Romano (83).

53. 30.09.1917 **URUGUAY - CHILE** **4-0(2-0)** 2nd Copa América
Estadio Parque Pereira, Montevideo; Referee: Germán Guassone (Argentina), Attendance: 23,000
URU: Cayetano Saporiti (39/0), Antonio Urdinarán (6/0), Manuel Varela (9/0), Jorge Germán Pacheco (26/0), Gregorio Rodríguez (4/0), José Vanzzino (8/0), José Pérez (13/1), Héctor Pedro Scarone (2/0), Ángel Romano (20/7), Carlos Scarone (17/11), Pascual Somma (11/0). Trainer: Ramón Platero (3).
Goals: Carlos Scarone (20), Ángel Romano (44), Carlos Scarone (62), Ángel Romano (75).

54. 07.10.1917 **URUGUAY - BRAZIL** **4-0(2-0)** 2nd Copa América
Estadio Parque Pereira, Montevideo; Referee: Germán Guassone (Argentina), Attendance: 21,000
URU: Cayetano Saporiti (40/0), Manuel Varela (10/0), Alfredo Foglino (20/0), Jorge Germán Pacheco (27/0), Gregorio Rodríguez (5/0), José Vanzzino (9/0), José Pérez (14/1), Héctor Pedro Scarone (3/1), Ángel Romano (21/9), Carlos Scarone (18/12), Pascual Somma (12/0). Trainer: Ramón Platero (4).
Goals: Héctor Pedro Scarone (8), Ángel Romano (17, 77), Carlos Scarone (86).

55. 14.10.1917 **URUGUAY - ARGENTINA** **1-0(0-0)** 2nd Copa América
Estadio Parque Pereira, Montevideo; Referee: Juan Livingstone (Chile), Attendance: 40,000
URU: Cayetano Saporiti (41/0), Manuel Varela (11/0), Alfredo Foglino (21/0), Jorge Germán Pacheco (28/0), Gregorio Rodríguez (6/0), José Vanzzino (10/0), José Pérez (15/1), Héctor Pedro Scarone (4/2), Ángel Romano (22/9), Carlos Scarone (19/12), Pascual Somma (13/0). Trainer: Ramón Platero (5).
Goal: Héctor Pedro Scarone (62).

56. 16.10.1917 **URUGUAY - BRAZIL** **3-1(3-1)**
Estadio Parque Pereira, Montevideo; Referee: Carlos Fanta (Chile)
URU: Alfredo Balmelli (2/0), José Benincasa (23/0), Miguel Benincasa (4/0), Pedro Olivieri (5/0), Abdón Porta (2/1), Nelson Montes (1/0), Pedro Etchart (1/0), Raúl Garrido (1/0), Luis Grecco (1/0), Isabelino Gradín (10/7), Rodolfo Marán (7/0). Trainer: Ramón Platero (6).
Goals: Luis Grecco (20, 30), Isabelino Gradín (43).

57. 18.07.1918 **URUGUAY - ARGENTINA** **1-1(1-1,1-1)** Premio de Honor Uruguayo
Estadio Parque Pereira, Montevideo; Referee: Álvaro Saralegui (Uruguay), Attendance: 30,000
URU: Cayetano Saporiti (42/0), José Benincasa (24/0), Alfredo Foglino (22/0), Ricardo Medina (1/0), Alfredo Zibechi (4/0), José Vanzzino (11/0), Américo Carbone (2/0), Ángel Romano (23/9), José Piendibene (28/13), Isabelino Gradín (11/8), Antonio Cámpolo (1/0). Trainer: Severino Castillo (1).
Goal: Isabelino Gradín (7).
**After 39 mins extra-time, the match was stopped due to nightfall*

58. 28.07.1918 **URUGUAY - ARGENTINA** **3-1(2-1)** Premio de Honor Uruguayo
Estadio Parque Pereira, Montevideo; Referee: Ángel Minoli (Uruguay), Attendance: 20,000
URU: Cayetano Saporiti (43/0), José Benincasa (25/0), Alfredo Foglino (23/0), Ricardo Medina (2/0), Alfredo Zibechi (5/0), José Vanzzino (12/0), Américo Carbone (3/0), Héctor Pedro Scarone (5/3), Ángel Romano (24/11), Isabelino Gradín (12/8), Pascual Somma (14/0). Trainer: Severino Castillo (2).
Goals: Héctor Pedro Scarone (7), Ángel Romano (9, 64).

59. 15.08.1918 **ARGENTINA - URUGUAY** **0-0** Premio de Honor Argentino
Estadio Club Gymnasia y Esgrima, Buenos Aires; Referee: Calixto Gardi (Argentina), Attendance: 18,000
URU: Cayetano Saporiti (44/0), José Benincasa (26/0), Alfredo Foglino (24/0), Juan Delgado (9/0), Alfredo Zibechi (6/0), José Vanzzino (13/0), José Pérez (16/1), Héctor Pedro Scarone (6/3), Ángel Romano (25/11), Isabelino Gradín (13/8), Pascual Somma (15/0). Trainer: Severino Castillo (3).

60. 25.08.1918 **ARGENTINA - URUGUAY** **2-1(2-1)** Premio de Honor Argentino
Estadio Club Gymnasia y Esgrima, Buenos Aires; Referee: Calixto Gardi (Argentina), Attendance: 12,000
URU: Cayetano Saporiti (45/0), José Benincasa (27/0), Alfredo Foglino (25/0), Juan Delgado (10/0), Alfredo Zibechi (7/0), Sadi Couture (1/0), José Pérez (17/1), Héctor Pedro Scarone (7/3), Ángel Romano (26/11), Isabelino Gradín (14/8), Pascual Somma (16/1). Trainer: Severino Castillo (4).
Goal: Pascual Somma (18).

61. 20.09.1918 **URUGUAY - ARGENTINA** **1-1(0-0)** Copa Lipton
Estadio Parque Pereira, Montevideo; Referee: Emilio Scoteguazza (Uruguay), Attendance: 15,000
URU: Cayetano Saporiti (46/0), José Benincasa (28/0), Alfredo Foglino (26/0), Juan Delgado (11/0), Alfredo Zibechi (8/0), José Vanzzino (14/0), José Pérez (18/1), Héctor Pedro Scarone (8/3), Carlos Scarone (20/13), Isabelino Gradín (15/8), Ángel Romano (27/11). Trainer: Severino Castillo (5).
Goal: Carlos Scarone (61).

62. 29.09.1918 **ARGENTINA - URUGUAY** **2-0(2-0)** Copa Newton
Estadio Club Gymnasia y Esgrima, Buenos Aires; Referee: Germán Guassone (Argentina), Attendance: 9,000
URU: Cayetano Saporiti (47/0), Santiago Anzuberro (1/0), Alfredo Foglino (27/0), Sadi Couture (2/0), Alfredo Zibechi (9/0), José Vanzzino (15/0), José Pérez (19/1), Héctor Pedro Scarone (9/3), Ángel Romano (28/11), Isabelino Gradín (16/8), Antonio Cámpolo (2/0). Trainer: Severino Castillo (6).

63. 13.05.1919 **URUGUAY – ARGENTINA** **3-2(2-1)** 3rd Copa América
Estádio das Estádio Laranjeiras, Rio de Janeiro (Brazil); Referee: Robert L. Todd (England), Attendance: 18,000
URU: Cayetano Saporiti (48/0), Manuel Varela (12/0), Alfredo Foglino (28/0), Juan Delgado (12/0), Alfredo Zibechi (10/0), José Vanzzino (16/0), José Pérez (20/1), Héctor Pedro Scarone (10/4), Carlos Scarone (21/14), Isabelino Gradín (17/9), Ángel Romano (29/11). Trainer: Severino Castillo (7).
Goals: Carlos Scarone (19), Héctor Pedro Scarone (23), Isabelino Gradín (85).

64. 17.05.1919 **URUGUAY – CHILE** **2-0(2-0)** 3rd Copa América
Estádio das Estádio Laranjeiras, Rio de Janeiro (Brazil); Referee: Adilon Ponteado (Brazil), Attendance: 7,000
URU: Roberto Chery (1/0), Manuel Varela (13/0), Alfredo Foglino (29/0), Rogelio Naguil (1/0), Alfredo Zibechi (11/0), José Vanzzino (17/0), José Pérez (21/2), Héctor Pedro Scarone (11/4), Carlos Scarone (22/15), Isabelino Gradín (18/9), Ángel Romano (30/11). Trainer: Severino Castillo (8).
Goals: Carlos Scarone (31), José Pérez (43).

65. 25.05.1919 **BRAZIL – URUGUAY** **2-2(1-2)** 3rd Copa América
Estádio das Estádio Laranjeiras, Rio de Janeiro; Referee: Robert L. Todd (England), Attendance: 23,000
URU: Cayetano Saporiti (49/0), Manuel Varela (14/0), Alfredo Foglino (30/0), Rogelio Naguil (2/0), Alfredo Zibechi (12/0), José Vanzzino (18/0), José Pérez (22/2), Héctor Pedro Scarone (12/4), Carlos Scarone (23/16), Isabelino Gradín (19/10), Rodolfo Marán (8/0). Trainer: Severino Castillo (9).
Goals: Isabelino Gradín (13), Carlos Scarone (17).

66. 29.05.1919 **BRAZIL - URUGUAY** **1-0(0-0,0-0*)** 3rd Copa América
Estádio das Estádio Laranjeiras, Rio de Janeiro; Referee: Juan Pedro Barbera (Argentina), Attendance: 35,000
URU: Cayetano Saporiti (50/0), Manuel Varela (15/0), Alfredo Foglino (31/0), Rogelio Naguil (3/0), Alfredo Zibechi (13/0), José Vanzzino (19/0), José Pérez (23/2), Héctor Pedro Scarone (13/4), Ángel Romano (31/11), Isabelino Gradín (20/10), Rodolfo Marán (9/0). Trainer: Severino Castillo (10).
**After 60 minutes extra time*

67. 18.07.1919 **URUGUAY – ARGENTINA** **4-1(4-0)** Premio de Honor Uruguayo
Estadio Parque Pereira, Montevideo; Referee: Martín Aphesteguy (Uruguay), Attendance: 15,000
URU: Vicente Clavijo (1/0), Manuel Varela (16/0), Alfredo Foglino (32/0), Juan Delgado (13/0), Alfredo Zibechi (14/0), Pascual Ruotta (1/0), Pascual Somma (17/1), Héctor Pedro Scarone (14/6), José María Villar (1/0), Ángel Romano (32/12), Omar Pérez (1/1). Trainer: Ernesto Fígoli (1).
Goals: Héctor Pedro Scarone (1), Omar Pérez (17), Héctor Pedro Scarone (22), Ángel Romano (24).

68. 24.08.1919 **URUGUAY – ARGENTINA** **2-1(2-0)** Copa Newton
Estadio Parque Pereira, Montevideo; Referee: Ángel Minoli (Uruguay), Attendance: 30,000
URU: Vicente Clavijo (2/0), Abraham Rébori (1/0), Alfredo Foglino (33/0), Pascual Ruotta (2/0), Alfredo Zibechi (15/0), José Vanzzino (20/0), José Pérez (24/2), Ángel Romano (33/12), José Piendibene (29/13), José María Villar (2/0), Omar Pérez (2/1). Trainer: Ernesto Fígoli (2).
Goals: Humberto Juan Recanatini (16 own goal), Roberto Castagnola (27 own goal).

69. 07.09.1919 **ARGENTINA - URUGUAY** **1-2(0-2)*** Copa Lipton
Estadio Club Gymnasia y Esgrima, Buenos Aires; Referee: Ricardo Palma (Argentina), Attendance: 17,000
URU: Vicente Clavijo (3/0), Manuel Varela (17/0), Alfredo Foglino (34/0), Pascual Ruotta (3/0), Alfredo Zibechi (16/0), José Vanzzino (21/0), Américo Carbone (4/0), Héctor Pedro Scarone (15/8), Ángel Romano (34/12), Isabelino Gradín (21/10), Pascual Somma (18/1). Trainer: Ernesto Fígoli (3).
Goals: Héctor Pedro Scarone (30, 42).
**Abandoned after 86 mins.*

70. 19.10.1919 **ARGENTINA - URUGUAY** **6-1(1-0)** Premio de Honor Argentino
Estadio Club Gymnasia y Esgrima, Buenos Aires; Referee: Juan José Rithner (Argentina), Attendance: 18,000
URU: Manuel Beloutas (1/0), Atilio Minoli (1/0), Alfredo Foglino (35/0), Desiderio Seijas (1/0), Alfredo Zibechi (17/0), Pascual Ruotta (4/0), Pascual Somma (19/1), Américo Carbone (5/0), Arturo Fraga (1/1), Ángel Romano (35/12), Rodolfo Marán (10/0). Trainer: Ernesto Fígoli (4).
Goal: Arturo Fraga (72).

71. 07.12.1919 **URUGUAY – ARGENTINA** **4-2(1-0)** Copa Prensa
Estadio Parque Pereira, Montevideo; Referee: Ricardo Vallarino (Uruguay), Attendance: 12,000
URU: Vicente Clavijo (4/0), José Benincasa (29/0), Alfredo Foglino (36/0), Pascual Ruotta (5/0), Alfredo Zibechi (18/0), José Vanzzino (22/0), José Pérez (25/2), Héctor Pedro Scarone (16/9), José Piendibene (30/16), Ángel Romano (36/12), Antonio Cámpolo (3/0). Trainer: Ernesto Fígoli (5).
Goals: José Piendibene (18, 47), Héctor Pedro Scarone (58), José Piendibene (79).

72. 18.07.1920 **URUGUAY - ARGENTINA** **2-0(1-0)** Premio de Honor Uruguayo
Estadio Parque Central, Montevideo; Referee: Martín Aphesteguy (Uruguay), Attendance: 25,000
URU: Juan Legnazzi (1/0), José Benincasa (30/0), Alfredo Foglino (37/0), Pascual Ruotta (6/0), Juan Delgado (14/0), Andrés Ravera (1/0), Pascual Somma (20/1), Héctor Pedro Scarone (17/10), José Piendibene (31/16), Ángel Romano (37/13), Antonio Cámpolo (4/0). Trainer: Ernesto Fígoli (6).
Goals: Héctor Pedro Scarone (18), Ángel Romano (56).

73. 25.07.1920 **ARGENTINA - URUGUAY** **1-3(1-2)** Copa Newton
Estadio Sportivo Barracas, Buenos Aires; Referee: Calixto Gardi (Argentina), Attendance: 18,000
URU: Juan Legnazzi (2/0), José Benincasa (31/0), Alfredo Foglino (38/0), Pascual Ruotta (7/0), Juan Delgado (15/0), Andrés Ravera (2/0), Pascual Somma (21/2), Héctor Pedro Scarone (18/10), José Piendibene (32/17), Ángel Romano (38/14), Antonio Cámpolo (5/0). Trainer: Ernesto Fígoli (7).
Goals: Ángel Romano (6), Pascual Somma (33), José Piendibene (85).

74. 08.08.1920 **ARGENTINA - URUGUAY** **1-0(0-0)** Premio de Honor Argentino
Estadio Sportivo Barracas, Buenos Aires; Referee: Fernando Díez (Argentina), Attendance: 15,000
URU: Juan Legnazzi (3/0), Antonio Urdinarán (7/0), Alfredo Foglino (39/0), Pascual Ruotta (8/0), Juan Delgado (16/0), Andrés Ravera (3/0), Pascual Somma (22/2), Ángel Romano (39/14), José Piendibene (33/17), Isabelino Gradín (22/10), Antonio Cámpolo (6/0). Trainer: Ernesto Fígoli (8).

75. 12.09.1920 **URUGUAY – ARGENTINA** **1-1(1-0)** 4th Copa América
Estadio Sporting Club, Valparaíso (Chile); Referee: Francisco Jiménez (Chile), Attendance: 17,000
URU: Juan Legnazzi (4/0), Antonio Urdinarán (8/0), Alfredo Foglino (40/0), Pascual Ruotta (9/0), Alfredo Zibechi (19/0), Andrés Ravera (4/0), Pascual Somma (23/2), José Pérez (26/2), José Piendibene (34/18), Ángel Romano (40/14), Antonio Cámpolo (7/0). Trainer: Ernesto Fígoli (9).
Goal: José Piendibene (10).

76. 18.09.1920 **URUGUAY - BRAZIL** **6-0(3-0)** 4th Copa América
Estadio Sporting Club, Valparaíso (Chile); Referee: Carlos Fanta (Chile), Attendance: 9,000
URU: Juan Legnazzi (5/0), Antonio Urdinarán (9/1), Alfredo Foglino (41/0), Pascual Ruotta (10/0), Alfredo Zibechi (20/0), Andrés Ravera (5/0), Pascual Somma (24/2), José Pérez (27/4), José Piendibene (35/18), Ángel Romano (41/16), Antonio Cámpolo (8/1). Trainer: Ernesto Fígoli (10).
Goals: Ángel Romano (23), Antonio Urdinarán (26), José Pérez (29), Antonio Cámpolo (48), Ángel Romano (60), José Pérez (65).

77. 26.09.1920 **CHILE – URUGUAY** **1-2(0-1)** 4th Copa América
Estadio Sporting Club, Valparaíso; Referee: Carlos Fanta (Chile), Attendance: 16,000
URU: Juan Legnazzi (6/0), Antonio Urdinarán (10/1), Alfredo Foglino (42/0), Pascual Ruotta (11/0), Alfredo Zibechi (21/0), Andrés Ravera (6/0), Pascual Somma (25/2), José Pérez (28/5), José Piendibene (36/18), Ángel Romano (42/17), Antonio Cámpolo (9/1). Trainer: Ernesto Fígoli (11).
Goals: Ángel Romano (37), José Pérez (65).

78. 09.10.1921 **PARAGUAY - URUGUAY** **2-1(1-0)** 5th Copa América
Estadio Sportivo Barracas, Buenos Aires (Argentina); Referee: Gerónimo Rapossi (Argentina), Attendance: 12,000
URU: Pedro Casella (1/0), José Benincasa (32/0), Alfredo Foglino (43/0), Fausto Broncini (4/0), Alfredo Zibechi (22/0), Sebastián Marroche (1/0), Pascual Somma (26/2), Luis Villazú (1/0), José Piendibene (37/19), Ángel Romano (43/17), Antonio Cámpolo (10/1). Trainer: Ernesto Fígoli (12).
Goal: José Piendibene (70).

79. 23.10.1921 **URUGUAY - BRAZIL** **2-1(2-0)** 5th Copa América
Estadio Sportivo Barracas, Buenos Aires (Argentina); Referee: Víctor Cabañas Saguier (Paraguay), Attendance: 10,000
URU: Manuel Beloutas (2/0), José Benincasa (33/0), Alfredo Foglino (44/0), Juan Molinari (1/0), Alfredo Zibechi (23/0), Fausto Broncini (5/0), Pascual Somma (27/2), Ángel Romano (44/19), José Piendibene (38/19), Norberto Cassanello (1/0), Antonio Cámpolo (11/1). Trainer: Ernesto Fígoli (13).
Goals: Ángel Romano (1, 8).

80. 30.10.1921 **ARGENTINA - URUGUAY** **1-0(0-0)**
Estadio Sportivo Barracas, Buenos Aires; Referee: Pedro Santos (Brazil), Attendance: 35,000
URU: Manuel Beloutas (3/0), José Benincasa (34/0), Alfredo Foglino (45/0), Juan Molinari (2/0), Alfredo Zibechi (24/0), José Vanzzino (23/0), Pascual Somma (28/2), Ángel Romano (45/19), José Piendibene (39/19), Norberto Cassanello (2/0), Antonio Cámpolo (12/1). Trainer: Ernesto Fígoli (14).

81. 02.11.1921 **URUGUAY – PARAGUAY** **4-2(2-1)**
Estadio Parque Central, Montevideo; Referee: Aurelio San Martín (Uruguay), Attendance: 8,000
URU: Manuel Beloutas (4/0), Marcos Lietti (1/0), Alfredo Foglino (46/0), Fausto Broncini (6/0), Armando Zibechi (1/0), Pedro Cabrera (1/0), Ladislao Pérez (1/0), Ángel Romano (46/19), Felipe Buffoni (2/4), Roberto Figueroa (1/0), Antonio Cámpolo (13/2). Trainer: Ernesto Fígoli (15).
Goals: Felipe Buffoni (14, 22), Antonio Cámpolo (49), Felipe Buffoni (53).

82. 23.09.1922 **URUGUAY - CHILE** **2-0(2-0)** 6th Copa América
Estádio das Estádio Laranjeiras, Rio de Janeiro (Brazil); Referee: Francisco Andreu Balcó (Paraguay), Attendance: 6,000
URU: Fausto Batignani (1/0), Antonio Urdinarán (11/2), Domingo Tejera (1/0), Antonio Aguerre (1/0), Alfredo Zibechi (25/0), José Vanzzino (24/0), Pascual Somma (29/2), Juan Carlos Heguy (1/1), Felipe Buffoni (3/4), Ángel Romano (47/19), Rodolfo Marán (11/0). Trainer: Pedro Olivieri (1).
Goals: Juan Carlos Heguy (10), Antonio Urdinarán (19).

83. 01.10.1922 **BRAZIL - URUGUAY** **0-0** 6th Copa América
Estádio das Estádio Laranjeiras, Rio de Janeiro; Referee: Servando Pérez (Argentina), Attendance: 30,000
URU: Fausto Batignani (2/0), Antonio Urdinarán (12/2), Domingo Tejera (2/0), Antonio Aguerre (2/0), Alfredo Zibechi (26/0), José Vanzzino (25/0), Pascual Somma (30/2), Juan Carlos Heguy (2/1), Ángel Romano (48/19), Norberto Cassanello (3/0), Rodolfo Marán (12/0). Trainer: Pedro Olivieri (2).

84. 08.10.1922 **URUGUAY - ARGENTINA** **1-0(1-0)** 6th Copa América
Estádio das Estádio Laranjeiras, Rio de Janeiro (Brazil); Referee: Pedro Santos (Brazil), Attendance: 14,000
URU: Fausto Batignani (3/0), Antonio Urdinarán (13/2), Domingo Tejera (3/0), Antonio Aguerre (3/0), Alfredo Zibechi (27/0), José Vanzzino (26/0), Pascual Somma (31/2), Ángel Romano (49/19), Felipe Buffoni (4/5), Norberto Cassanello (4/0), Juan Otero (1/0). Trainer: Pedro Olivieri (3).
Goal: Felipe Buffoni (43).

85. 12.10.1922 **PARAGUAY - URUGUAY** **1-0(1-0)** 6th Copa América
Estádio das Estádio Laranjeiras, Rio de Janeiro (Brazil); Referee: Pedro Santos (Brazil), Attendance: 3,000
URU: Fausto Batignani (4/0), Antonio Urdinarán (14/2), Domingo Tejera (4/0), Antonio Aguerre (4/0), Alfredo Zibechi (28/0), José Vanzzino (27/0), Pascual Somma (32/2), Ángel Romano (50/19), Felipe Buffoni (5/5), Norberto Cassanello (5/0), Juan Otero (2/0). Trainer: Pedro Olivieri (4).

86. 12.11.1922 **URUGUAY - ARGENTINA** **1-0(1-0)** Copa Lipton
Estadio Parque Central, Montevideo; Referee: Ricardo Vallarino (Uruguay), Attendance: 12,000
URU: Fausto Batignani (5/0), Antonio Urdinarán (15/2), Domingo Tejera (5/0), Antonio Aguerre (5/0), Alfredo Zibechi (29/0), Rogelio Naguil (4/0), Pascual Somma (33/2), Ángel Romano (51/20), Felipe Buffoni (6/5), Norberto Cassanello (6/0), Rodolfo Marán (13/0). Trainer: Rafael Galli (1).
Goal: Ángel Romano (26).

87. 10.12.1922 **URUGUAY - ARGENTINA** **1-0(1-0)** Premio de Honor Uruguayo
Estadio Parque Central, Montevideo; Referee: Aurelio San Martín (Uruguay), Attendance: 8,000
URU: Manuel Beloutas (5/0), Antonio Urdinarán (16/2), Domingo Tejera (6/0), Antonio Aguerre (6/0), Alfredo Zibechi (30/0), Orestes Del Cioppo (1/0), Pascual Somma (34/2), Héctor Pedro Scarone (19/10), Carlos Scarone (24/17), Norberto Cassanello (7/0), Zoilo Saldombide (1/0). Trainer: Rafael Galli (2).
Goal: Carlos Scarone (5).

88. 17.12.1922 **ARGENTINA - URUGUAY** **2-2(2-1)** Copa Newton
Estadio Sportivo Barracas, Buenos Aires. Ref: Gerónimo Rapossi (Argentina), Attendance: 16,000
URU: Manuel Beloutas (6/0), Antonio Urdinarán (17/2), Domingo Tejera (7/0), Antonio Aguerre (7/0), Gregorio Rodríguez (7/0), Jaime Bérgolo (1/1), Héctor Pedro Scarone (20/10), Héctor Olivieri (1/0), Carlos Scarone (25/18), Norberto Cassanello (8/0), Zoilo Saldombide (2/0). Trainer: Rafael Galli (3).
Goals: Carlos Scarone (13), Jaime Bérgolo (56).

89. 24.06.1923 **ARGENTINA - URUGUAY** **0-0** Copa Lipton
Estadio Sportivo Barracas, Buenos Aires; Referee: Gerónimo Rapossi (Argentina), Attendance: 30,000
URU: Manuel Beloutas (7/0), Alberto Nogués (1/0), Fermín Uriarte (1/0), Gregorio Rodríguez (8/0), Alfredo Zibechi (31/0), Jaime Bérgolo (2/1), Atilio Patiño (1/0), José Leandro Andrade (1/0), Héctor Olivieri (2/0), Ángel Romano (52/20), Pascual Somma (35/2). Trainer: Leonardo de Lucca (1).

90. 15.07.1923 **ARGENTINA - URUGUAY** **2-2(1-0)** Premio de Honor Argentino
Estadio Sportivo Barracas, Buenos Aires; Referee: Héctor Alfano (Argentina), Attendance: 25,000
URU: Pedro Casella (2/0), Alberto Nogués (2/0), Fermín Uriarte (2/0), Gregorio Rodríguez (9/0), Alfredo Zibechi (32/1), Jaime Bérgolo (3/1), Pascual Somma (36/2), Vital Ruffati (1/0), Héctor Olivieri (3/0), Ángel Romano (53/21), Rodolfo Marán (14/0). Trainer: Leonardo de Lucca (2).
Goals: Alfredo Zibechi (65), Ángel Romano (72).

91. 22.07.1923 **URUGUAY - ARGENTINA** **2-2(2-0)** Premio de Honor Uruguayo
Estadio Parque Central, Montevideo; Referee: Ricardo Vallarino (Uruguay), Attendance: 10,000
URU: Pedro Casella (3/0), Alberto Nogués (3/0), Alfredo Foglino (47/0), Gregorio Rodríguez (10/0), Alfredo Zibechi (33/1), José Vanzzino (28/0), Pascual Somma (37/2), Héctor Pedro Scarone (21/10), Felipe Buffoni (7/5), Ángel Romano (54/22), Zoilo Saldombide (3/1). Trainer: Leonardo de Lucca (3).
Goals: Ángel Romano (9), Zoilo Saldombide (15).

92. 30.09.1923 **URUGUAY - ARGENTINA** **0-2(0-2)** Premio de Honor Uruguayo
Estadio Parque Central, Montevideo; Referee: José Rami (Uruguay), Attendance: 7,000
URU: Pedro Casella (4/0), Juan Santero (1/0), Fermín Uriarte (3/0), Pedro Zingone (1/0), Alfredo Zibechi (34/1), Gregorio Rodríguez (11/0), Santos Urdinarán (1/0), Héctor Pedro Scarone (22/10), Héctor Olivieri (4/0), Ángel Romano (55/22), Pascual Somma (38/2). Trainer: Leonardo de Lucca (4).

93. 04.11.1923 **URUGUAY – PARAGUAY** **2-0(1-0)** 7th Copa América
Estadio Parque Central, Montevideo; Referee: Servando Pérez (Argentina), Attendance: 20,000
URU: Pedro Casella (5/0), José Nasazzi Yarza (1/0), Fermín Uriarte (4/0), José Leandro Andrade (2/0), José Vidal (1/0), Alfredo Juan Ghierra (1/0), Ladislao Pérez (2/0), Héctor Pedro Scarone (23/11), Pedro Petrone (1/1), José Pedro Cea (1/0), Pascual Somma (39/2). Trainer: Leonardo de Lucca (5).
Goals: Héctor Pedro Scarone (11), Pedro Petrone (88).

94. 25.11.1923 **URUGUAY - BRAZIL** **2-1(0-0)** 7th Copa América
Estadio Parque Central, Montevideo; Referee: Servando Pérez (Argentina), Attendance: 20,000
URU: Pedro Casella (6/0), José Nasazzi Yarza (2/0), Fermín Uriarte (5/0), José Leandro Andrade (3/0), José Vidal (2/0), Alfredo Juan Ghierra (2/0), Ladislao Pérez (3/0), Héctor Pedro Scarone (24/11), Pedro Petrone (2/2), José Pedro Cea (2/1), Pascual Somma (40/2). Trainer: Leonardo de Lucca (6).
Goals: Pedro Petrone (59), José Pedro Cea (75).

95. 25.11.1923 **URUGUAY – CHILE** **2-1(1-1)**
Estadio Pocitos, Montevideo; Referee: Juan Reybaud (Uruguay), Attendance: 10,000
URU: Alfonso Brugnoli (1/0), Pascual Bonchiani (1/0), Domingo Tejera (8/0), Manuel Méndez (1/0), Gildeón Silva (1/0), Horacio Acuña (1/0), Lorenzo Varoli (1/0), Norberto Cassanello (9/0), José Piendibene (40/20), Héctor Castro (1/1), Antonio Cámpolo (14/2). Trainer: Alberto Horacio Suppici (1).
Goals: Héctor Castro (22), José Piendibene (72).

96. 02.12.1923 **URUGUAY - ARGENTINA** **2-0(1-0)** 7th Copa América
Estadio Parque Central, Montevideo; Referee: Antônio Carneiro de Campos (Brazil), Attendance: 22,000
URU: Pedro Casella (7/0), José Nasazzi Yarza (3/0), Fermín Uriarte (6/0), José Leandro Andrade (4/0), José Vidal (3/0), Alfredo Juan Ghierra (3/0), Pascual Somma (41/3), Héctor Pedro Scarone (25/11), Pedro Petrone (3/3), José Pedro Cea (3/1), Ladislao Pérez (4/0). Trainer: Leonardo de Lucca (7).
Goals: Pedro Petrone (28), Pascual Somma (88).

97. 08.12.1923 **ARGENTINA - URUGUAY** **2-3(2-1)** Copa Ministro
Estadio Racing Club, Avellaneda; Referee: Pascual Gilio (Argentina), Attendance: 8,000
URU: Juan Legnazzi (7/0), Luis Merli (1/0), Domingo Tejera (9/0), Antonio Aguerre (8/0), Gildeón Silva (2/0), Ricardo Miramontes (1/0), Juan Pedro Arremón (1/0), Héctor Castro (2/3), René Borjas (1/1), Norberto Cassanello (10/0), Antonio Cámpolo (15/2). Trainer: Alberto Horacio Suppici (2).
Goals: Héctor Castro (18), René Borjas (55), Héctor Castro (63).

98. 25.05.1924 **URUGUAY - ARGENTINA** **2-0(1-0)** Copa Newton
Estadio Parque Central, Montevideo; Referee: José Rami (Uruguay), Attendance: 12,000
URU: Máximo Maturell (1/0), Alberto Nogués (4/0), Manuel Varela (18/0), Alberto Melogno (1/0), Emilio Bertone (1/0), Acevedo Alvarez (1/0), Atilio Patiño (2/0), Arturo Suffiotti (1/1), Camilo Bondanza (1/0), Roberto Figueroa (2/1), Juan Gemelli (1/0). Trainer: Manuel Varela (1).
Goals: Roberto Figueroa (24), Arturo Suffiotti (69).

99. 25.05.1924 **ARGENTINA - URUGUAY** **4-0(3-0)** Copa Newton
Estadio Sportivo Barracas, Buenos Aires; Referee: Lorenzo Muzzio (Argentina), Attendance: 6,000
URU: Vicente Clavijo (5/0), Juan Santero (2/0), José Pardiñas (1/0), Juan Carlos Alzugaray (1/0), Gregorio Rodríguez (12/0), Pascual Cabrera (1/0), Manuel Pardiñas (1/0), Luis Villazú (2/0), Atilio Barlocco (1/0), José Carballal (1/0), Julio López (1/0). Trainer: Alberto Horacio Suppici (3).

100. 26.05.1924 **URUGUAY - YUGOSLAVIA** **7-0(3-0)** 8th OG. Group Stage
Stade Olympique „Yves de Manoir", Colombes, Paris (France); Referee: Georges Vallat (France), Attendance: 3,025
URU: Andrés Mazali (1/0), José Nasazzi Yarza (4/0), Humberto Tomassina (1/0), José Leandro Andrade (5/0), José Vidal (4/1), Alfredo Juan Ghierra (4/0), Santos Urdinarán (2/0), Héctor Pedro Scarone (26/12), Pedro Petrone (4/5), José Pedro Cea (4/3), Ángel Romano (56/23). Trainer: Ernesto Fígoli (16).
Goals: José Vidal (20), Héctor Pedro Scarone (23), Pedro Petrone (35), José Pedro Cea (50), Ángel Romano (58), Pedro Petrone (61), José Pedro Cea (80).

101. 29.05.1924 **URUGUAY – UNITED STATES** **3-0(3-0)** 8th OG.2nd Round.
Stade de Bergèyre, Paris (France); Referee: Charles Barette (Belgium), Attendance: 10,455
URU: Andrés Mazali (2/0), José Nasazzi Yarza (5/0), Pedro Arispe (1/0), José Leandro Andrade (6/0), José Vidal (5/1), Humberto Tomassina (2/0), José Naya (1/0), Héctor Pedro Scarone (27/13), Pedro Petrone (5/7), José Pedro Cea (5/3), Ángel Romano (57/23). Trainer: Ernesto Fígoli (17).
Goals: Pedro Petrone (10), Héctor Pedro Scarone (15), Pedro Petrone (44).

102. 01.06.1924 **FRANCE - URUGUAY** **1-5(1-2)** 8th OG. Quarter-Finals
Stade Olympique „Yves de Manoir", Colombes, Paris; Referee: Lauritz Andersen (Denmark), Attendance: 30,868
URU: Andrés Mazali (3/0), José Nasazzi Yarza (6/0), Pedro Arispe (2/0), José Leandro Andrade (7/0), Alfredo Zibechi (35/1), Alfredo Juan Ghierra (5/0), José Naya (2/0), Héctor Pedro Scarone (28/15), Pedro Petrone (6/9), José Pedro Cea (6/3), Ángel Romano (58/24). Trainer: Ernesto Fígoli (18).
Goals: Héctor Pedro Scarone (2, 24), Pedro Petrone (58, 68), Ángel Romano (83).

103. 06.06.1924 **URUGUAY - HOLLAND** **2-1(0-1)** 8th OG. Semi-Finals
Stade Olympique „Yves de Manoir", Colombes, Paris (France); Referee: Georges Vallat (France), Attendance: 7,088
URU: Andrés Mazali (4/0), José Nasazzi Yarza (7/0), Pedro Arispe (3/0), José Leandro Andrade (8/0), José Vidal (6/1), Alfredo Juan Ghierra (6/0), Santos Urdinarán (3/0), Héctor Pedro Scarone (29/16), Pedro Petrone (7/9), José Pedro Cea (7/4), Ángel Romano (59/24). Trainer: Ernesto Fígoli (19).
Goals: José Pedro Cea (62), Héctor Pedro Scarone (81 penalty).

104. 09.06.1924 **URUGUAY - SWITZERLAND** **3-0(1-0)** 8th OG. Final
Stade Olympique „Yves de Manoir", Colombes, Paris (France); Referee: Marcel Slawick (France), Attendance: 40,522
URU: Andrés Mazali (5/0), José Nasazzi Yarza (8/0), Pedro Arispe (4/0), José Leandro Andrade (9/0), José Vidal (7/1), Alfredo Juan Ghierra (7/0), Santos Urdinarán (4/0), Héctor Pedro Scarone (30/16), Pedro Petrone (8/10), José Pedro Cea (8/5), Ángel Romano (60/25). Trainer: Ernesto Fígoli (20).
Goals: Pedro Petrone (9), José Pedro Cea (65), Ángel Romano (82).

105. 10.08.1924 **ARGENTINA - URUGUAY** **0-0** Copa Ministro de relaciones exteriors
Estadio River Plate, Buenos Aires; Referee: Vicente Vitterito (Uruguay), Attendance: 30,000
URU: Alfonso Brugnoli (2/0), José Benincasa (35/0), Domingo Tejera (10/0), Antonio Aguerre (9/0), Gildeón Silva (3/0), Alfredo Juan Ghierra (8/0), Juan Pedro Arremón (2/0), Antonio Sacco (1/0), René Borjas (2/1), Norberto Cassanello (11/0), Ladislao Pérez (5/0). Trainer: Leonardo de Lucca (8).

106. 31.08.1924 **URUGUAY – ARGENTINA** **2-3(0-0)** Premio de Honor Uruguayo
Estadio Pocitos, Montevideo; Referee: José Galli (Argentina), Attendance: 15,000
URU: Alfonso Brugnoli (3/0), José Benincasa (36/0), Alfredo Granja (6/0), Pascual Ruotta (12/2), Gildeón Silva (4/0), Alfredo Juan Ghierra (9/0), Ladislao Pérez (6/0), Antonio Sacco (2/0), Vicente Capuccio (1/0), Isabelino Gradín (23/10), Pascual Somma (42/3). Trainer: Leonardo de Lucca (9).
Goals: Pascual Ruotta (75, 89).

107. 21.09.1924 **URUGUAY - ARGENTINA** **1-1(1-0)**
Estadio Parque Central, Montevideo; Referee: Servando Pérez (Argentina), Attendance: 30,000
URU: Andrés Mazali (6/0), José Nasazzi Yarza (9/0), Fermín Uriarte (7/0), José Leandro Andrade (10/0), Alfredo Zibechi (36/1), Humberto Tomassina (3/0), Santos Urdinarán (5/1), Héctor Pedro Scarone (31/16), Pedro Petrone (9/10), José Pedro Cea (9/5), Ángel Romano (61/25). Trainer: Andrés Mazali (1).
Goal: Santos Urdinarán (29).

108. 28.09.1924 **ARGENTINA - URUGUAY** **0-0***
Estadio Sportivo Barracas, Buenos Aires; Referee: Ricardo Vallarino (Uruguay), Attendance: 60,000
URU: Andrés Mazali (7/0), José Nasazzi Yarza (10/0), Fermín Uriarte (8/0), José Leandro Andrade (11/0), Alfredo Zibechi (37/1), Alfredo Juan Ghierra (10/0), Santos Urdinarán (6/1), Héctor Pedro Scarone (32/16), Pedro Petrone (10/10), José Pedro Cea (10/5), Ángel Romano (62/25). Trainer: Andrés Mazali (2).
**Abandoned after only 4 mins!*

109. 02.10.1924 **ARGENTINA - URUGUAY** **2-1(1-1)***
Estadio Sportivo Barracas, Buenos Aires; Referee: Ricardo Vallarino (Uruguay), Attendance: 20,000
URU: Andrés Mazali (8/0), José Nasazzi Yarza (11/0), Fermín Uriarte (9/0), José Leandro Andrade (12/0), Alfredo Zibechi (38/1), Pedro Zingone (2/0), Santos Urdinarán (7/1), Héctor Pedro Scarone (33/16), Pedro Petrone (11/10), José Pedro Cea (11/6), Ángel Romano (63/25). Trainer: Andrés Mazali (3).
Goal: José Pedro Cea (30).
**Abandoned after 86 mins, after Uruguayan team left the field.*

110. 19.10.1924 **URUGUAY - CHILE** **5-0(1-0)** 8th Copa América
Estadio Parque Central, Montevideo; Referee: Eduardo Jara (Paraguay), Attendance: 15,000
URU: Andrés Mazali (9/0), José Nasazzi Yarza (12/0), Pedro Arispe (5/0), Ramón Bucetta (1/0), Pedro Zingone (3/1), Alfredo Juan Ghierra (11/0), Santos Urdinarán (8/1), Héctor Pedro Scarone (34/16), Pedro Petrone (12/13), José Pedro Cea (12/6), Ángel Romano (64/26). Trainer: Ernesto Meliante (1).
Goals: Pedro Petrone (40, 53), Pedro Zingone (73), Ángel Romano (78), Pedro Petrone (88).

111. 26.10.1924 **URUGUAY – PARAGUAY** **3-1(2-0)** 8th Copa América
Estadio Parque Central, Montevideo; Referee: Alberto Parodi (Chile), Attendance: 14,000
URU: Andrés Mazali (10/0), José Nasazzi Yarza (13/0), Pedro Arispe (6/0), Juan Carlos Alzugaray (2/0), Pedro Zingone (4/1), Alfredo Juan Ghierra (12/0), Santos Urdinarán (9/1), Héctor Pedro Scarone (35/16), Pedro Petrone (12/14), José Pedro Cea (13/7), Ángel Romano (65/27). Trainer: Ernesto Meliante (2).
Goals: Pedro Petrone (28), Ángel Romano (37), José Pedro Cea (53).

112. 02.11.1924 **URUGUAY - ARGENTINA** **0-0** 8th Copa América
Estadio Parque Central, Montevideo; Referee: Carlos Fanta Tomaszewski (Chile), Attendance: 20,000
URU: Andrés Mazali (11/0), José Nasazzi Yarza (14/0), Pedro Arispe (7/0), Juan Carlos Alzugaray (3/0), Alfredo Zibechi (39/1), Alfredo Juan Ghierra (13/0), Santos Urdinarán (10/1), Atilio Barlocco (2/0), Pedro Petrone (13/14), José Pedro Cea (14/7), Ángel Romano (66/27). Trainer: Ernesto Meliante (3).

113. 14.07.1925 **URUGUAY - PARAGUAY** **0-1(0-1)** Copa Bossio
Estadio Parque Central, Montevideo; Referee: Aníbal Tejada (Uruguay), Attendance: 18,000
URU: Máximo Maturell (2/0), Adhemar Canavessi (1/0), Fermín Uriarte (10/0), Juan Carlos Alzugaray (4/0), Pascual Cabrera (2/0), Luis Alfredo Sciutto (1/0), Juan Valverde (1/0), Vital Ruffati (2/0), Fermín Medina (1/0), Alfredo Mazzone (1/0), Zoilo Saldombide (4/1). Trainer: Alberto Horacio Suppici (4).

114. 18.07.1925 **URUGUAY - PARAGUAY** **0-1(0-0)** Copa Bossio
Estadio Parque Central, Montevideo; Referee: Agustín Imbriago (Uruguay), Attendance: 15,000
URU: Máximo Maturell (3/0), Adhemar Canavessi (2/0), Fermín Uriarte (11/0), Lorenzo Fernández (1/0), Pascual Cabrera (3/0), Luis Alfredo Sciutto (2/0), Juan Valverde (2/0), Vital Ruffati (3/0), Fermín Medina (2/0), Alfredo Mazzone (2/0), Zoilo Saldombide (5/1). Trainer: Alberto Horacio Suppici (5).

115. 16.08.1925 **PARAGUAY - URUGUAY** **1-0(0-0)** Copa Bossio
Estadio Puerto Sajonia, Asunción; Referee: Manuel Chaparro (Paraguay), Attendance: 20,000
URU: Máximo Maturell (4/0), Adhemar Canavessi (3/0), Fermín Uriarte (12/0), Miguel Ángel Melogno (1/0), Pascual Cabrera (4/0), Juan Carlos Alzugaray (5/0), Juan Valverde (3/0), Lorenzo Fernández (2/0), Roque Sosa (1/0), Alfredo Mazzone (3/0), Conrado Bidegain (1/0). Trainer: Alberto Horacio Suppici (6).

116. 19.08.1925 **PARAGUAY - URUGUAY** **0-1(0-1)** Copa Bossio
Estadio Puerto Sajonia, Asunción; Referee: Roque Centurión Miranda (Paraguay), Attendance: 18,000
URU: Máximo Maturell (5/0), Adhemar Canavessi (4/0), Fermín Uriarte (13/0), Miguel Ángel Melogno (2/0), Pascual Cabrera (5/0), Juan Carlos Alzugaray (6/0), Juan Valverde (4/0), Lorenzo Fernández (3/0), Roque Sosa (2/0), Alberto Aizpur (1/0), Conrado Bidegain (2/1). Trainer: Alberto Horacio Suppici (7).
Goal: Conrado Bidegain (25).

117. 22.08.1925 **PARAGUAY - URUGUAY** **0-0** Copa Bossio
Estadio Puerto Sajonia, Asunción; Referee: José Cabañas Saguier (Paraguay), Attendance: 20,000
URU: Máximo Maturell (6/0), Adhemar Canavessi (5/0), Fermín Uriarte (14/0), Américo Carbone (6/0), Pascual Cabrera (6/0), Miguel Ángel Melogno (3/0), Juan Valverde (5/0), Lorenzo Fernández (4/0), Roque Sosa (3/0), Pedro Minoli (1/0), Zoilo Saldombide (6/1). Trainer: Alberto Horacio Suppici (8).

118. 17.10.1926 **CHILE - URUGUAY** **1-3(0-2)** 10th Copa América
Estadio Sport de Nuñoa, Santiago; Referee: Pedro José Malbrán (Chile), Attendance: 11,152
URU: Fausto Batignani (6/0), José Nasazzi Yarza (15/0), Emilio Recoba (1/0), José Leandro Andrade (13/0), Lorenzo Fernández (5/0), José Vanzzino (29/0), Santos Urdinarán (11/1), Héctor Pedro Scarone (36/17), René Borjas (3/2), Héctor Castro (3/4), Zoilo Saldombide (7/1). Trainer: Andrés Mazali (4).
Goals: René Borjas (22), Héctor Castro (32), Héctor Pedro Scarone (55).

119. 24.10.1926 **URUGUAY - ARGENTINA** **2-0(1-0)** 10th Copa América
Estadio Sport de Nuñoa, Santiago (Chile); Referee: Miguel Barba (Paraguay), Attendance: 15,000
URU: Fausto Batignani (7/0), José Nasazzi Yarza (16/0), Emilio Recoba (2/0), José Leandro Andrade (14/0), Lorenzo Fernández (6/0), José Vanzzino (30/0), Santos Urdinarán (12/1), Héctor Pedro Scarone (37/17), René Borjas (4/3), Héctor Castro (4/5), Zoilo Saldombide (8/1). Trainer: Andrés Mazali (5).
Goals: René Borjas (22), Héctor Castro (73).

120. 28.10.1926 **URUGUAY - BOLIVIA** **6-0(4-0)** 10th Copa América
Estadio Sport de Nuñoa, Santiago (Chile); Referee: Juan Pedro Barbera (Argentina), Attendance: 8,000
URU: Fausto Batignani (8/0), José Nasazzi Yarza (17/0), Emilio Recoba (3/0), Alfredo Juan Ghierra (14/0), Lorenzo Fernández (7/0), José Vanzzino (31/0), Santos Urdinarán (13/1), Héctor Pedro Scarone (38/22), Héctor Castro (5/5), Ángel Romano (67/28), Zoilo Saldombide (9/1). Trainer: Andrés Mazali (6).
Goals: Héctor Pedro Scarone (9, 12, 28, 39), Ángel Romano (67), Héctor Pedro Scarone (81).

121. 01.11.1926 **URUGUAY - PARAGUAY** **6-1(3-0)** 10th Copa América
Estadio Sport de Nuñoa, Santiago (Chile); Referee: Francisco Jiménez (Chile), Attendance: 12,000
URU: Fausto Batignani (9/0), José Nasazzi Yarza (18/0), Emilio Recoba (4/0), José Leandro Andrade (15/0), Lorenzo Fernández (8/0), José Vanzzino (32/0), Santos Urdinarán (14/1), Héctor Pedro Scarone (39/22), Héctor Castro (6/9), Ángel Romano (68/28), Zoilo Saldombide (10/3). Trainer: Andrés Mazali (7).
Goals: Héctor Castro (14), Zoilo Saldombide (19), Héctor Castro (40, 59, 63), Zoilo Saldombide (80).

122. 14.07.1927 **URUGUAY - ARGENTINA** **0-1(0-0)** Copa Newton
Estadio Parque Central, Montevideo; Referee: Domingo Lombardi (Uruguay), Attendance: 12,000
URU: Miguel Capuccini (1/0), José Nasazzi Yarza (19/0), Pedro Arispe (8/0), Pascual Ruotta (13/2), Álvaro Antonio Gestido (1/0), José Vanzzino (33/0), Luis Deagustini (1/0), Ángel Romano (69/28), René Borjas (5/3), Isabelino Gradín (24/10), Juan Pedro Arremón (3/0). Trainer: Luis Grecco (1).

123. 30.08.1927 **ARGENTINA - URUGUAY** **0-1(0-0)** Copa Lipton
Estadio Boca Juniors, Buenos Aires; Referee: Servando Pérez (Argentina), Attendance: 25,000
URU: Miguel Capuccini (2/0), José Nasazzi Yarza (20/0), Pedro Arispe (9/0), José Leandro Andrade (16/0), Álvaro Antonio Gestido (2/0), José Vanzzino (34/0), Juan Pedro Arremón (4/0), Héctor Pedro Scarone (40/23), Pedro Petrone (14/14), José Pedro Cea (15/7), Zoilo Saldombide (11/3). Trainer: Luis Grecco (2).
Goal: Héctor Pedro Scarone (75).

124. 01.11.1927 **PERU - URUGUAY** **0-4(0-0)** 11th Copa América
Estadio Nacional, Lima; Referee: Consolato Nay Foino (Argentina), Attendance: 19,367
URU: Miguel Capuccini (3/0), Adhemar Canavessi (6/0), Domingo Tejera (11/0), José Leandro Andrade (17/0), Lorenzo Fernández (9/0), José Vanzzino (35/0), Juan Pedro Arremón (5/0), Antonio Sacco (3/2), Héctor Castro (7/10), Juan Peregrino Anselmo (1/0), Roberto Figueroa (3/2). Trainer: Luis Grecco (3).
Goals: Roberto Figueroa (49), Antonio Sacco (52, 71), Héctor Castro (75).

125. 06.11.1927 **URUGUAY - BOLIVIA** **9-0(3-0)** 11th Copa América
Estadio Nacional, Lima (Peru); Referee: Benjamín Fuentes Sánchez (Peru), Attendance: 6,000
URU: Miguel Capuccini (4/0), Domingo Tejera (12/0), Ramón Bucetta (2/0), José Leandro Andrade (18/0), Lorenzo Fernández (10/0), José Vanzzino (36/0), Juan Pedro Arremón (6/1), Héctor Pedro Scarone (41/24), Pedro Petrone (15/17), Héctor Castro (8/11), Roberto Figueroa (4/5). Trainer: Luis Grecco (4).
Goals: Pedro Petrone (18), Roberto Figueroa (19), Juan Pedro Arremón (43), Pedro Petrone (65), Roberto Figueroa (67), Héctor Castro (68), Roberto Figueroa (69), Pedro Petrone (81), Héctor Pedro Scarone (86).

126. 20.11.1927 **ARGENTINA - URUGUAY** **3-2(0-1)** 11th Copa América
Estadio Nacional, Lima (Peru); Referee: David Thurner (England), Attendance: 26,000
URU: Miguel Capuccini (5/0), Adhemar Canavessi (7/0), Domingo Tejera (13/0), José Leandro Andrade (19/0), Lorenzo Fernández (11/0), José Vanzzino (37/0), Juan Pedro Arremón (7/1), Héctor Pedro Scarone (42/26), Pedro Petrone (16/17), Héctor Castro (9/11), Roberto Figueroa (5/5). Trainer: Luis Grecco (5).
Goals: Héctor Pedro Scarone (33, 79).

127. 10.12.1927 **CHILE - URUGUAY** **2-3(1-1)**
Estadio Valparaíso, Viña del Mar; Referee: Sabugo (Chile), Attendance: 8,000
URU: Miguel Capuccini (6/0), Adhemar Canavessi (8/0), Domingo Tejera (14/0), José Leandro Andrade (20/0), Lorenzo Fernández (12/0), Venancio Bartibás (1/0), Juan Pedro Arremón (8/1), Héctor Pedro Scarone (43/27), Pedro Petrone (17/18), Héctor Castro (10/12), Roberto Figueroa (6/5). Trainer: Luis Grecco (6).
Goals: Pedro Petrone (18), Héctor Castro (60), Héctor Pedro Scarone (63).

128. 30.05.1928 **HOLLAND - URUGUAY** **0-2(0-1)** 9th OG. Group Stage
Olympisch Stadion, Amsterdam; Referee: John Langenus (Belgium), Attendance: 27.730
URU: Andrés Mazali (12/0), José Nasazzi Yarza (21/0), Pedro Arispe (10/0), José Leandro Andrade (21/0), Lorenzo Fernández (13/0), Álvaro Antonio Gestido (3/0), Santos Urdinarán (15/2), Héctor Pedro Scarone (44/28), René Borjas (6/3), José Pedro Cea (16/7), Juan Pedro Arremón (9/1). Trainer: Primo Gianotti (1).
Goals: Héctor Pedro Scarone (20), Santos Urdinarán (86).

129. 03.06.1928 **URUGUAY - GERMANY** **4-1(2-0)** 9th OG. Quarter-Finals
Olympisch Stadion, Amsterdam (Holland); Referee: Youssof Mohamed (Egypt), Attendance: 25,131
URU: Andrés Mazali (13/0), José Nasazzi Yarza (22/0) [*sent off 87*], Pedro Arispe (11/0), Juan Píriz (1/0), Lorenzo Fernández (14/0), Álvaro Antonio Gestido (4/0), Santos Urdinarán (16/2), Héctor Castro (11/13), Pedro Petrone (18/21), José Pedro Cea (17/7), Antonio Cámpolo (16/2). Trainer: Primo Gianotti (2).
Goals: Pedro Petrone (35, 39), Héctor Castro (63), Pedro Petrone (84).

130. 07.06.1928 **URUGUAY - ITALY** **3-2(3-1)** 9th OG. Semi-Finals
Olympisch Stadion, Amsterdam (Holland); Referee: Willem Eymers (Holland), Attendance: 15,230
URU: Andrés Mazali (14/0), Adhemar Canavessi (9/0), Pedro Arispe (12/0), José Leandro Andrade (22/0), Lorenzo Fernández (15/0), Álvaro Antonio Gestido (5/0), Santos Urdinarán (17/2), Héctor Pedro Scarone (45/29), Pedro Petrone (19/21), José Pedro Cea (18/8), Antonio Cámpolo (17/3). Trainer: Primo Gianotti (3).
Goals: José Pedro Cea (17), Antonio Cámpolo (28), Héctor Pedro Scarone (31).

131. 10.06.1928 **URUGUAY - ARGENTINA** **1-1(1-0,1-1)** 9th OG. Final
Olympisch Stadion, Amsterdam (Holland); Referee: Johannes Mutters (Holland), Attendance: 28,000
URU: Andrés Mazali (15/0), José Nasazzi Yarza (23/0), Pedro Arispe (13/0), José Leandro Andrade (23/0), Lorenzo Fernández (16/0), Álvaro Antonio Gestido (6/0), Santos Urdinarán (18/2), Héctor Castro (12/13), Pedro Petrone (20/22), José Pedro Cea (19/8), Antonio Cámpolo (18/3). Trainer: Primo Gianotti (4).
Goal: Pedro Petrone (23).

132. 13.06.1928 **URUGUAY – ARGENTINA** **2-1(1-1)** 9th OG.Final (Replay)
Olympisch Stadion, Amsterdam (Holland); Referee: Johannes Mutters (Holland), Attendance: 28,000
URU: Andrés Mazali (16/0), José Nasazzi Yarza (24/0), Pedro Arispe (14/0), José Leandro Andrade (24/0), Juan Píriz (2/0), Álvaro Antonio Gestido (7/0), Juan Pedro Arremón (10/1), Héctor Pedro Scarone (46/30), René Borjas (7/3), José Pedro Cea (20/8), Roberto Figueroa (7/6). Trainer: Primo Gianotti (5).
Goals: Roberto Figueroa (17), Héctor Pedro Scarone (68).

133. 15.08.1928 **PARAGUAY - URUGUAY** **3-1(2-0)**
Estadio Puerto Sajonia, Asunción; Referee: Miguel Barba (Paraguay), Attendance: 15,000
URU: Ángel Marini (1/0), José Benincasa (37/0), Humberto Tomassina (4/0), Juan Carlos Corazo (1/0), Raúl Romero (1/0), Francisco Occhiuzzi (1/0), Juan Igarzábal (1/0), Luis Mata (1/1), Juan González (1/0), Arturo Hohl (1/0), Zoilo Saldombide (12/3).
Goal: Luis Mata (65).

134. 19.08.1928 **PARAGUAY - URUGUAY** **1-1(1-1)**
Estadio Puerto Sajonia, Asunción; Referee: Miguel Barba (Paraguay), Attendance: 12,000
URU: Ángel Marini (2/0), José Benincasa (38/0), Humberto Tomassina (5/0), Juan Carlos Corazo (2/0), Raúl Romero (2/0), Francisco Occhiuzzi (2/0), Arturo Hohl (2/0), Antonio Castaldo (1/0), Juan González (2/1), Luis Mata (2/1), Zoilo Saldombide (13/3).
Goal: Juan González (29).

135. 30.08.1928 **ARGENTINA - URUGUAY** **1-0(1-0)** Copa Newton
Estadio Independiente, Avellaneda; Referee: Gerónimo Rapossi (Argentina), Attendance: 50,000
URU: Fausto Batignani (10/0), Ramón Bucetta (3/0), Domingo Tejera (15/0), Carlos Riolfo (1/0), Raúl Romero (3/0), Francisco Occhiuzzi (3/0), Juan Emilio Píriz (1/0), Francisco Fedullo (1/0), Pedro Petrone (21/22), Antonio Sacco (4/2), Zoilo Saldombide (14/3). Trainer: Primo Gianotti (6).

136. 21.09.1928 **URUGUAY - ARGENTINA** **2-2(0-1)** Copa Lipton
Estadio Parque Central, Montevideo; Referee: Aníbal Tejada (Uruguay), Attendance: 18,000
URU: Fausto Batignani (11/0), Ramón Bucetta (4/0), Domingo Tejera (16/0), Carlos Riolfo (2/0), Raúl Romero (4/0), Francisco Occhiuzzi (4/0), Juan Emilio Píriz (2/1), Antonio Sacco (5/2), Pedro Petrone (22/23), Juan Peregrino Anselmo (2/0), Zoilo Saldombide (15/3). Trainer: Primo Gianotti (7).
Goals: Juan Emilio Píriz (56), Pedro Petrone (89).

137. 16.06.1929 **ARGENTINA - URUGUAY** **2-0(0-0)** Copa Cámara de Diputados
Estadio Gasómetro de Boedo, Buenos Aires; Referee: Aníbal Tejada (Uruguay), Attendance: 50,000
URU: Andrés Mazali (17/0), José Nasazzi Yarza (25/0), Emilio Recoba (5/0), Julio Martínez (1/0), Gildeón Silva (5/0), Miguel Ángel Melogno (4/0), Juan Pedro Arremón (11/1), Conduelo Píriz (1/0), Pedro Petrone (23/23), Luis Gaitán (1/0), Roberto Figueroa (8/6). Trainer: Alberto Horacio Suppici (9).

138. 16.06.1929 **URUGUAY - ARGENTINA** **1-1(1-0)**
Estadio Parque Central, Montevideo; Referee: José Galli (Argentina), Attendance: 30,000
URU: Cirilo Estívez (1/0), Rodolfo Deagustini (1/0), Domingo Tejera (17/0), José Leandro Andrade (25/0), Francisco Occhiuzzi (5/0), Alberto Ibarra (1/0), Luis Deagustini (2/0), Héctor Pedro Scarone (47/30), Oscar Carbone (1/1), Pedro Lago (1/0), Pablo Dorado (1/0). Trainer: Ernesto Fígoli (21).
Goal: Oscar Carbone (42).

139. 20.09.1929 **URUGUAY – ARGENTINA** **2-1(1-0)** Copa Newton
Estadio Parque Central, Montevideo; Referee: Domingo Lombari (Uruguay), Attendance: 30,000
URU: Andrés Mazali (18/0), José Nasazzi Yarza (26/0), Pedro Arispe (15/0), José Leandro Andrade (26/0), Lorenzo Fernández (17/1), Álvaro Antonio Gestido (8/0), Santos Urdinarán (19/2), Héctor Castro (13/14), Pedro Petrone (24/23), Juan Peregrino Anselmo (3/0), Juan Pedro Arremón (12/1). Trainer: Alberto Horacio Suppici (10).
Goals: Héctor Castro (4), Lorenzo Fernández (65).

140. 28.09.1929 **ARGENTINA - URUGUAY** **0-0** Copa Lipton
Estadio Gasómetro de Boedo, Buenos Aires; Referee: Servando Pérez (Argentina), Attendance: 60,000
URU: Eduardo García (1/0), José Nasazzi Yarza (27/0), Pedro Arispe (16/0), José Leandro Andrade (27/0), Lorenzo Fernández (18/1), Álvaro Antonio Gestido (9/0), Santos Urdinarán (20/2), Conduelo Píriz (2/0), Pedro Petrone (25/23), Héctor Castro (14/14), Juan Pedro Arremón (13/1). Trainer: Alberto Horacio Suppici (11).

141. 01.11.1929 **PARAGUAY - URUGUAY** **3-0(2-0)** 12th Copa América
Estadio Alvear y Tagle, Buenos Aires (Argentina); Referee: José Galli (Argentina), Attendance: 40,000
URU: Andrés Mazali (19/0), Ramón Bucetta (5/0), Pedro Arispe (17/0) , José Leandro Andrade (28/0), Gildeón Silva (6/0), José Magallanes (1/0), Conduelo Píriz (3/0), Héctor Castro (15/14), Pedro Petrone (26/23), José Pedro Cea (21/8), Antonio Cámpolo (19/3). Trainer: Alberto Horacio Suppici (12).

142. 11.11.1929 **URUGUAY - PERU** **4-1(3-0)** 12th Copa América
Estadio River Plate, Buenos Aires (Argentina); Referee: Miguel Barba (Paraguay), Attendance: 22,000
URU: Andrés Mazali (20/0), José Nasazzi Yarza (28/0), Pedro Arispe (18/0), José Leandro Andrade (29/1), Gildeón Silva (7/0), José Magallanes (2/0), Juan Pedro Arremón (14/1), Conduelo Píriz (4/0), Lorenzo Fernández (19/4), Héctor Castro (16/14), Antonio Cámpolo (20/3). Trainer: Alberto Horacio Suppici (13).
Goals: Lorenzo Fernández (21, 29, 43), José Leandro Andrade (69).

143. 17.11.1929 **ARGENTINA - URUGUAY** **2-0(1-0)** 12th Copa América
Estadio Gasómetro de Boedo, Buenos Aires; Referee: Miguel Barba (Paraguay), Attendance: 60,000
URU: Andrés Mazali (21/0), José Nasazzi Yarza (29/0), Pedro Arispe (19/0), Gildeón Silva (8/0), Lorenzo Fernández (20/4), Álvaro Antonio Gestido (10/0), Conduelo Píriz (5/0), Héctor Pedro Scarone (48/30), Héctor Castro (17/14), José Pedro Cea (22/8), Antonio Cámpolo (21/3). Trainer: Alberto Horacio Suppici (14).

144. 25.05.1930 **ARGENTINA - URUGUAY** **1-1(1-1)** Copa Newton
Estadio Gasómetro de Boedo, Buenos Aires; Referee: Miguel Barba (Paraguay), Attendance: 60,000
URU: Enrique Ballestrero (1/0), Rodolfo Areco (1/0), Domingo Tejera (18/0), José Leandro Andrade (30/1), Lorenzo Fernández (21/4), Francisco Occhiuzzi (6/0), Conduelo Píriz (6/0), Héctor Pedro Scarone (49/30), Pedro Petrone (27/24), Héctor Castro (18/14), Pablo Dorado (2/0). Trainer: Alberto Horacio Suppici (15).
Goal: Pedro Petrone (61).

145. 18.07.1930 **URUGUAY – PERU** **1-0(0-0)** 1st FIFA WC. Group Stage
Estadio Centenario, Montevideo; Referee: John Langenus (Belgium), Attendance: 45,000
URU: Enrique Ballestrero (2/0), José Nasazzi Yarza (30/0), Domingo Tejera (19/0), José Leandro Andrade (31/1), Lorenzo Fernández (22/4), Álvaro Antonio Gestido (11/0), Santos Urdinarán (21/2), Héctor Castro (19/15), Pedro Petrone (28/24), José Pedro Cea (23/8), Victoriano Santos Iriare (1/0). Trainer: Alberto Horacio Suppici (16).
Goal: Héctor Castro (60).

146. 21.07.1930 **URUGUAY - ROMANIA** **4-0(4-0)** 1st FIFA WC. Group Stage
Estadio Centenario, Montevideo; Referee: Gilberto de Álmeida Rego (Brazil), Attendance: 50,000
URU: Enrique Ballestrero (3/0), José Nasazzi Yarza (31/0), Ernesto Mascheroni (1/0), José Leandro Andrade (32/1), Lorenzo Fernández (23/4), Álvaro Antonio Gestido (12/0), Pablo Dorado (3/1), Héctor Pedro Scarone (50/31), Juan Peregrino Anselmo (4/1), José Pedro Cea (24/9), Victoriano Santos Iriare (2/0). Trainer: Alberto Horacio Suppici (17).
Goals: Pablo Dorado (7), Héctor Pedro Scarone (16), Juan Peregrino Anselmo (30), José Pedro Cea (35).

147. 27.07.1930 **URUGUAY - YUGOSLAVIA** **6-1(3-1)** 1st FIFA WC. Semi-Finals
Estadio Centenario, Montevideo; Referee: Gilberto de Álmeida Rego (Brazil), Attendance: 55,000
URU: Enrique Ballestrero (4/0), Ernesto Mascheroni (2/0), José Nasazzi Yarza (32/0), José Leandro Andrade (33/1), Lorenzo Fernández (24/4), Álvaro Antonio Gestido (13/0), Pablo Dorado (4/1), Héctor Pedro Scarone (51/31), Juan Peregrino Anselmo (5/3), José Pedro Cea (25/12), Victoriano Santos Iriare (3/1). Trainer: Alberto Horacio Suppici (18).
Goals: José Pedro Cea (19), Juan Peregrino Anselmo (21, 31), Victoriano Santos Iriare (63), José Pedro Cea (66, 72).

148. 30.07.1930 **URUGUAY – ARGENTINA** **4-2(1-2)** 1st FIFA WC. Final
Estadio Centenario, Montevideo; Referee: John Langenus (Belgium), Attendance: 60,000
URU: Enrique Ballestrero (5/0), Ernesto Mascheroni (3/0), José Nasazzi Yarza (33/0), José Leandro Andrade (34/1), Lorenzo Fernández (25/4), Álvaro Antonio Gestido (14/0), Pablo Dorado (5/2), Héctor Pedro Scarone (52/31), Héctor Castro (20/16), José Pedro Cea (26/13), Victoriano Santos Iriare (4/2). Trainer: Alberto Horacio Suppici (19).
Goals: Pablo Dorado (12), José Pedro Cea (58), Victoriano Santos Iriare (68), Héctor Castro (89).

149. 06.09.1931 **BRAZIL - URUGUAY** **2-0(1-0)** Copa Rio Branco
Estádio Laranjeiras, Rio de Janeiro; Referee: Gilberto de Álmeida Rêgo (Brazil), Attendance: 16,000
URU: Enrique Ballestrero (6/0), José Nasazzi Yarza (34/0), Ernesto Mascheroni (4/0), Lorenzo Fernández (26/4), Álvaro Antonio Gestido (15/0), Francisco Occhiuzzi (7/0), Pablo Dorado (6/2), Arturo Frioni (1/0) [46.Conrado Haeberli (1/0)], Luis Alberto Rodríguez (1/0), Victoriano Santos Iriare (5/2). Trainer: Alberto Horacio Suppici (20).

150. 15.05.1932 **ARGENTINA - URUGUAY** **2-0(2-0)** Copa Comiteto Olimpico
Estadio Sportivo Barracas, Buenos Aires; Referee: Emilio Solari (Argentina), Attendance: 15,000
URU: Enrique Ballestrero (7/0), Santos Urdinarán (22/2), Domingo Tejera (20/0), Guillermo Campos (1/0), Alberto Legarburo (1/0), Abraham Lobos (1/0), Juan Miguel Labraga (1/0), Juan José García (1/0), Ignacio Nieto (1/0), Antonio Sacco (6/2), Eduardo Ithurbide (1/0). Trainer: Alberto Horacio Suppici (21).

151. 19.05.1932 **URUGUAY - ARGENTINA** **1-0(0-0)** Copa Comiteto Olimpico
Estadio Centenario, Montevideo; Referee: Domingo Lombardi (Uruguay), Attendance: 30,000
URU: Enrique Ballestrero (8/0), José Nasazzi Yarza (35/0), Ernesto Mascheroni (5/0), Arsenio Fernández (1/0), Álvaro Antonio Gestido (16/0), Francisco Occhiuzzi (8/0), Braulio Castro (1/0), Luis Mata (3/1), Pedro Duhart (1/0), Conduelo Píriz (7/0), Pablo Dorado (7/3). Trainer: Alberto Horacio Suppici (22).
Goal: Pablo Dorado (65).

152. 04.12.1932 **URUGUAY - BRAZIL** **1-2(0-1)** Copa Rio Branco
Estadio Centenario, Montevideo; Referee: Aníbal Tejada (Uruguay), Attendance: 13,000
URU: Héctor Macchiavello (1/0), José Nasazzi Yarza (36/0) [46.Pedro Aguirre (1/0)], Ernesto Mascheroni (6/0), Arsenio Fernández (2/0), Álvaro Antonio Gestido (17/0), Abraham Lobos (2/0), Braulio Castro (2/0), Juan José García (2/1), Pedro Duhart (2/0), José Pedro Cea (27/13), Eduardo Ithurbide (2/0) [46.Juan Emilio Píriz (3/1)]. Trainer: Alberto Horacio Suppici (23).
Goal: Juan José García (66).

153. 21.01.1933 **URUGUAY - ARGENTINA** **2-1(1-0)**
Estadio Centenario, Montevideo; Referee: Aníbal Tejada (Uruguay), Attendance: 45,000
URU: Enrique Ballestrero (9/0), Pedro Aguirre (2/0), Ernesto Mascheroni (7/0), Arsenio Fernández (3/0), Félix Magno (1/0), Ricardo Gregorio Faccio (1/0), Juan Miguel Labraga (2/0) [46.Juan Emilio Píriz (4/1)], Enrique Fernández (1/1), Conrado Haeberli (2/1), Juan Peregrino Anselmo (6/3), Atilio Fernández (1/0). Trainer: Alberto Horacio Suppici (24).
Goals: Conrado Haeberli (15), Enrique Fernández (66).

154. 05.02.1933 **ARGENTINA - URUGUAY** **4-1(1-1)**
Estadio Independiente, Avellaneda; Referee: Eduardo Forte (Argentina), Attendance: 60,000
URU: Enrique Ballestrero (10/0), Pedro Aguirre (3/0), Ernesto Mascheroni (8/0), Arsenio Fernández (4/0), Ricardo Gregorio Faccio (2/0) [46.Raúl Romero (5/0)], Abraham Lobos (3/0), Juan Emilio Píriz (5/1), Luis Mata (4/1) [46.Francisco Arispe (1/0)], Conrado Haeberli (3/2) [46.Pedro Young (1/0)], Enrique Fernández (2/1), Atilio Fernández (2/0). Trainer: Alberto Horacio Suppici (25).
Goal: Conrado Haeberli (29).

155. 14.12.1933 **URUGUAY - ARGENTINA** **0-1(0-0)**
Estadio Centenario, Montevideo; Referee: Martín Aphesteguy (Uruguay), Attendance: 35,000
URU: Eduardo García (2/0), José Nasazzi Yarza (37/0), Agenor Muñiz (1/0), Erebo Zunino (1/0), Álvaro Antonio Gestido (18/0), Marcelino Pérez (1/0), Braulio Castro (3/0), Luis Mata (5/1), Juan Peregrino Anselmo (7/3) [46.Oliver Icardi (1/0)], Enrique Fernández (3/1), Roberto Figueroa (9/6). Trainer: Alberto Horacio Suppici (26).

156. 18.07.1934 **URUGUAY - ARGENTINA** **2-2(1-1)**
Estadio Centenario, Montevideo; Referee: Martín Aphesteguy (Uruguay), Attendance: 60,000
URU: Eduardo García (3/0), Lorenzo Fernández (27/4), Agenor Muñiz (2/0), Ulises Chifflet (1/0) [46.Manuel Figliola (1/0)], Álvaro Antonio Gestido (19/0), Galileo Chanes (1/0), Vicente Carrère (1/0) [50.Juan Emilio Píriz (6/1)], Juan José García (3/2), Aníbal Ciocca (1/1) [75.Antonio Castaldo (2/0)], Enrique Fernández (4/1), Braulio Castro (4/0). Trainer: Alberto Horacio Suppici (27).
Goals: Juan José García (9), Aníbal Ciocca (58).

157. 15.08.1934 **ARGENTINA - URUGUAY** **1-0(0-0)**
Estadio Independiente, Avellaneda; Referee: Alberto Neme (Argentina), Attendance: 75,000
URU: Enrique Ballestrero (11/0), Lorenzo Fernández (28/4), Agenor Muñiz (3/0), Erebo Zunino (2/0), Álvaro Antonio Gestido (20/0), Luis María Denis (1/0), Juan Emilio Píriz (7/1), Francisco Arispe (2/0), Juan Peregrino Anselmo (8/3), Enrique Fernández (5/1), Braulio Castro (5/0). Trainer: Alberto Horacio Suppici (28).

158. 13.01.1935 **PERU - URUGUAY** **0-1(0-0)** 13th Copa América
Estadio Nacional, Lima; Referee: Humberto Reginatto (Chile), Attendance: 24,892
URU: Enrique Ballestrero (12/0), José Nasazzi Yarza (38/0), Agenor Muñiz (4/0), Erebo Zunino (3/0), Lorenzo Fernández (29/4), Luis María Denis (2/0), Juan Emilo Píriz (8/1) [46.Alberto Taboada (1/0)], Aníbal Ciocca (2/1), Héctor Castro (21/17), Enrique Fernández (6/1), Braulio Castro (6/0). Trainer: Raúl Blanco (1).
Goal: Héctor Castro (60).

159. 18.01.1935 **URUGUAY - CHILE** **2-1(1-0)** 13th Copa América
Estadio Nacional, Lima (Peru); Referee: José Serra (Peru), Attendance: 13,000
URU: Enrique Ballestrero (13/0) [46.Héctor Macchiavello (2/0)], José Nasazzi Yarza (39/0) [65.Miguel Olivera (1/0)], Agenor Muñiz (5/0), Erebo Zunino (4/0), Lorenzo Fernández (30/4), Marcelino Pérez (2/0) [46.Luis María Denis (3/0)], Alberto Taboada (2/0), Aníbal Ciocca (3/3), Héctor Castro (22/17), Enrique Fernández (7/1), Braulio Castro (7/0). Trainer: Raúl Blanco (2).
Goals: Aníbal Ciocca (33, 55).

160. 27.01.1935 **URUGUAY - ARGENTINA** **3-0(3-0)** 13th Copa América
Estadio Nacional, Lima (Peru); Referee: Humberto Reginatto Balbo (Chile), Attendance: 30,000
URU: Enrique Ballestrero (14/0), José Nasazzi Yarza (40/0), Agenor Muñiz (6/0), Erebo Zunino (5/0) [46.Luis María Denis (4/0)], Lorenzo Fernández (31/4), Marcelino Pérez (3/0), Alberto Taboada (3/1), Aníbal Ciocca (4/4), Héctor Castro (23/18), Enrique Fernández (8/1), Braulio Castro (8/0). Trainer: Raúl Blanco (3).
Goals: Héctor Castro (18), Alberto Taboada (28), Aníbal Ciocca (36).

161. 18.07.1935 **URUGUAY - ARGENTINA** **1-1(0-0)** Copa Héctor Gómez
Estadio Centenario, Montevideo; Referee: Martín Aphesteguy (Uruguay), Attendance: 20,000
URU: Enrique Ballestrero (15/0), Jorge Enrique Clulow (1/0), Agenor Muñiz (7/0), Rodolfo Carreras (1/0), Eugenio Galvalisi (1/0), Luis María Denis (5/0), Alberto Taboada (4/1), Aníbal Ciocca (5/4), Héctor Castro (24/18), Luis Alberto Rodríguez (2/0) [46.Daniel Aguiar (1/0)], Juan Emilio Píriz (9/2) [75.Arturo De León (1/0)]. Trainer: Raúl Blanco (4).
Goal: Juan Emilio Píriz (60).

162. 15.08.1935 **ARGENTINA - URUGUAY** **3-0(2-0)** Copa Juan Mignaburu
Estadio Independiente, Avellaneda; Referee: José Galli (Argentina), Attendance: 40,000
URU: Enrique Ballestrero (16/0), Jorge Enrique Clulow (2/0) [46.Pedro Aguirre (4/0)], Agenor Muñiz (8/0), Erebo Zunino (6/0) [46.Rodolfo Carreras (2/0)], Álvaro Antonio Gestido (21/0), Oscar Delbono (1/0), Alberto Taboada (5/1) [60.Juan Alberti (1/0)], Aníbal Ciocca (6/4), Héctor Castro (25/18), Severino Varela (1/0) [75.Daniel Aguiar (2/0)], Eduardo Ithurbide (3/0). Trainer: Alberto Horacio Suppici (29).

163. 09.08.1936 **ARGENTINA - URUGUAY** **1-0(0-0)** Copa Juan Mignaburu
Estadio Independiente, Avellaneda; Referee: Domingo Salari (Argentina), Attendance: 40,000
URU: Juan Bautista Besuzzo (1/0), Carlos Scandroglio (1/0) [5.Arturo Seoane (1/0)], Agenor Muñiz (9/0), Vicente Albanese (1/0), Leofar Cámera (1/0), Gumersindo Puentes (1/0) [46.Erebo Zunino (7/0)], Felipe Longo (1/0), Carlos Servetti (1/0), Aníbal Ciocca (7/4), Severino Varela (2/0), Euclides Franco (1/0). Trainer: José María Pedreia (1).

164. 20.09.1936 **URUGUAY - ARGENTINA** **2-1(0-1)** Copa Héctor R. Gómez
Estadio Centenario, Montevideo; Referee: Carlos Cerón (Uruguay), Attendance: 45,000
URU: Juan Bautista Besuzzo (2/0), José Nasazzi Yarza (41/0), Agenor Muñiz (10/0), Erebo Zunino (8/0), Álvaro Antonio Gestido (22/0) [46.Eugenio Galvalisi (2/0)], Galileo Chanes (2/0), Francisco Arispe (3/0) [46.Alberto Taboada (6/1)], Aníbal Ciocca (8/4) [55.Severino Varela (3/0)], Pedro Lago (2/1), Segundo Villadóniga (1/1), Eduardo Ithurbide (4/0). Trainer: Alberto Horacio Suppici (30).
Goals: Pedro Lago (67), Segundo Villadóniga (86).

165. 02.01.1937 **PARAGUAY - URUGUAY** **4-2(3-2)** 14th Copa América
Estadio Gasómetro de Boedo, Buenos Aires (Argentina); Referee: Virgílio Antônio Fedrighi (Brazil), Attendance: 35,000
URU: Juan Bautista Besuzzo (3/0), Arturo Seoane (2/0), Agenor Muñiz (11/0), Raymundo Andriolo (1/0) [46.Miguel Olivera (2/0)], Eugenio Galvalisi (3/0), Galileo Chanes (3/0), Braulio Castro (9/0), Severino Varela (4/2), Ulises Borges (1/0), Segundo Villadóniga (2/1), Eduardo Ithurbide (5/0) [46.Adelaido Camaití (1/0)]. Trainer: Alberto Horacio Suppici (31).
Goals: Severino Varela (16, 28).

166. 06.01.1937 **URUGUAY - PERU** **4-2(2-2)** 14th Copa América
Estadio Gasómetro de Boedo, Buenos Aires (Argentina); Referee: Alfredo Vargas (Chile), Attendance: 20,000
URU: Enrique Ballestrero (17/0) [46.Juan Bautista Besuzzo (4/0)], Avelino Cadilla (1/0), Agenor Muñiz (12/0), Carlos Martínez (1/0), Miguel Olivera (3/0), Galileo Chanes (4/0), Braulio Castro (10/0) [46.Juan Emilio Píriz (10/3)], Oscar Chirimini (1/0), José Pedro Roselli (1/0), Severino Varela (5/4), Adelaido Camaití (2/1). Trainer: Alberto Horacio Suppici (32).
Goals: Adelaido Camaití (16), Severino Varela (31, 56), Juan Emilio Píriz (79).

167. 10.01.1937 **CHILE - URUGUAY** **3-0(1-0)** 14th Copa América
Estadio Gasómetro de Boedo, Buenos Aires (Argentina); Referee: José Bartolomé Macías (Argentina), Attendance: 18,000
URU: Juan Bautista Besuzzo (5/0), Arturo Seoane (3/0), Agenor Muñiz (13/0), Rodolfo Carreras (3/0), Miguel Olivera (4/0) [46.Galileo Chanes (5/0)], Carlos Martínez (2/0), Juan Emilio Píriz (11/3), Severino Varela (6/4), Oscar Chirimini (2/0) [46.José Pedro Roselli (2/0)], Segundo Villadóniga (3/1), Adelaido Camaití (3/1). Trainer: Alberto Horacio Suppici (33).

168. 19.01.1937 **BRAZIL – URUGUAY** **3-2(1-1)** 14th Copa América
Estadio Gasómetro de Boedo, Buenos Aires (Argentina); Referee: José Bartolomé Macías (Argentina), Attendance: 35,000
URU: Enrique Ballestrero (18/0), Avelino Cadilla (2/0), Agenor Muñiz (14/0), Rodolfo Carreras (4/0), Eugenio Galvalisi (4/0), Carlos Martínez (3/0), Adelaido Camaití (4/1) [46.Juan Emilio Píriz (12/4)], Severino Varela (7/4), José Pedro Roselli (3/0), Segundo Villadóniga (4/2), Eduardo Ithurbide (6/0). Trainer: Alberto Horacio Suppici (34).
Goals: Segundo Villadóniga (1), Juan Emilio Píriz (66).

169. 23.01.1937 **ARGENTINA - URUGUAY** **2-3(0-1)** 14th Copa América
Estadio Gasómetro de Boedo, Buenos Aires; Referee: Alfredo Vargas Ascui (Chile), Attendance: 60,000
URU: Enrique Ballestrero (19/0) [46.Juan Bautista Besuzzo (6/0)], Avelino Cadilla (3/0), Agenor Muñiz (15/0), Rodolfo Carreras (5/0), Eugenio Galvalisi (5/0), Carlos Martínez (4/0), Adelaido Camaití (5/1) [46.Juan Emilio Píriz (13/5)], Severino Varela (8/5), José Pedro Roselli (4/0), Segundo Villadóniga (5/3) [70.Ulises Borges (2/0)], Eduardo Ithurbide (7/0). Trainer: Alberto Horacio Suppici (35).
Goals: Segundo Villadóniga (5), Juan Emilio Píriz (51), Severino Varela (58).

170. 10.10.1937 **URUGUAY - ARGENTINA** **0-3(0-0)** Copa Newton
Estadio Centenario, Montevideo; Referee: Aníbal Tejada (Uruguay), Attendance: 38,000
URU: Juan Bautista Besuzzo (7/0), Jorge Enrique Clulow (3/0), Agenor Muñiz (16/0), Rodolfo Carreras (6/0), Álvaro Antonio Gestido (23/0), Leofar Cámera (2/0), Roberto Porta (1/0), Aníbal Ciocca (9/4), Roberto Fager (1/0), Severino Varela (9/5), Andrés Amarillo (1/0). Trainer: Alberto Horacio Suppici (36).

171. 11.11.1937 **ARGENTINA - URUGUAY** **5-1(2-1)** Copa Lipton
Estadio Independiente, Avellaneda; Referee: Isaac Caswell (England), Attendance: 50,000
URU: Juan Bautisto Besuzzo (8/0), Alejandro Morales (1/0), Agenor Muñiz (17/1), Juan Peláez (1/0), Eugenio Galvalisi (6/0), Carlos Martínez (5/0), Roberto Porta (2/0), Oscar Chirimini (3/0), Francisco Arispe (4/0), Segundo Villadóniga (6/3), Adelaido Camaití (6/1). Trainer: Alberto Horacio Suppici (37).
Goal: Agenor Muñiz (42).

172. 18.06.1938 **ARGENTINA - URUGUAY** **1-0(1-0)** Copa Juan Mignaburu
Estadio Monumental „Antonio Vespucio Liberti“, Buenos Aires; Referee: Alberto Neme (Argentina), Attendance: 40,000
URU: Juan Bautisto Besuzzo (9/0), Agustín Prado (1/0), Agenor Muñiz (18/1), Mario Rodríguez (1/0), Ricardo Gregorio Faccio (3/0), Luis María Denis (6/0), Roberto Porta (3/0), Francisco Arispe (5/0), Lucio Gorla (1/0), Enrique Hernández (1/0), Arturo De León (2/0). Trainer: Alberto Horacio Suppici (38).

173. 12.10.1938 **URUGUAY - ARGENTINA** **2-3(2-1)** Copa Héctor Gómez
Estadio Centenario, Montevideo; Referee: Aníbal Tejada (Uruguay), Attendance: 45,000
URU: Eduardo Larrosa (1/0), Manuel Sanguinetti (1/0), Ernesto Mascheroni (9/0), Mario Rodríguez (2/0), Álvaro Antonio Gestido (24/0), Carlos Martínez (6/0), Roberto Porta (4/0), Severino Varela (10/6), Aníbal Ciocca (10/5), Enrique Hernández (2/0), Juan Emilio Píriz (14/5). Trainer: Alberto Horacio Suppici (39).
Goals: Severino Varela (22), Aníbal Ciocca (30).

174. 22.01.1939 **URUGUAY - ECUADOR** **6-0(1-0)** 15th Copa América
Estadio Nacional, Lima (Peru); Referee: Enrique Cuenca (Peru), Attendance: 10,000
URU: Horacio Granero (1/0), Manuel Sanguinetti (2/0), Ernesto Mascheroni (10/0), Erebo Zunino (9/0), Eugenio Galvalisi (7/0), General Viana (1/0) [46.Abdón Reyes (1/0)], Roberto Porta (5/1), Aníbal Ciocca (11/5), Pedro Lago (3/3), Severino Varela (11/9), Adelaido Camaití (7/1). Trainer: Alberto Horacio Suppici (40).
Goals: Roberto Porta (22), Severino Varela (53, 55), Pedro Lago (65, 70), Severino Varela (81).

175. 29.01.1939 **URUGUAY - CHILE** **3-2(2-2)** 15th Copa América
Estadio Nacional, Lima (Peru); Referee: Enrique Cuenca (Peru), Attendance: 15,000
URU: Horacio Granero (2/0), Manuel Sanguinetti (3/0), Ernesto Mascheroni (11/0), Erebo Zunino (10/0), Eugenio Galvalisi (8/0), Abdón Reyes (2/0) [46.Obdulio Jacinto Varela (1/0)], Roberto Porta (6/1), Aníbal Ciocca (12/5) [46.Oscar Chirimini (4/1)], Pedro Lago (4/3) [70.Roberto Fager (2/0)], Severino Varela (12/10), Adelaido Camaití (8/2). Trainer: Alberto Horacio Suppici (41).
Goals: Severino Varela (19), Adelaido Camaití (30), Oscar Chirimini (73).

176. 05.02.1939 **URUGUAY - PARAGUAY** **3-1(2-0)** 15th Copa América
Estadio Nacional, Lima (Peru); Referee: Enrique Cuenca (Peru), Attendance: 10,000
URU: Horacio Granero (3/0), Manuel Sanguinetti (4/0) [46.Félix Zaccour (1/0)], Ernesto Mascheroni (12/0), Erebo Zunino (11/0), Eugenio Galvalisi (9/0) [46.Obdulio Jacinto Varela (2/0)], General Viana (2/0), Roberto Porta (7/2), Aníbal Ciocca (13/5), Pedro Lago (5/4) [65.Roberto Fager (3/0)], Severino Varela (13/11), Adelaido Camaití (9/2). Trainer: Alberto Horacio Suppici (42).
Goals: Pedro Lago (14), Severino Varela (40), Roberto Porta (66).

177. 12.02.1939 **PERU - URUGUAY** **2-1(2-1)** 15th Copa América
Estadio Nacional, Lima; Referee: Alfredo Vargas (Chile), Attendance: 40,000
URU: Horacio Granero (4/0), Manuel Sanguinetti (5/0) [46.Félix Zaccour (2/0)], Ernesto Mascheroni (13/0), Erebo Zunino (12/0), Eugenio Galvalisi (10/0), General Viana (3/0), Roberto Porta (8/3), Aníbal Ciocca (14/5) [46.Adelaido Camaití (10/2)], Pedro Lago (6/4), Severino Varela (14/11) [46.Oscar Chirimini (5/1)], Plácido Rodríguez. Trainer: Alberto Horacio Suppici (43).
Goal: Roberto Porta (44).

178. 24.03.1940 **BRAZIL - URUGUAY** **3-4(0-1)** Copa Barón de Rio Branco
Estádio São Januário, Rio de Janeiro; Referee: Nobel Valentini (Uruguay)
URU: Julio Barrios (1/0), Héctor Romero (1/0), Agenor Muñiz (19/1), Carlos Martínez (7/0), Sixto González (1/1), Raúl Rodríguez (1/0), Ricardo Pérez (1/0), Oscar Chirimini (6/1) [Luis Mata (1/0)], Pedro Lago (7/4), Severino Varela (15/13), Adelaido Camaití (11/2). Trainer: José Pedro Cea (1).
Goals: Ricardo Pérez (36), Sixto González (63), Severino Varela (64, 90).

179. 31.03.1940 **BRAZIL – URUGUAY** **1-1(0-1)** Copa Barón de Rio Branco
Estádio São Januário, Rio de Janeiro; Referee: José Ferreira Lemos (Brazil)
URU: Julio Barrios (2/0) [Aníbal Luis Paz (1/0)], Héctor Romero (2/0), Agenor Muñiz (20/1), Carlos Martínez (8/0), Sixto González (2/1), Raúl Rodríguez (2/0), Ricardo Pérez (2/0), Oscar Chirimini (7/1) [Luis Mata (2/0)], Pedro Lago (8/4), Severino Varela (16/14), Adelaido Camaití (12/2). Trainer: José Pedro Cea (2).
Goal: Severino Varela (42).

180. 18.07.1940 **URUGUAY - ARGENTINA** **3-0(1-0)** Copa Héctor Gómez
Estadio Centenario, Montevideo; Referee: Aníbal Tejada (Uruguay), Attendance: 35,000
URU: Aníbal Luis Paz (2/0), Juan Ramón Cabrera (1/0), Agenor Muñiz (21/1), Salomé Beracoechea (1/0) [Luis María Denis (7/0)], Álvaro Antonio Gestido (25/0), Raúl Rodríguez (3/0), Luis Tomás Volpi (1/0), Roberto Porta (9/4), Ismael Rivero (1/2), Manuel Antúnez (1/0) [Juan Pedro Riephoff (1/0), José Antonio Vázquez (1/0)], Adelaido Camaití (13/2). Trainer: José Pedro Cea (3).
Goals: Roberto Porta (17), Ismael Rivero (52, 87).

181. 15.08.1940 **ARGENTINA - URUGUAY** **5-0(1-0)** Copa Juan Mignaburu
Estadio Monumental „Antonio Vespucio Liberti", Buenos Aires; Referee: Ubaldo Ruíz (Argentina), Attendance: 25,000
URU: Aníbal Luis Paz (3/0), Juan Ramón Cabrera (2/0), Agenor Muñiz (22/1), Luis Vecino (1/0), Álvaro Antonio Gestido (26/0), Raúl Rodríguez (4/0), Luis Tomás Volpi (2/0), Roberto Porta (10/4) [Juan Antonio Vázquez (2/0)], Ismael Rivero (2/2), Severino Varela (17/14) [Manuel Antúnez (2/0)], Héctor Magliano (1/0). Trainer: José Pedro Cea (4).

182. 09.02.1941 **URUGUAY - ECUADOR** **6-0(4-0)** 16th Copa América
Estadio Nacional, Santiago (Chile); Referee: Alfredo Vargas (Chile), Attendance: 70,000
URU: Aníbal Luis Paz (4/0), Avelino Cadilla (4/0), Juan Ramón Cabrera (3/0), Alberto Delgado (1/0) [59.Carlos Martínez (9/0)], Sixto González (3/1) [46.Obdulio Jacinto Varela (3/0)], Schubert Gambetta (1/1), Roberto Porta (11/5), Oscar Chirimini (8/1), Ismael Rivero (3/5), Antonio Alvarez (1/0), Héctor Magliano (2/0). Trainer: José Pedro Cea (5).
Goals: Ismael Rivero (9), Schubert Gambetta (16), Ismael Rivero (23), Roberto Porta (39), Jorge Laurido (75 own goal), Ismael Rivero (87).

183. 16.02.1941 **CHILE – URUGUAY** **0-2(0-1)** 16th Copa América
Estadio Nacional, Santiago; Referee: José Bartolomé Macías (Argentina), Attendance: 70,000
URU: Aníbal Luis Paz (5/0), Avelino Cadilla (5/0), Héctor Romero (3/0), Carlos Martínez (10/0), Obdulio Jacinto Varela (4/0) [85.Sixto González (4/1)], Schubert Gambetta (2/1), Roberto Porta (12/5), Ubaldo Cruche (1/1) [80.Oscar Chirimini (9/2)], Ismael Rivero (4/5), Juan Pedro Riephoff (2/0), Héctor Magliano (3/0). Trainer: José Pedro Cea (6).
Goals: Ubaldo Cruche (35), Oscar Chirimini (78).

184. 23.02.1941 **ARGENTINA - URUGUAY** **1-0(0-0)** 16th Copa América
Estadio Nacional, Santiago (Chile); Referee: Alfredo Vargas Ascui (Chile), Attendance: 48,000
URU: Aníbal Luis Paz (6/0), Avelino Cadilla (6/0), Héctor Romero (4/0), Carlos Martínez (11/0), Obdulio Jacinto Varela (5/0) [76.Sixto González (5/1)], Schubert Gambetta (3/1), José María Medina (1/0) [73.Oscar Chirimini (10/2)], Roberto Porta (13/5), Ismael Rivero (5/5), Juan Pedro Riephoff (3/0), Héctor Magliano (4/0). Trainer: José Pedro Cea (7).

185. 26.02.1941 **URUGUAY - PERU** **2-0(1-0)** 16th Copa América
Estadio Nacional, Santiago (Chile); Referee: José Bartolomé Macías (Argentina), Attendance: 20,000
URU: Aníbal Luis Paz (7/0) [88.Juan José Carvidón (1/0)], Avelino Cadilla (7/0), Héctor Romero (5/0), Carlos Martínez (12/0), Obdulio Jacinto Varela (6/1), Schubert Gambetta (4/1), Oscar Chirimini (11/2) [22.Ubaldo Cruche (2/1)], Roberto Porta (14/5), Ismael Rivero (6/5), Juan Pedro Riephoff (4/1), Héctor Magliano (5/0). Trainer: José Pedro Cea (8).
Goals: Juan Pedro Riephoff (37), Obdulio Jacinto Varela (70).

186. 10.01.1942 **URUGUAY - CHILE** **6-1(4-1)** 17th Copa América
Estadio Centenario, Montevideo; Referee: José Bartolomé Macías (Argentina), Attendance: 40,000
URU: Aníbal Luis Paz (8/0), Joaquín Bermúdez (1/0), Agenor Muñiz (23/1), Raúl Rodríguez (5/0), Obdulio Jacinto Varela (7/2) [81.Sixto González (6/1)], Schubert Gambetta (5/1), Luis Ernesto Castro (1/2), Severino Varela (18/14) [76.Oscar Chirimini (12/2)], Aníbal Ciocca (15/6), Roberto Porta (15/6), Bibiano Zapirain (1/1). Trainer: José Pedro Cea (9).
Goals: Luis Ernesto Castro (7), Obdulio Jacinto Varela (12), Aníbal Ciocca (15), Bibiano Zapirain (37), Roberto Porta (54), Luis Ernesto Castro (76).

187. 18.01.1942 **URUGUAY – ECUADOR** **7-0(7-0)** 17th Copa América
Estadio Centenario, Montevideo; Referee: Marcos Gerinaldo Rojas (Paraguay), Attendance: 45,000
URU: Aníbal Luis Paz (9/0), Joaquín Bermúdez (2/0), Agenor Muñiz (24/1), Raúl Rodríguez (6/0), Obdulio Jacinto Varela (8/2) [65.Sixto González (7/1)], Schubert Gambetta (6/2), Luis Ernesto Castro (2/2) [46.Enrique Castro (1/0)], Severino Varela (19/17) [80.Oscar Chirimini (13/2)], Aníbal Ciocca (16/6), Roberto Porta (16/8), Bibiano Zapirain (2/2). Trainer: José Pedro Cea (10).
Goals: Bibiano Zapirain (1), Schubert Gambetta (13), Severino Varela (16), Roberto Porta (23), Severino Varela (24, 29), Roberto Porta (42).

188. 24.01.1942 **URUGUAY - BRAZIL** **1-0(1-0)** 17th Copa América
Estadio Centenario, Montevideo; Referee: Marcos Gerinaldo Rojas (Paraguay), Attendance: 55,000
URU: Aníbal Luis Paz (10/0), Héctor Romero (6/0), Agenor Muñiz (25/1), Raúl Rodríguez (7/0), Obdulio Jacinto Varela (9/2), Schubert Gambetta (7/2), Luis Ernesto Castro (3/2), Severino Varela (20/18), Aníbal Ciocca (17/6), Roberto Porta (17/8), Bibiano Zapirain (3/2). Trainer: José Pedro Cea (11).
Goal: Severino Varela (32).

189. 28.01.1942 **URUGUAY - PARAGUAY** **3-1(2-0)** 17th Copa América
Estadio Centenario, Montevideo; Referee: Enrique Cuenca (Peru), Attendance: 40,000
URU: Aníbal Luis Paz (11/0), Joaquín Bermúdez (3/0), Agenor Muñiz (26/1), Raúl Rodríguez (8/0), Obdulio Jacinto Varela (10/2), Schubert Gambetta (8/2), Luis Ernesto Castro (4/2), Severino Varela (21/19), Aníbal Ciocca (18/7), Roberto Porta (18/9), Bibiano Zapirain (4/2). Trainer: José Pedro Cea (12).
Goals: Severino Varela (9), Roberto Porta (26), Aníbal Ciocca (65).

190. 01.02.1942 **URUGUAY - PERU** **3-0(0-0)** 17th Copa América
Estadio Centenario, Montevideo; Referee: José Bartolomé Macías (Argentina), Attendance: 40,000
URU: Aníbal Luis Paz (12/0), Héctor Romero (7/0), Agenor Muñiz (27/1), Raúl Rodríguez (9/0), Obdulio Jacinto Varela (11/2) [75.Eugenio Galvalisi (11/0)], Schubert Gambetta (9/2), Luis Ernesto Castro (5/3), Severino Varela (22/19) [20.Oscar Chirimini (14/3)], Aníbal Ciocca (19/7), Roberto Porta (19/10), Bibiano Zapirain (5/2). Trainer: José Pedro Cea (13).
Goals: Oscar Chirimini (47), Luis Ernesto Castro (54), Roberto Porta (77).

191. 07.02.1942 **URUGUAY - ARGENTINA** **1-0(0-0)** 17th Copa América
Estadio Centenario, Montevideo; Referee: Marcos Gerinaldo Rojas (Paraguay), Attendance: 70,000
URU: Aníbal Luis Paz (13/0), Héctor Romero (8/0), Agenor Muñiz (28/1), Raúl Rodríguez (10/0), Obdulio Jacinto Varela (12/2), Schubert Gambetta (10/2), Luis Ernesto Castro (6/3), Severino Varela (23/19) [21.Oscar Chirimini (15/3), 84.José María Correa (1/0)], Aníbal Ciocca (20/7), Roberto Porta (20/10), Bibiano Zapirain (6/3). Trainer: José Pedro Cea (14).
Goal: Bibiano Zapirain (57).

192. 25.05.1942 **ARGENTINA - URUGUAY** **4-1(3-0)** Copa Newton
Estadio Monumental „Antonio Vespucio Liberti", Buenos Aires; Referee: Juan José Alvarez (Argentina), Attendance: 40,000
URU: Aníbal Luis Paz (14/0), Joaquín Bermúdez (4/0), Secundino Arrascaeta (1/0) [Hugo Bagnulo (1/0)], Schubert Gambetta (11/2), Obdulio Jacinto Varela (13/2), Raúl Rodríguez (11/0), Luis Tomás Volpi (3/0), Juan Antonio Vázquez (3/0), José María Correa (2/0) [Oscar Chirimini (16/3)], Roberto Porta (21/10), Bibiano Zapirain (7/4). Trainer: José Pedro Cea (15).
Goal: Bibiano Zapirain.

193. 25.08.1942 **URUGUAY - ARGENTINA** **1-1(1-0)** Copa Lipton
Estadio Centenario, Montevideo; Referee: Aníbal Tejada (Uruguay), Attendance: 49,850
URU: Juan José Carvidón (2/0), Héctor Romero (9/0) [Blas Baz (1/0)], Secundino Arrascaeta (2/0), Schubert Gambetta (12/2), Obdulio Jacinto Varela (14/2), Raúl Rodríguez (12/0), Luis Ernesto Castro (7/3), Oscar Chirimini (17/3), José Antonio Vázquez (4/1), Manuel Antúnez (3/0) [Roberto Porta (22/10)], Bibiano Zapirain (8/4). Trainer: José Pedro Cea (16).
Goal: José Antonio Vázquez.

194. 28.03.1943 **ARGENTINA - URUGUAY** **3-3(2-1)** Copa Juan Mignaburu
Estadio Monumental „Antonio Vespucio Liberti", Buenos Aires; Referee: José Bartolomé Macías (Argentina), Attendance: 40,000
URU: Juan José Carvidón (3/0) [Flavio Pereyra Natero (1/0)], Blas Baz (2/0), Agenor Muñiz (29/1), Schubert Gambetta (13/2), Obdulio Jacinto Varela (15/2), Raúl Rodríguez (13/0), Luis Ernesto Castro (8/4) [Luis Tomás Volpi (4/0)], Oscar Chirimini (18/3) [Héctor Magliano (6/0)], José María Medina (2/2), Roberto Porta (23/10), Bibiano Zapirain (9/4). Trainer: Héctor Castro (1).
Goals: Luis Ernesto Castro, José María Medina 2.

195. 04.04.1943 **URUGUAY - ARGENTINA** **0-1(0-0)** Copa Héctor Gómez
Estadio Centenario, Montevideo; Referee: Aníbal Tejada (Uruguay), Attendance: 50,320
URU: Juan José Carvidón (4/0), Blas Baz (3/0), Agenor Muñiz (30/1), Schubert Gambetta (14/2), Obdulio Jacinto Varela (16/2), Raúl Rodríguez (14/0) [José Pedro Colturi (1/0)], Luis Ernesto Castro (9/4) [Luis Tomás Volpi (5/0)], Oscar Chirimini (19/3), José María Medina (3/2) [Aníbal Ciocca (21/7)], Roberto Porta (24/10), Bibiano Zapirain (10/4). Trainer: Héctor Castro (2).

196. 14.05.1944 **BRAZIL - URUGUAY** **6-1(4-1)**
Estádio São Januário, Rio de Janeiro; Referee: Genaro Cirillo (Uruguay)
URU: Flavio Pereyra Natero (2/0), Mario Lorenzo (1/0), Secundino Arrascaeta (3/0), José Pedro Colturi (2/0), Ubire Durán (1/0), Julio Sagastume (1/0), Luis Tomás Volpi (6/0) [Juan Santiago (1/0)], Juan Antonio Vázquez (5/1), José María Medina (4/2), Juan Pedro Riephoff (5/1) [Roberto Porta (25/10)], Juan Tejera (1/1). Trainer: Ricardo Acosta (1).
Goal: Juan Tejera (31).

197. 17.05.1944 **BRAZIL - URUGUAY** **4-0(1-0)**
Estádio Pacaembú, São Paulo; Referee: Mário Gonçalves Viana (Brazil)
URU: Juan José Carvidón (5/0), Alejandro Morales (2/0) [Mario Lorenzo (2/0)], Secundino Arrascaeta (4/0), José Pedro Colturi (3/0), Rodolfo Pini (1/0) [Ubire Durán (2/0)], Raúl Rodríguez (15/0), Juan Tejera (2/1), Roberto Porta (26/10), Juan Antonio Vázquez (6/1), Juan Pedro Riephoff (6/1) [José María Medina (5/2)], Juan Santiago (2/0). Trainer: Ricardo Acosta (2).

198. 24.01.1945 **URUGUAY - ECUADOR** **5-1(2-1)** 18th Copa América
Estadio Nacional, Santiago (Chile); Referee: Mário Silveira Vianna (Brazil), Attendance: 70,000
URU: Roque Gastón Máspoli (1/0), Raúl Pini (1/0), Eusebio Ramón Tejera (1/0), José Pedro Colturi (4/0), Obdulio Jacinto Varela (17/3), General Viana (4/0), Luis Ernesto Castro (10/4), José María Ortiz (1/0), José García (1/0) [46.Juan Pedro Riephoff (7/1)], Atilio García (1/3), Roberto Porta (27/11). Trainer: José Nasazzi Yarza (1).
Goals: Atilio García (1), Roberto Porta (28), Atilio García (60), Obdulio Jacinto Varela (69), Atilio García (83).

199. 28.01.1945 **URUGUAY - COLOMBIA** **7-0(3-0)** 18th Copa América
Estadio Nacional, Santiago (Chile); Referee: Mário Silveira Vianna (Brazil), Attendance: 28,000
URU: Roque Gastón Máspoli (2/0), Raúl Pini (2/0), Agustín Prado (2/0), José Pedro Colturi (5/0) [63.Schubert Gambetta (15/2)], Obdulio Jacinto Varela (18/3), General Viana (5/0), Bibiano Zapirain (11/4) [60.Luis Ernesto Castro (11/4)], José María Ortiz (2/1), Atilio García (2/5), Roberto Porta (28/12), Juan Pedro Riephoff (8/2) [30 José García (2/2)]. Trainer: José Nasazzi Yarza (2).
Goals: Atilio García (22), Juan Pedro Riephoff (25), José García (37), José María Ortiz (75), José García (80), Roberto Porta (86), Atilio García (89).

200. 07.02.1945 **BRAZIL - URUGUAY** **3-0(3-0)** 18th Copa América
Estadio Nacional, Santiago (Chile); Referee: José Bartolomé Macías (Argentina), Attendance: 28,000
URU: Roque Gastón Máspoli (3/0), Raúl Pini (3/0) [46.Eusebio Ramón Tejera (2/0)], Agustín Prado (3/0), Schubert Gambetta (16/2), Obdulio Jacinto Varela (19/3), General Viana (6/0), Bibiano Zapirain (12/4), José María Ortiz (3/1), Atilio García (3/5) [65.Nicolás Falero (1/0)], Roberto Porta (29/12), José García (3/2) [46.Raúl Sarro (1/0)]. Trainer: José Nasazzi Yarza (3).

201. 15.02.1945 **URUGUAY - BOLIVIA** **2-0(1-0)** 18th Copa América
Estadio Nacional, Santiago (Chile); Referee: Mário Gonçalves Vianna (Brazil), Attendance: 65,000
URU: Roque Gastón Máspoli (4/0), Agustín Prado (4/0), Eusebio Ramón Tejera (3/0), Schubert Gambetta (17/2) [*sent off 57*], Raúl Sarro (2/0), General Viana (7/0), Luis Ernesto Castro (12/4), Juan Santiago (3/0), Nicolás Falero (2/1), Roberto Porta (30/13), José García (4/2). Trainer: José Nasazzi Yarza (4).
Goals: Nicolás Falero (26), Roberto Porta (75).

202. 18.02.1945 **CHILE - URUGUAY** **1-0(1-0)** 18th Copa América
Estadio Nacional, Santiago; Referee: José Bartolomé Macías (Argentina), Attendance: 53,663
URU: Roque Gastón Máspoli (5/0), Agustín Prado (5/0), Eusebio Ramón Tejera (4/0), Schubert Gambetta (18/2), Raúl Sarro (3/0), General Viana (8/0), Luis Ernesto Castro (13/4) [70.José María Ortiz (4/1)], Atilio García (4/5), Bibiano Zapirain (13/4), Roberto Porta (31/13), Juan Pedro Riephoff (9/2) [18.José García (5/2)]. Trainer: José Nasazzi Yarza (5).

203. 25.02.1945 **ARGENTINA - URUGUAY** **1-0(0-0)** 18th Copa América
Estadio Nacional, Santiago (Chile); Referee: Juan Las Heras Marrodan (Chile), Attendance: 40,000
URU: Roque Gastón Máspoli (6/0), Agustín Prado (6/0), Eusebio Ramón Tejera (5/0), Obdulio Jacinto Varela (20/3), Raúl Sarro (4/0), General Viana (9/0), José María Ortiz (5/1), Atilio García (5/5) [80.Nicolás Falero (3/1)], Bibiano Zapirain (14/4), Roberto Porta (32/13), José García (6/2) [65.Luis Ernesto Castro (14/4)]. Trainer: José Nasazzi Yarza (6).

204. 18.07.1945 **URUGUAY - ARGENTINA** **2-2(0-2)** Copa Lipton
Estadio Centenario, Montevideo; Referee: Juan Carlos Armental (Uruguay), Attendance: 40,000
URU: Aníbal Luis Paz (15/0), Raúl Pini (4/0), Secundino Arrascaeta (5/0), Alfredo Young (1/0) [General Viana (10/0)], Obdulio Jacinto Varela (21/5), José Cajiga (1/0), Luis Ernesto Castro (15/4), Raúl Antonio Schiaffino (1/0) [Nicolás Falero (4/1)], José María Medina (6/0), Juan Pedro Riephoff (10/2) [Raúl Sarro (5/0)], Bibiano Zapirain (15/4). Trainer: José Pedro Cea (17).
Goals: Obdulio Jacinto Varela 2

205. 15.08.1945 **ARGENTINA - URUGUAY** **6-2(4-1)** Copa Newton
Estadio Gasómetro de Boedo, Buenos Aires; Referee: Eduardo Forte (Argentina), Attendance: 55,000
URU: Aníbal Luis Paz (16/0), Pedro Salazar (1/0), Secundino Arrascaeta (6/0), Alfredo Young (2/0) [Alcides Mañay (1/0)], Ubire Durán (3/0), José Cajiga (2/0) [Luis Abelleria (1/0)], José María Ortiz (6/2), Walter Gómez (1/0) [Domingo Gelpi (1/0)], Nicolás Falero (5/2) , Juan Pedro Riephoff (11/2) [Roberto Porta (33/13)], Bibiano Zapirain (16/4). Trainer: José Pedro Cea (18).
Goals: José María Ortiz, Nicolás Falero.

206. 05.01.1946 **URUGUAY - BRAZIL** **4-3(1-2)** Copa Rio Branco
Estadio Centenario, Montevideo; Referee: Mário Gonçalves Vianna (Brazil)
URU: Roque Gastón Máspoli (7/0), Mario Lorenzo (3/0) [Raúl Pini (5/0)], Eusebio Ramón Tejera (6/0), Ubire Durán (4/0), Obdulio Jacinto Varela (22/5), Luis Prais (1/0), Ramón Castro (1/1) [José María Ortiz (7/2)], José María Medina (7/0), Raúl Antonio Schiaffino (2/1), Juan Pedro Riephoff (12/3), Ramón Ferrés (1/0) [Luis Tomás Volpi (7/1)]. Trainer: Aníbal Tejada (1).
Goals: Juan Riephoff (18), Ramón Castro (49), Raúl Antonio Schiaffino (87), Luis Tomás Volpi (90).

207. 09.01.1946 **URUGUAY - BRAZIL** **1-1(1-1)** Copa Rio Branco
Estadio Centenario, Montevideo; Referee: Juan Carlos Amental (Uruguay)
URU: Roque Gastón Máspoli (8/0), Raúl Pini (6/0), Eusebio Ramón Tejera (7/0), Ubire Durán (5/0), Obdulio Jacinto Varela (23/5), Luis Prais (2/0), José María Ortiz (8/2), José María Medina (8/1) [Walter Gómez (2/0)], Juan Alberto Schiaffino (1/0), Juan Pedro Riephoff (13/3), Luis Tomás Volpi (8/1). Trainer: Aníbal Tejada (2).
Goal: José María Medina (34).

208. 16.01.1946 **URUGUAY - CHILE** **1-0(1-0)** 19th Copa América
Estadio Gasómetro de Boedo, Buenos Aires (Argentina); Referee: Mário Silveira Vianna (Brazil), Attendance: 50,000
URU: Roque Gastón Máspoli (9/0), Raúl Pini (7/0), Eusebio Ramón Tejera (8/0), Ubire Durán (6/0), Alcides Mañay (2/0) [46.Obdulio Jacinto Varela (24/5)], Luis Prais (3/0), Ramón Castro (2/1), José María Medina (9/2), Raúl Antonio Schiaffino (3/1), Juan Pedro Riephoff (14/3) [74.Juan Antonio Vázquez (7/1)], Bibiano Zapirain (17/4). Trainer: Aníbal Tejada (3).
Goal: José María Medina (34).

209. 23.01.1946 **BRAZIL - URUGUAY** **4-3(4-2)** 19th Copa América
Estadio Gasómetro de Boedo, Buenos Aires (Argentina); Referee: Cayetano de Nicola (Paraguay), Attendance: 40,000
URU: Roque Gastón Máspoli (10/0), Raúl Pini (8/0), Eusebio Ramón Tejera (9/0), Luis Sabatel (1/0), Obdulio Jacinto Varela (25/5), Luis Prais (4/0) [46.José Cajiga (3/0)], Luis Tomás Volpi (9/1), José María Medina (10/4), Raúl Antonio Schiaffino (4/1) [46.José García (7/2)], Juan Antonio Vázquez (8/2), Bibiano Zapirain (18/4). Trainer: Aníbal Tejada (4).
Goals: José María Medina (25), Juan Antonio Vázquez (37), José María Medina (70).

210. 29.01.1946 **URUGUAY - BOLIVIA** **5-0(3-0)** 19th Copa América
Estadio Independiente, Avellaneda (Argentina); Referee: Higinio Madrid (Chile), Attendance: 30,000
URU: Roque Gastón Máspoli (11/0), Raúl Pini (9/0), Sixto Valentín Possamai (1/0), Luis Sabatel (2/0), Ubire Durán (7/0) [46.Alcides Mañay (3/0)], José Cajiga (4/0), Luis Tomás Volpi (10/1), José María Medina (11/8), José García (8/3) [80.Walter Gómez (3/0)], Juan Pedro Riephoff (15/3), Bibiano Zapirain (19/4) [46.Ramón Castro (3/1)]. Trainer: Guzmán Vila Gomensoro (1).
Goals: José María Medina (1, 25, 30), José García (75), José María Medina (78).

211. 02.02.1946 **ARGENTINA - URUGUAY** **3-1(1-0)** 19th Copa América
Estadio Gasómetro de Boedo, Buenos Aires; Referee: Mário Silveira Vianna (Brazil), Attendance: 80,000
URU: Roque Gastón Máspoli (12/0), Raúl Pini (10/0), Eusebio Ramón Tejera (10/0), Luis Sabatel (3/0), Obdulio Jacinto Varela (26/5) [73.Ubire Durán (8/0)], José Cajiga (5/0), Luis Tomás Volpi (11/1), José María Medina (12/8) [73.Walter Gómez (4/0)], José García (9/3) [75.Raúl Antonio Schiaffino (5/1)], Juan Pedro Riephoff (16/4), Bibiano Zapirain (20/4). Trainer: Guzmán Vila Gomensoro (2).
Goal: Juan Pedro Riephoff (59).

212. 08.02.1946 **PARAGUAY - URUGUAY** **2-1(1-0)** 19th Copa América
Estadio Gasómetro de Boedo, Buenos Aires (Argentina); Referee: Mário Silveira Vianna (Brazil), Attendance: 18,000
URU: Roque Gastón Máspoli (13/0), Raúl Pini (11/0), Sixto Valentín Possamai (2/0), Luis Sabatel (4/0), Obdulio Jacinto Varela (27/5) [46.Ubire Durán (9/0)], José Cajiga (6/0) [Luis Prais (5/0)], Ramón Castro (4/1) [46.José María Medina (13/8)], José García (10/3), Juan Pedro Riephoff (17/4), Luis Tomás Volpi (12/1), Raúl Antonio Schiaffino (6/2). Trainer: Guzmán Vila Gomensoro (3).
Goal: Raúl Antonio Schiaffino (57).

213. 29.03.1947 **URUGUAY - BRAZIL** **0-0** Copa Rio Branco
Estadio Centenario, Montevideo; Referee: Juan Carlos Armental (Uruguay)
URU: Roque Gastón Máspoli (14/0), Mario Lorenzo (4/0), Eusebio Ramón Tejera (11/0), Schubert Gambetta (19/2), Alcides Mañay (4/0) [Lorenzo Barreto (1/0)], José Cajiga (7/0), Luis Ernesto Castro (16/4), José García (11/3), José María Medina (14/8), Juan Burgueño (1/0) [Luis Alberto Pérez Luz (1/0)], José Godart (1/0). Trainer: Marcelino Pérez (1).

214. 01.04.1947 **BRAZIL - URUGUAY** **3-2(2-0)** Copa Rio Branco
Estádio São Januário, Rio de Janeiro; Referee: João Etzel Filho (Brazil)
URU: Roque Gastón Máspoli (15/0), Raúl Pini (12/0), Eusebio Ramón Tejera (12/0), Schubert Gambetta (20/2), Rodolfo Pini (2/1) [José De Lucca (1/0)], Luis Alberto Pérez Luz (2/0), Luis Ernesto Castro (17/4), Juan Burgueño (2/0) [Juan Alberto Schiaffino (2/0)], José García (12/3), José María Medina (15/9), José Godart (2/0). Trainer: Marcelino Pérez (2).
Goals: José María Medina (52), Rodolfo Pini (80)

215. 02.12.1947 **URUGUAY – COLOMBIA** **2-0(1-0)** 20th Copa América
Estadio „George Capwell", Guayaquil (Ecuador); Referee: Juan José Alvarez (Argentina), Attendance: 20,000
URU: Juan José Tulic (1/0), Mario Lorenzo (5/0), Eusebio Ramón Tejera (13/0), Schubert Gambetta (21/2) [85.Víctor Pablo Rodríguez Andrade (1/0)], Hosiriz Romero (1/0), José Cajiga (8/0), Julio César Britos (1/1), José García (13/3) [70.Oscar Chelle (1/0)], Nicolás Falero (6/3), Raúl Sarro (6/0) [50. Juan Pedro Riephoff (18/4)], Héctor Magliano (7/0). Trainer: Juan López Fontana (1).
Goals: Nicolás Falero (26), Julio César Britos (61).

216. 06.12.1947 **URUGUAY – CHILE** **6-0(3-0)** 20th Copa América
Estadio „George Capwell", Guayaquil (Ecuador); Referee: Juan José Alvarez (Argentina), Attendance: 20,000
URU: Juan José Tulic (2/0), Mario Lorenzo (6/0) [46.Julio Ulises Terra (1/0)], Eusebio Ramón Tejera (14/0), Schubert Gambetta (22/3), Hosiriz Romero (2/0), José Cajiga (9/0), Julio César Britos (2/1) [46.Washington Puente (1/0)], José García (14/3), Nicolás Falero (7/5), Raúl Sarro (7/1) [46.Juan Pedro Riephoff (19/4)], Héctor Magliano (8/2). Trainer: Juan López Fontana (2).
Goals: Raúl Sarro (9), Nicolás Falero (39, 42), Schubert Gambetta (68), Héctor Magliano (88, 89).

217. 09.12.1947 **URUGUAY – BOLIVIA** **3-0(1-0)** 20th Copa América
Estadio „George Capwell", Guayaquil (Ecuador); Referee: Mario Rubén Heyn (Paraguay), Attendance: 15,000
URU: Juan José Tulic (3/0), Mario Lorenzo (7/0), Eusebio Ramón Tejera (15/0), Schubert Gambetta (23/3), Luis Alberto Pérez Luz (3/0), Julio César Britos (3/1), Lorenzo Barreto (2/0), Nicolás Falero (8/7), Juan Pedro Riephoff (20/4) [26.Washington Stula (1/0)], José García (15/3), Héctor Magliano (9/3). Trainer: Juan López Fontana (3).
Goals: Héctor Magliano (9), Nicolás Falero (50, 79).

218. 13.12.1947 **PARAGUAY – URUGUAY** **4-2(0-1)** 20th Copa América
Estadio „George Capwell", Guayaquil (Ecuador); Referee: Juan José Alvarez (Argentina), Attendance: 18,000
URU: Juan José Tulic (4/0), Mario Lorenzo (8/0), Eusebio Ramón Tejera (16/0), Schubert Gambetta (24/3), Hosiriz Romero (3/0) [80.Lorenzo Barreto (3/0)], José Cajiga (10/0), Julio César Britos (4/2), José García (16/3) [73.Oscar Chelle (2/0)], Nicolás Falero (9/7), Raúl Sarro (8/1) [28.Washington Stula (2/0)], Héctor Magliano (10/4). Trainer: Juan López Fontana (4).
Goals: Héctor Magliano (3), Julio César Britos (47).

219. 16.12.1947 **ECUADOR – URUGUAY** **1-6(0-5)** 20th Copa América
Estadio „George Capwell", Guayaquil; Referee: Víctor Francisco Rivas (Chile), Attendance: 30,000
URU: Juan José Tulic (5/0) [46.Francisco Sabini (1/0)], Mario Lorenzo (9/0), Eusebio Ramón Tejera (17/0) [46.José Riobó (1/0)], Schubert Gambetta (25/3), Hosiriz Romero (4/0) [46.Lorenzo Barreto (4/0)], José Cajiga (11/0), Washington Puente (2/2), José García (17/4), Nicolás Falero (10/9), Raúl Sarro (9/2), Héctor Magliano (11/4). Trainer: Juan López Fontana (5).
Goals: Nicolás Falero (19, 21), Washington Puente (24), José García (28), Raúl Sarro (35), Washington Puente (88).

220. 26.12.1947 **URUGUAY – PERU** **1-0(0-0)** 20th Copa América
Estadio „George Capwell", Guayaquil (Ecuador); Referee: Víctor Francisco Rivas (Chile), Attendance: 6,000
URU: Juan José Tulic (6/0), Julio Ulises Terra (2/0), Eusebio Ramón Tejera (18/0), Schubert Gambetta (26/3), Hosiriz Romero (5/0), José Cajiga (12/0), Julio César Britos (5/2) [46.Washington Puente (3/2)], José García (18/4), Nicolás Falero (11/10), Raúl Sarro (10/2), Héctor Magliano (12/4) [46.Washington Stula (3/0)]. Trainer: Juan López Fontana (6).
Goal: Nicolás Falero (74).

221. 28.12.1947 **ARGENTINA – URUGUAY** **3-1(1-0)** 20th Copa América
Estadio „George Capwell", Guayaquil (Ecuador); Referee: Mario Rubén Heyn (Paraguay), Attendance: 25,000
URU: Juan José Tulic (7/0), Julio Ulises Terra (3/0), Eusebio Ramón Tejera (19/0), Schubert Gambetta (27/3) [46.Víctor Pablo Rodríguez Andrade (2/0)], Hosiriz Romero (6/0), José Cajiga (13/0), Julio César Britos (6/3), José García (19/4), Nicolás Falero (12/10) [79.Oscar Chelle (3/0)], Raúl Sarro (11/2) [46.Juan Pedro Riephoff (21/4)], Héctor Magliano (13/4). Trainer: Juan López Fontana (7).
Goal: Julio César Britos (74).

222. 04.04.1948 **URUGUAY – BRAZIL** **1-1(1-0)** Copa Rio Branco
Estadio Centenario, Montevideo; Referee: Alberto Monard de Gama Malcher (Brazil), Attendance: 49,143
URU: Roque Gastón Máspoli (16/0), Mario Lorenzo (10/0), Eusebio Ramón Tejera (20/0), Schubert Gambetta (28/3), Obdulio Jacinto Varela (28/5), José Cajiga (14/0), Julio César Britos (7/3), José García (20/4) [Víctor Rodríguez Andrade (3/0)], Nicolás Falero (13/11), Raúl Sarro (12/2) [Juan Pedro Riephoff (22/4)], Juan Ramón Orlandi (1/0). Trainer: Juan López Fontana (8).
Goal: Nicolás Falero (1).

223. 11.04.1948 **URUGUAY – BRAZIL** **4-2(2-1)** Copa Rio Branco
Estadio Centenario, Montevideo; Referee: Luis Alberto Fernández (Uruguay), Attendance: 29,374
URU: Roque Gastón Máspoli (17/0), Mario Lorenzo (11/0), Eusebio Ramón Tejera (21/0), Schubert Gambetta (29/3), Obdulio Jacinto Varela (29/6), José Cajiga (15/0), Julio César Britos (8/4) [Washington Puente (4/2)], José García (21/4), Nicolás Falero (14/12) [Oscar Chelle (4/0)], Juan Alberto Schiaffino (3/0), Héctor Magliano (14/5). Trainer: Juan López Fontana (9).
Goals: Nicolás Falero (8), Obdulio Jacinto Varela (11), Julio César Britos (46), Héctor Magliano (52).

224. 13.04.1949 **URUGUAY – ECUADOR** **3-2(2-2)** 21st Copa América
Estádio São Januário, Rio de Janeiro (Brazil); Referee: Alberto Da Gama Malcher (Brazil), Attendance: 30,000
URU: Jorge La Paz (1/0), Matías González (1/0), Roberto Gadea (1/0), Julio César Villarreal (1/0), Roberto García (1/0), Simón García (1/0), Ramón Castro (5/3), Nelson Moreno (1/1) [Dagoberto Moll (1/0)], Juan Ayala (1/0) [José María García (1/0)], Ernesto Bentancour (1/0), Miguel Martínez (1/0). Trainer: Oscar Marcenaro (1).
Goals: Ramón Castro (15), Nelson Moreno (30), Ramón Castro (85).

225. 17.04.1949 **BOLIVIA – URUGUAY** **3-2(0-0)** 21st Copa América
Estádio São Januário, Rio de Janeiro (Brazil); Referee: Alberto Monard da Gama Malcher (Brazil), Attendance: 8,000
URU: Jorge La Paz (2/0), Matías González (2/0), Roberto Gadea (2/0), Julio César Villarreal (2/0), Roberto García (2/0), Simón García (2/0) [Esteban Suárez (1/0)], Ramón Castro (6/3), Nelson Moreno (2/1) [Dagoberto Moll (2/1)], Juan Ayala (2/0), Ernesto Bentancour (2/1), Miguel Martínez (2/0). Trainer: Oscar Marcenaro (2).
Goals: Dagoberto Moll (49), Ernesto Bentancour (70).

226. 20.04.1949 **URUGUAY - PARAGUAY** **2-1(1-0)** 21st Copa América

Estádio Pacaembú, São Paulo (Brazil); Referee: Cyril John Barrick (England), Attendance: 20,000

URU: Raúl Arizábalo (1/0), Matías González (3/0), Roberto Gadea (3/0), Julio César Villarreal (3/0), Roberto García (3/0), Simón García (3/0), Ramón Castro (7/3), Nelson Moreno (3/1), José María García (2/2), Ernesto Bentancour (3/1), Esteban Suárez (2/0). Trainer: Oscar Marcenaro (3).

Goals: José María García (22, 69).

227. 24.04.1949 **URUGUAY - COLOMBIA** **2-2(0-1)** 21st Copa América

Estádio Pacaembú, São Paulo (Brazil); Referee: Alberto da Gama Malcher (Brazil), Attendance: 14,000

URU: Raúl Arizábalo (2/0), Matías González (4/0), Roberto Gadea (4/0), Julio César Villarreal (4/0), Roberto García (4/0), Simón García (4/0), José María García (3/2), Nelson Moreno (4/1) [Dagoberto Moll (3/1)], Ramón Castro (8/3) [Juan Ayala (3/1)], Ernesto Bentancour (4/1), Esteban Suárez (3/0) [Miguel Martínez (3/1)]. Trainer: Oscar Marcenaro (4).

Goals: Miguel Martínez (57), Juan Ayala (86).

228. 30.04.1949 **BRAZIL - URUGUAY** **5-1(3-1)** 21st Copa América

Estádio São Januário, Rio de Janeiro; Referee: Alberto Monard de Gama Malcher (Brazil), Attendance: 45,000

URU: Jorge La Paz (3/0), Matías González (5/0), Roberto Gadea (5/0), Julio César Villarreal (5/0), Roberto García (5/0), Simón García (5/0), José María García (4/2) [Juan Ayala (4/1)], Nelson Moreno (5/1), Ramón Castro (9/4), Ernesto Bentancour (5/1) [Dagoberto Moll (4/1)], Esteban Suárez (4/0) [Miguel Martínez (4/1)]. Trainer: Oscar Marcenaro (5).

Goal: Ramón Castro (12).

229. 04.05.1949 **PERU - URUGUAY** **4-3(2-0)** 21st Copa América

Estádio Botafogo, Rio de Janeiro (Brazil); Referee: Alfredo Álvarez (Bolivia), Attendance: 30,000

URU: Jorge La Paz (4/0), Matías González (6/0), Roberto Gadea (6/0), Julio César Villarreal (6/0), Roberto García (6/0), Simón García (6/0), Nelson Moreno (6/1) [Dagoberto Moll (5/2)], Ramón Castro (10/5), Juan Ayala (5/2), Ernesto Bentancour (6/1), Miguel Martínez (5/1) [José María García (5/2)]. Trainer: Oscar Marcenaro (6).

Goals: Dagoberto Moll (58), Ramón Castro (60), Juan Ayala (85).

230. 08.05.1949 **CHILE - URUGUAY** **3-1(0-1)*** 21st Copa América

Estádio América, Belo Horizonte (Brazil); Referee: Mario Gardelli (Brazil), Attendance: 5,000

URU: Jorge La Paz (5/0), Matías González (7/0), Roberto Gadea (7/0), Julio César Villarreal (7/0), Roberto García (7/0), Simón García (7/0), Juan Ayala (6/3), Miguel Martínez (6/1) [José María García (6/2)], Dagoberto Moll (6/2) [Nelson Moreno (7/1)], Ramón Castro (11/5), Ernesto Bentancour (7/1). Trainer: Oscar Marcenaro (7).

Goal: Juan Ayala (35).

Uruguay left the field after 83 minutes

231. 07.04.1950 **CHILE - URUGUAY** **1-5(1-3)**

Estadio Nacional, Santiago; Referee: Mario Gardelli (Brazil), Attendance: 40,000

URU: Aníbal Luis Paz (17/0), William Rubén Martínez (1/0), Héctor Vilches (1/0), Víctor Pablo Rodríguez Andrade (4/0), Rodolfo Pini (3/2) [Ubire Durán (10/0)], José Cajiga (16/0) [Luis De Angelis (1/0)], Santos Carámbula (1/1), Carlos Romero (1/0), Nelson Cancela (1/0) [Juan Burgueño (3/0)], Julio Gervasio Pérez (1/2) [Ramón Cantou (1/0)], Rúben Morán (1/1). Trainer: Romeo Vázquez (1).

Goals: Rodolfo Pini (15), Julio Gervasio Pérez (35), Rúben Morán (36), Julio Gervasio Pérez (73), Santos Carámbula (89).

232. 09.04.1950 **CHILE - URUGUAY** **2-1(2-1)**

Estadio Nacional, Santiago; Referee: Mario Gardelli (Brazil), Attendance: 40,000

URU: Aníbal Luis Paz (18/0), William Rubén Martínez (2/0), Héctor Vilches (2/0) [Felipe Carrizo (1/0)], Víctor Pablo Rodríguez Andrade (5/0) [Domingo Rodríguez (1/0)], Rodolfo Pini (4/2) [Ubire Durán (11/0)], José Cajiga (17/0) [Luis De Angelis (2/0)], Santos Carámbula (2/1), Carlos Romero (2/1), Nelson Cancela (2/0) [Ramón Cantou (2/0)], Julio Gervasio Pérez (2/2) [Juan Burgueño (4/0), José María Ortiz (9/2)], Rúben Morán (2/1). Trainer: Romeo Vázquez (2).

Goals: Carlos Romero (25).

233. 30.04.1950 **PARAGUAY - URUGUAY** **3-2** Copa Trompowski

Estádio São Januário, Rio de Janeiro; Referee: Mário Vianna (Brazil)

URU: Aníbal Luis Paz (19/0), William Rubén Martínez (3/0) [Matías González (8/0)], Héctor Vilches (3/0) [Eusebio Ramón Tejera (22/0)], Víctor Pablo Rodríguez Andrade (6/0), Obdulio Jacinto Varela (30/6) [Rodolfo Pini (5/2)], Luis De Angelis (3/0), Julio César Britos (9/5), Julio Gervasio Pérez (3/3), Oscar Omar Míguez (1/0), Juan Alberto Schiaffino (4/0), Hugo Villamide (1/0). Trainer: Romeo Vázquez (3).

Goals: Julio César Britos, Julio Gervasio Pérez.

234. 06.05.1950 **BRAZIL - URUGUAY** **3-4(2-3)** Copa Rio Branco

Estádio Pacaembú, São Paulo; Referee: Cyril John Barrick (England)

URU: Roque Gastón Máspoli (18/0), Matías González (9/0), Héctor Vilches (4/0), Juan Carlos González (1/0), Obdulio Jacinto Varela (31/6), Víctor Pablo Rodríguez Andrade (7/0) [Schubert Gambetta (30/3)], Julio César Britos (10/5), Julio Gervasio Pérez (4/4), Oscar Omar Míguez (2/1), Juan Alberto Schiaffino (5/2), Hugo Villamide (2/0) [Alcides Edgardo Ghiggia (1/0)]. Trainer: Romeo Vázquez (4).

Goals: Julio Gervasio Pérez (23), Oscar Omar Míguez (27), Juan Alberto Schiaffino (29, 49).

235. 14.05.1950 **BRAZIL - URUGUAY** **3-2(3-2)** Copa Rio Branco

Estádio São Januário, Rio de Janeiro; Referee: Cyril John Barrick (England)

URU: Roque Gastón Máspoli (19/0), Matías González (10/0), Héctor Vilches (5/0) [Schubert Gambetta (31/3)], Juan Carlos González (2/0), Obdulio Jacinto Varela (32/6), Víctor Pablo Rodríguez Andrade (8/0), Alcides Edgardo Ghiggia (2/0), Julio Gervasio Pérez (5/4), Oscar Omar Míguez (3/1) [Eusebio Ramón Tejera (23/0)], Juan Alberto Schiaffino (6/2) [Carlos Romero (3/1)], Hugo Villamide (3/1) [Juan Ramón Orlandi (2/0)]. Trainer: Romeo Vázquez (5).

Goals: Nílton Santos (24 own goal), Hugo Villamide (43).

236. 17.05.1950 **BRAZIL - URUGUAY** **1-0(0-0)** Copa Rio Branco

Estádio São Januário, Rio de Janeiro; Referee: Cyril John Barrick (England)

URU: Roque Gastón Máspoli (20/0), Matías González (11/0), Eusebio Ramón Tejera (24/0), Juan Carlos González (3/0) [Schubert Gambetta (32/3)], Obdulio Jacinto Varela (33/6) [Rodolfo Pini (6/2)], Víctor Pablo Rodríguez Andrade (9/0), Alcides Edgardo Ghiggia (3/0), Julio Gervasio Pérez (6/4), Oscar Omar Míguez (4/1), Juan Alberto Schiaffino (7/2) [Carlos Romero (4/1)], Hugo Villamide (4/1) [Juan Ramón Orlandi (3/0)]. Trainer: Romeo Vázquez (6).

237. 02.07.1950 **URUGUAY - BOLIVIA** **8-0(4-0)** 4th FIFA WC. Group Stage
Estádio Independencia, Belo Horizonte (Brazil); Referee: George Reader (England), Attendance: 5,284
URU: Roque Gastón Máspoli (21/0), Matías González (12/0), Eusebio Ramón Tejera (25/0), Juan Carlos González (4/0), Obdulio Jacinto Varela (34/6), Víctor Pablo Rodríguez Andrade (10/0), Alcides Edgardo Ghiggia (4/1), Julio Gervasio Pérez (7/5), Oscar Omar Míguez (5/4), Juan Alberto Schiaffino (8/4), Ernesto José Vidal (1/1). Trainer: Juan López Fontana (10).
Goals: Oscar Omar Míguez (12), Ernesto José Vidal (18), Juan Alberto Schiaffino (20), Oscar Omar Míguez (37, 51), Juan Alberto Schiaffino (54), Julio Gervasio Pérez (78), Alcides Edgardo Ghiggia (83).

238. 09.07.1950 **URUGUAY - SPAIN** **2-2(1-2)** 4th FIFA WC. Final Round
Estádio Pacaembú, São Paulo (Brazil); Referee: Mervyn Griffiths (Wales), Attendance: 44,000
URU: Roque Gastón Máspoli (22/0), Matías González (13/0), Eusebio Ramón Tejera (26/0), Juan Carlos González (5/0), Obdulio Jacinto Varela (35/7), Víctor Pablo Rodríguez Andrade (11/0), Alcides Edgardo Ghiggia (5/2), Julio Gervasio Pérez (8/5), Oscar Omar Míguez (6/4), Juan Alberto Schiaffino (9/4), Ernesto José Vidal (2/1). Trainer: Juan López Fontana (11).
Goals: Alcides Edgardo Ghiggia (29), Obdulio Jacinto Varela (72).

239. 13.07.1950 **URUGUAY - SWEDEN** **3-2(1-2)** 4th FIFA WC. Final Round
Estádio „Cicero Pompeu de Toledo“ (Morumbí), São Paulo (Brazil); Referee: Giovanni Galeati (Italy), Attendance: 7,987
URU: Anibal Luis Paz (20/0), Matías González (14/0), Eusebio Ramón Tejera (27/0), Schubert Gambetta (33/3), Obdulio Jacinto Varela (36/7), Víctor Pablo Rodríguez Andrade (12/0), Alcides Edgardo Ghiggia (6/3), Julio Gervasio Pérez (9/5), Oscar Omar Míguez (7/6), Juan Alberto Schiaffino (10/4), Ernesto José Vidal (3/1). Trainer: Juan López Fontana (12).
Goals: Alcides Edgardo Ghiggia (39), Oscar Omar Míguez (77, 84)

240. 16.07.1950 **BRAZIL - URUGUAY** **1-2(0-0)** 4th FIFA WC. Final Round
Estádio „Jornalista Mário Filho“ (Maracanã), Rio de Janeiro; Referee: George A. Reader (England)), Attendance: 202,772
URU: Roque Gastón Máspoli (23/0), Matías González (15/0), Eusebio Ramón Tejera (28/0), Schubert Gambetta (34/3), Obdulio Jacinto Varela (37/7), Víctor Pablo Rodríguez Andrade (13/0), Alcides Edgardo Ghiggia (7/4), Julio Gervasio Pérez (10/5), Oscar Omar Míguez (8/6), Juan Alberto Schiaffino (11/5), Rúben Morán (3/1). Trainer: Juan López Fontana (13).
Goals: Juan Alberto Schiaffino (58), Alcides Edgardo Ghiggia (61).

241. 23.03.1952 **URUGUAY - MEXICO** **3-1(2-1)** Panamerican Championship
Estadio Nacional, Santiago; Referee: William Crawford (England)
URU: Roque Gastón Máspoli (24/0), Matías González (16/0), Schubert Gambetta (35/3) [Héctor Vilches (6/0)], Víctor Pablo Rodríguez Andrade (14/0), Ubire Durán (12/0), Obdulio Jacinto Varela (38/7), Alcides Edgardo Ghiggia (8/4), Julio Gervasio Pérez (11/5) [Javier Ambrois (1/0)], Oscar Omar Míguez (9/7), Julio César Abbadie (1/1), Ernesto José Vidal (4/1). Trainer: Juan López Fontana (14).
Goals: Sergio Bravo (27 own goal), Oscar Omar Míguez (40), Julio César Abbadie (87).

242. 30.03.1952 **URUGUAY - PERU** **5-2(3-1)** Panamerican Championship
Estadio Nacional, Santiago; Referee: William Crawford (England)
URU: Luis Radiche (1/0), Matías González (17/0), Héctor Vilches (7/0), Víctor Pablo Rodríguez Andrade (15/0) [Juan Carlos González (6/0)], Obdulio Jacinto Varela (39/7) [Osvaldo Balseiro (1/0)], Omar Ferreira (1/0), Alcides Edgardo Ghiggia (9/4), Julio Gervasio Pérez (12/6), Oscar Omar Míguez (10/10), Julio César Abbadie (2/1), Ernesto José Vidal (5/2). Trainer: Juan López Fontana (15).
Goals: Julio Gervasio Pérez (22), Oscar Omar Míguez (39, 54), Ernesto José Vidal (70), Oscar Omar Míguez (83).

243. 06.04.1952 **URUGUAY - PANAMA** **6-1(3-1)** Panamerican Championship
Estadio Nacional, Santiago; Referee: Walter Manning (England), Attendance: 27,333
URU: Roque Gastón Máspoli (25/0), Matías González (18/0) [José Emilio Santamaría (1/0)], Héctor Vilches (8/0), Víctor Pablo Rodríguez Andrade (16/0), Osvaldo Balseiro (2/0), Ubire Durán (13/0), Alcides Edgardo Ghiggia (10/4) [Julio César Britos (11/6)], Javier Ambrois (2/0), Oscar Omar Míguez (11/11), Julio César Abbadie (3/4) [Washington Loureiro (1/1)], Ernesto José Vidal (6/2). Trainer: Juan López Fontana (16).
Goals: Julio César Abbadie (6, 13, 30), Julio César Britos (63), Oscar Omar Míguez (69), Washington Loureiro (85).

244. 13.04.1952 **CHILE - URUGUAY** **2-0(1-0)** Panamerican Championship
Estadio Nacional, Santiago; Referee: Charles Dean (England), Attendance: 50,000
URU: Roque Gastón Máspoli (26/0), Matías González (19/0), Héctor Vilches (9/0), Juan Carlos González (7/0) [Víctor Pablo Rodríguez Andrade (17/0)], Obdulio Jacinto Varela (40/7) [Osvaldo Balseiro (3/0)], Omar Ferreira (2/0), Alcides Edgardo Ghiggia (11/4), Julio Gervasio Pérez (13/6) [Javier Ambrois (3/0)], Oscar Omar Míguez (12/11), Julio César Abbadie (4/4), Ernesto José Vidal (7/2). Trainer: Juan López Fontana (17).

245. 16.04.1952 **BRAZIL - URUGUAY** **4-2(2-0)** Panamerican Championship
Estadio Nacional, Santiago; Referee: Geoffrey Sunderland (England)
URU: Roque Gastón Máspoli (27/0), Matías González (20/0), Héctor Vilches (10/0), Víctor Pablo Rodríguez Andrade (18/0), Ubire Durán (14/0), Omar Ferreira (3/0), Egardo Alcides Ghiggia (12/4), Julio Gervasio Pérez (14/6) [Washington Loureiro (2/1)], Oscar Omar Míguez (13/12) [Ramón Ferrés (2/0)], Julio César Abbadie (5/4) [Nelson Cancela (3/1)], Ernesto José Vidal (8/2). Trainer: Juan López Fontana (18).
Goals: Oscar Omar Míguez (55), Nelson Cancela (90 penalty).

246. 25.02.1953 **URUGUAY - BOLIVIA** **2-0(1-0)** 22nd Copa América
Estadio Nacional, Lima (Peru); Referee: Charles Dean (England), Attendance: 45,000
URU: Luis Radiche (2/0), Matías González (21/0), Domingo Rodríguez (2/0), Humberto Cardozo (1/0), Carlos María Carranza (1/0) [66.Hosiriz Romero (7/0)], Rúben Vanoli (1/0), Washington Puente (5/3), Carlos Romero (5/2), Omar Pedro Méndez (1/0) [46.Walter Morel (1/0)], Raúl Bentancor (1/0), Donald Peláez (1/0). Trainer: Romeo Vázquez (7).
Goals: Washington Puente (11), Carlos Romero (88).

247. 01.03.1953 **CHILE - URUGUAY** **3-2(1-0)** 22nd Copa América
Estadio Nacional, Lima (Peru); Referee: Charles Dean (England), Attendance: 38,591
URU: Luis Radiche (3/0), Matías González (22/0), Domingo Rodríguez (3/0) [46.William Rubén Martínez (4/0)], Urbano Rivera (1/0), Néstor Carballo (1/0), Luis Alberto Cruz (1/0), Washington Puente (6/3), Carlos Romero (6/2) [46.Julio Quiroga (1/0)], Walter Morel (2/1), Rafael Arturo Souto (1/0), Donald Peláez (2/0) [46.Osvaldo Balseiro (4/1)]. Trainer: Romeo Vázquez (8).
Goals: Walter Morel (70), Osvaldo Balseiro (81).

248. 12.03.1953 **PARAGUAY – URUGUAY** **2-2(1-1)** 22nd Copa América
Estadio Nacional, Lima (Peru); Referee: David Gregory (England), Attendance: 35,000
URU: Luis Radiche (4/0) [32.Pedro Rodríguez (1/0)], Matías González (23/0), William Rubén Martínez (5/0), Urbano Rivera (2/0), Néstor Carballo (2/0), Luis Alberto Cruz (2/0) [17.Rúben Vanoli (2/0)], Washington Puente (7/3), Carlos Romero (7/2), Walter Morel (3/1) [15.Omar Pedro Méndez (2/0)], Osvaldo Balseiro (5/3), Donald Peláez (3/0). Trainer: Romeo Vázquez (9).
Goals: Osvaldo Balseiro (36, 55).

249. 15.03.1953 **BRAZIL – URUGUAY** **1-0(0-0)** 22nd Copa América
Estadio Nacional, Lima (Peru); Referee: Charles MacKenna (England), Attendance: 45,000
URU: Luis Radiche (5/0), Matías González (24/0), William Rubén Martínez (6/0), Urbano Rivera (3/0), Néstor Carballo (3/0), Rúben Vanoli (3/0), Washington Puente (8/3) [72.Rafael Arturo Souto (2/0)], Carlos Romero (8/2), Walter Morel (4/1) [74.Raúl Bentancor (2/0)], Osvaldo Balseiro (6/3), Donald Peláez (4/0) [83.Rúben Morán (4/1)]. Trainer: Romeo Vázquez (10).

250. 23.03.1953 **URUGUAY – ECUADOR** **6-0(1-0)** 22nd Copa América
Estadio Nacional, Lima (Peru); Referee: David Gregory (England), Attendance: 35,000
URU: Luis Radiche (6/0), Matías González (25/0), William Rubén Martínez (7/0), Urbano Rivera (4/0), Néstor Carballo (4/0), Rúben Vanoli (4/0) [46.Luis Alberto Cruz (3/0)], Washington Puente (9/4), Carlos Romero (9/3), Omar Pedro Méndez (3/1) [49.Walter Morel (5/2)], Osvaldo Balseiro (7/4), Donald Peláez (5/1). Trainer: Romeo Vázquez (11).
Goals: Omar Pedro Méndez (12), Washington Puente (51), Donald Peláez (58), Walter Morel (60), Carlos Romero (86), Osvaldo Balseiro (88).

251. 28.03.1953 **PERU - URUGUAY** **0-3(0-1)** 22nd Copa América
Estadio Nacional, Lima; Referee: Mário Silveira Vianna (Brazil), Attendance: 45,000
URU: Luis Radiche (7/0), Matías González (26/0), William Rubén Martínez (8/0), Urbano Rivera (5/0), Néstor Carballo (5/0), Luis Alberto Cruz (4/0), Carlos Romero (10/4), Rafael Arturo Souto (3/0), Walter Morel (6/2) [61.Raúl Bentancor (3/0)], Osvaldo Balseiro (8/4), Donald Peláez (6/3). Trainer: Romeo Vázquez (12).
Goals: Donald Peláez (23, 67), Carlos Romero (71).

252. 31.05.1953 **URUGUAY – ENGLAND** **2-1(1-0)**
Estadio Centenario, Montevideo; Referee: Arthur Edward Ellis (England), Attendance: 66,072
URU: Roque Gastón Máspoli (28/0), Matías González (27/0), William Rubén Martínez (9/0), Víctor Pablo Rodríguez Andrade (19/0), Néstor Carballo (6/0), Luis Alberto Cruz (5/0), Julio César Abbadie (6/5), Julio Gervasio Pérez (15/6), Oscar Omar Míguez (14/13), Juan Alberto Schiaffino (12/5), Juan Carlos Cabrera (1/0). Trainer: Juan López Fontana (19).
Goals: Julio César Abbadie (27), Oscar Omar Míguez (70).

253. 10.04.1954 **URUGUAY – PARAGUAY** **1-4**
Estadio Centenario, Montevideo; Referee: Marcos Rojas (Paraguay)
URU: Roque Gastón Máspoli (29/0), Matías González (28/0), Eusebio Ramón Tejera (29/0) [Héctor Argenti (1/0)], Urbano Rivera (6/0), Néstor Carballo (7/0), Roberto Rafael Leopardi (1/0), Julio César Abbadie (7/5), Javier Ambrois (4/0) [Juan Eduardo Hohberg (1/0)], Omar Oscar Míguez (15/14), Juan Alberto Schiaffino (13/5), Américo Natalio Galván (1/0). Trainer: Juan López Fontana (20).
Goal: Oscar Omar Míguez.

254. 18.04.1954 **PARAGUAY – URUGUAY** **1-1**
Estadio Libertad, Asunción; Referee: Juan Carlos Armental (Uruguay)
URU: Roque Gastón Máspoli (30/0), Mirto Lenin Davoine (1/0) [José Emilio Santamaría (2/0)], Eusebio Ramón Tejera (30/0), Víctor Pablo Rodríguez Andrade (20/0) [Urbano Rivera (7/0)], Néstor Carballo (8/0), Roberto Rafael Leopardi (2/0), Julio César Abbadie (8/6), Juan Eduardo Hohberg (2/0) [Javier Ambrois (5/0)], Omar Oscar Míguez (16/14), Juan Alberto Schiaffino (14/5), Luis Ernesto Castro (18/4) [Américo Natalio Galván (2/0)]. Trainer: Juan López Fontana (21).
Goal: Julio César Abbadie.

255. 23.05.1954 **SWITZERLAND – URUGUAY** **3-3(1-1)**
Stade Olympique de la Pontaise, Lausanne; Referee: Leopold Sylvain Horn (Holland), Attendance: 43,000
URU: Julio César Maceiras (1/0), José Emilio Santamaría (3/0), William Rubén Martínez (10/1), Víctor Pablo Rodríguez Andrade (21/0), Néstor Carballo (9/0), Roberto Rafael Leopardi (3/0) [Luis Alberto Cruz (6/0)], Julio César Abbadie (9/6) [Rafael Arturo Souto (4/0)], Juan Eduardo Hohberg (3/0) [Javier Ambrois (6/0)], Omar Oscar Míguez (17/14), Juan Alberto Schiaffino (15/6), Carlos Ariel Borges (1/1). Trainer: Juan López Fontana (22).
Goals: Carlos Ariel Borges, Juan Alberto Schiaffino, William Rubén Martínez.

256. 05.06.1954 **SAAR – URUGUAY** **1-7(1-3)**
Ludwigspark-Stadion, Saarbrücken; Referee: Albert Dusch (West Germany), Attendance: 15,000
URU: Roque Gastón Máspoli (31/0), José Emilio Santamaría (4/0), William Rubén Martínez (11/1) [Eusebio Ramón Tejera (31/0)], Víctor Pablo Rodríguez Andrade (22/0) [Urbano Rivera (8/0)], Obdulio Jacinto Varela (41/8) [Néstor Carballo (10/0)], Luis Alberto Cruz (7/0), Rafael Arturo Souto (5/0), Javier Ambrois (7/3), Omar Pedro Méndez (4/1) [Julio Gervasio Pérez (16/7)], Juan Alberto Schiaffino (16/8), Carlos Ariel Borges (2/1). Trainer: Juan López Fontana (23).
Goals: Julio Gervasio Pérez (10), Obdulio Jacinto Varela (19), Juan Alberto Schiaffino (36, 57), Javier Ambrois (65, 67, 80).

257. 16.06.1954 **URUGUAY – CZECHOSLOVAKIA** **2-0(0-0)** 5th FIFA WC. Group Stage
Wankdorf Stadion, Bern (Switzerland); Referee: Arthur Edward Ellis (England), Attendance: 30,000
URU: Roque Gastón Máspoli (32/0), José Emilio Santamaría (5/0), William Rubén Martínez (12/1), Víctor Pablo Rodríguez Andrade (23/0), Obdulio Jacinto Varela (42/8), Luis Alberto Cruz (8/0), Julio César Abbadie (10/6), Javier Ambrois (8/3), Oscar Omar Míguez (18/15), Juan Alberto Schiaffino (17/9), Carlos Ariel Borges (3/1). Trainer: Juan López Fontana (24).
Goals: Oscar Omar Míguez (70), Juan Alberto Schiaffino (84).

258. 19.06.1954 **URUGUAY – SCOTLAND** **7-0(2-0)** 5th FIFA WC. Group Stage
St. Jakob Stadion, Basel (Switzerland); Referee: Vincenzo Orlandini (Italy), Attendance: 34,000
URU: Roque Gastón Máspoli (33/0), José Emilio Santamaría (6/0), William Rubén Martínez (13/1), Víctor Pablo Rodríguez Andrade (24/0), Obdulio Jacinto Varela (43/8), Luis Alberto Cruz (9/0), Julio César Abbadie (11/8), Javier Ambrois (9/3), Oscar Omar Míguez (19/17), Juan Alberto Schiaffino (18/9), Carlos Ariel Borges (4/4). Trainer: Juan López Fontana (25).
Goals: Carlos Ariel Borges (17), Oscar Omar Míguez (31), Carlos Ariel Borges (48), Julio César Abbadie (55), Carlos Ariel Borges (58), Oscar Omar Míguez (82), Julio César Abbadie (84).

259. 26.06.1954 **URUGUAY - ENGLAND** **4-2(2-1)** 5th FIFA WC. Group Stage
St. Jakob Stadion, Basel (Switzerland); Referee: Carl Erich Steiner (Austria), Attendance: 35,000
URU: Roque Gastón Máspoli (34/0), José Emilio Santamaría (7/0), William Rubén Martínez (14/1), Víctor Pablo Rodríguez Andrade (25/0), Obdulio Jacinto Varela (44/9), Luis Alberto Cruz (10/0), Julio César Abbadie (12/8), Javier Ambrois (10/4), Oscar Omar Míguez (20/17), Juan Alberto Schiaffino (19/10), Carlos Ariel Borges (5/5). Trainer: Juan López Fontana (26).
Goals: Carlos Ariel Borges (5), Obdulio Jacinto Varela (44), Juan Alberto Schiaffino (47), Javier Ambrois (78)

260. 30.06.1954 **HUNGARY - URUGUAY** **4-2(1-0,2-2)** 5th FIFA WC. Semi-Finals
Stade Olympique de la Pontaise, Lausanne (Switzerland); Referee: Bryan Griffiths (Wales), Attendance: 50,000
URU: Roque Gastón Máspoli (35/0), José Emilio Santamaría (8/0), William Rubén Martínez (15/1), Víctor Pablo Rodríguez Andrade (26/0), Néstor Carballo (11/0), Luis Alberto Cruz (11/0), Rafael Arturo Souto (6/0), Javier Ambrois (11/4), Juan Eduardo Hohberg (4/2), Juan Alberto Schiaffino (20/10), Carlos Ariel Borges (6/5). Trainer: Juan López Fontana (27).
Goals: Juan Eduardo Hohberg (76, 87).

261. 03.07.1954 **AUSTRIA - URUGUAY** **3-1(1-1)** 5th FIFA WC. Bronze Medal
Hardturm Stadion, Zürich (Switzerland); Referee: Paul Wyssling (Switzerland), Attendance: 35,000
URU: Roque Gastón Máspoli (36/0), José Emilio Santamaría (9/0), William Rubén Martínez (16/1), Víctor Pablo Rodríguez Andrade (27/0), Néstor Carballo (12/0), Luis Alberto Cruz (12/0), Julio César Abbadie (13/8), Omar Pedro Méndez (5/1), Juan Eduardo Hohberg (5/3), Juan Alberto Schiaffino (21/10), Carlos Ariel Borges (7/5). Trainer: Juan López Fontana (28).
Goal: Juan Eduardo Hohberg (21).

262. 09.03.1955 **URUGUAY - PARAGUAY** **3-1(2-1)** 23rd Copa América
Estadio Nacional, Santiago (Chile); Referee: Juan Regis Brozzi (Argentina), Attendance: 48,000
URU: Roque Gastón Máspoli (37/0), William Rubén Martínez (17/1), Omar Tejera (1/0), Víctor Pablo Rodríguez Andrade (28/0), Néstor Carballo (13/0) [81.Carlos María Carranza (2/0)], Celedonio Rey (1/0), Carlos Ariel Borges (8/6), Julio Gervasio Pérez (17/7), Omar Oscar Míguez (21/18), Julio César Abbadie (14/9), Américo Natalio Galván (3/0). Trainer: Juan Carlos Corazzo (1).
Goals: Carlos Ariel Borges (2), Julio César Abbadie (5), Oscar Omar Míguez (86 penalty).

263. 13.03.1955 **CHILE - URUGUAY** **2-2(1-2)** 23rd Copa América
Estadio Nacional, Santiago; Referee: Juan Regis Brozzi (Argentina), Attendance: 44,238
URU: Roque Gastón Máspoli (38/0), William Rubén Martínez (18/1), Omar Tejera (2/0), Víctor Pablo Rodríguez Andrade (29/0), Néstor Carballo (14/0) [61.Carlos María Carranza (3/0)], Celedonio Rey (2/0), Carlos Ariel Borges (9/6), Julio Gervasio Pérez (18/7), Omar Oscar Míguez (22/18) [71.Héctor Demarco (1/0)], Julio César Abbadie (15/9), Américo Natalio Galván (4/2). Trainer: Juan Carlos Corazzo (2).
Goals: Américo Natalio Galván (24, 41).

264. 23.03.1955 **URUGUAY - ECUADOR** **5-1(3-1)** 23rd Copa América
Estadio Nacional, Santiago (Chile); Referee: Roberto González (Paraguay), Attendance: 25,000
URU: Walter Taibo Martínez (1/0), William Rubén Martínez (19/1), Omar Tejera (3/0) [46.Roberto Rafael Leopardi (4/0)], Víctor Pablo Rodríguez Andrade (30/0), Carlos María Carranza (4/0), Celedonio Rey (3/0), Carlos Ariel Borges (10/6), Julio Gervasio Pérez (19/8), Omar Oscar Míguez (23/19) [85.Walter Morel (7/2)], Julio César Abbadie (16/11) [80.Omar Abreo (1/0)], Américo Natalio Galván (5/3). Trainer: Juan Carlos Corazzo (3).
Goals: Américo Natalio Galván (4), Oscar Omar Míguez (12), Julio César Abbadie (26), Julio Gervasio Pérez (54), Julio César Abbadie (80).

265. 27.03.1955 **ARGENTINA - URUGUAY** **6-1(2-1)** 23rd Copa América
Estadio Nacional, Santiago (Chile); Referee: Juan Carlos Robles (Chile), Attendance: 35,241
URU: Walter Taibo Martínez (2/0), Matías González (29/0), Roberto Rafael Leopardi (5/0) [82.Omar Tejera (4/0)], Víctor Pablo Rodríguez Andrade (31/0), Carlos María Carranza (5/0) [65.Néstor Carballo (15/0)], Celedonio Rey (4/0), Carlos Ariel Borges (11/6), Julio Gervasio Pérez (20/8) [62.Héctor Demarco (2/0)], Omar Oscar Míguez (24/20), Julio César Abbadie (17/11), Américo Natalio Galván (6/3). Trainer: Juan Carlos Corazzo (4).
Goal: Oscar Omar Míguez (32).

266. 30.03.1955 **PERU - URUGUAY** **2-1(1-0)** 23rd Copa América
Estadio Nacional, Santiago (Chile); Referee: Juan Carlos Robles (Chile), Attendance: 65,000
URU: Roque Gastón Máspoli (39/0), Waldemar González (1/0), Omar Tejera (5/0), Carlos María Carranza (6/0), Néstor Carballo (16/0), Celedonio Rey (5/0), Carlos Ariel Borges (12/6), Héctor Demarco (3/0), Omar Oscar Míguez (25/20) [70.Walter Morel (8/3)], Julio César Abbadie (18/11) [78.Omar Abreo (2/0)], Américo Natalio Galván (7/3) [46.Guillermo Escalada (1/0)]. Trainer: Juan Carlos Corazzo (5).
Goal: Walter Morel (72).

267. 21.01.1956 **URUGUAY - PARAGUAY** **4-2(3-0)** 24th Copa América
Estadio Centenario, Montevideo; Referee: Juan Regis Brozzi (Argentina), Attendance: 55,000
URU: Julio César Maceiras (2/0), William Rubén Martínez (20/1), Roberto Rafael Leopardi (6/0) [72.Ladislao Brazionis (1/0)], Víctor Pablo Rodríguez Andrade (32/0), Carlos María Carranza (7/0), Luis Alberto Miramontes (1/0), Carlos Ariel Borges (13/6), Javier Ambrois (12/4), Oscar Omar Míguez (26/21) [66.Héctor Demarco (4/0)], Guillermo Escalada (2/2), José Walter Roque (1/1). Trainer: Hugo Bagnulo (1).
Goals: Oscar Omar Míguez (12), Guillermo Escalada (25, 32), José Walter Roque (65).

268. 28.01.1956 **URUGUAY - PERU** **2-0(1-0)** 24th Copa América
Estadio Centenario, Montevideo; Referee: Cayetano De Nicola (Paraguay), Attendance: 70,000
URU: Julio César Maceiras (3/0), William Rubén Martínez (21/1), Ladislao Brazionis (2/0), Víctor Pablo Rodríguez Andrade (33/0), Carlos María Carranza (8/0) [85.Alfonso Auscarriaga (1/0)], Washington Manghini (1/0), Carlos Ariel Borges (14/6) [87.Luis Pírez (1/0)], Javier Ambrois (13/4), Oscar Omar Míguez (27/22), Guillermo Escalada (3/3), José Walter Roque (2/1). Trainer: Hugo Bagnulo (2).
Goals: Guillermo Escalada (42), Oscar Omar Míguez (73).

269. 06.02.1956 **URUGUAY - CHILE** **2-1(1-0)** 24th Copa América
Estadio Centenario, Montevideo; Referee: Juan Regis Brozzi (Argentina), Attendance: 61,204
URU: Julio César Maceiras (4/0), William Rubén Martínez (22/1), Ladislao Brazionis (3/0), Víctor Pablo Rodríguez Andrade (34/0), Carlos María Carranza (9/0), Washington Manghini (2/0), Carlos Ariel Borges (15/7), Javier Ambrois (14/4), Oscar Omar Míguez (28/23), Oscar Daniel Melgarejo (1/0), José Walter Roque (3/1). Trainer: Hugo Bagnulo (3).
Goals: Oscar Omar Míguez (12), Carlos Ariel Borges (58).

270. 10.02.1956 **URUGUAY - BRAZIL** **0-0** 24th Copa América

Estadio Centenario, Montevideo; Referee: Juan Regis Brozzi (Argentina), Attendance: 80,000

URU: Julio César Maceiras (5/0), William Rubén Martínez (23/1), Ladislao Brazionis (4/0), Víctor Pablo Rodríguez Andrade (35/0), Carlos María Carranza (10/0), Luis Alberto Miramontes (2/0), Carlos Ariel Borges (16/7), Javier Ambrois (15/4), Oscar Omar Míguez (29/23), Oscar Daniel Melgarejo (2/0) [72.Héctor Demarco (5/0)], José Walter Roque (4/1). Trainer: Hugo Bagnulo (4).

271. 15.02.1956 **URUGUAY - ARGENTINA** **1-0(1-0)** 24th Copa América

Estadio Centenario, Montevideo; Referee: Cayetano de Nicola (Paraguay), Attendance: 80,000

URU: Julio César Maceiras (6/0), William Rubén Martínez (24/1), Ladislao Brazionis (5/0), Víctor Pablo Rodríguez Andrade (36/0), Carlos María Carranza (11/0), Luis Alberto Miramontes (3/0), Carlos Ariel Borges (17/7) [71.Luis Pírez (2/0)], Javier Ambrois (16/5), Oscar Omar Míguez (30/23), Guillermo Escalada (4/3) [75.Alfonso Auscarriaga (2/0)], José Walter Roque (5/1). Trainer: Hugo Bagnulo (5).

Goal: Javier Ambrois (23).

272. 24.06.1956 **BRAZIL - URUGUAY** **2-0(0-0)** Copa Atlántico

Estádio „Jornalista Mário Filho“ (Maracanã), Rio de Janeiro; Referee: Frederico Lopes (Brazil)

URU: Julio César Maceiras (7/0), William Rubén Martínez (25/1) [Walter Davoine (1/0)], José Emilio Santamaría (10/0), Víctor Pablo Rodríguez Andrade (37/0), Carlos María Carranza (12/0), Roberto Rafael Leopardi (7/0), Julio César Abbadie (19/11), Javier Ambrois (17/5) [Héctor Ramos (1/0)], Oscar Omar Míguez (31/23), José Francisco Sasía (1/0), Guillermo Escalada (5/3). Trainer: Hugo Bagnulo (6).

273. 01.07.1956 **URUGUAY - ARGENTINA** **1-2(0-0)** Copa Atlántico

Estadio Centenario, Montevideo; Referee: Erwin Hieger (Austria), Attendance: 51,927

URU: Julio César Maceiras (8/0), Walter Davoine (2/0), José Emilio Santamaría (11/0), Víctor Pablo Rodríguez Andrade (38/0), Héctor Ramos (2/0), Luis Alberto Miramontes (4/0), Julio César Abbadie (20/12), Javier Ambrois (18/5) [Carlos Romero (11/4)], José Francisco Sasía (2/0), Omar Oscar Míguez (32/23) [Alfonso Auscarriaga (3/0)], Guillermo Escalada (6/3). Trainer: Hugo Bagnulo (7).

Goal: Julio César Abbadie (56).

274. 15.07.1956 **PARAGUAY - URUGUAY** **2-2**

Estadio Libertad, Asunción; Referee: Cayetano de Nicola (Paraguay)

URU: Rodger Bernardico (1/0), Walter Davoine (3/0), José Emilio Santamaría (12/0), Roque Fernández (1/0), Carlos María Carranza (13/0), Washington Manghini (3/0), Alfredo Moscarelli (1/1), Alfonso Auscarriaga (4/1) [Osvaldo Balseiro (9/4)], José Francisco Sasía (3/0), Omar Pedro Méndez (6/1), Carlos Ariel Borges (18/7). Trainer: Roque Gastón Máspoli (1).

Goals: Alfredo Moscarelli, Alfonso Auscarriaga

275. 12.08.1956 **URUGUAY - CZECHOSLOVAKIA** **2-1(0-0)**

Estadio Centenario, Montevideo; Referee: Sten Ahlner (Sweden), Attendance: 70,000

URU: Rodger Bernardico (2/0), William Rubén Martínez (26/1), José Emilio Santamaría (13/0), Víctor Pablo Rodríguez Andrade (39/0), Héctor Ramos (3/0) [Carlos María Carranza (14/0)], Washington Manghini (4/0), Alfredo Moscarelli (2/1) [Omar Pedro Méndez (7/2)], Juan Eduardo Hohberg (6/3), José Francisco Sasía (4/0), Julio César Abbadie (21/12), Carlos Ariel Borges (19/8). Trainer: Roque Gastón Máspoli (2).

Goals: Carlos Ariel Borges (55), Omar Pedro Méndez (57).

276. 10.10.1956 **URUGUAY - ARGENTINA** **1-2(1-1)**

Estadio „José Artigas“, Paysandú; Referee: Erich Steiner (Austria), Attendance: 25,000

URU: Rodger Bernardico (3/0), William Rubén Martínez (27/1), Matías González (30/0), Víctor Pablo Rodríguez Andrade (40/0), Héctor Ramos (4/0) [Carlos María Carranza (15/0)], Luis Alberto Miramontes (5/0), Carlos Ariel Borges (20/8) [Alfredo Moscarelli (3/1)], Juan Eduardo Hohberg (7/3), José Francisco Sasía (5/0), Javier Ambrois (19/6), Oscar Leitch (1/0). Trainer: Lorenzo Fernández (1).

Goal: Javier Ambrois (40).

277. 14.11.1956 **ARGENTINA - URUGUAY** **2-2(2-1)**

Estadio „Alberto Armando“, Buenos Aires; Referee: Bertley Cross (England), Attendance: 40,000

URU: Rodger Bernardico (4/0), William Rubén Martínez (28/1), José Emilio Santamaría (14/0), Manuel Verdes (1/0), Héctor Ramos (5/0) [José Pedro Lezcano (1/0)], Luis Alberto Miramontes (6/0), Carlos Ariel Borges (21/8), Julio Gervasio Pérez (21/8) [Javier Ambrois (20/7)], Omar Oscar Míguez (33/24), Carlos María Carranza (16/0) [José Francisco Sasía (6/0)], Oscar Leitch (2/0). Trainer: Lorenzo Fernández (2).

Goals: Oscar Omar Míguez (8 penalty), Javier Ambrois (53).

278. 07.03.1957 **URUGUAY - ECUADOR** **5-2(2-2)** 25th Copa América

Estadio Nacional, Lima (Peru); Referee: Erwin Hieger (Austria), Attendance: 50,000

URU: Rodger Bernardico (5/0), Walter Marichal (1/0), José Emilio Santamaría (15/0), Edgardo Nilson González (1/0), José Pedro Lezcano (2/0), Luis Alberto Miramontes (7/0), Ariel Fernández (1/0), Javier Ambrois (21/11), Omar Pedro Méndez (8/2) [46.José Francisco Sasía (7/1)], Carlos María Carranza (17/0) [74 Rodolfo Pippo (1/0)], José Walter Roque (6/1). Trainer: Juan López Fontana (29).

Goals: Javier Ambrois (26, 29 penalty, 57, 74), José Francisco Sasía (87).

279. 17.03.1957 **COLOMBIA - URUGUAY** **1-0(1-0)** 25th Copa América

Estadio Nacional, Lima (Peru); Referee: Pedro di Leo (Italy), Attendance: 50,000

URU: Rodger Bernardico (6/0), Walter Marichal (2/0), José Emilio Santamaría (16/0), Edgardo Nilson González (2/0), José Pedro Lezcano (3/0), Jesús Castro (1/0), Ariel Fernández (2/0) [46.Luis Norberto Campero (1/0)], Javier Ambrois (22/11), Omar Pedro Méndez (9/2), José Francisco Sasía (8/1), José Walter Roque (7/1). Trainer: Juan López Fontana (30).

280. 20.03.1957 **ARGENTINA - URUGUAY** **4-0(1-0)** 25th Copa América

Estadio Nacional, Lima (Peru); Referee: Erwin Hieger (Austria), Attendance: 40,000

URU: Rodger Bernardico (7/0), Carlos Correa (1/0), José Emilio Santamaría (17/0), Edgardo Nilson González (3/0), José Pedro Lezcano (4/0), Luis Alberto Miramontes (8/0), Luis Norberto Campero (2/0), Rodolfo Pippo (2/0) [61.Omar Pedro Méndez (10/2)], Javier Ambrois (23/11), Carlos María Carranza (18/0) [65.José Francisco Sasía (9/1)], José Walter Roque (8/1). Trainer: Juan López Fontana (31).

281. 23.03.1957 **PERU - URUGUAY** **3-5(1-2)** 25th Copa América

Estadio Nacional, Lima; Referee: Bertley Cross (England), Attendance: 55,000

URU: Walter Taibo Martínez (3/0), Carlos Correa (2/0), José Emilio Santamaría (18/0), Edgardo Nilson González (4/0) [54.Roque Fernández (2/0)], Néstor Gonçalves (1/0), Luis Alberto Miramontes (9/0), Luis Norberto Campero (3/0), Rodolfo Pippo (3/0) [46.José Francisco Sasía (10/1)], Javier Ambrois (24/15), Carlos María Carranza (19/1), José Walter Roque (9/1). Trainer: Juan López Fontana (32).

Goals: Javier Ambrois (5, 21, 41), Carlos María Carranza (66), Javier Ambrois (78).

282. 28.03.1957 **URUGUAY - BRAZIL** **3-2(3-0)** 25th Copa América
Estadio Nacional, Lima (Peru); Referee: Erwin Hieger (Austria), Attendance: 50,000
URU: Walter Taibo Martínez (4/0), Carlos Correa (3/0), José Emilio Santamaría (19/0), Edgardo Nilson González (5/0), Néstor Gonçalves (2/0) [78.José Pedro Lezcano (5/0)], Luis Alberto Miramontes (10/0), Luis Norberto Campero (4/2), Rodolfo Pippo (4/0) [75.José Francisco Sasía (11/1)], Javier Ambrois (25/16), Carlos María Carranza (20/1), José Walter Roque (10/1). Trainer: Juan López Fontana (33).
Goals: Luis Norberto Campero (15), Javier Ambrois (17), Luis Norberto Campero (23).

283. 01.04.1957 **URUGUAY - CHILE** **2-0** 25th Copa América
Estadio Nacional, Lima (Peru); Referee: Erwin Hieger (Austria), Attendance: 40,000
URU: Walter Taibo Martínez (5/0), Carlos Correa (4/0), José Emilio Santamaría (20/0), Edgardo Nilson González (6/0), Néstor Gonçalves (3/0), Luis Alberto Miramontes (11/0), Luis Norberto Campero (5/3), Rodolfo Pippo (5/0), Javier Ambrois (26/16), Carlos María Carranza (21/1), José Walter Roque (11/2). Trainer: Juan López Fontana (34).
Goals: Luis Norberto Campero (28), José Walter Roque (40).
Suspended at 43rd min due to crowd invasion

284. 23.05.1957 **URUGUAY - ARGENTINA** **0-0** Copa Newton
Estadio Centenario, Montevideo; Referee: Erwin Hieger (Austria), Attendance: 32,764
URU: Walter Taibo Martínez (6/0), Carlos Correa (5/0), William Rubén Martínez (29/1), Víctor Pablo Rodríguez Andrade (41/0) [Edgardo Nilson González (7/0)], Néstor Gonçalves (4/0), Luis Alberto Miramontes (12/0), Carlos Ariel Borges (22/8), Javier Ambrois (27/16), Oscar Omar Míguez (34/24) [Julio Acosta (1/0)], José Francisco Sasía (12/1) [Rodolfo Pippo (6/0)], José Walter Roque (12/2). Trainer: Juan López Fontana (35).

285. 05.06.1957 **ARGENTINA - URUGUAY** **1-1(0-0)** Copa Lipton
Estadio El Palacio, Buenos Aires; Referee: Estebán Marino (Uruguay), Attendance: 35,950
URU: Walter Taibo Martínez (7/0), Carlos Correa (6/1), William Rubén Martínez (30/1), Víctor Pablo Rodríguez Andrade (42/0) [Edgardo Nilson González (8/0)], Néstor Gonçalves (5/0), Luis Alberto Miramontes (13/0), Carlos Ariel Borges (23/8), Rodolfo Pippo (7/0), Oscar Omar Míguez (35/24) [Julio Acosta (2/0)], Javier Ambrois (28/16), José Walter Roque (13/2). Trainer: Juan López Fontana (36).
Goal: Carlos Correa.

286. 16.06.1957 **COLOMBIA - URUGUAY** **1-1(1-0)** 6th FIFA WC. Qualifiers
Estadio „Nemesio Camacho“ ‘El Campín’, Bogotá; Referee: James Husband (England), Attendance: 15,000
URU: Walter Taibo Martínez (8/0), Carlos Correa (7/1), William Rubén Martínez (31/1), Edgardo Nilson González (9/0), Néstor Gonçalves (6/0), Luis Alberto Miramontes (14/0), Carlos Ariel Borges (24/8), Rodolfo Pippo (8/0), Luis Norberto Campero (6/3), Javier Ambrois (29/17), Héctor Rodríguez (1/0). Trainer: Juan López Fontana (37).
Goal: Javier Ambrois (46).

287. 30.06.1957 **URUGUAY - COLOMBIA** **1-0(0-0)** 6th FIFA WC. Qualifiers
Estadio Centenario, Montevideo; Referee: James Husband (England), Attendance: 35,000
URU: Walter Taibo Martínez (9/0), Carlos Correa (8/1), William Rubén Martínez (32/1), Edgardo Nilson González (10/0), Néstor Gonçalves (7/0), Luis Alberto Miramontes (15/0), Carlos Ariel Borges (25/8), Javier Ambrois (30/17), Oscar Omar Míguez (36/25), Héctor Rodríguez (2/0), José Walter Roque (14/2). Trainer: Juan López Fontana (38).
Goal: Oscar Omar Míguez (89 penalty).

288. 14.07.1957 **PARAGUAY - URUGUAY** **5-0(1-0)** 6th FIFA WC. Qualifiers
Estadio Puerto Sajonia, Asunción; Referee: John Husband (England), Attendance: 16,289
URU: Walter Taibo Martínez (10/0), William Rubén Martínez (33/1), Oscar Vilariño (1/0), Edgardo Nilson González (11/0), Néstor Gonçalves (8/0), Luis Alberto Miramontes (16/0), Carlos Ariel Borges (26/8), Javier Ambrois (31/17), Oscar Omar Míguez (37/25), Héctor Rodríguez (3/0), José Walter Roque (15/2). Trainer: Juan López Fontana (39).

289. 28.07.1957 **URUGUAY - PARAGUAY** **2-0(1-0)** 6th FIFA WC. Qualifiers
Estadio Centenario, Montevideo; Referee: John Husband (England), Attendance: 30,000
URU: Walter Taibo Martínez (11/0), William Rubén Martínez (34/2), Edgardo Nilson González (12/0), Carlos Correa (9/1), Néstor Gonçalves (9/0), Luis Alberto Miramontes (17/0), Carlos Ariel Borges (27/8), Héctor Núñez (1/0), Héctor Demarco (6/0), Julio Acosta (3/0), Eladio Benítez (1/1). Trainer: Juan López Fontana (40).
Goals: Eladio Benítez (8), William Rubén Martínez (89).

290. 06.04.1958 **URUGUAY - ARGENTINA** **1-0(1-0)**
Estadio Centenario, Montevideo; Referee: José María Codesal (Uruguay), Attendance: 40,000
URU: Walter Taibo Martínez (12/0), William Rubén Martínez (35/2), Climaco Rodríguez (1/0), Roque Fernández (3/0), Néstor Carballo (17/0) [Alberto Kulys (1/0)], Luis Alberto Miramontes (18/0) [Rubén Soria (1/0)], Héctor Núñez (2/0), Héctor Demarco (7/0), Oscar Omar Míguez (38/26), José Francisco Sasía (13/1) [Eladio Benítez (2/1)], Carlos Ariel Borges (28/8) [Carlos Chávez (1/0)]. Trainer: Lorenzo Fernández (3).
Goal: Oscar Omar Míguez.

291. 30.04.1958 **ARGENTINA - URUGUAY** **2-0(0-0)**
Estadio El Palacio, Buenos Aires; Referee: Robert Turner (England), Attendance: 25,000
URU: Walter Taibo Martínez (13/0), Esteban Alvarez (1/0) [Walter Marichal (3/0), Alberto Kulys (2/0)], Climaco Rodríguez (2/0), Roque Fernández (4/0), Néstor Carballo (18/0), Luis Alberto Miramontes (19/0), Héctor Núñez (3/0), Héctor Demarco (8/0) [Héctor Rodríguez (4/0)], José Francisco Sasía (14/1), Eladio Benítez (3/1) [Oscar Omar Míguez (39/26)], Carlos Ariel Borges (29/8). Trainer: Lorenzo Fernández (4).

292. 08.03.1959 **URUGUAY - BOLIVIA** **7-0(3-0)** 26th Copa América
Estadio Monumental „Antonio Vespucio Liberti“, Buenos Aires (Argentina); Referee: Alberto Monard da Gama Malcher (Brazil), Attendance: 35,000
URU: Walter Taibo Martínez (14/0), William Rúben Martínez (36/2), Climaco Rodríguez (3/0), Roque Fernández (5/0), Néstor Gonçalves (10/0), Luis Alberto Miramontes (20/0), Héctor Núñez (4/0) [46 Domingo Salvador Pérez (1/1)], Zelmar Aguilera (1/0), Víctor Homero Guglianone (1/1) [46.Vladas Douksas (1/1)], José Francisco Sasía (15/2), Guillermo Escalada (7/4) [46.Carlos Ariel Borges (30/10)]. Trainer: Héctor Castro (3).
Goals: José Francisco Sasía (5), Guillermo Escalada (12), Víctor Homero Guglianone (17), Carlos Ariel Borges (60, 65), Vladas Douksas (69), Domingo Salvador Pérez (89).

293. 14.03.1959 **PERU – URUGUAY** **5-3(3-1)** 26th Copa América
Estadio Monumental „Antonio Vespucio Liberti", Buenos Aires (Argentina); Referee: Juan Carlos Robles (Chile), Attendance: 40,000
URU: Walter Taibo Martínez (15/0), William Rúben Martínez (37/2), Climaco Rodríguez (4/0), Roque Fernández (6/0) [46.Walter Davoine (4/0)], Néstor Gonçalves (11/0), Luis Alberto Miramontes (21/0) [46.Juan Carlos Mesías (1/0)], Héctor Núñez (5/0), Héctor Demarco (9/1), Vladas Douksas (2/2) [72.Zelmar Aguilera (2/0)], José Francisco Sasía (16/3), Carlos Ariel Borges (31/10). Trainer: Héctor Castro (4).
Goals: Héctor Demarco (17), José Francisco Sasía (40), Vladas Douksas (76).

294. 18.03.1959 **URUGUAY – PARAGUAY** **3-1(2-0)** 26th Copa América
Estadio Monumental „Antonio Vespucio Liberti", Buenos Aires (Argentina); Referee: Juan Carlos Robles (Chile), Attendance: 70,000
URU: Juan Carlos Leiva (1/0), Esteban Alvarez (2/0) [29.William Rúben Martínez (38/2)], Alcides Silveira (1/0), Walter Davoine (5/0), Néstor Gonçalves (12/0), Juan Carlos Mesías (2/0), Carlos Ariel Borges (32/10), Héctor Demarco (10/2), Vladas Douksas (3/3), José Francisco Sasía (17/4), Guillermo Escalada (8/4). Trainer: Héctor Castro (5).
Goals: Héctor Demarco (2), Vladas Douksas (37), José Francisco Sasía (85).

295. 26.03.1959 **BRAZIL – URUGUAY** **3-1(0-1)** 26th Copa América
Estadio Monumental „Antonio Vespucio Liberti", Buenos Aires (Argentina); Referee: Juan Carlos Robles (Chile), Attendance: 70,000
URU: Juan Carlos Leiva (2/0), William Rúben Martínez (39/2), Alcides Silveira (2/0), Walter Davoine (6/0), Néstor Gonçalves (13/0), Juan Carlos Mesías (3/0), Carlos Ariel Borges (33/10) [46.Roque Fernández (7/0)], Héctor Demarco (11/2), Vladas Douksas (4/3), José Francisco Sasía (18/4), Guillermo Escalada (9/5) [46.Zelmar Aguilera (3/0)]. Trainer: Héctor Castro (6).
Goal: Guillermo Escalada (36).

296. 30.03.1959 **ARGENTINA – URUGUAY** **4-1(1-0)** 26th Copa América
Estadio Monumental „Antonio Vespucio Liberti", Buenos Aires; Referee: Isidro Ramírez Alvarez (Paraguay), Attendance: 80,000
URU: Walter Taibo Martínez (16/0), William Rúben Martínez (40/2), Alcides Silveira (3/0), Juan Carlos Mesías (4/0), Julio Castillo (1/0), Luis Alberto Miramontes (22/0), Domingo Salvador Pérez (2/1) [56.Héctor Núñez (6/0)], Héctor Demarco (12/3), Vladas Douksas (5/3), Guillermo Escalada (10/5), Carlos Ariel Borges (34/10). Trainer: Héctor Castro (7).
Goal: Héctor Demarco (85).

297. 02.04.1959 **CHILE – URUGUAY** **1-0(0-0)** 26th Copa América
Estadio Monumental „Antonio Vespucio Liberti", Buenos Aires (Argentina); Referee: Alberto Tejada Burga (Peru), Attendance: 5,000
URU: Walter Taibo Martínez (17/0), William Rúben Martínez (41/2), Alcides Silveira (4/0), Walter Davoine (7/0), Julio Castillo (2/0), Juan Carlos Mesías (5/0), Carlos Ariel Borges (35/10) [74.Zelmar Aguilera (4/0)], Héctor Demarco (13/3), Vladas Douksas (6/3) [46.Víctor Homero Guglianone (2/1)], Eladio Benítez (4/1) [46.Héctor Núñez (7/0)], Guillermo Escalada (11/5). Trainer: Héctor Castro (8).

298. 01.05.1959 **URUGUAY – PARAGUAY** **1-3**
Estadio Centenario, Montevideo; Referee: Esteban Marino (Uruguay)
URU: Luis María Maidana (1/0), Julio Dalmao (1/0), Omar Vilariño (2/0) [Climaco Rodríguez (5/0)], Walter Davoine (8/0) [Tomás Rolan (1/0)], Rubén Adán González (1/0) [Otto Vázquez (1/0)], Juan Carlos Mesías (6/0) [Héctor Inchauspe (1/0)], Antonio Vázquez (1/0) [Manuel Rumbo (1/0)], Luis Alberto Cubilla Almeida (1/0) [Héctor Demarco (14/3)], Juan Eduardo Hohberg (8/3) [Víctor Homero Guglianone (3/1), Eladio Benítez (5/1)], José Pedro Lezcano (6/0), Guillermo Escalada (12/6) [Carlos Chávez (2/0)]. Trainer: Juan Carlos Corazzo (6).
Goal: Guillermo Escalada.

299. 06.12.1959 **ECUADOR – URUGUAY** **0-4(0-2)** 27th Copa América
Estadio Modelo, Guayaquil; Referee: José Luis Praddaude (Argentina), Attendance: 55,000
URU: Roberto Eduardo Sosa (1/0), Florencio Horacio Troche Herrera (1/0), Alcides Silveira (5/1), Mario Omar Méndez (1/0), Rúben Adán González (2/0), Juan Carlos Mesías (7/0), Domingo Salvador Pérez (3/2), Mario Ludovico Bergara (1/1) [65.Víctor Homero Guglianone (4/1)], Vladas Douksas (7/3) [80.Eladio Benítez (6/1)], José Francisco Sasía (19/4), Guillermo Escalada (13/7). Trainer: Juan Carlos Corazzo (7).
Goals: Alcides Silveira (1 penalty), Guillermo Escalada (28), Mario Ludovico Bergara (46), Domingo Salvador Pérez (52).
The match was suspended after 83 minutes due to crowd problems

300. 12.12.1959 **URUGUAY – BRAZIL** **3-0(0-0)** 27th Copa América
Estadio Modelo, Guayaquil (Ecuador); Referee: José Luis Praddaude (Argentina), Attendance: 55,000
URU: Roberto Eduardo Sosa (2/0), Florencio Horacio Troche Herrera (2/0), Alcides Silveira (6/1), Mario Omar Méndez (2/0), Rúben Adán González (3/0), Juan Carlos Mesías (8/0), Domingo Salvador Pérez (4/2) [46.William Píriz (1/0)], Mario Ludovico Bergara (2/2), Vladas Douksas (8/3), José Francisco Sasía (20/5), Guillermo Escalada (14/8). Trainer: Juan Carlos Corazzo (8).
Goals: Guillermo Escalada (49), Mario Ludovico Bergara (67), José Francisco Sasía (75).

301. 16.12.1959 **URUGUAY – ARGENTINA** **5-0(3-0)** 27th Copa América
Estadio Modelo, Guayaquil (Ecuador); Referee: José María Gomes Sobrinho (Brazil), Attendance: 50,000
URU: Roberto Eduardo Sosa (3/0), Florencio Horacio Troche Herrera (3/0), Alcides Silveira (7/3), Mario Omar Méndez (3/0), Rúben Adán González (4/0), Juan Carlos Mesías (9/0), Domingo Salvador Pérez (5/2), Mario Ludovico Bergara (3/4), Vladas Douksas (9/3), José Francisco Sasía (21/6), Guillermo Escalada (15/8). Trainer: Juan Carlos Corazzo (9).
Goals: Alcides Silveira (9 penalty), Mario Ludovico Bergara (15), José Francisco Sasía (25), Alcides Silveira (55 penalty), Mario Ludovico Bergara (64).

302. 22.12.1959 **URUGUAY – PARAGUAY** **1-1(0-1)** 27th Copa América
Estadio Modelo, Guayaquil (Ecuador); Referee: José Luis Praddaude (Argentina), Attendance: 45,000
URU: Roberto Eduardo Sosa (4/0), Florencio Horacio Troche Herrera (4/0), Alcides Silveira (8/3), Mario Omar Méndez (4/0) [60.Walter Davoine (9/0)], Rúben Adán González (5/0), Juan Carlos Mesías (10/0), Domingo Salvador Pérez (6/2), Mario Ludovico Bergara (4/4) [67.Eladio Benítez (7/1)], Vladas Douksas (10/3), José Francisco Sasía (22/7), Guillermo Escalada (16/8). Trainer: Juan Carlos Corazzo (10).
Goal: José Francisco Sasía (88).

303. 01.06.1960 **CHILE – URUGUAY** **2-3(1-0)**
Estadio Nacional, Santiago; Referee: Juan Carlos Robles (Chile), Attendance: 45,000
URU: Roberto Eduardo Sosa (5/0), Esteban Alvarez (3/0), Emilio Walter Álvarez (1/0) [Jorge Gómez (1/0)], Mario Omar Méndez (5/0), Néstor Gonçalves (14/0), Juan Carlos Mesías (11/0), Luis Alberto Cubilla Almeida (2/0) [Héctor Salvá González (1/0)], Mario Ludovico Bergara (5/6), Víctor Homero Guglianone (5/2), Héctor Rodríguez (5/0), Guillermo Escalada (17/8). Trainer: Juan Carlos Corazzo (11).
Goals: Mario Ludovico Bergara (52), Víctor Homero Guglianone (64), Mario Ludovico Bergara (75).

304. 05.06.1960 **URUGUAY - CHILE** **2-2(0-1)**
Estadio Centenario, Montevideo; Referee: Estebán Marino (Uruguay), Attendance: 45,000
URU: Roberto Eduardo Sosa (6/0), Esteban Alvarez (4/0), Emilio Walter Álvarez (2/0), Mario Omar Méndez (6/0), Angel Rodríguez (1/0) [Jorge Gómez (2/0)], Juan Carlos Mesías (12/0), Héctor Salvá González (2/0), Mario Ludovico Bergara (6/6) [Luis Alberto Cubilla Almeida (3/0)], Víctor Homero Guglianone (6/4), Héctor Rodríguez (6/0) [Jorge Campanella (1/0)], Guillermo Escalada (18/8). Trainer: Juan Carlos Corazzo (12).
Goals: Víctor Homero Guglianone (59, 67).

305. 09.07.1960 **URUGUAY - BRAZIL** **1-0(0-0)** Copa Atlántico
Estadio Centenario, Montevideo; Referee: Juan Regis Brozzi (Argentina)
URU: Luis María Maidana (2/0), Santiago Pino (1/0), Florencio Horacio Troche Herrera (5/0), Jorge Gómez (3/0) , Rúben Adán González (6/0) [Néstor Gonçalves (15/0)], Juan Carlos Mesías (13/0), Domingo Salvador Pérez (7/3), Mario Ludovico Bergara (7/6) [Siegfried Khun (1/0)], Víctor Homero Guglianone (7/4), Héctor Rodríguez (7/0), Guillermo Escalada (19/8). Trainer: Juan Carlos Corazzo (13).
Goal: Domingo Salvador Pérez (55).

306. 13.07.1960 **URUGUAY - PARAGUAY** **2-1** Copa Atlántico
Estadio Centenario, Montevideo; Referee: Juan Regis Brozzi (Argentina)
URU: Luis María Maidana (3/0), Florencio Horacio Troche Herrera (6/0), Jorge Gómez (4/0), Santiago Pino (2/0), Rúben Adán González (7/0) [Néstor Gonçalves (16/0)], Juan Carlos Mesías (14/0), Domingo Salvador Pérez (8/3), Mario Ludovico Bergara (8/6) [Carlos Rosas Riolfo (1/0)], Víctor Homero Guglianone (8/4) [Siegfried Khun (2/0)], Héctor Rodríguez (8/1), Guillermo Escalada (20/9). Trainer: Juan Carlos Corazzo (14).
Goals: Héctor Rodríguez, Guillermo Escalada.

307. 17.08.1960 **ARGENTINA - URUGUAY** **4-0(0-0)** Copa Atlántico
Estadio Monumental „Antonio Vespucio Liberti", Buenos Aires; Referee: João Etzel Filho (Brazil), Attendance: 40,000
URU: Luis María Maidana (4/0), Florencio Horacio Troche Herrera (7/0), Jorge Gómez (5/0), Santiago Pino (3/0), Rúben Adán González (8/0) [Néstor Gonçalves (17/0)], Juan Carlos Mesías (15/0), Domingo Salvador Pérez (9/3) [Luis Alberto Cubilla Almeida (4/0)], Mario Ludovico Bergara (9/6), Oscar Cobos (1/0) [Siegfried Khun (3/0)], Héctor Rodríguez (9/1), Guillermo Escalada (21/9). Trainer: Juan Carlos Corazzo (15).

308. 15.07.1961 **BOLIVIA - URUGUAY** **1-1(0-1)** 7th FIFA WC. Qualifiers
Estadio „Hernándo Siles Zuazo", La Paz; Referee: Juan Carlos Robles (Chile)
URU: Luis María Maidana (5/0), William Rubén Martínez (42/2), Núber Cano (1/0), Eladio De Souza (1/0), Estanislao Francisco Malinowski (1/0), Walter Aguerre (1/0), Luis Alberto Cubilla Almeida (5/1), Mario Ludovico Bergara (10/6), Angel Rubén Cabrera (1/0), Jose Francisco Sasía (23/7), Guillermo Escalada (22/9). Trainer: Enrique Fernández Viola (1).
Goal: Luis Alberto Cubilla Almeida (23).

309. 30.07.1961 **URUGUAY - BOLIVIA** **2-1(2-0)** 7th FIFA WC. Qualifiers
Estadio Centenario, Montevideo; Referee: Juan Carlos Robles (Chile)
URU: Luis María Maidana (6/0), William Rubén Martínez (43/2), Núber Cano (2/0), Eladio De Souza (2/0), Rúben Adán González (9/0), Walter Aguerre (2/0), Luis Alberto Cubilla Almeida (6/1), Mario Ludovico Bergara (11/6), Angel Rubén Cabrera (2/1), Jose Francisco Sasía (24/7), Guillermo Escalada (23/10). Trainer: Enrique Fernández Viola (2).
Goals: Angel Rubén Cabrera (3), Guillermo Escalada (39).

310. 12.10.1961 **CHILE - URUGUAY** **2-3(2-2)**
Estadio Nacional, Santiago; Referee: Alberto Tejada Burga (Peru), Attendance: 40,000
URU: Luis Dogliotti (1/0), Florencio Horacio Troche Herrera (8/0), Rubén Soria (2/0), Edgardo Nilson González (130) [Eladio De Souza (3/0)], Néstor Gonçalves (18/0), Pedro Ramón Cubilla (1/0), Luis Alberto Cubilla Almeida (7/2), Héctor Jesús Silva (1/0), Jose Francisco Sasía (25/7), Vladas Douksas (11/3), Juan Pintos (1/2). Trainer: Juan Carlos Corazzo (16).
Goals: Juan Pintos (39, 42), Luis Alberto Cubilla Almeida (47).

311. 29.11.1961 **URUGUAY - SOVIET UNION** **1-2(1-2)**
Estadio Centenario, Montevideo; Referee: José Luis Praddaude (Argentina), Attendance: 75,000
URU: Luis María Maidana (7/0) [Luis Dogliotti (2/0)], Florencio Horacio Troche Herrera (9/0), Emilio Walter Álvarez (3/0), Edgardo Nilson González (14/0), Néstor Gonçalves (19/0) [Rúben Adán González (10/0)], Eladio De Souza (4/0), Luis Alberto Cubilla Almeida (8/3), Héctor Jesús Silva (2/0) [Pedro Virgilio Rocha Franchetti (1/0)], José Francisco Sasía (26/7) [Ronald Arturo Langón (1/0)], Vladas Douksas (12/3), Juan Pintos (2/2). Trainer: Juan Carlos Corazzo (17).
Goal: Luis Alberto Cubilla Almeida (29).

312. 23.12.1961 **URUGUAY - HUNGARY** **1-1(1-0)**
Estadio Centenario, Montevideo; Referee: Luis Ventre (Argentina), Attendance: 22,000
URU: Luis Dogliotti (3/0), Florencio Horacio Troche Herrera (10/0), Emilio Walter Álvarez (4/0), Mario Omar Méndez (7/0), Estanislao Francisco Malinowski (2/0) [Jorge Gómez (6/0)], Eladio de Souza (5/0), José Mattera (1/0), Jorge Oyarbide (1/0), José Francisco Sasía (27/7), Vladas Douksas (13/3), Guillermo Escalada (24/11) [Juan Pintos (3/2)]. Trainer: Juan Carlos Corazzo (18).
Goal: Guillermo Escalada (25).

313. 13.03.1962 **URUGUAY - ARGENTINA** **1-1(0-1)**
Estadio Centenario, Montevideo; Referee: Sergio Bustamante (Chile), Attendance: 35,000
URU: Roberto Eduardo Sosa (7/0), Florencio Horacio Troche Herrera (11/0), Emilio Walter Álvarez (5/1), Edgardo Nilson González (15/0) [Eladio de Souza (6/0)], Néstor Gonçalves (20/0), Pedro Ramón Cubilla (2/0), Domingo Salvador Pérez (10/3), Mario Ludovico Bergara (12/6), José Francisco Sasía (28/7), Vladas Douksas (14/3), Guillermo Escalada (25/11). Trainer: Juan Carlos Corazzo (19).
Goal: Emilio Walter Álvarez.

314. 11.04.1962 **WEST GERMANY - URUGUAY** **3-0(1-0)**
Volksparkstadion, Hamburg; Referee: Leopold Sylvain Horn (Holland), Attendance: 71,000
URU: Roberto Eduardo Sosa (8/0), Florencio Horacio Troche Herrera (12/0), Alejandro Majewski (1/0), Edgardo Nilson González (16/0), Néstor Gonçalves (21/0), Pedro Ramón Cubilla (3/0), Luis Alberto Cubilla Almeida (9/3), Héctor Jesús Silva (3/0) [José Francisco Sasía (29/7)], Angel Rubén Cabrera (3/1) [Ronald Arturo Langón (2/0)], Pedro Virgilio Rocha Franchetti (2/0) [Vladas Douksas (15/3)], Guillermo Escalada (26/11). Trainer: Juan Carlos Corazzo (20).

315. 18.04.1962 **HUNGARY - URUGUAY** **1-1(0-0)**
Népstadion, Budapest; Referee: Branko Tešanić (Yugoslavia), Attendance: 80,000
URU: Roberto Eduardo Sosa (9/0) [Luis María Maidana (8/0)], Florencio Horacio Troche Herrera (13/0), Alejandro Majewski (2/0), Edgardo Nilson González (17/0), Néstor Gonçalves (22/0), Pedro Ramón Cubilla (4/0) [Eladio de Souza (7/0)], Luis Alberto Cubilla Almeida (10/3) [Ronald Arturo Langón (3/0)], Héctor Jesús Silva (4/1), José Francisco Sasía (30/7), Vladas Douksas (16/3), Guillermo Escalada (27/11). Trainer: Juan Carlos Corazzo (21).
Goal: Héctor Jesús Silva (58).

316. 22.04.1962 **CZECHOSLOVAKIA - URUGUAY** **3-1(1-1)**
Strahov Štadion, Praha; Referee: Johannes Martens (Holland), Attendance: 45,000
URU: Luis María Maidana (9/0), Florencio Horacio Troche Herrera (14/0), Alejandro Majewski (3/0), Edgardo Nilson González (18/0), Néstor Gonçalves (23/0), Eladio De Souza (8/0) [72.Rúbens Dávila (1/0)], Ronald Arturo Langón (4/0), Héctor Jesús Silva (5/1), José Francisco Sasía (31/8) [72.Angel Rubén Cabrera (4/1)], Vladas Douksas (17/3) [76.Pedro Virgilio Rocha Franchetti (3/0)], Guillermo Escalada (28/11). Trainer: Juan Carlos Corazzo (22).
Goal: José Francisco Sasía (40).

317. 27.04.1962 **SOVIET UNION - URUGUAY** **5-0(3-0)**
Lenin Stadium, Moskva; Referee: Einar Johan Boström (Sweden), Attendance: 102,000
URU: Roberto Eduardo Sosa (10/0), Florencio Horacio Troche Herrera (15/0), Alejandro Majewski (4/0), Edgardo Nilson González (19/0), Néstor Gonçalves (24/0), Pedro Ramón Cubilla (5/0) [31.Edil Manrique (1/0)], Ronald Arturo Langón (5/0), Héctor Jesús Silva (6/1) [46.Pedro Virgilio Rocha Franchetti (4/0)], José Francisco Sasía (32/8), Vladas Douksas (18/3), Guillermo Escalada (29/11) [46. Luis Alberto Cubilla Almeida (11/3)]. Trainer: Juan Carlos Corazzo (23).

318. 02.05.1962 **SCOTLAND - URUGUAY** **2-3(0-2)**
Hampden Park, Glasgow; Referee: Arthur Holland (England), Attendance: 67,181
URU: Roberto Eduardo Sosa (11/0), Florencio Horacio Troche Herrera (16/0), Rubén Soria (3/0), Edgardo Nilson González (20/0), Néstor Gonçalves (25/0), Pedro Ramón Cubilla (6/0), Ronald Arturo Langón (6/0), Julio César Cortés (1/0), José Francisco Sasía (33/9), Vladas Douksas (19/3), Luis Alberto Cubilla Almeida (12/5). Trainer: Juan Carlos Corazzo (24).
Goals: José Francisco Sasía (33), Luis Alberto Cubilla Almeida (44, 48).

319. 30.05.1962 **URUGUAY - COLOMBIA** **2-1(0-1)** 7th FIFA WC. Group Stage
Estadio „Carlos Dittborn", Arica (Chile); Referee: Andor Dorogi (Hungary), Attendance: 7,908
URU: Roberto Eduardo Sosa (12/0), Florencio Horacio Troche Herrera (17/0), Emilio Walter Álvarez (6/1), Eliseo Álvarez (1/0), Mario Omar Méndez (8/0), Néstor Gonçalves (26/0), Luis Alberto Cubilla Almeida (13/6), Pedro Virgilio Rocha Franchetti (5/0), Ronald Arturo Langón (7/0), José Francisco Sasía (34/10), Domingo Salvador Pérez (11/3). Trainers: Hugo Bagnulo - Juan López Fontana - Roberto Scarone (1).
Goals: Luis Alberto Cubilla Almeida (67), José Francisco Sasía (75).

320. 02.06.1962 **YUGOSLAVIA - URUGUAY** **3-1(2-1)** 7th FIFA WC. Group Stage
Estadio „Carlos Dittborn", Arica (Chile); Referee: Karol Galba (Czechoslovakia), Attendance: 8,829
URU: Roberto Eduardo Sosa (13/0), Florencio Horacio Troche Herrera (18/0), Emilio Walter Álvarez (7/1), Eliseo Álvarez (2/0), Mario Omar Méndez (9/0), Néstor Gonçalves (27/0), Mario Ludovico Bergara (13/6), Pedro Virgilio Rocha Franchetti (6/0), Angel Rubén Cabrera (5/2) [*sent off 71*], José Francisco Sasía (35/10), Domingo Salvador Pérez (12/3). Trainers: Hugo Bagnulo - Juan López Fontana - Roberto Scarone (2).
Goal: Angel Rubén Cabrera (19).

321. 06.06.1962 **URUGUAY - SOVIET UNION** **1-2(0-1)** 7th FIFA WC. Group Stage
Estadio „Carlos Dittborn", Arica (Chile); Referee: Cesare Jonni (Italy), Attendance: 9,973
URU: Roberto Eduardo Sosa (14/0), Florencio Horacio Troche Herrera (19/0), Emilio Walter Álvarez (8/1), Eliseo Álvarez (3/0), Mario Omar Méndez (10/0), Néstor Gonçalves (28/0), Julio César Cortés (2/0), Luis Alberto Cubilla Almeida (14/6), Angel Rubén Cabrera (6/2), José Francisco Sasía (36/11), Domingo Salvador Pérez (13/3). Trainers: Hugo Bagnulo - Juan López Fontana - Roberto Scarone (3).
Goal: José Francisco Sasía (54).

322. 19.06.1962 **URUGUAY - CZECHOSLOVAKIA** **3-1(1-0)**
Estadio Centenario, Montevideo; Referee: José María Codesal (Uruguay), Attendance: 52,559
URU: Luis María Maidana (10/0), Florencio Horacio Troche Herrera (20/0), Climaco Rodríguez (6/0) [Edil Manrique (2/0)], Rubén Adán González (11/0), Mario Omar Méndez (11/2), Ricardo Elvio Pavoni Cúneo (1/0), Domingo Salvador Pérez (14/4), Juan José Rodríguez (1/0) [Angel Rubén Cabrera (7/2)], Alberto Pedro Spencer (1/0), Julio César Cortés (3/0) [Pedro Virgilio Rocha Franchetti (7/0)], Guillermo Escalada (30/11). Trainers: Hugo Bagnulo - Juan López Fontana - Roberto Scarone (4).
Goals: Domingo Salvador Pérez (31), Mario Méndez (57 penalty, 84 penalty).

323. 15.08.1962 **ARGENTINA - URUGUAY** **3-1(1-0)** Copa Lipton
Estadio Monumental „Antonio Vespucio Liberti", Buenos Aires; Referee: Juan Regis Brozzi (Argentina), Attendance: 30,000
URU: Roberto Eduardo Sosa (15/0), Jorge Carlos Manicera (1/0), Emilio Walter Álvarez (9/1), Luis Benítez (1/0), Rúben Adán González (12/0), Ricardo Elvio Pavoni Cúneo (2/0), José Mattera (2/1), Héctor Jesús Silva (7/1), Vladas Douksas (20/3), Mario Ludovico Bergara (14/6) [52.Eladio Benítez (10/1)], Guillermo Escalada (31/11) [28.Walter Gimenez (1/0)]. Trainer: Walter Taibo Martínez (1).
Goal: José Mattera (83 penalty).

324. 23.03.1963 **URUGUAY - CHILE** **3-2(2-0)** Copa Juan Pinto Durán
Estadio Centenario, Montevideo; Referee: Paterlini (Uruguay), Attendance: 30,000
URU: Roberto Eduardo Sosa (16/0), Florencio Horacio Troche Herrera (21/0), Roberto Matosas Postiglione (1/0), Luis Benítez (2/0), Darcy Pereira (1/0), Rubén Soria (4/0), Ronald Arturo Langón (8/0), Julio César Cortés (4/0), José Francisco Sasía (37/12), Pedro Virgilio Rocha Franchetti (8/0), Juan Pintos (4/4). Trainer: Washington Etchamendi (1).
Goals: Juan Pintos (38, 42), José Francisco Sasía (57).

325. 24.07.1963 **CHILE - URUGUAY** **0-0** Copa Juan Pinto Durán
Estadio Nacional, Santiago; Referee: Domingo Massaro (Chile), Attendance: 40,000
URU: Roberto Eduardo Sosa (17/0), Jorge Carlos Manicera (2/0), Emilio Walter Álvarez (10/1), Héctor Carlos Cincunegui (1/0), Eliseo Álvarez (4/0), Roberto Matosas Postiglione (2/0), Julio César Abbadie (22/12), Pedro Virgilio Rocha Franchetti (9/0), Ronald Arturo Langón (9/0), Vladas Douksas (21/3), Domingo Salvador Pérez (15/4). Trainer: Washington Etchamendi (2).

326. 25.04.1964 **MOROCCO – URUGUAY** **0-1**

Stade “Marcel Cerdan”, Casablanca; Referee: José María Ortiz de Mendibil (Spain)

URU: Walter Taibo Martínez (18/0), William Rubén Martínez (44/2), Nelson Díaz (1/0), Héctor Carlos Cincunegui (2/0), Darcy Pereira (2/0), Ricardo Elvio Pavoni Cúneo (3/0), Nelson Flores (1/0) [Abayubá Ibañez (1/0)], Julio César Cortés (5/1), Mario Castro (1/0), Eduardo Restivo (1/0) [Alberto Ferrero (1/0)], Juan Pintos (5/4). Trainer: Rafael Milans (1).

Goal: Julio César Cortés.

327. 29.04.1964 **NORTHERN IRELAND – URUGUAY** **3-0(1-0)**

Windsor Park, Belfast; Referee: Ken Nawley (England), Attendance: 23,000

URU: Walter Taibo Martínez (19/0), William Rubén Martínez (45/2), Nelson Díaz (2/0), Héctor Carlos Cincunegui (3/0), Darcy Pereira (3/0), Ricardo Elvio Pavoni Cúneo (4/0), Nelson Flores (2/0) [Alberto Ferrero (2/0)], Julio César Cortés (6/1), Mario Castro (2/0) [Néstor Soria (1/0)], Abayubá Ibañez (2/0), Juan Pintos (6/4). Trainer: Rafael Milans (2).

328. 06.05.1964 **ENGLAND – URUGUAY** **2-1(1-0)**

Wembley Stadium, London; Referee: István Zsolt (Hungary), Attendance: 55,000

URU: Walter Taibo Martínez (20/0), William Rubén Martínez (46/2), Nelson Díaz (3/0), Héctor Carlos Cincunegui (4/0), Darcy Pereira (4/0), Ricardo Elvio Pavoni Cúneo (5/0), Nelson Flores (3/0), Julio César Cortés (7/1), Alberto Pedro Spencer (2/1), Roberto Gil (1/0), Juan Pintos (7/4). Trainer: Rafael Milans (3).

Goal: Alberto Pedro Spencer (78).

329. 14.05.1964 **AUSTRIA – URUGUAY** **0-2(0-1)**

Prater Stadion, Wien; Referee: Miroslav Kusak (Czechoslovakia), Attendance: 42,000

URU: Walter Taibo Martínez (21/0) [46.Rodger Bernardico (8/0)], William Rubén Martínez (47/2), Nelson Díaz (4/0), Héctor Cincunegui (5/0), Darcy Pereira (5/0), Ricardo Elvio Pavoni Cúneo (6/0) [*sent off*], Nelson Flores (4/0) [46.Nelson Chabay (1/0)], Julio César Cortés (8/1) [58.Abayubá Ibañez (3/0)], Alberto Pedro Spencer (3/1), Roberto Gil (2/0), Mario Castro (3/2). Trainer: Rafael Milans (4).

Goals: Mario Castro (11, 68).

330. 20.05.1964 **SOVIET UNION – URUGUAY** **1-0(0-0)**

Lenin Stadium, Moskva; Referee: Friedrich Köpke (East Germany), Attendance: 25,000

URU: Rodger Bernardico (9/0), William Rubén Martínez (48/2), Nelson Díaz (5/0), Héctor Carlos Cincunegui (6/0), Darcy Pereira (6/0), Ricardo Elvio Pavoni Cúneo (7/0), Nelson Flores (5/0) [Abayubá Ibañez (4/0)], Julio César Cortés (9/1) [43.Francisco Cámera (1/0)], Alberto Pedro Spencer (4/1), Roberto Gil (3/0), Mario Castro (4/2). Trainer: Rafael Milans (5).

331. 03.01.1965 **URUGUAY – EAST GERMANY** **0-2(0-0)**

Estadio Centenario, Montevideo; Referee: José Maria Codesal (Uruguay), Attendance: 50,000

URU: Walter Taibo Martínez (22/0), Elgar Baeza (1/0) [Miguel Moreno (1/0)], Nelson Díaz (6/0), Edgardo Nilson González (21/0) [Luis Ignacio Ubiñas (1/0)], Roberto Gil (4/0) [Héctor Carlos Cincunegui (7/0), Mario Omar Méndez (12/2), Julio César Abbadie (23/12), Pedro Virgilio Rocha Franchetti (10/0), José Francisco Sasía (38/12), Héctor Jesús Silva (8/1), Juan Joya (1/0) [Raúl Núñez (1/0)]. Trainer: Rafael Milans (6).

332. 24.04.1965 **PARAGUAY – URUGUAY** **2-1** Copa Artigas

Estadio „Manuel Ferreira“, Asunción; Referee: Angel Eduardo Pazos (Uruguay)

URU: Walter Taibo Martínez (23/0), William Rubén Martínez (49/2), Eliseo Álvarez (5/0), Héctor Carlos Cincunegui (8/0), Roberto Gil (5/0), Mario Omar Méndez (13/2), Domingo Salvador Pérez (16/4) [Ronaldo Arturo Langón (10/0)], Héctor Salvá González (3/0), Julio Toja (1/1), Vladas Douksas (22/3), Danilo Meneses (1/0). Trainer: Rafael Milans (7).

Goal: Julio Toja.

333. 02.05.1965 **URUGUAY – PARAGUAY** **4-0** Copa Artigas

Estadio Centenario, Montevideo; Referee: José Dimas Larrosa (Paraguay)

URU: Walter Taibo Martínez (24/0), William Rubén Martínez (50/2), Jorge Carlos Manicera (3/0), Héctor Carlos Cincunegui (9/0), Néstor Gonçalves (29/0), Omar Caetano Otero (1/0), José Eusebio Urruzmendi Aycaguer (1/2), Pedro Virgilio Rocha Franchetti (11/0), Héctor Jesús Silva (9/3), Vladas Douksas (23/3), Danilo Meneses (2/0). Trainer: Rafael Milans (8).

Goals: Héctor Silva 2, José Eusebio Urruzmendi Aycaguer 2.

334. 09.05.1965 **CHILE – URUGUAY** **0-0** Copa Juan Pinto Durán

Estadio Nacional, Santiago; Referee: Francisco Pardiñas (Uruguay), Attendance: 59,316

URU: Walter Taibo Martínez (25/0), William Rubén Martínez (51/2), Jorge Carlos Manicera (4/0), Héctor Carlos Cincunegui (10/0), Néstor Gonçalves (30/0), Omar Caetano Otero (2/0), José Eusebio Urruzmendi Aycaguer (2/2), Pedro Virgilio Rocha Franchetti (12/0), Héctor Jesús Silva (10/3) [Julio Toja (2/1)], Vladas Douksas (24/3), Danilo Meneses (3/0). Trainer: Rafael Milans (9).

335. 16.05.1965 **URUGUAY – CHILE** **1-1(1-1)** Copa Juan Pinto Durán

Estadio Centenario, Montevideo; Referee: Domingo Massaro (Chile), Attendance: 16,991

URU: Walter Taibo Martínez (26/0) [Ladislao Mazurkiewicz Iglesias (1/0)], William Rubén Martínez (52/2), Jorge Carlos Manicera (5/0), Héctor Carlos Cincunegui (11/0), Néstor Gonçalves (31/0), Omar Caetano Otero (3/0), José Eusebio Urruzmendi Aycaguer (3/2), Pedro Virgilio Rocha Franchetti (13/0), Julio Toja (3/2), Vladas Douksas (25/3), Danilo Meneses (4/0). Trainer: Rafael Milans (10).

Goal: Julio Toja (42).

336. 23.05.1965 **URUGUAY – VENEZUELA** **5-0(2-0)** 8th FIFA WC. Qualifiers

Estadio Centenario, Montevideo; Referee: José Dimas Larrosa (Paraguay), Attendance: 18,000

URU: Ladislao Mazurkiewicz Iglesias (2/0), William Rubén Martínez (53/2), Jorge Carlos Manicera (6/0), Héctor Carlos Cincunegui (12/0), Néstor Gonçalves (32/0), Omar Caetano Otero (4/0), José Eusebio Urruzmendi Aycaguer (4/2), Pedro Virgilio Rocha Franchetti (14/1), Héctor Jesús Silva (11/6), Vladas Douksas (26/3), Danilo Meneses (5/1). Trainer: Rafael Milans (11).

Goals: Pedro Virgilio Rocha Franchetti (18), Héctor Jesús Silva (23, 52), Danilo Meneses (61), Héctor Jesús Silva (69).

337. 30.05.1965 **VENEZUELA – URUGUAY** **1-3(1-0)** 8th FIFA WC. Qualifiers

Estadio Universitario, Caracas; Referee: Roberto Goicoechea (Argentina), Attendance: 12,649

URU: Ladislao Mazurkiewicz Iglesias (3/0), William Rubén Martínez (54/2), Jorge Carlos Manicera (7/0), Luis Benítez (3/0), Néstor Gonçalves (33/0), Omar Caetano Otero (5/0), Jose Eusebio Urruzmendi (5/3), Pedro Virgilio Rocha Franchetti (15/3), Héctor Jesús Silva (12/6), Vladas Douksas (27/3), Danilo Meneses (6/1). Trainer: Rafael Milans (12).

Goals: Pedro Virgilio Rocha Franchetti (10, 47), José Eusebio Urruzmendi Aycaguer (88).

338. 06.06.1965 **PERU – URUGUAY** **0-1(0-0)** 8th FIFA WC. Qualifiers
Estadio Nacional, Lima; Referee: Claudio Vicuña (Chile), Attendance: 44,033
URU: Walter Taibo Martínez (27/0), Nelson Chabay (2/0), Jorge Carlos Manicera (8/0), Mario Omar Méndez (14/2), Roberto Gil (6/0), Omar Caetano Otero (6/0), José Eusebio Urruzmendi Aycaguer (6/4), Pedro Virgilio Rocha Franchetti (16/3), Héctor Jesús Silva (13/6), Vladas Douksas (28/3), Danilo Meneses (7/1). Trainer: Rafael Milans (13).
Goal: José Eusebio Urruzmendi Aycaguer (78).

339. 13.06.1965 **URUGUAY – PERU** **2-1(1-1)** 8th FIFA WC. Qualifiers
Estadio Centenario, Montevideo; Referee: Armando Nunes Castanheiras da Rosa Marques (Brazil), Attendance: 58,413
URU: Walter Taibo Martínez (28/0), Nelson Chabay (3/0), Jorge Carlos Manicera (9/0), Mario Omar Méndez (15/2), Roberto Gil (7/0), Omar Caetano Otero (7/0), José Eusebio Urruzmendi Aycaguer (7/4), Pedro Virgilio Rocha Franchetti (17/4), Héctor Jesús Silva (14/7), Vladas Douksas (29/3), Danilo Meneses (8/1). Trainer: Rafael Milans (14).
Goals: Héctor Jesús Silva (20), Pedro Virgilio Rocha Franchetti (65).

340. 07.09.1965 **BRAZIL – URUGUAY** **3-0(2-0)**
Estádio Mineirão, Belo Horizonte; Referee: Eunápio Gouveia de Queiroz (Brazil)
URU: Walter Taibo Martínez (29/0) [Carlos Bogni (1/0)], Héctor Carlos Cincunegui (13/0) [Miguel De Britos (1/0)], Jorge Carlos Manicera (10/0), Luis Alberto Varela (1/0), Omar Caetano Otero (8/0), Raúl Núñez (2/0) [Homero Lorda (1/0)], Vladas Douksas (30/3) [Víctor Rodolfo Espárrago Videla (1/0)], Horacio Franco (1/0), Héctor Salvá González (4/0), Sergio Silva (1/0) [Orlando Virgili (1/0)], Julio César Araújo Morales (1/0). Trainer: Juan López (41).

341. 04.12.1965 **URUGUAY – SOVIET UNION** **1-3(1-2)**
Estadio Centenario, Montevideo; Referee: Miguel Comesana (Argentina), Attendance: 35,000
URU: Roberto Eduardo Sosa (18/0), Emilio Walter Álvarez (11/1), Jorge Carlos Manicera (11/0), Mario Omar Méndez (16/2), Néstor Gonçalves (34/0), Omar Caetano Otero (9/0), Julio César Abbadie (24/12), Mario Ludovico Bergara (15/6) [46.Vladas Douksas (31/3)], Orlando Virgili (2/0) [Héctor Jesús Silva (15/7)], Pedro Virgilio Rocha Franchetti (18/5), Víctor Rodolfo Espárrago Videla (2/0) [José Eusebio Urruzmendi Aycaguer (8/4)]. Trainer: Juan López Fontana (42).
Goal: Pedro Virgilio Rocha Franchetti (32).

342. 15.05.1966 **PARAGUAY – URUGUAY** **2-2** Copa Artigas
Estadio Puerto Sajonia, Asunción; Referee: José María Codesal (Uruguay)
URU: Pedro González Acuña (1/0), Carlos Martínez (1/0), Nelson Chabay (4/0), Eliseo Álvarez (6/0), Roberto Gil (8/0), Mario Omar Méndez (17/2), Victor Rodolfo Espárrago (3/0), Héctor Salvá González (5/2), Ronald Arturo Langón (11/0), Vladas Douksas (32/3), Jorge Acuña (1/0) [Sergio Silva (2/0)]. Trainer: Ondino Leonel Viera Palaserez (1).
Goals: Héctor Salvá González 2.

343. 18.05.1966 **URUGUAY – PARAGUAY** **3-1** Copa Artigas
Estadio Centenario, Montevideo; Referee: Rodolfo Pérez Osorio (Paraguay)
URU: Roberto Eduardo Sosa (19/0), Florencio Horacio Troche Herrera (22/0), Jorge Carlos Manicera (12/0), Luis Ignacio Ubiñas (2/0), Milton Viera Rivero (1/1), Juan Martín Mujica (1/0), Domingo Salvador Pérez (17/5), Luis Eduardo Ramos (1/0), José Francisco Sasía (39/12), José Eusebio Urruzmendi Aycaguer (9/4) [Emilio Walter Álvarez (12/1)], Julio César Araújo Morales (2/1). Trainer: Ondino Leonel Viera Palaserez (2).
Goals: Milton Viera Rivero, Julio César Araújo Morales, Domingo Salvador Pérez

344. 15.06.1966 **ISRAEL – URUGUAY** **1-2(0-0)**
National Stadium, Ramat-Gan, Tel Aviv; Referee: Menachem Ashkenazi (Israel), Attendance: 40,000
URU: Ladislao Mazurkiewicz Iglesias (4/0), Florencio Horacio Troche Herrera (23/0), Nelson Díaz (7/0), Luis Ignacio Ubiñas (3/0), Jorge Carlos Manicera (13/0) [Pedro Virgilio Rocha Franchetti (19/5)], Omar Caetano Otero (10/0), Néstor Gonçalves (35/0), Julio César Abbadie (25/14), José Francisco Sasía (40/12) [Héctor Jesús Silva (16/7)], Julio César Cortés (10/1) [Vladas Douksas (33/3)], Domingo Salvador Pérez (18/5). Trainer: Ondino Leonel Viera Palaserez (3).
Goals: Julio César Abbadie (67, 72).

345. 19.06.1966 **ROMANIA – URUGUAY** **1-0(1-0)**
Stadion 23 August, Bucureşti; Referee: Alexandru Pîrvu (Romania), Attendance: 60,000
URU: Walter Taibo Martínez (30/0), Pablo Justo Forlán Lamarque (1/0), Florencio Horacio Troche Herrera (24/0), Emilio Walter Álvarez (13/1) [73 Jorge Carlos Manicera (14/0)], Omar Caetano Otero (11/0), Néstor Gonçalves (36/0), Pedro Virgilio Rocha Franchetti (20/5), José Eusebio Urruzmendi Aycaguer (10/4), Héctor Jesús Silva (17/7) [79 Héctor Salvá González (6/2)], Vladas Douksas (34/3) [46 Julio César Cortés (11/1)], Víctor Rodolfo Espárrago Videla (4/0) [46 Domingo Salvador Pérez (19/5)]. Trainer: Ondino Leonel Viera Palaserez (4).

346. 23.06.1966 **SPAIN – URUGUAY** **1-1(0-1)**
Estadio Riazor, La Coruña; Referee: Anibal da Silva Oliveira (Portugal), Attendance: 43,000
URU: Ladislao Mazurkiewicz Iglesias (5/0), Florencio Horacio Troche Herrera (25/0), Néstor Gonçalves (37/0), Nelson Díaz (8/0), Pablo Justo Forlán Lamarque (2/0), Omar Caetano Otero (12/0), Julio César Cortés (12/1), Julio César Abbadie (26/14) [46.José Eusebio Urruzmendi Aycaguer (11/4)], Héctor Jesús Silva (18/7) [86.Víctor Rodolfo Espárrago Videla (5/0)], Pedro Virgilio Rocha Franchetti (21/5) [46.Héctor Salvá González (7/2)], Domingo Salvador Pérez (20/6). Trainer: Ondino Leonel Viera Palaserez (5).
Goal: Domingo Salvador Pérez (44).

347. 26.06.1966 **PORTUGAL – URUGUAY** **3-0(1-0)**
Estádio Nacional, Lisboa; Referee: Karl Keller (Switzerland), Attendance: 35,000
URU: Walter Taibo Martínez (31/0), Carlos Martínez (2/0), Jorge Carlos Manicera (15/0), Luis Ignacio Ubiñas (4/0), Emilio Walter Álvarez (14/1), Juan Martín Mujica (2/0), Milton Viera Rivero (2/1) [Luis Eduardo Ramos (2/0)], Eliseo Álvarez (7/0), José Francisco Sasía (41/12), José Eusebio Urruzmendi Aycaguer (12/4), Víctor Rodolfo Espárrago Videla (6/0). Trainer: Ondino Leonel Viera Palaserez (6).

348. 11.07.1966 **ENGLAND – URUGUAY** **0-0** 8th FIFA WC. Group Stage
Wembley Stadium, London; Referee: István Zsolt (Hungary), Attendance: 87,148
URU: Ladislao Mazurkiewicz Iglesias (6/0), Florencio Horacio Troche Herrera (26/0), Jorge Carlos Manicera (16/0), Luis Ignacio Ubiñas (5/0), Néstor Gonçalves (38/0), Omar Caetano Otero (13/0), Julio César Cortés (13/1), Milton Viera Rivero (3/1), Héctor Jesús Silva (19/7), Pedro Virgilio Rocha Franchetti (22/5), Domingo Salvador Pérez (21/6). Trainer: Ondino Leonel Viera Palaserez (7).

349. 15.07.1966 **URUGUAY - FRANCE** **2-1(2-1)** 8th FIFA WC. Group Stage
White Harte Lane Stadium, London (England); Referee: Dr. Karol Galba (Czechoslovakia), Attendance: 45,662
URU: Ladislao Mazurkiewicz Iglesias (7/0), Florencio Horacio Troche Herrera (27/0), Jorge Carlos Manicera (17/0), Luis Ignacio Ubiñas (6/0), Néstor Gonçalves (39/0), Omar Caetano Otero (14/0), Julio César Cortés (14/2), Milton Viera Rivero (4/1), José Francisco Sasía (42/12), Pedro Virgilio Rocha Franchetti (23/6), Domingo Salvador Pérez (22/6). Trainer: Ondino Leonel Viera Palaserez (8).
Goals: Pedro Virgilio Rocha Franchetti (27), Julio César Cortés (32).

350. 19.07.1966 **URUGUAY - MEXICO** **0-0** 8th FIFA WC. Group Stage
Wembley Stadium, London (England); Referee: Bertil Lööw (Sweden), Attendance: 50,451
URU: Ladislao Mazurkiewicz Iglesias (8/0), Florencio Horacio Troche Herrera (28/0), Jorge Carlos Manicera (18/0), Luis Ignacio Ubiñas (7/0), Néstor Gonçalves (40/0), Omar Caetano Otero (15/0), Julio César Cortés (15/2), Milton Viera Rivero (5/1), José Francisco Sasía (43/12), Pedro Virgilio Rocha Franchetti (24/6), Domingo Salvador Pérez (23/6). Trainer: Ondino Leonel Viera Palaserez (9).

351. 23.07.1966 **WEST GERMANY - URUGUAY** **4-0(1-0)** 8th FIFA WC. Quarter-Finals
Hillsbrough Stadium, Sheffield (England); Referee: James Finney (England), Attendance: 33,751
URU: Ladislao Mazurkiewicz Iglesias (9/0), Florencio Horacio Troche Herrera (29/0) [*sent off 49*], Luis Ignacio Ubiñas (8/0), Néstor Gonçalves (41/0), Jorge Carlos Manicera (19/0), Omar Caetano Otero (16/0), Héctor Salvá González (8/2), Pedro Virgilio Rocha Franchetti (25/6), Héctor Jesús Silva (20/7) [*sent off 54*], Julio César Cortés (16/2), Domingo Salvador Pérez (24/6). Trainer: Ondino Leonel Viera Palaserez (10).

352. 04.01.1967 **URUGUAY -ROMANIA** **1-1(0-1)**
Estadio Centenario, Montevideo; Referee: Francisco Pardinas (Uruguay), Attendance: 7,000
URU: Jacinto Callero (1/0) [Miguel Angel Bazzano (1/0)], Elgar Baeza (2/0), Luis Alberto Varela (2/0), Héctor Carlos Cincunegui (14/0), Julio Walter Montero Castillo (1/0) [75.Rúben Techera (1/0)], Omar Caetano Otero (17/0), Domingo Salvador Pérez (25/6), Jorge Oyarbide (2/0), Jorge Acuña (2/0) [46.Luis Alberto Vera (1/0)], Héctor Salvá González (9/2) [46.Abayubá Ibañez (5/0)], José Eusebio Urruzmendi Aycaguer (13/5). Trainer: Juan Carlos Corazzo (25).
Goal: José Eusebio Urruzmendi Aycaguer (66).

353. 17.01.1967 **URUGUAY - BOLIVIA** **4-0(2-0)** 29th Copa América
Estadio Centenario, Montevideo; Referee: Isidro Ramírez Álvarez (Paraguay), Attendance: 15,000
URU: Miguel Angel Bazzano (2/0), Elgar Baeza (3/0), Luis Alberto Varela (3/0), Héctor Carlos Cincunegui (15/0), Julio Walter Montero Castillo (2/1), Omar Caetano Otero (18/0), Domingo Salvador Pérez (26/6) [24.Héctor Salvá González (10/2)], Jorge Oyarbide (3/1), Luis Alberto Vera (2/0), Pedro Virgilio Rocha Franchetti (26/7), José Eusebio Urruzmendi Aycaguer (14/5). Trainer: Juan Carlos Corazzo (26).
Goals: Pedro Virgilio Rocha Franchetti (5), Julio Walter Montero Castillo (44), Roberto Troncoso (55 own goal), Jorge Oyarbide (81).

354. 21.01.1967 **URUGUAY - VENEZUELA** **4-0(2-0)** 29th Copa América
Estadio Centenario, Montevideo; Referee: Eunápio de Queiroz (Brazil), Attendance: 7,000
URU: Miguel Angel Bazzano (3/0), Elgar Baeza (4/0) [55.Carlos Martínez (3/0)], Luis Alberto Varela (4/0), Héctor Carlos Cincunegui (16/0), Julio Walter Montero Castillo (3/1), Juan Martín Mujica (3/0), Héctor Salvá González (11/2), Jorge Oyarbide (4/3), Luis Alberto Vera (3/0) [81.Jorge Acuña (3/0)], Pedro Virgilio Rocha Franchetti (27/7), José Eusebio Urruzmendi Aycaguer (15/7). Trainer: Juan Carlos Corazzo (27).
Goals: José Eusebio Urruzmendi Aycaguer (5, 34), Jorge Oyarbide (62, 68).

355. 26.01.1967 **URUGUAY - CHILE** **2-2(1-2)** 29th Copa América
Estadio Centenario, Montevideo; Referee: Isidro Ramírez Alvarez (Paraguay), Attendance: 30,000
URU: Miguel Angel Bazzano (4/0), Carlos Martínez (4/0), Luis Alberto Varela (5/0), Héctor Carlos Cincunegui (17/0) [82.Pablo Justo Forlán Lamarque (3/0)], Julio Walter Montero Castillo (4/1) [46.Rúben Techera (2/0)], Omar Caetano Otero (19/0), Héctor Salvá González (12/2), Jorge Oyarbide (5/4), Luis Alberto Vera (4/0) [61.Domingo Salvador Pérez (27/6)], Pedro Virgilio Rocha Franchetti (28/8), José Eusebio Urruzmendi Aycaguer (16/7). Trainer: Juan Carlos Corazzo (28).
Goals: Pedro Virgilio Rocha Franchetti (15 penalty), Jorge Oyarbide (68).

356. 29.01.1967 **URUGUAY - PARAGUAY** **2-0(1-0)** 29th Copa América
Estadio Centenario, Montevideo; Referee: Mario Gasc (Chile), Attendance: 17,000
URU: Ladislao Mazurkiewicz Iglesias (10/0), Elgar Baeza (5/0) [73.Juan Carlos Paz (1/0)], Luis Alberto Varela (6/0), Héctor Carlos Cincunegui (18/0), Julio Walter Montero Castillo (5/1) [43.Rúben Techera (3/0)], Juan Martín Mujica (4/0), Domingo Salvador Pérez (28/7), Pedro Virgilio Rocha Franchetti (29/8), Jorge Oyarbide (6/4) [46.Luis Alberto Vera (5/0)], Héctor Salvá González (13/2), José Eusebio Urruzmendi Aycaguer (17/8). Trainer: Juan Carlos Corazzo (29).
Goals: Domingo Salvador Pérez (32), José Eusebio Urruzmendi Aycaguer (66).

357. 02.02.1967 **URUGUAY - ARGENTINA** **1-0(0-0)** 29th Copa América
Estadio Centenario, Montevideo; Referee: Mario Gasc (Chile), Attendance: 65,000
URU: Ladislao Mazurkiewicz Iglesias (11/0), Elgar Baeza (6/0), Luis Alberto Varela (7/0), Héctor Carlos Cincunegui (19/0) [82.Pablo Justo Forlán Lamarque (4/0)], Juan Carlos Paz (2/0), Juan Martín Mujica (5/0), Domingo Salvador Pérez (29/7), Pedro Virgilio Rocha Franchetti (30/9), Jorge Oyarbide (7/4) [46.Luis Alberto Vera (6/0)], Héctor Salvá González (14/2) [63.Rúben Techera (4/0)], José Eusebio Urruzmendi Aycaguer (18/8). Trainer: Juan Carlos Corazzo (30).
Goal: Pedro Virgilio Rocha Franchetti (75).

358. 25.06.1967 **URUGUAY - BRAZIL** **0-0** Copa Rio Branco
Estadio Centenario, Montevideo; Referee: Aurelio Domingo Bossolino (Argentina)
URU: Roberto Eduardo Sosa (20/0), Pablo Justo Forlán Lamarque (5/0), Jorge Carlos Manicera (20/0), Emilio Walter Álvarez (15/1), Omar Caetano Otero (20/0), Néstor Gonçalves (42/0), Pedro Virgilio Rocha Franchetti (31/9), Horacio Franco (2/0) [Alberto Urbano (1/0)], Jorge Acuña (4/0) [Rafael Leites (1/0)], Héctor Salvá González (15/2), José Eusebio Urruzmendi Aycaguer (19/8). Trainer: Juan Carlos Corazzo (31).

359. 28.06.1967 **URUGUAY - BRAZIL** **2-2(0-1)** Copa Rio Branco
Estadio Centenario, Montevideo; Referee: Aurelio Domingo Bossolino (Argentina)
URU: Roberto Eduardo Sosa (21/0), Pablo Justo Forlán Lamarque (6/0), Jorge Carlos Manicera (21/0), Emilio Walter Álvarez (16/1), Omar Caetano Otero (21/0), Néstor Gonçalves (43/0), Pedro Virgilio Rocha Franchetti (32/11), Horacio Franco (3/0) [Alberto Urbano (2/0), Luis Gómez Lugo (1/0)], Héctor Jesús Silva (21/7), Héctor Salvá González (16/2), José Eusebio Urruzmendi Aycaguer (20/8). Trainer: Juan Carlos Corazzo (32).
Goals: Pedro Virgilio Rocha Franchetti (58, 73).

360. 01.07.1967 **URUGUAY - BRAZIL** **1-1(1-1)** Copa Rio Branco
Estadio Centenario, Montevideo; Referee: Esteban Marino (Uruguay)
URU: Roberto Eduardo Sosa (22/0), Pablo Justo Forlán Lamarque (7/0), Jorge Carlos Manicera (22/0), Emilio Walter Álvarez (17/1), Omar Caetano Otero (22/0), Néstor Gonçalves (44/0), Pedro Virgilio Rocha Franchetti (33/12), Alberto Urbano (3/0), Héctor Jesús Silva (22/7) [Rafael Leites (2/0), Hamilton Rivero (1/0)], Héctor Salvá González (17/2), José Eusebio Urruzmendi Aycaguer (21/8). Trainer: Juan Carlos Corazzo (33).
Goal: Pedro Virgilio Rocha Franchetti (30).

361. 28.07.1967 **PERU - URUGUAY** **0-1(0-0)**
Estadio Nacional, Lima; Referee: Erwin Hiegger (Austria)
URU: Miguel Angel Bazzano (5/0), Pablo Justo Forlán Lamarque (8/0), Omar Caetano Otero (23/0), Julio Dalmao (2/0), Juan Carlos Masnik (1/0), Néstor Gonçalves (45/0), Alberto Urbano (4/0), Pedro Virgilio Rocha Franchetti (34/13), Alberto Pedro Spencer (5/1) [73.Julio César Cortés (17/2)], Héctor Salvá González (18/2), Rubén Laudelino Bareño (1/0). Trainer: Juan Carlos Corazzo (34).
Goal: Pedro Virgilio Rocha Franchetti (71).

362. 30.07.1967 **PERU - URUGUAY** **1-2(1-1)**
Estadio Nacional, Lima; Referee: Erwin Hiegger (Austria)
URU: Miguel Angel Bazzano (6/0), Pablo Justo Forlán Lamarque (9/0), Omar Caetano Otero (24/0), Julio Dalmao (3/0), Juan Carlos Masnik (2/0), Néstor Gonçalves (46/0), Alberto Urbano (5/0), Pedro Virgilio Rocha Franchetti (35/14), Alberto Pedro Spencer (6/1) [20.Julio César Cortés (18/2)], Héctor Salvá González (19/2), Rubén Laudelino Bareño (2/1) [76.Jorge Acuña (5/0)]. Trainer: Juan Carlos Corazzo (35).
Goals: Pedro Virgilio Rocha Franchetti (24), Rubén Laudelino Bareño (58).

363. 21.05.1968 **MEXICO - URUGUAY** **3-3(0-2)**
Estadio Azteca, Ciudad de México; Referee: Arturo Máximo Yamasaki Maldonado (Peru), Attendance: 50,000
URU: Ladislao Mazurkiewicz Iglesias (12/0), Julio Dalmao (4/0), Julio Walter Montero Castillo (6/1), Mario Omar Méndez (18/2), Dagoberto Fontes (1/0), Juan Martín Mujica (6/1), Orlando Virgili (3/0), Pedro Virgilio Rocha Franchetti (36/15), Héctor Jesús Silva (23/7) [Jorge Prestes (1/0)], Abayubá Ibañez (6/0) [Víctor Rodolfo Espárrago Videla (7/0)], Julio César Araújo Morales (3/2). Trainer: Juan Carlos Corazzo (36).
Goals: Julio César Araújo Morales (13), Juan Martín Mujica (22 penalty), Pedro Virgilio Rocha Franchetti (83).

364. 28.05.1968 **MEXICO - URUGUAY** **2-2(1-1)**
Estadio Azteca, Ciudad de México; Referee: Arturo Máximo Yamasaki Maldonado (Peru)
URU: Ladislao Mazurkiewicz Iglesias (13/0), Julio Dalmao (5/0), Julio Walter Montero Castillo (7/1), Mario Omar Méndez (19/3) [Pablo Justo Forlán Lamarque (10/0)], Juan Martín Mujica (7/1), Néstor Gonçalves (47/0), Orlando Virgili (4/1) [88.Angel Brunel (1/0)], Pedro Virgilio Rocha Franchetti (37/15), Héctor Jesús Silva (24/7) [72.Oscar Daniel Zubía (1/0)], Abayubá Ibañez (7/0) [59.Víctor Rodolfo Espárrago Videla (8/0)], Julio César Araújo Morales (4/2). Trainer: Juan Carlos Corazzo (37).
Goals: Orlando Virgili (17), Mario Omar Méndez (80).

365. 02.06.1968 **PARAGUAY - URUGUAY** **0-0** Copa Artigas
Estadio Puerto Sajonia, Asunción; Referee: Salvador Valenzuela (Paraguay)
URU: Ladislao Mazurkiewicz Iglesias (14/0), Julio Dalmao (6/0), Julio Walter Montero Castillo (8/1), Mario Omar Méndez (20/3) [Pablo Justo Forlán Lamarque (11/0)], Néstor Gonçalves (48/0), Juan Martín Mujica (8/1), Orlando Virgili (5/1) [Dagoberto Fontes (2/0)], Pedro Virgilio Rocha Franchetti (38/15), Héctor Jesús Silva (25/7), Víctor Rodolfo Espárrago Videla (9/0), Julio César Araújo Morales (5/2). Trainer: Juan Carlos Corazzo (38).
Uruguay left the field after 70 minutes.

366. 05.06.1968 **ARGENTINA - URUGUAY** **2-0(1-0)** Copa Lipton
Estadio Monumental „Antonio Vespucio Liberti", Buenos Aires; Referee: Guillermo Nimo (Argentina), Attendance: 20,000
URU: Ladislao Mazurkiewicz Iglesias (15/0), Julio Dalmao (7/0), Julio Walter Montero Castillo (9/1), Mario Omar Méndez (21/3), Néstor Gonçalves (49/0), Juan Martín Mujica (9/1), Orlando Virgili (6/1), Víctor Rodolfo Espárrago Videla (10/0) [Jorge Prestes (2/0)], Pedro Virgilio Rocha Franchetti (39/15), Abayubá Ibañez (9/0), Julio César Araújo Morales (6/2). Trainer: Juan Carlos Corazzo (39).

367. 09.06.1968 **BRAZIL - URUGUAY** **2-0(1-0)**
Estádio Pacaembú, São Paulo; Referee: Romualdo Arppi Filho (Brazil)
URU: Ladislao Mazurkiewicz Iglesias (16/0), Julio Dalmao (8/0), Julio Walter Montero Castillo (10/1), Mario Omar Méndez (22/3), Dagoberto Fontes (3/0), Juan Martín Mujica (10/1), Orlando Virgili (7/1), Pedro Virgilio Rocha Franchetti (40/15), Luis Del Rio (1/0) [Oscar Daniel Zubía (2/0)], Abayubá Ibañez (10/0) [Víctor Rodolfo Espárrago Videla (11/0)], Julio César Araújo Morales (7/2). Trainer: Juan Carlos Corazzo (40).

368. 12.06.1968 **BRAZIL - URUGUAY** **4-0(1-0)**
Estádio „Jornalista Mário Filho" (Maracanã), Rio de Janeiro; Referee: Aurelio Domingo Bossolino (Argentina)
URU: Miguel Angel Bazzano (7/0), Julio Dalmao (9/0), Julio Walter Montero Castillo (11/1), Mario Omar Méndez (23/3), Dagoberto Fontes (4/0), Juan Martín Mujica (11/1) [Angel Brunel (2/0)], Orlando Virgili (8/1), Pedro Virgilio Rocha Franchetti (41/15), Luis Del Rio (2/0), Abayubá Ibañez (11/0), Julio César Araújo Morales (8/2) [Víctor Rodolfo Espárrago Videla (12/0)]. Trainer: Juan Carlos Corazzo (41).

369. 20.06.1968 **URUGUAY - ARGENTINA** **2-1(1-0)** Copa Newton
Estadio Centenario, Montevideo; Referee: Ramón Ivannoe Barreto Ruíz (Uruguay), Attendance: 9,706
URU: Miguel Angel Bazzano (8/0), Julio Dalmao (10/0), Julio Walter Montero Castillo (12/1), Pablo Justo Forlán Lamarque (12/0), Dagoberto Fontes (5/0), Juan Martín Mujica (12/1), Orlando Virgili (9/1) [Oscar Daniel Zubía (3/1)], Pedro Virgilio Rocha Franchetti (42/15), Rubén Laudelino Bareño (3/1) [Víctor Rodolfo Espárrago Videla (13/0)], Abayubá Ibañez (12/0), Julio César Araújo Morales (9/3) [Luis Del Rio (3/0)]. Trainer: Juan Carlos Corazzo (42).
Goals: Julio César Araújo Morales (1), Oscar Daniel Zubía (64).

370. 26.10.1968 **URUGUAY - MEXICO** **0-2(0-2)**
Estadio Centenario, Montevideo; Referee: Esteban Marino (Uruguay)
URU: Ladislao Mazurkiewicz Iglesias (17/0), Julio Dalmao (11/0), Julio Walter Montero Castillo (13/1), Luis Ignacio Ubiñas (9/0), Dagoberto Fontes (6/0) [Alfredo Lamas (1/0)], Juan Martín Mujica (13/1), Juan Maldonado (1/0) [Oscar Daniel Zubía (4/1)], Pedro Virgilio Rocha Franchetti (43/15), Rubén Laudelino Bareño (4/1) [Víctor Rodolfo Espárrago Videla (14/0)], Abayubá Ibañez (13/0), Julio César Araújo Morales (10/3). Trainer: Juan Carlos Corazzo (43).

371. 08.06.1969 **URUGUAY - ENGLAND** **1-2(0-1)**
Estadio Centenario, Montevideo; Referee: Armando Marques (Brazil), Attendance: 54,161
URU: Luis María Maidana (11/0), Arilio Genaro Ancheta (1/0), Juan Carlos Paz (3/0), Luis Ignacio Ubiñas (10/0), Julio Walter Montero Castillo (14/1), Juan Martín Mujica (14/1), Luis Alberto Cubilla Almeida (15/7), Julio César Cortés (19/2), Héctor Jesús Silva (26/7), Roberto Matosas Postiglione (3/0), Julio César Araújo Morales (11/3). Trainer: Juan Eduardo Hohberg (1).
Goal: Luis Alberto Cubilla Almeida (53).

372. 27.06.1969 **PERU - URUGUAY** **1-0(0-0)**
Estadio Nacional, Lima; Referee: Erwin Hiegger (Austria), Attendance: 42,754
URU: Ladislao Mazurkiewicz Iglesias (18/0), Atilio Genaro Ancheta Weigel (2/0), Roberto Matosas Postiglione (4/0), Omar Caetano Otero (25/0), Luis Ignacio Ubiñas (11/0), Julio Walter Montero Castillo (15/1), Luis Alberto Cubilla Almeida (16/7), Pedro Virgilio Rocha Franchetti (44/15), Héctor Jesús Silva (27/7) [80.Sergio Silva (3/0)], Julio César Cortés (20/2), Rubén Laudelino Bareño (5/1) [68.Oscar Daniel Zubía (5/1)]. Trainer: Juan Eduardo Hohberg (2).

373. 02.07.1969 **COLOMBIA - URUGUAY** **0-1(0-0)**
Estadio „Pascual Guerrero", Cali; Referee: Iván de Jesús Barrios (Venezuela), Attendance: 24,351
URU: Ladislao Mazurkiewicz Iglesias (19/0), Atilio Genaro Ancheta Weigel (3/0), Roberto Matosas Postiglione (5/0), Luis Ignacio Ubiñas (12/0), Julio Walter Montero Castillo (16/1), Omar Caetano Otero (26/0) [Juan Martín Mujica (15/1)], Luis Alberto Cubilla Almeida (17/7) [Oscar Daniel Zubía (6/1)], Pedro Virgilio Rocha Franchetti (45/15), Héctor Jesús Silva (28/7), Julio César Cortés (21/2) [Rúben Techera (5/0)], Rubén Laudelino Bareño (6/2). Trainer: Juan Eduardo Hohberg (3).
Goal: Rubén Laudelino Bareño (59 penalty).

374. 06.07.1969 **ECUADOR - URUGUAY** **0-2(0-1)** 9th FIFA WC. Qualifiers
Estadio Modelo, Guayaquil; Referee: Romualdo Arpi Filho (Brazil), Attendance: 55,783
URU: Ladislao Mazurkiewicz Iglesias (20/0), Atilio Genaro Ancheta Weigel (4/0), Roberto Matosas Postiglione (6/0), Luis Ignacio Ubiñas (13/0), Julio Walter Montero Castillo (17/1), Omar Caetano Otero (27/0), Julio César Cortés (22/2), Pedro Virgilio Rocha Franchetti (46/15), Luis Alberto Cubilla Almeida (18/7), Oscar Daniel Zubía (7/2), Rubén Laudelino Bareño (7/3). Trainer: Juan Eduardo Hohberg (4).
Goals: Rubén Laudelino Bareño (31), Oscar Daniel Zubía (60).

375. 13.07.1969 **CHILE - URUGUAY** **0-0** 9th FIFA WC. Qualifiers
Estadio Nacional, Santiago; Referee: Aurelio Domingo Bossolino (Argentina), Attendance: 71,982
URU: Ladislao Mazurkiewicz Iglesias (21/0), Atilio Genaro Ancheta Weigel (5/0), Roberto Matosas Postiglione (7/0), Luis Ignacio Ubiñas (14/0), Julio Walter Montero Castillo (18/1), Omar Caetano Otero (28/0), Julio César Cortés (23/2), Pedro Virgilio Rocha Franchetti (47/15) [46.Dagoberto Fontes (7/0)], Luis Alberto Cubilla Almeida (19/7), Oscar Daniel Zubía (8/2), Rubén Laudelino Bareño (8/3). Trainer: Juan Eduardo Hohberg (5).

376. 20.07.1969 **URUGUAY - ECUADOR** **1-0(0-0)** 9th FIFA WC. Qualifiers
Estadio Centenario, Montevideo; Referee: Rodolfo Pérez Osorio (Paraguay), Attendance: 39,387
URU: Ladislao Mazurkiewicz Iglesias (22/0), Atilio Genaro Ancheta Weigel (6/1), Roberto Matosas Postiglione (8/0), Luis Ignacio Ubiñas (15/0), Julio Walter Montero Castillo (19/1), Omar Caetano Otero (29/0), Julio César Cortés (24/2), Luis Alberto Cubilla Almeida (20/7), Sergio Silva (4/0), Héctor Jesús Silva (29/7), Rubén Laudelino Bareño (9/3). Trainer: Juan Eduardo Hohberg (6).
Goal: Atilio Genaro Ancheta Weigel (76).

377. 10.08.1969 **URUGUAY - CHILE** **2-0(1-0)** 9th FIFA WC. Qualifiers
Estadio Centenario, Montevideo; Referee: Armando Nunes Castanheiras da Rosa Marques (Brazil), Attendance: 62,693
URU: Ladislao Mazurkiewicz Iglesias (23/0), Atilio Genaro Ancheta Weigel (7/1), Roberto Matosas Postiglione (9/0), Luis Ignacio Ubiñas (16/0), Julio Walter Montero Castillo (20/1), Omar Caetano Otero (30/0), Sergio Silva (5/0) [73.Nilo Acuña (1/0)], Julio César Cortés (25/3), Pedro Virgilio Rocha Franchetti (48/16), Luis Alberto Cubilla Almeida (21/7), Rubén Laudelino Bareño (10/3). Trainer: Juan Eduardo Hohberg (7).
Goals: Julio César Cortés (44), Pedro Virgilio Rocha Franchetti (90).

378. 31.03.1970 **URUGUAY - PERU** **2-0(2-0)**
Estadio Centenario, Montevideo; Referee: Pablo Víctor Vaga (Uruguay)
URU: Ladislao Mazurkiewicz Iglesias (24/0), Atilio Genaro Ancheta Weigel (8/1), Roberto Matosas Postiglione (10/0), Luis Ignacio Ubiñas (17/0), Julio Walter Montero Castillo (21/1) [Dagoberto Fontes (8/0)), Ángel Brunel (3/0), Julio Daniel Losada (1/0), Alberto Gómez (1/0), Luis Alberto Cubilla Almeida (22/8), Ildo Enrique Maneiro Ghezzi (1/1), Rubén Laudelino Bareño (11/3) [Oscar Daniel Zubía (9/2)]. Trainer: Juan Eduardo Hohberg (8).
Goals: Ildo Enrique Maneiro Ghezzi (27), Luis Alberto Cubilla Almeida (40).

379. 08.04.1970 **ARGENTINA - URUGUAY** **2-1(1-1)**
Estadio „Alberto Armando", Buenos Aires; Referee: Luis Pestarino (Argentina), Attendance: 35,000
URU: Ladislao Mazurkiewicz Iglesias (25/0), Atilio Genaro Ancheta Weigel (9/1), Luis Ignacio Ubiñas (18/0), Ángel Brunel (4/0), Roberto Matosas Postiglione (11/0), Ildo Enrique Maneiro Ghezzi (2/1), Víctor Rodolfo Espárrago Videla (15/0) [Alberto Gómez (2/0)], Julio Daniel Losada (2/0), Dagoberto Fontes (9/0), Rubén Laudelino Bareño (12/3), Oscar Daniel Zubía (10/3). Trainer: Juan Eduardo Hohberg (9).
Goal: Oscar Daniel Zubía (4).

380. 15.04.1970 **URUGUAY - ARGENTINA** **2-1(1-1)**
Estadio Centenario, Montevideo; Referee: Alejandro Otero (Uruguay), Attendance: 50,000
URU: Ladislao Mazurkiewicz Iglesias (26/0) [46.Héctor Santos (1/0)], Atilio Genaro Ancheta Weigel (10/1), Luis Ignacio Ubiñas (19/1), Juan Martín Mujica (16/1), Roberto Matosas Postiglione (12/0), Julio Walter Montero Castillo (22/1), Ildo Enrique Maneiro Ghezzi (3/1), Pedro Virgilio Rocha Franchetti (49/17) [46.Oscar Daniel Zubía (11/3)], Rubén Laudelino Bareño (13/3), Luis Alberto Cubilla Almeida (23/8) [77.Alberto Gómez (3/0)], Julio Daniel Losada (3/0). Trainer: Juan Eduardo Hohberg (10).
Goals: Pedro Virgilio Rocha Franchetti (20), Luis Ignacio Ubiñas (80).

381. 02.06.1970 **URUGUAY - ISRAEL** **2-0(1-0)** 9th FIFA WC. Group Stage
Estadio Cuauhtémoc, Puebla (Mexico); Referee: Robert Holley Davidson (Scotland), Attendance: 20,654
URU: Ladislao Mazurkiewicz Iglesias (27/0), Luis Ignacio Ubiñas (20/1), Juan Martín Mujica (17/2), Julio Walter Montero Castillo (23/1), Atilio Genaro Ancheta Weigel (11/1), Roberto Matosas Postiglione (13/0), Luis Alberto Cubilla Almeida (24/8), Víctor Rodolfo Espárrago Videla (16/0), Ildo Enrique Maneiro Ghezzi (4/2), Pedro Virgilio Rocha Franchetti (50/17) [13.Julio César Cortés (26/3)], Julio Daniel Losada (4/0). Trainer: Juan Eduardo Hohberg (11).
Goals: Ildo Enrique Maneiro Ghezzi (23), Juan Martín Mujica (51).

382. 06.06.1970 **ITALY – URUGUAY** **0-0** 9th FIFA WC. Group Stage

Estadio Cuauhtémoc, Puebla (Mexico); Referee: Rudolf Glöckner (East Germany), Attendance: 29,968

URU: Ladislao Mazurkiewicz Iglesias (28/0), Luis Ignacio Ubiñas (21/1), Juan Martín Mujica (18/2), Julio Walter Montero Castillo (24/1), Atilio Genaro Ancheta Weigel (12/1), Roberto Matosas Postiglione (14/0), Luis Alberto Cubilla Almeida (25/8), Víctor Rodolfo Espárrago Videla (17/0), Ildo Enrique Maneiro Ghezzi (5/2), Julio César Cortés (27/3), Rubén Laudelino Bareño (14/3) [71.Oscar Daniel Zubía (12/3)]. Trainer: Juan Eduardo Hohberg (12).

383. 10.06.1970 **SWEDEN – URUGUAY** **1-0(0-0)** 9th FIFA WC. Group Stage

Estadio Cuauhtémoc, Puebla (Mexico); Referee: Henry Landauer (United States), Attendance: 18,163

URU: Ladislao Mazurkiewicz Iglesias (29/0), Luis Ignacio Ubiñas (22/1), Juan Martín Mujica (19/2), Julio Walter Montero Castillo (25/1), Atilio Genaro Ancheta Weigel (13/1), Roberto Matosas Postiglione (15/0), Víctor Rodolfo Espárrago Videla (18/0) [62 Dagoberto Fontes (10/0)], Ildo Enrique Maneiro Ghezzi (6/2), Julio César Cortés (28/3), Oscar Daniel Zubía (13/3), Julio Daniel Losada (5/0). Trainer: Juan Eduardo Hohberg (13).

384. 14.06.1970 **SOVIET UNION – URUGUAY** **0-1(0-0,0-0)** 9th FIFA WC. Quarter-Finals

Estadio Azteca, Ciudad de México (Mexico); Referee: Laurens van Ravens (Holland), Attendance: 75,000

URU: Ladislao Mazurkiewicz Iglesias (30/0), Luis Ignacio Ubiñas (23/1), Atilio Genaro Ancheta Weigel (14/1), Roberto Matosas Postiglione (16/0), Juan Martín Mujica (20/2), Ildo Enrique Maneiro Ghezzi (7/2), Julio César Cortés (29/3), Julio Walter Montero Castillo (26/1), Luis Alberto Cubilla Almeida (26/8), Dagoberto Fontes (11/0) [114.Víctor Rodolfo Espárrago Videla (19/1)], Julio César Araújo Morales (12/3) [96.Alberto Gómez (4/0)]. Trainer: Juan Eduardo Hohberg (14).

Goal: Víctor Rodolfo Espárrago Videla (117).

385. 17.06.1970 **BRAZIL – URUGUAY** **3-1(1-1)** 9th FIFA WC. Semi-Finals

Estadio Monumental Jalisco, Guadalajara (Mexico); Referee: José María Ortiz de Mendibil Monasterio (Spain), Attendance: 51,261

URU: Ladislao Mazurkiewicz Iglesias (31/0), Luis Ignacio Ubiñas (24/1), Atilio Genaro Ancheta Weigel (15/1), Roberto Matosas Postiglione (17/0), Juan Martín Mujica (21/2), Ildo Enrique Maneiro Ghezzi (8/2) [74.Víctor Rodolfo Espárrago Videla (20/1)], Julio César Cortés (30/3), Julio Walter Montero Castillo (27/1), Luis Alberto Cubilla Almeida (27/9), Dagoberto Fontes (12/0), Julio César Araújo Morales (13/3). Trainer: Juan Eduardo Hohberg (15).

Goal: Luis Alberto Cubilla Almeida (19).

386. 20.06.1970 **WEST GERMANY – URUGUAY** **1-0(1-0)** 9th FIFA WC. Bronze Medal

Estadio Azteca, Ciudad de México (Mexico); Referee: Antonio Sbardella (Italy), Attendance: 105,000

URU: Ladislao Mazurkiewicz Iglesias (32/0), Luis Ignacio Ubiñas (25/1), Atilio Genaro Ancheta Weigel (16/1), Roberto Matosas Postiglione (18/0), Juan Martín Mujica (22/2), Ildo Enrique Maneiro Ghezzi (9/2) [69.Rodolfo Ariel Sandoval (1/0)], Julio César Cortés (31/3), Julio Walter Montero Castillo (28/1), Luis Alberto Cubilla Almeida (28/9), Dagoberto Dagoberto Fontes (13/0) [46.Víctor Rodolfo Espárrago Videla (21/1)], Julio César Araújo Morales (14/3). Trainer: Juan Eduardo Hohberg (16).

387. 08.02.1971 **URUGUAY – EAST GERMANY** **0-3(0-2)**

Estadio Centenario, Montevideo; Referee: Ramón Ivannoe Barreto Ruíz (Uruguay), Attendance: 20,000

URU: Walter Luis Corbo Burmia (1/0), Rodolfo Ariel Sandoval (2/0) [Atilio Genaro Ancheta Weigel (17/1)], Néstor Gonçalves (50/0) [Roberto Matosas Postiglione (19/0)], Jorge Vázquez (1/0) [Enrique Varela (1/0)], Julio Walter Montero Castillo (29/1), Juan Carlos Aparicio (1/0), Luis Villalba (1/0), Wálter Daniel Mantegazza (1/0) [Oscar Daniel Zubía (14/3)], Pierino Lattuada (1/0), Ildo Enrique Maneiro Ghezzi (10/2), Rubén Romeo Corbo Burmia (1/0). Trainer: Juan Ricardo Faccio (1).

388. 10.02.1971 **URUGUAY – EAST GERMANY** **1-1(0-1)**

Estadio Centenario, Montevideo; Referee: Alejandro Otero (Uruguay), Attendance: 10,000

URU: Luis Aguerre (1/0), Atilio Genaro Ancheta Weigel (18/1), Roberto Matosas Postiglione (20/0), Enrique Varela (2/0), Julio Walter Montero Castillo (30/1), Juan Carlos Aparicio (2/0), Luis Villalba (2/0) [Robinson Retamar (1/0)], Pierino Lattuada (2/0) [Miguel Leiva (1/0)], Oscar Daniel Zubía (15/4), Ildo Enrique Maneiro Ghezzi (11/2), Rubén Romeo Corbo Burmia (2/0) [Nelson Bonifacio Acosta (1/0)]. Trainer: Juan Ricardo Faccio (2).

Goal: Oscar Daniel Zubía (67).

389. 14.07.1971 **ARGENTINA – URUGUAY** **1-0(0-0)** Copa Lipton

Estadio „Alberto Armando", Buenos Aires; Referee: Ramón Ivannoe Barreto Ruíz (Uruguay), Attendance: 30,000

URU: Luis Aguerre (2/0) [Eduardo García (1/0)], Atilio Genaro Ancheta Weigel (19/1), Francis Campo (1/0), Juan Carlos Blanco (1/0), Julio Walter Montero Castillo (31/1), Juan Carlos Aparicio (3/0), Walter Pisano (1/0), Abayubá Ibañez (14/0), Francisco Bertocchi (1/0), Víctor Rodolfo Espárrago Videla (22/1), Carlos Rodríguez (1/0) [Pierino Lattuada (3/0)]. Trainer: Rodolfo Zamora (1).

390. 18.07.1971 **URUGUAY – ARGENTINA** **1-1(0-1)** Copa Lipton

Estadio Centenario, Montevideo; Referee: Luis Pestarino (Argentina), Attendance: 40,000

URU: Ladislao Mazurkiewicz Iglesias (33/0), Atilio Genaro Ancheta Weigel (20/1), Francis Campo (2/0), Juan Carlos Blanco (2/0), Julio Walter Montero Castillo (32/1), Juan Carlos Aparicio (4/0), Walter Pisano (2/0) [Angel Ferreira (1/0)], Abayubá Ibañez (15/0) [Roberto Repetto (1/0)], Francisco Bertocchi (2/1), Víctor Rodolfo Espárrago Videla (23/1), Carlos Rodríguez (2/0). Trainer: Rodolfo Zamora (2).

Goal: Francisco Bertocchi (59).

391. 27.10.1971 **URUGUAY – CHILE** **3-0(2-0)** Copa Juan Pinto Durán

Estadio Centenario, Montevideo; Referee: Armando Peña Rocha (Uruguay), Attendance: 30,000

URU: Luis Aguerre (3/0), Julían Bonifacino (1/0), Juan Carlos Masnik (3/0), Agapito Rivero (1/0), Julio Walter Montero Castillo (33/1), Juan Carlos Aparicio (5/0), Angel Ferreira (2/1), Julio César Jiménez (1/0) [Luis Villalba (3/0)], Roberto Repetto (2/1), Ildo Enrique Maneiro Ghezzi (12/2), Fernando Morena Belaro (1/1) [Rubén Romeo Corbo Burmia (3/0)]. Trainer: Rodolfo Zamora (3).

Goals: Roberto Repetto (13), Fernando Morena Belaro (44), Angel Ferreira (88).

392. 03.11.1971 **CHILE – URUGUAY** **5-0(3-0)** Copa Juan Pinto Durán

Estadio Nacional, Santiago; Referee: Juan Ambrosio Silvagno Cavanna (Chile), Attendance: 27,564

URU: Luis Aguerre (4/0), Julían Bonifacino (2/0), Juan Carlos Masnik (4/0), Agapito Rivero (2/0), Julio Walter Montero Castillo (34/1), Juan Carlos Aparicio (6/0), Roberto Repetto (3/1), Néstor Soria (3/0), Pierino Lattuada (4/0) [Hugo Fernández (1/0)], Ildo Enrique Maneiro Ghezzi (13/2), Rubén Romeo Corbo Burmia (4/0) [Luis Villalba (4/0)]. Trainer: Rodolfo Zamora (4).

393. 23.05.1972 **SPAIN – URUGUAY** **2-0(1-0)**

Estadio „Vicente Calderón", Madrid; Referee: Károly Palotai (Hungary), Attendance: 60,000

URU: Alberto Carrasco (1/0) [Villalba (1/0)], Mario González (1/0), Juan Carlos Masnik (5/0), Juan Pedro Ascery (1/0), Juan Carlos Blanco (3/0), Julio Walter Montero Castillo (35/1), Víctor Rodolfo Espárrago Videla (24/1), Ildo Enrique Maneiro Ghezzi (14/2), Angel Ferreira (3/1) [46.Luis Villalba (5/0)], Pierino Lattuada (5/0) [72.Luis Montero (1/0)], Fernando Morena Belaro (2/1) [55.Rubén Romeo Corbo Burmia (5/0)]. Trainer: Washington Etchamendi (3).

394. 27.05.1972 **EAST GERMANY - URUGUAY** **1-0(0-0)**
Zentralstadion, Leipzig; Referee: Bohumil Smejkal (Czechoslovakia), Attendance: 20,000
URU: Alberto Carrasco (2/0), Juan Pedro Ascery (2/0), Juan Carlos Masnik (6/0), Mario González (2/0), Julio Walter Montero Castillo (36/1), Juan Carlos Blanco (4/0), Luis Montero (2/0) [Luis Villalba (6/0)], Ildo Enrique Maneiro Ghezzi (15/2) [Angel Ferreira (4/1)], Pierino Lattuada (6/0) [Agapito Rivero (3/0)], Víctor Rodolfo Espárrago Videla (25/1), Rubén Romeo Corbo Burmia (6/0). Trainer: Washington Etchamendi (4).

395. 31.05.1972 **EAST GERMANY - URUGUAY** **0-0**
Ostsee-Stadion, Rostock; Referee: Erik Axelryd (Sweden), Attendance: 15,000
URU: Alberto Carrasco (3/0), Baudilio Jorge Jáuregui (1/0), Juan Carlos Masnik (7/0), Agapito Rivero (4/0), Julio Carlos Blanco (5/0), Mario González (3/0), Julio César Jiménez (2/0), Alberto Víctor Cardaccio (1/0), Pierino Lattuada (7/0) [Ildo Enrique Maneiro Ghezzi (16/2)], Víctor Rodolfo Espárrago Videla (26/1), Rubén Romeo Corbo Burmia (7/0). Trainer: Washington Etchamendi (5).

396. 14.06.1972 **NORWAY - URUGUAY** **0-1(0-0)**
Ullevaal Stadion, Oslo; Referee: Rolf Arnshed (Sweden), Attendance: 16,900
URU: Alberto Carrasco (4/0), Baudilio Jorge Jáuregui (2/0), Juan Carlos Masnik (8/0), Mario González (4/0), Julio Walter Montero Castillo (37/1), Juan Carlos Blanco (6/0), Luis Villalba (7/0), Ildo Enrique Maneiro Ghezzi (17/2), Pierino Lattuada (8/1), Víctor Rodolfo Espárrago Videla (27/1), Rubén Romeo Corbo Burmia (8/0) [Fernando Morena Belaro (3/1)]. Trainer: Washington Etchamendi (6).
Goal: Pierino Lattuada (87).

397. 29.06.1972 **SOVIET UNION - URUGUAY** **1-0(0-0)** Brazil Independence Cup
Estádio „Cicero Pompeu de Toledo“ (Morumbí), São Paulo; Referee: Abraham Klein (Israel), Attendance: 10,000
URU: Alberto Carrasco (5/0), Baudilio Jorge Jáuregui (3/0), Juan Carlos Masnik (9/0), Juan Carlos Blanco (7/0), Julio Walter Montero Castillo (38/1), Ricardo Elvio Pavoni Cúneo (8/0), Julio César Jiménez (3/0) [Fernando Morena Belaro (4/1)], Ildo Enrique Maneiro Ghezzi (18/2), Pierino Lattuada (9/1), Víctor Rodolfo Espárrago Videla (28/1), Luis Villalba (8/0) [Francisco Bertocchi (3/1)]. Trainer: Washington Etchamendi (7).

398. 02.07.1972 **URUGUAY - PORTUGAL** **1-1(1-1)** Brazil Independence Cup
Estádio „Jornalista Mário Filho“ (Maracanã), Rio de Janeiro; Referee: Rudolf Scheurer (Switzerland)
URU: Alberto Carrasco (6/0), Baudilio Jorge Jáuregui (4/0), Juan Carlos Masnik (10/0), Luis Ignacio Ubiñas (26/1), Julio Walter Montero Castillo (39/1), Ricardo Elvio Pavoni Cúneo (9/1), Luis Villalba (9/0), Ildo Enrique Maneiro Ghezzi (19/2) [Alberto Víctor Cardaccio (2/0)], Pierino Lattuada (10/1), Víctor Rodolfo Espárrago Videla (29/1), Fernando Morena Belaro (5/1) [Rubén Romeo Corbo Burmia (9/0)]. Trainer: Washington Etchamendi (8).
Goal: Ricardo Elvio Pavoni Cúneo (19).

399. 06.07.1972 **ARGENTINA - URUGUAY** **1-0(0-0)** Brazil Independence Cup
Estádio Beira-Rio, Porto Alegre; Referee: Edwin Keith Walker (England), Attendance: 3,000
URU: Alberto Carrasco (7/0), Baudilio Jorge Jáuregui (5/0), Juan Carlos Masnik (11/0), Luis Ignacio Ubiñas (27/1), Julio Walter Montero Castillo (40/1) [Ildo Enrique Maneiro Ghezzi (20/2)], Ricardo Elvio Pavoni Cúneo (10/1), Pierino Lattuada (11/1), Alberto Víctor Cardaccio (3/0), Fernando Morena Belaro (6/1), Víctor Rodolfo Espárrago Videla (30/1), Francisco Bertocchi (4/1). Trainer: Washington Etchamendi (9).

400. 17.05.1973 **ARGENTINA - URUGUAY** **1-1(0-1)** Copa Lipton
Estadio „José Amalfitani“, Buenos Aires; Referee: Oscar Veiró (Argentina), Attendance: 25,000
URU: Héctor Santos (2/0), Walter Daniel Olivera (1/0), Juan Carlos Masnik (12/0), Mario González (5/0), Alberto Víctor Cardaccio (4/0), Mario Zoryez (1/0), Luis Alberto Cubilla Almeida (29/9), Víctor Rodolfo Espárrago Videla (31/1), Fernando Morena Belaro (7/2) [Rubén Omar Rey Cucaro (1/0)], Ildo Enrique Maneiro Ghezzi (21/2), Rubén Romeo Corbo Burmia (10/0) [Francisco Bertocchi (5/1)]. Trainer: Hugo Bagnulo (12).
Goal: Fernando Morena Belaro (39).

401. 23.05.1973 **URUGUAY - ARGENTINA** **1-1(0-0)** Copa Newton
Estadio Centenario, Montevideo; Referee: Luis Gregorio Da Rosa (Uruguay), Attendance: 20,000
URU: Héctor Santos (3/0), Walter Daniel Olivera (2/0), Juan Carlos Masnik (13/0), Mario González (6/0), Alberto Víctor Cardaccio (5/0), Mario Zoryez (2/0), Luis Alberto Cubilla Almeida (30/9), Víctor Rodolfo Espárrago Videla (32/1), Fernando Morena Belaro (8/2) [Rubén Omar Rey Cucaro (2/1)], Ildo Enrique Maneiro Ghezzi (22/2), Rubén Romeo Corbo Burmia (11/0) [Francisco Bertocchi (6/1)]. Trainer: Hugo Bagnulo (13).
Goal: Rubén Omar Rey Cucaro (82).

402. 06.06.1973 **HAITI - URUGUAY** **0-0**
Stade „Sylvio Cator“, Port-au-Prince; Referee: Halford Navis (Jamaica)
URU: Héctor Santos (4/0), Walter Daniel Olivera (3/0), Juan Carlos Masnik (14/0), Luis Ignacio Ubiñas (28/1), Mario Zoryez (3/0), Alberto Víctor Cardaccio (6/0), Luis Alberto Cubilla Almeida (31/9), Víctor Rodolfo Espárrago Videla (33/1), Denis Alfredo Milar Otero (1/0), Ildo Enrique Maneiro Ghezzi (23/2) [Rubén Omar Rey Cucaro (3/1)], Rubén Romeo Corbo Burmia (12/0). Trainer: Hugo Bagnulo (14).

403. 24.06.1973 **COLOMBIA - URUGUAY** **0-0** 10th FIFA WC. Qualifiers
Estadio „Nemesio Camacho“ 'El Campín', Bogotá; Referee: Roberto Goicoechea (Argentina), Attendance: 30,000
URU: Héctor Santos (5/0), Walter Daniel Olivera (4/0) [*sent off 22*], Juan Carlos Masnik (15/0), Luis Ignacio Ubiñas (29/1), Alberto Víctor Cardaccio (7/0), Mario Zoryez (4/0), Luis Alberto Cubilla Almeida (32/9), Víctor Rodolfo Espárrago Videla (34/1), Rubén Omar Rey Cucaro (4/1) [Fernando Morena Belaro (9/2)], Ildo Enrique Maneiro Ghezzi (24/2), Rubén Romeo Corbo Burmia (13/0) [Francisco Bertocchi (7/1)]. Trainer: Hugo Bagnulo (15).

404. 01.07.1973 **ECUADOR - URUGUAY** **1-2(1-1)** 10th FIFA WC. Qualifiers
Estadio Olimpico „Atahualpa“, Quito; Referee: Romualdo Arppi Filho (Brazil), Attendance: 43,075
URU: Héctor Santos (6/0), Gustavo Daniel de Simone Horn (1/0), Juan Carlos Masnik (16/0), Luis Ignacio Ubiñas (30/1), Alberto Víctor Cardaccio (8/0), Mario Zoryez (5/0), Luis Alberto Cubilla Almeida (33/10), Víctor Rodolfo Espárrago Videla (35/1), Fernando Morena Belaro (10/3), Ildo Enrique Maneiro (25/2) [Denis Alfredo Milar Otero (2/0)], Francisco Bertocchi (8/1) [Néstor Soria (4/0)]. Trainer: Hugo Bagnulo (16).
Goals: Luis Alberto Cubilla Almeida (41), Fernando Morena Belaro (74).

405. 05.07.1973 **URUGUAY - COLOMBIA** **0-1(0-0)** 10th FIFA WC. Qualifiers
Estadio Centenario, Montevideo; Referee: Alberto Martínez González (Chile), Attendance: 54,917
URU: Héctor Santos (7/0), Gustavo Daniel de Simone Horn (2/0), Juan Carlos Masnik (17/0), Luis Ignacio Ubiñas (31/1), Alberto Víctor Cardaccio (9/0), Mario Zoryez (6/0), Luis Alberto Cubilla Almeida (34/10), Víctor Rodolfo Espárrago Videla (36/1), Fernando Morena Belaro (11/3), Rubén Romeo Corbo Burmia (14/0) [Denis Alfredo Milar Otero (3/0)], Francisco Bertocchi (9/1). Trainer: Hugo Bagnulo (17).

406. 08.07.1973 **URUGUAY - ECUADOR** **4-0(3-0)** 10th FIFA WC. Qualifiers
Estadio Centenario, Montevideo; Referee: José Romei Canete (Paraguay), Attendance: 33,033
URU: Héctor Santos (8/0), Gustavo Daniel de Simone Horn (3/0), Juan Carlos Masnik (18/0), Luis Ignacio Ubiñas (32/1), Alberto Víctor Cardaccio (10/0), Mario Zoryez (7/0), Luis Alberto Cubilla Almeida (35/11), Víctor Rodolfo Espárrago Videla (37/1), Fernando Morena Belaro (12/5), Denis Alfredo Milar Otero (4/1), Francisco Bertocchi (10/1). Trainer: Hugo Bagnulo (18).
Goals: Fernando Morena Belaro (4, 27), Luis Alberto Cubilla Almeida (30), Denis Alfredo Milar Otero (62).

407. 19.07.1973 **ISRAEL - URUGUAY** **1-2(0-1)**
National Stadium, Ramat-Gan, Tel Aviv; Referee: John Taylor (England), Attendance: 40,000
URU: Héctor Santos (9/0), Walter Daniel Olivera (5/0), Juan Carlos Masnik (19/0), Mario González (7/0), Alberto Víctor Cardaccio (11/0), Mario Zoryez (8/0), Víctor Rodolfo Espárrago Videla (38/1), Nito De Lima (1/0), Denis Alfredo Milar Otero (5/2), Luis Alberto Cubilla Almeida (36/11), Fernando Morena Belaro (13/6). Trainer: Hugo Bagnulo (19).
Goals: Denis Alfredo Milar Otero (28), Fernando Morena Belaro (74).

408. 23.03.1974 **HAITI - URUGUAY** **0-1**
Stade "Sylvio Cator", Port-au-Prince; Referee: Leslie Lawrence (Jamaica)
URU: Gustavo Daniel Fernández (1/0), Mario González (8/0), Walter Daniel Olivera (6/0), Juan Carlos Masnik (20/0), Mario Zoryez (9/0), Alberto Víctor Cardaccio (12/0), Richard Forlán Resova (1/0) [Pedro Alvarez (1/0)], Denis Alfredo Milar Otero (6/2), Wálter Daniel Mantegazza (2/0), Fernando Morena Belaro (14/7), Juan Ramón Silva (1/0). Trainer: Roberto Porta (1).
Goal: Fernando Morena.

409. 25.03.1974 **HAITI - URUGUAY** **0-0**
Stade "Sylvio Cator", Port-au-Prince; Referee: Leslie Lawrence (Jamaica)
URU: Gustavo Daniel Fernández (2/0), Mario González (9/0), Walter Daniel Olivera (7/0), Juan Carlos Masnik (21/0), Mario Zoryez (10/0), Alberto Víctor Cardaccio (13/0), Richard Forlán Resova (2/0) [Rubén Romeo Corbo Burmia (15/0)], Denis Alfredo Milar Otero (7/2) [Saúl Lorenzo Rivero (1/0)], Wálter Daniel Mantegazza (3/0) [Julio César Jiménez (4/0)], Fernando Morena Belaro (15/7), Juan Ramón Silva (2/0). Trainer: Roberto Porta (2).

410. 28.03.1974 **JAMAICA - URUGUAY** **0-3(0-1)**
National Stadium, Kingston; Referee: Leslie Lawrence (Jamaica)
URU: Walter Luis Corbo Burmia (2/0), Gustavo Daniel de Simone Horn (4/0), Luis Garisto Pan (1/0), Mario Zoryez (11/0) [Mario González (10/0)], Saúl Lorenzo Rivero (2/0), Roberto Burgos (1/0), Richard Forlán Resova (3/0) [Pedro Alvarez (2/0)], Julio César Jiménez (5/0) [Wálter Daniel Mantegazza (4/1)], José Gervasio Gómez (1/0), Fernando Morena Belaro (16/9) [Omar Mondada (1/0)], Rubén Romeo Corbo Burmia (16/0). Trainer: Roberto Porta (3).
Goals: Fernando Morena Belaro (27 penalty,75), Wálter Daniel Mantegazza (56).

411. 21.04.1974 **INDONESIA - URUGUAY** **2-3**
Gelora Bung Karno Stadium, Jakarta,
URU: Gustavo Daniel Fernández (3/0), Mario González (11/0) [Roberto Burgos (2/0)], Walter Daniel Olivera (8/0), Gustavo Daniel de Simone Horn (5/0), Mario Zoryez (12/0), Alberto Víctor Cardaccio (14/0), Pedro Alvarez (3/0) [Julio César Jiménez (6/0)], Denis Alfredo Milar Otero (8/3) [Juan Ramón Silva (3/0)], José César Gómez (1/0) [Wálter Daniel Mantegazza (5/1)], Fernando Morena Belaro (17/11), Rubén Romeo Corbo Burmia (17/0). Trainer: Roberto Porta (4).
Goals: Fernando Morena Belaro 2, Denis Alfredo Milar Otero.

412. 24.04.1974 **AUSTRALIA - URUGUAY** **0-0**
Olympic Park, Melbourne; Referee: Peter Ramplay (Australia), Attendance: 20,283
URU: Héctor Santos (10/0), Mario González (12/0), Walter Daniel Olivera (9/0) [Gustavo Daniel de Simone Horn (6/0)], Juan Carlos Masnik (22/0), Mario Zoryez (13/0), Julio César Jiménez (7/0), Denis Alfredo Milar Otero (9/3) [Wálter Daniel Mantegazza (6/1)], Alberto Víctor Cardaccio (15/0), Juan Ramón Silva (4/0), Fernando Morena Belaro (18/11), Rubén Romeo Corbo Burmia (18/0). Trainer: Roberto Porta (5).

413. 27.04.1974 **AUSTRALIA - URUGUAY** **2-0(0-0)**
Cricket Ground, Sydney, Sydney; Referee: Don Campbell (Australia)
URU: Gustavo Daniel Fernández (4/0), Gustavo Daniel de Simone Horn (7/0), Mario González (13/0), Luis Garisto Pan (2/0), Mario Zoryez (14/0) [Walter Daniel Olivera (10/0)], Alberto Víctor Cardaccio (16/0), Julio César Jiménez (8/0), Wálter Daniel Mantegazza (7/1), José César Gómez (2/0), Fernando Morena Belaro (19/11), Rubén Romeo Corbo Burmia (19/0). Trainer: Roberto Porta (6).

414. 08.05.1974 **URUGUAY - REPUBLIC OF IRELAND** **2-0(2-0)**
Estadio Centenario, Montevideo; Referee: Ramón Ivannoe Barreto Ruíz (Uruguay), Attendance: 37,760
URU: Gustavo Daniel Fernández (5/0), Baudilio Jorge Jáuregui (6/0), Juan Carlos Masnik (23/0), Pablo Justo Forlán Lamarque (13/0), Alberto Víctor Cardaccio (17/0), Ricardo Elvio Pavoni Cúneo (11/1), José César Gómez (3/0) [Pedro Alvarez (4/0)], Julio César Jiménez (9/0), Fernando Morena Belaro (20/13), Wálter Daniel Mantegazza (8/1) [Denis Alfredo Milar Otero (10/3)], Rubén Romeo Corbo Burmia (20/0). Trainer: Roberto Porta (7).
Goals: Fernando Morena Belaro (16, 26).

415. 15.06.1974 **HOLLAND - URUGUAY** **2-0(1-0)** 10th FIFA WC. Group Stage
Niedersachsen-Stadion, Hannover (West Germany); Referee: Károly Palotai (Hungary), Attendance: 55,000
URU: Ladislao Mazurkiewicz Iglesias (34/0), Baudilio Jorge Jáuregui (7/0), Juan Carlos Masnik (24/0), Pablo Justo Forlán Lamarque (14/0), Ricardo Elvio Pavoni Cúneo (12/1), Víctor Rodolfo Espárrago Videla (39/1), Julio Walter Montero Castillo (41/1), Pedro Virgilio Rocha Franchetti (51/17), Luis Alberto Cubilla Almeida (37/11) [68.Denis Alfredo Milar Otero (11/3)], Fernando Morena Belaro (21/13) [*sent off 89*], Wálter Daniel Mantegazza (9/1). Trainer: Roberto Porta (8).

416. 19.06.1974 **BULGARIA - URUGUAY** **1-1(0-0)** 10th FIFA WC. Group Stage
Niedersachsen-Stadion, Hannover (West Germany); Referee: John Keith Taylor (England), Attendance: 13,000
URU: Ladislao Mazurkiewicz Iglesias (35/0), Baudilio Jorge Jáuregui (8/0), Denis Alfredo Milar Otero (12/3), Pablo Justo Forlán Lamarque (15/0), Ricardo Elvio Pavoni Cúneo (13/2), Víctor Rodolfo Espárrago Videla (40/1), Pedro Virgilio Rocha Franchetti (52/17), Luis Garisto Pan (3/0) [72.Juan Carlos Masnik (25/0)], Fernando Morena Belaro (22/13), Wálter Daniel Mantegazza (10/1) [83.Alberto Víctor Cardaccio (18/0)], Rubén Romeo Corbo Burmia (21/0). Trainer: Roberto Porta (9).
Goal: Ricardo Elvio Pavoni Cúneo (87).

417. 23.06.1974 **SWEDEN – URUGUAY** **3-0(0-0)** 10th FIFA WC. Group Stage

Rheinstadion, Düsseldorf (West Germany); Referee: Erich Linemayr (Austria), Attendance: 28,000

URU: Ladislao Mazurkiewicz Iglesias (36/0), Baudilio Jorge Jáuregui (9/0), Denis Alfredo Milar Otero (13/3), Pablo Justo Forlán Lamarque (16/0), Ricardo Elvio Pavoni Cúneo (14/2), Víctor Rodolfo Espárrago Videla (41/1), Pedro Virgilio Rocha Franchetti (53/17), Luis Garisto Pan (4/0) [46.Juan Carlos Masnik (26/0)], Fernando Morena Belaro (23/13), Wálter Daniel Mantegazza (11/1), Rubén Romeo Corbo Burmia (22/0) [43.Luis Alberto Cubilla Almeida (38/11)). Trainer: Roberto Porta (10).

418. 04.06.1975 **URUGUAY – CHILE** **1-0(0-0)** Copa Juan Pinto Durán

Estadio Centenario, Montevideo; Referee: José Luis Martínez Bazán (Uruguay), Attendance: 23,000

URU: Héctor Santos (11/0) [Walter Luis Corbo Burmia (3/0)], Edison González (1/0), Gerardo Pelusso (1/0), Eduardo Del Capellán (1/0) [Juan Vicente Morales (1/0)], Saúl Lorenzo Rivero (3/0), Hugo Fernández (2/0), Nery Castillo (1/0) [Alfonso Darío Pereyra Bueno (1/0)], Lorenzo Unanue (1/1), Fernando Morena Belaro (24/13), Denis Alfredo Milar Otero (14/3), Juan Carlos Ocampo (1/0). Trainer: Carlos Silva Cabrera (1).

Goal: Lorenzo Unanue (65).

419. 12.06.1975 **PARAGUAY – URUGUAY** **0-1** Copa Artigas

Estadio Defensores del Chaco, Asunción; Referee: Angel Norberto Coerezza (Argentina)

URU: Héctor Santos (12/0), Carlos Cabrera (1/0), Hugo Fernández (3/0), Nil Roque Chagas (1/0), Héctor Roux (1/0), Ricardo Ortiz (1/0), Nery Castillo (2/0) [Edison González (2/0)], Daniel Bartolotta (1/0), Hebert Carlos Revetria (1/0) [Alberto Raúl Santelli Fernández (1/0)], Juan Ramón Silva (5/0), Julio César Jiménez (10/1). Trainer: Carlos Silva Cabrera (2).

Goal: Julio César Jiménez.

420. 19.06.1975 **URUGUAY – PARAGUAY** **0-1** Copa Artigas

Estadio Centenario, Montevideo; Referee: Alberto José Ducatelli (Argentina)

URU: Héctor Santos (13/0), Edison González (3/0), Gerardo Pelusso (2/0) [Hugo Fernández (4/0)], Héctor Roux (2/0), Saúl Lorenzo Rivero (4/0) [Ricardo Ortiz (2/0)], Juan Vicente Morales (2/0), Nery Castillo (3/0), Daniel Bartolotta (2/0) [José Lorenzo (1/0)], Fernando Morena Belaro (25/13) [Hebert Carlos Revetria (2/0)], Juan Ramón Silva (6/0), Julio César Jiménez (11/1). Trainer: Carlos Silva Cabrera (3).

421. 25.06.1975 **CHILE – URUGUAY** **1-3(1-2)** Copa Juan Pinto Durán

Estadio „Santa Laura", Santiago; Referee: Víctor Sergio Vásquez Sánchez (Chile), Attendance: 16,473

URU: Omar Correa (1/0), Carlos Peruena (1/1), Hugo Fernández (5/0), Juan Vicente Morales (3/0), Saúl Lorenzo Rivero (5/0), Eduardo Del Capellán (2/0), Nery Castillo (4/0), Juan Muhlethaler (1/0), Hebert Carlos Revetria (3/1), Juan Ramón Silva (7/0), Juan Carlos Ocampo (2/0). Trainer: Carlos Silva Cabrera (4).

Goals: Hebert Carlos Revetria (32), Carlos Peruena (45), Daniel Díaz (77 own goal).

422. 18.07.1975 **URUGUAY – ARGENTINA** **2-3(0-1)** Copa Newton

Estadio Centenario, Montevideo; Referee: Luis Gregorio Da Rosa (Uruguay), Attendance: 40,000

URU: Walter Luis Corbo Burmia (4/0), Carlos Peruena (2/1), Rafael Villazán (1/0), Juan Vicente Morales (4/0), Saúl Lorenzo Rivero (6/0) [Alfonso Darío Pereyra Bueno (2/0)], Ricardo Santiago Mier (1/0), José Lorenzo (2/0), Lorenzo Unanue (2/1), Fernando Morena Belaro (26/15), Juan Ramón Silva (8/0), Juan Carlos Ocampo (3/0) [Hebert Carlos Revetria (4/1)]. Trainer: Carlos Silva Cabrera (5).

Goals: Fernando Morena Belaro (62, 85).

423. 21.09.1975 **COLOMBIA – URUGUAY** **3-0(1-0)** 30th Copa América. Semi-Finals

Estadio „Nemesio Camacho" 'El Campín', Bogotá; Referee: César Augusto Orozco Guerrero (Peru), Attendance: 55,000

URU: Walter Luis Corbo Burmia (5/0), Alfredo De los Santos (1/0) [*sent off 17*], Walter Daniel Olivera (11/0), Mario González (14/0), Nelson Bonifacio Acosta (2/0), Ricardo Santiago Mier (2/0), Richard Forlán Resova (4/0) [75.José Lorenzo (3/0)], Lorenzo Unanue (3/1), Juan Ramón Silva (9/0), Fernando Morena Belaro (27/15), Juan Carlos Ocampo (4/0) [70.Juan Vicente Morales (5/0)]. Trainer: Juan Alberto Schiaffino (1).

424. 01.10.1975 **URUGUAY – COLOMBIA** **1-0(1-0)** 30th Copa América. Semi-Finals

Estadio Centenario, Montevideo; Referee: Rafael Hormazábal (Chile), Attendance: 70,000

URU: Walter Luis Corbo Burmia (6/0), Carlos Peruena (3/1) [86.Alfonso Darío Pereyra Bueno (3/0)], Nil Roque Chagas (2/0), Mario González (15/0), Nelson Bonifacio Acosta (3/0), Ricardo Santiago Mier (3/0), Richard Forlán Resova (5/0), Juan Ramón Carrasco Torres (1/0), Fernando Morena Belaro (28/16) [*sent off 80*], Juan Ramón Silva (10/0), José Lorenzo (4/0) [63.Hebert Carlos Revetria (5/1)]. Trainer: Juan Alberto Schiaffino (2).

Goal: Fernando Morena Belaro (17 penalty).

425. 25.02.1976 **URUGUAY – BRAZIL** **1-2** Copa Atlántico

Estadio Centenario, Montevideo; Referee: Roque Tito Cerullo Giuliano (Uruguay),

URU: Héctor Santos (14/0), Alfredo De Los Santos (2/0), Nil Roque Chagas (3/0), Sergio Ramírez (1/0), Nelson Bonifacio Acosta (4/0), Juan Vicente Morales (6/0), José María Muñiz (1/0), Julio César Jiménez (12/1), Fernando Morena Belaro (29/16), Alfonso Darío Pereyra Bueno (4/0), Juan Carlos Ocampo (5/1) [Washington Olivera (1/0)]. Trainer: José María Rodríguez (1).

Goal: Juan Carlos Ocampo.

426. 10.03.1976 **URUGUAY – PARAGUAY** **2-2** Copa Atlántico

Estadio Centenario, Montevideo; Referee: José Luis Martínez Bazán (Uruguay)

URU: Walter Luis Corbo Burmia (7/0), Alfredo De Los Santos (3/0), Rafael Villazán (2/0), Pablo Justo Forlán Lamarque (17/0), Alfonso Darío Pereyra Bueno (5/1), Juan Vicente Morales (7/0), José María Muñiz (2/0), Julio César Jiménez (13/1), Fernando Morena Belaro (30/16), Juan Ramón Silva (11/0) [Saúl Lorenzo Rivero (7/0)], Juan Carlos Ocampo (6/2). Trainer: José María Rodríguez (2).

Goals: Juan Carlos Ocampo, Alfonso Darío Pereyra Bueno.

427. 08.04.1976 **ARGENTINA – URUGUAY** **4-1(1-0)** Copa Atlántico

Estadio „José Amalfitani", Buenos Aires; Referee: Arturo Andrés Ithurralde (Argentina)

URU: Walter Luis Corbo Burmia (8/0), Alfredo De Los Santos (4/0), Rafael Villazán (3/0), Pablo Justo Forlán Lamarque (18/0), Saúl Lorenzo Rivero (8/0), Juan Vicente Morales (8/0) [Manuel Gregorio Keosseián (1/0)], José Cruz (1/0), Julio César Jiménez (14/1), Fernando Morena Belaro (31/16), Alfonso Darío Pereyra Bueno (6/2), Jorge Laclau (1/0) [Daniel Torres (1/0)]. Trainer: José María Rodríguez (3).

Goal: Alfonso Darío Pereyra Bueno (79).

428. 28.04.1976 **BRAZIL – URUGUAY** **2-1** Copa Atlántico
Estádio „Jornalista Mário Filho“ (Maracanã), Rio de Janeiro; Referee: José Faville Neto (Brazil)
URU: Walter Luis Corbo Burmia (9/0), Alfredo De Los Santos (5/0), Nil Roque Chagas (4/0), Mario González (16/0), Nelson Bonifacio Acosta (5/0), Sergio Ramírez (2/0), Rudy Rodríguez (1/0) [Hebert Carlos Revetria (6/1)], Julio César Jiménez (15/1), Fernando Morena Belaro (32/16), Alfonso Darío Pereyra Bueno (7/2), Daniel Torres (2/1) [Manuel Gregorio Keosseián (2/0)]. Trainer: José María Rodríguez (4).
Goal: Daniel Torres.

429. 19.05.1976 **PARAGUAY – URUGUAY** **1-0** Copa Atlántico
Estadio Defensores del Chaco, Asunción; Referee: José Romei Cañete (Paraguay), Attendance: 28,000
URU: Walter Luis Corbo Burmia (10/0), Alfredo De Los Santos (6/0), Francisco Salomón (1/0), Héctor Roux (3/0), Alfonso Darío Pereyra Bueno (8/2), Sergio Ramírez (3/0), José María Muñiz (3/0) [Rodolfo Enrique Rodríguez (1/0), Nelson Pedetti (1/0)], Juan José Duarte (1/0), Hebert Carlos Revetria (7/1), Juan Ramón Carrasco Torres (2/0), Rodolfo Abalde (1/0). Trainer: José María Rodríguez (5).

430. 09.06.1976 **URUGUAY – ARGENTINA** **0-3(0-3)** Copa Atlántico
Estadio Centenario, Montevideo; Referee: Ramón Ivannoe Barreto Ruíz (Uruguay), Attendance: 30,000
URU: Walter Luis Corbo Burmia (11/0), Nil Roque Chagas (5/0), Alfredo De Los Santos (7/0), Sergio Ramírez (4/0), Manuel Gregorio Keosseián (3/0), Gustavo Faral (1/0), José Hermes Moreira (1/0) [Waldemar Barreto Victorino (1/0)], Julio César Jiménez (16/1), Fernando Morena Belaro (33/16), Lorenzo Unanue (4/1), Rudy Rodríguez (2/0). Trainer: José María Rodríguez (6).

431. 06.10.1976 **CHILE – URUGUAY** **0-0** Copa Juan Pinto Durán
Estadio Nacional, Santiago; Referee: Juan Carvajal (Chile), Attendance: 35,000
URU: Rodolfo Sergio Rodríguez (1/0), Walter Daniel Olivera (12/0) [Julio César Jiménez (17/1)], Rafael Villazán (4/0), Héctor Roux (4/0), Alfonso Darío Pereyra Bueno (9/2), Beethoven Javier (1/0), José María Muñiz (4/0), Pedro Graffigna (1/0), Fernando Morena Belaro (34/16), Rodolfo Abalde (2/0) [Lorenzo Unanue (5/1)], Carlos Puppo (1/0). Trainer: Juan Eduardo Hohberg (17).

432. 12.10.1976 **PERU – URUGUAY** **0-0**
Estadio Nacional, Lima; Referee: César Pagano (Peru)
URU: Rodolfo Sergio Rodríguez (2/0), Sergio Ramírez (5/0), Alfredo De Los Santos (8/0), Rafael Villazán (5/0), Beethoven Javier (2/0) [74.Héctor Roux (5/0)], Alfonso Darío Pereyra Bueno (10/2), Julio César Jiménez (18/1), Lorenzo Unanue (6/1), José María Muñiz (5/0) [53.Rodolfo Abalde (3/0)], Fernando Morena Belaro (35/16), Rodolfo Enrique Rodríguez (2/0) [65.Waldemar Barreto Victorino (2/0)]. Trainer: Juan Eduardo Hohberg (18).

433. 15.10.1976 **COLOMBIA – URUGUAY** **1-2(1-0)**
Estadio „Nemesio Camacho“ 'El Campín', Bogotá; Referee: Arturo Andrés Ithurralde (Argentina), Attendance: 39,219
URU: Rodolfo Sergio Rodríguez (3/0), Héctor Roux (6/0), Alfredo De los Santos (9/0), Alfonso Darío Pereyra Bueno (11/2), Rafael Villazán (6/0), Sergio Ramírez (6/0), Rodolfo Abalde (4/0) [Carlos Puppo (2/0)], Pedro Graffigna (2/0), José María Muñiz (6/0) [Rodolfo Enrique Rodríguez (3/1)], Fernando Morena Belaro (36/16) [Lorenzo Unanue (7/1)], Waldemar Barreto Victorino (3/1). Trainer: Juan Eduardo Hohberg (19).
Goals: Waldemar Barreto Victorino (79), Rodolfo Enrique Rodríguez (84).

434. 20.10.1976 **ECUADOR – URUGUAY** **2-2(1-0)**
Estadio Olimpico „Atahualpa“, Quito; Referee: Oscar Veiró (Argentina), Attendance: 50,000
URU: Rodolfo Sergio Rodríguez (4/0), Alfredo De Los Santos (10/0), Rafael Villazán (7/0), Héctor Roux (7/0) [Beethoven Javier (3/0), Walter Daniel Olivera (13/0)], Alfonso Darío Pereyra Bueno (12/2), Sergio Ramírez (7/0), Waldemar Barreto Victorino (4/3), Pedro Graffigna (3/0), Fernando Morena Belaro (37/16), Lorenzo Unanue (8/1), Rodolfo Enrique Rodríguez (4/1) [José María Muñiz (7/0)]. Trainer: Juan Eduardo Hohberg (20).
Goals: Waldemar Barreto Victorino (21, 66).

435. 24.11.1976 **URUGUAY – PERU** **0-0**
Estadio Centenario, Montevideo; Referee: Roque Tito Cerullo Giuliano (Uruguay), Attendance: 15,000
URU: Rodolfo Sergio Rodríguez (5/0), Walter Daniel Olivera (14/0), Alfredo De Los Santos (11/0), Héctor Roux (8/0), Sergio Ramírez (8/0), Alfonso Darío Pereyra Bueno (13/2), Julio César Jiménez (19/1), Pedro Graffigna (4/0), José María Muñiz (8/0) [64.Rodolfo Enrique Rodríguez (5/1)], Fernando Morena Belaro (38/16), Waldemar Barreto Victorino (5/3). Trainer: Juan Eduardo Hohberg (21).

436. 04.01.1977 **URUGUAY – ECUADOR** **1-1(0-1)**
Estadio Centenario, Montevideo; Referee: Héctor Pedro Rodríguez (Uruguay), Attendance: 35,000
URU: Rodolfo Sergio Rodríguez (6/0), Sergio Ramírez (9/0), Walter Daniel Olivera (15/0), Francisco Salomón (2/0), Juan Vicente Morales (9/0), Juan Ramón Carrasco Torres (3/0) [José Luis Amaro (1/0)], Ricardo Ortiz (3/0), Pedro Graffigna (5/0), Alberto Raúl Santelli Fernández (2/0), Fernando Morena Belaro (39/17), Jorge Yanes (1/0) [Washington Olivera (2/0)]. Trainer: Juan Eduardo Hohberg (22).
Goal: Fernando Morena Belaro (57).
Match abandoned at 78 mins, as Ecuador had only five players left on the field.

437. 12.01.1977 **PARAGUAY – URUGUAY** **1-1** Copa Artigas
Estadio Defensores del Chaco, Asunción; Referee: Artemio Martínez (Paraguay), Attendance: 25,000
URU: Rodolfo Sergio Rodríguez (7/0), Héctor Roux (9/0), Alfredo De los Santos (12/0), Rafael Villazán (8/0), Juan Vicente Morales (10/0), Juan Ramón Carrasco Torres (4/1), Pedro Graffigna (6/0), Alfonso Darío Pereyra Bueno (14/2), Laddy Nittder Pizzani (1/0), Fernando Morena Belaro (40/17), Washington Olivera (3/0) [*sent off*]. Trainer: Juan Eduardo Hohberg (23).
Goal: Juan Ramón Carrasco Torres.

438. 23.01.1977 **URUGUAY – PARAGUAY** **2-1** Copa Artigas
Estadio Centenario, Montevideo; Referee: Luis Gregorio Da Rosa (Uruguay), Attendance: 40,000
URU: Rodolfo Sergio Rodríguez (8/0) [Artigas Araújo (1/0)], Sergio Ramírez (10/0), Alfredo De los Santos (13/0), Rafael Villazán (9/0), Juan Vicente Morales (11/1), Juan Ramón Carrasco Torres (5/1) [Lorenzo Unanue (9/1)], Pedro Graffigna (7/0), Alfonso Darío Pereyra Bueno (15/2), Jorge Yanes (2/0) [Alberto Raúl Santelli Fernández (3/1)], Laddy Nittder Pizzani (2/0), Fernando Morena Belaro (41/17). Trainer: Juan Eduardo Hohberg (24).
Goals: Juan Vicente Morales, Alberto Raúl Santelli Fernández

439. 30.01.1977 **URUGUAY – CHILE** **3-0(0-0)** Copa Juan Pinto Durán
Estadio Centenario, Montevideo; Referee: Ángel Norberto Coerezza (Argentina), Attendance: 20,000
URU: Rodolfo Sergio Rodríguez (9/0), Sergio Ramírez (11/0), Alfredo De Los Santos (14/0), Rafael Villazán (10/0), Juan Vicente Morales (12/1), Juan Ramón Carrasco Torres (6/1), Pedro Graffigna (8/0), Alfonso Darío Pereyra Bueno (16/3), Laddy Nittder Pizzani (3/1) [Waldemar Barreto Victorino (6/3)], Fernando Morena Belaro (42/18), Washington Olivera (4/0). Trainer: Juan Eduardo Hohberg (25).
Goals: Laddy Nittder Pizzani (53), Fernando Morena Belaro (62), Alfonso Darío Pereyra Bueno (75).

440. 09.02.1977 **VENEZUELA - URUGUAY** **1-1(1-0)** 11th FIFA WC. Qualifiers
Estadio „Brígido Iriarte“, Caracas; Referee: Guillermo Velázquez Ramírez (Colombia), Attendance: 5,000
URU: Rodolfo Sergio Rodríguez (10/0), Sergio Ramírez (12/0), Alfredo De los Santos (15/0), Rafael Villazán (11/0), Juan Vicente Morales (13/1), Juan Ramón Carrasco Torres (7/1), Pedro Graffigna (9/0), Alfonso Darío Pereyra Bueno (17/3) [77.Lorenzo Unanue (10/1)], Laddy Nittder Pizzani (4/1) [59.Alberto Raúl Santelli Fernández (4/1)], Fernando Morena Belaro (43/18), Washington Olivera (5/1). Trainer: Juan Eduardo Hohberg (26).
Goal: Washington Olivera (5).

441. 27.02.1977 **BOLIVIA - URUGUAY** **1-0(0-0)** 11th FIFA WC. Qualifiers
Estadio „Libertador Simón Bolívar“, La Paz; Referee: Romualdo Arppi Filho (Brazil), Attendance: 20,306
URU: Rodolfo Sergio Rodríguez (11/0), Sergio Ramírez (13/0), Alfredo De los Santos (16/0), Francisco Salomón (3/0), Juan Vicente Morales (14/1), Juan Ramón Carrasco Torres (8/1) [61.Lorenzo Unanue (11/1)], Pedro Graffigna (10/0), Alfonso Darío Pereyra Bueno (18/3), Waldemar Barreto Victorino (7/3), Fernando Morena Belaro (44/18), Washington Olivera (6/1) [61.Miguel Rosifredo Caillava (1/0)]. Trainer: Juan Eduardo Hohberg (27).

442. 17.03.1977 **URUGUAY - VENEZUELA** **2-0(1-0)** 11th FIFA WC. Qualifiers
Estadio Centenario, Montevideo; Referee: Armando Marques (Brazil),Att : 4,383
URU: Rodolfo Sergio Rodríguez (12/0), Sergio Ramírez (14/0), Raúl Moller (1/0), Martin Taborda (1/0), Manuel Santana (1/0), Miguel Rosifredo Caillava (2/0), Pedro Graffigna (11/0) [65.Juan José Duarte (2/0)], Lorenzo Unanue (12/1), Laddy Nittder Pizzani (5/3), Alberto Raúl Santelli Fernández (5/1) [69.Juan Ramón Carrasco Torres (9/1)], Washington Olivera (7/1). Trainer: Raúl Bentancor (1).
Goals: Laddy Nittder Pizzani (11, 83).

443. 27.03.1977 **URUGUAY - BOLIVIA** **2-2(1-1)** 11th FIFA WC. Qualifiers
Estadio Centenario, Montevideo; Referee: Arturo Andrés Ithurralde (Argentina), Attendance: 7,477
URU: Rodolfo Sergio Rodríguez (13/0), Eduardo del Capellán (3/0), Raúl Moller (2/0), Martin Taborda (2/0), Manuel Santana (2/0), Lorenzo Unanue (13/1), Pedro Graffigna (12/0) [77.Juan Muhlethaler (2/0)], Alfonso Darío Pereyra Bueno (19/5), Laddy Nittder Pizzani (6/3), Alberto Raúl Santelli Fernández (6/1), Jorge Rodríguez Cantero (1/0). Trainer: Raúl Bentancor (2).
Goals: Alfonso Darío Pereyra Bueno (25, 49).

444. 08.06.1977 **URUGUAY - WEST GERMANY** **0-2(0-1)**
Estadio Centenario, Montevideo; Referee: Angel Norberto Coerezza (Argentina), Attendance: 50,000
URU: Omar Correa (2/0) [Freddy Clavijo (1/0)], Alfredo de Los Santos (17/0), Julio Rivadavia (1/0), Francisco Salomón (4/0), Beethoven Javier (4/0), Juan Ramón Carrasco Torres (10/1), Alfonso Darío Pereyra Bueno (20/5), Ildo Enrique Maneiro Ghezzi (26/2), Rudy Rodríguez (3/0), Alberto Raúl Santelli Fernández (7/1), Washington Olivera (8/1) [Juan Muhlethaler (3/0)]. Trainer: Omar Borrás (1).

445. 15.06.1977 **URUGUAY - ENGLAND** **0-0**
Estadio Centenario, Montevideo; Referee: Miguel Comesana (Argentina), Attendance: 25,000
URU: Freddy Clavijo (2/0), Julio Rivadavia (2/0), Francisco Salomón (5/0), Alfredo de los Santos (18/0), Alfonso Darío Pereyra Bueno (21/5), Beethoven Javier (5/0), Rudy Rodríguez (4/0), Juan Ramón Carrasco Torres (11/1), Alberto Raúl Santelli Fernández (8/1), Ildo Enrique Maneiro Ghezzi (27/2), Washington Olivera (9/1) [Juan Muhlethaler (4/0)]. Trainer: Omar Borrás (2).

446. 25.04.1978 **URUGUAY - ARGENTINA** **2-0(0-0)**
Estadio Centenario, Montevideo; Referee: Jorge Eduardo Romero (Argentina), Attendance: 26,000
URU: Rodolfo Sergio Rodríguez (14/0), Carlos Peruena (4/1) [Rúben Giménez (1/0)], Alfredo De los Santos (19/0), Francisco Salomón (6/0), Eduardo Di Bartolomeo (1/0), Juan Ramón Carrasco Torres (12/1), Pedro Graffigna (13/0) [69.Lorenzo Unanue (14/1)], Ildo Enrique Maneiro Ghezzi (28/3), Antonio Alzamendi Casas (1/0) [81.Daniel Godoy (1/0)], Fernando Morena Belaro (45/19), Juan Carlos Ocampo (7/2). Trainer: Hugo Bagnulo (20).
Goals: Ildo Enrique Maneiro Ghezzi (64), Fernando Morena Belaro (80).

447. 03.05.1978 **ARGENTINA - URUGUAY** **3-0(1-0)**
Estadio „Alberto Armando“, Buenos Aires; Referee: José Luis da Rosa Barbosa (Uruguay), Attendance: 60,000
URU: Rodolfo Sergio Rodríguez (15/0), Carlos Peruena (5/1) [46.Rúben Giménez (2/0)], Alfredo De los Santos (20/0), Francisco Salomón (7/0), Eduardo Di Bartolomeo (2/0), Juan Ramón Carrasco Torres (13/1) [61.Julio Walter Montero Castillo (42/1)], Pedro Graffigna (14/0) [46.Lorenzo Unanue (15/1)], Ildo Enrique Maneiro Ghezzi (29/3), Antonio Alzamendi Casas (2/0), Fernando Morena Belaro (46/19), Juan Carlos Ocampo (8/2). Trainer: Hugo Bagnulo (21).

448. 24.05.1978 **URUGUAY - SPAIN** **0-0**
Estadio Centenario, Montevideo; Referee: Héctor Pedro Rodríguez (Uruguay), Attendance: 24,836
URU: Rodolfo Sergio Rodríguez (16/0), Alfredo De los Santos (21/0), Walter Daniel Olivera (16/0), Rúben Giménez (3/0), Washington González (1/0), Juan Ramón Carrasco Torres (14/1) [76.Miguel Rosifredo Caillava (3/0)], Lorenzo Unanue (16/1), Ildo Enrique Maneiro Ghezzi (30/3), Antonio Alzamendi Casas (3/0), Fernando Morena Belaro (47/19), Venancio Ariel Ramos Villanueva (1/0) [76.Rúben Umpiérrez (1/0)]. Trainer: Hugo Bagnulo (22).

449. 31.05.1979 **BRAZIL - URUGUAY** **5-1(4-1)**
Estádio „Jornalista Mário Filho“ (Maracanã), Rio de Janeiro; Referee: Oscar Scolfaro (Brazil)
URU: Rodolfo Sergio Rodríguez (17/0), Néstor Mario Montelongo (1/0), José Luis Russo (1/0), Jorge González (1/0), Washington González (2/0) [José Hermes Moreira (2/0)], Mario Daniel Saralegui (1/0), Jorge Rodríguez de Deus (1/0), Lorenzo Unanue (17/1), Alberto Willers Bica (1/0) [Gary Castillo (1/0)], Waldemar Barreto Victorino (8/4) [Carlos Lezcué (1/0)], Juan Carlos Ocampo (9/2). Trainer: Raúl Bentancor (3).
Goal: Waldemar Barreto Victorino (21).

450. 11.07.1979 **CHILE - URUGUAY** **1-0(1-0)** Copa Juan Pinto Durán
Estadio Nacional, Santiago; Referee: José Luis Martínez Bazán (Uruguay), Attendance: 23,000
URU: Rodolfo Sergio Rodríguez (18/0), Néstor Mario Montelongo (2/0) [Jorge González (2/0)], Julio Rivadavia (3/0), Hugo Eduardo De León (1/0), Mario Zoryez (15/0), Eduardo De la Peña (1/0), Julio Rodríguez (1/0) [Ariel José Krasouski (1/0)], Lorenzo Unanue (18/1), Alberto Willers Bica (2/0), Waldemar Barreto Victorino (9/4), Juan Carlos Ocampo (10/2) [Gary Castillo (2/0)]. Trainer: Raúl Bentancor (4).

451. 18.07.1979 **URUGUAY - CHILE** **2-1(0-0)** Copa Juan Pinto Durán
Estadio Centenario, Montevideo; Referee: Alberto Martínez (Chile), Attendance: 31,000
URU: Rodolfo Sergio Rodríguez (19/0), José Hermes Moreira (3/0), José Luis Russo (2/0), Hugo Eduardo De León (2/0), Washington González (3/0), Lorenzo Unanue (19/2), Ariel José Krasouski (2/0), Denis Alfredo Milar Otero (15/3), Alberto Willers Bica (3/0), Waldemar Barreto Victorino (10/5), Gary Castillo (3/0). Trainer: Raúl Bentancor (5).
Goals: Lorenzo Unanue (46), Waldemar Barreto Victorino (71).

452. 30.08.1979 **PERU – URUGUAY** **2-0(1-0)**

Estadio Nacional, Lima; Referee: César Pagano (Peru)

URU: Rodolfo Sergio Rodríguez (20/0), José Hermes Moreira (4/0), Nelson Marcenaro (1/0), Hugo Eduardo De León (3/0), Mario Zoryez (16/0), Lorenzo Unanue (20/2), Mario Daniel Saralegui (2/0) [56.Ildo Enrique Maneiro Ghezzi (31/3)] [*sent off 90*], Eduardo De la Peña (2/0) [61.Nelson Agresta (1/0)], Gary Castillo (4/0) [69.Daniel Alonso (1/0)], Waldemar Barreto Victorino (11/5), Washington Olivera (10/1). Trainer: Roque Gastón Máspoli (3).

453. 05.09.1979 **ECUADOR – URUGUAY** **2-1(2-0)** 31st Copa América. Group Stage

Estadio Olímpico „Atahualpa“, Quito; Referee: Romualdo Arppi Filho (Brazil), Attendance: 30,000

URU: Rodolfo Sergio Rodríguez (21/0), José Hermes Moreira (5/0), Nelson Marcenaro (2/0), Hugo Eduardo De León (4/0), Mario Zoryez (17/0), Mario Daniel Saralegui (3/0), Nelson Agresta (2/0), Lorenzo Unanue (21/2) [Ildo Enrique Maneiro Ghezzi (32/3)], Gary Castillo (5/0) [*sent off 65*], Waldemar Barreto Victorino (12/6), Daniel Alonso (2/0). Trainer: Roque Gastón Máspoli (4).

Goal: Waldemar Barreto Victorino (79 penalty).

454. 16.09.1979 **URUGUAY – ECUADOR** **2-1(1-0)** 31st Copa América. Group Stage

Estadio Centenario, Montevideo; Referee: Oscar Scolfaro (Brazil), Attendance: 25,000

URU: Rodolfo Sergio Rodríguez (22/0), José Hermes Moreira (6/0), Nelson Marcenaro (3/0), Hugo Eduardo De León (5/0), Mario Zoryez (18/0), Mario Daniel Saralegui (4/0) [Lorenzo Unanue (22/2)], Nelson Agresta (3/0), Ildo Enrique Maneiro Ghezzi (33/3) [*sent off 77*], Rúben Walter Paz Márquez (1/0), Alberto Willers Bica (4/1) [Daniel Alonso (3/0)], Waldemar Barreto Victorino (13/7). Trainer: Roque Gastón Máspoli (5).

Goals: Alberto Willers Bica (4), Waldemar Barreto Victorino (57 penalty).

455. 20.09.1979 **PARAGUAY – URUGUAY** **0-0** 31st Copa América. Group Stage

Estadio Defensores del Chaco, Asunción; Referee: Sergio Vásquez (Chile), Attendance: 25,000

URU: Rodolfo Sergio Rodríguez (23/0), Víctor Hugo Diogo Silva (1/0), Domingo Rufino Cáceres (1/0), Hugo Eduardo De León (6/0), Washington González (4/0), Eduardo De la Peña (3/0), Nelson Agresta (4/0), Denis Alfredo Milar Otero (16/3) [Lorenzo Unanue (23/2)], Rúben Walter Paz Márquez (2/0), Alberto Willers Bica (5/1), Waldemar Barreto Victorino (14/7). Trainer: Roque Gastón Máspoli (6).

456. 26.09.1979 **URUGUAY – PARAGUAY** **2-2(0-1)** 31st Copa América. Group Stage

Estadio Centenario, Montevideo; Referee: Édison Pérez Núñez (Peru), Attendance: 18,000

URU: Rodolfo Sergio Rodríguez (24/0), Víctor Hugo Diogo Silva (2/0), Domingo Rufino Cáceres (2/0), Hugo Eduardo De León (7/0), Washington González (5/0), Eduardo De la Peña (4/0), Nelson Agresta (5/0), Denis Alfredo Milar Otero (17/4), Rúben Walter Paz Márquez (3/1), Alberto Willers Bica (6/1), Daniel Alonso (4/0) [Ernesto Vargas (1/0)]. Trainer: Roque Gastón Máspoli (7).

Goals: Denis Alfredo Milar Otero (54 penalty), Rúben Walter Paz Márquez (83).

457. 15.03.1980 **ITALY – URUGUAY** **1-0(1-0)**

Stadio „Giuseppe Meazza“, Milano; Referee: Ivan Iosifov (Bulgaria), Attendance: 33,284

URU: Rodolfo Sergio Rodríguez (25/0), Víctor Hugo Diogo Silva (3/0) [46.José Hermes Moreira (7/0)], Washington González (6/0), Nelson Agresta (6/0), Nelson Marcenaro (4/0), Domingo Rufino Cáceres (3/0), Alberto Willers Bica (7/1) [58.Venancio Ariel Ramos Villanueva (2/0)], Eduardo De la Peña (5/0), Waldemar Barreto Victorino (15/7), Miguel Rosifredo Caillava (4/0), Rúben Walter Paz Márquez (4/1). Trainer: Roque Gastón Máspoli (8).

458. 18.03.1980 **BELGIUM – URUGUAY** **2-0(0-0)**

Stade Heysel, Bruxelles; Referee: Robert Wurtz (France), Attendance: 3,974

URU: Rodolfo Sergio Rodríguez (26/0), Domingo Rufino Cáceres (4/0), Nelson Marcenaro (5/0), Víctor Hugo Diogo Silva (4/0), Nelson Agresta (7/0), Washington González (7/0), Venancio Ariel Ramos Villanueva (3/0), Eduardo De la Peña (6/0), Waldemar Barreto Victorino (16/7) [70.Alfredo Arias (1/0)], Miguel Rosifredo Caillava (5/0), Rúben Walter Paz Márquez (5/1). Trainer: Roque Gastón Máspoli (9).

459. 22.03.1980 **YUGOSLAVIA – URUGUAY** **2-1(1-0)**

Koševo Stadion, Sarajevo; Referee: Nikolaos Lagoyannis (Greece), Attendance: 30,000

URU: Rodolfo Sergio Rodríguez (27/0), Víctor Hugo Diogo Silva (5/0) [57.José Hermes Moreira (8/0)], Washington González (8/0), Domingo Rufino Cáceres (5/0) [Jorge González (3/0)], Nelson Marcenaro (6/0), Nelson Agresta (8/0), Venancio Ariel Ramos Villanueva (4/0), Eduardo De la Peña (7/0), Waldemar Barreto Victorino (17/7), Miguel Rosifredo Caillava (6/0) [60 Carlos Reyes (1/0)], Rúben Walter Paz Márquez (6/1). Trainer: Roque Gastón Máspoli (10).

Goal: Boro Primorac (75 own goal).

460. 26.03.1980 **LUXEMBOURG – URUGUAY** **0-1(0-0)**

Stade de la Frontière, Esch-sur-Alzette; Referee: Walter Eschweiler (West Germany), Attendance: 1,500

URU: Carlos Mario Goyén Prieto (1/0), José Hermes Moreira (9/0), Washington González (9/0), Domingo Rufino Cáceres (6/0), Jorge González (4/0), Ricardo Ortiz (4/0), Alberto Willers Bica (8/1) [Waldemar Barreto Victorino (18/8)], Eduardo De la Peña (8/0), Alfredo Arias (2/0), Carlos Reyes (2/0) [Miguel Rosifredo Caillava (7/0)], Venancio Ariel Ramos Villanueva (5/0) [Rúben Walter Paz Márquez (7/1)]. Trainer: Roque Gastón Máspoli (11).

Goal: Waldemar Barreto Victorino (89).

461. 18.07.1980 **URUGUAY – PERU** **0-0** 50 years of Centenario

Estadio Centenario, Montevideo; Referee: Edison Pérez Núñez (Peru)

URU: Fernando Harry Álvez Mosquera (1/0), Víctor Hugo Diogo Silva (6/0), Domingo Rufino Cáceres (7/0) [38.Daniel Felipe Revelez (1/0)], Nelson Marcenaro (7/0), Daniel Martínez (1/0) [60.Juan Vicente Morales (15/1)], Jorge Wálter Barrios Balestrasse (1/0), Nelson Agresta (9/0), Sergio Rodolfo Santín (1/0) [60.Julio César Núñez (1/0)], Ernesto Vargas (2/0), Carlos Acevedo (1/0), Venancio Ariel Ramos Villanueva (6/0). Trainer: Roque Gastón Máspoli (12).

462. 21.08.1980 **URUGUAY – CHILE** **0-0**

Estadio Centenario, Montevideo; Referee: Teodoro Nitti (Argentina), Attendance: 18,000

URU: Rodolfo Sergio Rodríguez (28/0), Víctor Hugo Diogo Silva (7/0) [José Hermes Moreira (10/0)], Walter Daniel Olivera (17/0), Hugo Eduardo De León (8/0), Washington González (10/0), Jorge Wálter Barrios Balestrasse (2/0), Nelson Agresta (10/0) [Ariel José Krasouski (3/0)], Roberto Arsenio Luzardo (1/0), Ernesto Vargas (3/0) [Heber Bueno (1/0)], Carlos Acevedo (2/0), Venancio Ariel Ramos Villanueva (7/0). Trainer: Roque Gastón Máspoli (13).

463. 27.08.1980 **BRAZIL – URUGUAY** **1-0**

Estádio „Plácido Castelão“, Fortaleza; Referee: Luís Carlos Félix Ferrara (Brazil)

URU: Rodolfo Sergio Rodríguez (29/0), Víctor Hugo Diogo Silva (8/0), Walter Daniel Olivera (18/0), Hugo Eduardo De León (9/0), José Hermes Moreira (11/0) [Julio Aníbal Rodríguez (1/0)], Jorge Wálter Barrios Balestrasse (3/0), Nelson Agresta (11/0) [Ariel José Krasouski (4/0)], Eduardo De la Peña (9/0) [Roberto Arsenio Luzardo (2/0)], Ernesto Vargas (4/0), Waldemar Barreto Victorino (19/8), Venancio Ariel Ramos Villanueva (8/0). Trainer: Roque Gastón Máspoli (14).

464. 09.11.1980 **BOLIVIA - URUGUAY** **1-3(1-0)**
Estadio „Félix Capriles", Cochabamba; Referee: Luis Barrancos Alvarez (Bolivia), Attendance: 10,000
URU: Rodolfo Sergio Rodríguez (30/0), José Hermes Moreira (12/0), Walter Daniel Olivera (19/0), Hugo Eduardo De León (10/0), Daniel Martínez (2/0) [Víctor Hugo Diogo Silva (9/0)], Jorge Wálter Barrios Balestrasse (4/0), Nelson Agresta (12/0) [Ariel José Krasouski (5/0)], Eduardo De la Peña (10/1), Julio César Araújo Morales (15/4), Venancio Ariel Ramos Villanueva (9/0) [Rúben Walter Paz Márquez (8/1)], Waldemar Barreto Victorino (20/9). Trainer: Roque Gastón Máspoli (15).
Goals: Eduardo De la Peña (80), Julio César Araújo Morales (87), Waldemar Barreto Victorino (90).

465. 12.11.1980 **PERU - URUGUAY** **1-1(1-1)**
Estadio „Alejandro Villanueva", Lima; Referee: Artemio Santiago Sención (Uruguay)
URU: Rodolfo Sergio Rodríguez (31/0), José Hermes Moreira (13/0), Walter Daniel Olivera (20/0), Hugo Eduardo De León (11/0), Víctor Hugo Diogo Silva (10/0), Jorge Wálter Barrios Balestrasse (5/0), Ariel José Krasouski (6/1), Eduardo De la Peña (11/1) [*sent off 53*], Julio César Araújo Morales (16/4) [70.Roberto Arsenio Luzardo (3/0)], Waldemar Barreto Victorino (21/9), Rúben Walter Paz Márquez (9/1) [60.Venancio Ariel Ramos Villanueva (10/0)]. Trainer: Roque Gastón Máspoli (16).
Goal: Ariel José Krasouski (25).

466. 08.12.1980 **URUGUAY - FINLAND** **6-0(0-0)**
Estadio Centenario, Montevideo; Referee: José Luis Martínez Bazán (Uruguay), Attendance: 10,000
URU: Rodolfo Sergio Rodríguez (32/0), José Hermes Moreira (14/0) [Víctor Hugo Diogo Silva (11/0)], Daniel Martínez (3/0), Hugo Eduardo De León (12/0), Walter Daniel Olivera (21/0), Ariel José Krasouski (7/2) [Miguel Falero (1/1)], Jorge Wálter Barrios Balestrasse (6/0) [Ernesto Vargas (5/1)], Julio César Araújo Morales (17/6), Waldemar Barreto Victorino (22/9) [Jorge Siviero (1/1)], Roberto Arsenio Luzardo (4/0), Rúben Walter Paz Márquez (10/1). Trainer: Roque Gastón Máspoli (17).
Goals: Ariel José Krasouski (56), Julio César Araújo Morales (63, 64), Ernesto Vargas (75), Jorge Siviero (83), Miguel Falero (86).

467. 11.12.1980 **URUGUAY - BOLIVIA** **5-0(3-0)**
Estadio Campo Municipal, Maldonado; Referee: Artemio Santiago Sención (Uruguay), Attendance: 8,000
URU: Rodolfo Sergio Rodríguez (33/0), José Hermes Moreira (15/0), Walter Daniel Olivera (22/0), Hugo Eduardo De León (13/0), Daniel Martínez (4/0) [Ricardo Meroni (1/0)], Eduardo De la Peña (12/1), Ariel José Krasouski (8/2) [Nelson Agresta (13/0)], Rúben Walter Paz Márquez (11/2), Julio César Araújo Morales (18/8), Ernesto Vargas (6/1) [Venancio Ariel Ramos Villanueva (11/1)], Waldemar Barreto Victorino (23/10). Trainer: Roque Gastón Máspoli (18).
Goals: Waldemar Barreto Victorino (27), Julio César Araújo Morales (31, 40), Rúben Walter Paz Márquez (53), Venancio Ariel Ramos Villanueva (64).

468. 18.12.1980 **URUGUAY - SWITZERLAND** **4-0(1-0)**
Estadio „Luis Tróccoli", Montevideo; Referee: Jorge Eduardo Romero (Argentina), Attendance: 6,000
URU: Rodolfo Sergio Rodríguez (34/0), José Hermes Moreira (16/0), Daniel Martínez (5/0), Hugo Eduardo De León (14/0), Walter Daniel Olivera (23/1), Ariel José Krasouski (9/2), Ernesto Vargas (7/1) [Venancio Ariel Ramos Villanueva (12/1)], Eduardo De la Peña (13/1) [Roberto Arsenio Luzardo (5/0)], Waldemar Barreto Victorino (24/10), Rúben Walter Paz Márquez (12/5), Julio César Araújo Morales (19/8). Trainer: Roque Gastón Máspoli (19).
Goals: Walter Daniel Olivera (21), Rúben Walter Paz Márquez (66, 83, 89).

469. 30.12.1980 **URUGUAY - HOLLAND** **2-0(0-0)** Gold Cup
Estadio Centenario, Montevideo; Referee: Enrique Labó (Peru), Attendance: 65,000
URU: Rodolfo Sergio Rodríguez (35/0), José Hermes Moreira (17/0), Daniel Martínez (6/0), Hugo Eduardo De León (15/0), Walter Daniel Olivera (24/1), Ariel José Krasouski (10/2), Venancio Ariel Ramos Villanueva (13/2), Eduardo De la Peña (14/1), Waldemar Barreto Victorino (25/11), Rúben Walter Paz Márquez (13/5), Julio César Araújo Morales (20/8) [Ernesto Vargas (8/1)]. Trainer: Roque Gastón Máspoli (20).
Goals: Venancio Ariel Ramos Villanueva (31), Waldemar Barreto Victorino (45).

470. 03.01.1981 **URUGUAY - ITALY** **2-0(0-0)** Gold Cup
Estadio Centenario, Montevideo; Referee: Emilio Carlos Guruceta Muro (Spain), Attendance: 90,000
URU: Rodolfo Sergio Rodríguez (36/0), José Hermes Moreira (18/0), Daniel Martínez (7/0), Hugo Eduardo De León (16/0), Walter Daniel Olivera (25/1), Ariel José Krasouski (11/2), Venancio Ariel Ramos Villanueva (14/2), Eduardo De la Peña (15/1), Waldemar Barreto Victorino (26/12), Rúben Walter Paz Márquez (14/5), Julio César Araújo Morales (21/9) [Víctor Hugo Diogo Silva (12/0)]. Trainer: Roque Gastón Máspoli (21).
Goals: Julio César Araújo Morales (67 penalty), Waldemar Barreto Victorino (81).

471. 10.01.1981 **URUGUAY - BRAZIL** **2-1(0-0)** Gold Cup. Final
Estadio Centenario, Montevideo; Referee: Erich Linemayr (Austria), Attendance: 70,000
URU: Rodolfo Sergio Rodríguez (37/0), Víctor Hugo Diogo Silva (13/0), Daniel Martínez (8/0), Hugo Eduardo De León (17/0), Walter Daniel Olivera (26/1), Ariel José Krasouski (12/2), Venancio Ariel Ramos Villanueva (15/2), Eduardo De la Peña (16/1) [36.Jorge Wálter Barrios Balestrasse (7/1)], Waldemar Barreto Victorino (27/13), Rúben Walter Paz Márquez (15/5), Julio César Araújo Morales (22/9). Trainer: Roque Gastón Máspoli (22).
Goals: Jorge Wálter Barrios Balestrasse (50), Waldemar Barreto Victorino (80).

472. 29.04.1981 **CHILE - URUGUAY** **1-2(0-0)** Copa Juan Pinto Durán
Estadio Nacional, Santiago; Referee: Teodoro Nitti (Argentina), Attendance: 27,105
URU: Rodolfo Sergio Rodríguez (38/0), José Hermes Moreira (19/0), Daniel Enríquez (1/0), José Luis Russo (3/0), Washington González (11/0), Jorge Wálter Barrios Balestrasse (8/1), Nelson Agresta (14/1), Julio César Núñez (2/1) [Roberto Arsenio Luzardo (6/0)], Alberto Willers Bica (9/1) [Julio Franco (1/0)], Waldemar Barreto Victorino (28/13), Jorge Torres (1/0). Trainer: Roque Gastón Máspoli (23).
Goals: Julio César Núñez (65 penalty), Nelson Agresta (78).

473. 15.07.1981 **URUGUAY - CHILE** **0-0** Copa Juan Pinto Durán
Estadio Centenario, Montevideo; Referee: Abel Gnecco (Argentina), Attendance: 18,000
URU: Rodolfo Sergio Rodríguez (39/0), José Hermes Moreira (20/0), Daniel Felipe Revelez (2/0), José Luis Russo (4/0), Daniel Martínez (9/0) [Washington González (12/0)], Jorge Wálter Barrios Balestrasse (9/1), Ariel José Krasouski (13/2), Rúben Walter Paz Márquez (16/5), Ernesto Vargas (9/1) [Heber Bueno (2/0)], Waldemar Barreto Victorino (29/13), Jorge Torres (2/0). Trainer: Roque Gastón Máspoli (24).

474. 09.08.1981 **URUGUAY - COLOMBIA** **3-2(1-1)** 12th FIFA WC. Qualifiers
Estadio Centenario, Montevideo; Referee: Oscar Scolfaro (Brazil), Attendance: 71,000
URU: Rodolfo Sergio Rodríguez (40/0), José Hermes Moreira (21/0), Juan Carlos Blanco (8/0), Hugo Eduardo De León (18/0), Daniel Martínez (10/0), Eduardo De la Peña (17/1) [60.Jorge Wálter Barrios Balestrasse (10/1)), Ariel José Krasouski (14/2), Rúben Walter Paz Márquez (17/6), Ernesto Vargas (10/1), Julio César Araújo Morales (23/11), Waldemar Barreto Victorino (30/13). Trainer: Roque Gastón Máspoli (25).
Goals: Rúben Walter Paz Márquez (20), Julio César Araújo Morales (78, 87 penalty).

475. 23.08.1981 **URUGUAY - PERU** **1-2(0-1)** 12th FIFA WC. Qualifiers

Estadio Centenario, Montevideo; Referee: Juan Ambrosio Silvagno Cavanna (Chile), Attendance: 67,938

URU: Rodolfo Sergio Rodríguez (41/0), José Hermes Moreira (22/0), Juan Carlos Blanco (9/0), Hugo Eduardo De León (19/0), Daniel Martínez (11/0), Jorge Wálter Barrios Balestrasse (11/1) [50.Eduardo De la Peña (18/1)], Ariel José Krasouski (15/2), Rúben Walter Paz Márquez (18/6), Ernesto Vargas (11/1) [53.Heber Bueno (3/0)], Waldemar Barreto Victorino (31/14), Julio Cesar Morales (24/11). Trainer: Roque Gastón Máspoli (26).

Goal: Waldemar Barreto Victorino (64).

476. 06.09.1981 **PERU - URUGUAY** **0-0** 12th FIFA WC. Qualifiers

Estadio Nacional, Lima; Referee: Arnaldo David César Coelho (Brazil), Attendance: 45,000

URU: Rodolfo Sergio Rodríguez (42/0), José Hermes Moreira (23/0), Juan Carlos Blanco (10/0), Hugo Eduardo De León (20/0), Daniel Martínez (12/0), Jorge Wálter Barrios Balestrasse (12/1) [60.Julio César Araújo Morales (25/11)], Eduardo De la Peña (19/1), Nelson Agresta (15/1) [73.Ariel José Krasouski (16/2)], Rúben Walter Paz Márquez (19/6), Heber Bueno (4/0), Waldemar Barreto Victorino (32/14). Trainer: Roque Gastón Máspoli (27).

477. 13.09.1981 **COLOMBIA - URUGUAY** **1-1(1-1)** 12th FIFA WC. Qualifiers

Estadio „Nemesio Camacho“ 'El Campín', Bogotá; Referee: José Roberto Ramiz Wright (Brazil), Attendance: 10,000

URU: Rodolfo Sergio Rodríguez (43/0), José Hermes Moreira (24/0), Nelson Marcenaro (8/0), Juan Carlos Blanco (11/0), Daniel Martínez (13/0) [58.Washington González (13/0)], Jorge Wálter Barrios Balestrasse (13/1), Ariel José Krasouski (17/2) [46.José Luis Russo (5/0)], Rúben Walter Paz Márquez (20/6), Ernesto Vargas (12/1), Heber Bueno (5/0), Waldemar Barreto Victorino (33/15). Trainer: Roque Gastón Máspoli (28).

Goal: Waldemar Barreto Victorino (43).

478. 20.02.1982 **SOUTH KOREA - URUGUAY** **2-2(0-2)** Nehru Cup

Eden Gardens, Calcutta (India); Referee: Syed Shaid Hakim (Indonesia), Attendance: 70,000

URU: Rodolfo Sergio Rodríguez (44/0), Néstor Mario Montelongo (3/0), José Luis Russo (6/0), José Luis Ferrari (1/0), Nelson Agresta (16/1), Washington González (14/0), Jorge Wálter Barrios Balestrasse (14/1), Enzo Francéscoli Uriarte (1/0), Venancio Ariel Ramos Villanueva (16/3) [Julio Franco (2/0)], Carlos Amaro Nadal (1/1) [Mario Daniel Saralegui (5/0)], Jorge Orosmán da Silva Echeverrito (1/0). Trainer: Omar Borrás (3).

Goals: Venancio Ariel Ramos Villanueva (48 penalty), Carlos Amaro Nadal (65).

479. 22.02.1982 **CHINA - URUGUAY** **0-0** Nehru Cup

Eden Gardens, Calcutta (India); Referee: Sudhin Chatterjee (Indonesia), Attendance: 50,000

URU: Rodolfo Sergio Rodríguez (45/0), Néstor Mario Montelongo (4/0), José Luis Russo (7/0), José Luis Ferrari (2/0), Nelson Agresta (17/1), Washington González (15/0), Jorge Wálter Barrios Balestrasse (15/1), Enzo Francéscoli Uriarte (2/0), Venancio Ariel Ramos Villanueva (17/3) [Mario Daniel Saralegui (6/0)], Carlos Amaro Nadal (2/1) [Carlos Alberto Aguilera Nova (1/0)], Jorge Orosmán da Silva Echeverrito (2/0). Trainer: Omar Borrás (4).

480. 25.02.1982 **INDIA - URUGUAY** **1-3(1-2)** Nehru Cup

Eden Gardens, Calcutta (India); Referee: Zang Zhilin (China), Attendance: 75,000

URU: Rodolfo Sergio Rodríguez (46/0), Néstor Mario Montelongo (5/0), José Luis Russo (8/0), José Luis Ferrari (3/0), Nelson Agresta (18/1), Washington González (16/0), Jorge Wálter Barrios Balestrasse (16/1), Enzo Francéscoli Uriarte (3/0), Venancio Ariel Ramos Villanueva (18/3) [Carlos Alberto Aguilera Nova (2/0)], Carlos Amaro Nadal (3/1) [Mario Daniel Saralegui (7/1)], Jorge Orosmán da Silva Echeverrito (3/2). Trainer: Omar Borrás (5).

Goals: Jorge Orosmán da Silva Echeverrito (8, 23), Mario Daniel Saralegui (70).

481. 04.03.1982 **CHINA - URUGUAY** **0-2(0-1)** Nehru Cup

Eden Gardens, Calcutta (India); Referee: Pietro d'Elia (Italy), Attendance: 80,000

URU: Rodolfo Sergio Rodríguez (47/0), Néstor Mario Montelongo (6/0), José Luis Russo (9/0), José Luis Ferrari (4/0), Nelson Agresta (19/1), Washington González (17/0), Jorge Wálter Barrios Balestrasse (17/1), Enzo Francéscoli Uriarte (4/0), Venancio Ariel Ramos Villanueva (19/3) [Carlos Alberto Aguilera Nova (3/0)], Carlos Amaro Nadal (4/2), Jorge Orosmán da Silva Echeverrito (4/3) [Mario Daniel Saralegui (8/1)]. Trainer: Omar Borrás (6).

Goals: Jorge Orosmán da Silva Echeverrito (23), Carlos Amaro Nadal (84).

482. 02.06.1983 **PARAGUAY - URUGUAY** **0-0** Copa Artigas

Estadio Defensores del Chaco, Asunción; Referee: Carlos Rojas Martins (Brazil), Attendance: 25,000

URU: Rodolfo Sergio Rodríguez (48/0), Néstor Mario Montelongo (7/0), Nelson Daniel Gutiérrez Luongo (1/0), José Luis Russo (10/0), Washington González (18/0), Jorge Wálter Barrios Balestrasse (18/1), Nelson Agresta (20/1), Víctor Manuel Rabuñal (1/0) [Mario Daniel Saralegui (9/1)], Venancio Ariel Ramos Villanueva (20/3) [Jorge Villazán (1/0)], Fernando Morena Belaro (48/19), Wilmar Rubens Cabrera Sappa (1/0). Trainer: Omar Borrás (7).

483. 09.06.1983 **URUGUAY - PARAGUAY** **3-0** Copa Artigas

Estadio Centenario, Montevideo; Referee: Teodoro Nitti (Argentina), Attendance: 2,900

URU: Rodolfo Sergio Rodríguez (49/0), Néstor Mario Montelongo (8/0), José Luis Russo (11/0), Nelson Daniel Gutiérrez Luongo (2/0), Washington González (19/0), Jorge Wálter Barrios Balestrasse (19/1), Nelson Agresta (21/1), Víctor Manuel Rabuñal (2/0) [Roberto Arsenio Luzardo (7/0)], Venancio Ariel Ramos Villanueva (21/3), Fernando Morena Belaro (49/20), Wilmar Rubens Cabrera Sappa (2/2) [Jorge Villazán (2/0)]. Trainer: Omar Borrás (8).

Goals: Wilmar Rubens Cabrera Sappa 2, Fernando Morena.

484. 18.07.1983 **URUGUAY - PERU** **1-1(0-1)**

Estadio Centenario, Montevideo; Referee: Claudio Aquiles Busca (Chile), Attendance: 55,000

URU: Rodolfo Sergio Rodríguez (50/0), Néstor Mario Montelongo (9/0), Raúl Esnal (1/0), Nelson Daniel Gutiérrez Luongo (3/0), Washington González (20/0), Jorge Wálter Barrios Balestrasse (20/1), Nelson Agresta (22/1) [83.Mario Daniel Saralegui (10/1)], Víctor Manuel Rabuñal (3/0) [46.Roberto Arsenio Luzardo (8/1)], Wilmar Rubens Cabrera Sappa (3/2), Fernando Morena Belaro (50/20), Luis Alberto Acosta (1/0) [Carlos Alberto Aguilera Nova (4/0)]. Trainer: Omar Borrás (9).

Goal: Roberto Arsenio Luzardo (50).

485. 11.08.1983 **PERU - URUGUAY** **1-1(1-1)**

Estadio Nacional, Lima; Referee: Sergio Leiblinger (Peru), Attendance: 2,000

URU: Rodolfo Sergio Rodríguez (51/0), Carlos Eduardo Vázquez (1/0), Raúl Esnal (2/0), Eduardo Mario Acevedo Cardozo (1/0), Washington González (21/0), Jorge Wálter Barrios Balestrasse (21/1), Nelson Agresta (23/1), Juan Muhlethaler (5/1) [60.Alfredo De los Santos (22/0)], Carlos Alberto Aguilera Nova (5/0) [Antonio Alzamendi Casas (4/0)] [*sent off 64*], Wilmar Rubens Cabrera Sappa (4/2), Luis Alberto Acosta (2/0) [Jorge Villazán (3/0)]. Trainer: Omar Borrás (10).

Goal: Juan Muhlethaler (29).

486. 25.08.1983 **URUGUAY - PARAGUAY** **0-0**
Estadio Centenario, Montevideo; Referee: Ramón Ivannoe Barreto Ruíz (Uruguay), Attendance: 16,159
URU: Rodolfo Sergio Rodríguez (52/0), Carlos Eduardo Vázquez (2/0) [46.Eliseo Roque Rivero Pérez (1/0)], Raúl Esnal (3/0), Eduardo Mario Acevedo Cardozo (2/0), Washington González (22/0), Jorge Wálter Barrios Balestrasse (22/1), Nelson Agresta (24/1), Juan Muhlethaler (6/1) [70.Víctor Manuel Rabuñal (4/0)], Alberto Raúl Santelli Fernández (9/1) [61.Carlos Alberto Aguilera Nova (6/0)], Wilmar Rubens Cabrera Sappa (5/2), Luis Alberto Acosta (3/0) [70.Jorge Villazán (4/0)]. Trainer: Omar Borrás (11).

487. 01.09.1983 **URUGUAY - CHILE** **2-1(1-0)** 32nd Copa América. Group Stage
Estadio Centenario, Montevideo; Referee: Arnaldo David César Coelho (Brazil), Attendance: 30,000
URU: Rodolfo Sergio Rodríguez (53/0), Néstor Mario Montelongo (10/0), Nelson Daniel Gutiérrez Luongo (4/0) [*sent off 77*], Eduardo Mario Acevedo Cardozo (3/1), Washington González (23/0), Jorge Wálter Barrios Balestrasse (23/1), Nelson Agresta (25/1), Roberto Arsenio Luzardo (9/1) [76.Mario Daniel Saralegui (11/1)], Wilmar Rubens Cabrera Sappa (6/2), Fernando Morena Belaro (51/21), Luis Alberto Acosta (4/0) [81.Carlos Alberto Aguilera Nova (7/0)]. Trainer: Omar Borrás (12).
Goals: Eduardo Mario Acevedo Cardozo (45), Fernando Morena Belaro (63 penalty).

488. 04.09.1983 **URUGUAY - VENEZUELA** **3-0(1-0)** 32nd Copa América. Group Stage
Estadio Centenario, Montevideo; Referee: Gabriel González (Paraguay), Attendance: 52,567
URU: Rodolfo Sergio Rodríguez (54/0), Néstor Mario Montelongo (11/0), Raúl Esnal (4/0), Eduardo Mario Acevedo Cardozo (4/1), Washington González (24/0), Jorge Wálter Barrios Balestrasse (24/1), Nelson Agresta (26/1), Roberto Arsenio Luzardo (10/2), Wilmar Rubens Cabrera Sappa (7/3), Fernando Morena Belaro (52/22) [71.Carlos Alberto Aguilera Nova (8/0)], Luis Alberto Acosta (5/0) [*sent off 70*]. Trainer: Omar Borrás (13).
Goals: Wilmar Rubens Cabrera Sappa (35), Fernando Morena Belaro (51 penalty), Roberto Arsenio Luzardo (68).

489. 11.09.1983 **CHILE - URUGUAY** **2-0(1-0)** 32nd Copa América. Group Stage
Estadio Nacional, Santiago; Referee: Teodoro Nitti (Argentina), Attendance: 47,403
URU: Rodolfo Sergio Rodríguez (55/0), Néstor Mario Montelongo (12/0), Walter Daniel Olivera (27/1), Eduardo Mario Acevedo Cardozo (5/1), Washington González (25/0), Jorge Wálter Barrios Balestrasse (25/1), Nelson Agresta (27/1), Roberto Arsenio Luzardo (11/2), Alfredo De los Santos (23/0) [70.Carlos Alberto Aguilera Nova (9/0)], Wilmar Rubens Cabrera Sappa (8/3), Jorge Villazán (5/0). Trainer: Omar Borrás (14).

490. 18.09.1983 **VENEZUELA - URUGUAY** **1-2(0-0)** 32nd Copa América. Group Stage
Estadio Nacional „Brígido Iriarte", Caracas; Referee: Carlos Montalván (Peru), Attendance: 3,000
URU: Rodolfo Sergio Rodríguez (56/0), Néstor Mario Montelongo (13/0), Walter Daniel Olivera (28/1), Eduardo Mario Acevedo Cardozo (6/1), Washington González (26/0), Jorge Wálter Barrios Balestrasse (26/1), Nelson Agresta (28/1) [70.Alberto Raúl Santelli Fernández (10/2)], Mario Daniel Saralegui (12/1) [58.Víctor Hugo Diogo Silva (14/0)], Carlos Alberto Aguilera Nova (10/1), Wilmar Rubens Cabrera Sappa (9/3), Luis Alberto Acosta (6/0). Trainer: Omar Borrás (15).
Goals: Alberto Raúl Santelli Fernández (74), Carlos Alberto Aguilera Nova (87).

491. 21.09.1983 **SCOTLAND - URUGUAY** **2-0(1-0)**
Hampden Park, Glasgow; Referee: David Richardson (England), Attendance: 20,545
URU: Rodolfo Sergio Rodríguez (57/0), Víctor Hugo Diogo Silva (15/0), Washington González (27/0), Nelson Daniel Gutiérrez Luongo (5/0), Eduardo Mario Acevedo Cardozo (7/1), Nelson Agresta (29/1), Venancio Ariel Ramos Villanueva (22/3) [70.Néstor Mario Montelongo (14/0)], Mario Daniel Saralegui (13/1), Alberto Raúl Santelli Fernández (11/2) [70.Carlos Alberto Aguilera Nova (11/1)], Jorge Wálter Barrios Balestrasse (27/1), Luis Alberto Acosta (7/0) [Alfredo De los Santos (24/0)]. Trainer: Omar Borrás (16).

492. 26.09.1983 **ISRAEL - URUGUAY** **2-2(0-1)**
Bloomfield Stadium, Jaffa, Tel-Aviv; Referee: Nicolae Rainea (ROMANIA), Attendance: 5,000
URU: Rodolfo Sergio Rodríguez (58/0), Néstor Mario Montelongo (15/0) [Víctor Hugo Diogo Silva (16/0)], Washington González (28/0), Walter Daniel Olivera (29/1), Eduardo Mario Acevedo Cardozo (8/1), Jorge Wálter Barrios Balestrasse (28/1), Nelson Agresta (30/1), Mario Daniel Saralegui (14/1) [Alfredo De Los Santos (25/0)], Carlos Alberto Aguilera Nova (12/3) [Mauricio Joselito Silvera (1/0)], Alberto Raúl Santelli Fernández (12/2), Venancio Ariel Ramos Villanueva (23/3) [Luis Alberto Acosta (8/0)]. Trainer: Omar Borrás (17).
Goals: Carlos Alberto Aguilera Nova (10, 83).

493. 13.10.1983 **PERU - URUGUAY** **0-1(0-0)** 32nd Copa América. Semi-Finals
Estadio Nacional, Lima; Referee: Sergio Vázquez (Chile), Attendance: 28,000
URU: Rodolfo Sergio Rodríguez (59/0), Víctor Hugo Diogo Silva (17/0), Nelson Daniel Gutiérrez Luongo (6/0), Eduardo Mario Acevedo Cardozo (9/1), Washington González (29/0), Jorge Wálter Barrios Balestrasse (29/1), Nelson Agresta (31/1), Enzo Francéscoli Uriarte (5/0), Carlos Alberto Aguilera Nova (13/4) [80.Mario Daniel Saralegui (15/1)], Wilmar Rubens Cabrera Sappa (10/3), Luis Alberto Acosta (9/0) [77.Venancio Ariel Ramos Villanueva (24/3)]. Trainer: Omar Borrás (18).
Goal: Carlos Alberto Aguilera Nova (65).

494. 20.10.1983 **URUGUAY - PERU** **1-1(0-1)** 32nd Copa América. Semi-Finals
Estadio Centenario, Montevideo; Referee: Arturo Andrés Ithurralde (Argentina), Attendance: 58,000
URU: Rodolfo Sergio Rodríguez (60/0), Víctor Hugo Diogo Silva (18/0), Nelson Daniel Gutiérrez Luongo (7/0), Eduardo Mario Acevedo Cardozo (10/1), Washington González (30/0), Jorge Wálter Barrios Balestrasse (30/1), Nelson Agresta (32/1), Enzo Francéscoli Uriarte (6/0), Carlos Alberto Aguilera Nova (14/4) [75.Mario Daniel Saralegui (16/1)] [*sent off 79*], Wilmar Rubens Cabrera Sappa (11/4), Luis Alberto Acosta (10/0) [71.Venancio Ariel Ramos Villanueva (25/3)]. Trainer: Omar Borrás (19).
Goal: Wilmar Rubens Cabrera Sappa (49).

495. 27.10.1983 **URUGUAY - BRAZIL** **2-0(1-0)** 32nd Copa América. Final
Estadio Centenario, Montevideo; Referee: Héctor Froilan Ortíz Ramírez (Paraguay), Attendance: 65,000
URU: Rodolfo Sergio Rodríguez (61/0), Víctor Hugo Diogo Silva (19/1), Nelson Daniel Gutiérrez Luongo (8/0), Eduardo Mario Acevedo Cardozo (11/1), Washington González (31/0), Jorge Wálter Barrios Balestrasse (31/1), Nelson Agresta (33/1), Enzo Francéscoli Uriarte (7/1), Carlos Alberto Aguilera Nova (15/4) [85.Miguel Angel Bossio Bastianini (1/0)], Wilmar Rubens Cabrera Sappa (12/4), Luis Alberto Acosta (11/0) [75.Venancio Ariel Ramos Villanueva (26/3)]. Trainer: Omar Borrás (20).
Goals: Enzo Francéscoli Uriarte (41), Víctor Hugo Diogo Silva (80).

496. 04.11.1983 **BRAZIL - URUGUAY** **1-1(1-0)** 32nd Copa América. Final

Estádio Fonte Nova, Salvador; Referee: Edison Pérez Núñez (Peru), Attendance: 95,000

URU: Rodolfo Sergio Rodríguez (62/0), Víctor Hugo Diogo Silva (20/1), Nelson Daniel Gutiérrez Luongo (9/0), Eduardo Mario Acevedo Cardozo (12/1), Washington González (32/0), Jorge Wálter Barrios Balestrasse (32/1), Nelson Agresta (34/1), Enzo Francéscoli Uriarte (8/1), Carlos Alberto Aguilera Nova (16/5) [82.Miguel Angel Bossio Bastianini (2/0)], Wilmar Rubens Cabrera Sappa (13/4), Luis Alberto Acosta (12/0) [46.Venancio Ariel Ramos Villanueva (27/3)]. Trainer: Omar Borrás (21).

Goal: Carlos Alberto Aguilera Nova (77).

497. 13.06.1984 **URUGUAY - ENGLAND** **2-0(1-0)** Copa William Poole

Estadio Centenario, Montevideo; Referee: Lucio González (Paraguay), Attendance: 34,500

URU: Rodolfo Sergio Rodríguez (63/0), Nelson Daniel Gutiérrez Luongo (10/0), Eduardo Mario Acevedo Cardozo (13/1), Néstor Mario Montelongo (16/0) [Carlos Eduardo Vázquez (3/0)], Miguel Angel Bossio Bastianini (3/0), Daniel Martínez (14/0), Carlos Alberto Aguilera Nova (17/5), Ricardo Javier Perdomo (1/0), Wilmar Rubens Cabrera Sappa (14/5), Juan Ramón Carrasco Torres (15/1) [José Luis Zalazar Rodríguez (1/0)], Luis Alberto Acosta (13/1) [Rubén Sosa Ardáiz (1/0)]. Trainer: Omar Borrás (22).

Goals: Luis Alberto Acosta (8 penalty), Wilmar Rubens Cabrera Sappa (68).

498. 21.06.1984 **BRAZIL - URUGUAY** **1-0(0-0)**

Estádio „Antônio Couto Pereira", Curitiba; Referee: Gastón Edmundo Castro Makuc (Chile), Attendance: 41,000

URU: Rodolfo Sergio Rodríguez (64/0), Néstor Mario Montelongo (17/0), Nelson Daniel Gutiérrez Luongo (11/0), Eduardo Mario Acevedo Cardozo (14/1), Daniel Martínez (15/0), Ricardo Javier Perdomo (2/0) [José Luis Zalazar Rodríguez (2/0)], Miguel Angel Bossio Bastianini (4/0), Sergio Rodolfo Santín (2/0), Carlos Alberto Aguilera Nova (18/5), Roberto Inzúa (1/0), Luis Alberto Acosta (14/1) [Rubén Sosa Ardáiz (2/0)]. Trainer: Omar Borrás (23).

499. 18.07.1984 **URUGUAY - ARGENTINA** **1-0(0-0)**

Estadio Centenario, Montevideo; Referee: Edison Pérez Núñez (Peru), Attendance: 56,000

URU: José Luis Sosa (1/0), Néstor Mario Montelongo (18/0), Nelson Daniel Gutiérrez Luongo (12/0), Eduardo Mario Acevedo Cardozo (15/1), Daniel Martínez (16/0), Jorge Wálter Barrios Balestrasse (33/2), Miguel Angel Bossio Bastianini (5/0), Miguel Rosifredo Caillava (8/0) [José Luis Zalazar Rodríguez (3/0)], Carlos Alberto Aguilera Nova (19/5), Carlos Amaro Nadal (5/2), Wilmar Rubens Cabrera Sappa (15/5). Trainer: Omar Borrás (24).

Goal: Jorge Wálter Barrios Balestrasse (63).

500. 02.08.1984 **ARGENTINA - URUGUAY** **0-0**

Estadio Monumental „Antonio Vespucio Liberti", Buenos Aires; Referee: Juan Francisco Escobar Váldez (Paraguay), Attendance: 15,000

URU: José Luis Sosa (2/0), Néstor Mario Montelongo (19/0), Nelson Daniel Gutiérrez Luongo (13/0), Eduardo Mario Acevedo Cardozo (16/1) [*sent off 70*], Daniel Martínez (17/0) [*sent off 89*], Jorge Wálter Barrios Balestrasse (34/2), Miguel Angel Bossio Bastianini (6/0), Ricardo Javier Perdomo (3/0) [Mario Daniel Saralegui (17/1)], José Luis Zalazar Rodríguez (4/0), Carlos Alberto Aguilera Nova (20/5) [José Villareal (1/0)], Rubén Sosa Ardáiz (3/0) [César Javier Vega (1/0)]. Trainer: Omar Borrás (25).

501. 19.09.1984 **URUGUAY - PERU** **2-0(1-0)**

Estadio Centenario, Montevideo; Referee: Carlos Rojas Martins (Brazil), Attendance: 560

URU: José Luis Sosa (3/0), Néstor Mario Montelongo (20/0), Nelson Daniel Gutiérrez Luongo (14/0), César Javier Vega (2/0), José Alberto Batista González (1/0), Jorge Wálter Barrios Balestrasse (35/2), Miguel Angel Bossio Bastianini (7/0), Miguel Rosifredo Caillava (9/0) [72.José Luis Zalazar Rodríguez (5/1)], Carlos Alberto Aguilera Nova (21/6), Carlos Amaro Nadal (6/2), Rubén Sosa Ardáiz (4/0) [José Villareal (2/0)]. Trainer: Omar Borrás (26).

Goals: Carlos Alberto Aguilera Nova (7), José Luis Zalazar Rodríguez (90).

502. 03.10.1984 **PERU - URUGUAY** **1-3(0-1)**

Estadio Nacional, Lima; Referee: Abel Gnecco (Argentina), Attendance: 15,000

URU: José Luis Sosa (4/0), Néstor Mario Montelongo (21/0), Nelson Daniel Gutiérrez Luongo (15/0), Eduardo Mario Acevedo Cardozo (17/1), Daniel Martínez (18/0), Jorge Wálter Barrios Balestrasse (36/3), Miguel Angel Bossio Bastianini (8/0), Sergio Rodolfo Santín (3/0) [71.José Luis Zalazar Rodríguez (6/1)], Carlos Alberto Aguilera Nova (22/7) [77.José Villareal (3/0)], Carlos Amaro Nadal (7/3), Rubén Sosa Ardáiz (5/0) [77.Ricardo Javier Perdomo (4/0)]. Trainer: Omar Borrás (27).

Goals: Jorge Wálter Barrios Balestrasse (5), Carlos Alberto Aguilera Nova (53), Carlos Amaro Nadal (71 penalty).

503. 31.10.1984 **URUGUAY - MEXICO** **1-1(0-0)**

Estadio Centenario, Montevideo; Referee: Jorge Eduardo Romero (Argentina), Attendance: 50,950

URU: José Luis Sosa (5/0), Néstor Mario Montelongo (22/0), Nelson Daniel Gutiérrez Luongo (16/0), Eduardo Mario Acevedo Cardozo (18/1), Daniel Martínez (19/0), Jorge Wálter Barrios Balestrasse (37/3), Miguel Angel Bossio Bastianini (9/0), Enzo Francéscoli Uriarte (9/1), Carlos Alberto Aguilera Nova (23/7), Carlos Amaro Nadal (8/4), Rubén Sosa Ardáiz (6/0) [72.JoséVillareal (4/0)]. Trainer: Omar Borrás (28).

Goal: Carlos Amaro Nadal (82).

504. 29.01.1985 **URUGUAY - EAST GERMANY** **3-0(1-0)**

Estadio Centenario, Montevideo; Referee: Juan Cardellino do San Vincente (Uruguay), Attendance: 80,000

URU: Rodolfo Sergio Rodríguez (65/0), Néstor Mario Montelongo (23/0) [Víctor Hugo Diogo Silva (21/1)], Daniel Martínez (20/0), Nelson Daniel Gutiérrez Luongo (17/0), Eduardo Mario Acevedo Cardozo (19/1), Miguel Angel Bossio Bastianini (10/0) [Alfonso Darío Pereyra Bueno (22/5)], Carlos Alberto Aguilera Nova (24/8), Jorge Wálter Barrios Balestrasse (38/3) [Mario Daniel Saralegui (18/1)], Carlos Amaro Nadal (9/4) [Sergio Rodolfo Santín (4/0)], Enzo Francéscoli Uriarte (10/2), Jorge Orosmán da Silva Echeverrito (5/4). Trainer: Omar Borrás (29).

Goals: Carlos Alberto Aguilera Nova (37), Jorge Orosmán da Silva Echeverrito (78), Enzo Francéscoli Uriarte (84).

505. 03.02.1985 **URUGUAY - PARAGUAY** **1-0** Copa Artigas

Estadio Centenario, Montevideo; Referee: Artemio Santiago Seneción (Uruguay), Attendance: 55,794

URU: Rodolfó Sergio Rodríguez (66/0), Néstor Mario Montelongo (24/0) [Víctor Hugo Diogo Silva (22/1)], Nelson Daniel Gutiérrez Luongo (18/0), Eduardo Mario Acevedo Cardozo (20/1), Daniel Martínez (21/0) [José Alberto Batista González (2/0)], Jorge Wálter Barrios Balestrasse (39/3), Miguel Angel Bossio Bastianini (11/0), Enzo Francéscoli Uriarte (11/3), Carlos Alberto Aguilera Nova (25/8) [José Luis Zalazar Rodríguez (7/1)], Carlos Amaro Nadal (10/4), Jorge Orosmán da Silva Echeverrito (6/4) [*sent off*]. Trainer: Omar Borrás (30).

Goal: Enzo Francéscoli Uriarte.

506. 06.02.1985 **BOLIVIA – URUGUAY** **0-1(0-0)**
Estadio „Félix Capriles“, Cochabamba; Referee: Armando Aliaga (Bolivia), Attendance: 20,000
URU: Rodolfo Sergio Rodríguez (67/0), Néstor Mario Montelongo (25/0) [Víctor Hugo Diogo Silva (23/1)], Nelson Daniel Gutiérrez Luongo (19/0), Eduardo Mario Acevedo Cardozo (21/1), Daniel Martínez (22/0), Jorge Wálter Barrios Balestrasse (40/3), Alfonso Darío Pereyra Bueno (23/5), Miguel Angel Bossio Bastianini (12/0) [Mario Daniel Saralegui (19/1)], Sergio Rodolfo Santín (5/0) [José Luis Zalazar Rodríguez (8/1)], Carlos Amaro Nadal (11/4), Enzo Francéscoli Uriarte (12/4). Trainer: Omar Borrás (31).
Goal: Enzo Francéscoli Uriarte (89).

507. 10.02.1985 **PARAGUAY – URUGUAY** **1-3(0-2)** Copa Artigas
Estadio Defensores del Chaco, Asunción; Referee: Gabriel González (Paraguay), Attendance: 20,000
URU: Rodolfó Sergio Rodríguez (68/0), Néstor Mario Montelongo (26/0) [Víctor Hugo Diogo Silva (24/1)], Nelson Daniel Gutiérrez Luongo (20/0), Eduardo Mario Acevedo Cardozo (22/1), Daniel Martínez (23/0), Jorge Wálter Barrios Balestrasse (41/3), Miguel Angel Bossio Bastianini (13/0) [Alfonso Darío Pereyra Bueno (24/5)], Enzo Francéscoli Uriarte (13/4) [*sent off*], Carlos Alberto Aguilera Nova (26/8) [Mario Daniel Saralegui (20/1)] [*sent off*], Carlos Amaro Nadal (12/7), Jorge Orosmán da Silva Echeverrito (7/4) [Sergio Rodolfo Santín (6/0)]. Trainer: Omar Borrás (32).
Goals: Carlos Amaro Nadal (14, 44, 65).

508. 14.02.1985 **URUGUAY – FINLAND** **2-1(2-1)**
Estadio Centenario, Montevideo; Referee: Ramón Ivannoe Barreto Ruíz (Uruguay), Attendance: 29,735
URU: Rodolfo Sergio Rodríguez (69/0), Néstor Mario Montelongo (27/0) [José Alberto Batista González (3/0)], Daniel Martínez (24/0), Nelson Daniel Gutiérrez Luongo (21/0), Eduardo Mario Acevedo Cardozo (23/1), Miguel Angel Bossio Bastianini (14/0) [Alfonso Darío Pereyra Bueno (25/5)], Carlos Alberto Aguilera Nova (27/9) [José Luis Zalazar Rodríguez (9/1)], Jorge Wálter Barrios Balestrasse (42/3), Carlos Amaro Nadal (13/8), Sergio Rodolfo Santín (7/0), Jorge Orosmán da Silva Echeverrito (8/4). Trainer: Omar Borrás (33).
Goals: Carlos Alberto Aguilera Nova (30), Carlos Amaro Nadal (35).

509. 24.02.1985 **URUGUAY – COLOMBIA** **3-0(2-0)**
Estadio Centenario, Montevideo; Referee: José Luis Martínez Bazán (Uruguay), Attendance: 42,585
URU: Rodolfó Sergio Rodríguez (70/0), Néstor Mario Montelongo (28/0), Nelson Daniel Gutiérrez Luongo (22/0), Eduardo Mario Acevedo Cardozo (24/1), Daniel Martínez (25/0), Jorge Wálter Barrios Balestrasse (43/3), Miguel Angel Bossio Bastianini (15/0) [Alfonso Darío Pereyra Bueno (26/5)], Enzo Francéscoli Uriarte (14/5) [Sergio Rodolfo Santín (8/0)], Carlos Alberto Aguilera Nova (28/10) [Venancio Ariel Ramos Villanueva (28/3)], Carlos Amaro Nadal (14/9), Jorge Orosmán da Silva Echeverrito (9/4) [Wilmar Rubens Cabrera Sappa (16/5)]. Trainer: Omar Borrás (34).
Goals: Carlos Alberto Aguilera Nova (19), Enzo Francéscoli Uriarte (42), Carlos Amaro Nadal (89 penalty).

510. 27.02.1985 **URUGUAY – PERU** **2-2(1-1)**
Estadio Centenario, Montevideo; Referee: Ernesto Filippi (Uruguay), Attendance: 48,699
URU: Rodolfó Sergio Rodríguez (71/0), Néstor Mario Montelongo (29/0) [53.Víctor Hugo Diogo Silva (25/1)], Nelson Daniel Gutiérrez Luongo (23/0), Eduardo Mario Acevedo Cardozo (25/1), Daniel Martínez (26/0), Jorge Wálter Barrios Balestrasse (44/3), Miguel Angel Bossio Bastianini (16/0) [65.Alfonso Darío Pereyra Bueno (27/5)], Enzo Francéscoli Uriarte (15/5), Carlos Alberto Aguilera Nova (29/10) [69.Venancio Ariel Ramos Villanueva (29/3)], Carlos Amaro Nadal (15/10) [53.Jorge Orosmán da Silva Echeverrito (10/4)], Wilmar Rubens Cabrera Sappa (17/6). Trainer: Omar Borrás (35).
Goals: Carlos Amaro Nadal (44), Wilmar Rubens Cabrera Sappa (90).

511. 10.03.1985 **URUGUAY – ECUADOR** **2-1(1-0)** 13th FIFA WC. Qualifiers
Estadio Centenario, Montevideo; Referee: Édison Pérez (Peru), Attendance: 65,000
URU: Rodolfó Sergio Rodríguez (72/0), Néstor Mario Montelongo (30/0), Nelson Daniel Gutiérrez Luongo (24/0), Eduardo Mario Acevedo Cardozo (26/1), Daniel Martínez (27/0), Jorge Wálter Barrios Balestrasse (45/3) [65.Venancio Ariel Ramos Villanueva (30/4)], Miguel Angel Bossio Bastianini (17/0), Enzo Francéscoli Uriarte (16/5), Carlos Alberto Aguilera Nova (30/11), Carlos Amaro Nadal (16/10), Jorge Orosmán da Silva Echeverrito (11/4) [59.Wilmar Rubens Cabrera Sappa (18/6)]. Trainer: Omar Borrás (36).
Goals: Carlos Alberto Aguilera Nova (34), Venancio Ariel Ramos Villanueva (90).

512. 24.03.1985 **CHILE – URUGUAY** **2-0(1-0)** 13th FIFA WC. Qualifiers
Estadio Nacional, Santiago; Referee: Jesús Díaz Palacios (Colombia), Attendance: 79,911
URU: Rodolfó Sergio Rodríguez (73/0), Néstor Mario Montelongo (31/0), Nelson Daniel Gutiérrez Luongo (25/0), Eduardo Mario Acevedo Cardozo (27/1), Víctor Hugo Diogo Silva (26/1), Jorge Wálter Barrios Balestrasse (46/3) [58.Venancio Ariel Ramos Villanueva (31/4)], Miguel Angel Bossio Bastianini (18/0), Sergio Rodolfo Santín (9/0), Enzo Francéscoli Uriarte (17/5), Carlos Alberto Aguilera Nova (31/11) [58.Carlos Amaro Nadal (17/10)], Wilmar Rubens Cabrera Sappa (19/6). Trainer: Omar Borrás (37).

513. 31.03.1985 **ECUADOR – URUGUAY** **0-2(0-0)** 13th FIFA WC. Qualifiers
Estadio Olimpico „Atahualpa“, Quito; Referee: Juan Francisco Escobar Váldez (Paraguay), Attendance: 30,000
URU: Rodolfó Sergio Rodríguez (74/0), Víctor Hugo Diogo Silva (27/1), Nelson Daniel Gutiérrez Luongo (26/0), Alfonso Darío Pereyra Bueno (28/5), José Alberto Batista González (4/0), Mario Daniel Saralegui (21/2), Miguel Angel Bossio Bastianini (19/0), Sergio Rodolfo Santín (10/0), Enzo Francéscoli Uriarte (18/6), Venancio Ariel Ramos Villanueva (32/4) [72.Wilmar Rubens Cabrera Sappa (20/6)], Carlos Amaro Nadal (18/10) [55.Jorge Orosmán da Silva Echeverrito (12/4)]. Trainer: Omar Borrás (38).
Goals: Mario Daniel Saralegui (71), Enzo Francéscoli Uriarte (87).

514. 07.04.1985 **URUGUAY – CHILE** **2-1(1-1)** 13th FIFA WC. Qualifiers
Estadio Centenario, Montevideo; Referee: Carlos Alfonso Espósito (Argentina), Attendance: 66,500
URU: Rodolfó Sergio Rodríguez (75/0), Néstor Mario Montelongo (32/0), Nelson Daniel Gutiérrez Luongo (27/0), Alfonso Darío Pereyra Bueno (29/5), José Alberto Batista González (5/1), Mario Daniel Saralegui (22/2), Miguel Angel Bossio Bastianini (20/0), Sergio Rodolfo Santín (11/0), Enzo Francéscoli Uriarte (19/6), Venancio Ariel Ramos Villanueva (33/5) [89.Wilmar Rubens Cabrera Sappa (21/6)], Carlos Amaro Nadal (19/10) [70.Jorge Orosmán da Silva Echeverrito (13/4)]. Trainer: Omar Borrás (39).
Goal: José Alberto Batista González (10), Venancio Ariel Ramos Villanueva (57 penalty).

515. 23.04.1985 **PERU – URUGUAY** **2-1(1-1)**
Estadio Nacional, Lima; Referee: Edison Pérez Núñez (Peru), Attendance: 70,000
URU: Gualberto Velichco (1/0), Néstor Mario Montelongo (33/0), César Javier Vega (3/0) [*sent off 55*], Eduardo Mario Acevedo Cardozo (28/1), Daniel Martínez (28/0), Jorge Wálter Barrios Balestrasse (47/3), Abraham Yeladián (1/0), Juan Ramón Carrasco Torres (16/2) [70.Jesús Alzugaray (1/0)], Julio César Ribas (1/0) [58.Ricardo Javier Perdomo (5/0)], Carlos Alberto Aguilera Nova (32/11) [65.Jacinto Javier Cabrera López (1/0)], Jorge Orosmán da Silva Echeverrito (14/4). Trainer: Omar Borrás (40).
Goal: Juan Ramón Carrasco Torres (24).

516. 28.04.1985 **COLOMBIA – URUGUAY** **2-1(1-0)**
Estadio „Nemesio Camacho" 'El Campín', Bogotá; Referee: Alirio Blanquiceth Montoya (Colombia), Attendance: 15.,000
URU: Gualberto Velichco (2/0), Néstor Mario Montelongo (34/0), César Javier Vega (4/0), Eduardo Mario Acevedo Cardozo (29/1), Daniel Martínez (29/0), Jorge Wálter Barrios Balestrasse (48/3), Abraham Yeladián (2/0), Juan Ramón Carrasco Torres (17/2) [Jesús Alzugaray (2/0)], Julio César Ribas (2/0) [Ricardo Javier Perdomo (6/0), Juan Pedro Rabino (1/0)], Carlos Alberto Aguilera Nova (33/12) [Jacinto Javier Cabrera López (2/0)], Jorge Orosmán da Silva Echeverrito (15/4). Trainer: Omar Borrás (41).
Goal: Carlos Alberto Aguilera Nova (47).

517. 02.05.1985 **BRAZIL – URUGUAY** **2-0(1-0)**
Estádio Arruda, Recife; Referee: Elías Victoriano Jácome Guerreiro (Ecuador), Attendance: 60,000
URU: Gualberto Velichco (3/0), Néstor Mario Montelongo (35/0), José Luis Russo (12/0), Eduardo Mario Acevedo Cardozo (30/1), Daniel Martínez (30/0), Jorge Wálter Barrios Balestrasse (49/3), Abraham Yeladián (3/0) [Ricardo Javier Perdomo (7/0)], Juan Ramón Carrasco Torres (18/2) [*sent off 48*], Julio César Ribas (3/0) [*sent off 58*], Carlos Alberto Aguilera Nova (34/12) [Jacinto Javier Cabrera López (3/0)], Jorge Orosmán da Silva Echeverrito (16/4). Trainer: Omar Borrás (42).

518. 26.05.1985 **JAPAN – URUGUAY** **1-4(1-1)** Kirin Cup
National Stadium, Tokyo; Referee: Henrik van Ettekoven (Holland), Attendance: 30,000
URU: Gualberto Velichco (4/0), Néstor Mario Montelongo (36/0), José Luis Russo (13/0), Eduardo Mario Acevedo Cardozo (31/1), Julio César Pereira (1/0), Abraham Yeladián (4/0), Jorge Wálter Barrios Balestrasse (50/3), Julio César Ribas (4/0) [Jacinto Javier Cabrera López (4/0)], Carlos Alberto Aguilera Nova (35/14), Juan Ramón Carrasco Torres (19/2), Jorge Orosmán da Silva Echeverrito (17/6) [Jesús Alzugaray (3/0)]. Trainer: Omar Borrás (43).
Goals: Carlos Alberto Aguilera Nova (44), Jorge Orosmán da Silva Echeverrito (51), Carlos Alberto Aguilera Nova (73), Jorge Orosmán da Silva Echeverrito (69).

519. 01.06.1985 **URUGUAY – MALAYSIA** **6-0(2-0)** Kirin Cup
Nagai Stadium, Osaka
URU: Gualberto Velichco (5/0), Néstor Mario Montelongo (37/0), José Luis Russo (14/0), Eduardo Mario Acevedo Cardozo (32/1), Julio César Pereira (2/1), Heber Silva Cantera (1/0) [César Javier Vega (5/0)], Jorge Wálter Barrios Balestrasse (51/4), Juan Ramón Carrasco Torres (20/3) [Julio César Ribas (5/0)], Carlos Alberto Aguilera Nova (36/15), Jacinto Javier Cabrera López (5/1), Jesús Alzugaray (4/1). Trainer: Omar Borrás (44).
Goals: Juan Ramón Carrasco Torres (20), Julio César Pereira (42), Jesús Alzugaray (50), Jorge Wálter Barrios Balestrasse (64), Carlos Alberto Aguilera Nova (66), Jacinto Javier Cabrera López (87).

520. 21.08.1985 **FRANCE – URUGUAY** **2-0(1-0)** Artemio Franchi Cup
Stade Parc des Princes, Paris; Referee: Abel Gnecco (Argentina), Attendance: 20,405
URU: Rodolfo Sergio Rodríguez (76/0), Víctor Hugo Diogo Silva (28/1), José Alberto Batista González (6/1), Nelson Daniel Gutiérrez Luongo (28/0), Alfonso Darío Pereyra Bueno (30/5), Miguel Angel Bossio Bastianini (21/0), Venancio Ariel Ramos Villanueva (34/5), Jorge Wálter Barrios Balestrasse (52/4) [Mario Daniel Saralegui (23/2)], Enzo Francéscoli Uriarte (20/6), Sergio Rodolfo Santín (12/0), Wilmar Rubens Cabrera Sappa (22/6) [Gustavo Dalto (1/0)]. Trainer: Omar Borrás (45).

521. 17.10.1985 **CHILE – URUGUAY** **1-0(1-0)**
Estadio Nacional, Santiago; Referee: Víctor Ojeda (Chile), Attendance: 25,000
URU: Fernando Harry Álvez Mosquera (2/0), Julio César Pereira (3/1), César Javier Vega (6/0), Eduardo Mario Acevedo Cardozo (33/1), Eliseo Roque Rivero Pérez (2/0), Santiago Javier Ostolaza Sosa (1/0), Miguel Angel Bossio Bastianini (22/0), José Luis Zalazar Rodríguez (10/1), Mauricio Joselito Silvera (2/0), Rogelio Néstor Ramírez (1/0) [Daniel Sergio Oddine (1/0)], Gustavo Dalto (2/0) [Abraham Yeladián (5/0)]. Trainer: Omar Borrás (46).

522. 02.02.1986 **URUGUAY – CANADA** **3-1(1-1)** Marlboro Cup
Orange Bowl, Miami (United States); Referee: Angelo Bratsis (United States), Attendance: 15,054
URU: Fernando Harry Álvez Mosquera (3/0), Mario Menchaca (1/0), Eliseo Roque Rivero Pérez (3/0), José Luis Russo (15/0), Eduardo Mario Acevedo Cardozo (34/1), Miguel Angel Bossio Bastianini (23/0), Carlos Alberto Aguilera Nova (37/16), Santiago Javier Ostolaza Sosa (2/1), Rogelio Néstor Ramírez (2/0) [Enrique Raúl Báez (1/0)], José Luis Zalazar Rodríguez (11/2) [Pablo Javier Bengoechea Dutra (1/0)], Mauricio Joselito Silvera (3/0). Trainer: Omar Borrás (47).
Goals: Carlos Alberto Aguilera Nova (26), Santiago Javier Ostolaza Sosa (53), José Luis Zalazar Rodríguez (60).

523. 07.02.1986 **UNITED STATES – URUGUAY** **1-1(1-0)** Marlboro Cup
Orange Bowl, Miami; Referee: Marco Dorantes (Mexico), Attendance: 15,852
URU: Fernando Harry Álvez Mosquera (4/0), Mario Menchaca (2/0) [Julio César Pereira (4/1)], Eliseo Roque Rivero Pérez (4/0), José Luis Russo (16/0), Eduardo Mario Acevedo Cardozo (35/1), Miguel Angel Bossio Bastianini (24/0), Carlos Alberto Aguilera Nova (38/17), Santiago Javier Ostolaza Sosa (3/1) [Pablo Javier Bengoechea Dutra (2/0)], Rogelio Néstor Ramírez (3/0) [Enrique Raúl Báez (2/0)], José Luis Zalazar Rodríguez (12/2), Mauricio Joselito Silvera (4/0). Trainer: Omar Borrás (48).
Goal: Carlos Alberto Aguilera Nova (79).

524. 16.02.1986 **URUGUAY – POLAND** **2-2(0-1)**
Estadio Centenario, Montevideo; Referee: Juan Daniel Cardellino de San Vicente (Uruguay), Attendance: 44,000
URU: Fernando Harry Álvez Mosquera (5/0), Mario Menchaca (3/0), Eliseo Roque Rivero Pérez (5/0), César Javier Vega (7/0), Eduardo Mario Acevedo Cardozo (36/1), Miguel Angel Bossio Bastianini (25/1), Carlos Alberto Aguilera Nova (39/17), Santiago Javier Ostolaza Sosa (4/1) [55.Pablo Javier Bengoechea Dutra (3/0)], Enrique Raúl Báez (3/0), José Luis Zalazar Rodríguez (13/3), Mauricio Joselito Silvera (5/0). Trainer: Omar Borrás (49).
Goals: Miguel Angel Bossio Bastianini (61), José Luis Zalazar Rodríguez (78).

525. 13.04.1986 **MEXICO – URUGUAY** **1-0(1-0)**
Memorial Coliseum, Los Angeles; Referee: Angelo Bratsis (United States), Attendance: 46,000
URU: Rodolfo Sergio Rodríguez (77/0), Mario Daniel Saralegui (24/2) [46.Víctor Hugo Diogo Silva (29/1)], Nelson Daniel Gutiérrez Luongo (29/0), Eduardo Mario Acevedo Cardozo (37/1), José Alberto Batista González (7/1), Sergio Rodolfo Santín (13/0), Miguel Angel Bossio Bastianini (26/1), José Luis Zalazar Rodríguez (14/3) [46.Enzo Francéscoli Uriarte (21/6)], Antonio Alzamendi Casas (5/0) [67.Venancio Ariel Ramos Villanueva (35/5)], Wilmar Rubens Cabrera Sappa (23/6) [46.Jorge Orosmán da Silva Echeverrito (18/6)], Mauricio Joselito Silvera (6/0) [24.Rubén Sosa Ardáiz (7/0)]. Trainer: Omar Borrás (50).

526. 21.04.1986 **WALES - URUGUAY** **0-0**
Racecourse Stadium, Wrexham; Referee: Thomas O'Donnelly (Northern Ireland), Attendance: 11,154
URU: Rodolfo Sergio Rodríguez (78/0), Víctor Hugo Diogo Silva (30/1), José Alberto Batista González (8/1), Nelson Daniel Gutiérrez Luongo (30/0), Eduardo Mario Acevedo Cardozo (38/1), Miguel Angel Bossio Bastianini (27/1) [Mario Daniel Saralegui (25/2)], Antonio Alzamendi Casas (6/0), Jorge Wálter Barrios Balestrasse (53/4), Enzo Francéscoli Uriarte (22/6), Sergio Rodolfo Santín (14/0), Jorge Orosmán da Silva Echeverrito (19/6). Trainer: Omar Borrás (51).

527. 23.04.1986 **REPUBLIC OF IRELAND - URUGUAY** **1-1(1-1)**
Landsdowne Road, Dublin; Referee: John Martin (England), Attendance: 15,000
URU: Fernando Harry Álvez Mosquera (6/0), Víctor Hugo Diogo Silva (31/1), César Javier Vega Perrone (8/0), Nelson Daniel Gutiérrez Luongo (31/0), Eliseo Roque Rivero Pérez (6/0), Jorge Wálter Barrios Balestrasse (54/4), Venancio Ariel Ramos Villanueva (36/5), Mario Daniel Saralegui (26/2), Wilmar Rubens Cabrera Sappa (24/6), José Luis Zalazar Rodríguez (15/3), Rúben Walter Paz Márquez (21/6). Trainer: Omar Borrás (52).
Goal: Michael Joseph McCarthy (23 own goal).

528. 04.06.1986 **URUGUAY - WEST GERMANY** **1-1(1-0)** 13th FIFA WC. Group Stage
Estadio La Corregidora, Querétaro (Mexico); Referee: Vojtech Christov (Czechoslovakia), Attendance: 30,500
URU: Fernando Harry Álvez Mosquera (7/0), Víctor Hugo Diogo Silva (32/1), Eduardo Mario Acevedo Cardozo (39/1), Nelson Daniel Gutiérrez Luongo (32/0), José Alberto Batista González (9/1), Miguel Angel Bossio Bastianini (28/1), Jorge Wálter Barrios Balestrasse (55/4) [56.Mario Daniel Saralegui (27/2)], Sérgio Rodolfo Santín Spinelli (15/0), Enzo Francéscoli Uriarte (23/6), Antonio Alzamendi Casas (7/1) [82.Venancio Ariel Ramos Villanueva (37/5)], Jorge Orosmán da Silva Echeverrito (20/6). Trainer: Omar Borrás (53).
Goal: Antonio Alzamendi Casas (5).

529. 08.06.1986 **DENMARK - URUGUAY** **6-1(2-1)** 13th FIFA WC. Group Stage
Estadio Neza, Nezahualcoyotl (Mexico); Referee: Antonio Márquez (Mexico), Attendance: 26,500
URU: Fernando Harry Álvez Mosquera (8/0), Víctor Hugo Diogo Silva (33/1), Eduardo Mario Acevedo Cardozo (40/1), Nelson Daniel Gutiérrez Luongo (33/0), José Alberto Batista González (10/1), Miguel Angel Bossio Bastianini (29/1) [*sent off 20*], Mario Daniel Saralegui (28/2), Sérgio Rodolfo Santín Spinelli (16/0) [57.José Luis Zalazar Rodríguez (16/3)], Enzo Francéscoli Uriarte (24/7), Antonio Alzamendi Casas (8/1) [57.Venancio Ariel Ramos Villanueva (38/5)], Jorge Orosmán da Silva Echeverrito (21/6). Trainer: Omar Borrás (54).
Goal: Enzo Francéscoli Uriarte (45 penalty).

530. 13.06.1986 **URUGUAY - SCOTLAND** **0-0** 13th FIFA WC. Group Stage
Estadio Neza, Nezahualcoyotl (Mexico); Referee: Joël Quiniou (France), Attendance: 20,000
URU: Fernando Harry Álvez Mosquera (9/0), Víctor Hugo Diogo Silva (34/1), Eduardo Mario Acevedo Cardozo (41/1), Nelson Daniel Gutiérrez Luongo (34/0), José Alberto Batista González (11/1), Alfonso Darío Pereyra Bueno (31/5), Jorge Wálter Barrios Balestrasse (56/4), Sérgio Rodolfo Santín Spinelli (17/0), Enzo Francéscoli Uriarte (25/7) [84 Antonio Alzamendi Casas (9/1)], Venancio Ariel Ramos Villanueva (39/5) [71.Mario Daniel Saralegui (29/2)], Wilmar Rubens Cabrera Sappa (25/6). Trainer: Omar Borrás (55).

531. 16.06.1986 **ARGENTINA - URUGUAY** **1-0(1-0)** 13th FIFA WC. 2nd Round
Estadio Cuauhtémoc, Puebla (Mexico); Referee: Luigi Agnolin (Italy), Attendance: 26,000
URU: Fernando Harry Álvez Mosquera (10/0), Nelson Daniel Gutiérrez Luongo (35/0), Eduardo Mario Acevedo Cardozo (42/1) [61.Rúben Walter Paz Márquez (22/6)], Eliseo Roque Rivero Pérez (7/0), Sérgio Rodolfo Santín Spinelli (18/0), Venancio Ariel Ramos Villanueva (40/5), Miguel Angel Bossio Bastianini (30/1), Jorge Wálter Barrios Balestrasse (57/4), Alfonso Darío Pereyra Bueno (32/5), Wilmar Rubens Cabrera Sappa (26/6) [46.Jorge Orosmán da Silva Echeverrito (22/6)], Enzo Francéscoli Uriarte (26/7). Trainer: Omar Borrás (56).

532. 19.06.1987 **URUGUAY - ECUADOR** **2-1(1-0)**
Estadio Centenario, Montevideo; Referee: José Luis Martínez Bazan (Uruguay), Attendance: 5,000
URU: Jorge Fernando Seré (1/0), Gonzalo Lizardo Díaz (1/0), Obdulio Eduardo Trasante (1/0), Nelson Daniel Gutiérrez Luongo (36/0), Alfonso Enrique Domínguez (1/0), Gustavo Cristian Matosas (1/0), José Batlle Perdomo (1/2), Enzo Francéscoli Uriarte (27/7), José Enrique Peña (1/0) [Pablo Javier Bengoechea Dutra (4/0)], Antonio Alzamendi Casas (10/1), Rubén Sosa Ardáiz (8/0) [Mauricio Joselito Silvera (7/0)]. Trainer: Roberto Fleitas (1).
Goals: José Batlle Perdomo (5, 66).

533. 23.06.1987 **URUGUAY - BOLIVIA** **2-1(1-1)**
Estadio Centenario, Montevideo; Referee: Roberto Otelo (Uruguay), Attendance: 8,000
URU: Eduardo Pereira Martínez (1/0), Alfonso Enrique Domínguez (2/0), Obdulio Eduardo Trasante (2/0), Nelson Daniel Gutiérrez Luongo (37/0), José Luis Pintos Saldanha (1/0), Gustavo Cristian Matosas (2/1), José Batlle Perdomo (2/2), Enzo Francéscoli Uriarte (28/7), José Enrique Peña (2/0) [Pablo Javier Bengoechea Dutra (5/0)], Antonio Alzamendi Casas (11/2), Rubén Sosa Ardáiz (9/0). Trainer: Roberto Fleitas (2).
Goals: Gustavo Cristian Matosas (41), Antonio Alzamendi Casas (51).

534. 09.07.1987 **ARGENTINA - URUGUAY** **0-1(0-1)** 33rd Copa América. Semi-Finals
Estadio Monumental „Antonio Vespucio Liberti“, Buenos Aires; Referee: Elías Victoriano Jácome Guerreiro (Ecuador), Attendance: 65,000
URU: Eduardo Pereira Martínez (2/0), Alfonso Enrique Domínguez (3/0), Nelson Daniel Gutiérrez Luongo (38/0), Obdulio Eduardo Trasante (3/0), José Luis Pintos Saldanha (2/0), Gustavo Cristian Matosas (3/1), José Batlle Perdomo (3/2), Enzo Francéscoli Uriarte (29/7), Pablo Javier Bengoechea Dutra (6/0) [80.José Enrique Peña (3/0)], Antonio Alzamendi Casas (12/3), Rubén Sosa Ardáiz (10/0) [77.Eduardo Da Silva (1/0)]. Trainer: Roberto Fleitas (3).
Goal: Antonio Alzamendi Casas (43).

535. 12.07.1987 **URUGUAY - CHILE** **1-0(0-0)** 33rd Copa América. Final
Estadio Monumental „Antonio Vespucio Liberti“, Buenos Aires (Argentina); Referee: Romualdo Arppi Filho (Brazil), Attendance: 35,000
URU: Eduardo Pereira Martínez (3/0), Alfonso Enrique Domínguez (4/0), Nelson Daniel Gutiérrez Luongo (39/0), Obdulio Eduardo Trasante (4/0), José Luis Pintos Saldanha (3/0), Gustavo Cristian Matosas (4/1), José Batlle Perdomo (4/2) [*sent off 89*], Enzo Francéscoli Uriarte (30/7) [*sent off 27*], Pablo Javier Bengoechea Dutra (7/1), Antonio Alzamendi Casas (13/3) [86.José Enrique Peña (4/0)], Rubén Sosa Ardáiz (11/0). Trainer: Roberto Fleitas (4).
Goal: Pablo Javier Bengoechea Dutra (56).

536. 07.08.1988 **COLOMBIA - URUGUAY** **2-1(0-0)** Gonzalo Jiménez de Quesada Cup
Estadio „Nemesio Camacho“ 'El Campín', Bogotá; Referee: Octavio Sierra (Colombia), Attendance: 18,497
URU: Jorge Fernando Seré (2/0) [Celso Otero (1/0)], José Oscar Herrera Corominas (1/1), Jorge Miguel Gonçalves (1/0), Daniel Felipe Revelez (3/0), Nelson Cabrera (1/0), Gustavo Cristian Matosas (5/1) [Edison Omar Suárez (1/0)], José Batlle Perdomo (5/2), Rubén Fabián Pereira (1/0), Héctor Morán (1/0) [Gustavo Dalto (3/0)], Daniel Alejandro Vidal (1/0), Enrique Raúl Báez (4/0). Trainer: Gregorio Pérez (1).
Goal: José Oscar Herrera Corominas (73).

537. 27.09.1988 **URUGUAY - ECUADOR** **2-1(1-0)** Boqueron Cup Semi-Finals
Estadio Defensores del Chaco, Asunción; Referee: Gabriel González (Paraguay), Attendance: 8,580
URU: Adolfo Javier Zeoli (1/0), José Oscar Herrera Corominas (2/2), Daniel Florencio Sánchez (1/0), Sergio Panzardo (1/0) [Mario Rebollo (1/0)], Nelson Cabrera (2/0), Edison Omar Suárez (2/0), Rubén Fabián Pereira (2/0), Eber Alejandro Moas Silvera (1/0), Sergio Daniel Martínez Alzuri (1/0) [Edgar Borges (1/0) [*sent off*]], Rubén Fernando da Silva Echeverrito (1/0), Gustavo Dalto (4/1). Trainer: Óscar Wáshington Tabárez Silva (1).
Goals: Gustavo Dalto (15), José Oscar Herrera Corominas (85).

538. 29.09.1988 **PARAGUAY - URUGUAY** **3-1(3-0)** Boqueron Cup Final
Estadio Defensores del Chaco, Asunción; Referee: Luis Carlos Félix (Brazil), Attendance: 35,000
URU: Adolfo Javier Zeoli (2/0), José Oscar Herrera Corominas (3/2), Daniel Florencio Sánchez (2/0), Mario Rebollo (2/0), Nelson Cabrera (3/0), Edison Omar Suárez (3/0) [Sergio Daniel Martínez Alzuri (2/0)], Rubén Fabián Pereira (3/0), Eber Alejandro Moas Silvera (2/0), Enrique Raúl Báez (5/0), Rubén Fernando da Silva Echeverrito (2/1), Gustavo Dalto (5/1). Trainer: Óscar Wáshington Tabárez Silva (2).
Goal: Rubén Fernando da Silva Echeverrito (77).

539. 12.10.1988 **URUGUAY - PARAGUAY** **2-0(2-0)**
Estadio Centenario, Montevideo; Referee: Jorge Nieves (Uruguay), Attendance: 10,540
URU: Fernando Harry Álvez Mosquera (11/0), José Oscar Herrera Corominas (4/2), Jorge Miguel Gonçalves (2/0), Mario Rebollo (3/0), Nelson Cabrera (4/0), José Batlle Perdomo (6/2), Rubén Fabián Pereira (4/1), Rúben Walter Paz Márquez (23/6) [Edison Omar Suárez (4/0)], Daniel Alejandro Vidal (2/0) [Sergio Daniel Martínez Alzuri (3/0)], Rubén Fernando da Silva Echeverrito (3/2), Gustavo Dalto (6/1). Trainer: Óscar Wáshington Tabárez Silva (3).
Goals: Rubén Fernando da Silva Echeverrito (14 penalty), Rubén Fabián Pereira (20).

540. 01.11.1988 **CHILE - URUGUAY** **1-1(0-0)** Copa Juan Pinto Durán
Estadio Regional, Concepción; Referee: Carlos Manuel Robles Mella (Chile), Attendance: 16,301
URU: Fernando Harry Álvez Mosquera (12/0), José Oscar Herrera Corominas (5/2), Jorge Miguel Gonçalves (3/0), Mario Rebollo (4/0), Nelson Cabrera (5/0), Edison Omar Suárez (5/0) [74.Enrique Raúl Báez (6/0)], Carlos Gabriel Correa (1/0) [*sent off 89*], Rubén Fabián Pereira (5/1), Daniel Alejandro Vidal (3/1), Rubén Fernando da Silva Echeverrito (4/2), Gustavo Dalto (7/1) [46.Luis Alberto Acosta (15/1)]. Trainer: Óscar Wáshington Tabárez Silva (4).
Goal: Daniel Alejandro Vidal (87).

541. 09.11.1988 **URUGUAY - CHILE** **3-1(0-0)** Copa Juan Pinto Durán
Estadio Centenario, Montevideo; Referee: Juan Daniel Cardellino de San Vicente (Uruguay), Attendance: 6,470
URU: Oscar Ferro (1/0), José Oscar Herrera Corominas (6/2), Jorge Miguel Gonçalves (4/0), Mario Rebollo (5/0), Nelson Cabrera (6/0), José Batlle Perdomo (7/2), Rubén Fabián Pereira (6/1), Rúben Walter Paz Márquez (24/6), Daniel Alejandro Vidal (4/1) [75.Sergio Daniel Martínez Alzuri (4/1)], Rubén Fernando da Silva Echeverrito (5/3) [75.Enrique Raúl Báez (7/1)], Gustavo Dalto (8/1) [46.Edison Omar Suárez (6/0)]. Trainer: Óscar Wáshington Tabárez Silva (5).
Goals: Rubén Fernando da Silva Echeverrito (72 penalty), Enrique Raúl Báez (79), Sergio Daniel Martínez Alzuri (87).

542. 14.12.1988 **URUGUAY - PERU** **3-0(3-0)** MUFP Cup
Estadio Centenario, Montevideo; Referee: Ricardo Carlos Calabria (Argentina), Attendance: 9,000
URU: Oscar Ferro (2/0), José Oscar Herrera Corominas (7/2), Obdulio Eduardo Trasante (5/0), Nelson Daniel Gutiérrez Luongo (40/0), Nelson Cabrera (7/0), Pablo Javier Bengoechea Dutra (8/1) [80.Sergio Daniel Martínez Alzuri (5/1)], José Batlle Perdomo (8/2), Rubén Fabián Pereira (7/1), Enzo Francéscoli Uriarte (31/9) [Edison Omar Suárez (7/0)], Daniel Alejandro Vidal (5/1) [57.Rubén Fernando da Silva Echeverrito (6/3)], Rubén Sosa Ardáiz (12/1). Trainer: Óscar Wáshington Tabárez Silva (6).
Goals: Enzo Francéscoli Uriarte (13, 30), Rubén Sosa Ardáiz (43).

543. 22.04.1989 **ITALY - URUGUAY** **1-1(0-0)**
Stadio „Marco Antonio Bentegodi“, Verona; Referee: George Courtney (England), Attendance: 13,891
URU: Jorge Fernando Seré (3/0), José Oscar Herrera Corominas (8/2), Daniel Felipe Revelez (4/0), Hugo Eduardo De León (21/0), Alfonso Enrique Domínguez (5/0), Carlos Gabriel Correa (2/0) [72.Santiago Javier Ostolaza Sosa (5/1)], José Batlle Perdomo (9/2), Enzo Francéscoli Uriarte (32/9), Pablo Javier Bengoechea Dutra (9/1) [78.Carlos Alberto Aguilera Nova (40/18)], Antonio Alzamendi Casas (14/3), Rubén Sosa Ardáiz (13/1). Trainer: Óscar Wáshington Tabárez Silva (7).
Goal: Carlos Alberto Aguilera Nova (83).

544. 03.05.1989 **URUGUAY - ECUADOR** **3-1(1-0)**
Estadio Centenario, Montevideo; Referee: Jorge Eduardo Romero (Argentina), Attendance: 15,000
URU: Jorge Fernando Seré (4/0), José Oscar Herrera Corominas (9/2), Daniel Felipe Revelez (5/0), Hugo Eduardo De León (22/0), Alfonso Enrique Domínguez (6/0), Carlos Gabriel Correa (3/0) [Santiago Javier Ostolaza Sosa (6/1)], José Batlle Perdomo (10/2), Rúben Walter Paz Márquez (25/6), Sergio Daniel Martínez Alzuri (6/2) [Eduardo Da Silva (2/0)], Carlos Alberto Aguilera Nova (41/20), William Adrián Castro (1/0) [Adolfo Barán (1/0)]. Trainer: Óscar Wáshington Tabárez Silva (8).
Goals: Sergio Daniel Martínez Alzuri (8), Carlos Alberto Aguilera Nova (55, 89).

545. 23.05.1989 **ECUADOR - URUGUAY** **1-1(0-0)**
Estadio Olimpico „Atahualpa“, Quito; Referee: Adolfo Quirola (Ecuador), Attendance: 17,000
URU: Adolfo Javier Zeoli (3/0), José Oscar Herrera Corominas (10/3), Daniel Felipe Revelez (6/0), Hugo Eduardo De León (23/0), José Luis Pintos Saldanha (4/0), Rubén Fabián Pereira (8/1), José Batlle Perdomo (11/2), Edison Omar Suárez (8/0), Sergio Daniel Martínez Alzuri (7/2) [Edgar Borges (2/0)], Carlos Alberto Aguilera Nova (42/20), Gustavo Dalto (9/1) [Rubén Fernando da Silva Echeverrito (7/3)]. Trainer: Óscar Wáshington Tabárez Silva (9).
Goal: José Oscar Herrera Corominas (89).

546. 08.06.1989 **BOLIVIA - URUGUAY** **0-0**
Estadio „Ramón 'Tahuichi' Aguilera“, Santa Cruz de la Sierra; Referee: Pablo Peña (Bolivia), Attendance: 45,000
URU: Adolfo Javier Zeoli (4/0), José Oscar Herrera Corominas (11/3), Daniel Felipe Revelez (7/0), Hugo Eduardo De León (24/0), Alfonso Enrique Domínguez (7/0), Rubén Fabián Pereira (9/1), José Batlle Perdomo (12/2), Edison Omar Suárez (9/0) [Carlos Gabriel Correa (4/0)], Carlos Alberto Aguilera Nova (43/20), Rubén Fernando da Silva Echeverrito (8/3), William Adrián Castro (2/0) [Gustavo Dalto (10/1)]. Trainer: Óscar Wáshington Tabárez Silva (10).

547. 14.06.1989 **URUGUAY - BOLIVIA** **1-0(1-0)**

Estadio Centenario, Montevideo; Referee: Roberto Otello (Uruguay), Attendance: 10,000

URU: Adolfo Javier Zeoli (5/0), José Oscar Herrera Corominas (12/3) [*sent off 22*], Daniel Felipe Revelez (8/0), Hugo Eduardo De León (25/0), Alfonso Enrique Domínguez (8/0), Santiago Javier Ostolaza Sosa (7/1), Rubén Fabián Pereira (10/1) [Carlos Gabriel Correa (5/0)], Edison Omar Suárez (10/0) [Sergio Daniel Martínez Alzuri (8/2)], Carlos Alberto Aguilera Nova (44/21), Rubén Fernando da Silva Echeverrito (9/3) [Gustavo Dalto (11/1)], William Adrián Castro (3/0). Trainer: Óscar Wáshington Tabárez Silva (11).

Goal: Carlos Alberto Aguilera Nova (17 penalty).

548. 19.06.1989 **URUGUAY - CHILE** **2-2(0-1)**

Estadio Centenario, Montevideo; Referee: Ernesto Filippi Cavani (Uruguay), Attendance: 20,982

URU: Adolfo Javier Zeoli (6/0), Alfonso Enrique Domínguez (9/0), Daniel Felipe Revelez (9/0), Hugo Eduardo De León (26/0), José Luis Pintos Saldanha (5/0), Santiago Javier Ostolaza Sosa (8/1), Rubén Fabián Pereira (11/1) [Carlos Gabriel Correa (6/2)], Rúben Walter Paz Márquez (26/6), Sergio Daniel Martínez Alzuri (9/2), Carlos Alberto Aguilera Nova (45/21), Gustavo Dalto (12/1) [William Adrián Castro (4/0)]. Trainer: Óscar Wáshington Tabárez Silva (12).

Goals: Carlos Gabriel Correa (55, 73).

549. 02.07.1989 **ECUADOR - URUGUAY** **1-0(0-0)** 34th Copa América. Group Stage

Estádio Serra Dourada, Goiânia (Brazil); Referee: Carlos Maciel (Paraguay), Attendance: 19,000

URU: Adolfo Javier Zeoli (7/0), José Oscar Herrera Corominas (13/3) [58.Pablo Javier Bengoechea Dutra (10/1)], Daniel Felipe Revelez (10/0), Hugo Eduardo De León (27/0), Alfonso Enrique Domínguez (10/0), Santiago Javier Ostolaza Sosa (9/1), Carlos Gabriel Correa (7/2), Rúben Walter Paz Márquez (27/6), Antonio Alzamendi Casas (15/3) [75.Sergio Daniel Martínez Alzuri (10/2)], Carlos Alberto Aguilera Nova (46/21), Rubén Sosa Ardáiz (14/1). Trainer: Óscar Wáshington Tabárez Silva (13).

550. 04.07.1989 **URUGUAY - BOLIVIA** **3-0(2-0)** 34th Copa América. Group Stage

Estádio Serra Dourada, Goiânia (Brazil); Referee: Arnaldo David César Coelho (Brazil), Attendance: 8,000

URU: Adolfo Javier Zeoli (8/0), José Oscar Herrera Corominas (14/3), Nelson Daniel Gutiérrez Luongo (41/0), Hugo Eduardo De León (28/0), Alfonso Enrique Domínguez (11/0), Santiago Javier Ostolaza Sosa (10/3), Carlos Gabriel Correa (8/2), Pablo Javier Bengoechea Dutra (11/1) [*sent off 13*], Rúben Walter Paz Márquez (28/6) [79.Rubén Fabián Pereira (12/1)], Antonio Alzamendi Casas (16/3), Rubén Sosa Ardáiz (15/2) [79.Carlos Alberto Aguilera Nova (47/21)]. Trainer: Óscar Wáshington Tabárez Silva (14).

Goals: Santiago Javier Ostolaza Sosa (30), Rubén Sosa Ardáiz (33), Santiago Javier Ostolaza Sosa (60).

551. 06.07.1989 **URUGUAY - CHILE** **3-0(1-0)** 34th Copa América. Group Stage

Estádio Serra Dourada, Goiânia (Brazil); Referee: José Ramírez Calle (Peru), Attendance: 2,029

URU: Adolfo Javier Zeoli (9/0), José Oscar Herrera Corominas (15/3), Nelson Daniel Gutiérrez Luongo (42/0), Hugo Eduardo De León (29/0), Alfonso Enrique Domínguez (12/0), Santiago Javier Ostolaza Sosa (11/3), José Batlle Perdomo (13/2), Enzo Francéscoli Uriarte (33/10) [79.Carlos Alberto Aguilera Nova (48/21)], Rúben Walter Paz Márquez (29/6) [65.Carlos Gabriel Correa (9/2)], Antonio Alzamendi Casas (17/4), Rubén Sosa Ardáiz (16/3). Trainer: Óscar Wáshington Tabárez Silva (15).

Goals: Rubén Sosa Ardáiz (44), Antonio Alzamendi Casas (73), Enzo Francéscoli Uriarte (78).

552. 08.07.1989 **ARGENTINA - URUGUAY** **1-0(0-0)** 34th Copa América. Group Stage

Estádio Serra Dourada, Goiânia (Brazil); Referee: Jesús Díaz Palacios (Colombia), Attendance: 18,000

URU: Adolfo Javier Zeoli (10/0), José Oscar Herrera Corominas (16/3), Nelson Daniel Gutiérrez Luongo (43/0), Hugo Eduardo De León (30/0), Alfonso Enrique Domínguez (13/0), Santiago Javier Ostolaza Sosa (12/3) [72.Pablo Javier Bengoechea Dutra (12/1)], José Batlle Perdomo (14/2), Enzo Francéscoli Uriarte (34/10), Rúben Walter Paz Márquez (30/6) [72.Carlos Alberto Aguilera Nova (49/21)], Antonio Alzamendi Casas (18/4), Rubén Sosa Ardáiz (17/3). Trainer: Óscar Wáshington Tabárez Silva (16).

553. 12.07.1989 **URUGUAY - PARAGUAY** **3-0(1-0)** 34th Copa América. Final Round

Estádio „Jornalista Mário Filho" (Maracanã), Rio de Janeiro (Brazil); Referee: Juan Carlos Loustau (Argentina), Attendance: 60,000

URU: Adolfo Javier Zeoli (11/0), José Oscar Herrera Corominas (17/3), Nelson Daniel Gutiérrez Luongo (44/0), Hugo Eduardo De León (31/0), Alfonso Enrique Domínguez (14/0), Santiago Javier Ostolaza Sosa (13/3), José Batlle Perdomo (15/2), Enzo Francéscoli Uriarte (35/11) [70.Carlos Gabriel Correa (10/2)], Rúben Walter Paz Márquez (31/7), Antonio Alzamendi Casas (19/5), Rubén Sosa Ardáiz (18/3) [88.Rubén Fernando da Silva Echeverrito (10/3)]. Trainer: Óscar Wáshington Tabárez Silva (17).

Goals: Enzo Francéscoli Uriarte (28), Antonio Alzamendi Casas (82), Rúben Walter Paz Márquez (89).

554. 14.07.1989 **URUGUAY - ARGENTINA** **2-0(1-0)** 34th Copa América. Final Round

Estádio „Jornalista Mário Filho" (Maracanã), Rio de Janeiro (Brazil); Referee: Arnaldo David César Coelho (Brazil), Attendance: 45,000

URU: Adolfo Javier Zeoli (12/0), José Oscar Herrera Corominas (18/3), Nelson Daniel Gutiérrez Luongo (45/0), Hugo Eduardo De León (32/0), Alfonso Enrique Domínguez (15/0), Santiago Javier Ostolaza Sosa (14/3), José Batlle Perdomo (16/2) [46.Carlos Gabriel Correa (11/2)], Enzo Francéscoli Uriarte (36/11), Rúben Walter Paz Márquez (32/7) [77.Rubén Fabián Pereira (13/1)], Antonio Alzamendi Casas (20/5), Rubén Sosa Ardáiz (19/5). Trainer: Óscar Wáshington Tabárez Silva (18).

Goals: Rubén Sosa Ardáiz (38, 81).

555. 16.07.1989 **BRAZIL - URUGUAY** **1-0(0-0)** 34th Copa América. Final Round

Estádio „Jornalista Mário Filho" (Maracanã), Rio de Janeiro; Referee: Hernán Silva Arce (Chile), Attendance: 148,068

URU: Adolfo Javier Zeoli (13/0), José Oscar Herrera Corominas (19/3), Nelson Daniel Gutiérrez Luongo (46/0), Hugo Eduardo De León (33/0), Alfonso Enrique Domínguez (16/0), Santiago Javier Ostolaza Sosa (15/3) [69.Carlos Gabriel Correa (12/2)], José Batlle Perdomo (17/2), Enzo Francéscoli Uriarte (37/11), Rúben Walter Paz Márquez (33/7) [69.Rubén Fernando da Silva Echeverrito (11/3)], Antonio Alzamendi Casas (21/5), Rubén Sosa Ardáiz (20/5). Trainer: Óscar Wáshington Tabárez Silva (19).

556. 06.08.1989 **URUGUAY - COLOMBIA** **0-0**

Estadio Centenario, Montevideo; Referee: Ernesto Filippi (Uruguay), Attendance: 20,000

URU: Eduardo Pereira Martínez (4/0), José Oscar Herrera Corominas (20/3), Nelson Daniel Gutiérrez Luongo (47/0), Hugo Eduardo De León (34/0), Alfonso Enrique Domínguez (17/0), Santiago Javier Ostolaza Sosa (16/3), Carlos Gabriel Correa (13/2), Rubén Fabián Pereira (14/1) [William Adrián Castro (5/0)], Rúben Walter Paz Márquez (34/7), Antonio Alzamendi Casas (22/5), Rubén Sosa Ardáiz (21/5). Trainer: Óscar Wáshington Tabárez Silva (20).

557. 27.08.1989 **PERU – URUGUAY** **0-2(0-0)** 14th FIFA WC. Qualifiers
Estadio Nacional, Lima; Referee: Carlos Espósito (Argentina), Attendance: 35,000
URU: Eduardo Pereira Martínez (5/0), José Oscar Herrera Corominas (21/3), Nelson Daniel Gutiérrez Luongo (48/0), Hugo Eduardo De León (35/0), Alfonso Enrique Domínguez (18/0), Santiago Javier Ostolaza Sosa (17/3) [79.Carlos Gabriel Correa (14/2)], José Batlle Perdomo (18/2), Enzo Francéscoli Uriarte (38/11), Rúben Walter Paz Márquez (35/7) [75.Pablo Javier Bengoechea Dutra (13/1)], Antonio Alzamendi Casas (23/6), Rubén Sosa Ardáiz (22/6). Trainer: Óscar Wáshington Tabárez Silva (21).
Goals: Rubén Sosa Ardáiz (46), Antonio Alzamendi Casas (69).

558. 03.09.1989 **BOLIVIA – URUGUAY** **2-1(1-1)** 14th FIFA WC. Qualifiers
Estadio „Hernándo Siles Zuazo", La Paz; Referee: José Antonio Vergara Guerrero (Venezuela), Attendance: 52,000
URU: Eduardo Pereira Martínez (6/0), José Oscar Herrera Corominas (22/3) [78.Pablo Javier Bengoechea Dutra (14/1)], Nelson Daniel Gutiérrez Luongo (49/0), Hugo Eduardo De León (36/0), Alfonso Enrique Domínguez (19/0), Santiago Javier Ostolaza Sosa (18/3), José Batlle Perdomo (19/2), Enzo Francéscoli Uriarte (39/11), Rúben Walter Paz Márquez (36/7), Antonio Alzamendi Casas (24/6), Rubén Sosa Ardáiz (23/7). Trainer: Óscar Wáshington Tabárez Silva (22).
Goal: Rubén Sosa Ardáiz (49).

559. 17.09.1989 **URUGUAY – BOLIVIA** **2-0(2-0)** 14th FIFA WC. Qualifiers
Estadio Centenario, Montevideo; Referee: Gastón Castro Makuc (Chile), Attendance: 70,000
URU: Eduardo Pereira Martínez (7/0), José Oscar Herrera Corominas (23/3), Nelson Daniel Gutiérrez Luongo (50/0), Hugo Eduardo De León (37/0), Alfonso Enrique Domínguez (20/0), Santiago Javier Ostolaza Sosa (19/3), José Batlle Perdomo (20/2) [78.Carlos Gabriel Correa (15/2)], Enzo Francéscoli Uriarte (40/12), Rúben Walter Paz Márquez (37/7) [67.Pablo Javier Bengoechea Dutra (15/1)], Antonio Alzamendi Casas (25/6), Rubén Sosa Ardáiz (24/8). Trainer: Óscar Wáshington Tabárez Silva (23).
Goals: Rubén Sosa Ardáiz (31), Enzo Francéscoli Uriarte (38).

560. 24.09.1989 **URUGUAY – PERU** **2-0(1-0)** 14th FIFA WC. Qualifiers
Estadio Centenario, Montevideo; Referee: José Roberto Wright (Brazil), Attendance: 57,000
URU: Eduardo Pereira Martínez (8/0), José Oscar Herrera Corominas (24/3), Nelson Daniel Gutiérrez Luongo (51/0), Hugo Eduardo De León (38/0), Alfonso Enrique Domínguez (21/0), Santiago Javier Ostolaza Sosa (20/3), Carlos Gabriel Correa (16/2), Pablo Javier Bengoechea Dutra (16/1), Rúben Walter Paz Márquez (38/7), Antonio Alzamendi Casas (26/6), Rubén Sosa Ardáiz (25/10). Trainer: Óscar Wáshington Tabárez Silva (24).
Goals: Rubén Sosa Ardáiz (43, 57).

561. 02.02.1990 **URUGUAY – COLOMBIA** **2-0(0-0)** Marlboro Cup
Orange Bowl, Miami (United States); Referee: Vincent Mauro (United States), Attendance: 9,000
URU: Fernando Harry Álvez Mosquera (13/0), José Luis Pintos Saldanha (6/0), Jorge Miguel Gonçalves (5/0) [Daniel Felipe Revelez (11/0)], Hugo Eduardo De León (39/0), Alfonso Enrique Domínguez (22/0), Rubén Fabián Pereira (15/1), Santiago Javier Ostolaza Sosa (21/3), Edison Omar Suárez (11/0) [46.Pedro Pedrucci (1/1)], William Adrián Castro (6/1), Daniel Fonseca (1/0) [63.Néstor Gabriel Cedrés Vera (1/0)], Sergio Daniel Martínez Alzuri (11/2) [77.Johnny Miqueiro (1/0)]. Trainer: Óscar Wáshington Tabárez Silva (25).
Goals: Pedro Pedrucci (78), William Adrián Castro (84).

562. 04.02.1990 **COSTA RICA – URUGUAY** **0-2(0-2)** Marlboro Cup
Orange Bowl, Miami (United States); Referee: Antonio Evangelista (Canada), Attendance: 15,231
URU: Fernando Harry Álvez Mosquera (14/0), Jorge Miguel Gonçalves (6/0), Rubén Fabián Pereira (16/1), Hugo Eduardo De León (40/0), José Luis Pintos Saldanha (7/0), Alfonso Enrique Domínguez (23/0), Sergio Daniel Martínez Alzuri (12/2) [75.Johnny Miqueiro (2/0)], Santiago Javier Ostolaza Sosa (22/3), Daniel Fonseca (2/0) [46.Néstor Gabriel Cedrés Vera (2/0)], Pedro Pedrucci (2/1) [85.Carlos Gabriel Correa (17/2)], William Adrián Castro (7/2). Trainer: Óscar Wáshington Tabárez Silva (26).
Goals: William Adrián Castro (6 penalty), Mauricio Montero (12 own goal).

563. 20.03.1990 **MEXICO – URUGUAY** **2-1(2-1)**
Memorial Coliseum, Los Angeles; Referee: Majid Jay (United States), Attendance: 22,000
URU: Fernando Harry Álvez Mosquera (15/0), José Luis Pintos Saldanha (8/0), Jorge Miguel Gonçalves (7/0) [46.Daniel Felipe Revelez (12/0)], Hugo Eduardo De León (41/0), Alfonso Enrique Domínguez (24/0), Rubén Fabián Pereira (17/1), Carlos Gabriel Correa (18/2), Edison Omar Suárez (12/1), Néstor Gabriel Cedrés Vera (3/0) [46.Diego Martín Dorta (1/0)], Daniel Fonseca (3/0), William Adrián Castro (8/2) [73.Nelson Cabrera (8/0)]. Trainer: Óscar Wáshington Tabárez Silva (27).
Goal: Édison Omar Suárez (40).

564. 25.04.1990 **WEST GERMANY – URUGUAY** **3-3(0-0)**
Neckarstadion, Stuttgart; Referee: Bo Karlsson (Sweden), Attendance: 35,000
URU: Eduardo Pereira Martínez (9/0), Daniel Felipe Revelez (13/1), Hugo Eduardo De León (42/0), José Oscar Herrera Corominas (25/3), José Batlle Perdomo (21/2), Alfonso Enrique Domínguez (25/0), Rubén Fabián Pereira (18/1), Carlos Alberto Aguilera Nova (50/22) [80.Sergio Daniel Martínez Alzuri (13/2)], Rúben Walter Paz Márquez (39/7) [70.Daniel Fonseca (4/0)], Santiago Javier Ostolaza Sosa (23/4), Rubén Sosa Ardáiz (26/10). Trainer: Óscar Wáshington Tabárez Silva (28).
Goals: Carlos Alberto Aguilera Nova (49), Santiago Javier Ostolaza Sosa (73), Daniel Felipe Revelez (78).

565. 18.05.1990 **NORTHERN IRELAND – URUGUAY** **1-0(1-0)** Stanley Rous Cup
Windsor Park, Belfast; Referee: Keith Cooper (Wales), Attendance: 3,500
URU: Adolfo Javier Zeoli (14/0), Nelson Daniel Gutiérrez Luongo (52/0), Hugo Eduardo De León (43/0), José Oscar Herrera Corominas (26/3) [73.José Luis Pintos Saldanha (9/0)], José Batlle Perdomo (22/2), Alfonso Enrique Domínguez (26/0), Antonio Alzamendi Casas (27/6) [63.Carlos Alberto Aguilera Nova (51/22)], Santiago Javier Ostolaza Sosa (24/4), Enzo Francéscoli Uriarte (41/12), Pablo Javier Bengoechea Dutra (17/1) [60.Rúben Walter Paz Márquez (40/7)], Rubén Sosa Ardáiz (27/10). Trainer: Óscar Wáshington Tabárez Silva (29).

566. 22.05.1990 **ENGLAND – URUGUAY** **1-2(0-1)** Stanley Rous Cup
Wembley Stadium, London; Referee: Pietro D'Elia (Italy), Attendance: 38,751
URU: Eduardo Pereira Martínez (10/0), Nelson Daniel Gutiérrez Luongo (53/0), Hugo Eduardo De León (44/0), José Oscar Herrera Corominas (27/3), José Batlle Perdomo (23/3), Alfonso Enrique Domínguez (27/0), Antonio Alzamendi Casas (28/6), Santiago Javier Ostolaza Sosa (25/5), Enzo Francéscoli Uriarte (42/12), Rubén Sosa Ardáiz (28/10) [80.Sergio Daniel Martínez Alzuri (14/2)], Rúben Walter Paz Márquez (41/7). Trainer: Óscar Wáshington Tabárez Silva (30).
Goals: Santiago Javier Ostolaza Sosa (27), José Batlle Perdomo (61).

567. 13.06.1990 **URUGUAY - SPAIN** **0-0** 14th FIFA WC. Group Stage
Stadio Friuli, Udine (Italy); Referee: Helmut Kohl (Austria), Attendance: 35,713
URU: Fernando Harry Álvez Mosquera (16/0), Nelson Daniel Gutiérrez Luongo (54/0), Hugo Eduardo De León (45/0), José Oscar Herrera Corominas (28/3), José Batlle Perdomo (24/3), Alfonso Enrique Domínguez (28/0), Antonio Alzamendi Casas (29/6) [65.Carlos Alberto Aguilera Nova (52/22)], Rubén Fabián Pereira (19/1) [68.Carlos Gabriel Correa (19/2)], Enzo Francéscoli Uriarte (43/12), Rúben Walter Paz Márquez (42/7), Rubén Sosa Ardáiz (29/10). Trainer: Óscar Wáshington Tabárez Silva (31).

568. 17.06.1990 **BELGIUM - URUGUAY** **3-1(2-0)** 14th FIFA WC. Group Stage
Stadio „Marco Antonio Bentegodi", Verona (Italy); Referee: Siegfried Kirschen (East Germany), Attendance: 33,759
URU: Fernando Harry Álvez Mosquera (17/0), Nelson Daniel Gutiérrez Luongo (55/0), Hugo Eduardo De León (46/0), José Oscar Herrera Corominas (29/3), José Batlle Perdomo (25/3), Alfonso Enrique Domínguez (29/0), Antonio Alzamendi Casas (30/6) [46.Carlos Alberto Aguilera Nova (53/22)], Santiago Javier Ostolaza Sosa (26/5) [56.Pablo Javier Bengoechea Dutra (18/2)], Enzo Francéscoli Uriarte (44/12), Rúben Walter Paz Márquez (43/7), Rubén Sosa Ardáiz (30/10). Trainer: Óscar Wáshington Tabárez Silva (32).
Goal: Pablo Javier Bengoechea Dutra (74).

569. 21.06.1990 **URUGUAY - SOUTH KOREA** **1-0(0-0)** 14th FIFA WC. Group Stage
Stadio Friuli, Udine (Italy); Referee: Tullio Lanese (Italy), Attendance: 29,039
URU: Fernando Harry Álvez Mosquera (18/0), Nelson Daniel Gutiérrez Luongo (56/0), Hugo Eduardo De León (47/0), José Oscar Herrera Corominas (30/3), José Batlle Perdomo (26/3), Alfonso Enrique Domínguez (30/0), Sergio Daniel Martínez Alzuri (15/2), Santiago Javier Ostolaza Sosa (27/5) [46.Carlos Alberto Aguilera Nova (54/22)], Enzo Francéscoli Uriarte (45/12), Rúben Walter Paz Márquez (44/7), Rubén Sosa Ardáiz (31/10) [64.Daniel Fonseca (5/1)]. Trainer: Óscar Wáshington Tabárez Silva (33).
Goal: Daniel Fonseca (90).

570. 25.06.1990 **ITALY - URUGUAY** **2-0(0-0)** 14th FIFA WC. 2nd Round
Stadio Olimpico, Roma; Referee: George Courtney (England), Attendance: 73,303
URU: Fernando Harry Álvez Mosquera (19/0), Nelson Daniel Gutiérrez Luongo (57/0), Hugo Eduardo De León (48/0), José Luis Pintos Saldanha (10/0), José Batlle Perdomo (27/3), Alfonso Enrique Domínguez (31/0), Carlos Alberto Aguilera Nova (55/22) [67.Rubén Sosa Ardáiz (32/10)], Santiago Javier Ostolaza Sosa (28/5) [80.Antonio Alzamendi Casas (31/6)], Enzo Francéscoli Uriarte (46/12), Rubén Fabián Pereira (20/1), Daniel Fonseca (6/1). Trainer: Óscar Wáshington Tabárez Silva (34).

571. 05.05.1991 **UNITED STATES - URUGUAY** **1-0(1-0)**
Mile High Stadium, Denver; Referee: Antonio Evangelista (Canada), Attendance: 35,772
URU: Fernando Harry Álvez Mosquera (20/0), Guillermo Oscar Sanguinetti Giordano (1/0), Daniel Florencio Sánchez (3/0), Eber Alejandro Moas Silvera (3/0), Ronald Paolo Montero (1/0) [79.Leonardo Ramos (1/0)], César Silvera (1/0), Rubén Fabián Pereira (21/1), Henry López Báez (1/0) (59.Néstor Gabriel Cedrés Vera (4/0)], Sergio Daniel Martínez Alzuri (16/2), Gustavo Ferreyra (1/0) [79.William Gutiérrez (1/0)], Víctor López (1/0) [*sent off 90*]. Trainer: Pedro Ramón Cubilla (1).

572. 07.05.1991 **URUGUAY - MEXICO** **2-0(0-0)** Camel Cup
Memorial Coliseum, Los Angeles; Referee: Arturo Angeles (United States), Attendance: 10,000
URU: Fernando Harry Álvez Mosquera (21/0), Guillermo Oscar Sanguinetti Giordano (2/0), Eber Alejandro Moas Silvera (4/0), Ronald Paolo Montero (2/0), Daniel Florencio Sánchez (4/0), César Silvera (2/0), Rubén Fabián Pereira (22/1), Henry López Báez (2/0), Sergio Daniel Martínez Alzuri (17/2), Gustavo Ferreyra (2/1), Víctor López (2/1) [90.Álvaro Gutiérrez Pelscher (1/0)]. Trainer: Pedro Ramón Cubilla (2).
Goals: Víctor López (61), Gustavo Ferreyra (89).

573. 14.05.1991 **COSTA RICA - URUGUAY** **0-1(0-0)**
Estadio Nacional, San José; Referee: Rónald Gutiérrez (Costa Rica), Attendance: 3,500
URU: Fernando Harry Álvez Mosquera (22/0), Guillermo Oscar Sanguinetti Giordano (3/0), Eber Alejandro Moas Silvera (5/0), Ronald Paolo Montero (3/0) [18.Rúben Fernando Dos Santos (1/0)], Daniel Florencio Sánchez (5/0), César Silvera (3/0) [63.Álvaro Gutiérrez Pelscher (2/0)], Rubén Fabián Pereira (23/1), Henry López Báez (3/0) [74.Héctor Rodríguez Peña (1/0)], Sergio Daniel Martínez Alzuri (18/2) [63.William Gutiérrez (2/0)], Gustavo Ferreyra (3/1) [63.Néstor Gabriel Cedrés Vera (5/1)], Víctor López (3/1). Trainer: Pedro Ramón Cubilla (3).
Goal: Néstor Gabriel Cedrés Vera (89).

574. 30.05.1991 **CHILE - URUGUAY** **2-1(1-0)**
Estadio „Santa Laura", Santiago; Referee: Iván Enrique Guerrero Levancini (Chile), Attendance: 4,500
URU: Fernando Harry Álvez Mosquera (23/0), Leonardo Ramos (2/0), Daniel Felipe Revelez (14/1), Eber Alejandro Moas Silvera (6/0), Ronald Paolo Montero (4/0) [46.Rúben Fernando Dos Santos (2/0) [*sent off 84*]], Rubén Fabián Pereira (24/1) [*sent off 85*], César Silvera (4/0), Héctor Morán (2/0), Edgar Borges (3/0) [66.Venancio Ariel Ramos Villanueva (41/5)], Gustavo Ferreyra (4/1) [64.William Gutiérrez (3/0)], Víctor López (4/1). Trainer: Pedro Ramón Cubilla (4).
Goal: Luis Abarca (89 own goal).

575. 12.06.1991 **PERU - URUGUAY** **1-0(0-0)**
Estadio Nacional, Lima; Referee: José Ramírez Calle (Peru), Attendance: 16,500
URU: Fernando Harry Álvez Mosquera (24/0), José Luis Pintos Saldanha (11/0), Daniel Felipe Revelez (15/1), Eber Alejandro Moas Silvera (7/0), Rúben Fernando Dos Santos (3/0), Héctor Morán (3/0) [60.César Silvera (5/0)], Álvaro Gutiérrez Pelscher (3/0), Ramón Víctor Castro (1/0), Henry López Báez (4/0), Peter Méndez (1/0), William Gutiérrez (4/0) [79.Edgar Borges (4/0)]. Trainer: Luis Alberto Cubilla Almeida Almeida (1).

576. 20.06.1991 **URUGUAY - PERU** **0-0**
Estadio Centenario, Montevideo; Referee: Roberto Otello (Uruguay), Attendance: 12,000
URU: Fernando Harry Álvez Mosquera (25/0), Guillermo Oscar Sanguinetti Giordano (4/0), Daniel Florencio Sánchez (6/0), Eber Alejandro Moas Silvera (8/0), Rúben Fernando Dos Santos (4/0), Héctor Morán (4/0) [71.César Silvera (6/0)], Álvaro Gutiérrez Pelscher (4/0), Henry López Báez (5/0) [65.Ramón Víctor Castro (2/0)], Sergio Daniel Martínez Alzuri (19/2) [65.Néstor Gabriel Cedrés Vera (6/1)], Peter Méndez (2/0), Víctor López (5/1). Trainer: Luis Alberto Cubilla Almeida Almeida (2).

577. 26.06.1991 **URUGUAY - CHILE** **2-1(1-1)**
Estadio Centenario, Montevideo; Referee: Jorge Luis Nieves Parra (Uruguay), Attendance: 6,000
URU: Fernando Harry Álvez Mosquera (26/0), Guillermo Oscar Sanguinetti Giordano (5/0), Daniel Florencio Sánchez (7/0), Eber Alejandro Moas Silvera (9/0), Rúben Fernando Dos Santos (5/0), Héctor Morán (5/0), Rubén Fabián Pereira (25/1) [46.Álvaro Gutiérrez Pelscher (5/0)], Marcelo Fracchia (1/0), Henry López Báez (6/1) [46.Edgar Borges (5/0)], Peter Méndez (3/1), Víctor López (6/1) [80.Néstor Gabriel Cedrés Vera (7/1)]. Trainer: Luis Alberto Cubilla Almeida Almeida (3).
Goals: Henry López Báez (11), Peter Méndez (64 penalty).

578. 07.07.1991 **URUGUAY - BOLIVIA** **1-1(0-1)** 35th Copa América. Group Stage
Estadio Playa Ancha, Valparaíso (Chile); Referee: Carlos Alberto Maciel (Paraguay), Attendance: 15,000
URU: Fernando Harry Álvez Mosquera (27/0), Guillermo Oscar Sanguinetti Giordano (6/0), Daniel Felipe Revelez (16/1), Eber Alejandro Moas Silvera (10/0), José Luis Pintos Saldanha (12/0), Héctor Morán (6/0), Ramón Víctor Castro (3/1), Marcelo Fracchia (2/0), Peter Méndez (4/1), Henry López Báez (7/1) [70.William Gutiérrez (5/0)], Víctor López (7/1) [46.Edgar Borges (6/0)]. Trainer: Luis Alberto Cubilla Almeida Almeida (4).
Goal: Ramón Víctor Castro (73).

579. 09.07.1991 **ECUADOR - URUGUAY** **1-1(1-0)** 35th Copa América. Group Stage
Estadio Sausalito, Viña del Mar (Chile); Referee: Gastón Castro (Chile), Attendance: 18,000
URU: Fernando Harry Álvez Mosquera (28/0), Guillermo Oscar Sanguinetti Giordano (7/0), Daniel Felipe Revelez (17/1), Eber Alejandro Moas Silvera (11/0), Rúben Fernando Dos Santos (6/0), Héctor Morán (7/0), Álvaro Gutiérrez Pelscher (6/0), Ramón Víctor Castro (4/1), Marcelo Fracchia (3/0), Peter Méndez (5/2), Edgar Borges (7/0). Trainer: Luis Alberto Cubilla Almeida Almeida (5).
Goal: Peter Méndez (47 penalty).

580. 11.07.1991 **BRAZIL - URUGUAY** **1-1(1-0)** 35th Copa América. Group Stage
Estadio Sausalito, Viña del Mar (Chile); Referee: Juan Carlos Loustau (Argentina), Attendance: 15,000
URU: Fernando Harry Álvez Mosquera (29/0), Guillermo Oscar Sanguinetti Giordano (8/0), Daniel Felipe Revelez (18/1), Eber Alejandro Moas Silvera (12/0), Rúben Fernando Dos Santos (7/0), Héctor Morán (8/0), Álvaro Gutiérrez Pelscher (7/0), Ramón Víctor Castro (5/1), Marcelo Fracchia (4/0) [88.William Gutiérrez (6/0)], Peter Méndez (6/3), Edgar Borges (8/0) [46.Néstor Gabriel Cedrés Vera (8/1)]. Trainer: Luis Alberto Cubilla Almeida Almeida (6).
Goal: Peter Méndez (66).

581. 15.07.1991 **URUGUAY - COLOMBIA** **1-0(1-0)** 35th Copa América. Group Stage
Estadio Sausalito, Viña del Mar (Chile); Referee: Juan Carlos Loustau (Argentina), Attendance: 15,721
URU: Fernando Harry Álvez Mosquera (30/0), Guillermo Oscar Sanguinetti Giordano (9/0), Daniel Felipe Revelez (19/1), Eber Alejandro Moas Silvera (13/0), Rúben Fernando Dos Santos (8/0), Héctor Morán (9/0), Álvaro Gutiérrez Pelscher (8/0) [*sent off 40*], Ramón Víctor Castro (6/1) [66.Henry López Báez (8/1)], Marcelo Fracchia (5/0), Peter Méndez (7/4), Néstor Gabriel Cedrés Vera (9/1) [46.Daniel Florencio Sánchez (8/0)]. Trainer: Luis Alberto Cubilla Almeida Almeida (7).
Goal: Peter Méndez (19).

582. 04.09.1991 **SPAIN - URUGUAY** **2-1(2-0)**
Estadio „Carlos Tartiere", Oviedo; Referee: Jacobus Uilenberg (Holland), Attendance: 21,600
URU: Fernando Harry Álvez Mosquera (31/0), Fernando Rosa (1/0), Daniel Felipe Revelez (20/1), Eber Alejandro Moas Silvera (14/0), Rúben Fernando Dos Santos (9/0), Santiago Javier Ostolaza Sosa (29/5), Marcelo Fracchia (6/0) [79.Néstor Gabriel Cedrés Vera (10/1)], Gustavo Cristian Matosas (6/1), William Adrián Castro (9/2) [65.Álvaro Gutiérrez Pelscher (9/1)], Peter Méndez (8/4), Raphael Aguerre (1/0). Trainer: Luis Alberto Cubilla Almeida Almeida (8).
Goal: Álvaro Gutiérrez Pelscher (66).

583. 20.11.1991 **MEXICO - URUGUAY** **1-1(0-0)**
Estadio „Luis de la Fuente", Veracruz; Referee: Angelo Bratsis (United States), Attendance: 18,000
URU: Fernando Harry Álvez Mosquera (32/0), Cesilio De los Santos (1/0), Daniel Felipe Revelez (21/1), Eber Alejandro Moas Silvera (15/0), Rúben Fernando Dos Santos (10/0), Héctor Morán (10/0), Santiago Javier Ostolaza Sosa (30/5), Marcelo Fracchia (7/0), Ramón Víctor Castro (7/1) [75.Álvaro Gutiérrez Pelscher (10/1)], Néstor Gabriel Cedrés Vera (11/2) [75.Marcelo Tejera (1/0)], William Gutiérrez (7/0) [75.Gustavo Ferreyra (5/1)]. Trainer: Luis Alberto Cubilla Almeida Almeida (9).
Goal: Néstor Gabriel Cedrés Vera (72).

584. 30.04.1992 **URUGUAY - BRAZIL** **1-0(0-0)**
Estadio Centenario, Montevideo; Referee: Juan Antonio Bava (Argentina), Attendance: 20,000
URU: Luis Alberto Barbat (1/0), Leonardo Ramos (3/0), Daniel Florencio Sánchez (9/0), Fernando Alfredo Kanapkis García (1/0), Nelson Cabrera (9/0), Luis Carlos Sánchez (1/0), Jorge Wálter Barrios Balestrasse (58/4), José Luis Zalazar Rodríguez (17/3), Walter Peletti (1/0), Hugo Romeo Guerra (1/0), Adrián Gustavo Paz (1/1). Trainer: Luis Alberto Cubilla Almeida Almeida (10).
Goal: Adrián Gustavo Paz (70).

585. 21.06.1992 **URUGUAY - AUSTRALIA** **2-0(0-0)**
Estadio Centenario, Montevideo; Referee: Juan Carlos Loustau (Argentina), Attendance: 18,000
URU: Robert Dante Siboldi Badiola (1/0), Cesilio De los Santos (2/0), Daniel Florencio Sánchez (10/0), Fernando Alfredo Kanapkis García (2/0), Nelson Cabrera (10/0), Jorge Wálter Barrios Balestrasse (59/4), José Luis Zalazar Rodríguez (18/3), Marcelo Saralegui Arregín (1/0), Adrián Gustavo Paz (2/1) [78.Diego Martín Dorta (2/0)], Alejandro Javier Larrea Marzol (1/1), Claudio Morena (1/0) [46.Sergio Daniel Martínez Alzuri (20/3)]. Trainer: Luis Alberto Cubilla Almeida Almeida (11).
Goals: Sergio Daniel Martínez Alzuri (64), Alejandro Javier Larrea Marzol (84).

586. 04.07.1992 **URUGUAY - ECUADOR** **3-1(1-0)**
Estadio Centenario, Montevideo; Referee: Juan Carlos Crespi (Argentina), Attendance: 15,000
URU: Robert Dante Siboldi Badiola (2/0), Julio César ‚Tony' Gómez (1/0), Daniel Florencio Sánchez (11/0), Fernando Alfredo Kanapkis García (3/1), Nelson Cabrera (11/0), Jorge Wálter Barrios Balestrasse (60/4), Santiago Javier Ostolaza Sosa (31/5), José Luis Zalazar Rodríguez (19/4), Marcelo Saralegui Arregín (2/0) [75.Diego Martín Dorta (3/0)], Alejandro Javier Larrea Marzol (2/1), Adrián Gustavo Paz (3/2) [76.Sergio Daniel Martínez Alzuri (21/3)]. Trainer: Luis Alberto Cubilla Almeida Almeida (12).
Goals: Fernando Alfredo Kanapkis García (6), Adrián Gustavo Paz (55), José Luis Zalazar Rodríguez (67).

587. 01.08.1992 **URUGUAY - COSTA RICA** **2-1(2-0)**
Estadio Centenario, Montevideo; Referee: Francisco Lamolina (Argentina), Attendance: 16,000
URU: Luis Alberto Barbat (2/0), Guillermo Oscar Sanguinetti Giordano (10/1), Fernando Alfredo Kanapkis García (4/1), Daniel Florencio Sánchez (12/0), Nelson Cabrera (12/0), Marcelo Saralegui Arregín (3/0) [82.Diego Martín Dorta (4/0)], Jorge Wálter Barrios Balestrasse (61/4), Eber Alejandro Moas Silvera (16/0) [72.Yubert Lemos (1/0)], Walter Peletti (2/0), Hugo Romeo Guerra (2/0), Adrián Gustavo Paz (4/3) [*sent off 54*]. Trainer: Luis Alberto Cubilla Almeida Almeida (13).
Goals: Guillermo Oscar Sanguinetti Giordano (30), Adrián Gustavo Paz (42).

588. 23.09.1992 **URUGUAY - ARGENTINA** **0-0** Copa Lipton
Estadio Centenario, Montevideo; Referee: Félix Ramón Benegas Caballero (Paraguay), Attendance: 35,000
URU: Robert Dante Siboldi Badiola (3/0), Guillermo Oscar Sanguinetti Giordano (11/1), Daniel Florencio Sánchez (13/0), Fernando Alfredo Kanapkis García (5/1) [*sent off 71*], Nelson Cabrera (13/0), Gustavo Cristian Matosas (7/1) [46.Héctor Morán (11/0)], Santiago Javier Ostolaza Sosa (32/5), Gerardo Miranda (1/0) [72.Diego Martín Dorta (5/0)], José Luis Zalazar Rodríguez (20/4), Walter Peletti (3/0), Hugo Romeo Guerra (3/0). Trainer: Luis Alberto Cubilla Almeida Almeida (14).

589. 25.11.1992 **BRAZIL - URUGUAY** **1-2(1-1)**
Estádio „Ernâni Sátiro", Campina Grande; Referee: José Cristóvão da Silva França (Brazil), Attendance: 18,000
URU: Robert Dante Siboldi Badiola (4/0), Luis Da Luz (1/0), Daniel Florencio Sánchez (14/0), Eber Alejandro Moas Silvera (17/0), Nelson Cabrera (14/1), Héctor Morán (12/0), Santiago Javier Ostolaza Sosa (33/5), Marcelo Saralegui Arregín (4/0), José Enrique García (1/0) [87.Luis Carlos Sánchez (2/0)], Hugo Romeo Guerra (4/1), Walter Peletti (4/0). Trainer: Luis Alberto Cubilla Almeida Almeida (15).
Goals: Nelson Cabrera (42), Hugo Romeo Guerra (65).

590. 29.11.1992 **URUGUAY - POLAND** **0-1(0-0)**
Estadio Centenario, Montevideo; Referee: Javier Alberto Castrilli (Argentina), Attendance: 25,000
URU: Robert Dante Siboldi Badiola (5/0), Julio César ‚Tony' Gómez (2/0), Fernando Alfredo Kanapkis García (6/1), Daniel Florencio Sánchez (15/0), Nelson Cabrera (15/1), Marcelo Saralegui Arregín (5/0), Diego Martín Dorta (6/0) [75.Gerardo Rodríguez (1/0)], Luis Carlos Sánchez (3/0), Andrés Martínez (1/0) [70.Gerardo Miranda (2/0)], Peter Méndez (9/4) [46.José Enrique García (2/0)], Ricardo Dos Santos (1/0). Trainer: Luis Alberto Cubilla Almeida Almeida (16).

591. 20.12.1992 **URUGUAY - GERMANY** **1-4(0-1)**
Estadio Centenario, Montevideo; Referee: Juan Carlos Lousteau (Argentina), Attendance: 37,800
URU: Robert Dante Siboldi Badiola (6/0), Julio César ‚Tony' Gómez (3/0), Daniel Florencio Sánchez (16/0), Eber Alejandro Moas Silvera (18/0), Nelson Cabrera (16/1), Marcelo Saralegui Arregín (6/0) [58.José Enrique García (3/0)], Álvaro Gutiérrez Pelscher (11/1), Héctor Morán (13/1), José Luis Zalazar Rodríguez (21/4), Walter Peletti (5/0), Hugo Romeo Guerra (5/1). Trainer: Luis Alberto Cubilla Almeida Almeida (17).
Goal: Héctor Morán (84).

592. 16.06.1993 **URUGUAY - UNITED STATES** **1-0(0-0)** 36th Copa America. Group Stage
Estadio Bellavista, Ambato (Ecuador); Referee: Alberto Tejada (Peru), Attendance: 25,000
URU: Robert Dante Siboldi Badiola (7/0), Guillermo Oscar Sanguinetti Giordano (12/1), Daniel Florencio Sánchez (17/0), Fernando Alfredo Kanapkis García (7/1), Cesilio De los Santos (3/0), Santiago Javier Ostolaza Sosa (34/6), Héctor Morán (14/1) [73.Eber Alejandro Moas Silvera (19/0)], Marcelo Saralegui Arregín (7/0), Walter Peletti (6/0), Jorge Orosmán da Silva Echeverrito (23/6), Adrián Gustavo Paz (5/3) [83.Fabián Alberto O'Neill Domínguez (1/0)]. Trainer: Luis Alberto Cubilla Almeida Almeida (18).
Goal: Santiago Javier Ostolaza Sosa (50).

593. 19.06.1993 **URUGUAY - VENEZUELA** **2-2(1-1)** 36th Copa America. Group Stage
Estadio Bellavista, Ambato (Ecuador); Referee: Pablo Peña (Bolivia), Attendance: 15,000
URU: Robert Dante Siboldi Badiola (8/0), Guillermo Oscar Sanguinetti Giordano (13/1), Daniel Florencio Sánchez (18/0), Fernando Alfredo Kanapkis García (8/2), Cesilio De los Santos (4/0), Santiago Javier Ostolaza Sosa (35/6), Héctor Morán (15/1) [76.Hugo Romeo Guerra (6/1)], Marcelo Saralegui Arregín (8/1), Walter Peletti (7/0) [62.Eber Alejandro Moas Silvera (20/0)], Jorge Orosmán da Silva Echeverrito (24/6), Adrián Gustavo Paz (6/3). Trainer: Luis Alberto Cubilla Almeida Almeida (19).
Goals: Marcelo Saralegui Arregín (23), Fernando Alfredo Kanapkis García (79).

594. 22.06.1993 **ECUADOR - URUGUAY** **2-1(1-0)** 36th Copa America. Group Stage
Estadio Olimpico „Atahualpa", Quito; Referee: Francisco Lamolina (Argentina), Attendance: 45,000
URU: Robert Dante Siboldi Badiola (9/0), Guillermo Oscar Sanguinetti Giordano (14/1), Daniel Florencio Sánchez (19/0), Fernando Alfredo Kanapkis García (9/3), Cesilio De los Santos (5/0), Eber Alejandro Moas Silvera (21/0), Santiago Javier Ostolaza Sosa (36/6), Héctor Morán (16/1), Marcelo Saralegui Arregín (9/1), Hugo Romeo Guerra (7/1), Adrián Gustavo Paz (7/3). Trainer: Luis Alberto Cubilla Almeida Almeida (20).
Goal: Fernando Alfredo Kanapkis García (64).

595. 26.06.1993 **COLOMBIA - URUGUAY** **1-1(0-0,1-1); 5-3 on penalties** 36th Copa América. Quarter-Finals
Estadio Monumental, Guayaquil (Ecuador); Referee: Juan Francisco Escobar (Paraguay), Attendance: 15,000
URU: Robert Dante Siboldi Badiola (10/0), Nelson Cabrera (17/1), Daniel Florencio Sánchez (20/0), Fernando Alfredo Kanapkis García (10/3), Cesilio De los Santos (6/0), Eber Alejandro Moas Silvera (22/0), Santiago Javier Ostolaza Sosa (37/6), Héctor Morán (17/1), Marcelo Saralegui Arregín (10/2), Hugo Romeo Guerra (8/1) [57.Jorge Orosmán da Silva Echeverrito (25/6)], Walter Peletti (8/0). Trainer: Luis Alberto Cubilla Almeida Almeida (21).
Goal: Marcelo Saralegui Arregín (63).
Penalties: Walter Peletti, Marcelo Saralegui Arregín, Eber Alejandro Moas Silvera (miss), Robert Dante Siboldi Badiola

596. 13.07.1993 **PERU - URUGUAY** **1-2(0-1)**
Estadio Nacional, Lima; Referee: Luis Ángel Seminario (Peru), Attendance: 16,050
URU: Robert Dante Siboldi Badiola (11/0), José Oscar Herrera Corominas (31/3), Daniel Florencio Sánchez (21/0), Fernando Alfredo Kanapkis García (11/3), Nelson Cabrera (18/1), Héctor Morán (18/1), Santiago Javier Ostolaza Sosa (38/6), Gustavo Augusto Poyet Domínguez (1/0) [67.Carlos Alberto Aguilera Nova (56/22)], José Luis Zalazar Rodríguez (22/4), Daniel Fonseca (7/1), Rubén Sosa Ardáiz (33/12) [62.Eber Alejandro Moas Silvera (23/0)]. Trainer: Luis Alberto Cubilla Almeida Almeida (22).
Goals: Rubén Sosa Ardáiz (29, 56).

597. 17.07.1993 **URUGUAY - PERU** **3-0(3-0)**
Estadio Centenario, Montevideo; Referee: Daniel Bello (Uruguay), Attendance: 60,000
URU: Robert Dante Siboldi Badiola (12/0), José Oscar Herrera Corominas (32/3), Daniel Florencio Sánchez (22/0) [46.Héctor Rodríguez Peña (2/0)], Fernando Alfredo Kanapkis García (12/3), Nelson Cabrera (19/1) [79.Cesilio De los Santos (7/0)], Héctor Morán (19/2), Santiago Javier Ostolaza Sosa (39/6), Enzo Francéscoli Uriarte (47/12) [62.Carlos Alberto Aguilera Nova (57/22)], José Luis Zalazar Rodríguez (23/4), Daniel Fonseca (8/3) [72.Gustavo Augusto Poyet Domínguez (2/0)], Rubén Sosa Ardáiz (34/12). Trainer: Luis Alberto Cubilla Almeida Almeida (23).
Goals: Daniel Fonseca (10), Héctor Morán (27), Daniel Fonseca (32).

598. 25.07.1993 **VENEZUELA - URUGUAY** **0-1(0-0)** 15th FIFA WC. Qualifiers

Estadio Pueblo Nuevo, San Cristóbal; Referee: José Joaquín Torres Cádena (Colombia), Attendance: 10,000

URU: Robert Dante Siboldi Badiola (13/0), José Oscar Herrera Corominas (33/4) [72.Cesilio De los Santos (8/0)], Fernando Alfredo Kanapkis García (13/3), Daniel Florencio Sánchez (23/0), Nelson Cabrera (20/1), Héctor Morán (20/2), Santiago Javier Ostolaza Sosa (40/6), José Luis Zalazar Rodríguez (24/4), Enzo Francéscoli Uriarte (48/12), Daniel Fonseca (9/3), Rubén Sosa Ardáiz (35/12) [85.Carlos Alberto Aguilera Nova (58/22)]. Trainer: Luis Alberto Cubilla Almeida Almeida (24).

Goal: José Oscar Herrera Corominas (59).

599. 01.08.1993 **URUGUAY - ECUADOR** **0-0** 15th FIFA WC. Qualifiers

Estadio Centenario, Montevideo; Referee: Alberto Tejada Noriega (Peru), Attendance: 45,000

URU: Robert Dante Siboldi Badiola (14/0), José Oscar Herrera Corominas (34/4), Daniel Florencio Sánchez (24/0), Fernando Alfredo Kanapkis García (14/3), Nelson Cabrera (21/1), Héctor Morán (21/2) [78.Jorge Orosmán da Silva Echeverrito (26/6)], Santiago Javier Ostolaza Sosa (41/6), José Luis Zalazar Rodríguez (25/4), Enzo Francéscoli Uriarte (49/12), Daniel Fonseca (10/3) [46.Carlos Alberto Aguilera Nova (59/22)], Rubén Sosa Ardáiz (36/12). Trainer: Luis Alberto Cubilla Almeida Almeida (25).

600. 08.08.1993 **BOLIVIA - URUGUAY** **3-1(0-0)** 15th FIFA WC. Qualifiers

Estadio „Hernándo Siles Zuazo", La Paz; Referee: Iván Enrique Guerrero Levancini (Chile), Attendance: 45,000

URU: Robert Dante Siboldi Badiola (15/0), José Oscar Herrera Corominas (35/4), Daniel Florencio Sánchez (25/0), Fernando Alfredo Kanapkis García (15/3), Nelson Cabrera (22/1), Héctor Morán (22/2), Álvaro Gutiérrez Pelscher (12/1) [*sent off 27*], José Luis Zalazar Rodríguez (26/4), Enzo Francéscoli Uriarte (50/13), Daniel Fonseca (11/3) [67.Eber Alejandro Moas Silvera (24/0)], Rubén Sosa Ardáiz (37/12) [60.Carlos Alberto Aguilera Nova (60/22)]. Trainer: Luis Alberto Cubilla Almeida Almeida (26).

Goal: Enzo Francéscoli Uriarte (90).

601. 15.08.1993 **URUGUAY - BRAZIL** **1-1(0-1)** 15th FIFA WC. Qualifiers

Estadio Centenario, Montevideo; Referee: Juan Antonio Bava (Argentina), Attendance: 55,000

URU: Robert Dante Siboldi Badiola (16/0), Guillermo Oscar Sanguinetti Giordano (15/1), Daniel Florencio Sánchez (26/0), Fernando Alfredo Kanapkis García (16/3), Nelson Cabrera (23/1), Héctor Morán (23/2), Santiago Javier Ostolaza Sosa (42/6) [72.José Luis Zalazar Rodríguez (27/4)], Enzo Francéscoli Uriarte (51/13), Carlos Alberto Aguilera Nova (61/22), Daniel Fonseca (12/4), Rubén Sosa Ardáiz (38/12) [57.Adrián Gustavo Paz (8/3)]. Trainer: Luis Alberto Cubilla Almeida Almeida (27).

Goal: Daniel Fonseca (79).

602. 29.08.1993 **URUGUAY - VENEZUELA** **4-0(3-0)** 15th FIFA WC. Qualifiers

Estadio Centenario, Montevideo; Referee: Juan Francisco Escobar (Paraguay), Attendance: 20,000

URU: Robert Dante Siboldi Badiola (17/0), Gustavo Emilio Méndez Techera (1/0), José Oscar Herrera Corominas (36/4), Fernando Alfredo Kanapkis García (17/5), Carlos Soca (1/0) [37.Cesilio De los Santos (9/0)], Diego Martín Dorta (7/0), Álvaro Gutiérrez Pelscher (13/1), Enzo Francéscoli Uriarte (52/13), Carlos Alberto Aguilera Nova (62/22) [61.Adrián Gustavo Paz (9/3)], Néstor Gabriel Cedrés Vera (12/3), Rubén Sosa Ardáiz (39/13). Trainer: Ildo Enrique Maneiro Ghezzi (1).

Goals: Fernando Alfredo Kanapkis García (7, 31), Néstor Gabriel Cedrés Vera (41), Rubén Sosa Ardáiz (64).

603. 05.09.1993 **ECUADOR - URUGUAY** **0-1(0-1)** 15th FIFA WC. Qualifiers

Estadio „Isidro Romero Carbo", Guayaquil; Referee: Enrique Marín Gallo (Chile), Attendance: 65,000

URU: Robert Dante Siboldi Badiola (18/0), Gustavo Emilio Méndez Techera (2/0), José Oscar Herrera Corominas (37/4), Ricardo Canals (1/0), Fernando Alfredo Kanapkis García (18/5), José Alberto Batista González (12/1), Álvaro Gutiérrez Pelscher (14/1), Diego Martín Dorta (8/0), Enzo Francéscoli Uriarte (53/13) [69.Daniel Fonseca (13/4)], Carlos Alberto Aguilera Nova (63/22) [64.Marcelo Saralegui Arregín (11/2)], Rubén Sosa Ardáiz (40/14) [*sent off 89*]. Trainer: Ildo Enrique Maneiro Ghezzi (2).

Goal: Rubén Sosa Ardáiz (9).

604. 12.09.1993 **URUGUAY - BOLIVIA** **2-1(1-1)** 15th FIFA WC. Qualifiers

Estadio Centenario, Montevideo; Referee: Armando Pérez Hoyos (Colombia), Attendance: 58,000

URU: Robert Dante Siboldi Badiola (19/0), Gustavo Emilio Méndez Techera (3/0), José Oscar Herrera Corominas (38/4), Ricardo Canals (2/0), José Alberto Batista González (13/1), Diego Martín Dorta (9/0), Álvaro Gutiérrez Pelscher (15/1) [46.José Luis Zalazar Rodríguez (28/4)], Enzo Francéscoli Uriarte (54/14), Carlos Alberto Aguilera Nova (64/22) [*sent off 43*], Néstor Gabriel Cedrés Vera (13/3), Daniel Fonseca (14/5) [75.Marcelo Saralegui Arregín (12/2)]. Trainer: Ildo Enrique Maneiro Ghezzi (3).

Goals: Enzo Francéscoli Uriarte (3 penalty), Daniel Fonseca (51).

605. 19.09.1993 **BRAZIL - URUGUAY** **2-0(0-0)** 15th FIFA WC. Qualifiers

Estádio „Jornalista Mário Filho" (Maracanã), Rio de Janeiro; Referee: Alberto Tejada (Peru), Attendance: 101,533

URU: Robert Dante Siboldi Badiola (20/0), Gustavo Emilio Méndez Techera (4/0), José Oscar Herrera Corominas (39/4), Ricardo Canals (3/0) [68.José Luis Zalazar Rodríguez (29/4)], Fernando Alfredo Kanapkis García (19/5), José Alberto Batista González (14/1), Diego Martín Dorta (10/0), Álvaro Gutiérrez Pelscher (16/1), Enzo Francéscoli Uriarte (55/14) [68.Adrián Gustavo Paz (10/3)], Daniel Fonseca (15/5), Rubén Sosa Ardáiz (41/14). Trainer: Ildo Enrique Maneiro Ghezzi (4).

606. 13.10.1993 **GERMANY - URUGUAY** **5-0(3-0)**

Wildpark-Stadion, Karlsruhe; Referee: Gerd Grabher (Austria), Attendance: 29,000

URU: Oscar Ferro (3/0), José González (1/0) [46.Ricardo Bitancourt (1/0)], Ronald Paolo Montero (5/0), Fernando Alfredo Kanapkis García (20/5), Luis María Romero (1/0), Julio César Rodríguez (1/0), Gustavo Augusto Poyet Domínguez (3/0), Santiago Javier Ostolaza Sosa (43/6), Juan Ferreri (1/0), Jacinto Javier Cabrera López (6/1) [63.Osvaldo Canobbio (1/0)], Ricardo dos Santos (2/0) [55.Julio César Albino (1/0)]. Trainer: Roberto Fleitas (5).

607. 19.10.1994 **PERU - URUGUAY** **0-1(0-1)** Parra del Riego Cup

Estadio Nacional, Lima; Referee: Antonio Arnao Ortega (Peru), Attendance: 8,000

URU: Claudio Arbiza (1/0), Raúl Omar Otero (1/0), Luis Diego López Breijo (1/0), Álvaro Gutiérrez Pelscher (17/1), Edgardo Alberto Adinolfi Duarte (1/0), Nelson Javier Abeijón Pessi (1/0), Diego Martín Dorta (11/0) [82.Diego Tito (1/0)], Andrés Martínez (2/0) [73.Tabaré Abayubá Silva (1/0)], Pablo Javier Bengoechea Dutra (19/2) [73.Gustavo Emilio Méndez Techera (5/0)], Marcelo Alejandro Otero (1/0) [69.Darío Delgado (1/0)], Debray Darío Silva Pereira (1/1) [78.Fernando Edgardo Correa Ayala (1/0)]. Trainer: Héctor Núñez Bello (1).

Goal: Debray Darío Silva Pereira (8).

608. 18.01.1995 **SPAIN – URUGUAY** **2-2(1-2)**
Estadio Riazor, La Coruña; Referee: Atanas Uzunov (Bulgaria), Attendance: 22,000
URU: Claudio Arbiza (2/0), Rúben Alzueta (1/0) [46.Washington Eduardo Tais Videgaín (1/0)], Óscar Aguirregaray Acosta (1/0), Álvaro Gutiérrez Pelscher (18/1) [46.Debray Darío Silva Pereira (2/1)], Ronald Paolo Montero (6/0), Diego Martín Dorta (12/0), Eber Alejandro Moas Silvera (25/0), Pablo Javier Bengoechea Dutra (20/3) [85.Marcelo Alejandro Otero (2/0)], Gustavo Augusto Poyet Domínguez (4/0), Daniel Fonseca (16/6) [65.Ricardo Canals (4/0)], Enzo Francéscoli Uriarte (56/14) [65.Álvaro Alexander Recoba Rivero (1/0)]. Trainer: Héctor Núñez Bello (2).
Goals: Daniel Fonseca (18), Pablo Javier Bengoechea Dutra (39).

609. 01.02.1995 **MEXICO – URUGUAY** **1-0(1-0)**
"Jack Murphy" Stadium, San Diego; Referee: Arturo Angeles (United States), Attendance: 19,000
URU: Oscar Ferro (4/0), Washington Eduardo Tais Videgaín (2/0) [65.Diego Tito (2/0)], Álvaro Gutiérrez Pelscher (19/1), Eber Alejandro Moas Silvera (26/0), Tabaré Abayubá Silva (2/0), Nelson Javier Abeijón Pessi (2/0), Diego Martín Dorta (13/0), Raúl Omar Otero (2/0) [65.Álvaro Alexander Recoba Rivero (2/0)], Pablo Javier Bengoechea Dutra (21/3), Sergio Daniel Martínez Alzuri (22/3), Debray Darío Silva Pereira (3/1) [65.Edgardo Alberto Adinolfi Duarte (2/0)]. Trainer: Héctor Núñez Bello (3).

610. 22.03.1995 **COLOMBIA – URUGUAY** **2-1(1-0)**
Estadio „Atanasio Girardot", Medellín; Referee: Felipe Russi (Colombia), Attendance: 30,000
URU: Rúben Rodríguez (1/0), Gustavo Emilio Méndez Techera (6/0), Luis Diego López Breijo (2/0), Álvaro Gutiérrez Pelscher (20/1), Tabaré Abayubá Silva (3/0) [46.Edgardo Alberto Adinolfi Duarte (3/0)], Claudio Elías (1/0), Nelson Javier Abeijón Pessi (3/0), Gustavo Augusto Poyet Domínguez (5/0) [46.Marcelo Tejera (2/0)], Marcelo Alejandro Otero (3/0) [60.Raúl Omar Otero (3/0)], Osvaldo Canobbio (2/1), Debray Darío Silva Pereira (4/1). Trainer: Héctor Núñez Bello (4).
Goal: Osvaldo Canobbio (53).

611. 25.03.1995 **UNITED STATES – URUGUAY** **2-2(1-0)**
Cotton Bowl, Dallas; Referee: Antonio Marrufo Mendóza (Mexico), Attendance: 12,242
URU: Oscar Ferro (5/0), Gustavo Emilio Méndez Techera (7/0), Luis Diego López Breijo (3/0), Álvaro Gutiérrez Pelscher (21/1), Edgardo Alberto Adinolfi Duarte (4/0), Claudio Elías (2/0), Raúl Omar Otero (4/0) [64.Nelson Javier Abeijón Pessi (4/0)], Gustavo Augusto Poyet Domínguez (6/1), Marcelo Tejera (3/0) [64.Debray Darío Silva Pereira (5/1)], Marcelo Alejandro Otero (4/1), Osvaldo Canobbio (3/1). Trainer: Héctor Núñez Bello (5).
Goals: Marcelo Alejandro Otero (75), Gustavo Augusto Poyet Domínguez (83).
Abandoned after 84 minutes due to severe weather.

612. 29.03.1995 **ENGLAND – URUGUAY** **0-0**
Wembley Stadium, London; Referee: Hellmut Krug (Germany), Attendance: 34,894
URU: Oscar Ferro (6/0), Luis Diego López Breijo (4/0), Óscar Aguirregaray Acosta (2/0), Álvaro Gutiérrez Pelscher (22/1), Ronald Paolo Montero (7/0), Diego Martín Dorta (14/0), Pablo Javier Bengoechea Dutra (22/3), Gustavo Augusto Poyet Domínguez (7/1), Néstor Gabriel Cedrés Vera (14/3), Daniel Fonseca (17/6), Enzo Francéscoli Uriarte (57/14) [85.Debray Darío Silva Pereira (6/1)]. Trainer: Héctor Núñez Bello (6).

613. 31.03.1995 **YUGOSLAVIA – URUGUAY** **1-0(0-0)**
Crvena zvezda Stadion, Beograd; Referee: Sándor Puhl (Hungary), Attendance: 28,288
URU: Oscar Ferro (7/0), Gustavo Emilio Méndez Techera (8/0), Óscar Aguirregaray Acosta (3/0), Ronald Paolo Montero (8/0), Tabaré Abayubá Silva (4/0) [62.Edgardo Alberto Adinolfi Duarte (5/0)], Diego Martín Dorta (15/0) [27.Nelson Javier Abeijón Pessi (5/0)], Claudio Elías (3/0), Pablo Javier Bengoechea Dutra (23/3) (62.Marcelo Tejera (4/0)], Marcelo Otero (5/1) [77.Osvaldo Canobbio (4/1)], Enzo Francéscoli Uriarte (58/14) [46.Néstor Gabriel Cedrés Vera (15/3)], Debray Darío Silva Pereira (7/1). Trainer: Héctor Núñez Bello (7).

614. 05.04.1995 **URUGUAY – PERU** **1-0(0-0)** El Inca Cup
Estadio Centenario, Montevideo; Referee: Gustavo Gallesio (Uruguay), Attendance: 10,000
URU: Oscar Ferro (8/0), Luis Diego López Breijo (5/0), Óscar Aguirregaray Acosta (4/0), Álvaro Gutiérrez Pelscher (23/1), Edgardo Alberto Adinolfi Duarte (6/0), Gustavo Emilio Méndez Techera (9/0) [59.Marcelo Tejera (5/0)], Nelson Javier Abeijón Pessi (6/0), Raúl Omar Otero (5/0) [59.Tabaré Abayubá Silva (5/0)], Pablo Javier Bengoechea Dutra (24/4), Marcelo Alejandro Otero (6/1), Debray Darío Silva Pereira (8/1) [69.Osvaldo Canobbio (5/1)]. Trainer: Héctor Núñez Bello (8).
Goal: Pablo Javier Bengoechea Dutra (58 penalty).

615. 25.06.1995 **URUGUAY – NEW ZEALAND** **7-0(3-0)**
Estadio „General José Artigas", Paysandú; Referee: Daniel Adolfo Bello Rotunno (Uruguay), Attendance: 20,000
URU: Claudio Arbiza (3/0), José Oscar Herrera Corominas (40/4), Luis Diego López Breijo (6/0), Eber Alejandro Moas Silvera (27/0), Tabaré Abayubá Silva (6/0), Gustavo Augusto Poyet Domínguez (8/1), Álvaro Gutiérrez Pelscher (24/1) [46.Osvaldo Canobbio (6/2)], Rubén Fernando da Silva Echeverrito (13/3) [46.Nelson Javier Abeijón Pessi (7/1)], Rubén Sosa Ardáiz (42/15) [63.Sergio Daniel Martínez Alzuri (23/4)], Marcelo Alejandro Otero (7/1) [56.Debray Darío Silva Pereira (9/2)], Daniel Fonseca (18/8) [47.Marcelo Saralegui Arregín (13/2)]. Trainer: Héctor Núñez Bello (9).
Goals: Daniel Fonseca (1, 30), Rubén Sosa Ardáiz (37), Nelson Javier Abeijón Pessi (60), Debray Darío Silva Pereira (80), Osvaldo Canobbio (83), Sergio Daniel Martínez Alzuri (88).

616. 28.06.1995 **URUGUAY – NEW ZEALAND** **2-2(1-1)**
Estadio „Atilio Paiva Olivera", Rivera; Referee: Julio Matto (Uruguay), Attendance: 27,000
URU: Fernando Harry Álvez Mosquera (33/0), José Oscar Herrera Corominas (41/4), Óscar Aguirregaray Acosta (5/0), Eber Alejandro Moas Silvera (28/0), Edgardo Alberto Adinolfi Duarte (7/0) [46.Tabaré Abayubá Silva (7/0)], Gustavo Augusto Poyet Domínguez (9/1) [46.Rubén Sosa Ardáiz (43/15)], Álvaro Gutiérrez Pelscher (25/1), Pablo Javier Bengoechea Dutra (25/4) [55.Marcelo Saralegui Arregín (14/2)], Enzo Francéscoli Uriarte (59/15) (55.Nelson Javier Abeijón Pessi (8/1)], Osvaldo Canobbio (7/2) [46.Sergio Daniel Martínez Alzuri (24/5)], Daniel Fonseca (19/8) [76.Debray Darío Silva Pereira (10/2)]. Trainer: Héctor Núñez Bello (10).
Goals: Enzo Francéscoli Uriarte (10), Sergio Daniel Martínez Alzuri (55).

617. 05.07.1995 **URUGUAY – VENEZUELA** **4-1(2-0)** 37th Copa América. Group Stage
Estadio Centenario, Montevideo; Referee: Salvador Imperatore (Chile), Attendance: 32,000
URU: Fernando Harry Álvez Mosquera (34/0), José Oscar Herrera Corominas (42/4), Eber Alejandro Moas Silvera (29/0), Tabaré Abayubá Silva (8/0), Óscar Aguirregaray Acosta (6/0) [71.Luis Diego López Breijo (7/0)], Pablo Javier Bengoechea Dutra (26/4) [75.Rubén Sosa Ardáiz (44/15)], Álvaro Gutiérrez Pelscher (26/1), Gustavo Augusto Poyet Domínguez (10/2), Enzo Francéscoli Uriarte (60/16) (84.Diego Martín Dorta (16/0)], Daniel Fonseca (20/9), Marcelo Alejandro Otero (8/2). Trainer: Héctor Núñez Bello (11).
Goals: Daniel Fonseca (9), Marcelo Alejandro Otero (25), Enzo Francéscoli Uriarte (75 penalty), Gustavo Augusto Poyet Domínguez (84).

618. 09.07.1995 **URUGUAY - PARAGUAY** **1-0(1-0)** 37th Copa América. Group Stage

Estadio Centenario, Montevideo; Referee: Márcio Rezende de Freitas (Brazil), Attendance: 40,000

URU: Fernando Harry Álvez Mosquera (35/0), Gustavo Emilio Méndez Techera (10/0), José Oscar Herrera Corominas (43/4), Eber Alejandro Moas Silvera (30/0), Tabaré Abayubá Silva (9/0), Diego Martín Dorta (17/0), Álvaro Gutiérrez Pelscher (27/1), Gustavo Augusto Poyet Domínguez (11/2), Enzo Francéscoli Uriarte (61/17) [76.Marcelo Saralegui Arregín (15/2)], Marcelo Alejandro Otero (9/2) [46.Rubén Sosa Ardáiz (45/15)], Daniel Fonseca (21/9) [71.Sergio Daniel Martínez Alzuri (25/5)]. Trainer: Héctor Núñez Bello (12).

Goal: Enzo Francéscoli Uriarte (14).

619. 13.07.1995 **URUGUAY - MEXICO** **1-1(0-0)** 37th Copa América. Group Stage

Estadio Centenario, Montevideo; Referee: Javier Castrilli (Argentina), Attendance: 10,000

URU: Fernando Harry Álvez Mosquera (36/0), Gustavo Emilio Méndez Techera (11/0), José Oscar Herrera Corominas (44/4), Eber Alejandro Moas Silvera (31/0), Edgardo Alberto Adinolfi Duarte (8/0), Marcelo Saralegui Arregín (16/3), Diego Martín Dorta (18/0), Pablo Javier Bengoechea Dutra (27/4) [66.Nelson Javier Abeijón Pessi (9/1)], Rubén Fernando da Silva Echeverrito (14/3), Sergio Daniel Martínez Alzuri (26/5), Rubén Sosa Ardáiz (46/15) [66.Marcelo Alejandro Otero (10/2)]. Trainer: Héctor Núñez Bello (13).

Goal: Marcelo Saralegui Arregín (79).

620. 16.07.1995 **URUGUAY - BOLIVIA** **2-1(2-0)** 37th Copa América. Quarter-Finals

Estadio Centenario, Montevideo; Referee: Alfredo Rodas (Ecuador), Attendance: 45,000

URU: Fernando Harry Álvez Mosquera (37/0), Gustavo Emilio Méndez Techera (12/0), José Oscar Herrera Corominas (45/4), Eber Alejandro Moas Silvera (32/0), Tabaré Abayubá Silva (10/0), Diego Martín Dorta (19/0), Álvaro Gutiérrez Pelscher (28/1), Gustavo Augusto Poyet Domínguez (12/2) [66.Marcelo Saralegui Arregín (17/3)], Enzo Francéscoli Uriarte (62/17), Daniel Fonseca (22/10) [34.Rubén Sosa Ardáiz (47/15)], Marcelo Alejandro Otero (11/3) [71.Nelson Javier Abeijón Pessi (10/1)]. Trainer: Héctor Núñez Bello (14).

Goals: Marcelo Alejandro Otero (2), Daniel Fonseca (30).

621. 19.07.1995 **URUGUAY - COLOMBIA** **2-0(0-0)** 37th Copa América. Semi-Finals

Estadio Centenario, Montevideo; Referee: Félix Ramón Benegas (Paraguay), Attendance: 20,000

URU: Fernando Harry Álvez Mosquera (38/0), Gustavo Emilio Méndez Techera (13/0), José Oscar Herrera Corominas (46/4), Eber Alejandro Moas Silvera (33/0), Tabaré Abayubá Silva (11/0), Diego Martín Dorta (20/0), Álvaro Gutiérrez Pelscher (29/1), Edgardo Alberto Adinolfi Duarte (9/1) [79.Nelson Javier Abeijón Pessi (11/1)], Gustavo Augusto Poyet Domínguez (13/2) [84.Marcelo Saralegui Arregín (18/3)], Marcelo Alejandro Otero (12/4), Enzo Francéscoli Uriarte (63/17) (75.Sergio Daniel Martínez Alzuri (27/5)]. Trainer: Héctor Núñez Bello (15).

Goals: Edgardo Alberto Adinolfi Duarte (51), Marcelo Alejandro Otero (70).

622. 23.07.1995 **URUGUAY - BRAZIL** **1-1(0-1,1-1,1-1); 5-3 on penalties** 37th Copa América. Final

Estadio Centenario, Montevideo; Referee: Arturo Brizio Carter (Mexico), Attendance: 60,000

URU: Fernando Harry Álvez Mosquera (39/0), Gustavo Emilio Méndez Techera (14/0), José Oscar Herrera Corominas (47/4), Eber Alejandro Moas Silvera (34/0), Álvaro Gutiérrez Pelscher (30/1), Tabaré Abayubá Silva (12/0) [35.Edgardo Alberto Adinolfi Duarte (10/1)], Diego Martín Dorta (21/0) [45.Pablo Javier Bengoechea Dutra (28/5)], Gustavo Augusto Poyet Domínguez (14/2), Enzo Francéscoli Uriarte (64/17), Daniel Fonseca (23/10) [46.Sergio Daniel Martínez Alzuri (28/5)], Marcelo Alejandro Otero (13/4). Trainer: Héctor Núñez Bello (16).

Goal: Pablo Javier Bengoechea Dutra (51).

Penalties: Enzo Francéscoli Uriarte, Pablo Javier Bengoechea Dutra, José Oscar Herrera Corominas, Álvaro Gutiérrez Pelscher, Sergio Daniel Martínez Alzuri.

623. 20.09.1995 **ISRAEL - URUGUAY** **3-1(1-0)**

"Teddy Kollek" Stadium, Jerusalem; Referee: Amit Klein (Israel), Attendance: 9,000

URU: Leonardo Romay (1/0), Gustavo Emilio Méndez Techera (15/0), José Oscar Herrera Corominas (48/4), Claudio Elías (4/0), Juan Morán (1/0) [85.Luis Diego López Breijo (8/0)], Álvaro Gutiérrez Pelscher (31/1), Hebert Dos Santos (1/0) [52.Marco Vanzini (1/0)], Rubén Fernando da Silva Echeverrito (15/3) [69.Clever Marcelo Romero Silva (1/0)], Edgardo Alberto Adinolfi Duarte (11/1) [46.Yary Silvera (1/0)], Marcelo Alejandro Otero (14/5), Gerardo Federico Magallanes González (1/0) [46.Diego Seoane (1/0)]. Trainer: Héctor Núñez Bello (17).

Goal: Marcelo Alejandro Otero (65).

624. 11.10.1995 **BRAZIL - URUGUAY** **2-0(2-0)**

Estádio Fonte Nova, Salvador; Referee: José Joaquín Torres Cádena (Colombia), Attendance: 110,000

URU: Oscar Ferro (9/0), Gustavo Emilio Méndez Techera (16/0), José Oscar Herrera Corominas (49/4), Eber Alejandro Moas Silvera (35/0), Ronald Paolo Montero (9/0) [46.Edgardo Alberto Adinolfi Duarte (12/1)], Álvaro Gutiérrez Pelscher (32/1) [65.Juan González (1/0)], Pablo Javier Bengoechea Dutra (29/5), Gustavo Augusto Poyet Domínguez (15/2), Marcelo Saralegui Arregín (19/3) [85.Marco Vanzini (2/0)], Fabián Alberto O'Neill Domínguez (2/0) [75.Nelson Javier Abeijón Pessi (12/1)], Sergio Daniel Martínez Alzuri (29/5) [80.Gerardo Federico Magallanes González (2/0)]. Trainer: Héctor Núñez Bello (18).

625. 24.04.1996 **VENEZUELA - URUGUAY** **0-2(0-0)** 16th FIFA WC. Qualifiers

Estadio „Brígido Iriarte", Caracas; Referee: Alberto Tejada (Peru), Attendance: 6,839

URU: Claudio Arbiza (4/0), José Oscar Herrera Corominas (50/4), Eber Alejandro Moas Silvera (36/0), Nelson Artigas Olveira (1/0), Álvaro Gutiérrez Pelscher (33/1), Ronald Paolo Montero (10/0), Marcelo Alejandro Otero (15/6) [88.Néstor Gabriel Cedrés Vera (16/3)], Marcelo Saralegui Arregín (20/3), Daniel Fonseca (24/10) [*sent off 67*], Pablo Javier Bengoechea Dutra (30/5) [89.Nelson Javier Abeijón Pessi (13/1)], Gustavo Augusto Poyet Domínguez (16/3). Trainer: Héctor Núñez Bello (19).

Goals: Marcelo Alejandro Otero (54), Gustavo Augusto Poyet Domínguez (71).

626. 02.06.1996 **URUGUAY - PARAGUAY** **0-2(0-1)** 16th FIFA WC. Qualifiers

Estadio Centenario, Montevideo; Referee: Márcio Rezende de Freitas (Brazil), Attendance: 44,127

URU: Claudio Arbiza (5/0), José Oscar Herrera Corominas (51/4), Eber Alejandro Moas Silvera (37/0), Gustavo Emilio Méndez Techera (17/0), Álvaro Gutiérrez Pelscher (34/1) [65.Diego Martín Dorta (22/0)], Ronald Paolo Montero (11/0), Marcelo Alejandro Otero (16/6), Marcelo Saralegui Arregín (21/3) [46.Luis Alberto Romero (1/0)], Pablo Javier Bengoechea Dutra (31/5), Sergio Daniel Martínez Alzuri (30/5) [57.Néstor Gabriel Cedrés Vera (17/3)], Gustavo Augusto Poyet Domínguez (17/3). Trainer: Héctor Núñez Bello (20).

627. 07.07.1996 **COLOMBIA - URUGUAY** **3-1(2-0)** 16th FIFA WC. Qualifiers

Estadio Metropolitano „Roberto Meléndez", Barranquilla; Referee: Roberto Rúben Ruscio (Argentina), Attendance: 36,169

URU: Claudio Arbiza (6/0), Nelson Artigas Olveira (2/0) [35.Pablo Javier Bengoechea Dutra (32/5)], Eber Alejandro Moas Silvera (38/0), Óscar Aguirregaray Acosta (7/0), Robert Lima (1/0) [54.Tabaré Abayubá Silva (13/0)], Diego Martín Dorta (23/0) [70.Heberley Sosa (1/0)], Gustavo Augusto Poyet Domínguez (18/3), Marcelo Saralegui Arregín (22/3), Néstor Gabriel Cedrés Vera (18/3), Rubén Fabián Pereira (26/1) [*sent off 88*], Luis Alberto Romero (2/0). Trainer: Héctor Núñez Bello (21).

Goal: Gabriel Cedrés (57).

628. 17.07.1996 **CHINA - URUGUAY** **1-1(0-1)**
Workers Stadium, Beijing; Referee: Jun Lu (China), Attendance: 40,000
URU: Leonardo Romay (2/0) [46.Carlos Nicola (1/0)], Luis Diego López Breijo (9/0) [85.Jorge Miguel Gonçalves (8/0)], Fernando Picún (1/0), Pablo Hernández (1/0), Tabaré Abayubá Silva (14/0), Clever Marcelo Romero Silva (2/0), Rubén Fabián Pereira (27/1), Rodrigo Javier Lemos Rosende (1/0) [74.Rodrigo López (1/0)], Javier Omar Delgado Papariello (1/0), Álvaro Alexander Recoba Rivero (3/1), Juan González (2/0) [46.Washington Sebastián Abreu Gallo (1/0)]. Trainer: Héctor Núñez Bello (22).
Goal: Álvaro Alexander Recoba Rivero (17).

629. 25.08.1996 **JAPAN - URUGUAY** **5-3(3-1)**
Nagai Stadium, Osaka; Referee: Russamee Jindamai (Thailand), Attendance: 40,876
URU: Robert Dante Siboldi Badiola (21/0), Fernando Picún (2/0), Jorge Miguel Gonçalves (9/0) [46.Nelson Artigas Olveira (3/0)], Pablo Hernández (2/0), Clever Marcelo Romero Silva (3/0), Gonzalo de los Santos da Rosa (1/0), Tabaré Abayubá Silva (15/0) [70.Marco Vanzini (3/0)], Luis Jonne (1/0) [46.Rodrigo Javier Lemos Rosende (2/0)], Álvaro Alexander Recoba Rivero (4/3), Javier Omar Delgado Papariello (2/0) [46.Washington Sebastián Abreu Gallo (2/1)], Juan González (3/0). Trainer: Héctor Núñez Bello (23).
Goals: Álvaro Alexander Recoba Rivero (23), Washington Sebastián Abreu Gallo (73), Álvaro Alexander Recoba Rivero (77).

630. 08.10.1996 **URUGUAY - BOLIVIA** **1-0(0-0)** 16th FIFA WC. Qualifiers
Estadio Centenario, Montevideo; Referee: Paolo Borgosano (Venezuela), Attendance: 60,000
URU: Robert Dante Siboldi Badiola (22/0), Guillermo Oscar Sanguinetti Giordano (16/1), Ronald Paolo Montero (12/0), José Oscar Herrera Corominas (52/4), Gustavo Emilio Méndez Techera (18/0), Marcelo Alejandro Otero (17/6) [81.Pablo Javier Bengoechea Dutra (33/5)], Marcelo Saralegui Arregín (23/3) [82.Álvaro Gutiérrez Pelscher (35/1)], Gustavo Augusto Poyet Domínguez (19/3) [62.Luis Alberto Romero (3/0)], Néstor Gabriel Cedrés Vera (19/3), Daniel Fonseca (25/10), Enzo Francéscoli Uriarte (65/17). Trainer: Héctor Núñez Bello (24).
Goal: Juan Manuel Peña (64 own goal).

631. 12.11.1996 **CHILE - URUGUAY** **1-0(0-0)** 16th FIFA WC. Qualifiers
Estadio Nacional, Santiago; Referee: Ángel Guevara (Ecuador), Attendance: 73,547
URU: Robert Dante Siboldi Badiola (23/0), Guillermo Oscar Sanguinetti Giordano (17/1), Ronald Paolo Montero (13/0), José Oscar Herrera Corominas (53/4), Gustavo Emilio Méndez Techera (19/0), Álvaro Gutiérrez Pelscher (36/1), Marcelo Saralegui Arregín (24/3) [68.Pablo Javier Bengoechea Dutra (34/5)], Néstor Gabriel Cedrés Vera (20/3) [72.Álvaro Alexander Recoba Rivero (5/3)], Enzo Francéscoli Uriarte (66/17) [46.Luis Alberto Romero (4/0)], Gustavo Augusto Poyet Domínguez (20/3), Marcelo Alejandro Otero (18/6). Trainer: Héctor Núñez Bello (25).

632. 15.12.1996 **URUGUAY - PERU** **2-0(2-0)** 16th FIFA WC. Qualifiers
Estadio Centenario, Montevideo; Referee: Felipe Eduardo Russi Páez (Colombia), Attendance: 42,630
URU: Robert Dante Siboldi Badiola (24/0), Guillermo Oscar Sanguinetti Giordano (18/1), Ronald Paolo Montero (14/1), José Oscar Herrera Corominas (54/4), Washington Eduardo Tais Videgaín (3/0), Eber Alejandro Moas Silvera (39/0) [78.Gonzalo de los Santos da Rosa (2/0)], Pablo Javier Bengoechea Dutra (35/6), Nelson Javier Abeijón Pessi (14/1) [85.Marcelo Saralegui Arregín (25/3)], Daniel Fonseca (26/10) [60.Fabian O'Neill (3/0)], Enzo Francéscoli Uriarte (67/17), Marcelo Alejandro Otero (19/6) [*sent off 80*]. Trainer: Juan Ahuntchaín (1).
Goals: Ronald Paolo Montero (2), Pablo Javier Bengoechea Dutra (38).

633. 12.01.1997 **URUGUAY - ARGENTINA** **0-0** 16th FIFA WC. Qualifiers
Estadio Centenario, Montevideo; Referee: Márcio Rezende de Freitas (Brazil), Attendance: 62,000
URU: Robert Dante Siboldi Badiola (25/0), Ronald Paolo Montero (15/1), Washington Eduardo Tais Videgaín (4/0), José Oscar Herrera Corominas (55/4), Eber Alejandro Moas Silvera (40/0), Gustavo Emilio Méndez Techera (20/0), Nelson Javier Abeijón Pessi (15/1), Pablo Javier Bengoechea Dutra (36/6), Néstor Gabriel Cedrés Vera (21/3) , Enzo Francéscoli Uriarte (68/17) [59.Álvaro Alexander Recoba Rivero (6/3)], Daniel Fonseca (27/10) [58.Washington Sebastián Abreu Gallo (3/1)]. Trainer: Juan Ahuntchaín (2).

634. 12.02.1997 **ECUADOR - URUGUAY** **4-0(1-0)** 16th FIFA WC. Qualifiers
Estadio Olimpico „Atahualpa", Quito; Referee: Javier Alberto Castrilli (Argentina), Attendance: 18,000
URU: Robert Dante Siboldi Badiola (26/0), Washington Eduardo Tais Videgaín (5/0), Ronald Paolo Montero (16/1), José Oscar Herrera Corominas (56/4), Gustavo Emilio Méndez Techera (21/0) [*sent off 77*], Eber Alejandro Moas Silvera (41/0), Nelson Javier Abeijón Pessi (16/1) [sent off 90], Néstor Gabriel Cedrés Vera (22/3) [53.Debray Darío Silva Pereira (11/2)], Fabián Alberto O'Neill Domínguez (4/0), Enzo Francéscoli Uriarte (69/17) (63.Marcelo Saralegui Arregín (26/3)], Washington Sebastián Abreu Gallo (4/1) [53.Daniel Fonseca (28/10)][sent off 87]. Trainer: Juan Ahuntchaín (3).

635. 02.04.1997 **URUGUAY - VENEZUELA** **3-1(1-0)** 16th FIFA WC. Qualifiers
Estadio Centenario, Montevideo; Referee: René Ortubé (Bolivia), Attendance: 37,000
URU: Robert Dante Siboldi Badiola (27/0), Washington Eduardo Tais Videgaín (6/0), Ronald Paolo Montero (17/2) [*sent off 76*], Eber Alejandro Moas Silvera (42/0), Gonzalo de los Santos da Rosa (3/1), Pablo Javier Bengoechea Dutra (37/6), Marcelo Saralegui Arregín (27/3), Marcelo Alejandro Otero (20/7) [78.Pablo Hernández (3/0)], Enzo Francéscoli Uriarte (70/17) [68.Andrés Martínez (3/0)], Washington Sebastián Abreu Gallo (5/1) [42.Luis Alberto Romero (5/0)], Rúben Fernando Dos Santos (11/0). Trainer: Juan Ahuntchaín (4).
Goals: Gonzalo de los Santos da Rosa (29), Ronald Paolo Montero (46), Marcelo Alejandro Otero (59).

636. 30.04.1997 **PARAGUAY - URUGUAY** **3-1(1-0)** 16th FIFA WC. Qualifiers
Estadio Defensores del Chaco, Asunción; Referee: Antônio Pereira (Brazil), Attendance: 34,101
URU: Robert Dante Siboldi Badiola (28/0), Gustavo Emilio Méndez Techera (22/0), Eber Alejandro Moas Silvera (43/0), José Oscar Herrera Corominas (57/4), Gonzalo de los Santos da Rosa (4/1), Leonardo Ramos (4/0), Álvaro Gutiérrez Pelscher (37/1) [*sent off 17*], Marcelo Alejandro Otero (21/7) [60.Debray Darío Silva Pereira (12/3)], Enzo Francéscoli Uriarte (71/17), Gustavo Augusto Poyet Domínguez (21/3) [80.Rubén Fernando da Silva Echeverrito (16/3)], Sergio Daniel Martínez Alzuri (31/5) [41.Pablo Javier Bengoechea Dutra (38/6)]. Trainer: Juan Ahuntchaín (5).
Goal: Debray Darío Silva Pereira (87).

637. 08.06.1997 **URUGUAY - COLOMBIA** **1-1(1-0)** 16th FIFA WC. Qualifiers
Estadio Centenario, Montevideo; Referee: Francisco Mourão Dacildo (Brazil), Attendance: 37,655
URU: Fernando Harry Álvez Mosquera (40/0), Gustavo Emilio Méndez Techera (23/0), Eber Alejandro Moas Silvera (44/0), Ronald Paolo Montero (18/2), Gonzalo de los Santos da Rosa (5/1), Leonardo Ramos (5/0), Pablo Javier Bengoechea Dutra (39/6), Nelson Javier Abeijón Pessi (17/1) [60.Rubén Fernando da Silva Echeverrito (17/3)], Fabián Alberto O'Neill Domínguez (5/0) [81.Luis Alberto Romero (6/0)], Álvaro Alexander Recoba Rivero (7/3) [60.Sergio Daniel Martínez Alzuri (32/5)], Debray Darío Silva Pereira (13/4). Trainer: Juan Ahuntchaín (6).
Goal: Debray Darío Silva Pereira (6).

638. 12.06.1997 **PERU – URUGUAY** **1-0(0-0)** 38th Copa América. Group Stage
Estadio Patria, Sucre (Bolivia); Referee: Antonio Marrufo Mendóza (Mexico), Attendance: 6,000
URU: Robert Dante Siboldi Badiola (29/0), Julio César ‚Tony' Gómez (4/0), Héctor Rodríguez Peña (3/0), Eber Alejandro Moas Silvera (45/0), Leonardo Ramos (6/0), Nelson Javier Abeijón Pessi (18/1), Clever Marcelo Romero Silva (4/0) [56.Gonzalo de los Santos da Rosa (6/1)], Marcelo Saralegui Arregín (28/3), Álvaro Alexander Recoba Rivero (8/3) [46.Rubén Fernando da Silva Echeverrito (18/3)], Sergio Daniel Martínez Alzuri (33/5) [62.Josemir Lujambio (1/0)], Luis Alberto Romero (7/0). Trainer: Juan Ahuntchaín (7).

639. 15.06.1997 **URUGUAY – VENEZUELA** **2-0(1-0)** 38th Copa América. Group Stage
Estadio Patria, Sucre (Bolivia); Referee: Eduardo Gamboe (Chile), Attendance: 1,000
URU: Robert Dante Siboldi Badiola (30/0), Julio César ‚Tony' Gómez (5/0), Héctor Rodríguez Peña (4/0), Eber Alejandro Moas Silvera (46/0), Tabaré Abayubá Silva (16/0), Gonzalo de los Santos da Rosa (7/1), Javier Omar Delgado Papariello (3/0) [80.Yary Silvera (2/0)], Marcelo Saralegui Arregín (29/4), Rubén Fernando da Silva Echeverrito (19/3), Álvaro Alexander Recoba Rivero (9/4) [69.Clever Marcelo Romero Silva (5/0)], Luis Alberto Romero (8/0) [60.Washington Sebastián Abreu Gallo (6/1)]. Trainer: Juan Ahuntchaín (8).
Goals: Álvaro Alexander Recoba Rivero (20), Marcelo Saralegui Arregín (48).

640. 18.06.1997 **BOLIVIA – URUGUAY** **1-0(1-0)** 38th Copa América. Group Stage
Estadio „Hernándo Siles Zuazo", La Paz; Referee: Antonio Marrufo Mendóza (Mexico), Attendance: 30,000
URU: Robert Dante Siboldi Badiola (31/0), Julio César ‚Tony' Gómez (6/0), Héctor Rodríguez Peña (5/0), Eber Alejandro Moas Silvera (47/0), Tabaré Abayubá Silva (17/0), Gonzalo de los Santos da Rosa (8/1), Clever Marcelo Romero Silva (6/0), Marcelo Saralegui Arregín (30/4) [77.Nelson Javier Abeijón Pessi (19/1)], Javier Omar Delgado Papariello (4/0) [60.Rubén Fernando da Silva Echeverrito (20/3)], Álvaro Alexander Recoba Rivero (10/4), Luis Alberto Romero (9/0) [60.Sergio Daniel Martínez Alzuri (34/5)]. Trainer: Juan Ahuntchaín (9).

641. 20.07.1997 **BOLIVIA – URUGUAY** **1-0(0-0)** 16th FIFA WC. Qualifiers
Estadio „Hernándo Siles Zuazo", La Paz; Referee: Arturo Pablo Brizio Carter (Mexico), Attendance: 27,874
URU: Robert Dante Siboldi Badiola (32/0), Héctor Rodríguez Peña (6/0), Eber Alejandro Moas Silvera (48/0), Gonzalo de los Santos da Rosa (9/1), Óscar Aguirregaray Acosta (8/0), Leonardo Ramos (7/0) [83.Clever Marcelo Romero Silva (7/0)], Julio César ‚Tony' Gómez (7/0), Marcelo Saralegui Arregín (31/4), Pablo Javier Bengoechea Dutra (40/6), Enzo Francéscoli Uriarte (72/17) (55.Josemir Lujambio (2/0)], Sergio Daniel Martínez Alzuri (35/5) [74.Rubén Fernando da Silva Echeverrito (21/3)]. Trainer: Roque Gastón Máspoli (29).

642. 20.08.1997 **URUGUAY – CHILE** **1-0(1-0)** 16th FIFA WC. Qualifiers
Estadio Centenario, Montevideo; Referee: Antônio Pereira Da Silva (Brazil), Attendance: 40,000
URU: Robert Dante Siboldi Badiola (33/0), Ronald Paolo Montero (19/2) [*sent off 78*], Gustavo Emilio Méndez Techera (24/0), Tabaré Abayubá Silva (18/0), Héctor Rodríguez Peña (7/0), Pablo Javier Bengoechea Dutra (41/6) [74.Clever Marcelo Romero Silva (8/0)], Marcelo Alejandro Otero (22/8), Álvaro Gutiérrez Pelscher (38/1), Enzo Francéscoli Uriarte (73/17) [81.Óscar Aguirregaray Acosta (9/0)], Josemir Lujambio (3/0) [56.Daniel Fonseca (29/10)], Gustavo Augusto Poyet Domínguez (22/3). Trainer: Roque Gastón Máspoli (30).
Goal: Marcelo Alejandro Otero (20).

643. 10.09.1997 **PERU – URUGUAY** **2-1(0-1)** 16th FIFA WC. Qualifiers
Estadio Nacional, Lima; Referee: Esfandiar Baharmast (United States), Attendance: 34,721
URU: Robert Dante Siboldi Badiola (34/0), Óscar Aguirregaray Acosta (10/0) [68.Marcelo Saralegui Arregín (32/4)], Gustavo Emilio Méndez Techera (25/0), Héctor Rodríguez Peña (8/0), Luis Diego López Breijo (10/0), Gonzalo de los Santos da Rosa (10/1), Clever Marcelo Romero Silva (9/0), Pablo Javier Bengoechea Dutra (42/6) [77.Josemir Lujambio (4/0)], Tabaré Abayubá Silva (19/0), Álvaro Alexander Recoba Rivero (11/5), Daniel Fonseca (30/10) [*sent off 83*]. Trainer: Roque Gastón Máspoli (31).
Goal: Álvaro Alexander Recoba Rivero (43).

644. 12.10.1997 **ARGENTINA – URUGUAY** **0-0** 16th FIFA WC. Qualifiers
Estadio Monumental „Antonio Vespucio Liberti", Buenos Aires; Referee: Claudio Vinicius Cerdeira (Brazil), Attendance: 52,000
URU: Carlos Nicola (2/0), Ronald Paolo Montero (20/2), Guillermo Oscar Sanguinetti Giordano (19/1), Edgardo Alberto Adinolfi Duarte (13/1), Gonzalo de los Santos da Rosa (11/1), Líber Ernesto Vespa (1/0), Héctor Rodríguez Peña (9/0), Mario Barilko (1/0), Pablo Javier Bengoechea Dutra (43/6) [67.José Andrés Fleurquin Rubio (1/0)], Álvaro Alexander Recoba Rivero (12/5), Josemir Lujambio (5/0) [54.Antonio Pacheco (1/0)]. Trainer: Roque Gastón Máspoli (32).

645. 16.11.1997 **URUGUAY – ECUADOR** **5-3(2-1)** 16th FIFA WC. Qualifiers
Estadio „Domingo Burgueño", Maldonado; Referee: Antonio Marrufo Mendoza (Mexico), Attendance: 4,000
URU: Carlos Nicola (3/0), Guillermo Oscar Sanguinetti Giordano (20/1), Edgardo Alberto Adinolfi Duarte (14/1) [72.Julio César ‚Tony' Gómez (8/0)], Héctor Rodríguez Peña (10/0) [86.Rúben Silva (1/0)], Rúben Alzueta (2/0), Marcelo Saralegui Arregín (33/6), Víctor López (8/1), Mario Barilko (2/0), Diego Tito (3/0), Carlos Alberto Aguilera Nova (65/23), Washington Sebastián Abreu Gallo (7/3) [75.Osvaldo Canobbio (8/2)]. Trainer: Roque Gastón Máspoli (33).
Goals: Marcelo Saralegui Arregín (3, 12), Washington Sebastián Abreu Gallo (48, 52), Carlos Alberto Aguilera Nova (63).

646. 13.12.1997 **UNITED ARAB EMIRATES – URUGUAY** **0-2(0-1)** 3rd FIFA Confederations Cup. Group Stage
„King Fahd" International Stadium, Riyadh (Saudi Arabia); Referee: Ramesh Ramdhan (Trinidad Tobago), Attendance: 2,500
URU: Claudio Flores (1/0), Luis Diego López Breijo (11/0), Ronald Paolo Montero (21/2), Gustavo Emilio Méndez Techera (26/0), Gonzalo de los Santos da Rosa (12/1), Edgardo Alberto Adinolfi Duarte (15/1), Pablo Gabriel García Pérez (1/0), Líber Ernesto Vespa (2/0) [90.Pablo Hernández (4/0)], Marcelo Danubio Zalayeta (1/0), Andrés Nicolás Olivera (1/1) [75.Antonio Pacheco (2/1)], Álvaro Alexander Recoba Rivero (13/5) [54.Debray Darío Silva Pereira (14/4)]. Trainer: Víctor Haroldo Púa Sosa (1).
Goals: Andrés Nicolás Olivera (45), Antonio Pacheco (90).

647. 15.12.1997 **CZECH REPUBLIC – URUGUAY** **1-2(0-1)** 3rd FIFA Confederations Cup. Group Stage
„King Fahd" International Stadium, Riyadh (Saudi Arabia); Referee: Saad Kamell Manei (Kuwait), Attendance: 8,000
URU: Claudio Flores (2/0), Luis Diego López Breijo (12/0), Ronald Paolo Montero (22/2), Gustavo Emilio Méndez Techera (27/0), Gonzalo de los Santos da Rosa (13/1), Edgardo Alberto Adinolfi Duarte (16/1), Pablo Gabriel García Pérez (2/0), Líber Ernesto Vespa (3/0) [86.Pablo Hernández (5/0)], Debray Darío Silva Pereira (15/4) [75.Christian Fabián Callejas (1/0)], Marcelo Danubio Zalayeta (2/1), Andrés Nicolás Olivera (2/2) [65.Álvaro Alexander Recoba Rivero (14/5)]. Trainer: Víctor Haroldo Púa Sosa (2).
Goals: Andrés Nicolás Olivera (26), Marcelo Danubio Zalayeta (89).

648. 17.12.1997 **SOUTH AFRICA - URUGUAY** **3-4(1-2)** 3rd FIFA Confederations Cup. Group Stage

„King Fahd" International Stadium, Riyadh (Saudi Arabia); Referee: Ramesh Ramdhan (Trinidad Tobago), Attendance: 15,000

URU: Carlos Nicola (4/0), Luis Diego López Breijo (13/0) [68.Gonzalo de los Santos da Rosa (14/1)], Pablo Hernández (6/0), Carlos Díaz (1/0), César Pellegrín (1/0), Walter Fabián Coelho (1/0) [78.Líber Ernesto Vespa (4/0)], Martín Rivas (1/0), Antonio Pacheco (3/1) [68.Pablo Gabriel García Pérez (3/0)], Debray Darío Silva Pereira (16/6), Christian Fabián Callejas (2/1), Álvaro Alexander Recoba Rivero (15/6). Trainer: Víctor Haroldo Púa Sosa (3).

Goals: Debray Darío Silva Pereira (12), Álvaro Alexander Recoba Rivero (42), Debray Darío Silva Pereira (66), Christian Fabián Callejas (90).

649. 19.12.1997 **AUSTRALIA - URUGUAY** **1-0(0-0,0-0); Golden Goal** 3rd FIFA Confederations Cup. Semi-Finals

„King Fahd" International Stadium, Riyadh (Saudi Arabia); Referee: Nikolai Levnikov (Russia), Attendance: 22,000

URU: Claudio Flores (3/0), Luis Diego López Breijo (14/0), Ronald Paolo Montero (23/2), Gustavo Emilio Méndez Techera (28/0), Gonzalo de los Santos da Rosa (15/1), Edgardo Alberto Adinolfi Duarte (17/1), Pablo Gabriel García Pérez (4/0), Líber Ernesto Vespa (5/0), Álvaro Alexander Recoba Rivero (16/6) [80.Debray Darío Silva Pereira (17/6)], Marcelo Danubio Zalayeta (3/1), Andrés Nicolás Olivera (3/2). Trainer: Víctor Haroldo Púa Sosa (4).

650. 21.12.1997 **CZECH REPUBLIC - URUGUAY** **1-0(0-0)** 3rd FIFA Confederations Cup. Bronze.Medal

„King Fahd" International Stadium, Riyadh (Saudi Arabia); Referee: Lucien Bouchardeau (Niger), Attendance: 25,000

URU: Claudio Flores (4/0), Luis Diego López Breijo (15/0) [68.Pablo Hernández (7/0)], Ronald Paolo Montero (24/2), Gustavo Emilio Méndez Techera (29/0), Gonzalo de los Santos da Rosa (16/1) [46.Christian Fabián Callejas (3/1)], Edgardo Alberto Adinolfi Duarte (18/1), Pablo Gabriel García Pérez (5/0), Líber Ernesto Vespa (6/0) [79.Debray Darío Silva Pereira (18/6)], Marcelo Danubio Zalayeta (4/1), Andrés Nicolás Olivera (4/2), Álvaro Alexander Recoba Rivero (17/6). Trainer: Víctor Haroldo Púa Sosa (5).

651. 24.05.1998 **CHILE - URUGUAY** **2-2(2-0)**

Estadio Nacional, Santiago; Referee: José Antonio Arana Villamonte (Peru), Attendance: 61,528

URU: Gustavo Adolfo Munúa (1/0), Gustavo Emilio Méndez Techera (30/0), Luis Diego López Breijo (16/0), Ronald Paolo Montero (25/2), Mario Gastán (1/0), Juan Ferreri (2/0) [46.Andrés Nicolás Olivera (5/3)], Pablo Gabriel García Pérez (6/0), Líber Ernesto Vespa (7/0), Gerardo Federico Magallanes González (3/0), Marcelo Danubio Zalayeta (5/2), Fernando Edgardo Correa Ayala (2/0) [61.Christian Fabián Callejas (4/1)]. Trainer: Víctor Haroldo Púa Sosa (6).

Goals: Andrés Nicolás Olivera (62 penalty), Marcelo Danubio Zalayeta (81).

652. 17.06.1999 **PARAGUAY - URUGUAY** **2-3(1-3)**

Estadio „Antonio Oddone Sarubbi", Ciudad del Este; Referee: Angel Sánchez (Argentina), Attendance: 30,000

URU: Héctor Fabián Carini Hernández (1/0), Leonel Pilipauskas (1/0), Daniel Alejandro Lembo Bentancor (1/0), Luis Diego López Breijo (17/0), Raúl Federico Bergara (1/0), Líber Ernesto Vespa (8/0) [65. Inti Podestá Mezzetta (1/0)], José Andrés Fleurquin Rubio (2/0) [80.Fernando Picún (3/0)], Walter Fabián Coelho (2/0), Gerardo Federico Magallanes González (4/2) [46.Christian Fabián Callejas (5/1)], Jorge Gabriel Alvez (1/1) [55.Diego Martín Alonso López (1/0)], Marcelo Danubio Zalayeta (6/2) [70.Antonio Pacheco (4/1)]. Trainer: Víctor Haroldo Púa Sosa (7).

Goals: Jorge Gabriel Alvez (12), Gerardo Federico Magallanes González (13, 20).

653. 01.07.1999 **COLOMBIA - URUGUAY** **1-0(1-0)** 39th Copa America. Group Stage

Estadio „General Pablo Rojas", Asunción (Paraguay); Referee: Wilson De Souza Mendonça (Brazil), Attendance: 3,000

URU: Héctor Fabián Carini Hernández (2/0), Leonel Pilipauskas (2/0), Luis Diego López Breijo (18/0) [*sent off 67*], Daniel Alejandro Lembo Bentancor (2/0), Raúl Federico Bergara (2/0) [58.Christian Fabián Callejas (6/1)], Líber Ernesto Vespa (9/0) [46.Gianni Bismark Guigou Martínez (1/0)], José Andrés Fleurquin Rubio (3/0) [70.Fernando Picún (4/0)], Walter Fabián Coelho (3/0), Gerardo Federico Magallanes González (5/2) [*sent off 90*], Jorge Gabriel Alvez (2/1), Marcelo Danubio Zalayeta (7/2). Trainer: Víctor Haroldo Púa Sosa (8).

654. 04.07.1999 **URUGUAY - ECUADOR** **2-1(0-0)** 39th Copa America. Group Stage

Estadio „Feliciano Cáceres", Luque (Paraguay); Referee: Mario Sánchez (Chile), Attendance: 18,000

URU: Héctor Fabián Carini Hernández (3/0), Leonel Pilipauskas (3/0), Fernando Picún (5/0), Daniel Alejandro Lembo Bentancor (3/0), Raúl Federico Bergara (3/0) [66.Gianni Bismark Guigou Martínez (2/0)], Walter Fabián Coelho (4/0) [78.Líber Ernesto Vespa (10/0)], José Andrés Fleurquin Rubio (4/0), Pablo Gabriel García Pérez (7/0), Antonio Pacheco (5/1) [65.Christian Fabián Callejas (7/1)], Jorge Gabriel Alvez (3/1), Marcelo Danubio Zalayeta (8/4). Trainer: Víctor Haroldo Púa Sosa (9).

Goals: Marcelo Danubio Zalayeta (72, 74).

655. 07.07.1999 **ARGENTINA - URUGUAY** **2-0(1-0)** 39th Copa America. Group Stage

Estadio „Feliciano Cáceres", Luque (Paraguay); Referee: Gilberto Hidalgo Zamora (Peru), Attendance: 18,000

URU: Héctor Fabián Carini Hernández (4/0), Martín Del Campo (1/0), Daniel Alejandro Lembo Bentancor (4/0), Fernando Picún (6/0), Raúl Federico Bergara (4/0) [58.Clever Marcelo Romero Silva (10/0)], Líber Ernesto Vespa (11/0), José Andrés Fleurquin Rubio (5/0) [46.Gianni Bismark Guigou Martínez (3/0)], Walter Fabián Coelho (5/0), Gerardo Federico Magallanes González (6/2), Jorge Gabriel Alvez (4/1) [46.Antonio Pacheco (6/1)], Marcelo Danubio Zalayeta (9/4). Trainer: Víctor Haroldo Púa Sosa (10).

656. 10.07.1999 **PARAGUAY - URUGUAY** **1-1(1-0,1-1), 5-3 on penalties** 39th Copa América. Quarter-Finals

Estadio Defensores del Chaco, Asunción; Referee: Oscar Julián Ruíz Acosta (Colombia), Attendance: 30,767

URU: Héctor Fabián Carini Hernández (5/0), Martín Del Campo (2/0), Fernando Picún (7/0), Daniel Alejandro Lembo Bentancor (5/0) [89.Luis Diego López Breijo (19/0)], Raúl Federico Bergara (5/0) [62.Gianni Bismark Guigou Martínez (4/0)], Walter Fabián Coelho (6/0), José Andrés Fleurquin Rubio (6/0), Pablo Gabriel García Pérez (8/0), Gerardo Federico Magallanes González (7/2), Jorge Gabriel Alvez (5/1) [57.Diego Martín Alonso López (2/0)], Marcelo Danubio Zalayeta (10/5). Trainer: Víctor Haroldo Púa Sosa (11).

Goal: Marcelo Danubio Zalayeta (65).

Penalties: José Andrés Fleurquin Rubio, Gianni Bismark Guigou Martínez, Diego Martín Alonso López, Marcelo Danubio Zalayeta, Gerardo Federico Magallanes González

657. 13.07.1999 **URUGUAY - CHILE** **1-1(1-0,1-1), 5-3 on penalties** 39th Copa América. Semi-Finals

Estadio Defensores del Chaco, Asunción (Paraguay); Referee: Ubaldo Aquino Valenzano (Paraguay), Attendance: 7,000

URU: Héctor Fabián Carini Hernández (6/0), Martín Del Campo (3/0), Daniel Alejandro Lembo Bentancor (6/1), Fernando Picún (8/0), Raúl Federico Bergara (6/0) [81.Christian Fabián Callejas (8/1)], Pablo Gabriel García Pérez (9/0), José Andrés Fleurquin Rubio (7/0) [65.Gianni Bismark Guigou Martínez (5/0)], Walter Fabián Coelho (7/0), Gerardo Federico Magallanes González (8/2), Jorge Gabriel Alvez (6/1) [53.Diego Martín Alonso López (3/0)], Marcelo Danubio Zalayeta (11/5). Trainer: Víctor Haroldo Púa Sosa (12).

Goal: Daniel Alejandro Lembo Bentancor (23).

Penalties: Martín Del Campo, Gianni Bismark Guigou Martínez, Diego Martín Alonso López, Marcelo Danubio Zalayeta, Gerardo Federico Magallanes González

658. 18.07.1999 **BRAZIL – URUGUAY** **3-0(2-0)** 39th Copa América. Final

Estadio Defensores del Chaco, Asunción (Paraguay); Referee: Oscar Julián Ruíz Acosta (Colombia), Attendance: 30,000

URU: Héctor Fabián Carini Hernández (7/0), Martín Del Campo (4/0), Fernando Picún (9/0), Daniel Alejandro Lembo Bentancor (7/1), Raúl Federico Bergara (7/0) [74.Gianni Bismark Guigou Martínez (6/0)], Walter Fabián Coelho (8/0) [56.Jorge Gabriel Alvez (7/1)], José Andrés Fleurquin Rubio (8/0), Líber Ernesto Vespa (12/0) [46.Antonio Pacheco (7/1)], Christian Fabián Callejas (9/1), Gerardo Federico Magallanes González (9/2), Marcelo Danubio Zalayeta (12/5). Trainer: Víctor Haroldo Púa Sosa (13).

659. 18.08.1999 **URUGUAY – COSTA RICA** **5-4(2-1)**

Estadio Centenario, Montevideo; Referee: Robert Troxler (Paraguay), Attendance: 16,000

URU: Héctor Fabián Carini Hernández (8/0), Martín Del Campo (5/0), Daniel Alejandro Lembo Bentancor (8/1), Ronald Paolo Montero (26/2), Gianni Bismark Guigou Martínez (7/0), Clever Marcelo Romero Silva (11/0), Juan González (4/0), Walter Fabián Coelho (9/1), Fabián Alberto O'Neill Domínguez (6/1), Antonio Pacheco (8/2) [62.Álvaro Alexander Recoba Rivero (18/6)], Marcelo Alejandro Otero (23/10). Trainer: Daniel Alberto Passarella (1).

Goals: Marcelo Otero (21), Walter Fabián Coelho (30), Fabián Alberto O'Neill Domínguez (47), Antonio Pacheco (54), Marcelo Alejandro Otero (72).

660. 08.09.1999 **URUGUAY – VENEZUELA** **2-0(1-0)**

Estadio Centenario, Montevideo; Referee: Angel Osvaldo Sánchez (Argentina), Attendance: 12,000

URU: Héctor Fabián Carini Hernández (9/0), Gustavo Emilio Méndez Techera (31/0), Luis Diego López Breijo (20/0), Ronald Paolo Montero (27/2), Gianni Bismark Guigou Martínez (8/0), Clever Marcelo Romero Silva (12/0), Walter Fabián Coelho (10/1) [89.Walter Horacio Peralta Saracho (1/0)], Fabián Alberto O'Neill Domínguez (7/1), Gustavo Augusto Poyet Domínguez (23/3) [46.Andrés Nicolás Olivera (6/3)], Marcelo Alejandro Otero (24/10) [70.Marcelo Danubio Zalayeta (13/6)], Antonio Pacheco (9/3). Trainer: Daniel Alberto Passarella (2).

Goals: Antonio Pacheco (25), Marcelo Danubio Zalayeta (89).

661. 12.10.1999 **URUGUAY – ECUADOR** **0-0**

Estadio Centenario, Montevideo; Referee: Carlos Amarilla (Paraguay), Attendance: 8,000

URU: Héctor Fabián Carini Hernández (10/0), Gustavo Emilio Méndez Techera (32/0), Luis Diego López Breijo (21/0), Ronald Paolo Montero (28/2), Gianni Bismark Guigou Martínez (9/0), Clever Marcelo Romero Silva (13/0) [73.Walter Fabián Coelho (11/1)], Pablo Gabriel García Pérez (10/0), Andrés Nicolás Olivera (7/3), Rubén Fernando da Silva Echeverrito (22/3) [*sent off 90*], Álvaro Alexander Recoba Rivero (19/6) [78.Antonio Pacheco (10/3)], Marcelo Danubio Zalayeta (14/6). Trainer: Daniel Alberto Passarella (3).

662. 17.11.1999 **URUGUAY – PARAGUAY** **0-1(0-1)**

Estadio „Domingo Burgueño", Maldonado; Referee: Carlos Simón (Brazil), Attendance: 18,000

URU: Álvaro Núñez (1/0), Leonel Pilipauskas (4/0) [63.Daniel Alejandro Lembo Bentancor (9/1)], Luis Diego López Breijo (22/0), Ronald Paolo Montero (29/2), Raúl Federico Bergara (8/0) [63.Antonio Pacheco (11/3)], Gianni Bismark Guigou Martínez (10/0), Gustavo Augusto Poyet Domínguez (24/3) [73.Pablo Gabriel García Pérez (11/0)], Néstor Gabriel Cedrés Vera (23/3), Fabián Alberto O'Neill Domínguez (8/1), Marcelo Alejandro Otero (25/10) [*sent off 23*], Marcelo Danubio Zalayeta (15/6). Trainer: Daniel Alberto Passarella (4).

663. 29.03.2000 **URUGUAY – BOLIVIA** **1-0(1-0)** 17th FIFA WC. Qualifiers

Estadio Centenario, Montevideo; Referee: Antônio Pereira Da Silva (Brazil), Attendance: 49,811

URU: Héctor Fabián Carini Hernández (11/0), Gustavo Emilio Méndez Techera (33/0), Luis Diego López Breijo (23/0), Ronald Paolo Montero (30/2), Octavio Darío Rodríguez Peña (1/0), Pablo Gabriel García Pérez (12/1), Fabián Alberto O'Neill Domínguez (9/1), Néstor Gabriel Cedrés Vera (24/3) [57.Andrés Nicolás Olivera (8/3)], Walter Fabián Coelho (12/1), Álvaro Alexander Recoba Rivero (20/6) [89.Gustavo Augusto Poyet Domínguez (25/3)], Diego Martín Alonso López (4/0) [77.Marcelo Danubio Zalayeta (16/6)]. Trainer: Daniel Alberto Passarella (5).

Goal: Pablo Gabriel García Pérez (26).

664. 26.04.2000 **PARAGUAY – URUGUAY** **1-0(1-0)** 17th FIFA WC. Qualifiers

Estadio Defensores del Chaco, Asunción; Referee: Ángel Osvaldo Sánchez (Argentina), Attendance: 18,350

URU: Héctor Fabián Carini Hernández (12/0), Gustavo Emilio Méndez Techera (34/0), Leonardo Ramos (8/0), Daniel Alejandro Lembo Bentancor (10/1), Tabaré Abayubá Silva (20/0) [67.Gianni Bismark Guigou Martínez (11/0)], Walter Fabián Coelho (13/1), Pablo Gabriel García Pérez (13/1), Gonzalo de los Santos da Rosa (17/1) [*sent off 69*], Gustavo Augusto Poyet Domínguez (26/3) [60.Andrés Nicolás Olivera (9/3)], Álvaro Alexander Recoba Rivero (21/6), Debray Darío Silva Pereira (19/6) [77.Jorge Gabriel Alvez (8/1)]. Trainer: Daniel Alberto Passarella (6).

665. 03.06.2000 **URUGUAY – CHILE** **2-1(2-1)** 17th FIFA WC. Qualifiers

Estadio Centenario, Montevideo; Referee: Robert Troxler Ayala (Paraguay), Attendance: 60,000

URU: Héctor Fabián Carini Hernández (13/0), Gustavo Emilio Méndez Techera (35/0), Daniel Alejandro Lembo Bentancor (11/1), Ronald Paolo Montero (31/3), Octavio Darío Rodríguez Peña (2/0), Fabián Alberto O'Neill Domínguez (10/1), Pablo Gabriel García Pérez (14/1), Andrés Nicolás Olivera (10/3), Gianni Bismark Guigou Martínez (12/0), Álvaro Alexander Recoba Rivero (22/6) [89.Guillermo Gonzalo Giacomazzi Suárez (1/0)], Debray Darío Silva Pereira (20/7) [80.Diego Martín Alonso López (5/0)]. Trainer: Daniel Alberto Passarella (7).

Goal: Debray Darío Silva Pereira (36), Ronald Paolo Montero (42).

666. 28.06.2000 **BRAZIL – URUGUAY** **1-1(0-1)** 17th FIFA WC. Qualifiers

Estádio „Jornalista Mário Filho" (Maracanã), Rio de Janeiro; Referee: Oscar Julián Ruíz Acosta (Colombia), Attendance: 50,000

URU: Héctor Fabián Carini Hernández (14/0), Washington Eduardo Tais Videgaín (7/0), Daniel Alejandro Lembo Bentancor (12/1), Ronald Paolo Montero (32/3), Octavio Darío Rodríguez Peña (3/0), Pablo Gabriel García Pérez (15/1), Gianni Bismark Guigou Martínez (13/0), Andrés Nicolás Olivera (11/3), Fabián Alberto O'Neill Domínguez (11/1) [82.Guillermo Gonzalo Giacomazzi Suárez (2/0)], Álvaro Alexander Recoba Rivero (23/6) [58.Walter Fabián Coelho (14/1)], Debray Darío Silva Pereira (21/8). Trainer: Daniel Alberto Passarella (8).

Goal: Debray Darío Silva Pereira (6).

667. 18.07.2000 **URUGUAY – VENEZUELA** **3-1(1-1)** 17th FIFA WC. Qualifiers

Estadio Centenario, Montevideo; Referee: René Ortubé (Bolivia), Attendance: 58,000

URU: Héctor Fabián Carini Hernández (15/0), Washington Eduardo Tais Videgaín (8/0), Daniel Alejandro Lembo Bentancor (13/1), Ronald Paolo Montero (33/3) (83.Leonardo Ramos (9/0)], Octavio Darío Rodríguez Peña (4/1), Pablo Gabriel García Pérez (16/1), Gianni Bismark Guigou Martínez (14/0), Andrés Nicolás Olivera (12/5), Fabián Alberto O'Neill Domínguez (12/1), Álvaro Alexander Recoba Rivero (24/6) [90.Marcelo Danubio Zalayeta (17/6)], Debray Darío Silva Pereira (22/8) [*sent off 59*]. Trainer: Daniel Alberto Passarella (9).

Goals: Andrés Nicolás Olivera (30), Octavio Darío Rodríguez Peña (53), Andrés Nicolás Olivera (90).

668. 26.07.2000 **URUGUAY - PERU** **0-0** 17th FIFA WC. Qualifiers

Estadio Centenario, Montevideo; Referee: Oscar Godoi (Brazil), Attendance: 54,345

URU: Héctor Fabián Carini Hernández (16/0), Washington Eduardo Tais Videgaín (9/0), Daniel Alejandro Lembo Bentancor (14/1), Ronald Paolo Montero (34/3), Octavio Darío Rodríguez Peña (5/1), Fabián Alberto O'Neill Domínguez (13/1), Pablo Gabriel García Pérez (17/1), Gianni Bismark Guigou Martínez (15/0) [66.Marcelo Danubio Zalayeta (18/6)], Andrés Nicolás Olivera (13/5), Álvaro Alexander Recoba Rivero (25/6) [79.Walter Fabián Coelho (15/1)], Gerardo Federico Magallanes González (10/2). Trainer: Daniel Alberto Passarella (10).

669. 15.08.2000 **COLOMBIA - URUGUAY** **1-0(0-0)** 17th FIFA WC. Qualifiers

Estadio „Nemesio Camacho" 'El Campín', Bogotá; Referee: Daniel Giménez (Argentina), Attendance: 31,000

URU: Héctor Fabián Carini Hernández (17/0), Gustavo Emilio Méndez Techera (36/0), Daniel Alejandro Lembo Bentancor (15/1), Gonzalo Sorondo Amaro (1/0), Octavio Darío Rodríguez Peña (6/1), Fabián Alberto O'Neill Domínguez (14/1), Pablo Gabriel García Pérez (18/1), Gianni Bismark Guigou Martínez (16/0) [56.Guillermo Gonzalo Giacomazzi Suárez (3/0)], Andrés Nicolás Olivera (14/5), Debray Darío Silva Pereira (23/8) [85.Gerardo Federico Magallanes González (11/2)], Marcelo Alejandro Otero (26/10) [50.Rubén Fernando da Silva Echeverrito (23/3)]. Trainer: Daniel Alberto Passarella (11).

670. 03.09.2000 **URUGUAY - ECUADOR** **4-0(2-0)** 17th FIFA WC. Qualifiers

Estadio Centenario, Montevideo; Referee: Henry Cervantes (Colombia), Attendance: 62,000

URU: Héctor Fabián Carini Hernández (18/0), Washington Eduardo Tais Videgaín (10/0), Daniel Alejandro Lembo Bentancor (16/1), Oscar Damián Rodríguez Cantos (1/0), Gustavo Emilio Méndez Techera (37/0), Néstor Gabriel Cedrés Vera (25/4), Pablo Gabriel García Pérez (19/1) (81.José Andrés Fleurquin Rubio (9/0)], Gianni Bismark Guigou Martínez (17/0), Andrés Nicolás Olivera (15/6), Debray Darío Silva Pereira (24/9) [73.Álvaro Alexander Recoba Rivero (26/6)], Gerardo Federico Magallanes González (12/3) [63.Washington Sebastián Abreu Gallo (8/3)]. Trainer: Daniel Alberto Passarella (12).

Goal: Gerardo Federico Magallanes González (15), Debray Darío Silva Pereira (38), Andrés Nicolás Olivera (51), Néstor Gabriel Cedrés Vera (87).

671. 08.10.2000 **ARGENTINA - URUGUAY** **2-1(2-0)** 17th FIFA WC. Qualifiers

Estadio Monumental „Antonio Vespucio Liberti", Buenos Aires; Referee: Márcio Rezende de Freitas (Brazil), Attendance: 48,792

URU: Héctor Fabián Carini Hernández (19/0), Washington Eduardo Tais Videgaín (11/0), Daniel Alejandro Lembo Bentancor (17/1), Gonzalo Sorondo Amaro (2/0), Octavio Darío Rodríguez Peña (7/1), Néstor Gabriel Cedrés Vera (26/4) [65.Mario Ignacio Regueiro Pintos (1/0)], Pablo Gabriel García Pérez (20/1), Gianni Bismark Guigou Martínez (18/0), Andrés Nicolás Olivera (16/6), Álvaro Alexander Recoba Rivero (27/5) [71.Washington Sebastián Abreu Gallo (9/3)], Gerardo Federico Magallanes González (13/4) [87.Diego Martín Alonso López (6/0)]. Trainer: Daniel Alberto Passarella (13).

Goal: Gerardo Federico Magallanes González (50).

672. 15.11.2000 **BOLIVIA - URUGUAY** **0-0** 17th FIFA WC. Qualifiers

Estadio „Hernándo Siles Zuazo", La Paz; Referee: Horacio Marcelo Elizondo (Argentina), Attendance: 29,112

URU: Héctor Fabián Carini Hernández (20/0), Gustavo Antonio Varela Rodríguez (1/0), Daniel Alejandro Lembo Bentancor (18/1), Gonzalo Sorondo Amaro (3/0), Octavio Darío Rodríguez Peña (8/1), Clever Marcelo Romero Silva (14/0), Pablo Gabriel García Pérez (21/1), Walter Fabián Coelho (16/1) [65.Christian Fabián Callejas (10/1)], Mario Ignacio Regueiro Pintos (2/0), Gerardo Federico Magallanes González (14/4) [56.Debray Darío Silva Pereira (25/9)], José María Franco Ramallo (1/0) [75.Néstor Gabriel Cedrés Vera (27/4)]. Trainer: Daniel Alberto Passarella (14).

673. 28.02.2001 **SLOVENIA - URUGUAY** **0-2(0-1)**

SRC Bonifika Stadium, Koper; Referee: Anton Stredák (Slovakia), Attendance: 4,200

URU: Héctor Fabián Carini Hernández (21/0), Gustavo Emilio Méndez Techera (38/0), Gonzalo Sorondo Amaro (4/0), Ronald Paolo Montero (35/3), Octavio Darío Rodríguez Peña (9/1) [89.Gustavo Antonio Varela Rodríguez (2/0)], José Andrés Fleurquin Rubio (10/0), Pablo Gabriel García Pérez (22/1), Gianni Bismark Guigou Martínez (19/0), Álvaro Alexander Recoba Rivero (28/6), Andrés Nicolás Olivera (17/7), Debray Darío Silva Pereira (26/9) [59.Marcelo Danubio Zalayeta (19/7)]. Trainer: Víctor Haroldo Púa Sosa (14).

Goals: Andrés Nicolás Olivera (23), Marcelo Danubio Zalayeta (87).

674. 28.03.2001 **URUGUAY - PARAGUAY** **0-1(0-0)** 17th FIFA WC. Qualifiers

Estadio Centenario, Montevideo; Referee: José María García Aranda-Encinar (Spain), Attendance: 50,000

URU: Héctor Fabián Carini Hernández (22/0), Gustavo Antonio Varela Rodríguez (3/0), Gonzalo Sorondo Amaro (5/0), Ronald Paolo Montero (36/3), Gonzalo de los Santos da Rosa (18/1), Octavio Darío Rodríguez Peña (10/1), Gianni Bismark Guigou Martínez (20/0) [48.Walter Gerardo Pandiani Urquiza (1/0)], José Andrés Fleurquin Rubio (11/0) [68.Fabián Alberto O'Neill Domínguez (15/1)], Debray Darío Silva Pereira (27/9) [75.Marcelo Danubio Zalayeta (20/7)], Álvaro Alexander Recoba Rivero (29/6), Andrés Nicolás Olivera (18/7). Trainer: Víctor Haroldo Púa Sosa (15).

675. 24.04.2001 **CHILE - URUGUAY** **0-1(0-1)** 17th FIFA WC. Qualifiers

Estadio Nacional, Santiago; Referee: Horacio Marcelo Elizondo (Argentina), Attendance: 45,676

URU: Héctor Fabián Carini Hernández (23/0), Gustavo Emilio Méndez Techera (39/0), Gonzalo Sorondo Amaro (6/0), Daniel Alejandro Lembo Bentancor (19/1), Pablo Gabriel García Pérez (23/1), Octavio Darío Rodríguez Peña (11/1), Gianni Bismark Guigou Martínez (21/0), Andrés Nicolás Olivera (19/7) [82.Mario Ignacio Regueiro Pintos (3/0)], Debray Darío Silva Pereira (28/9) [77.Gustavo Antonio Varela Rodríguez (4/0)], Álvaro Alexander Recoba Rivero (30/6) [71.Clever Marcelo Romero Silva (15/0)], Gerardo Federico Magallanes González (15/4). Trainer: Víctor Haroldo Púa Sosa (16).

Goal: Italo Díaz (12 own goal).

676. 01.07.2001 **URUGUAY - BRAZIL** **1-0(1-0)** 17th FIFA WC. Qualifiers

Estadio Centenario, Montevideo; Referee: Hugh Dallas (Scotland), Attendance: 61,249

URU: Héctor Fabián Carini Hernández (24/0), Gustavo Emilio Méndez Techera (40/0), Gonzalo Sorondo Amaro (7/0), Ronald Paolo Montero (37/3), Pablo Gabriel García Pérez (24/1), Gianni Bismark Guigou Martínez (22/0), Clever Marcelo Romero Silva (16/0), Gonzalo de los Santos da Rosa (19/1), Debray Darío Silva Pereira (29/9) [63.Mario Ignacio Regueiro Pintos (4/0)], Gerardo Federico Magallanes González (16/5) [71.Guillermo Gonzalo Giacomazzi Suárez (4/0)], Álvaro Alexander Recoba Rivero (31/6) [75.Daniel Alejandro Lembo Bentancor (20/1)]. Trainer: Víctor Haroldo Púa Sosa (17).

Goal: Gerardo Federico Magallanes González (33 penalty).

677. 13.07.2001 **URUGUAY - BOLIVIA** **1-0(0-0)** 40th Copa América. Group Stage

Estadio „Atanasio Girardot", Medellín (Colombia); Referee: Mauricio Navarro (Canada), Attendance: 20,027

URU: Gustavo Adolfo Munúa (2/0), Carlos Díaz (2/0), Gonzalo Sorondo Amaro (8/0), Joe Emerson Bizera Bastos (1/0), Pablo Martín Lima Olid (1/0), Christian Fabián Callejas (11/1), Diego Fernando Pérez Aguado (1/0), Andrés Martínez (4/0) [56.Jorge Luis Anchén Cajiga (1/0)], Rodrigo Javier Lemos Rosende (3/0) [63.Sebastián Eguren Ledesma (1/0)], Ernesto Javier Chevantón Espinosa (1/1) [79.Carlos María Morales Maeso (1/0)], Richard Javier Morales Aguirre (1/0). Trainer: Víctor Haroldo Púa Sosa (18).

Goal: Javier Ernesto Chevanton (64).

678. 16.07.2001 **URUGUAY - COSTA RICA** **1-1(0-1)** 40th Copa América. Group Stage
Estadio „Atanasio Girardot“, Medellín (Colombia); Referee: Carlos Simón (Brazil), Attendance: 17,273
URU: Gustavo Adolfo Munúa (3/0), Carlos Díaz (3/0), Gonzalo Sorondo Amaro (9/0), Joe Emerson Bizera Bastos (2/0), Christian Fabián Callejas (12/1), Diego Fernando Pérez Aguado (2/0), Andrés Martínez (5/0) [51.Jorge Luis Anchén Cajiga (2/0)], Rodrigo Javier Lemos Rosende (4/0) [58.Sebastián Eguren Ledesma (2/0)], Carlos María Morales Maeso (2/1) [88.Carlos Gutiérrez (1/0)], Alejandro César Curbelo Aguete (1/0), Richard Javier Morales Aguirre (2/0). Trainer: Víctor Haroldo Púa Sosa (19).
Goal: Carlos María Morales Maeso (54)

679. 19.07.2001 **URUGUAY - HONDURAS** **0-1(0-0)** 40th Copa América. Group Stage
Estadio „Atanasio Girardot“, Medellín (Colombia); Referee: Roger Zambrano (Ecuador), Attendance: 20,233
URU: Adrián Berbia Pose (1/0), Carlos Díaz (4/0), Joe Emerson Bizera Bastos (3/0) [*sent off 52*], Andrés Martínez (6/0) [70.Diego Fernando Pérez Aguado (3/0)], Rodrigo Javier Lemos Rosende (5/0) [82.Jorge Luis Anchén Cajiga (3/0)], Carlos María Morales Maeso (3/1), Alejandro César Curbelo Aguete (2/0), Sebastián Eguren Ledesma (3/0) [*sent off 80*], Claudio Martín Dadómo Minervini (1/0), Carlos Gutiérrez (2/0), Walter Guglielmone Gómez (1/0) [67.Richard Javier Morales Aguirre (3/0)]. Trainer: Víctor Haroldo Púa Sosa (20).

680. 22.07.2001 **URUGUAY - COSTA RICA** **2-1(0-0)** 40th Copa América. Quarter-Finals
Estadio Centenario, Arménia (Colombia); Referee: Oscar Julián Ruíz Acosta (Colombia), Attendance: 8,876
URU: Gustavo Adolfo Munúa (4/0), Jorge Luis Anchén Cajiga (4/0), Carlos Gutiérrez (3/0), Gonzalo Sorondo Amaro (10/0), Alejandro César Curbelo Aguete (3/0), Pablo Martín Lima Olid (2/1), Diego Fernando Pérez Aguado (4/0), Christian Fabián Callejas (13/1), Rodrigo Javier Lemos Rosende (6/1) [90.Andrés Martínez (7/0)], Carlos María Morales Maeso (4/1) [70.Rubén Ariel Olivera da Rosa (1/0)], Richard Javier Morales Aguirre (4/0). Trainer: Víctor Haroldo Púa Sosa (21).
Goals: Rodrigo Javier Lemos Rosende (61 penalty), Pablo Martín Lima Olid (87).

681. 25.07.2001 **URUGUAY - MEXICO** **1-2(1-1)** 40th Copa América. Semi-Finals
Estadio „Hernán Ramírez Villegas“, Pereira (Colombia); Referee: Angel Osvaldo Sánchez (Argentina), Attendance: 11,797
URU: Gustavo Adolfo Munúa (5/0), Gonzalo Sorondo Amaro (11/0), Joe Emerson Bizera Bastos (4/0) [75.Fabián Larry Estoyanoff Poggio (1/0)], Pablo Martín Lima Olid (3/1), Christian Fabián Callejas (14/1), Diego Fernando Pérez Aguado (5/0), Rodrigo Javier Lemos Rosende (7/1) [67.Rubén Ariel Olivera da Rosa (2/0)], Carlos María Morales Maeso (5/1) [*sent off 45*], Carlos Gutiérrez (4/0), Richard Javier Morales Aguirre (5/1) [*sent off 90*], Jorge Luis Anchén Cajiga (5/0) [60.Carlos Díaz (5/0)]. Trainer: Víctor Haroldo Púa Sosa (22).
Goal: Richard Javier Morales Aguirre (32).

682. 29.07.2001 **URUGUAY - HONDURAS** **2-2(2-2,2-2), 4-5 on penalties** 40th Copa América. Bronze Medal
Estadio „Nemesio Camacho“ 'El Campín', Bogotá (Colombia); Referee: Gilberto Hidalgo (Peru), Attendance: 43,198
URU: Adrián Berbia Pose (2/0), Carlos Díaz (6/0), Carlos Gutiérrez (5/0), Gonzalo Sorondo Amaro (12/0), Joe Emerson Bizera Bastos (5/1), Claudio Martín Dadómo Minervini (2/0) [85.Pablo Martín Lima Olid (4/1)], Andrés Martínez (8/1) [65.Julio Pablo Rodríguez Cristóbal (1/0)], Diego Fernando Pérez Aguado (6/0), Rodrigo Javier Lemos Rosende (8/1), Fabián Larry Estoyanoff Poggio (2/0), Walter Guglielmone Gómez (2/0) [56.Rubén Ariel Olivera da Rosa (3/0)]. Trainer: Víctor Haroldo Púa Sosa (23).
Goals: Joe Emerson Bizera Bastos (22), Andrés Martínez (45).
Penalties: Gonzalo Sorondo Amaro, Carlos Gutiérrez (save), Julio Pablo Rodríguez Cristóbal, Rodrigo Javier Lemos Rosende, Rubén Ariel Olivera da Rosa.

683. 14.08.2001 **VENEZUELA - URUGUAY** **2-0(0-0)** 17th FIFA WC. Qualifiers
Estadio „José 'Pachencho' Romero“, Maracaibo; Referee: Antonio Marrufo Mendoza (Mexico), Attendance: 8,500
URU: Héctor Fabián Carini Hernández (25/0), Gustavo Emilio Méndez Techera (41/0) [*sent off 69*], Gonzalo Sorondo Amaro (13/0), Ronald Paolo Montero (38/3), Gonzalo de los Santos da Rosa (20/1), Gianni Bismark Guigou Martínez (23/0), Clever Marcelo Romero Silva (17/0) [64.Carlos María Morales Maeso (6/1)], Guillermo Gonzalo Giacomazzi Suárez (5/0) [53.Mario Ignacio Regueiro Pintos (5/0)], Debray Darío Silva Pereira (30/9) [58.Marcelo Danubio Zalayeta (21/7)], Andrés Nicolás Olivera (20/7), Álvaro Alexander Recoba Rivero (32/6). Trainer: Víctor Haroldo Púa Sosa (24).

684. 04.09.2001 **PERU - URUGUAY** **0-2(0-2)** 17th FIFA WC. Qualifiers
Estadio Nacional, Lima; Referee: Anders Frisk (Sweden), Attendance: 40,524
URU: Héctor Fabián Carini Hernández (26/0), Joe Emerson Bizera Bastos (6/1), Daniel Alejandro Lembo Bentancor (21/1), Washington Eduardo Tais Videgaín (12/0), Pablo Gabriel García Pérez (25/1), Octavio Darío Rodríguez Peña (12/1), Gianni Bismark Guigou Martínez (24/0), Gonzalo de los Santos da Rosa (21/1), Debray Darío Silva Pereira (31/10) [72.Mario Ignacio Regueiro Pintos (6/0)], Ernesto Javier Chevantón Espinosa (2/1) [65.Gerardo Federico Magallanes González (17/5)], Álvaro Alexander Recoba Rivero (33/7) [88.Diego Fernando Pérez Aguado (7/0)]. Trainer: Víctor Haroldo Púa Sosa (25).
Goals: Debray Darío Silva Pereira (12), Álvaro Alexander Recoba Rivero (45).

685. 07.10.2001 **URUGUAY - COLOMBIA** **1-1(1-0)** 17th FIFA WC. Qualifiers
Estadio Centenario, Montevideo; Referee: Pierluigi Collina (Italy), Attendance: 60,000
URU: Gustavo Adolfo Munúa (6/0), Washington Eduardo Tais Videgaín (13/0), Daniel Alejandro Lembo Bentancor (22/1), Ronald Paolo Montero (39/3), Pablo Gabriel García Pérez (26/1), Octavio Darío Rodríguez Peña (13/1), Gianni Bismark Guigou Martínez (25/0) [79.Néstor Fabián Canobbio Bentaberry (1/0)], Gonzalo de los Santos da Rosa (22/1), Debray Darío Silva Pereira (32/10) [75.Richard Javier Morales Aguirre (6/1)], Gerardo Federico Magallanes González (18/6) [46.Ernesto Javier Chevantón Espinosa (3/1)], Álvaro Alexander Recoba Rivero (34/7). Trainer: Víctor Haroldo Púa Sosa (26).
Goal: Gerardo Federico Magallanes González (35 penalty).

686. 07.11.2001 **ECUADOR - URUGUAY** **1-1(0-1)** 17th FIFA WC. Qualifiers
Estadio Olimpico „Atahualpa“, Quito; Referee: Felipe Ramos Rizzo (Mexico), Attendance: 40,000
URU: Héctor Fabián Carini Hernández (27/0), Washington Eduardo Tais Videgaín (14/0), Daniel Alejandro Lembo Bentancor (23/1), Ronald Paolo Montero (40/3), Pablo Gabriel García Pérez (27/1), Gianni Bismark Guigou Martínez (26/0), Clever Marcelo Romero Silva (18/0), Gonzalo de los Santos da Rosa (23/1), Debray Darío Silva Pereira (33/10) [74.Carlos María Morales Maeso (7/1)], Andrés Nicolás Olivera (21/8) [52.Vicente Martín Sánchez Bragunde (1/0)], Álvaro Alexander Recoba Rivero (35/7) [84.Diego Fernando Pérez Aguado (8/0)]. Trainer: Víctor Haroldo Púa Sosa (27).
Goal: Andrés Nicolás Olivera (44 penalty).

687. 14.11.2001 **URUGUAY - ARGENTINA** **1-1(1-1)** 17th FIFA WC. Qualifiers
Estadio Centenario, Montevideo; Referee: Dr. Markus Merk (Germany), Attendance: 48,100
URU: Héctor Fabián Carini Hernández (28/0), Washington Eduardo Tais Videgaín (15/0) [63.Richard Javier Morales Aguirre (7/1)], Daniel Alejandro Lembo Bentancor (24/1), Ronald Paolo Montero (41/3), Pablo Gabriel García Pérez (28/1), Octavio Darío Rodríguez Peña (14/1) [81.Mario Ignacio Regueiro Pintos (7/0)], Gianni Bismark Guigou Martínez (27/0), Gonzalo de los Santos da Rosa (24/1), Debray Darío Silva Pereira (34/11) [46.Diego Martín Alonso López (7/0)], Gerardo Federico Magallanes González (19/6), Álvaro Alexander Recoba Rivero (36/7). Trainer: Víctor Haroldo Púa Sosa (28).
Goal: Debray Darío Silva Pereira (18).

688. 20.11.2001 **AUSTRALIA - URUGUAY** **1-0(0-0)** 17th FIFA WC. Qualifiers. Play-offs
Cricket Ground, Melbourne; Referee: Graziano Cesari (Italy), Attendance: 84,656
URU: Héctor Fabián Carini Hernández (29/0), Washington Eduardo Tais Videgaín (16/0), Daniel Alejandro Lembo Bentancor (25/1), Ronald Paolo Montero (42/3), Octavio Darío Rodríguez Peña (15/1), Gianni Bismark Guigou Martínez (28/0), Pablo Gabriel García Pérez (29/1), Gonzalo de los Santos da Rosa (25/1), Álvaro Alexander Recoba Rivero (37/7), Ernesto Javier Chevantón Espinosa (4/1) [77.Mario Ignacio Regueiro Pintos (8/0)], Gerardo Federico Magallanes González (20/6), Guillermo Gonzalo Giacomazzi Suárez (6/0). Trainer: Víctor Haroldo Púa Sosa (29).

689. 25.11.2001 **URUGUAY - AUSTRALIA** **3-0(1-0)** 17th FIFA WC. Qualifiers. Play-offs
Estadio Centenario, Montevideo; Referee: Ali Mohamed Bujsaim (United Arab Emirates), Attendance: 62,000
URU: Héctor Fabián Carini Hernández (30/0), Washington Eduardo Tais Videgaín (17/0), Daniel Alejandro Lembo Bentancor (26/1), Ronald Paolo Montero (43/3), Octavio Darío Rodríguez Peña (16/1), Pablo Gabriel García Pérez (30/1), Gianni Bismark Guigou Martínez (29/0), Mario Ignacio Regueiro Pintos (9/0) [74.Gonzalo de los Santos da Rosa (26/1)], Álvaro Alexander Recoba Rivero (38/7), Debray Darío Silva Pereira (35/12) [82.Gonzalo Sorondo Amaro (14/0)], Gerardo Federico Magallanes González (21/6) [66.Richard Javier Morales Aguirre (8/3)]. Trainer: Víctor Haroldo Púa Sosa (30).
Goals: Debray Darío Silva Pereira (12), Richard Javier Morales Aguirre (70, 90).

690. 13.02.2002 **URUGUAY - SOUTH KOREA** **2-1(1-1)**
Estadio Centenario, Montevideo; Referee: Horacio Elizondo (Argentina), Attendance: 45,000
URU: Héctor Fabián Carini Hernández (31/0), Daniel Alejandro Lembo Bentancor (27/1), Gonzalo Sorondo Amaro (15/0) [63.Joe Emerson Bizera Bastos (7/1)], Octavio Darío Rodríguez Peña (17/1), Washington Eduardo Tais Videgaín (18/0) [69.Gustavo Antonio Varela Rodríguez (5/0)], Pablo Gabriel García Pérez (31/1) [78.Sebastián Eguren Ledesma (4/0)], Gianni Bismark Guigou Martínez (30/0), Andrés Nicolás Olivera (22/8) [66.Rubén Ariel Olivera da Rosa (4/0)], Mario Ignacio Regueiro Pintos (10/0), Richard Javier Morales Aguirre (9/3), Washington Sebastián Abreu Gallo (10/5). Trainer: Víctor Haroldo Púa Sosa (31).
Goals: Washington Sebastián Abreu Gallo (7, 55).

691. 27.03.2002 **SAUDI ARABIA - URUGUAY** **3-2(3-1)**
„Prince Mohammad Bin Fahd Bin Abdoulaziz" Stadium, Damman; Referee: Farid Ali Al Marzuki (United Arab Emirates), Attendance: 17,000
URU: Héctor Fabián Carini Hernández (32/0), Daniel Alejandro Lembo Bentancor (28/1), Oscar Damián Rodríguez Cantos (2/0), Pablo Martín Lima Olid (5/1), Gustavo Antonio Varela Rodríguez (6/0), Pablo Gabriel García Pérez (32/1), Fabián Alberto O'Neill Domínguez (16/2) [73.Rubén Ariel Olivera da Rosa (5/0)], Gianni Bismark Guigou Martínez (31/0) [61.Clever Marcelo Romero Silva (19/0)], Gerardo Federico Magallanes González (22/6), Álvaro Alexander Recoba Rivero (39/7) [46.Richard Javier Morales Aguirre (10/3)], Diego Martín Forlán Corazo (1/1). Trainer: Víctor Haroldo Púa Sosa (32).
Goals: Diego Martín Forlán Corazo (4), Fabián Alberto O'Neill Domínguez (59).

692. 17.04.2002 **ITALY - URUGUAY** **1-1(0-0)**
Stadio „Giuseppe Meazza", Milano; Referee: Stéphane Bré (France), Attendance: 16,773
URU: Héctor Fabián Carini Hernández (33/0) [63.Gustavo Adolfo Munúa (7/0)], Gustavo Emilio Méndez Techera (42/0) [74.Mario Ignacio Regueiro Pintos (11/0)], Joe Emerson Bizera Bastos (8/1), Daniel Alejandro Lembo Bentancor (29/1) [46.Gianni Bismark Guigou Martínez (32/0)], Octavio Darío Rodríguez Peña (18/1) [86.Sebastián Eguren Ledesma (5/0)], Pablo Gabriel García Pérez (33/1) [57.Gonzalo de los Santos da Rosa (27/1)], Gustavo Antonio Varela Rodríguez (7/0) [74.Diego Martín Forlán Corazo (2/1)], Fabián Alberto O'Neill Domínguez (17/2) [66.Rubén Ariel Olivera da Rosa (6/0)], Gerardo Federico Magallanes González (23/6) [66.Diego Fernando Pérez Aguado (9/0)], Álvaro Alexander Recoba Rivero (40/7) [57.Richard Javier Morales Aguirre (11/3)], Debray Darío Silva Pereira (36/12) [57.Washington Sebastián Abreu Gallo (11/6)]. Trainer: Víctor Haroldo Púa Sosa (33).
Goal: Washington Sebastián Abreu Gallo (77).

693. 12.05.2002 **UNITED STATES - URUGUAY** **2-1(2-0)**
"Robert F. Kennedy" Memorial Stadium, Washington; Referee: Fredy Burgos (Guatemala), Attendance: 30,413
URU: Gustavo Adolfo Munúa (8/0), Gustavo Emilio Méndez Techera (43/0), Daniel Alejandro Lembo Bentancor (30/1), Gonzalo Sorondo Amaro (16/0), Octavio Darío Rodríguez Peña (19/1) [68.Rubén Ariel Olivera da Rosa (7/0)], Pablo Gabriel García Pérez (34/1), Andrés Nicolás Olivera (23/8) [46.Mario Ignacio Regueiro Pintos (12/0)], Fabián Alberto O'Neill Domínguez (18/2), Gerardo Federico Magallanes González (24/6) [46.Gianni Bismark Guigou Martínez (33/0)], Álvaro Alexander Recoba Rivero (41/7), Washington Sebastián Abreu Gallo (12/7). Trainer: Víctor Haroldo Púa Sosa (34).
Goal: Washington Sebastián Abreu Gallo (60).

694. 16.05.2002 **CHINA - URUGUAY** **0-2(0-0)** Phillips Cup
Wulihe Stadium, Shenyang; Referee: Piromnya Chalah (Thailand), Attendance: 40,000
URU: Héctor Fabián Carini Hernández (34/0), Gustavo Emilio Méndez Techera (44/0) [82.Diego Fernando Pérez Aguado (10/0)], Gonzalo Sorondo Amaro (17/0), Ronald Paolo Montero (44/3) [67.Andrés Nicolás Olivera (24/8)], Octavio Darío Rodríguez Peña (20/1) [87.Sebastián Eguren Ledesma (6/0)], Pablo Gabriel García Pérez (35/1) [61.Clever Marcelo Romero Silva (20/0)], Gianni Bismark Guigou Martínez (34/0), Fabián Alberto O'Neill Domínguez (19/2) [46.Gonzalo de los Santos da Rosa (28/1)], Álvaro Alexander Recoba Rivero (42/7), Mario Ignacio Regueiro Pintos (13/0) [57.Diego Martín Forlán Corazo (3/1)], Washington Sebastián Abreu Gallo (13/9). Trainer: Víctor Haroldo Púa Sosa (35).
Goals: Washington Sebastián Abreu Gallo (74, 88).

695. 21.05.2002 **SINGAPORE - URUGUAY** **1-2(0-1)** Tiger Beer Challenge Trophy
National Stadium, Singapore; Referee: Subkhiddin Mohd Salleh (Malaysia), Attendance: 23,834
URU: Héctor Fabián Carini Hernández (35/0) [46.Federico Martín Elduayén Saldaña (1/0)], Gianni Bismark Guigou Martínez (35/0), Gonzalo Sorondo Amaro (18/0) [54.Sebastián Eguren Ledesma (7/0)], Joe Emerson Bizera Bastos (9/1), Mario Ignacio Regueiro Pintos (14/0), Clever Marcelo Romero Silva (21/0) [54.Diego Fernando Pérez Aguado (11/0)], Gonzalo de los Santos da Rosa (29/1), Andrés Nicolás Olivera (25/8), Gustavo Antonio Varela Rodríguez (8/0) [49.Rubén Ariel Olivera da Rosa (8/0)], Diego Martín Forlán Corazo (4/1), Richard Javier Morales Aguirre (12/5). Trainer: Víctor Haroldo Púa Sosa (36).
Goals: Richard Javier Morales Aguirre (27, 76).

696. 01.06.2002 **DENMARK - URUGUAY** **2-1(1-0)** 17th FIFA WC. Group Stage
Munsu Football Stadium, Ulsan (South Korea); Referee: Saad Kamell Manei (Kuwait), Attendance: 30,157
URU: Héctor Fabián Carini Hernández (36/0), Gustavo Emilio Méndez Techera (45/0), Gonzalo Sorondo Amaro (19/0), Ronald Paolo Montero (45/3), Octavio Darío Rodríguez Peña (21/2) [87.Gerardo Federico Magallanes González (25/6)], Pablo Gabriel García Pérez (36/1), Gustavo Antonio Varela Rodríguez (9/0), Gianni Bismark Guigou Martínez (36/0), Álvaro Alexander Recoba Rivero (43/7) [80.Mario Ignacio Regueiro Pintos (15/0)], Debray Darío Silva Pereira (37/12), Washington Sebastián Abreu Gallo (14/9) [88.Richard Javier Morales Aguirre (13/5)]. Trainer: Víctor Haroldo Púa Sosa (37).
Goal: Octavio Darío Rodríguez Peña (47).

697. 06.06.2002 **FRANCE – URUGUAY** **0-0** 17th FIFA WC. Group Stage
Asiad Main Stadium, Busan (South Korea); Referee: Felipe Ramos Rizo (Mexico), Attendance: 38,289
URU: Héctor Fabián Carini Hernández (37/0), Daniel Alejandro Lembo Bentancor (31/1), Ronald Paolo Montero (46/3), Pablo Gabriel García Pérez (37/1), Octavio Darío Rodríguez Peña (22/2) [72.Gianni Bismark Guigou Martínez (37/0)], Gustavo Antonio Varela Rodríguez (10/0), Debray Darío Silva Pereira (38/12) [60.Gerardo Federico Magallanes González (26/6)], Washington Sebastián Abreu Gallo (15/9), Gonzalo Sorondo Amaro (20/0), Clever Marcelo Romero Silva (22/0) [71.Gonzalo de los Santos da Rosa (30/1)], Álvaro Alexander Recoba Rivero (44/7). Trainer: Víctor Haroldo Púa Sosa (38).

698. 11.06.2002 **URUGUAY – SENEGAL** **3-3(0-3)** 17th FIFA WC. Group Stage
Suwon World Cup Stadium, Suwon (South Korea); Referee: Jan Wegereef (Holland), Attendance: 33,681
URU: Héctor Fabián Carini Hernández (38/0), Daniel Alejandro Lembo Bentancor (32/1), Ronald Paolo Montero (47/3), Pablo Gabriel García Pérez (38/1), Octavio Darío Rodríguez Peña (23/2), Gustavo Antonio Varela Rodríguez (11/0), Debray Darío Silva Pereira (39/12), Washington Sebastián Abreu Gallo (16/9) [46.Diego Martín Forlán Corazo (5/2)], Gonzalo Sorondo Amaro (21/0) [32.Mario Ignacio Regueiro Pintos (16/0)], Clever Marcelo Romero Silva (23/0) [46.Richard Javier Morales Aguirre (14/6)], Álvaro Alexander Recoba Rivero (45/8). Trainer: Víctor Haroldo Púa Sosa (39).
Goals: Richard Javier Morales Aguirre (46), Diego Martín Forlán Corazo (69), Álvaro Alexander Recoba Rivero (88 penalty).

699. 20.11.2002 **VENEZUELA – URUGUAY** **1-0(0-0)**
Estadio Olímpico „Ciudad Universitaria", Caracas; Referee: Luis Solórzano (Venezuela), Attendance: 26,000
URU: Gustavo Adolfo Munúa (9/0), Jorge Luis Anchén Cajiga (6/0) [85.Ronald Andrés Ramírez Villa (1/0)], Joe Emerson Bizera Bastos (10/1), Cristian Mario González Aidinovich (1/0), Pablo Martín Lima Olid (6/1), Sebastián Eguren Ledesma (8/0), Óscar Javier Morales Albornoz (1/0) [77.Marcelo Carlo Broli Gorgoroso (1/0)], Martín Ricardo Ligüera López (1/0) [57.Néstor Fabián Canobbio Bentaberry (2/0)], Rubén Ariel Olivera da Rosa (9/0) [*sent off 90*], Germán Andrés Hornos Correa (1/0) [67.Gonzalo Vargas Abella (1/0)], Richard Javier Morales Aguirre (15/6). Trainer: Jorge Da Silva (1).

700. 04.02.2003 **IRAN – URUGUAY** **1-1(1-0,1-1); 2-4 on penalties** Carlsberg Cup
Hong Kong Stadium, Hong Kong; Referee: Fong Yau-fat (Hong Kong), Attendance: 17,877
URU: Mauricio Daniel Nanni Lima (1/0), Diego Alfredo Lugano Morena (1/0), Bruno Ramón Silva Barone (1/0), Williams Guillermo Martínez Fracchia (1/0), Pablo Martín Lima Olid (7/1), Claudio Martín Dadómo Minervini (3/0) [46.Fabián Larry Estoyanoff Poggio (3/1)], Julio Pablo Rodríguez Cristóbal (2/0), Marcelo Fabián Sosa Farías (1/0) [69.Sebastián Taborda Ramos (1/0)], Martín Ricardo Ligüera López (2/0) [80.Julio Fabián Mozzo Valdéz (1/0)], Germán Andrés Hornos Correa (2/0) [91.Sergio Rubén Blanco Soto (1/0)], Mario Evaristo Leguizamón Martínez (1/0) [29.Walter Horacio Peralta Saracho (2/0) [*sent off 87*]]. Trainer: Gustavo Ferrín (1).
Goal: Fabián Larry Estoyanoff Poggio (84).
Penalties: Julio Pablo Rodríguez Cristóbal, Fabián Larry Estoyanoff Poggio, Pablo Martín Lima Olid, Bruno Ramón Silva Barone.

701. 28.03.2003 **JAPAN – URUGUAY** **2-2(1-2)**
Kasumigaoka National Stadium, Tokyo; Referee: Tae-Young Kim (South Korea), Attendance: 54,039
URU: Héctor Fabián Carini Hernández (39/0), Bruno Ramón Silva Barone (2/0) [81.Carlos Andrés Diogo Enseñat (1/0)], Daniel Alejandro Lembo Bentancor (33/2), Gonzalo Sorondo Amaro (22/0), Octavio Darío Rodríguez Peña (24/2), Sebastián Eguren Ledesma (9/0) [90.Juan Ramón Curbelo Garis (1/0)], Marcelo Fabián Sosa Farías (2/0), Pablo Martín Lima Olid (8/1), Álvaro Alexander Recoba Rivero (46/8), Diego Martín Forlán Corazo (6/3) [84.Fabián Larry Estoyanoff Poggio (4/1)], Ernesto Javier Chevantón Espinosa (5/1) [64.Walter Horacio Peralta Saracho (3/0)]. Trainer: Gustavo Ferrín (2).
Goals: Diego Martín Forlán Corazo (21), Daniel Alejandro Lembo Bentancor (25).

702. 08.06.2003 **SOUTH KOREA – URUGUAY** **0-2(0-1)**
Sangam World Cup Stadium, Seoul; Referee: Yoshida Toshimitsu (Japan), Attendance: 63,691
URU: Gustavo Adolfo Munúa (10/0), Cristian Mario González Aidinovich (2/0) [59.Jesús Cono Aguiar Moreira (1/0)], Daniel Alejandro Lembo Bentancor (34/2), Joe Emerson Bizera Bastos (11/1), Eduardo Alejandro Lago Correa (1/0), Álvaro Alexander Recoba Rivero (47/8) [71.Jorge Andrés Martínez Barrios (1/0)], Marcelo Fabián Sosa Farías (3/0), Martín Ricardo Ligüera López (3/0), Diego Martín Forlán Corazo (7/3) [46.Walter Horacio Peralta Saracho (4/0)], Washington Sebastián Abreu Gallo (17/10) [82.Fabián Larry Estoyanoff Poggio (5/1)], Germán Andrés Hornos Correa (3/1) [90.Diego Rafael Perrone Vienes (1/0)]. Trainer: Juan Ramón Carrasco Torres (1).
Goals: Germán Andrés Hornos Correa (13), Washington Sebastián Abreu Gallo (53).

703. 16.07.2003 **ARGENTINA – URUGUAY** **2-2(2-2)**
Estadio Unico, La Plata; Referee: Epifanio González Chávez (Paraguay), Attendance: 35,000
URU: Luis Alberto Barbat (3/0), Gianni Bismark Guigou Martínez (38/0), Luis Diego López Breijo (24/0) [74.Joe Emerson Bizera Bastos (12/1)], Gonzalo Sorondo Amaro (23/0) [5.Eduardo Alejandro Lago Correa (2/0)], Mario Ignacio Regueiro Pintos (17/0), Guillermo Gonzalo Giacomazzi Suárez (7/0) [80.Jorge Andrés Martínez Barrios (2/0)], Marcelo Fabián Sosa Farías (4/0), Martín Ricardo Ligüera López (4/0), Ernesto Javier Chevantón Espinosa (6/2), Walter Gerardo Pandiani Urquiza (2/0) [90.Diego Rafael Perrone Vienes (2/0)], Vicente Martín Sánchez Bragunde (2/0) [70.Carlos Éber Bueno Suárez (1/0)]. Trainer: Juan Ramón Carrasco Torres (2).
Goals: Ernesto Javier Chevantón Espinosa (6), Gabriel Milito (36 own goal).

704. 24.07.2003 **PERU – URUGUAY** **3-4(1-1)**
Estadio Nacional, Lima; Referee: Manuel Garay (Peru), Attendance: 7,500
URU: Ignacio Leonardo De León Jacue (1/0), Adrián Marcelo Romero González (1/0) [87.Carlos Andrés Diogo Enseñat (2/0)], Jesús Cono Aguiar Moreira (2/0), Joe Emerson Bizera Bastos (13/1), Eduardo Alejandro Lago Correa (3/0) [54.Bruno Ramón Silva Barone (3/0)], Jorge Andrés Martínez Barrios (3/0) [89.Juan Ramón Curbelo Garis (2/0)], Marcelo Fabián Sosa Farías (5/1) [82.Marcelo Carlo Broli Gorgoroso (2/0)], Martín Ricardo Ligüera López (5/2), Fabián Larry Estoyanoff Poggio (6/1), Carlos Éber Bueno Suárez (2/0), Diego Rafael Perrone Vienes (3/0) [60.Nicolás Ignacio Vigneri Cetrulo (1/1)]. Trainer: Juan Ramón Carrasco Torres (3).
Goals: Martín Ricardo Ligüera López (11), Marcelo Fabián Sosa Farías (50), Martín Ricardo Ligüera López (73), Nicolás Ignacio Vigneri Cetrulo (79).

705. 30.07.2003 **URUGUAY – PERU** **1-0(0-0)**
Estadio Centenario, Montevideo; Referee: Gustavo Méndez (Uruguay), Attendance: 6,800
URU: Gustavo Adolfo Munúa (11/0), Cristian Mario González Aidinovich (3/0), Joe Emerson Bizera Bastos (14/1), Eduardo Alejandro Lago Correa (4/0), Martín Ricardo Ligüera López (6/3), Marcelo Fabián Sosa Farías (6/1), Álvaro Alexander Recoba Rivero (48/8), Rubén Ariel Olivera da Rosa (10/0), Fabián Larry Estoyanoff Poggio (7/1) [57.Nicolás Ignacio Vigneri Cetrulo (2/1)], Jorge Andrés Martínez Barrios (4/0) [46.Diego Rafael Perrone Vienes (4/0)], Walter Horacio Peralta Saracho (5/0). Trainer: Juan Ramón Carrasco Torres (4).
Goal: Martín Ricardo Ligüera López (54).

706. 15.08.2003 **URUGUAY - IRAQ** **5-2(2-0)** LG Peace Cup
Azadi Stadium, Tehran; Referee: Azhar Rahim Moghadam Rahimi (Iran), Attendance: 7,000
URU: Gustavo Adolfo Munúa (12/0) [75.Luis Alberto Barbat (4/0)], Adrián Marcelo Romero González (2/0) [58.Juan Ramón Curbelo Garis (3/0)], Cristian Mario González Aidinovich (4/0), Eduardo Alejandro Lago Correa (5/0), Bruno Ramón Silva Barone (4/0) [68. Jesús Cono Aguiar Moreira (3/0)], Carlos Andrés Diogo Enseñat (3/0), Marcelo Fabián Sosa Farías (7/1) [72.Marcelo Carlo Broli Gorgoroso (3/0)], Martín Ricardo Ligüera López (7/6), Fabián Larry Estoyanoff Poggio (8/1), Carlos Éber Bueno Suárez (3/2), Walter Horacio Peralta Saracho (6/0) [32.Nicolás Ignacio Vigneri Cetrulo (3/1)]. Trainer: Juan Ramón Carrasco Torres (5).
Goals: Martín Ricardo Ligüera López (31, 36), Carlos Éber Bueno Suárez (67, 70), Martín Ricardo Ligüera López (82 penalty).

707. 20.08.2003 **URUGUAY - ARGENTINA** **2-3(1-1)**
Stadio "Artemio Franchi", Firenze (Italy); Referee: Massimo De Santis (Italy), Attendance: 8,000
URU: Gustavo Adolfo Munúa (13/0), Gianni Bismark Guigou Martínez (39/0), Daniel Alejandro Lembo Bentancor (35/2), Luis Diego López Breijo (25/0), Mario Ignacio Regueiro Pintos (18/0), Guillermo Gonzalo Giacomazzi Suárez (8/0) [56.Rubén Ariel Olivera da Rosa (11/0)], Nelson Javier Abeijón Pessi (20/1) [37.Marcelo Fabián Sosa Farías (8/1)], Álvaro Alexander Recoba Rivero (49/8), Ernesto Javier Chevantón Espinosa (7/2) [48.Martín Ricardo Ligüera López (8/7)], Washington Sebastián Abreu Gallo (18/10), Diego Martín Forlán Corazo (8/4) [69.Carlos Éber Bueno Suárez (4/2)]. Trainer: Juan Ramón Carrasco Torres (6).
Goals: Diego Martín Forlán Corazo (2), Martín Ricardo Ligüera López (57).

708. 07.09.2003 **URUGUAY - BOLIVIA** **5-0(2-0)** 18th FIFA WC. Qualifiers
Estadio Centenario, Montevideo; Referee: Gilberto Hidalgo Zamora (Peru), Attendance: 39,253
URU: Gustavo Adolfo Munúa (14/0), Cristian Mario González Aidinovich (5/0), Luis Diego López Breijo (26/0), Eduardo Alejandro Lago Correa (6/0), Richard Darío Núñez Pereyra (1/0), Martín Ricardo Ligüera López (9/7) [77.Rubén Ariel Olivera da Rosa (12/0)], Marcelo Fabián Sosa Farías (9/1) [69.Nelson Javier Abeijón Pessi (21/2)], Álvaro Alexander Recoba Rivero (50/8), Ernesto Javier Chevantón Espinosa (8/4), Carlos Éber Bueno Suárez (5/3), Diego Martín Forlán Corazo (9/5) [76.Vicente Martín Sánchez Bragunde (3/0)]. Trainer: Juan Ramón Carrasco Torres (7).
Goals: Diego Martín Forlán Corazo (18), Ernesto Javier Chevantón Espinosa (40, 62), Nelson Javier Abeijón Pessi (83), Carlos Éber Bueno Suárez (88).

709. 10.09.2003 **PARAGUAY - URUGUAY** **4-1(1-1)** 18th FIFA WC. Qualifiers
Estadio Defensores del Chaco, Asunción; Referee: Oscar Julián Ruíz Acosta (Colombia), Attendance: 7,918
URU: Gustavo Adolfo Munúa (15/0), Cristian Mario González Aidinovich (6/0), Jesús Cono Aguiar Moreira (4/0), Gonzalo Sorondo Amaro (24/0), Mario Ignacio Regueiro Pintos (19/0) [78.Richard Darío Núñez Pereyra (2/0)], Nelson Javier Abeijón Pessi (22/2), Guillermo Gonzalo Giacomazzi Suárez (9/0) [46.Martín Ricardo Ligüera López (10/7)], Rubén Ariel Olivera da Rosa (13/0), Ernesto Javier Chevantón Espinosa (9/5), Carlos Éber Bueno Suárez (6/3) [60.Álvaro Alexander Recoba Rivero (51/8)], Diego Martín Forlán Corazo (10/5). Trainer: Juan Ramón Carrasco Torres (8).
Goal: Ernesto Javier Chevantón Espinosa (23).

710. 15.10.2003 **URUGUAY - MEXICO** **2-0(1-0)**
Soldier Field, Chicago; Referee: Michael Kennedy (United States), Attendance: 41,587
URU: Luis Alberto Barbat (5/0), Adrián Marcelo Romero González (3/0) [83.Nery Damián Paz (1/0)], Joe Emerson Bizera Bastos (15/1), Eduardo Alejandro Lago Correa (7/0), Williams Daniel Hernández Spinelli (1/0) [80.Pablo Rodrigo Melo (1/0)], Jorge Andrés Martínez Barrios (5/0), Marcelo Fabián Sosa Farías (10/1), Carlos Javier Grossmüller (1/0) [68.Pablo Roberto Munhoz Rodríguez (1/0)], Walter Horacio Peralta Saracho (7/0) [53.Fabián Larry Estoyanoff Poggio (9/1)], Diego Rafael Perrone Vienes (5/2) [85.Nicolás Ignacio Vigneri Cetrulo (4/1)], Vicente Martín Sánchez Bragunde (4/0) [77.Cristian Gabriel Rodríguez Barotti (1/0)]. Trainer: Juan Ramón Carrasco Torres (9).
Goals: Diego Rafael Perrone Vienes (27, 63).

711. 15.11.2003 **URUGUAY - CHILE** **2-1(1-1)** 18th FIFA WC. Qualifiers
Estadio Centenario, Montevideo; Referee: Claudio Mario Martín (Argentina), Attendance: 70,000
URU: Gustavo Adolfo Munúa (16/0), Cristian Mario González Aidinovich (7/0), Luis Diego López Breijo (27/0), Eduardo Alejandro Lago Correa (8/0), Richard Darío Núñez Pereyra (3/0), Pablo Roberto Munhoz Rodríguez (2/0) [46.Adrián Marcelo Romero González (4/1)], Marcelo Fabián Sosa Farías (11/1), Martín Ricardo Ligüera López (11/7) [70.Álvaro Alexander Recoba Rivero (52/8)], Ernesto Javier Chevantón Espinosa (10/6), Carlos Éber Bueno Suárez (7/3), Diego Martín Forlán Corazo (11/5) [46.Germán Andrés Hornos Correa (4/1)]. Trainer: Juan Ramón Carrasco Torres (10).
Goals: Ernesto Javier Chevantón Espinosa (31), Adrián Marcelo Romero González (49).

712. 19.11.2003 **BRAZIL - URUGUAY** **3-3(2-0)** 18th FIFA WC. Qualifiers
Estádio „Baixada Pinheirão", Curitiba; Referee: Horacio Marcelo Elizondo (Argentina), Attendance: 28,000
URU: Gustavo Adolfo Munúa (17/0), Adrián Marcelo Romero González (5/1) [46.Álvaro Alexander Recoba Rivero (53/8)], Joe Emerson Bizera Bastos (16/1), Luis Diego López Breijo (28/0), Eduardo Alejandro Lago Correa (9/0), Marcelo Danubio Zalayeta (22/7), Nelson Javier Abeijón Pessi (23/2) [36.Richard Darío Núñez Pereyra (4/0)], Marcelo Fabián Sosa Farías (12/1), Martín Ricardo Ligüera López (12/7), Germán Andrés Hornos Correa (5/1) [55.Ernesto Javier Chevantón Espinosa (11/6)], Diego Martín Forlán Corazo (12/7). Trainer: Juan Ramón Carrasco Torres (11).
Goals: Diego Martín Forlán Corazo (57, 76), Gilberto da Silva (78 own goal).

713. 18.02.2004 **JAMAICA - URUGUAY** **2-0(1-0)**
National Stadium, Kingston; Referee: Edward Gordon (Trinidad Tobago), Attendance: 25,000
URU: Gustavo Adolfo Munúa (18/0) [46.Luis Alberto Barbat (6/0)], Jorge Winston Curbelo Garis (1/0), Pablo Rodrigo Melo (2/0), Pablo Martín Lima Olid (9/1), Richard Darío Núñez Pereyra (5/0), Martín Ricardo Ligüera López (13/7), Jorge Andrés Martínez Barrios (6/0), Rubén Ariel Olivera da Rosa (14/0), Diego Martín Forlán Corazo (13/7) [46.Fernando Edgardo Correa Ayala (3/0)], Marcelo Danubio Zalayeta (23/7) [44.Germán Andrés Hornos Correa (6/1)], Ernesto Javier Chevantón Espinosa (12/6) [59.Fabián Larry Estoyanoff Poggio (10/1)]. Trainer: Juan Ramón Carrasco Torres (12).

714. 31.03.2004 **URUGUAY - VENEZUELA** **0-3(0-1)** 18th FIFA WC. Qualifiers
Estadio Centenario, Montevideo; Referee: René Ortubé (Bolivia), Attendance: 42,131
URU: Gustavo Adolfo Munúa (19/0), Luis Diego López Breijo (29/0) [*sent off 75*], Gonzalo Sorondo Amaro (25/0), Octavio Darío Rodríguez Peña (25/2), Richard Darío Núñez Pereyra (6/0), Martín Ricardo Ligüera López (14/7), Marcelo Fabián Sosa Farías (13/1), Álvaro Alexander Recoba Rivero (54/8), Diego Martín Forlán Corazo (14/7) [73.Carlos Éber Bueno Suárez (8/3)], Germán Andrés Hornos Correa (7/1) [46.Walter Gerardo Pandiani Urquiza (3/0)], Ernesto Javier Chevantón Espinosa (13/6) [60.Fernando Edgardo Correa Ayala (4/0)]. Trainer: Juan Ramón Carrasco Torres (13).

715. 01.06.2004 **URUGUAY - PERU** **1-3(0-2)** 18th FIFA WC. Qualifiers
Estadio Centenario, Montevideo; Referee: Rubén Selman (Chile), Attendance: 23,329
URU: Gustavo Adolfo Munúa (20/0), Gonzalo Sorondo Amaro (26/0) [*sent off 33*], Daniel Alejandro Lembo Bentancor (36/2), Marcelo Alejandro De Souza (1/0), Gianni Bismark Guigou Martínez (40/0) [46.Adrián Marcelo Romero González (6/1)], Antonio Pacheco (12/3) [46.Diego Martín Forlán Corazo (15/8)], Pablo Gabriel García Pérez (39/1), Marcelo Fabián Sosa Farías (14/1), Richard Darío Núñez Pereyra (7/0), Walter Gerardo Pandiani Urquiza (4/0) [63.Debray Darío Silva Pereira (40/12)], Ernesto Javier Chevantón Espinosa (14/6). Trainer: Jorge Daniel Fossati Lurachi (1).
Goal: Diego Martín Forlán Corazo (72).

716. 06.06.2004 **COLOMBIA - URUGUAY** **5-0(3-0)** 18th FIFA WC. Qualifiers
Estadio Metropolitano „Roberto Meléndez“, Barranquilla; Referee: Carlos Amarilla (Paraguay), Attendance: 7,000
URU: Gustavo Adolfo Munúa (21/0), Adrián Marcelo Romero González (7/1) [46.Gonzalo de los Santos da Rosa (31/1)], Daniel Alejandro Lembo Bentancor (37/2), Marcelo Alejandro De Souza (2/0) [62.Eduardo Alejandro Lago Correa (10/0)], Cristian Mario González Aidinovich (8/0), Clever Marcelo Romero Silva (24/0), Pablo Gabriel García Pérez (40/1), Javier Omar Delgado Papariello (5/0), Néstor Fabián Canobbio Bentaberry (3/0) [46.Diego Martín Forlán Corazo (16/8)], Álvaro Alexander Recoba Rivero (55/8), Ernesto Javier Chevantón Espinosa (15/6). Trainer: Jorge Daniel Fossati Lurachi (2).

717. 07.07.2004 **URUGUAY - MEXICO** **2-2(1-1)** 41st Copa América. Group Stage
Estadio „Elías Aguirre“, Chiclayo (Peru); Referee: Gilberto Hidalgo (Peru), Attendance: 18,472
URU: Luis Alberto Barbat (7/0), Gustavo Antonio Varela Rodríguez (12/0), Joe Emerson Bizera Bastos (17/1), Ronald Paolo Montero (48/4), Octavio Darío Rodríguez Peña (26/2), Diego Martín Forlán Corazo (17/8) [74.Juan Martín Parodi González (1/0)], Marcelo Fabián Sosa Farías (15/1), Omar Heber Pouso Osores (1/0) [87.Vicente Martín Sánchez Bragunde (5/0)], Cristian Gabriel Rodríguez Barotti (2/0), Debray Darío Silva Pereira (41/12) [78.Richard Javier Morales Aguirre (16/6)], Carlos Éber Bueno Suárez (9/4). Trainer: Jorge Daniel Fossati Lurachi (3).
Goals: Carlos Éber Bueno Suárez (43), Ronald Paolo Montero (87).

718. 10.07.2004 **URUGUAY - ECUADOR** **2-1(0-0)** 41st Copa América. Group Stage
Estadio „Elías Aguirre“, Chiclayo (Peru); Referee: Gustavo Brand (Venezuela), Attendance: 25,000
URU: Luis Alberto Barbat (8/0), Gustavo Antonio Varela Rodríguez (13/0), Joe Emerson Bizera Bastos (18/1), Ronald Paolo Montero (49/4) [60.Eduardo Alejandro Lago Correa (11/0)], Octavio Darío Rodríguez Peña (27/2), Diego Martín Forlán Corazo (18/9) [68.Diego Fernando Pérez Aguado (12/0)], Marcelo Fabián Sosa Farías (16/1), Omar Heber Pouso Osores (2/0), Cristian Gabriel Rodríguez Barotti (3/0) [55.Vicente Martín Sánchez Bragunde (6/0)], Debray Darío Silva Pereira (42/12), Carlos Éber Bueno Suárez (10/5). Trainer: Jorge Daniel Fossati Lurachi (4).
Goals: Diego Martín Forlán Corazo (61), Carlos Éber Bueno Suárez (79).

719. 13.07.2004 **ARGENTINA - URUGUAY** **4-2(2-0)** 41st Copa América. Group Stage
Estadio „Miguel Grau“, Piura (Peru); Referee: Rubén Selman (Chile), Attendance: 19,865
URU: Luis Alberto Barbat (9/0), Carlos Andrés Diogo Enseñat (4/0), Joe Emerson Bizera Bastos (19/1) [*sent off 35*], Eduardo Alejandro Lago Correa (12/0), Octavio Darío Rodríguez Peña (28/2), Diego Fernando Pérez Aguado (13/0), Marcelo Fabián Sosa Farías (17/1) [86.Carlos Éber Bueno Suárez (11/5)], Javier Omar Delgado Papariello (6/0), Fabián Larry Estoyanoff Poggio (11/2) [43.Guillermo Daniel Rodríguez Pérez (1/0)], Diego Martín Forlán Corazo (19/9), Vicente Martín Sánchez Bragunde (7/1) [72.Cristian Gabriel Rodríguez Barotti (4/0)]. Trainer: Jorge Daniel Fossati Lurachi (5).
Goal: Fabián Larry Estoyanoff Poggio (8), Vicente Martín Sánchez Bragunde (39).

720. 18.07.2004 **URUGUAY - PARAGUAY** **3-1(1-1)** 41st Copa América. Quarter-Finals
Estadio „Jorge Basadre“, Tacna (Peru); Referee: Héctor Baldassi (Argentina), Attendance: 20,000
URU: Mario Sebastián Viera Galaín (1/0), Gustavo Antonio Varela Rodríguez (14/0) [*sent off 63*], Eduardo Alejandro Lago Correa (13/0), Ronald Paolo Montero (50/4), Octavio Darío Rodríguez Peña (29/2), Diego Martín Forlán Corazo (20/9) [69.Diego Fernando Pérez Aguado (14/0)], Marcelo Fabián Sosa Farías (18/1), Javier Omar Delgado Papariello (7/0), Cristian Gabriel Rodríguez Barotti (5/0) [85.Vicente Martín Sánchez Bragunde (8/1)], Debray Darío Silva Pereira (43/14), Carlos Éber Bueno Suárez (12/6) [75.Guillermo Daniel Rodríguez Pérez (2/0)]. Trainer: Jorge Daniel Fossati Lurachi (6).
Goals: Carlos Éber Bueno Suárez (40 penalty), Debray Darío Silva Pereira (66, 89).

721. 21.07.2004 **BRAZIL - URUGUAY** **1-1(0-1,1-1,1-1); 5-3 penalties** 41st Copa América. Semi-Finals
Estadio Nacional, Lima; Referee (Peru): Marco Antonio Rodríguez Moreno (Mexico), Attendance: 10,000
URU: Mario Sebastián Viera Galaín (2/0), Carlos Andrés Diogo Enseñat (5/0), Joe Emerson Bizera Bastos (20/1), Ronald Paolo Montero (51/4), Octavio Darío Rodríguez Peña (30/2), Diego Fernando Pérez Aguado (15/0) [81.Omar Heber Pouso Osores (2/0)], Marcelo Fabián Sosa Farías (19/2), Javier Omar Delgado Papariello (8/0), Cristian Gabriel Rodríguez Barotti (6/0) [70.Vicente Martín Sánchez Bragunde (9/1)], Debray Darío Silva Pereira (44/14), Carlos Éber Bueno Suárez (13/6) [62.Diego Martín Forlán Corazo (21/9)]. Trainer: Jorge Daniel Fossati Lurachi (7).
Goal: Marcelo Fabián Sosa Farías (22).
Penalties: Debray Darío Silva Pereira, Mario Sebastián Viera Galaín, Omar Heber Pouso Osores, Vicente Martín Sánchez Bragunde (saved).

722. 24.07.2004 **URUGUAY - COLOMBIA** **2-1(1-0)** 41st Copa América. Bronze Medal
Estadio Garcilaso de la Vega, Cuzco (Peru); Referee: René Ortubé (Bolivia), Attendance: 35,000
URU: Luis Alberto Barbat (10/0), Carlos Andrés Diogo Enseñat (6/0), Joe Emerson Bizera Bastos (21/1), Eduardo Alejandro Lago Correa (14/0), Guillermo Daniel Rodríguez Pérez (3/0), Jorge Andrés Martínez Barrios (7/0) [77.Gustavo Antonio Varela Rodríguez (15/0)], Omar Heber Pouso Osores (4/0), Juan Martín Parodi González (2/0) [77.Diego Martín Forlán Corazo (22/9)], Fabián Larry Estoyanoff Poggio (12/3) [59.Marcelo Fabián Sosa Farías (20/2)], Richard Javier Morales Aguirre (17/6), Vicente Martín Sánchez Bragunde (10/2). Trainer: Jorge Daniel Fossati Lurachi (8).
Goals: Fabián Larry Estoyanoff Poggio (3), Vicente Martín Sánchez Bragunde (81).

723. 05.09.2004 **URUGUAY - ECUADOR** **1-0(0-0)** 18th FIFA WC. Qualifiers
Estadio Centenario, Montevideo; Referee: Gilberto Hidalgo (Peru), Attendance: 28,000
URU: Mario Sebastián Viera Galaín (3/0), Carlos Andrés Diogo Enseñat (7/0), Joe Emerson Bizera Bastos (22/1), Ronald Paolo Montero (52/4), Octavio Darío Rodríguez Peña (31/2), Álvaro Alexander Recoba Rivero (56/8) [78.Diego Fernando Pérez Aguado (16/0)], Marcelo Fabián Sosa Farías (21/2), Javier Omar Delgado Papariello (9/0), Cristian Gabriel Rodríguez Barotti (7/0) [57.Fabián Larry Estoyanoff Poggio (13/3)], Carlos Éber Bueno Suárez (14/7), Debray Darío Silva Pereira (45/14) [25.Vicente Martín Sánchez Bragunde (11/2)]. Trainer: Jorge Daniel Fossati Lurachi (9).
Goal: Carlos Éber Bueno Suárez (57).

724. 09.10.2004 **ARGENTINA - URUGUAY** **4-2(3-0)** 18th FIFA WC. Qualifiers
Estadio Monumental „Antonio Vespucio Liberti“, Buenos Aires; Referee: Wilson Souza Mendonça (Brazil), Attendance: 50,000
URU: Mario Sebastián Viera Galaín (4/0), Carlos Andrés Diogo Enseñat (8/0), Daniel Alejandro Lembo Bentancor (38/2), Joe Emerson Bizera Bastos (23/1) [57.Eduardo Alejandro Lago Correa (15/0)], Octavio Darío Rodríguez Peña (32/2), Diego Fernando Pérez Aguado (17/0) [55.Pablo Gabriel García Pérez (41/1)], Marcelo Fabián Sosa Farías (22/2), Javier Omar Delgado Papariello (10/0), Cristian Gabriel Rodríguez Barotti (8/1), Debray Darío Silva Pereira (46/14) [55.Diego Martín Forlán Corazo (23/9)], Ernesto Javier Chevantón Espinosa (16/7). Trainer: Jorge Daniel Fossati Lurachi (10).
Goals: Cristian Gabriel Rodríguez Barotti (63), Ernesto Javier Chevantón Espinosa (86 penalty).

725. 12.10.2004 **BOLIVIA - URUGUAY** **0-0** 18th FIFA WC. Qualifiers
Estadio „Hernándo Siles Zuazo“, La Paz; Referee: Márcio Rezende de Freitas (Brazil), Attendance: 24,349
URU: Mario Sebastián Viera Galaín (5/0), Carlos Andrés Diogo Enseñat (9/0), Eduardo Alejandro Lago Correa (16/0), Octavio Darío Rodríguez Peña (33/2), Guillermo Daniel Rodríguez Pérez (4/0), Gustavo Antonio Varela Rodríguez (16/0), Pablo Gabriel García Pérez (42/1), Omar Heber Pouso Osores (5/0) [*sent off 74*], Mario Ignacio Regueiro Pintos (20/0) [72.Juan Martín Parodi González (3/0)], Vicente Martín Sánchez Bragunde (12/2) [76.Marcelo Fabián Sosa Farías (23/2)], Richard Javier Morales Aguirre (18/6) [78.Ernesto Javier Chevantón Espinosa (17/7)]. Trainer: Jorge Daniel Fossati Lurachi (11).

726. 17.11.2004 **URUGUAY - PARAGUAY** **1-0(0-0)** 18th FIFA WC. Qualifiers

Estadio Centenario, Montevideo; Referee: Carlos Simón (Brazil), Attendance: 35,000

URU: Mario Sebastián Viera Galaín (6/0), Luis Diego López Breijo (30/0), Diego Alfredo Lugano Morena (2/0), Ronald Paolo Montero (53/5), Guillermo Daniel Rodríguez Pérez (5/0), Gustavo Antonio Varela Rodríguez (17/0) [58.Fabián Larry Estoyanoff Poggio (14/3)], Pablo Gabriel García Pérez (43/1), Álvaro Alexander Recoba Rivero (57/8) [69.Vicente Martín Sánchez Bragunde (13/2)], Javier Omar Delgado Papariello (11/0), Debray Darío Silva Pereira (47/14) [46.Richard Javier Morales Aguirre (19/6)], Ernesto Javier Chevantón Espinosa (18/7). Trainer: Jorge Daniel Fossati Lurachi (12).

Goal: Ronald Paolo Montero (78).

727. 26.03.2005 **CHILE - URUGUAY** **1-1(0-1)** 18th FIFA WC. Qualifiers

Estadio Nacional, Santiago; Referee: Oscar Julián Ruíz Acosta (Colombia), Attendance: 56,684

URU: Mario Sebastián Viera Galaín (7/0), Diego Alfredo Lugano Morena (3/0), Ronald Paolo Montero (54/5), Luis Diego López Breijo (31/0), Carlos Andrés Diogo Enseñat (10/0), Pablo Gabriel García Pérez (44/1), Octavio Darío Rodríguez Peña (34/2), Rubén Ariel Olivera da Rosa (15/0) [59.Marcelo Fabián Sosa Farías (24/2)], Mario Ignacio Regueiro Pintos (21/1) [82.Vicente Martín Sánchez Bragunde (14/2)], Marcelo Danubio Zalayeta (24/7) [70.Richard Javier Morales Aguirre (20/6)], Diego Martín Forlán Corazo (24/9). Trainer: Jorge Daniel Fossati Lurachi (13).

Goal: Mario Ignacio Regueiro Pintos (4).

728. 30.03.2005 **URUGUAY - BRAZIL** **1-1(0-0)** 18th FIFA WC. Qualifiers

Estadio Centenario, Montevideo; Referee: Héctor Baldassi (Argentina), Attendance: 60,968

URU: Mario Sebastián Viera Galaín (8/0), Luis Diego López Breijo (32/0), Diego Alfredo Lugano Morena (4/0), Ronald Paolo Montero (55/5), Octavio Darío Rodríguez Peña (35/2), Pablo Gabriel García Pérez (45/1), Carlos Andrés Diogo Enseñat (11/0) [86.Gonzalo de los Santos da Rosa (32/1)], Rubén Ariel Olivera da Rosa (16/0) [73.Ernesto Javier Chevantón Espinosa (19/7)], Mario Ignacio Regueiro Pintos (22/1) [58.Javier Omar Delgado Papariello (12/0)], Diego Martín Forlán Corazo (25/10), Marcelo Danubio Zalayeta (25/7). Trainer: Jorge Daniel Fossati Lurachi (14).

Goal: Diego Martín Forlán Corazo (49).

729. 04.06.2005 **VENEZUELA - URUGUAY** **1-1(0-1)** 18th FIFA WC. Qualifiers

Estadio „José 'Pachencho' Romero", Maracaibo; Referee: Gabriel Brazenas (Argentina), Attendance: 27,000

URU: Mario Sebastián Viera Galaín (9/0), Luis Diego López Breijo (33/0), Diego Alfredo Lugano Morena (5/0), Ronald Paolo Montero (56/5), Carlos Andrés Diogo Enseñat (12/0), Marcelo Fabián Sosa Farías (25/2), Octavio Darío Rodríguez Peña (36/2) [63.Gonzalo de los Santos da Rosa (33/1)], Mario Ignacio Regueiro Pintos (23/1) [42.Diego Fernando Pérez Aguado (18/0)], Rubén Ariel Olivera da Rosa (17/0), Diego Martín Forlán Corazo (26/11) [78.Ernesto Javier Chevantón Espinosa (20/7)], Marcelo Danubio Zalayeta (26/7). Trainer: Jorge Daniel Fossati Lurachi (15).

Goal: Diego Martín Forlán Corazo (2).

730. 07.06.2005 **PERU - URUGUAY** **0-0** 18th FIFA WC. Qualifiers

Estadio Nacional, Lima; Referee: Héctor Baldassi (Argentina), Attendance: 31,515

URU: Mario Sebastián Viera Galaín (10/0), Guillermo Daniel Rodríguez Pérez (6/0), Luis Diego López Breijo (34/0) [32.Diego Fernando Pérez Aguado (19/0)], Diego Alfredo Lugano Morena (6/0), Octavio Darío Rodríguez Peña (37/2), Pablo Gabriel García Pérez (46/1), Rubén Ariel Olivera da Rosa (18/0), Javier Omar Delgado Papariello (13/0), Diego Martín Forlán Corazo (27/11), Marcelo Danubio Zalayeta (27/7) [83.Richard Javier Morales Aguirre (21/6)], Ernesto Javier Chevantón Espinosa (21/7) [71.Fabián Larry Estoyanoff Poggio (15/3)]. Trainer: Jorge Daniel Fossati Lurachi (16).

731. 17.08.2005 **SPAIN - URUGUAY** **2-0(2-0)**

Estadio El Molinón, Santander; Referee: Olegario Benquerenca (Portugal), Attendance: 25,885

URU: Héctor Fabián Carini Hernández (40/0), Gustavo Antonio Varela Rodríguez (18/0) [77.Diego Fernando Pérez Aguado (20/0)], Luis Diego López Breijo (35/0), Gonzalo Sorondo Amaro (27/0), Guillermo Daniel Rodríguez Pérez (7/0), Fabián Larry Estoyanoff Poggio (16/3) [46.Mario Ignacio Regueiro Pintos (24/1)], Pablo Gabriel García Pérez (47/1), Javier Omar Delgado Papariello (14/0) [59.Óscar Javier Morales Albornoz (2/0)], Gonzalo Castro Irizábal (1/0) [46.Álvaro Alexander Recoba Rivero (58/8)], Richard Javier Morales Aguirre (22/6) [70.Marcelo Danubio Zalayeta (28/7)], Diego Martín Forlán Corazo (28/11) [65.Marcelo Tejera (6/0)]. Trainer: Jorge Daniel Fossati Lurachi (17).

732. 04.09.2005 **URUGUAY - COLOMBIA** **3-2(1-0)** 18th FIFA WC. Qualifiers

Estadio Centenario, Montevideo; Referee: Horacio Elizondo (Argentina), Attendance: 50,054

URU: Héctor Fabián Carini Hernández (41/0), Gustavo Antonio Varela Rodríguez (19/0) [82.Vicente Martín Sánchez Bragunde (15/2)], Luis Diego López Breijo (36/0), Ronald Paolo Montero (57/5), Guillermo Daniel Rodríguez Pérez (8/0), Pablo Gabriel García Pérez (48/1), Diego Fernando Pérez Aguado (21/0), Álvaro Alexander Recoba Rivero (59/8) [78.Fabián Larry Estoyanoff Poggio (17/3)], Marcelo Danubio Zalayeta (29/10), Diego Martín Forlán Corazo (29/11), Richard Javier Morales Aguirre (23/6) [70.Marcelo Fabián Sosa Farías (26/2) [*sent off 87*]]. Trainer: Jorge Daniel Fossati Lurachi (18).

Goals: Marcelo Danubio Zalayeta (42, 51, 85).

733. 08.10.2005 **ECUADOR - URUGUAY** **0-0** 18th FIFA WC. Qualifiers

Estadio Olimpico „Atahualpa", Quito; Referee: Marcio Rezende de Freitas (Brazil), Attendance: 37,270

URU: Héctor Fabián Carini Hernández (42/0), Luis Diego López Breijo (37/0), Diego Alfredo Lugano Morena (7/0), Octavio Darío Rodríguez Peña (38/2), Guillermo Daniel Rodríguez Pérez (9/0), Gustavo Antonio Varela Rodríguez (20/0), Pablo Gabriel García Pérez (49/1), Omar Heber Pouso Osores (6/0), Álvaro Alexander Recoba Rivero (60/8) [82.Diego Martín Forlán Corazo (30/11)], Mario Ignacio Regueiro Pintos (25/1) [69.Richard Darío Núñez Pereyra (8/0)], Richard Javier Morales Aguirre (24/6) [76.Debray Darío Silva Pereira (48/14)]. Trainer: Jorge Daniel Fossati Lurachi (19).

734. 12.10.2005 **URUGUAY - ARGENTINA** **1-0(0-0)** 18th FIFA WC. Qualifiers

Estadio Centenario, Montevideo; Referee: Wilson Souza Mendonça (Brazil), Attendance: 55,000

URU: Héctor Fabián Carini Hernández (43/0), Carlos Andrés Diogo Enseñat (13/0), Diego Alfredo Lugano Morena (8/0), Ronald Paolo Montero (58/5), Octavio Darío Rodríguez Peña (39/2), Gustavo Antonio Varela Rodríguez (21/0), Pablo Gabriel García Pérez (50/1), Álvaro Alexander Recoba Rivero (61/9) [71.Fabián Larry Estoyanoff Poggio (18/3)], Diego Martín Forlán Corazo (31/11) [90.Luis Diego López Breijo (38/0)], Richard Javier Morales Aguirre (25/6), Marcelo Danubio Zalayeta (30/10) [62.Omar Heber Pouso Osores (7/0)]. Trainer: Jorge Daniel Fossati Lurachi (20).

Goal: Álvaro Alexander Recoba Rivero (46).

735. 26.10.2005 **MEXICO - URUGUAY** **3-1(1-1)**

Estadio Monumental Jalisco, Guadalajara; Referee: Hugo León Guajardo (Mexico), Attendance: 38,000

URU: Sergio William Navarro (1/0), Diego Roberto Godín Leal (1/0), Guillermo Daniel Rodríguez Pérez (10/0), Carlos Andrés García Cuña (1/0), Victorio Maximiliano Pereira Páez (1/0) [70.Darío Antonio Flores Bistolfi (1/0)], Omar Heber Pouso Osores (8/0) [74.Aníbal Gabriel Alcoba Rebollo (1/0)], Pablo Martín Lima Olid (10/1) [82.Pablo Rodrigo Melo (3/0)], Richard Darío Núñez Pereyra (9/0) [63.Sergio Rubén Blanco Soto (2/0)], Martín Ricardo Ligüera López (15/7) [46.Gonzalo Castro Irizábal (2/0)], Vicente Martín Sánchez Bragunde (16/2) [46.Rodrigo Sebastián Vázquez Maidana (1/0)], Washington Sebastián Abreu Gallo (19/11) [57.Pablo Mariano Granoche Louro (1/0)]. Trainer: Jorge Daniel Fossati Lurachi (21).

Goal: Washington Sebastián Abreu Gallo (18).

736. 12.11.2005 **URUGUAY – AUSTRALIA** **1-0(1-0)** 18th FIFA WC. Qualifiers. Play-offs
Estadio Centenario, Montevideo; Referee: Claus Bo Larsen (Denmark), Attendance: 58,000
URU: Héctor Fabián Carini Hernández (44/0), Luis Diego López Breijo (39/0) [63.Guillermo Daniel Rodríguez Pérez (11/0)], Ronald Paolo Montero (59/5), Octavio Darío Rodríguez Peña (40/3), Carlos Andrés Diogo Enseñat (14/0), Pablo Gabriel García Pérez (51/1), Diego Fernando Pérez Aguado (22/0), Álvaro Alexander Recoba Rivero (62/9), Diego Martín Forlán Corazo (32/11) [17.Debray Darío Silva Pereira (49/14)], Marcelo Danubio Zalayeta (31/10) [63.Fabián Larry Estoyanoff Poggio (19/3)], Richard Javier Morales Aguirre (26/6). Trainer: Jorge Daniel Fossati Lurachi (22).
Goal: Octavio Darío Rodríguez Peña (36).

737. 16.11.2005 **AUSTRALIA – URUGUAY** **1-0(1-0,1-0); 4-2 on penalties** 18th FIFA WC. Qualifiers. Play-offs
Telstra Stadium, Sydney; Referee: Luis Medina Cantalejo (Spain), Attendance: 82,698
URU: Héctor Fabián Carini Hernández (45/0), Carlos Andrés Diogo Enseñat (15/0), Diego Alfredo Lugano Morena (9/0), Ronald Paolo Montero (60/5) [82.Marcelo Fabián Sosa Farías (27/2)], Octavio Darío Rodríguez Peña (41/3), Guillermo Daniel Rodríguez Pérez (12/0), Pablo Gabriel García Pérez (52/1), Álvaro Alexander Recoba Rivero (63/9) [73.Marcelo Danubio Zalayeta (32/10)], Gustavo Antonio Varela Rodríguez (22/0), Richard Javier Morales Aguirre (27/6), Mario Ignacio Regueiro Pintos (26/1) [98.Fabián Larry Estoyanoff Poggio (20/3)]. Trainer: Jorge Daniel Fossati Lurachi (23).
Penalties: Octavio Darío Rodríguez Peña (miss), Gustavo Antonio Varela Rodríguez, Fabián Larry Estoyanoff Poggio, Marcelo Danubio Zalayeta (miss),

738. 01.03.2006 **ENGLAND – URUGUAY** **2-1(0-1)**
Anfield Road, Liverpool; Referee: Stefano Farina (Italy), Attendance: 40,013
URU: Héctor Fabián Carini Hernández (46/0) [46.Mario Sebastián Viera Galaín (11/0)], Carlos Andrés Diogo Enseñat (16/0), Diego Alfredo Lugano Morena (10/0), Diego Roberto Godín Leal (2/0), Pablo Martín Lima Olid (11/1), Diego Fernando Pérez Aguado (23/0) [88.Ignacio María González Gatti (1/0)], Omar Heber Pouso Osores (9/1), Gustavo Antonio Varela Rodríguez (23/0) [90.Carlos Adrián Valdez Suárez (1/0)], Gonzalo Vargas Abella (2/0) [76.Victorio Maximiliano Pereira Páez (2/0)], Diego Martín Forlán Corazo (33/11) [86.Alexander Jesús Medina Reobasco (1/0)], Mario Ignacio Regueiro Pintos (27/1) [83.Jorge Andrés Martínez Barrios (8/0)]. Trainer: Gustavo Ferrín (3).
Goal: Omar Heber Pouso Osores (26).

739. 21.05.2006 **URUGUAY – NORTHERN IRELAND** **1-0(1-0)**
Giants Stadium, East Rutherford, New York (United States); Referee: Arkadiusz Prus (United States), Attendance: 4,152
URU: Héctor Fabián Carini Hernández (47/0), Andrés Scotti Ponce de León (1/0), Carlos Adrián Valdez Suárez (2/0), Diego Roberto Godín Leal (3/0), Walter Alberto López Gasco (1/0), Diego Fernando Pérez Aguado (24/0), Pablo Gabriel García Pérez (53/1), Guillermo Gonzalo Giacomazzi Suárez (10/0), Fabián Larry Estoyanoff Poggio (21/4) [82.Juan Ignacio Surraco Lamé (1/0)], Washington Sebastián Abreu Gallo (20/11), Gonzalo Vargas Abella (3/0). Trainer: Óscar Wáshington Tabárez Silva (35).
Goal: Fabián Larry Estoyanoff Poggio (33).

740. 23.05.2006 **URUGUAY – ROMANIA** **2-0(0-0)**
Memorial Coliseum, Los Angeles; Referee: Kevin Stott (United States), Attendance: 4,000
URU: Héctor Fabián Carini Hernández (48/0), Jorge Ciro Fucile Perdomo (1/0), Carlos Adrián Valdez Suárez (3/0), Diego Roberto Godín Leal (4/0), Andrés Scotti Ponce de León (2/0), Diego Fernando Pérez Aguado (25/0) [72.Álvaro Rafael González Luengo (1/0)], Pablo Gabriel García Pérez (54/1), Guillermo Gonzalo Giacomazzi Suárez (11/0), Fabián Larry Estoyanoff Poggio (22/4) [86.Sebastián Bruno Fernández Miglierina (1/0)], Washington Sebastián Abreu Gallo (21/11), Gonzalo Vargas Abella (4/2) [80 Juan Ignacio Surraco Lamé (2/0)]. Trainer: Óscar Wáshington Tabárez Silva (36).
Goals: Gonzalo Vargas Abella (46, 59).

741. 27.05.2006 **SERBIA MONTENEGRO – URUGUAY** **1-1(1-0)**
Crvena zvezda Stadion, Beograd; Referee: Drago Kos (Slovenia), Attendance: 35,000
URU: Héctor Fabián Carini Hernández (49/0), Andrés Scotti Ponce de León (3/0), Carlos Adrián Valdez Suárez (4/0), Diego Roberto Godín Leal (5/1), Walter Alberto López Gasco (2/0) [68.Pablo Martín Lima Olid (12/1)], Victorio Maximiliano Pereira Páez (3/0), Omar Heber Pouso Osores (10/1), Guillermo Gonzalo Giacomazzi Suárez (12/0), Fabián Larry Estoyanoff Poggio (23/4) [90.Nicolás Ignacio Vigneri Cetrulo (5/1)], Washington Sebastián Abreu Gallo (22/11) [61.Andrés Nicolás Olivera (26/8)], Gonzalo Vargas Abella (5/2). Trainer: Óscar Wáshington Tabárez Silva (37).
Goal: Diego Roberto Godín Leal (82).

742. 31.05.2006 **LIBYA – URUGUAY** **1-2(0-2)** LG Cup. Semi-Finals
Stade 7 Novembre, Radès (Tunisia); Referee: Atef Yacoubi (Tunisia), Attendance: 5,000
URU: Héctor Fabián Carini Hernández (50/0), Jorge Ciro Fucile Perdomo (2/0) [73.Carlos Adrián Valdez Suárez (5/0)], Diego Roberto Godín Leal (6/1), Andrés Scotti Ponce de León (4/0), Pablo Martín Lima Olid (13/1), Omar Heber Pouso Osores (11/1), Álvaro Rafael González Luengo (2/0) [85.Walter Alejandro Gargano Guevara (1/0)], Guillermo Gonzalo Giacomazzi Suárez (13/0), Andrés Nicolás Olivera (27/8), Nicolás Ignacio Vigneri Cetrulo (6/2) [73.Fabián Larry Estoyanoff Poggio (24/4)], Washington Sebastián Abreu Gallo (23/12). Trainer: Óscar Wáshington Tabárez Silva (38).
Goals: Nicolás Ignacio Vigneri Cetrulo (16), Washington Sebastián Abreu Gallo (35).

743. 02.06.2006 **TUNISIA – URUGUAY** **0-0; 1-3 on penalties** LG Cup. Final
Stade 7 Novembre, Radès; Referee: Nasser Abbés Kabil (Egypt), Attendance: 25,000
URU: Héctor Fabián Carini Hernández (51/0), Andrés Scotti Ponce de León (5/0), Carlos Adrián Valdez Suárez (6/0), Diego Roberto Godín Leal (7/1), Walter Alberto López Gasco (3/0), Victorio Maximiliano Pereira Páez (4/0), Omar Heber Pouso Osores (12/1), Guillermo Gonzalo Giacomazzi Suárez (14/0), Andrés Nicolás Olivera (28/8), Fabián Larry Estoyanoff Poggio (25/4), Gonzalo Vargas Abella (6/2). Trainer: Óscar Wáshington Tabárez Silva (39).
Penalties: Andrés Scotti Ponce de León, Andrés Nicolás Olivera (saved), Fabián Larry Estoyanoff Poggio, Guillermo Gonzalo Giacomazzi Suárez.

744. 16.08.2006 **EGYPT – URUGUAY** **0-2(0-0)**
Municipal Stadium, Alexandria; Referee: Mohamed Benouza (Algeria), Attendance: 10,000
URU: Héctor Fabián Carini Hernández (52/0), Andrés Scotti Ponce de León (6/0), Carlos Adrián Valdez Suárez (7/0) [46.Carlos Andrés Diogo Enseñat (17/0)], Diego Roberto Godín Leal (8/2), Octavio Darío Rodríguez Peña (42/3), Pablo Gabriel García Pérez (55/1) [86.Omar Heber Pouso Osores (13/1)], Guillermo Gonzalo Giacomazzi Suárez (15/0), Ignacio María González Gatti (2/0) [64.Victorio Maximiliano Pereira Páez (5/0)], Fabián Larry Estoyanoff Poggio (26/4), Diego Martín Forlán Corazo (34/11) [76.Washington Sebastián Abreu Gallo (24/12)], Mario Ignacio Regueiro Pintos (28/1) [63.Néstor Fabián Canobbio Bentaberry (4/0)]. Trainer: Óscar Wáshington Tabárez Silva (40).
Goals: Diego Roberto Godín Leal (67), Abdulzaher El Saqqa (83 own goal).

745. 27.09.2006 **VENEZUELA – URUGUAY** **1-0(0-0)**
Estadio „José 'Pachencho' Romero", Maracaibo; Referee: Jorge Manzur (Venezuela), Attendance: 17,000
URU: Héctor Fabián Carini Hernández (53/0), Gonzalo Daniel Lemes Rodríguez (1/0), Mauricio Bernardo Victorino Dansilio (1/0), Ignacio Ithurralde Sáez (1/0), Gastón Filgueira (1/0), Victorio Maximiliano Pereira Páez (6/0), Walter Alejandro Gargano Guevara (2/0), Ignacio María González Gatti (3/0) [73.Egidio Raúl Arévalo Ríos (1/0)], Nicolás Ignacio Vigneri Cetrulo (7/2) [63.Mauro Adrián Vila Wilkins (1/0)], Washington Sebastián Abreu Gallo (25/12), Sergio Rubén Blanco Soto (3/0) [82.Diego Daniel Vera Méndez (1/0)]. Trainer: Óscar Wáshington Tabárez Silva (41).

746. 18.10.2006 **URUGUAY – VENEZUELA** **4-0(2-0)**
Estadio Centenario, Montevideo, Referee: Roberto Silvera (Uruguay), Attendance: 5,000
URU: Héctor Fabián Carini Hernández (54/0), Gonzalo Daniel Lemes Rodríguez (2/0), Mauricio Bernardo Victorino Dansilio (2/0), Diego Roberto Godín Leal (9/3), Gastón Filgueira (2/0) [78.Álvaro Rafael González Luengo (3/0)], Victorio Maximiliano Pereira Páez (7/0) [78.Carlos Javier Grossmüller (2/0)], Walter Alejandro Gargano Guevara (3/0), Ignacio María González Gatti (4/0) [63.Sergio Rubén Blanco Soto (4/1)], Mauro Adrián Vila Wilkins (2/0) [82.Diego Daniel Vera Méndez (2/0)], Washington Sebastián Abreu Gallo (26/13) [73.Jorge Adrián García Echeverría (1/0)], Vicente Martín Sánchez Bragunde (17/3). Trainer: Óscar Wáshington Tabárez Silva (42).
Goals: Vicente Martín Sánchez Bragunde (12), Diego Roberto Godín Leal (14), Washington Sebastián Abreu Gallo (51), Sergio Rubén Blanco Soto (88).

747. 15.11.2006 **GEORGIA – URUGUAY** **2-0(1-0)**
„Boris Paichadze" Stadium, Tbilisi; Referee: Vitaliy Godulyan (Ukraine); Attendance: 12,000
URU: Héctor Fabián Carini Hernández (55/0), Andrés Scotti Ponce de León (7/0) [64.Carlos Andrés Diogo Enseñat (18/0)], Diego Alfredo Lugano Morena (Cap) (11/0), Diego Roberto Godín Leal (10/3), Octavio Darío Rodríguez Peña (43/3), Gustavo Antonio Varela Rodríguez (24/0) [53.Victorio Maximiliano Pereira Páez (8/0)], Wálter Alejandro Gargano Guevara (4/0), Guillermo Gonzalo Giacomazzi Suárez (16/0) [68.Omar Heber Pouso Osores (14/1)], Fabián Larry Estoyanoff Poggio (27/4) [83.Gonzalo Vargas Abella (7/2)], Diego Martín Forlán Corazo (35/11), Néstor Fabián Canobbio Bentaberry (5/0) [46.Gonzalo Castro Irizábal (3/0)]. Trainer: Óscar Wáshington Tabárez Silva (43).

748. 07.02.2007 **COLOMBIA - URUGUAY** **1-3(0-1)**
Estadio "General Santander", Cúcuta; Referee: Jorge Hernán Hoyos (Colombia); Attendance: 22,105
URU: Héctor Fabián Carini Hernández (Cap) (56/0), Ignacio Ithurralde Sáez (2/0), Andrés Scotti Ponce de León (8/0), Diego Roberto Godín Leal (11/3), Álvaro Rafael González Luengo (4/0), Egidio Raúl Arévalo Ríos (2/0), Omar Heber Pouso Osores (15/1) [69.Julio Fabián Mozzo Valdéz (2/0)], Jorge Ciro Fucile Perdomo (3/0) [77.Pablo Adrián Castro Duret (1/0)], Luis Alberto Suárez Díaz (1/0) [*sent off 85*], Washington Sebastián Abreu Gallo (27/15) [75.Nicolás Ignacio Vigneri Cetrulo (8/2)], Gonzalo Vargas Abella (8/3) [87.Diego Daniel Vera Méndez (3/0)]. Trainer: Óscar Wáshington Tabárez Silva (44).
Goals: Washington Sebastián Abreu Gallo (17 penalty, 61 penalty), Gonzalo Vargas Abella (74).

749. 24.03.2007 **SOUTH KOREA - URUGUAY** **0-2(0-2)**
Seoul World Cup Stadium, Seoul; Referee: Kenji Ogiya (Japan), Attendance: 42,159
URU: Héctor Fabián Carini Hernández (57/0), Carlos Andrés Diogo Enseñat (19/0), Diego Alfredo Lugano Morena (Cap) (12/0), Octavio Darío Rodríguez Peña (44/3), Jorge Ciro Fucile Perdomo (4/0) [73.Pablo Martín Lima Olid (14/1)], Diego Fernando Pérez Aguado (26/0), Pablo Gabriel García Pérez (56/1) [83.Wálter Alejandro Gargano Guevara (5/0)], Néstor Fabián Canobbio Bentaberry (6/0) [64.Egidio Raúl Arévalo Ríos (3/0)], Fabián Larry Estoyanoff Poggio (28/4) [72.Gonzalo Vargas Abella (9/3)], Carlos Heber Bueno Suárez (15/9) [86.Nicolás Ignacio Vigneri Cetrulo (9/2)], Álvaro Alexandre Recoba Rivero (64/9) [89.Carlos Javier Grossmüller (3/0)]. Trainer: Óscar Wáshington Tabárez Silva (45).
Goals: Carlos Heber Bueno Suárez (19, 37).

750. 02.06.2007 **AUSTRALIA - URUGUAY** **1-2(1-1)**
Telstra Olympic Stadium, Sydney; Referee: Roberto Rosetti (Italy), Attendance: 61,795
URU: Héctor Fabián Carini Hernández (58/0), Carlos Andrés Diogo Enseñat (20/0), Diego Alfredo Lugano Morena (Cap) (13/0), Andrés Scotti Ponce de León (9/0) [28.Jorge Ciro Fucile Perdomo (5/0)], Octavio Darío Rodríguez Peña (45/3), Diego Fernando Pérez Aguado (27/0) [46.Guillermo Gonzalo Giacomazzi Suárez (17/0)], Pablo Gabriel García Pérez (57/1), Cristian Gabriel Rodríguez Barotti (9/1) [73.Néstor Fabián Canobbio Bentaberry (7/0)], Álvaro Alexandre Recoba Rivero (65/10) [82.Washington Sebastián Abreu Gallo (28/15)], Diego Martín Forlán Corazo (36/12) [89.Fabián Larry Estoyanoff Poggio (29/4)], Vicente Martín Sánchez Bragunde (18/3). Trainer: Óscar Wáshington Tabárez Silva (46).
Goals: Diego Martín Forlán Corazo (40), Álvaro Alexandre Recoba Rivero (77).

751. 26.06.2007 **URUGUAY - PERU** **0-3(0-1)** 42nd Copa América. Group Stage
Estadio Metropolitano, Mérida (Venezuela); Referee: Carlos Arecio Amarilla Demarqui (Paraguay); Attendance: 23,000
URU: Héctor Fabián Carini Hernández (59/0), Carlos Andrés Diogo Enseñat (21/0), Diego Alfredo Lugano Morena (Cap) (14/0), Diego Roberto Godín Leal (12/3), Octavio Darío Rodríguez Peña (46/3), Diego Fernando Pérez Aguado (28/0), Pablo Gabriel García Pérez (58/1), Néstor Fabián Canobbio Bentaberry (8/0) [46.Cristian Gabriel Rodríguez Barotti (10/1)], Fabián Larry Estoyanoff Poggio (30/4) [80.Gonzalo Vargas Abella (10/3)], Diego Martín Forlán Corazo (37/12), Vicente Martín Sánchez Bragunde (19/3) [66.Washington Sebastián Abreu Gallo (29/15)]. Trainer: Óscar Wáshington Tabárez Silva (47).

752. 30.06.2007 **BOLIVIA - URUGUAY** **0-1(0-0)** 42nd Copa América. Group Stage
Estadio Polideportivo de Pueblo Nuevo, San Cristóbal (Venezuela); Referee: Baldomero Toledo (United States); Attendance: 18,000
URU: Héctor Fabián Carini Hernández (60/0), Carlos Andrés Diogo Enseñat (22/0) [57.Ignacio María González Gatti (5/0)], Diego Alfredo Lugano Morena (Cap) (15/0), Andrés Scotti Ponce de León (10/0), Octavio Darío Rodríguez Peña (47/3), Victorio Maximiliano Pereira Páez (9/0), Diego Fernando Pérez Aguado (29/0), Pablo Gabriel García Pérez (59/1), Cristian Gabriel Rodríguez Barotti (11/1) [90.Wálter Alejandro Gargano Guevara (6/0)], Diego Martín Forlán Corazo (38/12) [82.Fabián Larry Estoyanoff Poggio (31/4)], Vicente Martín Sánchez Bragunde (20/4). Trainer: Óscar Wáshington Tabárez Silva (48).
Goal: Vicente Martín Sánchez Bragunde (58).

753. 03.07.2007 **VENEZUELA - URUGUAY** **0-0** 42nd Copa América. Group Stage
Estadio Metropolitano, Mérida; Referee: Carlos Eugênio Simon (Brazil), Attendance: 42,000
URU: Héctor Fabián Carini Hernández (61/0), Diego Alfredo Lugano Morena (Cap) (16/0), Andrés Scotti Ponce de León (11/0), Octavio Darío Rodríguez Peña (48/3), Victorio Maximiliano Pereira Páez (10/0), Diego Fernando Pérez Aguado (30/0), Pablo Gabriel García Pérez (60/1), Jorge Ciro Fucile Perdomo (6/0), Cristian Gabriel Rodríguez Barotti (12/1), Vicente Martín Sánchez Bragunde (21/4) [67.Álvaro Alexandre Recoba Rivero (66/10)], Diego Martín Forlán Corazo (39/12) [79.Washington Sebastián Abreu Gallo (30/15)]. Trainer: Óscar Wáshington Tabárez Silva (49).

754. 07.07.2007 **VENEZUELA - URUGUAY** **1-4(1-1)** 42nd Copa América. Quarter-Finals
Estadio Polideportivo de Pueblo Nuevo, San Cristóbal; Referee: Carlos Chandía Alarcón (Chile), Attendance: 42,000
URU: Héctor Fabián Carini Hernández (62/0), Diego Alfredo Lugano Morena (Cap) (17/0), Andrés Scotti Ponce de León (12/0), Octavio Darío Rodríguez Peña (49/3) [90.Diego Roberto Godín Leal (13/3)], Victorio Maximiliano Pereira Páez (11/0), Diego Fernando Pérez Aguado (31/0), Pablo Gabriel García Pérez (61/2), Jorge Ciro Fucile Perdomo (7/0), Cristian Gabriel Rodríguez Barotti (13/2), Álvaro Alexandre Recoba Rivero (67/10) [79.Ignacio María González Gatti (6/0)], Diego Martín Forlán Corazo (40/14). Trainer: Óscar Wáshington Tabárez Silva (50).
Goals: Diego Martín Forlán Corazo (38), Pablo Gabriel García Pérez (65), Cristian Gabriel Rodríguez Barotti (87), Diego Martín Forlán Corazo (90).

755. 10.07.2007 **URUGUAY - BRAZIL** **2-2(2-1,2-2,2-2); 4-5 on penalties** 42nd Copa América. Semi-Finals
Estadio "José Encarnación 'Pachencho' Romero", Maracaibo (Venezuela); Referee: Oscar Julián Ruíz Acosta (Colombia); Attendance: 40,000
URU: Héctor Fabián Carini Hernández (63/0), Diego Alfredo Lugano Morena (Cap) (18/0), Andrés Scotti Ponce de León (13/0), Octavio Darío Rodríguez Peña (50/3) [46.Ignacio María González Gatti (7/0)], Victorio Maximiliano Pereira Páez (12/0), Diego Fernando Pérez Aguado (32/0) [75.Wálter Alejandro Gargano Guevara (7/0)], Pablo Gabriel García Pérez (62/2), Jorge Ciro Fucile Perdomo (8/0), Cristian Gabriel Rodríguez Barotti (14/2), Álvaro Alexandre Recoba Rivero (68/10) [46.Washington Sebastián Abreu Gallo (31/16)], Diego Martín Forlán Corazo (41/15). Trainer: Óscar Wáshington Tabárez Silva (51).
Goals: Diego Martín Forlán Corazo (36), Washington Sebastián Abreu Gallo (70).
Penalties: Diego Martín Forlán Corazo (saved), Andrés Scotti Ponce de León, Ignacio María González Gatti, Cristian Gabriel Rodríguez Barotti, Washington Sebastián Abreu Gallo, Pablo Gabriel García Pérez (missed).

756. 14.07.2007 **URUGUAY - MEXICO** **1-3(1-1)** 42nd Copa América. 3rd Place play-off
Estadio Olímpico „Ciudad Universitaria", Caracas; Referee: Mauricio Reinoso (Ecuador), Attendance: 30,000
URU: Héctor Fabián Carini Hernández (64/0), Carlos Adrián Valdez Suárez (8/0), Diego Alfredo Lugano Morena (Cap) (19/0) [*sent off 36*], Andrés Scotti Ponce de León (14/0), Jorge Ciro Fucile Perdomo (9/0), Victorio Maximiliano Pereira Páez (13/0), Pablo Gabriel García Pérez (63/2) [79.Wálter Alejandro Gargano Guevara (8/0)], Ignacio María González Gatti (8/0) [74.Néstor Fabián Canobbio Bentaberry (9/0)], Cristian Gabriel Rodríguez Barotti (15/2), Diego Martín Forlán Corazo (42/15) [74.Vicente Martín Sánchez Bragunde (22/4)], Washington Sebastián Abreu Gallo (32/17). Trainer: Óscar Wáshington Tabárez Silva (52).
Goal: Washington Sebastián Abreu Gallo (22).

757. 12.09.2007 **SOUTH AFRICA - URUGUAY** **0-0**
Ellis Park, Johannesburg; Referee: Tendai Bwanya (Zimbabwe), Attendance: 7,500
URU: Juan Guillermo Castillo Iriart (1/0), Pablo Álvarez Menéndez (1/0) [58.José Martín Cáceres Silva (1/0)], Carlos Adrián Valdez Suárez (9/0), Diego Roberto Godín Leal (14/3), Jorge Ciro Fucile Perdomo (10/0) [84.Leandro Ezquerra de León (1/0)], Victorio Maximiliano Pereira Páez (14/0), Wálter Alejandro Gargano Guevara (9/0), Cristian Gabriel Rodríguez Barotti (16/2), Carlos Javier Grossmüller (4/0) [46.Julio Fabián Mozzo Valdéz (3/0)], Luis Alberto Suárez Díaz (2/0), Washington Sebastián Abreu Gallo (Cap) (33/17). Trainer: Óscar Wáshington Tabárez Silva (53).

758. 13.10.2007 **URUGUAY - BOLIVIA** **5-0(2-0)** 19th FIFA WC. Qualifiers
Estadio Centenario, Montevideo; Referee: Rubén Selmán Albornoz (Chile); Attendance: 25,200
URU: Héctor Fabián Carini Hernández (65/0), Victorio Maximiliano Pereira Páez (15/0), Andrés Scotti Ponce de León (15/0), Diego Roberto Godín Leal (15/3), Jorge Ciro Fucile Perdomo (11/0), Diego Fernando Pérez Aguado (33/0), Pablo Gabriel García Pérez (Cap) (64/2), Cristian Gabriel Rodríguez Barotti (17/2), Luis Alberto Suárez Díaz (3/1) [65.Vicente Martín Sánchez Bragunde (23/5)], Washington Sebastián Abreu Gallo (34/18) [73.Carlos Heber Bueno Suárez (16/10)], Diego Martín Forlán Corazo (43/16) [66.Mario Ignacio Regueiro Pintos (29/1)]. Trainer: Óscar Wáshington Tabárez Silva (54).
Goals: Luis Alberto Suárez Díaz (4), Diego Martín Forlán Corazo (38), Washington Sebastián Abreu Gallo (48), Vicente Martín Sánchez Bragunde (67), Carlos Heber Bueno Suárez (83).

759. 17.10.2007 **PARAGUAY - URUGUAY** **1-0(1-0)** 19th FIFA WC. Qualifiers
Estadio Defensores del Chaco, Asunción; Referee: Héctor Walter Baldassi (Argentina); Attendance: 25,000
URU: Héctor Fabián Carini Hernández (66/0), Diego Alfredo Lugano Morena (Cap) (20/0), Andrés Scotti Ponce de León (16/0), Diego Roberto Godín Leal (16/3), Victorio Maximiliano Pereira Páez (16/0), Diego Fernando Pérez Aguado (34/0) [68.Álvaro Rafael González Luengo (5/0)], Pablo Gabriel García Pérez (65/2), Jorge Ciro Fucile Perdomo (12/0), Cristian Gabriel Rodríguez Barotti (18/2) [79.Carlos Heber Bueno Suárez (17/10)], Luis Alberto Suárez Díaz (4/1) [62.Vicente Martín Sánchez Bragunde (24/5)], Diego Martín Forlán Corazo (44/16). Trainer: Óscar Wáshington Tabárez Silva (55).

760. 18.11.2007 **URUGUAY - CHILE** **2-2(1-0)** 19th FIFA WC. Qualifiers
Estadio Centenario, Montevideo; Referee: Sergio Fabián Pezzotta (Argentina); Attendance: 43,000
URU: Héctor Fabián Carini Hernández (67/0), Andrés Scotti Ponce de León (17/0) [61.Victorio Maximiliano Pereira Páez (17/0)], Diego Alfredo Lugano Morena (Cap) (21/0), Diego Roberto Godín Leal (17/3), Jorge Ciro Fucile Perdomo (13/0), Diego Fernando Pérez Aguado (35/0) [46.Egidio Raúl Arévalo Ríos (4/0)], Wálter Alejandro Gargano Guevara (10/0), Cristian Gabriel Rodríguez Barotti (19/2), Luis Alberto Suárez Díaz (5/2), Washington Sebastián Abreu Gallo (35/19), Vicente Martín Sánchez Bragunde (25/5) [64.Ignacio María González Gatti (9/0)]. Trainer: Óscar Wáshington Tabárez Silva (56).
Goals: Luis Alberto Suárez Díaz (42), Washington Sebastián Abreu Gallo (81).

761. 21.11.2007 **BRAZIL - URUGUAY** **2-1(1-1)** 19th FIFA WC. Qualifiers
Estádio „Cicero Pompeu de Toledo" Morumbi, São Paulo; Referee: Héctor Baldassi (Argentina); Attendance: 65,379
URU: Héctor Fabián Carini Hernández (68/0), Victorio Maximiliano Pereira Páez (18/0), Diego Alfredo Lugano Morena (Cap) (22/0), Diego Roberto Godín Leal (18/3), Jorge Ciro Fucile Perdomo (14/0), Álvaro Rafael González Luengo (6/0), Wálter Alejandro Gargano Guevara (11/0), Ignacio María González Gatti (10/0) [82.Carlos Heber Bueno Suárez (18/10)], Cristian Gabriel Rodríguez Barotti (20/2), Luis Alberto Suárez Díaz (6/2) [71.Vicente Martín Sánchez Bragunde (26/5)], Washington Sebastián Abreu Gallo (36/20). Trainer: Óscar Wáshington Tabárez Silva (57).
Goal: Washington Sebastián Abreu Gallo (9).

762. 06.02.2008 **URUGUAY - COLOMBIA** **2-2(0-1)**
Estadio Centenario, Montevideo; Referee: Liber Prudente (Uruguay); Attendance: 31,000
URU: Héctor Fabián Carini Hernández (69/0) [46.Juan Guillermo Castillo Iriart (2/0)], Victorio Maximiliano Pereira Páez (19/0), Diego Alfredo Lugano Morena (Cap) (23/0), Diego Roberto Godín Leal (19/3), Jorge Ciro Fucile Perdomo (15/0), Diego Fernando Pérez Aguado (36/0) [46.Cristian Gabriel Rodríguez Barotti (21/2)], Wálter Alejandro Gargano Guevara (12/0), Álvaro Rafael González Luengo (7/0) [67.José Martín Cáceres Silva (2/0)], Diego Martín Forlán Corazo (45/16) [75.Edinson Roberto Cavani Gómez (1/1)], Washington Sebastián Abreu Gallo (37/20), Luis Alberto Suárez Díaz (7/3). Trainer: Óscar Wáshington Tabárez Silva (58).
Goals: Edinson Roberto Cavani Gómez (78), Luis Alberto Suárez Díaz (86).

763. 25.05.2008 **TURKEY - URUGUAY** **2-3(1-1)**
rewirpower-Stadion, Bochum (Germany); Referee: Florian Meyer (Germany); Attendance: 13,786
URU: Héctor Fabián Carini Hernández (Cap) (70/0), Victorio Maximiliano Pereira Páez (20/0) [69.Bruno Ramón Silva Barone (5/0)], Gerardo Alcoba Rebollo (1/0), Diego Roberto Godín Leal (20/3), José Martín Cáceres Silva (3/0), Sebastián Eguren Ledesma (10/0), Wálter Alejandro Gargano Guevara (13/0), Ignacio María González Gatti (11/0) [74.Robert Mario Flores Bistolfi (1/0)], Henry Damián Giménez Báez (1/0) [56.Cristian Gabriel Rodríguez Barotti (22/3)], Edinson Roberto Cavani Gómez (2/1) [46.Sebastián Bruno Fernández Miglierina (2/0)], Luis Alberto Suárez Díaz (8/5). Trainer: Óscar Wáshington Tabárez Silva (59).
Goals: Luis Alberto Suárez Díaz (31 penalty, 78), Cristian Gabriel Rodríguez Barotti (85 penalty).

764. 28.05.2008 **NORWAY - URUGUAY** **2-2(0-1)**
Ullevaal Stadion, Oslo; Referee: Anthony Buttimer (Republic of Ireland); Attendance: 12,246
URU: Héctor Fabián Carini Hernández (Cap) (71/0), Bruno Ramón Silva Barone (6/0), Carlos Adrián Valdez Suárez (10/0), Diego Roberto Godín Leal (21/3), José Martín Cáceres Silva (4/0), Sebastián Eguren Ledesma (11/1), Wálter Alejandro Gargano Guevara (14/0) [73.Hugo Diego Arismendi Ciapparetta (1/0)], Ignacio María González Gatti (12/0) [78.Robert Mario Flores Bistolfi (2/0)], Henry Damián Giménez Báez (2/0) [56.Victorio Maximiliano Pereira Páez (21/0)], Diego Martín Forlán Corazo (46/16) [81.Sebastián Bruno Fernández Miglierina (3/0)], Luis Alberto Suárez Díaz (9/6). Trainer: Óscar Wáshington Tabárez Silva (60).
Goals: Luis Alberto Suárez Díaz (43), Sebastián Eguren Ledesma (69).

765. 14.06.2008 **URUGUAY - VENEZUELA** **1-1(1-0)** 19th FIFA WC. Qualifiers
Estadio Centenario, Montevideo; Referee: Alfredo Intriago (Ecuador), Attendance: 41,831
URU: Héctor Fabián Carini Hernández (72/0), Victorio Maximiliano Pereira Páez (22/0) [76.Bruno Ramón Silva Barone (7/0)], Diego Alfredo Lugano Morena (Cap) (24/1), Diego Roberto Godín Leal (22/3), José Martín Cáceres Silva (5/0), Diego Fernando Pérez Aguado (37/0), Wálter Alejandro Gargano Guevara (15/0), Ignacio María González Gatti (13/0), Diego Martín Forlán Corazo (47/16) [65.Carlos Heber Bueno Suárez (19/10)], Washington Sebastián Abreu Gallo (38/20), Luis Alberto Suárez Díaz (10/6) [65.Vicente Martín Sánchez Bragunde (27/5)]. Trainer: Óscar Wáshington Tabárez Silva (61).
Goal: Diego Alfredo Lugano Morena (12).

766. 17.06.2008 **URUGUAY - PERU** **6-0(2-0)** 19th FIFA WC. Qualifiers
Estadio Centenario, Montevideo; Referee: Pablo Antonio Pozo Quinteros (Chile); Attendance: 20,016
URU: Juan Guillermo Castillo Iriart (3/0), Bruno Ramón Silva Barone (8/0), Diego Alfredo Lugano Morena (Cap) (25/1), Diego Roberto Godín Leal (23/3), José Martín Cáceres Silva (6/0), Diego Fernando Pérez Aguado (38/0) [70.Sebastián Eguren Ledesma (12/1)], Wálter Alejandro Gargano Guevara (16/0), Ignacio María González Gatti (14/0) [73.Luis Alberto Suárez Díaz (11/6)], Cristian Gabriel Rodríguez Barotti (23/3), Diego Martín Forlán Corazo (48/19), Carlos Heber Bueno Suárez (20/12) [79.Washington Sebastián Abreu Gallo (39/21)]. Trainer: Óscar Wáshington Tabárez Silva (62).
Goals: Diego Martín Forlán Corazo (8, 38 penalty, 57), Carlos Heber Bueno Suárez (61, 69), Washington Sebastián Abreu Gallo (90).

767. 20.08.2008 **JAPAN - URUGUAY** **1-3(0-0)**
Sapporo Dome, Sapporo; Referee: Marcin Borski (Polonia), Attendance: 31,133
URU: Juan Guillermo Castillo Iriart (4/0), Bruno Ramón Silva Barone (9/0) [88.Gerardo Alcoba Rebollo (2/0)], Diego Alfredo Lugano Morena (Cap) (26/1), Carlos Adrián Valdez Suárez (11/0), Jorge Ciro Fucile Perdomo (16/0), Victorio Maximiliano Pereira Páez (23/0) [60.Álvaro Rafael González Luengo (8/0)], Diego Fernando Pérez Aguado (39/0) [69.Ignacio María González Gatti (15/1)], Sebastián Eguren Ledesma (13/2), Cristian Gabriel Rodríguez Barotti (24/3) [60.Vicente Martín Sánchez Bragunde (28/5)], Luis Alberto Suárez Díaz (12/6) [84.Jorge Marcelo Rodríguez Núñez (1/0)], Carlos Heber Bueno Suárez (21/12) [69.Washington Sebastián Abreu Gallo (40/22)]. Trainer: Óscar Wáshington Tabárez Silva (63).
Goals: Sebastián Eguren Ledesma (55), Ignacio María González Gatti (83), Washington Sebastián Abreu Gallo (90).

768. 06.09.2008 **COLOMBIA - URUGUAY** **0-1(0-1)** 19th FIFA WC. Qualifiers
Estadio „Nemesio Camacho“ 'El Campín', Bogotá; Referee: Leonardo Gaciba da Silva (Brazil); Attendance: 35,024
URU: Juan Guillermo Castillo Iriart (5/0), Bruno Ramón Silva Barone (10/0) [80.Álvaro Rafael González Luengo (9/0)], Diego Alfredo Lugano Morena (Cap) (27/1), Diego Roberto Godín Leal (24/3), Jorge Ciro Fucile Perdomo (17/0), Victorio Maximiliano Pereira Páez (24/0), Wálter Alejandro Gargano Guevara (17/0), Sebastián Eguren Ledesma (14/3) [90.Andrés Scotti Ponce de León (18/0)], Cristian Gabriel Rodríguez Barotti (25/3), Diego Martín Forlán Corazo (49/19), Luis Alberto Suárez Díaz (13/6) [68.Vicente Martín Sánchez Bragunde (29/5)]. Trainer: Óscar Wáshington Tabárez Silva (64).
Goal: Sebastián Eguren Ledesma (15).

769. 10.09.2008 **URUGUAY - ECUADOR** **0-0** 19th FIFA WC. Qualifiers
Estadio Centenario, Montevideo; Referee: Óscar Julián Ruiz Acosta (Colombia); Attendance: 43,392
URU: Juan Guillermo Castillo Iriart (6/0), Bruno Ramón Silva Barone (11/0), Diego Alfredo Lugano Morena (Cap) (28/1), Diego Roberto Godín Leal (25/3), José Martín Cáceres Silva (7/0), Sebastián Eguren Ledesma (15/3), Wálter Alejandro Gargano Guevara (18/0) [46.Victorio Maximiliano Pereira Páez (25/0)], Cristian Gabriel Rodríguez Barotti (26/3), Ignacio María González Gatti (16/1) [61.Luis Alberto Suárez Díaz (14/6)], Diego Martín Forlán Corazo (50/19), Carlos Heber Bueno Suárez (22/12) [70.Washington Sebastián Abreu Gallo (41/22)]. Trainer: Óscar Wáshington Tabárez Silva (65).

770. 11.10.2008 **ARGENTINA - URUGUAY** **2-1(2-1)** 19th FIFA WC. Qualifiers
Estadio Monumental „Antonio Vespucio Liberti“, Buenos Aires; Referee: Carlos Manuel Torres (Paraguay); Attendance: 42,421
URU: Juan Guillermo Castillo Iriart (7/0), Jorge Ciro Fucile Perdomo (18/0) [24.Edinson Roberto Cavani Gómez (3/1)], Diego Alfredo Lugano Morena (Cap) (29/2), Diego Roberto Godín Leal (26/3), José Martín Cáceres Silva (8/0), Victorio Maximiliano Pereira Páez (26/0), Sebastián Eguren Ledesma (16/3), Diego Fernando Pérez Aguado (40/0), Cristian Gabriel Rodríguez Barotti (27/3) [74.Carlos Heber Bueno Suárez (23/12)], Luis Alberto Suárez Díaz (15/6), Washington Sebastián Abreu Gallo (42/22) [74.Ernesto Javier Chevantón Espinosa (22/7)]. Trainer: Óscar Wáshington Tabárez Silva (66).
Goal: Diego Alfredo Lugano Morena (40).

771. 14.10.2008 **BOLIVIA - URUGUAY** **2-2(2-0)** 19th FIFA WC. Qualifiers
Estadio „Hernándo Siles Zuazo“, La Paz; Referee: Héctor Walter Baldassi (Argentina); Attendance: 21,075
URU: Juan Guillermo Castillo Iriart (8/0), Bruno Ramón Silva Barone (12/0), Diego Alfredo Lugano Morena (Cap) (30/2), Andrés Scotti Ponce de León (19/0), José Martín Cáceres Silva (9/0), Álvaro Rafael González Luengo (10/0) [55.Victorio Maximiliano Pereira Páez (27/0)], Hugo Diego Arismendi Ciapparetta (2/0), Wálter Alejandro Gargano Guevara (19/0), Cristian Gabriel Rodríguez Barotti (28/3) [71.Washington Sebastián Abreu Gallo (43/23)], Vicente Martín Sánchez Bragunde (30/5), Carlos Heber Bueno Suárez (24/13). Trainer: Óscar Wáshington Tabárez Silva (67).
Goals: Carlos Heber Bueno Suárez (64), Washington Sebastián Abreu Gallo (88).

772. 19.11.2008 **FRANCE - URUGUAY** **0-0**
Stade de France, Saint-Denis, Paris; Referee: Cyril Zimmermann (Switzerland); Attendance: 79,666
URU: Héctor Fabián Carini Hernández (73/0), Bruno Ramón Silva Barone (13/0), Diego Alfredo Lugano Morena (Cap) (31/2), Diego Roberto Godín Leal (27/3) [18.Carlos Adrián Valdez Suárez (12/0)], José Martín Cáceres Silva (10/0), Victorio Maximiliano Pereira Páez (28/0), Wálter Alejandro Gargano Guevara (20/0), Álvaro Daniel Pereira Barragán (1/0) [71.Mathías Adolfo Cardaccio Alaguich (1/0)], Cristian Gabriel Rodríguez Barotti (29/3) [82.Vicente Martín Sánchez Bragunde (31/5)], Luis Alberto Suárez Díaz (16/6) [69.Washington Sebastián Abreu Gallo (44/23)], Diego Martín Forlán Corazo (51/19) [46.Edinson Roberto Cavani Gómez (4/1)]. Trainer: Óscar Wáshington Tabárez Silva (68).

773. 11.02.2009 **LIBYA - URUGUAY** **2-3(1-1)**
Stade „11 Juin", Tripoli; Referee: Nasser Aouif (Tunisia), Attendance: 3,000
URU: Héctor Fabián Carini Hernández (74/0) [46.Mario Sebastián Viera Galaín (12/0)], Diego Roberto Godín Leal (28/3) [81.Carlos Adrián Valdez Suárez (13/0)], Diego Alfredo Lugano Morena (32/2), José Martín Cáceres Silva (11/0) [83.Jorge Ciro Fucile Perdomo (19/0)], Victorio Maximiliano Pereira Páez (29/0) [46.Bruno Ramón Silva Barone (14/0)], Álvaro Daniel Pereira Barragán (2/1), Sebastián Eguren Ledesma (17/4) [83.Jorge Marcelo Rodríguez Núñez (2/0)], Walter Alejandro Gargano Guevara (21/0), Cristian Gabriel Rodríguez Barotti (30/3) [59.Jorge Andrés Martínez Barrios (9/1)], Washington Sebastián Abreu Gallo (45/23) [59.Edinson Roberto Cavani Gómez (5/1)], Luis Alberto Suárez Díaz (17/6). Trainer: Óscar Wáshington Tabárez Silva (69).
Goals: Sebastián Eguren Ledesma (14), Álvaro Daniel Pereira Barragán (70), Jorge Andrés Martínez Barrios (73).

774. 28.03.2009 **URUGUAY - PARAGUAY** **2-0(1-0)** 19th FIFA WC. Qualifiers
Estadio Centenario, Montevideo; Referee: Carlos Eugênio Simon (Brazil); Attendance: 45,000
URU: Mario Sebastián Viera Galaín (13/0), Diego Roberto Godín Leal (29/3) [81.Bruno Ramón Silva Barone (15/0)], Diego Alfredo Lugano Morena (33/3), José Martín Cáceres Silva (12/0), Victorio Maximiliano Pereira Páez (30/0), Álvaro Daniel Pereira Barragán (3/1), Sebastián Eguren Ledesma (18/4), Diego Fernando Pérez Aguado (41/0), Cristian Gabriel Rodríguez Barotti (31/3) [72.Jorge Andrés Martínez Barrios (10/1)], Diego Martín Forlán Corazo (52/20) [79.Washington Sebastián Abreu Gallo (46/23)], Luis Alberto Suárez Díaz (18/6). Trainer: Óscar Wáshington Tabárez Silva (70).
Goals: Diego Martín Forlán Corazo (28), Diego Alfredo Lugano Morena (57).

775. 01.04.2009 **CHILE - URUGUAY** **0-0** 19th FIFA WC. Qualifiers
Estadio Nacional „Julio Martínez Prádanos", Santiago; Referee: Héctor Walter Baldassi (Argentina); Attendance: 55,000
URU: Mario Sebastián Viera Galaín (14/0), Diego Roberto Godín Leal (30/3), Diego Alfredo Lugano Morena (Cap) (34/3), José Martín Cáceres Silva (13/0), Victorio Maximiliano Pereira Páez (31/0), Álvaro Daniel Pereira Barragán (4/1) [70.Washington Sebastián Abreu Gallo (47/23)], Sebastián Eguren Ledesma (19/4), Diego Fernando Pérez Aguado (42/0) [40.Álvaro Fernández Gay (1/0)], Cristian Gabriel Rodríguez Barotti (32/3) [85.Edinson Roberto Cavani Gómez (6/1)], Diego Martín Forlán Corazo (53/20), Luis Alberto Suárez Díaz (19/6). Trainer: Óscar Wáshington Tabárez Silva (71).

776. 06.06.2009 **URUGUAY - BRAZIL** **0-4(0-2)** 19th FIFA WC. Qualifiers
Estadio Centenario, Montevideo; Referee: Saúl Esteban Laverni (Argentina); Attendance: 52,000
URU: Mario Sebastián Viera Galaín (15/0), Diego Roberto Godín Leal (31/3), Carlos Adrián Valdez Suárez (14/0), José Martín Cáceres Silva (14/0), Victorio Maximiliano Pereira Páez (32/0), Álvaro Daniel Pereira Barragán (5/1) [66.Álvaro Fernández Gay (2/0)], Sebastián Eguren Ledesma (20/4), Diego Fernando Pérez Aguado (43/0) [46.Washington Sebastián Abreu Gallo (48/23)], Jorge Andrés Martínez Barrios (11/1), Diego Martín Forlán Corazo (Cap) (54/20), Luis Alberto Suárez Díaz (20/6) [74.Edinson Roberto Cavani Gómez (7/1)]. Trainer: Óscar Wáshington Tabárez Silva (72).

777. 10.06.2009 **VENEZUELA - URUGUAY** **2-2(1-0)** 19th FIFA WC. Qualifiers
Estadio Polideportivo Cachamay, Puerto Ordaz; Referee: Sálvio Spínola Fagundes Filho (Brazil), Attendance: 37,000
URU: Juan Guillermo Castillo Iriart (9/0), Diego Roberto Godín Leal (32/3), Diego Alfredo Lugano Morena (Cap) (35/3), José Martín Cáceres Silva (15/0) [80.Edinson Roberto Cavani Gómez (8/1)], Jorge Ciro Fucile Perdomo (20/0), Álvaro Daniel Pereira Barragán (6/1), Miguel Ángel Amado Alanis (1/0), Diego Fernando Pérez Aguado (44/0), Álvaro Fernández Gay (3/0) [46.Cristian Gabriel Rodríguez Barotti (33/3)], Diego Martín Forlán Corazo (55/21), Luis Alberto Suárez Díaz (21/7) [65.Washington Sebastián Abreu Gallo (49/23)]. Trainer: Óscar Wáshington Tabárez Silva (73).
Goals: Luis Alberto Suárez Díaz (63), Diego Martín Forlán Corazo (72).

778. 12.08.2009 **ALGERIA - URUGUAY** **1-0(0-0)**
Stade „5 Juillet 1962", Algiers; Referee: Riadh Herzi (Tunisia), Attendance: 20,000
URU: Martín Andrés Silva Leites (1/0), Diego Roberto Godín Leal (33/3) [75.Carlos Adrián Valdez Suárez (15/0)], Diego Alfredo Lugano Morena (36/3) [46.Andrés Scotti Ponce de León (20/0)], Jorge Ciro Fucile Perdomo (21/0) [61.Miguel Ángel Amado Alanis (2/0)], Bruno Ramón Silva Barone (16/0), Álvaro Daniel Pereira Barragán (7/1), Sebastián Eguren Ledesma (21/4) [46.Álvaro Fernández Gay (4/0)], Walter Alejandro Gargano Guevara (22/0), Jorge Andrés Martínez Barrios (12/1) [61.Edinson Roberto Cavani Gómez (9/1)], Washington Sebastián Abreu Gallo (50/23) [46.Hernán Rodrigo López Mora (1/0)], Luis Alberto Suárez Díaz (22/7) [82.Sebastián Bruno Fernández Miglierina (4/0)]. Trainer: Óscar Wáshington Tabárez Silva (74).

779. 05.09.2009 **PERU - URUGUAY** **1-0(0-0)** 19th FIFA WC. Qualifiers
Estadio Monumental, Lima; Referee: Carlos Chandía Alarcón (Chile); Attendance: 15,000
URU: Juan Guillermo Castillo Iriart (10/0), Diego Roberto Godín Leal (34/3) [*sent off 59*], Diego Alfredo Lugano Morena (37/3), Jorge Ciro Fucile Perdomo (22/0), Álvaro Daniel Pereira Barragán (8/1), Sebastián Eguren Ledesma (22/4) [60.Álvaro Fernández Gay (5/0)], Walter Alejandro Gargano Guevara (23/0), Cristian Gabriel Rodríguez Barotti (34/3), Jorge Andrés Martínez Barrios (13/1) [80.Jorge Marcelo Rodríguez Núñez (3/0)], Washington Sebastián Abreu Gallo (51/23), Luis Alberto Suárez Díaz (23/7). Trainer: Óscar Wáshington Tabárez Silva (75).

780. 09.09.2009 **URUGUAY - COLOMBIA** **3-1(1-0)** 19th FIFA WC. Qualifiers
Estadio Centenario, Montevideo; Referee: Carlos Manuel Torres (Paraguay); Attendance: 30,000
URU: Juan Guillermo Castillo Iriart (11/0), Carlos Adrián Valdez Suárez (16/0) [*sent off 30*], Bruno Ramón Silva Barone (17/0), José Martín Cáceres Silva (16/0), Álvaro Daniel Pereira Barragán (9/1), Walter Alejandro Gargano Guevara (24/0), Diego Fernando Pérez Aguado (45/0), Cristian Gabriel Rodríguez Barotti (35/3) [81.Sebastián Eguren Ledesma (23/5)], Edinson Roberto Cavani Gómez (10/1) [35.Andrés Scotti Ponce de León (21/1)], Diego Martín Forlán Corazo (56/21), Luis Alberto Suárez Díaz (24/8) [90+1.Washington Sebastián Abreu Gallo (52/23)]. Trainer: Óscar Wáshington Tabárez Silva (76).
Goals: Luis Alberto Suárez Díaz (7), Andrés Scotti Ponce de León (77), Sebastián Eguren Ledesma (87).

781. 10.10.2009 **ECUADOR - URUGUAY** **1-2(0-0)** 19th FIFA WC. Qualifiers
Estadio Olimpico "Atahualpa", Quito; Referee: Sálvio Spínola Fagundes Filho (Brazil); Attendance: 42,700
URU: Néstor Fernando Muslera Micol (1/0), Diego Alfredo Lugano Morena (Cap) (38/3), José Martín Cáceres Silva (17/0), Victorio Maximiliano Pereira Páez (33/0), Álvaro Daniel Pereira Barragán (10/1), Andrés Scotti Ponce de León (22/1), Walter Alejandro Gargano Guevara (25/0), Diego Fernando Pérez Aguado (46/0) [73.Sebastián Eguren Ledesma (24/5)], Jorge Marcelo Rodríguez Núñez (4/0) [59.Jorge Ciro Fucile Perdomo (23/0)], Diego Martín Forlán Corazo (57/22), Luis Alberto Suárez Díaz (25/9) [85.Edinson Roberto Cavani Gómez (11/1)]. Trainer: Óscar Wáshington Tabárez Silva (77).
Goals: Luis Alberto Suárez Díaz (69), Diego Martín Forlán Corazo (90+3 penalty).

782. 14.10.2009 **URUGUAY - ARGENTINA** **0-1(0-0)** 19th FIFA WC. Qualifiers
Estadio Centenario, Montevideo; Referee: Carlos Arecio Amarilla Demarqui (Paraguay); Attendance: 60,000
URU: Néstor Fernando Muslera Micol (2/0), Diego Alfredo Lugano Morena (Cap) (39/3), José Martín Cáceres Silva (18/0) [*sent off 83*], Victorio Maximiliano Pereira Páez (34/0), Álvaro Daniel Pereira Barragán (11/1), Andrés Scotti Ponce de León (23/1), Walter Alejandro Gargano Guevara (26/0) [71.Cristian Gabriel Rodríguez Barotti (36/3) [*sent off 90+3*]], Diego Fernando Pérez Aguado (47/0), Jorge Marcelo Rodríguez Núñez (5/0) [59.Edinson Roberto Cavani Gómez (12/1)], Diego Martín Forlán Corazo (58/22), Luis Alberto Suárez Díaz (26/9) [77.Washington Sebastián Abreu Gallo (53/23)]. Trainer: Óscar Wáshington Tabárez Silva (78).

783. 14.11.2009 **COSTA RICA - URUGUAY** **0-1(0-0)** 19th FIFA WC. Qualifiers (Play-offs)
Estadio „Ricardo Saprissa Aymá", San José; Referee: Alberto Undiano Mallenco (Spain), Attendance: 19,500
URU: Néstor Fernando Muslera Micol (3/0), Diego Roberto Godín Leal (35/3), Diego Alfredo Lugano Morena (40/4), Mauricio Bernardo Victorino Dansilio (3/0), Álvaro Daniel Pereira Barragán (12/1), Sebastián Eguren Ledesma (25/5), Álvaro Rafael González Luengo (11/0), Marcelo Nicolás Lodeiro Benítez (1/0) [61.Jorge Marcelo Rodríguez Núñez (6/0)], Álvaro Fernández Gay (6/0), Diego Martín Forlán Corazo (59/22), Luis Alberto Suárez Díaz (27/9) [81.Sebastián Bruno Fernández Miglierina (5/0)]. Trainer: Óscar Wáshington Tabárez Silva (79).
Goal: Diego Alfredo Lugano Morena (11).

784. 18.11.2009 **URUGUAY – COSTA RICA** **1-1(0-0)** 19th FIFA WC. Qualifiers (Play-offs)
Estadio Centenario, Montevideo; Referee: Massimo Busacca (Switzerland), Attendance: 62,150
URU: Néstor Fernando Muslera Micol (4/0), Diego Roberto Godín Leal (36/3), Diego Alfredo Lugano Morena (41/4), Victorio Maximiliano Pereira Páez (35/0), Álvaro Daniel Pereira Barragán (13/1), Andrés Scotti Ponce de León (24/1) [72.Mauricio Bernardo Victorino Dansilio (4/0)], Sebastián Eguren Ledesma (26/5), Diego Fernando Pérez Aguado (48/0), Marcelo Nicolás Lodeiro Benítez (2/0) [84.Álvaro Fernández Gay (7/0)], Diego Martín Forlán Corazo (60/22), Luis Alberto Suárez Díaz (28/9) [65.Washington Sebastián Abreu Gallo (54/24)]. Trainer: Óscar Wáshington Tabárez Silva (80).
Goal: Washington Sebastián Abreu Gallo (70).

785. 03.03.2010 **SWITZERLAND - URUGUAY** **1-3(1-1)**
AFG Arena, St. Gallen; Referee: Nicola Rizzoli (Italy), Attendance: 12,500
URU: Néstor Fernando Muslera Micol (5/0), Diego Roberto Godín Leal (37/3), Jorge Ciro Fucile Perdomo (24/0), Victorio Maximiliano Pereira Páez (36/0), Álvaro Daniel Pereira Barragán (14/1) [72.Jorge Marcelo Rodríguez Núñez (7/0)], Andrés Scotti Ponce de León (25/1), Walter Alejandro Gargano Guevara (27/0) [63.Egidio Raúl Arévalo Ríos (5/0)], Diego Fernando Pérez Aguado (49/0), Marcelo Nicolás Lodeiro Benítez (3/0) [46.Jorge Andrés Martínez Barrios (14/1); 82.Sebastián Bruno Fernández Miglierina (6/0)], Diego Martín Forlán Corazo (61/23) [46.Washington Sebastián Abreu Gallo (55/24)], Luis Alberto Suárez Díaz (29/10) [63.Edinson Roberto Cavani Gómez (13/2)]. Trainer: Óscar Wáshington Tabárez Silva (81).
Goals: Diego Martín Forlán Corazo (34), Luis Alberto Suárez Díaz (49), Edinson Roberto Cavani Gómez (87).

786. 26.05.2010 **URUGUAY - ISRAEL** **4-1(2-1)**
Estadio Centenario, Montevideo; Referee: Enrique Marcos Osses Zencovich (Chile), Attendance: 47,734
URU: Néstor Fernando Muslera Micol (6/0), Andrés Scotti Ponce de León (26/1), Diego Alfredo Lugano Morena (Cap) (42/4), [46.Sebastián Eguren Ledesma (27/5)], Diego Roberto Godín Leal (38/3), Victorio Maximiliano Pereira Páez (37/0), Diego Fernando Pérez Aguado (50/0) [62.Egidio Raúl Arévalo Ríos (6/0)], Wálter Alejandro Gargano Guevara (28/0) [46.Marcelo Nicolás Lodeiro Benítez (4/0)], Álvaro Daniel Pereira Barragán (15/2) [71.José Martín Cáceres Silva (19/0)], Ignacio María González Gatti (17/1), Luis Alberto Suárez Díaz (30/10) [62.Edinson Roberto Cavani Gómez (14/2)], Diego Martín Forlán Corazo (62/24) [46.Washington Sebastián Abreu Gallo (56/26)]. Trainer: Óscar Wáshington Tabárez Silva (82).
Goals: Diego Martín Forlán Corazo (15), Álvaro Daniel Pereira Barragán (34), Washington Sebastián Abreu Gallo (75, 81).

787. 11.06.2010 **URUGUAY - FRANCE** **0-0** 19th FIFA WC. Group Stage
Cape Town Stadium, Cape Town (South Africa); Referee: Yuichi Nishimura (Japan), Attendance: 64,100
URU: Néstor Fernando Muslera Micol (7/0), Victorio Maximiliano Pereira Páez (38/0), Mauricio Bernardo Victorino Dansilio (5/0), Diego Alfredo Lugano Morena (Cap) (43/4), Diego Roberto Godín Leal (39/3), Álvaro Daniel Pereira Barragán (16/2), Diego Fernando Pérez Aguado (51/0) [87.Sebastián Eguren Ledesma (28/5)], Egidio Raúl Arévalo Ríos (7/0), Ignacio María González Gatti (18/1) [63.Marcelo Nicolás Lodeiro Benítez (5/0)], Luis Alberto Suárez Díaz (31/10) [74.Washington Sebastián Abreu Gallo (57/26)], Diego Martín Forlán Corazo (63/24). Trainer: Óscar Wáshington Tabárez Silva (83).

788. 16.06.2010 **SOUTH AFRICA - URUGUAY** **0-3(0-1)** 19th FIFA WC. Group Stage
Loftus Versfeld Stadium, Pretoria; Referee: Massimo Busacca (Switzerland), Attendance: 42,658
URU: Néstor Fernando Muslera Micol (8/0), Victorio Maximiliano Pereira Páez (39/0), Diego Alfredo Lugano Morena (Cap) (44/4), Diego Roberto Godín Leal (40/3), Jorge Ciro Fucile Perdomo (25/0) [71.Álvaro Fernández Gay (8/0)], Egidio Raúl Arévalo Ríos (8/0), Diego Fernando Pérez Aguado (52/0) [90.Wálter Alejandro Gargano Guevara (29/0)], Álvaro Daniel Pereira Barragán (17/3), Diego Martín Forlán Corazo (64/26), Luis Alberto Suárez Díaz (32/10), Edinson Roberto Cavani Gómez (15/2) (58/26) [89.Sebastián Bruno Fernández Miglierina (7/0)]. Trainer: Óscar Wáshington Tabárez Silva (84).
Goals: Diego Martín Forlán Corazo (24, 80 penalty), Álvaro Daniel Pereira Barragán (90).

789. 22.06.2010 **MEXICO - URUGUAY** **0-1(0-1)** 19th FIFA WC. Group Stage
Royal Bafokeng Stadium, Rustenburg (South Africa); Referee: Viktor Kassai (Hungary), Attendance: 33,425
URU: Néstor Fernando Muslera Micol (9/0), Victorio Maximiliano Pereira Páez (40/0), Diego Alfredo Lugano Morena (Cap) (45/4), Mauricio Bernardo Victorino Dansilio (6/0), Jorge Ciro Fucile Perdomo (26/0), Egidio Raúl Arévalo Ríos (9/0), Diego Fernando Pérez Aguado (53/0), Álvaro Daniel Pereira Barragán (18/3) [77.Andrés Scotti Ponce de León (27/1)], Diego Martín Forlán Corazo (65/26), Luis Alberto Suárez Díaz (33/11) [85.Álvaro Fernández Gay (9/0)], Edinson Roberto Cavani Gómez (16/2). Trainer: Óscar Wáshington Tabárez Silva (85).
Goal: Luis Alberto Suárez Díaz (43).

790. 26.06.2010 **URUGUAY – SOUTH KOREA** **2-1(1-0)** 19th FIFA WC. 2nd Round
„Nelson Mandela" Bay Stadium, Port Elizabeth (South Africa); Referee: Wolfgang Stark (Germany), Attendance: 30,597
URU: Néstor Fernando Muslera Micol (10/0), Victorio Maximiliano Pereira Páez (41/0), Diego Alfredo Lugano Morena (Cap) (46/4), Diego Roberto Godín Leal (41/3) [46.Mauricio Bernardo Victorino Dansilio (7/0)], Jorge Ciro Fucile Perdomo (27/0), Egidio Raúl Arévalo Ríos (10/0), Diego Fernando Pérez Aguado (54/0), Álvaro Daniel Pereira Barragán (19/3) [74.Marcelo Nicolás Lodeiro Benítez (6/0)], Diego Martín Forlán Corazo (66/26), Luis Alberto Suárez Díaz (34/13) [84.Álvaro Fernández Gay (10/0)], Edinson Roberto Cavani Gómez (17/2). Trainer: Óscar Wáshington Tabárez Silva (86).
Goals: Luis Alberto Suárez Díaz (8, 80).

791. 02.07.2010 **URUGUAY - GHANA** **1-1(0-1,1-1,1-1); 4-2 on penalties** 19th FIFA WC. Quarter-Finals
Soccer City, Johannesburg (South Africa); Referee: Olegário Manuel Bartolo Faustino Benquerença (Portugal), Attendance: 84,017
URU: Néstor Fernando Muslera Micol (11/0), Victorio Maximiliano Pereira Páez (42/0), Diego Alfredo Lugano Morena (Cap) (47/4) [38.Andrés Scotti Ponce de León (28/1)], Mauricio Bernardo Victorino Dansilio (8/0), Jorge Ciro Fucile Perdomo (28/0), Álvaro Fernández Gay (11/0) [46.Marcelo Nicolás Lodeiro Benítez (7/0)], Diego Fernando Pérez Aguado (55/0), Egidio Raúl Arévalo Ríos (11/0), Edinson Roberto Cavani Gómez (18/2) [76.Washington Sebastián Abreu Gallo (58/26)], Luis Alberto Suárez Díaz (35/13) [*sent off 120+1*], Diego Martín Forlán Corazo (67/27). Trainer: Óscar Wáshington Tabárez Silva (87).
Goal: Diego Martín Forlán Corazo (55).
Penalties: Diego Martín Forlán Corazo, Mauricio Bernardo Victorino Dansilio, Andrés Scotti Ponce de León, Washington Sebastián Abreu Gallo.

792. 06.07.2010 **URUGUAY - HOLLAND** **2-3(1-1)** 19th FIFA WC. Semi-Finals

Cape Town Stadium, Cape Town (South Africa); Referee: Ravshan Irmatov (Uzbekistan), Attendance: 62,479

URU: Néstor Fernando Muslera Micol (12/0), Victorio Maximiliano Pereira Páez (43/1), Mauricio Bernardo Victorino Dansilio (9/0), Diego Roberto Godín Leal (42/3), José Martín Cáceres Silva (20/0), Diego Fernando Pérez Aguado (56/0), Wálter Alejandro Gargano Guevara (30/0), Egidio Raúl Arévalo Ríos (12/0), Álvaro Daniel Pereira Barragán (20/3) [78.Washington Sebastián Abreu Gallo (59/26)], Edinson Roberto Cavani Gómez (19/2), Diego Martín Forlán Corazo (Cap) (68/28) [84.Sebastián Bruno Fernández Miglierina (8/0)]. Trainer: Óscar Wáshington Tabárez Silva (88).

Goals: Diego Martín Forlán Corazo (41), Victorio Maximiliano Pereira Páez (90+2).

793. 10.07.2010 **URUGUAY - GERMANY** **2-3(1-1)** 19th FIFA WC. 3rd Place play-off

„Nelson Mandela" Bay Stadium, Port Elizabeth (South Africa); Referee: Benito Armando Archundia Téllez (Mexico), Attendance: 36,254

URU: Néstor Fernando Muslera Micol (13/0), Jorge Ciro Fucile Perdomo (29/0), Diego Alfredo Lugano Morena (Cap) (48/4), Diego Roberto Godín Leal (43/3), José Martín Cáceres Silva (21/0), Victorio Maximiliano Pereira Páez (44/1), Diego Fernando Pérez Aguado (57/0) [77.Wálter Alejandro Gargano Guevara (31/0)], Egidio Raúl Arévalo Ríos (13/0), Edinson Roberto Cavani Gómez (20/3) [88.Washington Sebastián Abreu Gallo (60/26)], Luis Alberto Suárez Díaz (36/13), Diego Martín Forlán Corazo (69/29). Trainer: Óscar Wáshington Tabárez Silva (89).

Goals: Edinson Roberto Cavani Gómez (28), Diego Martín Forlán Corazo (51).

794. 11.08.2010 **ANGOLA - URUGUAY** **0-2(0-0)**

Estádio do Restelo, Lisboa (Portugal); Referee: Hugo Miguel (Portugal), Attendance: 1,500

URU: Néstor Fernando Muslera Micol (14/0), Andrés Scotti Ponce de León (29/1), Diego Alfredo Lugano Morena (Cap) (49/4) [63.Carlos Adrián Valdez Suárez (17/0)], Mauricio Bernardo Victorino Dansilio (10/0), Álvaro Daniel Pereira Barragán (21/3), Diego Fernando Pérez Aguado (58/0) [59.Wálter Alejandro Gargano Guevara (32/0)], Egidio Raúl Arévalo Ríos (14/0) [90.Ignacio María González Gatti (19/1)], Victorio Maximiliano Pereira Páez (45/1), Cristian Gabriel Rodríguez Barotti (37/3) [77.Sebastián Eguren Ledesma (29/5)], Sebastián Bruno Fernández Miglierina (9/0) [46.Edinson Roberto Cavani Gómez (21/4)], Washington Sebastián Abreu Gallo (61/26) [71.Abel Mathías Hernández Platero (1/1)]. Trainer: Juan José Verzeri (1).

Goals: Edinson Roberto Cavani Gómez (84 penalty), Abel Mathías Hernández Platero (90).

795. 08.10.2010 **INDONESIA - URUGUAY** **1-7(1-2)**

Stadion Utama Gelora Bung Karno, Djakarta; Referee: Abbas Bin Daud (Singapore), Attendance: 22,000

URU: Juan Guillermo Castillo Iriart (12/0), Jorge Ciro Fucile Perdomo (30/0) [46.Gastón Ezequiel Ramírez Pereyra (1/0)], Diego Alfredo Lugano Morena (Cap) (50/4) [46.Andrés Scotti Ponce de León (30/1)], Mauricio Bernardo Victorino Dansilio (11/0) [60.José Martín Cáceres Silva (22/0)], Álvaro Daniel Pereira Barragán (22/3), Victorio Maximiliano Pereira Páez (46/1), Diego Fernando Pérez Aguado (59/0) [46.Sebastián Eguren Ledesma (30/6)], Wálter Alejandro Gargano Guevara (33/0) [64.Álvaro Rafael González Luengo (12/0)], Cristian Gabriel Rodríguez Barotti (38/3) [60.Sebastián Bruno Fernández Miglierina (10/0)], Luis Alberto Suárez Díaz (37/16), Edinson Roberto Cavani Gómez (22/7). Trainer: Óscar Wáshington Tabárez Silva (90).

Goals: Edinson Roberto Cavani Gómez (35), Luis Alberto Suárez Díaz (43, 54), Sebastián Eguren Ledesma (58), Luis Alberto Suárez Díaz (69 penalty), Edinson Roberto Cavani Gómez (80, 84).

796. 12.10.2010 **CHINA P.R. - URUGUAY** **0-4(0-0)**

Wuhan Sports Center, Wuhan; Referee: Lee Dong-Jun (South Korea), Attendance: 20,000

URU: Néstor Fernando Muslera Micol (15/0), Victorio Maximiliano Pereira Páez (47/1), Diego Alfredo Lugano Morena (Cap) (51/4) [67.Mauricio Bernardo Victorino Dansilio (12/0)], José Martín Cáceres Silva (23/0), Jorge Ciro Fucile Perdomo (31/0) [46.Cristian Gabriel Rodríguez Barotti (39/4)], Diego Fernando Pérez Aguado (60/0) [64.Sebastián Eguren Ledesma (31/6)], Wálter Alejandro Gargano Guevara (34/0), Álvaro Daniel Pereira Barragán (23/3) [86.Andrés Scotti Ponce de León (31/1)], Luis Alberto Suárez Díaz (38/16) [81.Gastón Ezequiel Ramírez Pereyra (2/0)], Edinson Roberto Cavani Gómez (23/8), Diego Martín Forlán Corazo (70/29) [64.Sebastián Bruno Fernández Miglierina (11/1)]. Trainer: Óscar Wáshington Tabárez Silva (91).

Goals: Feng Xiaoting (70 own goal), Edinson Roberto Cavani Gómez (78), Cristian Gabriel Rodríguez Barotti (81), Sebastián Bruno Fernández Miglierina (84).

797. 17.11.2010 **CHILE - URUGUAY** **2-0(1-0)**

Estadio Monumental „David Arellano", Santiago; Referee: Carlos Manuel Torres (Paraguay), Attendance: 45,017

URU: Néstor Fernando Muslera Micol (16/0), Diego Alfredo Lugano Morena (Cap) (52/4), Mauricio Bernardo Victorino Dansilio (13/0), Jorge Ciro Fucile Perdomo (32/0), Victorio Maximiliano Pereira Páez (48/1) [78.José Martín Cáceres Silva (24/0)], Álvaro Daniel Pereira Barragán (24/3) [63.Sebastián Eguren Ledesma (32/6)], Egidio Raúl Arévalo Ríos (15/0) [63.Gastón Ezequiel Ramírez Pereyra (3/0)], Wálter Alejandro Gargano Guevara (35/0) [*sent off 40*], Edinson Roberto Cavani Gómez (24/8), Diego Martín Forlán Corazo (71/29) [78.Washington Sebastián Abreu Gallo (62/26)], Luis Alberto Suárez Díaz (39/16) [46.Cristian Gabriel Rodríguez Barotti (40/4)]. Trainer: Óscar Wáshington Tabárez Silva (92).

798. 25.03.2011 **ESTONIA - URUGUAY** **2-0(0-0)**

A. Le Coq Arena, Tallinn; Referee: Antti Munukka (Finland), Attendance: 6,817

URU: Juan Guillermo Castillo Iriart (13/0), Victorio Maximiliano Pereira Páez (49/1), Diego Alfredo Lugano Morena (Cap) (53/4), Mauricio Bernardo Victorino Dansilio (14/0), Jorge Ciro Fucile Perdomo (33/0) [69.Andrés Scotti Ponce de León (32/1)], Diego Fernando Pérez Aguado (61/0) [69.Sebastián Eguren Ledesma (33/6)], Egidio Raúl Arévalo Ríos (16/0), Gastón Ezequiel Ramírez Pereyra (4/0) [56.Álvaro Daniel Pereira Barragán (25/3)], Abel Mathías Hernández Platero (2/1), Washington Sebastián Abreu Gallo (63/26) [69.Sebastián Bruno Fernández Miglierina (12/1)], Diego Martín Forlán Corazo (72/29). Trainer: Óscar Wáshington Tabárez Silva (93).

799. 29.03.2011 **REPUBLIC OF IRELAND - URUGUAY** **2-3(1-3)**

Aviva Stadium, Dublin; Referee: Saïd Ennjimi (France), Attendance: 25,611

URU: Néstor Fernando Muslera Micol (17/0), Diego Alfredo Lugano Morena (Cap) (54/5), Diego Roberto Godín Leal (44/3), José Martín Cáceres Silva (25/0), Victorio Maximiliano Pereira Páez (50/1), Diego Fernando Pérez Aguado (62/0) [90.Andrés Scotti Ponce de León (33/1)], Egidio Raúl Arévalo Ríos (17/0) [63.Wálter Alejandro Gargano Guevara (36/0)], Álvaro Daniel Pereira Barragán (26/3), Abel Mathías Hernández Platero (3/2) [83.Sebastián Eguren Ledesma (34/6)], Diego Martín Forlán Corazo (73/29), Edinson Roberto Cavani Gómez (25/9). Trainer: Óscar Wáshington Tabárez Silva (94).

Goals: Diego Alfredo Lugano Morena (12), Edinson Roberto Cavani Gómez (22), Abel Mathías Hernández Platero (39).

800. 29.05.2011 **GERMANY - URUGUAY** **2-1(2-0)**

Rhein-Neckar-Arena, Sinsheim; Referee: Olegário Manuel Bártolo Faustino Benquerença (Portugal), Attendance: 25,655

URU: Néstor Fernando Muslera Micol (18/0), Victorio Maximiliano Pereira Páez (51/1), Diego Roberto Godín Leal (45/3), Diego Alfredo Lugano Morena (Cap) (55/5), José Martín Cáceres Silva (26/0), Egidio Raúl Arévalo Ríos (18/0) [76.Sebastián Eguren Ledesma (35/6)], Wálter Alejandro Gargano Guevara (37/1) [87.Washington Sebastián Abreu Gallo (64/26)], Edinson Roberto Cavani Gómez (26/9), Diego Martín Forlán Corazo (74/29), Álvaro Daniel Pereira Barragán (27/3) [55.Gastón Ezequiel Ramírez Pereyra (5/0)], Luis Alberto Suárez Díaz (40/16). Trainer: Óscar Wáshington Tabárez Silva (95).

Goal: Wálter Alejandro Gargano Guevara (49).

801. 08.06.2011 **URUGUAY - HOLLAND** **1-1(0-0); 4-3 on penalties** Copa Confraternidad Antel
Estadio Centenario, Montevideo; Referee: Néstor Fabián Pittana (Argentina), Attendance: 50,000
URU: Néstor Fernando Muslera Micol (19/0), Victorio Maximiliano Pereira Páez (52/1), Diego Alfredo Lugano Morena (Cap) (56/5) [78.Mauricio Bernardo Victorino Dansilio (15/0)], Diego Roberto Godín Leal (46/3), José Martín Cáceres Silva (27/0), Diego Fernando Pérez Aguado (63/0) [62.Sebastián Eguren Ledesma (36/6)], Egidio Raúl Arévalo Ríos (19/0), Gastón Ezequiel Ramírez Pereyra (6/0) [45.Marcelo Nicolás Lodeiro Benítez (8/0)], Luis Alberto Suárez Díaz (41/17) [88.Álvaro Daniel Pereira Barragán (28/3)], Diego Martín Forlán Corazo (75/29) [77.Abel Mathías Hernández Platero (4/2)], Edinson Roberto Cavani Gómez (27/9). Trainer: Óscar Wáshington Tabárez Silva (96).
Goal: Luis Alberto Suárez Díaz (82).
Penalties: Edinson Roberto Cavani Gómez, Abel Mathías Hernández Platero, Mauricio Bernardo Victorino Dansilio, Marcelo Nicolás Lodeiro Benítez (saved), Álvaro Daniel Pereira Barragán.

802. 23.06.2011 **URUGUAY - ESTONIA** **3-0(1-0)** Copa 100 años del Banco de Seguros del Estado
Estadio „Atilio Paiva Olivera", Rivera; Referee: Saúl Esteban Laverni (Argentina), Attendance: 22,800
URU: Néstor Fernando Muslera Micol (20/0), Victorio Maximiliano Pereira Páez (53/1), Diego Alfredo Lugano Morena (Cap) (57/5), Mauricio Bernardo Victorino Dansilio (16/0) [59.Sebastián Coates Nión (1/0)], José Martín Cáceres Silva (28/1), Diego Fernando Pérez Aguado (64/0) [59.Wálter Alejandro Gargano Guevara (38/1)], Egidio Raúl Arévalo Ríos (20/0) [84.Sebastián Eguren Ledesma (37/6)], Marcelo Nicolás Lodeiro Benítez (9/1) [72.Álvaro Rafael González Luengo (13/0)], Luis Alberto Suárez Díaz (42/17) [72.Abel Mathías Hernández Platero (5/2)], Diego Martín Forlán Corazo (76/29) [80.Washington Sebastián Abreu Gallo (65/26)], Edinson Roberto Cavani Gómez (28/9). Trainer: Óscar Wáshington Tabárez Silva (97).
Goals: José Martín Cáceres Silva (12), Mikk Reintam (55, own goal), Marcelo Nicolás Lodeiro Benítez (71).

803. 04.07.2011 **URUGUAY - PERU** **1-1(1-1)** 43rd Copa América. Group Stage
Estadio del Bicentenario, San Juan (Argentina); Referee: Wilmar Alexander Roldán Pérez (Colombia); Attendance: 25,000
URU: Néstor Fernando Muslera Micol (21/0), Victorio Maximiliano Pereira Páez (54/1), Diego Alfredo Lugano Morena (Cap) (58/5), Mauricio Bernardo Victorino Dansilio (17/0), José Martín Cáceres Silva (29/1), Diego Fernando Pérez Aguado (65/0), Egidio Raúl Arévalo Ríos (21/0), Marcelo Nicolás Lodeiro Benítez (10/1) [78.Cristian Gabriel Rodríguez Barotti (41/4)], Luis Alberto Suárez Díaz (43/18), Diego Martín Forlán Corazo (77/29), Edinson Roberto Cavani Gómez (29/9) [78.Abel Mathías Hernández Platero (6/2)]. Trainer: Óscar Wáshington Tabárez Silva (98).
Goal: Luis Alberto Suárez Díaz (45).

804. 08.07.2011 **URUGUAY - CHILE** **1-1(0-0)** 43rd Copa América. Group Stage
Estadio Malvinas Argentinas, Mendoza (Argentina); Referee: Carlos Arecio Amarilla Demarqui (Paraguay); Attendance: 38,000
URU: Néstor Fernando Muslera Micol (22/0), Victorio Maximiliano Pereira Páez (55/1) [79.Marcelo Nicolás Lodeiro Benítez (11/1)], Diego Alfredo Lugano Morena (Cap) (59/5), Sebastián Coates Nión (2/0), José Martín Cáceres Silva (30/1), Diego Fernando Pérez Aguado (66/0), Egidio Raúl Arévalo Ríos (22/0) [85.Sebastián Eguren Ledesma (38/6)], Álvaro Daniel Pereira Barragán (29/4), Luis Alberto Suárez Díaz (44/18), Diego Martín Forlán Corazo (78/29), Edinson Roberto Cavani Gómez (30/9) [46.Álvaro Rafael González Luengo (14/0)]. Trainer: Óscar Wáshington Tabárez Silva (99).
Goal: Álvaro Daniel Pereira Barragán (53).

805. 12.07.2011 **URUGUAY - MEXICO** **1-0(1-0)** 43rd Copa América. Group Stage
Estadio Ciudad de La Plata, La Plata (Argentina); Referee: Raúl Orosco Delgadillo (Bolivia), Attendance: 40,000
URU: Néstor Fernando Muslera Micol (23/0), Victorio Maximiliano Pereira Páez (56/1), Diego Alfredo Lugano Morena (Cap) (60/5), Sebastián Coates Nión (3/0), Álvaro Daniel Pereira Barragán (30/5), Álvaro Rafael González Luengo (15/0) [68.Marcelo Nicolás Lodeiro Benítez (12/1)], Diego Fernando Pérez Aguado (67/0), Egidio Raúl Arévalo Ríos (23/0), Cristian Gabriel Rodríguez Barotti (42/4) [83.Sebastián Eguren Ledesma (39/6)], Diego Martín Forlán Corazo (79/29) [89.Washington Sebastián Abreu Gallo (66/26)], Luis Alberto Suárez Díaz (45/18). Trainer: Óscar Wáshington Tabárez Silva (100).
Goal: Álvaro Daniel Pereira Barragán (14).

806. 16.07.2011 **ARGENTINA - URUGUAY** **1-1(1-1,1-1,1-1); 4-5 on penalties** 43rd Copa América. Quarter-Finals
Estadio „Brigadier Estanislao López", Santa Fé; Referee: Carlos Arecio Amarilla Demarqui (Paraguay), Attendance: 37,000
URU: Néstor Fernando Muslera Micol (24/0), Victorio Maximiliano Pereira Páez (57/1), Diego Alfredo Lugano Morena (Cap) (61/5), Mauricio Bernardo Victorino Dansilio (18/0) [19.Andrés Scotti Ponce de León (34/1)], José Martín Cáceres Silva (31/1), Álvaro Rafael González Luengo (16/0), Diego Fernando Pérez Aguado (68/1) [*sent off 38*], Egidio Raúl Arévalo Ríos (24/0) [109.Sebastián Eguren Ledesma (40/6)], Álvaro Daniel Pereira Barragán (31/5) [109.Wálter Alejandro Gargano Guevara (39/1)], Diego Martín Forlán Corazo (80/29), Luis Alberto Suárez Díaz (46/18). Trainer: Óscar Wáshington Tabárez Silva (101).
Goal: Diego Fernando Pérez Aguado (5).
Penalties: Diego Martín Forlán Corazo, Luis Alberto Suárez Díaz, Andrés Scotti Ponce de León, Wálter Alejandro Gargano Guevara, José Martín Cáceres Silva.

807. 19.07.2011 **PERU - URUGUAY** **0-2(0-0)** 43rd Copa América. Semi-Finals
Estadio Ciudad de La Plata, La Plata (Argentina); Referee: Raúl Orosco Delgadillo (Bolivia); Attendance: 35,000
URU: Néstor Fernando Muslera Micol (25/0), Victorio Maximiliano Pereira Páez (58/1), Diego Alfredo Lugano Morena (Cap) (62/5), Sebastián Coates Nión (4/0), José Martín Cáceres Silva (32/1), Álvaro Rafael González Luengo (17/0), Wálter Alejandro Gargano Guevara (40/1) [70.Sebastián Eguren Ledesma (41/6)], Egidio Raúl Arévalo Ríos (25/0), Álvaro Daniel Pereira Barragán (32/5), Diego Martín Forlán Corazo (81/29), Luis Alberto Suárez Díaz (47/20) [70.Abel Mathías Hernández Platero (7/2)]. Trainer: Óscar Wáshington Tabárez Silva (102).
Goals: Luis Alberto Suárez Díaz (52, 57).

808. 24.07.2011 **URUGUAY - PARAGUAY** **3-0(2-0)** 43rd Copa América. Final
Estadio Monumental „Antonio Vespucio Liberti", Buenos Aires (Argentina); Referee: Sálvio Spínola Fagundes Filho (Brazil); Attendance: 45,000
URU: Néstor Fernando Muslera Micol (26/0), Victorio Maximiliano Pereira Páez (59/1), Diego Alfredo Lugano Morena (Cap) (63/5), Sebastián Coates Nión (5/0), José Martín Cáceres Silva (33/1) [88.Diego Roberto Godín Leal (47/3)], Álvaro Rafael González Luengo (18/0), Diego Fernando Pérez Aguado (69/1) [70.Sebastián Eguren Ledesma (42/6)], Egidio Raúl Arévalo Ríos (26/0), Álvaro Daniel Pereira Barragán (33/5) [63.Edinson Roberto Cavani Gómez (31/9)], Diego Martín Forlán Corazo (82/31), Luis Alberto Suárez Díaz (48/21). Trainer: Óscar Wáshington Tabárez Silva (103).
Goals: Luis Alberto Suárez Díaz (12), Diego Martín Forlán Corazo (42, 89).

809. 02.09.2011 **UKRAINE - URUGUAY** **2-3(2-1)**
Sports Complex „Metallist", Kharkhiv; Referee: Björn Kuipers (Holland), Attendance: 33,000
URU: Néstor Fernando Muslera Micol (27/0), Victorio Maximiliano Pereira Páez (60/1), Diego Alfredo Lugano Morena (Cap) (64/6) [71.Sebastián Coates Nión (6/0)], Diego Roberto Godín Leal (48/3), José Martín Cáceres Silva (34/1), Álvaro Rafael González Luengo (19/1) [78.Abel Mathías Hernández Platero (8/3)], Diego Fernando Pérez Aguado (70/1) [62.Wálter Alejandro Gargano Guevara (41/1)], Sebastián Eguren Ledesma (43/6), Cristian Gabriel Rodríguez Barotti (43/4) [62.Gastón Ezequiel Ramírez Pereyra (7/0)], Edinson Roberto Cavani Gómez (32/9), Luis Alberto Suárez Díaz (49/21). Trainer: Óscar Wáshington Tabárez Silva (104).
Goals: Álvaro Rafael González Luengo (43), Diego Alfredo Lugano Morena (60), Abel Mathías Hernández Platero (86).

810. 07.10.2011 **URUGUAY - BOLIVIA** **4-2(3-1)** 20th FIFA WC. Qualifiers

Estadio Centenario, Montevideo; Referee: Víctor Hugo Carrillo Casanova (Peru); Attendance: 25,500

URU: Néstor Fernando Muslera Micol (28/0), José Martín Cáceres Silva (35/1), Diego Alfredo Lugano Morena (Cap) (65/8), Diego Roberto Godín Leal (49/3), Victorio Maximiliano Pereira Páez (61/1), Diego Fernando Pérez Aguado (71/1), Egidio Raúl Arévalo Ríos (27/0), Álvaro Daniel Pereira Barragán (34/5) [56.Jorge Ciro Fucile Perdomo (34/0)], Luis Alberto Suárez Díaz (50/22), Edinson Roberto Cavani Gómez (33/10) [70.Cristian Gabriel Rodríguez Barotti (44/4)], Diego Martín Forlán Corazo (83/31). Trainer: Óscar Wáshington Tabárez Silva (105).

Goals: Luis Alberto Suárez Díaz (3), Diego Alfredo Lugano Morena (25), Edinson Roberto Cavani Gómez (34), Diego Alfredo Lugano Morena (71).

811. 11.10.2011 **PARAGUAY - URUGUAY** **1-1(0-0)** 20th FIFA WC. Qualifiers

Estadio Defensores del Chaco, Asunción; Referee: Wilson Luiz Seneme (Brazil); Attendance: 12,922

URU: Néstor Fernando Muslera Micol (29/0), Victorio Maximiliano Pereira Páez (62/1), Diego Alfredo Lugano Morena (Cap) (66/8), Diego Roberto Godín Leal (50/3), José Martín Cáceres Silva (36/1), Diego Fernando Pérez Aguado (72/1) [58.Sebastián Eguren Ledesma (44/6)], Egidio Raúl Arévalo Ríos (28/0), Edinson Roberto Cavani Gómez (34/10), Álvaro Daniel Pereira Barragán (35/5) [65.Álvaro Rafael González Luengo (20/1)], Luis Alberto Suárez Díaz (51/22), Diego Martín Forlán Corazo (84/32) [83.Cristian Gabriel Rodríguez Barotti (45/4)]. Trainer: Óscar Wáshington Tabárez Silva (106).

Goal: Diego Martín Forlán Corazo (68).

812. 11.11.2011 **URUGUAY - CHILE** **4-0(2-0)** 20th FIFA WC. Qualifiers

Estadio Centenario, Montevideo; Referee: Héctor Walter Baldassi (Argentina); Attendance: 40,500

URU: Néstor Fernando Muslera Micol (30/0), José Martín Cáceres Silva (37/1), Diego Alfredo Lugano Morena (Cap) (67/8), Diego Roberto Godín Leal (51/3), Álvaro Daniel Pereira Barragán (36/5), Álvaro Rafael González Luengo (21/1) [69.Sebastián Eguren Ledesma (45/6)], Diego Fernando Pérez Aguado (73/1), Egidio Raúl Arévalo Ríos (29/0), Gastón Ezequiel Ramírez Pereyra (8/0) [57.Washington Sebastián Abreu Gallo (67/26)], Luis Alberto Suárez Díaz (52/26) [76.Cristian Gabriel Rodríguez Barotti (46/4)], Edinson Roberto Cavani Gómez (35/10). Trainer: Óscar Wáshington Tabárez Silva (107).

Goals: Luis Alberto Suárez Díaz (42, 45, 68, 73).

813. 15.11.2011 **ITALY - URUGUAY** **0-1(0-1)**

Stadio Olimpico, Roma; Referee: Duarte Nuno Pereira Gomes (Portugal), Attendance: 42,000

URU: Néstor Fernando Muslera Micol (31/0), José Martín Cáceres Silva (38/1), Diego Alfredo Lugano Morena (Cap) (68/8) [46.Sebastián Coates Nión (7/0)], Diego Roberto Godín Leal (52/3), Álvaro Daniel Pereira Barragán (37/5) [*sent off 81*], Victorio Maximiliano Pereira Páez (63/1) [90.Andrés Scotti Ponce de León (35/1)], Diego Fernando Pérez Aguado (74/1) [50.Sebastián Eguren Ledesma (46/6)], Egidio Raúl Arévalo Ríos (30/0), Cristian Gabriel Rodríguez Barotti (47/4) [83.Álvaro Rafael González Luengo (22/1)], Edinson Roberto Cavani Gómez (36/10), Sebastián Bruno Fernández Miglierina (13/2) [83.Emiliano Alfaro Toscano (1/0)]. Trainer: Óscar Wáshington Tabárez Silva (108).

Goal: Sebastián Bruno Fernández Miglierina (3).

814. 29.02.2012 **ROMANIA - URUGUAY** **1-1(0-1)**

Arena Naţională, Bucureşti; Referee: Viktor Kassai (Hungary), Attendance: 20,000

URU: Néstor Fernando Muslera Micol (32/0), Victorio Maximiliano Pereira Páez (64/1) [46.Jorge Ciro Fucile Perdomo (35/0)], Diego Alfredo Lugano Morena (69/8) (Cap), Diego Roberto Godín Leal (53/3), José Martín Cáceres Silva (39/1), Wálter Alejandro Gargano Guevara (42/1) [69.Álvaro Rafael González Luengo (23/1)], Egidio Raúl Arévalo Ríos (31/0) [78.Sebastián Eguren Ledesma (47/6)], Gastón Ezequiel Ramírez Pereyra (9/0), Luis Alberto Suárez Díaz (53/26), Edinson Roberto Cavani Gómez (37/11) [60.Washington Sebastián Abreu Gallo (68/26)], Diego Martín Forlán Corazo (85/32). Trainer: Óscar Wáshington Tabárez Silva (109).

Goal: Edinson Roberto Cavani Gómez (2).

815. 25.05.2012 **RUSSIA - URUGUAY** **1-1(0-0)**

Lokomotiv Stadium, Moskva; Referee: Kevin Blom (Holland); Attendance: 22,000

URU: Néstor Fernando Muslera Micol (33/0), Victorio Maximiliano Pereira Páez (65/1), Diego Alfredo Lugano Morena (Cap) (70/8), Diego Roberto Godín Leal (54/3), José Martín Cáceres Silva (40/1), Diego Fernando Pérez Aguado (75/1) [77.Wálter Alejandro Gargano Guevara (43/1)], Egidio Raúl Arévalo Ríos (32/0), Álvaro Daniel Pereira Barragán (38/5) [77.Gastón Ezequiel Ramírez Pereyra (10/0)], Edinson Roberto Cavani Gómez (38/11), Diego Martín Forlán Corazo (86/32), Luis Alberto Suárez Díaz (54/27). Trainer: Óscar Wáshington Tabárez Silva (110).

Goal: Luis Alberto Suárez Díaz (48).

816. 02.06.2012 **URUGUAY - VENEZUELA** **1-1(1-0)** 20th FIFA WC. Qualifiers

Estadio Centenario, Montevideo; Referee: Antonio Javier Arias Alvarenga (Paraguay); Attendance: 57,000

URU: Néstor Fernando Muslera Micol (34/0), Victorio Maximiliano Pereira Páez (66/1), Diego Alfredo Lugano Morena (Cap) (71/8) [78.Sebastián Coates Nión (8/0)], José Martín Cáceres Silva (41/1), Diego Roberto Godín Leal (55/3), Álvaro Daniel Pereira Barragán (39/5), Diego Fernando Pérez Aguado (76/1) [75.Álvaro Rafael González Luengo (24/1)], Egidio Raúl Arévalo Ríos (33/0), Luis Alberto Suárez Díaz (55/27), Diego Martín Forlán Corazo (87/33) [88.Washington Sebastián Abreu Gallo (69/26)], Edinson Roberto Cavani Gómez (39/11). Trainer: Óscar Wáshington Tabárez Silva (111).

Goal: Diego Martín Forlán Corazo (39).

817. 10.06.2012 **URUGUAY - PERU** **4-2(2-1)** 20th FIFA WC. Qualifiers

Estadio Centenario, Montevideo; Referee: Leandro Pedro Vuaden (Brazil), Attendance: 55,000

URU: Néstor Fernando Muslera Micol (35/0), Victorio Maximiliano Pereira Páez (67/2), José Martín Cáceres Silva (42/1), Sebastián Coates Nión (9/1), Diego Roberto Godín Leal (56/3), Álvaro Daniel Pereira Barragán (40/5) [60.Cristian Gabriel Rodríguez Barotti (48/5)], Diego Fernando Pérez Aguado (77/1), Egidio Raúl Arévalo Ríos (34/0), Luis Alberto Suárez Díaz (56/27) [90.Sebastián Eguren Ledesma (48/7)], Diego Martín Forlán Corazo (Cap) (88/33) [61.Gastón Ezequiel Ramírez Pereyra (11/0)], Edinson Roberto Cavani Gómez (40/11). Trainer: Óscar Wáshington Tabárez Silva (112).

Goals: Sebastián Coates Nión (15), Victorio Maximiliano Pereira Páez (30), Cristian Gabriel Rodríguez Barotti (63), Sebastián Eguren Ledesma (90+4).

818. 15.08.2012 **FRANCE - URUGUAY** **0-0**

Stade Océane, Le Havre; Referee: Daniele Orsato (Italy); Attendance: 25,000

URU: Néstor Fernando Muslera Micol (36/0), Diego Alfredo Lugano Morena (Cap) (72/8), Victorio Maximiliano Pereira Páez (68/2), Diego Roberto Godín Leal (57/3), Mauricio Bernardo Victorino Dansilio (19/0), Álvaro Daniel Pereira Barragán (41/5), Diego Fernando Pérez Aguado (78/1) [85.Sebastián Eguren Ledesma (49/7)], Cristian Gabriel Rodríguez Barotti (49/5), Walter Alejandro Gargano Guevara (44/1) [64.Álvaro Rafael González Luengo (25/1)], Diego Martín Forlán Corazo (89/33) [89.Sebastián Bruno Fernández Miglierina (14/2)], Washington Sebastián Abreu Gallo (70/26). Trainer: Óscar Wáshington Tabárez Silva (113).

819. 07.09.2012 **COLOMBIA - URUGUAY** **4-0(1-0)** 20th FIFA WC. Qualifiers

Estadio Metropolitano "Roberto Meléndez", Barranquilla; Referee: Héber Roberto Lopes (Brazil); Attendance: 45,000

URU: Néstor Fernando Muslera Micol (37/0), Diego Alfredo Lugano Morena (Cap) (73/8), Victorio Maximiliano Pereira Páez (69/2) [55.Gastón Ezequiel Ramírez Pereyra (12/0)], Diego Roberto Godín Leal (58/3), Mauricio Bernardo Victorino Dansilio (20/0) [46.Álvaro Rafael González Luengo (26/1)], Álvaro Daniel Pereira Barragán (42/5), Diego Fernando Pérez Aguado (79/1), Cristian Gabriel Rodríguez Barotti (50/5), Egidio Raúl Arévalo Ríos (35/0) [73.Walter Alejandro Gargano Guevara (45/1)], Diego Martín Forlán Corazo (90/33), Edinson Roberto Cavani Gómez (41/11). Trainer: Óscar Wáshington Tabárez Silva (114).

820. 11.09.2012 **URUGUAY - ECUADOR** **1-1(0-1)** 20th FIFA WC. Qualifiers

Estadio Centenario, Montevideo; Referee: Carlos Arecio Amarilla Demarqui (Paraguay); Attendance: 38,000

URU: Néstor Fernando Muslera Micol (38/0), Diego Alfredo Lugano Morena (Cap) (74/8), Victorio Maximiliano Pereira Páez (70/2), Diego Roberto Godín Leal (59/3), Álvaro Daniel Pereira Barragán (43/5) [46.Álvaro Rafael González Luengo (27/1)], Diego Fernando Pérez Aguado (80/1) [59.Cristian Gabriel Rodríguez Barotti (51/5)], Egidio Raúl Arévalo Ríos (36/0) [46.Walter Alejandro Gargano Guevara (46/1)], Gastón Ezequiel Ramírez Pereyra (13/0), Luis Alberto Suárez Díaz (57/27), Diego Martín Forlán Corazo (91/33), Edinson Roberto Cavani Gómez (42/12). Trainer: Óscar Wáshington Tabárez Silva (115).

Goal: Edinson Roberto Cavani Gómez (67).

821. 12.10.2012 **ARGENTINA - URUGUAY** **3-0(0-0)** 20th FIFA WC. Qualifiers

Estadio Malvinas Argentinas, Mendoza; Referee: Leandro Pedro Vuaden (Brazil); Attendance: 31,997

URU: Néstor Fernando Muslera Micol (39/0), Diego Alfredo Lugano Morena (Cap) (75/8) [64.Andrés Scotti Ponce de León (36/1)], Victorio Maximiliano Pereira Páez (71/2), José Martín Cáceres Silva (43/1), Diego Roberto Godín Leal (60/3), Walter Alejandro Gargano Guevara (47/1), Álvaro Rafael González Luengo (28/1) [68.Cristian Gabriel Rodríguez Barotti (52/5)], Egidio Raúl Arévalo Ríos (37/0), Luis Alberto Suárez Díaz (58/27), Diego Martín Forlán Corazo (92/33), Edinson Roberto Cavani Gómez (43/12). Trainer: Óscar Wáshington Tabárez Silva (116).

822. 16.10.2012 **BOLIVIA - URUGUAY** **4-1(2-0)** 20th FIFA WC. Qualifiers

Estadio "Hernando Siles Zuazo", La Paz; Referee: Víctor Hugo Rivera Chávez (Peru); Attendance: 25,402

URU: Néstor Fernando Muslera Micol (40/0), Andrés Scotti Ponce de León (37/1), Victorio Maximiliano Pereira Páez (72/2) [36.Edinson Roberto Cavani Gómez (44/12)], Mauricio Bernardo Victorino Dansilio (21/0), Álvaro Daniel Pereira Barragán (44/5), Cristian Gabriel Rodríguez Barotti (53/5), Walter Alejandro Gargano Guevara (48/1) [36.Marcelo Nicolás Lodeiro Benítez (13/1)], Álvaro Rafael González Luengo (29/1), Egidio Raúl Arévalo Ríos (38/0), Luis Alberto Suárez Díaz (59/28), Diego Martín Forlán Corazo (93/33) [66.Álvaro Fernández Gay (12/0)]. Trainer: Óscar Wáshington Tabárez Silva (117).

Goal: Luis Alberto Suárez Díaz (81).

823. 14.11.2012 **POLAND - URUGUAY** **1-3(0-2)**

PGE Arena, Gdańsk; Referee: William Collum (Scotland); Attendance: 39,460

URU: Néstor Fernando Muslera Micol (41/0), Diego Alfredo Lugano Morena (Cap) (76/8), José Martín Cáceres Silva (44/1), Diego Roberto Godín Leal (61/3), Matías Aguirregaray Guruceaga (1/0) [59.Walter Alejandro Gargano Guevara (49/1)], Cristian Gabriel Rodríguez Barotti (54/5) [74.Gonzalo Castro Irizábal (4/0)], Álvaro Rafael González Luengo (30/1), Egidio Raúl Arévalo Ríos (39/0) [70.Sebastián Eguren Ledesma (50/7)], Marcelo Nicolás Lodeiro Benítez (14/1) [79.Álvaro Daniel Pereira Barragán (45/5)], Luis Alberto Suárez Díaz (60/29) [85.Christian Ricardo Stuani Curbelo (1/0)], Edinson Roberto Cavani Gómez (45/13) [46.Gastón Ezequiel Ramírez Pereyra (14/0)]. Trainer: Óscar Wáshington Tabárez Silva (118).

Goals: Kamil Jacek Glik (22 own goal), Edinson Roberto Cavani Gómez (34), Luis Alberto Suárez Díaz (66).

824. 06.02.2013 **SPAIN - URUGUAY** **3-1(1-1)**

Khalifa International Stadium, Doha (Qatar); Referee: Fahad Jaber Al Marri (Qatar); Attendance: 48,000

URU: Néstor Fernando Muslera Micol (42/0), Diego Alfredo Lugano Morena (Cap) (77/8), Victorio Maximiliano Pereira Páez (73/2), José Martín Cáceres Silva (45/1), Diego Roberto Godín Leal (62/3), Diego Fernando Pérez Aguado (81/1) [65.Egidio Raúl Arévalo Ríos (40/0)], Cristian Gabriel Rodríguez Barotti (55/6) [69.Gonzalo Castro Irizábal (5/0)], Álvaro Rafael González Luengo (31/1) [80.Matías Aguirregaray Guruceaga (2/0)], Marcelo Nicolás Lodeiro Benítez (15/1) [77.Walter Alejandro Gargano Guevara (50/1)], Luis Alberto Suárez Díaz (61/29), Edinson Roberto Cavani Gómez (46/13) [70.Diego Martín Forlán Corazo (94/33)]. Trainer: Óscar Wáshington Tabárez Silva (119).

Goal: Cristian Gabriel Rodríguez Barotti (32).

825. 22.03.2013 **URUGUAY - PARAGUAY** **1-1(0-0)** 20th FIFA WC. Qualifiers

Estadio Centenario, Montevideo; Referee: Wilmar Alexander Roldán Pérez (Colombia); Attendance: 32,000

URU: Néstor Fernando Muslera Micol (43/0), Diego Alfredo Lugano Morena (Cap) (78/8), Victorio Maximiliano Pereira Páez (74/2) [68.Gastón Ezequiel Ramírez Pereyra (15/0)], Diego Roberto Godín Leal (63/3), Álvaro Daniel Pereira Barragán (46/5), Diego Fernando Pérez Aguado (82/1) [46.Egidio Raúl Arévalo Ríos (41/0)], Cristian Gabriel Rodríguez Barotti (56/6) [46.Edinson Roberto Cavani Gómez (47/13)], Álvaro Rafael González Luengo (32/1), Marcelo Nicolás Lodeiro Benítez (16/1), Luis Alberto Suárez Díaz (62/30), Diego Martín Forlán Corazo (95/33). Trainer: Óscar Wáshington Tabárez Silva (120).

Goal: Luis Alberto Suárez Díaz (82).

826. 26.03.2013 **CHILE - URUGUAY** **2-0(1-0)** 20th FIFA WC. Qualifiers

Estadio Nacional, Santiago; Referee: Néstor Fabián Pitana (Argentina); Attendance: 43,816

URU: Néstor Fernando Muslera Micol (44/0), Diego Alfredo Lugano Morena (Cap) (79/8), Diego Roberto Godín Leal (64/3), Álvaro Daniel Pereira Barragán (47/5), Matías Aguirregaray Guruceaga (3/0) [46.Alejandro Daniel Silva González (1/0)], Álvaro Rafael González Luengo (33/1), Egidio Raúl Arévalo Ríos (42/0), Marcelo Nicolás Lodeiro Benítez (17/1) [82.Cristian Gabriel Rodríguez Barotti (57/6)], Gastón Ezequiel Ramírez Pereyra (16/0) [70.Diego Martín Forlán Corazo (96/33)], Luis Alberto Suárez Díaz (63/30), Edinson Roberto Cavani Gómez (48/13). Trainer: Óscar Wáshington Tabárez Silva (121).

827. 05.06.2013 **URUGUAY - FRANCE** **1-0(0-0)**

Estadio Centenario, Montevideo; Referee: Julio César Quintana Rodríguez (Paraguay); Attendance: 35,000

URU: Néstor Fernando Muslera Micol (45/0), Diego Alfredo Lugano Morena (Cap) (80/8) [46.Andrés Scotti Ponce de León (38/1)], Victorio Maximiliano Pereira Páez (75/2), José Martín Cáceres Silva (46/1), Álvaro Daniel Pereira Barragán (48/5) [71.Cristian Gabriel Rodríguez Barotti (58/6)], Sebastián Coates Nión (10/1), Walter Alejandro Gargano Guevara (51/1), Egidio Raúl Arévalo Ríos (43/0) [46.Sebastián Eguren Ledesma (51/7)], Marcelo Nicolás Lodeiro Benítez (18/1) [46.Gastón Ezequiel Ramírez Pereyra (17/0)], Diego Martín Forlán Corazo (97/33) [46.Luis Alberto Suárez Díaz (64/31)], Edinson Roberto Cavani Gómez (49/13) [66.Abel Mathías Hernández Platero (9/3)]. Trainer: Óscar Wáshington Tabárez Silva (122).

Goal: Luis Alberto Suárez Díaz (50).

828. 11.06.2013 **VENEZUELA - URUGUAY** **0-1(0-1)** 20th FIFA WC. Qualifiers

Estadio Polideportivo Cachamay, Ciudad Guayana; Referee: Paulo César de Oliveira (Brazil); Attendance: 36,297

URU: Néstor Fernando Muslera Micol (46/0), Diego Alfredo Lugano Morena (Cap) (81/8), Victorio Maximiliano Pereira Páez (76/2), José Martín Cáceres Silva (47/1), Diego Roberto Godín Leal (65/3), Diego Fernando Pérez Aguado (83/1) [76.Sebastián Eguren Ledesma (52/7)], Cristian Gabriel Rodríguez Barotti (59/6) [85.Álvaro Daniel Pereira Barragán (49/5)], Walter Alejandro Gargano Guevara (52/1), Gastón Ezequiel Ramírez Pereyra (18/0) [60.Álvaro Rafael González Luengo (34/1)], Diego Martín Forlán Corazo (98/33), Edinson Roberto Cavani Gómez (50/14). Trainer: Óscar Wáshington Tabárez Silva (123).

Goal: Edinson Roberto Cavani Gómez (28).

829. 16.06.2013 **SPAIN - URUGUAY** **2-1(2-0)** 9th FIFA Confederations Cup, Group Stage

Arena Pernambuco, Recife (Brazil); Referee: Yuichi Nishimura (Japan); Attendance: 41,705

URU: Néstor Fernando Muslera Micol (47/0), Diego Alfredo Lugano Morena (Cap) (82/8), Victorio Maximiliano Pereira Páez (77/2), José Martín Cáceres Silva (48/1), Diego Roberto Godín Leal (66/3), Diego Fernando Pérez Aguado (84/1) [69.Diego Martín Forlán Corazo (99/33)], Cristian Gabriel Rodríguez Barotti (60/6), Walter Alejandro Gargano Guevara (53/1) [63.Marcelo Nicolás Lodeiro Benítez (19/1)], Gastón Ezequiel Ramírez Pereyra (19/0) [46.Álvaro Rafael González Luengo (35/1)], Luis Alberto Suárez Díaz (65/32), Edinson Roberto Cavani Gómez (51/14). Trainer: Óscar Wáshington Tabárez Silva (124).

Goal: Luis Alberto Suárez Díaz (88).

830. 20.06.2013 **NIGERIA - URUGUAY** **1-2(1-1)** 9th FIFA Confederations Cup, Group Stage

Arena Fonte Nova, Salvador (Brazil); Referee: Björn Kuipers (Holland); Attendance: 26,769

URU: Néstor Fernando Muslera Micol (48/0), Diego Alfredo Lugano Morena (Cap) (83/9), Victorio Maximiliano Pereira Páez (78/2), José Martín Cáceres Silva (49/1), Diego Roberto Godín Leal (67/3), Cristian Gabriel Rodríguez Barotti (61/6) [88.Álvaro Daniel Pereira Barragán (50/5)], Álvaro Rafael González Luengo (36/1), Egidio Raúl Arévalo Ríos (44/0), Luis Alberto Suárez Díaz (66/32) [83.Sebastián Coates Nión (11/1)], Diego Martín Forlán Corazo (**100**/34), Edinson Roberto Cavani Gómez (52/14). Trainer: Óscar Wáshington Tabárez Silva (125).

Goals: Diego Alfredo Lugano Morena (19), Diego Martín Forlán Corazo (51).

831. 23.06.2013 **URUGUAY - TAHITI** **8-0(4-0)** 9th FIFA Confederations Cup, Group Stage

Arena Pernambuco, Recife (Brazil); Referee: Pedro Proença Oliveira Alves Garcia (Portugal); Attendance: 22,047

URU: Martín Andrés Silva Leites (2/0), Andrés Scotti Ponce de León (39/1) [*sent off 51*], Álvaro Daniel Pereira Barragán (51/5), Sebastián Coates Nión (12/1), Matías Aguirregaray Guruceaga (4/0), Diego Fernando Pérez Aguado (Cap) (85/2), Sebastián Eguren Ledesma (53/7), Walter Alejandro Gargano Guevara (54/1), Marcelo Nicolás Lodeiro Benítez (20/2), Gastón Ezequiel Ramírez Pereyra (20/0) [69.Luis Alberto Suárez Díaz (67/34)], Abel Mathías Hernández Platero (10/7). Trainer: Óscar Wáshington Tabárez Silva (126).

Goals: Abel Mathías Hernández Platero (2, 24), Diego Fernando Pérez Aguado (27), Abel Mathías Hernández Platero (45+1), Marcelo Nicolás Lodeiro Benítez (61), Abel Mathías Hernández Platero (67 penalty), Luis Alberto Suárez Díaz (82, 90).

832. 26.06.2013 **BRAZIL - URUGUAY** **2-1(1-0)** 9th FIFA Confederations Cup, Semi-Finals

Estádio Mineirão, Belo Horizonte; Referee: Enrique Roberto Osses Zencovich (Chile); Attendance: 57,483

URU: Néstor Fernando Muslera Micol (49/0), Diego Alfredo Lugano Morena (Cap) (84/9), Victorio Maximiliano Pereira Páez (79/2), José Martín Cáceres Silva (50/1), Diego Roberto Godín Leal (68/3), Cristian Gabriel Rodríguez Barotti (62/6), Álvaro Rafael González Luengo (37/1) [83.Walter Alejandro Gargano Guevara (55/1)], Egidio Raúl Arévalo Ríos (45/0), Luis Alberto Suárez Díaz (68/34), Diego Martín Forlán Corazo (101/34), Edinson Roberto Cavani Gómez (53/15). Trainer: Óscar Wáshington Tabárez Silva (127).

Goal: Edinson Roberto Cavani Gómez (48).

833. 30.06.2013 **URUGUAY - ITALY** **2-2(0-1,2-2,2-2); 2-3 on penalties** 9th FIFA Confederations Cup, Final

Arena Fonte Nova, Salvador (Brazil); Referee: Djamel Haimoudi (Algeria); Attendance: 43,382

URU: Néstor Fernando Muslera Micol (50/0), Diego Alfredo Lugano Morena (Cap) (85/9), Victorio Maximiliano Pereira Páez (80/2) [81.Álvaro Daniel Pereira Barragán (52/5)], José Martín Cáceres Silva (51/1), Diego Roberto Godín Leal (69/3), Cristian Gabriel Rodríguez Barotti (63/6) [56.Álvaro Rafael González Luengo (38/1)], Walter Alejandro Gargano Guevara (56/1), Egidio Raúl Arévalo Ríos (46/0) [107.Diego Fernando Pérez Aguado (86/2)], Luis Alberto Suárez Díaz (69/34), Diego Martín Forlán Corazo (102/34), Edinson Roberto Cavani Gómez (54/17). Trainer: Óscar Wáshington Tabárez Silva (128).

Goals: Edinson Roberto Cavani Gómez (58, 78).

Penalties: Diego Martín Forlán Corazo (missed), Edinson Roberto Cavani Gómez, Luis Alberto Suárez Díaz, José Martín Cáceres Silva (missed), Walter Alejandro Gargano Guevara (missed).

834. 14.08.2013 **JAPAN - URUGUAY** **2-4(0-2)**

Miyagi Stadium, Rifu; Referee: Szymon Marciniak (Poland), Attendance: 45,883

URU: Néstor Fernando Muslera Micol (51/0), Diego Alfredo Lugano Morena (Cap) (86/9), Victorio Maximiliano Pereira Páez (81/2), José Martín Cáceres Silva (52/1) [77.Jorge Ciro Fucile Perdomo (36/0)], Diego Roberto Godín Leal (70/3) [80.Sebastián Coates Nión (13/1)], Cristian Gabriel Rodríguez Barotti (64/6) [67.Álvaro Daniel Pereira Barragán (53/5)], Walter Alejandro Gargano Guevara (57/1) [61.Sebastián Eguren Ledesma (54/7)], Álvaro Rafael González Luengo (39/2) [68.Christian Ricardo Stuani Curbelo (2/0)], Marcelo Nicolás Lodeiro Benítez (21/2) [61.Gastón Ezequiel Ramírez Pereyra (21/0)], Luis Alberto Suárez Díaz (70/35), Diego Martín Forlán Corazo (103/36). Trainer: Óscar Wáshington Tabárez Silva (129).

Goals: Diego Martín Forlán Corazo (27, 29), Luis Alberto Suárez Díaz (52), Álvaro Rafael González Luengo (58).

835. 06.09.2013 **PERU - URUGUAY** **1-2(0-1)** 20th FIFA WC. Qualifiers

Estadio Monumental, Lima; Referee: Patricio Loustau (Argentina); Attendance: 39,222

URU: Néstor Fernando Muslera Micol (52/0), Diego Alfredo Lugano Morena (Cap) (87/9), Victorio Maximiliano Pereira Páez (82/2), José Martín Cáceres Silva (53/1) [81.Jorge Ciro Fucile Perdomo (37/0)], Diego Roberto Godín Leal (71/3), Cristian Gabriel Rodríguez Barotti (65/6), Walter Alejandro Gargano Guevara (58/1) [70.Álvaro Rafael González Luengo (40/2)], Egidio Raúl Arévalo Ríos (47/0), Luis Alberto Suárez Díaz (71/37), Diego Martín Forlán Corazo (104/36) [25.Christian Ricardo Stuani Curbelo (3/0)], Edinson Roberto Cavani Gómez (55/17). Trainer: Óscar Wáshington Tabárez Silva (130).

Goals: Luis Alberto Suárez Díaz (43 penalty, 67).

836. 10.09.2013 **URUGUAY - COLOMBIA** **2-0(0-0)** 20th FIFA WC. Qualifiers

Estadio Centenario, Montevideo; Referee: Antonio Javier Arias Alvarenga (Paraguay); Attendance: 51,000

URU: Néstor Fernando Muslera Micol (53/0), Jorge Ciro Fucile Perdomo (38/0), Andrés Scotti Ponce de León (Cap) (40/1), Victorio Maximiliano Pereira Páez (83/2), José María Giménez de Vargas (1/0), Cristian Gabriel Rodríguez Barotti (66/6) [71.Gastón Ezequiel Ramírez Pereyra (22/0)], Álvaro Rafael González Luengo (41/2) [46.Walter Alejandro Gargano Guevara (59/1)], Egidio Raúl Arévalo Ríos (48/0), Marcelo Nicolás Lodeiro Benítez (22/2) [46.Christian Ricardo Stuani Curbelo (4/1)], Luis Alberto Suárez Díaz (72/37), Edinson Roberto Cavani Gómez (56/18). Trainer: Óscar Wáshington Tabárez Silva (131).

Goals: Edinson Roberto Cavani Gómez (77), Christian Ricardo Stuani Curbelo (81).

837. 11.10.2013 **ECUADOR - URUGUAY** **1-0(1-0)** 20th FIFA WC. Qualifiers

Estadio Olimpico "Atahualpa", Quito; Referee: Sandro Meira Ricci (Brazil); Attendance: 32,996

URU: Néstor Fernando Muslera Micol (54/0), Diego Alfredo Lugano Morena (Cap) (88/9), Jorge Ciro Fucile Perdomo (39/0), Victorio Maximiliano Pereira Páez (84/2) [65.Diego Martín Forlán Corazo (105/36)], Diego Roberto Godín Leal (72/3), José María Giménez de Vargas (2/0), Cristian Gabriel Rodríguez Barotti (67/6) [78.Gastón Ezequiel Ramírez Pereyra (23/0)], Walter Alejandro Gargano Guevara (60/1) [72.Alejandro Daniel Silva González (2/0)], Egidio Raúl Arévalo Ríos (49/0), Luis Alberto Suárez Díaz (73/37), Edinson Roberto Cavani Gómez (57/18). Trainer: Óscar Wáshington Tabárez Silva (132).

838. 15.10.2013 **URUGUAY - ARGENTINA** **3-2(2-2)** 20th FIFA WC. Qualifiers

Estadio Centenario, Montevideo; Referee: Marcelo de Lima Henrique (Brazil); Attendance: 55,000

URU: Néstor Fernando Muslera Micol (55/0), Diego Alfredo Lugano Morena (Cap) (89/9), Jorge Ciro Fucile Perdomo (40/0), Victorio Maximiliano Pereira Páez (85/2), Diego Roberto Godín Leal (73/3), Diego Fernando Pérez Aguado (87/2) [46.Gastón Ezequiel Ramírez Pereyra (24/0)], Cristian Gabriel Rodríguez Barotti (68/7), Egidio Raúl Arévalo Ríos (50/0), Luis Alberto Suárez Díaz (74/38), Edinson Roberto Cavani Gómez (58/19), Christian Ricardo Stuani Curbelo (5/1) [90.José María Giménez de Vargas (3/0)]. Trainer: Óscar Wáshington Tabárez Silva (133).

Goals: Cristian Gabriel Rodríguez Barotti (6), Luis Alberto Suárez Díaz (34 penalty), Edinson Roberto Cavani Gómez (49).

839. 13.11.2013 **JORDAN - URUGUAY** **0-5(0-2)** 20th FIFA WC. Qualifiers, Play-offs

Amman International Stadium, Amman; Referee: Svein Oddvar Moen (Norway), Attendance: 17,370

URU: Martín Andrés Silva Leites (3/0), Diego Alfredo Lugano Morena (Cap) (90/9), Victorio Maximiliano Pereira Páez (86/3), José Martín Cáceres Silva (54/1), Diego Roberto Godín Leal (74/3), Cristian Gabriel Rodríguez Barotti (69/8), Egidio Raúl Arévalo Ríos (51/0), Marcelo Nicolás Lodeiro Benítez (23/3) [70.Álvaro Daniel Pereira Barragán (54/5)], Luis Alberto Suárez Díaz (75/38) [81.Diego Martín Forlán Corazo (106/36)], Edinson Roberto Cavani Gómez (59/20), Christian Ricardo Stuani Curbelo (6/2) [70.Gastón Ezequiel Ramírez Pereyra (25/0)]. Trainer: Óscar Wáshington Tabárez Silva (134).

Goals: Victorio Maximiliano Pereira Páez (22), Christian Ricardo Stuani Curbelo (42), Marcelo Nicolás Lodeiro Benítez (69), Cristian Gabriel Rodríguez Barotti (78), Edinson Roberto Cavani Gómez (90+2).

840. 20.11.2013 **URUGUAY - JORDAN** **0-0** 20th FIFA WC. Qualifiers, Play-offs

Estadio Centenario, Montevideo; Referee: Jonas Eriksson (Sweden), Attendance: 62,000

URU: Martín Andrés Silva Leites (4/0), Diego Alfredo Lugano Morena (Cap) (91/9), Victorio Maximiliano Pereira Páez (87/3), José Martín Cáceres Silva (55/1), Diego Roberto Godín Leal (75/3), Cristian Gabriel Rodríguez Barotti (70/8), Egidio Raúl Arévalo Ríos (52/0), Marcelo Nicolás Lodeiro Benítez (24/3) [61.Gastón Ezequiel Ramírez Pereyra (26/0)], Luis Alberto Suárez Díaz (76/38), Edinson Roberto Cavani Gómez (60/20) [82.Abel Mathías Hernández Platero (11/7)], Christian Ricardo Stuani Curbelo (7/2) [61.Diego Martín Forlán Corazo (107/36)]. Trainer: Óscar Wáshington Tabárez Silva (135).

INTERNATIONAL PLAYERS

FM/Nr	Name	DOB	Caps	Goals	Period, Club
(429/681)	ABALDE Rodolfo		4	0	1976, Liverpool FC Montevideo (4/0).
(241/413)	ABBADIE Julio César	07.09.1930	26	14	1952-1966, CA Peñarol Montevideo (18/11), Genoa CFC (3/1), CA Peñarol Montevideo (5/2)
(607/873)	ABEIJÓN PESSI Nelson Javier	21.07.1973	23	2	1994-2003, Club Nacional de Football Montevideo (19/1), Cagliari Calcio (1/0), Calcio Como (3/1).
(205/359)	ABELLERIA Luis		1	0	1946
(264/445)	ABREO Omar		2	0	1955, Liverpool FC Montevideo (2/0).
(628/903)	ABREU GALLO Washington Sebastián	17.10.1976	70	26	1996-2012, CA San Lorenzo de Almagro (9/3), CDSC Cruz Azul Ciudad de México (7/6), CF América Ciudad de México (2/1), CdyD Dorados de Sinaola (1/1), CF Monterrey (7/2), San Luís FC (3/2), Tigres de la Universidad Autónoma de Nuevo León (7/5), CA River Plate Buenos Aires (3/1), Beitar Jerusalem FC (2/1), CA Reiver Plate Buenos Aires (3/1), Real Sociedad de Fútbol San Sebastián (5/0), PAE Aris Thessaloníki (5/1), Botafogo FR Rio de Janeiro (15/2), Figueirense FC (1/0).
(485/759)	ACEVEDO CARDOZO Eduardo Mario	25.09.1959	42	1	1983-1986, Defensor Sporting Club Montevideo (42/1).
(461/735)	ACEVEDO Carlos		2	0	1980
(284/472)	ACOSTA Julio		3	0	1957
(484/757)	ACOSTA Luis Alberto	15.12.1952	15	1	1983-1988, Montevideo Wanderers FC (15/1).
(388/612)	ACOSTA Nelson Bonifacio	12.06.1944	5	0	1971-1976, CA Peñarol Montevideo (5/0).
(95/160)	ACUÑA Horacio		1	0	1923, Colón FC Montevideo (1/0).
(342/569)	ACUÑA Jorge		5	0	1966-1967, Institución Atlética Sud América Montevideo (4/0).
(377/595)	ACUÑA Nilo		1	0	1969, CA Peñarol Montevideo (1/0).
(607/872)	ADINOLFI DUARTE Edgardo Alberto	27.03.1974	18	1	1994-1997, CA River Plate Montevideo (10/1), Maccabi Haifa FC (2/0), CA Peñarol Montevideo (6/0).
(452/722)	AGRESTA Nelson	30.06.1955	34	1	1979-1983
(82/136)	AGUERRE Antonio		9	0	1922-1924, Liverpool FC Montevideo (7/0), CA Peñarol Montevideo (2/0).
(388/609)	AGUERRE Luis		4	0	1971
(582/836)	AGUERRE Raphael	31.07.1969	1	0	1991, Montevideo Wanderers FC (1/0).
(308/516)	AGUERRE Walter		2	0	1961, CA Peñarol Montevideo (2/0).
(161/269)	AGUIAR Daniel		2	0	1935, Montevideo Wanderers FC (2/0).
(702/983)	AGUIAR MOREIRA Jesús Cono	19.07.1968	4	0	2003, CtA Fénix Montevideo (4/0).
(479/751)	AGUILERA NOVA Carlos Alberto	21.09.1964	65	23	1982-1997, CA River Plate Montevideo (3/0), Club Nacional de Football Montevideo (33/15), Racing Club Avellaneda (3/2), Genoa CFC (16/5), Torino Calcio (9/0), CA Peñarol Montevideo (1/1).
(292/482)	AGUILERA Zelmar		4	0	1959, Institución Atlética Sud América Montevideo (4/0).
(152/247)	AGUIRRE Pedro		4	0	1932-1935, Rampla Juniors FC Montevideo (4/0).
(608/882)	AGUIRREGARAY ACOSTA Óscar	25.10.1959	10	0	1995-1997, CA Peñarol Montevideo (10/0).
(823/1054)	AGUIRREGARAY GURUCEAGA Matías	01.04.1989	4	0	2012-2013, CFR 1907 Cluj (1/0), CA Peñarol Montevideo (3/0).
(116/197)	AIZPUR Alberto		1	0	1925, CA Lito (1/0).
(163/276)	ALBANESE Vicente		1	0	1936, Central FC Montevideo (1/0).
(162/273)	ALBERTI Juan		1	0	1935, CA Bella Vista Montevideo (1/0).
(606/867)	ALBINO Julio César	28.04.1971	1	0	1993, CA Progreso Montevideo (1/0).
(735/1011)	ALCOBA REBOLLO Aníbal Gabriel	24.01.1980	1	0	2005, Montevideo Wanderers FC (1/0).
(763/1037)	ALCOBA REBOLLO Gerardo	25.11.1984	2	0	2008, CA Peñarol Montevideo (2/0).
(813/1053)	ALFARO TOSCANO Emiliano	28.04.1988	1	0	2011, Liverpool FC Montevideo (1/0).
(452/723)	ALONSO Daniel	18.04.1956	4	0	1979, Liverpool FC Montevideo (4/0).
(652/930)	ALONSO LÓPEZ Diego Martín	16.04.1975	7	0	1999-2001, CA Bella Vista Montevideo (3/0), CA Gimnasia y Esgrima La Plata (3/0), Club Atlético de Madrid (1/0).
(30/079)	ALTAMIRANO Luis		3	0	1913, Montevideo Wanderers FC (3/0).
(98/170)	ALVAREZ Acevedo		1	0	1924, Liverpool FC Montevideo (1/0).
(182/325)	ALVAREZ Antonio		2	0	1941-1942, Racing Club Montevideo (1/0).
(319/529)	ÁLVAREZ Eliseo	09.08.1940	7	0	1962-1966
(303/504)	ÁLVAREZ Emilio Walter	10.02.1939	17	1	1960-1967
(291/481)	ALVAREZ Esteban		4	0	1958-1960, Defensor Sporting Club Montevideo (4/0).
(757/1033)	ÁLVAREZ MENÉNDEZ Pablo	07.02.1985	1	0	2007, Reggina Calcio Reggio Calabria (1/0).
(408/641)	ALVAREZ Pedro		4	0	1974, Liverpool FC Montevideo (4/0).
(652/929)	ALVEZ Jorge Gabriel	26.12.1974	8	1	1999-2000, Club Nacional de Football Montevideo (8/1).
(461/731)	ÁLVEZ MOSQUERA Fernando Harry	04.09.1959	40	0	1980-1997, CA Peñarol Montevideo (32/0), CA River Plate Montevideo (7/0), CA Peñarol Montevideo (1/0)
(446/703)	ALZAMENDI CASAS Antonio	07.06.1956	31	6	1978-1990, CA Independiente Avellaneda (3/0), Club Nacional de Football Montevideo (1/0), CA Peñarol Montevideo (5/12), River Plate Buenos Aires (4/2), CD Logroñes (Spain) (18/3).
(608/880)	ALZUETA Rúben	25.03.1968	2	0	1995-1997, Danubio FC Montevideo (1/0), CSD Huracán Buceo Montevideo (1/0).
(515/775)	ALZUGARAY Jesús Noel	11.05.1963	4	1	1985, Club Nacional de Football Montevideo (4/1).
(99/175)	ALZUGARAY Juan Carlos		6	0	1924-1925, Rampla Juniors FC Montevideo (6/0).
(777/1045)	AMADO ALANIS Miguel Ángel	28.12.1984	2	0	2009-2010, Defensor SC Montevideo (2/0).
(170/293)	AMARILLO Andrés		1	0	1937, Montevideo Wanderers FC (1/0).
(436/692)	AMARO José Luis		1	0	1977
(241/414)	AMBROIS Javier	09.05.1932	31	17	1952-1957, Club Nacional de Football Montevideo (31/17)
(677/949)	ANCHÉN CAJIGA Jorge Luis	17.08.1980	6	0	2001-2002, Danubio FC Montevideo (6/0).
(371/594)	ANCHETA Atilio Genaro	19.07.1948	20	1	1969-1971, Club Nacional de Football Montevideo (20/1).

(89/146)	ANDRADE José Leandro	01.10.1901	**34**	**1**	1923-1930, CA Bella Vista Montevideo (15/0), Club Nacional de Football Montevideo (19/1).
(165/284)	ANDRIOLO Raymundo		**1**	**0**	1937, Club Nacional de Football Montevideo (1/0).
(124/203)	ANSELMO Juan Peregrino	30.04.1902	**8**	**3**	1927-1934, CA Peñarol Montevideo (8/3).
(180/318)	ANTÚNEZ Manuel		**3**	**0**	1940-1942, Liverpool FC Montevideo (3/0).
(62/111)	ANZUBERRO Santiago		**1**	**0**	1918, Montevideo Wanderers FC (1/0).
(387/603)	APARICIO Juan Carlos		**6**	**0**	1971
(5/026)	APHESTEGUY Martín	22.09.1888	**17**	**0**	1906-1915, Montevideo Wanderers FC (17/0).
(22/069)	APHESTEGUY Miguel		**3**	**0**	1911-1913, Montevideo Wanderers FC (3/0).
(438/694)	ARAÚJO Artigas		**1**	**0**	1977
(607/869)	ARBIZA Claudio	03.03.1967	**6**	**0**	1994-1996, Defensor Sporting Club Montevideo (1/0), CA Olimpia Asunción (2/0), CSD Colo Colo Santiago (3/0).
(144/230)	ARECO Rodolfo		**1**	**0**	1930, CA Cerro Montevideo (1/0).
(745/1027)	ARÉVALO RÍOS Egidio Raúl	01.01.1982	**52**	**0**	2006-2013, CA Peñarol Montevideo (3/0), CF Monterrey (1/0), CA Peñarol Montevideo (11/0), Botafogo FR Rio de Janeiro (5/0), Club Tijuana Xoloitzcuintles de Caliente (14/0), US Città di Palermo (12/0), Chicago Fire Soccer Club (6/0).
(253/436)	ARGENTI Héctor		**1**	**0**	1954
(458/728)	ARIAS Alfredo		**2**	**0**	1980
(1/003)	ARÍMALO Germán		**1**	**0**	1902, Club Nacional de Football Montevideo (1/0).
(764/1040)	ARISMENDI CIAPPARETTA Hugo Diego	25.01.1988	**2**	**0**	2008, Club Nacional de Football Montevideo (2/0).
(154/252)	ARISPE Francisco		**5**	**0**	1933-1938, Club Nacional de Football Montevideo (5/0).
(101/183)	ARISPE Pedro	30.09.1900	**19**	**0**	1924-1929, Rampla Juniors FC Montevideo (19/0).
(226/396)	ARIZÁBALO Raúl		**2**	**0**	1949, Defensor Sporting Club Montevideo (2/0).
(192/334)	ARRASCAETA Secundino		**6**	**0**	1942-1945, Rampla Juniors FC Montevideo (4/0).
(97/165)	ARREMÓN Juan Pedro	08.02.1899	**14**	**1**	1923-1929, CA Peñarol Montevideo (14/1).
(393/628)	ASCERY Juan Pedro	16.10.1950	**2**	**0**	1972, Danubio FC Montevideo (2/0).
(268/452)	AUSCARRIAGA Alfonso		**4**	**1**	1956, Danubio FC Montevideo (4/1).
(224/390)	AYALA Juan		**6**	**3**	1949, CA Peñarol Montevideo (6/3).
(522/784)	BÁEZ Enrique Raúl	16.01.1966	**7**	**1**	1986-1988, Montevideo Wanderers FC (7/1).
(331/549)	BAEZA Elgar		**6**	**0**	1965-1967
(192/335)	BAGNULO Hugo		**1**	**0**	1942
(144/229)	BALLESTRERO Enrique	18.01.1905	**19**	**0**	1930-1937, Rampla Juniors FC Montevideo (15/0), CA Peñarol Montevideo (4/0).
(51/106)	BALMELLI Alfredo		**2**	**0**	1917, Central FC Montevideo (2/0)
(242/417)	BALSEIRO Osvaldo		**9**	**4**	1952-1956
(544/815)	BARÁN Adolfo	22.11.1961	**1**	**0**	1989, CA Peñarol Montevideo (1/0).
(584/839)	BARBAT Luis Alberto	17.06.1968	**10**	**0**	1992-2004, Liverpool FC Montevideo (2/0), Danubio FC Montevideo (8/0).
(361/586)	BAREÑO Rubén Laudelino	23.01.1944	**14**	**3**	1967-1970
(644/910)	BARILKO Mario	19.11.1970	**2**	**0**	1997, Club Nacional de Football Montevideo (2/0).
(99/178)	BARLOCCO Atilio		**2**	**0**	1924, Club Nacional de Football Montevideo (2/0).
(213/369)	BARRETO Lorenzo		**4**	**0**	1947, Central FC Montevideo (4/0).
(430/686)	BARRETO VICTORINO Waldemar	22.05.1952	**33**	**15**	1976-1981, CA River Plate Montevideo (7/3), Club Nacional de Football Montevideo (18/8), Asociación Deportivo Cali (8/4).
(461/733)	BARRIOS BALESTRASSE Jorge Wálter	24.01.1961	**61**	**4**	1980-1992, Montevideo Wanderers FC (51/4), SFP Olympiakos Peiraiás (6/0), CA Peñarol Montevideo (4/0).
(178/308)	BARRIOS Julio		**2**	**0**	1940
(127/204)	BARTIBÁS Venancio		**1**	**0**	1927, Central FC Montevideo (1/0).
(419/660)	BARTOLOTTA Daniel	09.01.1955	**2**	**0**	1975, Defensor Sporting Club Montevideo (2/0).
(30/077)	BASTOS Carlos		**3**	**1**	1913-1916, Montevideo Wanderers FC (3/1).
(82/134)	BATIGNANI Fausto	02.07.1903	**11**	**0**	1922-1928, Liverpool FC Montevideo (11/0).
(501/770)	BATISTA GONZÁLEZ José Alberto	06.03.1962	**14**	**1**	1984-1993, CA Peñarol Montevideo (5/1), CD Español Buenos Aires (9/0).
(193/336)	BAZ Blas		**3**	**0**	1942-1943, Racing Club de Montevideo (3/0).
(352/577)	BAZZANO Miguel Angel		**8**	**0**	1967-1968, Danubio FC Montevideo (8/0).
(70/118)	BELOUTAS Manuel		**7**	**0**	1919-1923, Universal FC Montevideo (7/0).
(522/785)	BENGOECHEA DUTRA Pablo Javier	27.06.1965	**43**	**6**	1986-1997, Montevideo Wanderers FC (7/1), Sevilla CF (11/1), CA Peñarol Montevideo (25/4).
(15/058)	BENINCASA José		**38**	**0**	1910-1928, CA River Plate Montevideo (20/0), CA Boca Juniors Buenos Aires (2/0), CA Peñarol Montevideo (16/0).
(42/092)	BENINCASA Miguel		**4**	**0**	1916-1917, CA River Plate Montevideo (4/0).
(289/476)	BENÍTEZ Eladio		**10**	**1**	1957-1962
(323/534)	BENÍTEZ Luis		**3**	**0**	1962-1965
(246/424)	BENTANCOR Raúl		**3**	**0**	1953, Danubio FC Montevideo (3/0).
(224/391)	BENTANCOUR Ernesto		**7**	**1**	1949, CA Peñarol Montevideo (7/1).
(180/315)	BERACOECHEA Salomé		**1**	**0**	1940
(679/954)	BERBIA POSE Adrián	12.10.1977	**2**	**0**	2001, CA Peñarol Montevideo (2/0).
(299/502)	BERGARA Mario Ludovico	01.12.1937	**15**	**6**	1959-1965
(652/928)	BERGARA Raúl Federico	29.12.1971	**8**	**0**	1999, Club Nacional de Football Montevideo (8/0).
(88/141)	BÉRGOLO Jaime		**3**	**1**	1922-1923, Montevideo Wanderers FC (3/1).
(186/329)	BERMÚDEZ Joaquín		**4**	**0**	1942, CA Peñarol Montevideo (4/0).
(274/458)	BERNARDICO Rodger		**9**	**0**	1956-1964, CA Cerro Montevideo (7/0)
(389/616)	BERTOCCHI Francisco		**10**	**1**	1971-1973
(98/169)	BERTONE Emilio		**1**	**0**	1924, Rampla Juniors FC Montevideo (1/0).
(5/027)	BERTONE Juan Carlos		**11**	**1**	1906-1910, Montevideo Wanderers FC (11/1).
(163/274)	BESUZZO Juan Bautista		**9**	**0**	1936-1938, Montevideo Wanderers FC (9/0).
(3/022)	BETANCOR Cándido Hernández		**3**	**0**	1905, Montevideo Wanderers FC (3/0).
(449/714)	BICA Alberto Willers	11.02.1958	**9**	**1**	1979-1981, Club Nacional de Football Montevideo (9/1).

(115/196)	BIDEGAIN Conrado		2	1	1925, Rampla Juniors FC Montevideo (2/1).
(606/866)	BITANCOURT José	21.04.1972	1	0	1993, Danubio FC Montevideo (1/0).
(677/944)	BIZERA BASTOS Joe Emerson	17.05.1980	23	1	2001-2004, CA Peñarol Montevideo (23/1).
(389/614)	BLANCO Juan Carlos		11	0	1971-1981
(700/979)	BLANCO SOTO Sergio Rubén	25.11.1981	4	1	2003-2006, Montevideo Wanderers FC (4/1).
(340/562)	BOGNI Carlos		1	0	1965
(95/157)	BONCHIANI Pascual		1	0	1923, CA Rosario Central (1/0).
(98/172)	BONDANZA Camilo		1	0	1924, Rampla Juniors FC Montevideo (1/0).
(391/621)	BONIFACINO Julían		2	0	1971
(255/440)	BORGES Carlos Ariel	14.01.1932	35	10	1954-1959, CA Peñarol Montevideo (35/10).
(537/811)	BORGES Edgar	15.07.1969	8	0	1988-1991, Danubio FC Montevideo (2/0), Club Nacional de Football Montevideo (6/0).
(165/285)	BORGES Ulises		2	0	1937, Rampla Juniors FC Montevideo (2/0).
(97/166)	BORJAS René	23.12.1897	7	3	1923-1928, Montevideo Wanderers FC (7/3).
(495/762)	BOSSIO BASTIANINI Miguel Angel	10.02.1960	30	1	1983-1986, CA Peñarol Montevideo (30/1).
(9/046)	BRACHI José		12	3	1908-1916, Dublin FC Montevideo (9/3), Club Nacional de Football Montevideo (3/0).
(5/029)	BRANDA Francisco		3	0	1906-1907, Montevideo Wanderers FC (3/0).
(267/450)	BRAZIONIS Ladislao		5	0	1956, Rampla Juniors FC Montevideo (5/0).
(46/101)	BRIENZA Antonio		1	0	1916, CA Defensor Montevideo (1/0).
(215/374)	BRITOS Julio César	18.05.1926	11	6	1947-1952, CA Peñarol Montevideo (8/4).
(699/969)	BROLI GORGOROSO Marcelo Carlo	13.03.1978	3	0	2002-2003, CtA Fénix Montevideo (3/0).
(44/099)	BRONCINI Alberto		1	0	1916, Central FC Montevideo (1/0).
(35/086)	BRONCINI Fausto		6	0	1914-1921, Central FC Montevideo (6/0).
(95/156)	BRUGNOLI Alfonso		3	0	1923-1924, Olimpia FC Montevideo (3/0).
(364/590)	BRUNEL Angel		4	0	1968-1970
(110/187)	BUCETTA Ramón		5	0	1924-1929, CA Lito (1/0), Club Nacional de Football Montevideo (4/0).
(12/053)	BUCK Robert Sidney		3	2	1909-1910, Montevideo Wanderers FC (3/2).
(462/739)	BUENO Heber		5	0	1980-1981, CA Bella Vista Montevideo (5/0).
(703/986)	BUENO SUÁREZ Carlos Eber	10.05.1980	24	13	2003-2008, CA Peñarol Montevideo (14/7), Sporting Clube de Portugal Lisboa (1/2), CA Boca Juniors Buenos Aires (3/1), CA Peñarol Montevideo (6/3).
(48/103)	BUFFONI Felipe		7	5	1916-1923, Montevideo Wanderers FC (7/5).
(410/644)	BURGOS Roberto		2	0	1974
(213/367)	BURGUEÑO Juan	1923	4	0	1947-1950, Danubio FC Montevideo

(308/517)	CABRERA Angel Rúben	09.10.1939	7	2	1961-1962, CA Peñarol Montevideo (7/2).
(419/656)	CABRERA Carlos		1	0	1975
(252/433)	CABRERA Juan Carlos		1	0	1953
(180/314)	CABRERA Juan Ramón		3	0	1940-1941, Club Nacional de Football Montevideo (3/0).
(515/774)	CABRERA LÓPEZ Jacinto Javier	17.02.1962	6	1	1985-1993, (5/1), Liverpool FC Montevideo (1/0).
(536/798)	CABRERA Nelson	18.07.1967	23	1	1988-1993, Danubio FC Montevideo (23/1).
(99/176)	CABRERA Pascual		6	0	1924-1925, Rampla Juniors FC Montevideo (6/0).
(81/131)	CABRERA Pedro		1	0	1921, CA Peñarol Montevideo (1/0).
(482/754)	CABRERA SAPPA Wilmar Rubens	31.07.1959	26	6	1983-1986, Club Nacional de Football Montevideo (15/5), Valencia CF (11/1).
(455/726)	CÁCERES Domingo Rufino	07.09.1959	7	0	1979-1980, CA Peñarol Montevideo (7/0).
(757/1034)	CÁCERES SILVA José Martín	07.04.1987	55	1	2007-2013, RC Recreativo de Huelva (6/0), FC Barcelona (7/0), Juventus FC Torino (8/0), Sevilla FC (17/1), Juventus FC Torino (17/0).
(166/287)	CADILLA Avelino		7	0	1937-1941, CA River Plate Montevideo (7/0).
(333/557)	CAETANO Omar	08.11.1938	30	0	1965-1969, CA Peñarol Montevideo (30/0).
(441/695)	CAILLAVA Miguel Rosifredo	14.11.1953	9	0	1977-1984, CA Peñarol Montevideo (9/0).
(204/354)	CAJIGA José		17	0	1945-1950, Rampla Juniors FC Montevideo (13/0).
(647/918)	CALLEJAS Christian Fabián	17.05.1978	14	1	1997-2001, Danubio FC Montevideo (14/1).
(352/575)	CALLERO Jacinto		1	0	1967, Club Nacional de Football Montevideo (1/0).
(3/021)	CAMACHO Aniceto		3	0	1905-1907, CURCC Montevideo (3/0).
(3/017)	CAMACHO Ceferino		6	0	1905-1908, CURCC Montevideo (6/0).
(165/286)	CAMAITÍ Adelaido		13	2	1937-1940, CA Peñarol Montevideo (13/2).
(330/548)	CÁMERA Francisco	01.01.1944	1	0	1964
(163/277)	CÁMERA Leofar		2	0	1936-1937, Club Nacional de Football Montevideo (2/0).
(304/508)	CAMPANELLA Jorge		1	0	1960
(279/469)	CAMPERO Luis Norberto		6	3	1957, Liverpool FC Montevideo (6/3).
(389/613)	CAMPO Francis		2	0	1971, Liverpool FC Montevideo (2/0).
(57/109)	CÁMPOLO Antonio	07.02.1897	21	3	1918-1929, CA Peñarol Montevideo (21/3).
(150/236)	CAMPOS Guillermo		1	0	1932, Institución Atlética Sud América Montevideo (1/0).
(603/861)	CANALS Ricardo	26.09.1970	4	0	1993-1995, Club Nacional de Football Montevideo (4/0).
(113/188)	CANAVESSI Adhemar	18.08.1903	9	0	1925-1928, CA Bella Vista Montevideo (9/0).
(12/054)	CANAVESSI Felipe		6	2	1909-1911, CURCC Montevideo (6/2).
(231/401)	CANCELA Nelson		3	1	1950-1952
(308/513)	CANO Núber		2	0	1961, CA Peñarol Montevideo (2/0).
(685/960)	CANOBBIO BENTABERRY Néstor Fabián	08.03.1980	9	0	2001-2006, CA Peñarol Montevideo (2/0), Valencia CF (1/0), RC Celta de Vigo (6/0).
(606/868)	CANOBBIO Osvaldo	27.06.1965	8	2	1993-1997, CA River Plate Montevideo (1/0), Club Nacional de Football Montevideo (6/2), CD Español Buenos Aires (1/0).
(519/778)	CANTERA Heber Silva		1	0	1985, Rampla Juniors FC Montevideo (1/0).
(231/405)	CANTOU Ramón		2	0	1950
(7/039)	CANTURY Alberto		4	0	1907-1908, Club Nacional de Football Montevideo (4/0).
(122/200)	CAPUCCINI Miguel	05.01.1904	6	0	1927, Montevideo Wanderers FC (6/0).
(106/186)	CAPUCCIO Vicente		1	0	1924, CA Lito (1/0).

(231/399)	CARÁMBULA Santos		**2**	**1**	1950
(99/179)	CARBALLAL José		**1**	**0**	1924, Rampla Juniors FC Montevideo (1/0).
(247/428)	CARBALLO Néstor	03.02.1929	**18**	**0**	1953-1958, Club Nacional de Football Montevideo (18/0).
(50/105)	CARBONE Américo		**6**	**0**	1917-1925, Dublín FC Montevideo (5/0), Club Atlético Uruguay Onward (1/0).
(1/005)	CARBONE Luis		**6**	**0**	1902-1908, Club Nacional de Football Montevideo (2/0), CURCC Montevideo (1/0), Club Nacional de Football Montevideo (3/0).
(138/224)	CARBONE Oscar		**1**	**1**	1929, CA Bella Vista Montevideo (1/1).
(772/1043)	CARDACCIO ALAGUICH Mathías Adolfo	02.09.1987	**1**	**0**	2008, Milan AC (1/0).
(395/631)	CARDACCIO Alberto Víctor	26.08.1949	**18**	**0**	1972-1974
(246/420)	CARDOZO Humberto		**1**	**0**	1953, CA Cerro Montevideo (1/0).
(652/925)	CARINI HERRNÁNDEZ Héctor Fabián	26.12.1979	**74**	**0**	1999-2009, Danubio FC Montevideo (20/0), Juventus FC Torino (18/0), R Standard Liège (1/0), Internazionale FC Milano (1/0), Cagliari Calcio (11/0), Internazionale FC Milano (13/0), Real Murcia CF (10/0).
(246/421)	CARRANZA Carlos María		**21**	**1**	1953-1957, CA Cerro Montevideo (21/1).
(393/626)	CARRASCO Alberto		**7**	**0**	1972
(424/670)	CARRASCO TORRES Juan Ramón	15.09.1956	**20**	**3**	1975-1985, Club Nacional de Football Montevideo (11/1), CF River Plate Buenos Aires (3/0), Club Nacional de Football Montevideo (1/0), CN Cúcuta Deportivo (5/1).
(161/267)	CARRERAS Rodolfo		**6**	**0**	1935-1937, Central FC Montevideo (6/0).
(156/260)	CARRÈRE Vicente		**1**	**0**	1934, Racing Club Montevideo (1/0).
(232/406)	CARRIZO Felipe		**1**	**0**	1950
(5/028)	CARVE Luis Piñeyro		**2**	**0**	1906-1907, Montevideo Wanderers FC (2/0).
(185/328)	CARVIDÓN Juan José		**5**	**0**	1941-1944, Montevideo Wanderers FC (1/0).
(78/124)	CASELLA Pedro	31.10.1898	**7**	**0**	1921-1923, CA Belgrano (7/0).
(79/128)	CASSANELLO Norberto		**11**	**0**	1921-1924, Montevideo Wanderers FC (11/0).
(134/214)	CASTALDO Antonio		**2**	**0**	1928, CA Defensor Montevideo (2/0).
(28/071)	CASTELLINO Francisco		**2**	**0**	1912-1916, Club Nacional de Football Montevideo (2/0).
(449/715)	CASTILLO Gary		**5**	**0**	1979, Institución Atlética Sud América Montevideo (5/0).
(757/1032)	CASTILLO IRIART Juan Guillermo	17.04.1978	**13**	**0**	2007-2011, CA Peñarol Montevideo (1/0), Botafogo FR Rio de Janeiro (10/0), AC Deportivo Cali (1/0).
(296/489)	CASTILLO Julio		**2**	**0**	1959, Rampla Juniors FC Montevideo (2/0).
(418/651)	CASTILLO Nery		**4**	**0**	1975
(28/072)	CASTRO Antonio Marques		**4**	**0**	1912-1916, Bristol FC Montevideo (1/0), Dublin FC Montevideo (3/0).
(151/244)	CASTRO Braulio		**10**	**0**	1932-1937, CA Peñarol Montevideo (10/0).
(8/041)	CASTRO Carlos Marques		**1**	**0**	1908, Bristol FC Montevideo (1/0).
(748/1031)	CASTRO DURET Pablo Adrián	18.01.1985	**1**	**0**	2007, CA Bella Vista Montevideo (1/0).
(187/332)	CASTRO Enrique		**1**	**0**	1942, Club Nacional de Football Montevideo (1/0).
(95/162)	CASTRO Héctor	29.11.1905	**25**	**18**	1923-1935, CA Lito (2/3), Club Nacional de Football Montevideo (23/15).
(731/1003)	CASTRO IRIZÁBAL Gonzalo	14.09.1984	**5**	**0**	2005-2013, Club Nacional de Football Montevideo (3/0), Real Sociedad de Fútbol San Sebastián (2/0).
(279/468)	CASTRO Jesús		**1**	**0**	1957, Institución Atlética Sud América Montevideo (1/0).
(186/330)	CASTRO Luis Ernesto		**18**	**4**	1942-1954, Club Nacional de Football Montevideo (17/4), Defensor Sporting Club Montevideo (1/0).
(326/541)	CASTRO Mario		**4**	**2**	1964
(206/362)	CASTRO Ramón		**11**	**5**	1946-1949, Montevideo Wanderers FC (4/1), Defensor Sporting Club Montevideo (7/4).
(575/832)	CASTRO Ramón Víctor	13.06.1964	**7**	**1**	1991, Montevideo Wanderers FC (7/1).
(544/814)	CASTRO William Adrián	22.05.1962	**9**	**2**	1989-1991, (8/2), CD Cruz Azul Ciudad de México (1/0).
(13/056)	CAVALLOTTI Ángel		**2**	**0**	1909-1914, Bristol FC Montevideo (1/0), CA River Plate Montevideo (1/0).
(762/1036)	CAVANI GÓMEZ Edinson Roberto	14.02.1987	**60**	**20**	2008-2013, US Città di Palermo (20/3), SSC Napoli (34/14), Paris Saint-Germain FC (6/3).
(93/155)	CEA José Pedro	01.09.1900	**27**	**13**	1923-1932, CA Lito (14/7), Club Nacional de Football Montevideo (13/6).
(561/818)	CEDRÉS VERA Gabriel Nestor	03.03.1970	**27**	**4**	1990-1991, CA Peñarol Montevideo (13/3), CA River Plate Buenos Aires (7/0), CA Boca Juniors Buenos Aires (2/0), CA Peñarol Montevideo (5/1).
(2/012)	CÉSPEDES Amílcar		**1**	**0**	1903, Club Nacional de Football Montevideo (1/0).
(1/007)	CÉSPEDES Bolívar		**2**	**1**	1902-1903, Club Nacional de Football Montevideo (2/1).
(1/011)	CÉSPEDES Carlos		**2**	**2**	1902-1903, Club Nacional de Football Montevideo (2/2).
(329/547)	CHABAY Nelson		**4**	**0**	1964-1966
(419/657)	CHAGAS Nil Roque		**5**	**0**	1975-1976, Danubio FC Montevideo (5/0).
(156/259)	CHANES Galileo		**5**	**0**	1934-1937, CA Peñarol Montevideo (5/0).
(290/478)	CHÁVEZ Carlos		**2**	**0**	1958-1959
(215/375)	CHELLE Oscar		**4**	**0**	1947-1948
(64/112)	CHERY Roberto	16.02.1896	**1**	**0**	1919, CA Peñarol Montevideo (1/0).
(677/947)	CHEVANTÓN ESPINOSA Ernesto Javier	12.08.1980	**22**	**7**	2001-2008, Danubio FC Montevideo (1/1), US Lecce (14/5), AS Monaco (6/1), Sevilla CF (1/0).
(156/258)	CHIFFLET Ulises		**1**	**0**	1934, Club Nacional de Football Montevideo (1/0).
(166/289)	CHIRIMINI Oscar		**19**	**3**	1937-1943, CA River Plate Montevideo (19/3).
(325/538)	CINCUNEGUI Héctor Carlos		**19**	**0**	1963-1967
(156/261)	CIOCCA Aníbal		**21**	**7**	1934-1943, Club Nacional de Football Montevideo (21/7).
(444/701)	CLAVIJO Freddy		**2**	**0**	1977, Defensor Sporting Club Montevideo (2/0).
(67/114)	CLAVIJO Vicente		**5**	**0**	1919, Reformers FC Montevideo (4/0), Club Nacional de Football Montevideo (1/0).
(161/266)	CLULOW Jorge Enrique		**3**	**0**	1935-1937, CA Peñarol Montevideo (3/0).

(802/1052)	COATES NIÓN Sebastián	07.10.1990	13	1	2011-2013, Club Nacional de Football Montevideo (5/0), Liverpool FC (8/1).
(307/512)	COBOS Oscar		1	0	1960
(648/921)	COELHO Walter Fabián	20.01.1977	16	1	1997, Club Nacional de Football Montevideo (16/1).
(195/338)	COLTURI José Pedro		5	0	1943-1945, CA Peñarol Montevideo (4/0).
(133/207)	CORAZO Juan Carlos		2	0	1928, Institución Atlética Sud América Montevideo (2/0).
(387/607)	CORBO Rubén Romeo	20.01.1952	22	0	1971-1974, CA Peñarol Montevideo (22/0).
(387/601)	CORBO Walter Luis	02.05.1949	11	0	1971-1976, CA Peñarol Montevideo (11/0).
(2/014)	CORDERO Alejandro		3	0	1903, Club Nacional de Football Montevideo (3/0).
(607/879)	CORREA AYALA Fernando Edgardo	06.01.1974	4	0	1994-2004, CA River Plate Montevideo (1/0), Racing Club Santander (1/0), RCD Mallorca (2/0).
(280/470)	CORREA Carlos		9	1	1957, Danubio FC Montevideo (9/1).
(540/812)	CORREA Carlos Gabriel	13.01.1968	19	2	1988-1990, CA River Plate Montevideo (1/0), CA Peñarol Montevideo (12/2), Real Murcia CF (6/0).
(191/333)	CORREA José María		2	0	1942, Institución Atlética Sud América Montevideo (1/0).
(421/664)	CORREA Omar		2	0	1975-1977, CA River Plate Montevideo (2/0).
(318/528)	CORTÉS Julio César	29.03.1941	31	3	1962-1970
(60/110)	COUTURE Sadi		2	0	1918, Dublín FC Montevideo (2/0).
(10/048)	CROCKER Federico		2	0	1908-1910, Dublín FC Montevideo (2/0).
(18/063)	CROSSLEY Leonardo		1	0	1910, CURCC Montevideo (1/0).
(183/326)	CRUCHE Ubaldo		2	1	1941, CA Peñarol Montevideo (2/1).
(427/674)	CRUZ José		1	0	1976
(247/429)	CRUZ Luis Alberto	28.04.1925	12	0	1953-1954, Club Nacional de Football Montevideo (12/0).
(3/019)	CUADRA Carlos María		1	0	1905, Club Nacional de Football Montevideo (1/0).
(298/494)	CUBILLA Luis Alberto	28.03.1940	38	11	1960-1974, CA Peñarol Montevideo (8/3), FC Barcelona (6/3), Club Nacional de Football Montevideo (24/5).
(310/519)	CUBILLA Pedro Ramón	25.05.1933	6	0	1961-1962, Rampla Juniors FC Montevideo (6/0).
(678/952)	CURBELO AGUETE Alejandro César	19.09.1973	3	0	2001, Montevideo Wanderers FC (3/0).
(713/997)	CURBELO GARIS Jorge Winston	21.12.1981	1	0	2004, Danubio FC Montevideo (1/0).
(701/981)	CURBELO GARIS Juan Ramón	02.05.1979	3	0	2003, CtA Fénix Montevideo (3/0).

(589/852)	DA LUZ Luis	02.06.1968	1	0	1992, Danubio FC Montevideo (1/0).
(478/750)	DA SILVA ECHEVERRITO Jorge Orosmán	11.12.1961	26	6	1982-1993, Defensor Sporting Club Montevideo (4/3), Real Valladolid CF (13/3), Club Atlético de Madrid (5/0), CD América de Cali (4/0).
(537/809)	DA SILVA ECHEVERRITO Rúben Fernando	11.04.1968	23	3	1988-2000, Danubio FC Montevideo (11/3), CA Boca Juniors Buenos Aires (2/0), CA Rosario Central (7/0), UNAM Guadalajara (1/0), Club Nacional de Football Montevideo (1/0).
(534/795)	DA SILVA Eduardo	18.08.1966	2	0	1987-1989, CA Peñarol Montevideo (2/0).
(8/043)	DACAL Pablo	1890	28	6	1908-1916, CA River Plate Montevideo (11/1), Club Nacional de Football Montevideo (17/5).
(679/955)	DADÓMO MINERVINI Claudio Martín	10.02.1982	3	0	2001-2003, Montevideo Wanderers FC (2/0), Club Nacional de Football Montevideo (1/0).
(298/491)	DALMAO Julio		11	0	1959-1968
(520/779)	DALTO Gustavo	16.03.1963	12	1	1985-1989, Danubio FC Montevideo (12/1).
(316/526)	DÁVILA Rúbens		1	0	1962
(254/438)	DAVOINE Mirto Lenin		1	0	1954, CA Peñarol Montevideo (1/0).
(272/455)	DAVOINE Walter		9	0	1956-1959
(231/404)	DE ANGELIS Luis		3	0	1950
(340/563)	DE BRITOS Miguel		1	0	1965
(2/015)	DE CASTRO Eduardo		1	0	1903, Club Nacional de Football Montevideo (1/0).
(450/718)	DE LA PEÑA Eduardo María	07.06.1955	19	1	1979-1981, Club Nacional de Football Montevideo (19/1).
(7/038)	DE LA SIERRA Juan Fernández		1	0	1907, Montevideo Wanderers FC (1/0).
(161/270)	DE LEÓN Arturo		2	0	1935-1938, Club Nacional de Football Montevideo (2/0).
(450/717)	DE LEÓN Hugo Eduardo	27.02.1958	48	0	1979-1990, Club Nacional de Football Montevideo (17/0), Gremio Porto Alegre (3/0), Club Nacional de Football Montevideo (13/0), CA River Plate Buenos Aires (15/0).
(704/987)	DE LEÓN JACUE Ignacio Leonardo	15.11.1977	1	0	2003, CtA Fénix Montevideo (1/0).
(407/637)	DE LIMA Nito		1	0	1973
(423/669)	DE LOS SANTOS Alfredo		25	0	1975-1983
(583/837)	DE LOS SANTOS Cesilio	12.02.1965	9	0	1991-1993, CF América Ciudad de México (9/0).
(629/906)	DE LOS SANTOS DA ROSA Gonzalo	19.07.1976	33	1	1996-2005, CA Peñarol Montevideo (9/1), CP Mérida (7/0), Málaga CF (3/0), Valencia CF (11/0), Club Atlético de Madrid (1/0), RCD Mallorca (2/0).
(214/371)	DE LUCCA José				1947
(5/031)	DE MIQUELERENA Rafael		3	0	1906-1907, Montevideo Wanderers FC (3/0).
(404/636)	DE SIMONE Gustavo	23.04.1948	7	0	1973-1974, Defensor Sporting Club Montevideo (7/0).
(308/514)	DE SOUZA Eladio		8	0	1961-1962,
(715/998)	DE SOUZA Marcelo Alejandro	30.09.1975	2	0	2004, CA Vélez Sarsfield (2/0).
(122/202)	DEAGUSTINI Luis		2	0	1927-1929, Montevideo Wanderers FC (2/0).
(138/222)	DEAGUSTINI Rodolfo		1	0	1929, Montevideo Wanderers FC (1/0).
(655/933)	DEL CAMPO Martín	24.05.1975	5	0	1999, Club Nacional de Football Montevideo (5/0).
(418/650)	DEL CAPELLÁN Eduardo	05.07.1953	3	0	1975-1977
(87/139)	DEL CIOPPO Orestes		1	0	1922, CA Belgrano (1/0)
(367/591)	DEL RIO Luis		3	0	1968
(162/271)	DELBONO Oscar		1	0	1935, Club Nacional de Football Montevideo (1/0).
(182/323)	DELGADO Alberto		1	0	1941, Rampla Juniors FC Montevideo (1/0).
(607/877)	DELGADO Darío	03.12.1969	1	0	1994, Montevideo Wanderers FC (1/0).
(30/078)	DELGADO Juan		16	0	1913-1920, Central FC Montevideo (7/0), CA Peñarol Montevideo (9/0).

(628/901)	DELGADO PAPARIELLO Javier Omar	08.07.1975	14	0	1996-2005, Danubio FC Montevideo (4/0), FK Saturn-REN TV Ramenskoye (10/0).
(6/034)	DEMARCHI Santiago		4	0	1907-1916, Club Nacional de Football Montevideo (4/0).
(263/443)	DEMARCO Héctor		14	3	1955-1959, Defensor Sporting Club Montevideo (14/3).
(157/263)	DENIS Luis María		7	0	1934-1940, Montevideo Wanderers FC (6/0).
(446/702)	DI BARTOLOMEO Eduardo		2	0	1978
(648/919)	DÍAZ Carlos	04.02.1979	6	0	1997-2001, Defensor Sporting Club Montevideo (6/0).
(532/787)	DÍAZ Gonzalo Lizardo	14.04.1966	1	0	1987, Montevideo Wanderers FC (1/0).
(326/539)	DÍAZ Nelson	12.01.1942	8	0	1964-1966
(701/980)	DIOGO ENSEÑAT Carlos Andrés	18.07.1983	22	0	2003-2007, CA River Plate Montevideo (3/0), CA Peñarol Montevideo (6/0), CA River Plate Montevideo (3/0), Real Madrid CF (5/0), Real Zaragoza CD (5/0).
(455/725)	DIOGO SILVA Víctor Hugo	09.04.1958	34	1	1979-1986, CA Peñarol Montevideo (20/1), Palmeiras (14/0).
(310/518)	DOGLIOTTI Luis		3	0	1961
(532/789)	DOMÍNGUEZ Alfonso Enrique	24.09.1965	31	0	1987-1990, CA Peñarol Montevideo (31/0).
(138/226)	DORADO Pablo	22.06.1908	7	3	1929-1932, CA Bella Vista Montevideo (7/3).
(563/820)	DORTA Diego Martín	31.12.1971	23	0	1990-1996, Central Español FC Montevideo (1/0), CA Peñarol Montevideo (20/0), CA Independiente Avellaneda (2/0).
(623/888)	DOS SANTOS Hebert	03.04.1974	1	0	1995, CA River Plate Montevideo (1/0).
(590/856)	DOS SANTOS Ricardo	19.04.1965	2	0	1992, Defensor Sporting Club Montevideo (1/0), CA River Plate Montevideo (1/0).
(573/830)	DOS SANTOS Rúben Fernando	16.11.1969	11	0	1991-1997, CA Peñarol Montevideo (5/0), Central Español FC Montevideo (3/0), CA Peñarol Montevideo (2/0), Defensor Sporting Club Montevideo (1/0).
(292/484)	DOUKSAS Vladas		34	3	1959-1966
(429/680)	DUARTE Juan José		2	0	1976-1977, CA Peñarol Montevideo (2/0).
(151/245)	DUHART Pedro	1910	2	0	1932, Club Nacional de Football Montevideo (2/0).
(19/064)	DURÁN GUANI José Maria		9	0	1911-1913, Bristol FC Montevideo (9/0).
(196/340)	DURÁN Ubire		14	0	1944-1952, Rampla Juniors FC Montevideo (6/0).
(39/090)	EGUÍA Dionisio		1	0	1915, Reformers FC Montevideo (1/0).
(677/950)	EGUREN LEDESMA Sebastián	08.01.1981	54	7	2001-2013, Montevideo Wanderers FC (8/0), Club Nacional de Football Montevideo (1/0), Villarreal CF (17/5), AIK Fotboll Stockholm (2/0), Real Sporting de Gijón (20/2), Club Libertad Asunción (5/0), SE Palmeiras São Paulo (1/0).
(695/963)	ELDUAYÉN SALDAÑA Federico Martín	25.06.1977	1	0	2002, CA Peñarol Montevideo (1/0).
(610/885)	ELÍAS Claudio	23.09.1974	4	0	1995, CA Progreso Montevideo (4/0).
(472/744)	ENRÍQUEZ Daniel	20.05.1958	1	0	1981, Club Nacional de Football Montevideo (1/0).
(266/447)	ESCALADA Guillermo	24.04.1936	31	11	1955-1962, Club Nacional de Football Montevideo (31/11).
(484/756)	ESNAL Raúl	23.04.1956	4	0	1983, Montevideo Wanderers FC (4/0).
(340/561)	ESPÁRRAGO Víctor Rodolfo	06.10.1944	41	1	1965-1974, CA Cerro Montevideo (2/0), Club Nacional de Football Montevideo (33/1), Sevilla CF (6/0).
(138/221)	ESTÍVEZ Cirilo		1	0	1929, Central FC Montevideo (1/0).
(681/958)	ESTOYANOFF POGGIO Fabián Larry	27.09.1982	31	4	2001-2007, CtA Fénix Montevideo (2/0), CA Peñarol Montevideo (7/0), CtA Fénix Montevideo (6/3), Cádiz CF (10/1), RC Deportivo La Coruña (6/0).
(757/1035)	EZQUERRA DE LEÓN Leandro	05.06.1986	1	0	2007, CA River Plate Montevideo (1/0).
(153/249)	FACCIO Ricardo Gregorio	12.03.1907	3	0	1933-1938, Club Nacional de Football Montevideo (3/0).
(170/292)	FAGER Roberto		3	0	1937-1939, Montevideo Wanderers FC (3/0).
(10/047)	FALCO Aníbal Zapicán		4	0	1908-1909, Club Nacional de Football Montevideo
(466/741)	FALERO Miguel		1	1	1980
(200/352)	FALERO Nicolás		14	12	1945-1948, Central FC Montevideo (5/2), CA Peñarol Montevideo (9/10).
(430/684)	FARAL Gustavo	15.07.1950	1	0	1976, CA Peñarol Montevideo (1/0).
(29/076)	FARINASSO Antonio		6	1	1913-1916, Universal FC Montevideo (6/1).
(135/217)	FEDULLO Francisco	27.05.1905	1	0	1928, Institución Atlética Sud América Montevideo (1/0).
(278/466)	FERNÁNDEZ Ariel		2	0	1957, CA Cerro Montevideo (2/0).
(151/243)	FERNÁNDEZ Arsenio		4	0	1932-1933, Club Nacional de Football Montevideo (4/0).
(153/251)	FERNÁNDEZ Atilio		2	0	1933, Club Nacional de Football Montevideo (2/0).
(153/250)	FERNÁNDEZ Enrique		8	1	1933-1935, Club Nacional de Football Montevideo (8/1).
(775/1044)	FERNÁNDEZ GAY Álvaro	11.10.1985	12	0	2009-2012, Club Nacional de Football Montevideo (3/0), Vitória FC Setúbal (4/0), CF Universidad de Chile Santiago (4/0), Chicago Fire Soccer Club (1/0).
(408/638)	FERNÁNDEZ Gustavo Daniel	16.02.1952	5	0	1974, CA Rentistas Montevideo (5/0).
(392/625)	FERNÁNDEZ Hugo		5	0	1971-1975
(114/193)	FERNÁNDEZ Lorenzo	22.05.1900	31	4	1925-1935, CA Capurro (16/0), CA Peñarol Montevideo (15/4).
(740/1020)	FERNÁNDEZ MIGLIERINA Sebastián Bruno	23.05.1985	14	2	2006-2012, CS Miramar Misiones Montevideo (1/0), Defensor Sporting Club Montevideo (2/0), CA Banfield (5/0), Málaga CF (6/2).
(274/459)	FERNÁNDEZ Roque		7	0	1956-1959
(478/747)	FERRARI José Luis		4	0	1982
(390/619)	FERREIRA Angel		4	1	1971-1972
(242/416)	FERREIRA Omar		3	0	1952
(606/865)	FERRERI Juan	13.07.1970	2	0	1993-1998, Defensor Sporting Club Montevideo (2/0).
(326/544)	FERRERO Alberto		2	0	1964
(206/363)	FERRÉS Ramón		2	0	1946-1952
(571/824)	FERREYRA Gustavo	29.05.1972	5	1	1991, CA Peñarol Montevideo (5/1).
(541/813)	FERRO Oscar	02.03.1967	9	0	1988-1995, CA Peñarol Montevideo (8/0), CA Ferro Carril Oeste Buenos Aires (1/0).

(156/262)	FIGLIOLA Manuel		**1**	**0**	1934, Racing Club Montevideo (1/0).
(81/133)	FIGUEROA Roberto	20.03.1904	**9**	**6**	1921-1933, Montevideo Wanderers FC (1/0), Club Nacional de Football Montevideo (1/1), Montevideo Wanderers FC (7/5).
(745/1025)	FILGUEIRA Gastón	08.01.1986	**2**	**0**	2006, Central Español FC Montevideo (2/0).
(644/912)	FLEURQUIN RUBIO José Andrés	02.08.1975	**11**	**0**	1997-2001, Defensor Sporting Club Montevideo (8/0), SK Sturm Graz (3/0).
(735/1010)	FLORES BISTOLFI Darío Antonio	06.02.1984	**1**	**0**	2005, CA River Plate Montevideo (1/0).
(763/1039)	FLORES BISTOLFI Robert Mario	13.05.1986	**2**	**0**	2008, CA River Plate Montevideo (2/0).
(646/914)	FLORES Claudio	10.05.1976	**4**	**0**	1997, CA Peñarol Montevideo (4/0).
(326/540)	FLORES Nelson		**5**	**0**	1964
(24/070)	FOGLINO Alfredo	1893	**47**	**0**	1912-1923, Club Nacional de Football Montevideo (47/0).
(561/816)	FONSECA Daniel	13.09.1969	**30**	**10**	1990-1997, Club Nacional de Football Montevideo (6/1), SSC Napoli (9/4), AS Roma (13/5), Juventus FC Torino (2/0).
(363/587)	FONTES Dagoberto	06.06.1943	**13**	**0**	1968-1970, Defensor Sporting Club Montevideo (13/0).
(691/962)	FORLÁN CORAZO Diego Martín	19.05.1979	**107**	**36**	2002-2013, Manchester United FC (22/9), Villarreal FC (20/6), Club Atlético de Madrid (40/16), Internazionale FC Milano (6/2), SC Internacional Porto Alegre (19/3).
(345/574)	FORLÁN Pablo Justo	14.07.1945	**18**	**0**	1966-1976, CA Peñarol Montevideo (12/0), Sao Paulo FC (6/0)
(408/639)	FORLÁN RESOVA Richard		**5**	**0**	1974-1975, Montevideo Wanderers FC (5/0).
(577/834)	FRACCHIA Marcelo	04.01.1968	**7**	**0**	1991, Central Español FC Montevideo (7/0).
(70/121)	FRAGA Arturo		**1**	**1**	1919, Central FC Montevideo (1/1).
(478/748)	FRANCÉSCOLI URIARTE Enzo	12.11.1961	**73**	**17**	1982-1997, Montevideo Wanderers FC (4/0), CA River Plate Buenos Aires (22/7), FC Matra Racing Paris (11/4), Olympique de Marseille (9/1), Torino Calcio (9/2), CA River Plate Buenos Aires (18/3).
(163/281)	FRANCO Euclides		**1**	**0**	1936, Institución Atlética Sud América Montevideo (1/0).
(340/560)	FRANCO Horacio		**3**	**0**	1965-1967
(472/746)	FRANCO Julio		**2**	**0**	1981-1982
(672/942)	FRANCO RAMALLO José María	28.09.1978	**1**	**0**	2000, CA Peñarol Montevideo (1/0).
(149/233)	FRIONI Arturo		**1**	**0**	1931, Montevideo Wanderers FC (1/0).
(6/035)	FROMMEL Marcos		**3**	**0**	1907-1908, Club Nacional de Football Montevideo (3/0).
(740/1018)	FUCILE PERDOMO Jorge Ciro	19.11.1984	**40**	**0**	2006-2013, Liverpool FC Montevideo (2/0), FC do Porto (32/0), Santos FC (1/0), FC do Porto (5/0).

(224/385)	GADEA Roberto		**7**	**0**	1949, Miramar (7/0).
(137/220)	GAITÁN Luis		**1**	**0**	1929, Rampla Juniors FC Montevideo (1/0).
(161/268)	GALVALISI Eugenio		**11**	**0**	1935-1939, Rampla Juniors FC Montevideo (10/0), Club Nacional de Football Montevideo (1/0).
(253/435)	GALVÁN Américo Natalio		**7**	**3**	1954-1955, CA Peñarol Montevideo (7/3).
(182/324)	GAMBETTA Schubert	14.04.1920	**35**	**3**	1941-1952, Club Nacional de Football Montevideo (35/3).
(12/051)	GARCÍA Alberto		**2**	**0**	1909, CA River Plate Montevideo (2/0).
(198/350)	GARCÍA Atilio	26.08.1914	**5**	**5**	1945, Club Nacional de Football Montevideo (5/5).
(735/1006)	GARCÍA CUÑA Carlos Andrés	06.11.1979	**1**	**0**	2005, Liverpool FC Montevideo (1/0).
(746/1029)	GARCÍA ECHEVERRÍA Jorge Adrián	19.08.1986	**1**	**0**	2006, Danubio FC Montevideo (1/0).
(140/227)	GARCÍA Eduardo		**3**	**0**	1929-1934, Club Nacional de Football Montevideo (3/0).
(389/618)	GARCÍA Eduardo		**1**	**0**	1971
(198/349)	GARCÍA José		**21**	**4**	1945-1948, Defensor Sporting Club Montevideo (19/4).
(589/853)	GARCÍA José Enrique	23.12.1967	**3**	**0**	1992, Club Nacional de Football Montevideo (3/0).
(224/394)	GARCÍA José María		**6**	**2**	1949, Montevideo Wanderers FC (6/2).
(150/240)	GARCÍA Juan José		**3**	**2**	1932-1934, Rampla Juniors FC Montevideo (3/2).
(646/915)	GARCÍA PÉREZ Pablo Gabriel	11.05.1977	**65**	**2**	1997-2007, Wanderers FC Montevideo (5/0), Club Atlético de Madrid (14/1), Milan AC (6/0), AC Venezia (13/0), CA Osasuna Pamplona (8/0), Real Madrid CF (9/0), RC Celta de Vigo (8/1), Real Murcia CF (2/0).
(224/387)	GARCÍA Roberto		**7**	**0**	1949, Montevideo Wanderers FC (7/0).
(224/388)	GARCÍA Simón		**7**	**0**	1949, Montevideo Wanderers FC (7/0).
(742/1021)	GARGANO GUEVARA Walter Alejandro	27.07.1984	**60**	**1**	2006-2013, Danubio FC Montevideo (8/0), SSC Napoli (35/1), FC Internazionale Milano (13/0), Parma FC (4/0).
(410/643)	GARISTO PAN Luis	03.12.1945	**4**	**0**	1974, CA Peñarol Montevideo (4/0).
(651/924)	GASTÁN Mario	11.12.1969	**1**	**0**	1998, Defensor Sporting Club Montevideo (1/0).
(205/360)	GELPI Domingo		**1**	**0**	1946
(98/173)	GEMELLI Juan		**1**	**0**	1924, CA Fénix (1/0).
(122/201)	GESTIDO Álvaro Antonio	17.05.1907	**26**	**0**	1927-1940, Sporting Club Solferino (7/0), CA Peñarol Montevideo (19/0).
(93/153)	GHIERRA Alfredo Juan	31.08.1891	**14**	**0**	1923-1926, Universal FC Montevideo (13/0), Club Nacional de Football Montevideo (1/0).
(234/410)	GHIGGIA Alcides Edgardo	22.12.1926	**12**	**4**	1950-1952, CA Peñarol Montevideo (12/4).
(665/937)	GIACOMAZZI SUÁREZ Guillermo Gonzalo	21.11.1977	**17**	**0**	2000-2007, CA Peñarol Montevideo (4/0), US Lecce (13/0).
(328/546)	GIL Roberto		**8**	**0**	1964-1966
(763/1038)	GIMÉNEZ BÁEZ Henry Damián	13.03.1986	**2**	**0**	2008, CA River Plate Montevideo (2/0).
(836/1057)	GIMÉNEZ DE VARGAS José María	20.01.1995	**3**	**0**	2013, Club Atlético de Madrid (3/0).
(446/704)	GIMÉNEZ Rúben		**3**	**0**	1978
(323/535)	GIMENEZ Walter		**1**	**0**	1962
(213/368)	GODART José		**2**	**0**	1947
(735/1005)	GODÍN LEAL Diego Roberto	16.02.1986	**75**	**3**	2005-2013, CA Cerro Montevideo (7/1), Club Nacional de Football Montevideo (6/2), Villarreal CF (30/0), Club Atlético de Madrid (32/0).
(446/705)	GODOY Daniel		**1**	**0**	1978, Danubio FC Montevideo (1/0).
(378/597)	GÓMEZ Alberto	10.06.1944	**4**	**0**	1970, Liverpool FC Montevideo (4/0).
(303/505)	GÓMEZ Jorge		**6**	**0**	1960-1961

(411/647)	GÓMEZ José César	23.10.1949	**3**	**0**	1974, CA Cerro Montevideo (1/0).
(410/645)	GÓMEZ José Gervasio	23.10.1949	**1**	**0**	1974, CA Cerro Montevideo (1/0).
(586/849)	GÓMEZ Julio César 'Tony'	11.11.1972	**8**	**0**	1992-1997, Club Nacional de Football Montevideo (8/0).
(205/357)	GÓMEZ Walter		**4**	**0**	1945-1946, Central FC Montevideo (4/0).
(536/797)	GONÇALVES Jorge Miguel	05.02.1967	**9**	**0**	1988-1996, CA Peñarol Montevideo (7/0), CA Cerro Montevideo (2/0).
(281/471)	GONÇALVES Néstor	27.04.1936	**50**	**0**	1957-1971, CA Peñarol Montevideo (49/0), *unattached* (1/0).
(342/568)	GONZÁLEZ ACUÑA Pedro		**1**	**0**	1966
(699/964)	GONZÁLEZ AIDINOVICH Cristian Mario	19.12.1976	**8**	**0**	2002-2004, Defensor Sporting Club Montevideo (4/0), UD Las Palmas (4/0).
(278/465)	GONZÁLEZ Edgardo Nilson	30.09.1936	**21**	**0**	1957-1965, Liverpool FC Montevideo (21/0).
(418/648)	GONZÁLEZ Edison	23.02.1949	**3**	**0**	1975, Liverpool FC Montevideo (3/0).
(738/1013)	GONZÁLEZ GATTI Ignacio María	14.05.1982	**19**	**1**	2006-2010, Danubio FC Montevideo (10/0), AS Monaco (5/1), Newcastle United FC (1/0), Levadiakos FC Levadia (2/0), Levante UD Valencia (1/0).
(449/711)	GONZÁLEZ Jorge	26.09.1954	**4**	**0**	1979-1980
(606/862)	GONZÁLEZ José	02.11.1968	**1**	**0**	1993, Defensor Sporting Club Montevideo (1/0).
(133/212)	GONZÁLEZ Juan		**2**	**1**	1928, Uruguay Club (2/1).
(624/894)	GONZÁLEZ Juan	27.05.1972	**4**	**0**	1995-1999, Club Nacional de Football Montevideo (3/0), Real Oviedo CF (1/0).
(234/411)	GONZÁLEZ Juan Carlos	22.08.1924	**7**	**0**	1950-1952
(740/1019)	GONZÁLEZ LUENGO Álvaro Rafael	29.10.1984	**41**	**1**	2006-2013, Defensor Sporting Club Montevideo (4/0), CA Boca Juniors Buenos Aires (6/0), Club Nacional de Football Montevideo (1/0), SS Lazio Roma (30/1).
(393/627)	GONZÁLEZ Mario	27.05.1950	**16**	**0**	1972-1976, CA Peñarol Montevideo (16/0).
(224/384)	GONZÁLEZ Matías	06.08.1925	**30**	**0**	1949-1956, CA Cerro Montevideo (29/0).
(298/492)	GONZÁLEZ Rúben Adán	1939	**12**	**0**	1959-1962, Club Nacional de Football Montevideo (10/0).
(178/310)	GONZÁLEZ Sixto		**7**	**1**	1940-1942, Liverpool FC Montevideo (7/1).
(266/446)	GONZÁLEZ Waldemar		**1**	**0**	1955, Club Nacional de Football Montevideo (1/0).
(448/706)	GONZÁLEZ Washington		**32**	**0**	1978-1983, Defensor Sporting Club Montevideo (5/0), Club Nacional de Football Montevideo (27/0).
(29/075)	GORLA Lucio		**4**	**2**	1913, Club Nacional de Football Montevideo (4/2).
(172/298)	GORLA Lucio		**1**	**0**	1938, Liverpool FC Montevideo (1/0).
(460/730)	GOYÉN PRIETO Carlos Mario	14.08.1955	**1**	**0**	1980, CA River Plate Montevideo (1/0).
(37/088)	GRADÍN Isabelino	08.07.1897	**24**	**10**	1915-1927, CA Peñarol Montevideo (22/10), Olimpia FC Montevideo (2/0).
(431/689)	GRAFFIGNA Pedro	23.09.1945	**14**	**0**	1976-1978, Defensor Sporting Club Montevideo (14/0).
(174/302)	GRANERO Horacio		**4**	**0**	1939, Central FC Montevideo (4/0).
(29/073)	GRANJA Alfredo		**6**	**0**	1913-1924, Reformers FC Montevideo (2/0), CA Peñarol Montevideo (4/0).
(735/1009)	GRANOCHE LOURO Pablo Mariano	05.09.1983	**1**	**0**	2005, Deportivo Toluca FC (1/0).
(710/992)	GROSSMÜLLER Carlos Javier	04.05.1983	**2**	**0**	2003-2007, Danubio FC Montevideo (3/0), FC Schalke 04 Gelsenkirchen (1/0).
(584/843)	GUERRA Hugo Romeo	18.03.1966	**8**	**1**	1992-1993, Club Gimnasia y Esgrima de La Plata (8/1).
(292/483)	GUGLIANONE Víctor Homero	1937	**8**	**4**	1959-1960, Montevideo Wanderers FC (8/4).
(679/956)	GUGLIELMONE GÓMEZ Walter	11.04.1978	**2**	**0**	2001, Montevideo Wanderers FC (2/0).
(653/932)	GUIGOU MARTÍNEZ Gianni Bismark	22.02.1975	**40**	**0**	1999-2004, Club Nacional de Football Montevideo (12/0), AS Roma (27/0), AC Siena (1/0).
(678/953)	GUTIÉRREZ Carlos	25.12.1976	**5**	**0**	2001, CA River Plate Montevideo (5/0).
(482/752)	GUTIÉRREZ LUONGO Nelson Daniel	13.04.1962	**57**	**0**	1983-1990, CA Peñarol Montevideo (27/0), CA River Plate Buenos Aires (12/0), SS Lazio Roma (8/0), Hellas Verona (10/0).
(572/829)	GUTIÉRREZ PELSCHER Álvaro	21.07.1968	**38**	**1**	1991-1997, CA Bella Vista Montevideo (10/1), Club Nacional de Football Montevideo (20/0), Real Valladolid CF (8/0).
(571/827)	GUTIÉRREZ William	29.03.1963	**7**	**0**	1991, Defensor Sporting Club Montevideo (7/0).
(149/235)	HAEBERLI Conrado		**3**	**2**	1931-1933, Rampla Juniors FC Montevideo (3/2).
(12/052)	HARLEY Juan	05.03.1886	**17**	**0**	1909-1916, CURCC Montevideo (10/0), CA Peñarol Montevideo (7/0).
(82/137)	HEGUY Juan Carlos		**2**	**1**	1922, Central FC Montevideo (2/1)
(172/299)	HERNÁNDEZ Enrique		**2**	**0**	1938, Club Nacional de Football Montevideo (2/0).
(628/900)	HERNÁNDEZ Pablo	02.05.1975	**7**	**0**	1996-1997, Defensor Sporting Club Montevideo (7/0).
(794/1050)	HERNÁNDEZ PLATERO Abel Mathías	08.08.1990	**11**	**7**	2010-2013, US Città de Palermo (11/7).
(710/991)	HERNÁNDEZ SPINELLI Williams Daniel	20.01.1982	**1**	**0**	2003, CSyD Villa Española Montevideo (1/0).
(536/796)	HERRERA COROMINAS José Oscar	17.06.1965	**57**	**4**	1988-1997, CA Peñarol Montevideo (19/3), UE Figueres (11/0), Cagliari Calcio (17/1), Atalanta Bergamasca Calcio (7/0), CDSC Cruz Azul Ciudad de México (3/0).
(253/437)	HOHBERG Juan Eduardo	08.10.1926	**8**	**3**	1954-1959, CA Peñarol Montevideo (8/3).
(133/213)	HOHL Arturo		**2**	**0**	1928, CA Peñarol Montevideo (2/0).
(699/967)	HORNOS COREEA Germán Andrés	21.08.1982	**7**	**1**	2002-2004, CtA Fénix Montevideo (3/1), Sevilla CF (4/0).
(326/543)	IBAÑEZ Abayubá		**15**	**0**	1964-1971
(138/223)	IBARRA Alberto		**1**	**0**	1929, Misiones FC (1/0).
(155/257)	ICARDI Oliver		**1**	**0**	1933, Institución Atlética Sud América Montevideo (1/0).
(133/210)	IGARZÁBAL Juan		**1**	**0**	1928, Misiones FC (1/0)
(298/496)	INCHAUSPE Héctor		**1**	**0**	1959
(498/766)	INZÚA Roberto		**1**	**0**	1984
(145/231)	IRIARTE Victoriano Santos	02.11.1902	**5**	**2**	1930-1931, Racing Club Montevideo (5/2).
(150/242)	ITHURBIDE Eduardo		**7**	**0**	1932-1937, Montevideo Wanderers FC (2/0), Club Nacional de Football Montevideo (5/0).

(745/1024)	ITHURRALDE SÁEZ Ignacio	30.05.1983	2	0	2006-2007, Defensor Sporting Club Montevideo (2/0).
(395/630)	JÁUREGUI Baudilio Jorge	09.07.1945	9	0	1972-1974
(431/688)	JAVIER Beethoven	20.06.1947	5	0	1976-1977, Defensor Sporting Club Montevideo (5/0).
(391/623)	JIMÉNEZ Julio César	27.08.1954	19	1	1971-1976, CA Peñarol Montevideo (16/1).
(629/907)	JONNE Luis	18.07.1975	1	0	1996, CA Cerro Montevideo (1/0).
(331/550)	JOYA Juan		1	0	1965, CA Peñarol Montevideo (1/0).
(4/024)	JUÁREZ Carlos Cibils		1	0	1906, Club Nacional de Football Montevideo (1/0).
(584/840)	KANAPKIS GARCÍA Fernando Alfredo	06.06.1966	20	5	1992-1993, Club Nacional de Football Montevideo (3/1), Danubio FC Montevideo (3/0), CD Mandiyú (13/4), CA Mineiro Belo Horizonte (1/0).
(427/676)	KEOSSEIÁN Manuel Gregorio	17.08.1953	3	0	1976, Danubio FC Montevideo (3/0).
(305/510)	KHUN Siegfried		3	0	1960
(450/720)	KRASOUSKI Ariel José	31.05.1958	17	2	1979-1981, Montevideo Wanderers FC (17/2).
(290/479)	KULYS Alberto		2	0	1958
(224/383)	LA PAZ Jorge		5	0	1949, CA Peñarol Montevideo (5/0).
(150/239)	LABRAGA Juan Miguel		2	0	1932-1933, Rampla Juniors FC Montevideo (2/0).
(427/675)	LACLAU Jorge		1	0	1976, Club Nacional de Football Montevideo (1/0).
(702/982)	LAGO COREEA Eduardo Alejandro	28.06.1979	16	0	2003-2004, CA Peñarol Montevideo (9/0), CtA Fénix Montevideo (7/0).
(138/225)	LAGO Pedro		8	4	1929-1940, CA Bella Vista Montevideo (1/0), CA Peñarol Montevideo (5/4).
(370/593)	LAMAS Alfredo		1	0	1968
(32/083)	LANDEIRA Alberto		1	0	1913, Central FC Montevideo (1/0).
(311/522)	LANGÓN Ronald Arturo	06.08.1939	11	0	1961-1966
(585/847)	LARREA MARZOL Alejandro Javier	05.12.1966	2	1	1992, Central Español FC Montevideo (2/1).
(173/300)	LARROSA Eduardo		1	0	1938, CA River Plate Montevideo (1/0).
(387/606)	LATTUADA Pierino		11	1	1971-1972, Liverpool FC Montevideo (11/1).
(34/085)	LÁZARO Manuel		4	1	1913-1915, Club Nacional de Football Montevideo (4/1).
(150/237)	LEGARBURO Alberto		1	0	1932, CA Defensor Montevideo (1/0).
(72/122)	LEGNAZZI Juan		7	0	1920-1923, CA Peñarol Montevideo (7/0).
(700/976)	LEGUIZAMÓN MARTÍNEZ Mario Evaristo	07.07.1982	1	0	2003, CA Peñarol Montevideo (1/0).
(276/461)	LEITCH Oscar		2	0	1956
(358/582)	LEITES Rafael		2	0	1967
(294/487)	LEIVA Juan Carlos		2	0	1959, Rampla Juniors FC Montevideo (2/0).
(388/611)	LEIVA Miguel		1	0	1971
(652/927)	LEMBO Daniel Alejandro	15.02.1978	38	2	1999-2004, CA Bella Vista Montevideo (9/1), Club Nacional de Football Montevideo (25/1), Real Betis Balompié Sevilla (4/0).
(745/1022)	LEMES RODRÍGUEZ Gonzalo Daniel	28.05.1980	2	0	2006, Central Español FC Montevideo (2/0).
(628/902)	LEMOS ROSENDE Rodrigo Javier	03.10.1973	8	1	1996-2001, Club Nacional de Football Montevideo (2/0), CA Bella Vista Montevideo (6/1)
(587/850)	LEMOS Yubert	12.06.1962	1	0	1992, Club Nacional de Football Montevideo (1/0).
(253/434]	LEOPARDI Roberto Rafael	19.07.1933	7	0	1954-1956, Club Nacional de Football Montevideo (7/0).
(277/463)	LEZCANO José Pedro		6	0	1956-1959, Danubio FC Montevideo (6/0).
(449/716)	LEZCUÉ Carlos		1	0	1979
(81/129)	LIETTI Marcos		1	0	1921, Universal FC Montevideo (1/0).
(699/966)	LIGÜERA LÓPEZ Martín Ricardo	09.11.1980	15	7	2002-2005, CtA Fénix Montevideo (8/7), RCD Mallorca (6/0), Club Real San Luis FC Potosí (1/0).
(677/945)	LIMA OLID Pablo Martín	26.03.1981	14	1	2001-2007, Danubio FC Montevideo (14/1).
(627/897)	LIMA Robert	18.06.1972	1	0	1996, CA Peñarol Montevideo (1/0).
(150/238)	LOBOS Abraham		3	0	1932-1933, CA Lito (2/0), Montevideo Wanderers FC (1/0).
(783/1049)	LODEIRO BENÍTEZ Marcelo Nicolás	21.03.1989	24	3	2009-2013, Club Nacional de Football Montevideo (2/0), AFC Ajax Amsterdam (10/1), Botafogo de FR Rio de Janeiro (12/2).
(163/279)	LONGO Felipe		1	0	1936, Institución Atlética Sud América Montevideo (1/0).
(571/823)	LÓPEZ BÁEZ Henry	03.07.1967	8	1	1991, CA Bella Vista Montevideo (8/1).
(607/871)	LÓPEZ BREIJO Luis Diego	22.08.1974	39	0	1994-2005, CA River Plate Montevideo (8/0), Racing Club Santander (8/0), Cagliari Calcio (23/0).
(739/1016)	LÓPEZ GASCO Walter Alberto	15.10.1985	3	0	2006, CA River Plate Montevideo (3/0).
(99/180)	LÓPEZ Julio		1	0	1924, CA Lito (1/0).
(778/1047)	LÓPEZ MORA Hernán Rodrigo	21.01.1978	1	0	2009, CA Vélez Sarsfield Buenos Aires (1/0).
(628/905)	LÓPEZ Rodrigo	21.01.1978	1	0	1996, CA River Plate Montevideo (1/0).
(571/825)	LÓPEZ Víctor	09.04.1971	8	1	1991-1997, CA Peñarol Montevideo (7/1), CA Ferro Carril Oeste Buenos Aires (1/0).
(340/564)	LORDA Homero		1	0	1965
(420/663)	LORENZO José		4	0	1975, CA Cerro Montevideo (4/0).
(196/339)	LORENZO Mario		11	0	1944-1948, CA Peñarol Montevideo (6/0),
(378/596)	LOSADA Julio Daniel	16.06.1950	5	0	1970, CA Peñarol Montevideo (5/0).
(243/418)	LOUREIRO Washington		2	1	1952
(4/023)	LOURTET Félix		3	0	1906-1909, CA River Plate Montevideo (3/0).
(700/972)	LUGANO MORENA Diego Alfredo	02.11.1980	91	9	2003-2013, Club Nacional de Football Montevideo (1/0), São Paulo FC (9/0), Fenerbahçe SK Istanbul (53/5), Paris St. Germain FC (13/3), Málaga FC (9/1), West Bromwich Albion FC (6/0).
(359/583)	LUGO Luis Gómez		1	0	1967
(638/908)	LUJAMBIO Josemir	25.09.1971	5	0	1997, CA Huracán Corrientes (5/0).
(462/738)	LUZARDO Roberto Arsenio	04.09.1959	11	2	1980-1983, Club Nacional de Football Montevideo (11/2).
(152/246)	MACCHIAVELLO Héctor		2	0	1932-1935, Racing Club Montevideo (2/0).

(255/439)	MACEIRAS Julio César	22.04.1926	**8**	**0**	1954-1956, Danubio FC Montevideo (8/0).
(623/889)	MAGALLANES GONZÁLEZ Gerardo Federico	28.08.1976	**26**	**6**	1995-2002, CA Peñarol Montevideo (2/0), Racing Club Santander (7/2), Defensor Sporting Club Montevideo (5/2), Racing Club Santander (3/1), AC Venezia (9/1).
(141/228)	MAGALLANES José		**2**	**0**	1929, Rampla Juniors FC Montevideo (2/0).
(181/321)	MAGLIANO Héctor		**14**	**5**	1940-1948, Montevideo Wanderers FC (14/5).
(153/248)	MAGNO Félix		**1**	**0**	1933, Club Nacional de Football Montevideo (1/0).
(298/490)	MAIDANA Luis María	24.02.1934	**11**	**0**	1959-1969
(314/525)	MAJEWSKI Alejandro		**4**	**0**	1962
(370/592)	MALDONADO Juan		**1**	**0**	1968
(308/515)	MALINOWSKI Estanislao Francisco		**2**	**0**	1961
(6/037)	MANANA Eugenio		**1**	**0**	1907, CURCC Montevideo (1/0).
(205/358)	MAÑAY Alcides		**4**	**0**	1946-1947, Defensor Sporting Club Montevideo (4/0).
(378/598)	MANEIRO Ildo Enrique	04.08.1947	**33**	**3**	1970-1979, Club Nacional de Football Montevideo (25/2), CA Peñarol Montevideo (8/1).
(268/451)	MANGHINI Washington		**4**	**0**	1956, Danubio FC Montevideo (4/0).
(323/533)	MANICERA Jorge Carlos	04.11.1938	**22**	**0**	1962-1967, Club Nacional de Football Montevideo (19/0), Flamengo Rio de Janeiro (3/0).
(9/045)	MANITO Guillermo		**1**	**0**	1908, CURCC Montevideo (1/0).
(317/527)	MANRIQUE Edil		**2**	**0**	1962
(387/605)	MANTEGAZZA Walter Daniel	17.06.1952	**11**	**1**	1971-1974, Club Nacional de Football Montevideo (10/1).
(42/096)	MARÁN Rodolfo		**14**	**0**	1916-1923, Universal FC Montevideo (4/0), Club Nacional de Football Montevideo (10/0).
(452/721)	MARCENARO Nelson Luis	04.09.1952	**8**	**0**	1979-1981, CA Peñarol Montevideo (8/0).
(45/100)	MARENCO Manuel		**1**	**0**	1916, Montevideo Wanderers FC (1/0).
(278/464)	MARICHAL Walter		**3**	**0**	1957-1958, Club Nacional de Football Montevideo (3/0).
(133/206)	MARINI Ángel		**2**	**0**	1928, CA Lito (2/0).
(78/125)	MARROCHE Sebastián		**1**	**0**	1921, Club Nacional de Football Montevideo (1/0).
(537/808)	MARTÍNEZ ALZURI Sergio Daniel	15.02.1969	**35**	**5**	1988-1997, Defensor Sporting Club Montevideo (15/2), CA Peñarol Montevideo (6/1), CA Boca Juniors Buenos Aires (14/2).
(590/855)	MARTÍNEZ Andrés	16.10.1972	**8**	**1**	1992-2001, CA Peñarol Montevideo (2/0), Defensor Sporting Club Montevideo (6/1).
(702/984)	MARTÍNEZ BARRIOS Jorge Andrés	05.04.1983	**14**	**1**	2003-2010, Montevideo Wanderers FC (7/0), Club Nacional de Football Montevideo (1/0), Catania Calcio (6/1).
(166/288)	MARTÍNEZ Carlos		**12**	**0**	1937-1941, Rampla Juniors FC Montevideo (12/0).
(342/570)	MARTÍNEZ Carlos		**4**	**0**	1966-1967, CA Fénix Montevideo (4/0).
(461/732)	MARTÍNEZ Daniel	21.12.1959	**30**	**0**	1980-1985, Danubio FC Montevideo (30/0).
(700/974)	MARTÍNEZ FRACCHIA Williams Guillermo	18.12.1982	**1**	**0**	2003, Defensor Sporting Club Montevideo (1/0).
(137/218)	MARTÍNEZ Julio		**1**	**0**	1929, CA Capurro (1/0).
(224/392)	MARTÍNEZ Miguel		**6**	**1**	1949, CA Peñarol Montevideo (6/1).
(231/397)	MARTÍNEZ William Rubén	13.01.1928	**54**	**2**	1950-1965, Rampla Juniors FC Montevideo (16/1), CA Peñarol Montevideo (27/1), Rampla Juniors FC Montevideo (11/0).
(146/232)	MASCHERONI Ernesto	21.11.1907	**13**	**0**	1930-1939, Olimpia FC Montevideo (4/0), CA Peñarol Montevideo (9/0).
(361/585)	MASNIK Juan Carlos	02.03.1943	**26**	**0**	1967-1974, New York Skyliners (2/0), Club Nacional de Football Montevideo (24/0).
(198/346)	MÁSPOLI Roque Gastón	12.10.1917	**39**	**0**	1945-1955, CA Peñarol Montevideo (39/0).
(133/211)	MATA Luis		**7**	**1**	1928-1940, Colón FC Montevideo (2/1), CA Peñarol Montevideo (3/0), (2/0).
(532/790)	MATOSAS Gustavo Cristian	25.05.1967	**7**	**1**	1987-1991, CA Peñarol Montevideo (5/1), CA San Lorenzo de Almagro (1/0), Racing Club de Avellaneda (1/0).
(324/536)	MATOSAS Roberto	11.05.1940	**20**	**0**	1963-1971, CA Peñarol Montevideo (20/0).
(312/523)	MATTERA José		**2**	**1**	1961-1962
(98/167)	MATURELL Máximo		**6**	**0**	1924-1925, CA Fénix (1/0), Club Nacional de Football Montevideo (5/0).
(100/181)	MAZALI Andrés	22.07.1902	**21**	**0**	1924-1929, Club Nacional de Football Montevideo (21/0).
(335/558)	MAZURKIEWICZ IGLESIAS Ladislao	14.02.1945	**36**	**0**	1965-1974, CA Peñarol Montevideo (33/0), CA Mineiro Belo Horizonte (3/0).
(113/192)	MAZZONE Alfredo		**3**	**0**	1925, Racing Club Montevideo (3/0).
(113/191)	MEDINA Fermín		**2**	**0**	1925, Racing Club Montevideo (2/0).
(184/327)	MEDINA José María		**15**	**9**	1941-1947, Montevideo Wanderers FC (1/0), Club Nacional de Football Montevideo (9/9).
(738/1012)	MEDINA REOBASCO Alexander Jesús	08.08.1978	**1**	**0**	2006, Cádiz FC (1/0).
(57/108)	MEDINA Ricardo		**2**	**0**	1918, Central FC Montevideo (2/0).
(269/454)	MELGAREJO Oscar Daniel		**2**	**0**	1956, Danubio FC Montevideo (2/0).
(710/995)	MELO Pablo Rodrigo	07.04.1982	**3**	**0**	2003-2005, CA Cerro Montevideo (2/0), Danubio FC Montevideo (1/0).
(98/168)	MELOGNO Alberto		**1**	**0**	1924, CA Bella Vista Montevideo (1/0).
(42/095)	MELOGNO Domingo		**2**	**0**	1916, CA River Plate Montevideo (2/0).
(115/194)	MELOGNO Miguel Ángel	22.03.1905	**4**	**0**	1925-1929, CA Bella Vista Montevideo (4/0).
(522/783)	MENCHACA Mario		**3**	**0**	1986
(95/158)	MÉNDEZ Manuel		**1**	**0**	1923, CA Wanderers Montevideo (1/0).
(299/501)	MÉNDEZ Mario Omar	11.05.1938	**22**	**3**	1959-1968
(246/423)	MÉNDEZ Omar Pedro	07.08.1934	**10**	**2**	1953-1957, Central Español FC Montevideo (3/1), Club Nacional de Football Montevideo (7/1).
(575/833)	MÉNDEZ Peter	19.08.1964	**9**	**4**	1991-1992, Defensor Sporting Club Montevideo (7/4), RCD Mallorca (1/0), CD Millonários Bogotá (1/0).

(602/859)	MÉNDEZ TECHERA Gustavo Emilio	03.02.1971	45	0	1993-2002, Club Nacional de Football Montevideo (14/0), AC Vicenza (16/0), Torino Calcio (11/0), Club Nacional de Football Montevideo (4/0).
(332/554)	MENESES Danilo		8	1	1965
(97/163)	MERLI Luis		1	0	1923, CA River Plate Montevideo (1/0).
(467/743)	MERONI Ricardo		1	0	1980, Defensor Sporting Club Montevideo (1/0).
(293/486)	MESÍAS Juan Carlos		15	0	1959-1960, Club Nacional de Football Montevideo (15/0).
(422/668)	MIER Ricardo Santiago		3	0	1975, CSD Huracán Buceo Montevideo (3/0).
(233/409)	MÍGUEZ Oscar Omar	05.12.1927	39	26	1950-1958, CA Peñarol Montevideo (39/26).
(402/635)	MILAR OTERO Denis Alfredo	20.08.1952	17	4	1973-1979, Liverpool FC Montevideo (14/3), Club Nacional de Football Montevideo (3/1).
(70/119)	MINOLI Atilio		1	0	1919, Universal FC Montevideo (1/0).
(117/198)	MINOLI Pedro		1	0	1925, Racing Club Montevideo (1/0).
(561/819)	MIQUEIRO Johnny	18.07.1964	2	0	1990, Progreso Montevideo (2/0).
(267/448)	MIRAMONTES Luis Alberto		22	0	1956-1959, Defensor Sporting Club Montevideo (22/0).
(97/164)	MIRAMONTES Ricardo		1	0	1923, Central FC Montevideo (1/0).
(588/851)	MIRANDA Gerardo	30.08.1963	2	0	1992, Club Nacional de Football Montevideo (2/0).
(537/807)	MOAS SILVERA Eber Alejandro	21.03.1969	48	0	1988-1997, Danubio FC Montevideo (15/0), CA Independiente Avellaneda (9/0), CD América de Cali (10/0), CF Monterrey (14/0).
(8/042)	MÓDENA Vicente		15	0	1908-1913, CA River Plate Montevideo (15/0)
(79/127)	MOLINARI Juan		2	0	1921, Universal FC Montevideo (2/0).
(224/393)	MOLL Dagoberto		6	2	1949, Miramar (6/2).
(442/696)	MOLLER Raúl	09.10.1950	2	0	1977, Club Nacional de Football Montevideo (2/0).
(410/646)	MONDADA Omar		1	0	1974
(48/104)	MONGELAR Carlos		3	2	1916-1917, Universal FC Montevideo (3/2).
(449/709)	MONTELONGO Néstor Mario	20.02.1955	37	0	1979-1985
(352/576)	MONTERO CASTILLO Julio Walter	25.04.1944	42	1	1967-1978, Club Nacional de Football Montevideo (40/1), Granada CF (2/0).
(393/629)	MONTERO Luis		2	0	1972
(571/821)	MONTERO Paolo Ronald	03.09.1971	60	5	1991-2005, CA Peñarol Montevideo (4/0), Atalanta Bergamasca Calcio (7/0), Juventus FC Torino (45/5), CA San Lorenzo de Almagro (4/0)
(677/948)	MORALES AGUIRRE Richard Javier	21.02.1975	27	6	2001-2005, Club Nacional de Football Montevideo (15/6), CA Osasuna Pamplona (6/0), Málaga CF (6/0).
(699/965)	MORALES ALBORNOZ Óscar Javier	29.03.1975	2	0	2002-2005, Club Nacional de Football Montevideo (2/0).
(171/294)	MORALES Alejandro		2	0	1937-1944, CA Defensor Montevideo (1/0).
(418/654)	MORALES Juan Vicente	18.04.1956	15	1	1975-1980, CA Cerro Montevideo (14/1), CA Peñarol Montevideo (1/0).
(340/566)	MORALES Julio César	16.02.1945	25	11	1965-1981
(677/951)	MORALES MAESO Carlos María	01.03.1970	7	1	2001, Deportivo Toluca FC (7/1).
(536/800)	MORÁN Héctor	13.02.1962	23	2	1988-1993, Club Nacional de Football Montevideo (10/0), CD Mandiyú (13/2).
(623/887)	MORÁN Juan	31.05.1967	1	0	1995, Liverpool FC Montevideo (1/0).
(231/403)	MORÁN Rúben	06.08.1930	4	1	1950-1953, CA Cerro Montevideo (4/1).
(430/685)	MOREIRA José Hermes	30.09.1958	24	0	1976-1981
(246/426)	MOREL Walter		8	3	1953-1955, CA River Plate Montevideo (8/3).
(585/848)	MORENA Claudio	19.12.1969	1	0	1992, Racing Club de Montevideo (1/0).
(391/624)	MORENA Fernando	02.02.1952	52	22	1971-1983, (6/1), CA Peñarol Montevideo (46/21).
(331/551)	MORENO Miguel		1	0	1965
(224/389)	MORENO Nelson		7	1	1949, CA Peñarol Montevideo (7/1).
(274/460)	MOSCARELLI Alfredo		3	1	1956
(700/978)	MOZZO VALDÉZ Julio Fabián	20.04.1981	3	0	2003-2007, Central Español FC Montevideo (1/0), CA Peñarol Montevideo (2/0).
(421/666)	MUHLETHALER Juan	17.12.1954	6	1	1975-1983, CA Peñarol Montevideo (4/0), Rampla Juniors FC Montevideo (2/1).
(343/572)	MUJICA Juan Martín	22.12.1943	22	2	1966-1970, Club Nacional de Football Montevideo (22/2).
(710/993)	MUNHOZ RODRÍGUEZ Pablo Roberto	31.08.1982	2	0	2003, Defensor Sporting Club Montevideo (2/0).
(155/254)	MUÑIZ Agenor		31	1	1933-1944, Montevideo Wanderers FC (18/1), CA Peñarol Montevideo (9/0)
(425/672)	MUÑIZ José María		8	0	1976, Club Nacional de Football Montevideo (8/0).
(651/923)	MUNÚA Gustavo Adolfo	27.01.1978	21	0	1998-2004, Club Nacional de Football Montevideo (13/0), RC Deportivo La Coruña (8/0).
(781/1048)	MUSLERA MICOL Néstor Fernando	16.06.1986	55	0	2009-2013, SS Lazio Roma (24/0), SK Galatasaray Istanbul (31/0).
(478/749)	NADAL Carlos Amaro	16.03.1958	19	10	1982-1985, CA Bella Vista Montevideo (4/2), AC Deportico Cali (15/8).
(64/113)	NAGUIL Rogelio		4	0	1919-1922, Club Nacional de Football Montevideo (4/0).
(700/971)	NANNI LIMA Mauricio Daniel	12.07.1979	1	0	2003, Montevideo Wanderers FC (1/0).
(93/151)	NASAZZI José	24.05.1901	41	0	1923-1936, CA Bella Vista Montevideo (36/0), Club Nacional de Football Montevideo (5/0).
(735/1004)	NAVARRO Sergio William	14.03.1968	1	0	2005, CS Miramar Misiones Montevideo (1/0).
(101/184)	NAYA José	25.07.1896	2	0	1924, Liverpool FC Montevideo (2/0).
(1/004)	NEBEL Miguel		2	0	1902-1903, Club Nacional de Football Montevideo (2/0).
(628/904)	NICOLA Carlos	03.01.1973	4	0	1996-1997, Club Nacional de Football Montevideo (4/0).
(150/241)	NIETO Ignacio		1	0	1932, Central FC Montevideo (1/0).
(89/143)	NOGUÉS Alberto		4	0	1923-1924, CA Wanderers Montevideo (4/0)
(22/068)	NOVOA Edmundo		1	0	1911, Bristol FC Montevideo (1/0).
(662/935)	NÚÑEZ Álvaro	11.05.1973	1	0	1999, Numancia FC (1/0).
(289/475)	NÚÑEZ Héctor	08.05.1936	7	0	1957-1959, Club Nacional de Football Montevideo (7/0).
(461/737)	NÚÑEZ Julio César		2	1	1980-1981

(708/990)	NÚÑEZ PEREYRA Richard Darío	16.02.1976	**9**	**0**	2003-2005, Grasshopper-Club Zürich (7/0), CDSC Cruz Azul Ciudad de México (2/0).
(331/552)	NÚÑEZ Raúl		**2**	**0**	1965
(418/653)	OCAMPO Juan Carlos		**10**	**2**	1975-1979, Danubio FC Montevideo (4/0), Club Nacional de Football Montevideo (6/2).
(133/209)	OCCHIUZZI Francisco		**8**	**0**	1928, CA Cerro Montevideo (4/0), Montevideo Wanderers FC (4/0).
(521/782)	ODDINE Daniel Sergio	14.07.1960	**1**	**0**	1985, CA Peñarol Montevideo (1/0).
(646/917)	OLIVERA Andrés Nicolás	30.05.1978	**28**	**8**	1997-2006, Valencia CF (5/3), Sevilla CF (20/8), Defensor Sporting Club Montevideo (3/0).
(680/957)	OLIVERA DA ROSA Rúben Ariel	04.05.1983	**18**	**0**	2001-2005, Danubio FC Montevideo (8/0), Juventus FC Torino (5/0), Club Atlético de Madrid (1/0), Juventus FC Torino (4/0).
(159/265)	OLIVERA Miguel		**4**	**0**	1935-1937, CA River Plate Montevideo (4/0).
(400/632)	OLIVERA Walter Daniel	26.08.1952	**29**	**1**	1973-1983, CA Peñarol Montevideo (29/1).
(425/673)	OLIVERA Washington		**10**	**1**	1976-1979, CA Peñarol Montevideo (10/1).
(88/142)	OLIVIERI Héctor		**4**	**0**	1922-1923, CA Belgrano (4/0).
(42/093)	OLIVIERI Pedro		**5**	**0**	1916-1917, Club Nacional de Football Montevideo (5/0).
(625/895)	OLVEIRA Nelson Artigas	19.06.1974	**3**	**0**	1996, CA Peñarol Montevideo (3/0).
(592/857)	O'NEILL DOMÍNGUEZ Fabián Alberto	14.10.1973	**19**	**2**	1993-2002, Club Nacional de Football Montevideo (2/0), Cagliari Calcio (9/1), Juventus FC Torino (4/0), AC Perugia (4/1).
(222/382)	ORLANDI Juan Ramón		**3**	**0**	1948-1950
(198/348)	ORTIZ José María		**9**	**2**	1945-1950, CA Peñarol Montevideo (8/2)
(419/659)	ORTIZ Ricardo		**4**	**0**	1975-1980
(521/780)	OSTOLAZA SOSA Santiago Javier	10.07.1962	**43**	**6**	1985-1993, CA Bella Vista Montevideo (1/0), Club Nacional de Football Montevideo (27/5), CDSC Cruz Azul Ciudad de México (2/0), Querétaro FC (12/1), Club Gimnasia y Esgrima de La Plata (1/0).
(536/802)	OTERO Celso	01.02.1958	**1**	**0**	1988, Montevideo Wanderers FC (1/0).
(84/138)	OTERO Juan		**2**	**0**	1922, Central FC Montevideo (2/0).
(607/876)	OTERO Marcelo Alejandro	14.04.1971	**26**	**10**	1994-2000, CA Peñarol Montevideo (13/4), AC Vicenza (9/4), Sevilla CF (4/2).
(607/870)	OTERO Raúl Omar	15.01.1970	**5**	**0**	1994-1995, CA River Plate Montevideo (5/0).
(312/524)	OYARBIDE Jorge		**7**	**4**	1961-1967
(644/911)	PACHECO Antonio	11.04.1976	**12**	**3**	1997-2004, CA Peñarol Montevideo (11/3), Albacete Balompié (1/0).
(16/059)	PACHECO Jorge Germán		**28**	**0**	1910-1917, Club Nacional de Football Montevideo (3/0), Bristol FC Montevideo (17/0), CA Peñarol Montevideo (8/0).
(674/943)	PANDIANI URQUIZA Walter Gerardo	27.04.1976	**4**	**0**	2001-2004, RC Deportivo La Coruña (1/0), RCD Mallorca (1/0), RC Deportivo La Coruña (2/0).
(7/040)	PANIZZI Luis		**1**	**0**	1907, CA River Plate Montevideo (1/0).
(537/806)	PANZARDO Sergio	20.07.1965	**1**	**0**	1988, CA Bella Vista Montevideo (1/0)
(99/174)	PARDIÑAS José		**1**	**0**	1924, CA Belgrano (1/0).
(99/177)	PARDIÑAS Manuel		**1**	**0**	1924, CA Belgrano (1/0).
(717/1000)	PARODI GONZÁLEZ Juan Martín	22.09.1974	**3**	**0**	2004, Panionios Athína (3/0).
(44/098)	PASCUARIELLO Pascual		**3**	**0**	1916, Reformers FC Montevideo (3/0).
(89/145)	PATIÑO Atilio		**2**	**0**	1923-1924, Rampla Juniors FC Montevideo (2/0).
(322/530)	PAVONI Elbio Ricardo	08.07.1943	**14**	**2**	1962-1974, Defensor Sporting Club Montevideo (7/0), CA Independiente Avellaneda (7/2).
(584/844)	PAZ Adrián Gustavo	09.09.1966	**10**	**3**	1992-1993, CA Peñarol Montevideo (3/2), CA Estudiantes de La Plata (7/1).
(179/313)	PAZ Aníbal Luis	18.02.1918	**20**	**0**	1940-1950, Club Nacional de Football Montevideo (20/0).
(356/580)	PAZ Juan Carlos		**3**	**0**	1967-1969, Racing Club de Montevideo (3/0).
(454/724)	PAZ MÁRQUEZ Rubén Wálter	08.08.1959	**44**	**7**	1979-1990, CA Peñarol Montevideo (20/6), Internacional Porto Alegre (2/0), Racing Club Avellaneda (11/1), Genoa CFC (11/0).
(710/996)	PAZ Nery Damián	09.02.1983	**1**	**0**	2003, CtA Fénix Montevideo (1/0).
(429/683)	PEDETTI Nelson		**1**	**0**	1976
(561/817)	PEDRUCCI Pedro	30.09.1961	**2**	**1**	1990, Toshiba Kawasaki (2/1).
(1/006)	PEIXOTO Alberto		**1**	**0**	1902, Albion FC Montevideo (1/0).
(246/425)	PELÁEZ Donald		**6**	**3**	1953, CA Peñarol Montevideo (6/3).
(171/295)	PELÁEZ Juan		**1**	**0**	1937, Montevideo Wanderers FC (1/0).
(584/842)	PELETTI Walter	31.05.1966	**8**	**0**	1992-1993, CA Huracán Buenos Aires (8/0).
(648/920)	PELLEGRÍN César	05.03.1979	**1**	**0**	1997, Danubio FC Montevideo (1/0).
(418/649)	PELUSSO Gerardo	25.02.1954	**2**	**0**	1975, Liverpool FC Montevideo (2/0).
(532/792)	PEÑA José Enrique		**4**	**0**	1987, Montevideo Wanderers FC (4/0).
(3/020)	PENA Juan	1882	**10**	**0**	1905-1910, CURCC Montevideo (5/0), Oriental Montevideo (2/0), Club Nacional de Football Montevideo (3/0).
(5/032)	PERALTA Gilberto		**1**	**1**	1906, Montevideo Wanderers FC (1/1).
(660/934)	PERALTA SARACHO Walter Horacio	03.06.1982	**7**	**0**	1999-2003, Danubio FC Montevideo (1/0), Club Nacional de Football Montevideo (6/0).
(532/791)	PERDOMO José Batlle	05.01.1965	**27**	**3**	1987-1990, CA Peñarol Montevideo (17/2), Genoa CFC (10/1).
(497/763)	PERDOMO Ricardo	03.07.1960	**7**	**0**	1984-1985, Club Nacional de Football Montevideo (7/0).
(324/537)	PEREIRA "ICA" Darcy		**6**	**0**	1963-1964
(772/1042)	PEREIRA BARRAGÁN Álvaro Daniel	28.01.1985	**54**	**5**	2008-2013, CFR 1907 Cluj (6/1), FC do Porto (34/4), FC Internazionale Milano (14/0).
(518/777)	PEREIRA Julio César	08.07.1962	**4**	**1**	1985-1986, Central Español FC Montevideo (4/1).
(533/793)	PEREIRA MARTÍNEZ Eduardo	21.03.1954	**10**	**0**	1987-1990, CA Peñarol Montevideo (3/0), CA Independiente Avellaneda (7/0).
(735/1007)	PEREIRA PÁEZ Victorio Maximiliano	08.06.1984	**87**	**3**	2005-2013, Defensor Sporting Club Montevideo (13/0), Sport Lisboa e Benfica (74/3).

(536/799)	PEREIRA Rubén Fabián	28.01.1968	27	1	1988-1996, Danubio FC Montevideo (25/1), CA Peñarol Montevideo (2/0).
(418/655)	PEREYRA BUENO Alfonso Darío	19.10.1956	32	5	1975-1986, Club Nacional de Football Montevideo (21/5), São Paulo (11/0).
(194/337)	PEREYRA NATERO Flavio		2	0	1943,
(677/946)	PÉREZ AGUADO Diego Fernando	18.05.1980	87	2	2001-2013, Defensor Sporting Club Montevideo (11/0), CA Peñarol Montevideo (4/0), AS Monaco (42/0), Bologna FC (30/2).
(292/485)	PÉREZ Domingo Salvador	07.06.1936	29	7	1959-1967, Rampla Juniors FC Montevideo (9/3), Club Nacional de Football Montevideo (20/4).
(31/080)	PÉREZ José		28	5	1913-1920, CURCC Montevideo (2/0),), CA Peñarol Montevideo (26/5).
(231/402)	PÉREZ Julio Gervasio	19.06.1926	21	8	1950-1956, Club Nacional de Football Montevideo 54-55
(81/132)	PÉREZ Ladislao		6	0	1921-1924, Universal FC Montevideo (1/0), CA Wanderers Montevideo (5/0).
(213/370)	PÉREZ LUZ Luis Alberto		3	0	1947, CA River Plate Montevideo (3/0).
(155/256)	PÉREZ Marcelino		3	0	1933-1935, Club Nacional de Football Montevideo (3/0).
(67/117)	PÉREZ Omar		2	1	1919, Montevideo Wanderers FC (2/1).
(178/312)	PÉREZ Ricardo		2	0	1940
(702/985)	PERRONE VIENES Diego Rafael	19.11.1977	5	2	2003, Danubio FC Montevideo (4/0), FC Atlas Guadalajara (1/2).
(421/665)	PERUENA Carlos		5	1	1975-1978, CA Peñarol Montevideo (5/1).
(93/154)	PETRONE Pedro	11.05.1905	28	24	1923-1930, Charley FC Montevideo (8/10), Club Nacional de Football Montevideo (20/14).
(628/899)	PICÚN Fernando	14.02.1972	9	0	1996-1999, CA River Plate Montevideo (2/0), Defensor Sporting Club Montevideo (7/0)
(13/057)	PIENDIBENE José	05.06.1890	40	20	1909-1923, CURCC Montevideo (17/8), CA Peñarol Montevideo (23/12).
(2/013)	PIGNI Gaudencio		1	0	1903, Club Nacional de Football Montevideo (1/0).
(652/926)	PILIPAUSKAS Leonel	18.05.1975	4	0	1999, CA Bella Vista Montevideo (3/0), Club Atlético de Madrid (1/0).
(198/345)	PINI Raúl		12	0	1944-1947, Club Nacional de Football Montevideo (12/0).
(197/344)	PINI Rodolfo	1926	6	2	19441950, Club Nacional de Football Montevideo
(305/509)	PINO Santiago		3	0	1960, CA Peñarol Montevideo (3/0).
(533/794)	PINTOS SALDANHA José Luis	25.03.1964	12	0	1987-1991, Club Nacional de Football Montevideo (12/0).
(278/467)	PIPPO Rodolfo		8	0	1957, CA Cerro Montevideo (8/0).
(268/453)	PÍREZ Luis		2	0	1956, Racing Club de Montevideo (2/0).
(137/219)	PÍRIZ Conduelo	1905	7	0	1929-1932, Club Nacional de Football Montevideo (7/0).
(129/205)	PÍRIZ Juan		2	0	1928, Club Nacional de Football Montevideo (2/0)
(135/216)	PÍRIZ Juan Emilio	17.05.1902	14	5	1928-1938, CA Defensor Montevideo (14/5).
(300/503)	PÍRIZ William		1	0	1959, Defensor Sporting Club Montevideo (1/0).
(389/615)	PISANO Walter		2	0	1971
(437/693)	PIZZANI Laddy Nittder		6	3	1977, CA Peñarol Montevideo (6/3).
(652/931)	PODESTÁ MEZZETTA Inti	23.04.1978	1	0	1999, Danubio FC Montevideo (1/0).
(42/094)	PORTA Abdón		2	1	1916-1917, Club Nacional de Football Montevideo (2/1).
(170/291)	PORTA Roberto	07.06.1913	33	13	1937-1945, Club Nacional de Football Montevideo (33/13).
(210/366)	POSSAMAI Sixto Valentín		2	0	1946, CA Peñarol Montevideo (2/0).
(717/999)	POUSO OSORES Omar Heber	28.02.1980	15	1	2004-2007, Danubio FC Montevideo (8/1), CA Peñarol Montevideo (5/0), Charlton Athletic FC London (2/0).
(596/858)	POYET DOMÍNGUEZ Gustavo Augusto	15.11.1967	26	3	1993-2000, Real Zaragoza CD (21/3), Chelsea FC London (5/0).
(172/296)	PRADO Agustín		6	0	1938-1945, CA Peñarol Montevideo (6/0)
(206/361)	PRAIS Luis		5	0	1946, CA Peñarol Montevideo (5/0).
(363/588)	PRESTES Jorge		2	0	1968
(216/377)	PUENTE Washington		9	4	1947-1953, Rampla Juniors FC Montevideo (9/4).
(163/278)	PUENTES Gumersindo		1	0	1936, Institución Atlética Sud América Montevideo (1/0).
(431/690)	PUPPO Carlos		2	0	1976
(17/061)	QUAGLIA Luis		3	1	1910-1912, CURCC Montevideo (3/1).
(247/430)	QUIROGA Julio		1	0	1953, Liverpool FC Montevideo (1/0).
(516/776)	RABINO Juan Pedro		1	0	1985, Progreso Montevideo (1/0).
(482/753)	RABUÑAL Víctor Manuel	08.01.1962	4	0	1983, CA Bella Vista Montevideo (4/0).
(242/415)	RADICHE Luis		7	0	1952-1953
(795/1051)	RAMÍREZ PEREYRA Gastón Ezequiel	02.12.1990	26	0	2010-2013, Bologna FC (11/0), Southampton FC (15/0).
(521/781)	RAMÍREZ Rogelio Néstor	08.04.1959	3	0	1985-1986, Defensor Sporting Club Montevideo (1/0), Unión de Santa Fe (2/0).
(425/671)	RAMÍREZ Sergio	24.12.1951	14	0	1976-1977
(699/970)	RAMÍREZ VILLA Ronald Andrés	23.11.1976	1	0	2002, Montevideo Wanderers FC (1/0).
(272/456)	RAMOS Héctor		5	0	1956, Club Nacional de Football Montevideo (5/0).
(571/826)	RAMOS Leonardo	11.09.1969	9	0	1991-2000, CA Vélez Sarsfield Buenos Aires (3/0), CA Estudiantes de La Plata (5/0), UD Salamanca (1/0).
(343/573)	RAMOS Luis	09.10.1939	2	0	1966, Club Nacional de Football Montevideo (2/0).
(448/707)	RAMOS VILLANUEVA Venancio Ariel	20.06.1959	41	5	1978-1991, CA Peñarol Montevideo (27/3), RC Lens (13/2), Nacional de Football Montevideo (1/0).
(72/123)	RAVERA Andrés		6	0	1920, CA Peñarol Montevideo (6/0).
(12/055)	RAYMONDA Santiago		4	2	1909-1910, CA River Plate Montevideo (4/2).
(537/810)	REBOLLO Mario	08.12.1964	5	0	1988, Montevideo Wanderers FC (5/0).
(118/199)	RECOBA Emilio	03.11.1904	5	0	1926-1929, Club Nacional de Football Montevideo (5/0).
(608/883)	RECOBA RIVERO Álvaro Alexander	17.03.1976	68	10	1995-2007, Danubio FC Montevideo (2/0), Club Nacional de Football Montevideo (8/4), Internazionale FC Milano (58/6).

(671/940)	REGUEIRO PINTOS Mario Ignacio	14.09.1978	29	1	2000-2007, Club Nacional de Football Montevideo (2/0), Racing Club Santander (21/1), Valencia CF (5/0), Real Murcia CF (1/0).
(390/620)	REPETTO Roberto		3	1	1971
(326/542)	RESTIVO Eduardo		1	0	1964
(388/610)	RETAMAR Robinson		1	0	1971
(33/084)	RETTA Antonio		1	0	1913, Central FC Montevideo (1/0).
(461/736)	REVELEZ Daniel Felipe	30.09.1959	21	1	1980-1991, CA Bella Vista Montevideo (2/0), Club Nacional de Football Montevideo (19/1).
(419/661)	REVETRIA Hebert Carlos	27.08.1955	7	1	1975-1976, Club Nacional de Football Montevideo (7/1).
(262/442)	REY Celedonio		5	0	1955, CA River Plate (5/0).
(400/634)	REY Omar	03.09.1949	4	1	1973, Hércules Alicante (4/1).
(174/304)	REYES Abdón		2	0	1939, CA Bella Vista Montevideo (2/0).
(459/729)	REYES Carlos		2	0	1980
(1/010)	REYES Ernesto Boutón		4	0	1902-1906, Club Nacional de Football Montevideo (4/0).
(515/773)	RIBAS Julio César	08.01.1957	5	0	1985, CA River Plate Montevideo (5/0).
(8/044)	RIBEYRO Raúl		1	0	1908, CA River Plate Montevideo (1/0)
(180/319)	RIEPHOFF Juan Pedro		22	4	1940-1948, Rampla Juniors FC Montevideo (22/4).
(1/008)	RINCÓN Gonzalo		2	0	1902-1903, Club Nacional de Football Montevideo (2/0).
(219/381)	RIOBÓ José		1	0	1947, Defensor Sporting Club Montevideo (1/0).
(135/215)	RIOLFO Carlos	05.11.1905	2	0	1928, CA Peñarol Montevideo (2/0).
(306/511)	RIOLFO Carlos Rosas		1	0	1960
(19/065)	RÍOS Ramón		5	0	1911, CA River Plate Montevideo (5/0).
(444/700)	RIVADAVIA Julio		3	0	1977-1979
(648/922)	RIVAS Martín	17.02.1977	1	0	1997, Danubio FC Montevideo (1/0).
(247/427)	RIVERA Urbano		8	0	1953-1954, Danubio FC Montevideo (8/0).
(391/622)	RIVERO Agapito		4	0	1971-1972, Liverpool FC Montevideo (4/0).
(360/584)	RIVERO Hamilton		1	0	1967
(180/317)	RIVERO Ismael		6	5	1940-1941, Rampla Juniors FC Montevideo (6/5).
(486/760)	RIVERO PÉREZ Eliseo Roque	27.12.1957	7	0	1983-1986, Danubio FC Montevideo (1/0), CA Peñarol Montevideo (6/0).
(409/642)	RIVERO Saúl Lorenzo	23.07.1954	8	0	1974-1976
(311/521)	ROCHA Pedro Virgilio	03.12.1942	53	17	1961-1974, CA Peñarol Montevideo (50/17), Sao Paulo FC (3/0).
(215/376)	RODRÍGUEZ ANDRADE Víctor Pablo Carlos	14.02.1927	42	0	1947-1957, Central FC Montevideo (3/0), CA Peñarol Montevideo
(304/507)	RODRÍGUEZ Angel		1	0	1960
(710/994)	RODRÍGUEZ BAROTTI Cristian Gabriel	30.09.1985	70	8	2003-2013, CA Peñarol Montevideo (8/1), Paris St. Germain FC (7/1), Sport Lisboa e Benfica (8/1), FC do Porto (25/2), Club Atlético de Madrid (22/3).
(443/699)	RODRÍGUEZ CANTERO Jorge		1	0	1977
(670/939)	RODRÍGUEZ CANTOS Oscar Damián	27.07.1974	2	0	2000-2002, Club Nacional de Football Montevideo (2/0).
(389/617)	RODRÍGUEZ Carlos		2	0	1971
(290/477)	RODRÍGUEZ Climaco		6	0	1958-1962
(682/959)	RODRÍGUEZ CRISTÓBAL Julio Pablo	09.08.1977	2	0	2001, CSD Huracán Buceo Montevideo (1/0), Club Nacional de Football Montevideo (1/0).
(449/713)	RODRÍGUEZ DE DEUS Jorge		1	0	1979, CA Peñarol Montevideo (1/0).
(232/407)	RODRÍGUEZ Domingo		3	0	1950-1953, CA River Plate Montevideo (3/0).
(590/854)	RODRÍGUEZ Gerardo		1	0	1992, CA Peñarol Montevideo (1/0).
(48/102)	RODRÍGUEZ Gregorio		12	0	1916-1924, Universal FC Montevideo (12/0).
(286/473)	RODRÍGUEZ Héctor		9	1	1957-1962, Club Nacional de Football Montevideo (9/1).
(322/531)	RODRÍGUEZ Juan José		1	0	1962
(450/719)	RODRÍGUEZ Julio		1	0	1979
(463/740)	RODRÍGUEZ Julio Aníbal		1	0	1980, CA River Plate Montevideo (1/0).
(606/864)	RODRÍGUEZ Julio César	20.09.1968	1	0	1993, Danubio FC Montevideo (1/0).
(149/234)	RODRÍGUEZ Luis Alberto		2	0	1931-1935, Montevideo Wanderers FC (2/0).
(172/297)	RODRÍGUEZ Mario		2	0	1938, Club Nacional de Football Montevideo (2/0).
(767/1041)	RODRÍGUEZ NÚÑEZ Jorge Marcelo	13.01.1985	7	0	2008-2010, CA River Plate Montevideo (7/0).
(248/432)	RODRÍGUEZ Pedro		1	0	1953, Rampla Juniors FC Montevideo (1/0).
(573/831)	RODRÍGUEZ PEÑA Héctor	22.10.1968	10	0	1991-1997, Defensor Sporting Club Montevideo (2/0), CA Colón Santa Fé (8/0).
(663/936)	RODRÍGUEZ PEÑA Octavio Darío	17.09.1974	50	3	2000-2007, CA Peñarol Montevideo (23/0), FC Schalke 04 Gelsenkirchen (27/3).
(719/1001)	RODRÍGUEZ PÉREZ Guillermo Daniel	21.03.1984	12	0	2004-2005, Danubio FC Montevideo (5/0), CD Atlas Guadalajara (7/0).
(177/307)	RODRÍGUEZ Plácido		1	0	1939, Rampla Juniors FC Montevideo (1/0).
(178/311)	RODRÍGUEZ Raúl		15	0	1940-1944, CA Peñarol Montevideo (15/0).
(429/682)	RODRÍGUEZ Rodolfo Enrique		5	1	1976, Defensor Sporting Club Montevideo (5/1).
(431/687)	RODRÍGUEZ Rodolfo Sergio	20.01.1956	78	0	1976-1986, Club Nacional de Football Montevideo (62/0), FC Santos (16/0).
(610/884)	RODRÍGUEZ Rúben	26.10.1967	1	0	1995, CA Cerro Montevideo (1/0).
(428/678)	RODRÍGUEZ Rudy		4	0	1976-1977, Defensor Sporting Club Montevideo (4/0).
(298/495)	ROLAN Tomás		1	0	1959
(19/066)	ROMANO Ángel	02.08.1893	69	28	1911-1927, CURCC Montevideo (11/4), Club Nacional de Football Montevideo (58/24).
(623/886)	ROMAY Leonardo	29.04.1969	2	0	1995-1996, Defensor Sporting Club Montevideo (2/0).
(231/400)	ROMERO Carlos	07.09.1927	11	4	1950-1956, Danubio FC Montevideo 50-53
(704/988)	ROMERO GONZÁLEZ Adrián Marcelo	25.06.1977	7	1	2003-2004, CA Cerro Montevideo (5/1), Club Nacional de Football Montevideo (2/0).
(178/309)	ROMERO Héctor		9	0	1940-1942, Club Nacional de Football Montevideo (9/0).
(215/373)	ROMERO Hosiriz		7	0	1947-1953, Liverpool FC Montevideo (7/0).
(626/896)	ROMERO Luis Alberto	15.06.1968	9	0	1996-1997, CA Peñarol Montevideo (9/0).

(606/863)	ROMERO Luis María	27.07.1966	**1**	**0**	1993, Montevideo Wanderers FC (1/0).
(133/208)	ROMERO Raúl		**5**	**0**	1928-1933, CA Bella Vista Montevideo (5/0).
(623/893)	ROMERO SILVA Clever Marcelo	04.07.1976	**24**	**0**	1995-2004, Defensor Sporting Club Montevideo (3/0), CA Peñarol Montevideo (14/0), Málaga CF (7/0).
(11/049)	RONZONI Carlos		**4**	**0**	1909-1911, Colón FC Montevideo (1/0), CURCC Montevideo (3/0).
(267/449)	ROQUE José Walter		**15**	**2**	1956-1957, Rampla Juniors FC Montevideo (15/2).
(582/835)	ROSA Fernando	21.01.1966	**1**	**0**	1991, CA Peñarol Montevideo (1/0).
(166/290)	ROSELLI José Pedro		**4**	**0**	1937, Institución Atlética Sud América Montevideo (4/0).
(419/658)	ROUX Héctor		**9**	**0**	1975-1977
(3/018)	ROVEGNO Arturo		**1**	**0**	1905, Club Nacional de Football Montevideo (1/0).
(90/147)	RUFFATI Vital		**3**	**0**	1923-1925, Rampla Juniors FC Montevideo (3/0).
(298/497)	RUMBO Manuel		**1**	**0**	1959
(67/115)	RUOTTA Pascual		**13**	**2**	1919-1927, CA Peñarol Montevideo (13/2)
(449/710)	RUSSO José Luis	14.07.1958	**16**	**0**	1979-1986, CSD Huracán Buceo Montevideo (1/0), Defensor Sporting Club Montevideo (10/0), Club Atlético Bucamaranga (5/0)

(209/365)	SABATEL Luis		**4**	**0**	1946, Rampla Juniors FC Montevideo (4/0).
(219/380)	SABINI Francisco		**1**	**0**	1947, Central FC Montevideo (1/0)
(105/185)	SACCO Antonio		**6**	**2**	1924-1932, CA Peñarol Montevideo (5/2), Institución Atlética Sud América Montevideo (1/0).
(272/457)	SACÍA José Francisco	27.12.1933	**43**	**12**	1956-1966, Defensor Sporting Club Montevideo (22/7), CA Peñarol Montevideo (16/5), Defensor Sporting Club Montevideo (5/0).
(196/341)	SAGASTUME Julio		**1**	**0**	1944
(205/356)	SALAZAR Pedro		**1**	**0**	1945
(87/140)	SALDOMBIDE Zoilo	18.03.1905	**15**	**3**	1922-1928, Montevideo Wanderers FC (2/0), CA Wanderers Montevideo (8/3), Club Nacional de Football Montevideo (5/0).
(429/679)	SALOMÓN Francisco		**7**	**0**	1976-1978, Defensor Sporting Club Montevideo (7/0).
(303/506)	SALVÁ Héctor	27.11.1939	**19**	**2**	1960-1967
(686/961)	SÁNCHEZ BRAGUNDE Vicente Martín	07.12.1979	**31**	**5**	2001-2008, Deportivo Toluca FC (26/5), FC Schalke 04 Gelsenkirchen (5/0).
(537/805)	SÁNCHEZ Daniel Florencio	03.05.1961	**26**	**0**	1988-1993, Danubio FC Montevideo (26/0).
(584/841)	SÁNCHEZ Luis Carlos	17.05.1964	**3**	**0**	1992, CA Peñarol Montevideo (3/0).
(5/030)	SANDERSON Enrique		**1**	**0**	1906, Montevideo Wanderers FC (1/0).
(386/600)	SANDOVAL Rodolfo Ariel	04.10.1948	**2**	**0**	1970-1971
(571/828)	SANGUINETTI GIORDANO Guillermo Oscar	21.06.1966	**20**	**1**	1991-1997, Racing Club Avellaneda (9/0), CA Gimnasia y Esgrima de La Plata (11/1).
(173/301)	SANGUINETTI Manuel		**5**	**0**	1938, CA River Plate Montevideo (5/0).
(243/419)	SANTAMARÍA José Emilio	31.07.1929	**20**	**0**	1952-1957, Club Nacional de Football Montevideo (20/0).
(442/698)	SANTANA Manuel		**2**	**0**	1977
(419/662)	SANTELLI FERNÁNDEZ Alberto Raúl	14.06.1953	**12**	**2**	1975-1983
(92/148)	SANTERO Juan		**2**	**0**	1923-1924, Liverpool FC Montevideo (2/0).
(196/343)	SANTIAGO Juan		**2**	**0**	1944-1945, Liverpool FC Montevideo
(461/734)	SANTÍN SPINELLI Sergio Rodolfo	06.08.1956	**18**	**0**	1980-1986, Atlético Nacional Medellin (Colombia) 86
(380/599)	SANTOS Héctor	29.10.1944	**14**	**0**	1970-1976
(16/060)	SANZ Oscar		**1**	**0**	1910, CA River Plate Montevideo (1/0).
(3/016)	SAPORITI Cayetano		**50**	**0**	1905-1919, Montevideo Wanderers FC (50/0).
(585/846)	SARALEGUI ARREGÍN Marcelo	18.05.1971	**33**	**6**	1992-1997, Club Nacional de Football Montevideo (3/0), Torino FBC (9/2), Racing Club de Avellaneda (6/1), CA Colón de Santa Fé (15/3).
(449/712)	SARALEGUI Mario Daniel	24.04.1959	**29**	**2**	1979-1986, CA Peñarol Montevideo (23/2), Elche CF (6/0).
(1/001)	SARDESON Enrique		**1**	**0**	1902, Albion FC Montevideo (1/0).
(1/009)	SARDESON Juan		**1**	**0**	1902, Albion FC Montevideo (1/0).
(200/351)	SARRO Raúl		**12**	**2**	1945-1948, Defensor Sporting Club Montevideo (12/2).
(29/074)	SAVIO Bernardo		**7**	**0**	1913-1916, CURCC Montevideo (3/0), CA Peñarol Montevideo (4/0).
(163/275)	SCANDROGLIO Carlos		**1**	**0**	1936, CA Peñarol Montevideo (1/0).
(11/050)	SCARONE Carlos	11.12.1890	**25**	**18**	1909-1922, CURCC Montevideo (9/7), Club Nacional de Football Montevideo (16/11).
(52/107)	SCARONE Héctor Pedro	26.11.1898	**52**	**31**	1917-1930, Club Nacional de Football Montevideo (52/31).
(207/364)	SCHIAFFINO Juan Alberto	28.07.1925	**21**	**10**	1946-1954, CA Peñarol Montevideo (21/10).
(204/355)	SCHIAFFINO Raúl Antonio		**6**	**2**	1945-1946, CA Peñarol Montevideo (8/2).
(113/189)	SCIUTTO Luis Alfredo		**2**	**0**	1925, Club Nacional de Football Montevideo (2/0).
(739/1015)	SCOTTI PONCE DE LEÓN Andrés	14.12.1975	**40**	**1**	2006-2013, FK Rubin Kazan (7/0), AA Argentinos Juniors Buenos Aires (17/1), CSD Colo Colo Santiago (11/0), Club Nacional de Football Montevideo (5/0).
(70/120)	SEIJAS Desiderio		**1**	**0**	1919, Central FC Montevideo (1/0).
(163/282)	SEOANE Arturo		**3**	**0**	1936-1937, Montevideo Wanderers FC (3/0).
(623/890)	SEOANE Diego	10.01.1969	**1**	**0**	1995, Liverpool FC Montevideo (1/0).
(17/062)	SEOANE Pedro		**4**	**2**	1910-1913, CA River Plate Montevideo (4/2).
(532/786)	SERÉ Jorge Fernando	09.07.1961	**4**	**0**	1987-1989, Danubio FC Montevideo (1/0), Club Nacional de Football Montevideo (3/0).
(163/280)	SERVETTI Carlos		**1**	**0**	1936, CA Bella Vista Montevideo (1/0).
(585/845)	SIBOLDI BADIOLA Robert Dante	24.09.1965	**34**	**0**	1992-1997, Atlas FC Guadalajara (10/0), CDSC Cruz Azul Ciudad de México (10/0), CF Tigres de la Universidad Autónoma de Nuevo León (14/0).
(700/973)	SILVA BARONE Bruno Ramón	29.03.1980	**17**	**0**	2003-2009, Danubio FC Montevideo (4/0), AFC Ajax Amsterdam (13/0).
(95/159)	SILVA Gildeón	1903	**8**	**0**	1923-1929, CA Peñarol Montevideo (8/0).
(826/1056)	SILVA GONZÁLEZ Alejandro Daniel	04.09.1989	**2**	**0**	2013, Club Olimpia Asunción (2/0).

(310/520)	SILVA Héctor Jesús	01.02.1940	**29**	**7**	1961-1969, Danubio FC Montevideo (7/1), CA Peñarol Montevideo (22/6).
(408/640)	SILVA Juan Ramón	30.08.1948	**11**	**0**	1974-1976, CA Peñarol Montevideo (11/0).
(778/1046)	SILVA LEITES Martín Andrés	25.03.1983	**4**	**0**	2009-2013, Defensor SC Montevideo (1/0), Club Olimpia Asunción (3/0).
(607/878)	SILVA PEREIRA Debray Darío	02.11.1972	**49**	**14**	1994-2005, CA Peñarol Montevideo (10/2), Cagliari Calcio (8/4), CF Málaga (21/6), Sevilla CF (8/2), Portsmouth FC (2/0).
(645/913)	SILVA Rúben	20.08.1974	**1**	**0**	1997, CSD Huracán Buceo Montevideo (1/0).
(340/567)	SILVA Sergio		**5**	**0**	1965-1969
(607/875)	SILVA Tabaré Abayubá	30.08.1974	**20**	**0**	1994-2000, Defensor Sporting Club Montevideo (19/0), Sevilla CF (1/0).
(294/488)	SILVEIRA Alcides		**8**	**3**	1959, Institución Atlética Sud América Montevideo (8/3).
(571/822)	SILVERA César	08.01.1969	**6**	**0**	1991, CA Peñarol Montevideo (6/0).
(492/761)	SILVERA Mauricio Joselito	30.12.1964	**7**	**0**	1983-1987, CA River Plate Montevideo (6/0), Club Nacional de Football Montevideo (1/0).
(623/891)	SILVERA Yary	20.02.1976	**2**	**0**	1995-1997, CA River Plate Montevideo (2/0).
(466/742)	SIVIERO Jorge Luis	13.05.1952	**1**	**1**	1980, Institución Atlética Sud América Montevideo (1/0).
(602/860)	SOCA Carlos	24.01.1969	**1**	**0**	1993, AA Argentinos Juniors Buenos Aires (1/0).
(19/067)	SOMMA Pascual	07.02.1891	**42**	**3**	1911-1924, Club Nacional de Football Montevideo (41/3), CA Defensor Montevideo (1/0).
(327/545)	SORIA Nestor		**4**	**0**	1964-1973
(290/480)	SORIA Rúben	1935	**4**	**0**	1958-1963
(669/938)	SORONDO AMARO Gonzalo	09.10.1979	**27**	**0**	2000-2005, Defensor Sporting Club Montevideo (13/0), Internazionale FC Milano (10/0), R Standard Liège (3/0), Charlton Athletic FC London (1/0).
(497/764)	SOSA ARDÁIZ Rúben	25.04.1966	**47**	**15**	1984-1995, Danubio FC Montevideo (6/0), Real Zaragoza CD (5/0), SS Lazio Roma (21/10), Internazionale FC Milano (15/5).
(700/975)	SOSA FARÍAS Marcelo Fabián	06.02.1978	**27**	**2**	2003-2006, Danubio FC Montevideo (12/1), Spartak Moskva (8/1), Club Atlético de Madrid (5/0), CA Osasuna Pamplona (2/0).
(627/898)	SOSA Heberley	01.08.1973	**1**	**0**	1996, CA Peñarol Montevideo (1/0).
(499/767)	SOSA José Luis	01.01.1956	**5**	**0**	1984, Club Nacional de Football Montevideo (5/0).
(299/500)	SOSA Roberto Eduardo	14.06.1935	**22**	**0**	1959-1967
(115/195)	SOSA Roque		**3**	**0**	1925, Club Nacional de Football Montevideo (3/0).
(247/431)	SOUTO Rafael Arturo	24.10.1930	**6**	**0**	1953-1954, Club Nacional de Football Montevideo (6/0).
(322/532)	SPENCER Alberto Pedro	06.12.1937	**6**	**1**	1962-1967, Peñarol Montevideo (6/1).
(823/1055)	STUANI CURBELO Christian Ricardo	12.10.1986	**7**	**2**	2012-2013, RCD Espanyol Barcelona (7/2).
(217/379)	STULA Washington		**3**	**0**	1947, CA Cerro Montevideo (3/0).
(748/1030)	SUÁREZ DÍAZ Luis Alberto	24.01.1987	**76**	**38**	2007-2013, FC Groningen (1/0), AFC Ajax Amsterdam (38/16), Liverpool FC (37/22).
(536/803)	SUÁREZ Edison Omar	06.11.1966	**12**	**1**	1988-1990, Danubio FC Montevideo (12/1).
(225/395)	SUÁREZ Esteban		**4**	**0**	1949, CA Bella Vista Montevideo (4/0).
(98/171)	SUFFIOTTI Arturo		**1**	**1**	1924, Club Nacional de Football Montevideo (1/1).
(739/1017)	SURRACO LAMÉ Juan Ignacio	14.08.1987	**2**	**0**	2006, Central Español FC Montevideo (2/0).

(158/264)	TABOADA Alberto		**6**	**1**	1935-1936, Montevideo Wanderers FC (6/1).
(442/697)	TABORDA Martin	14.04.1956	**2**	**0**	1977, Club Nacional de Football Montevideo (2/0).
(700/977)	TABORDA RAMOS Sebastián	22.05.1981	**1**	**0**	2003, Defensor Sporting Club Montevideo (1/0).
(264/444)	TAIBO Walter	07.03.1931	**31**	**0**	1955-1966
(608/881)	TAIS VIDEGAÍN Washington Eduardo	21.12.1972	**18**	**0**	1995-2002, CA Peñarol Montevideo (6/0), Racing Club Santander (5/0), Real Betis Balompié Sevilla (7/0).
(352/579)	TECHERA Rúben		**5**	**0**	1967-1969, Club Nacional de Football Montevideo (5/0).
(82/135)	TEJERA Domingo	22.07.1899	**20**	**0**	1922-1930, Montevideo Wanderers FC (20/0).
(198/347)	TEJERA Eusebio Ramón	06.01.1922	**31**	**0**	1945-1954, CA River Plate Montevideo (5/0), Club Nacional de Football Montevideo (23/0), Defensor Sporting Club Montevideo (3/0).
(196/342)	TEJERA Juan		**2**	**1**	1944
(583/838)	TEJERA Marcelo	06.08.1973	**6**	**0**	1991-2005, Defensor Sporting Club Montevideo (5/0), CA Peñarol Montevideo (1/0).
(262/441)	TEJERA Omar		**5**	**0**	1955, Montevideo Wanderers FC (5/0).
(216/378)	TERRA Julio Ulises		**3**	**0**	1947, CA River Plate Montevideo (3/0).
(607/874)	TITO Diego	16.08.1971	**3**	**0**	1994-1997, CA Bella Vista Montevideo (1/0), Club Nacional de Football Montevideo (2/0).
(32/082)	TOGNOLA José		**4**	**1**	1913-1916, Reformers FC Montevideo (4/1).
(332/555)	TOJA Julio		**3**	**2**	1965, Montevideo Wanderers FC (3/2).
(100/182)	TOMASSINA Humberto	12.09.1898	**5**	**0**	1924-1928, Liverpool FC Montevideo (3/0), CA Lito (2/0).
(427/677)	TORRES Daniel		**2**	**1**	1976
(472/745)	TORRES Jorge		**2**	**0**	1981
(532/788)	TRASANTE Obdulio Eduardo	20.04.1960	**5**	**0**	1987-1988, CA Peñarol Montevideo (5/0)
(299/499)	TROCHE HERRERA Florencio Horacio	04.02.1935	**29**	**0**	1959-1966
(215/372)	TULIC Juan José		**7**	**0**	1947, CA River Plate Montevideo (7/0).

(331/553)	UBIÑA Ignacio Luis	07.06.1940	**31**	**1**	1965-1973, Rampla Juniors FC Montevideo 66, Club Nacional de Football Montevideo (23/1).
(448/708)	UMPIÉRREZ Rúben	25.10.1956	**1**	**0**	1978, CA Cerro Montevideo (1/0).
(418/652)	UNANUE Lorenzo		**23**	**2**	1975-1979, CA Peñarol Montevideo (23/2).
(358/581)	URBANO Alberto		**5**	**0**	1967
(44/097)	URDINARÁN Antonio	30.10.1898	**17**	**2**	1916-1922, CA Defensor Montevideo (3/0), Club Nacional de Football Montevideo (14/2).
(92/150)	URDINARÁN Santos	03.03.1900	**22**	**2**	1923-1932, Club Nacional de Football Montevideo (22/2).

(89/144)	URIARTE Fermín	1902	**14**	**0**	1923-1925, CA Lito (14/0).
(1/002)	URIOSTE Carlos Carve		**4**	**0**	1902-1906, Club Nacional de Football Montevideo (4/0).
(333/556)	URRUZMENDI José Eusebio	25.08.1944	**21**	**8**	1965-1967, Club Nacional de Football Montevideo (21/8).
(738/1014)	VALDEZ SUÁREZ Carlos Adrian	02.05.1983	**17**	**0**	2006-2010, FBC Treviso (8/0), Reggina Calcio Reggio Calabria (8/0), AC Siena (1/0).
(31/081)	VALLARINO Ricardo		**5**	**3**	1913-1914, Club Nacional de Football Montevideo (5/3).
(113/190)	VALVERDE Juan		**5**	**0**	1925, CA Bella Vista Montevideo (5/0).
(246/422)	VANOLI Rúben		**4**	**0**	1953, CA River Plate Montevideo (4/0).
(623/892)	VANZINI Marco	19.04.1976	**3**	**0**	1995-1996, Danubio FC Montevideo (3/0).
(38/089)	VANZZINO José		**37**	**0**	1915-1927, Club Nacional de Football Montevideo (37/0).
(387/608)	VARELA Enrique		**2**	**0**	1971
(340/559)	VARELA Luis Alberto		**7**	**0**	1965-1967, CA Peñarol Montevideo (7/0).
(37/087)	VARELA Manuel		**18**	**0**	1915-1924, CA Peñarol Montevideo (11/0), Club Nacional de Football Montevideo (7/0).
(175/305)	VARELA Obdulio Jacinto	20.09.1917	**44**	**9**	1939-1954, Montevideo Wanderers FC (14/2), CA Peñarol Montevideo (30/7).
(672/941)	VARELA RODRÍGUEZ Gustavo Antonio	14.05.1978	**24**	**0**	2000-2006, Club Nacional de Football Montevideo (11/0), FC Schalke 04 Gelsenkirchen (13/0).
(162/272)	VARELA Severino		**23**	**19**	1935-1942, CA Peñarol Montevideo (23/19).
(699/968)	VARGAS ABELLA Gonzalo	22.09.1981	**10**	**3**	2002-2007, Defensor Sporting Club Montevideo (1/0), CA Gimnasia y Esgrima La Plata (5/2), AS Monaco (4/1).
(456/727)	VARGAS Ernesto	01.05.1961	**12**	**1**	1979-1981, CA Peñarol Montevideo (12/1).
(95/161)	VAROLI Lorenzo		**1**	**0**	1923, CA Lito (1/0).
(298/493)	VÁZQUEZ Antonio		**1**	**0**	1959
(485/758)	VÁZQUEZ Carlos	12.03.1962	**3**	**0**	1983, CA Bella Vista Montevideo (3/0).
(387/602)	VÁZQUEZ Jorge		**1**	**0**	1971
(181/322)	VÁZQUEZ Juan Antonio		**8**	**2**	1940-1946, CA Peñarol Montevideo
(735/1008)	VÁZQUEZ MAIDANA Rodrigo Sebastián	04.11.1980	**1**	**0**	2005, Club Nacional de Football Montevideo (1/0).
(298/498)	VÁZQUEZ Otto		**1**	**0**	1959
(181/320)	VECINO Luis		**1**	**0**	1940
(500/769)	VEGA PERRONE César Javier	02.09.1959	**8**	**0**	1984-1986, Danubio FC Montevideo (8/0).
(515/771)	VELICHCO Gualberto	21.02.1958	**5**	**0**	1985, Club Nacional de Football Montevideo (5/0).
(352/578)	VERA Luis Alberto		**6**	**0**	1967, CA Fénix Montevideo (6/0).
(745/1128)	VERA MÉNDEZ Diego Daniel	05.01.1985	**3**	**0**	2006-2007, CA Bella Vista Montevideo (2/0), Club Nacional de Football Montevideo (1/0).
(277/462)	VERDES Manuel		**1**	**0**	1956
(644/909)	VESPA Liber Ernesto	18.10.1971	**12**	**0**	1997-1999, AA Argentinos Juniors Buenos Aires (6/0), CA Rosario Central (6/0).
(174/303)	VIANA General		**10**	**0**	1939-1945, Central FC Montevideo (3/0), Club Nacional de Football Montevideo (7/0).
(745/1023)	VICTORINO DANSILIO Mauricio Bernardo	11.10.1982	**21**	**0**	2006-2012, Club Tiburones de Veracruz (2/0), CF de la Universidad de Chile Santiago (11/0), Cruzeiro EC Belo Horizonte (8/0).
(536/801)	VIDAL Daniel Alejandro	01.04.1967	**5**	**1**	1988, CA Peñarol Montevideo (5/1).
(237/412)	VIDAL Ernesto José	15.11.1921	**8**	**2**	1950-1952
(93/152)	VIDAL José	15.12.1896	**7**	**1**	1923-1924, CA Belgrano (7/1).
(720/1002)	VIERA GALAÍN Mario Sebastián	07.03.1983	**11**	**0**	2004-2009, Club Nacional de Football Montevideo (10/0), Villarreal CF (5/0).
(343/571)	VIERA Milton	11.05.1946	**5**	**1**	1966, Club Nacional de Football Montevideo (5/1).
(704/989)	VIGNERI CETRULO Nicolás Ignacio	06.07.1983	**9**	**2**	2003-2007, CtA Fénix Montevideo (4/1), CA Peñarol Montevideo (5/1).
(745/1026)	VILA WILKINS Mauro Adrián	25.02.1986	**2**	**0**	2006, Defensor Sporting Club Montevideo (2/0).
(288/474)	VILARIÑO Oscar		**2**	**0**	1957-1959
(231/398)	VILCHES Héctor	14.02.1926	**10**	**0**	1950-1952
(164/283)	VILLADÓNIGA Segundo		**6**	**3**	1936-1937, CA Peñarol Montevideo (6/3).
(387/604)	VILLALBA Luis		**9**	**0**	1971-1972
(233/408)	VILLAMIDE Hugo		**4**	**1**	1950
(67/116)	VILLAR José María		**2**	**0**	1919, Universal FC Montevideo (2/0).
(500/768)	VILLAREAL José		**4**	**0**	1984
(224/386)	VILLARREAL Julio César		**7**	**0**	1949, Liverpool FC Montevideo (7/0).
(482/755)	VILLAZÁN Jorge	05.10.1962	**5**	**0**	1983, Club Nacional de Football Montevideo (5/0).
(422/667)	VILLAZÁN Rafael		**11**	**0**	1975-1977, Club Nacional de Football Montevideo (11/0).
(78/126)	VILLAZÚ Luis		**2**	**0**	1921, CA Lito (2/0).
(340/565)	VIRGILI Orlando		**9**	**1**	1965-1968
(180/316)	VOLPI Luis Tomás		**12**	**1**	1940-1946, Club Nacional de Football Montevideo (6/1).
(436/691)	YANES Jorge		**2**	**0**	1977
(515/772)	YELADIÁN Abraham	02.01.1958	**5**	**0**	1985, Danubio FC Montevideo (5/0).
(204/353)	YOUNG Alfredo		**2**	**0**	1945
(154/253)	YOUNG Pedro		**1**	**0**	1933, CA Peñarol Montevideo (1/0).
(176/306)	ZACCOUR Félix		**2**	**0**	1939, Institución Atlética Sud América Montevideo (1/0).
(646/916)	ZALAYETA Marcelo Danubio	05.12.1978	**32**	**10**	1997-2005, CA Peñarol Montevideo (4/1), Juventus FC Torino (1/1), Empoli FC (7/3), Sevilla CF (9/2), Juventus FC Torino (1/0), AC Perugia (1/0), Juventus FC Torino (9/3)
(497/765)	ZALAZAR RODRÍGUEZ José Luis	26.10.1963	**29**	**4**	1984-1993, CA Peñarol Montevideo (16/3), Albacete Balompié (13/1).
(186/331)	ZAPIRAIN Bibiano		**20**	**4**	1942-1946, Club Nacional de Football Montevideo (20/4).
(537/804)	ZEOLI Adolfo Javier	02.05.1962	**14**	**0**	1988-1990, Danubio FC Montevideo (13/0), CD Tenerife (1/0).

(39/091)	ZIBECHI Alfredo	30.10.1895	**39**	**1**	1915-1924, Montevideo Wanderers FC (3/0), Club Nacional de Football Montevideo (36/1).
(81/130)	ZIBECHI Armando		**1**	**0**	1921, Montevideo Wanderers FC (1/0).
(4/025)	ZIBECHI Pedro		**5**	**2**	1906-1913, CURCC Montevideo (5/2).
(92/149)	ZINGONE Pedro	1899	**4**	**1**	1923-1924, CA Lito (4/1).
(400/633)	ZORYEZ Mario		**18**	**0**	1973-1979
(6/036)	ZUAZÚ Pedro		**10**	**0**	1907-1910, Club Nacional de Football Montevideo (10/0).
(364/589)	ZUBÍA Oscar Daniel	08.02.1946	**15**	**4**	1968-1971
(5/033)	ZUMARÁN Alberto		**5**	**3**	1906-1909, Montevideo Wanderers FC (5/3).
(155/255)	ZUNINO Erebo		**12**	**0**	1933-1939, CA Peñarol Montevideo (12/0).

NATIONAL COACHES

Name	Period	Matches	P	W	D	L	GF	-	GA	
Ramón PLATERO	15.08.1917 – 16.10.1917	[51-56]	6	5	0	1	13	-	2	83.33 %
Severino CASTILLO	18.07.1918 – 29.05.1919	[57-66]	10	3	4	3	13	-	12	50.00 %
Ernesto FÍGOLI	18.07.1919 – 02.11.1921	[67-81]	15	10	1	4	34	-	21	70.00 %
Pedro OLIVIERI	23.09.1922 - 12.10.1922	[82-85]	4	2	1	1	3	-	1	62.50 %
Rafael GALLI	12.11.1922 – 17.12.1922	[86-88]	3	2	1	0	4	-	2	83.33 %
Leonardo DE LUCCA	24.06.1923 - 25.12.1923	[89-94]	6	2	3	1	8	-	7	58.33 %
Alberto Horacio SUPPICI	25.11.1923	[95]	1	1	0	0	2	-	1	100.00 %
Leonardo DE LUCCA	02.12.1923	[96]	1	1	0	0	2	-	0	100.00 %
Alberto Horacio SUPPICI	08.12.1923	[97]	1	1	0	0	3	-	2	100.00 %
Manuel VARELA	25.05.1924	[98]	1	1	0	0	2	-	0	100.00 %
Alberto Horacio SUPPICI	25.05.1924	[99]	1	0	0	1	0	-	4	0 %
Ernesto FÍGOLI	26.05.1924 - 09.06.1924	[100-104]	5	5	0	0	20	-	2	100.00 %
Leonardo DE LUCCA	10.08.1924 – 31.08.1924	[105-106]	2	0	1	1	2	-	3	25.00 %
Andrés MAZALI	21.09.1924 – 02.10.1924	[107-109]	3	0	2	1	2	-	3	33.33 %
Ernesto MELIANTE	19.10.1924 – 02.11.1924	[110-112]	3	2	1	0	8	-	1	83.33 %
Alberto Horacio SUPPICI	14.07.1925 – 22.08.1925	[113-117]	5	1	1	3	1	-	3	30.00 %
Andrés MAZALI	17.10.1926 – 01.11.1926	[118-121]	4	4	0	0	17	-	2	100.00 %
Luis GRECCO	14.07.1927 – 10.12.1927	[122-127]	6	4	0	2	19	-	6	66.66 %
Primo GIANOTTI	30.05.1928 - 13.06.1928	[128-132]	5	4	1	0	12	-	5	90.00 %
Primo GIANOTTI	30.08.1928 – 21.09.1928	[135-136]	2	0	1	1	2	-	3	25.00 %
Alberto Horacio SUPPICI	16.06.1929	[137]	1	0	0	1	0	-	2	0 %
Ernesto FÍGOLI	16.06.1929	[138]	1	0	1	0	1	-	1	50.00 %
Alberto Horacio SUPPICI	20.09.1929 – 15.08.1934	[139-157]	19	8	3	8	29	-	26	50.00 %
Raúl BLANCO	13.01.1935 – 18.07.1935	[158-161]	4	3	1	0	7	-	2	87.50 %
Alberto Horacio SUPPICI	15.08.1935	[162]	1	1	0	0	3	-	0	100.00 %
José María PEDREIA	09.08.1936	[163]	1	1	0	0	1	-	0	100.00 %
Alberto Horacio SUPPICI	20.11.1936 – 12.02.1939	[164-177]	14	6	0	8	29	-	32	42.85 %
José Pedro CEA	24.03.1940 – 25.08.1942	[178-193]	16	11	2	3	41	-	17	75.00 %
Héctor CASTRO	28.03.1943 – 04.04.1943	[194-195]	2	0	1	1	3	-	4	25.00 %
Ricardo ACOSTA	14.05.1944 – 17.05.1944	[196-197]	2	0	0	2	1	-	10	0 %
José NASAZZI YARZA	24.01.1945 – 25.02.1945	[198-203]	6	3	0	3	14	-	6	50.00 %
José Pedro CEA	18.07.1945 – 15.08.1945	[204-205]	2	0	1	1	4	-	8	25.00 %
Aníbal TEJADA	05.01.1946 – 23.01.1946	[206-209]	4	2	1	1	9	-	8	62.50 %
Guzmán VILA GOMENSORO	29.01.1946 - 08.02.1946	[210-212]	3	1	0	2	7	-	5	33.33 %
Marcelino PÉREZ	29.03.1947 – 01.04.1947	[213-214]	2	0	1	1	2	-	3	25.00 %
Juan LÓPEZ FONTANA	02.12.1947 – 11.04.1948	[215-223]	9	6	1	2	26	-	11	72.22 %
Oscar MARCENARO	13.04.1949 – 08.05.1949	[224-230]	7	2	1	4	14	-	20	35.71 %
Romeo VÁZQUEZ	07.04.1950 – 17.05.1950	[231-236]	6	2	0	4	14	-	13	33.33 %
Juan LÓPEZ FONTANA	02.07.1950 – 16.04.1952	[237-245]	9	6	1	2	31	-	15	72.22 %
Romeo VÁZQUEZ	25.02.1953 – 28.03.1953	[246-251]	6	3	1	2	15	-	6	58.33 %
Juan LÓPEZ FONTANA	31.05.1953 – 03.07.1954	[252-261]	10	5	2	3	30	-	19	60.00 %
Juan Carlos CORAZZO	09.03.1955 - 30.03.1955	[262-266]	5	2	1	2	12	-	12	50.00 %
Hugo BAGNULO	21.01.1956 – 01.07.1956	[267-273]	7	4	1	2	10	-	7	64.28 %
Roque Gastón MÁSPOLI	15.07.1956 – 12/08.1956	[274-275]	2	1	1	0	4	-	3	75.00 %
Lorenzo FERNÁNDEZ	10.10.1956 – 14.11.1956	[276-277]	2	0	1	1	3	-	4	25.00 %
Juan LÓPEZ FONTANA	07.03.1957 – 28.07.1957	[278-289]	12	6	3	3	20	-	19	62.50 %
Lorenzo FERNÁNDEZ	06.04.1958 – 30.04.1958	[290-291]	2	1	0	1	1	-	2	50.00 %
Héctor CASTRO	08.03.1959 – 02.04.1959	[292-297]	6	2	0	4	15	-	14	33.33 %
Juan Carlos CORAZZO	01.05.1959 – 17.08.1960	[298-307]	10	6	2	2	22	-	13	70.00 %
Enrique FERNÁNDEZ VIOLA	15.07.1961 – 30.07.1961	[308-309]	2	1	1	0	3	-	2	75.00 %
Juan Carlos CORAZZO	12.10.1961 – 02.05.1962	[310-318]	9	2	3	4	11	-	20	38.88 %
Hugo BAGNULO - Juan LÓPEZ FONTANA - Roberto SCARONE	30.05.1962 – 19.06.1962	[319-322]	4	2	0	2	7	-	7	50.00 %
Walter TAIBO	15.08.1962	[323]	1	0	0	1	1	-	3	0 %
Washington ETCHAMENDI	23.03.1963 – 24.07.1963	[324-325]	2	1	1	0	3	-	2	75.00 %
Rafael MILANS	25.04.1964 - 13.06.1965	[326-339]	14	7	2	5	21	-	13	57.14 %
Juan LÓPEZ FONTANA	07.09.1965 – 04.12.1965	[340-341]	2	0	0	2	1	-	6	0 %
Ondino Leonel VIERA PALASEREZ	15.05.1966 – 23.07.1966	[342-351]	10	3	4	3	10	-	14	50.00 %
Juan Carlos CORAZZO	04.01.1967 - 26.10.1968	[352-370]	19	7	8	4	27	-	23	57.89 %
Juan Eduardo HOHBERG	08.06.1969 - 20.06.1970	[371-386]	16	8	2	6	16	-	11	56.25 %
Juan Ricardo FACCIO	08.02.1971 – 10.02.1971	[387-388]	2	0	1	1	1	-	4	25.00 %
Rodolfo ZAMORA	14.07.1971 – 03.11.1971	[389-392]	4	1	1	2	4	-	7	37.50 %
Washington ETCHAMENDI	23.05.1972 - 06.07.1972	[393-399]	7	1	2	4	2	-	6	28.57 %
Hugo BAGNULO	17.05.1973 – 19.07.1973	[400-407]	8	3	4	1	10	-	5	62.50 %
Roberto PORTA	23.03.1974 – 23.06.1974	[408-417]	10	4	3	3	10	-	10	55.00 %
Carlos Silva CABRERA	04.06.1975 – 18.07.1975	[418-422]	5	3	0	2	7	-	5	60.00 %
Juan Alberto SCHIAFFINO	21.09.1975 – 01.10.1975	[423-424]	2	1	0	1	1	-	3	50.00 %
José María RODRÍGUEZ	25.02.1976 – 09.06.1976	[425-430]	6	0	1	5	5	-	14	8.33 %
Juan Eduardo HOHBERG	09.10.1976 - 27.02.1977	[431-441]	11	3	7	1	12	-	8	59.09 %
Raúl BENTANCOR	17.03.1977 – 27.03.1977	[442-443]	2	1	1	0	4	-	2	75.00 %
Omar BORRÁS	08.06.1977 – 15.06.1977	[444-445]	2	0	1	1	0	-	2	25.00 %
Hugo BAGNULO	25.04.1978 – 24.05.1978	[446-448]	3	1	1	1	2	-	3	50.00 %
Raúl BENTANCOR	31.05.1979 – 18.07.1979	[449-451]	3	1	0	2	3	-	7	33.33 %
Roque Gastón MÁSPOLI	30.08.1979 – 13.09.1981	[452-477]	26	11	8	7	39	-	22	57.69 %
Omar BORRÁS	20.02.1982 – 16.06.1986	[478-531]	54	24	18	12	77	-	50	61.11 %
Roberto FLEITAS	19.06.1987 – 12.07.1987	[532-535]	4	4	0	0	6	-	2	100.00 %
Gregorio PÉREZ	07.08.1988	[536]	1	0	0	1	1	-	2	0 %

Óscar Wáshington TABÁREZ SILVA	27.09.1988 – 25.06.1990	[537-570]	34	17	8	9	50	-	28	61.76 %
Pedro Ramón CUBILLA	05.05.1991 – 30.05.1991	[571-574]	4	2	0	2	4	-	3	50.00 %
Luis Alberto CUBILLA ALMEIDA	12.06.1991 – 15.08.1993	[575-601]	27	11	10	6	32	-	26	59.25 %
Ildo Enrique MANEIRO	29.08.1993 – 19.09.1993	[602-605]	4	3	0	1	7	-	3	75.00 %
Roberto FLEITAS	13.10.1993	[606]	1	0	0	1	0	-	5	0 %
Héctor NÚÑEZ BELLO	19.10.1994 - 12.11.1996	[607-631]	25	9	7	9	36	-	31	50.00 %
Juan AHUNTCHAÍN	15.12.1996 – 18.06.1997	[632-640]	9	3	2	4	9	-	11	44.44 %
Roque Gastón MÁSPOLI	20.07.1997 – 16.11.1997	[641-645]	5	2	1	2	7	-	6	50.00 %
Víctor Haroldo PÚA SOSA	13.12.1997 – 18.07.1999	[646-658]	13	5	3	5	17	-	19	50.00 %
Daniel Alberto PASSARELLA (*Argentina*)	18.08.1999 – 15.11.2000	[659-672]	14	6	4	4	19	-	12	57.14 %
Víctor Haroldo PÚA SOSA	28.02.2001 – 11.06.2002	[673-698]	26	10	8	8	33	-	27	53.84 %
Jorge Da SILVA	20.11.2002	[699]	1	0	0	1	0	-	1	0 %
Gustavo FERRÍN	04.02.2003 – 28.03.2003	[700-701]	2	0	2	0	3	-	3	50.00 %
Juan Ramón CARRASCO	08.06.2003 – 31.03.2004	[702-714]	13	7	2	4	32	-	26	61.53 %
Jorge Daniel FOSSATI LURACHI	01.06.2004 - 16.11.2005	[715-737]	23	8	8	7	26	-	33	52.17 %
Gustavo FERRÍN	01.03.2006	[738]	1	0	0	1	1	-	2	0 %
Juan José VERZERI	11.08.2010	[794]	1	1	0	0	2	-	0	100.00 %
Óscar Wáshington TABÁREZ SILVA	21.05.2006 –>	[739->*	101	47	30	24	175	-	112	

Uruguay played without national coach in following matches: [1-50], [133-134].
*replaced by Juan José Verzeri for Match [794]

National coaches several times in charge:

Name	How often	Matches	M	W	D	L	GF	-	GA	
Ernesto FÍGOLI	3x	[67-81],[100-104],[138]	21	15	2	4	55	-	24	76.19 %
Leonardo DE LUCCA	3x	[89-94],[96],[105-106]	9	3	4	2	12	-	10	55.55 %
Alberto Horacio SUPPICI	4x	[95],[97],[99],[113-117],[137], [139-157],[162],[164-177]	43	18	4	21	67	-	70	46.51 %
Andrés MAZALI	2x	[107-109],[118-121]	7	4	2	1	19	-	5	71.42 %
Primo GIANOTTI	2x	[128-132],[135-136]	7	4	2	1	14	-	8	71.42 %
José Pedro CEA	2x	[178-193],[204-205]	18	11	3	4	45	-	25	69.44 %
Héctor CASTRO	2x	[194-195],[292-297]	8	2	1	5	18	-	18	31.25 %
Juan LÓPEZ	5x	[215-223],[237-245],[252-261], [278-289],[340-341]	42	23	7	12	108		70	63.09 %
Romeo VÁZQUEZ	2x	[231-236],[246-251]	12	5	1	6	29	-	19	45.83 %
Juan Carlos CORAZZO	4x	[262-266],[298-307], [310-318], [352-370]	43	17	14	12	72	-	68	55.81 %
Hugo BAGNULO	4x	[267-273],[400-407], [446-448]	18	8	6	4	22	-	15	61.11 %
Roque Gastón MÁSPOLI	3x	[274-275],[452-477],[641-645]	33	14	10	9	50	-	31	57.57 %
Lorenzo FERNÁNDEZ	2x	[276-277],[290-291]	4	1	1	2	4	-	6	37.50 %
Washington ETCHAMENDI	2x	[324-325],[393-399]	9	2	3	4	5	-	8	38.88 %
Juan Eduardo HOHBERG	2x	[371-386],[431-441]	27	11	9	7	28	-	19	57.40 %
Raúl BENTANCOR	2x	[442-443],[449-451]	5	2	1	2	7	-	9	50.00 %
Omar BORRÁS	2x	[444-445],[478-531]	56	24	19	13	77	-	52	59.82 %
Roberto FLEITAS	2x	[532-535],[606]	5	4	0	1	6	-	7	80.00 %
Óscar Wáshington TABÁREZ SILVA	2x	[537-570],[739->	135	64	38	33	225	-	140	61.48 %
Víctor Haroldo PÚA SOSA	2x	[646-658],[673-698]	39	15	11	13	50	-	46	52.56 %
Gustavo FERRÍN	2x	[700-701],[738]	3	0	2	1	4	-	5	33.33 %

HEAD-TO-HEAD STATISTICS

	HOME							AWAY							NEUTRAL							TOTAL						
Algeria								1	0	0	1	0	:	1								1	0	0	1	0	:	1
Angola															1	1	0	0	2	:	0	1	1	0	0	2	:	0
Argentina	78	36	21	21	111	:	90	81	11	21	49	75	:	164	21	7	2	12	28	:	35	180	54	44	82	214	:	##
Australia	3	3	0	0	6	:	0	5	1	1	3	2	:	5	1	0	0	1	0	:	1	9	4	1	4	8	:	6
Austria								1	1	0	0	2	:	0	1	0	0	1	1	:	3	2	1	0	1	3	:	3
Belgium								1	0	0	1	0	:	2	1	0	0	1	1	:	3	2	0	0	2	1	:	5
Bolivia	14	13	1	0	38	:	8	13	2	5	6	10	:	16	13	11	1	1	50	:	4	40	26	7	7	98	:	28
Brazil	24	11	9	4	34	:	24	34	4	7	23	31	:	74	15	5	3	7	29	:	31	73	20	19	34	94	:	129
Bulgaria															1	0	1	0	1	:	1	1	0	1	0	1	:	1
Canada															1	1	0	0	3	:	1	1	1	0	0	3	:	1
Chile	27	20	7	0	64	:	22	31	10	9	12	35	:	40	17	11	2	4	34	:	15	75	41	18	16	133	:	77
China P.R.								3	2	1	0	7	:	1	2	1	1	0	2	:	0	5	3	2	0	9	:	1
Colombia	13	8	4	1	22	:	10	15	4	3	8	13	:	26	10	6	2	2	19	:	7	38	18	9	11	54	:	43
Costa Rica	3	2	1	0	8	:	6	2	2	0	0	2	:	0	3	2	1	0	5	:	2	8	6	2	0	15	:	8
Czechoslovakia	2	2	0	0	5	:	2								2	1	0	1	3	:	3	4	3	0	1	8	:	5
Czech Republic															2	1	0	1	2	:	2	2	1	0	1	2	:	2
Denmark															2	0	0	2	2	:	8	2	0	0	2	2	:	8
East Germany	4	1	1	2	4	:	6	2	0	1	1	0	:	1								6	1	2	3	4	:	7
Ecuador	16	12	4	0	36	:	10	15	7	4	4	25	:	16	12	10	1	1	43	:	11	43	29	9	5	104	:	37
Egypt								1	1	0	0	2	:	0								1	1	0	0	2	:	0
England	4	2	1	1	5	:	3	5	1	2	2	4	:	5	1	1	0	0	4	:	2	10	4	3	3	13	:	10
Estonia	1	1	0	0	3	:	0	1	0	0	1	0	:	2								2	1	0	1	3	:	2
Finland	2	2	0	0	8	:	1															2	2	0	0	8	:	1
France	1	1	0	0	1	:	0	4	1	2	1	5	:	3	3	1	2	0	2	:	1	8	3	4	1	8	:	4

Georgia								1	0	0	1	0	:	2								1	0	0	1	0	:	2
Germany	2	0	0	2	1	:	6	4	0	1	3	4	:	13	5	1	1	3	7	:	10	11	1	2	8	12	:	29
Ghana															1	0	1	0	1	:	1	1	0	1	0	1	:	1
Haiti								3	1	2	0	1	:	0								3	1	2	0	1	:	0
Holland	2	1	1	0	3	:	1	1	1	0	0	2	:	0	3	1	0	2	4	:	6	6	3	1	2	9	:	7
Honduras															2	0	1	1	2	:	3	2	0	1	1	2	:	3
Hungary	1	0	1	0	1	:	1	1	0	1	0	1	:	1	1	0	0	1	2	:	4	3	0	2	1	4	:	6
India								1	1	0	0	3	:	1								1	1	0	0	3	:	1
Indonesia								2	2	0	0	10	:	3								2	2	0	0	10	:	3
Iran															1	0	1	0	1	:	1	1	0	1	0	1	:	1
Iraq															1	1	0	0	5	:	2	1	1	0	0	5	:	2
Israel	1	1	0	0	4	:	1	4	2	1	1	7	:	7	1	1	0	0	2	:	0	6	4	1	1	13	:	8
Italy	1	1	0	0	2	:	0	5	1	2	2	3	:	5	3	1	2	0	5	:	4	9	3	4	2	10	:	9
Jamaica								2	1	0	1	3	:	2								2	1	0	1	3	:	2
Japan								5	3	1	1	16	:	11								5	3	1	1	16	:	11
Jordan	1	0	1	0	0	:	0	1	1	0	0	5	:	0								2	1	1	0	5	:	0
Libya								1	1	0	0	3	:	2	1	1	0	0	2	:	1	2	2	0	0	5	:	3
Luxembourg								1	1	0	0	1	:	0								1	1	0	0	1	:	0
Malaysia															1	1	0	0	6	:	0	1	1	0	0	6	:	0
Mexico	3	0	2	1	2	:	4	4	0	3	1	7	:	9	12	5	2	5	14	:	12	19	5	7	7	23	:	25
Morocco								1	1	0	0	1	:	0								1	1	0	0	1	:	0
New Zealand	2	1	1	0	9	:	2															2	1	1	0	9	:	2
Nigeria															1	1	0	0	2	:	1	1	1	0	0	2	:	1
Northern Ireland								2	0	0	2	0	:	4	1	1	0	0	1	:	0	3	1	0	2	1	:	4
Norway								2	1	1	0	3	:	2								2	1	1	0	3	:	2
Panama															1	1	0	0	6	:	1	1	1	0	0	6	:	1
Paraguay	29	17	4	8	47	:	28	25	4	11	10	22	:	36	17	8	2	7	37	:	28	71	29	17	25	106	:	92
Peru	23	14	7	2	40	:	12	27	15	5	7	39	:	23	12	6	1	5	26	:	21	62	35	13	14	105	:	56
Poland	2	0	1	1	2	:	3	1	1	0	0	3	:	1								3	1	1	1	5	:	4
Portugal								1	0	0	1	0	:	3	1	0	1	0	1		1	2	0	1	1	1	:	4
Republic of Ireland	1	1	0	0	2	:	0	2	1	1	0	4	:	3								3	2	1	0	6	:	3
Romania	2	1	1	0	5	:	1	2	0	1	1	1	:	2	1	1	0	0	2	:	0	5	2	2	1	8	:	3
Russia								1	0	1	0	1	:	1								1	0	1	0	1	:	1
Saar								1	1	0	0	7	:	1								1	1	0	0	7	:	1
Saudi Arabia								1	0	0	1	2	:	3								1	0	0	1	2	:	3
Scotland								2	1	0	1	3	:	4	2	1	1	0	7	:	0	4	2	1	1	10	:	4
Senegal															1	0	1	0	3	:	3	1	0	1	0	3	:	3
Serbia	1	1	0	0	6	:	1	3	0	1	2	2	:	4	2	1	0	1	8	:	3	6	2	1	3	16	:	8
Singapore								1	1	0	0	2	:	1								1	1	0	0	2	:	1
Slovenia								1	1	0	0	2	:	0								1	1	0	0	2	:	0
South Africa								2	1	1	0	3	:	0	1	1	0	0	4	:	3	3	2	1	0	7	:	3
Soouth Korea	1	1	0	0	2	:	1	2	2	0	0	4	:	0	3	2	1	0	5	:	3	6	5	1	0	11	:	4
Soviet Union	2	0	0	2	2	:	5	2	0	0	2	0	:	6	3	1	0	2	2	:	3	7	1	0	6	4	:	14
Spain	1	0	1	0	0	:	0	5	0	2	3	4	:	9	4	0	2	2	4	:	7	10	0	5	5	8	:	16
Sweden															3	1	0	2	3	:	6	3	1	0	2	3	:	6
Switzerland	1	1	0	0	4	:	0	2	1	1	0	6	:	4	1	1	0	0	3	:	0	4	3	1	0	13	:	4
Tahiti															1	1	0	0	8	:	0	1	1	0	0	8	:	0
Tunisia								1	0	1	0	0	:	0								1	0	1	0	0	:	0
Turkey															1	1	0	0	3	:	2	1	1	0	0	3	:	2
Ukraine								1	1	0	0	3	:	2								1	1	0	0	3	:	2
United Arab Emirates															1	1	0	0	2	:	0	1	1	0	0	2	:	0
United States								4	0	2	2	4	:	6	2	2	0	0	4	:	0	6	2	2	2	8	:	6
Venezuela	13	10	2	1	36	:	8	13	6	4	3	17	:	11	2	1	1	0	4	:	2	28	17	7	4	57	:	21
Wales								1	0	1	0	0	:	0								1	0	1	0	0	:	0
TOTAL	**281**	**164**	**71**	**46**	**513**	**:**	**256**	**357**	**100**	**100**	**157**	**412**	**:**	**538**	**202**	**103**	**34**	**65**	**417**	**:**	**258**	**840**	**367**	**205**	**268**	**1342**	**:**	**1050**

232

VENEZUELA

The Country:
República Bolivariana de Venezuela
(Bolivarian Republic of Venezuela)
Capital: Caracas
Surface: 916,445 km²
Inhabitants: 28,946,101
Time: UTC-4.30

The FA:
Federación Venezolana de Fútbol
Avenida Santos Erminy Ira, Calle las Delicias
Torre, Mega II P.H. Sabana Grande,
Caracas 1050
Year of Formation: 1926
Member of FIFA since: 1952
Member of CONMEBOL since: 1952

NATIONAL TEAM RECORDS

COPA AMÉRICA	
1916	Did not enter
1917	Did not enter
1919	Did not enter
1920	Did not enter
1921	Did not enter
1922	Did not enter
1923	Did not enter
1924	Did not enter
1925	Did not enter
1926	Did not enter
1927	Did not enter
1929	Did not enter
1935	Did not enter
1937	Did not enter
1939	Did not enter
1941	Did not enter
1942	Did not enter
1945	Did not enter
1946	Did not enter
1947	Did not enter
1949	Did not enter
1953	Did not enter
1955	Did not enter
1956	Did not enter
1957	Did not enter
1959	Did not enter
1959E	Did not enter
1963	Did not enter
1967	5th Place
1975	Round 1
1979	Round 1
1983	Round 1
1987	Round 1
1989	Round 1
1991	Round 1
1993	Round 1
1995	Round 1
1997	Round 1
1999	Round 1
2001	Round 1
2004	Round 1
2007	Quarter-Finals
2011	4th Place

WORLD CUP	
1930	Did not enter
1934	Did not enter
1938	Did not enter
1950	Did not enter
1954	Did not enter
1958	Withdrew
1962	Did not enter
1966	Qualifiers
1970	Qualifiers
1974	Withdrew
1978	Qualifiers
1982	Qualifiers
1986	Qualifiers
1990	Qualifiers
1994	Qualifiers
1998	Qualifiers
2002	Qualifiers
2006	Qualifiers
2010	Qualifiers
2014	Qualifiers

OLYMPIC GAMES 1900-2012
1980
FIFA CONFEDERATIONS CUP 1992-2013
None
PLAYER WITH MOST INTERNATIONAL CAPS
Juan Fernando Arango Sáenz – 120 caps (1999-2013)
PLAYER WITH MOST INTERNATIONAL GOALS
Giancarlo Gregorio Maldonado Marrero – 22 goals / 65 caps (2003-2011) &   Juan Fernando Arango Sáenz – 22 goals / 120 caps (1999-2013)

FULL INTERNATIONALS (1938-2013)

1. 12.02.1938 **PANAMA - VENEZUELA** **2-1(0-0)** 4th Juegos Centroamericanos y del Caribe
Estadio Nacional, Ciudad de Panamá
VEN: Ezequiel Machado (1/0), Teodardo Marcano (1/0), Ramón Morales (1/0), José María Ardila (1/0), Nicasio Camero (1/0), Hernán Mujica (1/0), Alberto Castillo (1/1), Francisco Marcano (1/0), Carlos Feo (1/0), Reinaldo Febrés Cordero (1/0), Fernando Ríos (1/0). Trainer: Vittorio Godigna (1).
Goal: Alberto Castillo.

2. 14.02.1938 **MEXICO - VENEZUELA** **1-0(1-0)** 4th Juegos Centroamericanos y del Caribe
Estadio Nacional, Ciudad de Panamá (Panama); Referee: Luis Ferré (El Salvador)
VEN: Ezequiel Machado (2/0), Teodardo Marcano (2/0), Ramón Morales (2/0), José María Ardila (2/0), Nicasio Camero (2/0), Mauricio Corao (1/0), Alberto Castillo (2/1), Francisco Marcano (2/0), Carlos Feo (2/0), Reinaldo Febrés Cordero (2/0), Fernando Ríos (2/0). Trainer: Vittorio Godigna (2).

3. 16.02.1938 **EL SALVADOR - VENEZUELA** **3-2** 4th Juegos Centroamericanos y del Caribe
Estadio Nacional, Ciudad de Panamá (Panama)
VEN: Ezequiel Machado (3/0), Teodardo Marcano (3/0), Ramón Morales (3/0), José María Ardila (3/0), Nicasio Camero (3/0), Mauricio Corao (2/0), Hernán Mujica (2/0), Francisco Marcano (3/1), Reinaldo Febrés Cordero (3/1), Alberto Castillo (3/1), Fernando Ríos (3/0). Trainer: Vittorio Godigna (3).
Goals: Francisco Marcano, Reinaldo Febrés Cordero.

4. 20.02.1938 **COSTA RICA - VENEZUELA** **3-0** 4th Juegos Centroamericanos y del Caribe
Estadio Nacional, Ciudad de Panamá (Panama)
VEN: José Luis Candiales (1/0), Teodardo Marcano (4/0), Francisco Ravard (1/0), Félix Ochoa (1/0), Nicasio Camero (4/0), Mauricio Corao (3/0), Leonardo Márquez (1/0), Reinaldo Febrés Cordero (4/1), Carlos Feo (3/0), Alberto Castillo (4/1), Fernando Ríos (4/0). Trainer: Vittorio Godigna (4).

5. 23.02.1938 **VENEZUELA - COLOMBIA** **2-1** 4th Juegos Centroamericanos y del Caribe
Estadio Nacional, Ciudad de Panamá (Panama); Referee: Luis Angel Mirabal (Uruguay)
VEN: José Luis Candiales (2/0), Teodardo Marcano (5/0), Ramón Morales (4/0), José María Ardila (4/0), Nicasio Camero (5/0), Mauricio Corao (4/0), Francisco Marcano (4/1), Reinaldo Febrés Cordero (5/1), Carlos Feo (4/0), Alberto Castillo (5/1), Fernando Ríos (5/2). Trainer: Vittorio Godigna (5).
Goals: Fernando Ríos 2 (one penalty).

6. 11.08.1938 **BOLIVIA - VENEZUELA** **3-1(1-1)** 1st Juegos Bolivarianos
Estadio Universitario, Bogotá (Colombia)
VEN: José Luis Candiales (3/0), Teodardo Marcano (6/0), Roberto Andara (1/0), José María Ardila (5/0), Nicasio Camero (6/0), Vaughan Salas Lozada (1/0), Hernán Mujica (3/1), Graciano Castillo (1/0), Alberto Márquez (1/0), Reinaldo Febrés Cordero (6/1), Fernando Ríos (6/2). Trainer: Vittorio Godigna (6).
Goal: Hernán Mujica.

7. 13.08.1938 **COLOMBIA - VENEZUELA** **2-0(1-0)** 1st Juegos Bolivarianos
Estadio Universitario, Bogotá
VEN: Ezequiel Machado (4/0), Teodardo Marcano (7/0), Roberto Andara (2/0), Ramón Morales (5/0), Nicasio Camero (7/0), Vaughan Salas Lozada (2/0), Hernán Mujica (4/1), Graciano Castillo (2/0), Alberto Márquez (2/0), Reinaldo Febrés Cordero (7/1), Fernando Ríos (7/2). Trainer: Vittorio Godigna (7).

8. 17.08.1938 **PERU - VENEZUELA** **2-1** 1st Juegos Bolivarianos
Estadio Universitario, Bogotá (Colombia); Referee: Carlos Esteva Tejada (Mexico)
VEN: José Luis Candiales (4/0), Teodardo Marcano (8/0), Roberto Andara (3/0), Félix Ochoa (2/0), Nicasio Camero (8/0), Mauricio Corao (5/0), Hernán Mujica (5/1), Graciano Castillo (3/0), Alberto Márquez (3/0), Pablo Corao (1/0), Fernando Ríos (8/3). Trainer: Vittorio Godigna (8).
Goal: Fernando Ríos (75).

9. 19.08.1938 **ECUADOR - VENEZUELA** **5-2(4-0)** 1st Juegos Bolivarianos
Estadio Universitario, Bogotá (Colombia)
VEN: José Luis Candiales (5/0), Teodardo Marcano (9/0), Roberto Andara (4/0), Graciano Castillo (4/0), Nicasio Camero (9/0), Mauricio Corao (6/0), Alberto Márquez (4/0), Pablo Corao (2/0), Reinaldo Febrés Cordero (8/1), Hernán Mujica (6/1), Fernando Ríos (9/5). Trainer: Vittorio Godigna (9).
Goals: Fernando Ríos (83, 88).

10. 12.12.1946 **COLOMBIA - VENEZUELA** **2-0(1-0)** 5th Juegos Centroamericanos y del Caribe
Estadio Municipal, Barranquilla; Attendance: 15,000
VEN: Miguel Sanabria (1/0), Nicasio Camero (10/0), Manuel Antonio Pérez (1/0), Germán Martínez (1/0), Ernesto Blanco (1/0), David Zamudio (1/0), Pedro Terán (1/0), Andrés Sucre (1/0), Rafael González (1/0), Asdrúbal Olivares (1/0) [Luis Jiménez (1/0)], José María Ardila (6/0) [Rosendo Aparicio (1/0)]. Trainer: Sixto Soler (1).

11. 14.12.1946 **COSTA RICA - VENEZUELA** **5-2(2-0)** 5th Juegos Centroamericanos y del Caribe
Estadio Municipal, Barranquilla (Colombia)
VEN: Miguel Sanabria (2/0), Nicasio Camero (11/0), Manuel Antonio Pérez (2/0), Germán Martínez (2/0) [Luis Jiménez (2/0)], Nerio Seijas (1/0), David Zamudio (2/0), Ernesto Blanco (2/1), Hernán Mujica (7/1), Andrés Sucre (2/1), Víctor García (1/0), José María Ardila (7/0). Trainer: Sixto Soler (2).
Goals: Ernesto Blanco (59), Andrés Sucre (85).

12. 17.12.1946 **PANAMA - VENEZUELA** **2-1(2-0)** 5th Juegos Centroamericanos y del Caribe
Estadio Municipal, Barranquilla (Colombia); Referee: Manuel Soto (Chile)
VEN: Miguel Sanabria (3/0), Hernán Mujica (8/1) [*sent off*], Manuel Antonio Pérez (3/0), Germán Martínez (3/0), Nerio Seijas (2/0), David Zamudio (3/0), Luis Jiménez (3/0) [Pedro Terán (2/0)], Andrés Sucre (3/1) [Rafael González (2/0)], Víctor García (2/1), Carlos Rodríguez (1/0) [Rosendo Aparicio (2/0)], Asdrúbal Olivares (2/0). Trainer: Sixto Soler (3).
Goal: Víctor García (90).

13. 19.12.1946 **CURAÇAO - VENEZUELA** **1-0(1-0)** 5th Juegos Centroamericanos y del Caribe
Estadio Municipal, Barranquilla (Colombia)
VEN: Miguel Sanabria (4/0), Jorge Nurse (1/0), Manuel Antonio Pérez (4/0), Germán Martínez (4/0), Nicasio Camero (12/0) [Nerio Seijas (3/0)], David Zamudio (4/0), Pedro Terán (3/0), Andrés Sucre (4/1), Rafael González (3/0), Carlos Rodríguez (2/0), Rafael Márquez (1/0). Trainer: Sixto Soler (4).

14. 23.12.1946 **VENEZUELA - GUATEMALA** **3-2(3-1)** 5th Juegos Centroamericanos y del Caribe
Estadio Municipal, Barranquilla (Colombia)
VEN: Miguel Sanabria (5/0), Rafael Márquez (2/0), Manuel Antonio Pérez (5/0), Germán Martínez (5/0), Nicasio Camero (13/0) [David Zamudio (5/0)], Nerio Seijas (4/0) [Pedro Terán (4/0)], Luis Jiménez (4/0), Rafael González (4/0), Andrés Sucre (5/4), Carlos Rodríguez (3/0), Asdrúbal Olivares (3/0). Trainer: Sixto Soler (5).
Goals: Andrés Sucre (10, 25, 28).

15. 26.12.1946 **VENEZUELA – PORTO RICO** **6-0(2-0)** 5th Juegos Centroamericanos y del Caribe
Estadio Municipal, Barranquilla (Colombia)
VEN: Miguel Sanabria (6/0), Jorge Nurse (2/0), Rafael Márquez (3/0), Germán Martínez (6/0), David Zamudio (6/0), Nerio Seijas (5/0), Luis Jiménez (5/0) [Rosendo Aparicio (3/2)], Rafael González (5/0), Andrés Sucre (6/4) [Víctor García (3/4)], Carlos Rodríguez (4/1), Asdrúbal Olivares (4/0). Trainer: Sixto Soler (6).
Goals: Carlos Rodríguez (23), Víctor García (37), Rosendo Aparicio (52), Víctor García (60), Rosendo Aparicio (62), Víctor García (68).

16. 05.01.1948 **VENEZUELA - BOLIVIA** **2-2** 2nd Juegos Bolivarianos
Lima (Peru); Referee: Juan Honores (Peru)
VEN: Miguel Sanabria (7/0), Rafael Márquez (4/0), Reinaldo Cervini (1/0), Germán Martínez (7/0), David Zamudio (7/0) [Luis Osorio (1/0)], Ernesto Blanco (3/1), Fábregas (1/0) [Manuel Leopoldo Pérez (1/0); Giraldo (1/0)], Carlos Morales (1/0), Rafael González (6/1), Gastón Monterola (1/1), Pedro Terán (5/0). Trainer: Alvaro Cartéa (1).
Goals: Rafael González, Gastón Monterola.

17. 05.03.1951 **COSTA RICA - VENEZUELA** **3-1(0-1)** 1st Juegos Panamericanos
Buenos Aires (Argentina)
VEN: Policarpio Espejo (1/0), Rafael Márquez (5/0), Manuel Antonio Pérez (6/0), Luis Osorio (2/0), Rafael Campos (1/0), Carlos González (1/0), Ernesto González (1/0) [Rafael González (7/1)], Ernesto Blanco (4/1), Gastón Monterola (2/1), César Díaz (1/1), Asdrúbal Olivares (5/0). Trainer: Orlando Fantoni (1).
Goal: César Díaz (39).

18. 17.03.1955 **VENEZUELA - CURAÇAO** **3-2(2-2)** 2nd Juegos Panamericanos
Estadio Monumental, Ciudad de México (Mexico)
VEN: Alberto Delgado (1/0) [Franklin Alleyne (1/0)], Joseba Lascurain (1/0), Carlos Medina (1/0), Agustín Matson (1/0), Heriberto Heredia (1/0), Alí Tovar (1/0), Rafael González (8/1), Aniello Alterio (1/0), Gastón Monterola (3/2), Carlos Rodríguez (5/1), Pedro Díaz (1/2). Trainer: Orlando Fantoni (2).
Goals: Pedro Díaz (13 penalty,21), Gastón Monterola (50).

19. 21.03.1955 **CURAÇAO - VENEZUELA** **3-1(3-0)** 2nd Juegos Panamericanos
Estadio Monumental, Ciudad de México (Mexico)
VEN: Alberto Delgado (2/0), Joseba Lascurain (2/0), Carlos Medina (2/0), Agustín Matson (2/0), Heriberto Heredia (2/0), Alí Tovar (2/0), Rafael González (9/1), Aniello Alterio (2/0), Gastón Monterola (4/2), Carlos Rodríguez (6/2), Pedro Díaz (2/2). Trainer: Orlando Fantoni (3).
Goal: Carlos Rodríguez (57 penalty).

20. 31.08.1964 **VENEZUELA - MEXICO** **0-5(0-3)**
Estadio Olímpico „Ciudad Universitaria", Caracas; Referee: Héctor Osorio (Venezuela); Attendance: 500
VEN: Felipe Mirabal (1/0) [Miguel Sanabria (8/0)], David Mota (1/0), José Luis Zarzalejo (1/0) [O. Serfaty (1/0)], Fréderic Ellie Arlet (1/0), Manuel Suárez (1/0) [Luciano Ettari (1/0)], Alí Tovar (3/0), Argenis Tortolero (1/0), Salvador Gala (1/0) [E. García (1/0)], Humberto Francisco Scovino (1/0), Rafael Santana (1/0), Carlos Orta (1/0). Trainer: Rafael Franco Reyes (1).

21. 16.05.1965 **PERU - VENEZUELA** **1-0(1-0)** 8th FIFA WC. Qualifiers
Estadio Nacional, Lima; Referee: Adolfo Reginato (Chile); Attendance: 43,990
VEN: Felipe Mirabal (2/0), David Mota (2/0), Fréderic Ellie Arlet (2/0), José Luis Zarzalejo (2/0), Octavio De Suze (1/0), Antonio Ravelo Rodríguez (1/0), Argenis Tortolero (2/0), José Ravelo (1/0), Luis Pineda (1/0), Rafael Santana (2/0), Luis Mendoza Benedetto (1/0). Trainer: Rafael Franco Reyes (2).

22. 23.05.1965 **URUGUAY - VENEZUELA** **5-0(2-0)** 8th FIFA WC. Qualifiers
Estadio Centenario, Montevideo; Referee: José Dimas Larrosa (Paraguay); Attendance: 16,439
VEN: Felipe Mirabal (3/0), David Mota (3/0), Fréderic Ellie Arlet (3/0), José Luis Zarzalejo (3/0), José Ravelo (2/0), Octavio De Suze (2/0), Atilano Anzola (1/0), Ernesto Blanco (1/0), Rafael Santana (3/0), Luis Mendoza Benedetto (2/0), Nicolás Font (1/0). Trainer: Rafael Franco Reyes (3).

23. 30.05.1965 **VENEZUELA - URUGUAY** **1-3(1-1)** 8th FIFA WC. Qualifiers
Estadio Olímpico „Ciudad Universitaria", Caracas; Referee: Roberto Héctor Goicoechea (Argentina); Attendance: 12,649
VEN: Juan Arocha (1/0), David Mota (4/0), Fréderic Ellie Arlet (4/0), Marcel Luis Montes (1/0), José Luis Zarzalejo (4/0), Octavio De Suze (3/0), Ernesto Blanco (2/0), Argenis Tortolero (3/1), Antonio Ravelo Rodríguez (2/0), José Ravelo (3/0), Rafael Santana (4/0). Trainer: Rafael Franco Reyes (4).
Goal: Argenis Tortolero (40).

24. 01.06.1965 **VENEZUELA - PERU** **3-6(1-3)** 8th FIFA WC. Qualifiers
Estadio Olímpico „Ciudad Universitaria", Caracas; Referee: José Antonio Sundheim (Colombia); Attendance: 6,245
VEN: Felipe Mirabal (4/0), David Mota (5/0), Fréderic Ellie Arlet (5/1), Marcel Luis Montes (2/0), José Luis Zarzalejo (5/0), Octavio De Suze (4/0), Ernesto Blanco (3/0), Argenis Tortolero (4/1), José Ravelo (4/0), Humberto Francisco Scovino (2/1), Rafael Santana (5/1). Trainer: Rafael Franco Reyes (5).
Goals: Rafael Santana (32), Humberto Francisco Scovino (46), Fréderic Ellie Arlet (89).

25. 18.01.1967 **CHILE - VENEZUELA** **2-0(2-0)** 29th Copa América
Estadio Centenario, Montevideo (Uruguay); Referee: Isidro Ramírez Alvarez (Paraguay); Attendance: 15,000
VEN: Víctor Fassano (1/0), David Mota (6/0), Fréderic Ellie Arlet (6/1), José Luis Zarzalejo (6/0), Antonio Ravelo Rodríguez (3/0), José Vidal (1/0) [Gustavo González (1/0)], Salvador Gala (2/0) [Rafael Ignacio Naranjo Silva (1/0)], Argenis Tortolero (5/1), Luis Mendoza Benedetto (3/0), Humberto Francisco Scovino (3/1), Rafael Santana (6/1). Trainer: Rafael Franco Reyes (6).

26. 21.01.1967 **URUGUAY - VENEZUELA** **4-0(1-0)** 29th Copa América
Estadio Centenario, Montevideo; Referee: Eunápio Gouveia de Queiroz (Brazil); Attendance: 9,000
VEN: Víctor Fassano (2/0), David Mota (7/0), José Luis Zarzalejo (7/0), Fréderic Ellie Arlet (7/1), Antonio Ravelo Rodríguez (4/0) [José Vidal (2/0)], Gustavo González (2/0), Salvador Gala (3/0), Argenis Tortolero (6/1), Luis Mendoza Benedetto (4/0) [Pedro Alfonso González (1/0)], Rafael Ignacio Naranjo Silva (2/0), Rafael Santana (7/1). Trainer: Rafael Franco Reyes (7).

27. 25.01.1967 **ARGENTINA - VENEZUELA** **5-1(2-0)** 29th Copa América
Estadio Centenario, Montevideo (Uruguay); Referee: Mario Gasc (Chile); Attendance: 12,000
VEN: Víctor Fassano (3/0) [Omar Colmenares (1/0)], David Mota (8/0), José Luis Zarzalejo (8/0), Antonio Ravelo Rodríguez (5/0), Fréderic Ellie Arlet (8/1), Gustavo González (3/0), Rafael Ignacio Naranjo Silva (3/0), Argenis Tortolero (7/1) [Pedro Alfonso González (2/0)], Humberto Francisco Scovino (4/1) [Salvador Gala (4/0)], Luis Mendoza Benedetto (5/0), Rafael Santana (8/2). Trainer: Rafael Franco Reyes (8).
Goal: Rafael Santana (72).

28. 28.01.1967 **VENEZUELA - BOLIVIA** **3-0(0-0)** 29th Copa América
Estadio Centenario, Montevideo (Uruguay); Referee: Mario Gasc (Chile); Attendance: 11,000
VEN: Omar Colmenares (2/0), David Mota (9/0), José Luis Zarzalejo (9/0), Gustavo González (4/0), Fréderic Ellie Arlet (9/1), Rafael Ignacio Naranjo Silva (4/0), Argenis Tortolero (8/1) [Pedro Alfonso González (3/0)], Antonio Ravelo Rodríguez (6/1), Humberto Francisco Scovino (5/2) [Salvador Gala (5/0)], Luis Mendoza Benedetto (6/0), Rafael Santana (9/3). Trainer: Rafael Franco Reyes (9).
Goals: Humberto Francisco Scovino (59), Rafael Santana (67), Antonio Ravelo Rodríguez (84).

29. 01.02.1967 **PARAGUAY - VENEZUELA** **5-3(4-1)** 29th Copa América
Estadio Centenario, Montevideo (Uruguay); Referee: Estebán Marino (Uruguay); Attendance: 1,500
VEN: Omar Colmenares (3/0) [Víctor Fassano (4/0)], David Mota (10/0), José Luis Zarzalejo (10/0), Gustavo González (5/0), Fréderic Ellie Arlet (10/1), Rafael Ignacio Naranjo Silva (5/0), Argenis Tortolero (9/1) [Omar González (1/0)], Salvador Gala (6/0) [Humberto Francisco Scovino (6/2)], Antonio Ravelo Rodríguez (7/2), Luis Mendoza Benedetto (7/1), Rafael Santana (10/4). Trainer: Rafael Franco Reyes (10).
Goals: Luis Mendoza Benedetto (3), Rafael Santana (77), Antonio Ravelo Rodríguez (89).

30. 27.07.1969 **COLOMBIA - VENEZUELA** **3-0(1-0)** 9th FIFA WC. Qualifiers
Estadio „Nemesio Camacho“ ‘El Campín’, Bogotá; Referee: René Torres (Ecuador); Attendance: 47,984
VEN: Omar Colmenares (4/0) [Víctor Fassano (5/0)], David Mota (11/0), Fréderic Ellie Arlet (11/1), Manuel Asdrúbal Sánchez (1/0), Salvador Delgado (1/0), Pedro Alfonso González (4/0), Luis Mendoza Benedetto (8/1), Argenis Tortolero (10/1) [Omar González (2/0)], Ramón Iriarte (1/0), Antonio Ravelo Rodríguez (8/2), Augusto Nitti (1/0). Trainer: Rafael Franco Reyes (11).

31. 02.08.1969 **VENEZUELA - COLOMBIA** **1-1(0-0)** 9th FIFA WC. Qualifiers
Estadio Olímpico „Ciudad Universitaria“, Caracas; Referee: Juan Oscar Ortubé Vargas (Bolivia); Attendance: 17,101
VEN: Víctor Fassano (6/0), David Mota (12/0), Fréderic Ellie Arlet (12/1), Manuel Asdrúbal Sánchez (2/0), Salvador Delgado (2/0), Pedro Alfonso González (5/0), Antonio Ravelo Rodríguez (9/2), Luis Mendoza Benedetto (9/2), Rafael Santana (11/4), Ramón Iriarte (2/0), Augusto Nitti (2/0) [Alvaro Salcedo (1/0)]. Trainer: Rafael Franco Reyes (12).
Goal: Luis Mendoza Benedetto (55).

32. 06.08.1969 **VENEZUELA - PARAGUAY** **0-2(0-1)** 9th FIFA WC. Qualifiers
Estadio Olímpico „Ciudad Universitaria“, Caracas; Referee: J. Palacios (Chile); Attendance: 9,110
VEN: Víctor Fassano (7/0), Carlos Enrique Marín (1/0), Fréderic Ellie Arlet (Cap) (13/1), Manuel Asdrúbal Sánchez (3/0), Salvador Delgado (3/0), Pedro Alfonso González (6/0) [58.Rafael Ignacio Naranjo Silva (6/0)], Delmán Useche Pérez (1/0), Luis Mendoza Benedetto (10/2), Argenis Tortolero (11/1) [46.Ramón Iriarte (3/0)], Antonio Ravelo Rodríguez (10/2), Augusto Nitti (3/0). Trainer: Rafael Franco Reyes (13).

33. 10.08.1969 **VENEZUELA - BRAZIL** **0-5(0-0)** 9th FIFA WC. Qualifiers
Estadio Olímpico „Ciudad Universitaria“, Caracas; Referee: Eduardo Rendón (Ecuador); Attendance: 30,063
VEN: Eddie Nelson García (1/0), David Mota (13/0), Fréderic Ellie Arlet (Cap) (14/1), Manuel Asdrúbal Sánchez (4/0), Salvador Delgado (4/0), Pedro Alfonso González (7/0), Delmán Useche Pérez (2/0), Luis Mendoza Benedetto (11/2), Ramón Iriarte (4/0), Antonio Ravelo Rodríguez (11/2) [Rafael Santana (12/4)], Augusto Nitti (4/0). Trainer: Rafael Franco Reyes (14).

34. 21.08.1969 **PARAGUAY - VENEZUELA** **1-0(1-0)** 9th FIFA WC. Qualifiers
Estadio Puerto Sajonia, Asunción; Referee: Alejandro Otero (Uruguay); Attendance: 11,059
VEN: Eddie Nelson García (2/0), David Mota (14/0), Fréderic Ellie Arlet (Cap) (15/1), Igor Orlando Torres (1/0), Salvador Delgado (5/0), Pedro Alfonso González (8/0), Manuel Asdrúbal Sánchez (5/0) [José Luis Zarzalejo (11/0)], Delmán Useche Pérez (3/0), Antonio Ravelo Rodríguez (12/2), Rafael Santana (13/4), Augusto Nitti (5/0). Trainer: Rafael Franco Reyes (15).

35. 24.08.1969 **BRAZIL - VENEZUELA** **6-0(5-0)** 9th FIFA WC. Qualifiers
Estádio „Jornalista Mário Filho“ (Maracanã), Rio de Janeiro; Referee: Juan Oscar Ortubé Vargas (Bolivia); Attendance: 122,841
VEN: Víctor Fassano (8/0), David Mota (15/0), Fréderic Ellie Arlet (Cap) (16/1), Manuel Asdrúbal Sánchez (6/0) [José Luis Zarzalejo (12/0)], Salvador Delgado (6/0), Rafael Ignacio Naranjo Silva (7/0), Delmán Useche Pérez (4/0), Manuel García (1/0) [Luis Mendoza Benedetto (12/2)], Antonio Ravelo Rodríguez (13/2), Ramón Iriarte (5/0), Augusto Nitti (6/0). Trainer: Rafael Franco Reyes (16).

36. 13.11.1971 **VENEZUELA – TRINIDAD & TOBAGO** **1-0**
Estadio Olímpico „Ciudad Universitaria“, Caracas
VEN: Gustavo Brito (1/0), Iván Camero (1/0), Efraín Maldonado (1/0), Luis Marquina (1/0), Carlos Rodríguez (1/0), Reinaldo Rangel (1/0), José Araque (1/0), Humberto Galeano (1/0), Ricardo Pérez Carbonell (1/0), Rolman Tavarez (1/0), William Ravelo (1/1). *Substitutes*: Delmán Useche Pérez (5/0), Luis Mendoza Benedetto (13/2).Trainer: Gregorio Gómez (1).
Goal: William Ravelo (68).

37. 02.06.1972 **VENEZUELA - COLOMBIA** **2-1(1-1)**
Estadio Olímpico „Ciudad Universitaria“, Caracas; Referee: Mario Fiorenza (Venezuela); Attendance: 8,000
VEN: Omar Colmenares (5/0), Carlos Enrique Marín (2/0), Raúl Stanich (1/0), Vicente Arruda (1/0), Igor Orlando Torres (2/0), Delmán Useche Pérez (6/0), Luis Mendoza Benedetto (14/3), Francisco Rodríguez (1/0) [Héctor Rodríguez (1/0)], Asdrúbal Olivares (1/0), Iván García (1/1), Ramón Iriarte (6/0). Trainer: Gregorio Gómez (2).
Goals: Iván García (33), Luis Mendoza Benedetto (54).

38. 11.06.1972 **PARAGUAY - VENEZUELA** **4-1(4-1)** Copa Independencia de Brasil
Estádio „Pedro Pedrossian“, Campo Grande (Brazil); Referee: George Lamptey (Ghana); Attendance: 41,000
VEN: Omar Colmenares (6/0), Carlos Enrique Marín (3/0), Raúl Stanich (2/0), Vicente Arruda (2/0), Igor Orlando Torres (3/0), Lorenzo Useche (1/0), Héctor Rodríguez (2/0), Luis Mendoza Benedetto (15/3), Iván García (2/1), Asdrúbal Olivares (2/1), Ramón Iriarte (7/0). Trainer: Gregorio Gómez (3).
Goal: Asdrúbal Olivares (26).

39. 14.06.1972 **YUGOSLAVIA - VENEZUELA** **10-0(5-0)** Copa Independencia de Brasil
Estádio Belfort Duarta, Curitiba (Brazil); Referee: Ove Dahlberg (Sweden); Attendance: 5,000
VEN: Omar Colmenares (7/0), Carlos Enrique Marín (4/0), Raúl Stanich (3/0), Vicente Arruda (3/0), Igor Orlando Torres (4/0), Lorenzo Useche (2/0) [Ricardo Pérez Carbonell (2/0)], Héctor Rodríguez (3/0), Antonio Marcano (1/0), Iván García (3/1), Asdrúbal Olivares (3/1), Ramón Iriarte (8/0). Trainer: Gregorio Gómez (4).

40. 18.06.1972 **PERU - VENEZUELA** **1-0(0-0)** Copa Independencia de Brasil
Estádio „Vivaldo Lima", Manaus (Brazil); Referee: Armando David César Coelho (Brazil); Attendance: 20,000
VEN: Víctor Fassano (9/0), Carlos Enrique Marín (5/0), Raúl Stanich (4/0), Vicente Arruda (4/0), Luis Marquina (2/0), Lorenzo Useche (3/0), Ricardo Pérez Carbonell (3/0), Richard Alfred Páez Monzón (1/0), Antonio Marcano (2/0), Ramón Iriarte (9/0), Héctor Rodríguez (4/0). Trainer: Gregorio Gómez (5).

41. 21.06.1972 **VENEZUELA - BOLIVIA** **2-2(1-1)** Copa Independencia de Brasil
Estádio „Vivaldo Lima", Manaus (Brazil); Referee: Hwa Po Dei (Malaysia)
VEN: Víctor Fassano (10/0) [Omar Colmenares (8/0)], Carlos Enrique Marín (6/0) [*sent off 78*], Raúl Stanich (5/0), Vicente Arruda (5/0), Luis Marquina (3/0), Lorenzo Useche (4/0), Delmán Useche Pérez (7/0), Richard Alfred Páez Monzón (2/1), Asdrúbal Olivares (4/1), Iván García (4/1), Ramón Iriarte (10/1). Trainer: Gregorio Gómez (6).
Goals: Ramón Iriarte (15), Richard Alfred Páez Monzón (49).

42. 16.12.1973 **VENEZUELA – DOMINICAN REPUBLIC** **1-0(0-0)**
Estadio „Farid Richa", Barquisimeto; Referee: Mario Fiorenza (Venezuela)
VEN: Osorio (1/0), Alexis Georges (1/1), Lucidio (1/0), Bermejo (1/0), Julio Hernández (1/0), Melo (1/0), Olegario Díaz (1/0), Vicente Flores (1/0), Martínez (1/0) [Ramón Orriols (1/0)], López (1/0), Amado (1/0) [Alejo González (1/0)]. Trainer: Gregorio Gómez (7).
Goal: Alexis Georges (89).

43. 30.07.1975 **VENEZUELA - BRAZIL** **0-4(0-1)** 30th Copa América
Estadio Olímpico „Ciudad Universitaria", Caracas; Referee: Rafael Labóro (Peru); Attendance: 20,000
VEN: Omar Colmenares (9/0), Omar Ochoa (1/0), Pedro Castro (1/0) [Néstor Vázquez (1/0)], Luis Marquina (4/0), Igor Orlando Torres (5/0), Delmán Useche Pérez (8/0), Richard Alfred Páez Monzón (3/1), Luis Mendoza Benedetto (16/3), Miguel Rivas (1/0), Ramón Iriarte (11/1), Iván García (5/1) [José Acurzio (1/0)]. Trainer: José Walter Roque (1).

44. 03.08.1975 **VENEZUELA - ARGENTINA** **1-5(1-3)** 30th Copa América
Estadio Olímpico „Ciudad Universitaria", Caracas; Referee: Rafael Hormozabál Díaz (Chile); Attendance: 15,000
VEN: Vicente Emilio Vega (1/0) [Andrés Arizaleta (1/0)], Rubén Darío Torres (1/0), Néstor Vázquez (2/0), Luis Marquina (5/0), Igor Orlando Torres (6/0), Delmán Useche Pérez (9/0), Richard Alfred Páez Monzón (4/1), Luis Mendoza Benedetto (17/3), Alejo González (2/0), Ramón Iriarte (12/2), Vicente Flores (2/0) [Iván García (6/1)]. Trainer: José Walter Roque (2).
Goal: Ramón Iriarte (14).

45. 10.08.1975 **ARGENTINA - VENEZUELA** **11-0(4-0)** 30th Copa América
Estadio Cor de León, Rosario; Referee: Pedro Reyes (Peru); Attendance: 50,000
VEN: Andrés Arizaleta (2/0), Omar Ochoa (2/0), Delmán Useche Pérez (10/0), Luis Marquina (6/0), Igor Orlando Torres (7/0), Richard Alfred Páez Monzón (5/1), Luis Mendoza Benedetto (18/3), Alejo González (3/0), Miguel Rivas (2/0), Ramón Iriarte (13/2) [Rubén Darío Torres (2/0)], Iván García (7/1) [José Acurzio (2/0)]. Trainer: José Walter Roque (3).

46. 13.08.1975 **BRAZIL - VENEZUELA** **6-0(3-0)** 30th Copa América
Estádio Mineirão, Belo Horizonte; Referee: Carlos Rivero Angeles (Peru); Attendance: 32,000
VEN: Andrés Arizaleta (3/0), Omar Ochoa (3/0), Delmán Useche Pérez (11/0), Luis Marquina (7/0), Igor Orlando Torres (8/0), Richard Alfred Páez Monzón (6/1), Luis Mendoza Benedetto (19/3), Alejo González (4/0), Miguel Rivas (3/0) [Rubén Darío Torres (3/0)], Ramón Iriarte (14/2), José Acurzio (3/0). Trainer: José Walter Roque (4).

47. 20.01.1977 **VENEZUELA - ECUADOR** **1-0(1-0)**
Estadio „José Antonio Páez", Acarigua; Referee: José Varrone (Venezuela); Attendance: 2,500
VEN: Andrés Jiménez (1/0), Omar Ochoa (4/0) [José Betancourt Toro (1/0)], Nelson Marcenaro (1/0), Carlos Enrique Marín (7/0), William Salas (1/0), José Ricardo Moss (1/1), Ramón Echenáusi (1/0), José Enrique Chiazzaro (1/0) [Nabor Fuenmayor (1/0)], Miguel Rivas (4/0), Vicente Flores (3/0), Rafael Iriarte (1/0). Trainer: Dan Georgiadis (1).
Goal: José Ricardo Moss (28).

48. 09.02.1977 **VENEZUELA - URUGUAY** **1-1(0-1)** 11th FIFA WC. Qualifiers
Estadio Nacional „Brígido Iriarte", Caracas; Referee: Guillermo Velásquez Ramírez (Colombia); Attendance: 5,000
VEN: Santiago Romero (1/0), Omar Ochoa (5/0), Fréderic Ellie Arlet (17/1), Carlos Betancourt (1/0), William Salas (2/0), Carlos Enrique Marín (Cap) (8/1) [85.Nabor Fuenmayor (2/0)], José Ricardo Moss (2/1), Ramón Echenáusi (2/0), Rafael Iriarte (2/0), Vicente Flores (4/0), José Mora (1/0) [40.Iván García (8/1)]. Trainer: Dan Georgiadis (2).
Goal: Carlos Enrique Marín (83).

49. 06.03.1977 **VENEZUELA - BOLIVIA** **1-3(0-1)** 11th FIFA WC. Qualifiers
Estadio Nacional „Brígido Iriarte", Caracas; Referee: Juan Ambrosio Silvagno Cavanna (Chile); Attendance: 5,034
VEN: Santiago Romero (2/0), Carlos Enrique Marín (9/1), Fréderic Ellie Arlet (18/1), Carlos Betancourt (2/0) [59.José Betancourt Toro (2/0)], William Salas (3/0), Nabor Fuenmayor (3/0), José Ricardo Moss (3/1), Ramón Echenáusi (3/0), José Enrique Chiazzaro (2/0), Rafael Iriarte (3/1), Vicente Flores (5/0) [38.Edgar Soto (1/0)]. Trainer: Dan Georgiadis (3).
Goal: Rafael Iriarte (87).

50. 13.03.1977 **BOLIVIA - VENEZUELA** **2-0(2-0)** 11th FIFA WC. Qualifiers
Estadio „Libertador Simón Bolívar", La Paz; Referee: Edison Pérez Nuñez (Peru); Attendance: 21,217
VEN: Andrés Jiménez (2/0), Carlos Enrique Marín (10/1), Fréderic Ellie Arlet (19/1), José Betancourt Toro (3/0) [46.Carlos Betancourt (3/0)], William Salas (4/0), José Ricardo Moss (4/1), Ramón Echenáusi (4/0), Rafael Iriarte (4/1) [46.Iván García (9/1)], Vicente Flores (6/0), Edgar Soto (2/0), José Enrique Chiazzaro (3/0). Trainer: Dan Georgiadis (4).

51. 17.03.1977 **URUGUAY - VENEZUELA** **2-0(1-0)** 11th FIFA WC. Qualifiers
Estadio Centenario, Montevideo; Referee: Armando Nunes Castanheiras da Rosa Marques (Brazil); Attendance: 4,383
VEN: Santiago Romero (3/0), Carlos Enrique Marín (11/1), Fréderic Ellie Arlet (20/1), José Betancourt Toro (4/0), Carlos Betancourt (4/0), José Ricardo Moss (5/1), Ramón Echenáusi (5/0), Gerardo Vielma (1/0), Rafael Iriarte (5/1), José Enrique Chiazzaro (4/0), Vicente Flores (7/0) [84.Edgar Soto (3/0)]. Trainer: Dan Georgiadis (5).

52. 01.08.1979 **VENEZUELA - COLOMBIA** **0-0** 31st Copa América. Group Stage
Estadio Pueblo Nuevo, San Cristóbal; Referee: Luis Barrancos Alvarez (Bolivia); Attendance: 18,000
VEN: Vicente Emilio Vega (2/0), José Ramón Contreras (1/0) [Pedro Javier Acosta Sánchez (1/0)], Pedro Castro (2/0), Juan José Vidal (1/0), Emilio Campos Rodríguez (1/0), Asdrúbal José Sánchez Urbina (1/0), Richard Alfred Páez Monzón (7/1), Luis Mendoza Benedetto (20/3), Ángel de Jesús Castillo (1/0), Pedro Juan Febles (1/0) [Alexis Peña (1/0)], Julio César Hernández (1/0). Trainer: José Julián Hernández (1).

53. 08.08.1979 **VENEZUELA - CHILE** **1-1(0-0)** 31st Copa América. Group Stage
Estadio Pueblo Nuevo, San Cristóbal; Referee: César Humberto Pagano Trucios (Peru); Attendance: 14,000
VEN: Vicente Emilio Vega (3/0), José Ramón Contreras (2/0), Pedro Castro (3/0), Juan José Vidal (2/0), Emilio Campos Rodríguez (2/0), Asdrúbal José Sánchez Urbina (2/0), Richard Alfred Páez Monzón (8/1), Luis Mendoza Benedetto (21/3), Rodolfo Carvajal (1/1), Alexis Peña (2/0) [Rafael Santana (14/4)], Julio César Hernández (2/0) [Ángel de Jesús Castillo (2/0)]. Trainer: José Julián Hernández (2).
Goal: Rodolfo Carvajal (70).

54. 22.08.1979 **COLOMBIA - VENEZUELA** **4-0(1-0)** 31st Copa América. Group Stage
Nemesio Camacho "El Campín", Bogotá; Referee: Carlos Alfonso Espósito (Argentina); Attendance: 30,000
VEN: Vicente Emilio Vega (4/0), Ordán Ramón Aguirre (1/0), Pedro Castro (4/0), Pedro Javier Acosta Sánchez (2/0), Emilio Campos Rodríguez (3/0), Juan José Vidal (3/0), Richard Alfred Páez Monzón (9/1) [Bernardo Añor (1/0)], Luis Mendoza Benedetto (22/3), Asdrúbal José Sánchez Urbina (3/0), Rodolfo Carvajal (2/1), Alexis Peña (3/0) [Pedro Juan Febles (2/0)]. Trainer: José Julián Hernández (3).

55. 29.08.1979 **CHILE - VENEZUELA** **7-0(3-0)** 31st Copa América. Group Stage
Estadio Nacional, Santiago; Referee: Enrique Labó Revoredo (Peru); Attendance: 67,491
VEN: Vicente Emilio Vega (5/0), Jhonny Castellanos (1/0), Pedro Castro (5/0), Emilio Campos Rodríguez (4/0), Juan José Vidal (4/0), Asdrúbal José Sánchez Urbina (4/0), Richard Alfred Páez Monzón (10/1) [*sent off 53*], Luis Mendoza Benedetto (23/3), Ángel de Jesús Castillo (3/0) [Rafael Cadenas (1/0)], Rodolfo Carvajal (3/1) [Pedro Juan Febles (3/0)], Rafael Santana (15/4). Trainer: José Julián Hernández (4).

56. 01.07.1980 **VENEZUELA – COSTA RICA** **2-0(1/0)**
Estadio „Guillermo Soto Rojas", Mérida
VEN: Eustorgio Sánchez (1/0), Ordán Ramón Aguirre (2/0), Mauro Cichero (1/0), Pedro Javier Acosta Sánchez (3/0), Emilio Campos Rodríguez (5/0), Asdrúbal José Sánchez Urbina (5/0), Nelson José Carrero Heras (1/0), Alexis Peña (4/0), Iker Joseba Zubizarreta (1/0) [Bernardo Añor (2/0)], Pedro Juan Febles (4/1), Rodolfo Carvajal (4/2). Trainer: José Walter Roque (5).
Goals: Pedro Juan Febles (1), Rodolfo Carvajal (72).

57. 05.07.1980 **VENEZUELA – COSTA RICA** **1-1(1-0)**
Estadio Olímpico, Valera
VEN: Eustorgio Sánchez (2/0), Ordán Ramón Aguirre (3/0), Mauro Cichero (2/0), Pedro Javier Acosta Sánchez (4/0), Emilio Campos Rodríguez (6/0), Asdrúbal José Sánchez Urbina (6/0), Nelson José Carrero Heras (2/0), Alexis Peña (5/0), Rodolfo Carvajal (5/2), Pedro Juan Febles (5/1), Iker Joseba Zubizarreta (2/1). Trainer: José Walter Roque (6).
Goal: Iker Joseba Zubizarreta (15).

58. 11.01.1981 **NETHERLANDS ANTILLES - VENEZUELA** **2-1(1-1)**
Estadio Olimpico, Willemstad; Attendance: 5,000
VEN: Vicente Emilio Vega (6/0), Omar Ochoa (6/0) [Ordán Ramón Aguirre (4/0)], Pedro Castro (6/0), Pedro Javier Acosta Sánchez (5/0) [Nicolás Simonelli (1/0)], William Salas (5/0), Carlos Enrique Marín (12/1) [Asdrúbal José Sánchez Urbina (7/0)], Oscar Torres (1/0), Ramón Echenáusi (6/0), Vicente Flores (8/0), Juan José Scarpeccio Sabattini (1/0) [Iván García (10/1)], Julio César Hernández (3/1). Trainer: José Walter Roque (7).
Goal: Julio César Hernández (25).

59. 18.01.1981 **VENEZUELA - NETHERLANDS ANTILLES** **1-0(1-0)**
Estadio „Misael Delgado", Valencia; Referee: Pascual Figliulo (Venezuela)
VEN: Vicente Emilio Vega (7/0), Omar Ochoa (7/0), Pedro Castro (7/0), Nicolás Simonelli (2/0) [Pedro Javier Acosta Sánchez (6/0)], Emilio Campos Rodríguez (7/0), Carlos Enrique Marín (13/1) [Asdrúbal José Sánchez Urbina (8/0)], Oscar Torres (2/0) [Rafael Cadenas (2/0)], Ramón Echenáusi (7/0), Vicente Flores (9/0) [Ángel de Jesús Castillo (4/0)], Juan José Scarpeccio Sabattini (2/0), Julio César Hernández (4/2). Trainer: José Walter Roque (8).
Goal: Julio César Hernández (3).

60. 08.02.1981 **VENEZUELA - BRAZIL** **0-1(0-0)** 12th FIFA WC. Qualifiers
Estadio Olímpico „Ciudad Universitaria", Caracas; Referee: Ramón Ivannoe Barreto Ruíz (Uruguay); Attendance: 35,000
VEN: Vicente Emilio Vega (8/0), Omar Ochoa (8/0), Pedro Castro (Cap) (8/0) [Nicolás Simonelli (3/0)], Pedro Javier Acosta Sánchez (7/0), Emilio Campos Rodríguez (8/0), Carlos Enrique Marín (14/1), Ramón Echenáusi (8/0), Oscar Torres (3/0), Juan José Scarpeccio Sabattini (3/0), Iván García (11/1), Julio César Hernández (5/2) [Ángel de Jesús Castillo (5/0)]. Trainer: José Walter Roque (9).

61. 15.02.1981 **BOLIVIA - VENEZUELA** **3-0(1-0)** 12th FIFA WC. Qualifiers
Estadio „Hernándo Siles Zuazo", La Paz; Referee: Juan Francisco Escobar Váldez (Paraguay), At: 40,000
VEN: Vicente Emilio Vega (9/0), Omar Ochoa (9/0), Pedro Castro (9/0), Pedro Javier Acosta Sánchez (8/0), Emilio Campos Rodríguez (9/0), Juan José Scarpeccio Sabattini (4/0) [69.Ordán Ramón Aguirre (5/0)], Oscar Torres (4/0), Asdrúbal José Sánchez Urbina (9/0), Ángel de Jesús Castillo (6/0) [*sent off 83*], Iván García (12/1), William Castillo (1/0) [90.Vicente Flores (10/0)]. Trainer: José Walter Roque (10).

62. 15.03.1981 **VENEZUELA - BOLIVIA** **1-0(1-0)** 12th FIFA WC. Qualifiers
Estadio Olímpico „Ciudad Universitaria", Caracas; Referee: Elías Victoriano Jácome Guerreiro (Ecuador); Attendance: 25,000
VEN: Vicente Emilio Vega (10/0), William Salas (6/0), Pedro Castro (10/0), Pedro Javier Acosta Sánchez (9/1), Emilio Campos Rodríguez (10/0), Carlos Enrique Marín (15/1) [59.Ordán Ramón Aguirre (6/0)], Víctor Filomeno (1/0), Pedro Juan Febles (6/1), Félix Gutiérrez (1/0), Iván García (13/1), Mario Luis Bosetti (1/0) [51.William Castillo (2/0)]. Trainer: José Walter Roque (11).
Goal: Pedro Javier Acosta Sánchez (24).

63. 29.03.1981 **BRAZIL - VENEZUELA** **5-0(1-0)** 12th FIFA WC. Qualifiers
Estádio Serra Dourada, Goiânia; Referee: Jorge Eduardo Romero (Argentina); Attendance: 35,000
VEN: Vicente Emilio Vega (11/0), Omar Ochoa (10/0), Pedro Castro (11/0), Pedro Javier Acosta Sánchez (10/1), William Salas (7/0), Nelson José Carrero Heras (3/0) [60.Ordán Ramón Aguirre (7/0)], Oscar Torres (5/0), Víctor Filomeno (2/0), Félix Gutiérrez (2/0) [65.William Castillo (3/0)], Iván García (14/1), Pedro Juan Febles (7/1). Trainer: José Walter Roque (12).

64. 28.06.1981 **VENEZUELA - SPAIN** **0-2(0-1)**
Estadio Olímpico „Ciudad Universitaria", Caracas; Referee: Guillermo Velázquez (Colombia); Attendance: 15,000
VEN: Vicente Emilio Vega (12/0), José Pacheco (1/0), Pedro Castro (12/0), Pedro Javier Acosta Sánchez (11/1), Emilio Campos Rodríguez (11/0), José Luis Castrillo (1/0), Pedro Juan Febles (8/1) [85.Rafael Iriarte (6/1)], Nelson José Carrero Heras (4/0) [61.César José Marcano (1/0)], Eduardo Regueiro (1/0) [77.Ernesto Chacón (1/0)], Bernardo Añor (3/0), Vicente Flores (11/0). Trainer: José Walter Roque (13).

65. 04.09.1983 **URUGUAY - VENEZUELA** **3-0(2-0)** 32nd Copa América. Group Stage
Estadio Centenario, Montevideo; Referee: Gabriel González Roa (Paraguay); Attendance: 60,000
VEN: César Renato Baéna (1/0), René Antonio Torres Lobo (1/0) [*sent off 70*], Carlos Betancourt (5/0), Pedro Javier Acosta Sánchez (12/1), Oscar Torres (6/0), Nelson José Carrero Heras (5/0) [46.Jhonny Castellanos (2/0)], Braulen Barboza (1/0), Robert Ellie (1/0), José Rodríguez (1/0) [71.Nicolás Simonelli (4/0) [*sent off 85*]], Rodolfo Carvajal (6/2), Pedro Juan Febles (9/1). Trainer: José Walter Roque (14).

66. 08.09.1983 **CHILE - VENEZUELA** **5-0(3-0)** 32nd Copa América. Group Stage
Estadio Nacional, Santiago; Referee: Enrique Labó Revoredo (Peru); Attendance: 11,372
VEN: Vicente Emilio Vega (13/0), Alberto Ramos (1/0) [Ildemaro Fernández (1/0)], Pedro Javier Acosta Sánchez (13/1), Robert Ellie (2/0), Carlos Betancourt (6/0), Nelson José Carrero Heras (6/0), Braulen Barboza (2/0), José Rodríguez (2/0), Rodolfo Carvajal (7/2), Pedro Juan Febles (10/1), Jhonny Castellanos (3/0) [José Milillo (1/0)]. Trainer: José Walter Roque (15).

67. 18.09.1983 **VENEZUELA - URUGUAY** **1-2(0-0)** 32nd Copa América. Group Stage
Estadio Nacional „Brígido Iriarte", Caracas; Referee: Carlos Montalbán Miranda (Peru); Attendance: 3,000
VEN: Vicente Emilio Vega (14/0), José Rodríguez (3/0), Pedro Javier Acosta Sánchez (14/1), Julio Omar Barboza (1/0), Carlos Betancourt (7/0), Franco Rizzi (1/0), Robert Ellie (3/0), Asdrúbal José Sánchez Urbina (10/0), Rodolfo Carvajal (8/2) [82.Douglas Cedeño (1/0)], Pedro Juan Febles (11/2), José Gamboa (1/0) [64.Nelson José Carrero Heras (7/0)]. Trainer: José Walter Roque (16).
Goal: Pedro Juan Febles (77).

68. 21.09.1983 **VENEZUELA - CHILE** **0-0** 32nd Copa América. Group Stage
Estadio Nacional „Brígido Iriarte", Caracas; Referee: Elías Victoriano Jácome Guerreiro (Ecuador); Attendance: 3,000
VEN: César Renato Baéna (2/0), José Rodríguez (4/0), Pedro Javier Acosta Sánchez (15/1), Julio Omar Barboza (2/0), Carlos Betancourt (8/0), Franco Rizzi (2/0), Nelson José Carrero Heras (8/0) [William Urdaneta (1/0)], Asdrúbal José Sánchez Urbina (11/0), Rodolfo Carvajal (9/2) [Oscar Torres (7/0)], Pedro Juan Febles (12/2), Douglas Cedeño (2/0), Trainer: José Walter Roque (17).

69. 24.01.1984 **MEXICO - VENEZUELA** **3-0(0-0)**
Estadio „Sergio León Chávez", Irapuato; Referee: Marco Antonio Dorantes García (Mexico); Attendance: 18,000
VEN: César Renato Baéna (3/0), René Antonio Torres Lobo (2/0), Hildubrando Useche (1/0), Carlos Aranguren (1/0), Carlos Betancourt (Cap) (1/0), Franco Rizzi (3/0), Iván Isea (1/0) [23.José Milillo (2/0); 76.Carlos Herrera (1/0)], José Ramón López (1/0) [*sent off 68*], José González (1/0) [51.Pedro Barco (1/0)], Bernardo Añor (4/0) [82.Arturo Olivares (1/0)], Franklin Álvarez (1/0) [62.José Membrilla (1/0)]. Trainer: José Walter Roque (18).

70. 24.02.1985 **VENEZUELA - BOLIVIA** **5-0**
Caracas; Referee: Bernardo Corujo Darríba (Venezuela); Attendance: 4,000
VEN: César Renato Baéna (4/0), Carlos Landaeta (1/0), René Antonio Torres Lobo (3/1), Pedro Javier Acosta Sánchez (16/1), Jorge Betancourt (1/0) [Emilio Campos Rodríguez (12/0)], Richard Nada (1/0), Laureano Jaimes (1/0), Asdrúbal José Sánchez Urbina (12/0), William Méndez (1/0) [Nelson José Carrero Heras (9/0)], Bernardo Añor (5/1) [Heberth Márquez (1/0)], Pedro Juan Febles (13/4) [Douglas Cedeño (3/1)]. Trainer: José Walter Roque (19).
Goals: Bernardo Añor, Pedro Juan Febles 2, René Antonio Torres Lobo, Douglas Cedeño.

71. 22.04.1985 **BOLIVIA - VENEZUELA** **4-1**
Estadio „Ramón 'Tahuichi' Aguilera", Santa Cruz de la Sierra; Referee: Luis Barrancos Alvarez (Bolivia) ; Attendance: 25,000
VEN: César Renato Baéna (5/0), Carlos Landaeta (2/0), René Antonio Torres Lobo (4/1), Robert Ellie (4/0), Emilio Campos Rodríguez (13/0), Nelson José Carrero Heras (10/0), Laureano Jaimes (2/0), Asdrúbal José Sánchez Urbina (13/0), Carlos Alberto Maldonado (1/0) [Jorge Betancourt (2/0)], Bernardo Añor (6/2), Pedro Juan Febles (14/4) [Douglas Cedeño (4/1)]. Trainer: José Walter Roque (20).
Goal: Bernardo Añor.

72. 26.05.1985 **VENEZUELA - ARGENTINA** **2-3(1-2)** 13th FIFA WC. Qualifiers
Estadio Pueblo Nuevo, San Cristóbal; Referee: Juan Daniel Cardellino de San Vicente (Uruguay); Attendance: 30,000
VEN: César Renato Baéna (6/0), René Antonio Torres Lobo (5/2), Nicolás Simonelli (5/0), Pedro Javier Acosta Sánchez (17/1), Emilio Campos Rodríguez (14/0), Asdrúbal José Sánchez Urbina (14/0), William Méndez (2/0) [46.Heberth Márquez (2/1)], Nelson José Carrero Heras (11/0), Bernardo Añor (7/2), Pedro Juan Febles (15/4), Douglas Cedeño (5/1) [76.Carlos Alberto Maldonado (2/0)]. Trainer: José Walter Roque (21).
Goals: René Antonio Torres Lobo (8), Heberth Márquez (59).

73. 02.06.1985 **VENEZUELA - PERU** **0-1(0-0)** 13th FIFA WC. Qualifiers
Estadio Pueblo Nuevo, San Cristóbal; Referee: Jorge Orellana (Ecuador); Attendance: 19,000
VEN: César Renato Baéna (7/0), René Antonio Torres Lobo (6/2), Arnulfo Becerra (1/0), Pedro Javier Acosta Sánchez (18/1), Emilio Campos Rodríguez (15/0), Nelson José Carrero Heras (12/0) [76.Douglas Cedeño (6/1)], William Méndez (3/0), Asdrúbal José Sánchez Urbina (15/0), Bernardo Añor (8/2), Carlos Alberto Maldonado (3/0) [65.Pedro Juan Febles (16/4)], Heberth Márquez (3/1). Trainer: José Walter Roque (22).

74. 09.06.1985 **ARGENTINA - VENEZUELA** **3-0(1-0)** 13th FIFA WC. Qualifiers
Estadio Monumental „Antonio Vespucio Liberti", Buenos Aires; Referee: Gastón Edmundo Castro Makuc (Chile); Attendance: 35,000
VEN: César Renato Baéna (8/0), René Antonio Torres Lobo (7/2), Arnulfo Becerra (2/0), Pedro Javier Acosta Sánchez (19/1), Emilio Campos Rodríguez (16/0), Nelson José Carrero Heras (13/0), Robert Ellie (5/0) [46.William Méndez (4/0); 66.Richard Nada (2/0)], Asdrúbal José Sánchez Urbina (16/0), Bernardo Añor (9/2), Pedro Juan Febles (17/4), Douglas Cedeño (7/1). Trainer: José Walter Roque (23).

75. 16.06.1985 **PERU - VENEZUELA** **4-1(2-1)** 13th FIFA WC. Qualifiers
Estadio Nacional, Lima; Referee: Luis Carlos Ferreira (Brazil); Attendance: 10,327
VEN: César Renato Baéna (9/0), René Antonio Torres Lobo (8/2), Nicolás Simonelli (6/0), Pedro Javier Acosta Sánchez (20/1), Emilio Campos Rodríguez (17/0), Carlos Landaeta (3/0) [74.Nelson José Carrero Heras (14/0)], Asdrúbal José Sánchez Urbina (17/0), William Méndez (5/0), Bernardo Añor (10/2), Heberth Márquez (4/1) [63.Carlos Alberto Maldonado (4/0)], Pedro Juan Febles (18/5). Trainer: José Walter Roque (24).
Goal: Pedro Juan Febles (29).

76. 23.06.1985 **VENEZUELA - COLOMBIA** **2-2(1-1)** 13th FIFA WC. Qualifiers
Estadio Pueblo Nuevo, San Cristóbal; Referee: Ramón Ivannoe Barreto Ruíz (Uruguay); Attendance: 30,000
VEN: César Renato Baéna (10/0), René Antonio Torres Lobo (9/2), Nicolás Simonelli (7/0), Pedro Javier Acosta Sánchez (21/1), Emilio Campos Rodríguez (18/0), Carlos Landaeta (4/0) [Carlos Alberto Maldonado (5/0)], Asdrúbal José Sánchez Urbina (18/0), William Méndez (6/0), Bernardo Añor (11/3), Heberth Márquez (5/1), Douglas Cedeño (8/2) [Nelson José Carrero Heras (15/0)]. Trainer: José Walter Roque (25).
Goals: Douglas Cedeño (6), Bernardo Añor (69).

77. 30.06.1985 **COLOMBIA - VENEZUELA** **2-0(2-0)** 13th FIFA WC. Qualifiers
Estadio „Nemesio Camacho“ 'El Campín', Bogotá; Referee: Víctor Vásquez Sánchez (Chile); Attendance: 10,000
VEN: Daniel Nikolac (1/0), René Antonio Torres Lobo (10/2), Cecilio González (1/0), Pedro Javier Acosta Sánchez (22/1), Carlos Betancourt (9/0), Nelson José Carrero Heras (16/0) [Emilio Campos Rodríguez (19/0)], Asdrúbal José Sánchez Urbina (19/0), Carlos Alberto Maldonado (6/0), Pedro Juan Febles (19/5), Heberth Márquez (6/1), Douglas Cedeño (9/2) [William Méndez (7/0)]. Trainer: José Walter Roque (26).

78. 28.06.1987 **BRAZIL - VENEZUELA** **5-0(2-0)** 33rd Copa América. Group Stage
Estadio Chateau Carreras, Córdoba (Argentina); Referee: Elías Victoriano Jácome Guerreiro (Ecuador); Attendance: 8,000
VEN: César Renato Baéna (11/0), René Antonio Torres Lobo (11/2), Zdenko Morović (1/0), Pedro Javier Acosta Sánchez (23/1), Héctor Enrique Rivas Brito (1/0), Nelson José Carrero Heras (17/0), José Francisco Nieto (1/0) [63.Asdrúbal José Sánchez Urbina (20/0)], Franco Rizzi (4/0), Gerardo Méndez (1/0) [46.Heberth Márquez (7/1)], Ildemaro Fernández (2/0), Wilton Arreaza (1/0). Trainer: Rafael Santana (1).

79. 30.06.1987 **CHILE - VENEZUELA** **3-1(1-1)** 33rd Copa América. Group Stage
Estadio Chateau Carreras, Córdoba (Argentina); Referee: Luis Barrancos Álvarez (Bolivia); Attendance: 532
VEN: Daniel Nikolac (2/0), René Antonio Torres Lobo (12/2), Julio Quinteros (1/0) [78.Pablo Mendoza (1/0)], Pedro Javier Acosta Sánchez (24/2), Héctor Enrique Rivas Brito (2/0), Franco Rizzi (5/0), Nelson José Carrero Heras (18/0) [*sent off 56*], Asdrúbal José Sánchez Urbina (21/0), Gerardo Méndez (2/0) [67.José Francisco Nieto (2/0)], Heberth Márquez (8/1), Wilton Arreaza (2/0). Trainer: Rafael Santana (2).
Goal: Pedro Javier Acosta Sánchez (24 penalty).

80. 26.03.1989 **VENEZUELA - PARAGUAY** **1-2(1-2)**
Estadio Nacional „Brígido Iriarte“ Caracas; Referee: Francisco Farías (Venezuela); Attendance: 8,000
VEN: Daniel Nikolac (3/0), René Antonio Torres Lobo (13/2), Javier Medina (1/0), Héctor Enrique Rivas Brito (3/0) [Zdenko Morović (2/0)], Jorge Betancourt (3/0) [Ceferino Bencomo (1/0)], Noël San Vicente Bethelmy (1/0), Wilmer Segovia (1/0) [Carlos Domínguez (1/0)], Franco Rizzi (6/0), Ildemaro Fernández (3/0), Heberth Márquez (9/2) [Giovanni Savarese (1/0)], Enrique Samuel (1/0) [Otilio Enrique Yantis (1/0)]. Trainer: Carlos Horacio Moreno (1).
Goal: Heberth Márquez.

81. 29.03.1989 **VENEZUELA - PARAGUAY** **0-0**
Estadio Municipal, Maturin; Referee: Antonio López (Venezuela); Attendance: 6,500
VEN: Daniel Nikolac (4/0) [Franco Fasciana (1/0)], René Antonio Torres Lobo (14/2), Zdenko Morović (3/0), Héctor Enrique Rivas Brito (4/0), Jorge Betancourt (4/0), Noël San Vicente Bethelmy (2/0), Luis Mendoza (1/0), Franco Rizzi (7/0), Wilmer García (1/0) [Carlos Domínguez (2/0)], Ildemaro Fernández (4/0) [Giovanni Savarese (2/0)], Heberth Márquez (10/2) [Enrique Samuel (2/0)]. Trainer: Carlos Horacio Moreno (2).

82. 18.05.1989 **PERU - VENEZUELA** **2-1(0-0)**
Estadio Nacional, Lima; Referee: Walter Barrios (Peru); Attendance: 4,065
VEN: César Renato Baéna (12/0), René Antonio Torres Lobo (15/2), Andrés Leonardo Paz (1/0), Pedro Javier Acosta Sánchez (25/2), Luis Rojas (1/0) [60.William Pacheco (1/0)], Noël San Vicente Bethelmy (3/0) [33.Nelson José Carrero Heras (19/0)], Laureano Jaimes (3/0), Héctor Enrique Rivas Brito (5/0), Carlos Alberto Maldonado (7/0) [64.Stalín José Rivas (1/0)], Ildemaro Fernández (5/0) [46.Carlos Domínguez (3/1)], Heberth Márquez (11/2). Trainer: Carlos Horacio Moreno (3).
Goal: Carlos Domínguez (74).

83. 25.06.1989 **VENEZUELA - PERU** **3-1(0-0)**
Estadio Pueblo Nuevo, San Cristóbal; Referee: Arnaldo Gómez (Colombia); Attendance: 8,000
VEN: César Renato Baéna (13/0), René Antonio Torres Lobo (16/2) [64.Luis Alberto Camacaro (1/0)], Andrés Leonardo Paz (2/0), Pedro Javier Acosta Sánchez (26/2), William Pacheco (2/0), Bernardo Añor (12/3) [88.Nelson José Carrero Heras (20/0)], Laureano Jaimes (4/0) [73.Noël San Vicente Bethelmy (4/0)], Héctor Enrique Rivas Brito (6/1), Stalín José Rivas (2/1), Ildemaro Fernández (6/0) [62.Carlos Alberto Maldonado (8/0)], Pedro Juan Febles (20/6) [77.Heberth Márquez (12/2)]. Trainer: Carlos Horacio Moreno (4).
Goals: Héctor Enrique Rivas Brito (55), Pedro Juan Febles (56), Stalín José Rivas (80).

84. 01.07.1989 **BRAZIL - VENEZUELA** **3-1(2-0)** 34th Copa América. Group Stage
Estádio Fonte Nova, Salvador; Referee: Juan Daniel Cardellino de San Vicente (Uruguay); Attendance: 35,000
VEN: César Renato Baéna (14/0), René Antonio Torres Lobo (17/2), Andrés Leonardo Paz (3/0), Pedro Javier Acosta Sánchez (27/2), William Pacheco (3/0), Carlos Alberto Maldonado (9/1), Laureano Jaimes (5/0), Bernardo Añor (13/3), Héctor Enrique Rivas Brito (7/1) [57.Roberto Cavallo de Robertis (1/0)], Pedro Juan Febles (21/6) [57.Heberth Márquez (13/2)], Stalín José Rivas (3/1). Trainer: Carlos Horacio Moreno (5).
Goal: Carlos Alberto Maldonado (63).

85. 03.07.1989 **COLOMBIA - VENEZUELA** **4-2(1-0)** 34th Copa América. Group Stage
Estádio Fonte Nova, Salvador (Brazil); Referee: Rodolfo Antonio Martínez Mejía (Honduras); Attendance: 4,000
VEN: César Renato Baéna (15/0), Luis Alberto Camacaro (2/0), Andrés Leonardo Paz (4/0), Pedro Javier Acosta Sánchez (28/2), William Pacheco (4/0), Carlos Alberto Maldonado (10/3), Laureano Jaimes (6/0), Bernardo Añor (14/3) [54.Ildemaro Fernández (7/0)], Roberto Cavallo de Robertis (2/0), Heberth Márquez (14/2), Stalín José Rivas (4/1) [54.Noël San Vicente Bethelmy (5/0)]. Trainer: Carlos Horacio Moreno (6).
Goals: Carlos Alberto Maldonado (73, 88).

86. 05.07.1989 **VENEZUELA - PERU** **1-1(1-1)** 34th Copa América. Group Stage
Estádio Fonte Nova, Salvador (Brazil); Referee: Vincent Mauro (United States); Attendance: 1,500
VEN: César Renato Baéna (16/0), Luis Alberto Camacaro (3/0), Héctor Enrique Rivas Brito (8/1), Pedro Javier Acosta Sánchez (29/2), William Pacheco (5/0) [41.Noël San Vicente Bethelmy (6/0)], Laureano Jaimes (7/0), Roberto Cavallo de Robertis (3/0), Heberth Márquez (15/2), Pedro Juan Febles (22/6), Carlos Alberto Maldonado (11/4), Stalín José Rivas (5/1) [69.Ildemaro Fernández (8/0)]. Trainer: Carlos Horacio Moreno (7).
Goal: Carlos Alberto Maldonado (73).

87. 07.07.1989 **PARAGUAY - VENEZUELA** **3-0(1-0)** 34th Copa América. Group Stage
Estádio Fonte Nova, Salvador (Brazil); Referee: Rodolfo Antonio Martínez Mejía (Honduras); Attendance: 3,000
VEN: César Renato Baéna (17/0), René Antonio Torres Lobo (18/2), Luis Alberto Camacaro (4/0), Pedro Javier Acosta Sánchez (30/2), William Pacheco (6/0), Laureano Jaimes (8/0), Héctor Enrique Rivas Brito (9/1) [46.Ildemaro Fernández (9/0)], Noël San Vicente Bethelmy (7/0), Roberto Cavallo de Robertis (4/0), Pedro Juan Febles (23/6) [57.Heberth Márquez (16/2)], Carlos Alberto Maldonado (12/4). Trainer: Carlos Horacio Moreno (8).

88. 30.07.1989 **VENEZUELA - BRAZIL** **0-4(0-1)** 14th FIFA WC. Qualifiers
Estadio Nacional „Brígido Iriarte", Caracas; Referee: Juan Oscar Ortubé Vargas (Bolivia); Attendance: 20,000
VEN: César Renato Baéna (18/0), William Pacheco (7/0), Zdenko Morović (4/0), Pedro Javier Acosta Sánchez (31/2), Jorge Betancourt (5/0), Roberto Cavallo de Robertis (5/0), Héctor Enrique Rivas Brito (10/1), Bernardo Añor (15/3) [70.Nelson José Carrero Heras (21/0)], Ildemaro Fernández (10/0), Carlos Alberto Maldonado (13/4), Pedro Juan Febles (24/6) [55.Wilton Arreaza (3/0)]. Trainer: Carlos Horacio Moreno (9).

89. 06.08.1989 **VENEZUELA - CHILE** **1-3(0-2)** 14th FIFA WC. Qualifiers
Estadio Nacional „Brígido Iriarte", Caracas; Referee: Carlos Montalván Miranda (Peru); Attendance: 13,000
VEN: César Renato Baéna (19/0), René Antonio Torres Lobo (19/2), Andrés Leonardo Paz (5/0), Pedro Javier Acosta Sánchez (32/2), Jorge Betancourt (6/0) [46.Bernardo Añor (16/3)], Héctor Enrique Rivas Brito (11/1), Roberto Cavallo de Robertis (6/0), Nelson José Carrero Heras (22/0), Pedro Gallardo (1/0), Carlos Alberto Maldonado (14/4), Pedro Juan Febles (25/6) [51.Ildemaro Fernández (11/1)]. Trainer: Carlos Horacio Moreno (10).
Goal: Ildemaro Fernández (65).

90. 20.08.1989 **BRAZIL - VENEZUELA** **6-0(4-0)** 14th FIFA WC. Qualifiers
Estádio „Cicero Pompeu de Toledo" Morumbi, São Paulo; Referee: Ernesto Filippi Cavani (Uruguay); Attendance: 106,462
VEN: César Renato Baéna (20/0), René Antonio Torres Lobo (20/2), Andrés Leonardo Paz (6/0), Pedro Javier Acosta Sánchez (33/2), William Pacheco (8/0), Héctor Enrique Rivas Brito (12/1), Nelson José Carrero Heras (23/0), Roberto Cavallo de Robertis (7/0), Pedro Gallardo (2/0) [46.Pedro Juan Febles (26/6)], Carlos Alberto Maldonado (15/4), Wilton Arreaza (4/0) [77.Martín José Tarazona (1/0)]. Trainer: Miguel Sabino (1/replacing Carlos Horacio Moreno suspended).

91. 27.08.1989 **CHILE - VENEZUELA** **5-0(3-0)** 14th FIFA WC. Qualifiers
Estadio Malvinas Argentinas, Mendoza (Argentina); Referee: Elías Victoriano Jácome Guerreiro (Ecuador); Attendance: 19,000
VEN: José Gregorio Gómez (1/0), René Antonio Torres Lobo (21/2), Andrés Leonardo Paz (7/0), Pedro Javier Acosta Sánchez (34/2) [59.Pedro Gallardo (3/0)], Zdenko Morović (5/0), Nelson José Carrero Heras (24/0), Roberto Cavallo de Robertis (8/0), José Ramón López (2/0), Ildemaro Fernández (12/1) [73.Pedro Juan Febles (27/6)], Carlos Alberto Maldonado (16/4), Wilton Arreaza (5/0). Trainer: Carlos Horacio Moreno (11).

92. 06.07.1991 **CHILE - VENEZUELA** **2-0(2-0)** 35th Copa América. Group Stage
Estadio Nacional, Santiago; Referee: Armando Pérez Hoyos (Colombia); Attendance: 45,000
VEN: Franco Fasciana (2/0), William Pacheco (9/0), César José Marcano (2/0), José Luis Jiménez (1/0), Miguel Ángel Echenáusi (1/0), Laureano Jaimes (9/0), Roberto Cavallo de Robertis (9/0), Carlos Alberto Maldonado (17/4), Stalín José Rivas (6/1), Pedro Gallardo (4/0) [57.Carlos Castro (1/0)], Ildemaro Fernández (13/1) [80.Otilio Enrique Yantis (2/0)]. Trainer: Víctor Pignanelli (1).

93. 08.07.1991 **ARGENTINA - VENEZUELA** **3-0(2-0)** 35th Copa América. Group Stage
Estadio Regional, Concepción (Chile); Referee: Milton Villavicencio Echeverría (Ecuador); Attendance: 7,000
VEN: Franco Fasciana (3/0), William Pacheco (10/0), César José Marcano (3/0), José Luis Jiménez (2/0), Miguel Ángel Echenáusi (2/0), Laureano Jaimes (10/0), Roberto Cavallo de Robertis (10/0), Otilio Enrique Yantis (3/0), Carlos Alberto Maldonado (18/4) [74.Carlos Castro (2/0)], Stalín José Rivas (7/1), Ildemaro Fernández (14/1) [47.Pedro Gallardo (5/0)]. Trainer: Víctor Pignanelli (2).

94. 10.07.1991 **PARAGUAY - VENEZUELA** **5-0(2-0)** 35th Copa América. Group Stage
Estadio Nacional, Santiago (Chile); Referee: José Joaquín Torres Cadena (Colombia); Attendance: 30,000
VEN: Franco Fasciana (4/0), William Pacheco (11/0), César José Marcano (4/0), José Luis Jiménez (3/0), Miguel Ángel Echenáusi (3/0), Laureano Jaimes (11/0), Roberto Cavallo de Robertis (11/0), Carlos Alberto Maldonado (19/4), Stalín José Rivas (8/1), Carlos Castro (3/0) [46.Alexander Bottini (1/0)], Pedro Gallardo (6/0) [56.Otilio Enrique Yantis (4/0)]. Trainer: Víctor Pignanelli (3).

95. 12.07.1991 **PERU - VENEZUELA** **5-1(2-1)** 35th Copa América. Group Stage
Estadio Nacional, Santiago (Chile); Referee: Armando Pérez Hoyos (Colombia); Attendance: 4,000
VEN: Franco Fasciana (5/0), William Pacheco (12/0), Andrés Leonardo Paz (8/0), José Luis Jiménez (4/0), Miguel Ángel Echenáusi (4/0), José Flores (1/0), Laureano Jaimes (12/0), Stalín José Rivas (9/1) [37.Robert Rodallegas (1/0)], Roberto Cavallo de Robertis (12/0), Carlos Alberto Maldonado (20/4), Otilio Enrique Yantis (5/0) [46.Pedro Gallardo (7/0)]. Trainer: Víctor Pignanelli (4).
Goal: José Del Solar (14 own goal).

96. 23.01.1993 **VENEZUELA - PERU** **0-0**
Estadio Polideportivo Cachamay, Puerto Ordaz; Referee: Juan José Torres (Venezuela); Attendance: 15,000
VEN: José Gregorio Gómez (2/0), Angelo Bonacorso (1/0) [Luis Manuel Filosa Astudillo (1/0)], Edson Argenis Tortolero Román (1/0), Leonardo Alberto González Antequera (1/0), Miguel Ángel Echenáusi (5/0), Carlos José García Mijares (1/0), Edson José Rodríguez (1/0) [Reinaldo Restifo (1/0)], Wilson Arcangel Chacón (1/0), Gerson Diomar Díaz (1/0), José Luis Dolgetta (1/0), Linder García (1/0) [Alexander Bottini (2/0)]. Trainer: Ratomir Dujković (1).

97. 24.02.1993 **VENEZUELA - COLOMBIA** **0-0**
Estadio Pueblo Nuevo, San Cristóbal; Referee: Elías Victoriano Jácome Guerreiro (Ecuador)
VEN: José Gregorio Gómez (Cap) (3/0), Carlos José García Mijares (2/0) [61.Luis Manuel Filosa Astudillo (2/0)], Edson Argenis Tortolero Román (2/0), Leonardo Alberto González Antequera (2/0), Elvis Alfonso Martínez Dugarte (1/0), Miguel Ángel Echenáusi (6/0), Sergio Alejandro Hernández (1/0), Marcos Elías Mathías (1/0), Wilson Arcangel Chacón (2/0) [87.Juan Enrique García Rivas (1/0)], Edson José Rodríguez (2/0) [66.Gerson Diomar Díaz (2/0)], José Luis Dolgetta (2/0) [75.Diony José Guerra Ford (1/0)]. Trainer: Ratomir Dujković (2).

98. 21.05.1993 **COLOMBIA - VENEZUELA** **1-1(1-1)**

Estadio „Nemesio Camacho" 'El Campín', Bogotá; Referee: Armando Pérez Hoyos (Colombia); Attendance: 38,000

VEN: Rafael Edgar Dudamel Ochoa (1/0), Elvis Alfonso Martínez Dugarte (2/0), Leonardo Alberto González Antequera (3/0), Leonardo Lupi (1/0), Carlos José García Mijares (3/0), Marcos Elías Mathías (2/0) [79.Juan Enrique García Rivas (2/0)], Wilson Arcangel Chacón (3/0), Sergio Alejandro Hernández (2/0), Ricardo Milillo (1/0), Oswaldo Palencia (1/0) [78.José Luis Dolgetta (3/0)], Stalín José Rivas (10/2). Trainer: Ratomir Dujković (3).

Goal: Stalín José Rivas (43).

99. 07.06.1993 **FRANCE „B" - VENEZUELA** **2-0(0-0)**

Stade Lés Abymes, Pointe-à-Pitre (Guadéloupe)

VEN: Rafael Edgar Dudamel Ochoa (2/0), Carlos José García Mijares (4/0), Leonardo Alberto González Antequera (4/0), Leonardo Lupi (2/0) [José Alexander Echenique (1/0)], Miguel Ángel Echenáusi (7/0), Marcos Elías Mathías (3/0) [Edson José Rodríguez (3/0)], Sergio Alejandro Hernández (3/0), Ricardo Milillo (2/0), Stalín José Rivas (11/2), José Luis Dolgetta (4/0) [Juan Enrique García Rivas (3/0)], Oswaldo Palencia (2/0) [Carlos Alberto Contreras (1/0)]. Trainer: Ratomir Dujković (4).

100. 11.06.1993 **PERU - VENEZUELA** **3-1(1-0)**

Estadio Centenario, Arequipa; Referee: Antonio Arnao Ortega (Peru); Attendance: 18,000

VEN: Rafael Edgar Dudamel Ochoa (3/0), Carlos José García Mijares (5/0), Leonardo Alberto González Antequera (5/0), Marcos Elías Mathías (4/0), Miguel Ángel Echenáusi (8/0), Ricardo Milillo (3/0), Sergio Alejandro Hernández (4/0) [Luis Manuel Filosa Astudillo (3/0)], Edson José Rodríguez (4/0) [Miguel Cordero (1/0)], Juan Enrique García Rivas (4/0) [Carlos Alberto Contreras (2/0)], José Luis Dolgetta (5/0) [Oswaldo Palencia (3/1)], Stalín José Rivas (12/2). Trainer: Ratomir Dujković (5).

Goal: Oswaldo Palencia (74).

101. 15.06.1993 **ECUADOR - VENEZUELA** **6-1(2-0)** 36th Copa América. Group Stage

Estadio Olímpico „Atahualpa", Quito; Referee: Francisco Oscar Lamolina (Argentina); Attendance: 45,000

VEN: Rafael Edgar Dudamel Ochoa (4/0), Carlos José García Mijares (6/0) [*sent off 62*], Marcos Elías Mathías (5/0), Leonardo Alberto González Antequera (6/0), Miguel Ángel Echenáusi (9/0), Sergio Alejandro Hernández (5/0), Ricardo Milillo (4/0), Edson José Rodríguez (5/0) [56.Carlos Alberto Contreras (3/0)], Stalín José Rivas (13/2), Juan Enrique García Rivas (5/0) [56.Oswaldo Palencia (4/1)], José Luis Dolgetta (6/1). Trainer: Ratomir Dujković (6).

Goal: José Luis Dolgetta (79).

102. 19.06.1993 **URUGUAY - VENEZUELA** **2-2(1-1)** 36th Copa América. Group Stage

Estadio Bella Vista, Ambato (Ecuador); Referee: Pablo Peña Durán (Bolivia); Attendance: 15,000

VEN: José Gregorio Gómez (Cap) (4/0), Luis Manuel Filosa Astudillo (4/0), Marcos Elías Mathías (6/0), Leonardo Alberto González Antequera (7/0), José Alexander Echenique (2/0), Sergio Alejandro Hernández (6/0), Ricardo Milillo (5/0), Miguel Ángel Echenáusi (10/0), Stalín José Rivas (14/3), Oswaldo Palencia (5/1) [85.Carlos Alberto Contreras (4/0)], José Luis Dolgetta (7/2) [75.Edson José Rodríguez (6/0)]. Trainer: Ratomir Dujković (7).

Goals: José Luis Dolgetta (10), Stalín José Rivas (72).

103. 22.06.1993 **VENEZUELA – UNITED STATES** **3-3(0-2)** 36th Copa América. Group Stage

Estadio Olímpico „Atahualpa", Quito (Ecuador); Referee: Alberto Tejada Noriega (Peru); Attendance: 45,000

VEN: José Gregorio Gómez (Cap) (5/0), Carlos José García Mijares (7/0), Marcos Elías Mathías (7/0), Sergio Alejandro Hernández (7/0), Miguel Ángel Echenáusi (11/1), Leonardo Alberto González Antequera (8/0), José Alexander Echenique (3/0) [84.Ricardo Milillo (6/0)], Luis Manuel Filosa Astudillo (5/0) [46.Edson José Rodríguez (7/0)], Stalín José Rivas (15/3) [*sent off 84*], José Luis Dolgetta (8/4), Oswaldo Palencia (6/1). Trainer: Ratomir Dujković (8).

Goals: José Luis Dolgetta (68, 80), Miguel Ángel Echenáusi (89).

104. 18.07.1993 **VENEZUELA - BOLIVIA** **1-7(1-3)** 15th FIFA WC. Qualifiers

Estadio Polideportivo Cachamay, Puerto Ordaz; Referee: Morera Benny Ulloa (Costa Rica); Attendance: 12,500

VEN: José Gregorio Gómez (6/0), Carlos José García Mijares (8/0), Marcos Elías Mathías (8/0) [61.Héctor Enrique Rivas Brito (13/1)], José Alexander Echenique (4/0) [31.Ricardo Milillo (7/0)], Leonardo Alberto González Antequera (9/0), Luis Morales (1/0), Sergio Alejandro Hernández (8/0), Edson José Rodríguez (8/0), Oswaldo Palencia (7/2), José Luis Dolgetta (9/4), Pedro Felipe Camacho (1/0). Trainer: Ratomir Dujković (9).

Goal: Oswaldo Palencia (14).

105. 25.07.1993 **VENEZUELA - URUGUAY** **0-1(0-0)** 15th FIFA WC. Qualifiers

Estadio Pueblo Nuevo, San Cristóbal; Referee: José Joaquín Torres Cadena (Colombia); Attendance: 12,000

VEN: José Gregorio Gómez (7/0), Luis Manuel Filosa Astudillo (6/0), Leonardo Alberto González Antequera (10/0), Héctor Enrique Rivas Brito (14/1), Marcos Elías Mathías (9/0) [79.Carlos José García Mijares (9/0)], Edson José Rodríguez (9/0), Sergio Alejandro Hernández (9/0), Miguel Ángel Echenáusi (12/1), Stalín José Rivas (16/3), Oswaldo Palencia (8/2), José Luis Dolgetta (10/4). Trainer: Ratomir Dujković (10).

106. 01.08.1993 **VENEZUELA - BRAZIL** **1-5(0-1)** 15th FIFA WC. Qualifiers

Estadio Pueblo Nuevo, San Cristóbal; Referee: Armando Pérez Hoyos (Colombia); Attendance: 26,000

VEN: José Gregorio Gómez (8/0), Luis Manuel Filosa Astudillo (7/0), Héctor Enrique Rivas Brito (15/1), Leonardo Alberto González Antequera (11/0), Marcos Elías Mathías (10/0), Miguel Ángel Echenáusi (13/1) [*sent off 34*], Edson José Rodríguez (10/0), Sergio Alejandro Hernández (10/0), Wilson Arcangel Chacón (4/0), Stalín José Rivas (17/3) [80.Carlos Alberto Contreras (5/0)], José Luis Dolgetta (11/4) [72.Juan Enrique García Rivas (6/1)]. Trainer: Ratomir Dujković (11).

Goal: Juan Enrique García Rivas (84).

107. 08.08.1993 **ECUADOR - VENEZUELA** **5-0(2-0)** 15th FIFA WC. Qualifiers

Estadio Olímpico „Atahualpa", Quito; Referee: Francisco Oscar Lamolina (Argentina); Attendance: 35,000

VEN: José Gregorio Gómez (9/0), Luis Manuel Filosa Astudillo (8/0), Héctor Enrique Rivas Brito (16/1), Leonardo Alberto González Antequera (12/0), Marcos Elías Mathías (11/0), Ricardo Milillo (8/0), Luis Morales (2/0) [54.Carlos José García Mijares (10/0)], Wilson Arcangel Chacón (5/0) [88.Carlos Alberto Contreras (6/0)], Stalín José Rivas (18/3), Juan Enrique García Rivas (7/1), José Luis Dolgetta (12/4). Trainer: Ratomir Dujković (12).

108. 22.08.1993 **BOLIVIA - VENEZUELA** **7-0(1-0)** 15th FIFA WC. Qualifiers

Estadio „Hernándo Siles Zuazo", La Paz; Referee: Sabino Farina Céspedes (Paraguay); Attendance: 40,000

VEN: José Gregorio Gómez (10/0), Luis Manuel Filosa Astudillo (9/0), Sergio Alejandro Hernández (11/0), Edson Argenis Tortolero Román (3/0), Leonardo Alberto González Antequera (13/0), Carlos Alberto Contreras (7/0), Edson José Rodríguez (11/0), Miguel Ángel Echenáusi (14/1), Juan Enrique García Rivas (8/1) [28.Carlos José García Mijares (11/0)], Leopoldo Páez-Pumar (1/0), Stalín José Rivas (19/3) [46.Luis Morales (3/0)]. Trainer: Ratomir Dujković (13).

109. 29.08.1993 **URUGUAY - VENEZUELA** **4-0(3-0)** 15th FIFA WC. Qualifiers
Estadio Centenario, Montevideo; Referee: Juan Francisco Escobar Valdéz (Paraguay); Attendance: 20,000
VEN: José Gregorio Gómez (11/0), Luis Manuel Filosa Astudillo (10/0), Leonardo Alberto González Antequera (14/0) [*sent off 28*], Héctor Enrique Rivas Brito (17/1), Marcos Elías Mathías (12/0), Carlos José García Mijares (12/0), Miguel Ángel Echenáusi (15/1) [81.Carlos Alberto Contreras (8/0)], Leopoldo Páez Pumar (2/0), Stalín José Rivas (20/3), Wilson Arcangel Chacón (6/0), Juan Enrique García Rivas (9/1) [46.Edson José Rodríguez (12/0)]. Trainer: Ratomir Dujković (14).

110. 05.09.1993 **BRAZIL - VENEZUELA** **4-0(3-0)** 15th FIFA WC. Qualifiers
Estádio Mineirão, Belo Horizonte; Referee: Francisco Oscar Lamolina (Argentina); Attendance: 64,000
VEN: José Gregorio Gómez (12/0), Luis Manuel Filosa Astudillo (11/0), Héctor Enrique Rivas Brito (18/1), Edson Argenis Tortolero Román (4/0), Luis Morales (4/0), Carlos José García Mijares (13/0), Leopoldo Páez-Pumar (3/0) [78.Ricardo Milillo (9/0)], Miguel Ángel Echenáusi (16/1), Wilson Arcangel Chacón (7/0) [83.Sergio Alejandro Hernández (12/0)], Juan Enrique García Rivas (10/1), Edson José Rodríguez (13/0). Trainer: Ratomir Dujković (15).

111. 12.09.1993 **VENEZUELA - ECUADOR** **2-1(1-1)** 15th FIFA WC. Qualifiers
Estadio Polideportivo Cachamay, Puerto Ordaz; Referee: Fernando Chappel Merino (Peru); Attendance: 2,000
VEN: José Gregorio Gómez (13/0), Luis Manuel Filosa Astudillo (12/0), Edson Argenis Tortolero Román (5/0), Luis Morales (5/1), Leonardo Alberto González Antequera (15/0), Leopoldo Páez-Pumar (4/0), Miguel Ángel Echenáusi (17/1) [*sent off 81*], Héctor Enrique Rivas Brito (19/1), Stalín José Rivas (21/3), Juan Enrique García Rivas (11/2) [46.Carlos Alberto Contreras (9/0)], Pedro Felipe Camacho (2/0) [80.Edson José Rodríguez (14/0)]. Trainer: Ratomir Dujković (16).
Goals: Juan Enrique García Rivas (5), Luis Morales (47).

112. 28.01.1994 **VENEZUELA - COLOMBIA** **1-2(0-1)**
Estadio La Carolina, Barinas; Referee: Nelson Rodríguez (Venezuela); Attendance: 10,000
VEN: Johnny Barreto (1/0) [Osnel Antonio García (1/0)], Leonardo Alberto González Antequera (16/0), Edson Argenis Tortolero Román (6/0), Edson José Rodríguez (15/1) [Alexander Flores (1/0)], Héctor Enrique Rivas Brito (20/1), Noël San Vicente Bethelmy (8/0), Gabriel Antonio Miranda (1/0), Marcos Elías Mathías (13/0), Bernardo Añor (17/3) [Carlos Alberto Contreras (10/0)], Stalín José Rivas (22/3), Heberth Márquez (17/2). Trainer: Ratomir Dujković (17).
Goal: Edson José Rodríguez (61).

113. 03.04.1995 **BOLIVIA - VENEZUELA** **0-0**
Estadio Patria del Morro, Sucre; Referee: Pedro Saucedo Rodríguez (Bolivia)
VEN: Rafael Edgar Dudamel Ochoa (5/0) [Danny Vigas (1/0)], Alexander Antonio Hezzel (1/0), Edson Argenis Tortolero Román (7/0), Elvis Alfonso Martínez Dugarte (3/0), Noël San Vicente Bethelmy (9/0), Andrés Leonardo Paz (9/0) [William González Ruíz (1/0)], Gabriel Antonio Miranda (2/0), Gerson Diomar Díaz (3/0), Stalín José Rivas (23/3), José Luis Dolgetta (13/4) [Luis Manuel Filosa Astudillo (13/0)], Juan Enrique García Rivas (12/2) [Edson José Rodríguez (16/1)]. Trainer: Rafael Santana (3).

114. 18.06.1995 **VENEZUELA - BOLIVIA** **1-3(1-1)**
Estadio "Luis Loreta Lira", Valera; Referee: Raúl Pírez (Venezuela); Attendance: 6,000
VEN: Rafael Edgar Dudamel Ochoa (6/0), Alexander Antonio Hezzel (2/0), Edson Argenis Tortolero Román (8/0), Jesús Ángel Valbuena (1/0), Elvis Alfonso Martínez Dugarte (4/0), Sergio Alejandro Hernández (13/0) [80.Héctor Enrique Rivas Brito (21/1)], Edson José Rodríguez (17/1), Gerson Diomar Díaz (4/0), Gabriel Antonio Miranda (3/0) [70.Leonardo Alberto González Antequera (17/0)], Diony José Guerra Ford (2/0), Juan Enrique García Rivas (13/3). Trainer: Rafael Santana (4).
Goal: Juan Enrique García Rivas (38).

115. 05.07.1995 **URUGUAY - VENEZUELA** **4-1(2-0)** 37th Copa América. Group Stage
Estadio Centenario, Montevideo; Referee: Salvador Imperatore (Chile); Attendance: 32,000
VEN: Rafael Edgar Dudamel Ochoa (7/0), Alexander Antonio Hezzel (3/0) [77.Héctor Enrique Rivas Brito (22/1)], Edson Argenis Tortolero Román (9/0), Carlos José García Mijares (14/0), Elvis Alfonso Martínez Dugarte (5/0) [27.Leonardo Alberto González Antequera (18/0)], Gerson Diomar Díaz (5/0), Sergio Alejandro Hernández (14/0), Jesús Ángel Valbuena (2/0), Gabriel Antonio Miranda (4/0) [85.Juan Enrique García Rivas (14/3)], Stalín José Rivas (24/3) [*sent off 56*], José Luis Dolgetta (14/5). Trainer: Rafael Santana (5).
Goal: José Luis Dolgetta (53).

116. 09.07.1995 **MEXICO - VENEZUELA** **3-1(1-0)** 37th Copa América. Group Stage
Estadio Campus Municipal, Maldonado (Uruguay); Referee: Raúl Domínguez (United States); Attendance: 700
VEN: Gilberto Angelucci (1/0), Carlos José García Mijares (15/0), Edson Argenis Tortolero Román (10/0) [*sent off 69*], Jesús Ángel Valbuena (3/0) [55.Héctor Enrique Rivas Brito (23/1)], Edson José Rodríguez (18/1), Wilson Arcangel Chacón (8/0) [70.Luis Manuel Filosa Astudillo (14/0)], Sergio Alejandro Hernández (15/0), Gerson Diomar Díaz (6/0), Gabriel Antonio Miranda (5/0) [73.Leonardo Alberto González Antequera (19/0) [*sent off 89*]], Juan Enrique García Rivas (15/3), José Luis Dolgetta (15/5). Trainer: Rafael Santana (6).
Goal: Jorge Campos Navarrete (65 own goal).

117. 12.07.1995 **PARAGUAY - VENEZUELA** **3-2(1-1)** 37th Copa América. Group Stage
Estadio Campus Municipal, Maldonado (Uruguay); Referee: Oscar Julián Ruíz Acosta (Colombia); Attendance: 2,000
VEN: Gilberto Angelucci (2/0), Elvis Alfonso Martínez Dugarte (6/0), Héctor Enrique Rivas Brito (24/1), Carlos José García Mijares (16/0), Marcos Elías Mathías (14/0) [80.Jesús Ángel Valbuena (4/0)], William González Ruíz (2/0), Sergio Alejandro Hernández (16/0) [85.Diony José Guerra Ford (3/0)], Gerson Diomar Díaz (7/0) [85.Wilson Arcangel Chacón (9/0)], Gabriel Antonio Miranda (6/1), Stalín José Rivas (25/3), José Luis Dolgetta (16/6). Trainer: Rafael Santana (7).
Goals: Gabriel Antonio Miranda (13), José Luis Dolgetta (68).

118. 21.12.1995 **ARGENTINA - VENEZUELA** **6-0(5-0)**
Estadio Malvinas Argentinas, Mendoza; Referee: Eduardo Gamboa Martínez (Chile); Attendance: 5,000
VEN: Gilberto Angelucci (3/0), Carlos José García Mijares (17/0), William González Ruíz (3/0) [33.Laureano Jaimes (13/0)], Sergio Alejandro Hernández (17/0), Jesús Ángel Valbuena (5/0), Leonardo Alberto González Antequera (20/0), Reinaldo Restifo (2/0) [45.Wilson Arcangel Chacón (10/0)], Gerson Diomar Díaz (8/0) [33.Marcos Elías Mathías (15/0)], Edson José Rodríguez (19/1) [73.William Hidalgo (1/0)], Stalín José Rivas (26/3), José Luis Dolgetta (17/6). Trainer: Rafael Santana (8).

119. 05.01.1996 **TRINIDAD & TOBAGO - VENEZUELA** **0-0**
Industry Park, Palo Seco; Attendance: 5,000
VEN: Danny Vigas (2/0), Luis Manuel Filosa Astudillo (15/0), Carlos José García Mijares (18/0), William González Ruíz (4/0), Jesús Ángel Valbuena (6/0) [Edson José Rodríguez (20/1)], Leonardo Alberto González Antequera (21/0), Marcos Elías Mathías (16/0), Sergio Alejandro Hernández (18/0) [Reinaldo Restifo (3/0)], Stalín José Rivas (27/3), José Luis Dolgetta (18/6), William Hidalgo (2/0). Trainer: Rafael Santana (9).

120. 07.01.1996 **TRINIDAD & TOBAGO - VENEZUELA** **0-0**

Queen's Park Oval, Port of Spain; Attendance: 10,000

VEN: Danny Vigas (3/0), Luis Manuel Filosa Astudillo (16/0), Carlos José García Mijares (19/0), William González Ruíz (5/0), Jesús Ángel Valbuena (7/0) [Edson José Rodríguez (21/1)], Leonardo Alberto González Antequera (22/0), Marcos Elías Mathías (17/0), Sergio Alejandro Hernández (19/0), Stalín José Rivas (28/3), José Luis Dolgetta (19/6), William Hidalgo (3/0) [Reinaldo Restifo (4/0)]. Trainer: Rafael Santana (10).

121. 02.02.1996 **VENEZUELA - ECUADOR** **0-1(0-0)**

Estadio Nacional "Brígido Iriarte", Caracas; Referee: Lenin David Rodríguez Aguilera (Venezuela); Attendance: 6,000

VEN: Rafael Edgar Dudamel Ochoa (8/0), Alexander Antonio Hezzel (4/0), Carlos José García Mijares (20/0), William González Ruíz (6/0), Luis Morales (6/1) [81.José Francisco González Quijada (1/0)], Edson Argenis Tortolero Román (11/0), Noël San Vicente Bethelmy (10/0) [81.Edson José Rodríguez (22/1)], Leonardo Alberto González Antequera (23/0) [58.Reinaldo Restifo (5/0)], Sergio Alejandro Hernández (20/0) [58.Oswaldo Palencia (9/2)], Stalín José Rivas (29/3), José Luis Dolgetta (20/6). Trainer: Rafael Santana (11).

122. 27.03.1996 **GUATEMALA - VENEZUELA** **3-0(2-0)**

Estadio Nacional, Ciudad de Guatemala; Referee: Mario Efrain Escobar López (Guatemala); Attendance: 5,000

VEN: Danny Vigas (4/0), Luis Manuel Filosa Astudillo (17/0) [Juan Carlos Quiñónez (1/0)], William González Ruíz (7/0), Leonardo Alberto González Antequera (24/0), Luis José Vallenilla Pacheco (1/0), Sergio Alejandro Hernández (21/0), Jesús Valiente (1/0), Dany D'Oliveira (1/0) [César Salazar (1/0)], Stalín José Rivas (30/3), Giovanni Savarese (3/0) [Wilson Arcangel Chacón (11/0)], Dickson Ruberth Morán Puleo (1/0). Trainer: Rafael Santana (12).

123. 24.04.1996 **VENEZUELA - URUGUAY** **0-2(0-0)** 16th FIFA WC. Qualifiers

Estadio Nacional „Brígido Iriarte", Caracas; Referee: Alberto Tejada Noriega (Peru); Attendance: 6,839

VEN: Gilberto Angelucci (4/0), Luis Manuel Filosa Astudillo (18/0), William González Ruíz (8/0), Edson Argenis Tortolero Román (12/0), Leonardo Alberto González Antequera (25/0), Luis José Vallenilla Pacheco (2/0) [83.David Andrew McIntosh Parra (1/0)], Jesús Valiente (2/0), Sergio Alejandro Hernández (22/0), Gerson Diomar Díaz (9/0) [55.Stalín José Rivas (31/3)], Rafael Ernesto Castellín García (1/0) [62.Dickson Ruberth Morán Puleo (2/0)], Diony José Guerra Ford (4/0). Trainer: Rafael Santana (13).

124. 02.06.1996 **VENEZUELA - CHILE** **1-1(1-0)** 16th FIFA WC. Qualifiers

Estadio La Carolina, Barinas; Referee: Epifanio González Chávez (Paraguay); Attendance: 8,074

VEN: Rafael Edgar Dudamel Ochoa (9/0), David Andrew McIntosh Parra (2/0), Jesús Valiente (3/0), Edson Argenis Tortolero Román (Cap) (13/0), Leonardo Alberto González Antequera (26/0), Sergio Alejandro Hernández (23/0), Gerson Diomar Díaz (10/0) [67.Alexander Antonio Hezzel (5/0); 85.Gabriel José Urdaneta Rangel (1/0)], Félix José Hernández (1/0), Rafael Ernesto Castellín García (2/0) [67.Giovanni Savarese (4/0)], Stalín José Rivas (32/3), Diony José Guerra Ford (5/1). Trainer: Rafael Santana (14).

Goal: Diony José Guerra Ford (8).

125. 22.06.1996 **HONDURAS - VENEZUELA** **1-0(0-0)**

Estadio „Francisco Morázon", San Pedro Sula; Referee: Argelio Sabillón (Honduras); Attendance: 5,000

VEN: Félix Armando Golindano (1/0) [83.Danny Vigas (5/0)], David Andrew McIntosh Parra (3/0), Carlos José García Mijares (21/0), Félix José Hernández (2/0), Sergio Alejandro Hernández (24/0), Luis José Vallenilla Pacheco (3/0) [73.Luis Manuel Filosa Astudillo (19/0)], Edson Argenis Tortolero Román (14/0), Jesús Valiente (4/0) [73.Leonardo Alberto González Antequera (27/0)], Luis Enrique Vera Martineau (1/0), Stalín José Rivas (33/3) [81.Gabriel José Urdaneta Rangel (2/0)], Gabriel Antonio Miranda (7/1) [46.Alexis José Chirinos (1/0)], Trainer: Rafael Santana (15).

126. 07.07.1996 **BOLIVIA - VENEZUELA** **6-1(2-0)** 16th FIFA WC. Qualifiers

Estadio „Hernándo Siles Zuazo", La Paz; Referee: José Luis Da Rosa Varela (Uruguay); Attendance: 43,822

VEN: Rafael Edgar Dudamel Ochoa (10/0), Luis Manuel Filosa Astudillo (20/0), David Andrew McIntosh Parra (4/0), Edson Argenis Tortolero Román (15/1), Leonardo Alberto González Antequera (28/0), Félix José Hernández (3/0), Sergio Alejandro Hernández (25/0) [46.Carlos José García Mijares (22/0)], Luis Enrique Vera Martineau (2/0), Stalín José Rivas (34/3) [46.Gerson Diomar Díaz (11/0)], Giovanni Savarese (5/0) [46.Gabriel José Urdaneta Rangel (3/0)], Diony José Guerra Ford (6/1). Trainer: Rafael Santana (16).

Goal: Edson Argenis Tortolero Román (65).

127. 21.07.1996 **PANAMA - VENEZUELA** **0-2(0-0)**

Estadio „Rommel Fernández", Ciudad de Panamá; Attendance: 8,000

VEN: Félix Armando Golindano (2/0), Luis Manuel Filosa Astudillo (21/0), David Andrew McIntosh Parra (5/0), Edson Argenis Tortolero Román (16/1), Sergio Alejandro Hernández (26/0), William González Ruíz (9/0), Jesús Valiente (5/0) [46.Félix José Hernández (4/0)], Luis José Vallenilla Pacheco (4/0) [90.Reinaldo Melo (1/0)], Gabriel José Urdaneta Rangel (4/0) [86.Alexis García (1/1)], Gabriel Antonio Miranda (8/2), Daniel Noriega Acosta (1/0) [46.Jorge Giraldo (1/0)]. Trainer: Rafael Santana (17).

Goals: Gabriel Antonio Miranda (65), Alexis García (90 penalty).

128. 01.09.1996 **ECUADOR - VENEZUELA** **1-0(1-0)** 16th FIFA WC. Qualifiers

Estadio Olímpico „Atahualpa", Quito; Referee: Carlos Manuel Robles Mella (Chile); Attendance: 36,889

VEN: Rafael Edgar Dudamel Ochoa (11/0), Luis Manuel Filosa Astudillo (22/0), William González Ruíz (10/0), Edson Argenis Tortolero Román (17/1), David Andrew McIntosh Parra (6/0), Sergio Alejandro Hernández (27/0), Jesús Valiente (6/0) [40.Gabriel José Urdaneta Rangel (5/0)], Luis Enrique Vera Martineau (3/0) [65.Gerson Diomar Díaz (12/0)], Gabriel Antonio Miranda (9/2), Juan Enrique García Rivas (16/3), Juan Carlos Socorro Vera (1/0) [75.Félix José Hernández (5/0)]. Trainer: Rafael Santana (18).

129. 18.09.1996 **EL SALVADOR - VENEZUELA** **0-1(0-0)**

Estadio Cuscatlán, San Salvador; Attendance: 6,000

VEN: Félix Armando Golindano (3/0), Luis Manuel Filosa Astudillo (23/0) [Jhonny Lucena (1/0)], Luis José Vallenilla Pacheco (5/0), Leonardo Alberto González Antequera (29/0), David Andrew McIntosh Parra (7/0), Noël San Vicente Bethelmy (11/0) [César Salazar (2/0)], Gerson Diomar Díaz (13/0) [Carlos José García Mijares (23/0)], Sergio Alejandro Hernández (28/0), Luis Enrique Vera Martineau (4/0), Dickson Ruberth Morán Puleo (3/0), Juan Enrique García Rivas (17/3) [Rafael Ernesto Castellín García (3/1)]. Trainer: Rafael Santana (19).

Goal: Rafael Ernesto Castellín García (70).

130. 02.10.1996 **VENEZUELA – COSTA RICA** **2-0(1-0)**

Estadio La Carolina, Barinas; Referee: Lenin David Rodríguez Aguilera (Venezuela); Attendance: 7,000

VEN: Félix Armando Golindano (4/0) [46.José Fasciana (1/0)], David Andrew McIntosh Parra (8/0), Leonardo Alberto González Antequera (30/0), William González Ruíz (11/0), Luis Manuel Filosa Astudillo (24/0) [68.Jhonny Lucena (2/0)], Sergio Alejandro Hernández (29/0), Luis José Vallenilla Pacheco (6/0), Félix José Hernández (6/0), Gerson Diomar Díaz (14/0), Dickson Ruberth Morán Puleo (4/1) [71.Rafael Ernesto Castellín García (4/1)], Juan Enrique García Rivas (18/4). Trainer: Rafael Santana (20).

Goals: Juan Enrique García Rivas (19), Dickson Ruberth Morán Puleo (59).

131. 09.10.1996 **VENEZUELA - ARGENTINA** **2-5(1-1)** 16th FIFA WC. Qualifiers

Estadio Pueblo Nuevo, San Cristóbal; Referee: Eduardo Dluzniewski Takoz (Uruguay); Attendance: 30,000

VEN: Rafael Edgar Dudamel Ochoa (12/1), David Andrew McIntosh Parra (9/0), Leonardo Alberto González Antequera (31/0), William González Ruíz (12/0), Félix José Hernández (7/0) [43.Gabriel José Urdaneta Rangel (6/0)], Gabriel Antonio Miranda (10/2) [60.Juan Enrique García Rivas (19/4)], Sergio Alejandro Hernández (30/0), Luis Enrique Vera Martineau (5/0), Dickson Ruberth Morán Puleo (5/1), Giovanni Savarese (6/1), Diony José Guerra Ford (7/1) [46.Luis Manuel Filosa Astudillo (25/0)]. Trainer: Rafael Santana (21).

Goals: Giovanni Savarese (7), Rafael Edgar Dudamel Ochoa (87).

132. 10.11.1996 **PERU - VENEZUELA** **4-1(2-0)** 16th FIFA WC. Qualifiers

Estadio Nacional, Lima; Referee: René Marcelo Ortubé Betancourt (Bolivia); Attendance: 31,036

VEN: Rafael Edgar Dudamel Ochoa (13/1), Luis Manuel Filosa Astudillo (26/0), David Andrew McIntosh Parra (10/0), Edson Argenis Tortolero Román (18/1), William González Ruíz (13/0), Gabriel Antonio Miranda (11/2) [62.Luis Enrique Vera Martineau (6/1)], Jesús Valiente (7/0), Félix José Hernández (8/0) [46.Gerson Diomar Díaz (15/0)], Miguel Ángel Echenáusi (18/1), Juan Enrique García Rivas (20/4), Giovanni Savarese (7/1) [46.Dickson Ruberth Morán Puleo (6/1)]. Trainer: Rafael Santana (22).

Goal: Luis Enrique Vera Martineau (78).

133. 15.12.1996 **VENEZUELA - COLOMBIA** **0-2(0-1)** 16th FIFA WC. Qualifiers

Estadio Pueblo Nuevo, San Cristóbal; Referee: Eduardo Gamboa Martinez (Chile); Attendance: 25,000

VEN: Rafael Edgar Dudamel Ochoa (14/1), Luis Manuel Filosa Astudillo (27/0), Edson Argenis Tortolero Román (19/1), William González Ruíz (14/0), Elvis Alfonso Martínez Dugarte (7/0), Sergio Alejandro Hernández (31/0), Luis Ramos (1/0), Andrew Páez (1/0), Félix José Hernández (9/0) [78.Gabriel José Urdaneta Rangel (7/0)], Rafael Ernesto Castellín García (5/1) [82.Didier Sanabria (1/0)], Giovanni Savarese (8/1) [74.Gerson Diomar Díaz (16/0)]. Trainer: Eduardo Borrero (1).

134. 12.01.1997 **VENEZUELA - PARAGUAY** **0-2(0-1)** 16th FIFA WC. Qualifiers

Estadio „Guillermo Soto Rosa“, Mérida; Referee: Ángel Osvaldo Sánchez (Argentina); Attendance: 7,981

VEN: Rafael Edgar Dudamel Ochoa (15/1), David Andrew McIntosh Parra (11/0), José Alexander Echenique (5/0), John Freddy Medina (1/0), Luis José Vallenilla Pacheco (7/0), Luis Ramos (2/0), Andrew Páez (2/0), Juan Carlos Castellanos (1/0) [46.Luis Tizamo (1/0)], José Nabollán (1/0) [62.Jesús Valiente (8/0)], Gabriel José Urdaneta Rangel (8/0), Giovanni Savarese (9/1). Trainer: Eduardo Borrero (2).

135. 12.02.1997 **JAMAICA - VENEZUELA** **0-0**

National Stadium, Kingston; Attendance: 5,000

VEN: César Espinoza (1/0) [Tulio Hernández (1/0)], David Andrew McIntosh Parra (12/0), José Alexander Echenique (6/0), John Freddy Medina (2/0), Luis José Vallenilla Pacheco (8/0), Luis Ramos (3/0), Jesús Rodríguez (1/0), Gabriel José Urdaneta Rangel (9/0) [Marcos Elías Mathías (18/0)], Félix José Hernández (10/0) [José Francisco González Quijada (2/0)], Oswaldo Palencia (10/2), Dickson Ruberth Morán Puleo (7/1) [Luis Tizamo (2/0)].Trainer: Eduardo Borrero (3).

136. 19.02.1997 **COSTA RICA - VENEZUELA** **5-2(2-1)**

Estadio „Rosabel Cordero“, Heredia; Referee: Víctor Rodríguez Ugalde (Costa Rica); Attendance: 5,100

VEN: César Renato Baéna (21/0), Luis José Vallenilla Pacheco (9/0), José Alexander Echenique (7/0), John Freddy Medina (3/0), Elvis Alfonso Martínez Dugarte (8/0), Luis Ramos (4/0) [*sent off 77*], Félix José Hernández (11/0) [65.Marcos Elías Mathías (19/0)], Carlos Alberto Contreras (11/0) [46.Rafael Ernesto Castellín García (6/1)], Gerson Diomar Díaz (17/1), Jesús Rodríguez (2/0) [80.José Nabollán (2/0)], Oswaldo Palencia (11/3) [85.Dickson Ruberth Morán Puleo (8/1)]. Trainer: Eduardo Borrero (4).

Goals: Gerson Diomar Díaz (29), Oswaldo Palencia (59).

137. 02.04.1997 **URUGUAY - VENEZUELA** **3-1(1-0)** 16th FIFA WC. Qualifiers

Estadio Centenario, Montevideo; Referee: René Marcelo Ortubé Betancourt (Bolivia); Attendance: 37,000

VEN: Rafael Edgar Dudamel Ochoa (16/1), William González Ruíz (15/0), José Alexander Echenique (8/0), Edson Argenis Tortolero Román (20/1), Elvis Alfonso Martínez Dugarte (9/0), Félix José Hernández (12/0), Jesús Rodríguez (3/0) [71.Andrew Páez (3/0)], Gerson Diomar Díaz (18/1), Luis Ramos (5/0), Rafael Ernesto Castellín García (7/2), Diony José Guerra Ford (8/1). Trainer: Eduardo Borrero (5).

Goals: Rafael Ernesto Castellín García (55).

138. 29.04.1997 **CHILE - VENEZUELA** **6-0(3-0)** 16th FIFA WC. Qualifiers

Estadio Nacional, Santiago; Referee: Gilberto Alcalá Piñeda (Mexico); Attendance: 42,034

VEN: Rafael Edgar Dudamel Ochoa (17/1), William González Ruíz (16/0), José Alexander Echenique (9/0), Edson Argenis Tortolero Román (21/1), Elvis Alfonso Martínez Dugarte (10/0), Luis Ramos (6/0), Jesús Rodríguez (4/0) [46.Andrew Páez (4/0)], Félix José Hernández (13/0), Gerson Diomar Díaz (19/1), Giovanni Savarese (10/1), Diony José Guerra Ford (9/1) [55.Rafael Ernesto Castellín García (8/2)]. Trainer: Eduardo Borrero (6).

139. 08.06.1997 **VENEZUELA - BOLIVIA** **1-1(0-0)** 16th FIFA WC. Qualifiers

Estadio „Luis Loreto Lira“, Valera; Referee: Fernando Panesso Zuluaga (Colombia); Attendance: 3,352

VEN: Rafael Edgar Dudamel Ochoa (18/1), David Andrew McIntosh Parra (13/0), José Alexander Echenique (10/0), José Manuel Rey Cortegoso (1/0), Luis José Vallenilla Pacheco (10/0), Leonardo Alberto González Antequera (32/0), Rafael Ernesto Castellín García (9/2), Giovanni Savarese (11/2), Gerson Diomar Díaz (20/1), Gabriel Antonio Miranda (12/2) [69.Andrew Páez (5/0)], Juan Carlos Socorro Vera (2/0) [75.Gabriel José Urdaneta Rangel (10/0)]. Trainer: Eduardo Borrero (7).

Goal: Giovanni Savarese (70).

140. 12.06.1997 **BOLIVIA - VENEZUELA** **1-0(0-0)** 38th Copa América. Group Stage

Estadio „Hernándo Siles Zuazo“, La Paz; Referee: Byron Aldemar Moreno Ruales (Ecuador); Attendance: 40,000

VEN: Rafael Edgar Dudamel Ochoa (19/1), David Andrew McIntosh Parra (14/0) [*sent off 73*], José Manuel Rey Cortegoso (2/0), José Alexander Echenique (11/0), Luis José Vallenilla Pacheco (11/0), Gerson Diomar Díaz (21/1), Leonardo Alberto González Antequera (33/0), Gabriel Antonio Miranda (13/2), Juan Carlos Socorro Vera (3/0) [76.William González Ruíz (17/0)], Rafael Ernesto Castellín García (10/2) [84.Gabriel José Urdaneta Rangel (11/0)], Oswaldo Palencia (12/3) [58.Robert Rodallegas (2/0)]. Trainer: Eduardo Borrero (8).

141. 15.06.1997 **URUGUAY - VENEZUELA** **2-0(1-0)** 38th Copa América. Group Stage

Estadio Patria del Morro, Sucre (Bolivia); Referee: Eduardo Gamboa Martínez (Chile); Attendance: 1,000

VEN: Rafael Edgar Dudamel Ochoa (20/1), Elvis Alfonso Martínez Dugarte (11/0), José Manuel Rey Cortegoso (3/0), José Alexander Echenique (12/0), Luis José Vallenilla Pacheco (12/0), Gerson Diomar Díaz (22/1), Robert Rodallegas (3/0) [*sent off 35*], Leonardo Alberto González Antequera (34/0), Juan Carlos Socorro Vera (4/0), Gabriel Antonio Miranda (14/2) [80.Andrew Páez (6/0)], Rafael Ernesto Castellín García (11/2). Trainer: Eduardo Borrero (9).

142. 18.06.1997 **PERU - VENEZUELA** **2-0(1-0)** 38th Copa América. Group Stage
Estadio Patria del Morro, Sucre (Bolivia); Referee: Byron Aldemar Moreno Ruales (Ecuador); Attendance: 1,500
VEN: Rafael Edgar Dudamel Ochoa (21/1), David Andrew McIntosh Parra (15/0), José Alexander Echenique (13/0), José Manuel Rey Cortegoso (4/0) [*sent off 54*], Luis José Vallenilla Pacheco (13/0), Leonardo Alberto González Antequera (35/0), Gerson Diomar Díaz (23/1) [83.Oswaldo Palencia (13/3)], Juan Carlos Socorro Vera (5/0) [67.Jesús Rodríguez (5/0)], Gabriel Antonio Miranda (15/2) [58.William González Ruíz (18/0)], Gabriel José Urdaneta Rangel (12/0), Rafael Ernesto Castellín García (12/2). Trainer: Eduardo Borrero (10).

143. 06.07.1997 **VENEZUELA - ECUADOR** **1-1(0-0)** 16th FIFA WC. Qualifiers
Estadio „José Encarnación 'Pachenco' Romero", Maracaibo; Referee: Arturo Angeles (United States); Attendance: 4,729
VEN: Rafael Edgar Dudamel Ochoa (22/1), David Andrew McIntosh Parra (16/0), José Alexander Echenique (14/0), José Manuel Rey Cortegoso (5/0), Luis José Vallenilla Pacheco (14/0), Leonardo Alberto González Antequera (36/0), Robert Rodallegas (4/0), Gerson Diomar Díaz (24/1) [55.Rafael Ernesto Castellín García (13/2)], Gabriel José Urdaneta Rangel (13/0) [89.Elvis Alfonso Martínez Dugarte (12/0)], Dickson Ruberth Morán Puleo (9/1) [55.Gabriel Antonio Miranda (16/3)], Giovanni Savarese (12/2). Trainer: Eduardo Borrero (11).
Goal: Gabriel Antonio Miranda (75).

144. 20.07.1997 **ARGENTINA - VENEZUELA** **2-0(1-0)** 16th FIFA WC. Qualifiers
Estadio Monumental „Antonio Vespucio Liberti", Buenos Aires; Referee: Wilson Souza Mendonça (Brazil); Attendance: 48,000
VEN: Rafael Edgar Dudamel Ochoa (23/1), David Andrew McIntosh Parra (17/0), José Alexander Echenique (15/0), José Manuel Rey Cortegoso (6/0), Elvis Alfonso Martínez Dugarte (13/0), Leonardo Alberto González Antequera (37/0), Gerson Diomar Díaz (25/1) [73.Oswaldo Palencia (14/3)], Robert Rodallegas (5/0), Gabriel Antonio Miranda (17/3), Dickson Ruberth Morán Puleo (10/1) [56.Jhonny Lucena (3/0)], Giovanni Savarese (13/2). Trainer: Eduardo Borrero (12).

145. 20.08.1997 **VENEZUELA - PERU** **0-3(0-1)** 16th FIFA WC. Qualifiers
Estadio La Carolina, Barinas; Referee: Peter Prendergast (Jamaica); Attendance: 10,000
VEN: Rafael Edgar Dudamel Ochoa (24/1), David Andrew McIntosh Parra (18/0), José Alexander Echenique (16/0), José Manuel Rey Cortegoso (7/0), Luis José Vallenilla Pacheco (15/0), Leonardo Alberto González Antequera (38/0), Robert Rodallegas (6/0) [46.Jhonny Lucena (4/0)], Alexis García (2/1) [80.Jorge Giraldo (2/0)], Gabriel José Urdaneta Rangel (14/0), Oswaldo Palencia (15/3) [57.Dickson Ruberth Morán Puleo (11/1)], Giovanni Savarese (14/2). Trainer: Eduardo Borrero (13).

146. 10.09.1997 **COLOMBIA - VENEZUELA** **1-0(0-0)** 16th FIFA WC. Qualifiers
Estadio Metropolitano „Roberto Meléndez", Barranquilla; Referee: Carlos Elías Barroso Pimentel (Brazil); Attendance: 35,000
VEN: Rafael Edgar Dudamel Ochoa (25/1), Carlos José García Mijares (24/0), José Alexander Echenique (17/0), William González Ruíz (19/0), Luis Ramos (7/0), Giovanny José Pérez Fernández (1/0), Luis José Vallenilla Pacheco (16/0), Luis Guillermo Madríz (1/0), Juan Enrique García Rivas (21/4) [81.Jhonny Lucena (5/0)], Dickson Ruberth Morán Puleo (12/1) [59.Alexis García (3/1)], Gabriel José Urdaneta Rangel (15/0). Trainer: Eduardo Borrero (14).

147. 12.10.1997 **PARAGUAY - VENEZUELA** **1-0(0-0)** 16th FIFA WC. Qualifiers
Estadio Defensores del Chaco, Asunción; Referee: Esfandiar Baharmast (United States); Attendance: 35,000
VEN: Rafael Edgar Dudamel Ochoa (26/1), William González Ruíz (20/0), José Alexander Echenique (18/0), José Manuel Rey Cortegoso (8/0), Luis José Vallenilla Pacheco (17/0), Luis Ramos (8/0) [57.Jesús Valiente (9/0)], Luis Guillermo Madríz (2/0), Juan Enrique García Rivas (22/4), Gabriel José Urdaneta Rangel (16/0) [70.Elvis Alfonso Martínez Dugarte (14/0)], José Luis Dolgetta (21/6), Giovanny José Pérez Fernández (2/0) [63.Jorge Giraldo (3/0)]. Trainer: Eduardo Borrero (15).

148. 27.01.1999 **VENEZUELA – DENMARK LEAGUE XI** **1-1(0-0)**
Estadio „José Encarnación 'Pachenco' Romero", Maracaibo; Referee: Oscar Julián Ruíz Acosta (Colombia); Attendance: 15,000
VEN: Danny Vigas (6/0), Rolando Álvarez Suárez (1/0), Jorge Alberto Rojas Méndez (1/0), David Andrew McIntosh Parra (19/0), Edson Argenis Tortolero Román (22/1), José Manuel Rey Cortegoso (9/1), Luis Enrique Vera Martineau (7/1) [61.Juan Fernando Arango Sáenz (1/0)], José Ricardo Duno (1/0), Gabriel José Urdaneta Rangel (17/0), Fernando Martínez Silva (1/0), Cristian Alfonso Cásseres Caseres (1/0). Trainer: José Omar Pastoriza (1).
Goal: José Manuel Rey Cortegoso (65).

149. 03.02.1999 **VENEZUELA - ARGENTINA** **0-2(0-0)**
Estadio „José Encarnación 'Pachenco' Romero", Maracaibo; Referee: Fernando Panesso Zuluaga (Colombia); Attendance: 32,000
VEN: Danny Vigas (7/0), David Andrew McIntosh Parra (20/0), José Manuel Rey Cortegoso (10/1), Jorge Alberto Rojas Méndez (2/0), Rolando Álvarez Suárez (2/0), Edson Argenis Tortolero Román (23/1), José Ricardo Duno (2/0), Félix José Hernández (14/0) [59.Alexander Rondón Heredia (1/0)], Fernando Martínez Silva (2/0), Gabriel José Urdaneta Rangel (18/0), Cristian Alfonso Cásseres Caseres (2/0) [62.Luis Enrique Vera Martineau (8/1)]. Trainer: José Omar Pastoriza (2).

150. 30.03.1999 **VENEZUELA - COLOMBIA** **0-0**
Estadio „José Encarnación 'Pachenco' Romero", Maracaibo; Referee: Paolo Borgosano (Venezuela); Attendance: 17,000
VEN: Manuel Alejandro Sanhouse Contreras (1/0), David Andrew McIntosh Parra (21/0), José Manuel Rey Cortegoso (11/1), Rolando Álvarez Suárez (3/0), Leopoldo Rafael Jiménez González (1/0), Edson Argenis Tortolero Román (Cap) (24/1), José Ricardo Duno (3/0), Pedro De Pablos (1/0) [32.José Rivas (1/0)], Gabriel José Urdaneta Rangel (19/0), Cristian Alfonso Cásseres Caseres (3/0) [60.Juan Enrique García Rivas (23/4)], Alexander Rondón Heredia (2/0). Trainer: José Omar Pastoriza (3).

151. 15.04.1999 **VENEZUELA - COLOMBIA** **1-1(0-1)**
Estadio Nacional „Brígido Iriarte", Caracas; Referee: Gustavo Alonso Brand (Venezuela); Attendance: 24,000
VEN: Manuel Alejandro Sanhouse Contreras (2/0), David Andrew McIntosh Parra (22/0), José Manuel Rey Cortegoso (12/1), Rolando Álvarez Suárez (4/0), Leopoldo Rafael Jiménez González (2/0), Edson Argenis Tortolero Román (25/1), José Ricardo Duno (4/0), Héctor Pablo Bidoglio (1/0), Gabriel José Urdaneta Rangel (20/0), Juan Enrique García Rivas (24/5) [62.Juan Fernando Arango Sáenz (2/0)], Alexander Rondón Heredia (3/0) [80.Andrée Aníbal González Frustacci (1/0)]. Trainer: José Omar Pastoriza (4).
Goal: Juan Enrique García Rivas (68).

152. 19.05.1999 **ECUADOR - VENEZUELA** **0-2(0-1)**
Estadio Reales Tamarindos, Porto Viejo; Referee: Byron Aldemar Moreno Ruales (Ecuador); Attendance: 25,000
VEN: Danny Vigas (8/0) [*sent off 80*], David Andrew McIntosh Parra (23/0), Edson Argenis Tortolero Román (Cap) (26/1), José Manuel Rey Cortegoso (13/1), Leopoldo Rafael Jiménez González (3/0), Rolando Álvarez Suárez (5/0), Héctor Pablo Bidoglio (2/0) [81.Renny Vicente Vega Hernández (1/0)], José Ricardo Duno (5/0) [46.Andrée Aníbal González Frustacci (2/0)], Juan Enrique García Rivas (25/5) [71.Miguel Ángel Mea Vitali (1/0)], Gabriel José Urdaneta Rangel (21/2), Alexander Rondón Heredia (4/0). Trainer: José Omar Pastoriza (5).
Goals: Gabriel José Urdaneta Rangel (8, 56).

153. 15.06.1999 **VENEZUELA - ECUADOR** **3-2(0-2)**
Estadio Pueblo Nuevo, San Cristóbal; Referee: Edison Ibarra (Venezuela); Attendance: 9,000
VEN: Renny Vicente Vega Hernández (2/0), Leopoldo Rafael Jiménez González (4/0), José Manuel Rey Cortegoso (14/2), Rolando Álvarez Suárez (6/0), Jorge Alberto Rojas Méndez (3/0), Edson Argenis Tortolero Román (27/1) [76.Gerzon Armando Chacón Varela (1/0)], José Ricardo Duno (6/0) [59.José de Jesús Vera Márquez (1/0)], Héctor Pablo Bidoglio (3/0), Félix José Hernández (15/0) [59.Dickson Ruberth Morán Puleo (13/2)], Gabriel José Urdaneta Rangel (22/2), Daniel Noriega Acosta (2/0) [72.Juan Enrique García Rivas (26/6)]. Trainer: José Omar Pastoriza (6).
Goals: José Manuel Rey Cortegoso (50), Juan Enrique García Rivas (90), Dickson Ruberth Morán Puleo (90+3).

154. 20.06.1999 **VENEZUELA - PERU** **3-0(2-0)**
Estadio Olímpico „Ciudad Universitaria", Caracas; Referee: Paolo Borgosano (Venezuela); Attendance: 10,853
VEN: Renny Vicente Vega Hernández (3/0), David Andrew McIntosh Parra (24/0), José Manuel Rey Cortegoso (15/3), Rolando Álvarez Suárez (7/0), Jorge Alberto Rojas Méndez (4/0), Edson Argenis Tortolero Román (28/2) [66.José Ricardo Duno (7/0)], José de Jesús Vera Márquez (2/0) [*sent off 88*], Héctor Pablo Bidoglio (4/0) [46.Fernando Franco De Ornelas (1/1)], Gabriel José Urdaneta Rangel (23/2) [60.Juan Fernando Arango Sáenz (3/0)], Félix José Hernández (16/0) [46.Dickson Ruberth Morán Puleo (14/2)], Daniel Noriega Acosta (3/0) [67.Juan Enrique García Rivas (27/6)]. Trainer: José Omar Pastoriza (7).
Goals: Edson Argenis Tortolero Román (28), José Manuel Rey Cortegoso (40), Fernando Franco De Ornelas (61).

155. 23.06.1999 **PERU - VENEZUELA** **3-0(0-0)**
Estadio Nacional, Lima; Referee: José Antonio Arana Villamonte (Peru); Attendance: 13,989
VEN: Renny Vicente Vega Hernández (4/0), David Andrew McIntosh Parra (25/0), Miguel Ángel Mea Vitali (2/0), José Manuel Rey Cortegoso (16/3), Jorge Alberto Rojas Méndez (5/0), José Ricardo Duno (8/0), Héctor Pablo Bidoglio (5/0) [82.Leopoldo Rafael Jiménez González (5/0)], Félix José Hernández (17/0) [57.Dickson Ruberth Morán Puleo (15/2)], Gerzon Armando Chacón Varela (2/0) [20.Miguel Ángel Echenáusi (19/1)], Alexander Rondón Heredia (5/0) [68.Cristian Alfonso Cásseres Caseres (4/0)], Daniel Noriega Acosta (4/0) [67.Juan Enrique García Rivas (28/6)]. Trainer: José Omar Pastoriza (8).

156. 30.06.1999 **BRAZIL - VENEZUELA** **7-0(2-0)** 39th Copa América. Group Stage
Estadio „Antonio Oddone Sarubbi", Ciudad del Este (Paraguay); Referee: Bonifacio Núñes (Paraguay); Attendance: 20,000
VEN: Renny Vicente Vega Hernández (5/0), David Andrew McIntosh Parra (26/0) [46.Leopoldo Rafael Jiménez González (6/0)], Rolando Álvarez Suárez (8/0), José Manuel Rey Cortegoso (17/3), Jorge Alberto Rojas Méndez (6/0), Edson Argenis Tortolero Román (29/2), José de Jesús Vera Márquez (3/0) [65.José Ricardo Duno (9/0)], Héctor Pablo Bidoglio (6/0), Gabriel José Urdaneta Rangel (24/2), Daniel Noriega Acosta (5/0), Félix José Hernández (18/0) [60.Dickson Ruberth Morán Puleo (16/2)]. Trainer: José Omar Pastoriza (9).

157. 03.07.1999 **CHILE - VENEZUELA** **3-0(2-0)** 39th Copa América. Group Stage
Estadio „Antonio Oddone Sarubbi", Ciudad del Este (Paraguay); Referee: Juan Luna Humérez (Bolivia); Attendance: 5,000
VEN: Renny Vicente Vega Hernández (6/0), Leopoldo Rafael Jiménez González (7/0), Rolando Álvarez Suárez (9/0) [*sent off 18*], José Manuel Rey Cortegoso (18/3), Miguel Ángel Echenáusi (20/1), Edson Argenis Tortolero Román (30/2), José de Jesús Vera Márquez (4/0), Héctor Pablo Bidoglio (7/0), Gabriel José Urdaneta Rangel (25/2) [60.Félix José Hernández (19/0)], Dickson Ruberth Morán Puleo (17/2) [55.Juan Enrique García Rivas (29/6)], Daniel Noriega Acosta (6/0) [55.Alexander Rondón Heredia (6/0)]. Trainer: José Omar Pastoriza (10).

158. 06.07.1999 **MEXICO - VENEZUELA** **3-1(3-0)** 39th Copa América. Group Stage
Estadio „Antonio Oddone Sarubbi", Ciudad del Este (Paraguay); Referee: Bonifacio Núñez (Paraguay); Attendance: 5,000
VEN: Manuel Alejandro Sanhouse Contreras (3/0), Héctor Pablo Bidoglio (8/0), José Manuel Rey Cortegoso (19/3), Leopoldo Rafael Jiménez González (8/0), Miguel Ángel Mea Vitali (3/0), José Ricardo Duno (10/0) [58.Juan Fernando Arango Sáenz (4/0)], Miguel Ángel Echenáusi (21/1), José de Jesús Vera Márquez (5/0), Gabriel José Urdaneta Rangel (26/3), Dickson Ruberth Morán Puleo (18/2) [77.Juan Enrique García Rivas (30/6)], Daniel Noriega Acosta (7/0) [62.Cristian Alfonso Cásseres Caseres (5/0)]. Trainer: José Omar Pastoriza (11).
Goal: Gabriel José Urdaneta Rangel (72).

159. 25.08.1999 **BOLIVIA - VENEZUELA** **0-0**
Estadio Patria del Morro, Sucre; Referee: Alfred Bernal (Bolivia); Attendance: 11,376
VEN: Manuel Alejandro Sanhouse Contreras (4/0), Leopoldo Rafael Jiménez González (9/0), Rolando Álvarez Suárez (10/0), Miguel Ángel Mea Vitali (4/0), Jorge Alberto Rojas Méndez (7/0), José Ricardo Duno (11/0) [Gerzon Armando Chacón Varela (3/0)], José de Jesús Vera Márquez (6/0), Héctor Pablo Bidoglio (9/0), Gabriel José Urdaneta Rangel (27/3) [Alexander Rondón Heredia (7/0)], Juan Enrique García Rivas (31/6) [Jorge Giraldo (4/0)], Cristian Alfonso Cásseres Caseres (6/0) [Juan Fernando Arango Sáenz (5/0)]. Trainer: José Omar Pastoriza (12).

160. 08.09.1999 **URUGUAY - VENEZUELA** **2-0(1-0)**
Estadio Centenario, Montevideo; Referee: Ángel Osvaldo Sánchez (Argentina); Attendance: 12,000
VEN: Rafael Edgar Dudamel Ochoa (Cap) (27/1), Leopoldo Rafael Jiménez González (10/0), Rolando Álvarez Suárez (11/0), Miguel Ángel Mea Vitali (5/0), Jorge Alberto Rojas Méndez (8/0), José de Jesús Vera Márquez (7/0), Gerzon Armando Chacón Varela (4/0) [56.Juan Fernando Arango Sáenz (6/0)], Héctor Pablo Bidoglio (10/0), Gabriel José Urdaneta Rangel (28/3), Juan Enrique García Rivas (32/6) [62.Cristian Alfonso Cásseres Caseres (7/0)], Dickson Ruberth Morán Puleo (19/2) [77.Alexander Rondón Heredia (8/0)]. Trainer: José Omar Pastoriza (13).

28.09.1999 **HAITI - VENEZUELA** **3-2**
Olympique, Port-au-Prince; Referee: Wilson Saint-Clair (Haiti)
Goals: Edwin Quilagury (20, 35).
This match was played by the Venezuelan olympic team, more informations (line-ups) were not to find. Also concrete references if this match is considered as a full international by the Venezoelan FA were missed too.

161. 16.03.2000 **VENEZUELA - BOLIVIA** **0-0**
Estadio „José Encarnación 'Pachenco' Romero", Maracaibo; Referee: Jorge Manzur (Venezuela); Attendance: 8,000
VEN: Rafael Edgar Dudamel Ochoa (28/1), Leonel Gerardo Vielma Peña (1/0), José Manuel Rey Cortegoso (20/3), Rolando Álvarez Suárez (12/0) [46.José Francisco González Quijada (3/0)], Alexander Becerra (1/0), José de Jesús Vera Márquez (8/0), Didier Sanabria (2/0) [62.Jorge Alberto Rojas Méndez (9/0)], Héctor Pablo Bidoglio (11/0), Gabriel José Urdaneta Rangel (29/3), Juan Enrique García Rivas (33/6) [46.Fernando Martínez Silva (3/0)], José Ochoa (1/0) [67.Jorge Giraldo (5/0)]. Trainer: José Omar Pastoriza (14).

162. 22.03.2000 **MEXICO Olympic - VENEZUELA** **1-0(0-0)**
Estadio Olímpico, Villa Hermosa; Referee: Alejandro Pérez (Mexico); Attendance: 13,000
VEN: Rafael Edgar Dudamel Ochoa (29/1), Alexander Becerra (2/0), Rolando Álvarez Suárez (13/0) [*sent off 73*], José Manuel Rey Cortegoso (21/3), José Ricardo Duno (12/0) [46.Miguel Ángel Mea Vitali (6/0)], Leonel Gerardo Vielma Peña (2/0) [46.Leopoldo Rafael Jiménez González (11/0)], Héctor Pablo Bidoglio (12/0), Jorge Alberto Rojas Méndez (10/0) [70.Jorge Giraldo (6/0)], Gabriel José Urdaneta Rangel (30/3) [79.José Javier Villafraz Quintero (1/0)], Dickson Ruberth Morán Puleo (20/2) [44.Elvis Alfonso Martínez Dugarte (15/0)], José Ochoa (2/0) [46.Didier Sanabria (3/0)]. Trainer: José Omar Pastoriza (15).

163. 29.03.2000 **ECUADOR - VENEZUELA** **2-0(1-0)** 17th FIFA WC.Qualifier

Estadio Casa Blanca, Quito; Referee: Eduardo Gamboa Martínez (Chile); Attendance: 37,288

VEN: Rafael Edgar Dudamel Ochoa (30/1), Rolando Álvarez Suárez (14/0), José Javier Villafraz Quintero (2/0) [62.Miguel Ángel Mea Vitali (7/0)], Alexander Becerra (3/0), José Manuel Rey Cortegoso (22/3), Gabriel José Urdaneta Rangel (31/3), Jorge Alberto Rojas Méndez (11/0) [55.Juan Fernando Arango Sáenz (7/0)], Héctor Pablo Bidoglio (13/0), José de Jesús Vera Márquez (9/0), Cristian Alfonso Cásseres Caseres (8/0), Juan Enrique García Rivas (34/6) [55.José Ochoa (3/0)]. Trainer: José Omar Pastoriza (16).

164. 26.04.2000 **VENEZUELA - ARGENTINA** **0-4(0-2)** 17th FIFA WC.Qualifier

Estadio „José Encarnación 'Pachenco' Romero", Maracaibo; Referee: Carlos Arencio Amarilla Demarqui (Paraguay); Attendance: 19,355

VEN: Rafael Edgar Dudamel Ochoa (31/1), José Javier Villafraz Quintero (3/0) [46.Gregory Luzardo (1/0)], José Manuel Rey Cortegoso (23/3), José Francisco González Quijada (4/0), Jorge Alberto Rojas Méndez (12/0), Miguel Ángel Mea Vitali (8/0), José de Jesús Vera Márquez (10/0), Héctor Pablo Bidoglio (14/0), Gabriel José Urdaneta Rangel (32/3), Juan Enrique García Rivas (35/6) [71.Fernando Martínez Silva (4/0)], Rafael Ernesto Castellín García (14/2). Trainer: José Omar Pastoriza (17).

165. 31.05.2000 **VENEZUELA - PANAMA** **3-1(2-1)**

Estadio Pueblo Nuevo, San Cristóbal; Referee: Edison Ibarra (Venezuela)

VEN: Rafael Edgar Dudamel Ochoa (32/1), Luis Manuel Filosa Astudillo (28/0), Wilfredo José Alvarado Lima (1/0), José Francisco González Quijada (5/0), Miguel Ángel Echenáusi (22/1) [71.Leonardo Lupi (3/0)], Luis Alberto Farías (1/0) [46.José de Jesús Vera Márquez (11/0)], Juan Fernando Arango Sáenz (8/0) [46.Gabriel José Urdaneta Rangel (33/3)], Miguel Ángel Mea Vitali (9/0), Héctor Pablo Bidoglio (15/0) [46.Fernando Franco De Ornelas (2/1)], Dickson Ruberth Morán Puleo (21/2) [21.Giovanni Savarese (15/3)], Rafael Ernesto Castellín García (15/4). Trainer: José Omar Pastoriza (18).

Goals: Rafael Ernesto Castellín García (12, 45), Giovanni Savarese (59).

166. 04.06.2000 **COLOMBIA - VENEZUELA** **3-0(2-0)** 17th FIFA WC.Qualifier

Esetadio "Nemesio Camacho" 'El Campín', Bogotá; Referee: Oscar Godoi (Brazil); Attendance: 20,584

VEN: Rafael Edgar Dudamel Ochoa (33/1), Luis Manuel Filosa Astudillo (29/0), José Francisco González Quijada (6/0), Wilfredo José Alvarado Lima (2/0), Miguel Ángel Echenáusi (23/1), José de Jesús Vera Márquez (12/0) [56.Luis Alberto Farías (2/0)], Miguel Ángel Mea Vitali (10/0), Héctor Pablo Bidoglio (16/0) [68.Fernando Franco De Ornelas (3/1)], Juan Fernando Arango Sáenz (9/0), Rafael Ernesto Castellín García (16/4) [53.Giovanni Savarese (16/3)], Dickson Ruberth Morán Puleo (22/2). Trainer: José Omar Pastoriza (19).

167. 21.06.2000 **PANAMA - VENEZUELA** **2-0(1-0)**

Estadio „Rommel Fernández", Ciudad de Panamá; Referee: Roberto Moreno (Panama); Attendance: 11,000

VEN: José Leonardo Morales Lares (1/0), José Manuel Rey Cortegoso (24/3) [73.Rolando Álvarez Suárez (15/0)], José Francisco González Quijada (7/0), Wilfredo José Alvarado Lima (3/0) [*sent off*], Miguel Ángel Echenáusi (24/1) [46.Elvis Alfonso Martínez Dugarte (16/0)], Edson Argenis Tortolero Román (31/2) [65.Juan Fernando Arango Sáenz (10/0)], Fernando Franco De Ornelas (4/1) [46.Leopoldo Rafael Jiménez González (12/0)], Miguel Ángel Mea Vitali (11/0), Giovanni Savarese (17/3), Gabriel José Urdaneta Rangel (34/3), Dickson Ruberth Morán Puleo (23/2). Trainer: José Omar Pastoriza (20).

168. 28.06.2000 **VENEZUELA - BOLIVIA** **4-2(2-0)** 17th FIFA WC.Qualifier

Estadio Pueblo Nuevo, San Cristóbal; Referee: Roger Zambrano Alcivár (Ecuador); Attendance: 7,000

VEN: Gilberto Angelucci (5/0), Leopoldo Rafael Jiménez González (13/0), José Francisco González Quijada (8/0), Wilfredo José Alvarado Lima (4/0), Elvis Alfonso Martínez Dugarte (17/0), Edson Argenis Tortolero Román (32/3), Gabriel José Urdaneta Rangel (35/3) [90.Miguel Ángel Echenáusi (25/1)], Luis Alberto Farías (3/0), Miguel Ángel Mea Vitali (12/1), Dickson Ruberth Morán Puleo (24/3) [*sent off 63*], Giovanni Savarese (18/4) [72.Joel Galán (1/0)]. Trainer: José Omar Pastoriza (21).

Goals: Miguel Ángel Mea Vitali (24), Dickson Ruberth Morán Puleo (38), Giovanni Savarese (61), Edson Argenis Tortolero Román (68 penalty).

169. 05.07.2000 **MEXICO - VENEZUELA** **2-1(1-1)**

Estadio Tecnológico, Monterrey; Referee: Benito Armando Archundia Téllez (Mexico); Attendance: 20,000

VEN: Gilberto Angelucci (6/0), Leopoldo Rafael Jiménez González (14/0) [46.Luis Manuel Filosa Astudillo (30/0)], José Francisco González Quijada (9/0), Wilfredo José Alvarado Lima (5/0) [*sent off 73*], Elvis Alfonso Martínez Dugarte (18/0), Luis Alberto Farías (4/0), Miguel Ángel Mea Vitali (13/1) [86.Joel Galán (2/0)], Edson Argenis Tortolero Román (33/3) [90.Miguel Ángel Echenáusi (26/1)], Fernando Franco De Ornelas (5/1), Juan Fernando Arango Sáenz (11/0) [61.José de Jesús Vera Márquez (13/0)], Dickson Ruberth Morán Puleo (25/4) [74.Rolando Álvarez Suárez (16/0)]. Trainer: José Omar Pastoriza (22).

Goal: Dickson Ruberth Morán Puleo (27).

170. 18.07.2000 **URUGUAY - VENEZUELA** **3-1(1-1)** 17th FIFA WC.Qualifier

Estadio Centenario, Montevideo; Referee: René Marcelo Ortubé Betancourt (Bolivia); Attendance: 58,000

VEN: Gilberto Angelucci (7/0), Leopoldo Rafael Jiménez González (15/0) [*sent off 60*], José Francisco González Quijada (10/0), Wilfredo José Alvarado Lima (6/0), Elvis Alfonso Martínez Dugarte (19/0), Miguel Ángel Mea Vitali (14/1), Edson Argenis Tortolero Román (34/3), Luis Alberto Farías (5/0) [62.José de Jesús Vera Márquez (14/0)], Gabriel José Urdaneta Rangel (36/3), Giovanni Savarese (19/4) [71.Giovanny José Pérez Fernández (3/0)], Daniel Noriega Acosta (8/1) [62.Rolando Álvarez Suárez (17/0)]. Trainer: José Omar Pastoriza (23).

Goal: Daniel Noriega Acosta (23).

171. 25.07.2000 **VENEZUELA - CHILE** **0-2(0-0)** 17th FIFA WC.Qualifier

Estadio Pueblo Nuevo, San Cristóbal; Referee: Héctor Walter Baldassi (Argentina); Attendance: 14,880

VEN: Gilberto Angelucci (8/0), Rolando Álvarez Suárez (18/0), Wilfredo José Alvarado Lima (7/0), Elvis Alfonso Martínez Dugarte (20/0), Luis Alberto Farías (6/0), Edson Argenis Tortolero Román (35/3), Miguel Ángel Mea Vitali (15/1) [72.Juan Fernando Arango Sáenz (12/0)], Fernando Franco De Ornelas (6/1), Gabriel José Urdaneta Rangel (37/3), Dickson Ruberth Morán Puleo (26/4), Giovanni Savarese (20/4) [86.Giovanny José Pérez Fernández (4/0)]. Trainer: José Omar Pastoriza (24).

172. 10.08.2000 **COSTA RICA - VENEZUELA** **1-5(1-3)**

Estadio „Alejandro Morera Soto", San José; Referee: Carlos Torres (Costa Rica); Attendance: 6,000

VEN: Gilberto Angelucci (9/0) [José Fasciana (2/0)], Leopoldo Rafael Jiménez González (16/0), José Manuel Rey Cortegoso (25/4) [José Francisco González Quijada (11/0)], Wilfredo José Alvarado Lima (8/0), Elvis Alfonso Martínez Dugarte (21/0), Luis Alberto Farías (7/0), José de Jesús Vera Márquez (15/0) [Rolando Álvarez Suárez (19/0)], Edson Argenis Tortolero Román (36/3) [Miguel Ángel Echenáusi (27/1)], Dickson Ruberth Morán Puleo (27/4) [Ricardo David Páez Gómez (1/1)], Cristian Alfonso Cásseres Caseres (9/0) [Fernando Franco De Ornelas (7/2)], Gabriel José Urdaneta Rangel (38/5). Trainer: José Omar Pastoriza (25).

Goals: Gabriel José Urdaneta Rangel (2), José Manuel Rey Cortegoso (5), Gabriel José Urdaneta Rangel (25), Fernando Franco De Ornelas (62), Ricardo David Páez Gómez (88).

173. 16.08.2000 **PERU - VENEZUELA** **1-0(0-0)** 17th FIFA WC.Qualifier
Estadio Nacional „José Díaz", Lima; Referee: Byron Aldemar Moreno Ruales (Ecuador); Attendance: 41,084
VEN: Gilberto Angelucci (10/0), Leopoldo Rafael Jiménez González (17/0), Wilfredo José Alvarado Lima (9/0), José Francisco González Quijada (12/0), Elvis Alfonso Martínez Dugarte (22/0), Miguel Ángel Mea Vitali (16/1) [80.Fernando Franco De Ornelas (8/2)], Luis Alberto Farías (8/0), Edson Argenis Tortolero Román (37/3), Gabriel José Urdaneta Rangel (39/5), Giovanni Savarese (21/4) [70.Cristian Alfonso Cásseres Caseres (10/0)], Dickson Ruberth Morán Puleo (28/4). Trainer: José Omar Pastoriza (26).

174. 02.09.2000 **PARAGUAY - VENEZUELA** **3-0(3-0)** 17th FIFA WC.Qualifier
Estadio Defensores del Chaco, Asunción; Referee: Juan Carlos Paniagua Arandia (Bolivia); Attendance: 40,000
VEN: Gilberto Angelucci (11/0), Leopoldo Rafael Jiménez González (18/0), Wilfredo José Alvarado Lima (10/0), José Francisco González Quijada (13/0) [46.José Manuel Rey Cortegoso (26/4)], Elvis Alfonso Martínez Dugarte (23/0), Luis Alberto Farías (9/0), Miguel Ángel Mea Vitali (17/1) [52.Juan Enrique García Rivas (36/6)], Edson Argenis Tortolero Román (38/3) [66.Ricardo David Páez Gómez (2/1)], Gabriel José Urdaneta Rangel (40/5), Fernando Franco De Ornelas (9/2), Dickson Ruberth Morán Puleo (29/4). Trainer: José Omar Pastoriza (27).

175. 08.10.2000 **VENEZUELA - BRAZIL** **0-6(0-5)** 17th FIFA WC.Qualifier
Estadio „José Encarnación 'Pachenco' Romero", Maracaibo; Referee: Ubaldo Aquino Valenzano (Paraguay); Attendance: 6,350
VEN: Gilberto Angelucci (12/0), José Francisco González Quijada (14/0), Wilfredo José Alvarado Lima (11/0), José Manuel Rey Cortegoso (27/4), Elvis Alfonso Martínez Dugarte (24/0), Leopoldo Rafael Jiménez González (19/0), Luis Alberto Farías (10/0), Miguel Ángel Echenáusi (28/1) [46.Juan Fernando Arango Sáenz (13/0)], Fernando Franco De Ornelas (10/2), Juan Enrique García Rivas (37/6) [76.Giovanni Savarese (22/4)], Dickson Ruberth Morán Puleo (30/4) [67.Ricardo David Páez Gómez (3/1)]. Trainer: José Omar Pastoriza (28).

176. 15.11.2000 **VENEZUELA - ECUADOR** **1-2(0-2)** 17th FIFA WC.Qualifier
Estadio „José Encarnación 'Pachenco' Romero", Maracaibo; Referee: Eduardo Abel Lecca Betancourt (Peru); Attendance: 6,500
VEN: Gilberto Angelucci (13/0), José Francisco González Quijada (15/0), Wilfredo José Alvarado Lima (12/0), Luis José Vallenilla Pacheco (18/0) [87.Ricardo David Páez Gómez (4/1)], Fernando Franco De Ornelas (11/2), Luis Alberto Farías (11/0), Miguel Ángel Mea Vitali (18/1) [46.Gregory Luzardo (2/0)], Juan Fernando Arango Sáenz (14/0), Gabriel José Urdaneta Rangel (41/5), Rafael Ernesto Castellín García (17/4) [55.Giovanny José Pérez Fernández (5/0)], Juan Enrique García Rivas (38/7). Trainer: José Omar Pastoriza (29).
Goal: Juan Enrique García Rivas (66).

177. 28.03.2001 **ARGENTINA - VENEZUELA** **5-0(2-0)** 17th FIFA WC.Qualifier
Estadio Monumental „Antonio Vespucio Liberti", Buenos Aires; Referee: Gilberto Hidalgo Zamora (Peru); Attendance: 32,000
VEN: Rafael Edgar Dudamel Ochoa (34/1), Wilfredo José Alvarado Lima (13/0), José Manuel Rey Cortegoso (28/4), Luis José Vallenilla Pacheco (19/0), Jorge Alberto Rojas Méndez (13/0) [66.Elvis Alfonso Martínez Dugarte (25/0)], Fernando Franco De Ornelas (12/2) [56.Giovanny José Pérez Fernández (6/0)], José de Jesús Vera Márquez (16/0) [73.Miguel Ángel Mea Vitali (19/1)], Luis Enrique Vera Martineau (9/1), Gabriel José Urdaneta Rangel (42/5), Daniel Noriega Acosta (9/1), Ricardo David Páez Gómez (5/1). Trainer: Richard Alfred Páez Monzón (1).

178. 19.04.2001 **COSTA RICA - VENEZUELA** **2-2(1-0)**
Estadio „Alejandro Morera Soto", Alajuela; Referee: Ronald Cedeño (Costa Rica); Attendance: 8,000
VEN: Manuel Alejandro Sanhouse Contreras (5/0) [46.Rafael Edgar Dudamel Ochoa (35/1)], Luis José Vallenilla Pacheco (20/0), Rafael Loreto Mea Vitali (1/0) [46.Rolando Álvarez Suárez (20/0)], José Manuel Rey Cortegoso (29/4), Jorge Alberto Rojas Méndez (14/0), Héctor Augusto González Guzmán (1/0), Luis Enrique Vera Martineau (10/1) [46.Alexander Rondón Heredia (9/1)], Miguel Ángel Mea Vitali (20/1) [46.José de Jesús Vera Márquez (17/0)], Giovanny José Pérez Fernández (7/0) [61.J. Rey (1/0)], Cristian Alfonso Cásseres Caseres (11/0), Alexis José Chirinos (2/0) [61.Leopoldo Rafael Jiménez González (20/0)]. Trainer: Richard Alfred Páez Monzón (2).
Goals: Alexander Rondón Heredia (61), Roberto Arías (8 own goal).

179. 24.04.2001 **VENEZUELA - COLOMBIA** **2-2(1-0)** 17th FIFA WC.Qualifier
Estadio Pueblo Nuevo, San Cristóbal; Referee: Guido Aros Alvarado (Chile); Attendance: 19,000
VEN: Rafael Edgar Dudamel Ochoa (36/1), Luis José Vallenilla Pacheco (21/0), José Manuel Rey Cortegoso (30/4), Rafael Loreto Mea Vitali (2/0), Jorge Alberto Rojas Méndez (15/0), Miguel Ángel Mea Vitali (21/1) [60.Fernando Franco De Ornelas (13/2)], Juan Fernando Arango Sáenz (15/1), Luis Enrique Vera Martineau (11/1), Gabriel José Urdaneta Rangel (43/5) [70.Ricardo David Páez Gómez (6/1)], Alexander Rondón Heredia (10/2), Giovanni Savarese (23/4) [54.José de Jesús Vera Márquez (18/0)]. Trainer: Richard Alfred Páez Monzón (3).
Goals: Alexander Rondón Heredia (22), Juan Fernando Arango Sáenz (82).

180. 03.06.2001 **BOLIVIA - VENEZUELA** **5-0(3-0)** 17th FIFA WC.Qualifier
Estadio „Hernándo Siles Zuazo", La Paz; Referee: José Patricio Carpio Guevara (Ecuador); Attendance: 25,000
VEN: Manuel Alejandro Sanhouse Contreras (6/0), Luis José Vallenilla Pacheco (22/0), Rafael Loreto Mea Vitali (3/0), José Manuel Rey Cortegoso (31/4), Elvis Alfonso Martínez Dugarte (26/0), Miguel Ángel Mea Vitali (22/1), Juan Fernando Arango Sáenz (16/1) [67.Cristian Alfonso Cásseres Caseres (12/0)], Luis Enrique Vera Martineau (12/1), Héctor Augusto González Guzmán (2/0) [54.Wilfredo José Alvarado Lima (14/0)], Ricardo David Páez Gómez (7/1) [42.Leopoldo Rafael Jiménez González (21/0)], Alexander Rondón Heredia (11/2). Trainer: Richard Alfred Páez Monzón (4).

181. 11.07.2001 **COLOMBIA - VENEZUELA** **2-0(1-0)** 40th Copa América. Group Stage
Estadio Metropolitano „Roberto Meléndez", Barranquilla; Referee: Gilberto Hidalgo Zamora (Peru); Attendance: 50,000
VEN: Rafael Edgar Dudamel Ochoa (37/1), Luis José Vallenilla Pacheco (23/0) [*sent off 47*], Wilfredo José Alvarado Lima (15/0), José Manuel Rey Cortegoso (32/4), Jorge Alberto Rojas Méndez (16/0), Miguel Ángel Mea Vitali (23/1), Daniel Noriega Acosta (10/1) [54.Leopoldo Rafael Jiménez González (22/0)], Luis Enrique Vera Martineau (13/1), Juan Fernando Arango Sáenz (17/1), Alexander Rondón Heredia (12/2) [79.Cristian Alfonso Cásseres Caseres (13/0)], Ricardo David Páez Gómez (8/1) [85.Giovanny José Pérez Fernández (8/0)]. Trainer: Richard Alfred Páez Monzón (5).

182. 14.07.2001 **CHILE - VENEZUELA** **1-0(0-0)** 40th Copa América. Group Stage
Estadio Metropolitano „Roberto Meléndez", Barranquilla (Colombia); Referee: Gilberto Alcala Piñeda (Mexico); Attendance: 33,000
VEN: Rafael Edgar Dudamel Ochoa (38/1), Leonel Gerardo Vielma Peña (3/0), José Manuel Rey Cortegoso (33/4), Wilfredo José Alvarado Lima (16/0), Elvis Alfonso Martínez Dugarte (27/0), Miguel Ángel Mea Vitali (24/1), Luis Enrique Vera Martineau (14/1), Gabriel José Urdaneta Rangel (44/5) [72.Giovanny José Pérez Fernández (9/0)], Juan Fernando Arango Sáenz (18/1), Daniel Noriega Acosta (11/1) [78.Héctor Augusto González Guzmán (3/0)], Ricardo David Páez Gómez (9/1) [63.Alexander Rondón Heredia (13/2)]. Trainer: Richard Alfred Páez Monzón (6).

183. 17.07.2001 **ECUADOR - VENEZUELA** **4-0(2-0)** 40th Copa América. Group Stage
Estadio Metropolitano „Roberto Meléndez", Barranquilla (Colombia); Referee: Gilberto Hidalgo Zamora (Peru); Attendance: 20,000
VEN: Rafael Edgar Dudamel Ochoa (39/1), Leonel Gerardo Vielma Peña (4/0), José Manuel Rey Cortegoso (34/4), Wilfredo José Alvarado Lima (17/0), Elvis Alfonso Martínez Dugarte (28/0), Miguel Ángel Mea Vitali (25/1) [74.Giovanny José Pérez Fernández (10/0)], Luis Enrique Vera Martineau (15/1), Juan Fernando Arango Sáenz (19/1) [46.Alexander Rondón Heredia (14/2)], Gabriel José Urdaneta Rangel (45/5), Daniel Noriega Acosta (12/1), Ricardo David Páez Gómez (10/1) [69.Leopoldo Rafael Jiménez González (23/0)]. Trainer: Richard Alfred Páez Monzón (7).

184. 14.08.2001 **VENEZUELA - URUGUAY** **2-0(0-0)** 17th FIFA WC.Qualifier

Estadio „José Encarnación 'Pachenco' Romero", Maracaibo; Referee: Antonio Marrufo Mendoza (Mexico); Attendance: 8,500

VEN: Rafael Edgar Dudamel Ochoa (40/1), Luis José Vallenilla Pacheco (24/0), José Manuel Rey Cortegoso (35/4), Wilfredo José Alvarado Lima (18/0), Jorge Alberto Rojas Méndez (17/0), Miguel Ángel Mea Vitali (26/1), Luis Enrique Vera Martineau (16/1), Juan Fernando Arango Sáenz (20/1), Daniel Noriega Acosta (13/1) [65.Alexander Rondón Heredia (15/3)], Ricardo David Páez Gómez (11/1) [86.Giovanny José Pérez Fernández (11/0)], Dickson Ruberth Morán Puleo (31/5) [76.Leopoldo Rafael Jiménez González (24/0)]. Trainer: Richard Alfred Páez Monzón (8).

Goals: Dickson Ruberth Morán Puleo (52), Alexander Rondón Heredia (90).

185. 04.09.2001 **CHILE - VENEZUELA** **0-2(0-0)** 17th FIFA WC.Qualifier

Estadio Nacional, Santiago; Referee: René Marcelo Ortubé Betancourt (Bolivia); Attendance: 25,000

VEN: Rafael Edgar Dudamel Ochoa (41/1), Luis José Vallenilla Pacheco (25/0), Rafael Loreto Mea Vitali (4/0), Wilfredo José Alvarado Lima (19/0), Jorge Alberto Rojas Méndez (18/0), Miguel Ángel Mea Vitali (27/1), Luis Enrique Vera Martineau (17/1), Juan Fernando Arango Sáenz (21/2), Daniel Noriega Acosta (14/1) [75.Leopoldo Rafael Jiménez González (25/0)], Ricardo David Páez Gómez (12/2) [79.Giovanny José Pérez Fernández (12/0)], Dickson Ruberth Morán Puleo (32/5) [86.Alexander Rondón Heredia (16/3)]. Trainer: Richard Alfred Páez Monzón (9).

Goals: Ricardo David Páez Gómez (56), Juan Fernando Arango Sáenz (62).

186. 06.10.2001 **VENEZUELA - PERU** **3-0(0-0)** 17th FIFA WC.Qualifier

Estadio Pueblo Nuevo, San Cristóbal; Referee: Mario Fernando Sánchez Yanten (Chile); Attendance: 17,220

VEN: Gilberto Angelucci (14/0), Luis José Vallenilla Pacheco (26/0), Rafael Loreto Mea Vitali (5/0), Jorge Alberto Rojas Méndez (19/0), Wilfredo José Alvarado Lima (20/2), Miguel Ángel Mea Vitali (28/1), Luis Enrique Vera Martineau (18/1) [10.Leopoldo Rafael Jiménez González (26/0)], Juan Fernando Arango Sáenz (22/2) [*sent off 55*], Daniel Noriega Acosta (15/1) [60.Elvis Alfonso Martínez Dugarte (29/0)], Ricardo David Páez Gómez (13/2) [80.Gabriel José Urdaneta Rangel (46/5)], Dickson Ruberth Morán Puleo (33/6). Trainer: Richard Alfred Páez Monzón (10).

Goals: Wilfredo José Alvarado Lima (54, 77), Dickson Ruberth Morán Puleo (80).

187. 08.11.2001 **VENEZUELA - PARAGUAY** **3-1(3-1)** 17th FIFA WC.Qualifier

Estadio Pueblo Nuevo, San Cristóbal; Referee: Horacio Marcelo Elizondo (Argentina); Attendance: 22,500

VEN: Gilberto Angelucci (15/0), Héctor Augusto González Guzmán (4/1), Rafael Loreto Mea Vitali (6/0), Wilfredo José Alvarado Lima (21/2), Jorge Alberto Rojas Méndez (20/0), Miguel Ángel Mea Vitali (29/1), Luis Enrique Vera Martineau (19/1), Gabriel José Urdaneta Rangel (47/5), Ricardo David Páez Gómez (14/2) [72.Elvis Alfonso Martínez Dugarte (30/0)], Daniel Noriega Acosta (16/2) [61.Alexander Rondón Heredia (17/3)], Dickson Ruberth Morán Puleo (34/7) [80.Giovanny José Pérez Fernández (13/0)]. Trainer: Richard Alfred Páez Monzón (11).

Goals: Dickson Ruberth Morán Puleo (2), Daniel Noriega Acosta (22), Héctor Augusto González Guzmán (40).

188. 14.11.2001 **BRAZIL - VENEZUELA** **3-0(3-0)** 17th FIFA WC.Qualifier

Estádio „João Castelo", São Luís; Referee: Daniel Orlando Giménez (Argentina); Attendance: 65,000

VEN: Rafael Edgar Dudamel Ochoa (42/1), Héctor Augusto González Guzmán (5/1), Rafael Loreto Mea Vitali (7/0), José Manuel Rey Cortegoso (36/4), Jorge Alberto Rojas Méndez (21/0), Miguel Ángel Mea Vitali (30/1), Luis Enrique Vera Martineau (20/1) [*sent off 48*], Gabriel José Urdaneta Rangel (48/5) [58.Luis José Vallenilla Pacheco (27/0)], Ricardo David Páez Gómez (15/2) [32.Elvis Alfonso Martínez Dugarte (31/0)], Daniel Noriega Acosta (17/2), Dickson Ruberth Morán Puleo (35/7) [50.Leopoldo Rafael Jiménez González (27/0)]. Trainer: Richard Alfred Páez Monzón (12).

189. 13.01.2002 **VENEZUELA – CAMEROON „U 21"** **1-1(1-0)**

Stade „Mohammed V", Casablanca (Morocco); Referee: Luis Solórzano Torres (Venezuela); Attendance: 20,000

VEN: César Renato Baéna (22/0) [16.Gilberto Angelucci (16/0)], Luis José Vallenilla Pacheco (28/1), Wilfredo José Alvarado Lima (22/2), José Manuel Rey Cortegoso (37/4), Jorge Alberto Rojas Méndez (22/0), Leopoldo Rafael Jiménez González (28/0), Leonel Gerardo Vielma Peña (5/0) [33.Alexis García (4/1)], Héctor Augusto González Guzmán (6/1) [80.Pedro Alfonso Fernández Camacho (1/0)], Giovanny José Pérez Fernández (14/0) [64.Elvis Alfonso Martínez Dugarte (32/0)], Dickson Ruberth Morán Puleo (36/7) [60.José Antonio Torrealba Acevedo (1/0)], Alexander Rondón Heredia (18/3) [60.Alexis José Chirinos (3/0)]. Trainer: Richard Alfred Páez Monzón (13).

Goal: Luis José Vallenilla Pacheco (22).

190. 01.03.2002 **IRAN - VENEZUELA** **1-0(1-0)** LG Cup

Stade „Mohammed V", Casablanca (Morocco); Referee: Khalil Rouissi (Morocco); Attendance: 20,000

VEN: Gilberto Angelucci (17/0), Luis José Vallenilla Pacheco (29/1) [22.Leonel Gerardo Vielma Peña (6/0); 60.Carlos Luis Bravo (1/0)], Rafael Loreto Mea Vitali (8/0), Wilfredo José Alvarado Lima (23/2), Jorge Alberto Rojas Méndez (23/0), Héctor Augusto González Guzmán (7/1), Leopoldo Rafael Jiménez González (29/0), Luis Enrique Vera Martineau (21/1) [83.Giácomo Di Giorgi Zerillo (1/0)], Giovanny José Pérez Fernández (15/0) [65.José Antonio Torrealba Acevedo (2/0)], Dickson Ruberth Morán Puleo (37/7), Daniel Noriega Acosta (18/2) [74.Alexander Rondón Heredia (19/3)]. Trainer: Richard Alfred Páez Monzón (14).

191. 03.03.2002 **MOROCCO Olympic - VENEZUELA** **2-0(2-0)** LG Cup

Stade „Mohammed V", Casablanca; Referee: Brahimi (Morocco); Attendance: 25,000

VEN: Rafael Ponzo García (1/0), Elvis Alfonso Martínez Dugarte (33/0), José Manuel Rey Cortegoso (38/4) [Rafael Loreto Mea Vitali (9/0)], Wilfredo José Alvarado Lima (24/2), Jorge Alberto Rojas Méndez (24/0), Leopoldo Rafael Jiménez González (30/0), Giácomo Di Giorgi Zerillo (2/0) [Leonel Gerardo Vielma Peña (7/0)], Héctor Augusto González Guzmán (8/1), Giovanny José Pérez Fernández (16/0) [Carlos Luis Bravo (2/0)], Dickson Ruberth Morán Puleo (38/7) [José Antonio Torrealba Acevedo (3/0)], Alexander Rondón Heredia (20/3) [Daniel Noriega Acosta (19/2)]. Trainer: Richard Alfred Páez Monzón (15).

192. 07.05.2002 **VENEZUELA - COLOMBIA** **0-0**

Estadio Olímpico „Ciudad Universitaria", Caracas; Referee: Luis Solórzano Torres (Venezuela); Attendance: 28,000

VEN: Gilberto Angelucci (18/0), Luis José Vallenilla Pacheco (30/1), Wilfredo José Alvarado Lima (25/2) [82.Alejandro Enrique Cichero Konarek (1/0)], Rafael Loreto Mea Vitali (10/0) [46.Leonel Gerardo Vielma Peña (8/0)], Jorge Alberto Rojas Méndez (25/0), Miguel Ángel Mea Vitali (31/1) [46.Giovanny José Pérez Fernández (17/0)], Héctor Augusto González Guzmán (9/1) [46.Leopoldo Rafael Jiménez González (31/0)], Luis Enrique Vera Martineau (22/1), Dickson Ruberth Morán Puleo (39/7), Juan Fernando Arango Sáenz (23/2) [73.Jobanny Rivero (1/0)], Daniel Noriega Acosta (20/2) [21.Juan Enrique García Rivas (39/7)]. Trainer: Richard Alfred Páez Monzón (16).

193. 21.08.2002 **VENEZUELA - BOLIVIA** **2-0(2-0)**

Estadio Olímpico „Ciudad Universitaria", Caracas; Referee: Edison Ibarra (Venezuela); Attendance: 25,000

VEN: Gilberto Angelucci (19/0), Luis José Vallenilla Pacheco (31/1), Leonel Gerardo Vielma Peña (9/0), Wilfredo José Alvarado Lima (26/2) [88.José Manuel Rey Cortegoso (39/4)], Jorge Alberto Rojas Méndez (26/0), Leopoldo Rafael Jiménez González (32/0), Luis Enrique Vera Martineau (23/1), Ricardo David Páez Gómez (16/2) [63.Carlos Luis Bravo (3/0)], Héctor Augusto González Guzmán (10/2) [46.Giovanny José Pérez Fernández (18/0)], Dickson Ruberth Morán Puleo (40/7) [73.Wilfredo Moreno (1/0)], Daniel Noriega Acosta (21/3) [65.Juan Enrique García Rivas (40/7)]. Trainer: Richard Alfred Páez Monzón (17).

Goals: Daniel Noriega Acosta (17), Héctor Augusto González Guzmán (20).

194. 20.10.2002 **VENEZUELA - ECUADOR** **2-0(1-0)**

Estadio Olímpico „Ciudad Universitaria“, Caracas; Referee: Gustavo Brand (Venezuela); Attendance: 24,000

VEN: Gilberto Angelucci (20/0) [85.Manuel Alejandro Sanhouse Contreras (7/0)], Luis José Vallenilla Pacheco (32/1), Leonel Gerardo Vielma Peña (10/0) [81.Frank Presilla (1/0)], José Manuel Rey Cortegoso (40/5), Jobanny Rivero (2/0) [81.Wiswell Isea (1/0)], Miguel Ángel Mea Vitali (32/1) [83.Giácomo Di Giorgi Zerillo (3/0)], Leopoldo Rafael Jiménez González (33/0), Giovanny José Pérez Fernández (19/0) [59.Wilfredo Moreno (2/1)], Gabriel José Urdaneta Rangel (49/5) [77.Enrique Andrés Rouga Rossi (1/0)], Juan Enrique García Rivas (41/7) [59.Carlos Luis Bravo (4/0)], Daniel Noriega Acosta (22/3) [69.Cristian Alfonso Cásseres Caseres (14/0)]. Trainer: Richard Alfred Páez Monzón (18).

Goals: José Manuel Rey Cortegoso (30), Wilfredo Moreno (79).

195. 20.11.2002 **VENEZUELA – URUGUAY LEAGUE XI** **1-0(0-0)**

Estadio Olímpico „Ciudad Universitaria“, Caracas; Referee: Luis Solórzano Torres (Venezuela); Attendance: 26,000

VEN: Gilberto Angelucci (21/0), Luis José Vallenilla Pacheco (33/1), Leonel Gerardo Vielma Peña (11/0), Rafael Loreto Mea Vitali (11/0) [38.José Manuel Rey Cortegoso (41/5)], Jorge Alberto Rojas Méndez (27/0) [80.Jobanny Rivero (3/0)], Luis Enrique Vera Martineau (Cap) (24/1), Leopoldo Rafael Jiménez González (34/0) [18.Miguel Ángel Mea Vitali (33/1)], Ricardo David Páez Gómez (17/3) [72.Juan Enrique García Rivas (42/7)], Juan Fernando Arango Sáenz (24/2) [62.Héctor Augusto González Guzmán (11/2)], Dickson Ruberth Morán Puleo (41/7) [46.Gabriel José Urdaneta Rangel (50/5)], Daniel Noriega Acosta (23/3) [62.Wilfredo Moreno (3/1)]. Trainer: Richard Alfred Páez Monzón (19).

Goal: Ricardo David Páez Gómez (49).

196. 29.03.2003 **UNITED STATES - VENEZUELA** **2-0(0-0)**

Seahawks Stadium, Seattle; Referee: Michael Seifert (Canada); Attendance: 17,819

VEN: Gilberto Angelucci (22/0) [*sent off 86*], Luis José Vallenilla Pacheco (34/1) [81.Wilfredo José Alvarado Lima (27/2)], José Manuel Rey Cortegoso (42/5), Leonel Gerardo Vielma Peña (12/0), Jorge Alberto Rojas Méndez (28/0), Luis Enrique Vera Martineau (25/1) (Cap) [46.José Javier Villafraz Quintero (4/0)], Leopoldo Rafael Jiménez González (35/0), Gabriel José Urdaneta Rangel (51/5) [68.Giovanny José Pérez Fernández (20/0)], Ricardo David Páez Gómez (18/3), Daniel Noriega Acosta (24/3) [68.Cristian Alfonso Cásseres Caseres (15/0)], Juan Enrique García Rivas (43/7) [46.Wilfredo Moreno (4/1)]. Trainer: Richard Alfred Páez Monzón (20).

197. 02.04.2003 **VENEZUELA - JAMAICA** **2-0(2-0)**

Estadio Olímpico „Ciudad Universitaria“, Caracas; Referee: Segundo Díaz (Ecuador); Attendance: 27,000

VEN: Gilberto Angelucci (23/0) [50.Manuel Alejandro Sanhouse Contreras (8/0)], Héctor Augusto González Guzmán (12/2) [81.Leonel Gerardo Vielma Peña (13/0)], Wilfredo José Alvarado Lima (28/2), Alejandro Enrique Cichero Konarek (2/0) [77.Enrique Andrés Rouga Rossi (2/0)], Luis José Vallenilla Pacheco (35/1) [66.Jobanny Rivero (4/0)], Miguel Ángel Mea Vitali (34/1), Leopoldo Rafael Jiménez González (36/0) [66.José Javier Villafraz Quintero (5/0)], Juan Fernando Arango Sáenz (25/2), Ricardo David Páez Gómez (19/4), Gabriel José Urdaneta Rangel (52/6) [59.Cristian Alfonso Cásseres Caseres (16/0)], Wilfredo Moreno (5/1) [59.Daniel Noriega Acosta (25/3)]. Trainer: Richard Alfred Páez Monzón (21).

Goals: Gabriel José Urdaneta Rangel (11 penalty), Ricardo David Páez Gómez (38).

198. 30.04.2003 **VENEZUELA – TRINIDAD & TOBAGO** **3-0(2-0)**

Estadio Pueblo Nuevo, San Cristóbal; Referee: Jorge Rivero (Venezuela); Attendance: 22,000

VEN: Gilberto Angelucci (24/0), Héctor Augusto González Guzmán (13/2) [61.Luis José Vallenilla Pacheco (36/1)], José Manuel Rey Cortegoso (43/5) [75.Alejandro Enrique Cichero Konarek (3/0)], Wilfredo José Alvarado Lima (29/2), Jorge Alberto Rojas Méndez (29/0), Miguel Ángel Mea Vitali (35/1), Leopoldo Rafael Jiménez González (37/0), Ricardo David Páez Gómez (20/4) [72.Giovanny José Pérez Fernández (21/0)], Gabriel José Urdaneta Rangel (53/6) [51.Daniel Noriega Acosta (26/4)], Juan Fernando Arango Sáenz (26/4), Wilfredo Moreno (6/1) [60.Juan Enrique García Rivas (44/7)]. Trainer: Richard Alfred Páez Monzón (22).

Goals: Juan Fernando Arango Sáenz (30, 38), Daniel Noriega Acosta (75).

199. 07.06.2003 **VENEZUELA - HONDURAS** **2-1(2-1)**

Orange Bowl, Miami (United States); Referee: Kevin Terry (United States); Attendance: 8,000

VEN: Gilberto Angelucci (25/0), Luis José Vallenilla Pacheco (37/1), José Manuel Rey Cortegoso (44/5), Wilfredo José Alvarado Lima (30/2) [62.Alejandro Enrique Cichero Konarek (4/0)], Jorge Alberto Rojas Méndez (30/0), Leopoldo Rafael Jiménez González (38/0), Luis Enrique Vera Martineau (26/1), Ricardo David Páez Gómez (21/4) [41.Cristian Alfonso Cásseres Caseres (17/0)], Gabriel José Urdaneta Rangel (54/7) [70.José Javier Villafraz Quintero (6/0)], Juan Fernando Arango Sáenz (27/5) [86.Giovanny José Pérez Fernández (22/0)], Daniel Noriega Acosta (27/4). Trainer: Richard Alfred Páez Monzón (23).

Goals: Gabriel José Urdaneta Rangel (14), Juan Fernando Arango Sáenz (36).

200. 26.06.2003 **PERU - VENEZUELA** **1-0(0-0)**

Orange Bowl, Miami (United States); Referee: Michael Kennedy (United States); Attendance: 7,000

VEN: Gilberto Angelucci (26/0) [78.Manuel Alejandro Sanhouse Contreras (9/0)], Luis José Vallenilla Pacheco (38/1), Alejandro Enrique Cichero Konarek (5/0) [80.Leonel Gerardo Vielma Peña (14/0)], Wilfredo José Alvarado Lima (31/2) [46.José Manuel Rey Cortegoso (45/5)], Jorge Alberto Rojas Méndez (31/0), Luis Enrique Vera Martineau (27/1) (Cap), Leopoldo Rafael Jiménez González (39/0), Gabriel José Urdaneta Rangel (55/7) [74.José Javier Villafraz Quintero (7/0)], Juan Fernando Arango Sáenz (28/5) [81.Cristian Alfonso Cásseres Caseres (18/0)], Daniel Noriega Acosta (28/4) [46.Ricardo David Páez Gómez (22/4)], Juan Enrique García Rivas (45/7) [46.Dickson Ruberth Morán Puleo (42/7)]. Trainer: Richard Alfred Páez Monzón (24).

201. 03.07.2003 **TRINIDAD & TOBAGO - VENEZUELA** **2-2(0-1)**

„Hasely Crawford“ Stadium, Port of Spain; Referee: Richard Piper (Trinidad & Tobago); Attendance: 7,500

VEN: Manuel Alejandro Sanhouse Contreras (10/0), Luis José Vallenilla Pacheco (39/1), José Manuel Rey Cortegoso (46/5) [*sent off 65*], Leonel Gerardo Vielma Peña (15/0), Jorge Alberto Rojas Méndez (32/0), José Javier Villafraz Quintero (8/0) [89.Luis Enrique Vera Martineau (28/1)], Leopoldo Rafael Jiménez González (40/0), Giovanny José Pérez Fernández (23/0) [75.Alejandro Enrique Cichero Konarek (6/0)], Gabriel José Urdaneta Rangel (56/7) [80.Ricardo David Páez Gómez (23/4)], Dickson Ruberth Morán Puleo (43/7) [69.Daniel Noriega Acosta (29/4)], Cristian Alfonso Cásseres Caseres (19/2) [78.Juan Fernando Arango Sáenz (29/5)]. Trainer: Richard Alfred Páez Monzón (25).

Goals: Cristian Alfonso Cásseres Caseres (1, 49).

202. 26.07.2003 **NIGERIA - VENEZUELA** **1-0(1-0)**

Vicarage Road, Watford (England); Attendance: 1,000

VEN: Gilberto Angelucci (27/0), Luis José Vallenilla Pacheco (40/1), Wilfredo José Alvarado Lima (32/2), Alejandro Enrique Cichero Konarek (7/0), Jonay Miguel Hernández Santos (1/0), Miguel Ángel Mea Vitali (36/1) [77.José Javier Villafraz Quintero (9/0)], Leopoldo Rafael Jiménez González (41/0), Juan Fernando Arango Sáenz (30/5) [82.Giovanny José Pérez Fernández (24/0)], Ricardo David Páez Gómez (24/4) [80.Wilfredo Moreno (7/1)], Dickson Ruberth Morán Puleo (44/7) [56.Gabriel José Urdaneta Rangel (57/7)], Cristian Alfonso Cásseres Caseres (20/2) [77.Daniel Noriega Acosta (30/4)]. Trainer: Richard Alfred Páez Monzón (26).

203. 20.08.2003 **VENEZUELA - HAITI** **3-2(0-0)**
Estadio „José Encarnación 'Pachenco' Romero", Maracaibo; Referee: Jorge Manzur (Venezuela); Attendance: 15,000
VEN: Gilberto Angelucci (28/0) [46.Manuel Alejandro Sanhouse Contreras (11/0)], Luis José Vallenilla Pacheco (41/1), Leonel Gerardo Vielma Peña (16/1), José Manuel Rey Cortegoso (47/5) [51.Alejandro Enrique Cichero Konarek (8/0)], Jorge Alberto Rojas Méndez (33/0), Luis Enrique Vera Martineau (29/1), Miguel Ángel Mea Vitali (37/1) [66.José Javier Villafraz Quintero (10/0)], Héctor Augusto González Guzmán (14/3), Giovanny José Pérez Fernández (25/0) [62.Jobanny Rivero (5/1)], Wilfredo Moreno (8/1), Alexander Rondón Heredia (21/3) [62.Giancarlo Gregorio Maldonado Marrero (1/0)]. Trainer: Richard Alfred Páez Monzón (27).
Goals: Leonel Gerardo Vielma Peña (77 penalty), Héctor Augusto González Guzmán (83), Jobanny Rivero (87).

204. 06.09.2003 **ECUADOR - VENEZUELA** **2-0(1-0)** 18th FIFA WC. Qualifiers
Estadio Olímpico „Atahualpa", Quito; Referee: Rubén Selmán Albornoz (Chile); Attendance: 14,997
VEN: Gilberto Angelucci (29/0), Luis José Vallenilla Pacheco (42/1), José Manuel Rey Cortegoso (48/5), Wilfredo José Alvarado Lima (33/2), Jorge Alberto Rojas Méndez (34/0), Miguel Ángel Mea Vitali (38/1), Leopoldo Rafael Jiménez González (42/0), Ricardo David Páez Gómez (25/4) [52.Daniel Noriega Acosta (31/4)], Gabriel José Urdaneta Rangel (58/7) [63.Héctor Augusto González Guzmán (15/3)], Dickson Ruberth Morán Puleo (45/7) [67.Cristian Alfonso Cásseres Caseres (21/2)], Juan Fernando Arango Sáenz (31/5). Trainer: Richard Alfred Páez Monzón (28).

205. 09.09.2003 **VENEZUELA - ARGENTINA** **0-3(0-3)** 18th FIFA WC. Qualifiers
Estadio Olímpico „Ciudad Universitaria", Caracas; Referee: Martín Vázquez Broquetas (Uruguay); Attendance: 24,783
VEN: Gilberto Angelucci (30/0), Héctor Augusto González Guzmán (16/3) [46.Luis José Vallenilla Pacheco (43/1)], José Manuel Rey Cortegoso (49/5), Wilfredo José Alvarado Lima (34/2), Jorge Alberto Rojas Méndez (35/0), Luis Enrique Vera Martineau (30/1), Leopoldo Rafael Jiménez González (43/0), Ricardo David Páez Gómez (26/4), Juan Fernando Arango Sáenz (32/5) [61.Wilfredo Moreno (9/1)], Dickson Ruberth Morán Puleo (46/7) [46.Gabriel José Urdaneta Rangel (59/7)], Daniel Noriega Acosta (32/4). Trainer: Richard Alfred Páez Monzón (29).

206. 15.11.2003 **COLOMBIA - VENEZUELA** **0-1(0-1)** 18th FIFA WC. Qualifiers
Estadio Metropolitano "Roberto Meléndez", Barranquilla; Referee: Carlos Luis Chandía Alarcón (Chile); Attendance: 20,000
VEN: Gilberto Angelucci (31/0), Luis José Vallenilla Pacheco (44/1), José Manuel Rey Cortegoso (50/5), Alejandro Enrique Cichero Konarek (9/0), Jonay Miguel Hernández Santos (2/0), Miguel Ángel Mea Vitali (39/1) [7.Leonel Gerardo Vielma Peña (17/1)], Leopoldo Rafael Jiménez González (44/0), Ricardo David Páez Gómez (27/4) [57.Jorge Alberto Rojas Méndez (36/0)], Gabriel José Urdaneta Rangel (60/7) [57.Héctor Augusto González Guzmán (17/3)], Daniel Noriega Acosta (33/4), Juan Fernando Arango Sáenz (33/6). Trainer: Richard Alfred Páez Monzón (30).
Goal: Juan Fernando Arango Sáenz (8).

207. 18.11.2003 **VENEZUELA - BOLIVIA** **2-1(0-0)** 18th FIFA WC. Qualifiers
Estadio „José Encarnación 'Pachenco' Romero", Maracaibo; Referee: Mauricio Reinoso Fabara (Ecuador); Attendance: 30,000
VEN: Gilberto Angelucci (32/0), Luis José Vallenilla Pacheco (45/1), José Manuel Rey Cortegoso (51/6), Alejandro Enrique Cichero Konarek (10/0), Jonay Miguel Hernández Santos (3/0) [61.Jorge Alberto Rojas Méndez (37/0)], Leopoldo Rafael Jiménez González (45/0), Juan Fernando Arango Sáenz (34/7), Ricardo David Páez Gómez (28/4), Gabriel José Urdaneta Rangel (61/7), Daniel Noriega Acosta (34/4) [51.Wilfredo Moreno (10/1)], Dickson Ruberth Morán Puleo (47/7) [59.Alexander Rondón Heredia (22/3)]. Trainer: Richard Alfred Páez Monzón (31).
Goals: José Manuel Rey Cortegoso (90), Juan Fernando Arango Sáenz (90+2).

208. 18.02.2004 **VENEZUELA - AUSTRALIA** **1-1(0-1)**
Estadio Olímpico „Ciudad Universitaria", Caracas; Referee: Oscar Julián Ruíz Acosta (Colombia); Attendance: 16,000
VEN: Gilberto Angelucci (33/0) [46.Rafael Edgar Dudamel Ochoa (43/1)], Luis José Vallenilla Pacheco (46/1) [60.Héctor Augusto González Guzmán (18/3)], José Manuel Rey Cortegoso (52/6) [*sent off* 72], Alejandro Enrique Cichero Konarek (11/0), Jonay Miguel Hernández Santos (4/0), Leopoldo Rafael Jiménez González (46/0), Luis Enrique Vera Martineau (31/1) [46.Andrée Aníbal González Frustacci (3/0)], Juan Fernando Arango Sáenz (35/8), Gabriel José Urdaneta Rangel (62/7) [46.Jorge Alberto Rojas Méndez (38/0)], Massimo Margiotta (1/0), Dickson Ruberth Morán Puleo (48/7) [46.Alejandro Enrique Moreno Riera (1/0)]. Trainer: Richard Alfred Páez Monzón (32).
Goal: Juan Fernando Arango Sáenz (90+1).

209. 10.03.2004 **VENEZUELA - HONDURAS** **2-1(1-1)**
Estadio „José Encarnación 'Pachenco' Romero", Maracaibo; Referee: Jorge Manzur (Venezuela); Attendance: 24,400
VEN: Gilberto Angelucci (34/0) [46.Rafael Edgar Dudamel Ochoa (44/1)], Luis José Vallenilla Pacheco (47/1), Enrique Andrés Rouga Rossi (3/0), Oswaldo Augusto Vizcarrondo Araujo (1/0), Jorge Alberto Rojas Méndez (39/0), Jobanny Rivero (6/1) [46.Giovanny José Pérez Fernández (26/0)], Leopoldo Rafael Jiménez González (47/0), Luis Enrique Vera Martineau (32/2), Juan Fernando Arango Sáenz (36/8) [80.Miguel Ángel Mea Vitali (40/1)], Daniel Noriega Acosta (35/5) [63.Juan Enrique García Rivas (46/7)], Alejandro Enrique Moreno Riera (2/0) [46.Dickson Ruberth Morán Puleo (49/7)]. Trainer: Richard Alfred Páez Monzón (33).
Goals: Luis Enrique Vera Martineau (35 penalty), Daniel Noriega Acosta (53).

210. 31.03.2004 **URUGUAY - VENEZUELA** **0-3(0-1)** 18th FIFA WC. Qualifiers
Estadio Olímpico „Ciudad Universitaria", Caracas; Referee: René Marcelo Ortubé Betancourt (Bolivia); Attendance: 40,094
VEN: Gilberto Angelucci (35/0), Luis José Vallenilla Pacheco (48/1), José Manuel Rey Cortegoso (53/6), Alejandro Enrique Cichero Konarek (12/0), Jonay Miguel Hernández Santos (5/0), Leopoldo Rafael Jiménez González (48/0), Luis Enrique Vera Martineau (33/2) (Cap), Gabriel José Urdaneta Rangel (63/8) [63.Jorge Alberto Rojas Méndez (40/0)], Juan Fernando Arango Sáenz (37/9) [84.Andrée Aníbal González Frustacci (4/0)], Ricardo David Páez Gómez (29/4) [63.Héctor Augusto González Guzmán (19/4)], Alexander Rondón Heredia (23/3). Trainer: Richard Alfred Páez Monzón (34).
Goals: Gabriel José Urdaneta Rangel (19), Héctor Augusto González Guzmán (63), Juan Fernando Arango Sáenz (78).

211. 28.04.2004 **JAMAICA - VENEZUELA** **2-1(2-1)**
National Stadium, Kingston; Referee: Mark Forde (Barbados); Attendance: 16,000
VEN: Manuel Alejandro Sanhouse Contreras (12/0) [46.Javier Eduardo Toyo Bárcenas (1/0)], Héctor Augusto González Guzmán (20/4), José Manuel Rey Cortegoso (54/6), Leonel Gerardo Vielma Peña (18/1), Jorge Alberto Rojas Méndez (41/0), Miguel Ángel Mea Vitali (41/1) [72.Pedro De Pablos (2/0)], José Javier Villafraz Quintero (11/0), Ricardo David Páez Gómez (30/4) [72.Jobanny Rivero (7/1)], Juan Fernando Arango Sáenz (38/10) [60.Luis José Vallenilla Pacheco (49/1)], Massimo Margiotta (2/0) [46.Daniel Noriega Acosta (36/5)], Alexander Rondón Heredia (24/3) [60.Alejandro Enrique Moreno Riera (3/0)]. Trainer: Richard Alfred Páez Monzón (35).
Goal: Juan Fernando Arango Sáenz (27).

212. 01.06.2004 **VENEZUELA - CHILE** **0-1(0-0)** 18th FIFA WC. Qualifiers
Estadio Pueblo Nuevo, San Cristóbal; Referee: Carlos Torres Fretés (Paraguay); Attendance: 23,040
VEN: Gilberto Angelucci (36/0), Luis José Vallenilla Pacheco (50/1) [65.Héctor Augusto González Guzmán (21/4)], José Manuel Rey Cortegoso (55/6), Alejandro Enrique Cichero Konarek (13/0), Jonay Miguel Hernández Santos (6/0), Leonel Gerardo Vielma Peña (19/1) [76.Andrée Aníbal González Frustacci (5/0)], Ricardo David Páez Gómez (31/4), Leopoldo Rafael Jiménez González (49/0), Juan Fernando Arango Sáenz (39/10), Gabriel José Urdaneta Rangel (64/8) [46.Massimo Margiotta (3/0)], Alexander Rondón Heredia (25/3). Trainer: Richard Alfred Páez Monzón (36).

213. 06.06.2004 **PERU - VENEZUELA** **0-0** 18th FIFA WC. Qualifiers
Estadio Nacional „José Díaz", Lima; Referee: Jorge Luis Larrionda Pietrafiesa (Uruguay); Attendance: 40,000
VEN: Gilberto Angelucci (37/0), Luis José Vallenilla Pacheco (51/1), José Manuel Rey Cortegoso (56/6), Alejandro Enrique Cichero Konarek (14/0), Jonay Miguel Hernández Santos (7/0), Miguel Ángel Mea Vitali (42/1), Ricardo David Páez Gómez (32/4) [67.Héctor Augusto González Guzmán (22/4)], Leopoldo Rafael Jiménez González (50/0), Juan Fernando Arango Sáenz (40/10), Gabriel José Urdaneta Rangel (65/8) [79.Massimo Margiotta (4/0)], Alexander Rondón Heredia (26/3) [61.Dickson Ruberth Morán Puleo (50/7)]. Trainer: Richard Alfred Páez Monzón (37).

214. 06.07.2004 **COLOMBIA - VENEZUELA** **1-0(1-0)** 41th Copa América. Group Stage
Estadio Nacional „José Díaz", Lima (Peru); Referee: Márcio Rezende de Freitas (Brazil); Attendance: 45,000
VEN: Gilberto Angelucci (38/0), Luis José Vallenilla Pacheco (52/1) [70.Héctor Augusto González Guzmán (23/4)], José Manuel Rey Cortegoso (57/6), Alejandro Enrique Cichero Konarek (15/0), Jonay Miguel Hernández Santos (8/0) [65.Jorge Alberto Rojas Méndez (42/0)], Miguel Ángel Mea Vitali (43/1), Ricardo David Páez Gómez (33/4), Leopoldo Rafael Jiménez González (51/0), Juan Fernando Arango Sáenz (41/10), Dickson Ruberth Morán Puleo (51/7), Alexander Rondón Heredia (27/3) [60.Massimo Margiotta (5/0)]. Trainer: Richard Alfred Páez Monzón (38).

215. 09.07.2004 **PERU - VENEZUELA** **3-1(1-0)** 41th Copa América. Group Stage
Estadio Nacional „José Díaz", Lima; Referee: Rubén Selmán Albornoz (Chile); Attendance: 42,054
VEN: Gilberto Angelucci (39/0), Luis José Vallenilla Pacheco (53/1), José Manuel Rey Cortegoso (58/6), Alejandro Enrique Cichero Konarek (16/0), Jonay Miguel Hernández Santos (9/0), Miguel Ángel Mea Vitali (44/1) [*sent off 66*], Ricardo David Páez Gómez (34/4) [67.Héctor Augusto González Guzmán (24/4)], Leopoldo Rafael Jiménez González (52/0), Jorge Alberto Rojas Méndez (43/0) [46.Dickson Ruberth Morán Puleo (52/7)], Alexander Rondón Heredia (28/3) [59.Massimo Margiotta (6/1)], Juan Fernando Arango Sáenz (42/10). Trainer: Richard Alfred Páez Monzón (39).
Goal: Massimo Margiotta (74).

216. 12.07.2004 **VENEZUELA - BOLIVIA** **1-1(1-1)** 41th Copa América. Group Stage
Estadio Mansiche, Trujillo (Peru); Referee: William Mattus Vega (Costa Rica); Attendance: 25,000
VEN: Gilberto Angelucci (40/0), Luis José Vallenilla Pacheco (54/1), José Manuel Rey Cortegoso (59/6), Alejandro Enrique Cichero Konarek (17/0), Jonay Miguel Hernández Santos (10/0), Andrée Aníbal González Frustacci (6/0) [75.Leonel Gerardo Vielma Peña (20/1)], Ricardo David Páez Gómez (35/4), Leopoldo Rafael Jiménez González (53/0), Juan Fernando Arango Sáenz (43/10), Dickson Ruberth Morán Puleo (53/8) [58.Alexander Rondón Heredia (29/3)], Massimo Margiotta (7/1) [65.Héctor Augusto González Guzmán (25/4)]. Trainer: Richard Alfred Páez Monzón (40).
Goal: Dickson Ruberth Morán Puleo (27).

217. 18.08.2004 **SPAIN - VENEZUELA** **3-2(1-1)**
Estadio Gran Canaria, Las Palmas; Referee: Pasquale Rodomonti (Italy); Attendance: 32,000
VEN: Gilberto Angelucci (41/0) [76.Rafael Ponzo García (2/0)], Leonel Gerardo Vielma Peña (21/1) [76.Fernando Franco De Ornelas (14/2)], José Manuel Rey Cortegoso (60/6), Alejandro Enrique Cichero Konarek (18/0), Jonay Miguel Hernández Santos (11/0) [65.Alexander Rondón Heredia (30/3)], Luis Enrique Vera Martineau (34/2) [65.Andrée Aníbal González Frustacci (7/0)], Leopoldo Rafael Jiménez González (54/0), Gabriel José Urdaneta Rangel (66/8), Ricardo David Páez Gómez (36/4) [72.Enrique Andrés Rouga Rossi (4/0)], Jorge Alberto Rojas Méndez (44/1), Massimo Margiotta (8/1) [68.Rafael Ernesto Castellín García (18/5)]. Trainer: Richard Alfred Páez Monzón (41).
Goals: Jorge Alberto Rojas Méndez (45+1), Rafael Ernesto Castellín García (90+2).

218. 05.09.2004 **PARAGUAY - VENEZUELA** **1-0(0-0)** 18th FIFA WC. Qualifiers
Estadio Defensores del Chaco, Asunción; Referee: Gustavo Méndez González (Uruguay); Attendance: 30,000
VEN: Gilberto Angelucci (42/0), Luis José Vallenilla Pacheco (55/1), José Manuel Rey Cortegoso (61/6), Alejandro Enrique Cichero Konarek (19/0), Jorge Alberto Rojas Méndez (45/1), Leopoldo Rafael Jiménez González (55/0), Luis Enrique Vera Martineau (35/2), Ricardo David Páez Gómez (37/4) [68.Alexander Rondón Heredia (31/3)], Gabriel José Urdaneta Rangel (67/8) [71.Héctor Augusto González Guzmán (26/4)], Rafael Ernesto Castellín García (19/5) [76.Wilfredo Moreno (11/1)], Juan Fernando Arango Sáenz (44/10). Trainer: Richard Alfred Páez Monzón (42).

219. 09.10.2004 **VENEZUELA - BRAZIL** **2-5(0-2)** 18th FIFA WC. Qualifiers
Estadio „José Encarnación 'Pachenco' Romero", Maracaibo; Referee: Carlos Luis Chandía Alarcón (Chile); Attendance: 26,113
VEN: Gilberto Angelucci (43/0), Luis José Vallenilla Pacheco (56/1), José Manuel Rey Cortegoso (62/6), Alejandro Enrique Cichero Konarek (20/0), Jonay Miguel Hernández Santos (12/0) [55.Leonel Gerardo Vielma Peña (22/1)], Jorge Alberto Rojas Méndez (46/1), Luis Enrique Vera Martineau (36/2) [68.César Eduardo González Amais (1/0)], Leopoldo Rafael Jiménez González (56/0), Juan Fernando Arango Sáenz (45/10), Massimo Margiotta (9/1) [46.Héctor Augusto González Guzmán (27/4)], Dickson Ruberth Morán Puleo (54/10). Trainer: Richard Alfred Páez Monzón (43).
Goals: Dickson Ruberth Morán Puleo (79, 90+1).

220. 14.10.2004 **VENEZUELA - ECUADOR** **3-1(1-1)** 18th FIFA WC. Qualifiers
Estadio Pueblo Nuevo, San Cristóbal; Referee: Eduardo Abel Lecca Betancourt (Peru); Attendance: 13,800
VEN: Rafael Edgar Dudamel Ochoa (45/1), Luis José Vallenilla Pacheco (57/1) [68.Héctor Augusto González Guzmán (28/4)], José Manuel Rey Cortegoso (63/6), Alejandro Enrique Cichero Konarek (21/0), Jorge Alberto Rojas Méndez (47/1), Luis Enrique Vera Martineau (37/2), Leopoldo Rafael Jiménez González (57/0) [64.Ricardo David Páez Gómez (38/4)], Gabriel José Urdaneta Rangel (68/9), Juan Fernando Arango Sáenz (46/10), Alexander Rondón Heredia (32/3) [61.Juan Enrique García Rivas (47/7)], Dickson Ruberth Morán Puleo (55/12). Trainer: Richard Alfred Páez Monzón (44).
Goals: Gabriel José Urdaneta Rangel (21 penalty), Dickson Ruberth Morán Puleo (72, 81).

221. 17.11.2004 **ARGENTINA - VENEZUELA** **3-2(2-1)** 18th FIFA WC. Qualifiers
Estadio Monumental „Antonio Vespucio Liberti", Buenos Aires; Referee: Gilberto Hidalgo Zamora (Peru); Attendance: 30,000
VEN: Rafael Edgar Dudamel Ochoa (46/1), Luis José Vallenilla Pacheco (58/1), José Manuel Rey Cortegoso (64/6), Alejandro Enrique Cichero Konarek (22/0), Jonay Miguel Hernández Santos (13/0) [52.Gabriel José Urdaneta Rangel (69/9)], Leopoldo Rafael Jiménez González (58/0) [78.Cristian Alfonso Cásseres Caseres (22/2)], Luis Enrique Vera Martineau (38/2), Ricardo David Páez Gómez (39/4) [71.Leonel Gerardo Vielma Peña (23/2)], Jorge Alberto Rojas Méndez (48/1), Dickson Ruberth Morán Puleo (56/13), Juan Fernando Arango Sáenz (47/10). Trainer: Richard Alfred Páez Monzón (45).
Goals: Dickson Ruberth Morán Puleo (32), Leonel Gerardo Vielma Peña (73).

222. 21.12.2004 **VENEZUELA - GUATEMALA** **0-1(0-0)**
Estadio Nacional „Brígido Iriarte", Caracas; Referee: Luis Solórzano Torres (Venezuela); Attendance: 6,000
VEN: Javier Eduardo Toyo Bárcenas (2/0), Fernando Franco De Ornelas (15/2) [46.César Eduardo González Amais (2/0)], Leonel Gerardo Vielma Peña (24/2), Enrique Andrés Rouga Rossi (5/0), Jorge Alberto Rojas Méndez (49/1) [46.Gabriel Alejandro Cichero Konarek (1/0)], Héctor Augusto González Guzmán (29/4), Leopoldo Rafael Jiménez González (59/0) [46.Miguel Ángel Mea Vitali (45/1)], Andrée Aníbal González Frustacci (8/0), Ricardo David Páez Gómez (40/4) [58.Evelio de Jesús Hernández Guedez (1/0)], Giancarlo Gregorio Maldonado Marrero (2/0) [67.Alexis Acuña (1/0)], José Antonio Torrealba Acevedo (4/0) [46.Rafael Ernesto Castellín García (20/5)]. Trainer: Richard Alfred Páez Monzón (46).

223. 09.02.2005 **VENEZUELA - ESTONIA** **3-0(2-0)**
Estadio „José Encarnación 'Pachenco' Romero", Maracaibo; Referee: Luis Vasco (Ecuador); Attendance: 8,000
VEN: Rafael Edgar Dudamel Ochoa (47/1) [46.Gilberto Angelucci (44/0)], Héctor Augusto González Guzmán (30/4), José Manuel Rey Cortegoso (65/6), Alejandro Enrique Cichero Konarek (23/0), Jorge Alberto Rojas Méndez (50/1), Leopoldo Rafael Jiménez González (60/0) [63.Miguel Ángel Mea Vitali (46/1)], Leonel Gerardo Vielma Peña (25/2) [46.Andrée Aníbal González Frustacci (9/0)], Ricardo David Páez Gómez (41/5) [63.Luis José Vallenilla Pacheco (59/1)], Gabriel José Urdaneta Rangel (70/9) [63.Jonay Miguel Hernández Santos (14/0)], Rafael Ernesto Castellín García (21/5), Massimo Margiotta (10/2) [69.Giancarlo Gregorio Maldonado Marrero (3/1)]. Trainer: Richard Alfred Páez Monzón (47).
Goals: Ricardo David Páez Gómez (20), Massimo Margiotta (33), Giancarlo Gregorio Maldonado Marrero (82).

224. 26.03.2005 **VENEZUELA - COLOMBIA** **0-0** 18th FIFA WC. Qualifiers
Estadio „José Encarnación 'Pachenco' Romero", Maracaibo; Referee: Carlos Eugênio Simon (Brazil); Attendance: 18,000
VEN: Rafael Edgar Dudamel Ochoa (48/1), Héctor Augusto González Guzmán (31/4), José Manuel Rey Cortegoso (66/6), Alejandro Enrique Cichero Konarek (24/0), Jonay Miguel Hernández Santos (15/0), Leopoldo Rafael Jiménez González (61/0), Leonel Gerardo Vielma Peña (26/2), Gabriel José Urdaneta Rangel (71/9) [65.Andrée Aníbal González Frustacci (10/0)], Giancarlo Gregorio Maldonado Marrero (4/1), Massimo Margiotta (11/2) [74.Daniel Noriega Acosta (37/5)], Rafael Ernesto Castellín García (22/5) [56.César Eduardo González Amais (3/0)]. Trainer: Richard Alfred Páez Monzón (48).

225. 29.03.2005 **BOLIVIA - VENEZUELA** **3-1(2-0)** 18th FIFA WC. Qualifiers
Estadio „Hernándo Siles Zuazo", La Paz; Referee: Eduardo Abel Lecca Betancourt (Peru); Attendance: 7,908
VEN: Rafael Edgar Dudamel Ochoa (49/1), Héctor Augusto González Guzmán (32/4), José Manuel Rey Cortegoso (67/6), Alejandro Enrique Cichero Konarek (25/0) [46.Daniel Noriega Acosta (38/5)], Jonay Miguel Hernández Santos (16/0), Fernando Franco De Ornelas (16/2) [72.Alexander Rondón Heredia (33/3)], Luis Enrique Vera Martineau (39/2), Juan José Fuenmayor Núñez (1/0), Andrée Aníbal González Frustacci (11/0), Gabriel José Urdaneta Rangel (72/9) [58.César Eduardo González Amais (4/0)], Giancarlo Gregorio Maldonado Marrero (5/2). Trainer: Richard Alfred Páez Monzón (49).
Goal: Giancarlo Gregorio Maldonado Marrero (71).

226. 25.05.2005 **VENEZUELA - PANAMA** **1-1(1-1)**
Estadio Olímpico „Ciudad Universitaria", Caracas; Referee: Gustavo Brand (Venezuela); Attendance: 5,500
VEN: Rafael Edgar Dudamel Ochoa (50/1) [46.Gilberto Angelucci (45/0)], Leonel Gerardo Vielma Peña (27/2), Juan José Fuenmayor Núñez (2/0), Fernando Franco De Ornelas (17/2), Jobanny Rivero (8/1), Luis Enrique Vera Martineau (40/2) [78.Miguel Ángel Mea Vitali (47/1)], Héctor Augusto González Guzmán (33/4) [74.Pedro Alfonso Fernández Camacho (2/0)], Andrée Aníbal González Frustacci (12/0), Ricardo David Páez Gómez (42/5) [59.Paúl Ramírez (1/0)], Giancarlo Gregorio Maldonado Marrero (6/3) [46.Cristian Alfonso Cásseres Caseres (23/2)], Dickson Ruberth Morán Puleo (57/13). Trainer: Richard Alfred Páez Monzón (50).
Goal: Giancarlo Gregorio Maldonado Marrero (4).

227. 04.06.2005 **VENEZUELA - URUGUAY** **1-1(0-1)** 18th FIFA WC. Qualifiers
Estadio „José Encarnación 'Pachenco' Romero", Maracaibo; Referee: Gabriel Brazenas (Argentina); Attendance: 12,504
VEN: Rafael Edgar Dudamel Ochoa (51/1), Héctor Augusto González Guzmán (34/4), Alejandro Enrique Cichero Konarek (26/0), José Manuel Rey Cortegoso (68/6), Jorge Alberto Rojas Méndez (51/1) [68.Jonay Miguel Hernández Santos (17/0)], Leonel Gerardo Vielma Peña (28/2) [38.Gabriel José Urdaneta Rangel (73/9)], Luis Enrique Vera Martineau (41/2), Ricardo David Páez Gómez (43/5) [63.Cristian Alfonso Cásseres Caseres (24/2)], Juan Fernando Arango Sáenz (48/10), Dickson Ruberth Morán Puleo (58/13), Giancarlo Gregorio Maldonado Marrero (7/4). Trainer: Richard Alfred Páez Monzón (51).
Goal: Giancarlo Gregorio Maldonado Marrero (74).

228. 08.06.2005 **CHILE - VENEZUELA** **2-1(1-0)** 18th FIFA WC. Qualifiers
Estadio Nacional, Santiago; Referee: Carlos Torres Fretés (Paraguay); Attendance: 35,506
VEN: Rafael Edgar Dudamel Ochoa (52/1), Fernando Franco De Ornelas (18/2) [46.Luis José Vallenilla Pacheco (60/1)], José Manuel Rey Cortegoso (69/6), Alejandro Enrique Cichero Konarek (27/0), Jonay Miguel Hernández Santos (18/0), Leopoldo Rafael Jiménez González (62/0), Andrée Aníbal González Frustacci (13/0) [71.Giovanny José Pérez Fernández (27/0)], Gabriel José Urdaneta Rangel (74/9), Juan Fernando Arango Sáenz (49/10), Cristian Alfonso Cásseres Caseres (25/2) [57.César Eduardo González Amais (5/0)], Dickson Ruberth Morán Puleo (59/14). Trainer: Richard Alfred Páez Monzón (52).
Goal: Dickson Ruberth Morán Puleo (82).

229. 17.08.2005 **ECUADOR - VENEZUELA** **3-1(2-0)**
Estadio Federativo, Loja; Referee: Luis Enrique Vasco (Ecuador); Attendance: 10,000
VEN: Rafael Edgar Dudamel Ochoa (53/1) [46.Javier Eduardo Toyo Bárcenas (3/0)], Héctor Augusto González Guzmán (35/4), Leonel Gerardo Vielma Peña (29/2) [84.Daniel Godoy (1/0)], Enrique Andrés Rouga Rossi (6/0), Jorge Alberto Rojas Méndez (52/1), César Eduardo González Amais (6/0) [46.Andrée Aníbal González Frustacci (14/0)], Miguel Ángel Mea Vitali (48/1) [46.Juan José Fuenmayor Núñez (3/0)], Luis Enrique Vera Martineau (42/2) [81.Evelio de Jesús Hernández Guedez (2/0)], José Antonio Torrealba Acevedo (5/1), Giancarlo Gregorio Maldonado Marrero (8/4) [46.Pedro Luis Boada Noya (1/0)], Dickson Ruberth Morán Puleo (60/14). Trainer: Richard Alfred Páez Monzón (53).
Goal: José Antonio Torrealba Acevedo (70).

230. 03.09.2005 **VENEZUELA - PERU** **4-1(1-0)** 18th FIFA WC. Qualifiers
Estadio „José Encarnación 'Pachenco' Romero", Maracaibo; Referee: Márcio Rezende de Freitas (Brazil); Attendance: 6,000
VEN: Gilberto Angelucci (46/0), Héctor Augusto González Guzmán (36/4), Leonel Gerardo Vielma Peña (30/2), Alejandro Enrique Cichero Konarek (28/0), Jorge Alberto Rojas Méndez (53/1), Luis Enrique Vera Martineau (43/2), Ricardo David Páez Gómez (44/5), Gabriel José Urdaneta Rangel (75/9), Juan Fernando Arango Sáenz (50/11) [81.Leopoldo Rafael Jiménez González (63/0)], Giancarlo Gregorio Maldonado Marrero (9/5) [72.José Antonio Torrealba Acevedo (6/3)], Dickson Ruberth Morán Puleo (61/14) [58.Andrée Aníbal González Frustacci (15/0)]. Trainer: Richard Alfred Páez Monzón (54).
Goals: Giancarlo Gregorio Maldonado Marrero (17), Juan Fernando Arango Sáenz (68), José Antonio Torrealba Acevedo (73, 79).

231. 08.10.2005 **VENEZUELA - PARAGUAY** **0-1(0-0)** 18th FIFA WC. Qualifiers
Estadio „José Encarnación 'Pachenco' Romero", Maracaibo; Referee: Horacio Marcelo Elizondo (Argentina); Attendance: 13,272
VEN: Gilberto Angelucci (47/0), Héctor Augusto González Guzmán (37/4), José Manuel Rey Cortegoso (70/6), Alejandro Enrique Cichero Konarek (29/0), Jorge Alberto Rojas Méndez (54/1), Luis Enrique Vera Martineau (44/2), Gabriel José Urdaneta Rangel (76/9) [69.Andrée Aníbal González Frustacci (16/0)], Ricardo David Páez Gómez (45/5), Juan Fernando Arango Sáenz (51/11), Giancarlo Gregorio Maldonado Marrero (10/5) [74.Alejandro Enrique Moreno Riera (4/0)], Dickson Ruberth Morán Puleo (62/14) [55.José Antonio Torrealba Acevedo (7/3)]. Trainer: Richard Alfred Páez Monzón (55).

232. 12.10.2005 **BRAZIL - VENEZUELA** **3-0(1-0)** 18th FIFA WC. Qualifiers
Estádio Olimpico „Mangueirão", Belém; Referee: Héctor Walter Baldassi (Argentina); Attendance: 45,000
VEN: Rafael Edgar Dudamel Ochoa (54/1), Luis José Vallenilla Pacheco (61/1), José Manuel Rey Cortegoso (71/6), Alejandro Enrique Cichero Konarek (30/0), Jonay Miguel Hernández Santos (19/0), Leonel Gerardo Vielma Peña (31/2), Leopoldo Rafael Jiménez González (64/0), Gabriel José Urdaneta Rangel (77/9) [61.Jorge Alberto Rojas Méndez (55/1)], Ricardo David Páez Gómez (46/5) [50.Héctor Augusto González Guzmán (38/4)], Juan Fernando Arango Sáenz (52/11), Giancarlo Gregorio Maldonado Marrero (11/5) [70.José Antonio Torrealba Acevedo (8/3)]. Trainer: Richard Alfred Páez Monzón

(56).

233. 01.03.2006 **VENEZUELA - COLOMBIA** **1-1(0-0)**
Estadio „José Encarnación 'Pachenco' Romero", Maracaibo; Referee: José Carpio (Ecuador); Attendance: 18,000
VEN: Renny Vicente Vega Hernández (7/0) [46.Rafael Ponzo García (3/0)], Héctor Augusto González Guzmán (39/4) [74.Julio César Machado Cesáreo (1/0)], Leonel Gerardo Vielma Peña (32/2), Alejandro Enrique Cichero Konarek (31/0), Jonay Miguel Hernández Santos (20/0), José Javier Villafraz Quintero (12/0) [*sent off 73*], Pedro Alfonso Fernández Camacho (3/0) [74.Dickson Manuel Díaz Romero (1/0)], Juan Fernando Arango Sáenz (Cap) (53/11), Ricardo David Páez Gómez (47/5) [78.Rubén Darío Arocha Hernández (1/0)], Giancarlo Gregorio Maldonado Marrero (12/5), Armando Maita (1/0) [46.Jesús Javier Gómez Mercado (1/1)]. Trainer: Richard Alfred Páez Monzón (57).
Goal: Jesús Javier Gómez Mercado (48).

234. 05.05.2006 **MEXICO - VENEZUELA** **1-0(0-0)**
Rose Bowl, Pasadena (United States); Referee: Terry Vaughn (United States); Attendance: 58,147
VEN: Renny Vicente Vega Hernández (8/0), Oswaldo Augusto Vizcarrondo Araujo (2/0), Leonel Gerardo Vielma Peña (33/2) [56.Pedro Alfonso Fernández Camacho (4/0)], Alejandro Enrique Cichero Konarek (32/0), Jonay Miguel Hernández Santos (21/0) [65.Enrique Andrés Rouga Rossi (7/0)], Héctor Augusto González Guzmán (40/4) [67.Gerzon Armando Chacón Varela (5/0)], Miguel Ángel Mea Vitali (49/1), Ricardo David Páez Gómez (48/5), Jorge Alberto Rojas Méndez (56/1) [59.Alejandro Abraham Guerra Morales (1/0)], Daniel Enrique Arismendi Marchán (1/0) [62.Armando Maita (2/0)], Giancarlo Gregorio Maldonado Marrero (13/5) [68.Jesús Javier Gómez Mercado (2/1)]. Trainer: Richard Alfred Páez Monzón (58).

235. 26.05.2006 **UNITED STATES - VENEZUELA** **2-0(1-0)**
Cleveland Browns Stadium, Cleveland; Referee: Mauricio Morales Valle (Mexico); Attendance: 29,745
VEN: Javier Eduardo Toyo Bárcenas (4/0), Héctor Augusto González Guzmán (41/4), Oswaldo Augusto Vizcarrondo Araujo (3/0), Alejandro Enrique Cichero Konarek (33/0) [65.Gabriel Alejandro Cichero Konarek (2/0)], Jorge Alberto Rojas Méndez (57/1) [70.Jonay Miguel Hernández Santos (22/0)], Leonel Gerardo Vielma Peña (34/2) [46.Edgar Hernán Jiménez González (1/0)], Miguel Ángel Mea Vitali (50/1) [46.Pedro Alfonso Fernández Camacho (5/0)], Ricardo David Páez Gómez (49/5), Alejandro Abraham Guerra Morales (2/0) [56.Jesús Javier Gómez Mercado (3/1)], Juan Fernando Arango Sáenz (Cap) (54/11), José Antonio Torrealba Acevedo (9/3) [57.Giancarlo Gregorio Maldonado Marrero (14/5)]. Trainer: Richard Alfred Páez Monzón (59).

236. 16.08.2006 **VENEZUELA - HONDURAS** **0-0**
Estadio „Hermanos Ghersy", Maracay; Referee: Gustavo Brand (Venezuela); Attendance: 9,000
VEN: Renny Vicente Vega Hernández (9/0), Gerzon Armando Chacón Varela (6/0) [79.Daybiger Morales (1/0)], Oswaldo Augusto Vizcarrondo Araujo (4/0) [46.Grenddy Adrián Perozo Rincón (1/0)], Julio César Machado Cesáreo (2/0) [46.Juan José Fuenmayor Núñez (4/0)], Enrique Andrés Rouga Rossi (8/0), Leonel Gerardo Vielma Peña (35/2) [46.Alain Giancarlo Giroletti Nadalí (1/0)], Edson Argenis Tortolero Román (39/3) [10.Engelberth Pérez (1/0); 46.Armando Maita (3/0)], Alejandro Abraham Guerra Morales (3/0) [61.César Eduardo González Amais (7/0)], Jorge Alberto Rojas Méndez (58/1), Juan Fernando Arango Sáenz (55/11), Nicolás Ladislao Fedor Flores (1/0). Trainer: Richard Alfred Páez Monzón (60).

237. 02.09.2006 **SWITZERLAND - VENEZUELA** **1-0(0-0)**
St. Jakob-Park, Basel; Referee: Alain Hamer (Luxembourg); Attendance: 12,500
VEN: Renny Vicente Vega Hernández (10/0), Luis José Vallenilla Pacheco (62/1), Oswaldo Augusto Vizcarrondo Araujo (5/0), José Manuel Rey Cortegoso (72/6), Enrique Andrés Rouga Rossi (9/0), Leonel Gerardo Vielma Peña (36/2) [46.Juan Fernando Arango Sáenz (56/11)], Miguel Ángel Mea Vitali (51/1), Alejandro Abraham Guerra Morales (4/0) [60.Alain Giancarlo Giroletti Nadalí (2/0)], Jorge Alberto Rojas Méndez (59/1) [71.Fernando Franco De Ornelas (19/2)], Ricardo David Páez Gómez (50/5) [83.Jesús Javier Gómez Mercado (4/1)], José Antonio Torrealba Acevedo (10/3) [79.Nicolás Ladislao Fedor Flores (2/0)]. Trainer: Richard Alfred Páez Monzón (61).

238. 06.09.2006 **AUSTRIA - VENEZUELA** **0-1(0-1)**
St. Jakob-Park, Basel (Switzerland); Referee: Carlo Bertolini (Switzerland); Attendance: 1,453
VEN: Renny Vicente Vega Hernández (11/0), Luis José Vallenilla Pacheco (63/1), José Manuel Rey Cortegoso (73/6), Oswaldo Augusto Vizcarrondo Araujo (6/0), Jorge Alberto Rojas Méndez (60/1), Miguel Ángel Mea Vitali (52/1) [82.Alejandro Enrique Cichero Konarek (34/0)], Alain Giancarlo Giroletti Nadalí (3/0), Ricardo David Páez Gómez (51/5) [67.Jesús Javier Gómez Mercado (5/1)], Juan Fernando Arango Sáenz (57/11), Fernando Franco De Ornelas (20/3) [46.Alejandro Abraham Guerra Morales (5/0)], Nicolás Ladislao Fedor Flores (3/0) [79.Leonel Gerardo Vielma Peña (37/2)]. Trainer: Richard Alfred Páez Monzón (62).
Goal: Fernando Franco De Ornelas (8).

239. 27.09.2006 **VENEZUELA - URUGUAY** **1-0(0-0)**
Estadio „José Encarnación 'Pachenco' Romero", Maracaibo; Referee: Jorge Manzur (Venezuela); Attendance: 17,000
VEN: Renny Vicente Vega Hernández (12/0), Luis José Vallenilla Pacheco (64/1) [54.Héctor Augusto González Guzmán (42/4)], José Manuel Rey Cortegoso (74/6), Oswaldo Augusto Vizcarrondo Araujo (7/0) [76.Enrique Andrés Rouga Rossi (10/0)], Jorge Alberto Rojas Méndez (61/1), Miguel Ángel Mea Vitali (53/1), Alain Giancarlo Giroletti Nadalí (4/0) [54.Leonel Gerardo Vielma Peña (38/2)], Ricardo David Páez Gómez (52/5), Alejandro Abraham Guerra Morales (6/0) [50.Edgar Fernando Pérez Greco (1/0); 72.Gregory Lancken (1/0)], Giancarlo Gregorio Maldonado Marrero (15/5), Alejandro Enrique Moreno Riera (5/0) [54.Daniel Enrique Arismendi Marchán (2/1)]. Trainer: Richard Alfred Páez Monzón (63).
Goal: Daniel Enrique Arismendi Marchán (81).

240. 18.10.2006 **URUGUAY – VENEZUELA** **4-0(2-0)**
Estadio Centenario, Montevideo; Referee: Roberto Silvera (Uruguay); Attendance: 5,000
VEN: Manuel Alejandro Sanhouse Contreras (13/0), Luis José Vallenilla Pacheco (65/1) [76.Daniel Godoy (2/0)], Oswaldo Augusto Vizcarrondo Araujo (8/0), Grenddy Adrián Perozo Rincón (2/0) [74.Gabriel Alejandro Cichero Konarek (3/0)], Gregory Lancken (2/0) [67.Edder Alfonso Pérez Consuegra (1/0)], Miguel Ángel Mea Vitali (54/1) [*sent off 89*], Alain Giancarlo Giroletti Nadalí (5/0), Luis Manuel Seijas Gunther (1/0) [46.Rubén Darío Arocha Hernández (2/0)], Alejandro Abraham Guerra Morales (7/0), Giancarlo Gregorio Maldonado Marrero (16/5), Daniel Enrique Arismendi Marchán (3/1) [56.Jhon Ospina (1/0)]. Trainer: Richard Alfred Páez Monzón (64).

241. 15.11.2006 **VENEZUELA - GUATEMALA** **2-1(1-0)**
Estadio Nacional „Brígido Iriarte", Caracas; Referee: Candelario Andarcia (Venezuela); Attendance: 9,000
VEN: Renny Vicente Vega Hernández (13/0) [46.Javier Eduardo Toyo Bárcenas (5/0)], Héctor Augusto González Guzmán (43/4) [64.Jesús Javier Gómez Mercado (6/1)], Alejandro Enrique Cichero Konarek (35/0), José Manuel Rey Cortegoso (75/7), Jorge Alberto Rojas Méndez (62/1) [46.Enrique Andrés Rouga Rossi (11/0)], José Javier Villafraz Quintero (13/1), Miguel Ángel Mea Vitali (55/1) [58.Alain Giancarlo Giroletti Nadalí (6/0)], Ricardo David Páez Gómez (53/5) [*sent off 20*], Alejandro Abraham Guerra Morales (8/0) [80.Grenddy Adrián Perozo Rincón (3/0)], Giancarlo Gregorio Maldonado Marrero (17/5) [46.Luis José Vallenilla Pacheco (66/1)], Fernando Franco De Ornelas (21/3) [55.Nicolás Ladislao Fedor Flores (4/0)]. Trainer: Richard Alfred Páez Monzón (65).
Goals: José Javier Villafraz Quintero (3), José Manuel Rey Cortegoso (52).

242. 14.01.2007 **VENEZUELA - SWEDEN** **2-0(1-0)**
Estadio José Encarnación "Pachenco" Romero, Maracaibo; Referee: José Hernando Buitrago Arango (Colombia); Attendance: 14,000
VEN: Renny Vicente Vega Hernández (14/0) [72.Javier Eduardo Toyo Bárcenas (6/0)], Luis José Vallenilla Pacheco (67/1), José Manuel Rey Cortegoso (76/7), Osvaldo Augusto Vizcarrondo Araujo (9/0), Jorge Alberto Rojas Méndez (63/1) [70.Enrique Andrés Rouga Rossi (12/0)], Miguel Ángel Mea Vitali (56/1), José Javier Villafraz Quintero (14/1) [64.Leonel Gerardo Vielma Peña (39/2)], Evelio de Jesús Hernández Guedez (3/0) [54.César Eduardo González Amais (8/0)], Alejandro Abraham Guerra Morales (9/1), Fernando Franco De Ornelas (22/3) [72.Andreé Aníbal González Frustacci (17/0)], Cristian Alfonso Cásseres Caseres (26/2) [54.Daniel Enrique Arismendi Marchán (4/2)]. Trainer: Richard Alfred Páez Monzón (66).
Goals: Alejandro Abraham Guerra Morales (17), Daniel Enrique Arismendi Marchán (90+1).

243. 07.02.2007 **VENEZUELA - CHILE** **0-1(0-1)**
Estadio „José Encarnación 'Pachenco' Romero", Maracaibo; Referee: José Hernando Buitrago Arango (Colombia); Attendance: 9,000
VEN: Renny Vicente Vega Hernández (15/0), Luis José Vallenilla Pacheco (68/1) [54.César Eduardo González Amais (9/0)], Alejandro Enrique Cíchero Konarek (36/0) [56.Osvaldo Augusto Vizcarrondo Araujo (10/0)], José Manuel Rey Cortegoso (77/7), Jorge Alberto Rojas Méndez (64/1), Miguel Ángel Mea Vitali (57/1) [67.Alain Giancarlo Giroletti Nadalí (7/0)], Pedro Alfonso Fernández Camacho (6/0) [59.Leonel Gerardo Vielma Peña (40/2)], Héctor Augusto González Guzmán (44/4), Alejandro Abraham Guerra Morales (10/1) [63.Enrique Andrés Rouga Rossi (13/0)], José Antonio Torrealba Acevedo (11/3) [54.Daniel Enrique Arismendi Marchán (5/2)], Giancarlo Gregorio Maldonado Marrero (18/5) [69.Fernando Franco De Ornelas (23/3)]. Trainer: Richard Alfred Páez Monzón (67).

244. 28.02.2007 **MEXICO - VENEZUELA** **3-1(2-0)**
Qualcomm Stadium, San Diego (United States); Referee: Kevin Stott (United States); Attendance: 63,328
VEN: Manuel Alejandro Sanhouse Contreras (14/0), Luis José Vallenilla Pacheco (69/1) [83.Franklin José Lucena Peña (1/0)], José Manuel Rey Cortegoso (78/7), Osvaldo Augusto Vizcarrondo Araujo (11/0), Jorge Alberto Rojas Méndez (65/1), Miguel Ángel Mea Vitali (58/1) [46.Leonel Gerardo Vielma Peña (41/2)], José Javier Villafraz Quintero (15/1) [46.Alejandro Abraham Guerra Morales (11/1)], Enrique Andrés Rouga Rossi (14/0), Giovanny José Pérez Fernández (28/0) [46.Pedro Alfonso Fernández Camacho (7/0)], Nicolás Ladislao Fedor Flores (5/0) [69.Daniel Enrique Arismendi Marchán (6/3)], Dickson Ruberth Morán Puelo (63/14) [49.Evelio de Jesús Hernández Guedez (4/0)]. Trainer: Richard Alfred Páez Monzón (68).
Goal: Daniel Enrique Arismendi Marchán (83).

245. 24.03.2007 **VENEZUELA - CUBA** **3-1(2-0)**
Estadio "Guillermo Soto Rosa", Mérida; Referee: Candelario Andarcía (Venezuela); Attendance: 12,000
VEN: Renny Vicente Vega Hernández (16/0) [46.Javier Eduardo Toyo Bárcenas (7/0)], Héctor Augusto González Guzmán (45/4) [*sent off 68*], José Manuel Rey Cortegoso (79/7), Enrique Andrés Rouga Rossi (15/0) [46.Alejandro Enrique Cíchero Konarek (37/0)], Jorge Alberto Rojas Méndez (66/1), Luis Enrique Vera Martineau (45/2) [61.Leonel Gerardo Vielma Peña (42/2)], Edder Alfonso Pérez Consuegra (2/0) [46.Jesús Manuel Meza Moreno (1/0)], Alejandro Abraham Guerra Morales (12/1) [46.César Eduardo González Amais (10/1)], Juan Fernando Arango Sáenz (58/12), Giancarlo Gregorio Maldonado Marrero (19/5) [46.Nicolás Ladislao Fedor Flores (6/0)], José Antonio Torrealba Acevedo (12/4) [46.Dickson Ruberth Morán Puelo (64/14)]. Trainer: Richard Alfred Páez Monzón (69).
Goals: Juan Fernando Arango Sáenz (11), José Antonio Torrealba Acevedo (33), César Eduardo González Amais (64).

246. 28.03.2007 **VENEZUELA – NEW ZEALAND** **5-0(2-0)**
Estadio „José Encarnación 'Pachenco' Romero", Maracaibo; Referee: Juan Soto (Venezuela); Attendance: 12,000
VEN: Renny Vicente Vega Hernández (17/0) [46.Rafael Edgar Dudamel Ochoa (55/1)], Rubén Ramón Yori (1/0) [46.José Javier Villafraz Quintero (16/1)], Juan José Fuenmayor Núñez (5/0), Grenddy Adrián Perozo Rincón (4/0) [71.Julio César Machado Cesáreo (3/0)], Luis José Vallenilla Pacheco (70/1) [72.Renier Alexander Rodríguez González (1/0)], Pedro Alfonso Fernández Camacho (8/0) [66.Alain Giancarlo Giroletti Nadalí (8/0)], Jesús Manuel Meza Moreno (2/0) [46.Roberto José Rosales Altuve (1/0)], Ricardo David Páez Gómez (54/6), Juan Fernando Arango Sáenz (59/12), Giancarlo Gregorio Maldonado Marrero (20/5) [46.Nicolás Ladislao Fedor Flores (7/1)], Fernando Franco De Ornelas (24/5) [60.Dickson Ruberth Morán Puelo (65/14)]. Trainer: Richard Alfred Páez Monzón (70).
Goals: Ricardo David Páez Gómez (8), Fernando Franco De Ornelas (31, 49), Nicolás Ladislao Fedor Flores (85 penalty), Noah Hickey (90+1 own goal).

247. 25.05.2007 **VENEZUELA - HONDURAS** **2-1(2-1)**
Estadio Metropolitano, Mérida; Referee: Mayker Gómez (Venezuela); Attendance: 42,000
VEN: Javier Eduardo Toyo Bárcenas (8/0) [46.Rafael Edgar Dudamel Ochoa (56/1)], Luis José Vallenilla Pacheco (71/1) [46.Héctor Augusto González Guzmán (46/4)], Osvaldo Augusto Vizcarrondo Araujo (12/0), Edder Alfonso Pérez Consuegra (3/0) [22.Jesús Manuel Meza Moreno (3/0)], Miguel Ángel Mea Vitali (59/1) [46.José Javier Villafraz Quintero (17/1)], Leonel Gerardo Vielma Peña (43/3) [53.José Manuel Rey Cortegoso (80/7)], César Eduardo González Amais (11/1) [46.Alejandro Abraham Guerra Morales (13/1)], Jesús Javier Gómez Mercado (7/1), Enrique Andrés Rouga Rossi (16/0) [46.Jorge Alberto Rojas Méndez (67/1)], Daniel Enrique Arismendi Marchán (7/4), Nicolás Ladislao Fedor Flores (8/1). Trainer: Richard Alfred Páez Monzón (71).
Goals: Leonel Gerardo Vielma Peña (18), Daniel Enrique Arismendi Marchán (38).

248. 01.06.2007 **VENEZUELA - CANADA** **2-2(2-1)**
Estadio „José Encarnación 'Pachenco' Romero", Maracaibo; Referee: Carlos Eduardo López (Colombia); Attendance: 20,000
VEN: Renny Vicente Vega Hernández (18/0) [46.Javier Eduardo Toyo Bárcenas (9/0)], José Manuel Rey Cortegoso (81/7), Alejandro Enrique Cíchero Konarek (38/1), Héctor Augusto González Guzmán (47/4) [46.Nicolás Ladislao Fedor Flores (9/1)], Jorge Alberto Rojas Méndez (68/1), Miguel Ángel Mea Vitali (60/1) [63.José Javier Villafraz Quintero (18/1) [*sent off 85*]], Luis Enrique Vera Martineau (46/2) [68.Pedro Alfonso Fernández Camacho (9/0)], Ricardo David Páez Gómez (55/6), César Eduardo González Amais (12/1) [46.Luis José Vallenilla Pacheco (72/1)], Juan Fernando Arango Sáenz (60/12) [82.Jesús Javier Gómez Mercado (8/1)], Giancarlo Gregorio Maldonado Marrero (21/6) [46.Daniel Enrique Arismendi Marchán (8/4)]. Trainer: Richard Alfred Páez Monzón (72).
Goals: Alejandro Enrique Cíchero Konarek (22), Giancarlo Gregorio Maldonado Marrero (25).

249. 26.06.2007 **VENEZUELA - BOLIVIA** **2-2(1-1)** 42nd Copa América. Group Stage
Estadio Polideportivo de Pueblo Nuevo, San Cristóbal (Venezuela); Referee: Mauricio Reinoso (Ecuador); Attendance: 42,000
VEN: Renny Vicente Vega Hernández (19/0), Héctor Augusto González Guzmán (48/4), José Manuel Rey Cortegoso (82/7), Alejandro Enrique Cíchero Konarek (39/1), Jorge Alberto Rojas Méndez (69/1), Luis Enrique Vera Martineau (47/2), Miguel Ángel Mea Vitali (61/1), Ricardo David Páez Gómez (56/7) [72.Leonel Gerardo Vielma Peña (44/3)], Juan Fernando Arango Sáenz (61/12), Fernando Franco De Ornelas (25/5) [59.Alejandro Abraham Guerra Morales (14/1)], Giancarlo Gregorio Maldonado Marrero (22/7) [77.José Antonio Torrealba Acevedo (13/4)]. Trainer: Richard Alfred Páez Monzón (73).
Goals: Giancarlo Gregorio Maldonado Marrero (20), Ricardo David Páez Gómez (55).

250. 30.06.2007 **VENEZUELA - PERU** **2-0(0-0)** 42nd Copa América. Group Stage

Estadio Polideportivo de Pueblo Nuevo, San Cristóbal; Referee: Benito Armando Archundia Téllez (Mexico); Attendance: 42,000

VEN: Renny Vicente Vega Hernández (20/0), Héctor Augusto González Guzmán (49/4), José Manuel Rey Cortegoso (83/7), Alejandro Enrique Cíchero Konarek (40/2), Enrique Andrés Rouga Rossi (17/0) [37.Edder Alfonso Pérez Consuegra (4/0)], Miguel Ángel Mea Vitali (62/1), Luis Enrique Vera Martineau (48/2), Ricardo David Páez Gómez (57/7), Juan Fernando Arango Sáenz (62/12) [74.César Eduardo González Amais (13/1)], Giancarlo Gregorio Maldonado Marrero (23/7), Fernando Franco De Ornelas (26/5) [63.Daniel Enrique Arismendi Marchán (9/5)]. Trainer: Richard Alfred Páez Monzón (74).

Goals: Alejandro Enrique Cíchero Konarek (49), Daniel Enrique Arismendi Marchán (79).

251. 03.07.2007 **VENEZUELA - URUGUAY** **0-0** 42nd Copa América. Group Stage

Estadio Metropolitano, Mérida; Referee: Carlos Eugênio Simon (Brazil), Attendance: 42,000

VEN: Renny Vicente Vega Hernández (21/0), Héctor Augusto González Guzmán (50/4), José Manuel Rey Cortegoso (84/7), Alejandro Enrique Cíchero Konarek (41/2), Edder Alfonso Pérez Consuegra (5/0), Luis Enrique Vera Martineau (49/2), Miguel Ángel Mea Vitali (63/1) [75.Pedro Alfonso Fernández Camacho (10/0)], César Eduardo González Amais (14/1), Juan Fernando Arango Sáenz (63/12), Giancarlo Gregorio Maldonado Marrero (24/7) [57.José Antonio Torrealba Acevedo (14/4)], Fernando Franco De Ornelas (27/5) [65.Alejandro Abraham Guerra Morales (15/1)]. Trainer: Richard Alfred Páez Monzón (75).

252. 07.07.2007 **VENEZUELA - URUGUAY** **1-4(1-1)** 42nd Copa América. Quarter-Finals

Estadio Polideportivo de Pueblo Nuevo, San Cristóbal; Referee: Carlos Chandía Alarcón (Chile), Attendance: 42,000

VEN: Renny Vicente Vega Hernández (22/0), Héctor Augusto González Guzmán (51/4), José Manuel Rey Cortegoso (85/7), Alejandro Enrique Cíchero Konarek (42/2), Jorge Alberto Rojas Méndez (70/1), Luis Enrique Vera Martineau (50/2), Miguel Ángel Mea Vitali (64/1) [76.Alejandro Abraham Guerra Morales (16/1)], Ricardo David Páez Gómez (58/7), Juan Fernando Arango Sáenz (64/13), Giancarlo Gregorio Maldonado Marrero (25/7) [71.César Eduardo González Amais (15/1)], Fernando Franco De Ornelas (28/5) [46.Daniel Enrique Arismendi Marchán (10/5)]. Trainer: Richard Alfred Páez Monzón (76).

Goal: Juan Fernando Arango Sáenz (41).

253. 22.08.2007 **PARAGUAY - VENEZUELA** **1-1(1-0)**

Estadio "Antonio Oddone Sarubbi", Ciudad del Este; Referee: Héctor Walter Baldassi (Argentina); Attendance: 3,500

VEN: José Leonardo Morales Lares (2/0), Luis José Vallenilla Pacheco (73/1) [69.Roberto José Rosales Altuve (2/0)], José Manuel Rey Cortegoso (86/7), Grenddy Adrián Perozo Rincón (5/0) [73.Juan José Fuenmayor Núñez (6/0)], Edder Alfonso Pérez Consuegra (6/0), Miguel Ángel Mea Vitali (65/1) [78.Edgar Hernán Jiménez González (2/0)], Leonel Gerardo Vielma Peña (45/3), César Eduardo González Amais (16/1) [78.José David Moreno Chacón (1/0)], Alejandro Abraham Guerra Morales (17/1) [84.Anderson Arias Zambrano (1/0)], Jorge Alberto Rojas Méndez (71/1), Nicolás Ladislao Fedor Flores (10/2) [71.Daniel Enrique Arismendi Marchán (11/5)]. Trainer: Richard Alfred Páez Monzón (77).

Goal: Nicolás Ladislao Fedor Flores (57).

254. 08.09.2007 **VENEZUELA - PARAGUAY** **3-2(0-1)**

Estadio Cachamay, Puerto Ordaz; Referee: Carlos López (Colombia); Attendance: 30,000

VEN: Renny Vicente Vega Hernández (23/0), Héctor Augusto González Guzmán (52/4) [57.Roberto José Rosales Altuve (3/0)], José Manuel Rey Cortegoso (87/7), Alejandro Enrique Cíchero Konarek (43/2), Luis José Vallenilla Pacheco (74/1) [57.Gabriel Alejandro Cíchero Konarek (4/0)], Miguel Ángel Mea Vitali (66/1), Leonel Gerardo Vielma Peña (46/3) [57.Luis Manuel Seijas Gunther (2/0)], Ricardo David Páez Gómez (59/7), Alejandro Abraham Guerra Morales (18/2), Juan Fernando Arango Sáenz (65/13) [46.Daniel Enrique Arismendi Marchán (12/6)], Giancarlo Gregorio Maldonado Marrero (26/8) [86.Heiber Eduardo Díaz Tovar (1/0)]. Trainer: Richard Alfred Páez Monzón (78).

Goals: Daniel Enrique Arismendi Marchán (66), Giancarlo Gregorio Maldonado Marrero (75), Alejandro Abraham Guerra Morales (90).

255. 12.09.2007 **VENEZUELA - PANAMA** **1-1(0-0)**

Estadio "General José Antonio Anzoategui", Puerto La Cruz; Referee: José Hernando Buitrago Arango (Colombia); Attendance: 25,000

VEN: José Leonardo Morales Lares (3/0) [60.Renny Vicente Vega Hernández (24/0)], Roberto José Rosales Altuve (4/0), Alejandro Enrique Cíchero Konarek (44/2), Leonel Gerardo Vielma Peña (47/3) [77.Grenddy Adrián Perozo Rincón (6/0)], Jorge Alberto Rojas Méndez (72/1), Luis Enrique Vera Martineau (51/2) [60.Miguel Ángel Mea Vitali (67/1)], Luis Manuel Seijas Gunther (3/0), Ricardo David Páez Gómez (60/7) [64.César Eduardo González Amais (17/1)], Alejandro Abraham Guerra Morales (19/2) [46.Daniel Enrique Arismendi Marchán (13/6)], Juan Fernando Arango Sáenz (66/13) [85.Gabriel Alejandro Cíchero Konarek (5/0)], Giancarlo Gregorio Maldonado Marrero (27/9). Trainer: Richard Alfred Páez Monzón (79).

Goal: Giancarlo Gregorio Maldonado Marrero (90+6 penalty).

256. 13.10.2007 **ECUADOR - VENEZUELA** **0-1(0-0)** 19th FIFA WC. Qualifiers

Estadio Olimpico "Atahualpa", Quito; Referee: René Ortubé Betancourt (Bolivia); Attendance: 37,000

VEN: Renny Vicente Vega Hernández (25/0), Luis José Vallenilla Pacheco (75/1), José Manuel Rey Cortegoso (88/8), Alejandro Enrique Cíchero Konarek (45/2), Enrique Andrés Rouga Rossi (18/0), Miguel Ángel Mea Vitali (68/1) [79.Leonel Gerardo Vielma Peña (48/3)], Luis Enrique Vera Martineau (52/2), Ricardo David Páez Gómez (61/7) [77.Héctor Augusto González Guzmán (53/4)], Jorge Alberto Rojas Méndez (73/1), Juan Fernando Arango Sáenz (67/13) [65.Alejandro Abraham Guerra Morales (20/2)], Giancarlo Gregorio Maldonado Marrero (28/9). Trainer: Richard Alfred Páez Monzón (80).

Goal: José Manuel Rey Cortegoso (67).

257. 16.10.2007 **VENEZUELA - ARGENTINA** **0-2(0-2)** 19th FIFA WC. Qualifiers

Estadio "José Encarnación 'Pachencho' Romero", Maracaibo; Referee: Carlos Eugênio Simon (Brazil); Attendance: 35,000

VEN: Renny Vicente Vega Hernández (26/0), Luis José Vallenilla Pacheco (76/1) [46.Roberto José Rosales Altuve (5/0)], José Manuel Rey Cortegoso (89/8), Alejandro Enrique Cíchero Konarek (46/2), Enrique Andrés Rouga Rossi (19/0), Miguel Ángel Mea Vitali (69/1), Jorge Alberto Rojas Méndez (74/1) [67.Daniel Enrique Arismendi Marchán (14/6)], Ricardo David Páez Gómez (62/7), Luis Manuel Seijas Gunther (4/0) [54.Alejandro Abraham Guerra Morales (21/2)], Juan Fernando Arango Sáenz (68/13), Giancarlo Gregorio Maldonado Marrero (29/9). Trainer: Richard Alfred Páez Monzón (81).

258. 17.11.2007 **COLOMBIA - VENEZUELA** **1-0(0-0)** 19th FIFA WC. Qualifiers

Estadio „Nemesio Camacho" 'El Campín', Bogotá; Referee: Rubén Marcos Selmán (Chile); Attendance: 28,273

VEN: José Leonardo Morales Lares (4/0), Luis José Vallenilla Pacheco (77/1), José Manuel Rey Cortegoso (90/8), Leonel Gerardo Vielma Peña (49/3), Enrique Andrés Rouga Rossi (20/0), Miguel Ángel Mea Vitali (70/1), Jorge Alberto Rojas Méndez (75/1), Ricardo David Páez Gómez (63/7) [66.César Eduardo González Amais (18/1)], Juan Fernando Arango Sáenz (69/13), Nicolás Ladislao Fedor Flores (11/2) [77.Gabriel Alejandro Cichero Konarek (6/0)], Giancarlo Gregorio Maldonado Marrero (30/9) [55.Alejandro Abraham Guerra Morales (22/2)]. Trainer: Richard Alfred Páez Monzón (82).

259. 20.11.2007 **VENEZUELA - BOLIVIA** **5-3(2-2)** 19th FIFA WC. Qualifiers

Estadio Polideportivo de Pueblo Nuevo, San Cristóbal; Referee: Sálvio Fagundes Filho (Brazil); Attendance: 24,000

VEN: José Leonardo Morales Lares (5/0), Roberto José Rosales Altuve (6/0), José Manuel Rey Cortegoso (91/8), Alejandro Enrique Cíchero Konarek (47/2), Jorge Alberto Rojas Méndez (76/1), Luis Enrique Vera Martineau (53/2) [59.Miguel Ángel Mea Vitali (71/1)], Ricardo David Páez Gómez (64/7) [74.Alejandro Abraham Guerra Morales (23/3)], Juan Fernando Arango Sáenz (70/13), Luis Manuel Seijas Gunther (5/0) [64.Edder Alfonso Pérez Consuegra (7/0)], Daniel Enrique Arismendi Marchán (15/8), Giancarlo Gregorio Maldonado Marrero (31/11). Trainer: Richard Alfred Páez Monzón (83).

Goals: Daniel Enrique Arismendi Marchán (20, 40), Alejandro Abraham Guerra Morales (82), Giancarlo Gregorio Maldonado Marrero (89, 90+1).

260. 03.02.2008 **VENEZUELA - HAITI** **1-0(1-0)**
Estadio Monumental, Maturín; Referee: Juan Soto (Venezuela); Attendance: 16,000
VEN: José Leonardo Morales Lares (6/0), Dickson Manuel Díaz Romero (2/0) [76.Giácomo Di Giorgi Zerillo (4/0)], Grenddy Adrián Perozo Rincón (7/0), Gabriel Alejandro Cíchero Konarek (7/0), José Luis Granados Asprilla (1/0), Franklin José Lucena Peña (2/0), Tomás Eduardo Rincón Hernández (1/0) [82.Edgar Hernán Jiménez González (3/0)], Evelio de Jesús Hernández Guedez (5/0) [67.Ronald Alejandro Vargas Aranguren (1/0)], Jorge Alberto Rojas Méndez (77/2), Emilio Rentería García (1/0) [64.José Salomón Rondón Giménez (1/0)], Armando Rafael Maita Urbáez (1/0) [88.Edgar Fernando Pérez Greco (2/0)]. Trainer: César Alejandro Farías Acosta (1).
Goal: Jorge Alberto Rojas Méndez (10).

261. 06.02.2008 **VENEZUELA - HAITI** **1-1(1-1)**
Estadio "General José Antonio Anzoategui", Puerto La Cruz; Referee: Giovanny Perluzzo (Venezuela); Attendance: 30,000
VEN: José Leonardo Morales Lares (7/0), Leonel Gerardo Vielma Peña (50/3), José Manuel Rey Cortegoso (92/8), Grenddy Adrián Perozo Rincón (8/0) [84.Evelio de Jesús Hernández Guedez (6/0)], Enrique Andrés Rouga Rossi (21/0), Franklin José Lucena Peña (3/0) [75.Giácomo Di Giorgi Zerillo (5/0)], Tomás Eduardo Rincón Hernández (2/0), Juan Fernando Arango Sáenz (71/13), Jorge Alberto Rojas Méndez (78/2) [46.Carlos Enrique Fernández (1/0)], Daniel Enrique Arismendi Marchán (16/8) [71.José Salomón Rondón Giménez (2/0)], Alexander Rondón Heredia (34/4) [62.Armando Rafael Maita Urbáez (2/0)]. Trainer: César Alejandro Farías Acosta (2).
Goal: Alexander Rondón Heredia (31).

262. 23.03.2008 **VENEZUELA – EL SALVADOR** **1-0(1-0)**
Estadio "General José Antonio Anzoategui", Puerto La Cruz; Referee: Mayker Gómez (Venezuela); Attendance: 5,000
VEN: Giancarlos Martínez (1/0), Gerzon Armando Chacón Varela (7/0), José Francisco González Quijada (16/0) [57.Leonardo Alberto González Antequera (39/0)], Gabriel Alejandro Cíchero Konarek (8/0), José Luis Granados Asprilla (2/0), Giácomo Di Giorgi Zerillo (6/0), Evelio de Jesús Hernández Guedez (7/0) [82.Louis Angelo Peña Puentes (1/0)], Tomás Eduardo Rincón Hernández (3/0), Cristian Alfonso Cásseres Caseres (27/2) [85.Ronald Alejandro Vargas Aranguren (2/0)], Edgar Fernando Pérez Greco (3/0) [68.Ángel Antonio Chourio Galíndez (1/0)], José Salomón Rondón Giménez (3/1) [76.Juan Falcón (1/0)]. Trainer: César Alejandro Farías Acosta (3).
Goal: José Salomón Rondón Giménez (33).

263. 26.03.2008 **VENEZUELA - BOLIVIA** **0-1(0-0)**
Estadio "General José Antonio Anzoátegui", Puerto La Cruz; Referee: José Hernando Buitrago Arango (Colombia); Attendance: 16,000
VEN: Renny Vicente Vega Hernández (27/0), Franklin José Lucena Peña (4/0) [64.Gerzon Armando Chacón Varela (8/0)], Gabriel Alejandro Cíchero Konarek (9/0), Grenddy Adrián Perozo Rincón (9/0), Jonay Miguel Hernández Santos (23/0) [73.José Luis Granados Asprilla (3/0)], Leonel Gerardo Vielma Peña (51/3) [83.Evelio de Jesús Hernández Guedez (8/0)], Luis Manuel Seijas Gunther (6/0) [71.Carlos Enrique Fernández (2/0)], Tomás Eduardo Rincón Hernández (4/0), Ronald Alejandro Vargas Aranguren (3/0), Cristian Alfonso Cásseres Caseres (28/2) [46.Daniel Enrique Arismendi Marchán (17/8)], Alexander Rondón Heredia (35/4). Trainer: César Alejandro Farías Acosta (4).

264. 30.04.2008 **COLOMBIA - VENEZUELA** **5-2(2-2)**
Estadio „Alfonso López", Bucaramanga; Referee: Victor Hugo Carrillo (Peru); Attendance: 30,000
VEN: Javier Eduardo Toyo Bárcenas (10/0), Franklin José Lucena Peña (5/1) [66.Gerzon Armando Chacón Varela (9/0)], Osvaldo Augusto Vizcarrondo Araujo (13/0) [68.José Manuel Rey Cortegoso (93/8)], Gabriel Alejandro Cíchero Konarek (10/1), José Luis Granados Asprilla (4/0), Leonel Gerardo Vielma Peña (52/3) [62.Miguel Ángel Mea Vitali (72/1)], Ronald Alejandro Vargas Aranguren (4/0) [73.Luis Manuel Seijas Gunther (7/0)], Tomás Eduardo Rincón Hernández (5/0) [77.Evelio de Jesús Hernández Guedez (9/0)], Jorge Alberto Rojas Méndez (79/2), Alexander Rondón Heredia (36/4) [56.Daniel Enrique Arismendi Marchán (18/8)], José Antonio Torrealba Acevedo (15/4). Trainer: César Alejandro Farías Acosta (5).
Goals: Gabriel Alejandro Cíchero Konarek (10), Franklin José Lucena Peña (43).

265. 30.05.2008 **HONDURAS - VENEZUELA** **1-1(0-0)**
Lockhart Stadium, Fort Lauderdale (United States); Referee: Allan Wiemckowski (United States); Attendance: 10,000
VEN: José Leonardo Morales Lares (8/0), Pedro Luis Boada Noya (2/0) [68.Roberto José Rosales Altuve (7/0)], José Manuel Rey Cortegoso (94/8), Leonel Gerardo Vielma Peña (53/3), Gabriel Alejandro Cíchero Konarek (11/1) [75.Juan José Fuenmayor Núñez (7/0)], César Alexander González (1/0) [46.Alexander Rondón Heredia (37/4)], Tomás Eduardo Rincón Hernández (6/0) [88.Evelio de Jesús Hernández Guedez (10/0)], Luis Manuel Seijas Gunther (8/0) [62.Miguel Ángel Mea Vitali (73/1)], Jorge Alberto Rojas Méndez (80/2), Juan Fernando Arango Sáenz (72/13), Giancarlo Gregorio Maldonado Marrero (32/12) [83.Daniel Enrique Arismendi Marchán (19/8)]. Trainer: César Alejandro Farías Acosta (6).
Goal: Giancarlo Gregorio Maldonado Marrero (78 penalty).

266. 06.06.2008 **VENEZUELA - BRAZIL** **2-0(2-0)**
Gillette Stadium, Foxborough (United States); Referee: Jair Marrufo (United States); Attendance: 54,045
VEN: Renny Vicente Vega Hernández (28/0), Gerzon Armando Chacón Varela (10/0), Pedro Luis Boada Noya (3/0), José Manuel Rey Cortegoso (95/8), Jonay Miguel Hernández Santos (24/0) [80.Juan José Fuenmayor Núñez (8/0)], Miguel Ángel Mea Vitali (74/1), Tomás Eduardo Rincón Hernández (7/0) [88.Evelio de Jesús Hernández Guedez (11/0)], Ronald Alejandro Vargas Aranguren (5/1) [63.Alexander Rondón Heredia (38/4)], Jorge Alberto Rojas Méndez (81/2) [82.Franklin José Lucena Peña (6/1)], Juan Fernando Arango Sáenz (73/13) [90+2.César Alexander González (2/0)], Giancarlo Gregorio Maldonado Marrero (33/13) [74.Daniel Enrique Arismendi Marchán (20/8)]. Trainer: César Alejandro Farías Acosta (7).
Goals: Giancarlo Gregorio Maldonado Marrero (5), Ronald Alejandro Vargas Aranguren (44).

267. 09.06.2008 **NETHERLANDS ANTILLES - VENEZUELA** **0-1(0-0)**
Ergilio Hato Stadion, Willemstad; Referee: Álvaro De Avila (Netherlands Antilles); Attendance: 6,000
VEN: José Leonardo Morales Lares (9/0), Franklin José Lucena Peña (7/1) [58.Miguel Ángel Mea Vitali (75/1)], Gabriel Alejandro Cíchero Konarek (12/1), Pedro Luis Boada Noya (4/0) [46.José Manuel Rey Cortegoso (96/8)], Juan José Fuenmayor Núñez (9/0), Roberto José Rosales Altuve (8/0), Evelio de Jesús Hernández Guedez (12/0), César Alexander González (3/0) [61.Ronald Alejandro Vargas Aranguren (6/1)], Juan Fernando Arango Sáenz (74/13) [46.Jorge Alberto Rojas Méndez (82/2)], José Antonio Torrealba Acevedo (16/4) [63.Alexander Rondón Heredia (39/4)], Daniel Enrique Arismendi Marchán (21/9) [81.Giancarlo Gregorio Maldonado Marrero (34/13)]. Trainer: César Alejandro Farías Acosta (8).
Goal: Daniel Enrique Arismendi Marchán (75).

268. 14.06.2008 **URUGUAY - VENEZUELA** **1-1(1-0)** 19th FIFA WC. Qualifiers
Estadio Centenario, Montevideo; Referee: Alfredo Intriago (Ecuador), Attendance: 41,831
VEN: Renny Vicente Vega Hernández (29/0), Gerzon Armando Chacón Varela (11/0), Leonel Gerardo Vielma Peña (54/3), José Manuel Rey Cortegoso (97/8), Jonay Miguel Hernández Santos (25/0), Miguel Ángel Mea Vitali (76/1), Tomás Eduardo Rincón Hernández (8/0), Ronald Alejandro Vargas Aranguren (7/2) [73.Alexander Rondón Heredia (40/4)], Jorge Alberto Rojas Méndez (83/2) [79.Luis Manuel Seijas Gunther (9/0)], Juan Fernando Arango Sáenz (75/13), Giancarlo Gregorio Maldonado Marrero (35/13) [87.Pedro Luis Boada Noya (5/0)]. Trainer: César Alejandro Farías Acosta (9).
Goal: Ronald Alejandro Vargas Aranguren (56).

269. 19.06.2008 **VENEZUELA - CHILE** **2-3(0-0)** 19th FIFA WC. Qualifiers

Estadio Olímpico "Luis Ramos", Puerto la Cruz; Referee: Roberto Carlos Silvera (Uruguay); Attendance: 38,000

VEN: Renny Vicente Vega Hernández (30/0), Gerzon Armando Chacón Varela (12/0), Leonel Gerardo Vielma Peña (55/3), José Manuel Rey Cortegoso (98/8), Jonay Miguel Hernández Santos (26/0), Miguel Ángel Mea Vitali (77/1) [80.Luis Manuel Seijas Gunther (10/0)], Ronald Alejandro Vargas Aranguren (8/2) [59.Tomás Eduardo Rincón Hernández (9/0)], Jorge Alberto Rojas Méndez (84/2), Juan Fernando Arango Sáenz (76/14), Alexander Rondón Heredia (41/4) [55.Daniel Enrique Arismendi Marchán (22/9)], Giancarlo Gregorio Maldonado Marrero (36/14). Trainer: César Alejandro Farías Acosta (10).

Goals: Giancarlo Gregorio Maldonado Marrero (59), Juan Fernando Arango Sáenz (80).

270. 20.08.2008 **VENEZUELA - SYRIA** **4-1(1-0)**

Estadio "General José Antonio Anzoategui", Puerto La Cruz; Referee: Mayker Gómez (Venezuela); Attendance: 2,500

VEN: José Leonardo Morales Lares (10/0) [83.Rafael Enrique Romo Pérez (1/0)], Gerzon Armando Chacón Varela (13/0) [65.Johnny Fair Mirabal (1/0)], Pedro Luis Boada Noya (6/0), José Manuel Rey Cortegoso (99/8), Jonay Miguel Hernández Santos (27/0), Leonel Gerardo Vielma Peña (56/4) [62.Francisco Javier Flores Sequera (1/0)], Miguel Ángel Mea Vitali (78/1) [69.Rafael Eduardo Acosta Cammarota (1/0)], Jorge Alberto Rojas Méndez (85/3) [55.Luis Manuel Seijas Gunther (11/0)], Alejandro Abraham Guerra Morales (24/3) [79.Guillermo Abel Ramírez (1/0)], Alejandro Enrique Moreno Riera (6/1), Giancarlo Gregorio Maldonado Marrero (37/15) [75.Yonathan Alexander del Valle Rodríguez (1/0)]. Trainer: César Alejandro Farías Acosta (11).

Goals: Leonel Gerardo Vielma Peña (14), Giancarlo Gregorio Maldonado Marrero (53), Jorge Alberto Rojas Méndez (56), Alejandro Enrique Moreno Riera (62).

271. 06.09.2008 **PERU - VENEZUELA** **1-0(1-0)** 19th FIFA WC. Qualifiers

Estadio Monumental, Lima; Referee: Óscar Maldonado (Bolivia); Attendance: 15,000

VEN: Renny Vicente Vega Hernández (31/0), Gerzon Armando Chacón Varela (14/0), José Manuel Rey Cortegoso (**100**/8), Pedro Luis Boada Noya (7/0), Jonay Miguel Hernández Santos (28/0), Miguel Ángel Mea Vitali (79/1) [71.Leonel Gerardo Vielma Peña (57/4)], Tomás Eduardo Rincón Hernández (10/0), Jorge Alberto Rojas Méndez (86/3) [55.Alejandro Enrique Moreno Riera (7/1)], Ronald Alejandro Vargas Aranguren (9/2) [66.Alejandro Abraham Guerra Morales (25/3)], Juan Fernando Arango Sáenz (77/14), Giancarlo Gregorio Maldonado Marrero (38/15). Trainer: César Alejandro Farías Acosta (12).

272. 09.09.2008 **PARAGUAY - VENEZUELA** **2-0(2-0)** 19th FIFA WC. Qualifiers

Estadio Defensores del Chaco, Asunción; Referee: Héctor Walter Baldassi (Argentina); Attendance: 25,909

VEN: Renny Vicente Vega Hernández (32/0), Gerzon Armando Chacón Varela (15/0) [35.Franklin José Lucena Peña (8/1)], José Manuel Rey Cortegoso (101/8), Pedro Luis Boada Noya (8/0), Jonay Miguel Hernández Santos (29/0) [55.Juan José Fuenmayor Núñez (10/0)], Alejandro Abraham Guerra Morales (26/3), Tomás Eduardo Rincón Hernández (11/0), Miguel Ángel Mea Vitali (80/1), Juan Fernando Arango Sáenz (78/14), Alejandro Enrique Moreno Riera (8/1), Giancarlo Gregorio Maldonado Marrero (39/15) [71.José Antonio Torrealba Acevedo (17/4)]. Trainer: César Alejandro Farías Acosta (13).

273. 12.10.2008 **VENEZUELA - BRAZIL** **0-4(0-3)** 19th FIFA WC. Qualifiers

Estadio Polideportivo de Pueblo Nuevo, San Cristóbal; Referee: Victor Hugo Rivera (Peru); Attendance: 38,000

VEN: Renny Vicente Vega Hernández (33/0), Gerzon Armando Chacón Varela (16/0), José Manuel Rey Cortegoso (102/8), Pedro Luis Boada Noya (9/0), Jorge Alberto Rojas Méndez (87/3), Miguel Ángel Mea Vitali (81/1) [70.Franklin José Lucena Peña (9/1)], Leonel Gerardo Vielma Peña (58/4), Alejandro Abraham Guerra Morales (27/3) [61.Alejandro Enrique Moreno Riera (9/1)], Ronald Alejandro Vargas Aranguren (10/2) [55.Luis Manuel Seijas Gunther (12/0)], Juan Fernando Arango Sáenz (79/14), Giancarlo Gregorio Maldonado Marrero (40/15). Trainer: César Alejandro Farías Acosta (14).

274. 15.10.2008 **VENEZUELA - ECUADOR** **3-1(0-1)** 19th FIFA WC. Qualifiers

Estadio "General José Antonio Anzoategui", Puerto La Cruz; Referee: Enrique Marcos Osses Zencovich (Chile); Attendance: 10,581

VEN: Renny Vicente Vega Hernández (34/0), Roberto José Rosales Altuve (9/0), Gabriel Alejandro Cichero Konarek (13/1), José Manuel Rey Cortegoso (103/8), Juan José Fuenmayor Núñez (11/0), Franklin José Lucena Peña (10/1), Tomás Eduardo Rincón Hernández (12/0), Alejandro Enrique Moreno Riera (10/2) [79.Pedro Luis Boada Noya (10/0)], César Eduardo González Amais (19/1) [70.Jorge Alberto Rojas Méndez (88/3)], Juan Fernando Arango Sáenz (80/15), Giancarlo Gregorio Maldonado Marrero (41/16) [74.Daniel Enrique Arismendi Marchán (23/9)]. Trainer: César Alejandro Farías Acosta (15).

Goals: Giancarlo Gregorio Maldonado Marrero (48), Alejandro Enrique Moreno Riera (56), Juan Fernando Arango Sáenz (67).

275. 19.11.2008 **VENEZUELA - ANGOLA** **0-0**

Estadio La Carolina, Barinas; Referee: José Argote (Venezuela); Attendance: 15,000

VEN: Renny Vicente Vega Hernández (35/0), José Manuel Velázquez Rodríguez (1/0), Wilfredo José Alvarado Lima (35/2) [6.Grenddy Adrián Perozo Rincón (10/0)], Gabriel Alejandro Cíchero Konarek (14/1), Juan José Fuenmayor Núñez (12/0) [78.José Jesús Yegüez Salgado (1/0)], Tomás Eduardo Rincón Hernández (13/0), Franklin José Lucena Peña (11/1) [87.José Mauricio Parra Perdomo (1/0)], César Eduardo González Amais (20/1) [65.Pedro Alfonso Fernández Camacho (11/0)], Jorge Alberto Rojas Méndez (89/3) [61.Alejandro Abraham Guerra Morales (28/3)], Daniel Enrique Arismendi Marchán (24/9), Richard José Blanco Delgado (1/0) [70.Alexander Rondón Heredia (42/4)]. Trainer: César Alejandro Farías Acosta (16).

276. 11.02.2009 **VENEZUELA - GUATEMALA** **2-1(0-0)**

Estadio Monumental, Maturín; Referee: Giovanni Pierluzzo (Venezuela); Attendance: 10,000

VEN: Renny Vicente Vega Hernández (36/0), Gabriel Alejandro Cichero Konarek (15/1) [46.Jorge Alberto Rojas Méndez (90/3)], Franklin José Lucena Peña (12/1) [35.Francisco Javier Flores Sequera (2/0)], José Manuel Rey Cortegoso (104/8) [62.José Manuel Velázquez Rodríguez (2/0)], Juan José Fuenmayor Núñez (13/0), Roberto José Rosales Altuve (10/0) [81.Pablo Jesús Camacho Figueira (1/0)], Tomás Eduardo Rincón Hernández (14/0), César Eduardo González Amais (21/1) [46.Carlos Alfredo Salazar Cumana (1/0)], Ronald Alejandro Vargas Aranguren (11/2) [74.Rafael Eduardo Acosta Cammarota (2/0)], Giancarlo Gregorio Maldonado Marrero (42/17) [89.José Salomón Rondón Giménez (4/2)], Alejandro Enrique Moreno Riera (11/2). Trainer: César Alejandro Farías Acosta (17).

Goals: Giancarlo Gregorio Maldonado Marrero (65), José Salomón Rondón Giménez (90+2).

277. 28.03.2009 **ARGENTINA - VENEZUELA** **4-0(1-0)** 19th FIFA WC. Qualifiers

Estadio Monumental „Antonio Vespucio Liberti", Buenos Aires; Referee: Victor Hugo Rivera (Peru); Attendance: 46,085

VEN: Renny Vicente Vega Hernández (37/0), Gabriel Alejandro Cichero Konarek (16/1), Jorge Alberto Rojas Méndez (91/3) [83.Rafael Eduardo Acosta Cammarota (3/0)], José Manuel Velázquez Rodríguez (3/0), Juan José Fuenmayor Núñez (14/0), Roberto José Rosales Altuve (11/0) [50.Alejandro Enrique Moreno Riera (12/2)], Gerzon Armando Chacón Varela (17/0), Tomás Eduardo Rincón Hernández (15/0), César Eduardo González Amais (22/1), Juan Fernando Arango Sáenz (81/15), Giancarlo Gregorio Maldonado Marrero (43/17) [78.Francisco Javier Flores Sequera (3/0)]. Trainer: César Alejandro Farías Acosta (18).

278. 31.03.2009 **VENEZUELA - COLOMBIA** **2-0(0-0)** 19th FIFA WC. Qualifiers

Estadio Polideportivo Cachamay, Puerto Ordaz; Referee: Pablo Antonio Pozo Quinteros (Chile); Attendance: 35,000

VEN: Renny Vicente Vega Hernández (38/0), Franklin José Lucena Peña (13/1), Carlos Alfredo Salazar Cumana (2/0), José Manuel Velázquez Rodríguez (4/0), Juan José Fuenmayor Núñez (15/0), Roberto José Rosales Altuve (12/0), Tomás Eduardo Rincón Hernández (16/0), César Eduardo González Amais (23/1) [65.Louis Angelo Peña Puentes (2/0)], Juan Fernando Arango Sáenz (82/16) [85.Rafael Eduardo Acosta Cammarota (4/0)], Giancarlo Gregorio Maldonado Marrero (44/17) [74.Nicolás Ladislao Fedor Flores (12/3)], Alejandro Enrique Moreno Riera (13/2). Trainer: César Alejandro Farías Acosta (19).

Goals: Nicolás Ladislao Fedor Flores (78), Juan Fernando Arango Sáenz (82).

279. 13.05.2009 **VENEZUELA – COSTA RICA** **1-1(1-1)**
Estadio Polideportivo de Pueblo Nuevo, San Cristóbal; Referee: Marlon Escalante (Venezuela); Attendance: n/a
VEN: Rafael Enrique Romo Pérez (2/0) [46.José Leonardo Morales Lares (11/0)], Pedro Luis Boada Noya (11/0), Grenddy Adrián Perozo Rincón (11/0), José Manuel Velázquez Rodríguez (5/1), José Jesús Yegüez Salgado (2/0), Giácomo Di Giorgi Zerillo (7/0) [66.Rubén Darío Arocha Hernández (3/0)], Francisco Javier Flores Sequera (4/0) [81.José Mauricio Parra Perdomo (2/0)], Louis Angelo Peña Puentes (3/0), Marlon Antonio Fernández Jiménez (1/0), Juan Enrique García Rivas (48/7) [83.Carlos Enrique Fernández (3/0)], Alexander Rondón Heredia (43/4) [71.Yonathan Alexander del Valle Rodríguez (2/0)]. Trainer: César Alejandro Farías Acosta (20).
Goal: José Manuel Velázquez Rodríguez (24).

280. 06.06.2009 **BOLIVIA - VENEZUELA** **0-1(0-1)** 19th FIFA WC. Qualifiers
Estadio „Hernándo Siles Zuazo“, La Paz; Referee: Carlos Vera (Ecuador); Attendance: 23,427
VEN: Rafael Enrique Romo Pérez (3/0), Pedro Luis Boada Noya (12/0), José Manuel Velázquez Rodríguez (6/1), Grenddy Adrián Perozo Rincón (12/0), José Jesús Yegüez Salgado (3/0) [63.Carlos Alfredo Salazar Cumana (3/0)], Louis Angelo Peña Puentes (4/0) [55.Pedro Alfonso Fernández Camacho (12/0)], Francisco Javier Flores Sequera (5/0), Giácomo Di Giorgi Zerillo (8/0), Luis Manuel Seijas Gunther (13/0), Giancarlo Gregorio Maldonado Marrero (45/17), Juan Enrique García Rivas (49/7) [69.Alexander Rondón Heredia (44/4)]. Trainer: César Alejandro Farías Acosta (21).
Goal: Ronald Taylor Rivero Khun (33 own goal).

281. 10.06.2009 **VENEZUELA - URUGUAY** **2-2(1-0)** 19th FIFA WC. Qualifiers
Estadio Polideportivo Cachamay, Puerto Ordaz; Referee: Sálvio Spínola Fagundes Filho (Brazil), Attendance: 37,000
VEN: Renny Vicente Vega Hernández (39/0), Gerzon Armando Chacón Varela (18/0) [57.José Manuel Velázquez Rodríguez (7/1)], José Manuel Rey Cortegoso (105/9), Carlos Alfredo Salazar Cumana (4/0), Juan José Fuenmayor Núñez (16/0), Franklin José Lucena Peña (14/1), Tomás Eduardo Rincón Hernández (17/0), César Eduardo González Amais (24/1) [70.Louis Angelo Peña Puentes (5/0)], Juan Fernando Arango Sáenz (83/16), Giancarlo Gregorio Maldonado Marrero (46/18) [62.Nicolás Ladislao Fedor Flores (13/3)], Alejandro Enrique Moreno Riera (14/2). Trainer: César Alejandro Farías Acosta (22).
Goals: Giancarlo Gregorio Maldonado Marrero (9), José Manuel Rey Cortegoso (74).

282. 24.06.2009 **MEXICO - VENEZUELA** **4-0(1-0)**
Georgia Dome, Atlanta (United States); Referee: Terry Vaughn (United States); Attendance: 40,000
VEN: Rafael Enrique Romo Pérez (4/0), Pedro Luis Boada Noya (13/0) [65.Gerzon Armando Chacón Varela (19/0)], Carlos Alfredo Salazar Cumana (5/0), Grenddy Adrián Perozo Rincón (13/0), José Jesús Yegüez Salgado (4/0) [55.Francisco Javier Fajardo (1/0)], Tomás Eduardo Rincón Hernández (18/0), Francisco Javier Flores Sequera (6/0), Giácomo Di Giorgi Zerillo (9/0) [86.Marlon Antonio Fernández Jiménez (2/0)], Luis Manuel Seijas Gunther (14/0), Alejandro Enrique Moreno Riera (15/2) [88.Adrián José Lezama Espanol (1/0)], Giancarlo Gregorio Maldonado Marrero (47/18) [81.José Salomón Rondón Giménez (5/2)]. Trainer: César Alejandro Farías Acosta (23).

283. 27.06.2009 **COSTA RICA - VENEZUELA** **1-0(1-0)**
Estadio „Ricardo Saprissa“, San José; Referee: Ricardo Zelaya (Honduras); Attendance: n/a
VEN: Rafael Enrique Romo Pérez (5/0), Gerzon Armando Chacón Varela (20/0) [81.Francisco Javier Fajardo (2/0)], Grenddy Adrián Perozo Rincón (14/0) [44.Pedro Luis Boada Noya (14/0)], Carlos Alfredo Salazar Cumana (6/0), José Jesús Yegüez Salgado (5/0) [66.Henry Pernía (1/0)], Tomás Eduardo Rincón Hernández (19/0), Giácomo Di Giorgi Zerillo (10/0) [74.Rafael Eduardo Acosta Cammarota (5/0)], Luis Manuel Seijas Gunther (15/0) [*sent off 53*], Marlon Antonio Fernández Jiménez (3/0) [60.Francisco Javier Flores Sequera (7/0)], José Salomón Rondón Giménez (6/2) [71.Adrián José Lezama Espanol (2/0)], Yonathan Alexander del Valle Rodríguez (3/0). Trainer: César Alejandro Farías Acosta (24).

284. 12.08.2009 **COLOMBIA - VENEZUELA** **1-2(1-1)**
Giants Stadium, East Rutherford (United States); Referee: Arkadiusz Prus (United States); Attendance: n/a
VEN: Renny Vicente Vega Hernández (40/0), Gerzon Armando Chacón Varela (21/0), José Manuel Rey Cortegoso (106/10), Oswaldo Augusto Vizcarrondo Araujo (14/1), José Luis Granados Asprilla (5/0), Franklin José Lucena Peña (15/1), Giácomo Di Giorgi Zerillo (11/0), Tomás Eduardo Rincón Hernández (20/0), Luis Manuel Seijas Gunther (16/0) [83.Pedro Alfonso Fernández Camacho (13/0)], Nicolás Ladislao Fedor Flores (14/3) [70.Emilio Rentería García (2/0)], Giancarlo Gregorio Maldonado Marrero (48/18) [68.Alejandro Enrique Moreno Riera (16/2)]. Trainer: César Alejandro Farías Acosta (25).
Goals: José Manuel Rey Cortegoso (34), Oswaldo Augusto Vizcarrondo Araujo (78).

285. 05.09.2009 **CHILE - VENEZUELA** **2-2(1-2)** 19th FIFA WC. Qualifiers
Estadio Monumental „David Arellano“, Santiago; Referee: René Ortubé Betancourt (Bolivia); Attendance: 44,000
VEN: Renny Vicente Vega Hernández (41/0), Gerzon Armando Chacón Varela (22/0) [67.Pedro Luis Boada Noya (15/0)], Oswaldo Augusto Vizcarrondo Araujo (15/1), José Manuel Rey Cortegoso (107/11), José Luis Granados Asprilla (6/0), Franklin José Lucena Peña (16/1), Tomás Eduardo Rincón Hernández (21/0), Giácomo Di Giorgi Zerillo (12/0) [75.Ronald Alejandro Vargas Aranguren (12/2)], Luis Manuel Seijas Gunther (17/0) [64.Alejandro Enrique Moreno Riera (17/2)], Juan Fernando Arango Sáenz (84/16), Giancarlo Gregorio Maldonado Marrero (49/19). Trainer: César Alejandro Farías Acosta (26).
Goals: Giancarlo Gregorio Maldonado Marrero (34), José Manuel Rey Cortegoso (45+1).

286. 09.09.2009 **VENEZUELA - PERU** **3-1(1-1)** 19th FIFA WC. Qualifiers
Estadio Olímpico „Luis Ramos“, Puerto la Cruz; Referee: Carlos Vera (Ecuador); Attendance: 31,703
VEN: Renny Vicente Vega Hernández (42/0), Pedro Luis Boada Noya (16/0), Oswaldo Augusto Vizcarrondo Araujo (16/1), José Manuel Rey Cortegoso (108/11), Juan José Fuenmayor Núñez (17/0), Franklin José Lucena Peña (17/1), Luis Manuel Seijas Gunther (18/0), Ronald Alejandro Vargas Aranguren (13/3), Juan Fernando Arango Sáenz (85/16) [81.Giácomo Di Giorgi Zerillo (13/0)], Nicolás Ladislao Fedor Flores (15/5) [83.Yonathan Alexander del Valle Rodríguez (4/0)], Alejandro Enrique Moreno Riera (18/2) [77.Alexander Rondón Heredia (45/4)]. Trainer: César Alejandro Farías Acosta (27).
Goals: Nicolás Ladislao Fedor Flores (33, 52), Ronald Alejandro Vargas Aranguren (65).

287. 10.10.2009 **VENEZUELA - PARAGUAY** **1-2(0-0)** 19th FIFA WC. Qualifiers
Estadio Polideportivo Cachamay, Puerto Ordaz; Referee: Carlos Chandía Alarcón (Chile); Attendance: 41,680
VEN: Renny Vicente Vega Hernández (43/0), Pedro Luis Boada Noya (17/0), Franklin José Lucena Peña (18/1), Oswaldo Augusto Vizcarrondo Araujo (17/1), Juan José Fuenmayor Núñez (18/0), Tomás Eduardo Rincón Hernández (22/0), Luis Manuel Seijas Gunther (19/0) [67.Roberto José Rosales Altuve (13/0)], César Eduardo González Amais (25/1) [82.Alexander Rondón Heredia (46/5)], Juan Fernando Arango Sáenz (86/16), Giancarlo Gregorio Maldonado Marrero (50/19) [65.Alejandro Enrique Moreno Riera (19/2)], Nicolás Ladislao Fedor Flores (16/5). Trainer: César Alejandro Farías Acosta (28).
Goal: Alexander Rondón Heredia (85).

288. 14.10.2009 **BRAZIL - VENEZUELA** **0-0** 19th FIFA WC. Qualifiers
Estádio Morenão (Universitário Pedro Pedrossian), Campo Grande; Referee: Victor Hugo Carrillo (Peru); Attendance: 23,746
VEN: Renny Vicente Vega Hernández (44/0), Gerzon Armando Chacón Varela (23/0), José Manuel Rey Cortegoso (109/11), Oswaldo Augusto Vizcarrondo Araujo (18/1), José Luis Granados Asprilla (7/0), Giácomo Di Giorgi Zerillo (14/0), Franklin José Lucena Peña (19/1), Tomás Eduardo Rincón Hernández (23/0) [68.Luis Manuel Seijas Gunther (20/0)], Juan Fernando Arango Sáenz (87/16) [83.Nicolás Ladislao Fedor Flores (17/5)], Giancarlo Gregorio Maldonado Marrero (51/19), Alejandro Enrique Moreno Riera (20/2) [74.Alexander Rondón Heredia (47/5)]. Trainer: César Alejandro Farías Acosta (29).

289. 02.02.2010 **JAPAN - VENEZUELA** **0-0**
Kyushu Oil Dome Stadium, Oita; Referee: Fan Qi (China P.R.); Attendance: 27,009
VEN: José Leonardo Morales Lares (12/0), Giovanny Michael Romero Armenio (1/0), José Manuel Rey Cortegoso (110/11), Gabriel Alejandro Cichero Konarek (17/1), Carlos Alfredo Salazar Cumana (7/0), Franklin José Lucena Peña (20/1) [85.Grenddy Adrián Perozo Rincón (15/0)], Giácomo Di Giorgi Zerillo (15/0), Ágnel José Flores Hernández (1/0) [73.Juan José Fuenmayor Núñez (19/0)], Alejandro Abraham Guerra Morales (29/3) [81.Jesús Javier Gómez Mercado (9/1)], Alejandro Enrique Moreno Riera (21/2) [90.Edder José Farías Martínez (1/0)], Fernando Luis Aristiguieta De Luca (1/0) [68.Alexander Rondón Heredia (48/5)]. Trainer: César Alejandro Farías Acosta (30).

290. 03.03.2010 **VENEZUELA - PANAMA** **1-2(0-1)**
E Estadio Metropolitano, Barquisimeto; Referee: José Hernando Buitrago Arango (Colombia); Attendance: 37,000
VEN: Rafael Edgar Dudamel Ochoa (57/1) [44.José Leonardo Morales Lares (13/0)], Roberto José Rosales Altuve (14/0) [76.Yohandri José Orozco Cujía (1/0)], Oswaldo Augusto Vizcarrondo Araujo (19/1), Carlos Alfredo Salazar Cumana (8/0) [46.Grenddy Adrián Perozo Rincón (16/0)], Juan José Fuenmayor Núñez (20/0), Francisco Javier Flores Sequera (8/0) [56.Giácomo Di Giorgi Zerillo (16/0)], Luis Manuel Seijas Gunther (21/0) [70.Louis Angelo Peña Puentes (6/0)], César Eduardo González Amais (26/2), Tomás Eduardo Rincón Hernández (24/0), Nicolás Ladislao Fedor Flores (18/5), Alejandro Enrique Moreno Riera (22/2) [70.Yonathan Alexander del Valle Rodríguez (5/0)]. Trainer: César Alejandro Farías Acosta (31).
Goal: César Eduardo González Amais (90+6 penalty).

291. 06.03.2010 **VENEZUELA – NORTH KOREA** **2-1(1-0)**
Estadio „General José Antonio Anzoátegui“, Puerto La Cruz; Referee: José Hernando Buitrago Arango (Colombia); Attendance: 5,000
VEN: José Leonardo Morales Lares (14/0), Henry Pernía (2/0), Grenddy Adrián Perozo Rincón (17/0), Juan José Fuenmayor Núñez (21/0), José Luis Granados Asprilla (8/1), Francisco Javier Flores Sequera (9/0), Giácomo Di Giorgi Zerillo (17/0), Ágnel José Flores Hernández (2/0) [79.Mario Andrés Sánchez (1/1)], Louis Angelo Peña Puentes (7/0) [72.Yonathan Alexander del Valle Rodríguez (6/0)], Alejandro Enrique Moreno Riera (23/2) [82.Juan Enrique García Rivas (50/7)], Yohandri José Orozco Cujía (2/0) [53.Edder José Farías Martínez (2/0)]. Trainer: César Alejandro Farías Acosta (32).
Goals: José Luis Granados Asprilla (7), Mario Andrés Sánchez (89).

292. 31.03.2010 **CHILE - VENEZUELA** **0-0**
Estadio Municipal „Germán Becker“, Temuco; Referee: Roberto Carlos Silvera (Uruguay); Attendance: 18,000
VEN: José Leonardo Morales Lares (15/0), Giovanny Michael Romero Armenio (2/0), Jaime Andrés Bustamante Suárez (1/0), Henry Pernía (3/0) [66.Luiyi José Erazo Villamizar (1/0)], José Luis Granados Asprilla (9/1), Giácomo Di Giorgi Zerillo (18/0), Francisco Javier Flores Sequera (10/0) [53.Edgar Hernán Jiménez González (4/0)], Ágnel José Flores Hernández (3/0), Ángel Antonio Chourio Galíndez (2/0) [85.Mario Andrés Sánchez (2/1)], Edder José Farías Martínez (3/0) [82.Fernando Aristiguieta (2/0)], Yohandri José Orozco Cujía (3/0) [61.Richard José Blanco Delgado (2/0)]. Trainer: César Alejandro Farías Acosta (33).

293. 21.04.2010 **HONDURAS - VENEZUELA** **0-1(0-0)**
Estadio Olimpico Metropolitano, San Pedro Sula; Referee: Roberto Moreno (Panama); Attendance: 40,000
VEN: José Leonardo Morales Lares (16/0), José Luis Granados Asprilla (10/1), Henry Pernía (4/0), Luiyi José Erazo Villamizar (2/0), Julio César Machado Cesáreo (4/0) [68.Grenddy Adrián Perozo Rincón (18/0)], Giácomo Di Giorgi Zerillo (19/0) [90+3.Eliézer Álvarez (1/0)], Francisco Javier Flores Sequera (11/1), Ágnel José Flores Hernández (4/0) [80.Mario Andrés Sánchez (3/1)], Ángel Antonio Chourio Galíndez (3/0) [77.Carlos Enrique Fernández (4/0)], Edder José Farías Martínez (4/0) [72.Víctor Pérez Zabala (1/0)], Yohandri José Orozco Cujía (4/0) [60.Luis Humberto Vargas Archila (1/0)]. Trainer: César Alejandro Farías Acosta (34).
Goal: Francisco Javier Flores Sequera (52).

294. 20.05.2010 **ARUBA - VENEZUELA** **0-3(0-2)**
Complejo Deportivo „Guillermo Prospero Trinidad“, Oranjestad; Referee: Javier Eduardo Jauregui Santillan (Netherlands Antilles); Attendance: n/a
VEN: José Leonardo Morales Lares (17/0) [46.Daniel Eduardo Valdéz (1/0)], Oswaldo Augusto Vizcarrondo Araujo (20/1), Grenddy Adrián Perozo Rincón (19/0), Henry Pernía (5/0) [55.Óscar Daniel Rojas Heredia (1/0)], Francisco Javier Flores Sequera (12/1), Giácomo Di Giorgi Zerillo (20/0), Ágnel José Flores Hernández (5/0) [66.Richard José Blanco Delgado (3/0)], Yohandri José Orozco Cujía (5/0) [60.Louis Angelo Peña Puentes (8/0)], Ángel Antonio Chourio Galíndez (4/2), Edgar José Mendoza Acosta (1/0) [53.Juan Pablo Villarroel Di Parsia (1/0)], Edder José Farías Martínez (5/1). Trainer: César Alejandro Farías Acosta (35).
Goals: Ángel Antonio Chourio Galíndez (10, 31), Edder José Farías Martínez (50).

295. 29.05.2010 **VENEZUELA - CANADA** **1-1(1-0)**
Estadio Metropolitano, Mérida; Referee: José Hernando Buitrago Arango (Colombia); Attendance: 20,000
VEN: José Leonardo Morales Lares (18/0), Grenddy Adrián Perozo Rincón (20/0), Osvaldo Augusto Vizcarrondo Araujo (21/1), Juan José Fuenmayor Núñez (22/0), Tomás Eduardo Rincón Hernández (25/0) [82.Henry Pernía (6/0)], Giácomo Di Giorgi Zerillo (21/0), Francisco Javier Flores Sequera (13/1), Ágnel José Flores Hernández (6/0) [56.Louis Angelo Peña Puentes (9/0)], Yohandry José Orozco Cujía (6/0) [75.Edder José Farías Martínez (6/1)], Ángel Antonio Chourio Galíndez (5/3) [86.Richard José Blanco Delgado (4/0)], Nicolás Ladislao Fedor Flores (19/5) [90+2.Gelmin Javier Rivas Boada (1/0)]. Trainer: César Alejandro Farías Acosta (36).
Goal: Ángel Antonio Chourio Galíndez (44).

296. 11.08.2010 **PANAMA - VENEZUELA** **3-1(0-0)**
Estadio „Rommel Fernández“, Ciudad de Panamá; Referee: William Castro Quesada (Costa Rica); Attendance: 2,000
VEN: José Leonardo Morales Lares (19/0), Jaime Andrés Bustamante Suárez (2/0), Franklin José Lucena Peña (21/1), Osvaldo Augusto Vizcarrondo Araujo (22/2), Roberto José Rosales Altuve (15/0) [75.Pablo Jesús Camacho Figueira (2/0)], José Luis Granados Asprilla (11/1), Tomás Eduardo Rincón Hernández (26/0) [72.Francisco Javier Flores Sequera (14/1)], Juan Fernando Arango Sáenz (88/16), Ángel Antonio Chourio Galíndez (6/3) [69.Yohandry José Orozco Cujía (7/0)], Nicolás Ladislao Fedor Flores (20/5) [69.Alejandro Enrique Moreno Riera (24/2)], Giancarlo Gregorio Maldonado Marrero (52/19) [69.José Salomón Rondón Giménez (7/2)]. Trainer: César Alejandro Farías Acosta (37).
Goal: Osvaldo Augusto Vizcarrondo Araujo (70).

297. 03.09.2010 **VENEZUELA - COLOMBIA** **0-2(0-0)**
Estadio „José Antonio Anzoategui“, Puerto La Cruz; Referee: Roberto Moreno (Panama); Attendance: 30,000
VEN: Renny Vicente Vega Hernández (45/0), Franklin José Lucena Peña (22/1), Osvaldo Augusto Vizcarrondo Araujo (23/2), Roberto José Rosales Altuve (16/0), José Luis Granados Asprilla (12/1) [79.Juan José Fuenmayor Núñez (23/0)], Tomás Eduardo Rincón Hernández (27/0), Alejandro Abraham Guerra Morales (30/3) [59.Luis Manuel Seijas Gunther (22/0)], Juan Fernando Arango Sáenz (89/16), Ángel Antonio Chourio Galíndez (7/3) [83.Giácomo Di Giorgi Zerillo (22/0)], Ronald Alejandro Vargas Aranguren (14/3) [59.César Eduardo González Amais (27/2)], José Salomón Rondón Giménez (8/2) [68.Emilio Rentería García (3/0)]. Trainer: César Alejandro Farías Acosta (38).

298. 07.09.2010 **VENEZUELA - ECUADOR** **1-0(0-0)**
Estadio Metropolitano, Barquisimeto; Referee: Juan Torres (Panama); Attendance: 37,262
VEN: Daniel Hernández Santos (1/0), Jaime Andrés Bustamante Suárez (3/0), Franklin José Lucena Peña (23/1), Grenddy Adrián Perozo Rincón (21/0), José Luis Granados Asprilla (13/1), Tomás Eduardo Rincón Hernández (28/0), Luis Manuel Seijas Gunther (23/0) [78.Alejandro Abraham Guerra Morales (31/3)], César Eduardo González Amais (28/2) [85.Roberto José Rosales Altuve (17/0)], Ángel Antonio Chourio Galíndez (8/3) [73.Giácomo Di Giorgi Zerillo (23/0)], Nicolás Ladislao Fedor Flores (21/6) [90.Francisco Javier Flores Sequera (15/1)], Emilio Rentería García (4/0) [66.José Salomón Rondón Giménez (9/2)]. Trainer: César Alejandro Farías Acosta (39).
Goal: Nicolás Ladislao Fedor Flores (86).

299. 07.10.2010 **BOLIVIA - VENEZUELA** **1-3(0-3)**
Estadio „Ramón 'Tahuichi' Aguilera", Santa Cruz de la Sierra; Referee: Ibrahim Chaibou (Niger); Attendance: 18,000
VEN: Manuel Alejandro Sanhouse Contreras (15/0), Jaime Andrés Bustamante Suárez (4/0), Gabriel Alejandro Cichero Konarek (18/1), Grenddy Adrián Perozo Rincón (22/0), Osvaldo Augusto Vizcarrondo Araujo (24/3), Tomás Eduardo Rincón Hernández (29/0), Luis Manuel Seijas Gunther (24/0) [73.Jesús Javier Gómez Mercado (10/1)], César Eduardo González Amais (29/2) [64.Roberto José Rosales Altuve (18/0)], Juan Fernando Arango Sáenz (90/16) [86.Francisco Javier Flores Sequera (16/1)], Ángel Antonio Chourio Galíndez (9/5) [80.Emilio Rentería García (5/0)], Alejandro Enrique Moreno Riera (25/2) [70.Richard José Blanco Delgado (5/0)]. Trainer: César Alejandro Farías Acosta (40).
Goals: Ángel Antonio Chourio Galíndez (9), Osvaldo Augusto Vizcarrondo Araujo (28), Ángel Antonio Chourio Galíndez (36).

300. 12.10.2010 **MEXICO - VENEZUELA** **2-2(1-2)**
Estadio Olímpico „Benito Juárez", Ciudad Juárez; Referee: Joel Antonio Aguilar Chicas (El Salvador); Attendance: 20,000
VEN: Daniel Hernández Santos (2/0), Giovanny Michael Romero Armenio (3/0), Osvaldo Augusto Vizcarrondo Araujo (25/3), Grenddy Adrián Perozo Rincón (23/0), Gabriel Alejandro Cichero Konarek (19/1) [*sent off 24*], Juan Fernando Arango Sáenz (91/18), Franklin José Lucena Peña (24/1), Luis Manuel Seijas Gunther (25/0) [27.José Luis Granados Asprilla (14/1)], César Eduardo González Amais (30/2) [71.Roberto José Rosales Altuve (19/0)], Ángel Antonio Chourio Galíndez (10/5) [88.Jaime Andrés Bustamante Suárez (5/0)], Alejandro Enrique Moreno Riera (26/2) [67.Emilio Rentería García (6/0)]. Trainer: César Alejandro Farías Acosta (41).
Goals: Juan Fernando Arango Sáenz (6, 40).

301. 17.11.2010 **ECUADOR - VENEZUELA** **4-1(3-1)**
Estadio Olimpico "Atahualpa", Quito; Referee: Ibrahim Chaibou (Niger); Attendance: 9,000
VEN: Manuel Alejandro Sanhouse Contreras (16/0), Jaime Andrés Bustamante Suárez (6/0), Franklin José Lucena Peña (25/1), Grenddy Adrián Perozo Rincón (24/0), Giovanny Michael Romero Armenio (4/0), José Luis Granados Asprilla (15/1) [78.Juan José Fuenmayor Núñez (24/0)], Alejandro Abraham Guerra Morales (32/3) [67.Jesús Javier Gómez Mercado (11/1)], Luis Manuel Seijas Gunther (26/0) [86.Edgar Fernando Pérez Greco (4/0)], César Eduardo González Amais (31/2) [60.Giácomo Di Giorgi Zerillo (24/0)], Giancarlo Gregorio Maldonado Marrero (53/20), Alejandro Enrique Moreno Riera (27/2) [70.Daniel Enrique Arismendi Marchán (25/9)]. Trainer: César Alejandro Farías Acosta (42).
Goal: Giancarlo Gregorio Maldonado Marrero (48 penalty).

302. 09.02.2011 **VENEZUELA – COSTA RICA** **2-2(1-1)**
Estadio „José Antonio Anzoategui", Puerto La Cruz; Referee: Henry Gambetta Ávalos (Peru); Attendance: 15,000
VEN: Daniel Hernández Santos (3/0), Roberto José Rosales Altuve (20/0) [90.Ángel Antonio Chourio Galíndez (11/5)], Osvaldo Augusto Vizcarrondo Araujo (26/3), Grenddy Adrián Perozo Rincón (25/0), Gabriel Alejandro Cichero Konarek (20/1), Tomás Eduardo Rincón Hernández (30/0), Luis Manuel Seijas Gunther (27/0) [67.Alejandro Abraham Guerra Morales (33/3)], Juan Fernando Arango Sáenz (92/19), César Eduardo González Amais (32/2) [71.Evelio de Jesús Hernández Guedez (13/0)], José Salomón Rondón Giménez (10/4), Nicolás Ladislao Fedor Flores (22/6) [71.Daniel Enrique Arismendi Marchán (26/9)]. Trainer: César Alejandro Farías Acosta (43).
Goals: José Salomón Rondón Giménez (24, 80).

303. 16.03.2011 **ARGENTINA - VENEZUELA** **4-1(2-1)**
Estadio del Bicentenario, San Juan; Referee: Claudio Alfredo Puga Briones (Chile); Attendance: 25,000
VEN: José Leonardo Morales Lares (20/0), Giovanny Michael Romero Armenio (5/0) [46.Alexander David González Sibulo (1/0)], Carlos Alfredo Salazar Cumana (9/0) [56.Giácomo Di Giorgi Zerillo (25/0)], Osvaldo Augusto Vizcarrondo Araujo (27/3), Gabriel Alejandro Cichero Konarek (21/1), Edgar Hernán Jiménez González (5/0) [73.Evelio de Jesús Hernández Guedez (14/0)], Luis Manuel Seijas Gunther (28/0), Franklin José Lucena Peña (26/1), Louis Angelo Peña Puentes (10/0) [59.José Miguel Reyes (1/0)], César Eduardo González Amais (33/2) [59.Jesús Javier Gómez Mercado (12/1)], Daniel Enrique Arismendi Marchán (27/10) [66.Ángel Antonio Chourio Galíndez (12/5)]. Trainer: César Alejandro Farías Acosta (44).
Goal: Daniel Enrique Arismendi Marchán (29).

304. 25.03.2011 **JAMAICA - VENEZUELA** **0-2(0-0)**
Catherine Hall Sports Complex, Montego Bay; Referee: Enrico Wijngaarde (Suriname); Attendance: 8,000
VEN: José Leonardo Morales Lares (21/0), Roberto José Rosales Altuve (21/0) [90.Franklin José Lucena Peña (27/1)], Osvaldo Augusto Vizcarrondo Araujo (28/3), Grenddy Adrián Perozo Rincón (26/0), Gabriel Alejandro Cichero Konarek (22/1) [90+2.Juan José Fuenmayor Núñez (25/0)], Giácomo Di Giorgi Zerillo (26/0), Tomás Eduardo Rincón Hernández (31/0), Luis Manuel Seijas Gunther (29/0) [60.Yohandry José Orozco Cujía (8/0)], Ángel Antonio Chourio Galíndez (13/5) [84.Jesús Javier Gómez Mercado (13/1)], Alejandro Enrique Moreno Riera (28/3) [78.Mário Júnior Rondón Fernández (1/0)], Nicolás Ladislao Fedor Flores (23/7) [81.Daniel Enrique Arismendi Marchán (28/10)]. Trainer: César Alejandro Farías Acosta (45).
Goals: Nicolás Ladislao Fedor Flores (64), Alejandro Enrique Moreno Riera (67).

305. 29.03.2011 **MEXICO - VENEZUELA** **1-1(0-0)**
Qualcomm Stadium, San Diego (United States); Referee: Ricardo Salazar (United States); Attendance: n/a
VEN: José Leonardo Morales Lares (22/0), Roberto José Rosales Altuve (22/0) [80.Franklin José Lucena Peña (28/1)], Osvaldo Augusto Vizcarrondo Araujo (29/4), Grenddy Adrián Perozo Rincón (27/0), Gabriel Alejandro Cichero Konarek (23/1), Giácomo Di Giorgi Zerillo (27/0), Tomás Eduardo Rincón Hernández (32/0), Luis Manuel Seijas Gunther (30/0) [66.Yohandry José Orozco Cujía (9/0)], Ángel Antonio Chourio Galíndez (14/5) [61.Jesús Javier Gómez Mercado (14/1)], Nicolás Ladislao Fedor Flores (24/7) [85.Evelio de Jesús Hernández Guedez (15/0)], Alejandro Enrique Moreno Riera (29/3) [78.Daniel Enrique Arismendi Marchán (29/10)]. Trainer: César Alejandro Farías Acosta (46).
Goal: Osvaldo Augusto Vizcarrondo Araujo (73).

306. 01.06.2011 **GUATEMALA - VENEZUELA** **0-2(0-1)**
Estadio „Mateo Flores", Ciudad de Guatemala; Referee: César Ruano (Guatemala); Attendance: n/a
VEN: Renny Vicente Vega Hernández (46/0), Gabriel Alejandro Cichero Konarek (24/1), Franklin José Lucena Peña (29/1), Grenddy Adrián Perozo Rincón (28/1), Roberto José Rosales Altuve (23/0), Tomás Eduardo Rincón Hernández (33/0) [90.Francisco Javier Flores Sequera (17/1)], Luis Manuel Seijas Gunther (31/0) [77.Edgar Hernán Jiménez González (6/0)], César Eduardo González Amais (34/2) [71.Jesús Manuel Meza Moreno (4/0)], Yohandry José Orozco Cujía (10/0) [78.Alexander David González Sibulo (2/0)], Giancarlo Gregorio Maldonado Marrero (54/20) [86.Louis Angelo Peña Puentes (11/0)], Nicolás Ladislao Fedor Flores (25/8) [66.Alejandro Enrique Moreno Riera (30/3)]. Trainer: César Alejandro Farías Acosta (47).
Goals: Nicolás Ladislao Fedor Flores (26), Grenddy Adrián Perozo Rincón (67).

307. 07.06.2011 **VENEZUELA - SPAIN** **0-3(0-3)**
Estadio „José Antonio Anzoategui“, Puerto La Cruz; Referee: Georges Buckley de Martens (Peru); Attendance: 36,000
VEN: Renny Vicente Vega Hernández (47/0), Roberto José Rosales Altuve (24/0) [89.Alexander David González Sibulo (3/0)], Franklin José Lucena Peña (30/1), Grenddy Adrián Perozo Rincón (29/1), Gabriel Alejandro Cichero Konarek (25/1), Luis Manuel Seijas Gunther (32/0) [46.Giácomo Di Giorgi Zerillo (28/0)], Tomás Eduardo Rincón Hernández (34/0), César Eduardo González Amais (35/2) [62.Jesús Manuel Meza Moreno (5/0)], Yohandry José Orozco Cujía (11/0) [46.Juan Fernando Arango Sáenz (93/18)], Giancarlo Gregorio Maldonado Marrero (55/20) [46.Nicolás Ladislao Fedor Flores (26/8)], Alejandro Enrique Moreno Riera (31/3) [70.Alejandro Abraham Guerra Morales (34/3)]. Trainer: César Alejandro Farías Acosta (48).

308. 11.06.2011 **MEXICO „B“ - VENEZUELA** **0-3(0-1)**
„Sam Boyd“ Stadium, Las Vegas (United States); Referee: Alejandro Mariscal (United States); Attendance:
VEN: Daniel Hernández Santos (4/0), José Manuel Rey Cortegoso (111/11), Oswaldo Augusto Vizcarrondo Araujo (30/5), Juan José Fuenmayor Núñez (26/0) [*sent off 32*], Alexander David González Sibulo (4/0) [64.William Díaz Gutiérrez (1/0)], Giácomo Di Giorgi Zerillo (29/0) [46.José Luis Granados Asprilla (16/1)], Alejandro Abraham Guerra Morales (35/4) [57.Jesús Manuel Meza Moreno (30/11)], Edgar Hernán Jiménez González (7/0), Juan Fernando Arango Sáenz (94/18) [46.Francisco Javier Flores Sequera (18/1)], Daniel Enrique Arismendi Marchán (1/0) [68.Ángel Antonio Chourio Galíndez (15/5)], Nicolás Ladislao Fedor Flores (27/8) [80.Louis Angelo Peña Puentes (12/0)]. Trainer: César Alejandro Farías Acosta (49).
Goals: Alejandro Abraham Guerra Morales (13), Daniel Enrique Arismendi Marchán (65), Oswaldo Augusto Vizcarrondo Araujo (90+2).

309. 03.07.2011 **BRAZIL - VENEZUELA** **0-0** 43rd Copa América. Group Stage
Estadio Ciudad de La Plata, La Plata (Argentina); Referee: Raúl Orosco Delgadillo (Bolivia); Attendance: 40,000
VEN: Renny Vicente Vega Hernández (48/0), Roberto José Rosales Altuve (25/0), Oswaldo Augusto Vizcarrondo Araujo (31/5), Grenddy Adrián Perozo Rincón (30/1), Gabriel Alejandro Cichero Konarek (26/1), César Eduardo González Amais (36/2) [86.Giácomo Di Giorgi Zerillo (30/0)], Franklin José Lucena Peña (31/1), Tomás Eduardo Rincón Hernández (35/0), Juan Fernando Arango Sáenz (95/18), José Salomón Rondón Giménez (11/4) [63.Alejandro Enrique Moreno Riera (32/3)], Nicolás Ladislao Fedor Flores (28/8) [77.Giancarlo Gregorio Maldonado Marrero (56/20)]. Trainer: César Alejandro Farías Acosta (50).

310. 09.07.2011 **VENEZUELA - ECUADOR** **1-0(0-0)** 43rd Copa América. Group Stage
Estadio "Padre Ernesto Martearena", Salta (Argentina); Referee: Wálter Enrique Quesada Cordero (Costa Rica); Attendance: n/a
VEN: Renny Vicente Vega Hernández (49/0), Roberto José Rosales Altuve (26/0), Oswaldo Augusto Vizcarrondo Araujo (32/5), Grenddy Adrián Perozo Rincón (31/1), Gabriel Alejandro Cichero Konarek (27/1), César Eduardo González Amais (37/3) [65.Jesús Manuel Meza Moreno (7/0)], Franklin José Lucena Peña (32/1), Tomás Eduardo Rincón Hernández (36/0), Juan Fernando Arango Sáenz (96/18), Giancarlo Gregorio Maldonado Marrero (57/20) [81.Giácomo Di Giorgi Zerillo (31/0)], Nicolás Ladislao Fedor Flores (29/8) [75.José Salomón Rondón Giménez (12/4)]. Trainer: César Alejandro Farías Acosta (51).
Goal: César Eduardo González Amais (61).

311. 13.07.2011 **PARAGUAY - VENEZUELA** **3-3(1-1)** 43rd Copa América. Group Stage
Estadio „Padre Ernesto Martearena“, Salta (Argentina); Referee: Enrique Roberto Osses Zencovich (Chile); Attendance: n/a
VEN: Renny Vicente Vega Hernández (50/0), Roberto José Rosales Altuve (27/0), Grenddy Adrián Perozo Rincón (32/2), Oswaldo Augusto Vizcarrondo Araujo (33/5), Gabriel Alejandro Cichero Konarek (28/1), Giácomo Di Giorgi Zerillo (32/0), Alexander David González Sibulo (5/0) [76.Giancarlo Gregorio Maldonado Marrero (58/20)], Tomás Eduardo Rincón Hernández (37/0), Yohandry José Orozco Cujía (12/0) [67.Nicolás Ladislao Fedor Flores (30/9)], Daniel Enrique Arismendi Marchán (31/11) [64.Juan Fernando Arango Sáenz (97/18)], José Salomón Rondón Giménez (13/5). Trainer: César Alejandro Farías Acosta (52).
Goals: José Salomón Rondón Giménez (5), Nicolás Ladislao Fedor Flores (90), Grenddy Adrián Perozo Rincón (90+3).

312. 17.07.2011 **CHILE - VENEZUELA** **1-2(0-1)** 43rd Copa América. Quarter-Finals
Estadio del Bicentenario, San Juan (Argentina); Referee: Carlos Alfredo Vera Rodríguez (Ecuador); Attendance: n/a
VEN: Renny Vicente Vega Hernández (51/0), Roberto José Rosales Altuve (28/0), Grenddy Adrián Perozo Rincón (33/2), Oswaldo Augusto Vizcarrondo Araujo (34/6), Gabriel Alejandro Cichero Konarek (29/2), Tomás Eduardo Rincón Hernández (38/0) [*sent off 90+4*], Franklin José Lucena Peña (33/1), César Eduardo González Amais (38/3) [89.Alejandro Enrique Moreno Riera (33/3)], Juan Fernando Arango Sáenz (98/18), Giancarlo Gregorio Maldonado Marrero (59/20) [63.Luis Manuel Seijas Gunther (33/0)], Nicolás Ladislao Fedor Flores (31/9) [59.José Salomón Rondón Giménez (14/5)]. Trainer: César Alejandro Farías Acosta (53).
Goals: Oswaldo Augusto Vizcarrondo Araujo (34), Gabriel Alejandro Cichero Konarek (80).

313. 20.07.2011 **PARAGUAY - VENEZUELA** **0-0; 5-3 on penalties** 43rd Copa América. Semi-Finals
Estadio Malvinas Argentinas, Mendoza (Argentina); Referee: Francisco Chacón Gutiérrez (Mexico); Attendance: n/a
VEN: Renny Vicente Vega Hernández (52/0), Grenddy Adrián Perozo Rincón (34/2) [46.José Manuel Rey Cortegoso (112/11)], Giácomo Di Giorgi Zerillo (33/0), Oswaldo Augusto Vizcarrondo Araujo (35/6), Gabriel Alejandro Cichero Konarek (30/2), Franklin José Lucena Peña (34/1), Roberto José Rosales Altuve (29/0), César Eduardo González Amais (39/3) [84.Giancarlo Gregorio Maldonado Marrero (60/20)], Juan Fernando Arango Sáenz (99/18), José Salomón Rondón Giménez (15/5), Alejandro Enrique Moreno Riera (34/3) [72.Nicolás Ladislao Fedor Flores (32/9)]. Trainer: César Alejandro Farías Acosta (54).
Penalties: Giancarlo Gregorio Maldonado Marrero, José Manuel Rey Cortegoso, Franklin José Lucena Peña (miss), Nicolás Ladislao Fedor Flores.

314. 23.07.2011 **PERU - VENEZUELA** **4-1(1-0)** 43rd Copa América. 3rd Place Play-off
Estadio Ciudad de La Plata, La Plata (Argentina); Referee: Wilmar Alexander Roldán Pérez (Colombia); Attendance: n/a
VEN: Renny Vicente Vega Hernández (53/0), Gabriel Alejandro Cichero Konarek (31/2), José Manuel Rey Cortegoso (113/11), Oswaldo Augusto Vizcarrondo Araujo (36/6), Roberto José Rosales Altuve (30/0), Tomás Eduardo Rincón Hernández (39/0) [*sent off 58*], Luis Manuel Seijas Gunther (34/0) [46.Franklin José Lucena Peña (35/1)], César Eduardo González Amais (40/3) [67.Juan Fernando Arango Sáenz (**100**/19)], Yohandry José Orozco Cujía (13/0), Giancarlo Gregorio Maldonado Marrero (61/20), Nicolás Ladislao Fedor Flores (33/9) [61.José Salomón Rondón Giménez (16/5)]. Trainer: César Alejandro Farías Acosta (55).
Goal: Juan Fernando Arango Sáenz (79).

315. 07.08.2011 **EL SALVADOR - VENEZUELA** **2-1(0-1)**
„Robert F. Kennedy Memorial“ Stadium, Washington (United States); Referee: Baldomero Toledo (United States); Attendance: 15,000
VEN: Rafael Enrique Romo Pérez (6/0), William Díaz Gutiérrez (2/0), Andrés Elionay Sánchez León (1/0), Alexander David González Sibulo (6/0), José Luis Granados Asprilla (17/1), Ágnel José Flores Hernández (7/0), Juan Francisco Guerra (1/0), Jesús Alberto Lugo Limpio (1/0) [63.José Mauricio Parra Perdomo (3/0)], Ángel Antonio Chourio Galíndez (16/5), Fernando Luis Aristeguieta de Luca (1/1) [82.Manuel Alejandro Arteaga Rubianes (1/0)], Yonathan Alexander del Valle Rodríguez (7/0) [76.Josef Alexander Martínez (1/0)]. Trainer: César Alejandro Farías Acosta (56).
Goal: Fernando Luis Aristeguieta de Luca (29).

316. 10.08.2011 **HONDURAS - VENEZUELA** **2-0(0-0)**

Lockhart Stadium, Fort Lauderdale (United States); Referee: Terry Vaughn (United States); Attendance: 20,000

VEN: Rafael Enrique Romo Pérez (7/0), William Díaz Gutiérrez (3/0), Andrés Elionay Sánchez León (2/0), Alexander David González Sibulo (7/0) [79.Rohel Antonio Briceño Carpio (1/0)], José Luis Granados Asprilla (18/1), Ágnel José Flores Hernández (8/0), Juan Francisco Guerra (2/0) [87.Víctor Hugo García Hernández (1/0)], Ángel Antonio Chourio Galíndez (17/5) [65.Arquímedes José Figuera Salazar (1/0)], Fernando Luis Aristeguieta de Luca (2/1), Yonathan Alexander del Valle Rodríguez (8/0) [72.Jesús Alberto Lugo Limpio (2/0)], Giancarlo Gregorio Maldonado Marrero (62/20) [79.Josef Alexander Martínez (2/0)]. Trainer: César Alejandro Farías Acosta (57).

317. 02.09.2011 **VENEZUELA - ARGENTINA** **0-1(0-0)**

Yuba Bharati Krirangan (Salt Lake Stadium), Calcutta (India); Referee: Arumughan Rowan (India); Attendance: 90,000

VEN: Rafael Enrique Romo Pérez (8/0), Fernando Gabriel Amorebieta Mardaras (1/0) [46.Andrés José Túñez Arceo (1/0)], Gabriel Alejandro Cichero Konarek (32/2), Oswaldo Augusto Vizcarrondo Araujo (37/6), Roberto José Rosales Altuve (31/0), Tomás Eduardo Rincón Hernández (40/0), Ágnel José Flores Hernández (9/0), César Eduardo González Amais (41/3) [89.Josmar Zambrano Suárez (1/0)], Frank Feltscher Martínez (1/0) [77.Yohandry José Orozco Cujía (14/0)], Nicolás Ladislao Fedor Flores (34/9), José Salomón Rondón Giménez (17/5). Trainer: César Alejandro Farías Acosta (58).

318. 06.09.2011 **VENEZUELA - GUINEA** **2-1(2-0)**

Estadio Olímpico „Ciudad Universitaria", Caracas; Referee: Henry Gambetta Ávalos (Peru); Attendance: 20,000

VEN: José Leonardo Morales Lares (23/0), Franklin José Lucena Peña (36/1), José Manuel Rey Cortegoso (114/11), Andrés José Túñez Arceo (2/0), Alexander David González Sibulo (8/0), José Luis Granados Asprilla (19/1), Giácomo Di Giorgi Zerillo (34/0) [84.Ágnel José Flores Hernández (10/0)], Yohandry José Orozco Cujía (15/0) [77.Raúl González Guzmán (1/0)], Ángel Antonio Chourio Galíndez (18/5) [88.Josmar Zambrano Suárez (2/0)], Giancarlo Gregorio Maldonado Marrero (63/22) [77.Frank Feltscher Martínez (2/0)], Alejandro Enrique Moreno Riera (35/3) [67.Fernando Luis Aristeguieta de Luca (3/1)]. Trainer: César Alejandro Farías Acosta (59).

Goals: Giancarlo Gregorio Maldonado Marrero (25 penalty, 39 penaty).

319. 07.10.2011 **ECUADOR - VENEZUELA** **2-0(2-0)** 20th FIFA WC. Qualifiers

Estadio Olimpico "Atahualpa", Quito; Referee: Enrique Roberto Osses Zencovich (Chile); Attendance: 32,278

VEN: Renny Vicente Vega Hernández (54/0), Franklin José Lucena Peña (37/1), José Manuel Rey Cortegoso (115/11) [*sent off 78*], José Manuel Velázquez Rodríguez (8/1), José Luis Granados Asprilla (20/1), Giácomo Di Giorgi Zerillo (35/0), Francisco Javier Flores Sequera (19/1) [58.Ágnel José Flores Hernández (11/0)], Luis Manuel Seijas Gunther (35/0), Jesús Manuel Meza Moreno (8/0), Fernando Luis Aristeguieta de Luca (4/1) [46.Alejandro Enrique Moreno Riera (36/3)], Giancarlo Gregorio Maldonado Marrero (64/22) [72.Frank Feltscher Martínez (3/0)]. Trainer: César Alejandro Farías Acosta (60).

320. 11.10.2011 **VENEZUELA - ARGENTINA** **1-0(0-0)** 20th FIFA WC. Qualifiers

Estadio „José Antonio Anzoátegui", Puerto La Cruz; Referee: Roberto Carlos Silvera Calcerrada (Uruguay); Attendance: 35,600

VEN: Renny Vicente Vega Hernández (55/0), Fernando Gabriel Amorebieta Mardaras (2/1), Gabriel Alejandro Cichero Konarek (33/2), Franklin José Lucena Peña (38/1), Oswaldo Augusto Vizcarrondo Araujo (38/6), Roberto José Rosales Altuve (32/0), Tomás Eduardo Rincón Hernández (41/0), Juan Fernando Arango Sáenz (101/19), César Eduardo González Amais (42/3) [83.Julio Álvarez Mosquera (1/0)], Nicolás Ladislao Fedor Flores (35/9) [89.Alejandro Enrique Moreno Riera (37/3)], José Salomón Rondón Giménez (18/5) [76.Frank Feltscher Martínez (4/0)]. Trainer: César Alejandro Farías Acosta (61).

Goal: Fernando Gabriel Amorebieta Mardaras (61).

321. 11.11.2011 **COLOMBIA - VENEZUELA** **1-1(1-0)** 20th FIFA WC. Qualifiers

Estadio Metropolitano "Roberto Meléndez", Barranquilla; Referee: Omar Andrés Ponce Manzo (Ecuador); Attendance: 49,612

VEN: Renny Vicente Vega Hernández (56/0), Fernando Gabriel Amorebieta Mardaras (3/1), Gabriel Alejandro Cichero Konarek (34/2), Oswaldo Augusto Vizcarrondo Araujo (39/6), Roberto José Rosales Altuve (33/0), Tomás Eduardo Rincón Hernández (42/0) [64.Juan Francisco Guerra (3/0)], Ágnel José Flores Hernández (12/0), Juan Fernando Arango Sáenz (102/19), César Eduardo González Amais (43/3), Nicolás Ladislao Fedor Flores (36/9) [58.José Salomón Rondón Giménez (19/5)], Alejandro Enrique Moreno Riera (38/3) [71.Frank Feltscher Martínez (5/1)]. Trainer: César Alejandro Farías Acosta (62).

Goal: Frank Feltscher Martínez (79).

322. 15.11.2011 **VENEZUELA - BOLIVIA** **1-0(1-0)** 20th FIFA WC. Qualifiers

Estadio Pueblo Nuevo, San Cristóbal; Referee: Georges Buckley De Maritens (Peru); Attendance: 33,351

VEN: Renny Vicente Vega Hernández (57/0), Fernando Gabriel Amorebieta Mardaras (4/1), Gabriel Alejandro Cichero Konarek (35/2), Oswaldo Augusto Vizcarrondo Araujo (40/7), Roberto José Rosales Altuve (34/0), Tomás Eduardo Rincón Hernández (43/0), Julio Álvarez Mosquera (2/0) [71.Franklin José Lucena Peña (39/1)], Juan Fernando Arango Sáenz (103/19), César Eduardo González Amais (44/3) [64.Frank Feltscher Martínez (6/1)], Giancarlo Gregorio Maldonado Marrero (65/22) [77.Rolf Günther Feltscher Martínez (1/0)], José Salomón Rondón Giménez (20/5). Trainer: César Alejandro Farías Acosta (63).

Goal: Oswaldo Augusto Vizcarrondo Araujo (24).

323. 22.12.2011 **VENEZUELA – COSTA RICA** **0-2(0-1)**

Estadio Metropolitano de Lara, Barquisimeto; Referee: Rudolph Angela (Aruba); Attendance: 35,000

VEN: Alan José Liebeskind Díaz (1/0), Gabriel Alejandro Cichero Konarek (36/2) [79.Enrique Andrés Rouga Rossi (22/0)], Grenddy Adrián Perozo Rincón (35/2), José Manuel Velázquez Rodríguez (9/1), Alexander David González Sibulo (9/0) [43.Carlos Gregorio Rivero González (1/0)], Francisco Javier Flores Sequera (20/1) [58.Ángel Antonio Chourio Galíndez (19/5)], Miguel Ángel Mea Vitali (82/1), Louis Angelo Peña Puentes (13/0) [58.Hermes Manuel Palomino Fariñes (1/0)], Edgar Fernando Pérez Greco (5/0), Emilio Rentería García (7/0) [73.Josef Alexander Martínez (3/0)], Darwin Machís (1/0) [59.Juan Francisco Guerra (4/0)]. Trainer: César Alejandro Farías Acosta (64).

324. 21.01.2012 **UNITED STATES - VENEZUELA** **1-0(0-0)**

University of Phoenix Stadium, Glendale; Referee: Roberto Gracía Orozco (Mexico); Attendance: 22,403

VEN: José Leonardo Morales Lares (24/0), Carlos Gregorio Rivero González (2/0), Enrique Andrés Rouga Rossi (23/0), Carlos Alfredo Salazar Cumana (10/0), José Manuel Velázquez Rodríguez (10/1) [*sent off 90+8*], Francisco Javier Flores Sequera (21/1), Ágnel José Flores Hernández (13/0), Alejandro Abraham Guerra Morales (36/4) [89.Diego Alejandro Guerrero Corredor (1/0)], Miguel Ángel Mea Vitali (83/1) [78.Emilio Rentería García (8/0)], Edgar Fernando Pérez Greco (6/0) [73.Ángel Antonio Chourio Galíndez (20/5)], Alejandro Enrique Moreno Riera (39/3) [86.Richard José Blanco Delgado (6/0)]. Trainer: César Alejandro Farías Acosta (65).

325. 25.01.2012 **MEXICO - VENEZUELA** **3-1(0-0)**

Reliant Stadium, Houston (United States); Referee: Edwin Jurisevic (United States); Attendance: 40,128

VEN: José Leonardo Morales Lares (25/0), José Manuel Velázquez Rodríguez (11/1), Carlos Alfredo Salazar Cumana (11/0), Rubert José Quijada Fasciana (1/0), Carlos Gregorio Rivero González (3/0), Francisco Javier Flores Sequera (22/1) [87.Rubén Darío Arocha Hernández (4/0)], Miguel Ángel Mea Vitali (84/1), Edgar Fernando Pérez Greco (7/1), José Miguel Reyes (2/0) [83.Ágnel José Flores Hernández (14/0)], Alejandro Abraham Guerra Morales (37/4), Darwin Machís (2/0) [75.Alejandro Enrique Moreno Riera (40/3)]. Trainer: César Alejandro Farías Acosta (66).

Goal: Edgar Fernando Pérez Greco (51).

326. 29.02.2012 **SPAIN - VENEZUELA** **5-0(2-0)**
Estadio La Rosaleda, Málaga; Referee: Andris Treimanis (Latvia); Attendance: 28,963
VEN: Daniel Hernández Santos (5/0), Roberto José Rosales Altuve (35/0), Oswaldo Augusto Vizcarrondo Araujo (41/7), Fernando Gabriel Amorebieta Mardaras (5/1) [*sent off 64*], Rubert José Quijada Fasciana (2/0) [71.Rolf Günther Feltscher Martínez (2/0)], Miguel Ángel Mea Vitali (85/1) [81.Francisco Javier Flores Sequera (23/1)], Tomás Eduardo Rincón Hernández (44/0), Julio Álvarez Mosquera (3/0) [59.César Eduardo González Amais (45/3)], Juan Fernando Arango Sáenz (104/19) [89.Edgar Fernando Pérez Greco (8/1)], Nicolás Ladislao Fedor Flores (37/9) [66.Andrés José Túñez Arceo (3/0)], José Salomón Rondón Giménez (21/5) [77.Frank Feltscher Martínez (7/1)]. Trainer: César Alejandro Farías Acosta (67).

327. 23.05.2012 **VENEZUELA - MOLDOVA** **4-0(1-0)**
Estadio Polideportivo Cachamay, Puerto Ordaz; Referee: Henry Gambetta Ávalos (Peru); Attendance: 20,000
VEN: José Leonardo Morales Lares (26/0), Oswaldo Augusto Vizcarrondo Araujo (42/8), Roberto José Rosales Altuve (36/0) [59.Carlos Gregorio Rivero González (4/0)], Gabriel Alejandro Cichero Konarek (37/2), Grenddy Adrián Perozo Rincón (36/2), Juan Fernando Arango Sáenz (Cap) (105/19) [46.Yohandry José Orozco Cujía (16/0)], Edgar Fernando Pérez Greco (9/1), Tomás Eduardo Rincón Hernández (45/0) [46.Francisco Javier Flores Sequera (24/1)], Luis Manuel Seijas Gunther (36/1) [59.Juan Francisco Guerra (5/0)], Nicolás Ladislao Fedor Flores (38/9) [46 .Yonathan Alexander Del Valle Rodríguez (9/0)], Mário Júnior Rondón Fernández (2/0) [46.José Salomón Rondón Giménez (22/7)]. Trainer: César Alejandro Farías Acosta (68).
Goals: Luis Manuel Seijas Gunther (45+1), José Salomón Rondón Giménez (50), Oswaldo Augusto Vizcarrondo Araujo (53), José Salomón Rondón Giménez (73).

328. 02.06.2012 **URUGUAY - VENEZUELA** **1-1(1-0)** 20th FIFA WC. Qualifiers
Estadio Centenario, Montevideo; Referee: Antonio Javier Arias Alvarenga (Paraguay); Attendance: 57,000
VEN: Renny Vicente Vega Hernández (58/0), Roberto José Rosales Altu (37/0), Oswaldo Augusto Vizcarrondo Araujo (43/8), Fernando Gabriel Amorebieta Mardaras (6/1), Gabriel Alejandro Cichero Konarek (38/2), Juan Fernando Arango Sáenz (106/19), Tomás Eduardo Rincón Hernández (46/0), Giácomo Di Giorgi Zerillo (36/0) [75.Yohandry José Orozco Cujía (17/0)], Frank Feltscher Martínez (8/1) [55.Nicolás Ladislao Fedor Flores (39/9)], Luis Manuel Seijas Gunther (37/1) [88.Grenddy Adrián Perozo Rincón (37/2)], José Salomón Rondón Giménez (23/8). Trainer: César Alejandro Farías Acosta (69).
Goal: José Salomón Rondón Giménez (84).

329. 09.06.2012 **VENEZUELA - CHILE** **0-2(0-0)** 20th FIFA WC. Qualifiers
Estadio „José Antonio Anzoátegui", Puerto La Cruz; Referee: José Hernando Buitrago Arango (Colombia); Attendance: 35,000
VEN: Renny Vicente Vega Hernández (59/0), Roberto José Rosales Altu (38/0), Oswaldo Augusto Vizcarrondo Araujo (44/8), Grenddy Adrián Perozo Rincón (38/2), Gabriel Alejandro Cichero Konarek (39/2), Juan Fernando Arango Sáenz (107/19), Giácomo Di Giorgi Zerillo (37/0), Luis Manuel Seijas Gunther (38/1) [82.Yohandry José Orozco Cujía (18/0)], Julio Álvarez Mosquera (4/0) [64.Juan Francisco Guerra (6/0)], José Salomón Rondón Giménez (24/8), Nicolás Ladislao Fedor Flores (40/9) [64.Yonathan Alexander Del Valle Rodríguez (10/0)]. Trainer: César Alejandro Farías Acosta (70).

330. 15.08.2012 **JAPAN - VENEZUELA** **1-1(1-0)**
Sapporo Dome, Sapporo; Referee: Lee Min-Hu (Korea Republic); Attendance: 39,396
VEN: Daniel Hernández Santos (6/0), Roberto José Rosales Altuve (39/0), Rolf Günther Feltscher Martínez (3/0), Gabriel Alejandro Cichero Konarek (40/2), Andrés José Túñez Arceo (4/0), Alexander David González Sibulo (10/0) [78.Frank Feltscher Martínez (9/1)], Ágnel José Flores Hernández (15/0) [54.Franklin José Lucena Peña (40/1)], Francisco Javier Flores Sequera (25/1) [70.José Manuel Velázquez Rodríguez (12/1)], Luis Manuel Seijas Gunther (39/1) [90.Yohandry José Orozco Cujía (19/0)], Nicolás Ladislao Fedor Flores (41/10), Mário Júnior Rondón Fernández (3/0) [61.Josef Alexander Martínez (4/0)]. Trainer: César Alejandro Farías Acosta (71).
Goal: Nicolás Ladislao Fedor Flores (62).

331. 07.09.2012 **PERU - VENEZUELA** **2-1(0-1)** 20th FIFA WC. Qualifiers
Estadio Nacional, Lima; Referee: Martín Emilio Vázquez Broquetas (Uruguay); Attendance: 34,703
VEN: Renny Vicente Vega Hernández (60/0), Oswaldo Augusto Vizcarrondo Araujo (45/8), Roberto José Rosales Altuve (40/0), Rolf Günther Feltscher Martínez (4/0), Gabriel Alejandro Cichero Konarek (41/2) [*sent off 67*], Andrés José Túñez Arceo (5/0), Juan Fernando Arango Sáenz (108/20), Ágnel José Flores Hernández (16/0), Francisco Javier Flores Sequera (26/1) [63.César Eduardo González Amais (46/3)], Luis Manuel Seijas Gunther (40/1) [74.Frank Feltscher Martínez (10/1)], Nicolás Ladislao Fedor Flores (42/10) [69.José Salomón Rondón Giménez (25/8)]. Trainer: César Alejandro Farías Acosta (72).
Goal: Juan Fernando Arango Sáenz (43).

332. 11.09.2012 **PARAGUAY - VENEZUELA** **0-2(0-1)** 20th FIFA WC. Qualifiers
Estadio Defensores del Chaco, Asunción; Referee: Enrique Roberto Osses Zencovich (Chile); Attendance: 13,680
VEN: Daniel Hernández Santos (7/0), Oswaldo Augusto Vizcarrondo Araujo (46/8), Roberto José Rosales Altuve (41/0), Andrés José Túñez Arceo (6/0), Alexander David González Sibulo (11/0), Juan Fernando Arango Sáenz (109/20), César Eduardo González Amais (47/3) [80.Edgar Fernando Pérez Greco (10/1)], Franklin José Lucena Peña (41/1), Luis Manuel Seijas Gunther (41/1) [87.Ágnel José Flores Hernández (17/0)], José Salomón Rondón Giménez (26/10), Josef Alexander Martínez (5/0) [73.Richard José Blanco Delgado (7/0)]. Trainer: César Alejandro Farías Acosta (73).
Goals: José Salomón Rondón Giménez (45, 68).

333. 16.10.2012 **VENEZUELA - ECUADOR** **1-1(1-1)** 20th FIFA WC. Qualifiers
Estadio "José Antonio Anzoátegui", Puerto La Cruz; Referee: Néstor Fabián Pitana (Argentina); Attendance: 35,076
VEN: Daniel Hernández Santos (8/0), Fernando Gabriel Amorebieta Mardaras (7/1), Roberto José Rosales Altuve (42/0), Grenddy Adrián Perozo Rincón (39/2), Alexander David González Sibulo (12/0) [82.Gabriel Alejandro Cichero Konarek (42/2)], Juan Fernando Arango Sáenz (110/21), Franklin José Lucena Peña (42/1), Evelio de Jesús Hernández Guedez (16/0), Edgar Fernando Pérez Greco (11/1) [57.Ronald Alejandro Vargas Aranguren (15/3)], José Salomón Rondón Giménez (27/10), Josef Alexander Martínez (6/0) [68.Nicolás Ladislao Fedor Flores (43/10)]. Trainer: César Alejandro Farías Acosta (74).
Goal: Juan Fernando Arango Sáenz (6).

334. 14.11.2012 **VENEZUELA - NIGERIA** **1-3(0-0)**
Marlins Park, Miami (United States); Referee: Terry Vaughn (United States); Attendance: n/a
VEN: Daniel Hernández Santos (9/0), Fernando Gabriel Amorebieta Mardaras (8/1) [34.Andrés José Túñez Arceo (7/0)], Oswaldo Augusto Vizcarrondo Araujo (47/8), Roberto José Rosales Altuve (43/0), Alexander David González Sibulo (13/0) [69.Franklin José Lucena Peña (43/1)], Juan Fernando Arango Sáenz (111/21), César Eduardo González Amais (48/3) [88.Francisco Carabalí Terán (1/0)], Ágnel José Flores Hernández (18/0) [62.Tomás Eduardo Rincón Hernández (47/0)], Luis Manuel Seijas Gunther (42/1), José Salomón Rondón Giménez (28/10) [87.Fernando Luis Aristeguieta de Luca (5/1)], Gelmin Javier Rivas Boada (2/0) [65.Frank Feltscher Martínez (11/2)]. Trainer: César Alejandro Farías Acosta (75).
Goal: Frank Feltscher Martínez (70).

335. 22.03.2013 **ARGENTINA - VENEZUELA** **3-0(2-0)** 20th FIFA WC. Qualifiers
Estadio Monumental "Antonio Vespucio Liberti", Buenos Aires; Referee: Víctor Hugo Carrillo (Peru); Attendance: 40,000
VEN: Daniel Hernández Santos (10/0), Oswaldo Augusto Vizcarrondo Araujo (48/8), Gabriel Alejandro Cichero Konarek (43/2), Andrés José Túñez Arceo (8/0), Alexander David González Sibulo (14/0), Juan Fernando Arango Sáenz (112/21) [75.César Eduardo González Amais (49/3)], Franklin José Lucena Peña (44/1), Tomás Eduardo Rincón Hernández (48/0), Luis Manuel Seijas Gunther (43/1) [57.Rómulo Otero Vásquez (1/0)], Frank Feltscher Martínez (12/2), José Salomón Rondón Giménez (29/10) [82.Nicolás Ladislao Fedor Flores (44/10)]. Trainer: César Alejandro Farías Acosta (76).

336. 26.03.2013 **VENEZUELA - COLOMBIA** **1-0(1-0)** 20th FIFA WC. Qualifiers

Estadio Polideportivo Cachamay, Ciudad Guayana; Referee: Antonio Javier Arias Alvarenga (Paraguay); Attendance: 41,250

VEN: Daniel Hernández Santos (11/0), Oswaldo Augusto Vizcarrondo Araujo (49/8), Gabriel Alejandro Cichero Konarek (44/2) [84.Rolf Günther Feltscher Martínez (5/0)], Andrés José Túñez Arceo (9/0) [61.Ágnel José Flores Hernández (19/0)], Alexander David González Sibulo (15/0), Juan Fernando Arango Sáenz (113/21), César Eduardo González Amais (1/0), Franklin José Lucena Peña (50/3), Tomás Eduardo Rincón Hernández (49/0), José Salomón Rondón Giménez (30/11), Fernando Luis Aristeguieta de Luca (6/1) [68.Nicolás Ladislao Fedor Flores (45/10)]. Trainer: César Alejandro Farías Acosta (77).

Goal: José Salomón Rondón Giménez (13).

337. 22.05.2013 **VENEZUELA - EL SALVADOR** **2-1(0-1)**

Estadio Olímpico Metropolitano, Mérida; Referee: Diego Jefferson Lara León (Ecuador); Attendance: 28,133

VEN: Renny Vicente Vega Hernández (61/0), Grenddy Adrián Perozo Rincón (40/2), Gabriel Alejandro Cichero Konarek (45/2), Alexander David González Sibulo (16/0), Juan Fernando Arango Sáenz (114/21) [89.Rómulo Otero Vásquez (2/0)], César Eduardo González Amais (51/4) [79.Louis Angelo Peña Puentes (14/0)], Ágnel José Flores Hernández (20/0) [63.Evelio de Jesús Hernández Guedez (17/0)], Tomás Eduardo Rincón Hernández (50/0) [79.Franklin José Lucena Peña (46/1)], Luis Manuel Seijas Gunther (44/1), Richard José Blanco Delgado (8/0) [72.Mário Júnior Rondón Fernández (4/0)], Josef Alexander Martínez (7/1) [72.Fernando Luis Aristeguieta de Luca (7/1)]. Trainer: César Alejandro Farías Acosta (78).

Goals: César Eduardo González Amais (56 penalty), Josef Alexander Martínez (68 penalty).

338. 07.06.2013 **BOLIVIA - VENEZUELA** **1-1(0-0)** 20th FIFA WC. Qualifiers

Estadio "Hernando Siles Zuazo", La Paz; Referee: Patricio Loustau (Argentina); Attendance: 10,155

VEN: Renny Vicente Vega Hernández (62/0), Roberto José Rosales Altuve (44/0), Grenddy Adrián Perozo Rincón (41/2), Gabriel Alejandro Cichero Konarek (46/2), Juan Fernando Arango Sáenz (115/22) [81.Rolf Günther Feltscher Martínez (6/0)], César Eduardo González Amais (52/4) [71.Alexander David González Sibulo (17/0)], Ágnel José Flores Hernández (21/0), Tomás Eduardo Rincón Hernández (51/0), Luis Manuel Seijas Gunther (45/1), Richard José Blanco Delgado (9/0) [65.Evelio de Jesús Hernández Guedez (18/0)], Josef Alexander Martínez (8/1). Trainer: César Alejandro Farías Acosta (79).

Goal: Juan Fernando Arango Sáenz (58).

339. 11.06.2013 **VENEZUELA - URUGUAY** **0-1(0-1)** 20th FIFA WC. Qualifiers

Estadio Polideportivo Cachamay, Ciudad Guayana; Referee: Paulo César de Oliveira (Brazil); Attendance: 36,297

VEN: Daniel Hernández Santos (12/0), Oswaldo Augusto Vizcarrondo Araujo (50/8), Roberto José Rosales Altuve (45/0), Gabriel Alejandro Cichero Konarek (47/2) [58.Luis Manuel Seijas Gunther (46/1)], Andrés José Túñez Arceo (10/0), Juan Fernando Arango Sáenz (116/22), César Eduardo González Amais (53/4) [74.Richard José Blanco Delgado (10/0)], Franklin José Lucena Peña (47/1), Tomás Eduardo Rincón Hernández (52/0) [*sent off 84*], Frank Feltscher Martínez (13/2) [56.Fernando Luis Aristeguieta de Luca (8/1)], José Salomón Rondón Giménez (31/11). Trainer: César Alejandro Farías Acosta (80).

340. 15.08.2013 **VENEZUELA - BOLIVIA** **2-2(1-1)**

Estadio Polideportivo de Pueblo Nuevo, San Cristóbal; Referee: Imer Lemuel Machado Barrera (Colombia); Attendance: 24,700

VEN: Daniel Hernández Santos (13/0), Oswaldo Augusto Vizcarrondo Araujo (51/8), Roberto José Rosales Altuve (46/0), Gabriel Alejandro Cichero Konarek (48/2), Alexander David González Sibulo (18/0), Juan Fernando Arango Sáenz (117/22) [*sent off 89*], César Eduardo González Amais (54/4) [62.Yohandry José Orozco Cujía (20/1)], Franklin José Lucena Peña (48/1) [71.Fernando Luis Aristeguieta de Luca (9/1)], Ágnel José Flores Hernández (22/0) [46.Tomás Eduardo Rincón Hernández (53/0)], José Salomón Rondón Giménez (32/11), Josef Alexander Martínez (9/2). Trainer: César Alejandro Farías Acosta (81).

Goals: Josef Alexander Martínez (16), Yohandry José Orozco Cujía (84).

341. 07.09.2013 **CHILE - VENEZUELA** **3-0(2-0)** 20th FIFA WC. Qualifiers

Estadio Nacional „Julio Martínez Prádanos“, Santiago; Referee: Sandro Meira Ricci (Brazil); Attendance: 46,500

VEN: Daniel Hernández Santos (14/0), Oswaldo Augusto Vizcarrondo Araujo (52/8), Roberto José Rosales Altuve (47/0), Grenddy Adrián Perozo Rincón (42/2), Gabriel Alejandro Cichero Konarek (49/0) [44.Alexander David González Sibulo (19/0)], Juan Fernando Arango Sáenz (118/22), César Eduardo González Amais (55/4) [70.Yohandry José Orozco Cujía (21/1)], Franklin José Lucena Peña (49/1), Luis Manuel Seijas Gunther (47/1) [79.Rómulo Otero Vásquez (3/0)], José Salomón Rondón Giménez (33/11), Josef Alexander Martínez (10/2). Trainer: César Alejandro Farías Acosta (82).

342. 11.09.2013 **VENEZUELA - PERU** **3-2(1-1)** 20th FIFA WC. Qualifiers

Estadio Olímpico "General José Antonio Anzoátegui", Puerto la Cruz; Referee: Néstor Fabián Pitana (Argentina); Attendance: 20,049

VEN: Daniel Hernández Santos (15/0), Fernando Gabriel Amorebieta Mardaras (9/1), Oswaldo Augusto Vizcarrondo Araujo (53/8), Roberto José Rosales Altuve (48/0), Alexander David González Sibulo (20/0), Juan Fernando Arango Sáenz (119/22) [86.Fernando Luis Aristeguieta de Luca (10/1)], César Eduardo González Amais (56/5) [68.Rómulo Otero Vásquez (4/1)], Yohandry José Orozco Cujía (22/1), Tomás Eduardo Rincón Hernández (54/0), José Salomón Rondón Giménez (34/12), Josef Alexander Martínez (11/2) [75.Franklin José Lucena Peña (50/1)]. Trainer: César Alejandro Farías Acosta (83).

Goals: José Salomón Rondón Giménez (37), César Eduardo González Amais (62 penalty), Rómulo Otero Vásquez (77).

343. 11.10.2013 **VENEZUELA - PARAGUAY** **1-1(0-1)** 20th FIFA WC. Qualifiers

Estadio Polideportivo de Pueblo Nuevo, San Cristóbal; Referee: Víctor Hugo Carrillo Casanova (Peru); Attendance: 27,227

VEN: Daniel Hernández Santos (16/0), Fernando Gabriel Amorebieta Mardaras (10/1), Oswaldo Augusto Vizcarrondo Araujo (54/8), Roberto José Rosales Altuve (49/0), Alexander David González Sibulo (21/0) [77.Luis Manuel Seijas Gunther (48/2)], Juan Fernando Arango Sáenz (120/22), Franklin José Lucena Peña (51/1), Yohandry José Orozco Cujía (23/1), Rómulo Otero Vásquez (5/1) [64.Fernando Luis Aristeguieta de Luca (11/1)], Nicolás Ladislao Fedor Flores (46/10), Josef Alexander Martínez (12/2) [71.Louis Angelo Peña Puentes (15/0)]. Trainer: César Alejandro Farías Acosta (84).

Goal: Luis Manuel Seijas Gunther (82).

INTERNATIONAL PLAYERS

FM/Nr	Name	DOB	Caps	Goals	Period, Club
(270/417)	ACOSTA CAMMAROTA Rafael Eduardo	20.02.1989	5	0	2008-2009, Cagliari Calcio (5/0).
(52/161)	ACOSTA SÁNCHEZ Pedro Javier	28.11.1959	34	2	1979-1989, Club Deportivo Galicia Caracas (15/1), Club Deportivo Portugués Caracas (7/0), Caracas FC (4/1), Club Sport Marítimo de Venezuela Caracas (8/0).
(222/372)	ACUÑA Alexis	08.11.1977	1	0	2004, Monagas SC Maturín (1/0).
(43/136)	ACURZIO José		3	0	1975, Club Deportivo Portugués Caracas (3/0).
(54/164)	AGUIRRE Ordán Ramón		7	0	1979-1981
(18/058)	ALLEYNE Franklin		1	0	1955
(18/056)	ALTERIO Aniello		2	0	1955
(165/344)	ALVARADO LIMA Wilfredo José	31.03.1973	35	2	2000-2008, Deportivo Táchira FC San Cristóbal (21/2), Club Deportivo Italchacao Caracas (4/0), Deportivo Táchira FC San Cristóbal (1/0), Club Deportivo Italchacao Caracas (8/0), Llaneros de Guanare FC (1/0).
(293/442)	ÁLVAREZ Eliézer	12.09.1987	1	0	2010, Unión Atlético Píar Aragua de Maturín
(69/203)	ÁLVAREZ Franklin		1	0	1984
(320/467)	ÁLVAREZ MOSQUERA Julio	01.05.1981	4	0	2011-2012, CD Numancia de Soria (4/0).
(148/321)	ÁLVAREZ SUÁREZ Rolando	14.12.1975	20	0	1999-2001, Club Internacional de Lara FC (9/0), Caracas FC (10/0), Club Deportivo Italchacao Caracas (1/0).
(42/129)	AMADO		1	0	1973
(317/462)	AMOREBIETA MARDARAS Fernando Gabriel	29.03.1985	10	1	2011-2013, Athletic Club Bilbao (8/1), Fulham FC London (2/0).
(6/017)	ANDARA Roberto		4	0	1938
(116/285)	ANGELUCCI Gilberto	07.08.1967	47	0	1995-2005, CA San Lorenzo de Almagro (4/0), Deportivo Táchira FC San Cristóbal (21/0), AD Mineros de Guayana (15/0), Unión Atlético Maracaibo (7/0).
(54/165)	AÑOR Bernardo		17	3	1979-1994,
(22/077)	ANZOLA Atilano		1	0	1965
(10/032)	APARICIO Rosendo		3	2	1946
(148/326)	ARANGO SÁENZ Juan Fernando	17.05.1980	120	22	1999-2013, SCA Nueva Cádiz Cumana (4/0), Caracas FC (2/0), CF Saltillo (1/0), CF Monterrey (15/2), Club Atlético Pachuca (6/3), CF Puebla de la Franja (15/5), RCD Mallorca (40/6), Borussia VfL Mönchengladbach (37/6).
(69/198)	ARANGURÉN Carlos		1	0	1984
(36/105)	ARAQUE José		1	0	1971, Estudiantes de Mérida FC (1/0).
(1/004)	ARDILA José María		7	0	1938-1946
(253/401)	ARIAS ZAMBRANO Anderson	20.04.1987	1	0	2007, Deportivo Táchira FC San Cristóbal (1/0).
(234/382)	ARISMENDI MARCHÁN Daniel Enrique	04.07.1982	31	11	2006-2011, Carabobo FC Valencia (4/2), Unión Atlético Maracaibo (11/6), CF Atlante Cancún (7/1), Unión Atlético Maracaibo (2/0), Deportivo Anzoátegui SC Puerto La Cruz (7/2).
(315/456)	ARISTEGUIETA DE LUCA Fernando Luis	09.04.1992	11	1	2011-2013, Caracas FC (5/1), FC Nantes (6/0).
(289/433)	ARISTIGUIETA DE LUCA Fernando Luis	09.04.1992	2	0	2010, Caracas FC (2/0).
(44/139)	ARIZALETA Andrés		3	0	1975, Club Deportivo Portugués Caracas (3/0).
(233/381)	AROCHA HERNÁNDEZ Rubén Darío	21.04.1987	4	0	2006-2012, Real Madrid CF (1/0), Namur (1/0), Zamora FC Barinas (1/0), Deportivo Táchira FC San Cristóbal (1/0).
(23/080)	AROCHA Juan		1	0	1965, Unión Deportivo Canarias Caracas (1/0).
(78/222)	ARREAZZA Wilton	12.08.1966	5	0	1987-1989, Caracas FC (5/0).
(37/111)	ARRUDA Vicente		5	0	1972
(315/458)	ARTEAGA RUBIANES Manuel Alejandro	17.06.1994	1	0	2011, Zulia FC Maracaibo (1/0).
(65/184)	BAÉNA César Renato	13.01.1961	22	0	1983-2002, Universidad de los Andes FC Mérida (2/0), Estudiantes de Mérida FC (8/0), Caracas FC (12/0).
(65/186)	BARBOZA Braulen		2	0	1983, Club Atlético San Cristóbal (2/0).
(67/192)	BARBOZA Julio Omar		2	0	1983, Club Deportivo Táchira (2/0).
(69/204)	BARCO Pedro	15.09.1961	1	0	1984
(112/277)	BARRETO Johnny	29.04.1969	1	0	1994, Caracas FC (1/0).
(161/340)	BECERRA Alexander		3	0	2000, El Vigía FC (3/0).
(73/215)	BECERRA Arnulfo	09.04.1962	2	0	1985, Deportivo Táchira FC San Cristóbal (2/0).
(80/229)	BENCOMO Ceferino	01.10.1970	1	0	1989
(42/122)	BERMEJO		1	0	1973
(48/150)	BETANCOURT Carlos	10.11.1957	9	0	1977-1985
(69/199)	BETANCOURT Carlos		1	0	1984
(70/209)	BETANCOURT Jorge		6	0	1985-1989, 1985 (2/0), Club Sport Marítimo de Venezuela Caracas (4/0).
(47/147)	BETANCOURT TORO José		4	0	1977
(151/332)	BIDOGLIO Héctor Pablo	05.02.1968	16	0	1999-2000, Caracas FC (16/0).
(275/422)	BLANCO DELGADO Richard José	21.01.1982	10	0	2008-2013, Estrella Roja FC Caracas (1/0), Deportivo Italia FC Caracas (4/0), CD O'Higgins Rancagua (1/0), AC CD Mineros de Guayana Puerto Ordaz (4/0).
(10/025)	BLANCO Ernesto		4	1	1946-1951
(22/078)	BLANCO Ernesto		3	0	1965
(229/376)	BOADA NOYA Pedro Luis	26.07.1977	17	0	2005-2009, Deportivo Táchira FC San Cristóbal (1/0), Deportivo Anzoátegui SC Puerto La Cruz (16/0).

(96/251)	BONACORSO Amleto	30.04.1967	1	0	1993, Unión Deportiva de Lara FC Barquisimeto (1/0).
(62/178)	BOSETTI Mario Luis		1	0	1981, Estudiantes de Mérida FC (2/0).
(94/248)	BOTTINI Alexander	07.05.1969	2	0	1991-1993, Monagas SC Maturín (2/0).
(190/354)	BRAVO Carlos Luis	06.02.1978	4	0	2002, Monagas SC Maturín (4/0).
(316/460)	BRICEÑO CARPIO Rohel Antonio	15.03.1984	1	0	2011, Caracas FC (1/0).
(36/099)	BRITO Gustavo		1	0	1971
(292/437)	BUSTAMANTE SUÁREZ Jaime Andrés	21.04.1980	6	0	2010, Caracas FC (6/0).

(55/167)	CADENAS Rafael		2	0	1979-1981, Universidad de los Andes FC Mérida (2/0).
(83/240)	CAMACARO Luis Alberto	15.07.1967	4	0	1989, Unión Atlético Táchira San Cristóbal (4/0).
(276/426)	CAMACHO FIGUEIRA Pablo Jesús	12.12.1990	2	0	2009-2010, Deportivo Italia FC Caracas (1/0), Caracas FC (1/0).
(104/275)	CAMACHO Pedro Felipe	26.12.1964	2	0	1993, Minervén FC El Callao (2/0).
(36/100)	CAMERO Iván		1	0	1971, Club Deportivo Galicia Caracas (1/0).
(1/005)	CAMERO Nicasio		13	0	1938-1946
(17/046)	CAMPOS Rafael		1	0	1951
(52/156)	CAMPOS RODRÍGUEZ Emilio		19	0	1979-1985
(4/013)	CANDIALES José Luis		5	0	1938
(334/475)	CARABALÍ TERÁN Francisco	21.02.1991	1	0	2012, Trujillanos FC Valera (1/0).
(56/170)	CARRERO HERAS Nelson José	06.06.1956	24	0	1980-1989
(53/163)	CARVAJAL Rodolfo		9	2	1978-1983, Universidad de los Andes FC Mérida (9/2).
(148/325)	CÁSSERES CASERES Cristian Alfonso	29.06.1977	28	2	1999-2008, Club Deportivo Italchacao Caracas (7/0), CD Atlas Guadalajara (1/0), CF La Piedad (2/0), CD Atlas Guadalajara (1/0), Club Deportivo Italchacao Caracas (10/2), Unión Atlético Maracaibo (1/0), CD Atlas Guadalajara (3/0), Unión Atlético Maracaibo (1/0), Deportivo Italia FC Caracas (2/0).
(55/166)	CASTELLANOS Jhonny		3	0	1979-1983, Club Atlético Zamora Barinas (3/0).
(134/312)	CASTELLANOS Juan Carlos	07.01.1975	1	0	1997, El Vígia FC (1/0).
(123/294)	CASTELLÍN GARCÍA Rafael Ernesto	02.09.1975	22	5	1996-2005, Minervén FC El Callao (2/0), Caracas FC (11/2), Club Deportivo Italchacao Caracas (4/2), Caracas FC (5/1).
(1/007)	CASTILLO Alberto		5	1	1938
(52/158)	CASTILLO Ángel de Jesús		6	0	1979-1981
(6/019)	CASTILLO Graciano		4	0	1938
(61/175)	CASTILLO William		3	0	1981
(64/180)	CASTRILLO José Luis		1	0	1981
(92/247)	CASTRO Carlos	18.03.1968	3	0	1991, Unión Atlético Táchira San Cristóbal (3/0).
(43/133)	CASTRO Pedro		12	0	1975-1981
(84/241)	CAVALLO de ROBERTIS Roberto	28.04.1967	12	0	1989-1991, Club Deportivo Italia Caracas (12/0).
(67/195)	CEDEÑO Douglas		9	2	1983-1985, Mineros de Guayana Puerto Ordáz (2/0), 1985 (7/2).
(16/038)	CERVINI Reinaldo		1	0	1948
(64/183)	CHACÓN Ernesto		1	0	1981
(153/337)	CHACÓN VARELA Gerzon Armando	27.10.1980	23	0	1999-2009, Unión Atlético Táchira San Cristóbal (4/0), Deportivo Táchira FC San Cristóbal (19/0).
(96/256)	CHACÓN Wilson Arcangel	11.05.1971	11	0	1993-1996, Unión Atlético Táchira San Cristóbal (11/0).
(47/145)	CHIAZZARO José Enrique		4	0	1977, Estudiantes de Mérida FC (4/0).
(125/300)	CHIRINOS Alexis José	26.10.1973	3	0	1996-2002, Minervén FC El Callao (1/0), Monagas SC Maturín (1/0), AD Mineros de Guayana (1/0).
(262/411)	CHOURIO GALÍNDEZ Ángel Antonio	05.05.1985	20	5	2008-2012, AC Aragua FC Maracay (1/0), Real Esppor Club Caracas (18/5), Deportivo Táchira FC San Cristóbal (1/0).
(192/358)	CICHERO KONAREK Alejandro Enrique	24.04.1977	47	2	2002-2007, Club Deportivo Italchacao Caracas (1/0), Club Atlético Cerro Montevideo (8/0), Club Nacional de Football Montevideo (13/0), FC Litex Lovetch (25/2).
(222/370)	CICHERO KONAREK Gabriel Alejandro	25.04.1984	49	2	2004-2013, Montevideo Wanderers FC (1/0), US Lecce (1/0), Montevideo Wanderers FC (1/0), Deportivo Italia FC Caracas (9/1), Red Bull New York (2/0), Caracas FC (3/0), CA Newell's Old Boys Rosario (14/1), RC Lens (4/0), Caracas FC (4/0), FC Nantes (10/0).
(56/169)	CICHERO Mauro		2	0	1980
(27/087)	COLMENARES Omar		9	0	1967-1975, Valencia FC (9/0).
(99/272)	CONTRERAS Carlos Alberto	17.08.1972	11	0	1993-1997, Unión Atlético Táchira San Cristóbal (10/0), Estudiantes de Mérida FC (1/0).
(52/154)	CONTRERAS José Ramón		2	0	1979, Club Deportivo Táchira (2/0).
(2/012)	CORAO Mauricio		6	0	1938
(8/021)	CORAO Pablo		2	0	1938
(100/273)	CORDERO Miguel	10.11.1971	1	0	1993, Portuguesa FC Acarigua (1/0).

(122/290)	D'OLIVEIRA Danny		1	0	1996
(154/338)	DE ORNELAS Fernando Franco	29.07.1976	28	5	1999-2007, South China FC (1/1), Celtic Glasgow FC (8/1), Club Deportivo Italchacao Caracas (2/0), South China FC (2/0), Olympiakos Nicosia (2/0), Odd Grenland (13/3).
(150/330)	DE PABLOS Pedro	02.01.1977	2	0	1999-2004, Caracas FC (1/0), Deportivo Táchira FC San Cristóbal (1/0).
(21/072)	DE SUZE Octavio		4	0	1965
(270/418)	DEL VALLE RODRÍGUEZ Yonathan Alexander	28.05.1990	10	0	2008-2012, Deportivo Táchira FC San Cristóbal (6/0), AJ Auxerre (4/0).
(18/050)	DELGADO Alberto		2	0	1955
(30/090)	DELGADO Salvador		6	0	1969
(190/355)	DI GIORGI ZERILLO Giácomo	24.02.1981	37	0	2002-2012, Caracas FC (2/0), Unión Deportivo Lara FC (1/0), Llaneros de Guanare FC (3/0), Deportivo Anzoátegui SC Puerto La Cruz (31/0).
(17/049)	DÍAZ César		1	1	1951
(96/257)	DÍAZ Gerson Diomar	11.02.1972	25	1	1993-1997, Caracas FC (25/1).

(308/452)	DÍAZ GUTIÉRREZ William	31.03.1985	**3**	**0**	2011, Deportivo Táchira FC San Cristóbal (3/0).
(42/125)	DÍAZ Olegario		**1**	**0**	1973
(18/057)	DÍAZ Pedro		**2**	**2**	1955
(233/380)	DÍAZ ROMERO Dickson Manuel	04.03.1980	**2**	**0**	2006-2008, Unión Atlético Maracaibo (1/0), Monagas SC Maturín (1/0).
(254/402)	DÍAZ TOVAR Heiber Eduardo	11.10.1984	**1**	**0**	2007, CD Lara Barquisimeto (1/0).
(96/258)	DOLGETTA José Luis	01.08.1970	**21**	**6**	1993-1997, Unión Atlético Táchira San Cristóbal (20/6), Atlético Zulia FC Maracaibo (1/0).
(80/230)	DOMÍNGUEZ Carlos	17.04.1966	**3**	**1**	1989
(98/267)	DUDAMEL OCHOA Rafael Edgar	07.01.1973	**57**	**1**	1993-2010, Universidad de los Andes FC Mérida (4/0), El Vigía FC (3/0), CD Atlético Huila Neiva (7/1), Club Independiente Santa Fé Bogotá (7/0), Quilmes AC Buenos Aires (5/0), Club Deportivo Cali (13/0), CD Los Millionarios Bogotá (3/0), Unión Atlético Maracaibo (2/0), CC Deportivo Tulúa (2/0), Deportivo Táchira FC San Cristóbal (6/0), Mamelodi Sundowns FC Pretoria (2/0), Estudiantes de Mérida FC (2/0), Real Esppor Club Caracas (1/0).
(148/323)	DUNO José Ricardo	19.03.1977	**12**	**0**	1999-2000, Minervén FC El Callao (3/0), SCA Nueva Cádiz Cumana (7/0), Club Zulianos FC Maracaibo (1/0), Deportivo Táchira FC San Cristóbal (1/0).
(92/246)	ECHENÁUSI Miguel Ángel	21.02.1968	**28**	**1**	1991-2000, Unión Atlético Táchira San Cristóbal (4/0), Caracas FC (12/1), Minervén FC El Callao (1/0), Estudiantes de Mérida FC (10/0).
(47/144)	ECHENÁUSI Ramón		**8**	**0**	1977-1981
(99/271)	ECHENIQUE José Alexander	11.11.1971	**18**	**0**	1993-1997, Unión Atlético Táchira San Cristóbal (18/0).
(20/062)	ELLIE ARLET Fréderic "Freddie"		**20**	**1**	1964-1977
(65/187)	ELLIE Robert		**5**	**0**	1983-1985, Universidad de los Andes FC Mérida (5/0).
(292/438)	ERAZO VILLAMIZAR Luiyi José	13.06.1988	**2**	**0**	2010, Real Esppor Club Caracas (2/0).
(17/045)	ESPEJO Policarpio		**1**	**0**	1951
(135/315)	ESPINOZA César	16.09.1968	**1**	**0**	1997, Estudiantes de Mérida FC (1/0).
(20/070)	ETTARI Luciano		**1**	**0**	1964
(16/039)	FÁBREGAS		**1**	**0**	1948
(282/428)	FAJARDO Francisco Javier	08.07.1990	**2**	**0**	2009, AC Aragua FC Maracay (2/0).
(262/412)	FALCÓN Juan	24.02.1989	**1**	**0**	2008, Llaneros de Guanare FC (1/0).
(165/345)	FARÍAS Luis Alberto	28.09.1973	**11**	**0**	2000, Carabobo FC Valencia (9/0), Deportivo Táchira FC San Cristóbal (2/0).
(289/434)	FARÍAS MARTÍNEZ Edder José	12.04.1988	**6**	**1**	2010, Monagas SC Maturín (6/1).
(81/235)	FASCIANA Franco	08.03.1960	**5**	**0**	1989-1991, 1989 (1/0), Club Atlético Zamora Barinas (4/0).
(130/307)	FASCIANA José	04.03.1971	**2**	**0**	1996-2000, Unión Atlético Táchira San Cristóbal (1/0), Club Deportivo Italchacao Caracas (1/0).
(25/082)	FASSANO Víctor "Vito"		**10**	**0**	1967-1972, Club Deportivo Italia Caracas (10/0).
(52/159)	FEBLES Pedro Juan	18.04.1958	**27**	**6**	1979-1989, Club Deportivo Italia Caracas (5/1), Club Deportivo Galicia Caracas (3/0), Club Atlético Táchira San Cristóbal (11/5), Club Sport Marítimo de Venezuela Caracas (8/0).
(1/010)	FEBRÉS CORDERO Reinaldo		**8**	**1**	1938
(236/385)	FEDOR FLORES Nicolás Ladislao "MIKU"	19.08.1985	**46**	**10**	2006-2013, Carabobo FC Valencia (4/0), Valencia CF "B" (6/2), Club Gimnàstic de Tarragona (1/0), UD Salamanca (6/3), Getafe CF (23/4), Celtic Glasgow FC (5/1), Al-Gharafa SC Doha (1/0).
(317/463)	FELTSCHER MARTÍNEZ Frank	17.05.1988	**13**	**2**	2011-2013, Grasshopper Club Zürich (13/2).
(322/468)	FELTSCHER MARTÍNEZ Rolf Günther	06.10.1990	**6**	**0**	2011-2013, Parma FC (2/0), Calcio Padova (4/0).
(1/009)	FEO Carlos		**4**	**0**	1938
(189/352)	FERNÁNDEZ CAMACHO Pedro Alfonso	27.07.1977	**13**	**0**	2002-2009, Deportivo Táchira FC San Cristóbal (1/0), Unión Atlético Maracaibo (9/0), Zulia FC Maracaibo (2/0), Deportivo Táchira FC San Cristóbal (1/0).
(261/409)	FERNÁNDEZ Carlos Enrique	01.09.1990	**4**	**0**	2008-2010, Deportivo Anzoátegui Puerto La Cruz (4/0).
(66/190)	FERNÁNDEZ Ildemaro	27.12.1961	**14**	**1**	1983-1991, Estudiantes de Mérida FC (12/1), Mineros de Guayana Puerto Ordáz (2/0).
(279/427)	FERNÁNDEZ JIMÉNEZ Marlon Antonio	16.01.1986	**3**	**0**	2009, Deportivo Táchira FC San Cristóbal (3/0).
(316/459)	FIGUERA SALAZAR Arquímedes José	06.10.1989	**1**	**0**	2011, Trujillanos FC Valera (1/0).
(62/176)	FILOMENO Víctor		**2**	**0**	1981
(96/260)	FILOSA ASTUDILLO Luis Manuel	15.02.1973	**30**	**0**	1993-2000, FC Deportivo Mineros de Guayana (27/0), AD Mineros de Guayana (3/0).
(112/280)	FLORES Alexander	21.09.1968	**1**	**0**	1994, AD Mineros de Guayana (1/0).
(289/432)	FLORES HERNÁNDEZ Ágnel José	25.05.1989	**22**	**0**	2010-2013, AC Mineros de Guayana Puerto Ordaz (14/0), Deportivo Táchira FC San Cristóbal (8/0).
(95/249)	FLORES José	28.06.1967	**1**	**0**	1991, Anzoategui FC Puerto La Cruz (1/0).
(270/415)	FLORES SEQUERA Francisco Javier	30.04.1990	**26**	**1**	2008-2012, Guaros de Lara FC/ CD Lara Barquisimeto (16/1), Deportivo Anzoátegui SC Puerto La Cruz (8/0), Deportivo Táchira FC San Cristóbal (2/0).
(42/126)	FLORES Vicente		**11**	**0**	1973-1981
(22/079)	FONT Nicolás		**1**	**0**	1965
(47/148)	FUENMAYOR Nabor		**3**	**0**	1977
(225/373)	FUENMAYOR NÚÑEZ Juan José	05.09.1979	**26**	**0**	2005-2011, Unión Atlético Maracaibo (9/0), Zulia FC Maracaibo (3/0), Vålerenga Fotball (10/0), Deportivo Anzoátegui SC Puerto La Cruz (4/0).
(20/065)	GALA Salvador		**6**	**0**	1964-1967, Litoral SC Caracas (6/0).

(168/347)	GALÁN Joel	25.03.1978	2	0	2000, Deportivo Táchira FC San Cristóbal (2/0).
(36/106)	GALEANO Humberto		1	0	1971
(89/242)	GALLARDO Pedro	02.05.1969	7	0	1989-1991, 1989 (3/0), Portuguesa FC Acarigua (4/0).
(67/194)	GAMBOA José		1	0	1983, Club Deportivo Portugués Caracas (1/0).
(127/303)	GARCÍA Alexis	26.07.1978	4	1	1996-2002, AD Mineros de Guayana (4/1).
(20/071)	GARCÍA E.		1	0	1964
(33/096)	GARCÍA Eddie Nelson		2	0	1969
(316/461)	GARCÍA HERNÁNDEZ Víctor Hugo	11.06.1994	1	0	2011, Real Esppor Club Caracas (1/0).
(38/116)	GARCÍA Iván		14	1	1972-1981, Estudiantes de Mérida FC (14/1).
(96/259)	GARCÍA Linder	02.11.1967	1	0	1993, Estudiantes de Mérida FC (1/0).
(35/098)	GARCÍA Manuel		1	0	1969
(96/254)	GARCÍA MIJARES Carlos José	12.11.1971	24	0	1993-1997, Unión Atlético Táchira San Cristóbal (13/0), Minervén FC El Callao (10/0), Atlético Zulia FC Maracaibo (1/0).
(112/279)	GARCÍA Osnel Antonio	22.06.1968	1	0	1994, Trujillanos FC Valera (1/0).
(97/266)	GARCÍA RIVAS Juan Enrique	16.04.1970	50	7	1993-2010, Minervén FC El Callao (15/3), Caracas FC (23/4), Nacional Táchira FC (1/0), Monagas SC Maturín (3/0), AD Mineros de Guayana (3/0), Caracas FC (1/0), AD Mineros de Guayana (1/0), Zamora FC Barinas (2/0), AC Mineros de Guayana FC Puerto Ordaz (1/0).
(11/034)	GARCÍA Víctor		3	4	1946
(81/234)	GARCÍA Wilmer		1	0	1989
(42/120)	GEORGES Alexis		1	1	1973
(16/044)	GIRALDO		1	0	1948
(127/302)	GIRALDO Jorge	24.01.1978	6	0	1996-2000, Caracas FC (6/0).
(236/388)	GIROLETTI NADALÍ Alain Giancarlo	08.09.1979	8	0	2006-2007, Aragua FC Maracay (8/0).
(229/375)	GODOY Daniel	13.06.1980	2	0	2005-2006, Caracas FC (2/0).
(125/298)	GOLINDANO Félix Armando	16.11.1969	4	0	1996
(91/244)	GÓMEZ José Gregorio	27.11.1963	13	0	1989-1993, Long Island Roughriders (1/0), FC Deportivo Mineros de Guayana (12/0).
(233/378)	GÓMEZ MERCADO Jesús Javier	06.08.1984	14	1	2006-2011, Estudiantes de Mérida FC (3/1), Raja Casablanca (5/0), Caracas FC (3/0), Wadi Degla FC Cairo (3/0).
(44/131)	GONZÁLEZ Alejo		4	0	1973-1975, Club Deportivo Galicia Caracas (4/0).
(219/369)	GONZÁLEZ AMAIS César Eduardo	01.10.1982	56	5	2004-2013, CD Atlético Huila Neiva (1/0), Club Deportivo Cali (4/0), Caracas FC (10/1), CA Colón de Santa Fé (3/0), CA Huracán Buenos Aires (6/0), San Luis FC Potosí (7/1), Club de Gimnasia y Esgrima La Plata (9/1), CA River Plate Buenos Aires (5/0), Deportivo Táchira FC San Cristóbal (11/2).
(96/253)	GONZÁLEZ ANTEQUERA Leonardo Alberto	05.12.1971	39	0	1993-2008, Trujillanos FC Valera (21/0), Caracas FC (17/0), Trujillanos FC Valera (1/0).
(17/047)	GONZÁLEZ Carlos		1	0	1951
(77/217)	GONZÁLEZ Cecilio		1	0	1985
(265/414)	GONZÁLEZ César Alexander	21.06.1990	3	0	2008, Deportivo Anzoátegui SC Puerto La Cruz (3/0).
(17/048)	GONZÁLEZ Ernesto		1	0	1951
(151/333)	GONZÁLEZ FRUSTACCI Andrée Aníbal	30.06.1975	17	0	1999-2007, Caracas FC (2/0), Club Plaza Colonia (1/0), Defensor Sporting Club Montevideo (3/0), Unión Atlético Maracaibo (11/0).
(25/084)	GONZÁLEZ Gustavo		5	0	1967, Club Deportivo Italia Caracas (5/0).
(178/350)	GONZÁLEZ GUZMÁN Héctor Augusto	04.11.1977	53	4	2001-2007, Caracas FC (9/1), Club Olimpo Bahia Blanca (4/2), CA Colón Santa Fé (12/1), Quilmes AC Buenos Aires (4/0), CSC Deportivo Cuenca (9/0), Unión Atlético Maracaibo (3/0), LDU de Quito (2/0), AEK Lárnaka FC (10/0).
(318/466)	GONZÁLEZ GUZMÁN Raúl	28.06.1985	1	0	2011, Anagennisi Deryneia (1/0).
(69/202)	GONZÁLEZ José		1	0	1984
(29/088)	GONZÁLEZ Omar		2	0	1967-1969, Valencia FC (2/0).
(26/086)	GONZÁLEZ Pedro Alfonso		8	0	1967-1969, Club Deportivo Portugués Caracas (8/0).
(121/287)	GONZÁLEZ QUIJADA José Francisco	21.07.1971	16	0	1996-2008, 1996 (1/0), AD Mineros de Guayana (1/0), Deportivo Táchira FC San Cristóbal (14/0).
(10/029)	GONZÁLEZ Rafael		9	1	1946-1955
(113/283)	GONZÁLEZ RUÍZ William	27.12.1969	20	0	1995-1997, AD Mineros de Guayana (20/0).
(303/449)	GONZÁLEZ SIBULO Alexander David	13.09.1992	21	0	2011-2013, Caracas FC (9/0), BSC Young Boys Bern (8/0), FC Aarau (4/0).
(260/403)	GRANADOS ASPRILLA José Luis	22.10.1986	20	1	2008-2011, Deportivo Táchira FC San Cristóbal (10/1), Real Esppor Club Caracas (10/0).
(97/265)	GUERRA FORD Diony José	27.09.1971	9	1	1993-1997, Minervén FC El Callao (3/0), 1996 (4/1), CD Concepción (2/0).
(315/454)	GUERRA Juan Francisco	16.02.1987	6	0	2011-2012, UD Las Palmas (4/0), Caracas FC (2/0).
(234/383)	GUERRA MORALES Alejandro Abraham	09.07.1985	37	4	2006-2012, Caracas FC (29/3), Deportivo Anzoátegui SC Puerto La Cruz (6/1), AC Mineros de Guayana Puerto Ordaz (2/0).
(324/473)	GUERRERO CORREDOR Diego Alejandro	26.06.1986	1	0	2012, Deportivo Táchira FC San Cristóbal (1/0).
(62/177)	GUTIÉRREZ Félix		2	0	1981

(18/054)	HEREDIA Heriberto		2	0	1955
(124/296)	HERNÁNDEZ Félix José	18.04.1973	19	0	1996-1999, Minervén FC El Callao (1/0), Unión Atlético Táchira San Cristóbal (12/0), Club Atlético Celaya (6/0).
(222/371)	HERNÁNDEZ GUEDEZ Evelio de Jesús	18.06.1984	18	0	2004-2013, Trujillanos FC Valera (1/0), Club Deportivo ItalMaracaibo (1/0), Zamora FC Barinas (10/0), Deportivo Petare FC Caracas (3/0), Deportivo Anzoátegui SC Puerto La Cruz (3/0).
(42/123)	HERNÁNDEZ Julio		1	0	1973
(52/160)	HERNÁNDEZ Julio César		5	2	1979-1981
(298/448)	HERNÁNDEZ SANTOS Daniel	29.10.1985	16	0	2010-2013, Real Murcia CF (4/0), Real Valladolid CF (8/0), PAE Asteras Tripolis (4/0).

(202/363)	HERNÁNDEZ SANTOS Jonay Miguel	15.02.1979	**29**	**0**	2003-2008, Dundee FC (13/0), Córdoba CF (5/0), CF Ciudad de Murcia (4/0), Pontevedra CF (7/0).
(97/263)	HERNÁNDEZ Sergio Alejandro	30.01.1971	**31**	**0**	1993-1996, Unión Atlético Táchira San Cristóbal (31/0).
(135/317)	HERNÁNDEZ Tulio	14.02.1974	**1**	**0**	1997, Minervén FC El Callao (1/0).
(69/206)	HERRERA Carlos		**1**	**0**	1984
(113/281)	HEZZEL Alexander Antonio	12.08.1964	**5**	**0**	1995-1996, Caracas FC (5/0).
(118/286)	HIDALGO William	07.12.1971	**3**	**0**	1995-1996
(47/146)	IRIARTE Rafael		**6**	**1**	1977-1981
(30/091)	IRIARTE Ramón		**14**	**2**	1969-1975
(69/200)	ISEA Iván	12.02.1964	**1**	**0**	1984
(194/361)	ISEA Wiswell	13.09.1982	**1**	**0**	2002, Trujillanos FC Valera (1/0).
(70/211)	JAIMES Laureano	13.07.1961	**13**	**0**	1985-1995, Deportivo Táchira FC San Cristóbal (2/0), Unión Atlético Táchira San Cristóbal (11/0).
(47/140)	JIMÉNEZ Andrés		**2**	**0**	1977
(235/384)	JIMÉNEZ GONZÁLEZ Edgar Hernán	19.10.1984	**7**	**0**	2006-2011, Caracas FC (7/0).
(150/329)	JIMÉNEZ GONZÁLEZ Leopoldo Rafael	22.05.1978	**64**	**0**	1999-2005, Club Deportivo Italchacao Caracas (45/0), Unión Atlético Maracaibo (8/0), CD Once Caldas Manizales (6/0), CF Córdoba (3/0), FK Alania Vladikavkaz (2/0).
(92/245)	JIMÉNEZ José Luis	07.10.1968	**4**	**0**	1991, Portuguesa FC Acarigua (4/0).
(10/031)	JIMÉNEZ Luis		**5**	**0**	1946
(239/391)	LANCKEN Gregory	07.05.1979	**2**	**0**	2006, Deportivo Táchira FC San Cristóbal (1/0).
(70/208)	LANDAETA Carlos		**4**	**0**	1985
(18/051)	LASCURAIN Joseba		**2**	**0**	1955
(282/429)	LEZAMA ESPANOL Adrián José	22.07.1989	**2**	**0**	2009, Deportivo Anzoátegui SC Puerto La Cruz (2/0).
(323/469)	LIEBESKIND DÍAZ Alan José	07.01.1985	**1**	**0**	2011, CD Lara Barquisimeto (1/0).
(42/128)	LÓPEZ		**1**	**0**	1973
(69/201)	LÓPEZ José Ramón	19.03.1960	**1**	**0**	1984-1989, Club Sport Marítimo de Venezuela Caracas (2/0).
(129/306)	LUCENA Jhonny	15.07.1975	**5**	**0**	1996-1997, Llaneros FC Guanare (5/0).
(244/395)	LUCENA PEÑA Franklin José	20.02.1981	**51**	**1**	2007-2013, Caracas FC (39/1), Real Esppor Club Caracas (12/0).
(42/121)	LUCIDIO		**1**	**0**	1973
(315/455)	LUGO LIMPIO Jesús Alberto	14.09.1991	**2**	**0**	2011, Aragua FC Maracay (2/0).
(98/268)	LUPI Leonardo	02.10.1972	**3**	**0**	1993-2000, Trujillanos FC Valera (3/0).
(164/343)	LUZARDO Gregory	09.09.1969	**2**	**0**	2000, Club Deportivo Italchacao Caracas (2/0).
(233/379)	MACHADO CESÁREO Julio César	19.06.1982	**4**	**0**	2006-2010, Carabobo FC Valencia (1/0), Unión Atlético Maracaibo (2/0), Deportivo Táchira FC San Cristóbal (1/0).
(1/001)	MACHADO Ezequiel		**4**	**0**	1938
(323/470)	MACHÍS Darwin	07.02.1993	**2**	**0**	2011-2012, AC Mineros de Guayana Puerto Ordaz (2/0).
(146/320)	MADRÍZ Luis Guillermo	22.07.1970	**2**	**0**	1997, Estudiantes de Mérida FC (2/0).
(233/377)	MAITA Armando	26.08.1981	**3**	**0**	2006, Carabobo FC Valencia (2/0), Aragua FC Maracay (1/0).
(260/406)	MAITA URBÁEZ Armando Rafael	26.08.1981	**2**	**0**	2008, Unión Atlético Maracaibo (2/0).
(71/214)	MALDONADO Carlos Alberto	30.07.1963	**20**	**4**	1985-1991, Deportivo Táchira FC San Cristóbal (6/0), Unión Atlético Táchira San Cristóbal (14/4).
(36/101)	MALDONADO Efraín "Issa"		**1**	**0**	1971
(203/364)	MALDONADO MARRERO Giancarlo Gregorio	29.06.1982	**65**	**22**	2003-2011, AD Mineros de Guayana (1/0), Unión Atlético Maracaibo (13/5), CD O'Higins Rancagua (12/3), CF Atlante Cancún (21/10), Xerez CD Jerez de la Frontera (4/1), CD Chivas Carson (2/1), CF Atlante Cancún (12/2).
(39/117)	MARCANO Antonio		**2**	**0**	1972
(64/182)	MARCANO César José	31.10.1957	**4**	**0**	1981-1991, Club Sport Marítimo de Venezuela Caracas (3/0).
(1/008)	MARCANO Francisco		**4**	**1**	1938
(1/002)	MARCANO Teodardo		**9**	**0**	1938
(47/141)	MARCENARO Nelson		**1**	**0**	1977
(208/36)	MARGIOTTA Massimo	27.10.1977	**11**	**2**	2004-2005, Vicenza Calcio (11/2).
(32/094)	MARÍN Carlos Enrique		**15**	**1**	1969-1981
(6/020)	MÁRQUEZ Alberto		**4**	**0**	1938
(70/213)	MÁRQUEZ Heberth	30.11.1964	**17**	**2**	1985-1994, Club Sport Marítimo de Venezuela Caracas (17/2).
(4/016)	MÁRQUEZ Leonardo		**1**	**0**	1938
(13/037)	MÁRQUEZ Rafael		**5**	**0**	1946-1951
(36/102)	MARQUINA Luis		**7**	**0**	1971-1975, Estudiantes de Mérida FC (7/0).
(42/127)	MARTÍNEZ		**1**	**0**	1973
(97/262)	MARTÍNEZ DUGARTE Elvis Alfonso	04.10.1970	**33**	**0**	1993-2002, Estudiantes de Mérida FC (2/0), Caracas FC (12/0), Deportivo Táchira FC San Cristóbal (12/0), Nacional Táchira FC San Cristóbal (7/0).
(10/024)	MARTÍNEZ Germán		**7**	**0**	1946-1948
(262/410)	MARTÍNEZ Giancarlos	21.05.1979	**1**	**0**	2008, Deportivo Italia FC Caracas (1/0).
(315/457)	MARTÍNEZ Josef Alexander	19.05.1993	**12**	**2**	2011-2013, Caracas FC (3/0), BSC Young Boys Bern (5/1), FC Thun (4/1).
(148/324)	MARTÍNEZ SILVA Fernando	08.06.1977	**4**	**0**	1999-2000, Minervén FC El Callao (2/0), Estudiantes de Mérida FC (2/0).
(97/264)	MATHÍAS Marcos Elías	12.05.1970	**19**	**0**	1993-1997, Trujillanos FC Valera (19/0).
(18/053)	MATSON Agustín		**2**	**0**	1955
(123/295)	McINTOSH PARRA David Andrew	17.02.1973	**26**	**0**	1996-1999, Minervén FC El Callao (18/0), Caracas FC (8/0).
(152/334)	MEA VITALI Miguel Ángel	19.02.1981	**85**	**1**	1999-2012, Caracas FC (17/1), UE Lleida (13/0), Poggibonsi Calcio (1/0), Caracas FC (2/0), CA Chacarita Juniors San Martín (2/0), Caracas FC (9/0), SS Lazio Roma (2/0), Sora Calcio (1/0), SS Lazio Roma (1/0), PAE Levadeiakos Levadeia (2/0), Unión Atlético Maracaibo (27/0), FC Vaduz (4/0), CD Lara Barquisimeto (4/0).

(178/349)	MEA VITALI Rafael Loreto	16.02.1975	**11**	**0**	2001-2002, Caracas FC (10/0), SV Waldhof Mannheim (1/0).
(18/052)	MEDINA Carlos		**2**	**0**	1955
(80/225)	MEDINA Javier	10.12.1963	**1**	**0**	1989
(134/311)	MEDINA John Freddy	29.09.1970	**3**	**0**	1997, Atlético Zulia FC Maracaibo (3/0).
(42/124)	MELO		**1**	**0**	1973
(127/304)	MELO Reinaldo	05.05.1977	**1**	**0**	1996
(69/205)	MEMBRILLA José		**1**	**0**	1984
(78/221)	MÉNDEZ Gerardo		**2**	**0**	1987, Unión Atlético Táchira San Cristóbal (2/0).
(70/212)	MÉNDEZ William	10.12.1958	**7**	**0**	1985, Deportivo Táchira FC San Cristóbal (7/0).
(294/443)	MENDOZA ACOSTA Edgar José	15.06.1991	**1**	**0**	2010, CD Lara Barquisimeto (1/0).
(21/076)	MENDOZA BENEDETTO Luis	1946	**23**	**3**	1965-1979
(81/233)	MENDOZA Luis	27.03.1970	**1**	**0**	1989
(79/224)	MENDOZA Pablo		**1**	**0**	1987, Club Deportivo Italia Caracas (1/0).
(245/396)	MEZA MORENO Jesús Manuel	06.01.1986	**8**	**0**	2007-2011, Estudiantes de Mérida FC (3/0), CD Atlas Guadalajara (5/0).
(66/191)	MILILLO José		**2**	**0**	1983-1984, Estudiantes de Mérida FC (2/0).
(98/269)	MILILLO Ricardo	19.09.1969	**9**	**0**	1993, Estudiantes de Mérida FC (9/0).
(20/059)	MIRABAL Felipe		**4**	**0**	1964-1965, Club Deportivo Portugués Caracas (4/0).
(270/416)	MIRABAL Johnny Fair	30.06.1990	**1**	**0**	2008, Caracas FC (1/0).
(112/278)	MIRANDA Gabriel Antonio	24.08.1968	**17**	**3**	1994-1997, Caracas FC (17/3).
(16/041)	MONTEROLA Gastón		**4**	**2**	1948-1955
(23/081)	MONTES Marcel Luis		**2**	**0**	1965
(48/151)	MORA José		**1**	**0**	1977
(16/040)	MORALES Carlos		**1**	**0**	1948
(236/389)	MORALES Daybiger		**1**	**0**	2006, Unión Deportivo Lara FC (1/0).
(167/346)	MORALES LARES José Leonardo	07.07.1978	**26**	**0**	2000-2012, Club Zulianos Maracaibo (1/0), Deportivo Anzoátegui SC Puerto La Cruz (25/0).
(104/274)	MORALES Luis	03.12.1964	**6**	**1**	1993-1996, Minervén FC El Callao (5/1), 1996 (1/0).
(1/003)	MORALES Ramón		**5**	**0**	1938
(122/291)	MORÁN PULEO Dickson Ruberth	11.08.1973	**65**	**14**	1996-2007, Club Deportivo Italchacao Caracas (2/0), Atlético Zulia FC Maracaibo (10/1), Estudiantes de Mérida FC (6/1), Córdoba CF (11/2), Club Deportivo Italchacao Caracas (1/0), Estudiantes de Mérida FC (9/3), Deportivo Táchira FC San Cristóbal (2/0), Unión Atlético Maracaibo (12/1), CD Atlético Bucaramanga (3/5), AA Argentinos Juniors Buenos Aires (3/1), Estudiantes de Mérida FC (3/0), Deportivo Táchira FC San Cristóbal (3/0).
(253/400)	MORENO CHACÓN José David	31.10.1982	**1**	**0**	2007, Deportivo Anzoátegui SC Puerto La Cruz (1/0).
(208/366)	MORENO RIERA Alejandro Enrique	08.07.1979	**40**	**3**	2004-2012, Los Angeles Galaxy (3/0), San José Earthquakes (1/0), Houston Dynamos (1/0), Columbus Crew (15/2), Philadelphia Union (7/0), CD Chivas Carson (13/1).
(193/359)	MORENO Wilfredo	19.04.1976	**11**	**1**	2002-2004, AD Mineros de Guayana (11/1).
(78/218)	MOROVIĆ Zdenko	31.08.1966	**5**	**0**	1987-1989, Club Deportivo Italia Caracas (1/0), Club Sport Marítimo de Venezuela Caracas (4/0).
(47/143)	MOSS José Ricardo		**5**	**1**	1977
(20/060)	MOTA David		**15**	**0**	1964-1969, Club Deportivo Galicia Caracas (15/0).
(1/006)	MUJICA Hernán		**8**	**1**	1938-1946

(134/313)	NABOLLÁN José	14.03.1974	**2**	**0**	1997, Atlético Zulia FC Maracaibo (2/0).
(70/210)	NADA Richard		**2**	**0**	1985
(25/085)	NARANJO SILVA Rafael Ignacio	1943	**7**	**0**	1967-1969
(78/220)	NIETO José Francisco		**2**	**0**	1987, Unión Atlético Táchira San Cristóbal (2/0).
(77/216)	NIKOLAC Daniel	11.05.1961	**4**	**0**	1985-1989, Club Sport Marítimo de Venezuela Caracas (4/0).
(30/092)	NITTI Augusto		**6**	**0**	1969, Club Deportivo Italia Caracas (6/0).
(127/301)	NORIEGA ACOSTA Daniel	30.03.1977	**38**	**5**	1996-2005, AD Mineros de Guayana (1/0), CA Unión Santa Fé (6/0), Club Sporting Cristal Lima (1/0), CA Unión Santa Fé (9/2), Club Deportivo Italchacao Caracas (3/0), AD Mineros de Guayana (3/1), Club Deportivo Italchacao Caracas (11/1), CD Independiente Medellin (2/1), Caracas FC (2/0).
(13/036)	NURSE Jorge		**2**	**0**	1946

(4/015)	OCHOA Félix		**2**	**0**	1938
(161/341)	OCHOA José	17.12.1978	**3**	**0**	2000, El Vigía FC (3/0).
(43/132)	OCHOA Omar		**10**	**0**	1975-1981
(69/207)	OLIVARES Arturo		**1**	**0**	1984
(37/112)	OLIVARES Asdrúbal		**4**	**1**	1972
(10/030)	OLIVARES Asdrúbal		**5**	**0**	1946-1951
(290/435)	OROZCO CUJÍA Yohandri José	19.03.1991	**23**	**1**	2010-2013, Zulia FC Maracaibo (7/0). VfL Wolfsburg (12/0), Deportivo Táchira FC San Cristóbal (4/1).
(42/130)	ORRIOLS Ramón		**1**	**0**	1973
(20/068)	ORTA Carlos		**1**	**0**	1964
(42/119)	OSORIO		**1**	**0**	1973
(16/042)	OSORIO Luis		**2**	**0**	1948-1951
(240/393)	OSPINA Jhon	06.06.1986	**1**	**0**	2006, Deportivo Táchira FC San Cristóbal (1/0).
(335/476)	OTERO VÁSQUEZ Rómulo	09.11.1992	**5**	**1**	2013, Caracas FC (5/1).

(64/179)	PACHECO José		**1**	**0**	1981
(82/238)	PACHECO William	18.04.1962	**12**	**0**	1989-1991, Unión Atlético Táchira San Cristóbal (8/0), Minervén FC El Callao (4/0).
(133/309)	PÁEZ Andrew	28.12.1968	**6**	**0**	1996-1997, AD Mineros de Guayana (6/0).

(172/348)	PÁEZ GÓMEZ Ricardo David	09.02.1979	64	7	2000-2007, Deportivo Táchira FC San Cristóbal (15/2), Estudiantes de Mérida FC (7/2), Unión Atlético Maracaibo (4/0), Bani Yas SC (3/0), Barcelona SC Guayaquil (6/0), CD América Cali (5/0), Club Deportivo Pereira (3/1), Politehnica-AEK Timişoara (3/0), Club Deportivo ItalMaracaibo (3/0), PAS Joánnina (4/0), AD Mineros de Guayana (5/2), Vería FC (6/0).
(40/118)	PÁEZ MONZÓN Richard	31.05.1952	10	1	1972-1979, Estudiantes de Mérida FC (6/1), Portuguesa FC Acarigua (4/0).
(108/276)	PÁEZ-PUMAR Leopoldo	29.03.1971	4	0	1993, Caracas FC (4/0).
(98/270)	PALENCIA Oswaldo	01.02.1970	15	3	1993-1997, Estudiantes de Mérida FC (8/2), 1996 (1/0), Universidad de los Andes FC Mérida (6/2).
(323/472)	PALOMINO FARIÑES Hermes Manuel	04.03.1988	1	0	2011, PFC Cherno More Varna (1/0).
(275/424)	PARRA PERDOMO José Mauricio	06.02.1990	3	0	2008-2011, Deportivo Táchira FC San Cristóbal (3/0).
(82/236)	PAZ Andrés Leonardo	30.11.1963	9	0	1989-1995, Unión Atlético Táchira San Cristóbal (8/0), 1995 (1/0).
(52/162)	PEÑA Alexis		5	0	1979-1980, Universidad de los Andes FC Mérida (5/0).
(262/413)	PEÑA PUENTES Louis Angelo	25.12.1989	15	0	2008-2013, Estudiantes de Mérida FC (5/0), Sporting Clube de Braga (4/0), Caracas FC (5/0), Clube Náutico Capibaribe Recife (1/0).
(39/107)	PÉREZ CARBONELL Ricardo		2	0	1971-1972
(240/394)	PÉREZ CONSUEGRA Edder Alfonso	03.07.1983	7	0	2006-2007, Caracas FC (5/0), CS Marítimo Funchal (2/0).
(236/386)	PÉREZ Engelberth	04.02.1986	1	0	2006, Atlético Zamora FC Barinas (1/0).
(146/319)	PÉREZ FERNÁNDEZ Giovanny José	14.10.1974	28	0	1997-2007, Deportivo Táchira FC San Cristóbal (2/0), Club Deportivo Italchacao Caracas (15/0), Estudiantes de Mérida FC (5/0), Unión Atlético Maracaibo (4/0), Deportivo Táchira FC San Cristóbal (1/0), Zamora FC Barinas (1/0).
(239/390)	PÉREZ GRECO Edgar Fernando	16.02.1982	11	1	2006-2012, Deportivo Táchira FC San Cristóbal (4/0), CD Lara Barquisimeto (7/1).
(10/023)	PÉREZ Manuel Antonio		6	0	1946-1951
(16/043)	PÉREZ Manuel Leopoldo		1	0	1948
(293/441)	PÉREZ ZABALA Víctor	14.03.1990	1	0	2010, Carabobo FC Valencia
(283/430)	PERNÍA Henry	09.11.1990	6	0	2009-2010, Llaneros de Guanare FC (6/0).
(236/387)	PEROZO RINCÓN Grenddy Adrián	28.02.1986	42	2	2006-2013, Deportivo Táchira FC San Cristóbal (20/0), Boyacá Chicó FC Tunja (15/2), Club Olimpo de Bahía Blanca (4/0), Deportivo Táchira FC San Cristóbal (2/0), AJ Ajaccio (1/0).
(21/075)	PINEDA Luis		1	0	1965
(191/356)	PONZO GARCÍA Rafael	18.10.1978	3	0	2002-2006, CD Tenerife (1/0), Real Oviedo CF (2/0).
(194/362)	PRESILLA Frank	28.07.1982	1	0	2002, Deportivo Táchira FC San Cristóbal (1/0).
(325/474)	QUIJADA FASCIANA Rubert José	10.02.1989	2	0	2012, Monagas SC Maturín (2/0).
(122/292)	QUIÑÓNEZ Juan Carlos	13.09.1975	1	0	1996, Unión Atlético Táchira San Cristóbal (1/0).
(79/223)	QUINTEROS Julio	31.10.1964	1	0	1987, Portuguesa FC Acarigua (1/0).
(270/419)	RAMÍREZ Guillermo Abel	10.11.1989	1	0	2008, Caracas FC (1/0).
(226/374)	RAMÍREZ Paúl	30.07.1986	1	0	2005, AC Bellinzona (1/0).
(66/189)	RAMOS Alberto		1	0	1983, Club Deportivo Italia Caracas (1/0).
(133/308)	RAMOS Luis	18.02.1966	8	0	1996-1997, Atlético Zulia FC Maracaibo (8/0).
(36/104)	RANGEL Reinaldo		1	0	1971
(4/014)	RAVARD Francisco		1	0	1938
(21/074)	RAVELO José		4	0	1965
(21/073)	RAVELO RODRÍGUEZ Antonio	02.04.1940	13	2	1965-1969
(36/109)	RAVELO William		1	1	1971
(64/181)	REGUEIRO Eduardo		1	0	1981
(260/405)	RENTERÍA GARCÍA Emilio	09.10.1984	8	0	2008-2012, Caracas FC (1/0), Columbus Crew (7/0).
(96/261)	RESTIFO Reinaldo	27.05.1969	5	0	1993-1996, Club Deportivo Italia Caracas (5/0).
(139/318)	REY CORTEGOSO José Manuel	20.05.1975	115	11	1997-2011, Caracas FC (11/1), Club Sport Emelec Guayaquil (8/2), Caracas FC (22/2), Club Sport Emelec Guayaquil (10/1), Caracas FC (8/0), Pontevedra CF (10/0), Caracas FC (2/0), CDC Atlético Nacional Medellin (4/1), Caracas FC (10/0), AEK Lárnaka FC (7/1), Caracas FC (16/3), CSD Colo Colo Santiago (2/0), CD Lara Barquisimeto (5/0).
(178/351)	REY J.		1	0	2001
(303/450)	REYES José Miguel	19.09.1992	2	0	2011-2012, Carabobo FC Valencia (1/0), Deportivo Anzoátegui SC Puerto La Cruz (1/0).
(260/404)	RINCÓN HERNÁNDEZ Tomás Eduardo	13.01.1988	54	0	2008-2013, Zamora FC Barinas (13/0), Hamburger SV (41/0).
(1/011)	RÍOS Fernando		9	5	1938-1946
(295/447)	RIVAS BOADA Gelmin Javier	23.03.1989	2	0	2010-2012, Deportivo Anzoátegui SC Puerto La Cruz (2/0).
(78/219)	RIVAS BRITO Héctor Enrique	27.09.1968	24	1	1987-1995, Club Sport Marítimo de Venezuela Caracas (24/1).
(150/331)	RIVAS José	05.01.1976	1	0	1999, Club Internacional de Lara FC (1/0).
(43/134)	RIVAS Miguel		4	0	1975-1977, Club Deportivo Galicia Caracas (4/0).
(82/239)	RIVAS Stalín José	05.08.1971	34	3	1989-1996, FC Deportivo Mineros de Guayana (9/2), R Standard Liège (6/1), Minervén FC Callao (7/0), Caracas FC (12/0).
(323/471)	RIVERO GONZÁLEZ Carlos Gregorio	27.11.1992	4	0	2011-2012, Deportivo Anzoátegui SC Puerto La Cruz (4/0).
(192/357)	RIVERO Jobanny	13.12.1980	8	1	2002-2004, Trujillanos FC Valera (1/0), Caracas FC (7/1).
(67/193)	RIZZI Franco	13.07.1964	7	0	1983-1989, Club Italo Venezolano (3/0), Club Sport Marítimo de Venezuela Caracas (4/0).
(95/250)	RODALLEGAS Robert	18.11.1969	6	0	1991-1997, Unión Atlético Táchira San Cristóbal (1/0), Minervén FC El Callao (5/0).
(11/035)	RODRÍGUEZ Carlos		6	2	1946-1955
(36/103)	RODRÍGUEZ Carlos		1	0	1971

(96/255)	RODRÍGUEZ Edson José	24.04.1970	22	1	1993-1996, Club Sport Marítimo de Venezuela Caracas (19/1), 1996 (3/0).
(37/113)	RODRÍGUEZ Francisco		1	0	1972, Anzoategui FC Puerto La Cruz (1/0).
(246/399)	RODRÍGUEZ GONZÁLEZ Renier Alexander	25.03.1984	1	0	2007, Unión Atlético Maracaibo (1/0).
(37/114)	RODRÍGUEZ Héctor		4	0	1972
(135/316)	RODRÍGUEZ Jesús	24.03.1968	5	0	1997, Estudiantes de Mérida FC (5/0).
(65/188)	RODRÍGUEZ José		4	0	1983, Unión Deportiva de Lara FC Barquisimeto (4/0).
(294/445)	ROJAS HEREDIA Óscar Daniel	16.01.1990	1	0	2010, Llaneros de Guanare FC (1/0).
(82/237)	ROJAS Luis	01.08.1963	1	0	1989
(148/322)	ROJAS MÉNDEZ Jorge Alberto	01.12.1977	91	3	1999-2009, CF Badajoz (2/0), Estudiantes de Mérida FC (6/0), Caracas FC (19/0), Club Sport Emelec Guayaquil (10/0), Caracas FC (6/1), CDC Atlético Nacional Medellin (8/0), Caracas FC (6/0), CDC Atlético Nacional Medellin (5/0), Caracas FC (8/0), CD América de Cali (6/0), Unión Atlético Maracaibo (8/1), Red Bull New York (7/1).
(289/431)	ROMERO ARMENIO Giovanny Michael	01.01.1984	5	0	2010-2011, Caracas FC (5/0).
(48/149)	ROMERO Santiago		3	0	1977, Portuguesa FC Acarigua (3/0).
(270/420)	ROMO PÉREZ Rafael Enrique	07.07.1990	5	0	2008-2011, Llaneros de Guanare FC (5/0), Udinese Calcio (3/0).
(304/451)	RONDÓN FERNÁNDEZ Mário Júnior	26.03.1986	4	0	2011-2013, FC Paços de Ferreira (1/0), CD Nacional Madeira (3/0).
(260/407)	RONDÓN GIMÉNEZ José Salomón	16.09.1989	34	12	2008-2013, AC Aragua FC Maracay (3/1), UD Las Palmas (3/1), Málaga FC (18/6), FK Rubin Kazan (10/4).
(149/327)	RONDÓN HEREDIA Alexander	03.08.1977	48	5	1999-2010, SCA Nueva Cádiz Cumana (6/0), Club Zulianos Maracaibo (2/0), Caracas FC (12/3), Deportivo Táchira FC San Cristóbal (6/0), São Paulo FC (6/0), Deportivo Táchira FC San Cristóbal (1/0), Deportivo Anzoátegui SC Puerto La Cruz (15/2).
(246/398)	ROSALES ALTUVE Roberto José	20.11.1988	45	0	2007-2013, Caracas FC (1/0), KAA Gent (13/0), FC Twente Enschede (31/0).
(194/360)	ROUGA ROSSI Enrique Andrés	03.02.1982	23	0	2002-2012, Caracas FC (7/0), CPD Atlético Junior Barranquilla (4/0), Caracas FC (6/0), Alki Lárnaka FC (4/0), Deportivo Táchira FC San Cristóbal (2/0).

(6/018)	SALAS LOZADA Vaughan		2	0	1938
(47/142)	SALAS William		7	0	1977-1981, Portuguesa FC Acarigua (7/0).
(122/293)	SALAZAR César		2	0	1996
(276/425)	SALAZAR CUMANA Carlos Alfredo	15.05.1989	11	0	2009-2012, AC Aragua FC Maracay (6/0), Deportivo Anzoátegui SC Puerto La Cruz (5/0).
(31/093)	SALCEDO Alvaro		1	0	1969
(80/228)	SAMUEL Enrique	16.11.1967	2	0	1989
(80/226)	SAN VICENTE Bethelmy Noël	21.12.1964	11	0	1989-1996, Club Sport Marítimo de Venezuela Caracas (7/0), 1994 (1/0), 1995 (1/0), Minervén FC El Callao (2/0).
(133/310)	SANABRIA Didier	26.11.1974	3	0	1996-2000, Unión Atlético Táchira San Cristóbal (1/0), Deportivo Táchira FC San Cristóbal (2/0).
(10/022)	SANABRIA Miguel		8	0	1946-1964
(56/168)	SÁNCHEZ Eustorgio		2	0	1980
(315/453)	SÁNCHEZ LEÓN Andrés Elionay	12.12.1987	2	0	2011, Deportivo Petare FC Caracas (2/0).
(30/089)	SÁNCHEZ Manuel Asdrúbal		6	0	1969
(291/436)	SÁNCHEZ Mario Andrés	19.06.1991	3	1	2010, Deportivo Anzoátegui SC Puerto La Cruz (3/1).
(52/157)	SÁNCHEZ URBINA Asdrúbal José		21	0	1979-1987, Universidad de los Andes FC Mérida (19/0), Estudiantes de Mérida FC (2/0).
(150/328)	SANHOUSE CONTRERAS Manuel Alejandro	16.07.1975	16	0	1999-2010, Club Deportivo Italchacao Caracas (6/0), Caracas FC (1/0), Espoli Club Quito (4/0), Deportivo Táchira FC San Cristóbal (1/0), Unión Atlético Maracaibo (2/0), Deportivo Táchira FC San Cristóbal (2/0).
(20/067)	SANTANA Rafael		15	4	1964-1979, Club Deportivo Galicia Caracas (13/4), Club Deportivo Portugués Caracas (2/0).
(80/231)	SAVARESE Giovanni	14.07.1971	23	4	1989-2001, Long Island Roughriders (2/0), New York/New Jersey MetroStars (12/2), Viterbese AC (7/2), San José Earthquakes (1/0), Swansea City FC (1/0).
(58/174)	SCARPECCIO SABATTINI Juan José	14.05.1952	4	0	1981, Estudiantes de Mérida FC (3/0).
(24/066)	SCOVINO Humberto Francisco		6	2	1964-1967, Valencia FC (6/2).
(80/227)	SEGOVIA Wilmer	26.04.1968	1	0	1989
(240/392)	SEIJAS GUNTHER Luis Manuel	23.06.1986	48	2	2006-2013, CA Banfield (1/0), Deportivo Táchira FC San Cristóbal (4/0), Independiente Santa Fé (7/0), Santa Fé CD Bogotá (22/0), R Standard Liège (12/1), Sociedad Deportivo Quito (2/1).
(11/033)	SEIJAS Nerio		5	0	1946
(20/069)	SERFATY O.		1	0	1964
(58/172)	SIMONELLI Nicolás		7	0	1981-1985
(128/305)	SOCORRO VERA Juan Carlos	13.05.1972	5	0	1996-1997, UD Las Palmas (5/0).
(49/152)	SOTO Edgar		3	0	1977
(37/110)	STANICH Raúl		5	0	1972, Valencia FC (5/0).
(20/063)	SUÁREZ Manuel		1	0	1964
(10/028)	SUCRE Andrés		6	4	1946

(90/243)	TARAZONA Martín José	20.03.1968	1	0	1989
(36/108)	TAVAREZ Rolman		1	0	1971
(10/027)	TERÁN Pedro		5	0	1946-1948
(134/314)	TIZAMO Luis	06.10.1975	2	0	1997, Minervén FC El Callao (2/0).
(189/353)	TORREALBA ACEVEDO José Antonio	13.06.1980	17	4	2002-2008, Estudiantes de Mérida FC (4/0), Mamelodi Sundowns FC Pretoria (9/4), Deportivo Táchira FC San Cristóbal (3/0), Kaizer Chiefs FC Johannesburg (1/0).

(34/097)	TORRES Igor Orlando		**8**	**0**	1969-1975
(65/185)	TORRES LOBO René Antonio	13.10.1960	**21**	**2**	1983-1989, Universidad de los Andes FC Mérida (1/0), Estudiantes de Mérida FC (11/2), Mineros de Guayana Puerto Ordáz (9/0).
(58/173)	TORRES Oscar		**7**	**0**	1981-1983, Estudiantes de Mérida FC (7/0).
(44/138)	TORRES Rubén Darío		**3**	**0**	1975, Anzoategui FC Puerto La Cruz (3/0).
(20/064)	TORTOLERO Argenis		**11**	**1**	1964-1969
(96/252)	TORTOLERO ROMÁN Edson Argenis	27.08.1971	**39**	**3**	1993-2006, Minervén FC El Callao (21/1), Universidad de los Andos FC Mérida (9/1), Deportivo Táchira FC San Cristóbal (5/1), CF Queretaro (3/0), no club (1/0).
(18/055)	TOVAR Alí		**3**	**0**	1955-1964
(211/368)	TOYO BÁRCENAS Javier Eduardo	12.10.1977	**10**	**0**	2004-2008, Caracas FC (9/0), CD Atlético Bucaramanga (1/0).
(317/464)	TÚÑEZ ARCEO Andrés José	15.03.1987	**10**	**0**	2011-2013, RC Celta de Vigo (10/0).
(124/297)	URDANETA RANGEL Gabriel José	07.01.1976	**77**	**9**	1996-2005, Caracas FC (2/0), Atlético Zulia FC Maracaibo (14/0), Universidad de los Andes FC Mérida (10/3), Caracas FC (15/2), FC Luzern (7/0), SV Waldhof Mannheim (2/0), FC Lugano (3/1), Caracas FC (4/1), SC Kriens (8/1), BSC Young Boys Bern (12/1).
(68/196)	URDANETA William		**1**	**0**	1983, Unión Deportiva de Lara FC Barquisimeto (1/0).
(69/197)	USECHE Hildubrando		**1**	**0**	1984
(38/115)	USECHE Lorenzo		**4**	**0**	1972
(32/095)	USECHE PÉREZ Delmán		**11**	**0**	1969-1975, Estudiantes de Mérida FC (11/0).
(114/284)	VALBUENA Jesús Ángel	28.07.1969	**7**	**0**	1995-1996, Trujillanos FC Valera (7/0).
(294/444)	VALDÉZ Daniel Eduardo	09.04.1985	**1**	**0**	2010, Zamora FC Barinas (1/0).
(122/289)	VALIENTE Jesús	28.08.1973	**9**	**0**	1996-1997, Trujillanos FC Valera (9/0).
(122/288)	VALLENILLA PACHECO Luis José	13.03.1974	**77**	**1**	1996-2007, Trujillanos FC Valera (17/0), Universidad de los Andos FC Mérida (6/0), Club Deportivo Italchacao Caracas (7/1), Deportivo Táchira FC San Cristóbal (3/0), Caracas FC (21/0), Club Olimpo Bahia Blanca (6/0), AD Mineros de Guayana (1/0), Unión Atlético Maracaibo (11/0), Nea Salamis Famagusta FC (5/0).
(260/408)	VARGAS ARANGUREN Ronald Alejandro	02.12.1986	**15**	**3**	2008-2012, Caracas FC (8/2), Club Brügge KV (5/1), RSC Anderlecht Bruxelles (1/0).
(293/440)	VARGAS ARCHILA Luis Humberto	15.04.1989	**1**	**0**	2010, Yaracuyanos FC (1/0).
(43/135)	VÁSQUEZ Néstor		**2**	**0**	1975, Club Deportivo Italia Caracas (2/0).
(152/335)	VEGA HERNÁNDEZ Renny Vicente	04.07.1979	**62**	**0**	1999-2012, Nacional Táchira FC San Cristóbal (6/0), Aragua FC Maracay (2/0), Carabobo FC Valencia (14/0), Bursaspor Kulübü (8/0), Denizlispor Kulübü (9/0), Caracas FC (18/0), CSD Colo Colo Santiago (3/0), Caracas FC (2/0).
(44/137)	VEGA Vicente Emilio		**14**	**0**	1975-1983, Club Deportivo San Cristóbal (1/0), Portuguesa FC Acarigua (13/0).
(275/421)	VELÁZQUEZ RODRÍGUEZ José Manuel	08.09.1990	**12**	**1**	2008-2012, Deportivo Anzoátegui SC Puerto La Cruz (1/0), Villarreal CF „B" (6/1), AC Mineros de Guayana Puerto Ordaz (4/0), Panathinaïkos AO Athína (1/0).
(153/336)	VERA MÁRQUEZ José de Jesús	09.02.1969	**18**	**0**	1999-2001, Estudiantes de Mérida FC (8/0), Club Independiente Santa Fé Bogotá (7/0), Estudiantes de Mérida FC (3/0).
(125/299)	VERA MARTINEAU Luis Enrique	09.03.1973	**53**	**2**	1996-2007, Minervén FC El Callao (6/1), Universidad de los Andes FC Mérida (2/0), Caracas FC (14/0), Monagas SC Maturín (2/0), Caracas FC (29/1).
(25/083)	VIDAL José		**2**	**0**	1967, Unión Deportiva de Lara FC Barquisimeto (2/0).
(52/155)	VIDAL Juan José		**4**	**0**	1979, Club Deportivo Italia Caracas (4/0).
(51/153)	VIELMA Gerardo		**2**	**0**	1977-1978
(161/339)	VIELMA PEÑA Leonel Gerardo	30.08.1978	**58**	**4**	2000-2008, Estudiantes de Mérida FC (11/0), Unión Atlético Maracaibo (6/1), Deportivo Táchira FC San Cristóbal (3/0), Club Deportivo Cali (4/1), Caracas FC (3/0), CD Once Caldas Manizales (2/0), Club Deportivo ItalMaracaibo (5/0), Caracas FC (15/1), Independiente Santa Fé (9/1).
(113/282)	VIGAS Danny	05.10.1973	**8**	**0**	1995-1999, Atlético Zulia FC Maracaibo (5/0), Universidad de los Andes FC Mérida (3/0).
(162/342)	VILLAFRAZ QUINTERO José Javier	01.01.1980	**18**	**1**	2000-2007, Estudiantes de Mérida FC (9/0), Unión Atlético Maracaibo (1/0), Estudiantes de Mérida FC (1/0), Deportivo Táchira FC San Cristóbal (7/1).
(294/446)	VILLARROEL DI PARSIA Juan Pablo	13.09.1991	**1**	**0**	2010, Deportivo Italia FC Caracas (1/0).
(209/367)	VIZCARRONDO ARAUJO Oswaldo Augusto	31.05.1984	**54**	**8**	2004-2013, Caracas FC (13/0), Club Olimpia Asunción (5/1), CD Once Caldas Manizales (7/2), Deportivo Anzoátegui SC Puerto La Cruz (11/3), Club Olimpo de Bahía Blanca (4/1), Club América Ciudad de México (4/1), CA Lanús (6/0), FC Nantes (4/0).
(80/232)	YANTIS Otilio Enrique	23.06.1967	**5**	**0**	1989-1991, 1989 (1/0), FC Deportivo Mineros de Guayana (4/0).
(275/423)	YEGÜEZ SALGADO José Jesús	19.09.1987	**5**	**0**	2008-2009, Deportivo Anzoátegui SC Puerto La Cruz (1/0), Deportivo Táchira FC San Cristóbal (4/0).
(246/397)	YORI Rubén Ramón	02.06.1976	**1**	**0**	2007, Deportivo Anzoátegui SC Puerto La Cruz (1/0).
(317/465)	ZAMBRANO SUÁREZ Josmar	09.06.1992	**2**	**0**	2011, CD Tenerife (2/0).
(10/026)	ZAMUDIO David		**7**	**0**	1946-1948
(20/061)	ZARZALEJO José Luis		**12**	**0**	1964-1969
(56/171)	ZUBIZARRETA Iker Joseba		**3**	**1**	1980

NATIONAL COACHES

Name	Period	Matches	P	W	D	L	GF	-	GA	
Vittorio GODIGNA (*Italy*)	12.02.1938 – 19.08.1938	[1-9]	9	1	0	8	9	-	22	11.11 %
Sixto SOLER (*Peru*)	12.12.1946 – 26.12.1946	[10-15]	6	2	0	4	12	-	12	33.33 %
Alvaro CARTÉA	05.01.1948	[16]	1	0	1	0	2	-	2	50.00 %
Orlando FANTONI (*Brazil*)	05.03.1951 – 21.03.1955	[17-19]	3	1	0	2	5	-	8	33.33 %
Rafael Franco REYES (*Argentina*)	31.08.1964 – 24.08.1969	[20-35]	16	1	1	14	12	-	54	9.37 %
Gregorio GÓMEZ (*Argentina*)	13.11.1971 – 16.12.1973	[36-42]	7	3	1	3	7	-	18	50.00 %
José Walter ROQUE (*Uruguay*)	30.07.1975 – 13.08.1975	[43-46]	4	0	0	4	1	-	26	0.00 %
Dan GEORGIADIS (*Greece*)	20.01.1977 – 17.03.1977	[47-51]	5	1	1	3	3	-	8	30.00 %
José Julián HERNÁNDEZ	01.08.1979 – 29.08.1979	[52-55]	4	0	2	2	1	-	12	25.00 %
José Walter ROQUE (*Uruguay*)	01.07.1980 – 30.06.1985	[56-77]	22	4	3	15	18	-	46	25.00 %
Rafael SANTANA (*Spain**)	28.06.1987 – 30.06.1987	[78-79]	2	0	0	2	1	-	8	0.00 %
Carlos Horacio MORENO (*Argentina*)	26.03.1989 – 27.08.1989	[80-91]	11	1	2	8	11	-	28	18.18 %
Miguel SABINO	20.08.1989	[90]	1	0	0	1	0	-	6	0.00 %
Víctor PIGNANELLI (*Uruguay*)	06.07.1991 – 12.07.1991	[92-95]	4	0	0	4	1	-	15	0.00 %
Ratomir DUJKOVIĆ (*Yugoslavia*)	23.01.1993 – 28.01.1994	[96-112]	17	1	5	11	13	-	53	20.58 %
Rafael SANTANA (*Spain**)	03.04.1995 – 10.11.1996	[113-132]	20	3	4	13	15	-	43	25.00 %
Eduardo BORRERO (*Colombia*)	15.12.1996 – 12.10.1997	[133-147]	15	0	3	12	5	-	32	10.00 %
José Omar PASTORIZA (*Argentina*)	27.01.1999 – 15.11.2000	[148-176]	29	6	5	18	26	-	59	29.31 %
Richard Alfred PÁEZ MONZÓN	28.03.2001 – 20.11.2007	[177-259]	83	29	18	36	101	-	117	45.78 %
César Alejandro FARÍAS ACOSTA	03.02.2008 –>	[260->	84	29	24	31	97	-	118	

(*) Originally Spanish citizen, later Venezoelan naturalized.

National coaches several times in charge:

Name	How often	Matches	M	W	D	L	GF	-	GA	
José Walter ROQUE (*Uruguay*)	2x	[43-46],[56-77]	26	4	3	19	19	-	72	21.15 %
Rafael SANTANA	2x	[78-79],[113-132]	22	3	4	15	16	-	51	22.72 %

HEAD-TO-HEAD STATISTICS

	HOME					AWAY					NEUTRAL					TOTAL				
Angola	1	0	1	0	0 : 0											1	0	1	0	0 : 0
Argentina	8	1	0	7	6 : 24	9	0	0	9	3 : 41	3	0	0	3	1 : 9	20	1	0	19	10 : 74
Aruba						1	1	0	0	3 : 0						1	1	0	0	3 : 0
Australia	1	0	1	0	1 : 1											1	0	1	0	1 : 1
Austria						1	1	0	0	1 : 0						1	1	0	0	1 : 0
Bolivia	15	7	4	4	28 : 24	13	2	3	8	8 : 33	5	1	3	1	9 : 8	33	10	10	13	45 : 65
Brazil	8	0	0	8	3 : 34	9	0	1	8	1 : 36	4	1	1	2	2 : 12	21	1	2	18	6 : 82
Cameroon "U21"											1	0	1	0	1 : 1	1	0	1	0	1 : 1
Canada	2	0	2	0	3 : 3											2	0	2	0	3 : 3
Chile	9	0	3	6	5 : 14	9	1	2	6	5 : 27	6	1	0	5	3 : 15	24	2	5	17	13 : 56
Colombia	16	3	10	3	13 : 14	13	1	2	10	5 : 27	4	2	0	2	6 : 7	33	6	12	15	24 : 48
Costa Rica	6	2	3	1	8 : 6	4	1	1	2	9 : 9	3	0	0	3	3 : 11	13	3	4	6	20 : 26
Cuba	1	1	0	0	3 : 1											1	1	0	0	3 : 1
Curaçao											3	1	0	2	4 : 6	3	1	0	2	4 : 6
Denmark League XI	1	0	1	0	1 : 1											1	0	1	0	1 : 1
Dominican Republic	1	1	0	0	1 : 0											1	1	0	0	1 : 0
Ecuador	11	7	2	2	18 : 10	10	2	0	8	6 : 25	3	1	0	2	3 : 9	24	10	2	12	27 : 44
El Salvador	2	2	0	0	3 : 1	1	1	0	0	1 : 0	2	0	0	2	3 : 5	5	3	0	2	7 : 6
Estonia	1	1	0	0	3 : 0											1	1	0	0	3 : 0
France "B"											1	0	0	1	0 : 2	1	0	0	1	0 : 2
Guatemala	3	2	0	1	4 : 3	2	1	0	1	2 : 3	1	1	0	0	3 : 2	6	4	0	2	9 : 8
Guinea	1	1	0	0	2 : 1											1	1	0	0	2 : 1
Haiti	3	2	1	0	5 : 3											3	2	1	0	5 : 3
Honduras	3	2	1	0	4 : 2	2	1	0	1	1 : 1	3	1	1	1	3 : 4	8	4	2	2	8 : 7
Iran											1	0	0	1	0 : 1	1	0	0	1	0 : 1
Jamaica	1	1	0	0	2 : 0	3	1	1	1	3 : 2						4	2	1	1	5 : 2
Japan						2	0	2	0	1 : 1						2	0	2	0	1 : 1
Mexico	1	0	0	1	0 : 5	3	0	1	2	3 : 7	8	0	1	7	5 : 19	12	0	2	10	8 : 31
Mexico „B“											1	1	0	0	3 : 0	1	1	0	0	3 : 0
Mexico Olympic						1	0	0	1	0 : 1						1	0	0	1	0 : 1
Moldova	1	1	0	0	4 : 0											1	1	0	0	4 : 0
Morocco Olympic						1	0	0	1	0 : 2						1	0	0	1	0 : 2
Netherlands Antilles	1	1	0	0	1 : 0	2	1	0	1	2 : 2						3	2	0	1	3 : 2
New Zealand	1	1	0	0	5 : 0											1	1	0	0	5 : 0
Nigeria											2	0	0	2	1 : 4	2	0	0	2	1 : 4
North Korea	1	1	0	0	2 : 1											1	1	0	0	2 : 1
Panama	4	1	2	1	6 : 5	4	1	0	3	4 : 7	1	0	0	1	1 : 2	9	2	2	5	11 : 14
Paraguay	9	2	2	5	9 : 13	7	1	1	5	3 : 9	7	0	2	5	9 : 23	23	3	5	15	21 : 45
Peru	11	7	1	3	24 : 15	11	0	1	10	6 : 24	7	0	1	6	4 : 16	29	7	3	19	34 : 55
Porto Rico											1	1	0	0	6 : 0	1	1	0	0	6 : 0
Spain	2	0	0	2	0 : 5	2	0	0	2	2 : 8						4	0	0	4	2 : 13
Sweden	1	1	0	0	2 : 0											1	1	0	0	2 : 0
Switzerland						1	0	0	1	0 : 1						1	0	0	1	0 : 1
Syria	1	1	0	0	4 : 1											1	1	0	0	4 : 1
Trinidad and Tobago	2	2	0	0	4 : 0	3	0	3	0	2 : 2						5	2	3	0	6 : 2
United States						3	0	0	3	0 : 5	1	0	1	0	3 : 3	4	0	1	3	3 : 8
Uruguay	12	2	4	6	10 : 17	13	1	2	10	8 : 36	2	0	1	1	2 : 4	27	3	7	17	20 : 57
Uruguay League XI	1	1	0	0	1 : 0											1	1	0	0	1 : 0
Yugoslavia											1	0	0	1	0 : 10	1	0	0	1	0 : 10
TOTAL	**142**	**54**	**38**	**50**	**185 : 204**	**130**	**17**	**20**	**93**	**79 : 309**	**71**	**11**	**12**	**48**	**75 : 173**	**343**	**82**	**70**	**191**	**339 : 686**